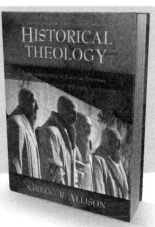

A COMPANION TO WAYNE GRUDEM'S *SYSTEMATIC THEOLOGY*

HISTORICAL THEOLOGY

AN INTRODUCTION TO CHRISTIAN DOCTRINE

FOREWORD BY WAYNE GRUDEM

GREGG R. ALLISON

ZONDERVAN
ACADEMIC

ZONDERVAN ACADEMIC

Historical Theology
Copyright © 2011 by Gregg R. Allison

Requests for information should be addressed to:
Zondervan, 3900 *Sparks Dr. SE, Grand Rapids, Michigan 49546*

Library of Congress Cataloging-in-Publication Data

Allison, Gregg R.
    Historical theology : an introduction to Christian doctrine : a companion to Wayne Grudem's Systematic theology /
Gregg R. Allison.
        p. cm.
    Includes indexes.
    ISBN 978-0-310-23013-7 (hardcover)
    1. Theology, Doctrinal—History. I. Title.
    BT21.3.A44 2011
    230.09—dc22   2010034658

Cover design: Tammy Johnson
Cover photography: age fotostock/SuperStock
Interior design: Mark Sheeres and Matthew Van Zomeren

Printed in the United States of America

23 24 25 26 27 28 29 30 31 32 33 34 35 36 /TRM/ 30 29 28 27 26 25 24 23 22 21 20 19 18 17 16 15

This book is dedicated to my three children,
whom God gave to my wife, Nora, and me—
Lauren Marie Schneringer,
Hanell Joy Schuetz,
and Luke Winford Allison
—three wonderful blessings in my life
as I was writing this book.
As committed followers of Jesus Christ,
you are heirs to the evangelical legacy
described in the following pages,
members of the great company of saints
whose study of Scripture, careful thinking,
fight against heresy, prayer,
worship, perseverance in the truth,
love for Christ, labor in the church,
and yielding to the Holy Spirit
led to the development of the evangelical doctrines
that you now embrace, and that embrace you.
May you follow the way of this truth throughout your life—
until you go to be with Jesus, or he comes for his church—
redeemed by the One who is "the Way, the Truth, and the Life."

CONTENTS

PART 3:
THE DOCTRINE OF HUMANITY

PART 4:
THE DOCTRINES OF CHRIST
AND THE HOLY SPIRIT

PART 5:
THE DOCTRINE OF THE
APPLICATION OF REDEMPTION

PART 6:
THE DOCTRINE OF THE CHURCH

PART 7:
THE DOCTRINE OF THE FUTURE

PERMISSIONS

By permission of Oxford University Press

St. Anselm of Canterbury: Major Works, edited by Brian Davies and G. R. Evans (OWC 1998)

Documents of the Christian Church, 3rd ed., edited by Henry Bettenson and Chris Mauer (1999)

Used by permission of Baker Academic, a division of Baker Publishing Group:

Michael W. Holmes, *The Apostolic Fathers* (Grand Rapids, 1999)

H. D. McDonald, *The Atonement of the Death of Christ* (Grand Rapids, 1985)

Ray C. Petry, ed., *A History of Christianity: Readings in the History of the Development of Doctrine,* Vol. 1: The Early and Medieval Church (Grand Rapids, 1990)

Reprinted by permission of HarperCollins Publishers:

Early Christian Doctrines, by J. N. D. Kelly, rev. ed., copyright © 1960, 1965, 1968, 1978 by John Norman Davidson Kelly

Reproduced by kind permission of Continuum International Publishing Group:

George Tavard, *Holy Writ or Holy Church: The Crisis of the Protestant Reformation* (London: Burns & Oates, 1959)

Karl Barth, *Church Dogmatics,* 13 vols., edited by G. W. Bromiley and T. F. Torrance (Edinburgh: T & T Clark, 1936)

FOREWORD

This book is an amazingly rich resource that traces the development of thirty-two major doctrines from the time of the New Testament to writers in the present day. Every chapter provides a fascinating story that is hard to put down because it shows how God has worked in Christians' lives over the centuries to allow one heresy after another to challenge the church, then to raise up courageous, wise teachers and writers to respond to the wrong teaching with a new and deeper understanding of Scripture, resulting in even stronger faith in God and his Word. Therefore this book is the story of how the Holy Spirit has guided and protected the people of God over many centuries, and how he is still doing so today.

Christians tend to make two mistakes when thinking about church history. The first mistake is to *ignore it* or think it unimportant. This view forgets that the Holy Spirit has been working in the church throughout the centuries to gift "shepherds and teachers" (Eph. 4:11) so that they would guide and teach the church. Gregg Allison quotes extensively from these gifted teachers that God raised up in every generation and shows how we can still learn a great deal from them today.

The second mistake is to *idolize* church history, or at least some part of it. I have met Christians who seem to think that there was some golden age of doctrinal understanding long ago, and our task today should be simply to "get back" to that understanding of the past, such as the views of the early church Fathers, or the early creeds of the church, or Augustine, or Luther, or Calvin, or the Puritans, or Wesley. But this view can neglect the fact that our only perfect source of doctrine is the Bible itself, and no one in history has understood it perfectly. Rather, Christ has been working in the church throughout the centuries to "sanctify" it, so that at the end "he might present the church to himself in splendor, without spot or wrinkle or any such thing, that she might be holy and without blemish" (Eph. 5:26–27). The history that this book traces is a history of the Christian church gradually growing in understanding, making progress toward the goal that we "may no longer be children, tossed to and fro by the waves and carried about by every wind of doctrine," but by "speaking the truth in love" we may "grow up in every way into him who is the head, into Christ" (Eph. 4:14–15).

Gregg Allison is one of the wisest, most articulate, and most knowledgeable theologians in the church today, and this is evident throughout this book. He is also a humble, godly man whose life adorns (Titus 2:10) the doctrine he teaches, and it is my privilege to count him as a friend. I am grateful that he wrote this book to be used alongside my *Systematic Theology* (as a supplement and sometimes a needed corrective to my brief historical summaries), and I am sure that his book will also find wide usefulness as a resource by itself. It is a privilege for me to commend this wonderful book for the strengthening of the church throughout the world.

Wayne Grudem, Ph.D.
Research Professor of Theology and Biblical Studies
Phoenix Seminary, Phoenix, Arizona, USA

PREFACE

This book is intended to be a companion volume to Wayne Grudem's *Systematic Theology: An Introduction to Biblical Doctrine* (Grand Rapids: Zondervan, 1994, 2000). Indeed, it was Wayne who called me one day with a proposal and a purpose: to write a book that would trace the development of the doctrines that his book covers, to help Christians understand how they have come to have the beliefs they have today. I did not realize at the time how daunting a task this project would be; at times I have been overwhelmed by the sense that no one person should have undertaken to accomplish it. Now, over a dozen years later, I am thankful to God (and Wayne) that I can present this book to you. Although it is a companion volume, my *Historical Theology* can be read on its own. Still, to receive the maximum benefit, it should be read in tandem with his *Systematic Theology*. One helpful plan would be to read his chapter on, for example, the Trinity and then read the corresponding chapter in my book to understand how that doctrine developed in the church over the course of time.[1]

Like Grudem's *Systematic Theology*, my *Historical Theology* was not written for teachers of historical theology and church history, but for students and for all Christians who desire to know how the church has come to believe what it believes today. As such, I have called it "An Introduction to the Development of Christian Doctrine." Entire books have been written about the progression of, for example, the inspiration of Scripture or justification, but this book is intended for Christians who have never studied such evolvement of doctrine. I have tried to recount this development in an understandable way by avoiding the use of technical terms without first explaining them, and by providing helpful glossaries of the people, writings, and events frequently encountered in the book. My hope is that the church, and evangelicals in particular, will become as familiar with the giants of the past—Clement of Rome, Justin Martyr, Irenaeus, Augustine, Thomas Aquinas, Martin Luther, Huldrych Zwingli, John Calvin, John Wesley, Karl Barth—as they are with Billy Graham, John Piper, J. I. Packer, Chuck Colson, Ravi Zacharias, Tim Keller, Al Mohler, and Mark Driscoll.

Several distinctive features have guided me as I have written *Historical Theology*:

1. Present Each Doctrine in Its Chronological Development.

Unlike the vast majority of other historical theology and church history books, which are organized chronologically, my book is organized topically. An example of the common approach is Jaroslav Pelikan's five-volume masterpiece, *The Christian Tradition: A History of the Development of Doctrine*.[2] This collection is organized chronologically: the first volume covers the early church period, from AD 100 to 600; the second volume

---

1. See p. 19 in this book for a helpful chart, "Reading the Companion Volumes for Greatest Benefit."

2. Jaroslav Pelikan, *The Christian Tradition: A History of the Development of Doctrine*, 5 vols. (Chicago: Univ. of Chicago Press, 1971–91): vol. 1, *The Emergence of the Catholic Tradition (100–600)*, 1971; vol. 2, *The Spirit of Eastern Christendom (600–1700)*, 1977; vol. 3, *The Growth of Medieval Theology (600–1300)*, 1980; vol. 4, *Reformation of Church and Dogma (1300–1700)*, 1985; vol. 5, *Christian Doctrine and Modern Culture (since 1700)*, 1991.

covers the development of Eastern Orthodoxy, from 600 to 1700; the third volume covers the medieval church, from 600 to 1300; the fourth volume covers Reformation developments, from 1300 to 1700; and the fifth volume covers the modern period, from 1700 to the present. Within each time period, the various doctrines and their development are treated. Accordingly, to understand the progression of the doctrines of, for example, the inerrancy of Scripture and the person of Jesus Christ, readers must track down those specific topics in each of the five volumes. This approach requires a fair bit of effort, first, to identify where the doctrine of Scripture and the doctrine of Christ are covered in each volume, and second, to read their entire coverage throughout five volumes.

My *Historical Theology* is organized in the opposite way: it is first arranged topically, then chronologically. Accordingly, to understand the progression of the two doctrines, readers simply turn to chapter 5 to trace the development of the inerrancy of Scripture and chapter 17 to trace the development of the doctrine of the person of Christ. Within each chapter, the progression of the topic starts with the early church (from its New Testament affirmations to 600), moves into the church of the Middle Ages or medieval era (from 600 to 1500), continues with Reformation and post-Reformation developments (1500–1750), and concludes with the modern period (1750 to the present day).[3] Although my book follows an atypical organizational plan, its topical-chronological approach brings together the development of each doctrine in one place for easy reading and reference.[4]

2. Let the Voices of the Past be Heard in Their Own Words.

Following Grudem's pattern of quoting biblical passages at length, I cite the actual words (in English translation, of course) of church leaders, biblical scholars, and theologians of the past. Unlike the words of Scripture, theirs are not—and never claimed to be—inspired by God. Nonetheless, I think it is important to let these towering figures speak for themselves and for readers to hear their voices ring out across the centuries. If it is true that with historical theology comes "a 'sensation of pastness,' the experience of touching right back to a past lived reality,"[5] I want to stimulate that sense of connection, and one way of doing so is to let the voices of the past be heard in their own words. Accordingly, I quote their most significant affirmations and proposals. For space purposes, I place their other important statements in footnotes; only when really pressed for space do I summarize in my own words what they wrote. I also carefully document the most accessible resources from which these citations are taken, for the purpose of making further study as easy as

---

3. This division of historical theology into four eras is a typical approach to periodization. The dates are not arbitrary, but neither are they rigid. That is, nothing in particular took place, for example, in the year 600 to mark the end of the early church age and the beginning of the medieval period. As Richard Muller explains: "Even if the lines between these periods cannot be rigidly drawn, there are identifiable characteristics of, for example, patristic [early church] theology that are not duplicated in the other periods of the history of the church. The Reformation did bring about major changes in the life of the church, indeed, in the whole of Western culture, that still have their impact on us today. And the perspectives on God, man, and the world that dominated the West through the Middle Ages and the Reformation and post-Reformation eras were altered profoundly in the Enlightenment of the eighteenth century, marking the dawn of the 'modern' era." Richard A. Muller, *The Study of Theology: From Biblical Interpretation to Contemporary Formulation*, Foundations of Contemporary Interpretation, vol. 7 (Grand Rapids: Zondervan, 1991), 103.

4. A similar topical-chronological approach can be found in John D. Hannah, *Our Legacy: the History of Christian Doctrine* (Colorado Springs: NavPress, 2001).

5. John F. McCarthy, *The Science of Historical Theology: Elements of a Definition* (Rome: Propaganda Mariana, 1976), 185.

possible. Without a lot of effort—collecting a reasonable number of books, utilizing computerized software, and accessing the Internet—readers may delve deeper into, for example, my presentation of Origen's interpretation of Scripture or Anselm's satisfaction theory of the atonement by finding easy access and clear reference to the former's *First Principles* or the latter's *Why God Became Man*. More than a discussion of the historical development of Christian doctrine, this book is also a helpful resource for further reading and study.

3. Exercise Restraint in Criticizing Historical Developments.

I am a Protestant, and unashamedly so. Moreover, I am a conservative evangelical, also without shame. As I studied the progression of doctrines, I at times found myself cringing at the church's careless interpretation of Scripture, unwarranted appeal to biblical passages, and confusing theological thinking in support of its doctrinal development. Despite my own assessment, I have attempted to refrain personally from criticizing these theological wrong turns. What I have done instead is to note other church voices from the past that have criticized those troubling developments. Sometimes these corrective voices were not sounded for centuries; even then, the church, or certain aspects of it, refused to hear these remedial expressions. This dynamic will be most clearly seen in my account of the development of doctrines (e.g., the authority, clarity, sufficiency, and necessity of Scripture) in the medieval church and the reactionary criticisms in the Reformation and post-Reformation period. Luther, Zwingli, Calvin, Turretin, Quenstedt, and a host of others adequately and firmly offered their "protestations" against misguided Catholic formulations in those areas, and I allow their criticisms to be heard rather than my own.

I do something similar in my rehearsal of doctrinal drift in the modern era, though at times I offer (briefly) my own personal assessment. This section of my book—the modern period—was the most difficult to write, because the last several centuries have been characterized by attacks—vicious at times, often based on misunderstandings of Scripture and sound doctrine, commonly growing out of an anti-Christian worldview—against every traditional doctrine that the church has cherished from its inception. So harmful have these attacks been that I wish I did not have to cover these assaults against the church. They have left many deep scars; many church members have been led astray and even abandoned their profession of Christ as a result. Churches continue to wrestle with these attacks today. Although I wish I could report successful resistance in every case, such is not the case. Still, Christians can take heart that God for the sake of Christ has always raised up, and continues to call, choice servants to fight back against these dark forces. By tracing the demise of traditional church beliefs during the modern period and illustrating apologetic responses to these assaults, I hope to stimulate others to step forward to defend the faith against current criticisms today.

4. Focus on Major Developments in Each Doctrine.

To offer a concise and introductory historical theology, I have focused on the major developments in thirty-three doctrines.[6] This approach has necessitated that I limit my references

---

6. I count my first chapter, "Introduction to Historical Theology," as one of these topics, just as Grudem has a chapter titled "Introduction to Systematic Theology."

14

to the most significant church leaders, biblical scholars, and theologians who have contributed to the development of these doctrines. Accordingly, readers will note the appearance of the same major figures in many, if not all, chapters. Even among these important contributors, I have often needed to make a difficult selection for purposes of space. This emphasis should not be taken to imply that other important figures, as well as many minor figures, did little to shape the contours of these doctrines; indeed, the opposite is usually the case. I encourage readers to use my book as a springboard to deeper exploration by finding monographs on those doctrines whose development they wish to trace in a more detailed manner.

Selection of topics to cover has also been part of writing this book. I treat thirty-three doctrines, corresponding to forty-three (out of fifty-seven) chapters in Grudem's *Systematic Theology*. At times I may combine several of his chapters into one (e.g., his three chapters on the incommunicable and communicable attributes of God become one chapter in my book). For purposes of space, I have not treated some of the doctrines he addresses.[7] In one case, I have included a topic—the interpretation of Scripture—that he does not cover.[8]

Such selection of materials, the concentration on major figures, and even the choice of which doctrines to cover will be criticized by some people. Let me assure these readers that I have felt the pain of having to make difficult selections. Choosing Irenaeus rather than Tertullian to illustrate the early church's rule of faith; picking between Augustine's various writings to present his doctrines of sin and grace; focusing much more on the Reformers (Luther, Zwingli, Calvin) than on their successors, the post-Reformers (Quenstedt, Turretin); and opting for a discussion of Schleiermacher's remaking of Christian doctrine rather than that of other important modern liberal figures—I have pondered every selection and second-guessed myself on most decisions. In many cases, I have opted to include the church leaders, biblical scholars, and theologians whose works are most readily accessible (both in terms of availability of resources and clarity of writing) to the general public, for ease of further reading and study. In the end, I humbly stand by my choices, acknowledging that other equally important ones could have been made.[9] Such selectivity means that, while I do tell the story of the historical development of Christians doctrines, it is not the whole story. Still, I hope and believe that my account is sufficient for an introductory book as this work intends to be.

5. Focus on the Development of Evangelical Doctrine.

While tracing the broad contours of the development of Christian doctrine, I concentrate on the development of doctrine within evangelicalism, especially as that movement

---

7. All of these doctrines are important and deserve treatment, but I did not have space to cover them. For the correspondence between the chapters in Grudem's *Systematic Theology* and my *Historical Theology*, see the helpful chart "Reading the Companion Volumes for Greatest Benefit," on p. 19.

8. In a conversation with Wayne, in which I asked him what he would change if he reworked his *Systematic Theology*, he answered that he would add a chapter on the interpretation of Scripture. Indeed, he noted that when he teaches the beginning theology course at Phoenix Seminary, he includes a section on biblical interpretation. Because of my interest in the

doctrine of Scripture, and due to its ongoing importance for the church, I include a chapter on the historical development of the church's interpretation of Scripture.

9. I thoroughly concur with Geoffrey Bromiley: "Writing a historical theology involves a venture and rests on a series of choices of aim, method, matter, and approach, choices which are in some sense arbitrary and all of which are open to dispute. Even at best, then, the author will do justice neither to the subject, nor to the intention of the author, nor to the expectations of readers." Geoffrey W. Bromiley, *Historical Theology: An Introduction* (Edinburgh: T & T Clark, 1978), xxi.

exists in North America. The term *evangelical* has come to refer to several things.[10] In one sense, *evangelical* refers to the Lutheran churches that emerged from the Reformation. The term focuses on the centrality of the gospel (Gr. εὐαγγελιον, *euangelion*) and has a corollary emphasis on Scripture as the normative statement of the gospel for these churches. Second, *evangelical* refers to the eighteenth-century revival movements associated with John Wesley in Great Britain; Jonathan Edwards in the northeastern colonies of America; George Whitefield, who assisted in both regions; and the German Pietists. All these movements emphasized conversion, piety, evangelism, and social reformation. In America the Great Awakening spawned a revival tradition that manifested itself in the Second Great Awakening (Charles Finney), the Third Great Awakening (Dwight Moody), Billy Graham, and others. In a third sense, *evangelical* is a catchall term for theologically conservative Protestants of whatever heritage who share a set of commitments. Primarily, these are (1) a high view of the Bible (its inspiration, inerrancy, clarity, sufficiency, necessity, and authority); (2) salvation by grace alone through faith in Christ alone as that salvation is communicated through the gospel and empowered by the Holy Spirit; (3) holiness of life; and (4) social engagement of some kind, whether that is championing the culture of life over the culture of death (abortion, euthanasia, infanticide) or involvement in political matters. *Evangelical*, fourthly, refers to the movement that arose out of fundamentalism around the middle of the twentieth century and that is characterized by a network of theological seminaries (e.g., Trinity Evangelical Divinity School, Gordon-Conwell Theological Seminary), publications (e.g., *Christianity Today*), ad hoc evangelistic and social agencies (e.g., Billy Graham Evangelistic Association, World Vision), and organizations (e.g., National Association of Evangelicals, Evangelical Theological Society). Finally, and most recently, *evangelical* refers to an ethos characterized "by social and cultural factors as much as by theological or historical ones. Indeed, a strong case has been made that social and cultural factors are the predominant shapers of current evangelical activity—a point that is raising serious concerns today."[11]

In this book, the term *evangelical* combines the third and fourth senses from above: It refers to theologically conservative Protestants with certain doctrinal commitments,[12] who are found in many different churches and denominations (Baptist, Presbyterian, Reformed, Lutheran, Methodist, Episcopalian, Congregational, Christian, Brethren,

---

10. Much of the following discussion is adapted from Mark Noll and David Wells, eds., *Christian Faith and Practice in the Modern World: Theology from an Evangelical Point of View* (Grand Rapids: Eerdmans, 1986). For further discussion, see the interchange between George M. Marsden and Donald W. Dayton in *Christian Scholar's Review* 23, no. 1 (1993). For a discussion of evangelicalism in Great Britain, see David W. Bebbington, *Evangelicals in Modern Britain: A History from the 1730s to the 1980s* (London: Unwin, 2008).

11. D. H. Williams, *Retrieving the Tradition and Renewing Evangelicalism: A Primer for Suspicious Protestants* (Grand Rapids: Eerdmans, 1999), 4.

12. An example of these common doctrinal elements is the statement of faith of the National Association of Evangelicals: "We believe the Bible to be the inspired, the only infal-

lible, authoritative Word of God. We believe that there is one God, eternally existent in three persons: Father, Son and Holy Spirit. We believe in the deity of our Lord Jesus Christ, in His virgin birth, in His sinless life, in His miracles, in His vicarious and atoning death through His shed blood, in His bodily resurrection, in His ascension to the right hand of the Father, and in His personal return in power and glory. We believe that for the salvation of lost and sinful people, regeneration by the Holy Spirit is absolutely essential. We believe in the present ministry of the Holy Spirit by whose indwelling the Christian is enabled to live a godly life. We believe in the resurrection of both the saved and the lost; they that are saved unto the resurrection of life and they that are lost unto the resurrection of damnation. We believe in the spiritual unity of believers in our Lord Jesus Christ."

independent, Pentecostal, Bible, Holiness, and inter- and nondenominational), and who are characterized by various networks of schools, publications, and the like. Even more specifically, while recognizing the amazing growth of churches worldwide due to extensive evangelical mission work, this book focuses on evangelical Christians and churches in North America. A result of this decision is that the historical development recounted here is primarily that of the theology of the Western church—the Roman Catholic Church and Protestant churches—and not Eastern Orthodoxy. Another result is that the book concentrates on theological developments in Europe and North America.

6. Discern "A Sense of the Urgent Need for Greater Doctrinal Understanding in the Whole Church."

This is one of the distinctive features of Grudem's *Systematic Theology*.[13] I concur wholeheartedly; thus, it is one of my guiding principles. One way of meeting this urgent need is to provide understandable, accessible systematic theologies like his. Another way is to provide understandable, accessible historical theologies like mine. As Christians and their churches are exposed to the development of doctrine, as they are able to trace the progression of their beliefs beginning with the early church, passing into the medieval period, moving into the Reformation and post-Reformation era, and through the modern period up to today, they "will find that understanding (and living) the doctrines of Scripture is one of their greatest joys."[14]

---

13. Wayne Grudem, *Systematic Theology: An Introduction to Biblical Doctrine* (Grand Rapids: Zondervan, 1994, 2000), 18.
14. Ibid.

ACKNOWLEDGMENTS

I wish to thank many people for their help in the writing of this book. First, Wayne Grudem took a risk when he asked me, a recently graduated systematic theologian without any publishing experience, to write a historical theology book that would cover everything he did not include in his *Systematic Theology*. He took the initiative in making the proposal to Zondervan and urging the editors to give me the opportunity to carry it out. Wayne has also given me encouragement over a dozen years to persevere in my writing. I am very grateful to him for his friendship.

Zondervan has been more patient with me than I ever could have hoped for, and certainly more than I deserve. Perhaps sensing the immensity of this project, no editor ever sought to rush me through the lengthy process. Even when I turned in the largest rough draft Zondervan had ever received, no one laughed at or chided me. Rather, a calm and simple suggestion was made that I revisit the length of the draft for the sake of keeping the book to one volume. I want to thank especially Jim Ruark, David Frees, and Laura Weller, my editors, for bearing with me in such a kind, gracious, and patient manner. Every one of your suggestions and comments has been on target and made this book better.

The majority of this book was written during three sabbaticals. For these concentrated periods of research and writing, I would like to thank the board of directors and the administration of two seminaries: Western Seminary, Portland, Oregon, which granted me a sabbatical for the fall semester, 2000, and The Southern Baptist Theological Seminary, Louisville, Kentucky, which granted me a sabbatical during the spring semester, 2006, and another for the fall semester, 2009. Library assistance at both seminaries also played an important role in collecting the many resources used in writing this book, so I extend thanks to the librarians and their assistants at both schools. Particular thanks goes to Karen Arvin, Matthew Barrett, and Hannah Wymer.

Numerous students have played a major role in the research and editing of this book through taking my course in historical theology at both Western Seminary and Southern Seminary. Participants in CHS 650/550 at Western Seminary were Th.M. students Clint Heacock and Jason Johansen, and M.Div. or M.A. students Nate Baxter, Marc Cortez, Grant Goins, Nate Gustafson, Danny Jenkins, Sandra Jenkins, and Jeff Morgan. Participants in CHS 652/552 at Western Seminary were Th.M. students Carmen Bryant, Bernard Maurer, Jeff Olson, and Molly Whitcomb, and M.Div. or M.A. students Todd Arnett, Kurt Gross, David Haigh, Brad Hayen, Troy Hicks, and Will Silmon. These students became involved at the initial stages of development of this book and contributed by doing extensive research and writing of the first drafts of some of the chapters. Participants in course 27885 at Southern Seminary were Joel Amunrud, Dave Campbell, Lenny Cheng, Bradley Cochran, Charles Davis, Patrick Gordon, Brian Hubert, Chuck Joiner, Joo Jung, Woosup Kim, Rony Kozman, Kudol Lee, Bryan Lilly, John Lopes, Joshua

Nelson, Christopher Newkirk, Eron Plevan, Brian Preston, Dave Richards, Isaac Sumner, and Eric Williamson. These students worked through the late-stage rough draft of the book, editing the text for misspellings, grammatical errors, lack of clarity, and content, and examining every footnote for accuracy. My thanks to each student for careful, meticulous, and time-consuming hard work and patient kindness toward me. Graduate assistants and Garrett Fellows not already named, but who helped with research and grading, were Chris Bosson, Micah Carter, Ryan Lister, John McKinley, Aaron O'Kelley, Gary Schultz, Michael Wren, Kenneth Reid, and Christopher Clemans.

Several colleagues gave me suggestions for parts of this book. For their help, I would like to thank Gerry Breshears, Bob Krupp, and Randy Roberts from Western Seminary, and Chad Brand, Michael Haykin, Tom Nettles, David Puckett, Mark Seifrid, Kevin Smith, Bruce Ware, Steve Wellum, Greg Wills, Shawn Wright, and Bob Vogel from Southern Seminary. I also extend special thanks to Tom Nettles and John Woodbridge for their foundational courses in church history and historical theology.

Many books have proved to be valuable resources, and these volumes are listed in the Abbreviations and Source References. Special mention needs to be made of one resource for the development of Christian doctrines in the early church: David W. Bercot, ed., *A Dictionary of Early Christian Beliefs: A Reference Guide to More than 700 Topics Discussed by the Early Church Fathers* (Peabody, Mass.: Hendrickson, 1998).

Most of all, I would like to thank my family for their love, support, and prayers. My wife, Nora, has championed my work through her encouraging words, personal example of dedication, and self-sacrifice on behalf of our family and me. I thank her also for composing the challenging index for this book. Our three children, Lauren, Hanell, and Luke, have grown up with their dad working on this lengthy project. They are excited and thankful that it is finally finished! To them I joyfully dedicate this book.

READING THE COMPANION VOLUMES FOR GREATEST BENEFIT

Grudem's *Systematic Theology* CHAPTER(S)	Allison's *Historical Theology* CHAPTER
1	1
2	3
3	2
4	4
5	5
6	6
7, 8	7
X	8*
9, 10	9
11, 12, 13	10
14	11
15	12
16	13
17	X
18	X
19, 20	14
21, 22,** 23	15
24	16
25	X

* I include a chapter on the history of the interpretation of Scripture that Grudem does not cover.

** I do not treat the history of man as male and female.

*** I treat the history of the debate over the baptism in and filling with the Holy Spirit together with the work of the Holy Spirit in ch. 20, which thus appears twice in this list.

ABBREVIATIONS AND SOURCE REFERENCES

ANF   *Ante-Nicene Fathers*, ed. Alexander Roberts, James Donaldson, Philip Schaff, and Henry Wace, 10 vols. (Peabody, Mass.: Hendrickson, 1994).

Anselm   *Anselm of Canterbury: The Major Works*, ed. Brian Davies and G. R. Evans (Oxford and New York: Oxford Univ. Press, 1998).

Bettenson   *Documents of the Christian Church*, ed. Henry Bettenson and Chris Maunder, 3rd ed. (Oxford: Oxford University Press, 1999).

BSac   *Bibliotheca sacra*

CD   Karl Barth, *Church Dogmatics*, ed. G. W. Bromiley and T. F. Torrance, 13 vols. (Edinburgh: T & T Clark, 1936).

Heppe   Heinrich Heppe, *Reformed Dogmatics*, ed. Ernst Bizer, trans. G. T. Thomson (London: Allen and Unwin, 1950).

Holmes   Michael W. Holmes, The Apostolic Fathers: Greek Texts and English Translations (Grand Rapids: Baker, 1999).

JBR   *Journal of Bible and Religion*

JETS   *Journal of the Evangelical Theological Society*

Kelly   J. N. D. Kelly, *Early Christian Doctrines*, rev. ed. (San Francisco: HarperSanFrancisco, 1978).

LCC   Library of Christian Classics, 26 vols. (Philadelphia: Westminster, 1960), diverse volumes.

LCC 1   John Calvin, *Institutes of the Christian Religion*, ed. John T. McNeill, trans. Ford Lewis Battles (Philadelphia: Westminster, 1960), in John Baillie, John T. McNeill, and Henry P. Van Dusen, gen. eds., Library of Christian Classics, 26 vols. (Philadelphia: Westminster, 1960), vol. 20.

LCC 2   John Calvin, *Institutes of the Christian Religion*, ed. John T. McNeill, trans. Ford Lewis Battles (Philadelphia: Westminster, 1960), in John Baillie, John T. McNeill, and Henry P. Van Dusen, gen. eds., Library of Christian Classics, 26 vols. (Philadelphia: Westminster, 1960), vol. 21.

Lumpkin   William L. Lumpkin, *Baptist Confessions of Faith*, rev. ed. (Valley Forge: Judson, 1969).

LW   Martin Luther, *Luther's Works*, eds., Jaroslav Pelikan, Hilton C. Oswald, and Helmut T. Lehmann, 55 vols. (St. Louis: Concordia, 1955–1986).

Mansi   Joannes Dominicus Mansi, *Sacrorum Conciliorum nova et amplissima collectio*, rev. ed., 31 vols. (Lyons: Petit and Martin, 1899–1927).

NPNF[1]   *Nicene- and Post-Nicene Fathers*, eds. Alexander Roberts, James Donaldson, Philip Schaff, and Henry Wace, 1st ser., 14 vols. (Peabody, Mass: Hendrickson, 1994).

NPNF[2]   *Nicene- and Post-Nicene Fathers*, ed. Alexander Roberts, James Donaldson, Philip Schaff, and Henry Wace, 2nd ser., 14 vols. (Peabody, Mass.: Hendrickson, 1994).

Pelikan   Jaroslav Pelikan, *The Christian Tradition: A History of the Development of Doctrine*, 5 vols. (Chicago and London: University of Chicago Press, 1971–1991).

Petry   *A History of Christianity: Readings in the History of the Church*, ed. Ray C. Petry, vol. 1: The Early and Medieval Church (Grand Rapids: Baker, 1990).

PG   *Patrologiae cursus completus: Series graeca*, ed. J.-P. Migne, 165 vols. (Paris: 1857–86).

PL   *Patrologiae cursus completus: Series latina*, ed. J.-P. Migne, 221 vols. (Paris: 1844–64).

Preus   Robert D. Preus, *The Theology of Post-Reformation Lutheranism: A Study of Theological Prolegomena* (St. Louis: Concordia, 1970).

Schaff   Philip Schaff, *Creeds of Christendom*, 3 vols. (New York: Harper, 1877–1905).

Schmid   Heinrich Schmid, *The Doctrinal Theology of the Evangelical Lutheran Church*, trans. Charles A. Hay and Henry E. Jacobs (Minneapolis: Augsburg, 1899).

SJT   *Scottish Journal of Theology*

Summa Contra Gentiles   Thomas Aquinas, *Summa Contra Gentiles*, 1.3, online ed., *An Annotated Translation (with Some Abridgement) of the Summa Contra Gentiles of Saint Thos Aquinas*, trans. Joseph Rickaby (The Catholic Primer, 2005).

Summa Theologica   Thomas Aquinas, *Summa Theologica*. Translated by Fathers of the English Dominican Province. Cincinnati, Ohio: Printers to the Holy Apostolic See, 1914.

Tavard   George H. Tavard, *Holy Writ or Holy Church: The Crisis of the Protestant Reformation* (London: Burns & Oates, 1959).

WLS   Martin Luther, *What Luther Says*, ed. Ewald M. Plass, 3 vols. in 1 (St. Louis: Concordia, 1959).

WTJ   *Westminster Theological Journal*

INTRODUCTION TO HISTORICAL THEOLOGY

What is historical theology? What benefits does it provide? How should we study it?

Historical theology is the study of the interpretation of Scripture and the formulation of doctrine by the church of the past.[1] Such concentration on the accumulated wisdom of the ages provides great benefit to Christians and churches today as they seek to live faithfully and obediently for Jesus Christ. This high value of historical theology, or church tradition, was underscored by Kenneth Kantzer, one of the founders of modern evangelicalism: "While it is not infallible, it must be acknowledged as God's guidance of his people in accordance with his promise to the church of all ages."[2] At the same time, church tradition must always have reference to Scripture; hence, historical theology must be either approved or chastened by the Word of God. As J. I. Packer, another leading evangelical, articulated: "Scripture must have the last word on all human attempts to state its meaning, and tradition, viewed as a series of such human attempts, has a ministerial

---

1. Jaroslav Pelikan, working from the *Formula of Concord*, defined historical theology as the study of what the church "believes, teaches, and confesses as it prays and suffers, serves and obeys, celebrates and awaits the coming of the Kingdom of God." Jaroslav Pelikan, *Development of Christian Doctrine: Some Historical Prolegomena* (New Haven: Yale Univ. Press, 1969), 143.

2. Kenneth S. Kantzer, "A Systematic Biblical Dogmatics: What Is It and How Is It to Be Done?" in *Doing Theology in Today's World: Essays in Honor of Kenneth S. Kantzer*, ed. John D. Woodbridge and Thomas Edward McComiskey (Grand Rapids: Zondervan, 1991), 466. Kantzer, like many others, distinguished between two senses of tradition. Church Tradition (with a capital *T*), from a Roman Catholic theology perspective, refers to one aspect of divine revelation. It consists of the teachings of Jesus that he communicated orally to his disciples but which were not written down, and which were transmitted orally from the apostles to their successors, the

bishops. This living Tradition continues in the church today and at times has been proclaimed as official Roman Catholic doctrine. Specifically, Pope Pius IX promulgated the dogma of the immaculate conception of Mary in his bull *Ineffabilis Deus* (December 8, 1854), and Pope Pius XII promulgated the dogma of the bodily assumption of Mary in his bull *Munificentissimus Deus* (November 1, 1950). The result of this view of divine revelation is "that the Church does not draw her certainty about all revealed truths from the holy Scriptures alone. Hence, both Scripture and Tradition must be accepted and honored with equal feelings of devotion and reverence." *Dogmatic Constitution on Divine Revelation* (Vatican II, *Dei Verbum*, November 18, 1965), 9. Church tradition (with a lowercase *t*) is the accumulated wisdom of the church of the past in terms of its interpretation of Scripture and its formulation of doctrine. This tradition is not part of divine revelation in the Roman Catholic sense but is of great benefit to evangelical churches today, as I argue in this chapter.

rather than a magisterial role."[3] In determining doctrine and practice, the magisterial, or authoritative, role belongs to Scripture, and Scripture alone. The ministerial, or helping, role accorded to historical theology means that it serves the church in many ways.

One benefit that historical theology offers the church today is helping it *distinguish orthodoxy from heresy*. The term *orthodoxy* here refers to that which the New Testament calls "sound doctrine" (1 Tim. 1:10; 2 Tim. 4:3; Titus 1:9; 2:1), that which rightly reflects in summary form all the teaching of Scripture and which the church is bound to believe and obey.[4] *Heresy*, then, is anything that contradicts sound doctrine. It is false belief that misinterprets Scripture or that ignores some of the teaching of Scripture, or that incorrectly puts together all the teaching of Scripture. The church is to shun heresy and seek to correct its errors (e.g., Titus 1:9). Expressed another way, historical theology helps the church recognize sound doctrine and distinguish it from false doctrine because, generally speaking, "that faith which has been believed everywhere, always, by everyone"[5]— that is, what the church has historically believed and held as its doctrine—corresponds to orthodoxy, and whatever has been traditionally rejected by the church corresponds to heresy. For example, the belief that the Word of God who became incarnate as Jesus Christ (John 1:1, 14) was a created being who was not eternal but had a beginning in time was condemned as a heresy by the early church. In accordance with all the teaching of Scripture, the church has always believed that the Son of God, the second person of the Trinity, was, is, and always will be fully God, equal in all respects to the Father and the Holy Spirit.[6] A study of historical theology that rehearses the development of doctrine helps churches today to identify and embrace orthodoxy and to reject and correct heresy.[7]

A second benefit of historical theology is that it *provides sound biblical interpretations and theological formulations*. In some cases, the immense effort and careful study exercised by the church in the past has resulted in such excellent biblical and theological understanding that the majority of the groundwork has been laid for the church as it engages in the study of theology today. For example, the early church's work on the doctrine of the Trinity (one divine essence, three persons) and the doctrine of the

---

3. J. I. Packer, "The Comfort of Conservatism," in *Power Religion: The Selling Out of the Evangelical Church?* ed. M. S. Horton (Chicago: Moody, 1992), 288. Alister McGrath concurred: "Tradition is to be honored where it can be shown to be justified and rejected where it cannot. This critical appraisal of tradition was an integral element of the Reformation, and was based on the foundational belief that tradition was ultimately about the interpretation of Scripture—an interpretation which had to be justified with reference to precisely that same authoritative source." Alister E. McGrath, "The Importance of Tradition for Modern Evangelicalism," in *Doing Theology for the People of God*, ed. Donald Lewis and Alister E. McGrath (Downers Grove, Ill.: InterVarsity, 1996), 160.

4. According to Packer, "The word [orthodoxy] expresses the idea that certain statements accurately embody the revealed truth content of Christianity and are therefore in their own nature normative for the universal church." J. I.

Packer, "Orthodoxy," in *Evangelical Dictionary of Theology*, ed. Walter A. Elwell, 2nd ed. (Grand Rapids: Baker, 2001), 875.

5. Vincent of Lerins, *Commonitory*, 2.6, in *NPNF*[2], 11:132.

6. For further discussion, see chap. 17.

7. Indeed, as D. H. Williams pointedly asserted with regard to historical theology, specifically of the early church, "If the aim of contemporary evangelicalism is to be doctrinally orthodox and exegetically faithful to Scripture, it cannot be accomplished without recourse to and integration of the foundational Tradition of the early church.... Tradition is not something evangelicals can take or leave." D. H. Williams, *Retrieving the Tradition and Renewing Evangelicalism*, 13. From a hopeful perspective, historical theology "will help us avoid repeating the doctrinal errors that have arisen at earlier times." J. Kenneth Grider, "Historical Theology," in *Beacon Dictionary of Theology*, ed. Richard Taylor, Willard H. Taylor, and J. Kenneth Grider (Kansas City: Beacon Hill, 1983), 258.

incarnation (two unchanging natures, divine and human, united in one person) has set forth the essential elements that any current expression of these doctrines will (and must) reflect. Although the present context may raise specific challenges and demand interaction with different issues not faced by the early church as it hammered out these doctrines, its thoughtful work on the Trinity and the incarnation provides a solid foundation from which to face these contemporary tests.[8] Colloquially speaking, though the church may refine and strengthen the proverbial wheel, it has no need to reinvent it. The basic contours of cardinal doctrines have been shaped by the church of the past and thus help churches do theology today.[9]

A third benefit of historical theology is that it *presents stellar examples of faith, love, courage, hope, obedience, and mercy.* Early Christians such as Polycarp, Perpetua, and Felicitas were threatened with death if they would not renounce their faith in Jesus Christ—and they died as martyrs rather than deny the Lord who had saved them.[10] They are examples of perseverance to the point of death for Christians facing persecution today. Athanasius, a mere twenty-nine-year-old secretary at the first ecumenical, or general, council of the church convened at Nicea in 325, understood the importance of sound doctrine. He championed the Nicene confession of the deity of the Son of God and fought against devastating heresy while enduring five exiles for this doctrine of Christ.[11] He is a model of costly commitment to the truth for the church today. A theological interpretation of Scripture enabled Augustine to produce a rich commentary on the gospel of John, which in turn reinforced and helped develop the orthodox doctrine of the Trinity.[12] *The Confessions of St. Augustine,* an account of his early life and conversion to Christianity, stands as one of the bestsellers in the history of the world and has cheered on many to consider the gospel of Jesus Christ.[13] His grace-filled life, theological acumen, and careful study of Scripture are patterns for Christians today. Olympias, a widowed deaconess of the church in Constantinople, leveraged her immense wealth to become a generous patron of the church. She donated many of her estates to the church, supported the ministries of such church leaders as John Chrysostom and Gregory of Nazianzus, ransomed exiled captives, sustained a community of 250 virgins, and cared for the

---

8. An example of this benefit can be seen in many of the responses of evangelicals to the contemporary viewpoint called "open theism." This heresy had an important forerunner in the movement named Socinianism in the sixteenth and seventeenth centuries, which embraced a similar limitation on the divine knowledge. The responses offered by post-Reformers like Francis Turretin to that Socinian version of the heresy have been echoed by contemporary opponents of open theism. See Francis Turretin, *Institutes of Elenctic Theology,* ed. James T. Dennison Jr., trans. George Musgrave Giger, 3 vols. in 1 (Phillipsburg, N.J.: P & R, 1997), 3rd topic, 12th q., 1:206–12.

9. A corollary of this benefit is that historical theology can ascertain "the traditional exegetical foundation for certain dogmas." With this research in hand, evangelicals can examine whether the foundational passages (1) are interpreted properly, (2) constitute legitimate grounding for those

doctrines, (3) encourage further work on (even modification of) those theological formulations, and (4) prompt consideration of other passages as better warrants for those beliefs. For further discussion, see Jaroslav Pelikan, *Historical Theology: Continuity and Change in Christian Doctrine* (London: Hutchinson; New York: Corpus, 1971), 135–36.

10. See *The Martyrdom of Polycarp,* in Holmes, 226–45; *ANF,* 1:39–44. For the martyrdom of Perpetua and Felicitas, see *The Passion of the Holy Martyrs Perpetua and Felicitas,* in *ANF,* 3:699–706.

11. See, e.g., his *Four Discourses against the Arians,* in *NPNF²,* vol. 4.

12. See his *Tractates on the Gospel of John,* in *NPNF¹,* vol. 7.

13. See Augustine, *The Confessions of St. Augustine,* in *NPNF¹,* vol. 1.

poor. She is a model of generous giving, hospitality, and mercy.[14] Martin Luther, though excommunicated by the pope and threatened with execution for heresy, was sequestered by his protective friends and hid in the Wartburg Castle for eight months. Dressed as a knight, letting his hair and beard grow long, and going by the alias of Junker Jörg (Knight George), while suffering from loneliness, constipation, insomnia, and satanic attacks, he wrote nearly a dozen books and, as if that accomplishment were not enough, translated the entire New Testament into German.[15] He is an example for today's churches of faith and courage and exhausting labor for the cause of Christ. Such examples from church history could be multiplied thousands of times over.

A fourth benefit that historical theology renders the church is *to protect against the individualism that is rampant today* among Christians. Tragically, numerous factors — a consumerist mentality, an insistence on individual rights, an emphasis on personal autonomy, a pronounced sense of entitlement — have converged to foster an atmosphere in which too many Christians pick and choose their doctrines like they pick and choose their clothes or fast-food meals. If they feel uncomfortable about the sovereignty of God or are upset by the thought of an eternal conscious punishment of the wicked, they opt to overlook or dismiss those doctrines. If their worldly lifestyle is confronted by the demands of sanctification, or if the authority of Scripture challenges their stylish doubts about truth and certainty, they choose to minimize or set aside those doctrines. Thankfully, historical theology can act as a corrective to this regrettable situation. It reminds believers that theirs is a corporate faith that has always affirmed divine sovereignty, hell, holiness, and biblical authority. This rich heritage protects against the tendency to select the doctrines one likes and to reject those one does not like, thus giving in to one's sinful propensities.

Similarly, historical theology can guard Christians and churches from the penchant for the novel,[16] the yearning for relevancy, and the tendency to follow strong leaders who are biblically and theologically shallow. Lamenting evangelicalism's radical proneness to destabilization, Alister McGrath urged this solution: "Rediscovering the corporate and historic nature of the Christian faith reduces the danger of entire communities of faith being misled by charismatic individuals and affirms the ongoing importance of the Christian past as a stabilizing influence in potentially turbulent times."[17] Coining bizarre new doctrines (such as the health, wealth, and prosperity gospel), tampering with traditional doctrines (such as minimizing the need for repentance from sin as part of the response to

---

14. See Wendy Mayer, "Poverty and Generosity toward the Poor in the Time of John Chrysostom," in *Wealth and Poverty in Early Church and Society*, ed. Susan R. Holman, Holy Cross Studies in Patristic Theology and History (Grand Rapids: Baker, 2008), 140–58. The book offers many examples of early Christian hospitality and concern for the poor. See also Christine D. Pohl, *Making Room: Recovering Hospitality as a Christian Tradition* (Grand Rapids: Eerdmans, 1999). Disturbingly, the radical new atheism, which is quick to point out the evils foisted on society by Christians, seems to be completely unaware of the immense good that Christians have done for the poor, the sick, the marginalized, and the needy. Their ignorance or, more sinister yet, their intentional neglect of these countless acts of mercy, makes their case against Christianity ring hollow.

15. See Roland H. Bainton, *Here I Stand: A Life of Martin Luther* (Peabody, Mass.: Hendrickson, 1977).

16. As Timothy George explained, "The assumption is that recent modes of knowing truth are vastly superior to older ways, that the best equals the latest." He, too, insisted that historical theology can "serve as a bulwark against ... theological faddism." Timothy George, "Dogma Beyond Anathema: Historical Theology in the Service of the Church," *Review and Expositor* 84 (Fall 1987): 697.

17. McGrath, "Importance of Tradition," 166.

the gospel), and following dynamic leaders who boastfully minimize the importance of sound doctrines, are exposed as dangerous developments by a consideration of what the church has historically believed—or not believed.[18] Again, McGrath offers wise council:

> Tradition is like a filter, which allows us to identify suspect teachings immediately. To protest that "We have never believed this before!" is not necessarily to deny the correctness of the teaching in question. But it is to raise a fundamental question: why have Christians not believed this before? And, on further investigation, it usually turns out that there are often very good reasons for not accepting that belief. The past here acts as both a resource and a safeguard, checking unhelpful and unorthodox doctrinal developments by demanding that their supporters explain their historical and theological credentials.[19]

A fifth benefit of historical theology is that it not only helps the church understand the historical development of its beliefs, but enables it *to express those beliefs in contemporary form.* As Richard Muller explained, "Not only does doctrine necessarily arise in a historical context and take its basic conceptual framework and linguistic forms from that context, it also arrives at contemporary expression only by way of a meditation *on,* and even more importantly a meditation *through,* earlier stages of historical expression."[20] For example, the early church's doctrine of human nature was formulated in a context affected by Platonic thinking. This philosophy exalted the human spirit while it denigrated the human body; the former aspect is inherently good, asserted Platonism, while the latter aspect is inherently evil. Tragically, a significant part of the early church was negatively

---

18. Pelikan, quoting Lord Acton, underscored this important "redemptive" role of historical theology: " 'History must be our deliverer not only from the undue influence of other times, but from the undue influence of our own, from the tyranny of environment and the pressure of the air we breathe. It ... promotes the faculty of resistance to contemporary surroundings by familiarity with other ages and other orbits of thought.' This humanizing and civilizing force of historical study can give the systematic theologian a healthy detachment from the transiency of dogmatic fashion." Pelikan, *Historical Theology*, 150. Similarly, B. A. Gerrish urged that historical theology "is a determination to make one's theological decisions in the best company; and it assumes that proven durability is at least as good a criterion of the best company as is current fashion. As the Anglican divine Richard Hooker shrewdly remarked, 'There are few things known to be good, till such time as they grow to be ancient.' This means that in the work of theology we show our highest respect not for the present best-seller, but for the established classics, which have done most to shape the tradition." B. A. Gerrish, "Theology and the Historical Consciousness," in *Revisioning the Past: Prospects in Historical Theology*, ed. Mary Potter Engel and Walter E. Wyman Jr. (Minneapolis: Fortress, 1992), 290. His citation is from Richard Hooker, *Ecclesiastical Polity*, 5.7.3 (London: Everyman's Library, 1907), 11, 29.

19. McGrath, "Importance of Tradition," 167. In a stunning thesis, Williams envisioned two tragic outcomes if evangelical churches would not give heed to their doctrinal tradition. He predicted they "(1) will increasingly proliferate a sectarian approach to Christian faith, characterized by an ahistorical and spiritual subjectivism, which Philip Schaff aptly called 'the great disease which has fastened itself upon the heart of Protestantism,' and (2) will be more susceptible to the influences of accommodating the church to a pseudo-Christian culture such that the uniqueness of the Christian identity is quietly and unintentionally traded way in the name of effective ministry." Williams, *Retrieving the Tradition and Renewing Evangelicalism*, 14. Elsewhere, he noted that evangelicalism "cannot avoid the problem of how far we should accommodate the Christian message to the surrounding culture without losing Christian identity.... The formation of a distinct Christian identity in years to come will not be successful unless we deliberately reestablish the link to those resources that provide us with the defining 'center' of Christian belief and practice." Ibid., 12–13. Historical theology can stave off this frightening future.

20. Richard Muller, "The Role of Church History in the Study of Systematic Theology," in Woodbridge and McComiskey, *Doing Theology in Today's World*, 79.

influenced by this disregard for, and even contempt of, the body. As a result, Christians placed much of the blame for their sinfulness on the fact of human embodiment, insisted that even sexual intercourse between a husband and wife is tinged with sinful lust, and engaged in ruthless asceticism, denying themselves the good physical gifts of God, such as food, drink, and sleep. Understanding that Platonic context and its influence on the early church's theology helps Christians today reformulate the doctrine of humanity so as to avoid the negative impact of that philosophy.[21] As Timothy George noted, "We must not simply repeat the classical doctrines of the faith with precision and clarity; we must also reflect upon these doctrines in such a way that we can expound them as our own. In this sense historical theology has both a normative and a descriptive role to play."[22]

A sixth benefit of historical theology is that it encourages the church *to focus on the essentials*, that is, to major on those areas that have been emphasized repeatedly throughout the history of the church. For good reason, the church has concentrated much study of Scripture and expended significant theological effort developing doctrines such as the Trinity, the person and work of Jesus Christ, human dignity and depravity, the inspiration and inerrancy of Scripture, salvation, and other cardinal beliefs. These doctrines are the foundation of the gospel, the core of the Christian faith and worldview, and constitute the repeated themes of divine revelation. Fascination with "new truth" and an inordinate attachment to minor beliefs has produced churches that are not centered, not unified, and not missional — "infants, tossed back and forth by the waves, and blown here and there by every wind of teaching and by the cunning and craftiness of men in their deceitful scheming" (Eph. 4:14). Recognizing and committing themselves to what the church has traditionally emphasized spares churches today from such disasters and helps them become gospel-focused communities.[23]

A seventh benefit of historical theology is that it gives the church *hope by providing assurance that Jesus is fulfilling his promise to his people*. One of the most important biblical passages throughout the history of the church has been Matthew 16:13–20. Peter, by means of divine revelation, grasped the identity of his friend Jesus and confessed, "You are the Christ, the Son of the living God." At this confession, Jesus promised, "On this rock I will build my church, and the gates of Hades will not overcome it." Throughout its nearly two-thousand-year pilgrimage, the church has advanced through periods of great faithfulness, obedience, dedication, and missional endeavors, and it has persevered through other periods of carnality, political posturing, disengagement, and heresy. If Luther's sinner-saint label is true of individual Christians, it is equally true of the church

---

21. They may also note that some leaders in the early church acknowledged this corrupting influence and sought to avoid it, emphasizing the goodness of the material creation, recognizing that the embodiment of the Son of God in the incarnation did not result in him being sinful, and embracing the hope of the future resurrection of the body. For further discussion, see chap. 15. For a contemporary example of the reformulation of the doctrine of humanity, with an emphasis on holistic dualism or dualistic holism, see John Cooper, *Body, Soul and Life Everlasting: Biblical Anthropology and the Monism-Dualism Debate* (Grand Rapids: Eerdmans; Leicester: Apollos, 1989, 2000).

22. Timothy George, "Dogma Beyond Anathema," 693. He added, "It is always proper and necessary to rethink and reformulate the classic expressions of the faith; but we must do so in a way that does not do violence to the intention of those expressions, insofar as they faithfully reflect the primary witness of Scripture itself." Ibid., 700.

23. A corollary of this emphasis on the major doctrines is that "there must be, in thoughtful minds, different degrees, different depths of conviction: of some things we can be more sure than others." John Stoughton, *An Introduction to Historical Theology* (London: Religious Tract Society, n.d.), 9.

itself. Even today, as churches find themselves in the midst of perhaps the most tumultuous period of their history—external attacks by a new and virulent form of atheism, internal confusion over the gospel and worship, cultural doubts about the relevancy of the Christian faith, postmodern questioning of truth and authority, and rampant revisioning of many cardinal doctrines—they experience both victory and defeat. Historical theology provides hope by reminding them that God for Christ's sake has always been faithful to his promise to build his church.[24] Certainly the development of doctrine is a thoroughly human process, carried out by the church. But such development has a divine origin—it is the church *of Jesus Christ,* and he is at work to build his church.[25]

Finally, as beneficiaries of the heritage of doctrinal development sovereignly overseen by Jesus Christ, the church of today is privileged *to enjoy a sense of belonging to the church of the past.* In words reflective of a more literary past, John Stoughton affirmed concerning historical theology: "It attaches us to former generations, and inspires us with satisfaction and joy to find, that in the substance of evangelical faith and sentiment we are one with the Church of all ages. To feel this is a prelibation [celebratory foretaste] of heaven, where our present-time relations will cease, ancestry and posterity will become contemporaneous, the faith of one will confirm the faith of another, and the joy of all will be the joy of each."[26] The church today is heir to a great legacy, a heritage that can provide a sense of rootedness, depth, certainty, and hope.[27]

Given all of these benefits, the question arises of how one studies historical theology.[28] Two basic approaches are commonly found: synchronic and diachronic. The *synchronic approach* engages in the study of the theology of a certain time period, a particular theologian, a specific theological school or tradition, and the like. Examples of this approach include the study of the doctrine of the Trinity in the third and fourth centuries, the development of Christology in the fourth and fifth centuries, the theology of John Calvin, and neoorthodox theologies of the Word of God. The *diachronic approach* engages in the study of the development of thought on a given doctrine throughout the periods of the church's history. Examples of

---

24. R. P. C. Hanson chastised detractors of church history, who "assume that it can throw no light on what the Christian faith is about, on the activity and character of God as seen in Christianity, or by Christians." R. P. C. Hanson, "Introduction to Volume 2," in *The Pelican Guide to Modern Theology,* vol. 2: *Historical Theology,* ed. Jean Danielou, A. H. Couratin, and John Kent (Baltimore: Penguin, 1969), 10.

25. Stoughton explained this development as "the growth of a human process, though starting from a Divine origin, and continued under Divine culture." Stoughton, *Introduction to Historical Theology,* 8.

26. Ibid., 13.

27. As Muller noted, this benefit for the church becomes a benefit for the individual Christian: "The study of the history of the church and its teachings is not only an objective, external discipline, it is also a subjective, internal exercise by which and through which the life and mind of the church becomes an integral part of the life and mind of the individual Christian." Richard A. Muller, *The Study of Theology: From Biblical Interpretation to Contemporary Formulation,* Foundations of

Contemporary Interpretation, vol. 7 (Grand Rapids: Zondervan, 1991), 107.

28. Clearly, historical theology "must engage with literary sources just like other" historical disciplines. "Literary criticism is needed to establish authorship or provenance of books. Textual criticism must restore the text where copying errors have crept in. Once the historian has a good text and knows where it comes from, he can begin interpretation. Often that means translating from an ancient into a modern language to make it accessible to other theologians. But he must also explain the context, the thought-world of the writer being expounded, and especially the sources he used and the influence he had on others." Stuart G. Hall, "Theological History and Historical Theology," in *The Threshold of Theology,* ed. Paul Davis (Basingstoke, UK: Marshall Pickering, 1988), 107–8. Thus, numerous parallels are found between establishing and interpreting biblical texts and establishing and interpreting historical texts. As an introductory work on historical theology, this book does not delve into these issues.

this approach include the study of the doctrines of Scripture and sin as developed in the early church, the Middle Ages, the Reformation and post-Reformation period, and the modern period. As noted in the preface, this book follows the latter, diachronic approach.

Within this approach, two perspectives are commonly adopted. One is the relativist perspective; the other, the essentialist. According to the first, the development of doctrine over the course of the centuries exhibits such an immense diversity that it is not possible to identify a core, or essential center, of the Christian faith. The relativist perspective draws attention to "diversity, disagreement, discontinuity, loose ends, and wrong turnings" as the church developed its beliefs.[29] In its extreme form, "unrestrained relativism ... claims that no manifestation of Christianity enjoys any logical or theological priority over any other. Therefore the smallest sect has as much doctrinal authority as the longest-lived or [most] widely dispersed world church. As such, since Christianities are so different, they are all equally right and equally wrong."[30] Such relativism naturally leads to alarm and "the despair of finding no certainty, nothing fixed to believe."[31] This book does not accept the relativist perspective.

The second perspective holds that an essential Christian theology does exist. In its extreme form, "this view argues that, in truth, only one 'correct' Christianity has been handed down, and that all others are erroneous and deviant."[32] This radical position usually sustains itself by ignoring historical theology and its demonstration that doctrines have indeed developed over time. Alternatively, it considers every development of church tradition between the closing of the New Testament and the appearance of the group championing this extreme view as being defective. Variations of this essentialist perspective moderate this unsustainable extreme position. The viewpoint of this book is a moderate essentialist perspective: An essential center, a core, of Christian doctrine, does indeed exist, but it does not manifest itself in any one particular church or theological movement, for several reasons: (1) No pure church exists. This fact means that no tradition can legitimately claim complete doctrinal accuracy. (2) Scripture itself emphasizes the incompleteness of theological knowledge in this church age. As Paul affirms, "Now we see but a poor reflection as in a mirror; then we shall see face to face. Now I know in part; then I shall know fully, even as I am fully known" (1 Cor. 13:12). Complete theological knowledge awaits the return of Jesus Christ and thus cannot be attained in this age. (3) All doctrinal formulation "is deeply involved with the cultural background and the philosophical assumptions of the period during which it is taking place."[33] To the extent that this cultural context and philosophical framework cloud the proper interpretation of Scripture and theological understanding, such formulation diverges from the truth.[34] These and other factors work against achieving complete doctrinal purity,

---

29. Euan Cameron, *Interpreting Christian History: The Challenge of the Churches' Past* (Malden, Mass.: Blackwell, 2005), x.

30. Ibid., 6.

31. Ibid., x.

32. Ibid., 5–6.

33. Hanson, "Introduction to Volume 2," 14.

34. Indeed, historical theology "dispels the illusion that theologians of any school have drawn their opinions, entirely and exclusively, from the fountain of God. It throws light on the genesis of opinion. And we are brought to see how metaphysics and logic, tradition and Church authority, education, circumstances, and intellectual idiosyncrasy, have had to do with forming theological thought." Stoughton, *Introduction to Historical Theology*, 6.

and they counter any claim to possess it during the church's earthly pilgrimage. This is the negative side.

A positive side also exists. In addition to his work of disclosing and inscripturating divine revelation, the Holy Spirit illuminates Scripture, the Word of God (1 Cor. 2:6–16). Accordingly, Christians can prayerfully engage in careful exegesis in reliance on the Spirit to bring more proper understanding of the Bible. Moreover, as noted above, Jesus Christ has promised to build his church (Matt. 16:13–20), so churches can take heart that he is at work to bring about greater theological correctness. Indeed, he has equipped the church with all the resources it needs to move toward greater and greater doctrinal purity. Specifically, Christ has endowed the church with gifted leaders "to prepare God's people for works of service, so that the body of Christ may be built up until we all reach unity in the faith and in the knowledge of the Son of God and become mature, attaining to the whole measure of the fullness of Christ. Then we will no longer be infants, tossed back and forth by the waves, and blown here and there by every wind of teaching and by the cunning and craftiness of men in their deceitful scheming" (Eph. 4:12–14).[35] As church leaders teach and equip their members, and as everyone engages in "speaking the truth in love" (Eph. 4:15; clearly communicating sound doctrine so as to build up rather than tear down), the church will advance in theological purity. These and other reasons provide hope, not only that an essential core of Christian doctrine exists, but also that churches can move progressively closer to recognizing and affirming this sound doctrine. Historical theology aids in this effort as well, as it "shows how the church and its word, moving across the centuries and continents, have come from there to here with an ongoing continuity in spite of every discontinuity."[36] This ongoing continuity is the core, or essential center, of the Christian faith. It is given expression by the church in different shapes and forms throughout the ages, and though each expression is culturally and historically conditioned, it can nevertheless be an adequate expression of the truth for the church during its earthly pilgrimage.[37]

---

35. As this passage implies, some doctrinal formulations are incorrect and must be rejected. Cameron, repudiating the relativist perspective, noted that "if there is an essential Christianity ... there must necessarily be forms that are *so* deviant that they do not represent a valid interpretation of Christian teaching and belief, in effect 'right' and 'wrong' ways to adapt Christianity to its conditions.... A cultural adaptation which spins on too eccentric an orbit may come to appear ... as not just an adaptation but a deviation, perversion, or distortion of the Christian message. Even within what could broadly be called the Christian mainstream ... at various times beliefs and practices have arisen which *all* subsequent churches have declared to be misapprehensions, exaggerations, or distortions of what Christianity ought to mean." Cameron, *Interpreting Christian History*, 236–37. Because of, and in response to, these aberrations, "there are times in the life of the church when it is necessary to say, 'Be accursed, be delivered up to the wrath of God and destroyed,' for that is what anathema means in the original Pauline sense: 'If anyone preaches another gos-

pel, let him [be] anathema!' [Gal. 1:8, 9].... Karl Barth was surely right when he said, 'If we do not have the confidence of *damnamus* [we anathametize], we ought to omit *credimus* [we believe], and go back to doing theology as usual.'" George, "Dogma beyond Anathema," 704. His citation of Barth is from *CD*, I/1, 630.

36. Geoffrey W. Bromiley, *Historical Theology: An Introduction* (Edinburgh: T & T Clark, 1978), xxvi.

37. To insist on some level of absolute perfection for doctrinal expression in this church age is to chase after a phantom, and such perfection is not necessary—nor required by God. He himself, in his communication to human beings, accommodated his revelation so that it would be intelligible to us. In so doing, he did not invent some perfect heavenly language but employed instead common human languages—Hebrew, Aramaic, and Greek. When the Son of God taught his disciples and the crowds as the incarnate God-man, he used figures of speech and illustrations drawn from everyday life. If such communication is adequate for divine revelation, it is

Although a discipline in itself, historical theology is also related to several other important biblical and theological disciplines, namely, exegetical theology, biblical theology, systematic theology, and practical theology. The following diagram and discussion represent and explain the integration of these disciplines:[38]

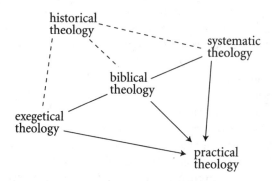

Let the solid line connecting exegetical, biblical, and systematic theology represent the line of authority, because each of these disciplines works directly with Scripture, the inspired Word of God. Exegetical theology seeks to determine the meaning of biblical texts. Biblical theology describes the progressive revelation found in Scripture by examining the theology of its various groupings (e.g., the theology of the Pentateuch and the theology of the Synoptic Gospels). It also traces the many themes in these biblical groupings and notes their development over time. Systematic theology expresses what Christians and churches are to believe, do, and be today in accordance with all the teaching of Scripture. Having identified the key passages concerning the worship of God, for example, exegetical theology unpacks the meaning of those passages, biblical theology notes the progressive development in the ways God ordered his people to worship (e.g., building altars, worshiping in the tabernacle and the temple, worshiping in spirit and truth), and systematic theology prescribes worship as celebrating the covenant relationship that Christians enjoy with God and that is made possible through the Son of God, Jesus Christ, and directed by the Spirit of God according to the Word of God. Work in

certainly adequate for the church's theological formulation. Furthermore, as Muller affirmed in regard to the inescapable historical and cultural conditioning of all expressions of Christian doctrine (a reason often given for rejecting them), "every statement that we make is conditioned by the social, cultural, political, and religious context out of which we have come and in which we make the statement—but this fundamental fact of our intellectual and spiritual life does not lead us to cease and desist from making statements.... What is more, it is hardly the case that the cultural and historical conditionedness of a statement places a barrier in the way of understanding. Quite to the contrary, it is the historical and cultural location of a particular statement or doctrine or

theory that makes it intelligible to a particular culture at a particular time in history. Normative theological statements must be historically and culturally conditioned—indeed, the way in which they belong to and reflect the culture and the time to which they speak accounts for their normative status." Muller, "Role of Church History," 91–92.

38. The genesis of the following model is two articles by D. A. Carson: "The Role of Exegesis in Systematic Theology," in Woodbridge and McComiskey, *Doing Theology in Today's World*, 39–76; and "Unity and Diversity in the New Testament: The Possibility of Systematic Theology," in *Scripture and Truth*, ed. D. A. Carson and John D. Woodbridge (Grand Rapids: Zondervan, 1983), 65–95.

exegetical, biblical, and systematic theology, all of which deal directly with Scripture (thus, placed on the solid line), constitutes the important interpretive and organizational process in constructing theology.

The important role that historical theology (represented by the dashed lines) plays in this interpretive and organizing process is to inform each of the three disciplines with wisdom from the past. Because this discipline does not deal with Scripture directly, I have placed it behind the line of authority, not on it. This placement reflects what Packer noted earlier: Historical theology is ministerial, not magisterial. It does not possess the authority to determine doctrine and practice like the other disciplines, but it still has a very important role to play as an aid to the other three. For example, historical theology helps exegetical theology by providing interpretive insights for the determination of the meaning of Jesus' affirmation that "[God's] worshipers must worship in spirit and in truth" (John 4:24). Historical theology helps biblical theology by noting various approaches to the relationship between the worship of God in the tabernacle and temple (under the old covenant) and the worship of God in the church (under the new covenant). Historical theology helps systematic theology by offering different formulations of the theology of worship and how the church of the past actually engaged in services of worship. Contemporary Christians, then, are aided by historical theology as they interpret Scripture, do biblical theology, and construct their systematic theology.[39]

Ultimately, this entire biblical and theological process is oriented toward practical theology (represented by the arrowed lines coming out toward the readers).[40] Practical theology consists of the communication of the Word of God to churches today through preaching, teaching, discipling, mentoring, counseling, and so forth. Accordingly, what is heard from pulpits, discussed in small group Bible studies, offered in counseling sessions, and the like reflects the wisdom of the church of the past—historical theology.

Thankfully, the last several decades have witnessed a growing interest in historical theology on the part of many in the church.[41] Wonderful new tools now make the biblical

---

39. Muller cautioned about two possible errors in constructing a systematic theology: "When systematic theology in the larger sense—the contemporary discipline of theological statement—fails to take seriously the foundational materials provided by biblical and historical study, it not only brings down on itself the charge of methodological ineptitude and of failure to recognize its own historical conditionedness, it also gives itself over to increasingly arbitrary and rootless speculations. In other words, systematic theology cannot either simply repeat the doctrinal, philosophical, and phenomenological results of previous generations or argue its own case, whether doctrinally, philosophically, or phenomenologically, in the present, without reference to the foundational disciplines. On the other hand, systematic theology cannot afford to be merely the repetition of the results of biblical theology and the history of doctrine. A systematic theology that duplicates the materials of either one of these essentially historical disciplines will fail to address the present and will appear like a relic of the past taken from a museum." Muller, *Study of Theology*, 162.

40. Working with a slightly different model, Schubert Ogden explained, "The critical interpretation of the past provided by historical theology is never simply an end in itself, but also always the means, even if the indispensable means, to the ulterior end of critical validation, which systematic theology and practical theology are constituted to attain. In this sense, doing historical theology, from its end, anticipates the work of its sister disciplines, even as they, for their part, necessarily presuppose its work." Schubert M. Ogden, "Prolegomena to Historical Theology," in Engel and Wyman, *Revisioning the Past*, 27.

41. D. H. Williams has been a major contributor to this growing interest. His book *Retrieving the Tradition and Renewing Evangelicalism* targeted evangelicals, especially those in the Free Church or "believers' church," the nonmagisterial wing of the Reformation ("magisterial" refers to those churches—Lutheran, Reformed, Anglican—that accepted the centuries old church-state situation). "Free" refers to the conviction that true churches must be liberated from state control and

and theological insights of the church of the past available not only to scholars, but also to pastors, Sunday school teachers, and laypeople.[42] This book is offered in the hope of continuing this trend of making historical theology accessible to believers and their churches.

---

influence. Examples abound: Mennonites, Baptists, Congregationalists, Evangelical Free churches, Methodists, and Holiness and Restorationist churches (Nazarene, Disciples of Christ/Christian Church, Brethren, Pentecostal, Bible churches). He has followed up that book with work as editor of an important series: Evangelical Ressourcement: Ancient Sources for the Church's Future (Grand Rapids: Baker Academic). He has two books in that series: *Evangelicals and Tra-* *dition: The Formative Influence of the Early Church* (2005) and *Tradition, Scripture, and Interpretation: A Sourcebook of the Ancient Church* (2006).

42. E.g., Thomas Oden is the general editor of an important series that makes the early church's interpretation of all the books of the Bible (and the Apocrypha) available: *The Ancient Christian Commentary on Scripture*, 29 vols. (Downers Grove, Ill.: InterVarsity, 2000–10).

Part 1

THE DOCTRINE OF THE WORD OF GOD

Chapter 2

THE CANON OF SCRIPTURE

How has the church come to believe what belongs in the Bible and what does not belong?

STATEMENT OF BELIEF

The church has historically believed that a specific set of writings — called the *canon of Scripture* — composes the Old and New Testaments. This list of divinely inspired and authoritative narratives, prophecies, gospels, letters, and other writings that make up the Word of God developed in the early church. The canon of the Protestant church differs from that of the Roman Catholic Church. The Protestant canon is composed of sixty-six books, while the Catholic canon is more extensive. It includes the *Apocrypha*, extra books in the Old Testament (e.g., Tobit, Judith), and additions to certain Old Testament writings as found in the Protestant Bible (e.g., additions to Esther, Bell and the Dragon). Evangelical churches follow the Protestant canon.[1]

THE CANON IN THE EARLY CHURCH

From its beginning on the day of Pentecost, the church considered the Hebrew Bible to be the Word of God (2 Tim. 3:16–17; 2 Peter 1:19–21). The writings that composed the Jewish Scriptures — now called the Old Testament — were fixed and had been so for several centuries prior to the coming of Jesus Christ. The eminent Jewish historian Josephus (AD 37–100) noted: "From Artaxerxes [464–423 BC] to our own time the complete history has been written, but has not been deemed worthy of equal credit with the earlier records, because of the failure of the exact succession of the prophets."[2] Thus, although other writings (e.g., 1 and 2 Maccabees, a history of the Jews in the second century before Christ) were in circulation among the Jewish people at the time of the early church, none of these had been inserted into the canon of the Hebrew Bible and recognized as part

---

1. My thanks to Lenny Cheng for his help with this chapter.

2. Josephus, *Against Apion*, 1.41. A similar sentiment is expressed in rabbinical literature: "After the latter prophets Haggai, Zechariah, and Malachi had died, the Holy Spirit departed from Israel, but they still availed themselves of the *bath qol* (or *bath kol*, a voice from heaven)." Babylonian Talmud, *Yomah* 9b, repeated in *Sotah* 48b, *Sanhedrin* 11a, and Midrash *Rabbah* on Song of Songs, 8.9.3.

of the authoritative Word of God. Indeed, the canon of the Jewish Scriptures had come to a close at the time of the writing of Ezra, Nehemiah, and Esther (435 BC). No other writings had been—nor could have been—added to the Hebrew Bible in the intervening period, because divine inspiration of the prophets had ceased.

What did the Hebrew Bible look like? Josephus noted twenty-two divinely inspired books in the Hebrew canon: the five books of Moses, thirteen prophetic books, and four books containing hymns and precepts.[3] Later Jewish reckonings of the Hebrew Bible typically listed twenty-four books distributed in three divisions: the Law, the Prophets, and the Writings.[4]

The Hebrew Canon (according to the Talmud)

The Law	The Prophets	The Writings
Genesis	Joshua	Ruth
Exodus	Judges	Psalms
Leviticus	Samuel	Job
Numbers	Kings	Proverbs
Deuteronomy	Jeremiah	Ecclesiastes
	Ezekiel	Song of Songs
	Isaiah	Lamentations
	Twelve Minor Prophets	Daniel
		Esther
		Ezra–Nehemiah
		Chronicles

This Hebrew Bible, with its fixed canon, was the Bible of the early church.[5] Although it contained obvious differences in order and grouping from the Old Testament with which

---

3. Josephus, *Against Apion*, 1.37. The books of Moses were the traditional Pentateuch. The prophetic books were Joshua, Judges–Ruth, Samuel, Kings, Isaiah, Jeremiah–Lamentations, Ezekiel, the Minor Prophets (Hosea, Joel, Amos, Obadiah, Jonah, Micah, Nahum, Habakkuk, Zephaniah, Haggai, Zechariah, and Malachi), Job, Daniel, Ezra–Nehemiah, Chronicles, and Esther. The last category consisted of Psalms, Proverbs, Ecclesiastes, and Song of Songs. Note that the books of Samuel, Kings, and Chronicles, while appearing as two books in our Old Testament, were considered one book each in the Hebrew canon of Josephus. Also, Judges and Ruth, Jeremiah and Lamentations, and Ezra and Nehemiah, while separated in our Old Testament, were joined together and considered one book in this ordering.

4. *Baba Bathra* 14b–15a. The Minor Prophets are the same as in Josephus. Samuel, Kings, and Chronicles are not divided but considered one book each. Ezra and Nehemiah are joined

together and considered one book. The difference between this rendering of the canon and that of Josephus, besides the change in the ordering of the books, is the separation of Ruth from Judges and Jeremiah from Lamentations. This adds two more books to the total, raising Josephus's twenty-two-book canon to a twenty-four-book canon.

5. The Council of Jamnia, a meeting of rabbinic scholars about AD 90, was once thought to be the focal point for deciding the canon of Hebrew Scripture. Current thought views the council as discussing the inspiration of several of the books in the canon, but not as deciding which books to include or exclude from the canon. The closure of the Hebrew canon had been set for quite some time prior to Jamnia. Jack P. Lewis, "What Do We Mean by Jabneh?" *JBR* 32 (1964): 125–32; Robert C. Newman, "The Council of Jamnia and the Old Testament Canon," *WTJ* 38 (1976): 319–49.

today's church is familiar, all of the books that we consider to be canonical were present and together composed the Word of God for the Jewish people — and the early church.

Following the death, resurrection, and ascension of Jesus Christ, together with the outpouring of the Holy Spirit on the day of Pentecost to initiate the church, a new phase of revelation began. While relying on the authority of the divinely inspired Hebrew Scriptures, the church was conscious of being the recipient of new truth concerning the person and work of Jesus Christ and the Christian mission in the world.

The ultimate source of this truth was God himself. Justin Martyr resolutely affirmed, "For I choose to follow not men or men's doctrines, but God and the doctrines [delivered] by him."[6] God the Father passed on this truth to his Son; thus, he should be followed as "the only true and steadfast Teacher, the Word of God, our Lord Jesus Christ."[7] Jesus Christ, in turn, entrusted this truth to certain faithful people, custodians and communicators of the revelation. Chief among these were the apostles, the eyewitnesses of Christ and his ministry and the architects of the church itself. The revelation entrusted to these apostles could not be separated, however, from the earlier revelation given through the prophets. The Spirit of Christ had been active within the prophets as they foretold his coming, and that same Spirit was active in the apostles to give inspired understanding of Christ's coming. Thus, Polycarp urged obedience to Jesus Christ, "just as he himself has commanded us, as did the apostles who preached the gospel to us, and the prophets, who announced in advance the coming of our Lord."[8]

Not everyone agreed with this harmony, however. Beginning in the second century, heretics emphasized an apparent conflict between the prophets and the new Christian truth. To counter this, the apologists (Christian writers who defended the faith) underscored the unity of the prophetic and apostolic revelation. Tertullian, speaking of the church, noted: "The law and the prophets she unites in one volume with the writings of the evangelists and apostles; from which she drinks in [receives] her faith."[9] Although the Hebrew Scriptures prophesied of the coming of Christ and the new revelation to the church explained that coming after the fact, this difference in perspectives did not destroy the unity of the truth. Irenaeus noted: "I have pointed out the truth, and shown the preaching of the church, which the prophets proclaimed but which Christ brought to perfection, and the apostles have handed down. From which the church, receiving [these truths], and throughout all the world alone preserving them in their integrity, has transmitted them to her sons."[10] The old and new revelations composed a unity. Thus, Tertullian accused Marcion, a leading heretic, of being the "author of the breach of peace between the gospel and the law," whereas the church found no distinction between the predictions of the prophets and the declarations of the Lord.[11]

Our discussion may give the wrong impression that the early church possessed a written Bible readily available to all its members (much like each of us taking our own copy of

---

6. Justin Martyr, *Dialogue with Trypho, a Jew*, 80.3, in *ANF*, 1:239.

7. Irenaeus, *Against Heresies*, 5.preface, in *ANF*, 1:526.

8. Polycarp, *Letter to the Philippians*, 6.3, in Holmes, 213; *ANF*, 1:34.

9. Tertullian, *Prescription against Heretics*, 36, in *ANF*, 3:260.

10. Irenaeus, *Against Heresies*, 5.preface, in *ANF*, 1:526.

11. Tertullian, *Against Marcion*, 1.19; 4.39, in *ANF*, 3:285, 416.

the Bible to church and Bible study). This, however, was not the case. Indeed, for the first few decades of its existence, the church had only oral stories that it could pass on. Even when the last writings of what was to become the New Testament were being penned, the church was still largely dependent on unwritten tradition, which continued for the first several centuries of the church.

These written records and unwritten tradition were seen as two parts of a unified whole, and the early church appealed to both to express its doctrine and to fight heresy. "The only true and life-giving faith, which the church has received from the apostles and imparted to her sons,"[12] was referred to as "the glorious and holy rule of our tradition," "the rule of faith," and "the rule (or canon) of truth."[13] This tradition was essentially fixed and agreed upon by all the churches,[14] with its content being a succinct statement of essential Christian doctrine.[15] Whatever was believed in the church had to conform to this rule of faith. Indeed, true doctrine could be distinguished from false by tracing its origin to "the tradition of the apostles."[16] Moreover, this rule of faith was public knowledge, accessible to everyone. Thus, it stood in contrast to certain heresies that claimed a "secret knowledge" of the truths of the Christian faith. This hidden wisdom was reserved for the elite of these erring movements and often went against biblical teaching. Not so for apostolic tradition: It was public knowledge in conformity with Scripture.

The recipients and transmitters of this tradition were, in particular, the successors of the apostles, the bishops who led the churches. They were the guarantee that what was believed and practiced by the churches was in accord with this apostolic rule of faith. These bishops were not a source of new revelation that stood alongside of written Scripture. They were, instead, faithful transmitters of the truth received from the apostles — and ultimately from God himself. Tertullian held that "all doctrine which agrees with the apostolic churches — those molds and original sources of the faith — must be reckoned for truth, as undoubtedly containing that which the churches received from the apostles, the apostles from Christ, and Christ from God."[17]

Eventually, some of this apostolic tradition was written down. In this way "the gospel has come down to us, which [the apostles] did at one time proclaim in public, and, at a later period, by the will of God, handed down to us in the Scriptures, to be the ground and pillar of our faith."[18] As noted earlier, the apostolic tradition and the written apostolic records were a unified whole in the early church; the tension between these two that we will witness later was not present. This was due to the harmony that existed between them: Tradition was a summary of biblical truth, and when heretics twisted Scripture, the apologists would turn to the tradition to underscore how Scripture was and should be understood in the church. This unity of unwritten and written truth — together with the harmony between Hebrew Scripture and apostolic revelation — was

12. Irenaeus, *Against Heresies*, 3.preface, in *ANF*, 1:414.

13. Clement of Rome, *Letter of the Romans to the Corinthians*, 7.2, in Holmes, 37; *ANF*, 1:7; Tertullian, *Prescription against Heretics*, 12, in *ANF*, 3:249; Irenaeus, *Against Heresies* 1.22.2, in *ANF*, 1:347. Irenaeus also calls it "the sure tradition from the apostles." *Against Heresies* 5.20.1, in *ANF*, 1:548.

14. Irenaeus, *Against Heresies*, 1.10.2, in *ANF*, 1:331.

15. Tertullian, *Prescription against Heretics*, 13, in *ANF*, 3:249; cf. *Against Praxeas*, 2, in *ANF*, 3:598–99. Irenaeus, *Against Heresies*, 1.10.1, in *ANF*, 1:330.

16. Tertullian, *Prescription against Heretics*, 21, in *ANF*, 3:252.

17. Ibid.; cf. 37, in *ANF*, 3:252, 261.

18. Irenaeus, *Against Heresies*, 3.1.1, in *ANF*, 1:414.

keenly expressed by Irenaeus in his appeal to "the preaching of the apostles, the authoritative teaching of the Lord, the announcements of the prophets, the dictated utterances [i.e., written records] of the apostles, and the administration of the law."[19] Together, Scripture and tradition provided the foundation of truth for the early church. Heretics, those outside of the church, were criticized because they "consent neither to Scripture nor to tradition."[20]

To the collection of authoritative Hebrew Scripture were eventually added some additional writings in the form of gospels, a historical account, letters, and an apocalypse (a revelation of future events). Some of these writings themselves pointed to an expansion of the canon of Scripture. For example, Peter spoke of the letters of the apostle Paul in the context of "the other Scriptures" (2 Peter 3:14–16), and Paul himself connected a saying of Jesus ("The laborer is worthy of his wages") with Deuteronomy 25:4, referring to both as "Scripture" (1 Tim. 5:18).[21]

The earliest Christian writings outside of our New Testament continued this practice of elevating the words of Jesus and the writings of the apostles, recognizing in them the authority of divine revelation. One example was a reference by Polycarp to a portion of Paul's letter to the Ephesians (4:26) as "Scripture."[22] Another came from an anonymous work that noted the complementary authority of "the Books" (the Old Testament) and "the Apostles."[23] Moreover, the *Letter of Barnabas* quoted Jesus' words ("Many are invited, but few are chosen"; Matt. 22:14) with the introductory formula "it is written," an expression that was reserved for citations from Old Testament Scripture.[24]

A crucial question arose: Which of the writings from the early church should be included in this expanding canon—consisting of both the Hebrew Bible (our Old Testament) and the New Testament? (Irenaeus was the first to call the two parts of this collection the Old and New Testaments.)[25] The letters of Paul, written by an apostle clearly invested with divine authority, were easily recognized as belonging to canonical Scripture. But what about the anonymous letter to the Hebrews? Why should Mark and Luke be placed alongside the gospels written by the apostles Matthew and John? And what about the *Letter of Barnabas* and the *Shepherd of Hermas*, two very early writings that enjoyed widespread circulation in the early church?

This issue of the canon of Scripture became particularly critical when false teachers and prophets appeared. Marcion, for example, was a leader of a heretical movement whose views were obviously wrong. His "canon" of Scripture consisted of "the Gospel and the Apostle" (a mutilated version of the gospel of Luke and ten letters of Paul). Marcion rejected the entire Old Testament and all parts of the growing New Testament that

---

19. Ibid., 2.35.4, in *ANF*, 1:413.

20. Ibid., 3.2.2, in *ANF*, 1:415.

21. Whether Paul quoted Luke 10:7 or an oral teaching of Jesus Christ is disputed.

22. Polycarp, *Letter to the Philippians*, 12.1, in Holmes, 219; *ANF*, 1:35.

23. *2 Clement*, 14.2. The writing was misnamed Clement's *Second Letter to the Corinthians*, in Holmes, 121; *ANF*, 10:255.

24. *Letter of Barnabas*, 4.14, in Holmes, 283; *ANF*, 1:139.

25. Irenaeus, *Against Heresies*, 4.9.1, in *ANF*, 1:472. Irenaeus, referring to Matthew 13:52, explained: "Now without contradiction the Lord means by those things which are brought forth from the treasure new and old, the two covenants; the old, that giving of the law which took place formerly; and he points out as the new that manner of life required by the gospel.... But one and the same householder produced both covenants, the Word of God, our Lord Jesus Christ."

reflected favorably upon the Old.[26] The early church was rightly concerned by Marcion's views and recognized that his restricted canon of Scripture fostered his heretical theology. His "canon" was wrong—obviously. But what writings *should be included* in the true canon?

The church turned to defining the canon of Scripture. Two key criteria emerged to determine which writings to include in the canon: (1) *apostolicity*: Does this writing have an apostle for its author (e.g., Paul's letters, the gospels of Matthew and John)? If not, is an apostle associated with this writing (e.g., Mark's gospel records the account of the apostle Peter)? (2) *antiquity*: Has the church historically recognized the voice of God speaking to his people in this writing? Although equipped with these criteria, the church did not set out to *determine* the canon of Scripture as much as to *recognize* and *affirm* those authoritative, inspired writings that God intended for inclusion in his Word.

Several attempts at this have come down to us. The following lists set forth the views of the biblical canon by key individuals of the early church. Some are formal lists; others are compiled by an analysis of the individual's writings. One should keep in mind that a particular list (e.g., Eusebius's canon) may reflect its author's personal convictions regarding the canon, and these may be different from the consensus of the church at the time. (Writings that are not in our New Testament are in italics.)

The first list dates to about AD 170. The *Muratorian Canon* consisted of the following:

The Muratorian Canon (AD 170)

Canonical writings	Missing from this list	Rejected writings
The four Gospels	Hebrews	*Paul to the Laodiceans*
Acts of the Apostles	James	*Paul to the Alexandrians*
Thirteen letters of Paul	1 and 2 Peter	*Shepherd of Hermas*
Jude	3 John	(Other Gnostic writings)
1 and 2 John		
Revelation of John		
Wisdom of Solomon		
Revelation of Peter		

---

26. From the gospel of Luke, Marcion removed the account of Jesus' birth as well as any reference to Jesus acknowledging the Creator God to be his Father. From the Pauline corpus he removed all of the apostle's references to Old Testament prophecies of Christ's advent as well as any reference to the Creator God as the Father of Jesus. Moreover, he did not include 1 and 2 Timothy and Titus. See Irenaeus, *Against Heresies*, 1.27.2, in *ANF*, 1:352.

27. The *Muratorian Canon* is named for the Italian archae-

ologist L. A. Muratori (1672–1750), who discovered and published the document in *Antiquitates Italicae Medii Aevi*, III (Milan, 1740). The document is a fragment and begins with a concluding discussion of Mark's gospel and continues with a discussion of "the third book of the Gospel, that according to Luke." Some emendations of the corrupted text restore 1 Peter and even 2 Peter. For the complete text, see Alexander Souter, *The Text and Canon of the New Testament*, 2nd ed. (London: Duckworth, 1954), 191ff.

Because of the fragmentary nature of the *Muratorian Canon*, we cannot be absolutely certain that some or all of the "missing" writings were not indeed considered canonical.[27]

About this same time, another heretical group arose. Called Montanism after its founder, Montanus, this movement encouraged an eager anticipation of the Lord's quick return by appealing to new revelations given by the Holy Spirit. The church responded to this emphasis on revelation outside of the Bible by underscoring the closed canon of Scripture. Eusebius, in confronting this heresy, carefully avoided formulating a response that would seem to carry authority like that of Scripture—the very heresy he was attacking! He spoke of "the doctrine of the New Testament, to which it is impossible that any thing should be added or diminished, by one who has resolved to live according to the gospel."[28] Although he did not provide a list of the New Testament writings, he did confirm the church's sense that one could not add to or subtract from the closed canon of Scripture.

By the middle of the third century, Origen was using this New Testament:[29]

Origen's Canon (Mid Third Century)

Canonical writings	Disputed writings
The four Gospels	Hebrews
Acts of the Apostles	2 Peter (?)
Thirteen letters of Paul	2 and 3 John
James	
Jude (?)	
1 Peter	
2 Peter (?)	
1 John	
Jude (?)	
Revelation	

28. Eusebius, *Ecclesiastical History*, 5.16, in *Eusebius' Ecclesiastical History*, trans. Christian Frederick Cruse (Grand Rapids: Baker, 1962), 195. Eusebius seems to be quoting an apologist for church orthodoxy.

29. Several comments are called for: (1) In his *Commentary on the Gospel of John*, 19.6, Origen referred to the second chapter of James and noted that the words are from "the letter bearing (the name of) James." Some scholars have taken this to be an indication of Origen's doubt about the letter's canonicity. This view, however, is wrong. Origen referred to the letter as Scripture in *Selection on Psalms*, 30.6, and called James "the apostle" in his *Commentary on the Gospel of John*, frag. 126. (2) The placement of 2 Peter is in doubt because of conflicting evidence. On one hand, Origen quoted Peter at least six times in his writings and seemed to consider the letter to be canonical. For example, he spoke of Peter sounding aloud with the two trumpets of his letters (*Homilies on Joshua*, 7.1). On the other hand, according to a comment by Eusebius, Origen believed that "Peter, upon whom the church of Christ is built, against which the gates of hell shall not prevail, has left one epistle undisputed. Suppose, also, the second was left by him, for on this there is some doubt." Eusebius, *Ecclesiastical History*, 6.25, in Cruse, *Eusebius' Ecclesiastical History*, 246. (3) Origen seemed to consider Jude to be canonical ("filled with words of heavenly grace"; *Commentary on Matthew*, 10.17), but he acknowledged that the writing was not received as such by all the churches (ibid., 30).

In the early part of the fourth century, Eusebius divided his classification of biblical books into four categories:[30]

Eusebius's Canon (Early Fourth Century)

Accepted books	Disputed books (yet known to most)	Spurious works	Absurd works (heretical works)
The four Gospels	James	*Acts of Paul*	*Gospel of Peter*
Acts of the Apostles	2 Peter	*Shepherd of Hermas*	*Gospel of Thomas*
13 letters of Paul	2 and 3 John	*Didache*	*Gospel of Matthias*
1 John	Jude	*Letter of Barnabas*	*Acts of Andrew*
1 Peter		*Revelation of Peter*	*Acts of John*
Revelation of John (may be spurious)		*Gospel according to the Hebrews*	*Acts of others*
		Revelation of John (may be accepted)	

It should be clear that nearly all of the New Testament writings that we consider canonical were viewed similarly by the early church: the four Gospels, the Acts of the Apostles, thirteen letters of the apostle Paul, 1 Peter, 1 John, and (at least in many circles) the Revelation of John. Several writings that are now considered canonical—James, 2 Peter, 2 and 3 John, Jude, and Hebrews—were on the "fringe" of the early church's canon.

- *James.* Being certain of the author of this letter has been a difficulty: Was it James the apostle, James the half brother of Jesus, or some other James of the early church? Also, its Jewish-Christian address ("To the twelve tribes scattered among the nations [the Diaspora]") and flavor rendered it less attractive to the largely Gentile churches.
- *2 Peter.* Although it claimed to be authored by the apostle, so did several other writings (the Acts of Peter, the Revelation of Peter) that were clearly not to be placed with the canonical writings. Thus, some churches hesitated to accept it.
- *2 and 3 John.* These letters were so brief and seemingly unimportant that the church easily overlooked them; citations from these in early writings are very scarce. Determining authorship was also a problem with these letters.

---

30. Several comments are in order: (1) Although Eusebius placed the letter of James among the "disputed books," he held that it was canonical. This placement, therefore, was due to his recognition that some churches had doubts about the letter's canonicity. (2) Regarding 2 Peter, Eusebius noted that "one of his epistles called the first is acknowledged as genuine. For this was anciently used by the ancient fathers in their writings, as an undoubted work of the apostle. But that which is called the second, we have not, indeed, understood to be embodied with the sacred books ... yet as it appeared useful to many, it was studiously read with the other Scriptures.... These, however, are those that are called Peter's epistles, of which I have understood only one epistle to be genuine, and admitted by the ancient fathers." *Ecclesiastical History,* 3.3, in Cruse, *Eusebius' Ecclesiastical History*, 83.

Both begin with the writer designating himself as "the elder." At least some in the early church took this person to be someone other than John the apostle. Attributed to some unknown "John the elder" and thus lacking apostolic authority, the two letters failed to pass a key test for inclusion in the canon.

- *Jude.* Questions about Jude's canonical status arose because of its citations from extrabiblical sources (Jude 9 quotes *The Assumption of Moses,* and Jude 14 cites *1 Enoch*).
- *Hebrews.* Inclusion or exclusion of this letter was tied to its association with the apostle Paul. Some of the churches (primarily those in the East) attributed it to Paul or at least found Pauline thoughts behind the non-Pauline style. This secured its place in the biblical canon for those churches. Other churches (primarily those in the West) disputed this Pauline authorship or association and thus excluded Hebrews from their canon.[31]

Still other writings were on the margins of the early church's canon but ultimately were not included in the New Testament. The *Letter of Barnabas,* the *Shepherd of Hermas,* the *Didache* (or the *Teaching [of the Twelve Apostles]*), and several other works appeared with some consistency in some of the lists of canonical writings. The church eventually recognized that none of these passed the tests of apostolicity and antiquity, and thus they could not be part of the canonical Scriptures composing the New Testament.

The first appearance of a list of New Testament writings that corresponds exactly with the canon as is known today was Athanasius's *Thirty-ninth (Easter) Letter* in AD 367.[32] After setting forth the list of the canonical Old Testament books, Athanasius presented this New Testament canon:[33]

---

31. Pantaenus and Clement of Alexandria considered Paul to be the author of Hebrews. According to Eusebius's *Ecclesiastical History* (6.14), Clement believed that the letter "was written by Paul, to the Hebrews, in the Hebrew tongue; but that it was carefully translated by Luke, and published among the Greeks." Apparently, Clement developed this view from Pantaenus: "But now as the blessed presbyter [i.e., Pantaenus] used to say, 'since the Lord who was the apostle of the Almighty was sent to the Hebrews, Paul by reason of his inferiority, as if sent to the Gentiles, did not subscribe himself an apostle of the Hebrews; both out of reverence for the Lord, and because he wrote of his abundance to the Hebrews, as a herald and apostle of the Gentiles.'" Cruse, *Eusebius' Ecclesiastical History,* 234. Origen nuanced this view: "But I would say that the thoughts are the apostle's but the dictation [writing style] and phraseology belong to someone who has recorded what the apostle said, and as one who noted down at his leisure what his master dictated. If, then, any church considers this epistle as coming from Paul, let it be commended for this, for neither did those ancient men [i.e., the church fathers] deliver it as such without cause. But who it was that really wrote the epistle, God only knows." *Ecclesiastical History,* 6.25, in Cruse, *Eusebius' Ecclesiastical History,* 246–47.

32. Athanasius, *Thirty-ninth Letter,* 3, in *NPNF²,* 4:551–52. As bishop of Alexandria, Egypt, Athanasius had the responsibility to determine the date of Easter each year. To communicate his decision, Athanasius wrote letters to the churches. It was in his Easter letter of AD 367 that he undertook the task of spelling out the canon of Scripture. His introduction underscored the seriousness of his task: "In proceeding to make mention of these things, I shall adopt, to commend my undertaking, the pattern of Luke the Evangelist, saying on my own account: 'Forasmuch as some have taken in hand,' to reduce into order for themselves the books termed apocryphal, and to mix them up with the divinely inspired Scriptures, concerning which we have been fully persuaded, as they who from the beginning were eyewitnesses and ministers of the Word, delivered to the fathers; it seemed good to me also, having been urged thereto by true brothers, and having learned from the beginning, to set before you the books included in the canon, and handed down, and accredited as divine."

33. Ibid., 5, 7, in *NPNF²,* 4:552.

Athanasius's Canon (367)

Canonical writings	Canonical writings (cont.)	Noncanonical writings
Four Gospels	Fourteen letters of Paul	Wisdom of Solomon
Matthew	Romans	Wisdom of Sirach
Mark	1 and 2 Corinthians	Esther
Luke	Galatians	Judith
John	Ephesians	Tobit
	Philippians	Didache
Acts of the Apostles	Colossians	Shepherd of Hermas
	1 and 2 Thessalonians	
Seven general letters	Hebrews	
James	1 and 2 Timothy	
1 and 2 Peter	Titus	
1, 2, and 3 John	Philemon	
Jude		
	Revelation of John	

Although the seven general letters were placed before the Pauline letters, and the letter to the Hebrews was included in the Pauline writings, no other differences existed between Athanasius's canon and the New Testament as we read it today. As for the noncanonical writings, Athanasius explained that they are "not indeed included in the canon, but are appointed by the fathers to be read by those who newly join us and who wish for instruction in the word of godliness."[34] They were merely read by new believers in the church for further progress in the faith and were not part of the canon of Scripture.

Athanasius's New Testament canon was officially endorsed by the Council of Hippo in AD 393. Now Paul's writings (which do not include Hebrews) appeared before the general letters: "The canonical Scriptures ... of the New Testament: Four books of the Gospels, the Acts of the Apostles (one book), thirteen letters of Paul the apostle, one of the same to the Hebrews, two of Peter, three of John, one of James, one of Jude, the Revelation of John."[35] Two other important church meetings endorsed this same list: the Third Council of Carthage in 397 and the Fourth Council of Carthage in 419.[36] The church—both Catholic and Protestant—has recognized this canon ever since.

Although the canon of the New Testament has remained unchanged since the latter part of the fourth century, that is not the case with the Old Testament canon. Developments in the fifth century led to the insertion of other writings into the list of books

---

34. Ibid., 7, in *NPNF*[2], 4:552. Athanasius added one more category of writings: the apocryphal books. Since these were "an invention of heretics," they were to be avoided completely.
35. The Council of Hippo, canon 36; cited in James J.

Megivern, *Bible Interpretation* (Wilmington, N.C.: McGrath, 1978), 48.
36. The Third Council of Carthage, canon 47; the Fourth Council of Carthage, canon 29.

recognized by the church as divinely inspired and authoritative. Beginning in the third century before Christ, a Greek translation of the Hebrew Bible was undertaken.[37] The term *Septuagint* (seventy) became attached to this Greek translation; it is often noted by the Roman numerals LXX. This Bible became widely circulated among Greek-speaking Jews, and as the church expanded into Gentile areas, the LXX became its Old Testament.

The Septuagint (LXX)

- The first division:
    Genesis
    Exodus
    Leviticus
    Numbers
    Deuteronomy

- The second division:
    Joshua
    Judges
    Ruth
    The Book of Four Kingdoms: 1 and 2 Samuel; 1 and 2 Kings
    Paraleipomena (literally, "things left over"): 1 and 2 Chronicles
    1 Esdras: a variant account of 2 Chronicles 35:1–Nehemiah 8:12
    Esther: considerably expanded with a preface, a conclusion, three additional
        narrative sections at 3:13; 4:17; 8:12, and one additional sentence at 9:19
    Judith: a godly, beautiful, and resourceful woman defeats the arrogant
        enemies of Israel
    Tobit: an obedient son receives miraculous help from an angel

- The third division:
    Psalms: expanded to include Psalm 151
    Proverbs
    Ecclesiastes
    Song of Songs
    Job
    The Book of Wisdom (or The Wisdom of Solomon): a writing in praise
        of wisdom, and the story of Israel's earliest history and the exodus told
        from the viewpoint of Wisdom
    Ecclesiasticus (or Wisdom of Jesus Ben Sirach): a guide to wise and virtu-
        ous living, and a eulogy of great Old Testament saints

---

37. Fanciful legends became associated with the translation process: Seventy or seventy-two Jews were supposedly brought to Alexandria, Egypt, for this work. Although isolated from one another in separate cells, they produced identical translations (of the Pentateuch; later legends claimed they did the entire Hebrew Bible) in seventy-two days! One such legend is found in the *Letter of Aristeas*. Moreover, the Jewish philosopher Philo, from Alexandria, Egypt, claimed that all the translators wrote the same words "as if some unseen prompter had suggested all their language to them." Philo, *Life of Moses*, 2.7.37, in *The Works of Philo Judaeus*, trans. Charles Duke Yonge (London: H. G. Bohn, 1854, repr. 1993), bk. 25.

- The fourth division:
  The twelve Minor Prophets
  Isaiah
  Jeremiah
  Lamentations
  Baruch: a prayer, a poem about wisdom, and a prophecy of Israel's future
    hope
  Letter of Jeremiah: a letter from Jeremiah to the exiles, warning against
    idolatry
  Ezekiel
  Daniel: with The Song of the Three Children (the prayer of Azariah/Abed-
    nego in the midst of the fire, and the song of Daniel's three friends in
    the furnace) at 3:23; The History of Susanna (a victim of false accusa-
    tions is rescued by Daniel's wisdom) as chapter 13; and Bel and the
    Dragon (Daniel exposes false gods) as chapter 14

- Appendix
  1 and 2 Maccabees: a history of Jewish revolts in the second century BC

The Septuagint is more extensive than Hebrew Scripture, and its additions are called
the *apocryphal* (or hidden) *writings*, or the *Apocrypha* for short. The writers of the New
Testament were familiar with the Septuagint and indeed used it as the source for a number of their citations of the Old Testament. However, at no point did they quote from
the apocryphal writings; at best they may have alluded to them. The earliest list of "the
books of the old covenant" that the church drew up (AD 170) included all the books of
Hebrew Scripture with the exception of Esther, but it did not include any of the apocryphal writings.[38] This practice continued into the third century with Origen (though
he included the apocryphal Letter of Jeremiah in his Old Testament canon) and into the
fourth century with Athanasius (though he included the Letter of Jeremiah and Baruch
in his canonical list).

Beginning in the second century after Christ, a Latin translation of the entire Bible
was undertaken, reflecting the shift from Greek to Latin as the universal language of the
Roman Empire. The version of the Old Testament originally translated was the Septuagint, not the Hebrew Bible. As the church began to adopt Latin as its language, the Latin
translation *including the Apocrypha* became its Bible. In 382 the bishop of Rome invited
Jerome to embark on a new Latin translation of the Bible. As he commenced his work on
the Old Testament, Jerome realized that a proper translation required a Hebrew original
and not the Greek Septuagint. Thus, he began to translate from the Hebrew Bible and had
to confront the obvious differences between it and the Septuagint.

Jerome first translated Samuel and Kings, and in his preface to these books he composed a list of canonical Scripture. It included only the writings in the Hebrew Bible;

---

38. The list appeared in a letter from Melito, the bishop of
Sardis, to his friend Onesimus and was preserved by Eusebius
in his *Ecclesiastical History*, 4.26. See Cruse, *Eusebius' Ecclesiastical History*, 164.

these alone were Scripture. He then commented: "This preface to the Scriptures may serve as a 'helmeted' [general] introduction to all the books which we turn [translate] from Hebrew into Latin, so that we may be assured that what is not found in our list must be placed among the apocryphal writings."[39] These were Wisdom (of Solomon), the Book of Jesus Ben Sirach (Ecclesiasticus), Judith, Tobit, and 1 and 2 Maccabees.[40] Elsewhere, Jerome indicated his rejection of Baruch, and though he did translate the additional stories in Daniel of the LXX, he placed them in an appendix to the book. Thus, he relegated the Apocrypha to secondary status in comparison with canonical Scripture.

In commenting on two of the apocryphal writings (Wisdom of Solomon and Ecclesiasticus), Jerome indicated the role or purpose of the Apocrypha: "As then the church reads Judith, Tobit, and the books of Maccabees, but does not admit them among the canonical Scriptures, so let it read these two volumes for the edification of the people, not to give authority to doctrines of the church."[41] That is, the church could read the apocryphal writings for its growth, but they could not be consulted in the establishment of church doctrine. (This function for the Apocrypha, as Jerome conceived it, will be invoked later by the Reformers as the question of the canon of Scripture is reopened over a millennium later in the sixteenth century.)[42]

Jerome exerted an immense influence through his Latin translation of the Bible, called the *Latin Vulgate*.[43] We might anticipate that his attitude toward the Apocrypha became the prevailing view in the church, but this was not the case. One of his contemporaries, Augustine, exercised an even greater influence on the church's perspective toward the apocryphal writings.

The foundation of Augustine's view toward the canon of Scripture was his belief that "one and the same Spirit" had spoken through both the writers of the Hebrew Scripture and the translators of the Septuagint. Even when the two versions differed significantly, the Spirit's work of inspiration had been active in both. This must have been the case, because the apostles cited both the Hebrew Bible and the Septuagint. If the founders of the church held this view, it must continue to be Augustine's view—and thus the church's view—of Scripture: "I also, according to my capacity, following the footsteps of the apostles, who themselves have quoted prophetic testimonies from both, that is, from the Hebrew Bible and the Septuagint, have thought that both should be used as authoritative, since both are one and divine."[44] In a series of letters between them, Augustine urged Jerome to translate the Old Testament into Latin from the Septuagint rather than the Hebrew.[45] As Jerome included translations of the apocryphal writings in his Latin

39. Jerome, *Preface to the Books of Samuel and Kings*, in *NPNF²*, 6:490. He described the contents of the Old Testament in his letter to Paulinus (*Letter 53*), dated 394. Again, he made no mention of the apocryphal writings.

40. Ibid. He also included the *Shepherd of Hermas* in this list of Old Testament Apocrypha, but it is out of place; it should be listed as a New Testament apocryphal writing. For the sake of simplicity and so as not to confuse, I have left it out of his list.

41. Jerome, *Preface to the Books of Proverbs, Ecclesiastes, and the Song of Songs*, *NPNF²*, 6:492.

42. See later discussion.

43. The name *Vulgate* became the common way of referring to Jerome's translation in the sixteenth century. E. F. Sutcliffe, "Jerome," in G. W. H. Lampe, ed., *The West from the Fathers to the Reformation*, vol. 2, Cambridge History of the Bible (Cambridge: Cambridge Univ. Press, 1969), 80–101 (esp. 99).

44. Augustine, *The City of God*, 18.43–44, in *NPNF¹*, 2:386–87.

45. Augustine, *Letter 28.2*; *Letter 71*, in *NPNF¹*, 1:251; 1:326–28. Jerome, *Letter 105*; *Letter 112*, in *NPNF²*, 6:189, 214.

Vulgate, these became widely known. The church had previously looked to the Hebrew Bible for its canon of the Old Testament. As the Vulgate became the new Bible of the church, however, the Apocrypha was regarded as part of canonical Scripture.

The Council of Hippo in 393, the Third Council of Carthage in 397, and the Fourth Council of Carthage in 419 all ratified the canon of Augustine.[46] Thus, the Old Testament with the Apocrypha (composed of Tobit, Judith, additions to Esther, 1 and 2 Maccabees, the Book of Wisdom, Ecclesiasticus, Baruch, and additions to Daniel), together with the New Testament canon described above, would be the Scripture of the church. This view would go without significant challenge until the Reformation of the sixteenth century.

THE CANON IN THE MIDDLE AGES

For over a millennium, the church pressed on with the Latin Vulgate—consisting of the Old Testament with the Apocrypha and the New Testament—as its Bible. Two major developments arose during the medieval period that would eventually result in reopening the question of what writings legitimately belong in the canon of Scripture.

The first of these developments[47] was the elevation of the Roman Catholic Church to possess supreme authority—an authority that was even greater than that of Scripture. This development led to the claim that the Roman Catholic Church possessed the authority to determine the canon of Scripture. As Guido Terreni affirmed: "From the church's authority the canonical books derive their power of authority. Through the church the books of the Bible were accepted as authoritative. On her [the church's] authority the faithful firmly believe that they [the canonical Scriptures] infallibly contain the truth. That we must firmly believe in them can be proved only on the basis of the church's authority."[48] Moreover, according to Gabriel Biel: "The truth that holy mother church defines or accepts as catholic is to be believed with the same veneration as if it were expressed in Holy Scripture."[49] Because the Catholic Church had defined the canon of Scripture, its determination of the canon had to be embraced by all Christians.

A second development was the rise of the important movement called *humanism* in the latter half of the Middle Ages. This movement should not be confused with the secular humanism of the twentieth and twenty-first centuries, a secularizing ethos that is largely anti-Christian in nature. The humanism of the fourteenth, fifteenth, and sixteenth centuries was primarily a cultural and educational movement focused on promoting eloquence in speaking and writing.[50] Born in the Italian Renaissance and extending to northern Europe, humanism was not anti-Christian but was embraced by many leading figures in the church.

Humanism's motto was "*ad fontes*": "back to the sources." For the church, this meant a return to its foundational writings: the Hebrew Old Testament, the Greek New Testament,

---

46. Council of Hippo, canon 36. Megivern, *Bible Interpretation*, 48. Cf. Third Council of Carthage, canon 47; Fourth Council of Carthage, canon 29.

47. Recounted in more detail in chap. 4.

48. Guido Terreni, *Questio de Magisterio Infallibili*, in Tavard, 32.

49. Gabriel Biel, *In Defense of Apostolic Obedience*, 1, in Pelikan, 3:125.

50. For an excellent introduction to humanism, see Alister E. McGrath, *Reformation Thought: An Introduction*, 3rd ed. (Oxford, UK, and Cambridge, Mass.: Blackwell, 1999), 39–65.

and the works of the early church. This led to several developments and questions: First, the difference between the Hebrew Bible and the Latin Vulgate, which included the Apocrypha, became evident once again. The question arose anew: Should the church's Old Testament be based on the shorter Hebrew Bible or the Septuagint with its additional apocryphal writings?

Second, Jerome's ancient distinction between canonical and apocryphal writings was revived. The translator of the Vulgate had urged that the Apocrypha could be read "for the edification of the people" but could not be used "to give authority to doctrines of the church."[51] The church could appeal to canonical Scripture alone to establish its doctrine. Augustine had blurred this distinction, and thus the church, following his influence, had established certain beliefs and practices on the authority of apocryphal writings. For example, the classic proof text for the belief in purgatory and the practice of praying for the dead was 2 Maccabees 12:38–45. The question arose: Should the church continue to base its beliefs and practices on the Apocrypha, or should canonical Scripture alone be used to establish them?

Third, a comparison of the Latin translation with the Greek New Testament revealed that the Vulgate was a poor rendering of the original in certain places. This discovery was particularly important for several passages, because certain church beliefs and practices were based on the Latin version. For example, the Vulgate version of Jesus' evangelistic preaching (Matt. 4:17) had "do penance." This command of the Lord was used as the biblical foundation of the church's sacrament of penance, a means of receiving God's grace after sinning by praying, giving to the poor, forgoing certain physical pleasures, and so forth. Erasmus, a leading humanist scholar, insisted that the Greek should be translated "repent," a strong call to an inner change of heart rather than an external, church-imposed practice. The question arose: Should the church base its beliefs and practices from the New Testament on the poorly translated Latin Vulgate, or should it appeal to the original Greek text?

THE CANON IN THE REFORMATION AND POST-REFORMATION

The Reformers, influenced by humanism, followed these developments and responded to these questions in the following way: First, the church's Old Testament should be based on the shorter Hebrew Bible, not on the Septuagint with its additional apocryphal writings. This decision was based on the fact that Jewish Scripture, with its twenty-two (or twenty-four) books, had been the Word of God used by Jesus and the disciples; thus, that shorter version must be considered the Bible of the church. Also, some of the apocryphal writings included incorrect historical or chronological information, and many of them had not been considered sound by the early church.[52] Thus, the Reformers dismissed the Apocrypha from the canonical Old Testament.

51. Jerome, *Preface to the Books of Proverbs, Ecclesiastes, and the Song of Songs*, in *NPNF*[2], 6:492.

52. E.g., Luther rejected 1 Maccabees and the additions to Esther and Daniel because they did not appear in the Hebrew Bible. He dismissed Judith and Tobit for their inaccurate historical accounts and Baruch for its chronological inconsistencies. He rejected the Wisdom of Solomon and Ecclesiasticus because of their lack of support in the early church. Martin Luther, *Prefaces to the Apocrypha*, LW, 35:337–54.

Second, adopting Jerome's classical distinction, the Reformers urged that the church could appeal to canonical Scripture alone to establish its beliefs and practices. Because the Apocrypha was noncanonical, it could not be used as the basis of church doctrine. This meant that belief in purgatory and the practice of praying for the dead were without *biblical* support and should be discontinued. At least for some of the Reformers, however, the Apocrypha was not worthless. Martin Luther said that Judith was "a fine, good, holy, useful book, well worth reading by us Christians."[53] He also praised the Wisdom of Solomon: "It pleases me beyond measure that the author here extols the Word of God so highly and ascribes to the Word all the wonders God has performed, both on enemies and in his saints."[54] Thus, the reading of the Apocrypha was encouraged, but the establishment of church doctrine on its authority was discouraged. The Reformers returned to Jerome's distinction and championed it.

Third, the Reformers urged that, just as the church's Old Testament should be based on the Hebrew Bible, so its New Testament should be based on the original Greek. Where the church's beliefs and practices were based on the poorly translated Latin Vulgate, they must be modified or abolished. Thus, when Luther sparked the Reformation with his Ninety-five Theses, posted on the door of the university church in Wittenberg, Germany, on October 31, 1517, he opened with these two points:

- When our Lord and Master Jesus Christ said, "Repent" (Matt. 4:17), he willed the entire life of believers to be one of repentance.
- This word cannot be understood as referring to the sacrament of penance, that is, confession and satisfaction, as administered by the clergy.[55]

In his explanation of these points, Luther appealed to "the Greek word *metanoeite* itself, which means 'repent' and could be translated more exactly by the Latin *transmentamini*, which means 'assume another mind and feeling, recover one's senses, make a transition from one state of mind to another, have a change of spirit.'"[56] This discovery began a process that culminated in Luther's dismissal of penance as a sacrament of the church.[57] More importantly, it established that the foundation for the church's canonical New Testament had to be the original Greek and not the Latin Vulgate.

Over against the medieval period's elevation of the authority of the Roman Catholic Church, the Reformers rejected its claim to possess authority over Scripture. The formal principle of Protestantism was *sola Scriptura* — Scripture alone. Among other things, this meant "the holy, biblical Scripture, because it is the Word of God, has standing and credibility enough in and of itself."[58] Thus, the Bible does not require the church to confer authority on it. For the issue of canonicity, this meant the church did not *establish* the canon of Scripture. Indeed, John Calvin offered a biting critique of this position,[59] challenging the Roman Catholic hierarchy to demonstrate that the church was the one

53. Ibid., 339.
54. Ibid., 343.
55. *The Ninety-five Theses*, LW, 31:25–33.
56. *Explanations of the Ninety-five Theses*, LW, 31:83–84.
57. *The Babylonian Captivity of the Church*, LW, 36:5–126.

58. Heinrich Bullinger, *The Opposition of Evangelical and Papal Doctrine*, 1.A.1 (Zurich, 1551), in Pelikan, 4:208.
59. John Calvin, *Institutes of the Christian Religion*, 4.9.14, LCC, 2:1178–79.

that had fixed the canon of Scripture.[60] Quoting Paul, Calvin affirmed that the church is "built on the foundation of the apostles and prophets" (Eph. 2:20); thus, Scripture preceded the church, and it cannot owe its existence to church authority.[61] The church *recognized* and *affirmed* the divinely inspired writings that God intended for placement in the canon, but it did not *create* or *determine* the canon of Scripture.

How, then, does the church know canonical Scripture? Calvin pointed to "the secret testimony of the Spirit" and Scripture's own "clear evidence of its own truth":[62]

> Let this point therefore stand: that those whom the Holy Spirit has inwardly taught truly rest upon Scripture, and that Scripture indeed is self-authenticated.... And the certainty it deserves with us, it attains by the testimony of the Spirit.... Therefore, illumined by his power, we believe neither by our own nor by anyone else's judgment that Scripture is from God; but above human judgment we affirm with utter certainty (just as if we were gazing upon the majesty of God himself) that it has flowed to us from the very mouth of God by the ministry of men.[63]

Both the Holy Spirit and Scripture itself attest to canonical Scripture, which consists of the Old Testament based on the Hebrew Bible, not the Septuagint, and the New Testament. Thus, the apocryphal writings must be excluded from the canon.

The Protestant confessions underscored this. For example, the *French Confession of Faith* of 1559, after listing the Old and New Testament canonical books, stated: "We know these books to be canonical and the sure rule of our faith not so much by the common accord and consent of the church as by the testimony and inward illumination of the Holy Spirit, which enables us to distinguish them from other ecclesiastical books upon which, however useful, we can not found any articles of faith."[64] The *Westminster Confession of Faith*, after listing the canonical writings, added: "The books commonly called Apocrypha, not being of divine inspiration, are no part of the canon of the Scripture, and therefore are of no authority in the church of God, not to be any otherwise approved, or made use of, than other human writings."[65] Thus, the Protestant Church embraced sixty-six books in its canonical Scripture and rejected the Apocrypha.[66]

---

60. Ibid., 1.7.3, LCC, 1:76–78.

61. Ibid., 1.7.2, LCC, 1:75–76. This was Luther's point as well: "Scripture is the womb from which arises divine truth and the church." *First Lectures on the Psalms*, LW, 10:397.

62. Calvin, *Institutes*, 1.7.4; 1.7.2, LCC, 1:78, 76.

63. Ibid., 1.7.5, LCC, 1:80.

64. John Calvin and Antoine de la Roche Chandieu, *Gallican Confession*, art. 4, in Schaff, 3:361–62. Similarly, Guy de Bray's *Belgic Confession* (1561), after listing the canonical Scriptures, added: "We receive all these books, and these only, as holy and canonical, for the regulation, foundation, and confirmation of our faith; believing without any doubt all things contained in them, not so much because the church receives and approves them as such, but more especially because the Holy Spirit witnesses in our hearts that they are from God, whence they carry the evidence in themselves." *Belgic Confes-*

sion, art. 5–6, in Schaff, 3:386–87.

65. *Westminster Confession of Faith*, 1.2–3. Similarly, the *Belgic Confession*, speaking of the apocryphal writings, noted: "All which the church may read and take instruction from, so far as they agree with the canonical books; but they are far from having such power and efficacy as that we may from their testimony confirm any point of faith or of the Christian religion; much less to detract from the authority of the other sacred books." *Belgic Confession*, art. 6, in Schaff, 3:387.

66. The celebrated case of Martin Luther's problem with the letter of James was not at all typical of Protestantism in general. He called it "an epistle of straw" (LW, 35:362) and threatened, "Away with James. I almost feel like throwing Jimmy into the stove...." (LW, 34:317). Actually, Luther placed Hebrews, James, Jude, and Revelation at the end of his New Testament because he had strong doubts about their apostolicity.

The Roman Catholic Church reacted to this Protestant rejection of the Apocrypha at the Council of Trent. It sought to correct the Protestant "errors" by reaffirming the Catholic canon of Scripture, which included the apocryphal writings. A conciliary decree gave this warning: "If anyone does not receive, as sacred and canonical, these books, with all their parts, as they have been read in the Catholic Church and as they are contained in the old Latin Vulgate edition, and knowingly and deliberately rejects the above mentioned traditions, let him be anathema [cursed]."[67] Thus, Protestants were threatened with church condemnation for using a Bible without the Apocrypha.

Despite these threats, the Protestant churches continued to insist on a canonical Scripture that did not contain the Apocrypha.[68] Moreover, the authority of these canonical writings was derived from three important yet unequally weighted sources: "The Scripture ... has its canonical authority chiefly from the Holy Spirit, by whose impulse and inspiration it was brought forth; thereafter from the writers to whom God gave sure and special testimonies of the truth. After this it has authority from the primitive church as a witness at whose time these writings were published and approved."[69] Beyond these three sources that confirm the canonicity of the biblical writings is the inner witness of the Holy Spirit himself to their canonical authority: "The canonical authority of Scripture, considered as to its doctrines, is proved by external and internal criteria, but especially by the internal testimony of the Holy Spirit illuminating the minds of men, through the Scriptures attentively read or heard from the mouth of a teacher."[70] Thus, the post-Reformers continued the defense of the Protestant canon of Scripture begun by Luther, Calvin, and the other Reformers.

THE CANON IN THE MODERN PERIOD

Generally speaking, this Protestant–Roman Catholic division of conviction as to what constitutes the canon of Scripture continues even to our day. Not to be overlooked, however, is their agreement that both the Old Testament and the New Testament compose the

He also recognized the struggle waged in the early church for including these writings in the canon. Thus, he considered twenty-three books as "the true and certain chief books of the New Testament" while he relegated these four writings to a lower level. He denied that Paul was the author of Hebrews and found difficulty with some of its passages that seemed "contrary to all the gospels and to St. Paul's epistles." Not only did James lack apostolic authorship; it also failed the most crucial test: It did not "press Christ." "All the genuine sacred books agree in this, that all of them preach and inculcate [German *treiben*: press, drive home] Christ. And that is the true test by which to judge all books, when we see whether or not they inculcate Christ." James also ran into conflict with the rest of the Bible: "It is flatly against St. Paul and all the rest of Scripture in ascribing justification to works (James 2:24)." Jude was found wanting in that "it is an extract or copy of St. Peter's second epistle" and "cites sayings and incidents that are found nowhere else in the Scriptures (Jude 9, 14)." Luther's problems with Revelation stemmed from its lack of clarity: "The apostles do not deal with visions, but prophesy in clear and plain words.... For it befits the apostolic office to speak clearly of Christ and his deeds, without images and visions.... I can in no way detect that the Holy Spirit produced it." *Prefaces to the New Testament*, LW, 35:394–99.

67. *Canons and Decrees of the Council of Trent*, 4th session (April 8, 1546), *Decree Concerning the Canonical Scriptures*, in Schaff, 2:80. The text has been rendered clearer.

68. Martin Chemnitz, *Examination of the Council of Trent*, trans. Fred Kramer, pt. 1, sec. 6 (St. Louis: Concordia, 1971), 168–95.

69. Ibid., 176.

70. David Hollaz, *Examen Theologicum Acroamaticum* (1707), 126, in Schmid, 84.

biblical canon. Occasionally in the early modern period, this agreement was challenged. For example, Friedrich Schleiermacher relegated the Old Testament to secondary status. He noted the common consensus among Christians that a great difference exists between the Old and New Testaments, and he denied that Christian maturity could be helped even by the Prophets and the Psalms. He asserted that when Christians give heed to the Old Testament, their Christianity is infected with legalism and they can find little support for Christian doctrines. Furthermore, Schleiermacher denied that the use of the Old Testament by Christ and the apostles was a precedent set by them for Christians to follow; indeed, he spoke of the "gradual retirement" of the Old Testament as the New Testament appeared and proposed that "the real meaning of the facts would be clearer if the Old Testament followed the New as an appendix."[71] Thus, for Schleiermacher, "the Old Testament Scriptures do not ... share the normative dignity or the inspiration of the New."[72] This denial of the canonicity of the Old Testament was exceptional, not normative.

The greatest challenges to the church's historical understanding of the canon began with haste and intensity as the modern period progressed. With the rise of historical criticism came a thoroughgoing suspicion of the authorship of most biblical writings, leading to the demise of the traditional view of canonization. For example, Hugo Grotius doubted the authorship of 2 Peter by the apostle Peter and the authorship of Ecclesiastes by Solomon. Similarly, Baruch Spinoza (followed by Jean LeClerc and many others) argued against Mosaic authorship of the Pentateuch. Also, the (alleged) division between the Bible and the Word of God, another key tenet of historical criticism, wreaked havoc with the traditional consensus. In his important work *Treatise on the Free Investigation of the Canon* (1771–75), Johann Salomo Semler explained: "Holy Scripture and the Word of God are clearly to be distinguished, for we know the difference.... To Holy Scripture (using the particular historical expression that originated among the Jews) belong Ruth, Esther, the Song of Songs, etc., but not all the books that are called holy belong to the Word of God, which at all times makes all men wise unto salvation."[73]

As historical criticism drove scholars in the direction of treating the Bible just like any other human book, the notion of the canonization of the biblical writings came to be viewed as a completely human action with a denial of any divine superintendence of the process. The seminal work in this regard was the *Introduction to the Old Testament* by Johann Gottfried Eichhorn.[74] Bemoaning the fact that the term *canon* had ever been used, Eichhorn approached the process of collecting the various writings of the Old Testament as a purely historical development. Many who have followed Eichhorn have accepted his basic premise and discussed the Old (and New) Testament canon as the result of a merely human effort.[75]

---

71. Friedrich Schleiermacher, *The Christian Faith*, ed. H. R. Mackintosh and J. S. Stewart (Edinburgh: T & T Clark, 1928, repr. 1960), 610–11.

72. Ibid., 608.

73. Johann Salomo Semler, *Treatise on the Free Investigation of the Canon*, cited in David G. Dunbar, "The Biblical Canon," in *Hermeneutics, Authority and Canon*, ed. D. A. Carson and John D. Woodbridge (Grand Rapids: Zondervan, 1986; Baker, 1995), 344–45.

74. Johann Gottfried Eichhorn, *Einleitung in das Alte Testament* (Introduction to the Old Testament), 3 vols. (Leipzig: Weidmanns, 1803).

75. A recent example of this trend is James Barr, *The Bible in the Modern World* (London: SCM, 1973, 1990), 118–20.

Standing against this tide, evangelicals echoed the traditional view of canonicity with some modifications. B. B. Warfield, for example, rehearsed the common Protestant view of the historical development by which the church recognized certain writings as being canonical. In particular, he affirmed that "in every case the principle on which a book was accepted, or doubts against it laid aside, was the historical tradition of apostolicity."[76] Yet Warfield expressed a novel notion of apostolicity: it should not be understood to refer to the *writing* of New Testament canonical books by the apostles, but instead to the *determination* of the exact canon of Scripture by the apostles themselves.[77]

Employing a salvation-historical approach to the canonicity of Scripture, Herman Ridderbos began his discussion with a presupposition of faith in Jesus Christ and his delegation of authority to the apostles, the foundation of his church: "The authority of God is in no way limited to his mighty works in Jesus Christ, but ... it also extends to their proclamation in the words and writings of those who have been especially appointed as the authorized bearers and instruments of divine revelation. The written tradition established by the apostles, in analogy with the writings of the Old Testament, thereby acquires the significance of being the foundation and standard of the future church."[78] From this presupposition of christological and apostolic authority flows the principle of christological and apostolic priority in discussions of the canon: Jesus Christ authorized the apostles to be his witnesses and to write the authoritative foundational documents on which the church was founded. Thus, "the canon in its redemptive historical sense is not the product of the church; rather the church itself is the product of the canon."[79] A second key principle that flows from this presupposition is that the canon is closed.[80]

As historical criticism grew, and with it the historical-critical approach to the canon of Scripture, opposition to it arose. Of particular note is the *canon consciousness* set forth by Brevard Childs. As far as this historical-critical approach to the Old Testament goes, Childs offered three biting critiques. The first focused on its misplaced emphasis on the history of Hebrew literature rather than the canonical text itself.[81] The second criticized the historical-critical approach's failure to see the role of canonical Scripture in Israel's life.[82] The final criticism pointed to the approach's disregard of any and all religious factors that influenced the shaping of the Old Testament canon. For Childs, rather, "It

76. B. B. Warfield, *The Inspiration and Authority of the Bible*, ed. Samuel G. Craig (Phillipsburg, N.J.: P & R, 1948), 415.

77. "Let it be clearly understood that it was not exactly apostolic *authorship* which in the estimation of the earliest churches, constituted a book a portion of the 'canon'.... From the beginning it was not so. The principle of canonicity was not apostolic authorship, but *imposition by the apostles as 'law.'*" Ibid.

78. Herman Ridderbos, *The Authority of the New Testament Scriptures* (Grand Rapids: Baker, 1963), 27. My discussion of Ridderbos follows the contours of David Dunbar's presentation in "Biblical Canon," 352–55.

79. Ridderbos, *Authority of the New Testament Scriptures*, 27.

80. Ridderbos's presuppositional approach did not over-

look the complex and at times halting process by which the biblical canon came into existence. Still, he ultimately emphasized the divine promise of Jesus to build his church upon the apostolic confession (Matt. 16:18) as key to understanding rightly this historical development: "The absoluteness of the canon is not to be separated from the relativity of history. It is true, however, that we shall have to view the history of the canon in the light of this a priori of faith; and we shall view it as a history in which not only the power of human sin and error, but, above all, the promise of Christ works itself out, in order to build and to establish His church upon the testimony of the apostles." Ibid., 41.

81. Brevard S. Childs, *Introduction to the Old Testament as Scripture* (Philadelphia: Fortress, 1979), 40.

82. Ibid.

is constitutive of Israel's history that the literature formed the identity of the religious community which in turn shaped the literature."[83] Childs extended this critique to New Testament canonical discussions influenced by historical criticism.[84] Moving beyond critique to a constructive proposal, Childs emphasized a canonical approach to Scripture that focuses biblical interpretation on the final, canonical form of the Old Testament and New Testament as those writings have been received by the church.[85]

The impact of Childs on evangelicals has been extensive. In particular, they have latched onto his emphasis on the final canonical form of the biblical text as the focus and justification for doing biblical theology.[86] But Childs has also influenced evangelical biblical scholars in their understanding of the development of the canon. For example, John Sailhamer, following Childs's lead, outlined three important developments leading to "the final shape" of the Old Testament:

- *Composition.* The notion of authorship represents a decisive moment in the history of a text. In this way of thinking about the final shape, composition is viewed neither in terms of a dynamic process nor a rigid status quo. The composition of a biblical book ... represents a creative and decisive moment in the history of the text.
- *Canonization.* Canonization ... looks at the point where a book becomes part of a larger collection and contributes to its overall shape.... This means that in classical terms of authorship, the shape of the OT canon as a whole must be taken seriously and integrated into our text model. Not only do the books of the Hebrew Bible have authors, but also the Hebrew Bible as a whole and as a canon is the product of composition and authorship.
- *Consolidation.* Here the issue is the further development of a canonical text within a community.... The notion of consolidation means that once texts become a part of a community, they take on essential characteristics of that community.[87]

Thus, Sailhamer attempted to work out the implications of Childs's groundbreaking work on canonical consciousness and apply those to an evangelical position on the development of the canon.

And so the evangelical movement today embraces various approaches to the issue of the canon. Representing a growing evangelical position, David Dunbar noted several important elements in a robust doctrine of the canonicity of Scripture. Like Ridderbos, Dunbar emphasized the christological or salvation-historical development of the

---

83. Ibid., 41.

84. Brevard S. Childs, *The New Testament as Canon: An Introduction* (Valley Forge, Pa.: Trinity Press International, 1994), 21.

85. Childs, *Introduction to the Old Testament*, 73; *New Testament as Canon*, 48. Childs was critiqued by James Barr, *The Concept of Biblical Theology: An Old Testament Perspective* (Minneapolis: Augsburg Fortress, 1999), 378–438.

86. An example of this is Paul House, whose *Old Testament*

Theology was, among other things, "devoted to the pursuit of the wholeness of the Old Testament message." Paul R. House, *Old Testament Theology* (Downers Grove, Ill.: InterVarsity, 1998), 57.

87. John H. Sailhamer, "Biblical Theology and the Composition of the Hebrew Bible," in *Biblical Theology: Retrospect and Prospect*, ed. Scott J. Hafemann (Downers Grove, Ill.: InterVarsity, 2002), 27–31.

canon: "The oral and written apostolic witness to Christ was that from which the primitive church drew its life. The process by which the written form of that witness rose to increasing prominence and was gradually defined in the canonical understanding of the church was both natural and spontaneous. The process was, to a great extent, under way before the Christian community was aware of its implications."[88] As for the criteria for canonicity, Dunbar explained:

> Broadly stated, the church regarded apostolicity as the qualifying factor for canonical recognition; however, this apostolicity should be understood not strictly in terms of authorship but in terms of content and chronology. That which was canon must embody the apostolic tradition, and this tradition was to be discerned in the most primitive documents: "the normative testimonies must derive from the period closest to Christ, namely that of Christian origins, the age of the apostles and their disciples." The recognition of this apostolicity, moreover, was based primarily on the tradition of the church. Those books that had functioned authoritatively for earlier Christians were received as an authentic apostolic tradition.[89]

An important implication for canonical discussions today is that "the canon is in principle closed."[90] Furthermore, for Dunbar, discussions of canonicity must move beyond historical considerations and include the affirmation of God's providential work in the canonical process.[91] In conclusion, Dunbar affirmed, "The early Christians believed that they knew where to find the canon of Christ and the apostles. Today we still so believe."[92] The importance that evangelicals attach to this issue can be seen in the fact that the theme of the 2008 Evangelical Theological Society national meeting was the canon of Scripture.[93]

In summary, the Protestant church, with its roots in the Reformation, and taking its clues from the early church, embraces a canon of thirty-nine Old Testament writings that do not include the Apocrypha and twenty-seven New Testament writings.

---

88. Dunbar, "Biblical Canon," 357.

89. Ibid., 358. Dunbar cited Hans F. von Campenhausen, *Formation of the Christian Bible* (Philadelphia: Fortress, 1972), 330.

90. Ibid., 358.

91. Ibid., 359.

92. Ibid., 360.

93. The plenary addresses appear in the following: Peter J. Gentry, "The Text of the Old Testament;" Stephen Dempster, "Canons on the Right and Canons on the Left: Finding a Resolution in the Canon Debate;" Daniel B. Wallace, "Challenges in New Testament Criticism for the Twenty-First Century," and C. E. Hill, "The New Testament Canon: *Deconstuctio ad Absurdum?*" *JETS* 52, no. 1 (March 2009): 19–119.

Chapter 3

THE INSPIRATION OF SCRIPTURE

How has the church come to believe that all the words of Scripture are "God-breathed" such that the Bible is the actual Word of God?

STATEMENT OF BELIEF

The church has historically acknowledged that "all Scripture is God-breathed" (2 Tim. 3:16) and that in the writing of Scripture the biblical authors "spoke from God as they were carried along by the Holy Spirit" (2 Peter 1:21).[1] Technical terms such as *verbal* and *plenary*, though coined in the midst of modern debates about this doctrine, accurately represent the historical position of the church that Scripture is fully inspired (plenary inspiration), even to its very words (verbal inspiration). Only in the modern period has this critical doctrine come under attack, yet for the most part evangelicals have clung to and defended the divine inspiration of all of Scripture.

THE INSPIRATION OF SCRIPTURE IN THE EARLY CHURCH

The writers of the New Testament clearly considered the Hebrew Bible (now the church's Old Testament) to be the Word of God. They inherited this perspective from Judaism and followed their Lord in this outlook. Just as Jesus Christ frequently quoted from and alluded to Hebrew Scripture during his earthly ministry, so did the authors of the Gospels, letters, and other writings that eventually became the church's New Testament.

Two New Testament passages explicitly set forth the inspiration of the Old Testament. Second Timothy 3:16 affirms that all Scripture is inspired by God; specifically,

---

1. My thanks to Jeff Olson, Troy Hicks, and Brian Hubert for their help on this chapter.

God "breathed out" the very words of Scripture so that "the Old Testament writings are regarded as God's Word in written form."[2] Second Peter 1:19–21 states that no part of the Old Testament (called "the word of the prophets," or "prophetic Scripture," by Peter) "had its origin in the will of man, but men spoke from God as they were carried along by the Holy Spirit." It was not by human initiative that Scripture came about, but it was the Spirit who worked through the biblical authors as they wrote. Thus, the Holy Spirit's work of inspiration extended to both the human authors of the Old Testament and their actual written words. This perspective was expanded to include the New Testament writings as they became part of canonical Scripture.

The early church fathers continued to quote frequently from and allude to the Old Testament and the expanding New Testament. They also explicitly affirmed belief in the inspiration of Scripture. As Clement of Rome noted about the church of Corinth, "You have searched the Scriptures, which are true, which were given by the Holy Spirit."[3] Clement applied this to the letter that Paul had earlier written to the same church (*First Corinthians*): "Take up the epistle of the blessed Paul the apostle. What did he first write to you in the 'beginning of the gospel?' Truly he wrote to you in the Spirit."[4] Justin Martyr attributed the ability of the prophets to foretell the future to the "Spirit of prophecy"[5] who inspired them, for "they only spoke those things which they saw and heard, being filled with the Holy Spirit."[6] Origen affirmed that "the Scriptures themselves are divine, i.e., were inspired by the Spirit of God."[7] Furthermore, Gregory of Nyssa explained: "The Scripture, 'inspired by God,' as the apostle [Paul] calls it, is the Scripture of the Holy Spirit, and its intention is the profit of men.... Thus it is by the power of the Spirit that the holy men who are under divine influence are inspired, and every Scripture is for this reason said to be 'inspired by God,' because it is the teaching of the divine breath."[8] The early church was completely united in its conviction that all of Scripture—both the Old and New Testaments—was divinely inspired by the Holy Spirit.

Affirming belief in the divine inspiration of Scripture was one matter; explaining how the Spirit inspired the biblical authors was another. Theologians of the early church tended to accentuate the divine authorship of the Bible. At times this emphasis resulted in neglect of the role of the human authors. It may have been due to the influence of Philo, who believed that the inspiring work of the Holy Spirit caused the biblical authors to lose consciousness and write in a state of ecstasy.[9] Echoes of Philo can be heard in the early church

---

2. Wayne Grudem, *Systematic Theology: An Introduction to Biblical Doctrine* (Grand Rapids: Zondervan, 1994, 2000), 74–75.

3. Clement of Rome, *Letter of the Romans to the Corinthians*, 45, in Holmes, 79; *ANF*, 1:17.

4. Ibid., 47, in Holmes, 83; *ANF*, 1:18.

5. Justin Martyr, *First Apology*, 38 (cf. 31), in *ANF*, 1:175; cf. 173.

6. Justin Martyr, *Dialogue with Trypho, a Jew*, 7, in *ANF*, 1:198. The text has been rendered clearer.

7. Origen, *First Principles*, 4.1 (from the Latin ed.), in *ANF*, 4:349.

8. Gregory of Nyssa, *Against Eunomius*, 7.1, in *NPNF*[2], 5:192–93. The text has been rendered clearer.

9. "Philo's explanation of the experience of the prophets was that, when God's Spirit seized them, they lost consciousness; they no longer knew what they were saying, or, rather, they no longer spoke but God spoke through their lips." In Kelly, 62. According to Philo's discussion of different types of ecstasy, "the best form of all is the divine possession or frenzy to which the prophets as a class are subject." He provided examples of this "inspired and God-possessed experience": "Now with every good man it is the holy Word which assures him his gift of prophecy. For a prophet (being

fathers as they sought to explain the inspiration of Scripture by the Holy Spirit. For example, Justin Martyr described the prophets by using the image of a stringed instrument that is strummed by a musician: The prophets "present themselves pure to the energy of the divine Spirit, in order that the divine pick itself, descending from heaven, and using righteous men as an instrument like a harp or lyre, might reveal to us the knowledge of divine and heavenly things."[10] Using the same metaphor, Athenagorus wrote about "the Spirit from God, who moved the mouths of the prophets like musical instruments." He described the prophets as being "lifted in ecstasy above the natural operations of their minds by the impulses of the divine Spirit." Thus, they "uttered the things with which they were inspired, the Spirit making use of them as a flute player breathes into a flute."[11]

At times the early church fathers seemed to embrace the idea of mechanical dictation: the biblical writers were mere secretaries recording word for word what the Holy Spirit told them to write. Irenaeus was one who noted that Scripture was "dictated" by the Holy Spirit.[12] Caius, perplexed by people who attempted to correct Scripture, reasoned: "Either they do not believe that the holy Scriptures were uttered [dictated] by the Holy Spirit, and they are thus infidels, or they deem themselves wiser than the Holy Spirit, and what alternative is there but to pronounce them demoniacs?"[13] And Augustine opposed those who complained that Jesus Christ had written nothing himself. The reality was that Christ, as head of his body, had used his disciples "as if they were his own hands" in composing the Gospels.[14]

Although the role of the Holy Spirit in the writing of Scripture was predominant in the early church's view of inspiration, the role of the human authors was not entirely overlooked. Speaking of the prophets, Hippolytus noted:

---

a spokesman) has no utterance of his own, but all his utterance came from elsewhere, the echoes of another's voice.... The name [prophet] only befits the wise, since he alone is the vocal instrument of God, smitten and played by his invisible hand." Comparing the human mind or reason with the sun that rises and sets, Philo continued: "For when the light of God shines, the human light sets; when the divine light sets, the human dawns and rises. This is what regularly befalls the fellowship of the prophets. The mind is evicted at the arrival of the divine Spirit, but when that departs the mind returns to its tenancy. Mortal and immortal may not share the same home. And therefore the setting of reason and the darkness which surrounds it produce ecstasy and inspired frenzy.... For indeed the prophet, even when he seems to be speaking, really holds his peace, and his organs of speech, mouth and tongue, are wholly in the employ of another, to show forth what he wills. Unseen by us that other beats on the chords with the skill of a master-hand and makes them instruments of sweet music, laden with every harmony." Philo, *Quis Rerum Divinarum Heres Sit* (Who Is the Heir of Divine Things?), 249–66, Loeb Classical Library, Philo 4:411–19. Elsewhere, Philo described "the divine and prophetic possession": "For no pronouncement of a prophet is ever his own; he is an

interpreter prompted by another in all his utterances, when knowing not what he does he is filled with inspiration, as the reason withdraws and surrenders the citadel of the soul to a new visitor and tenant, the divine Spirit which plays upon the vocal organism and dictates words which clearly express its prophetic message." Philo, *De Specialibus Legibus* (The Special Laws), bk. 4, 49, Loeb Classical Library, Philo 8:37–39.

10. Justin Martyr, *Hortatory Address to the Greeks*, 8, in *ANF*, 1:276. The text has been rendered clearer.

11. Athenagorus, *A Plea for the Christians*, 7, 9, in *ANF*, 2:132–33.

12. Irenaeus, *Against Heresies*, 2.28.2, in *ANF*, 1:399. The Latin text, discussing Scripture as the product of "the Word of God and Spirit," has *dictae*, which may be translated "spoken" (as the *ANF* text has rendered it) or "dictated." The Latin text is available at www.textexcavation.com/documents/images/ah2p054.jpg.

13. Caius, *Against the Heresy of Artemon*, 3. Preserved in Eusebius, *Ecclesiastical History*, 5.28, in *Eusebius' Ecclesiastical History*, trans. Christian Frederick Cruse (Grand Rapids: Baker, 1962), 216.

14. Augustine, *The Harmony of the Gospels*, 1.35.54, in *NPNF¹*, 6:101.

Just as it is with musical instruments, so they always had the Word, like the pick, in union with them, and when moved by him, the prophets announced what God willed. For they did not speak of their own power (let there be no mistake as to that), neither did they declare what pleased themselves. But first of all they were endowed with wisdom by the Word, and then again were rightly instructed in the future by means of visions. Finally, when they were fully convinced themselves, they spoke those things which were revealed by God to them alone, and concealed from everyone else.[15]

Thus, Hippolytus underscored the preparation, instruction, and persuasion that the biblical writers underwent before they engaged in the writing of Scripture. They were not entirely passive instruments being played by the divine musician with his pick. Furthering this discussion, Origen contrasted the effect of the prophetic spirit of the Greek gods with the effect of the inspiration of the Holy Spirit. As pagan priests and priestesses received oracles, they were driven into a state of ecstasy and madness, losing self-control. But "the Jewish prophets, who were enlightened as far as was necessary for their prophetic work by the Spirit of God, were the first to enjoy the benefit of the inspiration; and by the contact ... of the Holy Spirit they became clearer in mind, and their souls were filled with a brighter light."[16] Thus, the biblical writers were not "possessed" by God so as to become mere mouthpieces of the Holy Spirit.[17]

Whether produced by divine dictation or through the cooperative effort of the human authors and the Holy Spirit, all of Scripture—even its very words—is inspired. This was the unanimous consensus of the early church. For example, Origen urged that "great pains and labor are to be employed, until every reader [of Scripture] reverentially understands that he is dealing with divine and not human words inserted in the sacred books."[18] He emphasized that this is true of both the Old Testament and New Testament, for both were inspired by the same Holy Spirit: "That this Spirit inspired each one of the saints, whether prophets or apostles; and that there was not one Spirit in the men of the old covenant, and another in those who were inspired at the coming of Christ, is most clearly taught throughout the churches."[19] Inspiration meant that one may not make "any change one way or another" with the words of the Bible, as Hippolytus underscored. "Rather, we make the Scriptures in which these words are written public, and read them to those who can believe rightly."[20] It also meant that proof for one's position can be authoritatively established "from the very words of Scripture."[21] The early church clearly

15. Hippolytus, *Treatise on Christ and Antichrist*, 2.2, in *ANF*, 5:204–5. The text has been rendered clearer.

16. Origen, *Against Celsus*, 7.3–4, in *ANF*, 4:612.

17. John Chrysostom occasionally focused attention on the human authors of Scripture. E.g., he differentiated between Moses' account of Abram's departure from Haran and Stephen's rendition of the same event; in both cases he called them the "blessed author" of their narrative. *Homilies on Genesis*, Homily 31, in *The Fathers of the Church*, vol. 28: *St. John Chrysostom: Homilies on Genesis 18–45* (Washington, D.C.: Catholic Univ. of America Press, 1990), 242.

18. Origen, *First Principles*, 4.19, in *ANF*, 4:368.

19. Ibid., preface, 4, in *ANF*, 4:240. Indeed, for Origen, the fulfillment of all the Old Testament prophecies about the Messiah—the fulfillment as detailed by the New Testament—is proof "that the Scriptures themselves, which contained these predictions, were divinely inspired." Ibid., 4.1.6, in *ANF*, 4:353.

20. Hippolytus, *Treatise on Christ and Antichrist*, 2.2, in *ANF*, 5:205.

21. Irenaeus, *Against Heresies*, 2.27.2, in *ANF*, 1:398.

and unanimously affirmed the plenary and verbal inspiration of Scripture.[22] Representing the church's consensus, the Nicene-Constantinopolitan Creed, in its statement about the Holy Spirit, confessed "he spoke by the prophets."[23]

THE INSPIRATION OF SCRIPTURE IN THE MIDDLE AGES

Continuing this consensus, the medieval church reiterated the doctrine of the inspiration of Scripture with little advancement in thought. Simply put, "Whatever things are in Scripture are spoken by God."[24] Photius, patriarch of Constantinople, preached about the Spirit's inspiration of the biblical authors, making comments such as, "David announces in advance, inspired by God," and referring to "the great Paul" as "the trumpet of the Spirit."[25] For John Scotus Eriugena, inspiration by the Holy Spirit is the reason that Scripture presents Jesus Christ to his followers. In a stunning prayer, Scotus exclaimed: "O Lord Jesus, no other reward, no other blessedness, no other joy do I ask than a pure understanding, free of mistakes, of your words which were inspired by the Holy Spirit.... Nowhere else are you sought more effectively than in your words."[26] Even the controversialist Peter Abelard linked the biblical texts/authors with the "Spirit, by whose agency these writings were written and dictated, and communicated directly by it [the Spirit] to the writers."[27] Thomas Aquinas simply noted, "The author of Holy Scripture is God."[28] Specifically, he explained: "The Holy Spirit decides by what terms spiritual things are to be signified in certain passages of Scripture."[29] At the same time he expressed the divine authorship of Scripture, he also affirmed that "the literal sense is that which the author

22. According to some, the one exception to this was Theodore of Mopsuestia: "With the single exception of Theodore of Mopsuestia ... it has been found impossible to produce, in the long course of the eight first centuries of Christianity, a single doctor who has disowned the plenary inspiration of the Scriptures, unless it be in the bosom of the most violent heresies that have tormented the Christian Church." Louis Gaussen, *Theopneustia: The Plenary Inspiration of the Holy Scriptures*, trans. David Scott, rev. ed. (Chicago: Moody, 1840), 139–40. Even this evaluation may be misleading, however, because Theodore did not deny this doctrine but sought to differentiate between the various modes of inspiration detectable in Scripture. As Kelly comments: "Theodore of Mopsuestia, again, has some original speculations on the subject.... While accepting the inspiration of the whole Bible, he argues that the Holy Spirit's action varied from writer to writer; the special gift bestowed on the prophets, for example, was in a different category from the grace of prudence which Solomon possessed." Kelly, 64. Clearly, this position is far removed from a rejection of the doctrine of inspiration; thus, the early church consensus was complete.

23. Nicene-Constantinopolitan Creed, in Schaff, 2:59.

24. Hervaeus Natalis, *In quattuor Petri Lombardi Sen-tentiarum* (Venice, 1505), prologue, q. 1, cited in Richard A. Muller, *Post-Reformation Reformed Dogmatics: The Rise and Development of Reformed Orthodoxy, ca. 1520 to ca. 1725*, vol. 2; *Holy Scripture: The Cognitive Foundation of Theology*, 2nd ed. (Grand Rapids: Baker Academic, 2003), 45.

25. Photius, *Homily* 5.5; 6.7. *The Homilies of Photius Patriarch of Constantinople*, trans. Cyril Mango (Cambridge: Harvard Univ. Press, 1958), 119, 133.

26. John Scotus Eriugena, *De Divina Natura*, bk. 5, in Tavard, 12–13.

27. Peter Abelard, *Sic et Non (Yes and No)*, "On the Contrary," art. 10, cited in A. J. Minnis and A. B. Scott, eds., *Medieval Literary Theory and Criticism, c. 1100–c. 1375: The Commentary-Tradition* (Oxford: Clarendon, 1988), 87.

28. Thomas Aquinas, *Summa Theologica*, pt. 1, q. 1, art. 10. For Aquinas, foundational to the two senses of Scripture—the literal sense and the spiritual sense (further segmented into allegorical, tropological, and anagogical)—was the fact of God's powerful ability "to signify His meaning not by words only (as man also can do), but also by things themselves." Ibid.

29. Ibid., pt. 3a., q. 60, art. 5. The text has been rendered clearer.

intends."[30] Thus, Aquinas emphasized the divine and human cooperation in the writing of Scripture.

Gabriel Biel explained divine inspiration more fully: "All true instruction, all consolation, all exhortation, all devotion is understood through the Word that proceeds from the mouth of God, and it proceeds from hearing, from reading, from meditation, and from contemplation of the divine eloquence…. The Word of the eternal God, holy Scripture, also proceeds from the mouth of God and indicates his own will, without which no one is able to live rightly with understanding."[31] Speaking of Scripture, Biel noted: "It is sufficient for salvation to believe in general that everything revealed by God is true in the sense intended by the Holy Spirit (all of which is contained in the biblical canon)."[32] Even pre-Reformers like John Wycliffe, while criticizing certain doctrinal elements of the Catholic Church, continued to affirm the church's historical view of the divine inspiration of Scripture. Indeed, to emphasize the authority of the Bible, Wycliffe underscored its divine authorship. Scripture is in fact the Word of God, which Wycliffe at times called "the will" or "the testament" of God. If this is the case, Scripture cannot be broken: "If it is not lawful for a son to break his earthly father's testament, how much more is it not lawful for a catholic to break the unbreakable testament of God the Father?"[33] So identified is God with his Word that Wycliffe acknowledged, "[God] and his Word are all one, and they may not be separated."[34]

THE INSPIRATION OF SCRIPTURE IN THE REFORMATION AND POST-REFORMATION

The inspiration of Scripture was not one of the doctrinal clashes between Protestants and Catholics at the time of the Reformation, for both groups firmly believed the historic position of the church. It should come as no surprise, then, that neither Catholics nor Protestants dedicated important theological treatises to the issue. Rather, the doctrine of divine inspiration was assumed throughout the writings of the time.

Martin Luther made many casual, passing references to the divine authorship of Scripture, demonstrating that he held to biblical inspiration. He often referred to the Bible as "the Word of God" and as "Holy Scripture." At times he specifically equated the two, speaking of "Holy Scriptures as the Word of God."[35] At other times, he underscored Scripture as divine speech: "God does not deal with us in accordance with his majesty but

30. Ibid., pt. 1, q. 1, art. 10. Richard Muller cites Aquinas as affirming "God is the principal author of Scripture, man however is the instrument," but he gives no reference for the citation. Muller, *Post-Reformation Reformed Dogmatics*, vol. 2: *Holy Scripture*, 39, 45.

31. Gabriel Biel, *Sacri canonis misse expositio resolutissima* (Basel, 1510), lecture 71. Latin cited in Heiko A. Oberman, *The Harvest of Medieval Theology: Gabriel Biel and Late Medieval Nominalism*, Latin citation translated by Michael J. Harstad (Grand Rapids: Baker, 2000), 394.

32. Gabriel Biel, *Epithoma pariter et collectorium circa*

quattuor sententiarum libros (Tübingen, 1501), prologue q. 1, ans. 1, nota 3 D. Latin cited in Oberman, *Harvest of Medieval Theology*, 394; my trans.

33. John Wycliffe, *De Veritate Scriptura Sacra*, chap. 9, folio 21, col. 4. Latin cited in *John Wycliffe and His English Precursors* (London: Religious Tract Society, 1884), 236n3; my trans.

34. John Wycliffe, *Wycket* (Oxford, 1828), 5, in *John Wycliffe and His English Precursors*, 236n4.

35. Martin Luther, *Sermons on the Gospel of St. John*, LW, 22:470.

assumes human form and speaks with us throughout all Scripture as man speaks with man."[36] Thus, Scripture is "God's Book or Word."[37] Specifically, the Spirit was responsible for the writing of Scripture; indeed, "we attribute to the Holy Spirit all of Holy Scripture."[38] Even the seemingly "trivial" matters of Scripture are inspired by God, as Luther pondered in regard to one specific case: "Why, then, is it recorded? I reply: One must always keep in view what I emphasize so often, namely, that the Holy Spirit is the author of this book. He himself takes such delight in playing and trifling when describing things that are unimportant, puerile, and worthless; and he hands this down to be taught in the church as though it redounded to the greatest edification."[39] Similarly, Luther questioned the propriety of certain biblical statements concerning intimate details about its characters: "Why did the completely clean mouth of the Holy Spirit lower itself to the basest and most ignoble matters, yes, to matters that are even repulsive, filthy, and subject to damnation, as though these things were particularly profitable for the instruction of the church of God?"[40] Rather than deny inspiration at these "vulgar" points, Luther affirmed the Holy Spirit's authorship of even these portions of Scripture. For Luther, Scripture is the divinely inspired Word of God.

John Calvin had little to say systematically about the inspiration of Scripture because, as with Luther, in the context in which he found himself, this issue was not a point of debate between the Catholic Church and the Reformers. When he did address the doctrine, however, he emphasized the superintending work of the Holy Spirit in the production of the Word of God. Commenting on 2 Peter 1:20, Calvin urged:

> God speaks to us, and not mortal men. Then Peter especially bids us to believe the prophecies as the undoubted oracles of God, because they have not emanated from men's own private suggestions.... They did not of themselves, or according to their own will, foolishly deliver their own inventions.... He says that they were moved — not that they were out bereaved of mind ... but because they dared not to announce anything of their own, and obediently followed the Spirit as their guide, who ruled in their mouth as in his own sanctuary.[41]

In a similar vein, Calvin commented on the phrase "all Scripture is God-breathed" (2 Tim. 3:16): "Moses and the prophets did not utter at random what we have received from their hand, but, speaking at the suggestion of God, they boldly and fearlessly testified, what was actually true, that it was the mouth of the Lord that spoke.... We owe to the Scripture the same reverence which we owe to God; because it has proceeded from him alone, and has nothing belonging to man mixed with it."[42]

At first glance, Calvin's comments seem to verge on a mechanical dictation view of inspiration. Elsewhere, he declared that the apostles are "sure and genuine scribes of the

36. *Lectures on Genesis: Chapters 21–25*, LW, 4:61.

37. *The Catholic Epistles*, LW, 30:107.

38. *Last Words of David: Second Samuel 23:1–7*, LW, 15:275.

39. *Lectures on Genesis: Chapters 26–30*, LW, 5:352.

40. *Lectures on Genesis: Chapters 38–44*, LW, 7:35.

41. John Calvin, "The Second Epistle of Peter," 1:20–21,

in *Commentaries on the Catholic Epistles*, ed. and trans. John Owen (Grand Rapids: Baker, 2005), 390–91.

42. John Calvin, "The Second Epistle to Timothy," 3:16, in *Commentaries on the Epistles to Timothy, Titus, and Philemon*, trans. William Pringle (Grand Rapids: Baker, 2005), 249.

Holy Spirit and their writings are therefore to be considered oracles of God."[43] He also referred to the prophets as "organs of the Holy Spirit,"[44] even using the word *dictate* in conjunction with divine inspiration.[45] When making these statements, however, Calvin was attempting to distinguish the Christian faith from religions invented by mere humans; thus, he emphasized the uniquely divine authorship of the Bible. Elsewhere, he did affirm the contribution of the biblical authors to the writing of Scripture. For example, Calvin noted that Scripture "has flowed to us from the very mouth of God by the ministry of men."[46] He also expressed the active role of the apostles in teaching the Old Testament in their writings: "They were to expound the ancient Scripture and to show that what is taught there has been fulfilled in Christ. Yet they were not to do this except from the Lord, that is, with Christ's Spirit as precursor in a certain measure dictating the words."[47] Thus, at the same time that he underscored the dictation of words by the Holy Spirit—with the clarification that this occurred "in a certain measure"—Calvin insisted on the active role of the apostles to explain the Old Testament and demonstrate its fulfillment in Christ. B. B. Warfield correctly concluded that when Calvin used *dictated* in this context, he referred to the result, not the mode, of inspiration.[48] This belies the notion of a mechanical dictation theory of inspiration.

But how can Bible readers become convinced that God is responsible for what they are reading so they can gain wisdom leading to eternal salvation? For Calvin, only one reality could give the assurance that God himself was the author of Scripture: "Credibility of doctrine is not established until we are persuaded beyond doubt that God is its Author. Thus, the highest proof of Scripture derives in general from the fact that God in person speaks in it."[49] This testimony of the Spirit gives absolute certainty of the divine authorship of Scripture: "Illumined by his [the Spirit's] power, we believe neither by our own nor by anyone else's judgment that Scripture is from God; but above human judgment we

---

43. John Calvin, *Institutes of the Christian Religion*, 4.8.9, LCC, 2:1157.

44. Calvin, "Second Epistle to Timothy," 249.

45. Speaking of the Old Testament, Calvin explained: "Because the Lord was pleased to reveal a clearer and fuller doctrine in order better to satisfy weak consciences, he commanded that the prophecies also be committed to writing and be accounted part of his Word. At the same time, histories were added to these, also the labor of the prophets, but composed under the Holy Spirit's dictation. I include the psalms with the prophecies, since what we attribute to the prophecies is common to them." John Calvin, *Institutes*, 4.8.6, LCC, 2:1154. Of course, Calvin's entire theology of divine providence is the framework for this view of divine inspiration. As Kantzer explained: "Having a clear concept of God's absolute sovereignty in foreordaining and overruling free (that is, psychologically self-determined) human acts, so that people say and do things of whose place in God's plan they are quite unaware, Calvin could not with consistency have found any problem with the idea of verbal inspiration; it would have been an unprecedented lapse from his own theology had he done

so, and there is not the least evidence that he ever did so. He did not work with the concept of nondecisive divine influence in human action, as Arminians and process theologians do; he was, after all, a Calvinist, and all the evidence suggests that at that point, as at all others, he thought like one." Kenneth Kantzer, "John Calvin and the Inerrancy of Scripture," in *Inerrancy and the Church*, ed. John Hannah (Chicago: Moody, 1984), 157.

46. Calvin, *Institutes*, 1.7.5, LCC, 1:80.

47. Ibid., 4.8.8, LCC, 2:1155.

48. B. B. Warfield, "Calvin's Doctrine of the Knowledge of God," *Princeton Theological Review* 7, no. 2 (1909): 255. Even Dewey M. Beegle, an outspoken critic of modern evangelicalism's (alleged) mechanical dictation theory, admitted: "But he [Calvin] does not mean mechanical dictation, because in other contexts he is strongly opposed to the concept that conceived of the biblical writers as mere robots. The term 'dictation' was for Calvin the means of declaring the divine aspect of Scripture." Dewey M. Beegle, *Scripture, Tradition, and Infallibility* (Grand Rapids: Eerdmans, 1973), 140.

49. Calvin, *Institutes*, 1.7.4, LCC, 1:78.

affirm with utter certainty (just as if we were gazing upon the majesty of God himself) that it has flowed to us from the very mouth of God by the ministry of men."[50] Beyond this, Calvin and the other Reformers did not need to press the issue of biblical inspiration, because Catholics and Protestants were in agreement on the doctrine.

Protestants in the post-Reformation period introduced a careful, meticulous exploration of the doctrine of inspiration. Quenstedt and Gerhard articulated the distinction between the divine and human authors of Scripture. As for the former: "The *efficient* or principal *cause* of Scripture is the triune God."[51] Concerning the latter:

> The *instrumental causes* of Holy Scripture were holy men of God (2 Pet. 1:21), that is, men particularly and immediately elected and called by God for the purpose of committing to writing the divine revelations; such were the prophets of the Old Testament and the evangelists and apostles of the New Testament; whom, therefore, we properly call the *amanuenses* [secretaries] of God, the hand of Christ, and the scribes or notaries of the Holy Spirit, since they neither spoke nor wrote by their own human will, but, borne along by the Holy Spirit, were acted upon, led, driven, inspired, and governed by the Holy Spirit. They wrote not as men, but as men of God, i.e., as servants of God and particular organs of the Holy Spirit.[52]

Quenstedt clarified the concept of "secretary" so as not to be seen as embracing mechanical dictation: it is "not as though these divine amanuenses wrote ignorantly and unwillingly, beyond the reach of and contrary to their own will; for they wrote cheerfully, willingly and intelligently."[53]

Several results came about from this divine and human cooperative work. First was the verbal, plenary inspiration of Scripture. The inspiring work of the Holy Spirit extended to "all the words, without exception, contained in the holy manuscript."[54] Accordingly, inspiration extends to all of Scripture, not just to its theological truth:

> There are contained in Scripture historical, chronological, genealogical, astronomical, natural-historical, and political matters which, although the knowledge of them is not actually necessary to salvation, are nevertheless divinely revealed, because an acquaintance with them assists not a little in the interpretation of the Holy Scriptures, and in illustrating the doctrines and moral precepts. If only the mysteries of the faith, which are contained in the Holy Scriptures, depend on divine inspiration, and all the rest, which may be known by the light of nature, depend merely on the divine direction, then not all of Scripture is inspired. But Paul declares [2 Tim. 3:16–17] that the whole of

50. Ibid., 1.7.5, LCC, 1:80. It should be noted, however, that Calvin wrote a lengthy chapter on proofs for the divine authority of Scripture: "So Far as Human Reason Goes, Sufficiently Firm Proofs Are at Hand to Establish the Credibility of Scripture." Ibid., 1.8, LCC, 1:81–92.

51. John Andrew Quenstedt, *Theologia Didactico-Polemica sive Systema Theologicum* (Leipzig, 1715), 1.55, in Schmid, 42.

52. John Gerhard, *Loci Theologici* (1621), 2.26, in Schmid, 42–43.

53. Quenstedt, *Theologia Didactico-Polemica*, 1.52, in Schmid, 43.

54. David Hollaz, *Examen Theologicum Acroamaticum* (1707), 83, 85, in Schmid, 45.

Scripture is inspired. Therefore not only the mysteries of the faith, but also the remaining truths that may be known by the light of nature, which are contained in Scripture, are divinely suggested and inspired.[55]

A second result of the divine-human work in the writing of Scripture was the inerrancy of all of Scripture. Quenstedt underscored the resulting freedom from error produced by the Holy Spirit's inspiration of the biblical authors:

The canonical Holy Scriptures in the original text are the infallible truth and are free from every error; in other words, in the canonical sacred Scriptures there is found no lie, no falsity, no error, not even the least, whether in subject matter or expressions, but in all things and all the details that are handed down in them, they are most certainly true, whether they pertain to doctrines or morals, to history or chronology, to topography or nomenclature. No ignorance, no thoughtlessness, no forgetfulness, no lapse of memory can and are to be ascribed to the amanuenses of the Holy Spirit in their penning the sacred writings.[56]

The *Westminster Confession of Faith*, following its list of Old and New Testament books, concluded with this simple affirmation: "All which are given by inspiration of God, to be the rule of faith and life."[57] The *Confession* noted that the characteristics of this inspired Word of God include its "entire perfection" and "infallible truth."[58]

In a more technical discussion, the post-Reformers maintained that inspiration is especially true of the autographs, or the original texts written by the biblical authors. The *Westminster Confession* stated: "The Old Testament in Hebrew (which was the native language of the people of God of old), and the New Testament in Greek (which at the time of the writing of it was most generally known to the nations), being immediately inspired by God, and by his singular care and providence kept pure in all ages, are therefore authentic; so as, in all controversies of religion the church is finally to appeal unto them."[59] Thus, the autographs, or original texts in Hebrew and Greek, were directly inspired by God. Although not inspired, the process of copying those original texts was protected by God, as Turretin argued:

[We cannot] readily believe that God, who dictated and inspired each and every word to these inspired (*theopneustois*) men, would not take care of their entire

55. Hollaz, *Examen Theologicum Acroamaticum*, 83, in Schmid, 46. Similarly, Quenstedt denied that seemingly unimportant matters of Scripture are not inspired: "Many things in Scripture seem to be of small account (2 Tim. 4:13), in regard to which some suppose that our theory of inspiration derogates [detracts] from the dignity of the Holy Spirit; but they are, nevertheless, of great moment [importance] if we regard the end had [that was] in view (Rom. 15:4) and the all-wise design of God, in accordance with which these things were introduced into the Scriptures." Quenstedt, *Theologia Didactico-Polemica*, 1.71, in Schmid, 46.

56. Quenstedt, *Theologia Didactico-Polemica*, 1.112; cited in Beegle, *Scripture, Tradition, and Infallibility*, 143. Similarly

for Turretin, inspiration was the foundation for the truthfulness of all of Scripture: "The prophets did not fall into mistakes in those things which they wrote as inspired men (*theopneustōs*) and as prophets, not even in the smallest particulars; otherwise faith in the whole of Scripture would be rendered doubtful." Francis Turretin, *Institutes of Elenctic Theology*, ed. James T. Dennison Jr., trans. George Musgrave Giger, 3 vols. in 1 (Phillipsburg, N.J.: P & R, 1997), 2nd topic, 4th q., sec. 23, 1:69.

57. *Westminster Confession of Faith*, 1.2, in Schaff, 3:602.
58. Ibid., 1.5, in Schaff, 3:603.
59. Ibid., 1.8, in Schaff, 3:604–5.

preservation. If men use the utmost care diligently to preserve their words (especially if they are of any importance, as for example a testament [will] or contract) in order that it may not be corrupted, how much more, must we suppose, would God take care of his word which he intended as a testament [will] and seal of his covenant with us, so that it might not be corrupted; especially when he could easily foresee and prevent such corruptions in order to establish the faith of his church?[60]

Turretin carefully distinguished between this work of divine preservation and that of divine inspiration: "Although we give to the Scriptures absolute integrity, we do not therefore think that the copyists and printers were inspired (*theopneustous*), but only that the providence of God watched over the copying of the sacred books, so that although many errors might have crept in, it has not so happened (or they have not so crept into the manuscripts) but that they can be easily corrected by a collation of others (or with the Scriptures themselves)."[61] These two steps of divine inspiration and providentially protected transmission should be accompanied by a third step: translation. On behalf of the people of God, the *Westminster Confession* called for the translation of the Hebrew and Greek texts "into the vulgar [common] language of every nation unto which they come, that the Word of God dwelling plentifully in all, they may worship him in an acceptable manner, and through patience and comfort of the Scriptures, may have hope."[62] Through inspiration, providence, and translation, Scripture is the truthful and authoritative Word of God for people everywhere.

THE INSPIRATION OF SCRIPTURE IN THE MODERN PERIOD

Except for an occasional eccentric denial of the inspiration of Scripture, this church doctrine prevailed unscathed until the modern period; only then did the consensus come under attack and fall apart. Several factors contributed to this assault. First, a general antisupernatural attitude began to prevail in certain educated circles, leading to the dismissal of most if not all miraculous elements in the Bible. English Deists, such as Edward Herbert of Cherbury, Matthew Tindal, and Anthony Collins reduced Christianity to a basic ethical system and insisted that whatever is not in conformity with human reason cannot be true.[63] Given the fact that miracles are beyond human reason, these skeptics denounced the truthfulness of biblical accounts of healings, casting out of demons, and even the resurrection of Jesus; these stories amounted to nothing more than myth. The historical consensus that Scripture is inspired by God became weakened as some key church leaders acknowledged the mythological character of some portions of the Bible.

A second contribution to the demise of the church's historic position came with the advent of biblical criticism. Doubts began to arise about the authorship of certain biblical books (e.g., the Mosaic authorship of the Pentateuch). Also, theories proliferated

---

60. Turretin, *Institutes of Elenctic Theology*, 2nd topic, 5th q., sec. 7, 1:71.

61. Ibid., 2nd topic, 5th q., sec. 10, 1:72–73.

62. *Westminster Confession of Faith*, 1.8, in Schaff, 3:605.

63. For an extended discussion on these and other English Deists, see chap. 4.

about the stitching together of various sources to compose certain biblical books (e.g., the mosaic authorship of the Pentateuch, bringing together at least four diverse documents). As a result, the human contribution to the writing of Scripture came into focus. Based on the assumption that "to err is human," critics challenged the historical consensus that divine inspiration protected Scripture from all error. These critics scoffed that only a mechanical dictation theory of inspiration could account for an inerrant Bible. Employing their critical studies, they (rightly) pointed out that such a transcription theory was untenable. Given a genuinely human contribution to the writing of Scripture, these critics insisted on the presence of genuine human error throughout the Bible.

Friedrich Schleiermacher was pivotal in bringing an altered concept of the inspiration of Scripture into Protestantism. He completely reformulated the doctrine of inspiration to bring it in line with his view that the Christian religion is a feeling of absolute dependence on God. Furthermore, he presented a case that faith cannot be grounded on a foundation of Scripture proven to be inspired by God.[64] Accordingly, Schleiermacher had little patience for the "holy book" of Christianity.[65] Rather, genuine faith must arise from an experience of Jesus Christ related only minimally to the Bible: "The faith that makes alive may spring even from a message about Christ which is in no way bound up with the conviction that the books of Scripture possess a special character, but may rest on any other sort of witness that is accompanied by real perception of Christ's spiritual power."[66] Thus, Christian faith by no means depends on a truthful, inspired Bible. Indeed, for Schleiermacher, the biblical testimonies (which are merely the reflections of the apostles on their faith in Christ) "contained much in detail that had been misinterpreted, or inaccurately grasped, or set in a wrong light owing to confusions of memory."[67]

Dismissing the traditional understanding of "all Scripture is God-breathed" (2 Tim. 3:16) and focusing more on the biblical writers as men "carried along by the Holy Spirit" (2 Peter 1:21), Schleiermacher protested against the historic doctrine of inspiration.[68] Specifically, inspiration cannot be confined to the process of writing Scripture, for it belongs generally to all Christians and particularly to the apostles throughout their *entire* ministry: "The peculiar inspiration of the apostles is not something that belongs exclusively to the books of the New Testament."[69] And what of the Old Testament? Dividing it into Law, History, and Prophets, Schleiermacher explicitly denied that the Holy Spirit inspired the first two sections. He did the same with the legal and historical portions of the Prophets.[70] Almost reluctantly, Schleiermacher allowed for the inspiration of some prophetic portions of the Prophets: "Only Messianic prophecy would remain as capable of sharing in inspiration in our sense."[71] Thus, Schleiermacher relegated the Old Testament to secondary status, maintaining that "the Old Testament Scriptures do not ... share the normative dignity or the inspiration of the New."[72]

---

64. Friedrich Schleiermacher, *The Christian Faith*, ed. H. R. Mackintosh and J. S. Stewart (Edinburgh: T & T Clark, 1928, repr. 1960), 592.

65. Friedrich Schleiermacher, *On Religion: Speeches to Its Cultured Despisers*, ed. and trans. Richard Crouter (Cambridge: Cambridge Univ. Press, 1988), 50.

66. Schleiermacher, *Christian Faith*, 592.

67. Ibid., 593.
68. Ibid., 598.
69. Ibid., 599.
70. Ibid., 609.
71. Ibid.
72. Ibid., 608.

Several key ideas expressed by Schleiermacher became commonplace in Protestant criticism of the traditional doctrine of inspiration. One such theme was that the doctrine must not—indeed, cannot—serve as a foundation for Christian faith. William Clarke claimed that the inspiration of Scripture "is not vital to the truth of Christianity. It cannot be so, for any doctrine of divine influence in composing the Christian Scriptures presupposes the truth of Christianity. If Christianity were not historically true, no divine aid in the composition of its scriptures could make it true, nor would such aid be given."[73] Indeed, Benjamin Jowett averred: "If the term inspiration were to fall into disuse, no fact of nature, or history, or language, no event in the life of man or dealing of God with him, would be in any degree altered."[74]

Critics were attracted to this position because they had begun to question the truthfulness of all of Scripture. Accordingly, they were faced with this dilemma: Either continue to assert the inerrancy of Scripture and be embarrassed by attacks against its truthfulness by historical-critical scholars, or jettison the foundational doctrine of biblical inspiration. Horace Bushnell, for one, felt "constrained to admit" that "the inherent difficulties of the question of a punctually infallible and verbal inspiration ... are insuperable."[75] He maintained that "when the divine authority of the scriptures is made to depend thus on the question of their most rigid, strictest, most punctual infallibility ... the argument so stated must inevitably be lost; as, in fact, it always is."[76] William Robertson Smith followed this thinking and concluded: "Not on the Bible as an infallible book, but on the historic manifestation of God in Christ must our faith rest. And when this is understood we shall no longer be constantly uneasy at the progress of criticism in Scripture."[77]

In place of the church's historical position on inspiration, Protestant critics embraced what Bushnell called a theory of "a general, undefined inspiration."[78] Some asserted a strong continuity between the biblical authors' experience of inspiration by the Holy Spirit and common believers' experience of that same Spirit: "Inspiration to write was not different in kind from the general inspiration of the divine Spirit. The writing of the Scriptures was one of the higher and finer fruits of the influence of God upon the whole body of believing and receptive people. No promise can be cited of a divine influence differing from all other, given on purpose to prepare men to write."[79] Accordingly, there was no qualitative difference between the work of the Holy Spirit in inspiring the biblical writers and his work in the lives of ordinary believers. All experience a general inspiration of the Spirit, though in the scriptural authors this general inspiration was stronger and more heightened than is common.

One corollary of such a theory was that inspiration came in differing degrees. This idea led to the notion that some portions of Scripture are more inspired than others, and

73. William Newton Clarke, *Outline of Christian Theology*, 4th ed. (New York: Scribner, 1899), 38.

74. Benjamin Jowett, "On the Interpretation of Scripture," in *Essays and Reviews* (1860), 351. Reprinted in Benjamin Jowett, *The Interpretation of Scripture and Other Essays* (London: George Routledge & Sons, 1907), 16.

75. Horace Bushnell, *Nature and the Supernatural as Together Constituting the One System of God* (New York: Scribner, 1892), 33. Bushnell seems to use the term "punctually" to mean "precisely" or "exactly."

76. Ibid. Here "punctual" seems to mean "precise" or "exact."

77. William Robertson Smith, "Christianity and the Supernatural" (January 1869), in *Lectures and Essays of William Robertson Smith*, ed. J. S. Black and G. Chrystal (London: A. & C. Black, 1912), 134.

78. Bushnell, *Nature and the Supernatural*, 495.

79. Clarke, *Outline of Christian Theology*, 43.

some portions are not inspired at all. Of course, this meant that the biblical authors were not—indeed, could not be—protected from error as they wrote the Bible. When applied by Samuel Davidson, this idea was made to account for objectionable portions of Scripture, like the imprecatory psalms:[80] "Inspiration does not necessarily and always imply *suggestion by the Holy Spirit*. It does not exclude *individuality*, or suppress the exercise of the human faculties; and therefore an unmerciful sentiment may find entrance into a canonical work. Inspiration admits of degrees and does not usually reach the extent of *absolute infallibility*. Admitting of degrees, it necessarily partakes of imperfection."[81] Although formerly the church would have found such a sentiment to be highly dangerous and even heretical, for these Protestant critics, the general theory of inspiration was a vast improvement over the historical doctrine: "Christianity is grounded not in the inspiration of its documents, but in the reality of its fact. Therefore if the Scriptures should by sound evidence be reduced to the level of ordinary human records, possessed simply of ordinary human veracity and correctness, Christianity would not be altered thereby. A religion of facts cannot be dependent for its reality upon its documents."[82]

In the wake of these Protestant attacks, what was left was not a doctrine of the inspiration of the biblical *writings* themselves, but a doctrine of the inspiration of the biblical *writers* instead. Citing the definition of inspiration in the *Century Dictionary*, Clarke proposed:

> According to this [definition], inspiration (apart from any special or technical use of the word) is "a breathing or infusion of something into the mind or soul; an awakening or creation of thought or purpose, or any mental condition, by some specific influence; intellectual exaltation." Inspiration is exaltation, quickening of ability, stimulation of spiritual power; it is uplifting and enlargement of capacity for perception, comprehension, and utterance; and all under the influence of a thought, a truth, or an ideal which has taken possession of the soul. When such influence comes from God through the power of some truth of his imparted, a man should be larger, freer, richer-minded, with ability more prepared, and touched to diviner issues.[83]

This idea was a far cry from the historical doctrine of the divine inspiration of Scripture. Karl Barth reformulated the discussion in his neoorthodox direction, maintaining that the Bible is a witness to revelation and becomes the Word of God:

---

80. The imprecatory psalms (Pss. 7, 35, 55, 58, 59, 69, 79, 109, 137, 139) are so named because in them imprecations—or curses—are prayed against one's enemies (and/or their families).

81. Samuel Davidson, *The Text of the Old Testament Considered, with a Treatise on Sacred Interpretation, and a Brief Introduction to the Old Testament Books and the Apocrypha*, vol. 2 of Thomas Hartwell Horne, *An Introduction to the Critical Study and Knowledge of the Holy Scriptures* (London: Longmans, 1856), 766.

82. Clarke, *Outline of Christian Theology*, 38.

83. Ibid., 41. Clarke did not give the reference in the *Century Dictionary*, nor did he give a justification for using that

dictionary's definition rather than some other definition or rather than inductively researching the (perhaps technical) sense of inspiration as Scripture uses the term. As for the biblical notion of inspiration, Clarke maintained: "The word 'inspiration' is used in connection with the Scriptures solely on the authority of 2 Tim. 3:16, where it is said that 'Every scripture [of the Old Testament] is inspired,' or God-breathed, or else, and more probably, that 'Every inspired scripture,' or writing, 'is profitable.' There is no authority in the Scriptures for applying the word to the present Bible as a whole, and theology is not bound to employ this word in defining the quality of the Scriptures." Ibid., 37–38.

We have to call the Bible a witness of divine revelation. We have here an undoubted limitation: we distinguish the Bible as such from revelation. A witness is not absolutely identical with that to which it witnesses.... In the Bible we meet with human words written in human speech, and in these words, and therefore by means of them, we hear of the lordship of the triune God. Therefore when we have to do with the Bible, we have to do primarily with this means, with these words, with the witness which as such is not itself revelation, but only—and this is the limitation—the witness to it.[84]

In a sense, then, the Bible is a book like all other religious books.[85] If this is so, what allows Christians to regard this "relative" book as "absolute," thereby elevating a human reality to a status reserved only for God?

The answer is that there is indeed only one single absolute fundamental and indestructible priority, and that is the priority of God as Creator over the totality of His creatures and each of them without exception. Yet how strange it is that we learn of this very priority ... only through the Bible, and only through the Bible as it is read and understood and expounded as witness of revelation and therefore as itself the Word of God. We learn of it only through the Bible as it is itself apparently absolutised.[86]

Still, Barth insisted on the distinction between the Bible and God's Word: "Again it is quite impossible that there should be a direct identity between the human word of Holy Scripture and the Word of God, and therefore between the creaturely reality in itself and as such and the reality of God the Creator."[87]

Key for Barth was his insistence that God and God alone can reveal or disclose himself to people. Furthermore, God reveals himself *immediately*, or directly, without anything *mediating* or going between himself and those to whom he reveals himself. Again, speaking of the Bible, Barth asserted: "It witnesses to God's revelation, but that does not mean that God's revelation is now before us in any kind of divine revealedness. The Bible is not a book of oracles; it is not an instrument of direct impartation. It is genuine witness."[88] That which we need the most, according to Barth, is God to make a free choice to reveal himself to people through the Bible—the "book"—as it becomes the Word of God:

The presence of the Word of God itself, the real and present speaking and hearing of it, is not identical with the existence of the book as such. But in this presence something takes place in and with the book, for which the book as such does indeed give the possibility, but the reality of which cannot be anticipated or replaced by the existence of the book. A free divine decision is made. It then comes about that the Bible ... is taken and used as an instrument in the hand of God, i.e., it speaks to and is heard by us as the authentic witness to divine revelation and is therefore present as the Word of God.[89]

---

84. *CD*, I/2, 463.
85. Ibid., 495–96.
86. Ibid., 497–98.

87. Ibid., 499.
88. Ibid., 507.
89. Ibid., 530.

For Barth, an important corollary of the Bible being a witness, but not revelation itself, was its errancy. But this was not a problem, as he explained: "Verbal inspiration does not mean the infallibility of the biblical word in its linguistic, historical and theological character as a human word. It means that the fallible and faulty human word is as such used by God and has to be received and heard in spite of its human fallibility."[90]

Another neoorthodox theologian, Emil Brunner, was also glad for "the collapse of the orthodox system of doctrine, that is, the system based upon the doctrine of verbal inspiration."[91] For Brunner, "the orthodox doctrine of verbal inspiration has been finally destroyed. It is clear that there is no connection between it and scientific research and honesty: we are forced to make a decision for or against this view."[92] He closely associated this orthodox position with "the incubus of the old mechanical theory of inspiration."[93] Given that this theory had been overthrown, Brunner could only conclude that the orthodox view had been destroyed as well.

In summary, theologians of the nineteenth and twentieth centuries questioned and then abandoned the view of inspiration that the church had held from its inception.

Reaction to the attacks against the church's historic doctrine of inspiration came from both the Roman Catholic Church and Protestant churches. From the Catholic perspective, Pope Pius IX included attacks against divine revelation in general and Scripture in particular in his *Syllabus of Errors*.[94] Among other things, the pope condemned as heretical the viewpoints that divine revelation is progressing and that Scripture contains myths. Moreover, Pope Leo XIII denounced antisupernatural, rationalistic approaches to the Bible.[95] Specifically, he condemned those who sought to limit the inspiration of Scripture or to find errors in it, insisting instead "so far is it from being possible that any error can co-exist with inspiration, that inspiration not only is essentially incompatible with error, but excludes and rejects it as absolutely and necessarily as it is impossible that God himself, the Supreme Truth, can utter that which is not true."[96] Pope Pius X further condemned critics who ascribed only a general sense of inspiration to the Bible.[97]

On the Protestant side of the issue, theologians continued to champion the verbal, plenary inspiration of Scripture. For example, Basil Manly Jr., in *The Bible Doctrine of Inspiration*, affirmed both the divine and human authorship of the Bible: "This twofold authorship extends to every part of Scripture, and to the language as well as to the general ideas expressed.... Or it may be summed up in one single statement: the whole Bible is truly God's Word written by men."[98] A similar affirmation of the verbal, plenary inspira-

---

90. Ibid., 533.

91. Emil Brunner, *The Mediator: A Study of the Central Doctrine of the Christian Faith*, trans. Olive Wyon (London: Lutterworth, 1934), 104–5.

92. Ibid., 105.

93. Ibid., 181.

94. Pope Pius IX, *Syllabus of Errors* (1864).

95. Pope Leo XIII, *Providentissimus Deus*, 10 (1893).

96. Ibid., 20. On September 15, 1920, Pope Benedict XV issued *Spiritus Paraclitus*. By appealing to the great biblical translator and commentator Jerome, Benedict reaffirmed the ancient view of the church as to the doctrine of inspiration.

He also disavowed all current attempts to (mis)interpret Leo's *Providentissimus Deus* as permitting a more liberal approach to the doctrine. Specifically, Benedict denounced efforts to limit the inspiration (and hence inerrancy) of Scripture to those portions dealing with matters of faith and practice. See especially *Spiritus Paraclitus*, 19. On September 30, 1943, the fiftieth anniversary of *Providentissimus Deus*, Pope Pius XII issued *Divino Afflante Spiritu*, reaffirming Leo's statements on the divine inspiration of Scripture.

97. Pope Pius X, *Pascendi Dominici Gregis*, 22 (1907).

98. Basil Manly Jr., *The Bible Doctrine of Inspiration* (New York: A. C. Armstrong and Son, 1888).

tion of Scripture came from James Bannerman. He linked the doctrine of revelation, the doctrine of inspiration, and the doctrine of biblical inerrancy:

> Along then with, and over and above, a supernatural presentation of truth to the mind of the prophet by God, there must have been, in the case of an infallible Scripture, a supernatural inspiration from God, enabling the prophet unerringly and without failure to transfer the revelation given him, and in the purity and integrity in which it was given him, to the permanent page; so that thus it might be, in so far as the capacity of human language will allow of it, an adequate reproduction and image of the divine mind.[99]

By far the most formidable defense of the historic Protestant view on this issue came from B. B. Warfield in two articles: "The Church Doctrine of Inspiration" and "The Biblical Idea of Inspiration." He averred that "over against the numberless discordant theories of inspiration which vex our time, there stands a well-defined church-doctrine of inspiration."[100] Warfield raised the obvious question: "How shall we account for the immediate adoption of so developed a doctrine of inspiration in the very infancy of the church, and for the tenacious hold which the church has kept upon it through so many ages?" His reply was simple and straightforward: "This is the doctrine of inspiration which was held by the writers of the New Testament and by Jesus as reported in the Gospels. It is this simple fact that has commended it to the church of all ages as the true doctrine.... This church-doctrine of inspiration was the Bible doctrine before it was the church-doctrine, and is the church-doctrine only because it is the Bible doctrine."[101] For Warfield, without this doctrine of divine inspiration of Scripture, "we could not, or could only with difficulty, maintain the confidence of our faith and the surety of our hope."[102]

According to Warfield, the biblical idea of inspiration could be defined as "that particular operation of God in the production of Scripture which takes effect at the very point of the writing of Scripture ... with the effect of giving to the resultant Scripture a specifically supernatural character, and constituting it a Divine, as well as human, book."[103] It should be noted that Warfield, working from the Greek word *theopneustos* (2 Tim. 3:16), did not approve of the word "inspiration": "The Greek term has ... nothing to say of *in*spiring or of *in*spiration: it speaks only of a 'spiring' or 'spiration.' What it says of Scripture is, not that it is 'breathed into by God' or is the product of the divine 'inbreathing' into its human authors, but that it is breathed out by God, 'God-breathed,' the product of the creative breath of God."[104] Working from 2 Peter 1:19–21, he pointed out that Scripture not only was the product of the divine operation, but also came about "through the instrumentality of men who 'spoke from him'.... The men who spoke from God are here declared, therefore, to have been taken up by the Holy Spirit and brought by

99. James Bannerman, *Inspiration: The Infallible Truth and Divine Authority of the Holy Scriptures* (Edinburgh: T & T Clark, 1865), 214.

100. B. B. Warfield, "The Church Doctrine of Inspiration," in *The Inspiration and Authority of the Bible*, ed. Samuel G. Craig (Phillipsburg, N.J.: P & R, 1948), 106.

101. Ibid., 114.

102. Ibid., 127.

103. B. B. Warfield, "The Biblical Idea of Inspiration," in Craig, *Inspiration and Authority of the Bible*, 160.

104. Ibid., 133.

his power to the goal of his choosing."[105] Thus, Scripture is the product of a cooperative effort of God and its human authors.[106]

But Warfield rejected the notion that, say, 50 percent of Scripture is written by God while the other half is written by the human authors: "The whole of Scripture in all its parts and in all its elements, down to the last minutiae, in form of expression as well as in substance of teaching, is from God; but the whole of it has been given by God through the instrumentality of men. There is, therefore ... not, indeed, a human element or ingredient in Scripture, and much less human divisions or sections of Scripture, but a human side or aspect to Scripture."[107] His preferred term for this divine-human cooperation was *confluence*; by inspiration, "the Spirit of God, flowing confluently in with the providentially and graciously determined work of men, spontaneously producing under the Divine directions the writings appointed to them, gives the product a Divine quality unattainable by human powers alone."[108] Two corollaries flow from this: "the 'inspiration' by which Scripture is produced renders it trustworthy and authoritative."[109] In this manner, Warfield articulated the historic doctrine of inspiration and insisted on its foundational character for the Christian faith.[110]

Despite these and other well-reasoned defenses of the church's historical position, critics continued to launch scathing attacks against this doctrine. Jack Rogers and Donald McKim, in *The Authority and Interpretation of the Bible: An Historical Approach*, proposed that the doctrine of the verbal, plenary inspiration of the Bible, with its corollaries of biblical inerrancy and authority, was not the historic position of the church. According to their proposal, from its earliest period through the Reformation, the church "held that the authority of Scripture resided in its function of bringing people into a saving relationship with God through Jesus Christ. The Bible was to be interpreted as a document in which God had accommodated his ways and thoughts to our limited, human ways of thinking and speaking."[111] Because of this

---

105. Ibid., 137.
106. Ibid., 150.
107. Ibid.
108. Ibid., 158.
109. Ibid., 161.

110. William G. T. Shedd also took up the defense of the plenary and verbal inspiration of Scripture against its critics. Responding to the nonplenary view—what he called "the middle theory of partial inspiration"—Shedd offered three objections to it. First, he asserted that "the primary and secondary matter in Scripture, such as doctrine and history, are so indissolubly connected with each other that uncertainty in respect to the latter casts uncertainty upon the former." Second, Shedd held that "it is improbable that God would reveal a fact or doctrine to the human mind, and do nothing toward securing an accurate statement of it. This is particularly the case, when the doctrine is one of the mysteries of religion." Finally, he offered that "the middle theory of a partial inspiration is more difficult to be maintained, than is the theory of plenary inspiration. Because if only a part of Scripture is infallible, it becomes necessary to point out which part it is.

If any one asserts that there are errors in the Bible, he must demonstrate them. This is an arduous task." Against this partial view, Shedd defended the verbal, plenary inspiration of Scripture. He argued this from the tight, even inseparable "connection between thought and language." Thus, "when the Holy Spirit inspires a prophet, the mind of the prophet is so moved that he not merely thinks, but utters his thinking in language that is suitable and simultaneously inbreathed and prompted along with the thought." Accordingly, the Holy Spirit inspired both the biblical author's thinking and use of words as he, the human author, wrote. Still, Shedd noted: "This is wholly different from dictation. Dictation separates thought and language; verbal inspiration unites them. Verbal inspiration is the truth, if thought is prior to and suggests language; but not if language is prior to and suggests thought." William G. T. Shedd, *Dogmatic Theology*, 2.1, in *Dogmatic Theology*, ed. Alan W. Gomes, 3rd ed. (Phillipsburg, N.J.: P & R, 2003), 92–94, 103.

111. Jack B. Rogers and Donald K. McKim, *The Authority and Interpretation of the Bible: An Historical Approach* (San Francisco: Harper & Row, 1979), xvii.

divine accommodation, Scripture contains historical, geographical, genealogical, scientific, and other errors. However, these do no harm to the authority of Scripture, because this authority resides in its central thrust of saving people (and this cannot be affected by the presence of errors in the Bible). Thus, Rogers and McKim made a distinction between the *infallibility* of Scripture (the human authors of Scripture never "deliberately deceive in the religious realm")[112] and the *inerrancy* of Scripture (Scripture does not contain historical, geographical, genealogical, scientific, and other errors). They embraced the former as being a property of Scripture and rejected the latter because of its novelty.

According to Rogers and McKim, the idea of a verbally and fully inspired — and, hence, inerrant and authoritative — Bible is a relatively recent formulation. They claimed that it was introduced by the seventeenth-century theologian Francis Turretin and defended in the face of biblical criticism by Princeton Seminary (especially B. B. Warfield, A. A. Hodge, Charles Hodge, and Archibald Alexander) in the nineteenth and early twentieth centuries. Being a late addition, this doctrine is not the historical position of the church and, according to Rogers and McKim, should be tossed out. A formidable response was formulated by John Woodbridge. In his *Biblical Authority: A Critique of the Rogers/McKim Proposal*, Woodbridge painstakingly and minutely demonstrated that those authors had blatantly misrepresented the major figures of the church and their affirmation of the inspiration and inerrancy of Scripture.[113]

The evangelical consensus was expressed in the *Chicago Statement on Biblical Inerrancy*, which included several statements on the doctrine. The *Chicago Statement* upheld the verbal, plenary inspiration of Scripture:

> We affirm that the whole of Scripture and all its parts, down to the very words of the original, were given by divine inspiration. We deny that the inspiration of Scripture can rightly be affirmed of the whole without the parts, or of some parts but not the whole.[114]

While defining inspiration as a work of the Holy Spirit in the biblical writers, the *Chicago Statement* clearly distanced the evangelical view from the mechanical dictation theory of inspiration:

> We affirm that God in His work of inspiration utilized the distinctive personalities and literary styles of the writers whom He had chosen and prepared. We deny that God, in causing these writers to use the very words that He chose, overrode their personalities.[115]

---

112. Ibid., 127. Similarly Stephen T. Davis addressed the two issues: "The Bible is inerrant if and only if it makes no false or misleading statements on any topic whatsoever. The Bible is infallible if and only if it makes no false or misleading statements on any matter of faith and practice. In these senses, I personally hold that the Bible is infallible but not inerrant." Stephen T. Davis, *The Debate about the Bible: Inerrancy versus Infallibility* (Philadelphia: Westminster, 1977), 23.

113. John D. Woodbridge, *Biblical Authority: A Critique of the Rogers/McKim Proposal* (Grand Rapids: Zondervan, 1982).

114. *Chicago Statement on Biblical Inerrancy*, art. 6, in Grudem, *Systematic Theology*, 1205.

115. Ibid., art. 8, in Grudem, *Systematic Theology*, 1205.

A key corollary of inspiration is Scripture's inerrancy:

> We affirm that inspiration, though not conferring omniscience, guaranteed true and trustworthy utterance on all matters of which the Bible authors were moved to speak and write. We deny that the finitude or fallenness of these writers, by necessity or otherwise, introduced distortion or falsehood into God's Word.[116]

Indeed, the *Chicago Statement* affirmed "that the doctrine of inerrancy is grounded in the teaching of the Bible about inspiration."[117] In a technical point regarding what constitutes the inspired text, the *Chicago Statement* affirmed that the original writings (or autographs) of Scripture are, properly speaking, the inspired Word of God, while copies and translations are derivatively so:

> We affirm that inspiration, strictly speaking, applies to the autographic text of Scripture, which in the providence of God can be ascertained from available manuscripts with great accuracy. We further affirm that copies and translations of Scripture are the Word of God to the extent that they faithfully represent the original. We deny that any essential element of the Christian faith is affected by the absence of the autographs. We further deny that this absence renders the assertion of Biblical inerrancy invalid or irrelevant.[118]

Moreover, the *Chicago Statement* repudiated the Rogers and McKim proposal:

> We affirm that the doctrine of inerrancy has been integral to the church's faith throughout its history. We deny that inerrancy is a doctrine invented by Scholastic Protestantism, or is a reactionary position postulated in response to negative higher criticism.[119]

The *Chicago Statement on Biblical Inerrancy*, with these specific articles, became the standard and common expression of evangelicalism's doctrine of inspiration. Although some have shifted away from it, evangelicalism continues to uphold this position in light of biblical teaching and because it is the historic position of the church from its beginning. Concern for even the slightest drift away from the traditional doctrine has been expressed, most recently by Gregory Beale in *The Erosion of Inerrancy in Evangelicalism*.[120]

---

116. Ibid., in Grudem, *Systematic Theology*, 1205.

117. Ibid., art. 15, in Grudem, *Systematic Theology*, 1206.

118. Ibid., art. 10, in Grudem, *Systematic Theology*, 1205–6.

119. Ibid., art. 16, in Grudem, *Systematic Theology*, 1206.

120. Gregory K. Beale, *The Erosion of Inerrancy in Evangelicalism: Responding to New Challenges to Biblical Authority* (Wheaton: Crossway, 2008). Specifically, Beale responded to Peter Enns, *Inspiration and Incarnation: Evangelicals and the Problem of the Old Testament* (Grand Rapids: Baker, 2005).

Chapter 4

THE AUTHORITY OF SCRIPTURE

How has the church come to believe that the Bible is God's word?

STATEMENT OF BELIEF

The church has historically acknowledged that all the words in Scripture are God's words in such a way that to believe and obey the Bible is to believe and obey God himself.[1] For its first millennium and more, the church affirmed and practiced the supreme authority of Scripture. Even church tradition and its own authority played a ministerial role, being a servant to Scripture itself to weed out heresies and to maintain the unity of the church. But a change took place in the latter part of the Middle Ages. As the Roman Catholic Church permitted other sources to lay claim to the title of authoritative truth, a multiple-source notion arose, consisting of written Scripture, church tradition, and the teaching office of the church. Against this trend the Protestant motto *sola Scriptura* (Scripture alone) was sounded. More than a motto, however, this formal principle of Protestantism became a decisive point of division between Protestant churches and the Roman Catholic Church. Although this division persists to today, a new attack against the very concept of biblical authority itself developed in the modern period. The idea of authority as an inherent property or attribute of Scripture itself was challenged, and in its place critics championed an instrumental or functional notion of authority: Scripture is authoritative because of the way it functions. Because the Word of God reveals God and his acts, because Scripture places demands on its readers, because the Bible bears witness to revelation and becomes the Word of God—for this reason it is authoritative. Evangelicals for the most part still cling to the traditional doctrine of the authority of Scripture, but some have parted company and moved to an instrumental concept of biblical authority.[2]

---

1. This definition is adapted from the one given by Wayne Grudem, *Systematic Theology: An Introduction to Biblical Doctrine* (Grand Rapids: Zondervan, 1994, 2000), 73.

2. My thanks to Lenny Cheng for his help with this chapter.

THE AUTHORITY OF SCRIPTURE IN THE EARLY CHURCH

The early church embraced the authority of Scripture because it has God as its origin. Simply put:

DIVINE AUTHOR   DIVINE AUTHOR*ITY*

(GOD)   (SCRIPTURE)

This conviction was an inheritance from the church's Jewish roots, whose Scripture was characterized by the prophetic formula "Thus says the Lord." When the prophets used this phrase, they were "claiming to be messengers from the sovereign King of Israel, namely, God himself, and they are claiming that their words are the absolutely authoritative words of God."[3] This indefectible authority of Hebrew Scripture was at the heart of Jesus' pronouncement that "the Scripture cannot be broken" (John 10:35) and his promise that "not the smallest letter, not the least stroke of a pen, will by any means disappear from the Law until everything is accomplished" (Matt. 5:18). Moreover, in anticipation of the New Testament, Jesus authorized his disciples to be his bona fide witnesses through the empowerment of the Holy Spirit whom they would receive (John 14:26; 16:13). As the apostles composed their writings, they were conscious of speaking "by the authority of the Lord Jesus" (1 Thess. 4:1–2; cf. 1 Cor. 14:36–38). Thus, Scripture as the Word of God possessed divine authority.

Christians who wrote after the New Testament was completed continued to emphasize the authority of the entire Bible. For Justin Martyr, the authority of Scripture was due to its divine authorship; indeed, Scripture demands to "be believed for its own nobility and for the confidence due to him who sends it. Now the word of truth is sent from God.... For being sent with authority, it were not fit that it should be required to produce proof of what is said; since neither is there any proof beyond itself, which is God."[4] In addition to stemming from the identity of the author of Scripture, biblical authority was established by its antiquity; indeed, "the Scriptures of God ... are much more ancient than any secular literature."[5] Clement of Alexandria also viewed Scripture as authoritative, because in it the voice of God is heard: "He, then, who of himself believes the Scripture and the voice of the Lord, which by the Lord acts to the benefit of men, is rightly regarded [as] faithful. Certainly, we use it as a criterion in the discovery of things.... We are by the voice of the Lord trained up to the knowledge of the truth."[6]

As seen in the above citation, Clement of Alexandria made the additional point that, because it is authoritative, Scripture determines what the church is to believe. Indeed, Irenaeus called the Bible "the ground and pillar of our faith."[7] As Jesus did with the

---

3. Grudem, *Systematic Theology*, 74.

4. Justin Martyr, *Fragments of the Lost Work of Justin on the Resurrection*, 1, in *ANF*, 1:294. Similarly, Clement of Alexandria affirmed that "the Scriptures which we believe are valid from their omnipotent authority." Clement of Alexandria, *Elucidations*, in *ANF*, 2:409.

5. Tertullian, *The Soul's Testimony*, 5, in *ANF*, 3:178.

6. Clement of Alexandria, *Stromata*, 7.16, in *ANF*, 2:551.

7. Irenaeus, *Against Heresies*, 3.1.1, in *ANF*, 1:414. It may be that Irenaeus is referring to 1 Tim. 3:15, in which the apostle Paul describes the church as "the ground and pillar of the truth."

two disciples traveling on the road to Emmaus, the church was to instruct its members, "proving to them from the Scriptures themselves."[8] Truth, or orthodox doctrine, "is not found by changing the meanings [of the words of Scripture]—for so people subvert all true teaching—but in the consideration of what perfectly belongs to and becomes [is fitting of] the sovereign God, and in establishing each one of the points demonstrated in the Scriptures again from similar Scriptures."[9] Heresy—any belief that is to be rejected by the church—is in error precisely because it "lacks the authority of Scripture"[10] and because it does "violence to the Scriptures ... opposes the Scriptures ... [and] dismisses the Scriptures."[11] Still, heretics attempted to establish their erroneous views from Scripture. Because both the church and heretical groups appealed to Scripture in support of their doctrines, a standoff was in the making.

To defend and demonstrate the rightness of its doctrines, the church began to invoke its own authority and tradition. This practice of appealing to church authority, especially to the writings of the church fathers, was never intended to deprive Scripture of its rightful place of authority. In battles against heresy, the point of appeal was to provide support for true doctrines because they were the doctrines the church had always embraced; they were not the novel ideas of the false teachers. And of course, whatever the church believed had to be traced back to Scripture itself, because that was the ultimate authority in all matters. Vincent of Lerins clearly expressed this notion:

> But here someone perhaps will ask, since the canon of Scripture is complete, and sufficient of itself for everything, and more than sufficient, what need is there to join with it the authority of the church's interpretation? For this reason—because, owing to the depth of Holy Scripture, all do not accept it in one and the same sense, but one understands its words in one way, another in another; so that it seems to be capable of as many interpretations as there are interpreters. For Novatian expounds it one way, Sabellius another, Donatus another, Arius, Eunomius, Macedonius, another, Photinus, Apollinaris, Priscillian, another, Iovinian, Pelagius, Celestius, another, lastly, Nestorius another. Therefore, it is very necessary, on account of so great intricacies of such various error, that the rule for the right understanding of the prophets and apostles should be framed in accordance with the standard of ecclesiastical and catholic interpretation.[12]

For Vincent, the authority of the church, including its tradition and interpretation of Scripture, was not in opposition to the authority of Scripture. Rather, it functioned

---

8. Irenaeus, *Against Heresies*, 4.26.1, in *ANF*, 1:497. His reference was Luke 24:13–35.

9. Clement of Alexandria, *Stromata*, 7.16, in *ANF*, 2:551. In keeping with this, Origen urged this method of establishing true doctrine: "That we may not appear to build our assertions on subjects of such importance and difficulty on the ground of inference alone, or to require the assent of our hearers to what is only conjectural, let us see whether we can obtain any declarations from holy Scripture, by the authority of which these positions may be more credibly maintained." Origen, *First Principles*, 1.5, in *ANF*, 4:258.

10. Tertullian, *On Fasting*, 10, in *ANF*, 4:109.

11. Clement of Alexandria, *Stromata*, 7.16, in *ANF*, 2:552.

12. Vincent of Lerins, *Commonitory*, 2.5, in *NPNF²*, 11:132. All the names he mentions are the leaders or proponents of early heresies. Commonitory refers to an aid to memory.

as support for the proper understanding of authoritative Scripture against heretical claims.[13]

Augustine joined together the inspiration, canonicity, and authority of Scripture: "[God] produced the Scripture which is called canonical, which has paramount authority, and to which we yield assent in all matters of which we ought not to be ignorant, and yet cannot know of ourselves."[14] Accordingly, Augustine urged that divine truth "must undoubtedly be believed on the testimony of those witnesses by whom the Scriptures, justly called divine, were written; and who by divine assistance were enabled, either through bodily senses or intellectual perception, to see or to foresee the things in question."[15] Thus, truth is to be discovered "both by sure reason and authority of holy Scripture ... not by human judgment, but by authority of divine Scripture."[16] Indeed, "holy Scripture sets a rule to our teaching.... Therefore, let it not be for me to teach you any other thing except to expound to you the words of the Teacher, and to treat them as the Lord will have given to me."[17] As a proper response to Scripture, Augustine urged Christians to "give in and yield our assent to the authority of holy Scripture ... to the authority and truthfulness of the inspired pages."[18]

In summary, because of its divine authorship, inspired canonical Scripture was considered completely authoritative by the early church. Although in fighting against heresy, the church often appealed to its own authority and tradition, these were never regarded as supplements to or opponents of Scripture.

THE AUTHORITY OF SCRIPTURE IN THE MIDDLE AGES

This harmony between authoritative Scripture and the secondary contributions of church tradition and authority continued in the first part of the Middle Ages. This can be seen in Thomas Aquinas, who argued for the supremacy of Scripture over the writings of the church fathers in the formulation of correct theology: "Theology properly uses the authority of the canonical Scriptures as an incontrovertible proof, and the authority of the doctors of the church as one that may properly be used, yet merely as probable. For our faith rests upon the revelation made to the apostles and prophets who wrote the canonical books, and not on the revelations (if any such there are) made to other doctors."[19] In relationship to the formulation of theology, John Scotus Eriugena asserted

---

13. For further discussion, see chap. 7.

14. Augustine, *The City of God*, 11:3, in *NPNF*[1], 2:206.

15. Augustine, *The Enchiridion on Faith, Hope, and Love*, 4; in *St. Augustine: The Enchiridion on Faith, Hope, and Love* ed. Henry Paolucci (Washington, D.C.: Regnery, 1961), 4; in *NPNF*[1], 3:238.

16. Augustine, *Of Holy Virginity*, 19, 21, in *NPNF*[1], 3:423.

17. Augustine, *On the Good of Widowhood*, 2, in *NPNF*[1], 3:442.

18. Augustine, *On Forgiveness of Sins, and Baptism*, 1.33;

2.58, in *NPNF*[1], 5:28, 67.

19. Thomas Aquinas, *Summa Theologica*, pt. 1, q. 1, ans. 8. For support, Aquinas appealed to Augustine's *Letter to Jerome* (19:1): "Only those books of Scripture which are called canonical have I learned to hold in such honor as to believe their authors have not erred in any way in writing them. But other authors I so read as not to deem everything in their works to be true, merely on account of their having so thought and written, whatever may have been their holiness and learning."

simply, "In everything the authority of sacred Scripture is to be followed."[20] In terms of biblical interpretation, John Gerson's first hermeneutical rule was: "Holy Scripture is the rule of faith, against which no authority may be admitted."[21]

As philosophy became an important tool in scholastic theology, the issue of the authority of Scripture vis-à-vis the authority of human reason was raised. Again, Anselm championed the authority of Scripture as the highest authority:

> If I say anything that is not confirmed by a greater authority—even if I may seem to be proving it logically—it is not to be accepted as having any validity beyond the fact that it seems to me for the moment to be so, until God reveals to me something in any way better. For I am sure that if I say anything which is undoubtedly contradictory to holy Scripture, it is wrong; and if I become aware of such a contradiction, I do not wish to hold to that opinion.[22]

Thus, any theological opinion or conviction must have at least the implicit support of Scripture and not contradict it:

> If at times we assert by a process of reasoning a conclusion which we cannot explicitly cite from the sayings of Scripture or demonstrate from the bare wording, still it is by using Scripture that we know in the following way whether the affirmation should be accepted or rejected. If the conclusion is reached by straightforward reasoning and Scripture in no way contradicts it, then (since just as Scripture opposes no truth, so too it abets no falsehood) by the very fact that it does not deny what is inferred on the basis of reason, that conclusion is acceptable as authorized by Scripture.[23]

So, in the first part of the Middle Ages, scriptural authority was firmly entrenched as the supreme authority in the church.

In the latter part of the medieval period, the authority of the pope and the church's canon lawyers, making pronouncements on behalf of an increasingly corrupt, papal-dominated institution, clashed with the authority of Scripture. For example, William of Amidanis, after claiming that "the pope resembles God," explained: "Just as the heavens contained all types of inferior matter, in the same way the pope presided over all types of terrestrial power, which of necessity was inferior to his. Some writers had the temerity to declare that the pope could say of himself: all power is given unto me in heaven and on earth."[24] This development came to mean that the papal interpretation of Scripture was the highest authority in the church. Indeed, John of Turrecremata spoke of "a binding decision interpreting their [Scriptures'] sense … [that] … belongs to the Roman Pontiff, whose decision binds all."[25]

---

20. John Scotus Eriugena, *De Divina Natura*, bk. 1, chap. 64, PL, 122:509, in Tavard, 12.

21. John Gerson, *Tractatus contra Heresim de Communione Laicorum*, in Gerson, *Opera Omnia* (Antwerp, 1576), vol. 1, col. 457, in Tavard, 53.

22. Anselm, *Why God Became Man*, 1.18, in *Anselm*, 298.

23. Anselm, *The Compatibility of the Foreknowledge, Pre-*destination, and Grace of God with Human Freedom, 3.6, in *Anselm*, 460.

24. William of Amidanis, in Walter Ullmann, *Medieval Papalism* (London: Methuen, 1949), 55, 89.

25. John of Turrecremata, *De Ecclesia*, bk. 2, chap. 107, in Tavard, 60.

In reaction to this development, champions of biblical authority insisted on the supremacy of Scripture over all human authority, including the pope. Chief among these critics of growing papal authority was John Hus, who offered: "For this truth [of faith], on account of its certitude, a man ought to risk his life. And in this way a man is not bound to believe the sayings of the saints that are far from Scripture; nor should he believe papal bulls except insofar as what they say is founded on Scripture simply."[26] In a scathing rebuke of the pope and the church's hierarchy, Hus critiqued the idea that the pope "is able to dispense at variance with the apostles' teaching ... and no one has a right to say to him, 'Why do you do this?' For he himself may lawfully say: 'Thus I will, thus I command; let my will be the reason.'"[27] Hus and others stood firmly against the development of papal and ecclesiastical authority that stood over and even against scriptural authority.

But what had transpired since the first part of the Middle Ages, in which an ongoing, close correlation between the church and Scripture existed? The demise of this former harmony can be traced to a rather obscure and innocuous set of theoretical questions posed by Henry of Ghent,[28] the first of which created a theoretical yet sinister wedge between the authority of Scripture and the authority of the church: "Must we rather believe the authorities of this doctrine (i.e., Sacred Scripture) than those of the church, or the other way round?"[29] In keeping with those before him, Henry answered his question with an affirmation of harmonious agreement between the two authorities: "Concerning the things of faith, the church and holy Scripture agree in everything and testify to the same thing, namely, to the truth of faith. In this it is reasonable to believe both: Scripture on account of the authority of Christ, which valid reasons show as obviously residing in it; the church on account of what man sees in her."[30]

Not content to stop here, Henry pushed the point further: "Let us see which we should sooner believe in matters of faith, even though they are in perfect agreement. Should it happen that the community which is called the church, and Scripture, disagree on some point, we could then know to which of them it is safer to adhere."[31] In this case, by "church," Henry did not refer to a true church but to a community that is reputed to be the church and that has fallen away from the ideal and become heretical. He answered his question with this false church in mind: "In itself and absolutely speaking, one must believe holy Scripture rather than the church. For the truth as such is always kept in Scripture without alteration or change; and nobody may add to, subtract from, or change it.... In the persons, however, who are in the church, truth may evolve and vary; the majority can dissent and renounce faith by mistake or malice, although the church remains always in a few just men."[32] Unexpectedly, therefore, Henry drove a

26. John Hus, *De Ecclesia*, trans. David S. Schaff (New York: Scribner's, 1915), 71, in Tavard, 51. A "papal bull" is an official declaration by the pope.

27. Ibid., 175–76, in Tavard, 49.

28. Henry engaged in this theoretical exercise in the prologue to his *Commentary on the Sentences*. The *Four Books of Sentences*, written by Peter Lombard, was the standard theo-

logical textbook for the preparation of the medieval church's clergy.

29. Henry of Ghent, *Commentary on the Sentences*, art. 10, q. 1, n. 4, in Tavard, 23.

30. Ibid.

31. Ibid.

32. Ibid., art. 10, q. 1, n. 5, in Tavard, 23–24.

wedge between the authority of the church and the authority of Scripture. He solidified this in his explanation of the distinction between new believers and mature believers in terms of their differing relationship to the authority of the church and to the authority of Scripture. In terms of new Christians: "For the first birth and reception of faith, the authority of the church is more important than that of Scripture. It is therefore reasonable for a man who approaches faith for the first time to believe first and more in the church than in Scripture and to believe in Christ and his Scripture on account of the church."[33] The reverse is true of mature believers: "To confirm and substantiate, however, a faith already born, the authority of holy Scripture, when it is understood, has the higher value. For a believer would adhere to it even if he saw the men through whom he received the faith renounce it, and even if he saw the whole church in the others—which is impossible—abandon the faith."[34] Thus, Henry of Ghent's speculative questioning led to the unraveling of the church's previously close correlation between the church and Scripture.

Reaction to Henry was largely negative. In disagreeing with his speculations, however, Gerald of Bologna introduced a novel idea into the debate. Certainly, Gerald affirmed, Scripture enjoys ultimate authority, because knowledge of Scripture "transmits cognizance [understanding] of all the items that are necessary to salvation, and the truth of all that is to be believed explicitly or implicitly, not always explicitly."[35] However, while some of these implicit matters are derived necessarily from Scripture, others come "from the doctrine and tradition of the apostles ... without [outside of] Scripture."[36] Gerald's new element was a tradition expressed by the church fathers but that comes from apostolic sources that are unwritten—an "oral tradition," so to speak. At one point, Gerald even spoke about this tradition using the language of "revelation." Specifically, with reference to how the church knows which books belong in Scripture, Gerald asserted, "The primitive church understood from a special divine revelation which books she must receive or discard."[37]

Thomas Netter Waldensis elaborated on this notion of oral tradition. He introduced a controversial concept of "apostolic succession"—"the apostles ... their successors, and ... men of sound doctrine and catholic doctors"—as a guarantee of sound doctrine.[38] Among these successors of the apostles, special place belongs to the bishops: "The greatest authority in doubtful things belongs to the bishops and sees [ecclesiastical centers] that received the apostles themselves or their letters, like the churches of Rome, Jerusalem, Ephesus, Alexandria, Thessalonica, Crete, and the like, for authority was primary in them and was thus transferred to the other sees." Even beyond this lies a supreme authority: "In this authority of churches and bishops, however, the guardian of the Roman see [the Church of Rome] rightly claims for himself the highest authority and the most fruitful faith."[39] Thus, the authority of unwritten apostolic teachings was clearly articulated:

---

33. Ibid., art. 10, q. 1, n. 9, in Tavard, 24.

34. Ibid., art. 10, q. 1, n. 10, in Tavard, 24.

35. Gerald of Bologna, *Commentary on the Sentences*, 456, in Tavard, 27.

36. Ibid., 457, in Tavard, 27.

37. Ibid., 360, in Tavard, 27.

38. Thomas Netter Waldensis, *Doctrinale Antiquatum Fidei Catholicae Ecclesiae*, chap. 19, in Tavard, 57.

39. Ibid., chap. 23, in Tavard, 58.

"The church protects and keeps the unwritten words of the apostles and their unwritten traditions that would all belong to the canon of Scripture had they been written.... I believe that the catholic church still keeps like a treasure the greater part of the words of St. Paul in the traditions and the successive documents of the fathers." Thomas Netter Waldensis drew this conclusion: "Such is the dignity of the apostolic traditions which did not transmit in the Scriptures, that the same veneration and the same fervent faith is due to them as to the written ones.... If therefore, once we have studied the Scriptures, we see what the church universally accepts, either in the popular tradition or in the common agreement of the fathers, we must consider it as a full definition of faith as though it were found in the Scriptures.[40] As Gabriel Biel summarized, "Many things that are not in the canon of the Bible were communicated to the church by the apostles and have come down to us through episcopal succession."[41]

And so the church in the latter part of the medieval period affirmed in a novel way the reality of church tradition derived from unwritten apostolic sources and even of postapostolic divine revelation. To these unwritten apostolic sources and postapostolic divine revelations was added the teaching of general church councils (e.g., the Council of Nicea.).[42] Thus, the stage was set for either a continuation of the subordination of the authority of the church to the authority of Scripture—the historic position of the church up to this point—or a new development: the subordination of the authority of Scripture to the authority of the church.

New developments contributed to and ensured the subordination of biblical authority to the authority of the church. Moving beyond Gerald of Bologna's perspective that God had revealed which books compose canonical Scripture, Guido Terreni affirmed the church's authority to determine the canon: "From the church's authority the canonical books derive their power of authority. Through the church the books of the Bible were accepted as authoritative. On her [the church's] authority the faithful firmly believe that they [the canonical Scriptures] infallibly contain the truth. That we must firmly believe in them can be proved only on the basis of the church's authority."[43] Terreni also expanded the notion of what constitutes heresy, thereby expanding the sources of authority. He asserted that "the doctrine of the general councils confirmed by the apostolic see, and mainly the four Councils of Nicea, Constantinople, Ephesus, and Chalcedon, is in such harmony with the sacred doctrine and Scripture, that he who condemns those councils as heretical and holds doctrines that are counter to them, is to be avoided as a heretic."[44]

Changing the question somewhat—from what constitutes heresies to what constitutes catholic truths—William of Ockham listed five types of truths that the church must believe:

---

40. Ibid.

41. Gabriel Biel, *Collectorium super 4 Libros Sententiarum*, bk. 4, chap. 7, q. unica, in Tavard, 62.

42. As Marsilius of Padua explained: "It is not necessary to our eternal salvation that we believe or recognize as irrevocably true any scripture except those that are called canonical, or those that necessarily follow upon these, or the interpretations of determinations of what is obscure in the holy Scrip-

tures when they are taught by a general council of the faithful or Catholics. This applies especially to points like the articles of the Christian faith, error on which would bring to eternal damnation." *Defensor Pacis*, diccio 2, chap. 19, n. 1, in Tavard, 29.

43. Guido Terreni, *Questio de Magisterio Infallibili*, in Tavard, 32.

44. Guido Terreni, *Summa de Heresibus*, in Tavard, 33.

(1) with what is said in holy Scripture, or what can be inferred therefrom through necessary reasoning; (2) with the truths that have come from the apostles by word of mouth or in the writings of the faithful, even though they may not be found in the Sacred Scriptures and may not be concluded with certainty from the Scriptures alone; (3) with the contents of trustful chronicles and histories; (4) with what may be manifestly concluded from truths of the first and second kind only, or from one of them combined with a truth of the third category; (5) with the truths that God, besides the truths revealed to the apostles, has revealed or even inspired to others, or which he would again reveal or even inspire, once that revelation or inspiration has or would have reached, without possibility of doubt, the universal church.[45]

For his second type, Ockham formulated a category of truth that has "come down to us from the apostles by word of mouth." This orally transmitted tradition from the apostles to the postapostolic church was a novel idea introduced in the fourteenth century. And for his fifth type, Ockham articulated a category of truth that is revealed or inspired by God and that is not part of the canon of Scripture. Peter d'Ailly further explained: "God wanted these truths so that Catholics should believe. This is why he also wanted to reveal them to the church, that they might be determined by her. Thus, definitions by the church do not always proceed by way of evident conclusions from the Scriptures; they may also derive from a special revelation made to Catholics."[46] Following this line of thinking, Heinrich Totting von Oyta offered biblical support for this extrabiblical, postapostolic revelation or inspiration: Christ's promise to be with his church to the end of the world (Matt. 28:20) and Christ's words to his disciples, "I have much more to say to you, more than you can now bear" (John 16:12). As von Oyta commented: "Christ promised the apostles that there would be revealed some catholic truths which were not expressly in the Scriptures and did not formally follow from them. This was not only for them, but also for the church which was to last till the end."[47] Furthermore, von Oyta explained how to discern such postapostolic revelation: it had "to be acknowledged as such by the church's authority."[48]

Despite protests from pre-Reformers like John Wycliffe,[49] the church, in the person of William of Waterford, underscored its new position on authority: "There is an infinity of truly catholic doctrines that could not be evidently concluded even from the contents of Sacred Scripture.... We are bound to believe and to do [many things] that cannot be deduced from Sacred Scripture alone."[50] Thus, apostolic tradition and customs sanctioned by church authority were added to Scripture as authoritative sources of truth in the Roman Catholic Church.[51]

---

45. William of Ockham, *Dialogue against Heretics*, bk. 2, chap. 5, in Tavard, 35.

46. Peter d'Ailly, in *I Sententiarum*, q. 1, ans. 3, in Tavard, 55.

47. Heinrich Totting von Oyta, *Commentary on the Sentences,* in Tavard, 36.

48. Ibid.

49. John Wycliffe, *De Veritate S. Scriptura*, c. 21, vol. 2, p. 168, in Tavard, 41.

50. William of Waterford, *LXXII Quaestiones de Sacramento Altaris,* in Tavard, 43.

51. Ibid.

THE AUTHORITY OF SCRIPTURE IN THE REFORMATION AND POST-REFORMATION

On the issue of biblical authority, Martin Luther waged war against the Roman Catholic Church, championing the formal principle of the Reformation: *sola Scriptura*, or Scripture alone. On the one hand, this meant that Scripture, because it is the Spirit's writing, is the final judge of Christian doctrine and practice, standing above everything else: "Our endeavor must, therefore, not be to put aside Scripture and to direct our attention to the merely human writings of the fathers. On the contrary, putting aside all human writings, we should spend all the more and all the more persistent labor on Holy Scriptures alone."[52] As the highest authority, Scripture must be the touchstone for Christian beliefs; indeed, "nothing except the divine words are to be the first principles for Christians. All human words are conclusions drawn from them and must be brought back to them and approved by them."[53] Thus, the Word of God is to reign supreme, alone determining doctrine and practice: "In all articles, the foundation of our faith must be God's Word alone, and without God's Word there can be no article of faith."[54]

On the other hand, this meant that anything that lacks biblical warrant cannot be authoritative or binding for Christians. Biblical authority is such "that we are under no obligation to accept anything not asserted in it."[55] Luther specifically applied this to the extrabiblical doctrines of the Catholic Church:

> Since, then, God wants no one to feel obligated to hold to anything not offered by Scripture, we should likewise reject all non-Scriptural doctrine. This injunction can be used against the sacrilege of the pope and the papists who ... shamelessly declare that we must accept more than Scripture contains.... Beware of this, and be certain that all you need to accept is in Scripture. But concerning anything not found in Scripture, you should say...: When did God ever make that statement?[56]

Luther condemned this Catholic practice—which he described as "our search for auxiliary light besides such lucid and clear passages of Scripture"—as "a great punishment brought upon us by the wrath of God."[57] There was only one hope of escape: "We are of necessity obliged to flee for refuge to the solid rock of divine Scripture and not to have the hardihood to believe anything, no matter what it may be, that speaks, ordains, or does anything without this authority."[58] Thus, he urged the pope—as well as himself, or anyone else, for that matter: "My dear pope, you must not lord it over Scripture, nor must I or anybody else, according to our own ideas. The devil take that attitude! We should rather allow Scripture to rule and master us, and we ourselves should not be the masters, according to our own mad heads, setting ourselves above Scripture."[59]

---

52. Martin Luther, *WLS*, 1:87.
53. Ibid., 1:87–88.
54. Ibid., 1:405.
55. Ibid., 1:85.

56. Ibid., 1:85.
57. Ibid., 1:86.
58. Ibid., 1:89.
59. Ibid., 1:90.

But there was more, and more in terms of a constructive approach to biblical authority. For Luther, the authority of Scripture means that the preached word is to be regarded as the Word of God; that is, the preacher communicates on the part of God:

> Would to God that we could gradually train our hearts to believe that the preacher's words are God's Word.... As a matter of fact, it is ... the Divine Majesty Himself that is preaching here. To be sure, I do not hear this with my ears or see it with my eyes; all I hear is the voice of the preacher ... and I behold only a man before me. But I view the picture correctly if I add that the voice and words of ... pastor are not his own words and doctrine but those of our Lord and God.... "This is the place; here God is speaking through the voice of the preacher who brings God's Word."[60]

Thus, the pastor and his quality of preaching mean nothing at all. What is important is the authoritative Word of God that is communicated: "For a poor speaker may speak the Word of God just as well as he who is endowed with eloquence.... There is no difference between the Word when uttered by a schoolboy and when uttered by the angel Gabriel; they vary only in rhetorical ability."[61]

Although he denounced the Catholic propensity to add authoritative extrabiblical traditions and interpretations to Scripture, Luther and the Lutheran churches did not simply throw out the accumulated wisdom of nearly fifteen hundred years of church doctrine and practice. In keeping with the principle of *sola Scriptura*, the *Formula of Concord* articulated the supreme authority of Scripture: "We believe, confess, and teach that the only rule and norm, according to which all dogmas and all doctors ought to be esteemed and judged, is no other whatever than the prophetic and apostolic writings both of the Old and of the New Testament.... But other writings, whether of the fathers or of the moderns, with whatever name they come, are in no way to be equaled to the Holy Scriptures, but are all to be esteemed inferior to them."[62] Immediately following this affirmation, however, the *Formula* addressed the importance of certain church traditions "(such as are the *Apostles'*, the *Nicene*, and the *Athanasian Creeds*). We publicly profess that we embrace them, and reject all heresies and all dogmas that have ever been brought into the church of God contrary to their decision."[63] Thus, in a way reminiscent of the early church, Luther and the Lutheran churches insisted on the supreme authority of Scripture while embracing a harmonious relationship between authoritative Scripture and the historic creeds of the church.

Like others before him, John Calvin emphasized that the authority of Scripture is grounded in the authority of its divine Author. In addition, only one reality can provide the assurance that God himself is the authoritative author of Scripture: "If we desire to provide in the best way for our consciences—that they may not be perpetually beset by the instability of doubt or vacillation, and that they may not also boggle at the smallest quibbles—we ought to seek our conviction in a higher place than human reason,

---

60. Martin Luther, *Sermons on the Gospel of St. John*, LW, 22:526–27.

61. Ibid., LW, 22:529.

62. *Formula of Concord*, Epitome 1: "Of the Compendious Rule and Norm," in Schaff, 3:93–94.

63. Ibid., in Schaff, 3:95.

judgments, or conjectures, that is, in the secret testimony of the Spirit."[64] Specifically, for Calvin, this "testimony of the Spirit is more excellent than all reason. For as God alone is a fit witness of himself in his Word, so also the Word will not find acceptance in men's hearts before it is sealed by the inward testimony of the Spirit. The same Spirit, therefore, who has spoken through the mouths of the prophets must penetrate into our hearts to persuade us that they faithfully proclaimed what had been divinely commanded."[65] This testimony of the Spirit gives absolute certainty of the divine authorship, and hence authority, of Scripture: "Therefore, illumined by his [the Spirit's] power, we believe neither by our own nor by anyone else's judgment that Scripture is from God; but above human judgment we affirm with utter certainty (just as if we were gazing upon the majesty of God himself) that it has flowed to us from the very mouth of God by the ministry of men."[66] Thus, Scripture is authoritative because it has God for its author.

This being said, it should be noted as well that Calvin wrote a lengthy chapter on proofs for the divine authority of Scripture: "So Far as Human Reason Goes, Sufficiently Firm Proofs Are at Hand to Establish the Credibility of Scripture."[67] These proofs encompassed the superiority of Scripture to all human wisdom, the great antiquity of Scripture, the confirmation of biblical authority by "numerous and remarkable miracles," the fulfillment of prophecies, the preservation of Scripture against many attempts to destroy it, the simplicity and heavenly character and authority of the New Testament, the constant testimony of the church to the authority of Scripture, and the sacrifice of martyrs for the sake of Scripture. Although these proofs could not absolutely establish the authority of Scripture, they are nonetheless aids for Christians to embrace biblical authority.

Like Luther before him, Calvin denounced the usurpation of biblical authority by the Roman Catholic Church. He leveled a scathing attack against the church's claim to confer authority on Scripture: "A most pernicious error widely prevails that Scripture has only so much weight as is conceded to it by the consent of the church. As if the eternal and inviolable truth of God depended upon the decision of men!"[68] For Calvin, any kind of conferred authority, even the kind conferred by the church, is insufficient to establish the absolute certainty that is needed when it comes to Scripture.[69] Appealing to Scripture itself (Eph. 2:20), Calvin refuted this Roman Catholic contention: "If the teaching of the prophets and apostles is the foundation, this must have had authority before the church began to exist.... It is utterly vain, then, to pretend that the power of judging Scripture so lies with the church that its certainty depends upon churchly assent."[70] Not the church's approbation, but its recognition, of Scripture is, therefore, the key, for Scripture is self-authenticating: "Because the church recognizes Scripture to be the truth of its own God, as a pious duty it unhesitatingly venerates Scripture."[71] Thus, the church is to submit to the authority of Scripture rather than to exercise authority over Scripture.

---

64. John Calvin, *Institutes of the Christian Religion*, 1.7.4, LCC, 1:78.

65. Ibid., 1.7.4, LCC, 1:79.
66. Ibid., 1.7.5, LCC, 1:80.
67. Ibid., 1.8, LCC, 1:81–92.

68. Ibid., 1.7.1, LCC, 1:75.
69. Ibid.
70. Ibid., 1.7.2, LCC, 1:75–76.
71. Ibid., 1.7.2, LCC, 1:76.

Of course, this was exactly the opposite of what had occurred in the Roman Catholic Church in the latter part of the Middle Ages, and Calvin continued his critique of this development. He was particularly critical of the support offered by the church for its position, especially two key areas. The first was the church's claim to be infallibly led by the Holy Spirit.[72] Of course, Calvin agreed that the church should "be taught by the Holy Spirit through God's Word."[73] In saying this, however, he highlighted the difference between his position and that of the Roman Catholic Church: "Our opponents locate the authority of the church outside God's Word; but we insist that it be attached to the Word, and do not allow it to be separated from it."[74] Calvin also addressed the second key area of support—John 16:12—marshaled by the Roman Catholic Church to justify the authority of its traditions.[75] Furthermore, he presented a thoroughgoing refutation of the authority of church councils.[76] Thus, Calvin keenly defended the authority of Scripture over against the Roman Catholic Church's claims to confer authority on Scripture, to proclaim certain teaching as part of authoritative tradition, and to convene councils that were more authoritative than Scripture itself.

Of course, the Roman Catholic Church acted swiftly to counter this challenge to its own authority. John Eck, John Cochlaus, and Albert Pigge (among others) defended and expanded the church's position that honored both Scripture and tradition.[77] Interpretation of canonical Scripture, they asserted, belongs properly to the church, because the "true understanding of Scripture" is located in the church, which both precedes and is "superior to Scripture"; indeed, "Scripture is not authentic without the authority of the Church, since canonical writers are her members."[78] Thus, "How necessary to us is the authority of the most holy church and of the apostolic see to provide the whole meaning and the authority of Sacred Scripture."[79] This ecclesial authority is most readily seen in the church's determination of the biblical canon: "Without [apart from] the Scriptures we have received many things from the Church's tradition; we have received no Scripture at all without [apart from] the Church."[80] Specifically, it was the Holy Spirit guiding the church that enabled it to establish rightly the composition of Scripture: "For although the Word of God is beyond judgment, the grace of the Holy Spirit has given the Church the power to discern which books have the Word of God and which do not."[81]

---

72. Ibid., 4.8.11–13, LCC, 2:1159–62.

73. Ibid., 4.8.13, LCC, 2:1162.

74. Ibid.

75. "But what effrontery is this? I confess that the disciples were as yet untutored and well-nigh unteachable when they heard this from the Lord. But when they committed their doctrine to writing, were they even then beset with such dullness that they afterward needed to supply with a living voice what they had omitted from their writings through the fault of ignorance? Now, if they had already been led into all truth by the Spirit of truth [John 16:13] when they put forth their writings, what hindered them from embracing and leaving in written form a perfect and distinct knowledge of gospel doctrine?" Ibid., 4.8.14, LCC, 2:1163–64.

76. Ibid., 4.9.1–14, LCC, 2:1166–79.

77. E.g., John Cochlaus claimed: "There is no lesser impiety in disregarding and rejecting the living voice of the Church and its unwritten ancient traditions than in disregarding and rejecting canonical Scripture." John Cochlaus, *De Auctoritate Ecclesiae et Scripturae adversus Lutherum* (1524), chap. 4, in Tavard, 125.

78. John Eck, *Enchiridion Locorum Communium* (1525), folio 5r; folio 5v, in Tavard, 120.

79. Cochlaus, *De Auctoritate Ecclesiae et Scripturae adversus Lutherum* (1524), bk. 2, chap. 12, in Tavard, 126. Cf. Albert Pigge, *Hierarchiae Ecclesiasticae Assertio* (1538), 8b., in Tavard, 147.

80. Cochlaus, chap. 9., in Tavard, 127.

81. Eck, *Enchiridion Locorum Communium*, folio 233rb., in Tavard, 121.

Accordingly, "If the Church can discern the Scriptures, it can also, with better reason, know beyond doubt the true sense of Scripture, for the Scriptures are understood by the same Spirit that wrote them."[82] The same Spirit was invoked as the authoritative basis for tradition:

> The Holy Spirit, doctor and leader, consoler of the Church, is not tied down to the written Word of God. He has rightly taught the Church with an interior and inspired word many items that have not been explicitly included in the written Word of God.... For the Spirit was not only in the apostles. He has also spoken in their successors. Continuously he has remained in the Church to this day and he remains in her forever and ever. In her, therefore, he still speaks today as though in the seat and basis of truth, and he teaches all the very truth.[83]

In Pigge's view such tradition stands over Scripture as "the most certain rule of truth, wherewith the Scriptures and all the doubts arising from them must be weighed under pain of error."[84] Thus, "the authority of ecclesiastical tradition shines much farther than that of the Scriptures, be it only because it extends to the Scriptures themselves, and not vice versa."[85] As Eck concluded: "Great indeed, great is the authority of the Church, to which Scripture itself bows.... All this draws its force from the fact that the Church is assisted by her doctor and master, the Holy Spirit."[86]

In Eck, Cochlaus, Pigge, and others, the Roman Catholic Church reacted to the Protestant doctrine of the authority of Scripture. In so doing, it departed from its own traditional perspective of the coincidence of Scripture and its own historical understanding handed down throughout the ages. In its place, the Catholic Church affirmed a novel idea of its own supremacy over Scripture while insisting also on church tradition as another inspired revelation from the Holy Spirit of equal value to the Word of God.

The official Roman Catholic position was formulated at the Council of Trent. The Council decreed that authoritative divine revelation—"saving truth and moral discipline [instruction]"—comes in two forms: "This truth and discipline [instruction] are contained in the written books and the unwritten traditions which, received by the apostles from the mouth of Christ himself, or from the apostles themselves as the Holy Spirit dictated, have come down even unto us."[87] Furthermore, the council sanctioned the church's own interpretation of Scripture as the only authoritative interpretation.[88] Thus, according to the Roman Catholic Church, authoritative divine revelation comes from both Scripture and tradition, and only the church's interpretation of Scripture is to be considered authoritative. Protestant and Roman Catholic sentiments on the authority of Scripture could not be farther apart.

---

82. Eck, *Confutatio Scriptorum Protestantium contra Praefatum Librum*, in Tavard, 123.

83. Cochlaus, *Philippica* (1540), in Tavard, 128–29.

84. Pigge, *Elucidatio*, fol. 76r, in Tavard, 147.

85. Pigge, *Hierarchiae Ecclesiasticae Assertion*, 24c., in Tavard, 147.

86. Eck, *Enchiridion Locorum Communium*, fol. 233va., in Tavard, 122.

87. *Canons and Decrees of the Council of Trent*, 4th session (April 8, 1546), *Decree Concerning the Canonical Scriptures*, in Schaff, 2:79–80.

88. Ibid., in Schaff, 2:83.

These opposing positions became more firmly entrenched during the post-Reformation period, as Protestant doctrinal statements such as the *Westminster Confession of Faith*[89] and Protestant scholastic theologians such as Francis Turretin[90] and John Andrew Quenstedt[91] continued and advanced the formal principle of Protestantism: *sola Scriptura*.

THE AUTHORITY OF SCRIPTURE IN THE MODERN PERIOD

The Roman Catholic Church continued to affirm the dual nature of divine revelation and its own authority in relation to both Scripture and tradition. In a further development that officially cemented centuries of practice, Vatican Council I pronounced the doctrine of the infallibility of the pope:

> It is a dogma divinely revealed: that the Roman Pontiff, when he speaks *ex cathedra*, that is, when in discharge of the office of pastor and doctor of all Christians, by virtue of his supreme apostolic authority, he defines a doctrine regarding faith or morals to be held by the universal church, by the divine assistance promised to him in blessed Peter, is possessed of that infallibility with which the divine Redeemer will that his church should be endowed for defining doctrine regarding faith or morals; and that therefore such definitions of the Roman Pontiff are irreformable of themselves, and not from the consent of the church.[92]

Although the church had, from the time of the Council of Trent, officially sanctioned church tradition as being divine revelation, the declaration of papal infallibility ensured that all such tradition would possess divine authority. This means that the doctrines of the immaculate conception of Mary (promulgated December 8, 1854) and the bodily assumption of Mary (promulgated November 1, 1950) must be embraced by all Catholics because they are part of divine revelation and carry divine authority to be believed.

Modern Protestants continued to denounce this traditional Roman Catholic doctrine. Against its two-source notion of divine revelation, Charles Hodge offered this logical argument: "If there are two standards of doctrine of equal authority, the one the explanatory, and infallible interpreter of the other, it is of necessity the interpretation that determines the faith of the people. Instead, therefore, of our faith resting on the testimony of God as recorded in his Word, it rests on what poor, fallible, often fanciful, prejudiced, benighted men, tell us is the meaning of that Word. Man and his authority take the place of God."[93] Similarly, John Warwick Montgomery argued that

---

89. *Westminster Confession of Faith*, 4, 5, 10, in Schaff, 3:602 – 4.

90. Francis Turretin, *Institutes of Elenctic Theology*, ed. James T. Dennison Jr., trans. George Musgrave Giger, 3 vols. in 1 (Phillipsburg, N.J.: P & R, 1997), 2nd topic, 4th q., 6th q., 1:62 – 64, 86 – 91.

91. John Andrew Quenstedt, *Theologia Didactico-Polemica sive Systema Theologicum* (Leipzig, 1715), 1.93, 97 – 98, in Schmid, 55 – 60.

92. *Dogmatic Decrees of the Vatican Council Concerning the Catholic Faith and the Church of Christ*, 4th session (July 18, 1870), *First Dogmatic Constitution on the Church of Christ*, 4, in Schaff, 2:270 – 71.

93. Charles Hodge, *Systematic Theology*, 3 vols. (1872 – 73; Peabody, Mass.: Hendrickson, 1999), 1:128.

"all multiple-source views" of authority are "unstable," giving "preference to one source rather than to another." As seen in the Catholic Church, tradition takes preference over Scripture; thus, tradition becomes the church's "*final* authority."[94] So consistent has this position been that it may be said that a hallmark of evangelicalism, following its Protestant heritage, has been the rejection of Roman Catholic tradition as a source of authoritative divine revelation.

As important as this sustained clash between Protestants and Roman Catholics continued to be for Christianity, beyond this intramural debate a growing tide of biblical criticism gradually eroded people's traditional confidence in the authority of Scripture. The origin and development of biblical criticism, leading to the demise of the traditional doctrines of inspiration and inerrancy, is recounted elsewhere.[95] Suffice it to say here that a tragic yet logical result of attacks against the divine inspiration and truthfulness of Scripture was the demise of biblical authority. This was logical because of the intimate connection between the doctrines of biblical inspiration and biblical authority:

> The divine authority of the Scriptures and their inspiration are two distinct, but inseparable, truths. The authority of the Scriptures proceeds from their inspiration, and their inspiration establishes their authority.... If the authority of the Scriptures falls, their inspiration falls; if, on the contrary, it be the inspiration that is taken from us, the authority likewise vanishes away. The Scripture without inspiration is a cannon from which the charge has been removed.[96]

This was also tragic, for as Emil Brunner succinctly put it: "In earlier days this discussion used to be cut short by saying briefly, 'It is written'; that is, with the aid of the doctrine of verbal inspiration. Today we can no longer do this, even if we would."[97] The Bible as divinely authoritative became a principal target of attack in the modern world.

Examples of this abound. Friedrich Schleiermacher, referring to historical ideas of biblical inspiration, truthfulness, and authority, asserted that "in order to attain to faith, we need no such doctrine of Scripture."[98] Indeed, one of Schleiermacher's key proposals was that "the authority of holy Scripture cannot be the foundation of faith in Christ; rather must the latter be presupposed before a particular authority can be granted to holy Scripture."[99] But to place faith before biblical authority was to reverse the historical order of Scripture as leading to salvation, and it elevated personal experience above divinely authoritative revelation. In Schleiermacher's revolutionary turn-to-the-subject, the trajectory was set for the future disregard for biblical authority, with subjective experience enthroned as supremely authoritative.

---

94. John Warwick Montgomery, *The Suicide of Christian Theology* (Minneapolis: Bethany, 1970), 281.

95. See chaps. 3, 5.

96. J. H. Merle d'Aubigne, *The Authority of God* (New York: R. Carter, 1851), 48, cited in René Pache, *The Inspiration and Authority of Scripture*, trans. Helen I. Needham (Chicago: Moody, 1969; repr., Salem, Wis.: Sheffield, 1992), 305.

97. Emil Brunner, *The Mediator: A Study of the Central Doctrine of the Christian Faith*, trans. Olive Wyon (London: Lutterworth, 1934), 323. Although Brunner made this statement with reference to the doctrine of the virgin birth, it can be universally applied to the discussion of any Christian doctrine.

98. Friedrich Schleiermacher, *The Christian Faith*, ed. H. R. Mackintosh and J. S. Stewart (Edinburgh: T & T Clark, 1928, repr. 1960), 593.

99. Ibid., 591.

Emil Brunner substituted the authority of Scripture with the authority of Jesus Christ. He stated, "We believe in Christ, not because Scripture, or the apostles, teach us about him in such and such a way, but we believe in the Scriptures because, and in so far as, they teach Christ. The authority of Scripture is not formal but material: Christ, the revelation. Even subjectively, however, this authority is not based upon the Scriptures as such, but upon the encounter of faith with the Christ of Scripture."[100] In so stating, Brunner explicitly denied the formal principle of Protestantism. He replaced it with "a completely new conception of the authority of Scripture. We are not required to believe the Scriptures because they are the Scriptures; but because Christ, whom I am convinced in my conscience is the Truth, meets me in the Scriptures—therefore I believe. Scripture ... is an *instrumental* authority, in so far as it contains that element before which I must bow in the truth, which also itself awakens in me the certainty of truth."[101]

Karl Barth also took an instrumental approach to biblical authority, using the theme of "Scripture as a *witness* to divine revelation."[102] Summarizing what is discussed elsewhere,[103] according to Barth, "we distinguish the Bible as such from revelation. A witness is not absolutely identical with that to which it witnesses.... Therefore when we have to do with the Bible, we have to do primarily with this means, with these words, with the witness which as such is not itself revelation but only—and this is the limitation—the witness to it."[104] This meant for Barth that rather than saying that the Bible *is* the Word of God, one should rather say that it *becomes* the Word of God, when God condescends sovereignly and freely to reveal himself to people through the Bible.[105] Barth's exposition of the relationship between revelation, the Word of God, witnesses to revelation, and the Bible exerted a huge impact on the church. Authority became associated with the *function* of the Bible: Scripture exercises *instrumental* authority as it becomes the Word of God. The Bible is an *attestation* to the authority of the triune God, whose lordship becomes present only when God freely and sovereignly deigns to reveal himself personally to people through this witness.[106] This position was, of course, a far cry from the historic Protestant understanding of biblical authority.

---

100. Emil Brunner, *The Christian Doctrine of God: Dogmatics*, 2 vols., trans. Olive Wyon (London: Lutterworth, 1934), 1:110. Although Brunner claimed to be following Martin Luther in this, it is arguable that Luther never made such a definitive separation between the Word of God who is Jesus Christ and the Word of God that is Scripture to the point that the authority of the latter would be subject to the authority of the former.

101. Ibid.

102. *CD*, I/2, 457.

103. See chap. 3.

104. *CD*, I/2, 463.

105. Ibid., 507–8.

106. These instrumentalist approaches to biblical authority by Brunner, Barth, and others were summarized by Paul Achtemeier: "Obviously, if the Bible does not have its origins in some unique way in the will of God, if it is a book like any other book, then no more authority can be claimed for it than for any other book. The nature and locus of inspiration, in short, will determine the authority that we may claim for Scripture. Whatever authority Scripture will have, therefore, will depend on its relationship to God. Some have sought to define that relationship in terms of the use God makes of Scripture to awaken faith and obedience in those who hear its message. The Bible's authority will then lie not so much in the accuracy of its historical reporting or on its ability to anticipate discoveries of modern sciences. Rather, its authority will lie in the way in which it brings to bear in the contemporary world the significance of events and people about which it speaks. It will be authoritative as an instrument in accomplishing God's plan of salvation, bearing witness to God's will and to the way he has accomplished his purposes in the past." Paul J. Achtemeier, *The Inspiration of Scripture: Problems and Proposals*, Biblical Perspectives on Current Issues (Philadelphia: Westminster, 1980), 37.

But Scripture, and biblical authority as traditionally understood, was not without its defenders. Despite these attacks against the authority of Scripture, many evangelicals continued to affirm the historic doctrine. One approach used was to criticize the elevation of human critical reason above the authority of Scripture. (Remember: To a large degree, modern approaches to biblical authority were a response to the encroachment of biblical criticism, specifically the historical-critical method of interpretation.) J. I. Packer exposed the fallacy of those who elevate reason to an authority along with Scripture. Calling them "subjectivists in the matter of authority," he explained:

> Their position is based on an acceptance of the presuppositions and conclusions of ... critical Bible study, which are radically at variance with the Bible's own claims for itself. On this basis, they think it necessary to say—indeed, to insist—that some scriptural assertions are erroneous.... They say, we must use our Christian wits to discern beneath the fallible words of fallible men the eternal truth of God. But this makes it impossible to regard Scripture as authoritative without qualification; what is now authoritative is not Scripture as it stands, but Scripture as pruned by a certain type of scholarship—in other words, human opinions about Scripture.[107]

Packer continued his criticism:

> It is true that these critics pay lip-service to the principle of biblical authority, and, indeed, suppose themselves to accept it; but their view of the nature of Scripture effectively prevents them from doing so. It is evident that they have not thought out with sufficient seriousness what subjection to biblical authority means in practice. Their view really amounts to saying that the question of biblical authority is now closed; the supreme authority is undoubtedly Christian reason, which must hunt for the word of God in the Bible by the light of rationalistic critical principles.[108]

Thus, Packer defended the traditional doctrine of the authority of Scripture.

Yet evangelicals did more than just criticize critical approaches to Scripture and its authority. They also offered robust discussions of the topic. D. Martyn Lloyd-Jones, for example, outlined several general principles concerning biblical authority. One was that "Scripture must be viewed as a whole: There is nothing more important, if we are concerned about the authority of the Scriptures, than to start with the whole Bible first, and to consider the details in the light of the whole, and not in the reverse order." Furthermore, "the authority of the Scriptures is a matter of faith and not of argument.... There is a real value in these [namely, scientific, historical, archaeological, rational] arguments, but in the end (as the Protestant Fathers themselves taught) no man can truly believe in and submit himself to the authority of the Scriptures except as the result of the 'testimonium Spiritus internum' [internal witness of the Spirit]." Moreover, biblical authority is "a truth to be asserted" with reference to the principle that "the whole Bible is the Word

---

107. J. I. Packer, *Fundamentalism and the Word of God* (Grand Rapids: Eerdmans, 1958), 72.   108. Ibid., 72–73.

of God."[109] Lloyd-Jones bolstered this general outline of biblical authority with detailed arguments for it, including the uniqueness of Scripture, Scripture's own claims, Christ's teachings, the New Testament's view of the Old, and the authority of the apostles.[110]

Picking up on this argument from Christ's teachings, Abraham Kuyper expressed the idea that by calling Jesus Christ "Lord," Christians obligate themselves to accept their Lord's view of Scripture:

> When the Christ, whose Spirit witnessed beforehand in the prophets, attributes such authority to the Scripture of the Old Covenant, and by his apostles indicates the ground for that authority in the theopneusty [inspiration], there is no power that can prevent the recognition of that authority by him who believes in Jesus. Not to recognize it would avenge itself in the representation that in the very holiest things Christ had wholly mistaken himself. This would imply *the loss of his Savior.*[111]

Anticipating an objection, Edward J. Carnell gave an answer to critics who maintained that "Jesus was mistaken in his view of Scripture. The assumption is that if Jesus had enjoyed the benefits of modern criticism, he would have entertained a different attitude toward the Old Testament." Appealing to Scripture (John 5:24; 12:49; 14:10), Carnell offered this rejoinder: "Since Christ was so intimately united with the Father, we cannot impugn the judgment of Christ without impugning the judgment of the Father. Jesus and the Father were one in teaching as well as in essence."[112]

These robust evangelical discussions of the authority of Scripture at times recaptured the historic Reformation emphasis on the intimate link between the Word of God and the Spirit of God. Lloyd-Jones criticized the conflict in the minds of some people between the authority of Scripture and the authority of the Holy Spirit; such is a false and unnecessary conflict: "The Bible suggests, therefore, that the Holy Spirit normally speaks to us through the Word. He takes his own Word, he illumines it, and takes our minds and enlightens them, and we are thus made receptive to the Word.... It is not right, therefore, to speak of the Spirit *or* the Word, but rather of the Spirit *and* the Word, and especially the Spirit *through* the Word."[113] Other evangelicals insisted on this intersection of biblical authority with the ministry of the Holy Spirit. As Millard Erickson explained: "Actually, it is the combination of these two factors that constitutes authority. Both are needed. The written word, correctly interpreted, is the objective basis of authority. The inward illuminating and persuading work of the Holy Spirit is the subjective dimension.... Together, the two yield a maturity that is necessary in the Christian life."[114]

Just how difficult it is to maintain a balance between the Word of God and the Spirit of God, however, was seen in the theology of Stanley Grenz. Framing the doctrine of Scripture within his discussion of the work of the Holy Spirit, he offered a view of biblical

109. D. Martyn Lloyd-Jones, *Authority* (Chicago: InterVarsity, 1958), 37–47.

110. Ibid., 47–61.

111. Abraham Kuyper, *Principles of Sacred Theology* (Grand Rapids: Eerdmans, 1954), 551.

112. Edward J. Carnell, *The Case for Orthodox Theology* (Philadelphia: Westminster, 1959), 39–40.

113. Lloyd-Jones, *Authority*, 63–64.

114. Millard J. Erickson, *Christian Theology*, 2nd ed. (Grand Rapids: Baker, 1998), 278.

authority that located Scripture as a servant (thus playing a secondary role) to both divine revelation and the Spirit.[115] Thus, Grenz sketched out a view of the Bible as being the *instrument* of the Spirit and of divine revelation and on that basis authoritative for the church: "The Spirit speaking through its pages is our sole authority. Only the Bible is so intimately related to the historical revelation of God so as itself to be termed 'revelation.' Only the Bible constitutes the written record of the revelatory historical occurrences, together with the prophetic interpretation and application of these events. Only the Bible directs our attention to God in Christ, thereby bringing us face-to-face with the loving, Savior God."[116] The underpinnings of neoorthodox theology and its understanding of Scripture as possessing instrumental authority were clear with Grenz and others.

The classic formulation of contemporary evangelicalism on biblical authority came in the *Chicago Statement on Biblical Inerrancy*. Its opening affirmed that Scripture "is of infallible divine authority in all matters upon which it touches: it is to be believed as God's instruction, in all that it affirms; obeyed, as God's command, in all that it requires; embraced, as God's pledge, in all that it promises."[117] Specifically, it affirmed the self-evident nature of such authority while denying "that the Scriptures receive their authority from the Church, tradition, or any other human source."[118] Furthermore, it underscored the supremacy of biblical authority, maintaining "that the Scriptures are the supreme written norm by which God binds the conscience, and that the authority of the Church is subordinate to that of Scripture."[119] Moreover, it affirmed the Bible itself to be divine revelation and openly denied the neoorthodox view "that the Bible is merely a witness to revelation, or only becomes revelation in encounter, or depends on the response of men for its validity."[120] Certainly, the *Chicago Statement* stood in the classic Protestant legacy affirming authority as an intrinsic property of Scripture and ruled out viewing biblical authority in functionalist ways.

---

115. Stanley Grenz, *Theology for the Community of God* (Nashville: Broadman, 1994), 524.

116. Ibid., 525. His view echoes that of John Baillie, *The Idea of Revelation in Recent Thought* (New York: Columbia University Press, 1956).

117. *Chicago Statement on Biblical Inerrancy*, statement 2, in Grudem, *Systematic Theology*, 1204.

118. Ibid., art. 1, in Grudem, *Systematic Theology*, 1204.

119. Ibid., art. 2, in Grudem, *Systematic Theology*, 1205.

120. Ibid., art. 3, in Grudem, *Systematic Theology*, 1205.

Chapter 5

THE INERRANCY OF SCRIPTURE

How has the church come to believe that the Bible is completely true and without error in everything that it affirms?

STATEMENT OF BELIEF

The church has historically acknowledged that Scripture in its original manuscripts and properly interpreted is completely true and without any error in everything that it affirms, whether that has to do with doctrine, moral conduct, or matters of history, cosmology, geography, and the like.[1] Over time, the church has expressed this conviction by applying a number of terms to the Bible, such as *truthful*, *inerrant*, and *infallible*. No matter what term it used, the church from its outset was united in its belief that the Word of God is true and contains no error. The first significant challenge to this belief did not arise until the seventeenth century. Beginning with questions about Moses as the author of the Pentateuch, the situation is such that nearly three centuries later few if any affirmations of Scripture have not come under attack as to their truthfulness. Although evangelicals originally affirmed the historic church position, increasing attacks against the inerrancy of Scripture have necessitated a sustained defense of this doctrine over the last several decades. Most continue to support the complete truthfulness, or inerrancy, of Scripture, while some evangelicals maintain the infallibility of Scripture—it is not liable to fail in regard to accomplishing its divinely designed purpose.[2]

THE INERRANCY OF SCRIPTURE IN THE EARLY CHURCH

The early church fully accepted the complete truthfulness of Scripture, as did the Jewish people before them. Bruce Vawter summarized this:

---

1. This definition is adapted from the standard one given by Paul D. Feinberg, "The Meaning of Inerrancy," in *Inerrancy*, ed. Norman Geisler (Grand Rapids: Zondervan, 1982), 294.

See later discussion.

2. My thanks to Joo Jung for his help on this chapter.

It would be pointless to call into question that Biblical inerrancy in a rather absolute form was a common persuasion from the beginning of Christian times, and from Jewish times before that. For both the Fathers and the rabbis generally, the ascription of any error to the Bible was unthinkable.... If the word was God's it must be true, regardless of whether it made known a mystery of divine revelation or commented on a datum of natural science, whether it derived from human observation or chronicled an event of history.[3]

To cite two biblical examples of this attitude, the psalmist David noted that "the words of the LORD are flawless, like silver refined in a furnace of clay, purified seven times" (Ps. 12:6), and Jesus confirmed this, acknowledging to the Father, "Your word is truth" (John 17:17). The earliest Christians continued to express this same firm belief. Clement of Rome affirmed the complete truthfulness of the Old Testament: "You have searched the Scriptures, which are true, which were given by the Holy Spirit; you know that nothing unrighteous or counterfeit is written in them."[4] Hippolytus spoke of "the Scripture of truth,"[5] and Irenaeus declared that "the Scriptures are indeed perfect."[6]

The truthfulness of the Bible was understood in two ways by the early church. First, the affirmations of Scripture correspond to reality. That is, the Bible recounts the stories of people who really lived, it relates events that actually took place, it rehearses the works of God as they were performed historically, and so forth. As Tertullian noted, "The statements of Holy Scripture will never be discordant with truth."[7] And Origen criticized heretical views that the biblical writers were tellers of tall tales. He argued from the unfavorable and derogatory stories found in Scripture. It would be quite strange for the biblical authors to present such shameful and embarrassing acts—including those in which they themselves were involved—unless their accounts portrayed the actual facts.[8] Scripture tells the truth—even when the stories it recounts are ugly.

Second, truthfulness means Scripture does not contradict Scripture; thus, there is no disharmony within the Bible. Theophilus affirmed that "all the prophets spoke harmoniously and in agreement with one another."[9] This noncontradictory nature of the Bible has an important implication for interpreting Scripture, as Irenaeus emphasized: "All Scripture, which has been given to us by God, shall be found by us perfectly consistent: and the parables shall harmonize with those passages which are perfectly plain; and those statements the meaning of which is clear shall serve to explain the parables."[10] Because Scripture cannot contradict itself, its clearer passages can be used to shed light on the more difficult passages so they can be understood. Justin Martyr pointed out another important implication of biblical harmony for interpreting Scripture: "Since I am entirely convinced that no Scripture contradicts another, I shall admit rather that I

3. Bruce Vawter, *Biblical Inspiration* (Philadelphia: Westminster, 1972), 132–33.

4. Clement of Rome, *Letter of the Romans to the Corinthians*, 45, in Holmes, 79; *ANF*, 1:17.

5. Hippolytus, *Fragments from Commentaries*, 2.27, in *ANF*, 5:182.

6. Irenaeus, *Against Heresies*, 2.28.2, in *ANF*, 1:399.

7. Tertullian, *A Treatise on the Soul*, 21, in *ANF*, 3:202.

8. Origen, *Against Celsus*, 2.15, in *ANF*, 4:437.

9. Theophilus, *To Autolycus*, 3.17, in *ANF*, 2:116.

10. Irenaeus, *Against Heresies*, 2.28.3, in *ANF*, 1:400.

do not understand what is recorded, and shall strive to persuade those who imagine that the Scriptures are contradictory, to be rather of the same opinion as myself."[11]

Why is Scripture true? In one sense, the early church simply adopted as its own the Jewish view of Hebrew Scripture. But a theological reason lay at the heart of this position, according to Irenaeus: "The Scriptures are indeed perfect, since they were spoken by the Word of God and his Spirit."[12] As Athanasius explained: "It is the opinion of some that the Scriptures do not agree or that God who gave them is false. But there is no disagreement at all. Far from it! Neither can the Father, who is truth, lie; 'for it is impossible that God should lie' [Heb. 6:18]."[13] Because God speaks truth and cannot lie, the Bible, which is the Word of God, communicates truth without error.

This simple affirmation of the truthfulness of Scripture was accompanied by attempts to deal with the evident difficulties that the Bible presents. The church's opponents underscored these problem areas in an attempt to discredit the authority of Scripture, and so church leaders responded with a defense of the Bible's inerrancy. Arnobius addressed the charge that Scripture could not be true because it contains grammatical errors: "You accuse our writings of having disgraceful blemishes. However, do not your most perfect and wonderful books contain these grammatical errors as well?"[14] Thus, grammatical imperfections are common to most writings, but these do not render the writings untrue. Furthermore, John Chrysostom highlighted the importance of distinguishing between contradictions in Scripture and passages that offer different perspectives on the same event or teaching. For example, he explained the diversity between the two accounts of Jesus' genealogy as the result of the different purposes that Matthew and Luke had in writing their gospels.[15] Chrysostom also illustrated this by means of the complementary accounts—the Synoptic Gospels presenting one perspective, John's gospel another view—of the carrying of the cross to Jesus' place of crucifixion.[16] Thus, the early church

---

11. Justin Martyr, *Dialogue with Trypho, a Jew*, 65, in *ANF*, 4:230. Origen similarly offered: "A person becomes a peacemaker when he demonstrates that the things that appear to others to be a conflict in the Scriptures are actually no conflict at all. He demonstrates their harmony and peace—whether of the Old Scriptures with the New, or of the Law with the Prophets, or of the Gospels with the apostolic Scriptures, or of the apostolic Scriptures with each other. For he knows that all Scripture is the one perfect and harmonized instrument of God, from which different sounds give forth one saving voice to those who are willing to learn." Origen, *From the Second Book of the Commentary on the Gospel according to Matthew*, 2, in *ANF*, 10:413. The text has been rendered clearer.

12. Irenaeus, *Against Heresies*, 2.28.2, in *ANF*, 1:399.

13. Athanasius, *Easter Letter*, 19.3, in *NPNF*[2], 4:546. The text has been rendered clearer.

14. Arnobius, *Against the Heathen*, 59, in *ANF*, 6:430. The text has been rendered clearer.

15. John Chrysostom, *Homilies on the Gospel of St. Matthew*, "Homily 1," 7–8, in *NPNF*[1], 10:4. Jesus' genealogy in Matthew is found in 1:1–17; that in Luke, in 3:23–38.

16. "One of the evangelists has stated that Christ carried the cross, another that Simon of Cyrene carried it. But this causes no contradiction or strife. You ask, 'How is there no contradiction between the statements that he carried it and did not carry it?' Because both took place. When they went out of the Praetorium, Christ was carrying the cross. But as they proceeded, Simon took it from him and carried it." John Chrysostom, *Homily on the Paralytic Let Down through the Roof*, 3, in *NPNF*[1], 9:214. Chrysostom referred to John's account (John 19:17), which has Jesus "bearing his own cross," and the Synoptic Gospels (Matt. 27:32; Mark 15:21; Luke 23:26), which have Simon bearing the cross for Jesus. He underscored a simple solution to the apparent problem: John recounts the situation at the beginning of Jesus' march toward Calvary, and the Synoptics focus on a point later in that journey. But Chrysostom did not insist on this type of harmonization all the time. For example, he distinguished Jesus' healing of the paralytic in Matt. 9:1–8 from his healing of the paralytic in John 5. It seems that some people viewed these passages as recounting the same healing. Thus, they used the many divergent points between the accounts to argue for the contradictory nature of Scripture. Chrysostom rightly noted they are different accounts because they refer to different miracles of healing. Thus, they cannot be contradictory.

attempted to respond to criticism of the truthfulness of Scripture because of alleged difficulties in grammar and consistency.

Augustine expressed his complete trust in the Word of God, which he referred to as "infallible Scripture:"[17]

> I have learned to yield this [total] respect and honor only to the canonical books of Scripture. Of these alone do I most firmly believe that their authors were completely free from error. And if in these writings I am perplexed by anything which appears to me opposed to the truth, I do not hesitate to suppose that either the manuscript is faulty, or the translator has not caught the meaning of what was said, or I myself have failed to understand it.... Concerning which it would be wrong to doubt that they are free from error.[18]

So thoroughly convinced was he that Scripture was free from all error, Augustine dared to imagine what the presence of even one mistake in the Bible would lead to:

> It seems to me that most disastrous consequences must follow upon our believing that anything false is found in the sacred books; that is to say, that the men by whom the Scriptures have been given to us and committed to writing did put down in these books anything false.... For if you once admit into such a high sanctuary of authority one false statement as made in the way of duty, there will not be left a single sentence of those books which, if appearing to anyone difficult in practice or hard to believe, may not by the same fatal rule be explained away, as a statement in which, intentionally and under a sense of duty, the author declared what was not true.[19]

Augustine could envision only one scenario in which a view allowing for errors in Scripture could be countenanced, namely, if someone would "propose to furnish us with certain rules by which we may know when a falsehood might or might not become a duty."[20] The presence of just one error in Scripture would not mean that all of Scripture *is in error*, as some mistakenly understand Augustine to say. But it would lead to the suspicion that any part *could be in error*. Human judgment would have to be used to determine which portions are true and which contain errors, but no set rules can be established that enable the church to know infallibly this distinction. The church is left with hopelessly subjective opinion to act as the judge of Scripture's truthfulness.

This all-encompassing notion of the truthfulness of Scripture resulted in Augustine affirming the divine creation of the universe out of nothing;[21] the origin of humanity no more than six thousand years before his time;[22] the great age of people who lived before

---

17. Augustine, *The City of God*, 21.23, in *NPNF*[1], 2:469.

18. Augustine, *Letter* 82 (1.3), to Jerome, in *NPNF*[1], 1:350.

19. Augustine, *Letter* 28 (3), to Jerome, in *NPNF*[1], 1:251–52.

20. Augustine, *Letter* 28 (5), to Jerome, in *NPNF*[1], 1:252.

21. Augustine, *City of God*, 11.6, in *NPNF*[1], 2:208. Augustine noted that "the sacred and infallible Scriptures" indicate this divine creation.

22. Ibid., 12.10–12, in *NPNF*[1], 2:232–33. "Reckoning by the sacred writings, we find that not more than six thousand years have passed" from the creation of the first human beings. This is "the true account of the duration of the world as it is given by our documents, which are truly sacred," and any other notion stands in opposition "to the authority of our well-known and divine books."

the flood;[23] and the scientific possibility of the worldwide flood and of Noah's ark to save eight people and the animals on board.[24] Clearly, he believed that biblical inerrancy extended to matters of cosmology, human origins, genealogy, and the like. Scripture's infallibility also meant that no contradictions exist in the Bible. Accordingly, Augustine underscored that "we are bound to believe" everything in Scripture.[25]

THE INERRANCY OF SCRIPTURE IN THE MIDDLE AGES

As did the early church, the church of the Middle Ages affirmed overwhelmingly the truthfulness of all of Scripture. Herman Sasse summarizes this: "During all these [fifteen] centuries no one doubted that the Bible in its entirety was God's Word, that God was the principal author of the Scriptures, as their human authors had written under the inspiration of God the Holy Spirit, and that, therefore, these books were free from errors and contradictions, even when this did not seem to be the case. The Middle Ages had inherited this view from the Fathers who had established it in numerous exegetical and apologetical writings."[26]

Examples of this abound. Anselm clearly affirmed that the truthfulness of Scripture was the absolute touchstone for everything he believed: "For I am sure that if I say anything which is undoubtedly contradictory to holy Scripture, it is wrong; and if I become aware of such a contradiction, I do not wish to hold to that opinion."[27] Hervaeus, asserting that Scripture is spoken by God, concluded that Scripture must be true because "it is certain that God cannot speak falsehood."[28] Thomas Aquinas did not address the doctrine explicitly but held Scripture to be wholly true. In his discussion of biblical interpretation, he affirmed, "It is plain that nothing false can ever underlie the literal sense of Holy Scripture."[29] Although remembered most for his work with Aristotle's philosophy, Aquinas himself believed theology was more certain than any other discipline, including philosophy. This confidence was due to the fact that "other disciplines derive their certitude from the natural light of human reason, which can err, whereas theology derives its certitude from the light of the divine knowledge, which cannot be misled."[30] Specifically for Aquinas, theology is founded primarily on the Word of God, which never errs but is

23. Ibid., 15.9–14, in *NPNF*[1], 2:291–95. Augustine rejected the proposal that the long life spans of the patriarchs are in actuality ten times the actual number of years they lived, and he employed a biblical argument in his refutation.

24. Ibid., 15.26–27, in *NPNF*[1], 2:306–8. Augustine engaged in calculations of how a great number of animals could fit into the ark, and he sought to explain how the carnivorous animals on board could have survived the long ordeal.

25. Ibid., 21.6, in *NPNF*[1], 2:457.

26. Herman Sasse, "The Rise of the Dogma of Holy Scripture in the Middle Ages," *Reformed Theological Review* 18, no. 2 (June 1959): 45.

27. Anselm, *Why God Became Man*, 1.18, in *Anselm*, 298.

28. Hervaeus Natalis, *In Quattuor Petri Lombardi Sen-tentiarum*, prologue, q. 1, cited in Richard A. Muller, *Post-Reformation Reformed Dogmatics: The Rise and Development of Reformed Orthodoxy, ca. 1520 to ca. 1725*, vol. 2, *Holy Scripture: The Cognitive Foundation of Theology*, 2nd ed. (Grand Rapids: Baker, 2003), 45.

29. Thomas Aquinas, *Summa Theologica*, pt. 1, q. 1, art. 10.

30. Ibid., pt. 1, q. 1, art. 5. Alexander of Hales expressed a similar notion: "What is known by divine inspiration is recognized as more true than what is known by human reason, inasmuch as it is impossible for falsehood to be in inspiration while reason is infected with many. Therefore, when knowledge of theology is elevated by divine inspiration, such knowledge or science is more true than other sciences." Alexander of Hales, *Summa Theologica*, 2, q. 1, n. 1, cited in Muller, *Holy Scripture*, 43.

instead "infallible truth," and only secondarily on insights derived from leading theologians of the church: theology "properly uses the authority of the canonical Scriptures as an incontrovertible proof, and the authority of the doctors of the Church as one that may properly be used, yet merely as probable."[31] Indeed, for Aquinas, the salvation of fallen human beings depends on divine revelation being truthful and without error.

> Hence it was necessary for the salvation of man that certain truths which exceed human reason should be made known to him by divine revelation. Even as regards those truths about God which human reason could have discovered, it was necessary that man should be taught by a divine revelation; because the truth about God, such as reason could discover, would only be known by a few, and that after a long time, and with the admixture of many errors. Whereas man's whole salvation, which is in God, depends upon the knowledge of this truth.[32]

An exception to this medieval consensus was the controversialist Peter Abelard, whose *Sic et Non* (*Yes and No*) provocatively set the writings of one church father against those of another so as to demonstrate their disharmony. He traced this proneness to err to the biblical authors themselves, noting that "the prophets themselves sometimes lacked God's gift of prophecy and, by dint of their sheer practice in their craft, produced false prophecies, emanating from their own spirit, while all the time believing that they possessed the gift of prophecy." Yet Abelard softened the implications that could be derived from agreeing that "the very prophets and apostles were not altogether strangers to error": "But we must not accuse holy men of being liars if, holding opinions on some matters which were at variance with the truth, they speak, not out of a desire to deceive, but through ignorance. No statement which is prompted by charity, and aims at some sort of edification [of the hearer], should be put down to arrogance or sinfulness."[33] Given his propensity to pit seemingly mutually exclusive positions against each other, it should come as no surprise that elsewhere, in a complete reversal, Abelard echoed the traditional view of Scripture's inerrancy. That Scripture could not err had to be the case, according to Abelard, because it was produced "as though the finger of God had written it, that is, as though it were composed and written at the dictation of the Holy Spirit."[34]

More sophisticated discussions concerning the truthfulness of Scripture ensued among medieval theologians. For example, Alexander of Hales raised a concern about

---

31. Aquinas, *Summa Theologica*, pt. 1, q. 1, art. 8. Aquinas continued his discussion with a quote from Augustine in his letter to Jerome (cited in ch. 4, n. 19).

32. Ibid., pt. 1, q. 1, art. 1.

33. Peter Abelard, *Sic et Non* (*Yes and No*), prologue, cited in A. J. Minnis and A. B. Scott, *Medieval Literary Theory and Criticism, c. 1100–c. 1375: The Commentary-Tradition* (Oxford: Clarendon, 1988), 94–95. For examples of inferior prophecies in Ezekiel, Abelard relied on Gregory's *Homilies on Ezekiel the Prophet* (the first homily; 1.1; 2.6.9–11; trans.

Theodosia Tomkinson [Etna, Calif.: CTOS, 2008]). Although Abelard's reference to "holy men" may be primarily to the early church fathers, it would seem by his ascription of error to the prophets and apostles that the reference must be secondarily to those biblical authors themselves.

34. Peter Abelard, *Commentary on St. Paul's Epistle to the Romans*, 3.7.15, cited in Gillian Evans, *Language and Logic: The Earlier Middle Ages* (Cambridge: Cambridge Univ. Press, 1984), 138.

the truthfulness of Scripture when certain types of language are employed. His sophisticated answer explained that even figurative or parabolic language in Scripture can communicate the truth in relation to the referent to which that language points.[35] Henry of Ghent addressed the problem of lies reported in Scripture (e.g., the Hebrew midwives refused to inform their Egyptian masters of the birth of male babies, lying instead to avoid killing them; Ex. 1:17–19). Henry explained:

> We must reply that Holy Scripture sets before us not only the deeds and characters of the just, which it uses to encourage us to imitate them, but also men's weaknesses and sins, which it uses to instill fear into us. So, contrary to the assertion of some that such lies are not sins, Scripture sets before us a deceit as an example which it does not recommend us to imitate, but rather relates to show us what a severe punishment is incurred even by such a pious falsehood.... So, in brief, whatever lies are found in Scripture, it does not proffer to us as being true by positively asserting their truth and commending them, but in reporting them in the text solely for our instruction.[36]

Thus, medieval theologians and leaders affirmed the truthfulness of all of Scripture.

THE INERRANCY OF SCRIPTURE IN THE REFORMATION AND POST-REFORMATION

Although certain key aspects of the doctrine of Scripture were fiercely debated during the period of the Reformation, the truthfulness of Scripture (along with its inspiration) was a cardinal issue agreed upon by both Protestants and Catholics.[37] Even though it was not a point of contention, the Reformers did address the issue and uniformly upheld the historical position of the church that Scripture did not and could not err.

Martin Luther explicitly expressed this view: Not only has Scripture "*never* erred";[38] it "*cannot* err."[39] Luther meant two things by this affirmation: First, everything presented in Scripture corresponds to reality, the way things are. Second, no part of Scripture can contradict another part of Scripture: "It is certain that Scripture cannot disagree with

---

35. Alexander of Hales, *Summa Theologica*, q. 1, chap. 4, art. 4, cited in Minnis and Scott, *Medieval Literary Theory and Criticism*, 222–23.

36. Henry of Ghent, *The Sum of Ordinary Questions*, art. 16, q. 5, 4–5, cited in Minnis and Scott, *Medieval Literary Theory and Criticism*, 265–66. As for the "severe punishment" that the midwives incurred as a result of their falsehood, Henry cited a gloss on this passage by Gregory the Great: "Many try to assert that this kind of lie is not a sin because the Lord built them [i.e., the midwives] houses; in this reward it becomes clear rather what is deserved by the guilt of lying. For the reward of their kindly deed, which could have been stored up for them in the life hereafter, was commuted into a reward here on earth because of the guilt they had incurred

by lying." Ibid., 266.

37. The points of debate included the canonicity of the Apocrypha (addressed in chap. 2), biblical authority (chap. 4), the clarity of Scripture (chap. 6), its sufficiency and necessity (chap. 7), and the interpretation of Scripture (chap. 8). Agreement on the inspiration of Scripture is treated in chap. 3.

38. Martin Luther, *Samtliche Schriften*, 15.1481; 9.356; ed. J. G. Walch, 2nd ed. (St. Louis: Concordia, 1881–1930), cited in Robert D. Preus, "The View of the Bible Held by the Church," in Geisler, *Inerrancy*, 379.

39. Ibid., 14.1073, cited in Preus, "View of the Bible," 379; also in idem, "Luther and Biblical Infallibility," in *Inerrancy and the Church*, ed. John Hannah (Chicago: Moody, 1984), 135n140.

itself."[40] Luther grounded his affirmations of the inerrancy of Scripture on several points. The first was a theological reason: "You must follow straight after Scripture, accept it and not speak even one syllable against it, because it is God's mouth."[41] What has God said about himself? "It is established by God's Word that God does not lie, nor does his Word lie."[42] Thus, because God is truthful, the Word of God must be truthful as well. A second reason focused on the authors of Scripture: They were unable "to err and waver in the faith."[43] Thus, God who cannot lie gave his revelation through human writers who could not err; this resulted in an inerrant Bible. Luther noted an important implication of this: "In theology one must simply hear, believe, and hold firmly in his heart: 'God is faithful, no matter how absurd what he says in his Word may appear to our reason.'"[44]

But what of the difficulties in Scripture? At times, Luther dismissed them with little or no comment, so convinced was he of the truthfulness of Scripture. In explaining some of the difficulties, Luther appealed to errors introduced by poor copying; it is not Scripture itself that is in error, but rather, poor manuscripts create the problem. He also ascribed difficulties to poor interpretation of the Bible; thus, the Word of God is not wrong, but its readers offer incorrect interpretations of it. Commenting on the charge by some that Scripture errs because it contradicts itself (e.g., affirming at times that salvation is by faith and at other times that salvation is by works), Luther retorted, "But it is impossible that Scripture contradicts itself; it only seems so to foolish, coarse, and hardened hypocrites."[45] Occasionally, Luther wrestled with key scriptural difficulties. Yet, even when dealing with these problem passages, Luther was disturbed by his own pretentiousness that he, a mere mortal and sinful human being, could ever suspect that the Word of his infinite and perfectly holy God might be in error.[46]

John Calvin held a similar view, here summarized by J. I. Packer: "Calvin could never have consciously entertained the possibility that human mistakes, whether of reporting or of interpreting facts of any sort whatever, could have entered into the text of Scripture as the human writers gave it."[47] Indeed, in describing Scripture, Calvin called it "the eternal and inviolable truth of God."[48] For Calvin, the complete truthfulness of the Word of God is evident to all and does not stand in need of proof or authentication from any outside source: "Scripture exhibits fully as clear evidence of its own truth as white and black things do of their color, or sweet and bitter things do of their taste."[49]

Calvin's conviction of a wholly truthful Bible was founded on his belief that the Holy Spirit had inspired the human authors of Scripture, and this divine superintending work precluded any error on their part. Although in every other case human authors exhibit a tendency to err, this was not the case of the writers of Scripture:

40. Ibid., cited in Preus, "View of the Bible," 380; also in Preus, "Luther and Biblical Infallibility," 135n142.

41. Ibid., cited in Preus, "View of the Bible," 380; also in Preus, "Luther and Biblical Infallibility," 135n139.

42. Ibid., cited in Preus, "Luther and Biblical Infallibility," 135n144.

43. Martin Luther, *Theses Concerning Faith and Law*, LW, 34:113.

44. *Commentary on Psalm 45*, LW, 12:288.

45. Luther, *Samtliche Schriften*, cited in Preus, "Luther and Biblical Infallibility," 134n135.

46. Ibid., in Preus, "Luther and Biblical Infallibility," 138n155.

47. J. I. Packer, "John Calvin and the Inerrancy of Holy Scripture," in Hannah, *Inerrancy and the Church*, 178.

48. John Calvin, *Institutes of the Christian Religion*, 1.7.1, LCC, 1:75.

49. Ibid., 1.7.2, LCC, 1:76.

If we then ask how Calvin found it credible that sinful, fallible human beings should freely, spontaneously, and with all their idiosyncrasies showing, nonetheless have written material that was error-free and marked by divine wisdom in that way, his answer ... is: "They put forward nothing of their own." "They dared not announce anything of their own, and obediently followed the Spirit as their guide, who ruled in their mouth as in his own sanctuary."[50]

But what of the difficulties in Scripture? Like Luther before him, Calvin addressed the problem passages with a variety of responses. In some cases, Calvin attributed the difficulty to the accommodated language employed by God in his Word addressed to lowly human beings. This was the case, for example, with Moses in his composition of the Creation account in Genesis 1. For Calvin, as Moses wrote, he was "accommodating himself to the simplicity of ordinary people" and "speaking popularly." Indeed, "Moses wrote in a popular style things which, without instruction, all ordinary persons endued with common sense, are able to understand.... Had he spoken of things generally unknown, the uneducated might have pleaded in excuse that such subjects were beyond their capacity. Lastly, since the Spirit of God here opens a common school for all, it is not surprising that he should chiefly choose those subjects which would be intelligible to all."[51] Thus, Moses avoided a technical, scientific account of the creation (e.g., he referred to the sun and moon as "two great lights") because his intent was to teach average people. Such lack of precision, however, does not mean he erred in his account.

Calvin also noted instances when an apparent error in Scripture was actually the result of a copyist's mistake. This was his solution to Matthew's ascription of his quotation in Matthew 27:9 to Jeremiah: "by mistake" the wrong name "crept in" in the process of copying Matthew's gospel, but Matthew himself was not responsible for the textual error.[52] Another solution to scriptural difficulties was Calvin's proposal that the New Testament authors, when quoting the Old Testament, did not necessarily "translate word for word"; thus, the authors cannot be charged with error. This was his approach, for example, to Matthew's "loose" citation of Micah 5:2 in Matthew 2:6.[53] For Calvin, inexact biblical quotations, such as we might find in allusions, paraphrases, or citations of the general sense of a passage, cannot be equated with error.

Accordingly, by appealing to accommodated language, textual difficulties that arose from copyists' errors, and the reality of inexact citations of Old Testament Scripture by the New Testament authors, Calvin addressed the problem passages in Scripture. Clearly from these approaches, Calvin established himself as another Reformer who would not countenance the idea of error in Scripture.

Protestants who followed the Reformers continued to affirm the complete truthfulness of all Scripture. The *Westminster Confession of Faith* described the Word of God as

50. Packer, "John Calvin and the Inerrancy of Holy Scripture," in Hannah, *Inerrancy and the Church*, 158. Packer cites Calvin's twenty-fourth sermon on 2 Timothy and his commentary on 2 Peter 1:20.

51. John Calvin, *Commentaries on the First Book of Moses Called Genesis*, vol. 1, trans. John King (repr., Grand Rapids:

Baker, 2005), 86.

52. John Calvin, *Commentary on a Harmony of the Evangelists, Matthew, Mark, and Luke*, vol. 3, trans. William Pringle (repr., Grand Rapids: Baker, 2005), 272.

53. Ibid., 133–34.

"infallible truth"[54] and explained that by saving faith "a Christian believes to be true whatever is revealed in the Word because the authority of God himself speaks in it."[55] This post-Reformation affirmation of the truthfulness of all of Scripture was in good part a reaction to Socinianism. This heretical movement allowed for errors in portions of Scripture—specifically, parables, records of historical events, morals, and descriptions of natural or scientific matters. According to Socinus, the founder of the movement, because these are minor manners, errors in them have no effect on matters of salvation and doctrine; thus, they are inconsequential. The post-Reformer Abraham Calov explained the dangers inherent in such a belief: "But if error, or even the intimation of error, is admitted in these matters, then not even that which pertains to true doctrine is above the suspicion of error, since both historical sections and parables contribute greatly to the truth of doctrine."[56] In addition, Quenstedt denied that these so-called "minor matters" could contain error: "Each and every thing presented to us in Scripture is absolutely true, whether it pertains to doctrine, ethics, history, chronology, topography, or genealogies. No ignorance, no lack of understanding, no forgetfulness or lapse of memory can or should be ascribed to the amanuenses [secretaries] of the Holy Spirit in their writing of the Holy Scriptures."[57]

For the post-Reformers, the complete truthfulness of all Scripture is derived from the doctrine of inspiration. As Turretin explained: "The sacred writers were so acted upon and inspired by the Holy Spirit (as to the things themselves and as to the words) as to be kept free from all error and … their writings are truly authentic and divine.… The prophets did not fall into mistakes in those things which they wrote as inspired men (*theopneustôs*) and as prophets, not even in the smallest particulars; otherwise faith in the whole of Scripture would be rendered doubtful."[58] According to the post-Reformers, because biblical inspiration and its corollary, the truthfulness of Scripture, are a foundational matter, they only need to be affirmed, not proved. This did not stop them, however, from attempting to clear up scriptural problems, of which there were two types: (1) biblical records of historical events, genealogies, descriptions of natural phenomena, and so forth, that are problematic; and (2) alleged contradictions within Scripture itself.

As to the first type, the post-Reformers urged careful interpretation of the alleged problem passages. One interpretive principle is that Scripture often describes natural phenomena as they appear to us on earth. For example, Moses' characterization of the

---

54. *Westminster Confession of Faith*, 1.5, in Schaff, 3:603.

55. Ibid., 14.2, in Schaff, 3:630. The text has been rendered clearer.

56. Abraham Calov, *Systema Locorum Theologicorum* (Wittenberg, 1655), 1:552, in Preus, 347. His last name is also rendered as Calovius.

57. John Andrew Quenstedt, *Theologia Didactico-Polemica sive Systema Theologicum* (Leipzig, 1715), 1.4.2, q. 5, ekthesis (I.112), in Preus, 346. The text has been rendered clearer.

58. Francis Turretin, *Institutes of Elenctic Theology*, ed. James T. Dennison Jr., trans. George Musgrave Giger, 3 vols. in 1 (Phillipsburg, N.J.: P & R, 1997), 2nd topic, 4th q., sec. 5, sec. 23, 1:62, 69. Despite this statement, Turretin did not engage in a discussion of inerrancy as a separate topic under the doctrine of Scripture (though he extensively treated Scrip-

ture's necessity, authority, canon, purity, perfection, clarity, and interpretation). Quenstedt made a similar point: "The prophets and apostles spoke and wrote not from the decision and impulse of their own free will—or, as Scripture says, 'of themselves' (John 11:51; 16:13)—but they 'were led and moved by the Holy Spirit' (2 Pet. 1:21) or 'inspired' (2 Tim. 3:16). This being true, it then follows that they could in no manner make mistakes in their writing, and no falsification, no error, no danger of error, no untruth obtained or could obtain in their preaching or writing. This was because the Holy Spirit, who is the Spirit of truth and the Fountain of all wisdom, and who had as His hand and pen holy writers, cannot deceive or be deceived, neither can He err or have a lapse of memory." Quenstedt, *Theologia Didactico-Polemica*, 1.4.2, q. 5 (I.112), in Preus, 340.

moon as "a great light" (Gen. 1:16) uses the language of observation—how it appears to human observers.[59] Given the fact that Scripture speaks at times from this observational point of view and not from a scientifically technical perspective, it cannot be charged with error in its description of natural phenomena.

As to the second type of problem, the post-Reformers responded to the Socinian attack against the truthfulness of Scripture by denying that it contains numerous contradictions. As John Gerhard affirmed: "All Scripture is inspired, and accordingly all the things in Scripture are in agreement and are not contrary or opposed to one another."[60] Specific problematic passages were addressed, though the various post-Reformers differed among themselves as to their proposed solutions, and many offered various options for resolving the problems. For example, Matthew 27:9–10 apparently cites Zechariah 11:12–13 but attributes the quotation to Jeremiah. Among the eight possible solutions he listed, Gerhard proposed that Matthew cites from the Zechariah passage as well as Jeremiah 32:7–9. As another example, to clear up the question of how many blind men were healed by Jesus at Jericho (Matt. 20:29–34 indicates two men; Mark 10:46–52 names Bartimaeus as the one man; Luke 18:35–43 mentions one man), Calov proposed: "One of the men was better known than the other; therefore Mark and Luke made mention of only the one to whom without doubt the main circumstances of this story pertain; Matthew tells his story more comprehensively."[61] Other solutions to these problems were offered, indicating that no easy answer was forthcoming and so no forced harmonization should be proposed.[62]

To summarize, the attitude of Quenstedt reflected the honest recognition by the post-Reformers that the Bible contains some very difficult problems. However, this does not—indeed, cannot—overturn the doctrine of inerrancy: "God who speaks in Scripture does not reveal things that are in opposition to himself or contradictions (part of which are always false). But we grant that there are sometimes apparent contradictions found in Scripture—sayings that appear on the face of it to be contrary and contradictory."[63] Thus, while carefully and honestly working through these scriptural problems, the post-Reformers rested comfortably with the doctrine of inerrancy.

THE INERRANCY OF SCRIPTURE IN THE MODERN PERIOD

The early church, the church in the Middle Ages, and the divided church at the time of the Reformation were all united in their belief in the full truthfulness of Scripture. This

---

59. Friedemann Bechmann commented that the moon is a great light, "not because it is greater than the other stars in magnitude, but because it is closer to us. And because of its nearness to our point of vision, it appears to be greater.... The size of the moon appears greater to us than the stars because of its proximity and because, brightened by the sun, it is able to dispel the darkness of night, which the other stars cannot do." Friedemann Bechmann, *Annotationes Uberiores in Compendium Theologicum Leonhardi Hutteri* (Frankfort and Leipzig, 1703), 223, in Preus, 358–59.

60. John Gerhard, *Tractatus de Legitima Scripturae Sacrae Interpretatione* (Jena, 1663), 25, in Preus, 349.

61. Abraham Calov, *Biblia Novi Testamenti Illustrata* (Dresden and Leipzig, 1719), 1.383, in Preus, 352.

62. E.g., Matthew Poole refused to offer a definitive harmonization for the divergent accounts of the death of Judas. Matthew Poole, *Commentary on the Holy Bible* (repr., Edinburgh: Banner of Truth Trust, 1962), 3:135.

63. Quenstedt, *Theologia Didactico-Polemica*, 1.4.2, q. 5, *fontes solutionum*, 11 (I.118), in Preus, 353.

remarkable consensus, strongly held for over a millennium and a half, began to unravel at the beginning of the seventeenth century.[64]

To set the background for this development, the period spanning the sixteenth and seventeenth centuries was a time of unprecedented change. European (and thus Christian) society was in the midst of a scientific revolution. The ancient geocentric theory of the universe proposed by Ptolemy—that the earth was at the center of the universe and all other heavenly bodies, including the sun, revolved around it—was replaced by the heliocentric theory of Copernicus: the sun, not the earth, was at the center of our solar system. The impact on current thinking was immense. The church's view was that the Bible places humanity at the apex of divine Creation (Gen. 1:26–31). If this is so, then the earth, with its human population, must be at the center of the universe. But a scientific revolution was destroying this long-held notion and seemed to displace people, created in the image of God, from the center of attention. Similarly, the discovery of new worlds and new people—many of whom followed religions other than Christianity—raised questions about their origins, the rightness of their beliefs, and so forth.

Into this confusing world, biblical criticism was introduced. Isaac La Peyrère (1592–1676) offered a "pre-Adam" theory: There were people who existed before Adam was created by God. The major tenets of this theory were as follows: (1) the apostle Paul had revealed to La Peyrère that Adam was not the first man; (2) there were races of humans that had lived as far back as 50,000 BC (recall: most Europeans at this time believed the world to be less than five thousand years old, so La Peyrère's dating pushed back the age of the earth a huge amount of time); and (3) Moses did not discuss the origin of humanity in general; he only wrote about the beginning of the Jewish nation. La Peyrère's theory exerted an influence on the biblical critics who followed him. Indeed, his impact was quite significant, as Richard Popkin notes: "The whole enterprise of reconciling Scripture and the new science was blown apart by a mad genius, Isaac La Peyrère (Pereira), who ... really set off the warfare between theology and science."[65]

Hugo Grotius (1583–1645) a professor at the Remonstrant seminary in Amsterdam, held heretical views on the Trinity, Jesus Christ, and the atonement. He also diverged from the church's view of Scripture by holding the following ideas: (1) Peter did not author the second letter attributed to him (2 Peter), and Solomon did not write Ecclesiastes; (2) the people of Israel adopted the culture and idolatrous practices of the surrounding heathen nations, meaning that the Old Testament is merely a fallible record of this syncretism, or joining together, of biblical and nonbiblical religions; (3) the revealed parts of Scripture (e.g., its prophecies) must be distinguished from its nonrevealed parts (e.g., its historical narratives), which were simply the result of research rather than revelation; and (4) God's accommodation of himself in Scripture resulted in errors in the

---

64. The following discussion is a summary of material studied in a Ph.D. seminar, "The Origin and Development of Biblical Criticism in the Seventeenth and Eighteenth Centuries," conducted by John Woodbridge at Trinity Evangelical Divinity School.

65. Richard Popkin, "Skepticism, Theology, and the Scientific Revolution in the Seventeenth Century," *Problems in the Philosophy of Science*, ed. I. Lakatos and Alan Musgrave (Amsterdam: North Holland Publishing, 1968), 3:18, cited in John D. Woodbridge, *Biblical Authority: A Critique of the Rogers/McKim Proposal* (Grand Rapids: Zondervan, 1982), 89.

Bible (that is, God adjusted himself to the culture and worldview of the human authors of the Bible such that Scripture, being a human work, necessarily contains errors). Rather than viewing the entire Bible as God's truthful revelation of himself, Grotius detached some parts of it from revelation, leaving those portions to be merely human writings that contain errors.

Baruch Spinoza (1632–77), a Jewish philosopher, made a division of Scripture into primary and secondary matters. These secondary matters were then relegated to an inferior status. An example of this is found in his major work, *Tractatus Theologico-Politicus*, a significant purpose of which was to undermine the sovereign right of kings and queens to rule over European nations. But Spinoza developed this perspective in a European society that saw this rule as a "divine right," based on biblical passages such as Romans 13:1–7. He challenged this centuries-old belief by bracketing these passages, relegating them to the status of secondary matters. Scripture could be used to further primary matters such as obedience to God and moral development, but no appeal could be made to Scripture to further secondary purposes. Thus, the Bible could not be used in support of the divine right of kings and queens to rule.

Another key development introduced by Spinoza was his insistence that human reason stands above Scripture and even judges Scripture. In this, Spinoza was influenced by the philosophy of René Descartes. In his *Discourse on Method* (1637), Descartes had embarked on a search for absolute certainty for human knowledge. His search began with doubt. He proposed to accept nothing he had ever learned or thought he knew to be true, simply because it had always been believed. Rather, he would doubt everything until something became so evident to his thinking that he could not doubt it; he would have to believe it to be true. This, then, would be an unshakable foundation for human knowledge. The quest for absolute certainty would begin on sure footing.

What was that foundation of true knowledge that Descartes discovered? The phrase for which he is best known expresses it: *Cogito, ergo sum* (I think, therefore I am). Even when he doubted everything, Descartes could not doubt the fact that he was thinking; this led to the conclusion that he does indeed exist. Thus, man, as a thinking subject, is the starting point of human knowledge. Thinking, or human reason, receives priority in the quest for true knowledge. Later on Descartes developed examples demonstrating that human experience—what we see, hear, taste, touch, and smell—is an unreliable source of knowledge. Human reason, on the other hand, is a sure guide to what we can and do know. With Descartes we find the elevation of human reason as the key criterion for true knowledge.

Spinoza applied Descartes' methodology to the study of Scripture: He proposed to examine it "afresh in a careful, impartial and free spirit, making no assumptions about it." Strict reasoning would be applied to Scripture. What was the result of Spinoza's study?

> I found nothing expressly taught in Scripture that was not in agreement with the intellect or that contradicted it, and I also came to see that the prophets taught only very simple doctrines easily comprehensible by all, setting them forth in such a style and confirming them by such reasoning as would most likely induce the people's devotion to God. So I was completely convinced that

Scripture does not in any way inhibit reason and has nothing to do with philosophy, each standing on its own footing.[66]

Thus, reason applied to Scripture becomes the ultimate criterion of the truth of the Bible. And because the Bible leaves human reason totally untouched, reason stands above Scripture and judges Scripture. For Spinoza, then, Scripture is to be interpreted just like any other book, without regard for how the church and its interpretive tradition has historically understood it, and with reliance on human reason alone.

Applying reason to Scripture, Spinoza concluded that Moses was not the author of the Pentateuch. Spinoza offered three reasons for this: (1) The author writes in the third person ("he did such and such"). If Moses had written the Pentateuch, much of which involves him personally, he would have written in the first person ("I did such and such"). (2) In Numbers 12:3, the author praises Moses ("Now Moses was a very humble man, more humble than anyone else on the face of the earth"). Had Moses written the Pentateuch, his humility would have prevented him from making such a comment exalting himself. (3) The death of Moses is recounted in Deuteronomy 34. Obviously Moses could not have written it.

Looking at Spinoza's objections to Mosaic authorship of the Pentateuch, we may think them quite shallow and quickly offer a response. Indeed, traditional biblical scholars like Matthew Poole were actively engaged in addressing such issues at this very time.[67] What must be appreciated about Spinoza, however, is that he was the first serious critic in church history to challenge the traditional belief that Moses had written the Pentateuch. He was the first, but certainly not the last. Seeds of doubt were sown and began to bear fruit in critics who followed Spinoza. Indeed, he left an infamous legacy behind him.

One man upon whom Spinoza exerted a profound influence was Richard Simon (1638–1712), considered by many to be the "father of biblical criticism." He was a French priest and an expert in the languages and customs of the world of biblical times. In 1678 Simon wrote a highly controversial book, *Critical History of the Old Testament*.[68] He offered his "public scribes" hypothesis in response to Spinoza's attack on Mosaic authorship of the Pentateuch. He made two major points in "defending" Moses as its author: (1) The public scribes were officials in Israelite society who performed clerical duties. Because they had access to the records of the Jewish nation, they contributed to the writing of the Pentateuch. Indeed, they were responsible for additions to and alterations of the books of Moses. Because these scribes were inspired by the Holy Spirit, their changes did not undermine biblical authority. (2) The Pentateuch was written and conserved

66. Baruch Spinoza, *Tractatus Theologico-Politicus*, trans. Samuel Shirley, intro. Brad S. Gregory (Leiden: E. J. Brill, 1989), 54. Spinoza easily dismissed the church's dogmatic interpretation of Scripture: "We see nearly all men parade their own ideas as God's Word, their chief aim being to compel others to think as they do, while using religion as a pretext. We see, I say, that the chief concern of theologians on the whole has been to extort from Holy Scripture their own arbitrary invented ideas, for which they claim divine authority. In no other field do they display less scruple ... than in the interpretation of Scripture." Ibid., 141.

67. For an explanation of the comment about Moses' humility in Num. 12:3 and the account of his death, see Poole, *Commentary on the Holy Bible*, 1:286, 407. Poole's work was originally released as a two-volume publication entitled *Annotations on the Holy Bible*, with volume 1 (*Genesis to Isaiah*) appearing in 1683 and volume 2 (*Jeremiah to Revelation*) in 1685.

68. Richard Simon, *Histoire Critique du Vieux Testament* (*Critical History of the Old Testament*), 1678, 2nd ed. 1685.

on small rolls. As a result of the storage and periodic removal of these rolls, their order became mixed up. Therefore, the chronology that we now find in the Pentateuch reflects this confusion of the proper order. This was not the fault of Moses, but of the people who were to conserve the Pentateuch. These two points allowed Simon to maintain that Moses wrote most of the Pentateuch while admitting that authors other than Moses wrote some of it. In contrast with Spinoza, however, Simon held that God inspired even these non-Mosaic parts. Simon also maintained that no precise chronology of ancient Israelite history could be constructed from the Pentateuch. Chronological errors had been introduced by the displacement of the rolls.

Jean LeClerc (1657–1736), like his mentor Hugo Grotius, was a biblical critic who taught at the Remonstrant seminary in Amsterdam. One of his key principles was expressed in his writing *Entretiens* (1684): Human reason is an infallible guide in giving humankind all it needs to know for salvation. He entered into a bitter debate (1685–87) with Richard Simon in which he made these main points: (1) there is no evidence in support of Simon's "public scribes" hypothesis; (2) indeed, Mosaic authorship of the Pentateuch should be totally rejected; (3) a distinction must be made between inspired portions of Scripture (e.g., Old Testament prophecies and Christ's words) and noninspired parts (which are the product of human research, just like any other book); and (4) any idea of the Bible being fully inspired and therefore without error is misguided and should be dismissed. LeClerc's impact was immense. Key people who followed him began to waver in their belief in the absolute truthfulness of all of Scripture.

The Simon-LeClerc debate was followed intensely in Germany. Early response to their proposals was generally negative. Indeed, Simon and LeClerc were often lumped together with La Peyrère and Spinoza, and the whole group was condemned for its radical criticism of Scripture. Some, however, believed that this criticism should be more carefully considered before being condemned. Thus, Johann Salomo Semler (1725–91) came to agree with Simon's "public scribes" hypothesis. In his *Treatise on the Free Investigation of the Canon*, Semler distinguished between the Bible and the Word of God. The latter contains moral truths that are key for human existence. The former is God's accommodation in an attempt to teach humanity these crucial principles. Miracles, prophecies, Jesus' teaching on the resurrection, and the inspiration of Scripture all fall into this category. Thus, they merely reflect God condescending to the erroneous views of the people in biblical times. They are not true.

Biblical criticism spread to Great Britain as well and was particularly evident in English Deism. This eighteenth-century movement attacked the truthfulness of biblical statements as part of a larger attack on scriptural revelation itself as being subservient to reason. Edward Herbert of Cherbury (1583–1648) was influenced by Grotius. In his work *De Veritate* (*On Truth*), he rejected all knowledge that claims to have a supernatural origin. In a second writing, *De Religione Gentilium* (*On Gentile Religion*), he set forth the five tenets of Deism: (1) the existence of God; (2) human beings have a responsibility to worship God; (3) this worship is accomplished through moral living; (4) human beings must also repent of sins; and (5) there is a future judgment of good and bad works. Herbert emptied the Christian faith of all supernatural elements and replaced it with a code of ethical conduct.

Anthony Collins (1676–1729), influenced by LeClerc and Simon, continued the attack against Scripture. In his *Discourse on Freethinking*, he asserted that any belief that is not in harmony with human reason cannot be revelation. In his *Discourse on the Grounds and Reason of the Christian Religion*, Collins denied that Christianity has any valid proof of its truthfulness. John Toland (1670–1722) offered a similar view in *Christianity Not Mysterious*. Furthermore, like Spinoza before him, Toland insisted that the Bible be treated and interpreted just like any other (merely human) book: "All men will own the truth I defend if they read the sacred Writings with that equity and attention that is due to mere human works. Nor is there any different rule to be followed in the interpretation of Scripture from what is common to all other books."[69] And Matthew Tindal (1655–1733), in *Christianity as Old as Creation*, asserted that Christianity finds its essence in all religions; thus, there is nothing unique about the Christian faith.

Both English Deism and the early development of German biblical criticism were largely a theological attack against Scripture. Full-scale attacks against the truthfulness of Scripture awaited another development known as the documentary hypothesis. This series of theories proposed that the Pentateuch is a collection of selections from several written documents (abbreviated *JEDP*). These were composed by different authors at different places over a period of about five centuries. The hypothesis excludes any possibility that Moses wrote the first five books of the Bible.[70]

---

69. John Toland, *Christianity Not Mysterious* (repr., Stuttgart-Bad Cannstatt: Frommann-Holzboog, 1964), 49, cited in Roy A. Harrisbille, and Walter Sundberg, *The Bible in Modern Culture: Baruch Spinoza to Brevard Childs*, 2nd ed. (Grand Rapids: Eerdmans, 2002), 48. The text has been rendered clearer.

70. The documentary hypothesis originated with Jean Astruc's *Conjectures Concerning the Original Memoranda Which It Appears Moses Used to Compose the Book of Genesis* (1753). Astruc observed that the Hebrew word for God in Genesis 1 is different from that used in Genesis 2. He attempted to account for this difference by proposing that Moses used two different written sources when he wrote the opening of Genesis. One source was written by an author who only knew God by the name *Elohim*, while the other was written by an author who knew God as *Yahweh* (or *Jehovah*). Although Astruc's proposal was not favorably received, it expressed a basic assumption of the documentary hypothesis: different divine names indicate different sources. This idea was extended by Johann Gottfried Eichorn (1752–1827) in his *Introduction to the Old Testament* (1780–83). He divided up all of Genesis and the first two chapters of Exodus between the *Jahvist* document, abbreviated *J*, and the *Elohist* document, abbreviated *E*. A third document, *D*, was introduced by Wilhelm DeWette in *A Critical-Exegetical Dissertation* (1805). He maintained that none of the Pentateuch was written prior to the time of David. His reasoning: Genesis 49 tells of a king coming from Judah, a reference to David. Given that predictive prophecy is not possible, David must have already become king when that was written of him. Accordingly, the book of Deuteronomy was the Book of the Law discovered by the high priest Hilkiah in the Jerusalem temple at the time of King Josiah's reform (2 Kings 22). Thus, the *D* (*Deuteronomist*) document arose in 621 BC. Three documents—*J*, *E*, and *D*—were now in place in the hypothesis. Hermann Hupfeld (*The Sources of Genesis*; 1853) and Karl Heinrich Graf added several proposals for a fourth source for the Pentateuch. With Abraham Kuenen's *The Religion of Israel* (1869), this document became known as *P* (for *Priestly Code*). He proposed that this legislation on holiness was composed in various stages from the time of Ezekiel to the time of Ezra, who added the last sections to it about 570 BC. Thus, the full-fledged documentary hypothesis, *JEDP*, came into existence. The task of persuasively presenting and defending the theory was taken on by Julius Wellhausen in *The Composition of the Hexateuch* (1876) and *Introduction to the History of Israel* (1878). Banished from view was Moses as the author of the Pentateuch. In its place was installed an evolutionary view of the development of Israelite religion, progressing from primitive animism to sophisticated monotheism. For a more thorough discussion of the *JEDP* theory, see Gleason L. Archer Jr., *A Survey of Old Testament Introduction* (Chicago: Moody, 1974); Edgar Krentz, *The Historical-Critical Method* (Philadelphia: Fortress Press, 1975); *The End of the Historical-Critical Method* (Eugene, Ore.: Wipf & Stock, 2001).

The *JEDP* theory was commended to the English-speaking world by William Robertson Smith, particularly through his article entitled "Bible" in the *Encyclopedia Britannica* (9th ed., 1875) and his book *The Old Testament and the Jewish Church* (1912).[71] After an investigation, Smith was dismissed from his teaching position for failure to support "the doctrine of the immediate inspiration, infallible truth and Divine authority of the Holy Scriptures, as set forth in the Holy Scriptures themselves and in the *[Westminster] Confession of Faith*."[72]

About the same time the *JEDP* theory was developing, Darwin's *Origin of Species* was first published in 1859. More than any other writing, this work undermined people's confidence in the truthfulness of the creation account of Genesis. John Broadus, a leading nineteenth-century Southern Baptist, explained the reason:

> If the Darwinian theory of the origin of man has been accepted, then it becomes easy to conclude that the first chapter of Genesis is by no means true history. From this starting-point, and pressed by a desire to reconstruct the history on evolutionary principles, one might easily persuade himself that in numerous other cases of apparent conflict between Old Testament statements and the accredited results of various sciences the conflict is real, and the Old Testament is incorrect.[73]

A specific example of this development at the Southern Baptist Theological Seminary was the case of Old Testament professor Crawford H. Toy. When he joined the faculty in 1869, he affirmed and taught a high view of the inspiration and truthfulness of Scripture.[74] By 1876, however, influenced by higher criticism of the Bible and Darwinian evolutionary theory, Toy had drifted away from his original views. Among other things, he maintained that Genesis 1 and Genesis 2 are conflicting accounts of the creation and that Genesis 1 cannot be reconciled with the findings of modern science; indeed, the biblical account of a six-day creation is simply in error.[75] Toy resigned from the faculty because of the incompatibility of his views with those of the institution.[76]

Others drifted from the historic view of biblical inerrancy by taking a different approach. A distinction was erected between the *inerrancy* of Scripture and the *infallibility* of Scripture. The *inerrancy* of Scripture was the technical term retained to describe the historic position of the church toward the complete truthfulness of the Bible. William

---

71. William Robertson Smith, *The Old Testament and the Jewish Church: Twelve Lectures on Biblical Criticism* (London: Adam & Charles Black, 1912).

72. J. S. Black and G. Chrystal, *The Life of William Robertson Smith* (London: Adam & Charles Black, 1912), 241–42.

73. John A. Broadus, *Memoir of James Petigru Boyce* (New York: A. C. Armstrong & Son, 1893), 260.

74. This can be readily noted in Toy's inaugural address at the seminary: "The [grammatical-historical] method ... takes for granted a theory of inspiration, namely, that under the absolutely perfect guiding influence of the Holy Spirit, the writers of the Bible have preserved each his personality of character and intellect and surroundings. Here we do no more

than refer again to the fact that the theory of inspiration affects the system of interpretation, and that a fundamental principle of our hermeneutics must be that the Bible, its real assertions being known, is in every iota of its substance absolutely and infallibly true." Cited in L. Russ Bush and Tom J. Nettles, *Baptists and the Bible* (Chicago: Moody, 1980), 232–33.

75. Ibid., 229–31.

76. In his resignation letter, Toy said that "discrepancies and inaccuracies occur in the historical narrative [of Scripture]." Still, he maintained that "this does not invalidate the documents ... as expression of religious truth." Bush and Nettles, *Baptists and the Bible*, 233.

LaSor, no defender of the traditional view, noted: "Those who defend the 'inerrancy of the Bible' generally mean by that word that the Bible contains no error of any kind, whether religious, historical, geographical, numerical, or any other category."[77] Stephen T. Davis defined *infallibility* in this way: "The Bible is infallible if and only if it makes no false or misleading statements on any matter of faith and practice."[78] That is, Scripture does not contain any falsehoods in the areas of Christian doctrine—areas that impact salvation and holy living. But this leaves open the possibility—indeed, for most if not all of these critics, the actuality—of errors when the Bible addresses matters of history, geography, genealogy, cosmology, and so forth. Specifically, for Davis: "The Bible is infallible, as I define that term, but not inerrant. That is, there are historical and scientific errors in the Bible, but I have found none on matters of faith and practice."[79] In addition, critics of the traditional view who still needed to affirm belief in biblical inerrancy redefined error as *willful deception*. Given this definition, they could affirm the complete inerrancy of Scripture, because at no point does a biblical author willfully deceive his readers. Clearly, this notion was far removed from the traditional sense of the inerrancy of Scripture.

Perhaps the most notable institutional example of the drift from affirming the inerrancy of Scripture to affirming the infallibility of Scripture was Fuller Theological Seminary.[80] Its original statement of faith (written several years after its founding in 1947) contained the following article on Scripture: "The books which form the canon of the Old and New Testaments as originally given are plenarily [fully] inspired and free from all error in the whole and in the part. These books constitute the written Word of God, the only infallible rule of faith and practice."[81] Through the years, as faculty and trustees did not uphold the doctrine of biblical inerrancy, a revision of the original document became necessary. In 1971 the board of the school voted unanimously to adopt a new doctrinal statement in which the phrase "plenarily inspired and free from all error in the whole and in the part" had been removed: "Scripture is an essential part and trustworthy record of this divine self-disclosure. All the books of the Old and New Testaments, given by divine inspiration, are the written Word of God, the only infallible rule of faith and practice."[82] Clearly, Fuller Seminary moved away from the historic doctrine of the full inerrancy of Scripture and embraced a Bible that is infallible in matters of faith and practice but which can and does indeed contain errors in matters of history, science, geography, and the like. Reaction to this shift was pronounced. Harold O. J. Brown lamented Fuller's disconcerting drift from orthodoxy to liberalism, following similar swings at

---

77. William LaSor, "Life under Tension—Fuller Theological Seminary and 'The Battle for the Bible,'" *Theology, News and Notes*, special issue, Fuller Theological Seminary (1976), 23.

78. Stephen T. Davis, *Debate about the Bible* (Philadelphia: Westminster, 1977), 23.

79. Ibid., 115. Davis does not engender much confidence in his view, as he followed up his above-cited statement with the following: "Perhaps someday it will be shown that the Bible is not infallible. For now I can only affirm infallibility as the most probable interpretation of the evidence I see." Ibid., 116. See also ch. 3, n. 112.

80. For more discussion, see George Marsden, *Reforming Fundamentalism: Fuller Seminary and the New Evangelicalism* (Grand Rapids: Eerdmans, 1987).

81. Cited in Harold Lindsell, *The Battle for the Bible* (Grand Rapids: Zondervan, 1976), 107.

82. Fuller Theological Seminary, *Statement of Faith*, 3. http://www.fuller.edu/about-fuller/mission-and-history/statement-of-faith.aspx.

Harvard, Yale, and Princeton seminaries.[83] Harold Lindsell, in *The Battle for the Bible*, forcefully denounced this development at Fuller.[84]

Following a yet different approach, Karl Barth's reformulation of the doctrine of the Word of God included an explicit denial of scriptural inerrancy. For Barth, an important corollary of the Bible being a witness to but not revelation itself—it *becomes*, but not *is*, the Word of God—was its errancy.[85] Barth insisted on the errancy of the Bible because, as a witness written by real—and therefore sinful—human beings, it has to contain errors: "The prophets and apostles as such, even in their office, even in their function as witnesses, even in the act of writing down their witness, were real, historical men as we are, and therefore sinful in their action, and capable and actually guilty of error in their spoken and written word."[86] Breaking from the historic position of the church, Barth concluded: "Verbal inspiration does not mean the infallibility of the biblical word in its linguistic, historical and theological character as a human word. It means that the fallible and faulty human word is as such used by God and has to be received and heard in spite of its human fallibility."[87]

The *Chicago Statement on Biblical Inerrancy* (1978) was the written outcome of a consultation by leading evangelicals concerned about defection among Christians—even a significant number of evangelicals—from belief in Scripture's complete truthfulness. The impetus for this statement made clear the importance of this doctrine: "We are persuaded that to deny it is to set aside the witness of Jesus Christ and of the Holy Spirit and to refuse that submission to the claims of God's own word which marks true Christian faith."[88] The *Chicago Statement* championed belief in both the infallibility and the inerrancy of Scripture. Concerning infallibility, it stated: "We affirm that Scripture, having been given by divine inspiration, is infallible, so that, far from misleading us, it is true and reliable in all matters it addresses. We deny that it is possible for the Bible to be at the same time infallible and errant in its assertions. Infallibility and inerrancy may be distinguished, but not separated."[89] Concerning inerrancy, it noted: "We affirm that Scripture in its entirety is inerrant, being free from all falsehood, fraud, or deceit. We deny that Biblical infallibility and inerrancy are limited to spiritual, religious or redemptive themes, exclusive of assertions in the fields of history and science. We further deny that scientific hypotheses about earth history may properly be used to overturn the teaching of Scripture on creation and the flood."[90] Thus, the *Chicago Statement* stood against a limited view of inerrancy, denying that Scripture's truthfulness can be restricted to matters of faith and salvation alone.

---

83. Harold O. J. Brown, "Can a Seminary Stand Fast?" *Christianity Today* 19, no. 10 (February 14, 1975): 7–8. I have obtained personal correspondence from a key leader at Fuller (who respectfully requested that the letter not be published) that corrects Brown's statement that "several" conservative faculty members resigned from the seminary over this issue. The corrected number is two, yet in reality Brown's "several" is correct, because Charles Woodbridge, Wilbur Smith, Harold Lindsell, and Gleason Archer resigned their faculty positions over this issue. Also, this correspondence demonstrates a disconcerting naïveté concerning the doctrinal drift that was afoot at Fuller.

84. Lindsell, *The Battle for the Bible*, chap. 6.

85. *CD*, I/2, 507.

86. Ibid., 528–29.

87. Ibid., 533.

88. *The Chicago Statement on Biblical Inerrancy*, preface, in Wayne Grudem, *Systematic Theology* (Grand Rapids: Zondervan, 1994, 2000), 1204.

89. Ibid., art. 11, in Grudem, *Systematic Theology*, 1206.

90. Ibid., art. 12, in Grudem, *Systematic Theology*, 1206.

Furthermore, the *Chicago Statement* linked the inspiration of Scripture and its inerrancy: "We affirm that inspiration, though not conferring omniscience, guaranteed true and trustworthy utterance on all matters of which the Bible authors were moved to speak and write. We deny that the finitude or fallenness of these writers, by necessity or otherwise, introduced distortion or falsehood into God's Word."[91] Indeed, the *Chicago Statement* affirmed "that the doctrine of inerrancy is grounded in the teaching of the Bible about inspiration."[92] In response to criticism that the term *inerrancy* is a poor one—it is the negation of a negative idea ("without error")—the *Chicago Statement* urged the continued use of the term. It also emphasized that contemporary challenges to inerrancy have not defeated the doctrine.[93]

Reflecting the doctrine of inerrancy as expressed by the *Chicago Statement*, Paul Feinberg's discussion of the issue represented the conservative evangelical understanding.[94] Some of Feinberg's key points were the following: (1) "Inerrancy does not demand strict adherence to the rules of grammar."[95] Feinberg, like most evangelicals, noted the grammatical anomalies present in Scripture (e.g., Rev. 21:9)[96] yet argued that statements can be true even if grammatically incorrect. (2) "Inerrancy does not exclude the use either of figures of speech or of a given literary genre."[97] He explained: "Figures of speech are common to ordinary communication and cannot be said to express falsehoods simply because they are not literal."[98] As far as the use of different genre (poetry, narrative, prophecy, epistolary, apocalyptic, etc.) by the biblical authors, Feinberg noted: "The literary style or form has nothing to do with the *truth* or *falsity* of the content conveyed in that style."[99] (3) "Inerrancy does not demand historical or semantic precision."[100] That is, even though Scripture does not employ the historical or linguistic exactness commonly found in technical literature today, this lack of precision cannot be equated with error. (4) "Inerrancy does not demand the technical language of modern science."[101] Like the

---

91. Ibid., art. 9, in Grudem, *Systematic Theology*, 1205.

92. Ibid., art. 15, in Grudem, *Systematic Theology*, 1206.

93. Ibid., art. 13, in Grudem, *Systematic Theology*, 1206. In underscoring this, the *Chicago Statement* was keeping with a tradition among evangelicals that recognized this point. For example, John Murray affirmed: "In maintaining and defending biblical inerrancy it is necessary to bear in mind that our concept of inerrancy is to be derived from Scripture itself. A similar necessity appears in connection with the criteria of truth and of right. We may not impose upon the Bible our own standards of truthfulness or our own notions of right and wrong. It is easy for the proponents of inerrancy to set up certain canons of inerrancy which are arbitrarily conceived and which prejudice the whole question from the outset. And it is still easier for the opponents of inerrancy to set up certain criteria in terms of which the Bible could readily be shown to be in error. Both attempts must be resisted." John Murray, "Inspiration and Inerrancy," in *Collected Writings* (Carlisle, Pa.: Banner of Truth Trust, 1976), 4:25–26.

94. Paul D. Feinberg, "The Meaning of Inerrancy," in Geisler, *Inerrancy*, 267–304.

95. Ibid., 299.

96. The genitive plural as written must be an accusative plural in order to be grammatically correct. As the text of Rev. 21:9 is written, the seven angels (who had the seven bowls) were full of the seven last plagues. What John undoubtedly intended to affirm was that the seven angels had the seven bowls that were full of the seven last plagues. The bowls, not the angels, were full of the plagues, as Rev. 16 confirms.

97. Feinberg, "The Meaning of Inerrancy," 299.

98. Ibid.

99. Ibid. In emphasizing this, Feinberg was keeping with a tradition among evangelicals that recognized this literary point. E.g., John Murray affirmed: "Inerrancy in reference to Scripture is the inerrancy that accepts certain well-established and obviously recognized literary or verbal *usus loquendi* (figures of speech). It makes full allowance for the variety of literary devices which preserves language from stereotyped uniformity and monotony." Murray, "Inspiration and Inerrancy," 4:29.

100. Ibid., 299.

101. Ibid., 300.

preceding point, this qualification noted that the lack of scientific exactness by the biblical authors cannot be equated with error, for two reasons: "First, it was not their intention to provide a scientific explanation for all things. Second, popular or observational language is used even today by the common man."[102] Imprecise language (e.g., "the sun rises") cannot be equated with error. (5) "Inerrancy does not require verbal exactness in the citation of the Old Testament by the New."[103]Many other conventions—paraphrase, summary, general reference, for example—can be and were indeed used by the apostolic writers in referring to the Old Testament. These "looser" forms of citations cannot be equated with error. (6) "Inerrancy does not demand that the *Logia Jesu* (*the sayings of Jesus*) contain the *ipsissima verba* (*the exact words*) of Jesus, only the *ipsissima vox* (*the exact voice*)."[104] Because Jesus spoke many of his sayings in Aramaic, we do not have the exact words of Jesus. Rather, we have the faithful renderings into Greek of what Jesus spoke and taught in Aramaic, and he really did say and teach what the New Testament ascribes to him. The exact voice of Jesus cannot be equated with error.

Besides clarifying these issues, Feinberg formulated a definition of the doctrine that is both clear and defensible: "Inerrancy means that when all facts are known, the Scriptures in their original autographs and properly interpreted will be shown to be wholly true in everything that they affirm, whether that has to do with doctrine or morality or with the social, physical, or life sciences."[105] This formulation has become the standard view of conservative evangelicals in the twenty-first century. The debate, however, is far from being over.[106] Christians from all theological perspectives continue to give attention to the issue of the truthfulness of all Scripture, or its inerrancy.

---

102. Ibid.

103. Ibid.

104. Ibid., 301.

105. Ibid., 294.

106. E.g., Craig D. Allert, *A High View of Scripture? The Authority of the Bible and the Formation of the New Testament Canon*. Evangelical Resourcement (Grand Rapids: Baker Academic, 2007); A. T. B. McGowan, *The Divine Authenticity of Scripture: Retrieving an Evangelical Heritage* (Downers Grove, Ill.: InterVarsity Academic, 2007); Kenton L. Sparks, *God's Word in Human Words: An Evangelical Appropriation of Critical Biblical Scholarship* (Grand Rapids: Baker Academic, 2008).

Chapter 6

THE CLARITY OF SCRIPTURE

How has the church come to believe that the Bible is written in such a way that ordinary believers and not just Bible scholars are able to understand it rightly?

STATEMENT OF BELIEF

The church has historically recognized that "the Bible is written in such a way that its teachings are able to be understood by all who will read it, seeking God's help and being willing to follow it."[1] While affirming this generally, the church has also acknowledged that some parts of the Bible seem quite puzzling and hard to understand. The early church believed that these more obscure portions could be understood by reading them in the light of the clearer portions. The Roman Catholic Church emphasized the obscurity of Scripture for average believers and insisted that only its clergy—men who were trained to interpret the Bible—could understand it rightly. The Protestant Reformers responded with the doctrine of the clarity[2] of Scripture, insisting that the Bible is written in such a way that ordinary believers and not just Bible scholars are able to understand it correctly. Many churches today follow this Protestant doctrine, especially in their encouragement of personal reading of the Bible, discussion of Scripture in group Bible studies, and interaction with the Word as it is preached by pastors, ministers, and clergy.[3]

THE CLARITY OF SCRIPTURE IN THE EARLY CHURCH

The clarity of Scripture was the assumption of the early church. The New Testament writings are filled with hundreds of references and allusions to the Old Testament. In

---

1. Wayne Grudem, *Systematic Theology: An Introduction to Biblical Doctrine* (Grand Rapids: Zondervan, 1994, 2000), 108.

2. The old term for the clarity of Scripture was *perspicuity*,

but since this word itself is not clear to people today, the term *clarity* will also be used.

3. My thanks to Carmen Bryant for her help on this topic.

fact, the apostle Paul affirmed that "everything that was written in the past [i.e., the Old Testament] was written to teach us [i.e., Christians], so that through endurance and the encouragement of the Scriptures we might have hope" (Rom. 15:4). Similarly, he noted that the Israelites' experiences of sin and divine judgment "happened to them as examples and were written down as warnings for us, on whom the fulfillment of the ages has come" (i.e., believers in Jesus Christ; 1 Cor. 10:11). The authors of the New Testament assumed that their readers would be able to follow and benefit from the stories and teachings in the Old Testament. And this was despite the fact that these Christian readers were far removed from the political, economic, social, linguistic, and religious situations in which those stories and teachings originated. The Old Testament was thought to be clear and understandable.

In like manner, the New Testament was written in such a way that ordinary believers could understand it. Most of its letters were written not to church leaders but to entire congregations. Analogies to contemporary realities and situations were used to communicate spiritual truths. Thus, salvation from sin was described as reconciliation from enmity (e.g., Rom. 5:10), and Christians with their variety of gifts from the Holy Spirit were likened to members of the human body (e.g., 1 Cor. 12:12–30). Where difficulty in understanding was anticipated, the New Testament authors added explanations for the sake of clarity. Thus, specific background information about Jewish customs was supplied for a Gentile audience when needed (e.g., Mark 7:3–4), and editorial comments served to explain unusual features of stories (e.g., John 7:37–39). The New Testament was written to be clear and understandable.

At the same time, however, there was the frank admission that some of the New Testament was difficult to understand. Peter called his readers' attention to Paul's letters: "Our dear brother Paul also wrote you with the wisdom that God gave him. He writes the same way in all his letters, speaking in them of these matters. His letters contain some things that are *hard to understand*, which ignorant and unstable people distort, as they do the other Scriptures, to their own destruction" (2 Peter 3:15–16, emphasis added). Still, Peter's admission of the obscurity of Scripture was quite limited: He did not indicate that *all of Scripture*, or even *all of Paul's writings*, were hard to understand. Rather, only *some of the Pauline correspondence* was problematic. Even this portion was not unintelligible: It was *difficult to understand*, not *impossible*. And the key problem with these problem passages was not the difficulty in understanding them. It consisted instead in *the twisting and distortion of their true* (and understandable!) *meaning* by untaught and unstable people. As John Calvin later noted, "We must observe that we are not forbidden to read Paul's letters because they contain some things hard and difficult to understand. On the contrary, they are commended to us, provided we bring a calm and teachable mind."[4]

When the New Testament was completed, the leaders of the early church continued this assumption of the clarity of Scripture. Their writings are full of quotations and

---

4. John Calvin, *Commentaries on the Catholic Epistles*, ed. and trans. John Owen (Grand Rapids: Baker, 2005), 424. The text has been rendered clearer.

allusions to both the Old and New Testaments, appeals based on the conviction that the Bible is understandable. Clement of Rome noted simply: "For you know, and know well, the sacred Scriptures, dear friends, and you have searched into the oracles of God. We write these things, therefore, merely as a reminder."[5] Clement assumed that his readers would understand the Old Testament narrative because it was clear. Clarity of the New Testament was assumed as well, as Polycarp indicated in an address to the Philippians: "For I am convinced that you are all well trained in the sacred Scriptures and that nothing is hidden from you." He then proceeded to quote Ephesians 4:26 ("be angry but do not sin," and "do not let the sun set on your anger"), encouraging his readers to follow this clear instruction.[6]

Some of the early church fathers addressed this issue directly. Irenaeus encouraged believers to meditate on the truths that God has revealed to humanity: "These things ... fall [plainly] under our observation, and are clearly and unambiguously in express terms set forth in the Sacred Scriptures.... The entire Scriptures—the Prophets and the Gospels—can be clearly, unambiguously, and harmoniously understood by all, although all do not believe them."[7] Like Peter before him, Tertullian acknowledged that certain parts of Scripture are hard to understand and so formulated this principle: "Since some passages are more obscure than others, it is right ... that uncertain statements should be determined by certain ones, and obscure ones by statements that are clear and plain."[8] By this method the meaning of even the difficult portions of Scripture could be brought forth. Irenaeus offered a reasoned explanation for this approach: "No question can be solved by another which itself awaits solution. Nor ... can an ambiguity be explained by means of another ambiguity, or enigmas by means of another greater enigma. But things of this kind receive their solution from those which are manifest, consistent and clear."[9]

With Clement of Alexandria came an emphasis on the mysteries of Scripture. Writing at the time of Gnosticism—heretical movements that promoted a secret *gnosis*, or knowledge, that was reserved for their elite members—Clement was significantly influenced by this thinking. For him, any and all truth about God is inexpressible; thus, he wrote of the impossibility of expressing God: "For this [i.e., the divine] is by no means capable of expression."[10] God alone can communicate truth about himself, and this can only be conveyed "in enigmas, symbols, allegories, metaphors, and in similar figures."[11] Thus, Scripture is thoroughly like a parable: "For neither prophecy nor the Savior himself announced the divine mysteries simply so as to be easily understood by everyone, but expressed them in parables.... The holy mysteries ... are preserved for chosen men, selected for knowledge because of their faith; for the style of the Scriptures is that of a

5. Clement of Rome, *Letter of the Romans to the Corinthians*, 53, in Holmes, 87; *ANF*, 1:19.

6. Polycarp, *Letter to the Philippians*, 12, in Holmes, 219; *ANF*, 1:35. Of course, the first part of the quotation is from Ps. 4:4, but the two are found together in the Ephesian letter.

7. Irenaeus, *Against Heresies*, 2.27.1–2, in *ANF*, 1:398.

8. Tertullian, *On the Resurrection of the Flesh*, 21, in *ANF*, 3:560. The text has been rendered clearer.

9. Irenaeus, *Against Heresies*, 2.10.1, in *ANF*, 1:370. The text has been rendered clearer.

10. Clement of Alexandria, *Stromata*, 5.12, in *ANF*, 2:463.

11. Ibid., 5.4, in *ANF*, 2:449. The text has been rendered clearer.

parable."[12] Clement added that the truths of God are "transparent and bright to the gnostics … but they are dark to the multitude."[13] Thus, a two-tiered system of Christians was erected, with spiritual believers being able to understand the mysteries of Scripture that simple believers could not appreciate.

Clement's emphasis on a mysterious meaning of Scripture was developed by his successor, Origen. On the one hand, Origen held that the Bible was clear for all believers whenever it addressed crucial truths. These he listed as God, Christ, the Holy Spirit, the eternal destiny of people, angels, the creation of the world, and Scripture. In regard to these, Origen believed "that the holy apostles, in preaching the Christian faith, expressed themselves with the utmost clearness on certain points which they believed to be necessary for everyone, even to those who seemed somewhat dull in the study of divine knowledge."[14] He also emphasized the plain language of Scripture that anyone could understand.[15] On the other hand, he believed that Scripture contained much mystery — spiritual truth hidden under its words — that can only be understood by those "who by means of the Holy Spirit himself should obtain the gift of language, of wisdom, and of knowledge."[16] Indeed, Origen emphasized this hidden meaning of Scripture.[17] Only mature believers endowed with a "religious and holy spirit" and possessing "the key of knowledge," as those "skilled in the law," could probe this deeper, divine sense of the Bible.[18] Yet even these experts could not hope to understand fully

12. Ibid., 6.15, in *ANF*, 2:509. The text has been rendered clearer. Clement continued: "Prophecy does not employ figurative forms in its expressions for the sake of beautiful diction. But from the fact that truth does not pertain to everyone, it is veiled in various ways, causing the light to arise only on those who are initiated into knowledge, who seek the truth through love." Ibid., in *ANF*, 2:510. The text has been rendered clearer.

13. Ibid., in *ANF*, 2:507. The text has been rendered clearer. For Clement the term *gnostics* referred to spiritually mature Christians.

14. Origen, *First Principles*, preface, 3, in *ANF*, 4:239. The text has been rendered clearer. Writing against the heretic Celsus and his attack on the inferiority of Scripture to the writings of the Greek philosophers, Origen argued: "See, then, if Plato and the wise men among the Greeks, in the beautiful things they say, are not like those physicians who confine their attention to those who are called 'the better classes of society' and despise the multitude. In contrast, the prophets among the Jews and the disciples of Jesus scorn mere elegance of style and what is called in Scripture 'the wisdom of men' and 'the wisdom according to the flesh' which delights in what is obscure. They resemble those who study to provide the most wholesome food for the largest number of persons. For this purpose they adapt their language and style to the capacities of the common people and avoid whatever would seem foreign to them, for fear that the introduction of strange forms of expression should produce a distaste for their teaching." *Against Celsus*, 7.60, in *ANF*, 4:635. The text has been rendered clearer.

15. Several examples underscore this point. In his commentary on the gospel of John, Origen noted that this work had been "committed to the earthly treasure house of common speech, of writing which any passer-by can read, and which can be heard when read aloud by anyone who opens his ears." *Commentary on the Gospel of John*, 1.6, in *ANF*, 10:300. The text has been rendered clearer. Commenting to Celsus on Paul's letters, Origen urges: "For if anyone gives himself to their attentive study, I am well assured … that he will be amazed at the understanding of the man who can clothe great ideas in common language." *Against Celsus*, 3.20, in *ANF*, 4:471. The text has been rendered clearer. Again comparing Plato's writings with Scripture, Origen emphasized this contrast: "Observe now the difference between the fine phrases of Plato concerning the 'chief good' and the declarations of our prophets concerning the 'light' of the blessed. And notice that the truth contained in Plato concerning this subject failed to help his readers attain to a pure worship of God. Nor did it help Plato himself, who could philosophize so grandly about the 'chief good.' In contrast, the simple language of the holy Scriptures has led to their honest readers being filled with a divine spirit." *Against Celsus*, 6.5, in *ANF*, 4:575. The text has been rendered clearer.

16. Origen, *First Principles*, preface, 3, in *ANF*, 4:239.

17. For further discussion, see chap. 8.

18. Origen, *First Principles*, 4.1.9–10 (from the Latin ed.), in *ANF*, 4:357–58.

the divine mysteries.[19] Thus, the two-tiered system of Christians and their understanding of Scripture, begun by Clement, was reinforced by Origen. He also emphasized the inexhaustible depths of the divine mysteries hidden in Scripture and the consequent inability of Christians to understand them.

Augustine affirmed that God had clearly revealed in his Word whatever was necessary for Christians to know: "For among the things that are plainly laid down in Scripture are to be found all matters that concern faith and the manner of life."[20] To support this contention, he posed this series of rhetorical questions concerning the words of God: "Why were they spoken, but to be known? Why did they sound forth, but to be heard? Why were they heard, but to be understood?"[21] But Augustine also acknowledged the presence of "many and varied obscurities and ambiguities" in Scripture. Indeed, he admitted, "Some of the expressions are so obscure as to shroud the meaning in the thickest darkness."[22] He offered his thoughts on God's intention in this: "I do not doubt that all this was divinely arranged for the purpose of subduing pride by requiring hard effort, and of preventing a feeling of satisfaction in the intellect, which generally undervalues what is discovered without difficulty."[23] Two extremes, therefore, had to be avoided as Scripture came into being: (1) It could not be totally obscure, for that would lead to (spiritual) hunger on the part of its seeking readers, and (2) Scripture could not be totally clear, for that would result in laziness from overeating (to sustain the imagery) by its readers. God, however, avoided both extremes: "The Holy Spirit has, with admirable wisdom and care for our welfare, so arranged the Holy Scriptures as by the plainer passages to satisfy our hunger, and by the more obscure to stimulate our appetite."[24]

In a way reminiscent of Tertullian, Augustine articulated a principle to help believers grasp the obscure portions of Scripture: "When we have made ourselves to a certain extent familiar with the language of Scripture, we may proceed to open up and investigate the obscure passages, and in doing so draw examples from the plainer expressions to throw light upon the more obscure, and use the evidence of passages about which there is no doubt to remove all hesitation in regard to the doubtful passages."[25] Above all, the understanding of Scripture is dependent upon knowledge and utilization of certain principles of interpretation. Thus, Augustine engaged in setting forth those key principles so as to guide others in properly interpreting Scripture.[26] He then urged: "The man who is in possession of the rules which here I attempt to lay down, if he comes upon an obscure passage in the books which he reads, will not need an interpreter to uncover the secret for

19. Origen, *First Principles*, 4.26 (from the Latin ed.), in *ANF*, 4:375. Writing against his opponent Celsus, Origen added: "The prophets in particular ... are full of acknowledged difficulties, and of declarations that are obscure to the multitude.... Even we ourselves, who have devoted much study to these writings, would not say that 'we were acquainted with everything.'" *Against Celsus*, 1.12, in *ANF*, 4:401.

20. Augustine, *On Christian Doctrine*, 2.9.14, in *NPNF¹*, 2:539. The text has been rendered clearer.

21. Augustine, *Tractates on the Gospel of John*, Tractate 21.12 (John 5:20–23), in *NPNF¹*, 7:142.

22. Augustine, *On Christian Doctrine*, 2.6, in *NPNF¹*, 2:537.

23. Ibid. The text has been rendered clearer. Cf. Augustine, *Commentary on Psalm 11*, 8; *Commentary on Psalm 94*, 1; *Commentary on Psalm 147*, 10, 12, in *NPNF¹*, 8:43, 459, 667–68.

24. Augustine, *On Christian Doctrine*, 2.8, in *NPNF¹*, 2:537. Continuing his affirmation, Augustine added a principle that will be the focus of the next point: "For almost nothing is dug out of those obscure passages which may not be found set forth in the plainest language elsewhere." Ibid.

25. Ibid., 2.9, in *NPNF¹*, 2:539; cf. 2.12, in *NPNF¹*, 2:540.

26. For further discussion, see chap. 8.

him. Rather, holding to certain rules and following certain principles, he will arrive at the hidden sense without any error, or at least without falling into any terrible absurdity."[27]

Some leaders of the early church would not allow the deep things of Scripture to discourage all Christians from reading them with great benefit. John Chrysostom offered that "the Scriptures are so proportioned that even the most ignorant can understand them if they only read them studiously."[28] This is especially true of any and all Scripture that is necessary: "All things are clear and open that are in the divine Scriptures; the necessary things are all plain."[29] Still, for Chrysostom, some Scripture is obscure, and because of this, he urged careful study of Scripture, encouraging its readers to dig deeply through its obscurities like a miner digs for gold.[30] Cyril of Alexandria responded to a heretic who criticized the Scriptures for their common language, by explaining the reason for their simplicity: "That they might be understandable to all, small and great, they have for practical purposes been written in familiar language, so that they are not beyond anyone's comprehension."[31] Gregory the Great noted: "In its obvious sense, it [Scripture] has food to nourish little ones. In its secret meaning, it can command the admiration of the most learned minds. It is almost like a river, both shallow and deep, in which a lamb may walk and an elephant swim."[32]

THE CLARITY OF SCRIPTURE IN THE MIDDLE AGES

This emphasis on both the clarity and obscurity of Scripture continued as a major theme in the church of the Middle Ages. According to Rabanus Maurus:

> To be sure, Sacred Scripture is written on our account.... Indeed, many things in it are so open that they provide nourishment to little ones. Certain parts have more veiled sentences, sentences such as to put the stout-hearted through their paces [that challenge the bravest] and which are more gratifying insofar as it takes more work to understand them. Some things in Scripture, moreover, are so closed and impenetrable that, while we do not understand them, owing to our weakness and blindness, we find them to be of more profit to our sense of humility than to our understanding.[33]

---

27. Augustine, *On Christian Doctrine*, preface, 9, in *NPNF*[1], 2:521.

28. Chrysostom, *Concionis de Lazaro* 3, PG, 48:994, cited in Francis Turretin, *Institutes of Elenctic Theology*, ed. James T. Dennison Jr., trans. George Musgrave Giger, 3 vols. in 1 (Phillipsburg, N.J.: P & R, 1997), 1:145.

29. Chrysostom, *Homilies on Thessalonians*, homily 3 on 2 Thess. 1:9–10, in *NPNF*[1], 13:388. In this context, Chrysostom raised the issue of the need for preaching: If Scripture is clear, why is there any call for preaching? His answer affirmed both the perspicuity of Scripture and the depravity of its hearers/readers. In light of this latter reality, preaching is needed.

30. Chrysostom, *Homilies on St. John*, homily 40 on John 5:31–32, in *NPNF*[1], 14:143.

31. Cyril of Alexandria, *Against Julian the Apostate*, bk. 7, cited in Martin Chemnitz, *Examination of the Council of Trent*, pt. 1, trans. Fred Kramer (St. Louis: Concordia, 1971), 166. Chemnitz also cited the comments of Lactantius: "Should not God the maker of the mind and voice, and of language, be able to speak clearly? Yes, with the highest foresight he willed that divine things should be unadorned, in order that all might understand what he himself was saying to all." Ibid., 167.

32. Gregory the Great, "Epistle," 4, in *Moralia* (a commentary on the book of Job), trans. D. Herlihy.

33. Rabanus Maurus, in *Ezekiel*, bk. 15, PL, 110:910–11, cited in Henri de Lubac, *Medieval Exegesis: The Four Senses of Scripture*, vol. 1 (Grand Rapids: Eerdmans, 1998), 76n25.

Indeed, Scripture "is broadened by the immensity of the mysteries."[34] Of course, this viewpoint rendered the Bible a very obscure book for new believers and superficial readers, not to mention the many illiterate members of the church. Because the literate members of the church were primarily its priests, the solemn duty of studying and teaching the Bible to the laypeople fell almost exclusively upon their shoulders. A division between clergy and laity concerning the interpretation and understanding of Scripture was well under way.

Perhaps no better example of this comes from a contemporary of the fourteenth-century pre-Reformer John Wycliffe, in a criticism of his translation of the Bible into English:

> Christ delivered his gospel to the clergy and teachers of the church in order that they might minister to the laity and to weaker persons, according to their situations and needs. But this master John Wycliffe translated Scripture from Latin into English. Thus, he opened it up to the laity, and to women who can read, even more so than it had been formerly opened to the most educated and understanding clergy. In this way the pearl of the gospel is cast before swine and trampled under their feet. That which was previously valuable to both clergy and laity has become the laughingstock of both! The jewel of the church is turned into the joke of the people, and what was previously the principal gift of the clergy and teachers is made forever common to the laity.[35]

The church believed that the interpretation and understanding of the Bible belonged to the clergy, not to laypeople like Wycliffe and his followers.

This hierarchical structure brought a benefit to the church: With the interpretation of the Bible as the responsibility of the trained clergy, they could guard against false doctrine and stamp out heresy. But this clergy-laity distinction also ensured that the church could retain its authority over the people. Laypeople who took it upon themselves to interpret the Bible posed a threat to the power of the church. An example of this is a document written in 1270 against the Waldensians, a group originated by Peter Waldo and eventually excommunicated from the church (it would later merge with the Protestants at the time of the Reformation):

> And because they [the Waldensians] presumed to interpret the words of the gospel in a sense of their own, not perceiving that there were any other, they said that the entire gospel ought to be obeyed literally. And they boasted that they wished to do this, and that they only were the true imitators of Christ.... This was their first heresy, contempt of the power of the church.... In their zeal they lead many others astray along with them. They teach even little girls the words of the Gospels and Epistles, so that they may be trained in error from their childhood.... They teach their docile and fluent disciples to repeat the words of

---

34. Irimbert of Admont, in *Ruth*, prologue. Irimbert's reference was to the short book of Ruth. Cited in Lubac, *Medieval Exegesis*, 2:91.

35. John Dowling, *The History of Romanism* (New York: E. Walker's Son, 1881), 383. Dowling cited Knighton, a canon of Leicester.

the Gospels and the sayings of the apostles ... by heart, in their common language, so that they may know how to teach others and lead the faithful astray.[36]

Although the Waldensians held doctrines to which the church objected, the main concerns of the church were the movement's unauthorized preaching and use of unauthorized translations of the Bible. It was not uncommon, therefore, for various councils of the church during the Middle Ages to prohibit the laity from possessing Scripture in any language. One example was the Council of Toulouse (France) in 1229: "We prohibit ... that the laity should be permitted to have the books of the Old or the New Testament."[37] Without the Bible—either in Latin or translation—in the hands of laypeople, the church reinforced the notion that only its trained clergy could read and understand Scripture. In other words, the Word of God was an obscure book for the laity. If they would read it, they would only go astray and take others with them. For safety's sake—as well as for the sake of the church's authority—Scripture was to be a closed book for common folk.[38]

Dissenting from this position was John Wycliffe. In response to the church's insistence that translating the Bible was heretical, Wycliffe offered his reasons for providing Scripture in the language of the common people:

> It seems first that the knowledge of God's law should be taught in the language which is best known, because this knowledge is God's Word. When Christ says in the Gospel that both heaven and earth shall pass away but his words shall not pass away [Matt. 5:18], he means by his "words" his knowledge. Thus God's knowledge is Holy Scripture that may in no way be false. Also the Holy Spirit gave to the apostles at Pentecost knowledge to know all manner of languages to teach the people God's law by them; and so God willed that the people be taught his law in various languages. But what man on God's behalf should reverse God's ordinance and his will?... Thus Christ and his apostles taught the people in that language that was best known to them. Why should men not do so now?[39]

---

36. David of Augsburg, "On the Waldensians of Bavaria, 1270," in *Heresy and Authority in Medieval Europe: Documents in Translation*, ed. Edward Peters (Philadelphia: Univ. of Pennsylvania Press, 1980), 149–50. The text has been rendered clearer.

37. Canon 14 of the Council of Toulouse (1229), in Peters, *Heresy and Authority*, 195.

38. To be more accurate, these statements regarding the clergy-laity distinction need to be slightly nuanced. Jacopo Passavanti, a Dominican monk from fourteenth-century Florence, Italy, provides a helpful balance: "Each Christian is bound to have some knowledge of holy Scripture, and each according to the state and condition and rank that he holds; for in one manner should the priest and guide of souls know it, and in another manner the master and doctor and preacher, those who step down into the deep sea of Scripture, and know and understand the hidden mysteries, so as to be ready for the instruction of others.... And in yet another manner the laity and uneducated parish priests are bound to know it, to whom it is sufficient to know in general the Ten Commandments, the articles of the faith, the sacraments of the church, the sins, church ordinances, the doctrine of the holy gospel, as far as is necessary for their salvation, and as much as they hear from their rectors and the preachers of Scripture and the faith. They should not engage in subtle study of Scripture, nor put their foot down too deeply into the sea of Scripture, which not all people can do, nor ought they wish to scan it, because very often one slips and drowns oneself in incautious and curious and vain research. But each one ought to know, as much as befits his office, and the status which he holds." Jacopo Passavanti, *The Mirror of True Repentance*, in Peters, *Heresy and Authority*, 298. The text has been rendered clearer.

39. John Wycliffe, *On the Pastoral Office*, 2.2a., in LCC, 14:49–51.

Although the medieval church decried the use of the Bible by laypeople, John Wycliffe—as a proponent of the clarity of Scripture—made it available in the language of the English people.

THE CLARITY OF SCRIPTURE IN THE REFORMATION AND POST-REFORMATION

While the Reformation is most commonly known for its insistence on *sola Scriptura* (Scripture only), another key issue in the break between Protestants and Catholics was the doctrine of the clarity of Scripture. Early in his career as a Reformer, Martin Luther was confronted with current church positions that weighed against common laypeople being encouraged to hear and understand the Word of God. One of these positions was that the interpretation of Scripture belonged to the pope, and to the pope alone.[40] A second position was that the church's theology was formed with reference to Scripture, church tradition, and the interpretation of the Bible by the church fathers.[41] At the heart of these positions was the belief that Scripture was "obscure and ambiguous" and therefore in need of clarification by the church.[42]

Luther spelled out his view of the clarity of Scripture in this context, particularly in his writing *The Bondage of the Will* against the Christian humanist Erasmus. Luther summed up his position in this way: "For it should be settled as fundamental, and most firmly fixed in the minds of Christians, that the Holy Scriptures are a spiritual light far brighter even than the sun, especially in what relates to salvation and all essential matters."[43] Specifically, Luther affirmed a twofold clarity of Scripture: (1) The *external clarity* of Scripture itself: "The position is that nothing whatsoever is left obscure or ambiguous, but all that is in the Scripture is through the Word brought forth into the clearest light and proclaimed to the whole world."[44] (2) The *internal clarity* of the heart of the reader of Scripture: "If you speak of internal clarity, the truth is that nobody who does not have the Spirit of God sees a jot [bit] of what is in the Scriptures.... The Spirit is needed for the understanding of all Scripture and every part of Scripture."[45] For Luther the Bible is clear in and of itself, but the Holy Spirit is still absolutely necessary for the reader to understand clear Scripture. In

---

40. This issue was the second of the three walls that Luther attempted to tear down in his 1520 writing *To the Christian Nobility of the German Nation Concerning the Reform of the Christian Estate*, LW, 44:115–217.

41. Luther addressed this position in his third of a series of four writings against his former professor Jerome Emser of Leipzig, whose coat of arms was a shield and helmet adorned with a goat: *Answer to the Hyperchristian, Hyperspiritual, and Hyperlearned Book by Goat Emser in Leipzig — Including Some Thoughts Regarding His Companion, the Fool Murner*, LW, 39:143–224.

42. In a scathing denunciation of this notion, Luther offered: "On the same account I have thus far hounded the pope, in whose kingdom nothing is more commonly said or more widely accepted than this dictum: 'the Scriptures are

obscure and equivocal; we must seek the interpreting Spirit from the Apostolic See [i.e., the papal office] of Rome!' No more disastrous words could be spoken; for by this means ungodly men have exalted themselves above the Scriptures and done what they liked, till the Scriptures were completely trodden down and we could believe and teach nothing but maniacs' dreams. In a word, that dictum is no mere human invention; it is poison sent into the world by the inconceivably malevolent prince of all the devils himself!" Martin Luther, *The Bondage of the Will*, trans. James I. Packer and O. R. Johnston (Old Tappan, N.J.: Revell, 1957), 124.

43. Ibid., 125.

44. Ibid., 74.

45. Ibid., 73–74.

light of this, when the Word of God is not understood or is misunderstood, it is not due to any fault in itself. Rather, the problem lies with the readers of Scripture. They fail to grasp its meaning because of some spiritual defect in them. Thus, for Luther:

> I know that to many people a great deal remains obscure; but that is due, not to any lack of clarity in Scripture, but to their own blindness and dullness, in that they make no effort to see truth which, in itself, could not be plainer. As Paul said of the Jews..., "The veil remains on their heart" [2 Cor. 3:15]; and again, "If our gospel is hid, it is hid to them who are lost, whose heart the god of this world has blinded" [2 Cor. 4:3–4]. They are like men who cover their eyes, or go from daylight into darkness, and hide there, and then blame the sun, or the darkness of the day, for their inability to see. So let wretched men abjure [renounce] that blasphemous perversity which would blame the darkness of their own hearts to the plain Scriptures of God![46]

The doctrine of the clarity of Scripture was axiomatic for Luther. Indeed, he referred to it as "this very first principle of ours" and thus did not consider that the doctrine required any proof.[47] However, due to the attacks of his opponents, Luther offered support for Scripture's clarity. He noted Old Testament passages that refer to light or enlightenment (Deut. 17:8; Pss. 19:8; 119:105, 130; Isa. 8:20; Mal. 2:7).[48] Moreover, he argued from the fact that civil laws are "perfectly clear ... and more certain than anything else." If this is true of human laws, then God's laws must be much clearer.[49] Furthermore, Luther cited New Testament passages that applied the metaphor of light to Scripture (e.g., 2 Cor. 4:3–4; 2 Peter 1:19).[50] Finally, he used *reductio ad absurdum* arguments, trying to imagine the hopeless situation that would come about if Scripture were obscure instead of clear. In such a case, interpreters would become entangled in a never-ending process of trying to explain what the Bible means. Biblical passages that speak of the benefits of Scripture (2 Tim. 3:16) or that encourage the Word of God to be used as the standard against error (Titus 1:9) would be meaningless. Indeed, one would even wonder why God bothered to give a revelation that is obscure.[51]

So how much of Scripture is clear? As noted above, Luther believed that all of Scripture is clear. This attribute is especially true of biblical sections that address matters of salvation and living the Christian life. In particular, he used 2 Peter 1:19 to support his statement, "I would say of the whole of Scripture that I do not allow any part of it to be called obscure." Noting Peter's statement, "We have the word ... as ... a light shining in a dark place," Luther argued: "If part of the lamp does not shine, then it is a part of the dark place rather than of the lamp! When he enlightened us, Christ did not intend that part of the Word should be left obscure to us, for he commands us to mark the Word; and this command is pointless if the Word is not clear."[52]

---

46. Ibid., 73.

47. Ibid., 125.

48. Ibid., 125–26. The references are those in English versions of the Bible. Luther mistakenly identified the reference in Malachi as the book of Zechariah.

49. Ibid., 125–26.

50. Ibid., 127.

51. Ibid., 127–28.

52. Ibid., 129.

Luther carefully clarified his ideas on this doctrine. The clarity of Scripture does not imply that believers can understand everything about God. On the contrary, "Nobody questions that there is a great deal hid in God of which we know nothing."[53] But the obscurity that exists in God cannot be applied to Scripture. This was a critical error of Erasmus, who cited biblical passages that refer to the unfathomable depths of God (e.g., Rom. 11:33) and used them to argue for the obscurity of some parts of Scripture.[54]

Moreover, the clarity of Scripture does not imply that every text of Scripture is obvious. Luther made a distinction between the *text* of Scripture and the *subject matter* of Scripture. In the former case, he admitted that the text may be obscure, but with regard to the latter, the subject matter of Scripture is fully knowable. This clarity is linked to the resurrection of Christ:

> For what solemn truth can the Scriptures still be concealing, now that the seals are broken, the stone rolled away from the door of the tomb, and that greatest of all mysteries brought to light—that Christ, God's Son, became man, that God is three in one, that Christ suffered for us, and will reign forever? And are not these things known and sung in our streets? Take Christ from the Scriptures—and what will you find in them? You see, then, that the entire content of the Scriptures has now been brought to light, even though some passages that contain unknown words remain obscure.[55]

Even with the frank admission that some texts of Scripture are obscure due to linguistic and grammatical difficulties, Luther counted as few the actual number of these difficulties.[56] And these do not amount to insurmountable problems, because clearer passages of Scripture can be used to shine their light on the less clear ones: "If words are obscure in one place, they are clear in another. What God has so plainly declared to the world is in some parts of Scripture stated in plain words, while in other parts it still lies hidden under obscure words. But when something stands in broad daylight, and a mass

---

53. Ibid., 71. Philipp Melanchthon followed Luther in this view: "I have not the mistaken view that the holy can be penetrated through the industry of human talent. There is something in the holy that nobody can ever see unless it is shown to him by God. And Christ cannot be known to us without the Holy Spirit teaching us. But apart from prophecy, the meaning of the words must be known in which, as a shrine, the divine mysteries are hidden. For what is the use of reciting in a magic way words that have not been understood? Is it not like telling a story to a deaf person?" Philipp Melanchthon, *Corpus Reformatorum*, vol. 2, col. 64: *Encomium Eloquentiae*, cited in W. Schwarz, *Principles and Problems of Biblical Translations* (Cambridge: Cambridge Univ. Press, 1955), 195.

54. Ibid., 71. Erasmus classified Scripture into obscure portions and clear portions, and Luther objected to this division on the basis of the weakness of Erasmus's alleged biblical support. Luther understood Erasmus to have taken the referent of "his" in Romans 11:33 ("How unsearchable are his

judgments") to be "Scripture," but Luther pointed out that the correct referent is "God." Also, Luther noted that Erasmus had mistakenly applied Isa. 40:13 ("Who has known the mind of the Lord?") to Scripture, thus making the question undermine the clarity of the Bible. Ibid., 72–73.

55. Luther continued: "But the notion that in Scripture some things are obscure and all is not plain was spread by the godless philosophers (whom you now echo, Erasmus)—who have never yet cited a single item to prove their crazy view; nor can they. And Satan has used these phantom menaces to scare off men from reading the sacred text, and to destroy all sense of its value, so as to ensure that his own brand of poisonous philosophy reigns supreme in the church." Ibid. The text has been rendered clearer.

56. Ibid., 71. Actually, Luther said almost in the same breath that "many" passages contain linguistic and semantic difficulties and "some" such problems exist.

of evidence for it is in broad daylight, it does not matter whether there is any evidence for it in the dark."[57]

Finally, the clarity of Scripture does not imply that all the mysteries of the faith are now resolved. Even a clear Bible does not provide all the lofty details of these mysteries. But the obscurity of biblical mystery cannot be turned around and used against the clarity of Scripture. Thus, when Erasmus listed three mysteries as examples of Scripture's obscurity, Luther corrected him: "Scripture makes the straightforward affirmation that the Trinity, the Incarnation, and the unpardonable sin are facts. There is nothing obscure or ambiguous about that. You imagine that Scripture tells us *how* they are what they are; but it does not, nor do we need to know."[58] Thus, as to the *facts* of the mysteries of the faith, Scripture is clear. But it does not address the lofty details—the *how*—of such mysteries. Because Scripture was not designed to explain mysteries, however, it cannot be faulted and called obscure for failing to do what it never intended to do. Thus, Martin Luther was a staunch defender of the clarity of Scripture at the outset of the Reformation.

Huldrych Zwingli dedicated a sermon on this doctrine: *Of the Clarity and Certainty of the Word of God* (first delivered in 1522).[59] He defined clarity this way: "When the Word of God shines on the human understanding, it enlightens it in such a way that it understands and confesses the Word and knows the certainty of it."[60] He did not frame this doctrine in terms of an attribute or quality of Scripture.[61] Rather, the focus of his treatment was the effect that the Word of God has on the readers of the Bible. Clarity is an impact that brings enlightenment to the understanding and the assurance that what one understands is true and worthy of being trusted because it is from God.

This definition led Zwingli to make a distinction between two types of the Word of God, an *external* Word and an *internal* Word. The *external* Word is Scripture as it is read and preached before the church. It is not this Word that leads to faith, for if it did, every person who hears the Word would believe. But this idea is defeated by both Scripture (think of the parable of the sower) and experience: not everyone believes the Word. In contrast to this stands the *internal* Word. This is the Word that God proclaims in the hearts of people. It is by this Word that God illumines people so that understanding and assurance take place. It is this Word that leads to faith. Thus, the clarity of Scripture

---

57. Ibid., 70–71.

58. Ibid., 73.

59. Huldrych Zwingli, *Of the Clarity and Certainty of the Word of God*, LCC, 24:59–95.

60. Ibid., 75.

61. He did not deny this, though, and comments to this effect do appear in some of his other writings. For example, Zwingli referred to the gospel as "light" and claimed that it is "clearer than day." Huldreich Zwingli, *Commentary on True and False Religion*, in *The Latin Works of Huldreich Zwingli*, vol. 3, trans. Samuel Macauley Jackson (Philadelphia: Heidelberg, 1929), 220, 150. Some passages, such as Luke 12:52; John 14:6; and Rom. 6:5–11, are singled out by Zwingli as being particularly clear. Ibid., 129, 287, 134. Even the meaning of the words of Christ when he instituted the Lord's Supper (despite the controversy which this issue sparked not only between the Roman Catholic Church and the Reformers, but also between the Reformers themselves) is "perfectly clear" and "plain in itself." Ibid., 220, 227. Finally, the biblical teaching on certain important themes is also characterized by Zwingli as being clear. E.g., the matter of the prohibition of images "is set forth with such distinct and clear ordinances all through the Scriptures," the nature of the true church is "clearly taught" in the New Testament, and the teaching on the free grace of God is "clearer than day." Ibid., 334, 369–70, 391. Thus, comments as to the clarity of biblical passages or doctrines are to be found in Zwingli's writings, but in most cases, if not exclusively, such comments are casual ones.

refers to this internal Word only. Clarity is a function of the internal Word as it enlightens people's hearts, bringing understanding, response, and certainty.

Zwingli summarized his position on the clarity of Scripture: "The Word of God is certain and can never fail. It is clear, and will never leave us in darkness. It teaches its own truth. It arises and irradiates [illumines] the souls of people with full salvation and grace. It gives the soul sure comfort in God."[62] Again, this applies to Zwingli's internal Word, the Word of God that the Holy Spirit communicates to people's hearts. This is not true of his external Word, Scripture as it is read and preached in the people's hearing. It should be noted that the other Reformers and those who succeeded them did not follow Zwingli's division of the Word of God into external and internal realities.

Unlike Luther and Zwingli, at no point in his writings did John Calvin engage in a sustained discussion of the clarity of Scripture. Yet he repeatedly affirmed it. Commenting on Peter's use of the metaphor of light to refer to Scripture (2 Peter 1:19), Calvin highlighted some key aspects of Scripture's clarity:

> It deserves further notice that Peter comments on the clarity of Scripture. What is said [about the prophetic word being a lamp] would be a false statement if [in reality] Scripture were not fit and appropriate to show us with certainty the right way. Whoever, then, will open his eyes through faithful obedience shall know by experience that Scripture has not been mistakenly called a light. It is indeed obscure to unbelievers; but they who are going to be destroyed are willfully blind. Thus, the blasphemy of the Papists is damnable. They pretend that the light of Scripture does nothing other than dazzle the eyes, and they say this to keep the common people from reading the Bible.[63]

Calvin firmly rooted his perspective on the clarity of Scripture in the historical context of the Roman Catholic Church's denial that the Bible is understandable to laypeople. In opposition to this view, Calvin noted the apostolic affirmation of Scripture's clarity. He appealed to the purpose of the Bible — "to show us with certainty the right way" — as support. This light of Scripture is available only to those who possess certain characteristics and who approach it in a proper manner. To others — those who are "willfully blind" — Scripture is closed and obscure.

In commenting on Deuteronomy 30:11, Calvin underscored other aspects of this doctrine:

> Moses commends the Law because of its easiness. God does not set before us obscure mysteries to keep our minds in suspense and to torture us with difficulties, but teaches in a common way whatever is necessary to know, according to the intelligence — or rather ignorance — of the people.... Moses, therefore, declares that it is not hard to understand the Law, such that it must be studied to the point of absolute exhaustion. Rather, God speaks there distinctly and

62. Zwingli, *Of the Clarity and Certainty of the Word of God*, LCC, 24:93.

63. John Calvin, *Commentaries on the Catholic Epistles*, ed. and trans. John Owen (Grand Rapids: Baker, 2005), 388–89. The text has been rendered clearer.

explicitly, such that the only thing required is diligent application of oneself to the task.[64]

Calvin appealed to the accommodation of God as support for the clarity of Scripture: In consideration for the ignorance of humanity, God lowered himself to our level and delivered his revelation in an appropriate way. In terms of Scripture, this means that God adapted himself to human speech, and speech that would be understandable. "For who even of slight intelligence does not understand that, as nurses commonly do with infants, God also 'lisps' in speaking to us?"[65] In another striking image, Calvin compared God to a "mother stooping to her child, so to speak, so as not to leave us behind in our weakness."[66] Thus, divine communication is not obscure, but clear, and not difficult to understand if diligent study is employed. God wants to be understood, and so Scripture is understandable.

Calvin offered two other points to substantiate the doctrine of the clarity of Scripture. First, he noted that Scripture is clear because of the purpose and need for it. He rejected the adequacy of general revelation for people to know God. Thus, "it was necessary that another and better help be added" to lead people to God. "It was not in vain, then, that he [God] added the light of his Word by which to become known for salvation." Employing a powerful metaphor, Calvin explained: "Just as old or bleary-eyed men and those with weak vision, if you thrust before them a most beautiful volume [book], even if they recognize it to be some sort of writing, yet can scarcely construe [read] two words, but with the aid of glasses will begin to read distinctly; so Scripture, gathering up the otherwise confused knowledge of God in our minds, having dispersed our dullness, clearly shows us the true God."[67] It is precisely this purpose and need for Scripture—to provide and acquire the knowledge of God—that demands that Scripture is clear. Second, Calvin argued that Scripture is clear because of its simplicity of words and style. Certainly the subject matter of Scripture is glorious and involves "heavenly mysteries above human capacity."[68] The Bible, however, presents this content in a "humble and lowly style"[69] that is "simple and even homely."[70] This "elementary instruction"[71] is necessary because Scripture, "having regard for men's rude and stupid wit, customarily speaks in the manner of the common folk."[72] Thus, Scripture is clear for everyone, even untrained and uneducated laypeople.

In addition to his work on Scripture's clarity, Calvin also addressed the issue of its obscurity. He noted the relative obscurity of the Old Testament in comparison with the New. God's plan all along was to reveal his great salvation, but he did so in a veiled way in the Old Testament. This revelation became clearer in the New Testament.[73] Next, Calvin

---

64. John Calvin, *Commentaries on the Last Four Books of Moses*, vol. 1 (Grand Rapids: Baker, 2005), 412. The text has been rendered clearer.

65. John Calvin, *Institutes of the Christian Religion*, 1.13.1, LCC, 1:121.

66. Ibid., 3.21.4, LCC, 2:925–26. The imagery is from Augustine.

67. Ibid., 1.6.1, LCC, 1:70.

68. Ibid., 1.8.11, LCC, 1:90.

69. Ibid.

70. John Calvin, *Commentary on the Gospel of John* (Grand Rapids: Baker, 2005), 2:156; cf. idem, *Commentaries on the Book of Genesis* (Grand Rapids: Baker, 2005), 1:113.

71. Calvin, *Institutes*, 3.10.1, LCC, 1:719.

72. Ibid., 1.11.1, LCC, 1:99.

73. Ibid., 4.10.17, LCC, 2:1195–96. Cf. 3.2.6, LCC, 1:548.

drew attention to the temporary obscurity of Christ's teaching for the apostles, underscoring the disciples' inability to grasp the teachings of Jesus while he was among them. Although they were in his actual presence and directly heard his own words, still they could not understand his meaning. This inability was due to their lack of the enlightenment of the Holy Spirit at that time.[74] Furthermore, Calvin affirmed the obscurity of Scripture for nonbelievers. As noted above, the light of Scripture is available only to those whose eyes are open through faithful obedience. This is not the case for unbelievers; for them, the Bible is a closed book. In part, this is God's design: Scripture comes to them obscurely.[75] But this is also due to the blindness that Satan imposes on unbelievers so they cannot trust Christ because of the obscurity of the gospel.[76]

Interestingly, Calvin confessed the obscurity of parts of Scripture for believers. Scripture's clarity does not imply that believers will easily understand everything in the Bible. Patience and a willingness to obey should accompany the diligent study of difficult portions of Scripture. And the light of clearer passages should be used to clarify the more obscure passages. Moreover, he emphasized the relative obscurity of all Scripture during earthly existence. Although in one sense Calvin restricted the obscurity of Scripture for believers to only certain portions, there is another sense in which he maintained that the whole of Scripture is obscure. He addressed this in his comments on 1 Corinthians 13:12, beginning with a paraphrase of that verse:

> "The measure of knowledge, that we now have, is appropriate for our imperfect existence and [what one might call our] 'childhood,' as it were; for we do not as yet see clearly the mysteries of the heavenly kingdom, and we do not as yet enjoy a distinct view of them." To express this, he [Paul] uses a comparison—that *we now see only as in a mirror*, and therefore but obscurely.... The knowledge of God, which we now have from his Word, is indeed certain and true, and has nothing in it that is confused, or perplexed, or dark, but is spoken of as comparatively *obscure*, because it comes far short of that clear revelation to which we look forward; for then *we shall see face to face*.[77]

Thus, while affirming the clarity of Scripture, Calvin carefully provided several clarifications of the doctrine. In accommodating himself to human understanding, God communicated his Word in such a way that people may embrace an adequate knowledge of him. "For we have in the Word (in so far as is necessary for us) a naked and open revelation of God, and it has nothing obscure in it, to hold us in [a state of] uncertainty."[78]

The doctrine of Scripture's clarity was not simply a statement by the Reformers about a characteristic of the Word of God. The implications of affirming this attribute were enormous. One of the most obvious was a commitment to translating the Bible into the languages of the common people. Luther's translation of Scripture into the German language stands as one of his greatest legacies and remains a constant testimony to his

74. Ibid., 3.2.4, LCC, 1:546.

75. Ibid., 3.24.13, LCC, 2:979–81.

76. John Calvin, *Commentary on Isaiah* (Grand Rapids: Baker, 2005), 3:420–21.

77. John Calvin, *Commentary on the Epistles of Paul the Apostle to the Corinthians* (Grand Rapids: Eerdmans, 1948), 1:429–30.

78. Ibid., 431.

insistence on the clarity of Scripture.[79] Another implication of this doctrine was the encouragement of laypeople to hear, read, and understand the Bible.

In the face of the Reformers' affirmation of the clarity of Scripture, the Roman Catholic Church reacted on a number of fronts. One was to prohibit the translation of the Bible into the language of the people. Examples of this from the early years of the Reformation include a 1526 order in the Netherlands to burn all Gospels and Epistles translated into the common language; a 1530 prohibition by King Henry VIII of the reading of Scripture in the English language; a 1548 prohibition in France of all Bibles translated into French; and a 1551 prohibition in Spain of all Bibles in Spanish and popular dialects. Indeed, the Council of Trent decreed that the Latin Vulgate—not the Hebrew Old Testament, not the Greek New Testament, and certainly not any vernacular edition—was the official version of Scripture.[80] Then, to prevent Protestant biblical interpretation from challenging the Roman Catholic Church's interpretation of Scripture, the Council of Trent declared that only the Church possesses the right to interpret the Bible.[81] This affirmation continued the Catholic Church's centuries-old insistence that Scripture is too obscure for laypeople to rightly interpret it.

The Protestant doctrine of the clarity of Scripture, formulated by Luther, Zwingli, and Calvin, continued to be a major point of contention between Catholics and Protestants in subsequent centuries. As a renewed and more aggressive Catholic Church critically challenged Scripture's clarity, the post-Reformers were called upon to offer an apologetic for the doctrine. At stake was the translation of the Bible into the languages of the people, encouragement to read and study personally the Word of God, the authority of Catholic tradition in the interpretation of Scripture, and the power of the Catholic Church.

A new trend in post-Reformation discussions of the doctrine, as expressed by Matthew Poole, was to limit scriptural clarity to "things necessary to be believed or done in order for salvation."[82] This tendency can be seen in Francis Turretin's framing of

---

79. As Luther himself stated in his preface to the Old Testament in German: "Though I cannot boast of having achieved perfection, nevertheless I venture to say that this German Bible is clearer and more accurate at many points than the Latin. So it is true that if the printers do not, as usual, spoil it with their carelessness, the German language certainly has here a better Bible than the Latin language—and the readers will bear me out in this." *Preface to the Old Testament*, LW, 35:249.

80. "The same sacred and holy council—considering that no small advantage may accrue to the church of God, if it be made known which out of all the Latin editions, now in circulation, of the sacred books, is to be held as authentic—ordains and declares, that the old [Latin] Vulgate edition, which, by the long use of so many ages, has been approved of in the church, be, in public lectures, disputations, sermons, and expositions, held as authentic; and that no one dare or presume to reject it under any pretext whatsoever." *Canons and Decrees of the Council of Trent*, 4th session (April 8, 1546), *Decree Concerning the Canonical Scriptures*, in Schaff, 2:82.

81. "Furthermore, in order to restrain petulant spirits, it [the council] decrees that no one, relying on his own judgment,

shall—in matters of faith, and of morals pertaining to the edification of Christian doctrine—wresting [distorting] the sacred Scripture to his own senses, presume to interpret the holy Scripture contrary to that sense which holy mother church—to whom it belongs to judge of the true sense and interpretation of the holy Scriptures—has held and holds; or even contrary to the unanimous consent of the Fathers; even though such interpretations were never [intended] to be at any time published. Those who act contrary shall be made known by their ordinaries and be punished [in accordance with] the penalties established by law." Ibid., in Schaff, 2:83.

82. Matthew Poole, *Commentary on the Holy Bible* (Edinburgh: Banner of Truth Trust, 1962), vol. 1, preface, v. Poole's work was originally released as a two-volume publication entitled *Annotations on the Holy Bible*, with volume 1 (*Genesis to Isaiah*) appearing in 1683 and volume 2 (*Jeremiah to Revelation*) in 1685. Actually, Poole himself wrote only the commentary from Genesis through Isaiah 58; at that point in the project he died. Other scholars completed the work, relying heavily on Poole's massive five-volume Latin work *Synopsis Criticorum*. The following citations from the preface to Poole's

the issue: "Whether the Scriptures are so plain *in things essential to salvation* ... that without the external aid of tradition or the infallible judgment of the [Catholic] church, they may be read and understood profitably by believers? The papists [Catholics] deny this; we [Protestants] affirm this."[83] It can be further detected in John William Baier's substantive discussion:

> Clarity, or that *those things which are necessary to be believed and done by man in seeking to be saved*, are taught in Scripture in words and phrases so clear and conformed to normal communication, that any man acquainted with the language, possessed of a sound judgment, and paying close attention to the words, may learn the true sense of the words, so far as those things are concerned which must be known, and may embrace these essential doctrines by the simple grasp of his mind. As the mind of man is led, by the Scriptures themselves and their supernatural light, or the divine power joined with them, it yields the assent of faith to the Word understood and the things signified.[84]

All three representative discussions framed the doctrine in terms of the clarity of Scripture in matters that are essential for salvation. Focus was placed on the clarity of the actual words and expressions of Scripture, so much so that for Baier, even a nonbeliever who has acquired the normal ability of understanding language can comprehend intellectually at least the message of salvation. A second step — "the assent of faith" — is needed to bring a person who grasps the meaning of Scripture to the place of believing that message.[85]

Like their predecessors, the post-Reformers offered justification for this doctrine. Much of this was thoroughly biblical in nature. For example, passages affirming that Scripture is a light or a lamp (Pss. 19:9; 119:105; 2 Peter 1:19) were cited.[86] Theological support was also offered for the clarity of Scripture, focusing primarily on the divine inspiration of the Bible and on the design or purpose of Scripture. For example, Quenstedt argued that because Scripture has God for its author, and God can speak clearly (for he created language and the voice), the Bible must be clear.[87] And Calov questioned

Commentary on the Holy Bible, reissued in three volumes in 1962, were also written by the scholars who completed his work. It is arguable, however, that they represent Poole's own sympathies.

83. Francis Turretin, *Institutes of Elenctic Theology*, ed. James T. Dennison, trans. George Musgrave Giger, 3 vols. (Phillipsburg: N.J.: P & R, 1997), 2nd topic, 17th q., sec. 7, 1:144 (italics added).

84. John William Baier, *Compendium Theologiae Positivae* (1685), 138, in Schmid, 70 (italics added). The text has been rendered clearer.

85. According to David Hollaz: "An unregenerate man, opposing the illuminating grace of the Holy Spirit, cannot understand the true sense of the sacred writings. But when an unregenerate man, in a teachable spirit, attentively reads the Holy Scriptures, or hears them expounded by a teacher, the Holy Spirit illuminates him by the Scriptures, so that he may understand the true sense of the divine Word and rightly apply

it, thus understood, with saving effect." David Hollaz, *Examen Theologicum Acroamaticum* (1707), 155, in Schmid, 75.

86. E.g., "The divine Word is said to be a lamp and a light. Now whatever is a lamp for our feet and a light for our path is clear and perspicuous, and so it is true of Scripture. Major proof: Certainly a lamp is an instrument of illumination which, if it does not discharge its duty, loses its value as a lamp. A light cannot be called a light for our feet and path unless it is clear and unless it illuminates." Quenstedt, *Theologia Didactico-Polemica* (Wittenberg: Johanne Ludoph Quenstedt, 1696), 1.122 (my translation of the Latin text).

87. Ibid. Quenstedt's argument is discussed in Schmid, 70. Likewise, Turretin maintained that "the clarity of the Scriptures is further proved ... by their efficient cause (viz., God, the Father of men who cannot be said either to be unwilling or unable to speak plainly without impugning his perfect goodness and wisdom)." Turretin, *Institutes of Elenctic Theology*, 1:145.

the benefit of Scripture, which is designed to give eternal life, if it does not clearly communicate the knowledge that is necessary for salvation.[88]

According to the post-Reformers, clarity does not do away with the attentive study of Scripture, the teaching ministry of the church, and the illumination of the Holy Spirit. John Gerhard emphasized the need for careful Bible study to understand clear Scripture: "Observe that, in asserting clarity, we do not exclude the godly study of the Scriptures by reading and meditation, nor the use of the [Bible study] helps necessary for the interpretation of the Scripture."[89] These necessary elements include such matters as the right character and prayerful approach of the interpreter of Scripture, along with a correct mind-set, one that is not "prejudiced by preconceived erroneous opinions."[90]

Moreover, the post-Reformers insisted that Scripture's clarity did not do away with the teaching ministry of the church. This notion was the incorrect implication that Robert Bellarmine, the Roman Catholic apologist, drew from the doctrine of the Bible's clarity. But John Gerhard pointed out that God commanded both the right interpretation of clear Scripture by all Christians and the teaching ministry of the church. Indeed, God established pastors, elders, and other teachers in the church for the pursuit of the correct understanding of clear Scripture. Both the diligent study of Scripture by all believers, and instruction in the Bible by certain individuals in the church, are necessary.[91]

Furthermore, the doctrine does not eliminate the need for spiritual illumination of Scripture. John Owen emphasized the need for readers of Scripture to be "elevated, enlightened, guided, conducted, by an internal efficacious work of the Spirit of God upon them."[92] This illumination is necessary for the understanding of perspicuous Scripture:

> It is supposed, when we assert the *clearness* and *perspicuity* of the Scripture, that there is unto the understanding of it use made of that *aid* and *assistance* of the Spirit of God.... Without this the *clearest revelations* of divine supernatural things will appear as wrapped up in darkness and obscurity—not for lack of

---

88. Abraham Calov, *Systema Locorum Theologicorum* (Wittenberg, 1655), 1:634, in Preus, 156. Turretin argued similarly: "The clarity of the Scriptures is furthered proved by their design to be a canon and rule of faith and practice, which they could not be unless they were clear." Turretin, *Institutes of Elenctic Theology*, 1:145.

89. John Gerhard, *Loci Theologici* (1621), 2:329, in Schmid, 72.

90. Quenstedt, *Theologia Didactico-Polemica*, 1.119, in Schmid, 72. Likewise, Baier (146) noted: "For he who does not attend to the words themselves, but follows his own prejudices and makes the words of Scripture conform to them, can err even in clear passages and in investigating the true sense." John William Baier, *Compendium Theologiae Positivae*, 146, in Schmid, 72. Cf. John Owen, *The Causes, Ways, and Means of Understanding the Mind of God as Revealed in His Word, with Assurance Therein* (London, 1687), chap. 7, in *The Works of John Owen*, ed. William H. Goold, 16 vols. (Edinburgh: Banner of Truth Trust, 1967), 4:199–228.

91. Concerning the teaching ministry of the church, John Owen explained: "[This ministry] is not a means *co-ordinate* with the Scripture, but *subservient* unto it; and the great end of it is, that those who are called thereunto, and are furnished with gifts for the discharge of it, might diligently 'search the Scriptures' and teach others the mind of God revealed therein. It was, I say, the will of God that the church should ordinarily be always under the conduct of such a *ministry*; and his will it is that those who are called thereunto should be furnished with *particular spiritual gifts*, for the finding out and declaration of the truths that are treasured up in the Scripture.... The Scripture, therefore, is such a revelation as does suppose and make necessary this ordinance of the ministry, wherein and whereby God will also be glorified." John Owen, *Causes, Ways, and Means of Understanding the Mind of God*, chap. 6, in Goold, *Works of John Owen*, 4:190–91.

92. Owen, *Causes, Ways, and Means of Understanding the Mind of God*, chap. 1, in Goold, *Works of John Owen*, 4:126.

light in them, but for lack of *light in us*. Therefore, by asserting the necessity of supernatural illumination for the right understanding of divine revelation, we no way impugn the *perspicuity* of the Scripture.[93]

Thus, according to the post-Reformers, clarity does not do away with the attentive study of Scripture, the teaching ministry of the church, and the illumination of the Holy Spirit.

THE CLARITY OF SCRIPTURE IN THE MODERN PERIOD

In further application of this doctrine, the late eighteenth century and nineteenth century witnessed the impressive expansion of the Protestant missionary endeavor, accompanied by the rise of Bible societies that produced and distributed copies of Scripture. Scripture was made available to the people groups that were the focus of Protestant missionary activity, and this access to the Bible in the language of those groups was rooted in the conviction of Scripture's clarity.

The nineteenth century also featured two trends that undermined this doctrine. One was the development of the science of hermeneutics — the study of the rules of interpretation. Although principles of *biblical* interpretation had been around since the church began, this new science expanded the theory of interpretation to include *all literature*, not just the Bible. The clarity of Scripture gave way to the clarity of written works in general. Gone was the *confession of faith* — Scripture is clear — and in its place was put a *literary principle* — all literary works are clear. There is nothing particularly religious about this principle, and certainly nothing that is distinctively Protestant.

A second nineteenth-century development was the rise of biblical criticism and its attacks against the truthfulness of Scripture. As T. P. Weber noted: "Higher [biblical] criticism also took away the individual believer's ability to interpret the Bible for himself.... The findings of higher criticism forced many lay people to doubt their ability to understand anything."[94] More specifically, Gerhard Maier connected the historical-critical method with the demise of scriptural clarity:

> The representatives of the higher-critical method have given sharp opposition to the orthodox thoughts concerning the *perspicuitas* (clarity) and *sufficientia* (sufficiency) of the Scriptures. They have obscured the clarity by their "proof" of contradictions in the Bible, and they have clung to and deepened the obscurity by means of their fruitless search for a canon in a canon. They have undermined the sufficiency of the Scriptures by claiming that the historical-critical work was necessary in order to comprehend the Scriptures. To the degree that their views asserted themselves, a division set in between Scripture and congregation. However, the matter has not ended with Scripture. Since through

---

93. Ibid., chap. 6, in Goold, *Works of John Owen*, 4:194.
94. T. P. Weber, *Living in the Shadow of the Second Com-* ing: *American Premillennialism, 1875–1982* (Grand Rapids: Zondervan, 1983), 36.

Scripture we meet God and learn to know him, therefore by invalidating the clarity and sufficiency of Scripture, they have also destroyed the certainty of faith. If it is uncertain *where* the living God is speaking, then I no longer know *who* is speaking.[95]

Because of these and other developments, the conviction of Scripture's clarity passed into obscurity.

Rarely did this doctrine garner attention in evangelical writings of the twentieth and twenty-first centuries. Indeed, it has become a sorely neglected attribute of Scripture.[96] Exceptions to this were occasionally found, however, and the *Chicago Statement on Biblical Hermeneutics* happily addressed this issue:

> We affirm the clarity of Scripture and specifically of its message about salvation from sin. We deny that all passages of Scripture are equally clear or have equal bearing on the message of redemption.

> We affirm that a person is not dependent for understanding of Scripture on the expertise of biblical scholars. We deny that a person should ignore the fruits of the technical study of Scripture by biblical scholars.[97]

Kevin Vanhoozer combined linguistic philosophy (specifically speech-act theory) with an Augustinian strategy—faith seeking textual understanding—and the notion of covenantal communication to present a defense of the possibility of true understanding of the biblical text. For Vanhoozer Scripture's clarity enables the church to recover "the knowability of the literal sense" of Scripture and to affirm that Scripture has "something definite or determinate to say—about history, about God, about the human condition"—and to deny that Scripture can only "make an 'indistinct sound' [1 Cor. 14:8]."[98]

In my own doctoral studies, my dissertation was a reformulation of the Protestant doctrine of the clarity of Scripture.[99] According to Deuteronomy 29:29, whatever God

---

95. Gerhard Maier, *The End of the Historical-Critical Method*, trans. Edwin W. Leverenz and Rudolph F. Norden (St. Louis: Concordia, 1977), 48–49.

96. In this matter, few have heeded Berkouwer's plea: "In the struggle of the church, it becomes increasingly clear that the confessed perspicuity is not a mere notation of a 'quality' of Scripture in the manner in which we attribute certain qualities to other things, after which we can relax. This confession of the church will only be meaningful if it includes an insight into the power of the Spirit's way through the Word (divine and human) in its historical form. This occurs with such strong and prevailing force that it is not possible for man to relax. We are being challenged by ever-increasing responsibility in the face of new questions and tasks.... No confession concerning Scripture is more disturbing to the church than the confession of its perspicuity." G. C. Berkouwer, *Holy Scripture*, trans. Jack B. Rogers (Grand Rapids: Eerdmans, 1975), 269–70. Recent exceptions to this trend include James Callahan, *The Clarity of Scripture: History, Theology and Contemporary Literary Studies* (Downers Grove, Ill.: InterVarsity, 2001); Mark D. Thompson, *A Clear and Present Word: The Clarity of Scripture*, New Studies in Biblical Theology (Downers Grove, Ill.: InterVarsity, 2006).

97. *Chicago Statement on Biblical Hermeneutics*, arts. 23, 24, in *Hermeneutics, Inerrancy, and the Bible: Papers from ICBI Summit II*, ed. Earl D. Radmacher and Robert D. Preus (Grand Rapids: Zondervan, 1984), 886.

98. Kevin J. Vanhoozer, *Is There a Meaning in This Text? The Bible, the Reader, and the Morality of Literary Knowledge* (Grand Rapids: Zondervan, 1998), 314.

99. Gregg R. Allison, "The Protestant Doctrine of the Perspicuity of Scripture: A Reformulation on the Basis of Biblical Teaching," diss. PhD. (Deerfield, Ill.: Trinity Evangelical Divinity School, 1995). My sincere thanks to my readers—Wayne Grudem, John Feinberg, and Grant Osborne—for their encouragement to address a topic that is rarely discussed today.

has revealed to his people is accessible and intelligible; thus, all of Scripture must be considered to be perspicuous. This doctrine does not mean that each part of Scripture is *easily* understandable (2 Peter 3:14–16 contradicts this idea), only that it *is* intelligible. Moreover, in designating those people to whom Scripture is comprehensible, I maintain that the only requirement for understanding Scripture is that believers possess the normal acquired ability to understand what is read or heard.[100] If this ability is present, then the believers' gender, age, education, language, and cultural background do not present a barrier to understanding clear Scripture. However, this fact should not be taken to mean that all people will have the same level of comprehension of perspicuous Scripture. Generally speaking, spiritually mature believers understand Scripture better than do immature and new believers. The same is true generally speaking of adult believers as compared with children, believers with well-developed exegetical skills as compared with those who lack such training, and so forth.

Furthermore, Scripture envisions itself being read/heard and understood in a local church context in which both God-ordained, gifted leaders (elders, pastor-teachers) and other believers (1 Cor. 14:26; Col. 3:16) encourage and assist the members of the assembly in comprehending clear Scripture. Clear Scripture is also understood through the illumination of the Holy Spirit (1 Cor. 2:6–3:3), and this Spirit-guided comprehension entails a willing disposition on the part of the reader/hearer to appropriate and obey the message of Scripture. While the preceding details deal with the understanding of perspicuous Scripture by believers, I also affirm that Scripture is intelligible to some degree for nonbelievers.[101]

A key reason for my affirmation of the clarity of Scripture is that the biblical writings "are characterized by the presumption of continued intelligibility even as those writings travel far from their original audience and their original historical, literary and rhetorical settings."[102] Specific examples support this principle. From a forward-looking perspective, the deuteronomic covenant (Deut. 29:29; 30:11–14; 31:9–13) "anticipated its own intelligibility, abiding validity and applicability for the people of Israel throughout successive generations of people and time periods, in different socio-politico-cultural milieus, and in varying religious/spiritual climates."[103] From a backward-looking perspective, in certain New Testament passages (Rom. 5:4; 1 Cor. 10:1–11),

---

100. Nehemiah 8:2 notes that "men and women and all who were able to understand" listened to the reading of the Law of God.

101. Allison, "Protestant Doctrine of the Perspicuity of Scripture," 517–36. As for my definition of Scripture's clarity: "Perspicuity is a property of Scripture as a whole and of each portion of Scripture whereby it is comprehensible to all believers who possess the normal acquired ability to understand oral communication and/or written discourse, regardless of their gender, age, education, language, or cultural background. However, the level of people's comprehension of perspicuous Scripture is appropriate to and usually varies proportionately with various factors, including, but not limited to, spiritual

maturity. In addition, the doctrine of perspicuity is always affirmed in the context of a believing community, a context which assumes the assistance of others in attaining a more precise understanding of Scripture, and perspicuity requires a dependence on the Holy Spirit for Scripture to be grasped and calls for a responsive obedience to what is understood. Moreover, perspicuity includes the comprehensibility of the way of salvation to unbelievers who are aided by the Holy Spirit, and it does not exclude some type of cognition of Scripture in general by unbelievers." Ibid., 516–17.

102. Ibid., 556.

103. Ibid., 557.

the apostle Paul reflects on Old Testament Scripture and its utility for Christian believers. These are people far removed from those writings in terms of centuries of time and of political, economic, cultural and linguistic distance, to mention nothing of the tremendous religious transformation from Judaism to Christianity that had taken place. His unadorned allusions to Old Testament Scripture demonstrate Paul's assumption that, despite these vast changes and distances, his audience was still capable of grasping the meaning of the Old Testament writings. More importantly still, he notes that it is especially New Covenant believers who are capable of comprehending them.[104]

In summary, though some isolated evangelicals have treated the subject, the doctrine of the clarity of Scripture is an important though sorely overlooked doctrine in the Christian world today.

---

104. Ibid., 558.

Chapter 7

THE SUFFICIENCY AND NECESSITY OF SCRIPTURE

How has the church come to believe that the Bible is enough for knowing what God wants his people to believe and do? How has it come to believe that without the Bible the church could not trust and obey God as he has designed?

STATEMENT OF BELIEF

The church has historically acknowledged that God's revelation of himself, the way of salvation, and instructions for living a life of faith and obedience are found in the Bible. Because God has designed to reveal all this through his written Word, the people of God must know and live by Scripture. Thus, the church has affirmed the sufficiency of Scripture: "The sufficiency of Scripture means that Scripture contained all the words of God which he intended his people to have at each stage of redemptive history, and that it now contains everything we need God to tell us for salvation, for trusting him perfectly, and for obeying him perfectly."[1] The church has also recognized the necessity of Scripture: "The necessity of Scripture means that the Bible is necessary for knowing the gospel, for maintaining spiritual life, and for knowing God's will, but is not necessary for knowing that God exists or for knowing something about God's character and moral laws."[2]

Although true of the early church, this insistence on Scripture's sufficiency and necessity was abandoned as the church developed. During the Middle Ages the Roman Catholic Church denied that the Bible is the sole source of divine revelation. Rather, church tradition as conveyed by the pope and magisterium, or the teaching office of the church, is needed as a supplement to Scripture. The Catholic Church also held that the Bible is not necessary for the church's existence but only for its well-being. The Protestant Reformers disagreed and once again championed the sufficiency and necessity of the Bible. Scripture is sufficient to know God and to trust and obey him completely; therefore, the

---

1. Wayne Grudem, *Systematic Theology: An Introduction to Biblical Doctrine* (Grand Rapids: Zondervan, 1994, 2000), 127.   2. Ibid., 116.

church does not need anything (tradition, magisterium) or anyone (the pope) to supplement the Word of God. Also, Scripture is necessary; therefore, the church could not even exist apart from the Word of God. Evangelical churches follow the Protestant Reformers in affirming both of these attributes of Scripture, though they at times find it difficult to live these two realities.[3]

SCRIPTURE'S SUFFICIENCY AND NECESSITY IN THE EARLY CHURCH

The earliest Christians looked to the Jewish Bible as their sufficient source of doctrinal and practical instruction for a life of faith and obedience. The apostle Paul underscored this (2 Tim. 3:14–17) when affirming the inspiration of all of Scripture, or what would come to be called the Old Testament. These "sacred writings" were sufficient to lead the earliest Christians to salvation in Jesus Christ and to prepare them adequately for living the Christian life. Time and time again Jesus and the apostles relied on these writings to emphasize their teachings and to prove their doctrines because of the sufficiency of Scripture.

Eventually the New Testament was added as God saw fit to extend his revelation. From that point on, the Old and New Testaments together constitute his sufficient Word by which Christians are to live. To reinforce its own sufficiency, Scripture itself prohibits any human from adding to or subtracting from it. Moses had already addressed the people of Israel, warning, "Do not add to what I command you and do not subtract from it" (Deut. 4:2), and the apostle John echoed this in the conclusion of his Revelation (22:18–19).

The New Testament likewise affirmed the necessity of Scripture: Without Scripture people cannot trust and obey God as he has designed. Indeed, the biblical writers insisted that faith in Christ comes only by knowing the gospel (Rom. 10:13–17) and that progress in the Christian faith requires nourishing oneself on God's Word (Matt. 4:4; 1 Peter 2:2).

Christians who wrote after the New Testament was completed continued to emphasize the sufficiency and necessity of the Bible. With great simplicity, Tertullian stated, "I revere the fullness of His [God's] Scripture."[4] Vincent of Lerins emphasized that "the canon of Scripture is complete, and sufficient of itself for everything, and more than sufficient."[5] Practically speaking, Scripture's sufficiency makes it the sole standard for Christian belief. Clement of Alexandria underscored this point in a chapter entitled "On Scripture as the Criterion by Which Truth and Heresy Are Distinguished." His argument was simple: The source of Christian teaching is God, and he has instructed believers "through the prophets, the Gospel, and the blessed apostles" (i.e., the Old Testament, the four Gospels, and the rest of the New Testament). This teaching is like an axiom in math or a first principle in philosophy: It has no need of proof, nor is it capable of being corrected. Rather, it is the standard by which everything else is evaluated.[6]

---

3. My thanks to Todd Arnett, Bernard Maurer, and Kudol Lee for their help with this chapter.

4. Tertullian, *Treatise against Hermogenes*, 22, in *ANF*, 3:490.

5. Vincent of Lerins, *Commonitory*, 2.5, in *NPNF²*, 11:132. Commonitory is an aid to memory.

6. Clement of Alexandria, *Stromata*, 7.16, in *ANF*, 2:551.

In light of this, true belief has to be established by Scripture, as Cyril of Jerusalem noted: "For concerning the divine and holy mysteries of the faith, not even a casual statement must be delivered without the Holy Scriptures.... For this salvation which we believe depends not on ingenious reasoning, but on demonstration of the Holy Scriptures."[7] Heresy, on the contrary, is anything that does not conform to the touchstone of Scripture, as Clement of Alexandria explained:

> Heretics have it within their ability to provide themselves with proper proofs for the divine Scriptures from the Scriptures themselves. But they select only what contributes to their own pleasures. They have a craving for fame and so willfully evade by various means the things communicated by the blessed apostles and teachers, things that are wedded to inspired words. They oppose the divine tradition by human teachings in order to establish their heresy.[8]

Similarly, Athanasius attacked heresy by constant appeal to Scripture, affirming, "the sacred and inspired Scriptures are sufficient to declare the truth."[9] Appropriately, Tertullian warned any heretic who would tamper with Scripture: "If it is nowhere written, then let it fear the woe which impends on all who add to or take away from the written word."[10] The early church was united in its conviction that nothing could be considered true belief unless it could be demonstrated from the Bible. This was so because of the sufficiency of Scripture.

The early church also affirmed the necessity of Scripture. Hippolytus urged attention to the Bible because of its necessity:

> There is one God, the knowledge of whom we gain from the Holy Scriptures, and from no other source. For just as a man, if he wishes to be skilled in the wisdom of this world, will find himself unable to get at it in any other way than by mastering the dogmas [teachings] of philosophers, so all of us who wish to practice piety [holiness] will be unable to learn its practice from any other source than the oracles of God. Whatever things, then, the Holy Scriptures declare, at these let us look; and whatever they teach, these let us learn.... But even as He [God] has chosen to teach them by the Holy Scriptures, so let us discern them.[11]

---

7. Cyril of Jerusalem, *Catechetical Lectures*, 4.17, in *NPNF²*, 7:23. Similarly, Tertullian challenged Praxeas, the heretic whom he opposed: "It will be your duty to adduce your proofs out of the Scriptures as plainly as we do." Tertullian, *Against Praxeas*, 11, in *ANF*, 3:605.

8. Clement of Alexandria, *Stromata*, 7.16, in *ANF*, 2:553–54.

9. Athanasius, *Against the Heathen*, 1, in *NPNF²*, 4:4. Elsewhere he notes: "Holy Scripture is of all things most sufficient for us." *To the Bishops of Egypt*, 4, in *NPNF²*, 4:225. "Divine Scripture is sufficient above all things." *Councils of Ariminum and Seleucia*, pt. 1, 6, in *NPNF²*, 4:453. "The Scriptures are enough for instruction, but it is a good thing to encourage one another in the faith and to stir up with words." *Life of Antony*,

16, in *NPNF²*, 4:200.

10. Tertullian, *Treatise against Hermogenes*, 22, in *ANF*, 3:490. Cf. Irenaeus, *Against Heresies*, 5.30.1, in *ANF*, 1:559.

11. Hippolytus, *Against the Heresy of One Noetus*, 9, in *ANF*, 5:227. Just as Hippolytus believed that Scripture is necessary for knowledge of God the Father, so Origen affirmed its necessity for knowledge of God the Son: "We ... believe it is possible in no other way to explain and bring within the reach of human knowledge this higher and more divine reason [Logos; Word] as the Son of God, than by means of those Scriptures alone which were inspired by the Holy Spirit, i.e., the Gospels and Epistles, and the law and the prophets, according to the declaration of Christ himself." Origen, *First Principles*, 1.3.1, in *ANF*, 4:252.

Indeed, the necessity of Scripture means Christians must engage in daily Bible reading, as Theonas of Alexandria underscored: "Let no day pass by without reading some portion of the Sacred Scriptures, at such convenient hour as offers, and giving some space to meditation. And never cast off the habit of reading in the Holy Scriptures; for nothing feeds the soul and enriches the mind so well as those sacred studies do."[12] With the necessity of Scripture in mind, John Chrysostom rebuked Christians who thought they did not need the Bible because they were not monks (men who lived a religious life by withdrawing from involvement in the world): "This belief … has ruined you, because you need it much more than they do. For those who live in the world and each day are wounded are the ones who have the most need of medicine.… The things that are contained in Scripture—do you not think they are highly necessary?"[13] In other words, without the daily reading of Scripture, believers cut themselves off from the necessary cure for what ails them. Elsewhere, Chrysostom listed some of the ills—heresies, careless living, profitless work—that befall Christians who neglect Scripture: "Just as people who are deprived of daylight stumble about, so also those who do not look at the brilliant light of the Holy Scriptures must frequently and constantly sin because they walk in the worst darkness."[14] Scripture is necessary; thus, its neglect plunges the church into many evils. As Jerome strikingly summarized, "Ignorance of Scripture is ignorance of Christ."[15]

An important development took place in the early church that became the background for later controversies concerning the Bible. Without diminishing in any way the sufficiency and necessity of Scripture, the early church fathers made reference to other sources of Christian beliefs and practices. These were (1) apostolic tradition, the testimony of the apostles as it was handed down in the proclamation and teaching of the early churches (1 Cor. 11:23; 2 Thess. 2:15; 3:6); (2) the canon of truth, or the rule of faith, a summary of the growing doctrinal understanding of the early church;[16] and (3) church authority, especially the practice of appealing to the church fathers in support of theological positions.

---

12. Theonas of Alexandria, *The Epistle of Theonas, Bishop of Alexandria, to Lucianus, the Chief Chamberlain*, 9, in *ANF*, 6:161.

13. Chrysostom, *The Gospel of Matthew: Homily 2*, in *NPNF*[1], 10:13. The text has been rendered clearer.

14. Chrysostom, *Homilies on Romans: The Argument*, in *NPNF*[1], 11:335.

15. Jerome, *Commentary on the Book of Isaiah*, 18, prologue, PL, 24:17b.

16. An example of this comes from Irenaeus: "The Church, though dispersed throughout the whole world, even to the ends of the earth, has received from the apostles and their disciples this faith: [She believes] in one God, the Father Almighty, Maker of heaven, and earth, and the sea, and all things that are in them; and in one Christ Jesus, the Son of God, who became incarnate for our salvation; and in the Holy Spirit, who proclaimed through the prophets the dispensations of God, and the advents, and the birth from a virgin, and the passion, and the resurrection from the dead, and the ascension into heaven in the flesh of the beloved Christ Jesus, our Lord, and his [future] manifestation from heaven in the glory of the Father 'to gather all things in one,' and to raise up anew all flesh of the whole human race, in order that to Christ Jesus, our Lord, and God, and Savior, and King, according to the will of the invisible Father, 'every knee should bow, of things in heaven, and things in earth, and things under the earth, and that every tongue should confess' to him, and that he should execute just judgment towards all; that he may send 'spiritual wickednesses,' and the angels who transgressed and became apostates, together with the ungodly, and unrighteous, and wicked, and profane among men, into everlasting fire; but may, in the exercise of his grace, confer immortality on the righteous, and holy, and those who have kept his commandments, and have persevered in his love, some from the beginning [of their Christian course], and others from [the date of] their repentance, and may surround them with everlasting glory." Irenaeus, *Against Heresies*, 1.10.1, in *ANF*, 1:330.

In no case did any of these three oppose, correct, or supplement Scripture so as to endanger its sufficiency and necessity: (1) Apostolic tradition was eventually written down; indeed, the apostles, who at one time proclaimed the gospel publicly, "at a later period, by the will of God, handed [it] down to us [wrote it] in the Scriptures, to be the ground and pillar of our faith."[17] Prior to the composition of the New Testament canon (toward the end of the fourth century), however, the oral and written forms of the apostolic witness to Christ worked in tandem. Together, Scripture and apostolic tradition provided the foundation of truth for the early church. Heretics, those outside of the church, were criticized because they "consent neither to Scripture nor to tradition."[18] (2) The canon of truth, or the rule of faith, was a means of emphasizing what true churches believed and a way of exposing groups that promoted heresy. It was a succinct expression of early church beliefs and was derived from Scripture itself. These beliefs would later be expressed in written creeds or statements of faith. (3) Appeals to church authority, specifically to the writings of the early fathers, were never undertaken to divest the Bible of its authority and sufficiency. Rather, in its fight against heresy, the church underscored those earlier writings so as to bolster its case for the truth of the beliefs to which it held. Its teachings were sound because they were the truths to which the church had always clung; they were not the innovations of heretics. As Vincent of Lerins explained:

> But here someone perhaps will ask, because the canon of Scripture is complete and sufficient of itself for everything, and more than sufficient, what need is there to join with it the authority of the church's interpretation? For this reason — because, owing to the depth of Holy Scripture, all do not accept it in one and the same sense, but one understands its words in one way, another in another; so that it seems to be capable of as many interpretations as there are interpreters. For Novatian expounds it one way, Sabellius another, Donatus another, Arius, Eunomius, Macedonius, another, Photinus, Apollinaris, Priscillian, another, Iovinian, Pelagius, Celestius, another, lastly, Nestorius another. Therefore, it is very necessary, on account of so great intricacies of such various error, that the rule for the right understanding of the prophets and apostles should be framed in accordance with the standard of ecclesiastical and catholic interpretation.[19]

---

17. Ibid., 3.1.1, in *ANF*, 1:414.

18. Ibid., in *ANF*, 1:415.

19. Vincent of Lerins, *Commonitory*, 2.5, in *NPNF²*, 11:132. All the names he mentions are the leaders or proponents of intricate heresies. We must be very careful not to read back into Vincent's comments the latter development in the Roman Catholic Church that split tradition from Scripture (see later in this chapter). Vincent's concern was to protect the proper interpretation of Scripture from heretical distortions, as he indicated: "That whether I or anyone else should wish to detect the frauds and avoid the snares of heretics as they rise, and to continue sound and complete in the catholic faith, we must, the Lord helping, fortify our own belief in two ways; first, by the authority of the divine law, and then, by the tradition of the catholic church" Ibid., 2.4, in *NPNF²*, 11:132. Although Vincent indicates "two ways" — "the authority of the divine law and the tradition of the catholic church" — he is not pitting these two against one another or indicating that the latter supplements the former. Clearly, for Vincent, the authority of the divine law is profusely sufficient (Ibid., 2.5; in *NPNF²*, 11:132); therefore, tradition could not add anything to it. But tradition — understood as the early church's proper interpretation of Scripture — can safeguard it from the many errors of heretics.

Thus, the authority of the church's interpretation was not in opposition to the sufficiency of Scripture but functioned as support for the proper understanding of sufficient Scripture over against heretical interpretations of it. Accordingly, "in the Catholic Church itself, all possible care must be taken, that we hold that faith which has been believed everywhere, always, by all. For that is truly and in the strictest sense 'catholic,' which, as the name itself and the reason of the thing declare, comprehends all universally."[20] As Jerome warned: "The sword of God smites whatever they [heretics] draw and forge from a pretended apostolic tradition, without the authority and testimony of the Scriptures."[21] Whatever challenges to Scripture developed later from a changing relationship between the Bible, tradition, and church authority, these other sources of Christian beliefs and practices never threatened the sufficiency and necessity of Scripture in the early church.

SCRIPTURE'S SUFFICIENCY AND NECESSITY IN THE MIDDLE AGES

Ongoing affirmations and discussions of the sufficiency and necessity of Scripture were carried on in the medieval church. Concerning the necessity of Scripture, Gabriel Biel affirmed:

> All true instruction, all consolation, all exhortation, all devotion is understood through the Word that proceeds from the mouth of God, and it proceeds from hearing, from reading, from meditation, and from contemplation of the divine eloquence.... The Word of the eternal God, holy Scripture, also proceeds from the mouth of God and indicates his own will, without which no one is able to live rightly with understanding. In this we learn how far away we are when approaching God, and how far away we have strayed from God.... Only Holy Scripture teaches all that is to be believed and hoped and all other things necessary for salvation.[22]

Thomas Aquinas added further discussion. Although perhaps best known for his reliance on philosophy, he addressed the issue of the necessity of Scripture in light of the reality of assured philosophical knowledge. While acknowledging the importance of human reason, Aquinas argued for the necessity of theological science that, for him, is grounded on divine revelation: "It was necessary for man's salvation that there should be a knowledge revealed by God besides philosophical science built up by human reason.

---

20. Ibid., 2.6, in *NPNF*[2], 11:132.

21. Jerome, *Commentaries on the Prophets: Haggai*, 1.11, cited in Francis Turretin, *Institutes of Elenctic Theology*, ed. James T. Dennison Jr., trans. George Musgrave Giger, 3 vols. in 1 (Phillipsburg, N.J.: P & R, 1992), 1:143. For Irenaeus, it is precisely because of apostolic tradition that the church can supply biblical justification for its doctrine: "Since the tradition from the apostles does exist in the church and is perma-

nent among us, let us revert to the scriptural proof furnished by those apostles who also wrote the Gospels." Irenaeus, *Against Heresies*, 3.5.1, in *ANF*, 1:417.

22. Gabriel Biel, *Sacri Canonis Misse Expositio Resolutissima* (Basel, 1510), lecture 71. Latin cited in Heiko A. Oberman, *The Harvest of Medieval Theology: Gabriel Biel and Late Medieval Nominalism* (Grand Rapids: Baker, 2000), 394. Trans. Michael J. Harstad.

First, indeed, because man is directed to God, as to an end that surpasses the grasp of his reason.... Hence it was necessary for the salvation of man that certain truths which exceed human reason should be made known to him by divine revelation." He further acknowledged that reason is sufficient to discover some important divine matters. Still:

> Even as regards those truths about God which human reason can discover, it was necessary that man should be taught by a divine revelation; because the truth about God such as reason could discover would only be known by a few, and that after a long time, and with the admixture of many errors. But, man's whole salvation, which is in God, depends upon the knowledge of this truth. Therefore, in order that the salvation of men might be brought about more fitly and more surely, it was necessary that they should be taught divine truths by divine revelation. It was therefore necessary that besides philosophical science discovered by reason, there should be a sacred science obtained through revelation.[23]

Taking one more step, Aquinas asserted that this necessary divine revelation is that on which "sacred scripture or doctrine is based."[24] Thus, if divine revelation is necessary, then Scripture, which is based on divine revelation, must also be necessary.

Addressing the sufficiency of Scripture,[25] Duns Scotus drew attention to several reasons for rejecting this doctrine. One was the progressive nature of revelation: Scripture originally consisted only of the writings of Moses, later other Old Testament Scripture was added, and finally New Testament Scripture was added; these additional components seem to belie the notion of Scripture's sufficiency. Other reasons noted by Scotus were superfluous ceremonies and historical accounts found in Scripture, and the absence of scriptural judgment regarding the sinfulness or propriety of many issues. Responding to these objections, Scotus affirmed Scripture's sufficiency, citing Augustine's belief that canonical Scripture is supremely authoritative in "those things of which we must not be ignorant, but which we cannot know of ourselves."[26] For Scotus, then, "sufficient holy Scripture contains the doctrine necessary for Christian pilgrims."[27] Aquinas concurred: "The truth of faith is sufficiently explicit in the teaching of Christ and the apostles."[28]

Practically speaking, this doctrine meant that anything that is not stated in or derived from Scripture cannot be binding on the conscience of a believer, as Rupert of Deutz explained: "Whatever may be arrived at, or concluded from arguments, outside of that Holy Scripture ... does not in any way belong to the praise and confession of Almighty God.... Whatever may be arrived at outside of the rule of the Holy Scriptures, nobody can lawfully demand from a Catholic."[29] For Rupert, the sufficiency of Scripture provides the justification for this belief: "Let us search for wisdom, let us consult sacred Scripture

---

23. Thomas Aquinas, *Summa Theologica*, pt. 1, q. 1, art. 1.

24. Ibid., pt. 1, q. 1, art. 2.

25. Duns Scotus, *Ordinatio*, prologue, 2, q. 1, n. 95–97, discussed in Richard A. Muller, *Post-Reformation Reformed Dogmatics: The Rise and Development of Reformed Orthodoxy, ca. 1520 to ca. 1725*, vol. 2: *Holy Scripture: The Cognitive Foundation of Theology*, 2nd ed. (Grand Rapids: Baker, 2003), 49.

26. Ibid., prologue, 2, q. 1, n. 98. Scotus quoted Augustine, *The City of God*, 11.3. Cited in Muller, *Holy Scripture*, 49.

27. Ibid., prologue, q. 2, n. 14, cited in Muller, *Holy Scripture*, 50 (my translation of the Latin text).

28. Thomas Aquinas, *Summa Theologica*, 2nd pt. of pt. 2, q. 1, art. 10.

29. Rupert of Deutz, *De Omnipotentia Dei*, 27, in Tavard, 13.

itself, apart from which nothing can be found, nothing said which is solid or certain."[30] As Othlo of Sankt Emmeram concluded, "There is no need for us to add anything of doctrine to them [the Scriptures] nor to propound anything except what we have been taught by reading them."[31] After rehearsing the many benefits that derive from Scripture, John Hus emphasized: "From this it appears that wisdom is to be praised and, therefore, also in a formal sense, the sacred Scriptures, by which [this wisdom] perfects humanity."[32] Another practical application of this doctrine is the need to read Scripture regularly. As Adalger noted simply, "He who wishes to be with God always, must pray frequently and must read [the Bible] frequently; for when we pray, we speak with God, but when we read, God is speaking with us."[33]

This raises the question as to the proper reading and understanding of Scripture. The medieval church emphasized the reading of Scripture in accordance with the church's historical interpretation of it. In keeping with the trajectory set by Vincent of Lerins, Hugh of St. Victor cautioned those who would study the Bible without reference to the fathers of the church: "Do not attempt to learn by yourself lest, believing yourself introduced to knowledge, you be rather blinded. That introduction is to be sought for from men of doctrine and wisdom who may bring you in and open the matter to you as you need it, with the authorities of the holy Fathers and the testimonies of the Scripture."[34] By understanding the Bible in continuity with earlier interpretation of it, the church would be guarded from innovative—and, hence, incorrect—ideas. As Lanfranc of Canterbury explained: "Although these scriptures (ecclesiastical chronicles and acts of the church Fathers) do not enjoy the highest acme [pinnacle] of authority, which has been received by the Scriptures that are called prophetic or apostolic (the Old and New Testaments), they nevertheless suffice to prove the fact that all the faithful who have preceded us from pristine times have professed the faith which we now profess."[35]

Two currents should be emphasized: (1) the medieval church closely correlated Scripture and the historical interpretation of the church, and (2) it clearly acknowledged the supreme authority of the former in relation to the latter. Accordingly, Gratian's *Decree* affirmed the sufficiency of Scripture: "Who does not know that the holy canonical Scripture is contained within definite limits and that it has precedence over all letters of subsequent bishops, so that it is altogether impossible to doubt or question the truth or adequacy of what is written in it?"[36] Similarly, Hugh of St. Victor explained the relationship between canonical Scripture and "patristic" scripture:

> All divine Scripture is contained in the two Testaments, the Old and the New.
> Each testament is divided into three parts: The Old contains the Law, the

30. Rupert of Deutz, *Commentary on the Apocalypse*, cited in Clark Pinnock, *Biblical Revelation: The Foundation of Christian Theology* (Chicago: Moody, 1971), 152.

31. Othlo of Sankt Emmeram, *Dialogue on Three Questions*, 1, in Pelikan, 3:122.

32. John Hus, *Mag. Joannis Hus Super IV Sententiarum*, in *Opera Omnia*, 3 vols. (Prague: 1905; repr., Osnabruck: Biblio-Verlag, 1966), vol. 2: *Inceptio* 1.8, cited in Muller, *Holy Scripture*, 54.

33. Adalger, *Admonition to a Recluse*, 13, in Pelikan, 3:120.

34. Hugh of St. Victor, *Eruditio Didascalia*, bk. 6, chap. 4, in Tavard, 17.

35. Lanfranc of Canterbury, *Liber de Corpore et Sanguine Domini*, chap. 19, in Tavard, 17.

36. Gratian, *Decretum*, P. I, d. 9, c. 8, in Tavard, 16.

Prophets, the Historians. The New contains the Gospels, the Apostles, the Fathers.... In the last category [i.e., the Fathers] the first place belongs to the decretals which are called canonical, that is, regular. Then there comes the writings of the holy fathers—Jerome, Augustine, Ambrose, Gregory, Isidore, Origen, Bede and the other doctors; these are innumerable. Patristic writings, however, are not counted in the text of the divine Scriptures.[37]

Likewise, John Gerson affirmed the sufficiency of Scripture and the reality of "catholic truths." He underscored first that "Scripture has been given to us as a sufficient and infallible rule for the organization of all the ecclesiastical body and of its members to the end of the world." Gerson then acknowledged that some doctrines are not found in Scripture, yet he emphasized that these doctrines are related in some way to it: "Holy Scripture contains them according to one of the degrees of catholic truths."[38]

For the church in the early part of the medieval period, this correlation of Scripture and the church's traditional biblical interpretation was not problematic for the sufficiency and necessity of Scripture. Reading the Bible within this historical consensus was only reasonable, given the fact that the Holy Spirit leads the church into the right interpretation of the Bible that he inspired. Support for this was found in Christ's provision for his disciples, as found in Luke 24:45 and John 20:22. Because of the Spirit's gift of grasping Scripture, "until the end of this age, among all, weak or powerful, who sincerely announce the works of God, a sound understanding is developed."[39]

Tragically, the sufficiency and necessity of Scripture came under attack and began to fade into oblivion in the latter part of the Middle Ages. At this time, the notion of church tradition—the unwritten teaching of Christ that was communicated orally from him to his disciples, and from them to their successors, the bishops—gained ascendancy in the Roman Catholic Church. Specifically, Gerald of Bologna introduced a novel idea that some divine revelation could come "from the doctrine and tradition of the Apostles to their friends outside of Scripture ... from the tradition of the Apostles without [outside of] the Scriptures."[40] Thomas Netter Waldensis elaborated on this notion of oral tradition: "The church protects and keeps the unwritten words of the apostles and their unwritten traditions which would all belong to the Canon of Scripture had they been written.... I believe that the catholic church still keeps like a treasure the greater part of the words of St. Paul in the traditions and the successive documents of the fathers." This notion had two very important implications: "Such is the dignity of the apostolic traditions which did not transmit in the Scriptures, that the same veneration and the same fervent faith is due to them as to the written ones....

37. Hugh of St. Victor, *De Scriptura et Scriptoribus Sacris*, chap. 6, in Tavard, 16.

38. John Gerson, *De Examinatione Doctrinarum*, 2nd principal pt., 1st consideration, in Gerson, *Opera Omnia* (Antwerp, 1576), vol. 1, col. 12, in Tavard, 52. For Gerson, the six degrees of catholic truth all belong to Scripture. These are: (1) what is expressly written in the Bible; (2) apostolic tradition; (3) postapostolic revelations; (4) whatever can be derived from the first three degrees of truth; (5) probable conclusions from the first three degrees; (6) pious truths. Gerson, *Recommendatio Lic. in Decretis*, consideration 11, 4th genus, in Gerson, *Opera Omnia* (Antwerp, 1576), vol. 4, col. 891, in Tavard, 52–53.

39. Gerhoh, *Commentary on the Psalms*, P. 6, in Tavard, 19.

40. Gerald of Bologna, *Commentary on the Sentences*, 457, in Tavard, 27.

If therefore, once we have studied the Scriptures, we see what the church universally accepts, either in the popular tradition or in the common agreement of the fathers, we must consider it as a full definition of faith as though it were found in the Scriptures."[41] So the church in the latter part of the Middle Ages affirmed in a novel way the reality of church tradition derived from unwritten apostolic sources and even of postapostolic divine revelation. To these were added the teaching of general church councils (e.g., the Council of Nicea, AD 325).[42]

With these developments, the doctrine of the sufficiency and necessity of Scripture, so much a part of the church in its early years and the Middle Ages, was overthrown. The Roman Catholic Church came to affirm that Scripture is needed for the *bene esse* (well-being) but not the *esse* (existence) of the church. Because it possessed authoritative tradition, the church would exist even if Scripture would disappear or be destroyed. But this Scripture was beneficial for the church to become all that God intended it to become. However, the church denied the sufficiency and necessity of Scripture that it once had affirmed.

SCRIPTURE'S SUFFICIENCY AND NECESSITY IN THE REFORMATION AND POST-REFORMATION

A defense of the sufficiency and necessity of Scripture resurfaced when Martin Luther was faced by challenges from two very different groups: the Roman Catholic Church and the enthusiasts (or fanatics). Against Roman Catholicism and its insistence on tradition, postapostolic revelations, and general councils as another source of Christian belief, Luther emphasized the sufficiency of Scripture. He rejected the decrees of church councils as a supplement to the Bible. He also rejected the pope's decisions that stemmed from his sole right to interpret the Word of God. For example, in his criticism of indulgences (the selling of the remission of sins), Luther urged: "A simple layman armed with Scripture is to be believed above a pope or a council without it. As for the pope's decree on indulgences, I say that neither the Church nor the pope can establish articles of faith. These must come from Scripture. For the sake of Scripture, we should reject pope and councils."[43] This is so, because Scripture is different than all other alleged sources of revelation or instruction: "Those things that have been delivered to us by God in the holy Scriptures must be sharply distinguished from those that have been invented by men in the Church; it matters not how eminent they are for saintliness or scholarship."[44] Indeed, Scripture "is incomparably superior to the Church and in this Word, the Church, being a creature, has nothing to decree, ordain or make, but only to be decreed, ordained, and made."[45]

---

41. Thomas Netter Waldensis, *Doctrinale Antiquatum Fidei Catholicae Ecclesiae,* chap. 23, in Tavard, 58.

42. For more details concerning this development, see chap. 4.

43. The Leipzig Debate (July 1519). See, for example, Roland H. Bainton, *Here I Stand: A Life of Martin Luther* (Peabody, Mass.: Hendrickson, 1977), 90.

44. Martin Luther, *The Babylonian Captivity of the Church,* in *Three Treatises,* trans. A. T. W. Steinhauser (Minneapolis: Fortress, 1970), 223.

45. Ibid., 238.

When confronted by the Catholic Church and urged to change his mind on this issue, Luther responded with these very famous words: "Unless I am convicted [convinced] by Scripture and plain reason—I do not accept the authority of popes and councils, for they have contradicted each other—my conscience is captive to the Word of God. I cannot and I will not recant anything, for to go against conscience is neither right nor safe. God help me. Amen."[46] He was opposed by, among others, John Driedo, a Catholic who argued against the principle of *sola Scriptura* (Scripture alone). Yet even Driedo conceded, "We admit that the express doctrine of Christ and the apostles in the canonical books teaches us sufficiently all the dogmas necessary for man's salvation."[47]

As formulated by Luther and his followers in the *Augsburg Confession*, Scripture's sufficiency means that "it is against the Scripture to ordain or require the observation of any traditions, to the end that we may merit remission of sins and satisfaction for sins by them."[48] This emphasis on Scripture's sufficiency, however, did not mean that the Lutheran Church could dispense with or neglect the accumulated wisdom of the church throughout the centuries of its existence. Although Luther and his church repudiated Roman Catholic tradition, they did not do away with all tradition entirely. The *Formula of Concord* articulated the supreme authority of Scripture.[49] At the same time, it affirmed the importance of certain church traditions (or "symbols"):

> Inasmuch as immediately after the times of the apostles—indeed, even while they were yet alive—false teachers and heretics arose, against whom in the early church symbols were composed, that is to say, brief and explicit confessions, which contained the unanimous consent of the catholic Christian faith, and the confession of the orthodox and true church (such as the *Apostles'*, the *Nicene*, and the *Athanasian Creeds*). We publicly profess that we embrace them, and reject all heresies and all dogmas that have ever been brought into the church of God contrary to their decision.[50]

Thus, for Luther, Scripture was sufficient, but this did not entail disregard or contempt for the biblical and theological wisdom expressed by the historic church in its creeds.

Against a different group, the enthusiasts or fanatics, Luther insisted on the necessity of Scripture. The enthusiasts believed that the Spirit of God speaks directly to believers apart from the Word of God. Luther's response underscored a fine balance between the Spirit and the Word (which included both the gospel that was preached for the forgiveness of sins and the sacraments that portrayed the same promise of forgiveness). Explaining God's twofold work, Luther commented:

> Outwardly he deals with us through the oral [preached] Word of the gospel and through material signs of baptism and the sacrament of the altar [the Lord's Supper]. Inwardly he deals with us through the Holy Spirit, faith, and other

---

46. The Diet of Worms (April 18, 1521), in Bainton, *Here I Stand*, 144.

47. John Driedo, *The Writings and Dogmas of the Church* (*De ecclesiasticis scripturis et dogmatibus*, 1533), bk. 4, chap. 6, cited in Pinnock, *Biblical Revelation*, 152.

48. *Augsburg Confession*, "Of Ecclesiastical Power," art. 7, in Schaff, 3:64.

49. *Formula of Concord*, Epitome 1, "Of the Compendious Rule and Norm," in Schaff, 3:93–94.

50. Ibid., in Schaff, 3:94–95.

gifts. What ever their measure or order, the outward factors should and must precede. The inward experience follows and is effected by the outward. God has determined to give no one the Spirit or faith except through the outward [the Word and the sacraments].[51]

Thus, the Spirit of God only carries out his ministry in believers through the Word of God. And the Spirit of God is absolutely necessary for understanding the Word of God: "No one can correctly understand God or his Word unless he has received such understanding immediately from the Holy Spirit."[52] The enthusiasts could not enjoy the Spirit's saving and nurturing work apart from the Spirit's necessary Word.

In one brief passage, Calvin affirmed his belief in the sufficiency and necessity of Scripture: "Scripture is the school of the Holy Spirit. Just as nothing is omitted that is both necessary and useful to know, so nothing is taught except what is expedient to know."[53] Like Luther before him, Calvin linked closely together the Word of God and the Spirit of God so that the denial of the sufficiency of Scripture cuts against the Holy Spirit. Commenting on John 16:3, Calvin stated:

> That very *Spirit* had *led them* [the apostles] *into all truth*, when they committed to writing the substance of their doctrine. Whoever imagines that anything must be added to their doctrine, as if it were imperfect and but half-finished, not only accuses the apostles of dishonesty, but blasphemes against *the Spirit*. If the doctrine which they committed to writing had proceeded from mere learners or persons imperfectly taught, an addition to it would not have been superfluous; but now that their writings may be regarded as perpetual records of the revelation which was promised and given to them, nothing can be added to them without doing grievous injury to the Holy Spirit.[54]

Practically speaking for Calvin, this sufficiency of Scripture stood against the Roman Catholic view of apostolic tradition and other supplements to the Bible that were allegedly given to the church by the Spirit. Concerning tradition, the church pointed to the words of Jesus (John 16:12) to argue that Christ transmitted certain matters to the disciples that they did not write down in Scripture. Instead, they passed these on orally to their successors, the bishops of the church. This apostolic tradition is handed down in the church and constitutes another source of Christian beliefs. Concerning other supplements to the Bible, the church maintained that its councils were led directly by the Holy Spirit and therefore could not err. For Calvin, this had a serious implication: "Accordingly, if it should decree anything beyond or apart from God's Word, this must be taken as nothing but a sure oracle of God."[55] Thus, decisions of church councils constitute another true source of Christian beliefs.

---

51. Martin Luther, *Against the Heavenly Prophets in the Matter of Images and Sacraments*, LW, 40:83.

52. *The Magnificat*, LW, 21:299.

53. John Calvin, *Institutes of the Christian Religion*, 3.21.3, LCC, 2:924.

54. John Calvin, *Commentary on the Gospel according to John*, vol. 2, trans. William Pringle (Grand Rapids: Eerdmans, 1949), 143. Cf. *Institutes*, 1.6.2: "Now, in order that true religion may shine upon us, we ought to hold that it must take its beginning from heavenly doctrine and that no one can get even the slightest taste of right and sound doctrine unless he be a pupil of Scripture." LCC, 1:72, his emphasis.

55. Calvin, *Institutes*, 4.8.13, LCC, 2:1162.

Calvin objected to these points on the basis of the sufficiency of Scripture. Again, he insisted that the Spirit of God and the Word of God are inseparably linked, criticizing the Catholic Church for boasting "of the Holy Spirit solely to commend with his name strange doctrines foreign to God's Word—while the Spirit wills to be conjoined with God's Word by an indissoluble bond."[56] Calvin concluded that "we are to expect nothing more from his [God's] Spirit than that he will illumine our minds to perceive the truth of his [Christ's] teachings."[57] As for the alleged biblical basis (John 16:12) for the addition of traditions, Calvin exploded:

> But what effrontery is this? I confess that the disciples were as yet untutored and well-nigh unteachable when they heard this from the Lord. But when they committed their doctrine to writing, were they even then beset with such dullness that they afterward needed to supply with a living voice what they had omitted from their writings through the fault of ignorance? Now, if they had already been led into all truth by the Spirit of truth [cf. John 16:13] when they put forth their writings, what hindered them from embracing and leaving in written form a perfect and distinct knowledge of gospel doctrine?... For every schoolboy knows that in the writings of the apostles, which these fellows, as it were, maim and halve, there abides the fruit of that revelation which the Lord then promised to the apostles.[58]

Thus, the Spirit of God carries out his work of teaching only through the Word of God. The church is to learn its beliefs and practices from the Bible, and the Bible alone, without any recourse to apostolic tradition and church decrees. This principle is an application of Scripture's sufficiency.

Calvin also objected to the fanatics' insistence that the Spirit of God works apart from the Word of God; this, for Calvin, amounted to despising Scripture.[59] Again, he insisted that the Spirit and the Word are inseparably linked together: "For by a kind of mutual bond the Lord has joined together the certainty of his Word and of his Spirit so that the perfect religion of the Word may abide in our minds when the Spirit, who causes us to contemplate God's face, shines; and that we in turn may embrace the Spirit with no fear of being deceived when we recognize him in his own image, namely, in the Word."[60] He thus affirmed the necessity of Scripture.

For Calvin, the sufficiency of Scripture was confirmed by David's rule for living rightly (Ps. 19): "the law of God alone is perfectly sufficient for this purpose.... As soon as people depart from it, they are liable to fall into numerous errors and sins."[61] Calvin also pointed to Paul's description of a fully formed Christian (2 Tim. 3:15–17) in support: "Paul asserts absolutely, that the Scripture is sufficient for perfection. Accordingly, he who is not satisfied with Scripture desires to be wiser than is either proper or desir-

---

56. Ibid., 4.8.14, LCC, 2:1163.

57. Ibid., 4.8.13, LCC, 2:1162 63.

58. Ibid., 4.8.14, LCC, 2:1163.

59. Ibid., 1.9.1, LCC, 1:93.

60. Ibid., 1.9.3, LCC, 1:95.

61. John Calvin, *Commentary upon the Book of Psalms*, vol. 1, trans. James Anderson (Grand Rapids: Eerdmans, 1949), 325.

able."[62] Practically speaking, the sufficiency of Scripture means that Christians may not investigate those things about God that Scripture does not reveal. Appealing to the principle of Deuteronomy 29:29, Calvin cautioned not to engage in speculation about the "secret things" of God. Such vain thinking will inevitably lead to error. Rather, Christians should limit themselves to the divine revelation given in Scripture.

> Let us use great caution that neither our thoughts nor our speech go beyond the limits to which the Word of God itself extends. For how can the human mind measure off the measureless essence of God according to its own little measure…? Let us then willingly leave to God the knowledge of himself. But we shall be "leaving it to him" if we conceive him to be as he reveals himself to us, without inquiring about him elsewhere than from his Word. And let us not take it into our heads either to seek out God anywhere else than in his sacred Word, or to think anything about him that is not prompted by his Word, or to speak anything that is not taken from that Word.[63]

With this, Calvin expressed the "formal principle" of the Reformation: Scripture, and Scripture alone, is the source and standard for the Christian faith. This principle is due to its sufficiency.

Calvin argued for the necessity of written Scripture on the basis of the human tendency to forget or distort what is committed to memory or passed on orally:

> Suppose we ponder how slippery is the fall of the human mind into forgetfulness of God, how great the tendency to every kind of error, how great the lust to fashion constantly new and artificial religions. Then we may perceive how necessary was such written proof of the heavenly doctrine, that it should neither perish through forgetfulness nor vanish through error nor be corrupted by the audacity of men. It is therefore clear that God has provided the assistance of the Word for the sake of all those to whom he has been pleased to give useful instruction.[64]

In contrast with general revelation, Scripture gives a much clearer picture of God: "Just as old or bleary-eyed men and those with weak vision, if you thrust before them a most beautiful volume, even if they recognize it to be some sort of writing, yet can

---

62. John Calvin, *Commentaries on the Epistles to Timothy, Titus, and Philemon*, trans. William Pringle (Grand Rapids: Eerdmans, 1948), 250–51. Calvin also affirmed the sufficiency of the law for Israel, with appeals to Deut. 4:9; 12:28 and 32. *Institutes,* 2.8.5, LCC, 1:371.

63. Calvin, *Institutes*, 1.13.21, LCC, 1:146. Similarly, Calvin notes: "As then we cannot by our own faculties examine the secrets of God, so we are admitted into a certain and clear knowledge of them by the grace of the Holy Spirit: and if we ought to follow the guidance of the Spirit, where he leaves us, there we ought to stop and as it were to fix our standing. If anyone will seek to know more than what God has revealed,

he shall be overwhelmed with the immeasurable brightness of inaccessible light. But we must bear in mind the distinction … between the secret counsel of God and his will made known in Scripture; for though the whole doctrine of Scripture surpasses in its height the mind of man, yet an access to it is not closed against the faithful, who reverently and soberly follow the Spirit as their guide; but the case is different with regard to his hidden counsel, the depth and height of which cannot by any investigation be reached." *Commentaries on the Epistle of Paul the Apostle to the Romans*, trans. John Owen (Grand Rapids: Eerdmans, 1947), 446–47.

64. Calvin, *Institutes*, 1.6.3, LCC, 1:72.

scarcely construe two words, but with the aid of spectacles will begin to read distinctly; so Scripture, gathering up the otherwise confused knowledge of God in our minds, having dispersed our dullness, clearly shows us the true God."[65] Just as a pair of glasses is needed to see clearly, Scripture is necessary to know God as he has revealed himself.

Along with this emphasis on the sufficiency and necessity of Scripture, Calvin blended an urgent appeal to church members to recognize and submit to the divinely appointed preachers and teachers of the Word of God.[66] Although some might tend to find these two mutually exclusive, Calvin closely linked Scripture, which is both sufficient and necessary for believers, and teachers of Scripture, who communicate this sufficient and necessary instruction to believers.

The Roman Catholic Church reacted strongly to this Reformation doctrine of the sufficiency and necessity of Scripture. It did so because the Protestant position was a direct attack on the importance of church tradition and conciliar decrees as a supplement to the Bible. In support of the church's denial of the necessity of Scripture, John Driedo pointed to the beginning of the church and its early missionary endeavors to spread the gospel: "To found new churches and sow the seed of faith in the hearts of the Gentiles and pagans, there was no need of the Scriptures—which they did not consider holy—but of the living voice of the Holy Spirit."[67] Similarly Alonso de Castro denied the necessity of Scripture: "One must hold without any hesitancy that the traditions and definitions of the universal Church, even if no testimony of Sacred Scripture supports them, must be granted as much faith as is due to the holy Scriptures themselves. For the Holy Spirit moves her [i.e., the Church's] tongue now in the utterance of what is necessary to our salvation just as much as he moved the hands of writers in order to write the Sacred Scriptures."[68] This novel position also led to specific denials of the sufficiency of Scripture, as represented by this apparently contradictory affirmation of Josse Clichtove: "The gospel of Christ is indeed sufficient to lead a good life, and it contains precepts that suffice to salvation; yet not all things that we have to do to reach salvation are explained in it in all particulars and details."[69] The official Catholic objection was decreed at the Council of Trent,[70] which condemned Protestants for championing the sufficiency and necessity of Scripture.[71] As Robert Bellarmine explained, "We assert that the whole necessary doctrine, whether concerning faith or practice, is not clearly contained in Scripture; and thus besides the written word of God we assert that furthermore the unwritten word of God is required, i.e., divine and apostolic traditions."[72] He enumerated these other sources

---

65. Ibid., 1.6.1, LCC, 1:70.

66. Ibid., 4.1.5, LCC, 2:1018.

67. John Driedo, *De Ecclesiasticis Scripturis et Dogmatibus* (1533), pt. 4, folio 241v, in Tavard, 138.

68. Alonso de Castro, *Adversus omnes haereses*, bk. 1, chap. 4, folio 6v, in Tavard, 153. De Castro (1495–1558) was part of the theologian-lawyers constituting the School of Salamanca in Spain. He was a counselor to the emperor Charles V and a participant in the first two sessions of the Council of Trent, standing firmly against the Protestants.

69. Josse Clichtove, *Antilutherus*, folio 29v, in Tavard, 160.

Clichtove (1472–1543), a theologian and professor at the Sorbonne, attacked the doctrines of Martin Luther.

70. *Canons and Decrees of the Council of Trent*, 4th session (April 8, 1546), *Decree Concerning the Canonical Scriptures*, in Schaff, 2:80–83.

71. Ibid.

72. Robert Bellarmine, *De Verbo Dei*, 4.3, tome 1, p. 163 (Paris, 1608), cited in Latin in Charles Hodge, *Systematic Theology*, 3 vols. (Peabody, Mass.: Hendrickson, 1999), 1:105. Trans. Hanell Schuetz.

of theological truth: "Revelation contained in holy Scripture or in the tradition of the apostles or in the holy doctors, or reason reaching a firm conclusion from theological principles."[73] This viewpoint was a far cry from the Protestant doctrine of the sufficiency and necessity of Scripture.

The post-Reformation theologians defended their doctrine of Scripture against such attacks while further developing the Protestant position. Concerning the sufficiency of Scripture, John Owen offered this definition: "The Holy Spirit of God has prepared and disposed of the Scripture so as it might be a most sufficient and absolutely perfect way and means of communicating unto our minds that saving knowledge of God and his will that is needful which we may live unto him, and come unto the enjoyment of him in his glory."[74] Similarly, Turretin affirmed that Scripture is "a total and adequate rule of faith and practice."[75] Furthermore, Owen specified that Scripture is "sufficient with respect to the end of the revelation itself ... sufficient unto the end for which it is designed—that is, sufficient to generate, cherish, increase, and preserve faith, and love, and reverence, with holy obedience, in them, in such a way and manner as will assuredly bring them unto the end of all supernatural revelation in the enjoyment of God."[76] Calov similarly affirmed: "Given that Scripture is breathed by God toward this goal—that people might be made wise unto salvation—and given that its usefulness is directed toward this same goal, how can Scripture itself not be perfect and sufficient?"[77]

In support of the necessity of Scripture, William Whitaker appealed to the example of Christ's use of Scripture against the temptations of Satan: "If Christ defended himself against Satan with the Scriptures, how much more are the Scriptures needed by us against the same enemy! And it was for this purpose that Christ used the weapons of Scripture against Satan, that he might provide us with an example; for he could have repelled Satan with a single word."[78] Developing another approach, Gerhard reasoned from Scripture's usefulness and maintained that to such utility is "connected a certain necessity according to which God wants the Scriptures in the church."[79] The specific nature of the Scripture's necessity was a point of debate. Turretin noted that Protestantism holds to a relative, not absolute, necessity for Scripture:

> Scripture is not absolutely necessary with respect to God. For two thousand years before the time of Moses, God instructed his church by the spoken word alone. So he could—if he wished—have taught in the same manner afterwards, but only hypothetically—on account of the divine will—since God has seen fit for weighty reasons to commit his word to writing. Hence the divine ordination

---

73. Robert Bellarmine, *De auctoritate Papae et Concilii* (1511), in Tavard, 115.

74. John Owen, *The Causes, Ways, and Means of Understanding the Mind of God as Revealed in His Word, with Assurance Therein* (London, 1687), chap. 6, in *The Works of John Owen*, ed. William H. Goold, 16 vols. (Edinburgh: Banner of Truth Trust, 1967), 4:187.

75. Turretin, *Institutes of Elenctic Theology*, 2nd topic, 16th q., sec 16.2, 1:135.

76. Owen, *Causes, Ways, and Means of Understanding the Mind of God*, chap. 6, in Goold, *Works of John Owen*, 4:196.

77. Abraham Calov, *Biblia Novi Testamenti Illustrata* (Dresden and Leipzig, 1719), 2.1037, in Preus, 311.

78. William Whitaker, *Disputation on Holy Scripture*, cited in Philip Edgcumbe Hughes, *Theology of the English Reformers*, new ed. (Grand Rapids: Baker, 1965), 16–17.

79. John Gerhard, *Loci Theologici* (1621), 2:28, in Preus, 273.

has established, it [Scripture] was made necessary to the church, so that it pertains not only to the well being (*bene esse*) of the church, but also to its very being (*esse*). Without it the church could not now stand.[80]

It was the Roman Catholic position that Scripture is needed for the *bene esse* (well-being) but not the *esse* (existence) of the church. But the Protestant view stood against this idea, as Polanus asserted: "Ever since Holy Scripture was given by God to the Church, it has been and is and will be necessary not only to the Church's *bene esse* but also to the Church's *esse*." He reasoned that this is so "because true doctrine could not have been and could not be preserved amid so many heresies and scandals, had Scripture not been ordained for its preservation by God and commended to the Church." Thus, Polanus concluded that the church needs Scripture just as "the daily bread is necessary, which this life cannot do without."[81]

Baptist churches that developed in the post-Reformation period continued the Protestant emphasis on the sufficiency and necessity of Scripture.[82] Baptist theologian John Gill presented arguments for the perfection of Scripture, the term used by the post-Reformers to designate both the sufficiency and necessity of Scripture. By "perfection" was not meant "a perfect account of all that God has done from the beginning of time," but that the biblical writings "related all things necessary to salvation, every thing that ought to be believed and done; and are a complete, perfect standard of faith and practice."[83] Thus, the post-Reformers continued to embrace and defend the perfection—or sufficiency and necessity—of Scripture.

SCRIPTURE'S SUFFICIENCY AND NECESSITY IN THE MODERN PERIOD

Such affirmations and stellar defenses of Scripture's necessity and sufficiency continued to be offered by theologians in the modern period. For example, in his discussion of the finality of Scripture (i.e., Scripture is the touchstone or ultimate judge in all matters held by the church), John Murray echoed Turretin's idea (cited above):

There were periods in the history of God's redemptive revelation when the finality of Scripture had no meaning. There was no inscripturated revelatory Word. God's mind and will were communicated and transmitted by other methods. Even when revelation began to be committed to writing and was therefore to

---

80. Turretin, *Institutes of Elenctic Theology*, 2nd topic, 2nd q., sec. 2, 1:57. Reformer Johannes Heidegger articulated a similar idea about Scripture's relative rather than absolute necessity: "God might also have preserved the Church without Scripture: with God all things are possible.... [However,] once God had emitted proof of his grace and did not wish any other norm of his revelation to exist in the world, Scripture was so necessary to the Church, that she can no more do without it than the world without the sun, or indeed without God himself." Johannes Henricus Heidegger, *Corpus Theologiae*

(Zürich, 1700), 2.4, in Heppe, 32.

81. Amandus Polanus, *Syntagma Theologiae Christianae* (Hanover, 1624), 1.35, in Heppe, 32.

82. E.g., *Second London Confession of Faith* (1677, 1688), 1.1, in Lumpkin, 248; *The Orthodox Creed* (1678), 37, in ibid., 324–25.

83. John Gill, *A Body of Doctrinal Divinity; or, A System of Evangelical Truths, Deduced from the Sacred Scriptures* (1767; repr., Paris, Ark.: Baptist Standard Bearer, 1984), 18–21.

some extent inscripturated, there were centuries of redemptive history in which the finality of Scripture did not have for the church the precise import it has for us today.... It is apparent that revelation was not complete even with the advent of the Lord of glory himself. And so when he ascended on high there was not to extant Scripture the finality of which we speak now, the reason being that the revelatory process was still in operation.[84]

Now, however, that the period of revelation has concluded, Scripture in its entirety — both the Old and New Testaments as the church affirms — is the final and necessary revelation from God: "Unless we believe that revelation is still in process as it was in the days of the prophets, in the days of our Lord, and in the days of the apostles subsequent to our Lord's ascension, then Scripture occupies for us an exclusive place and performs an exclusive function as the only extant mode of revelation ... the only revelation of the mind and will of God available to us."[85] Thus, Murray affirmed Scripture's sufficiency and necessity.

Charles Hodge argued specifically against the Roman Catholic view of the incompleteness of Scripture, the view that "the Bible ... does not contain all the Church is bound to believe; nor are the doctrines which it does contain therein fully or clearly made known."[86] He observed, "What the doctrines are that are imperfectly revealed in the Scriptures, or merely implied or entirely omitted, has never been authoritatively decided by the Church of Rome."[87] Hodge did attempt to develop a list of key doctrines categorized by the majority of Roman Catholic theologians as being incompletely revealed in Scripture:

(1) The canon of Scripture. (2) The inspiration of the sacred writers. (3) The full doctrine of the Trinity. (4) The personality and divinity of the Holy Spirit. (5) Infant baptism. (6) The observance of Sunday as the Christian Sabbath. (7) The threefold orders of the ministry. (8) The government of the Church by bishops. (9) The perpetuity of the apostleship. (10) The grace of orders. (11) The sacrificial nature of the Eucharist. (12) The seven sacraments. (13) Purgatory.[88]

Hodge concluded that the Catholic advocacy of tradition leads the Church "to depreciate the Scriptures, and to show how much the Church would lose if she had no other source of knowledge of divine truth but the written word.... Tradition is always represented by Romanists as not only the interpreter, but the complement of the Scriptures."[89]

At the same time, Hodge qualified his discussion by emphasizing that the Protestant doctrine of Scripture's sufficiency does not completely do away with tradition of a certain type; after all, Protestants do champion the analogy of faith (i.e., Scripture itself repeats and often advances a certain tradition of truth through progressive revelation).[90] Beyond the analogy of faith, Hodge also pointed out that Protestants show great respect for traditional teaching — "a common faith of the church, which no man is at liberty to reject, and which no man can reject and be a Christian" — that has been handed down from generation to

84. John Murray, "The Finality and Sufficiency of Scripture," in *Collected Writings* (Carlisle, Pa.: Banner of Truth Trust, 1976), 1:18–19.

85. Ibid., 1:19.

86. Hodge, *Systematic Theology*, 1:106.

87. Ibid., 1:105.

88. Ibid., 1:106.

89. Ibid.

90. Ibid., 1:113.

generation of the church. Indeed, Protestants underscore two reasons for acknowledging "the authority of this common faith": "First, because what all the competent readers of a plain book take to be its meaning, must be its meaning. Secondly, because the Holy Spirit is promised to guide the people of God into the knowledge of the truth, and therefore that which they, under the teaching of the Spirit, agree in believing must be true."[91] Thus, while acknowledging the roles both the analogy of faith and traditional teaching play in Protestant doctrine and practice, Hodge clearly distinguished this from the Roman Catholic idea of infallible church tradition being a necessary supplement to Scripture.

This did not mean, however, that the doctrine of Scripture's sufficiency and necessity did not come under close scrutiny and even attack. One challenging development was the Wesleyan quadrilateral. Methodists embraced four sources for theological understanding: Scripture, tradition, experience, and reason. At first glance, this quadrilateral could be viewed as undermining the authority, sufficiency, and necessity of Scripture. However, the *Methodist Articles of Religion* (1784) focused squarely on the supremacy of Scripture: "The Holy Scriptures contain all things necessary to salvation; so that whatever is not read therein, nor may be proved thereby, is not to be required of any man that it should be believed as an article of faith or be thought requisite or necessary for salvation."[92] After affirming the supremacy of Scripture, Methodist theologian William Pope concluded that "every other final authority is absolutely or by implication interdicted."[93]

Another challenging situation for the doctrine of Scripture's sufficiency was one of the characteristic elements of Pentecostal/charismatic theology. With claims of direct guidance by the Holy Spirit and divine revelations through such continuing gifts as prophecy and the word of knowledge, proponents of this theology were accused of minimizing or even undermining Scripture's sufficiency.

J. Rodman Williams brought insight and balance to this discussion. He affirmed the existence and legitimacy of what he termed "subordinate revelation," appealing to Paul's prayer for "an enlarged revelation" of Jesus Christ (Eph. 1:17) and the gift of prophecy (prophecy being a revelation from God; 1 Cor. 14:26) to build up the church. Indeed, Williams averred: "God, the living God, is the God of revelation. He is ready to grant through His Spirit a spirit of revelation and wisdom for a deeper knowledge of Christ and also through revelation and prophecy to speak to His people."[94] Having said this, Williams urged that all other revelation is "wholly subordinate to special revelation": "God's truth

---

91. Ibid., 1:114.

92. *Methodist Articles of Religion*, art. 5, in Schaff, 3:808. Similarly, art. 5 of the *Reformed Episcopal Articles of Religion* (1875) affirmed the same thing; in Schaff, 3:815.

93. William Burt Pope, *A Compendium of Christian Theology*, vol. 1, 2nd ed., rev. and enlarged (New York: Phillips & Hunt, n.d.), 208. Pope qualified this statement about ultimate authority with a discussion of secondary authorities: "The supreme authority sanctions, however, other inferior standards in the form of creeds. Those Rules of Faith which were constructed from the beginning were based upon the formulas of Scripture itself: expressing in compendium the belief of the Church. But of these, in all their forms, earlier and later,

the Bible is the test: the court to which they must finally be brought.... The Rule also presupposes and harmonizes, as subordinate to itself, Public Ministerial Instruction and Private Judgment, under the guidance of the Holy Spirit. The Scriptures are the text-book of a living continuous teaching which is an ordinance of God in the congregation ... the appointed means in the Church for the continuation of the Apostles' doctrine. Moreover, the privilege, duty, and responsibility of private judgment are everywhere declared." Ibid., 208–9.

94. J. Rodman Williams, *Renewal Theology: Systematic Theology from a Charismatic Perspective*, 3 vols. in 1 (Grand Rapids: Zondervan, 1996), 1:43–44.

has been fully declared. Accordingly, what occurs in revelation within the Christian community is *not* new truth that goes beyond the special revelation (if so, it is spurious and not of God). It is only a deeper appreciation of what has already been revealed, or a disclosure of some message for the contemporary situation that adds nothing essentially to what he has before made known."[95] Thus, Williams affirmed the sufficiency of Scripture.

Wayne Grudem (from a third wave evangelical perspective)[96] articulated a traditional view of Scripture's sufficiency and necessity while maintaining the legitimacy of ongoing prophetic revelation. Specifically, he developed helpful applications of Scripture's sufficiency, including (1) the encouragement that comes from knowing "that everything God wants to tell us about [any particular doctrinal issue or personal situation] is to be found in Scripture"; (2) the reassurance "that God does not require us to believe anything about himself or his redemptive work which is not found in Scripture"; (3) the reminder "that nothing is sin which is not forbidden by Scripture (either explicitly or by implication)"; and (4) the comfort "that nothing is required of us by God that is not commanded in Scripture (either explicitly or by implication)."[97]

In terms of the practical outworking of the doctrine of Scripture's sufficiency, the last part of the twentieth century into the twenty-first century witnessed an ever-widening divide between evangelicals over the issue of counseling, church planting and church growth, church leadership and administration, even preaching. At the core of this debate were different notions and applications of the sufficiency of Scripture. Although the spectrum is broad and many practitioners defy easy categorization, a general division has grown and continues to grow between integrationists on the one hand and strict biblicists on the other hand. In the first camp are included Christians who seek to integrate biblical instruction about human beings, the church, leadership, preaching, and the like with the best insights of secular psychology, sociology and demographic studies, business theories, secular leadership principles, communication techniques, and much more. In the second group are Christians who insist that Scripture's sufficiency rules out any integration of biblical truth with humanly derived knowledge.[98]

Thus, as the third millennium of the church begins, evangelicals are faced with an important debate about the sufficiency of Scripture. One important scholarly work that could help with this is Timothy Ward's *Word and Supplement: Speech Acts, Biblical Texts, and the Sufficiency of Scripture*.[99] Much work still needs to be done on this topic as well as on the necessity of Scripture.

---

95. Ibid., 1:44, his emphasis.

96. Third wave evangelicalism agrees with Pentecostal/charismatic theology that all the spiritual gifts—including the so-called "sign" or "miraculous" gifts (e.g., prophecy, speaking in tongues, healing)—are operative in the church today. It also concurs with non-Pentecostal/charismatic theology that baptism with the Holy Spirit occurs at, rather than subsequent to, conversion. For further discussion, see chap. 20.

97. Grudem, *Systematic Theology*, 130–35.

98. To take only one area—counseling, or soul care—and only two examples, see Ed Hindson and Howard Eyrich, gen. eds., *Totally Sufficient: The Bible and Christian Counseling* (Ross-Shire, UK: Christian Focus, 2004), and Eric L. Johnson, *Foundations for Soul-Care: A Christian Psychology Proposal* (Downers Grove, Ill.: InterVarsity, 2007).

99. Timothy Ward, *Word and Supplement: Speech Acts, Biblical Texts, and the Sufficiency of Scripture* (Oxford: Oxford Univ. Press, 2002).

8

THE INTERPRETATION OF SCRIPTURE

How has the church come to interpret the Bible? How has the literal, or grammatical-historical, method of interpretation come to be used to understand the Word of God?

STATEMENT OF BELIEF

As the church historically has treasured the revelation of God in his inspired Word, it also has recognized the crucial need to interpret the Bible properly. In this regard, the church has sensed a tension between two essentially different methods of understanding Scripture. One of these is a literal approach, the other a spiritual or allegorical approach. In the latter case, the Bible is viewed as containing several meanings. One of these—the literal meaning—can be grasped by considering the words, grammar, and sentence structure of biblical passages. This is the literal method of interpretation. The other meanings—often referred to as the spiritual or mystical senses—demand an allegorical method: by a process of abstraction, the interpreter moves from the concrete realities of the biblical passages to concepts that lie hidden behind those texts. The Protestant Reformers, many of whom were trained in the plural meanings approach, rejected it in favor of the literal, or grammatical-historical, method of interpretation. Only by interpreting the Bible according to its one true meaning and avoiding allegorizing could the church hope to discover Jesus Christ, to whom Scripture pointed. For the most part, evangelicals follow this literal, or historical-grammatical, method of interpretation.[1]

THE INTERPRETATION OF SCRIPTURE IN THE EARLY CHURCH

The interpretation of Scripture did not begin with Christianity. Before the church began, the Jews read and interpreted the Hebrew Bible, or what we now call our Old

---

1. My thanks to Dave Richards for his help on this chapter.

Testament. Indeed, the Lord commanded the regular reading of his Word (Deut. 31:9–13), which at times the people of Israel were faithful in doing (e.g., Neh. 8). As a godly Jew, Jesus went to the temple and the synagogue and heard Scripture, and on occasions in the synagogue he himself read from and interpreted Scripture (Luke 4:16–22).

In the early church, the apostles followed the example of their Lord in interpreting the Hebrew Bible. Jesus had employed *typology*, a method that underscored the correspondence between what had gone on earlier in the Old Testament (called the *type*) and something in his own day (called the *antitype*). For example, Jonah's three days in the stomach of the great fish (Jonah 1:17) was a type of Jesus' burial (Matt. 12:38–41), and Moses' lifting of the serpent in the wilderness (Num. 21:4–9) was a type of Jesus' exaltation (John 3:14–15). In a similar manner, the authors of the New Testament used typology. Thus, Adam is a type of Jesus Christ, the two representing all of humanity (Rom. 5:12–21). The flood of Noah corresponds to Christian baptism, the two portraying escape from divine judgment (1 Peter 3:18–22). And the experiences of sin and condemnation of the Israelites serve as warning examples to Christians so they avoid similar destructive behavior (1 Cor. 10: 1–13).

After the writing of the New Testament, the early church continued to interpret Scripture typologically. But a new development arose that focused on the proper use of an allegorical method of interpreting the Bible, an approach that was common in Judaism. Indeed, the term *midrash* is often used for various techniques employed by the rabbis in writing commentaries on Hebrew Scripture. Some forms of midrash were allegorical, commenting on the text of Scripture but actually focusing on another, more spiritual subject matter. The purpose of an allegorical interpretation was to "draw out the 'deeper meaning' of the text, to explain its obscurities and difficulties, and to apply it to the contemporary situation."[2] In the early church, the debate over the use of allegorical interpretation played itself out in two different schools of biblical interpretation.[3]

The *school of Alexandria* (in Egypt) embraced an allegorical approach. To summarize this method of exegesis, or interpretation, of Scripture: "In allegorical exegesis the sacred text is treated as a mere symbol, or allegory, of spiritual truths. The literal, or historical sense, if it is regarded at all, plays a relatively minor role, and the aim of the exegete is to elicit the moral, theological or mystical meaning which each passage, indeed each verse and even each word, is presumed to contain."[4]

Although this method was used by Clement of Alexandria, headmaster of the school (190–203),[5] it was developed and popularized by Clement's successor, Origen. He was scandalized by any purported literal reading of the opening chapters of Genesis:

---

2. Gerald Bray, *Biblical Interpretation: Past and Present* (Downers Grove, Ill.: InterVarsity, 1996), 57.

3. The influence of Philo of Alexandria (20 BC–AD 54) was immense in this regard. Philo was a Greek-speaking Jewish scholar who attempted to apply the philosophy of Plato to the interpretation of the Old Testament (for Philo, this Bible was the *Septuagint*, the Greek translation of the Hebrew Scriptures; see chap. 2, pp. 47–50). Just as Plato had stressed the reality of a spiritual world lying hidden behind our tangible, visible world, so Philo emphasized the spiritual meaning lying

behind the words of Scripture. An allegorical method of interpretation was necessary to discern this deeper meaning.

4. Kelly, 70.

5. E.g., Clement explained: "Knowing well that the Savior teaches nothing in a merely human way, but teaches all things to his own [disciples] with divine and mystic wisdom, we must not listen to his utterances [communication] carnally; but with due investigation and intelligence must search out and learn the meaning hidden in them. For even those things which seem to have been simplified to the disciples by the

For who that has understanding will suppose that the first, and second, and third day, and the evening and the morning, existed without a sun, and moon, and stars? And that the first day was, as it were, also without a sky? And who is so foolish as to suppose that God, after the manner of a husbandman [farmer], planted a paradise in Eden, towards the east, and placed in it a tree of life, visible and palpable, so that one tasting of the fruit by the bodily teeth obtained life? And again, that one was a partaker of good and evil by masticating what was taken from the tree? And if God is said to walk in the paradise in the evening, and Adam to hide himself under a tree, I do not suppose that anyone doubts that these things figuratively indicate certain mysteries, the history having taken place in appearance, and not literally.[6]

According to Origen, the text of Genesis appears to be a historical narrative reporting actual realities. However, interpreters of Scripture cannot legitimately read this text literally. They must understand that it is metaphorical or figurative; that is, there is another meaning beyond the literal one. Specifically, Origen found three levels of meaning in Scripture, corresponding to the three parts of human beings (who are composed of body, soul, and spirit). These three senses are understood by Christians according to their progress in the faith; thus, everyone receives benefit from Scripture. As for the first sense: "In order that all the more simple individuals may be edified, so to speak, by the very body of Scripture; for such we term that common and historical sense." There is a second sense: "If some have commenced to make considerable progress [in the faith], and are able to see something more (than that [sense]), they may be edified by the very soul of Scripture." The third sense is the last: "Those, again, who are perfect [mature] ... may be edified by the spiritual law itself ... as if by the Spirit. For as man is said to consist of body, and soul, and spirit, so also does sacred Scripture, which has been granted by the divine bounty for the salvation of man."[7]

While not denying the literal sense of Scripture and its benefits for ordinary believers, Origen viewed this "body" as a covering or veil of spiritual truths. Indeed, he dismissed the idea that all of Scripture can be taken literally and emphasized its hidden meaning: "Now all this ... was done by the Holy Spirit in order that, seeing those events which lie on the surface [i.e., the literal sense] can be neither true nor useful, we may be led to the

Lord himself are found to require not less, even more, attention than what is expressed enigmatically, from the surpassing superabundance of wisdom in them." Clement of Alexandria, *Who Is the Rich Man Who Will Be Saved?* 5, in *ANF*, 2:592.

6. Origen, *First Principles*, 4.1.16 (from the Greek ed.), in *ANF*, 4:365.

7. Ibid., 4.1.11 (from the Latin ed.), in *ANF*, 4:359. He used a reference in Paul to define "the perfect [mature]" as Christians "who resemble those of whom the apostle says, 'We speak wisdom among them who are perfect [mature], but not the wisdom of this world, nor of the princes of this world, who will be brought to nothing; but we speak the wisdom of God, hidden in a mystery, which God has decreed before the ages to our glory' [1 Cor. 2:6–7]." Ibid. Origen also appealed to a biblical basis for this threefold level of meaning, citing Prov. 22:20–21

and its rule of treating Scripture "in a threefold manner, in counsel and knowledge, and that you may answer the words of truth." Ibid. An example of Origen's allegorical approach is his interpretation of the burnt offerings and sacrifices detailed in Leviticus. According to the literal sense, these offerings were the actual sacrifices prescribed by the Mosaic law. According to the sense of "the soul of Scripture," these offerings pointed to Christ's sacrifice on Calvary. Finally, according to the spiritual sense, these offerings symbolize the spiritual sacrifices that all Christians are called to offer in obedience to Jesus Christ. Origen, *Homilies in Leviticus*, 1.4–5, in Origen, *Homilies in Leviticus 1–16*, trans. Gary Wayne Barkley, *The Fathers of the Church: A New Translation* (Washington, D.C.: Catholic Univ. of America Press, 1990), 83:30–31.

investigation of that truth which is more deeply concealed, and to the ascertaining of a meaning worthy of God in those Scriptures which we believe to be inspired by him."[8] Thus, Origen was prone to interpret the Bible allegorically and discover a great deal of deeper meaning. As a result, the school of Alexandria that flourished in the second and third centuries became known for its allegorical interpretation. Much of this was quite fanciful, bordering at times on the bizarre.

In reaction to this allegorizing method, the *school of Antioch* (in Syria) underscored a different approach to Scripture that had elements of both literal interpretation and typology. Typological interpretation stood in stark contrast to the allegorical approach:

> Typological exegesis ... was a technique for bringing out the correspondence between the two Testaments, and took as its guiding principle the idea that the events and personages of the Old were "types" of, i.e., prefigured and anticipated, the events and personages of the New. The typologist took history seriously; it was the scene of the progressive unfolding of God's consistent redemptive purpose.... Typology, unlike allegory, had no temptation to undervalue, much less dispense with, the literal sense of Scripture.[9]

For example, the school of Antioch, in interpreting the Pentateuch, focused literally on Moses as the giver of the Law and typologically on Moses as the prophet who foreshadowed Jesus Christ (Deut. 18:15–19; Acts 3:17–23).

The major figures associated with the school of Antioch included Diodore of Tarsus, Theodore of Mopsuestia, Theodoret, and John Chrysostom. All were united in their critique of allegorical interpretation. Commenting on the appeal of the proponents of allegory to Paul's use of it (Gal. 4:24), Theodore of Mopsuestia complained:

> Countless students of scripture have played tricks with the plain sense of the Bible and want to rob it of any meaning it contains. In fact, they make up inept fables and call their inanities "allegories." They so abuse the apostle's paradigm as to make the holy texts incomprehensible and meaningless.... [Paul] neither dismisses the historical narrative nor is he adding new things to an old story. Instead, Paul is talking about events as they happened, then submits the story of those events to his present understanding.[10]

Theodore's concern was the tendency of the allegorical approach to overlook or even dismiss the literal meaning, and hence historical reality, of texts. The biblical authors themselves explicitly take the historical account of earlier writers as "unquestionably factual,"[11] and this method emphasized the necessity of a literal interpretation.

While insisting on a literal approach, members of the school of Antioch also employed typology in their interpretation of Scripture. Key to perceiving types in the Bible was a concept called *theoria*, or insight:

---

8. Origen, *First Principles*, 4.1.15 (from the Latin ed.), in *ANF*, 4:364.

9. Kelly, 71.

10. Theodore of Mopsuestia, *Commentary on Galatians*,

cited in Joseph W. Trigg, *Biblical Interpretation* (Wilmington, Del.: Glazier, 1988), 173.

11. Ibid., 175.

By this they meant the power of perceiving, in addition to the historical facts set out in the text, a spiritual reality to which they were designed to point. Thus they accepted typology proper ... but tried to rescue it from being exploited arbitrarily. For *theoria* to operate they considered it necessary (a) that the literal sense of the sacred narrative should not be abolished, (b) that there should be a real correspondence between the historical fact and the further spiritual object discerned, and (c) that these two objects should be apprehended together, though of course in different ways.[12]

In contrasting allegory and *theoria*, Severian of Gabala noted: "It is one thing to force allegory out of the history, and quite another thing to preserve the history intact while discerning a *theoria* over and above it."[13] And Diodore of Tarsus cautioned: "We do not forbid the higher interpretation and *theoria*, for the historical narrative does not exclude it, but is on the contrary the basis and substructure of loftier insights.... We must, however, be on guard against letting the *theoria* do away with the historical basis, for the result would be, not *theoria*, but allegory."[14] Thus, the school of Antioch opposed the fanciful allegorical method of the school of Alexandria, insisting instead on a literal approach to Scripture that allowed for the discovery of typology. Some representatives restricted typological interpretation to the types that the New Testament authors explicitly drew out of the Old Testament, while others encouraged a broader typology.[15]

In a different typological approach, Tyconius offered seven rules of biblical interpretation that aimed at linking Scripture with the church in its contemporary setting. Tyconius's *Book of Rules* was one of the earliest hermeneutical manuals in the church, and it exerted a powerful influence on future biblical interpretation.[16]

Tyconius's Seven Rules (from *The Book of Rules*)

I considered it necessary to write a book of rules and so to fashion keys and lamps, as it were, to the secrets of the law.... If the sense of these rules is accepted without ill will, as we impart it, whatever is closed will be opened and whatever

---

12. Kelly, 76. See esp. A. Vaccari, "La theoria nella scuola esegetica di Antiocha," *Biblica* 1 (1920): 3–36.

13. Severian of Gabala de creat, *On the Creation*, 4/2, in Kelly, 76.

14. Diodore of Tarsus, *Preface to the Psalms*, in Kelly, 76–77.

15. Thus, Theodore of Mopsuestia considered only four psalms (Pss. 2, 8, 45 [in Heb., Ps. 44], and 110 [in Heb., Ps. 109]) to be messianic, and he did not believe that the prophecy of the suffering servant in Isaiah 53:7 ("he shall be led as a sheep to the slaughter") was intended by Isaiah as referring to the crucifixion of Jesus Christ. Theodoret, on the other hand, allowed for messianic prophecy in passages such as Hos. 11:1;

Mic. 4:1–3; Hag. 2:9; Zech. 11:12–14; et al. The difference between these two can best be seen in their commentaries on the Song of Solomon. Theodore, emphasizing a literal approach (without discounting a further typological understanding), interpreted this writing as a wedding poem celebrating the love of Solomon and his princess. Theodoret, on the other hand, refused to interpret it as a story of human love but emphasized its typological meaning portraying Christ's love for his people.

16. This was especially true of Tyconius's impact on Augustine's *On Christian Doctrine*, which presented a modified summary of *The Book of Rules*.

is dark will be illumined; and anyone who walks the vast forest of prophecy guided by these rules, as by pathways of light, will be kept from straying into error. These are the rules:

1. the Lord and his body
2. the Lord's bipartite body
3. the promises and the law
4. the particular and the general
5. times
6. recapitulation
7. the devil and his body*

> *Tyconius: The Book of Rules, ed. and trans. William S. Babcock (Atlanta: Scholars, 1989). The rather strange-sounding references to the Lord's (bipartite) body and Satan's body reflect Tyconius's concern to provide a biblical warrant for his view that the church is composed of both believers (members of Christ's body) and unbelievers (members of Satan's body).

Although not a part of the Alexandrian school, Augustine continued to emphasize allegorical interpretation. This focus was part of his overall approach, which considered the understanding of Scripture to be dependent on the knowledge and utilization of certain principles of interpretation. Indeed, Augustine engaged in setting forth those key principles: a good interpreter must be humble and godly, become familiar with the entirety of Scripture, pay close attention to the words of Scripture (especially in the original languages), and recognize figures of speech.[17] In principle, Augustine urged interpreters to focus on the biblical author's meaning, warning that "whoever takes another meaning out of Scripture than the writer intended, goes astray."[18] Yet he embraced a fourfold meaning as the intention of the Scriptures: "In all the sacred books, we should consider eternal truths that are taught, the facts that are narrated, the future events that are predicted, and the precepts or counsels that are given."[19] As this interpretive paradigm developed, the four senses were the *literal* sense, the meaning of the text as the author intended it and expressed it in the words of the Bible; the *etiological* sense, the meaning that explains the reason for something written in the Bible (e.g., Jesus offers the reason for Moses' permission of divorce [Deut. 24:1–4] in Matt. 19:7–8);[20] the *analogical* sense, the meaning that demonstrates that the Old and New Testaments are in harmony with each other; and the *allegorical* sense, the meaning that looks upon the things written in Scripture in a figurative manner.

17. Augustine, *On Christian Doctrine*, preface, in *NPNF*¹, 2:519–21. Specifically: "The man who is in possession of the rules which here I attempt to lay down, if he comes upon an obscure passage in the books which he reads, will not need an interpreter to uncover the secret for him. Rather, holding to certain rules and following certain principles, he will arrive at the hidden sense without any error, or at least without falling into any terrible absurdity." Ibid., 521. Cf. *On Christian Doctrine*, 2.7, 9, 11, 13, 16.

18. Ibid., 1.36, in *NPNF*¹, 2:533.

19. Augustine, *On the Literal Meaning of Genesis*, 1.1, in *Ancient Christian Writers: The Literal Meaning of Genesis*, vol. 1, trans. John Hammond Taylor (New York: Newman, 1982), 19.

20. Etiology (also, aetiology) refers to the study of causes or reasons.

A classic example of allegorical interpretation is Augustine's understanding of the parable of the good Samaritan, in which each element of the story is a figure for something else.

Augustine's Allegorization of the Parable of the Good Samaritan

the traveler = Adam
Jerusalem = the heavenly city from which Adam fell
Jericho = Adam's resulting mortality
the robbers = the devil and his demons
stripping him = depriving Adam of his immortality
beating him = encouraging Adam to sin
leaving him half dead = Adam was dead spiritually but still retained some
    knowledge of God
the priest and the Levite = the ineffective ministry of the old covenant
the good Samaritan = Jesus Christ
binding the wounds = restraining from sin
the oil = the comfort of the Holy Spirit
the wine = exhortation to good works
the donkey = the body of Christ
the inn = the church
the two coins = the two commandments of love
the innkeeper = the apostle Paul
the return of the Samaritan = the resurrection of Christ.*

*Augustine, *Questiones Evangeliorum*, 2.19. For the text, see C. H. Dodd, *The Parables of the Kingdom* (New York: Scribner, 1961), 1–2.

Although this approach would seem to result in an unchecked interpretation of Scripture, Augustine established certain boundaries to the extent one could allegorize. Thus, all interpretations had to (1) correspond to the teachings of the church and (2) promote love for God and others.[21] Of course, whatever did not seem to foster love was to be taken figuratively. For example, texts describing the destruction of the Canaanites at God's command could only be understood allegorically because they had no literal meaning.[22]

While these developments were going on, Jerome championed in a stronger way biblical interpretation that focused on the authorial intention of Scripture: "My fixed purpose

---

21. "Whoever, then, thinks that he understands the Holy Scriptures, or any part of them, but puts such an interpretation upon them as does not tend to build up this two-fold love of God and our neighbor, does not yet understand them as he ought." Augustine, *On Christian Doctrine*, 1.36, in *NPNF*[1], 2:533. Cf. 3.10. Augustine also encouraged biblical interpretation that would promote the three Christian virtues, or graces,

of faith, hope, and love: "If a man fully understands that 'the end of the commandment is love out of a pure heart, a good conscience, and sincere love' (1 Timothy 1:5) and is bent upon making all his understanding of Scripture to bear upon these three graces, he may come to the interpretation of these books with an easy mind." *On Christian Doctrine*, 1.40, in *NPNF*[1], 2:534.

was not to bend the Scriptures to my own wishes but simply to say what I took to be their meaning. A commentator has no business to impose his own views; his duty is to make plain the meaning of the author whom he professes to interpret. For, if he contradicts the writer whom he is trying to expound, he will prove to be his opponent rather than his interpreter."[23] This focus on the intention of the authors of Scripture so as to interpret it rightly would become a major theme in Reformation and modern hermeneutics.

Another important development began in the early church that would exert an increasing influence over the church's subsequent interpretation of Scripture. The practice of appealing to church authority, especially to the writings of the church fathers, was intended to protect the church from the growing number of insidious heresies that threatened it. In battles against these heresies, the appeal to church tradition and church authority was intended to provide support for true beliefs because they were the truths the church had always embraced; they were not the novel ideas of the false teachers.[24] The practice of appealing to church authority, especially to the writings of the church fathers, would develop significantly in the medieval period.

THE INTERPRETATION OF SCRIPTURE IN THE MIDDLE AGES

Much of medieval interpretation was influenced by Origen and Augustine and their multiple-sense approach to Scripture. At the beginning of the Middle Ages, Gregory the Great did much to promote the allegorical method of interpretation, setting forth his desired approach: "That I should not only shake loose from the words of the historical narrative their allegorical meaning, but should also direct the allegorical interpretation towards moral edification." Accordingly, Gregory employed a threefold approach to interpretation: "The reader must realize that some things are expounded here as simple historical narrative, some things examined for their allegorical meaning, and some things discussed only for their moral import—but of course some things are explored carefully in all three ways."[25] Other medieval interpreters of Scripture found four meanings in biblical texts. John Cassian had placed the four possible categories of meaning into a popular rhyme that typified the biblical interpretation that was handed down to the church of the Middle Ages:

> The letter shows us what God and our fathers did;
> The allegory shows us where our faith is hid;
> The moral meaning gives us rules of daily life;
> The anagogy shows us where we end our strife.[26]

As the Venerable Bede explained: "Holy Scripture has four senses: history, which speaks of events; allegory, in which something other than the normal meaning is

---

22. Augustine, *On Christian Doctrine*, 3.10–12, in *NPNF*[1], 2:560–62.

23. Jerome, *Letter*, 48.17, in *NPNF*[2], 6:76–77.

24. For further discussion, see chap. 4.

25. Gregory the Great, "Introduction," in *Moralia* (a com-

mentary on the book of Job); available at http://ccat.sas. upenn.edu/jod/texts/moralia.html; PL, 75:515.

26. John Cassian, "Cassian's Conferences," 14, chap. 8, in *NPNF*[2], 11:437. In Lat.: *Litera, gesta docet; quid credas, allegoria; moralis, quid agas; quo tendas anagogia.*

understood; tropology, that is, the moral form of expression, in which the ordering of men's morals is the subject; anagogy, by means of which we are led to higher things when we intend to treat of the loftiest themes and matters celestial."[27]

The most influential scholar of the Middle Ages, Thomas Aquinas, continued this fourfold approach to Scripture, with some variation. He distinguished between (1) the *literal* sense, which is the meaning of the *words* of Scripture, and (2) the *spiritual* sense. This latter sense is based on the literal sense and gives an additional three meanings according to the *things* to which Scripture points: "The author of Holy Scripture is God, in whose power it is to signify his meaning not by words only (as man can do), but also by things themselves.... The things signified by the words have themselves also a meaning."[28] Thus, Aquinas's interpretive approach was the following:

- *literal*, or historical, sense: the meaning signified by the words of the Bible and intended by the biblical author;
- *spiritual* senses: the meanings signified by the things of the Bible and grounded on the literal sense:
  allegorical sense: the devotional meaning of the Bible, focusing on Christ and the church;
  tropological sense: the practical meaning of the Bible, focusing on the individual's conduct and behavior;
  anagogical sense: the eschatological meaning of the Bible, focusing on its future fulfillment.[29]

Medieval interpretation of the Bible largely continued the practice of identifying multiple meanings in Scripture and emphasizing the spiritual senses of the Word of God.

This focus, however, is only part of the story. In the twelfth century, another school of biblical interpretation developed that emphasized close attention to the literal meaning of Scripture. Working within the medieval framework of multiple senses, Hugh of St. Victor criticized the penchant of interpreters for underestimating or even neglecting the literal sense of Scripture in their rush to find its hidden meaning.[30] In contrast to this prevailing trend, Hugh urged interpreters to "read Scripture and first learn carefully what it tells you was done in the flesh" (i.e., according to the literal sense).[31] For Hugh, the literal sense does not replace the spiritual senses of Scripture, but his emphasis on it stood in contrast with other interpreters of the time. It also reflected the influence of Jewish biblical scholars with whom he consulted.

27. Venerable Bede, *Gl. ord. marg.*, Genesis, pro, cited by Alexander of Hales, *Summa Theologica*, introductory treatise, q. 1, chap. 4, art. 3. Cited in A. J. Minnis and A. B. Scott, eds., *Medieval Literary Theory and Criticism, c. 1100–c. 1375: The Commentary Tradition* (Oxford: Clarendon, 1988), 217–18. Bede's perspective was quite influential, as seen in the fact that Henry of Ghent quoted the same above-cited passage in his *Sum of Ordinary Questions*, art. 16. Cited in Minnis and Scott, 256–57.

28. Thomas Aquinas, *Summa Theologica*, pt. 1, q. 1, art. 10.

29. Ibid. "Tropological" is derived from the Greek word τρόπος (*tropos*), indicating manner or way; thus, by extension, it was related to a person's conduct. "Anagogical" is derived from the Greek word ἀναγω (*anagō*), indicating "to go up"; thus, by extension, it was related to future fulfillment.

30. Hugh of St. Victor, *De Sacramentis Christianae Fidei*, 1.8.6, 466, cited in Beryl Smalley, *The Study of the Bible in the Middle Ages* (Notre Dame, Ind.: Univ. of Notre Dame Press, 1964), 94.

31. Hugh of St. Victor, *De Scripturis*, 5:13–15, cited in Smalley, *Study of the Bible in the Middle Ages*, 94.

Hugh of St. Victor was the first of the school of the Victorines, interpreters who continued his emphasis on the literal meaning of Scripture. Of lesser note was Richard,[32] but Andrew of St. Victor made a significant contribution. Like his predecessor Hugh, Andrew relied heavily on Jewish literal interpretation, especially that of the school of Rashi (1040–1105), still considered one of the greatest Jewish exegetes of all time.[33] Particularly in prophetic passages, Andrew would acknowledge the traditional Christian understanding of a reference to the coming Messiah but would record the Jewish interpretation as the literal sense. For example, the "man of sorrows" (Isa. 53:3) referred either to the Jews of the Babylonian captivity or to the prophet Isaiah himself, but it was not a reference to the suffering Christ as the church had understood it.[34] His efforts to give a purely literal interpretation of the Old Testament were the first in the church's history and stood against the background of purely allegorical interpretations. Although some of his contemporaries criticized him for robbing the Bible of its messianic vision,[35] Andrew's reliance on Jewish interpreters and his consequent emphasis on the literal meaning of Scripture influenced later generations of biblical scholars.

Standing in continuity with this school of interpretation was one of the most influential medieval interpreters, Nicholas of Lyra. His most important writing was a commentary on the entire Bible.[36] Like others before him, Nicholas emphasized the literal sense of Scripture: "Just as a building that begins to part company with its foundation is inclined to collapse, so a mystical exposition which deviates from the literal sense must be considered unseemly and inappropriate, or at any rate less seemly and less appropriate, than other interpretations. So those who wish to make headway in the study of Holy Scripture must begin by understanding the literal sense."[37] Often, Nicholas took issue with his predecessors who had relied on an allegorical or spiritual sense of Scripture, thereby dispensing with its literal meaning.[38] Unique to Nicholas's interpretative approach was his view of what is called the "double-literal sense" of Scripture. All of the Old Testament signifies things literally, which in turn signify Jesus Christ. By insisting on this double-literal sense, Nicholas maintained a value for the Old Testament writings (and their literal significance) in and of themselves while also focusing on their ultimate

---

32. Although he was not the scholar like his predecessor Hugh and his contemporary Andrew were, Richard continued the Victorine emphasis on the literal sense of Scripture: "Many take much more pleasure in holy Scripture when they can perceive some suitable literal meaning. The building of the spiritual interpretation is more firmly established, so they think, when aptly grounded in the solid historical sense. Who can lay or firmly establish a solid foundation in a formless void? The mystical senses are extracted and formed from fitting comparisons of the things contained in the letter (i.e., the literal sense)." Richard of St. Victor, *Prologus in visionem Ezechielis*, 527–28, cited in Smalley, *Study of the Bible in the Middle Ages*, 108.

33. Principal members of the Rashi school included (1) Joseph Kara (1050–1125), who professed to emphasize the literal meaning of Scripture but in reality engaged in extensive allegorical interpretation; (2) Samuel ben Meir, or Rash-

bam, the grandson of Rashi; (3) Eliezer of Beaugency; and (4) Joseph Bekhor Shor of Orleans.

34. Andrew of St. Victor, *Comment* on Isaiah 53:2–12, cited in Smalley, *Study of the Bible in the Middle Ages*, 164–65.

35. E.g., Richard of St. Victor strongly criticized Andrew as undermining the Christian understanding of messianic passages in *De Tabernaculo* (214) and *De Emmanuele* (601–666). Cited in Smalley, *Study of the Bible in the Middle Ages*, 110.

36. *Postilla Litteralis in Vetus et Novum Testamentum* (written before 1350, published after 1450).

37. Nicholas of Lyra, *Postilla*, "Second Prologue," cited in Minnis and Scott, *Medieval Literary Theory*, 268.

38. See, e.g., ibid., cited in Minnis and Scott, *Medieval Literary Theory*, 269. In this prologue, Nicholas summarized seven rules of biblical interpretation, similar to the seven rules articulated by Tyconius's *The Book of Rules*.

value in pointing toward Christ.[39] Thus, Nicholas of Lyra championed the literal sense of Scripture while closely connecting the prefigurement of Christ to that sense of Old Testament passages.

In another development, medieval church leaders encouraged the reading of Scripture in continuity with the church's historical interpretation of it. Indeed, Hugh of St. Victor warned against reading the Bible apart from the early church fathers.[40] In interpreting Scripture in this way, the church would be protected from novelty leading to heresy; thus, continuity with the church's historical interpretation was highly valued. Indeed, Hugh of St. Victor offered an explanation of the relationship between canonical Scripture and "patristic" scripture:

> All divine Scripture is contained in the two testaments, the Old and the New. Each testament is divided into three parts: The Old contains the Law, the Prophets, the Historians. The New contains the Gospels, the Apostles, the Fathers.... In the last category the first place belongs to the decretals which are called canonical, that is, regular. Then there comes the writings of the holy fathers — Jerome, Augustine, Ambrose, Gregory, Isidore, Origen, Bede and the other doctors; these are innumerable. Patristic writings, however, are not counted in the text of the divine Scriptures.[41]

For the church in the early part of the medieval period, reading the Bible within this historical consensus was only reasonable, given the fact that the Holy Spirit leads the church into the right interpretation of the Bible that he inspired.[42]

This close-knit unity between the practice and the history of biblical interpretation began to unravel in the latter part of the Middle Ages. Increasingly, the church came to ground its "proper" interpretation on its own authority. John Gerson explained the process of interpretation that begins with the literal meaning, moves to the deeper interpretation provided by the early church fathers, and culminates in the authoritative definitions as determined by the church's ecumenical councils.[43] Commonly, appeal was made to the church's possession of the Holy Spirit for its authority to interpret Scripture in a multiple-sense way.[44] It would be but a small step from this to an affirmation of the supremacy and binding authority of the papal interpretation of Scripture.[45] Thus, the

---

39. See, e.g., Philip Krey, "The Apocalypse Commentary of 1329," in *Nicholas of Lyra: The Senses of Scripture*, ed. Philip D. W. Krey and Lesley Smith (Leiden: Brill, 2000), 191–92, 285.

40. "Do not attempt to learn by yourself lest, believing yourself introduced to knowledge, you be rather blinded. That introduction is to be sought for from men of doctrine and wisdom who may bring you in and open to you as you need it, with the authorities of the holy fathers and the testimonies of the Scripture." Hugh of St. Victor, *Eruditio Didascalia*, bk. 6, chap. 4, in Tavard, 17.

41. Hugh of St. Victor, *De Scriptura et Scriptoribus Sacris*, chap. 6., in Tavard, 16.

42. E.g., Gerhoh, *Commentary on the Psalms*, P. 6, in Tavard, 19.

43. John Gerson, *propositio* 6, col. 3, in Tavard, 54.

44. John Cochlaus, *De auctoritate Ecclesiae et Scripturae adversus Lutherum* (1524), chap. 9, in Tavard, 126.

45. As articulated by John of Turrecremata: "One must distinguish between two interpretations of the divine Law or of sacred Scripture. One proceeds by way of scholarly discussion and research; it enquires as to their true sense, and adds nothing to, or takes nothing away from, the words of the Law or of Scripture. The other proceeds by way of a binding decision interpreting their sense. The former belongs to scholars, whose interpretation, however, nobody is obligated to follow. The latter belongs to the Roman Pontiff, whose decision binds all." John of Turrecremata, *On the Church*, bk. 2, chap. 107, in Tavard, 60.

Catholic Church established itself as the supreme and authoritative guide to the proper interpretation of Scripture.

THE INTERPRETATION OF SCRIPTURE IN THE REFORMATION AND POST-REFORMATION

As was true of many of the Reformation controversies, Martin Luther was the first Reformer to question seriously the interpretive legacy he had inherited. Trained in the fourfold approach to Scripture, he was at first fascinated with it and consequently engaged in allegorical interpretation.[46] Luther changed his mind on the matter, however: "I finally realized that to my own great harm I had followed an empty shadow and had left unconsidered the heart and core of the Scriptures. Later on, therefore, I began to have a dislike for allegories."[47] He turned instead to an insistence upon the "literal" meaning, or as Luther preferred, the "grammatical, historical meaning."[48] This should replace the allegorical method, "for allegory is pernicious when it does not agree with the history, but especially when it takes the place of the history, from which the church is more correctly instructed."[49] Indeed, the literal meaning is "the highest, best, strongest, in short, the whole substance, nature and foundation of Holy Scripture."[50] Thus, "we should strive, so far as it is possible, to get one, simple, true, and grammatical meaning from the words of the text."[51]

Luther applied several other interpretive principles in his understanding and exposition of the Bible. One was a familiarity with Paul's letter to the Romans: "This epistle is really the chief part of the New Testament and is truly the purest gospel.... It is a bright light, almost sufficient to illuminate the entire holy Scripture."[52] This emphasis was

---

46. Martin Luther, *Lectures on Genesis: Chapters 6-19*, LW, 2:150.

47. Ibid. Other reasons he gave for rejecting this approach include the following: (1) It wreaks havoc with Scripture (LW, 39:177). (2) "It is not sufficiently supported by the authority of Scripture, by the custom of the fathers, or by grammatical principles" (LW, 27:311). (3) Because the Holy Spirit is "the simplest writer," Scripture can have only one simple sense (LW, 39:178). (4) The logic of effective communication demands that there be only one sense (LW, 39:178).

48. *Answers to the Hyperchristian, Hyperspiritual, Hyperlearned Book by Goat Emser in Leipzig*, LW, 39:181.

49. *Lectures on Genesis: Chapters 26–30*, LW, 5:345.

50. *Answer to the Hyperchristian, Hyperspiritual, and Hyperlearned Book by Goat Emser in Leipzig*, LW, 39:177.

51. *Lectures on Genesis: Chapters 45–50*, LW, 8:146. Perhaps the best example of this is Luther's understanding of Christ's words at the Last Supper: "This is my body" (Matt. 26:26). His insistence on a physical presence of Christ in the bread and wine, though putting him at odds with other Reformers, was consistent with his insistence on a literal interpretation of Scripture. Thus, Luther strongly opposed Zwingli

and Oecolampadius on this issue. They held that the words of Christ were better expressed as "This represents my body" or "This is a sign of my body." To this, Luther responded: "They wish first of all to change the natural words and meanings of the Scriptures into their own words and meanings. For anyone who ventures to interpret words in the Scriptures any other way than what they say, is under obligation to prove this contention out of the text of the very same passage or by an article of faith. But who will enable the fanatics to prove that 'body' is the equivalent of 'sign of the body,' and 'is' the equivalent of 'represents'?... The sum and substance of all this is that we have on our side the clear, distinct Scripture which reads, 'Take, eat; this is my body'...." The emphasis on "the natural words and meanings" of the "clear, distinct Scripture" is in keeping with Luther's literal approach to interpreting the Bible. Luther, *That These Words of Christ, "This Is My Body," Still Stand Firm against the Fanatics*, LW, 37:3–150 (citations from 32–33). Cf. *Confession Concerning Christ's Supper*, LW, 37:151–372.

52. *Preface to the Epistle of St. Paul to the Romans*, LW, 35:365.

undoubtedly due to the crucial role this book played in Luther's own conversion. It also was the writing that most clearly emphasized and articulated the doctrine of justification by grace through faith alone, a key principle in Luther's theology.[53]

A second key interpretive principle was a knowledge of the subject matter of Scripture, especially the New Testament. Immersing oneself generally in the Bible and its worldview would open up the understanding of the particular parts of Scripture.[54] His focus on the New Testament led to a third principle—a christological interpretation. For Luther, Christ was the focus of all of Scripture, and thus its proper understanding is that which "drives home Christ" (*Christum treibet*).[55]

A fourth key principle was a careful consideration of the context of the passage being interpreted. Luther recognized that many words have several connotations. In such cases, "the context and the construction must be considered"[56] to determine which meaning is the intended one in each particular instance. And the interpreter must not take biblical words out of their context; to do so is "tortures the Word of God according to his whim and fancy."[57]

Fifth, Luther insisted on the need to distinguish between law and gospel. By this distinction, Luther did not mean to differentiate between the Old and New Testaments. Rather, law is anything in Scripture that expresses the demands of God while emphasizing human inability to live up to those standards (e.g., Matt. 5:48, part of the teachings of Jesus), revealing people to be sinners. Opposed to this is gospel, anything in Scripture that expresses God's promises by underscoring that Jesus Christ has met all his demands. Gospel brings grace to save sinners awakened to their need by law. To interpret the Bible properly, a clear distinction between these two must be made.[58]

In addition to these principles of interpretation for a proper understanding of the Bible, Luther also insisted on the need to be the right kind of person to interpret Scripture. Chief among the right character qualities that one must possess are godliness, a righteous life, and being a true Christian.[59] Above all, one must have the Holy Spirit to illumine the Word of God: "The truth is that nobody who has not the Spirit of God sees a jot [bit] of what is in the Scriptures.... The Spirit is needed for the understanding of all Scripture and every part of Scripture."[60]

This emphasis on being dependent on the Holy Spirit, who inspired Scripture, for the proper interpretation of Scripture was a common theme among the Reformers. Another outstanding example of this was Huldrych Zwingli and his followers in Switzerland. Beginning in July 1525, every day (except Fridays and Sundays) at 7:00 a.m. (summer) or 8:00 a.m. (winter), all the pastors and theological students in Zürich met in the cathedral

53. Thus, for Luther: "And if you want to engage successfully in theology and the study of Holy Scripture and do not want to run into a Scripture that is closed or sealed, you should learn above all to understand sin correctly, and the Epistle to the Romans should be your door and key to Scripture. Otherwise you will never penetrate to an understanding and knowledge of it." *Lectures on Genesis: Chapters 38–44*, LW, 7:280.

54. Ibid.

55. *Prefaces to the New Testament*, LW, 35:396.

56. *Lectures on Genesis: Chapters 45–50*, LW, 8:209.

57. *Against the Heavenly Prophets in the Matter of Images and Sacraments*, LW, 40:156–57. Luther rebukes Karlstadt

in this passage.

58. Luther develops this law-gospel contrast in several writings, including *The Freedom of a Christian* (LW 31:344); *Answer to the Hyperchristian, Hyperspiritual, and Hyperlearned Book by Goat Emser in Leipzig* (LW 39:143–224); and *What to Look For and Expect in the Gospels* (LW, 35:117–24). My thanks to Mark Seifrid for pointing out these references.

59. LW, 44:134–35.

60. Martin Luther, *The Bondage of the Will*, trans. James I. Packer and O. R. Johnston (Old Tappan, N. J.: Revell, 1957), 73–74. Cf. LW, 33:28.

for an hour of intense exegesis and interpretation of Scripture (based on the Greek or Hebrew and Latin versions). Zwingli opened each meeting with this prayer: "Almighty, eternal and merciful God, whose Word is a lamp unto our feet and a light unto our path, open and illuminate our minds, that we may purely and perfectly understand your Word and that our lives may be conformed to what we have rightly understood, that in nothing we may be displeasing unto your majesty, through Jesus Christ our Lord. Amen."[61]

Like Luther, John Calvin championed a literal method of biblical interpretation. Familiar with the excesses of allegorical interpretation, he rejected that approach and emphasized "that the true meaning of Scripture is the natural and obvious meaning."[62] This meaning was the sense that the biblical author intended for his readers to grasp. Thus, the principal task of an interpreter is to discover the author's intent: "It is almost his only work to lay open the mind of the writer whom he undertakes to explain." In line with this, Calvin expressed his preference for a simple and naturally flowing interpretation: "I shall bring to a passage of Scripture an interpretation that is not subtle, not forced nor distorted, but one that is natural, fluent, and plain."[63]

Calvin developed other key elements for a proper interpretation. First, like Luther, he insisted on a familiarity with the letter to the Romans.[64] Second, he pointed to a proper theological framework, provided by his own *Institutes of the Christian Religion*. After many centuries of Roman Catholic error, Christians needed a new theological structure so they could understand Scripture correctly.[65] A third key principle for Calvin was a christological interpretation. Like Luther before him, he underscored "that we ought to

61. Gottfried W. Locher, *Zwingli's Thought: New Perspectives* (Leiden: Brill, 1981), 28.

62. John Calvin, *Commentaries on Galatians and Ephesians*, trans. William Pringle (repr., Grand Rapids: Baker, 2005), 136. In his commentary on 2 Cor. 3:6 ("the letter kills, but the Spirit gives life"), Calvin attacked the Catholic understanding that originated with Origen and led to justification for allegorical interpretation: "This passage was mistakenly perverted, first by Origen, and afterwards by others, to a spurious signification. From this arose a very pernicious error—that of imagining that the perusal of Scripture would be not merely useless, but even injurious, unless it were drawn out into allegories. This error was the source of many evils. For there was not merely a liberty allowed of adulterating the genuine meaning of Scripture, but the more of audacity anyone had in this manner of acting, so much the more eminent an interpreter of Scripture was he accounted. Thus many of the ancients recklessly played with the sacred word of God, as if it had been a ball to be tossed to and fro. In consequence of this, heretics had it more in their power to trouble the church; for as it had become general practice to make any passage whatever mean anything that one might choose, there was no frenzy so absurd or monstrous, as not to admit of being brought forward under some pretext of allegory. Even good men themselves were carried headlong, so as to contrive very many mistaken opinions, led astray through a fondness for allegory." John Calvin, *Commentaries on the Epistles of Paul

to the Corinthians*, 2 vols., trans. John Pringle (Grand Rapids: Baker, 1948), 2:174–75.

63. John Calvin, *Institutes of the Christian Religion*, 4.11.1, LCC, 2:1212.

64. "When anyone understands this epistle, he has a passage opened to him to the understanding of the whole Scripture." John Calvin, "The Epistle Dedicatory. John Calvin to Simon Gryneus," *Commentary on Romans*, trans. John Owen (repr., Grand Rapids: Baker, 2005), xxiv.

65. Calvin explained the purpose for his *Institutes*: "It has been my purpose in this labor to prepare and instruct candidates in sacred theology for the reading of the divine Word, in order that they may be able both to have easy access to it and to advance in it without stumbling." John Calvin, "John Calvin to the Reader," *Institutes*, 4, LCC, 1:4. Torrance's theory on Calvin's motive for this purpose is on target: "The Gospel had been heavily overlaid with the traditions of men and so obscured by extraneous ideas inculcated into people's minds that it was practically impossible for ordinary men and women struggling on their own to understand the way of salvation even by reading the Bible. What they required was a key to open up a good and right understanding of Holy Scripture, or a simple guide to its content so that they might know what to look for and how they were to relate the different teachings and apply them to their own lives." T. F. Torrance, *The Hermeneutics of John Calvin* (Edinburgh: Scottish Academic Press, 1988), 62.

read the Scriptures with the express design of finding Christ in them."[66] Fourth, Calvin urged attentiveness to the meaning of words and to the context in which passages are found.[67] Accordingly, we find him engaging in careful word studies to help determine the author's intent. By context Calvin had in mind knowing the recipients of the passage to be interpreted,[68] the circumstance of the writing,[69] the words surrounding the passage,[70] and the overall drift of the passage.[71] A fifth principle was respect for the analogy of faith. Calvin called attention to the responsibility to interpret any particular Scripture in conformity with all the truth, or entirety, of Scripture.[72] He also employed the analogy of faith to encourage the illumination of more obscure passages of Scripture by clearer passages. This principle explains his penchant for bringing together a large number of passages in marshaling support for a particular interpretation. Thus, Calvin commonly argued for his interpretation because it was "buttressed by firm testimonies" or "sufficiently pointed out through all God's Word."[73]

Like Luther, Calvin also insisted that the Bible reader should be the right kind of person to interpret Scripture. Specifically, he noted wisdom, soberness, humility, attentive listening, sound judgment and discernment, reverence and piety, willingness to learn and to obey, mature and persistent deliberation, and the attitude of engaging in interpretation for the purpose of edification.[74] Tied to this was the illumination of the Holy Spirit. Although this aspect of the Spirit's work means several things in the writings of Calvin, the role of the Spirit in enlightening the exegete of Scripture and in executing, or applying, that Scripture in the sphere of human lives is particularly important here.[75] Finally,

66. John Calvin, *Commentary on the Gospel according to John*, 2 vols., trans. William Pringle (Grand Rapids: Baker, 1948), 1:218.

67. Calvin succinctly stated his principle: "There are many statements in Scripture the meaning of which depends upon their context." Calvin, *Institutes*, 4.16.23, LCC, 2:1346.

68. Ibid., 4.13.13, LCC, 2:1267.

69. Ibid., 3.17.14; 4.16.23, LCC, 1:818–19; 2:1346–47.

70. Ibid., 4.12.24, LCC, 2:1250.

71. Ibid., 4.17.26, LCC, 2:1393–94.

72. This was the basis of Calvin's appeal to King Francis in his dedication of the *Institutes*: "When Paul wished all prophecy to be made to accord with the analogy of faith [Rom. 12:6], he set forth a very clear rule to test all interpretation of Scripture." Ibid., "Prefatory Address to King Francis I of France," 2, LCC, 1:12–13.

73. Ibid., 3.3.22; 3.4.32, LCC, 1:617, 660.

74. These points are peppered throughout the *Institutes*, e.g., 2.8.50; 2.14.4; 3.2.4; 3.4.29; 3.4.37; 3.11.9; 3.11.11; 3.15.7; 3.21.1; 3.23.2.

75. Calvin affirmed that the Holy Spirit must exercise his enlightening ministry if Scripture is to be understood: "The Spirit of God, from whom the doctrine of the gospel comes, is its only true interpreter, to open it up to us. Hence, in judging of it, men's minds must of necessity be in blindness until they are enlightened by the Spirit of God." Calvin, *Commentaries on the Epistles of Paul to the Corinthians*, 1:117. Specifically, the Spirit works by preparing the mind of the reader of Scripture to receive its meaning. As Calvin explained: "The soul, illumined by him [the Spirit of God], takes on a new keenness, as it were, to contemplate the heavenly mysteries, whose splendor had previously blinded it. And man's understanding, thus beamed by the light of the Holy Spirit, then at last truly begins to taste those things which belong to the Kingdom of God." Calvin, *Institutes*, 3.2.34, LCC, 1:582; cf. 4.14.11. Beyond this, the Spirit offers the meaning of Scripture. Ibid., 4.17.25, LCC, 2:1392. Specifically, he noted: "And as the seed, covered with earth, lies hidden for a time, so the Lord will illuminate us by his Spirit, and will cause that reading which, being barren and void of fruit, causes nothing but wearisomeness, to have plain light of understanding." John Calvin, *Commentary upon the Acts of the Apostles*, 2 vols., trans. Henry Beveridge (repr., Grand Rapids: Baker, 2005), 1:360; cf. 1:354. But even this illumination of the Holy Spirit is in itself inadequate: "Unless the power of God, by which he can do all things, confronts our eyes, our ears will barely receive the Word or not esteem it at its true value." Calvin, *Institutes*, 3.2.31, LCC, 1:577. The Holy Spirit gives this divine power for the execution, or application, of Scripture: "The Word of God is not received by faith if it flits about in the top of the brain, but when it takes root in the depth of the heart.... The Spirit accordingly serves as a seal, to seal up in our hearts those very promises the certainty of which it has previously impressed upon our minds." Ibid., 3.2.36, LCC, 1:583–84.

Calvin called attention to the teaching ministry of the church. Besides the internal ministry of the Holy Spirit to understand Scripture, God provides an external ministry for comprehending his Word—the teaching office of the church.[76]

In response to this Protestant approach to biblical interpretation, the Roman Catholic Church, meeting in the Council of Trent, made two official pronouncements. The first concerned the text of Scripture. Instead of the Hebrew Old Testament and Greek New Testament, the official version would be Jerome's Latin Vulgate.[77] Then, to prevent Protestant interpretation from challenging the church's interpretation of Scripture, the council declared that only the church possesses the right to interpret the Bible:

> Furthermore, in order to restrain petulant spirits, it [the council] decrees that no one, relying on his own judgment, shall—in matters of faith, and of morals pertaining to the edification of Christian doctrine—wresting [distorting] the sacred Scripture to his own senses, presume to interpret the holy Scripture contrary to that sense which holy mother church—to whom it belongs to judge of the true sense and interpretation of the holy Scriptures—has held and holds; or even contrary to the unanimous consent of the Fathers; even though such interpretations were never [intended] to be at any time published. Those who act contrary shall be made known by their ordinaries and be punished [in accordance with] the penalties established by law.[78]

Thus, a major point of separation between Protestants and Catholics during the Reformation was the interpretation of Scripture.

The post-Reformers carefully and thoroughly articulated the crucial principles for a proper interpretation of Scripture. Working from the doctrine of biblical inspiration, they emphasized that the same Spirit who gave Scripture by way of inspiration was needed to illumine the understanding of those seeking to grasp Scripture's meaning,[79] which was one meaning—the literal meaning.[80] This insistence on the one literal sense of Scripture as the target of interpretation stood in stark contrast to the Roman Catholic insistence on multiple meanings for biblical texts.[81] According to Johann August Ernesti, the specific way that the Holy Spirit spoke in the Scripture was by the inspired words of the text. Consequently, it is to the words of Scripture, not the things (historical events) recorded in Scripture, that biblical interpreters must give heed.[82] Allegorical,

---

76. "It is his [God's] will to teach us through human means. As he was of old not content with the law alone, but added priests as interpreters from whose lips the people might ask its true meaning [cf. Mal. 2:7], so today he not only desires us to be attentive to its reading, but also appoints instructors to help us by their efforts." Calvin, *Institutes*, 4.1.5, LCC, 2:1017–18.

77. *Canons and Decrees of The Council of Trent*, 4th session (April 8, 1546), *Decree Concerning the Canonical Scriptures*, in Schaff, 2:82.

78. Ibid., 2:83.

79. Abraham Calov, *Socinismus Profligatus* (Wittenberg, 1665), 89ff., in Preus, 319.

80. This literal sense could be expressed in one of two ways: "The *strict literal sense* obtains when the words are taken according to their ordinary and natural meaning.... A *figurative literal sense* obtains when the words are taken figuratively or in a modified sense, when very obviously in the writings and text of the Scriptures to be explained there occurs some sort of trope [figurative expression]." Salomon Glassius, *Philologia Sacra* (Leipzig, 1713), 370–71, in Preus, 322.

81. John Gerhard, *Loci Theologici* (1621), 1.67, in Preus, 326.

82. Johann August Ernesti, *Institutio*, 13, cited in John Sailhamer, "Johann August Ernesti: The Role of History in Biblical Interpretation," *JETS* 44, no. 2 (June 2001): 203.

tropological, and anagogical senses, because they are established on the things of Scripture rather than its words, are therefore illegitimate meanings. Further motivating this emphasis on the one literal sense of Scripture was the post-Reformers' conviction of the clarity of Scripture and a concern to avoid interpretive chaos should a multiple sense for Scripture reign as it did in the Roman Catholic Church.[83] The post-Reformers also had to combat Roman Catholic apologists like Robert Bellarmine, who insisted that Scripture could be interpreted rightly only by the church: "For truly Catholic Christians, it is wisdom to understand holy Scripture according to the interpretations of the holy doctors and of the sacred council having apostolic authority. Whoever rejects this way of knowing Christian truth is not Christian. He who forgoes it is found unfaithful."[84] The post-Reformers rejected this interpretive exclusivity. In its place, they elevated the perspicuity of Scripture and the analogy of faith as key interpretive principles.[85]

Despite this fine emphasis on Scripture and its proper interpretation, the post-Reformation period witnessed a general malaise in Protestant churches. Preaching gained the reputation of being sterile and arid, laxity in Bible study prevailed, and churches languished as a result. Part of Philip Jacob Spener's proposal for renewal of these churches, set forth in his *Pia Desideria* (*Pious Desire*), was the call for a "more extensive use of the Word of God among us."[86] He noted that "the reading and exposition of a certain text ... is not enough" and, appealing to 2 Timothy 3:16–17, urged that "all Scripture, without exception, should be known by the congregation if we are all to receive the necessary benefit.... It should therefore be considered whether the church would not be well advised to introduce the people to Scripture in still other ways than through the customary sermon on the appointed lesson."[87] His concrete suggestions for how to encourage Scripture study included fathers leading family Bible reading, personal reading of Scripture, public reading of Scripture during the church worship services, and small group meetings for discussion of Scripture.[88] Spener's vision was certainly a fulfillment of the Protestant doctrine of Scripture and its interpretation.

THE INTERPRETATION OF SCRIPTURE IN THE MODERN PERIOD

Even as Spener's vision was sparking renewal through German Pietism, forces were being unleashed against the church and its doctrine of Scripture that would contribute to the demise of biblical interpretation. Indeed, biblical criticism did much more than shake people's confidence in the truthfulness and authority of Scripture(see further on this in chapter 5). Along with it came the conviction that "in the interpretation of Scripture ... the same rules apply to the Old and New Testaments as to other books."[89] An important

83. Abraham Calov, *Apodixis Articulorum Fidei* (Lüneburg, 1684), 51, in Preus, 326.

84. Robert Bellarmine, *De divina institutione Romani Pontificis*, in Tavard, 115–16.

85. *Westminster Confession of Faith*, 1.9, in Schaff, 3:605-6.

86. Philip Jacob Spener, *Pia Desideria*, trans. Theodore G. Tappert (Philadelphia: Fortress, 1964), 87.

87. Ibid., 88.

88. Ibid., 88–90.

example of this trend was William Robertson Smith, who learned from his mentor A. B. Davidson that "the books of Scripture, so far as interpretation and general formal criticism are concerned, must be handled very much as other books are handled."[90] For Smith, this meant specifically that the Old Testament must be understood as presenting an evolutionary view of Israelite religion and that it must be interpreted using a historical-critical approach to Scripture. From an evolutionary perspective, he approached the Old Testament as a record of the gradual development of Judaism from a simplistic, primitive and childish faith to a mature, ethical-religious system.[91] The implication of this viewpoint was that the Israelite sacrificial system was barbaric and reprehensible, certainly no worthy basis for the Christian religion.[92]

Smith's article entitled "Bible" in the *Encyclopedia Britannica* (9th ed., 1875) was a groundbreaking piece. It set forth a historical-critical approach to Scripture based on the principle that the biblical writings "set before us the gradual development of the religion of revelation."[93] For Smith, then, much of the Bible presents an inferior, evolving religion that provides little or no help for genuine believers. Thus, he had to disconnect true Christian devotion from Scripture, or at least from the reigning and historical view of Scripture as the inspired, inerrant Word of God.[94] A subjective, personal relationship with God was key.[95] For Smith, this personal relationship with God, based on his historic revelation in Christ, did not—indeed, given his evolutionary and historical-critical views of Scripture, could not—depend on a fully inspired and inerrant Bible. This view provided a measure of comfort for Smith, but it would not for those who followed in his footsteps and interpreted Scripture like just another book.

Another development accompanying the rise of biblical criticism was the rejection of the Roman Catholic insistence that the church's magisterium was the sole interpreter of Scripture. In his *Tractatus Theologico-Politicus*, Baruch Spinoza championed the inalienable right of all people to interpret Scripture as they saw fit: "As the sovereign right to free opinion belongs to every man even in matters of religion, and it is inconceivable that any man can surrender this right, there also belongs to every man the sovereign right and supreme authority to judge freely with regard to religion, and consequently to explain it and interpret it for himself."[96] Accordingly, the Catholic Church's claim to be the only

89. Benjamin Jowett, "On the Interpretation of Scripture," in *Essays and Reviews* (1860; reprint, London, George Routledge & Sons, 1907), 337. Mallock, in a satirical piece, represented Jowett's view as the following: "We used to look upon the Bible as a book standing apart by itself, and to be interpreted by a peculiar canon of criticism. But now we have learned that it is to be studied just like all other books; and we are now, for the first time coming to understand what, in its true grandeur, a real revelation is." W. H. Mattlock, *The New Republic: Culture, Faith, and Philosophy in an English Country House* (Piccadilly: Chatto and Windus, 1877), 145–46.

90. A. B. Davidson, *A Commentary, Grammatical and Exegetical, on the Book of Job*, vol. 1 with a Translation (London: Williams and Norgate, 1862), ix.

91. William Robertson Smith, *The Old Testament in the Jewish Church: Twelve Lectures on Biblical Criticism* (London: Adam & Charles Black, 1912), 192.

92. William Robertson Smith, *Religion of the Semites* (New York: D. Appleton & Co., 1889), 418.

93. William Robertson Smith, "Bible," *Encyclopedia Britannica*, 9th ed. (1875), 3:548. Within the next few years following the publication of this article, Smith was tried for heresy and eventually removed from his teaching position.

94. J. S. Black and G. Chrystal, eds., *Lectures and Essays of William Robertson Smith* (London: Adam & Charles Black, 1912), 134.

95. Ibid., 157.

96. Baruch Spinoza, *Theological-Political Treatise*, 2nd ed., trans. Samuel Shirley (Indianapolis and Cambridge: Hackett, 2001), 103.

interpreter of Scripture was to be rejected.[97] Subjectivism in interpreting Scripture began to be an important characteristic of the modern period.

This completely subjective approach to biblical interpretation was strongly rejected by most Protestants, some of whom articulated and defended a "scientific" approach to Scripture. Influenced by both Bacon's inductive method of science (the so-called scientific method) and the philosophy of Scottish common sense realism, Charles Hodge paralleled Scripture and theology with the natural world and science: "The Bible is to the theologian what nature is to the man of science. It is his store-house of facts; and his method of ascertaining what the Bible teaches is the same as that which the natural philosopher adopts to ascertain what nature teaches."[98] This method was that of ascertaining and examining the facts of Scripture (biblical theology) and drawing conclusions and demonstrating harmony from this data (systematic theology).[99] Hodge averred that the divine will is for God's people to use the scientific method to grasp and appreciate the harmony and beauty of biblical truth.[100] Moreover, this scientific method is the same inductive method that is standard in the world of natural science.[101] At the same time, Hodge insisted on the important role of the Holy Spirit in theology.[102]

Following in the steps of William Robertson Smith and others, liberal Protestant scholarship concentrated its efforts on the historical-critical approach to biblical interpretation. In addition to the *JEDP* theory that gained ascendancy in Old Testament biblical studies,[103] New Testament studies focused on new types of critical approaches: source criticism, form criticism, and redaction criticism. All three of these critical approaches displaced attention from a study and interpretation of Scripture to something else — written traditions, oral units, or editorial redaction — that exists behind the text itself. The impact of source, form, and redaction criticism was devastating for biblical interpretation. In addition, traditional doctrines of Scripture were challenged and upended. Evangelicals were placed in a defensive position, with much of their energy needing to be devoted to a defense of biblical inspiration, truthfulness, and authority. Biblical interpretation was often focused on noting the truth value of the passage being discussed. According to Hans Frei's *The Eclipse of Biblical Narrative*, interpretation devolved into a question of "whether or not the [biblical] story is true history."[104] The key interpretative question "What does the Bible mean?" was replaced by the apologetic question "Is what the Bible says true?" While undoubtedly an important question — especially so, given the onslaught of biblical criticism against Scripture's truthfulness — the latter question was far removed from the question of meaning.

97. "The interpretation of religion is vested above all in each individual. And this again affords further proof that our method of Scriptural interpretation is the best. For since the supreme authority for the interpretation of Scripture is vested in each individual, the rule that governs interpretation must be nothing other than the natural light that is common to all, and not any supernatural right, nor any external authority." Ibid., 159–60.

98. Charles Hodge, *Systematic Theology*, 3 vols. (1872–73; Peabody, Mass.: Hendrickson, 1999), 1:10.

99. Ibid., 1:1–2.

100. Ibid., 1:3.

101. Ibid., 1:4–15, 17. Hodge's approach, wrenched out of its context and interpreted critically, has become the whipping boy for all that is bad with "modern" evangelical interpretation of Scripture. To a large degree, Hodge has been misunderstood and treated disrespectfully.

102. Ibid., 1:16.

103. For more on the *JEDP* theory, see chap. 5.

104. Hans Frei, *The Eclipse of Biblical Narrative: A Study in Eighteenth and Nineteenth Century Hermeneutics* (New Haven: Yale Univ. Press, 1974), 6; cf. 16.

The use of these critical methods in biblical interpretation became a concern for evangelicals. Alister McGrath summarized the two general evangelical responses to biblical criticism: "Some have concluded that the critical argument does indeed compel us to abandon the traditional Christian and evangelical view of Scripture, and that we must recognize Scripture as a fallible (though inspired) witness to divine revelation. Others have dismissed criticism as irresponsible and irrelevant, retreating into a dogmatic and simplistic fundamentalism."[105] Appealing to a middle course, McGrath expressed an attitude of welcoming critical methods while denying their overthrow of biblical authority.[106]

In addition to the challenges presented by the historical-critical approaches to an evangelical biblical hermeneutic, another challenge arose from the world of literary criticism. William Wimsatt and Monroe Beardsley published an important essay, "The Intentional Fallacy"[107] that, in the common (mis)understanding of it, argued that "what an author intended is irrelevant to the meaning of his text."[108] This sparked an intense discussion on whether *meaning* may properly be defined, in keeping with the historical notion, as "the author's intent." One scholar who stepped up in defense of the author was E. D. Hirsch. He first pointed out the unforeseen result of banishing authorial intention to the realm of irrelevance: "Once the author had been ruthlessly banished as the determiner of his text's meaning, it very gradually appeared that no adequate principle existed for judging the validity of an interpretation. By an inner necessity the study of 'what a text says' became the study of what it says to an individual critic.... For if the meaning of the text is not the author's, then no interpretation can possibly correspond to *the* meaning of the text."[109] He then clearly delineated between meaning and significance: "*Meaning* is that which is represented by a text; it is what the author meant by his use of a particular sign sequence; it is what the signs represent. *Significance*, on the other hand, names a relationship between that meaning and a person, or a conception, or a situation, or indeed anything imaginable."[110] For Hirsch, "failure to consider this simple and essential distinction has been the source of enormous confusion in hermeneutic theory."[111] Thus, he defended "the sensible view that a text means what its author meant"[112] because of a pragmatic reality: this meaning offers the only way of adjudicating between conflicting interpretations of a text. Hirsch's perspective resonated with evangelical interpreters of Scripture because of their conviction that God, through the biblical authors, had intended one and only one meaning.[113]

In 1982 key leaders of the evangelical movement developed a set of guidelines setting forth the principles and practices of Bible interpretation. This group, which had earlier (1978) tackled the doctrine of the inerrancy of Scripture, recognized that a commitment to

---

105. Alister McGrath, *A Passion for Truth: The Intellectual Coherence of Evangelicalism* (Downers Grove, Ill.: InterVarsity, 1996), 98.

106. Ibid., 98–99.

107. William K. Wimsatt and Monroe Beardsley, "The Intentional Fallacy," *Sewanee Review* 54 (1946): 468–88.

108. E. D. Hirsch, *Validity in Interpretation* (New Haven: Yale Univ. Press, 1967), 12.

109. Ibid., 3–5.

110. Ibid., 8.

111. Ibid.

112. Ibid., 1.

113. Rallying in defense of authorial intent was such a noted biblical scholar as Walter C. Kaiser Jr., *The Uses of the Old Testament in the New* (Chicago: Moody, 1985).

Scripture's truthfulness would only have proper value if the inerrant Word of God was properly understood. Two affirmations from their *Chicago Statement on Biblical Hermeneutics* are especially relevant to this chapter. The first is "that the meaning expressed in each biblical text is single, definite and fixed."[114] Accompanying this affirmation was a denial of a deeper or hidden meaning in Scripture, a meaning that goes beyond that expressed by the authors. This sense, or author's intent, is established by the author's text and is stable. At the same time, one meaning may engender multiple applications.[115] The second affirmation was "the necessity of interpreting the Bible according to its literal, or normal, sense. The literal sense is the grammatical-historical sense, that is, the meaning which the writer expressed."[116]

Following the ever-growing sophistication in hermeneutical theory, evangelicals modified their interpretative approaches to reflect the latest developments. For example, as the issue of genre and its importance for proper interpretation came to the forefront, evangelicals advanced in genre sensitivity for biblical interpretation.[117] A popular example of this was the bestselling book *How to Read the Bible for All Its Worth*, which identified the various genres found in Scripture—narrative, poetry, prophecy, apocalyptic, epistle, parable, law, wisdom, gospel—and explained the particular hermeneutical principles that apply to each different genre.[118] Furthermore, Kevin Vanhoozer focused on the importance of genre for proper biblical interpretation: "In Scripture there are many different kinds of communicate acts: assertions, warnings, promises, questions, songs, proverbs, commands, and so forth.... Each genre represents a 'mode of cognition' and offers a distinct perspective for conceiving God, humanity and the world."[119] As Vanhoozer took the lead, other evangelicals followed by paying close attention to biblical genre for the proper interpretation of Scripture.

Of interest to evangelicals was the question of whether the "single meaning" of Scripture, affirmed by the *Chicago Statement*, "may be fuller than the purview of the human author, since God had more in view" than did the biblical writers as they authored their material.[120] Certainly, evangelicals refused to take the Roman Catholic Church's multiple-senses approach to biblical interpretation. Still, as some noted, the historical understanding of Scripture's composition—the Bible was written by human authors who were inspired by the Holy Spirit—leads to the conclusion that Scripture has a dual

114. *Chicago Statement on Biblical Hermeneutics*, art. 7, in *Hermeneutics, Inerrancy, and the Bible: Papers from ICBI Summit II*, ed. Earl D. Radmacher and Robert D. Preus (Grand Rapids: Zondervan, 1984), 883, 884–85.

115. Norman Geisler, "Explaining Hermeneutics: A Commentary on the Chicago Statement on Biblical Hermeneutics Articles of Affirmation and Denial," in Radmacher and Preus, *Hermeneutics, Inerrancy, and the Bible*, 893.

116. *Chicago Statement on Biblical Hermeneutics*, art. 15, in Radmacher and Preus, *Hermeneutics, Inerrancy, and the Bible*, 884–85.

117. This had already been duly noted in the *Chicago Statement on Biblical Hermeneutics*. *Chicago Statement on Biblical Hermeneutics*, arts. 13–14, in Radmacher and Preus, *Hermeneutics, Inerrancy, and the Bible*, 884. And J. I. Packer had expressed the importance of these literary forms: "Valuable as an aid in determining the literal meaning of biblical passages is the discipline of genre criticism, which seeks to identify in terms of style, form and content, the various literary categories to which the biblical books and particular passages within them belong." J. I. Packer, "Exposition on Biblical Hermeneutics," in Radmacher and Preus, *Hermeneutics, Inerrancy, and the Bible*, 911.

118. Gordon D. Fee and Douglas Stuart, *How to Read the Bible for All Its Worth* (Grand Rapids: Zondervan, 1982).

119. Kevin J. Vanhoozer, "From Canon to Concept: 'Same' and 'Other' in the Relation between Biblical and Systematic Theology," *Scottish Bulletin of Evangelical Theology* 12 (1994): 111–12.

120. Norman Geisler, "Explaining Hermeneutics: A Commentary on the Chicago Statement on Biblical Hermeneutics Articles of Affirmation and Denial," in Radmacher and Preus, *Hermeneutics, Inerrancy, and the Bible*, 900.

(human and divine) authorship. In this way a discussion of *sensus plenior*, or a fuller sense, of Scripture was broached by such leading evangelical scholars as S. Lewis Johnson, J. I. Packer, Elliott Johnson, and Douglas Moo.[121] Evangelicals responded to this issue with a divergence of opinions. Many, like Walter Kaiser, denied the existence of a deeper meaning in biblical texts.[122] A few others, like James DeYoung, affirmed the presence of a deeper meaning of Scripture.[123] Kevin Vanhoozer called for a theological interpretation by reading Scripture in canonical context: "To interpret Scripture theologically is to read for the divine intention, and this means reading each part in light of the canonical whole. The canonical context alone forms the proper context for describing what God is doing in his word and for understanding the purpose for which God's word was sent (Isa. 55:11). To limit oneself to recovering only the human authorial intentions is to fall short of theological interpretation."[124] Indeed, theological interpretation of Scripture became an important discussion that brought evangelicals into dialogue with scholars strongly influenced by historical criticism as an approach that offered promise of reviving the reading of Scripture with theological convictions for theological growth.[125]

121. Darrell Bock, "Evangelicals and the Use of the Old Testament in the New," *BSac* 142 (1985): 213. Bock discussed the following evangelicals in his article: S. Lewis Johnson, *The Old Testament in the New* (Grand Rapids: Zondervan, 1980); J. I. Packer, "Biblical Authority, Hermeneutics and Inerrancy," in *Jerusalem and Athens: Critical Discussions on the Theology and Apologetics of Cornelius Van Til*, ed. E. R. Greehan (Phillipsburg, N.J.: P & R, 1971); Elliott E. Johnson, "Author's Intention and Biblical Interpretation," in Radmacher and Preus, *Hermeneutics, Inerrancy, and the Bible*. Added to this discussion was Douglas J. Moo, "The Problem of Sensus Plenior," in *Hermeneutics, Authority, and Canon*, ed. D. A. Carson and John D. Woodbridge (Grand Rapids: Zondervan, 1986), 175–211. In one way or another, these scholars worked with the foundational definition of *sensus plenior* offered earlier by the Roman Catholic scholar Raymond Brown: "The *sensus plenior* is that additional, deeper meaning, intended by God but not clearly intended by the human author, which is seen to exist in the words of a biblical text (or group of texts, or even a whole book) when they are studied in the light of further revelation or development in the understanding of revelation." Raymond E. Brown, *The Sensus Plenior of Sacred Scripture* (Baltimore: St. Mary's Univ. Press, 1955). This work was Brown's doctoral dissertation and launched his career as a leading Catholic theologian.

122. Walter C. Kaiser Jr., "A Response to Author's Intention and Biblical Interpretation," in Radmacher and Preus, *Hermeneutics, Inerrancy, and the Bible*, 444–45.

123. James DeYoung and Sarah Hurty, *Beyond the Obvious: Discover the Deeper Meaning of Scripture* (Gresham, Ore.: Vision House, 1995).

124. Kevin J. Vanhoozer, "Intention/Intentional Fallacy," in *Dictionary for Theological Interpretation of the Bible*, ed. Kevin J. Vanhoozer et al. (Grand Rapids: Baker; London: SPCK, 2005), 330.

125. Daniel J. Treier, *Introducing Theological Interpretation of Scripture: Recovering a Christian Practice* (Grand Rapids: Baker Academic, 2008); Vanhoozer et al., *Dictionary for Theological Interpretation of the Bible*; idem, ed., *Theological Interpretation of the Old Testament: A Book-by-Book Survey* (Grand Rapids: Baker Academic, 2005, 2008); idem, ed., *Theological Interpretation of the New Testament: A Book-by-Book Survey* (Grand Rapids: Baker Academic, 2005, 2008); A. K. M. Adam, Stephen E. Fowl, Kevin J. Vanhoozer, and Francis Watson, *Reading Scripture with the Church: Toward a Hermeneutic for Theological Interpretation* (Grand Rapids: Baker Academic, 2006); Stephen E. Fowl, ed., *The Theological Interpretation of Scripture: Classic and Contemporary Readings*. Blackwell Readings in Modern Theology (Cambridge: Blackwell, 1997); Markus Bockmuehl, *Seeing the Word: Refocusing New Testament Study*. Studies in Theological Interpretation (Grand Rapids: Baker, 2007); Joel B. Green, *Seized by Truth: Reading the Bible as Scripture* (Nashville: Abingdon, 2007); Ellen F. Davis and Richard B. Hays, eds., *The Art of Reading Scripture* (Grand Rapids: Eerdmans, 2003); D. Christopher Spinks, *The Bible and the Crisis of Meaning: Debates on the Theological Interpretation of Scripture*. T & T Clark Theology (London and New York: T & T Clark, 2007). Moreover, two study groups dedicated to TIS currently meet at the Society of Biblical Literature, and two series of biblical commentaries take a theological approach to the interpretation of Scripture: Brazos Theological Commentary on the Bible (Grand Rapids: Brazos) and The Two Horizons Commentary series (Grand Rapids: Eerdmans). Theological interpretation of Scripture was the topic of an entire volume of the *International Journal of Systematic Theology*, 12, no. 2 (April, 2010). For further discussion see Gregg R. Allison, "Theological Interpretation of Scripture: An Introduction and Preliminary Evaluation," *Southern Baptist Theological Journal* 14/2 (Summer 2010): 28–36.

Beyond addressing these individual issues related to the interpretation of Scripture, evangelicals made important strides in formulating a comprehensive approach to biblical interpretation. Examples included Grant Osborne's *The Hermeneutical Spiral*[126] and the multiauthored *Introduction to Biblical Interpretation*.[127] Evangelical efforts toward a comprehensive hermeneutical approach to Scripture were quite impressive.

One of the most recent developments in comprehensive evangelical biblical interpretation was the "redemptive-movement hermeneutic" offered by William Webb.[128] He called for evangelicals to move beyond what Scripture teaches and develop an ultimate ethic for the contemporary culture. Wayne Grudem argued that "Webb's trajectory hermeneutic nullifies in principle the moral authority of the entire New Testament ... creates an overly complex system of interpretation ... [and] creates a system that is overly liable to subjective influence and therefore is indeterminate and will lead to significant misuse."[129] Indeed, Grudem concluded that Webb's hermeneutical process was "entirely foreign to the way in which God intended the Bible to be read, understood, believed, and obeyed."[130] Clearly, the interpretation of Scripture, always of importance in the church and a matter of debate, continues to be an essential focus among Christians today.

---

126. Grant R. Osborne, *The Hermeneutical Spiral: A Comprehensive Introduction to Biblical Interpretation* (Downers Grove, Ill.: InterVarsity, 1991), 412.

127. William W. Klein, Craig C. Blomberg, and Robert L. Hubbard Jr., *Introduction to Biblical Interpretation* (Dallas: Word, 1993), 114.

128. William J. Webb, *Slaves, Women and Homosexuals: Exploring the Hermeneutics of Cultural Analysis* (Downers Grove, Ill.: InterVarsity, 2001).

129. Wayne Grudem, "Should We Move beyond the New Testament to a Better Ethic? An Analysis of William J. Webb, *Slaves, Women and Homosexuals: Exploring the Hermeneutics of Cultural Analysis,*" *JETS* 47, no. 2 (June 2004): 301, 318, 321.

130. Ibid., 346. For a response, see William J. Webb, "A Redemptive-Movement Hermeneutic: Encouraging Dialogue among Four Evangelical Views," *JETS* 48, no. 2 (June 2005): 331–49.

Part 2

THE DOCTRINE OF GOD

Chapter 9

THE EXISTENCE AND KNOWABILITY OF GOD

How has the church demonstrated the existence of God? How has it viewed the possibility of knowing God?

STATEMENT OF BELIEF

The church has historically believed in God's existence and that his existence can be demonstrated, perhaps even proven. Several lines of support for the existence of God have been put forward and generally are divided into two categories: general revelation and special revelation. General revelation is evidence available to all persons at all times and in all places, whereas special revelation is evidence available to some people at some times and in some places.

General revelation includes the innate sense of God that people possess, the revelation of God in the creation, the revelation of God through his providential care for all people, and the human conscience. Special revelation includes God's mighty works in history (like the Passover and exodus from Egypt), dreams and visions, the incarnation, and Scripture. In addition to these, the church has developed several "proofs" for the existence of God, which include the ontological, cosmological, teleological, and moral arguments. Still others in the church have held that God's existence cannot be demonstrated nor proven but must instead be accepted by faith or taken as a basic belief that needs no supporting evidence. While all Christians agree that God exists, they demonstrate or believe in his existence in many different ways.

Historically, the church has not only believed in the existence of God, but also that God can be known. This knowledge is not and cannot be exhaustive, for God is incomprehensible; thus, human beings can never know all there is to know about God or about any particular aspect of God. But God is knowable to the degree and in the way that is sufficient for human beings to have a personal relationship with him during their earthly lives. Indeed, one characteristic that distinguishes believers from unbelievers is that Christians know God relationally and non-Christians do not.[1]

---

1. My thanks to Woosup Kim for his help on this chapter.

THE EXISTENCE AND KNOWABILITY
OF GOD IN THE EARLY CHURCH

To say that Jesus and the apostles held that God exists and believed that he could be known states a very obvious fact. The reality of God was such a given fact that at no time in his ministry did Jesus pause to prove God's existence. On the contrary, he emphasized that the true knowledge of God is revealed through the Son, Jesus Christ himself (Matt. 11:27; John 17:3). In addition to pointing people to the Son of God, the apostles insisted that God has provided witnesses to his reality so that everyone everywhere and at all times can know that he exists. Specifically, these witnesses are the creation (Rom. 1:18–20), the moral consciousness of human beings (Rom. 2:12–16), God's providence in caring for the needs of people everywhere (Acts 14:17), and an innate sense of deity (Acts 17:22–31). This was the apostolic teaching as set forth in the New Testament.

The early church continued to assert the existence and knowability of God. Affirming both general and special revelation, Origen underscored that some knowledge of God can be "gained by means of the visible creation and the natural feelings of the human mind; and it is possible, moreover, for such knowledge to be confirmed from the sacred Scriptures."[2] Origin further explained that human understanding "knows the Father of the world from the beauty of his works and the comeliness of his creatures."[3] Making specific reference to the creation, Aristides "perceived that the world and all that is in it are moved by the power of another; and I understood that he who moves them is God, who is hidden in them, and veiled by them. And it is manifest that that which causes motion is more powerful than which is moved."[4] In this approach, Aristides echoed Aristotle's theory of motion: Whatever moves has been set in motion by something else. Thus, for Aristides, the observation of movement in the universe leads to the acknowledgment that a powerful Mover—that is, God—is the one responsible for such motion. Origen lamented the fact that, despite such convincing evidence of the existence of God in creation, many educated and sophisticated people misread the evidence and draw the wrong conclusion: They say that "its nature and power were the result of chance!" They imagine that "so great a work as the universe could exist without an architect or overseer."[5]

Others emphasized God's revelation in providence. Theophilus used the analogy of a ship being steered by its captain to explain that the providential work of God should lead people to "perceive that God is the pilot of the whole universe, although he is not visible to the eyes of the flesh."[6] For Theophilus, God's care for the world is evident in many ways: "the timely rotation of the seasons, and the changes of temperature; the regular orbit of the stars; the well-ordered course of days and nights, months and years; and the providence with which God provides nourishment for all creation."[7] Lactantius reasoned

---

2. Origen, *On First Principles*, 1.3.1, in *ANF*, 4:252.
3. Ibid., 1.1.6, in *ANF*, 4:243.
4. Aristides, *The Apology of Aristides*, 1, in *ANF*, 10:263.
5. Origen, *On First Principles*, 2.1.4, in *ANF*, 4:269.
6. Theophilus, *To Autolycus*, 1.5, in *ANF*, 2:90.

7. Ibid., 1.6, in *ANF*, 2:90. The text has been rendered clearer. For similar approaches, see Minucius Felix, *The Octavius*, 17, in *ANF*, 4:182; Athanasius, *Against the Heathen*, 3.35–36, in *NPNF*[2], 4:22–23.

as all Christians would: "If nothing can be done or produced without design, it is plain that there is a divine providence, to which the term 'design' particularly belongs."[8]

Still others urged that God has instilled an innate sense of himself within people's hearts; this too directs people to acknowledge God's existence. As Arnobius noted: "Is there any human being who has not entered on the first day of his life with an idea of that great God? In whom has it not been implanted by nature? On whom has it not been impressed, yes, stamped almost in his mother's womb? In whom is there not a natural instinct that he is King and Lord, the ruler of all things that exist?"[9] Tertullian was of the opinion that this innate sense within human hearts was a stronger witness to God's existence than even the testimony of creation.[10]

Yet Tertullian emphasized a better testimony to the existence of God—Scripture: "So that we might obtain an ampler and more authoritative knowledge at once of himself and of his plans and will, God has added a written revelation. This revelation is on behalf of everyone whose heart is set on seeking God, that seeking they may find, and finding they may believe, and believing they may obey."[11] Scripture as the written Word of God provides a clearer, fuller, and more commanding revelation of God's existence.

At the same time that the early church pointed to divine revelation to provide human beings with knowledge of God, it also emphasized the incomprehensibility of God. By this, it did not mean that God could not be known at all, but that God could never be exhaustively known. As Aristides explained: "If I would search out this mover of all things, to understand what is his nature, it seems to me that he is indeed unsearchable in his nature. And if I would study the stability of his providence, so as to grasp it fully—this is vain effort for me."[12] John Chrysostom—speaking of God as inexpressible, incomprehensible, invisible, and unknowable—underscored the fact that only God possesses exhaustive knowledge of himself.[13]

The reason for this limitation on the human knowledge of God is the infinite difference between God and human beings. As Lactantius affirmed: "The truth, that is the secret of the most high God, who created all things, cannot be attained by our own ability and perceptions. There would be no difference between God and human beings, if human thought could reach to the counsels and plans of that eternal majesty."[14] On the one hand, God's infinite nature makes full knowledge of him impossible, as Cyprian noted: "He cannot be seen, for he is too bright for vision. He cannot be comprehended, for he is too pure for our discernment. He cannot be measured, for he is too great for our perception. Therefore, we are only rightly measuring him when we say that he is inconceivable."[15] On the other hand, the fact that human beings are finite means that God "is beyond the power of human nature to take in [comprehend]."[16] Even the knowledge

---

8. Lactantius, *The Divine Institutes*, 2.12, in *ANF*, 7:61. The text has been rendered clearer.

9. Arnobius, *Against the Heathen*, 33, in *ANF*, 6:421.

10. Tertullian, *Apology*, 17, in *ANF*, 3:32.

11. Ibid., 18, in *ANF*, 3:32.

12. Aristides, *The Apology of Aristides*, 1, in *ANF*, 10:263. The text has been rendered clearer.

13. John Chrysostom, *On the Incomprehensibility of God*, 3,

cited in Alister McGrath, *Christian Spirituality: An Introduction* (Malden, Mass.: Blackwell, 1999), 118.

14. Lactantius, *The Divine Institutes*, preface, in *ANF*, 7:9.

15. Cyprian, *Treatise 6*, 9, in *ANF*, 5:467. The text has been rendered clearer.

16. Origen, *Commentary on the Gospel of John*, 2.23, in *ANF*, 10:339.

available to human beings pales in comparison with who and what God actually is, as Origen noted: "We must of necessity believe that he is by many degrees far better than what we perceive him to be."[17] Thus, as Lactantius pointed out, though human beings can know something about him, God is "incomprehensible and unspeakable, and fully known to no [one] other than himself."[18]

Lactantius's statement emphasized another key belief of the early church: Not only is God unknowable; he is inexpressible. Clement of Alexandria observed that both Plato and the apostle Paul indicated "the impossibility of expressing God.... [W]hat is divine is unutterable by human power."[19] An important element in this view is the limitation of human language to express adequately what can be known about God. Try as they might, the words, images, and symbols that are part and parcel of human existence always fall far short of being able to describe adequately who and what God is. Thus, though Arnobius described what God is like, he also recognized the near futility of his attempts to do so. Indeed, much of what he said about God is what God is not: "You are illimitable, unbegotten, immortal, enduring forever, God yourself alone! No bodily shape may represent you, nor any outline delineate you. Your virtues are inexpressible and your greatness is indefinable. You are unrestricted as to location, movement and condition. Nothing can be clearly expressed about you by the meaning of human words."[20]

Picking up on this idea of the inexpressibility of God, Dionysius the Pseudo-Areopagite employed the term *apophatic* (or negative) to describe his new approach to theology.[21] He was concerned to correct some theologians who—in Dionysius's opinion—believed too highly in their ability to use human language, ideas, and symbols to describe the reality of God. For Dionysius, one could not define the reality of God, because "the cause of all things" is beyond definition, "beyond privations, beyond every denial, beyond every assertion."[22] Thus, we cannot truly say "God is this" and "God is not that," for his reality goes far beyond the distinctions we make with our limited human language. Accordingly, Dionysius dismissed the kataphatic approach, which makes positive assertions about the attributes of God, and championed the apophatic approach, by which we "deny all things"[23] about God. This would seem to imply that little, if anything, can be truly and adequately said about God. On the one hand, this was Dionysius's point, who envisioned arriving at the point of "not simply running short of words but actually speechless and unknowing."[24] On the other hand, Dionysius did use his way of negation to express what God is not. This apophatic tradition initiated by Dionysius developed and continued to

17. Origen, *On First Principles*, 1, in *ANF*, 4:243.

18. Lactantius, *The Divine Institutes*, 1.8, in *ANF*, 7:18.

19. Clement of Alexandria, *Stromata*, 5.12, in *ANF*, 2:462–63.

20. Arnobius, *Against the Heathen*, 31, in *ANF*, 6:421. The text has been rendered clearer.

21. He is named the "Pseudo-Areopagite" to emphasize the fact that he was not the person—"Dionysius, a member of the Areopagus" (the council in Athens)—who is mentioned in Acts 17:34. Throughout most of the Middle Ages, the author was identified with this biblical character, thereby giving his writings significant authority. It was later discovered that his writings date from sometime in the sixth century; thus, he could not have been one of Paul's converts. His apophatic tradition stood in contrast to the *kataphatic* (or positive) tradition based on divine revelation that affirmed certain attributes of God.

22. Dionysius the Pseudo-Areopagite, *The Mystical Theology*, 1, in *Pseudo-Dionysius: The Complete Works*, trans. Colm Luibheid and Paul Rorem (New York: Paulist, 1987), 136.

23. Ibid., 2, in Luibheid and Rorem, *Pseudo-Dionysius*, 138.

24. Ibid., 3, in Luibheid and Rorem, *Pseudo-Dionysius*, 139.

make a contribution to the church's doctrine of the knowability and incomprehensibility of God. It stood as a reminder that no one can know God exhaustively, and that language, images, and symbols about him — even when taken from the Bible — have severe limitations in adequately describing or defining God.

Dionysius's Apophatic Expression of God

It is not soul or mind, nor does it possess imagination, conviction, speech, or understanding. Nor is it speech per se, understanding per se. It cannot be spoken of and it cannot be grasped by understanding. It is not number or order, greatness or smallness, equality or inequality, similarity or dissimilarity. It is not immovable, moving, or at rest. It has no power, it is not power, nor is it light. It does not live nor is it life. It is not a substance, nor is it eternity or time. It cannot be grasped by the understanding since it is neither knowledge nor truth. It is neither one nor oneness, divinity nor goodness. Nor is it a spirit, in the sense in which we understand that term.... There is no speaking of it, nor name nor knowledge of it. Darkness and light, error and truth — it is none of these. It is beyond assertion and denial.*

*Dionysius the Pseudo-Areopagite, *The Mystical Theology*, 5, in *Pseudo-Dionysius: The Complete Works*, 141.

More typical of the early church's view was Augustine's contribution to the matter. Citing Romans 1:18–23, Augustine insisted that all people know of God's existence through what exists in the created world.[25] But far more important than this is knowledge of God that comes through understanding "what true love is."[26] For Augustine, God has left a trace of himself — indeed, his triune nature — in humanity, which is created in his image. This trace can be discovered by contemplating the self when it loves someone: "When I, who make this inquiry, love anything, there are three things concerned — I myself, the one whom I love, and love itself. For I do not love love; rather, I love a lover; for there is no love where nothing is loved. Therefore there are three things — he who loves, and that which is loved, and love."[27] This analogy of the Trinity in humanity, the image of God, became for Augustine a clear proof not only of God's existence, but the reality of the Trinity. To this Augustine added other analogies, like the trinity of the mind: memory, understanding, and love.[28] In other words, God can be known by reflection on the traces of the Trinity in human beings.

Augustine also presented an interesting argument against those who held to the inexpressibility of God. Although recognizing the inadequacy of human language to speak of God in a worthy manner, he nonetheless distanced himself from those who maintained that nothing could be said of God. Augustine argued that to say that God is unspeakable

---

25. Augustine, *On the Spirit and the Letter*, 19, in *NPNF*[1], 5:91.

26. Augustine, *On the Trinity*, 8.7.10, in *NPNF*[1], 3:122.

27. Ibid., 9.2.2, in *NPNF*[1], 3:126. The text has been rendered clearer.

28. Ibid., 14.12.15, in *NPNF*[1], 3:191.

is to speak about him, plunging one into a contradiction, "because if the unspeakable is what cannot be spoken of, it is not unspeakable if it can be called unspeakable."[29]

THE EXISTENCE AND KNOWABILITY OF GOD IN THE MIDDLE AGES

The medieval church continued to underscore the availability of knowledge of the existence of God through the created order. For example, Peter of Poitiers, commenting on Romans 1:20, explained: "When man sees that this machine of the world, so great and spacious, could not have been made by some other creature, he understands that it was Another who produced this beautiful and spacious work; thus, with the guidance of reason, he comprehends God very well and very certainly."[30] But the church of the Middle Ages did not just mimic the findings of earlier times. Anselm and Thomas Aquinas offered formal proofs of God's existence from reason. These new initiatives made important contributions to the discussion of the knowability and existence of God.

Anselm developed the earliest form of the ontological argument in his *Proslogion*. An ontological argument is an *a priori* (to be prior to) argument, meaning that it is prior to human experience. Thus, an ontological argument focuses on thinking about the concept of God without making appeal to experience. According to Anselm's version, reflection on the idea of God leads to the conclusion that God must exist.

Anselm's Ontological Argument

1. God is *that being than which nothing greater can be conceived*.
2. It is one thing for an object to exist in the mind, and another thing to understand that an object actually exists. Thus, when a painter plans beforehand what he is going to execute, he has [the picture] in his mind, but he does not yet think that it actually exists because he has not yet executed it. However, when he has actually painted it, then he both has it in his mind and understands that it actually exists because he has now made it.
3. [It is greater for an object to exist both in the mind and in reality than for it to exist in the mind only.]
4. Surely *that being than which nothing greater can be conceived* cannot exist in the mind only. For if it exists solely in the mind, it can be thought to exist in reality also, which is greater.
5. If then *that being than which nothing greater can be conceived* exists in the mind alone, this same being than which nothing greater can be conceived is that being than which nothing greater can be conceived. But this is obviously impossible.

---

29. Augustine, *On Christian Doctrine*, 1.6.6, in *NPNF*[1], 2:524.

30. Peter of Poitiers, *Sentences* 1.1, in Pelikan, 3:288.

6. Therefore there is absolutely no doubt that *some being than which nothing greater can be conceived* exists both in the mind and in reality.*

*Anselm, *Proslogion*, 2, in *Anselm*, 87–88. I have made one change from the original text, both to simplify and to reflect the more common parlance with which Anselm's argument is presented: "something-than-which-nothing-greater-can-be-thought" has been rendered *that being than which nothing greater can be conceived*. I have also inserted step 3, which finds expression in the next section (3) of *Proslogion*. In so doing, I make explicit a key assumption in Anselm's argument.

In step 1, Anselm defined God: He is *that being than which nothing greater can be conceived*. In step 2, he expressed a key assumption: existence is an attribute. Just as love, truthfulness, justice, wisdom, and grace are attributes, so is existence. Step 3 articulated another assumption, that any object that exists both in the mind and in reality is greater than that object if it would exist in the mind only. Step 4 applied this assumption to the argument for God's existence: A being that is loving, truthful, just, wise, and gracious, and that exists in reality, is greater than a being that is loving, truthful, just, wise, and gracious, but exists in the mind only. In step 5, Anselm pointed out the absurd idea that *that being than which nothing greater can be conceived* exists in the mind only: A greater being—one that exists both in the mind and in reality—could be conceived. But the being that exists in the mind only has already been defined as *that being than which nothing greater can be conceived*. The contradiction is obvious. The conclusion is reached in step 6. The existence—both in the mind and in reality—of *that being than which nothing greater can be conceived* is certain. Thus, the existence of God was proven.

Thomas Aquinas offered two other kinds of arguments: the cosmological and teleological arguments. In contrast with Anselm's ontological argument, which is an *a priori* approach, both the cosmological and teleological arguments are *a posteriori* (to be after) demonstrations of God's existence. This means they are arguments that are based on some experience. In the case of cosmological arguments, the experience of the *cosmos*, or world, is the focus of attention. Thus, the argument flows from the experience of the world to the conclusion that God exists. In the case of teleological arguments, the experience of *telos*, or design or order in the world, is the focal point. Thus, the argument moves from the experience of purpose and design in the world to the conclusion that God exists. Specifically, "the existence of God can be proved in five ways."[31] Each of these arguments, in which Aquinas borrowed heavily from Aristotle's philosophy, makes an appeal to human reason.[32] And through the five ways, "human understanding is led to some knowledge of God, namely, of his existence and of other attributes that must necessarily be attributed to the First Cause."[33]

Aquinas's First Way is an argument from motion. It is based on Aristotle's distinction between a thing's *actuality* and its *potentiality*, with *motion* being the change between the two states. For example, the nut lying under the tree in my backyard is *in actuality* an

31. Thomas Aquinas, *Summa Theologica*, pt. 1, q. 2, art. 3.

32. Thomas Aquinas, *Summa Contra Gentiles*, 1.3.

33. Ibid., 1.3. See further *Summa Theologica*, pt. 1, q. 12, art. 12.

acorn, and it is *in potentiality* an oak tree. For the acorn to become an oak tree, something must set it in *motion*, because no potentiality becomes an actuality unless it is moved by something other than itself. Once it has become in actuality an oak tree, it is in potentiality lumber for some new oak cabinets. Again, however, for this potentiality to become an actuality, something most set it in motion, because no potentiality becomes an actuality unless it is moved by something other than itself. This idea of motion set forth by Aristotle was transformed into Aquinas's First Way: The fact that some things in the world are in motion — changing from potentiality to actuality — demonstrates that there was a First Mover who, according to Aquinas, is God.

Aquinas's First Way: The Argument from Motion

- It is certain, and evident to our senses, that in this world some things are in motion.
- Now whatever is in motion is put in motion by something else. For motion is nothing other than the change of something from potentiality to actuality. But nothing can be changed from potentiality to actuality except by something in a state of actuality.
- Now it is not possible that the same thing should be at once in actuality and potentiality in the same respect, but only in different respects. It is therefore impossible that in the same respect and in the same way a thing should be both mover and moved, that is, that it should move itself.
- Therefore, whatever is moved must be moved by something else. If that by which it is moved is itself moved, then this also must be moved by something else, and that in turn by something else again.
- But this cannot go on to infinity, because then there would be no first mover, and, consequently, no other mover, seeing that subsequent movers move only because they are moved by the first mover.
- Therefore it is necessary to arrive at a first mover, which is moved by nothing else.
- And this everyone understands to be God.*

*Thomas Aquinas, *Summa Theologica*, pt. 1, q. 2, art. 3. The text has been rendered clearer and divided conveniently into various steps.

Aquinas's Second Way used Aristotle's idea of *efficient cause*, or that which is responsible for bringing something else to be. For example, my parents are the efficient cause of me, my daughter is the efficient cause of her history papers, and my son is the efficient cause of winning the basketball game by sinking a last second shot. This idea of causation set forth by Aristotle was transformed into Aquinas's Second Way: From the fact that there are efficient causes, and the string of efficient causes cannot go on forever but must begin with a first efficient cause, the existence of God is proven.

Aquinas's Second Way: The Argument from Efficient Cause

- In the world of sense we find there are efficient causes.
- There is no case known, nor indeed is it possible, in which a thing is found to be the efficient cause of itself, because in that case it would have to be prior to itself, which is impossible.
- Now, in efficient causes it is not possible to go on to infinity, because in all efficient causes following in order, the first is the cause of the intermediate cause, and the intermediate is the cause of the ultimate cause, whether the intermediate cause is several or one only.
- Now, to take away the cause is to take away the effect. Therefore, if there is no first cause among efficient causes, there will be no ultimate [cause], nor any intermediate cause.
- But if in efficient causes it is possible to go on to infinity, there will be no first efficient cause, neither will there be an ultimate effect, nor any intermediate efficient causes, all of which are plainly false.
- Therefore it is necessary to admit [there is] a first efficient cause.
- To which everyone gives the name of God.*

*Thomas Aquinas, *Summa Theologica*, pt. 1, q. 2, art. 3. The text has been rendered clearer and divided conveniently into various steps.

For his Third Way, Aquinas relied on Aristotle's modes of existence. One mode is *necessary existence*. Something that exists necessarily must exist; its nonexistence is impossible. Another mode is *contingent* or *possible existence*. Something that exists contingently may or may not exist; its existence is only a possibility, and so is its nonexistence. For example, my existence was contingent on my parents. I was only a possibility, dependent on my father and my mother conceiving me. This Aristotelian distinction between modes of existence was transformed into Aquinas's Third Way: Aquinas assumed that, given an infinite number of possibilities in the universe, at one time or another each possibility would be actualized. Because one of these possibilities is that each being having contingent existence does not exist, one possibility is that nothing exists. If at some point nothing exists, then *nothing ever would exist* in the universe, because "nothing comes from nothing." Therefore, if the possibility of nothing at all existing were ever actualized in the universe—and at some point this possibility is actualized—then nothing at all would exist now, which is obviously absurd. Aquinas concluded that something exists whose existence is necessary, and this proves the existence of God.

Aquinas's Third Way: The Argument from Possibility and Necessity

- We find in nature things that are possible to be and not to be, since they are found to be generated and to degenerate. Consequently, they are possible to be and not to be.

- But it is impossible for these always to exist, for that which is possible not to be at some time is not. Therefore, if everything is possible not to be, then at one time there could have been nothing in existence.
- Now if this were true, even now there would be nothing in existence, because that which does not exist only begins to exist by something already existing. Therefore, if at one time nothing was in existence, it would have been impossible for anything to have begun to exist; thus, even now nothing would be in existence—which is absurd.
- Therefore, not all beings are merely possible, but there must exist something the existence of which is necessary.
- But every necessary thing either has its necessity caused by another, or not caused.
- Now it is impossible to go on to infinity in necessary things that have their necessity caused by another, as has been already proved in regard to efficient causes.
- Therefore we must posit the existence of some being having of itself its own necessity, and not receiving it from another. Rather, it causes in others their necessity.
- All people speak of this as God.*

*Thomas Aquinas, *Summa Theologica,* pt. 1, q. 2, art. 3. The text has been rendered clearer and divided conveniently into various steps.

Aquinas's Fourth Way was based on Aristotle's notion of hierarchy of being leading to the idea of perfection. If some things are better, truer, and nobler than other things, then there must be something that is the best, truest, and noblest. And this must be the cause of whatever shares such perfections; indeed, that thing must be perfect itself. This idea of hierarchy of being and perfection, set forth by Aristotle, was transformed into Aquinas's Fourth Way.

Aquinas's Fourth Way: The Argument from Hierarchy

- Among beings there are some more and some less good, true, noble, and the like.
- But "more" and "less" are used to describe different things, according to how they resemble in their different ways something that is the maximum.... So there is something that is truest, something best, and something noblest, and, consequently, something which is uttermost being. For those things that are greatest in truth are greatest in being.
- Now the maximum of any group is the cause of all in that group.
- Therefore, there must also be something which is to all beings the cause of their being, goodness, and every other perfection.

- And this we call God.*

   *Thomas Aquinas, *Summa Theologica*, pt. 1, q. 2, art. 3. The text has been rendered clearer and divided conveniently into various steps.

This Fourth Way completed Aquinas's *cosmological arguments* for the existence of God. All are a posteriori arguments, moving from some experience in the *cosmos*, or world—motion, efficient causes, beings that possess contingent or possible existence, and the hierarchy of being—and concluding with the existence of God.

The Fifth Way was Aquinas's only *teleological argument*, being based on the experience of *telos*—purpose and design—in the universe. At its heart is Aristotle's idea that all things are directed toward their telos, end, or purpose. If one thinks of the animal and plant world, the telos of a tadpole is a frog and the end of an acorn is an oak tree. This Aristotelian idea of teleology was transformed into Aquinas's Fifth Way: From the existence of purpose and design evident in the universe, Aquinas proved the existence of God.

Aquinas's Fifth Way: The Argument from Purposeful Direction and Ordering

- We see that things which lack intelligence, such as natural bodies, act for an end, and this is evident from their acting always, or nearly always, in the same way, so as to obtain the best result.
- Hence it is plain that they achieve their end not by chance, but by design.
- Now, whatever lacks intelligence cannot move toward an end, unless it is directed by some being endowed with knowledge and intelligence. An analogy is an arrow being shot to its target by the archer.
- Therefore some intelligent being exists by whom all natural things are directed to their end.
- And this being we call God.*

   *Thomas Aquinas, *Summa Theologica*, pt. 1, q. 2, art. 3. The text has been rendered clearer and divided conveniently into various steps.

Beyond these proofs for the existence of God, Aquinas developed the idea that human beings can see God through what he called the "beatific vision." He described this vision: "The created intellect cannot see the essence of God, unless God by his grace unites himself to the created intellect, as an object made intelligible to it."[34] Furthermore, Aquinas argued for the possibility of this vision.[35] Of course, the beatific vision is not something attainable through human means; rather, divine grace must function to bring about this reality.[36] As to which of these types of knowledge—knowledge of God by grace,

---

34. Ibid., pt. 1, q. 12, art. 4.
35. Ibid., pt. 1, q. 12, art. 1.
36. Ibid., pt. 1, q. 12, art. 5.

or knowledge by human reason (as demonstrated by his own "five ways")—is better, Aquinas left no room for misunderstanding: "We have a more perfect knowledge of God by grace than by natural reason."[37]

While the efforts of Anselm and Aquinas were contributing several major arguments for the existence of God, others in the Middle Ages continued the early church's habit of emphasizing the incomprehensibility of God. This apophatic tradition continued to underscore the inability of human beings to know God and to express knowledge about God in human language and symbols. Picking up on the writings of Dionysius the Pseudo-Areopagite in the early church, an unknown English writer of the fourteenth century, in a book entitled *The Cloud of Unknowing*, pointed out that the reality of God is hidden from human knowledge and feeling. Indeed, grasping God will never come about through the power of knowledge, but only through the power of love.[38]

Another approach to the knowledge of God was offered by Bonaventure in his writing *The Journey of the Mind to God*. Like Augustine, Bonaventure believed that the triune God has left remnants or traces of himself in the macrocosm of the created order; thus, reflection on the physical universe provides knowledge of God. Better still is contemplation of the revelation of God in the microcosm of the human mind, "where the divine image shines forth. Here the light of the truth, as from a candelabra, will shine upon the face of our mind, in which the image of the most blessed Trinity appears in splendor."[39] Thus, Bonaventure urged: "Enter into yourself. You will be able to see God through yourself as through an image; and this indeed is to see through a mirror in an obscure manner."[40] Through this mystical path of knowing God, people are "ecstatically carried far beyond the intellect" to experience God himself.[41] In the place of cognitive knowledge of God, an experiential embrace of him and by him was substituted, and this introspective method was the preferred path to God.

THE EXISTENCE AND KNOWABILITY OF GOD IN THE REFORMATION AND POST-REFORMATION

Like those before him, Martin Luther insisted that people everywhere can know God by observation of what has been created and is being sustained and directed by him.[42] The problem with this knowledge is that people respond with misguided worship: "Their error is this, that their trust is false and wrong; for it is not placed in the only God, besides whom there is truly no God in heaven or upon earth. Therefore the heathen really make their self-invented notions and dreams of God an idol, and put their trust in that which is altogether nothing."[43] So human observation and reasoning about God can at best know that he exists, but "there is a vast difference between knowing that there is a God and

37. Ibid., pt. 1, q. 12, art. 13.
38. *The Cloud of Unknowing*, trans. James Walsh, Classics of Western Spirituality (New York: HarperCollins, 2004).
39. Bonaventure, *The Journey of the Mind to God*, 3.1.
40. Ibid.
41. Ibid., 1.7.
42. Martin Luther, *Lecture on Romans 11:33–36*, LW, 25:432.
43. Martin Luther, *The Large Catechism*, 3.1, trans. F. Bente and W. H. T. Dan, in *Triglot Concordia: The Symbolical Books of the Evangelical Lutheran Church* (St. Louis: Concordia, 1921), 264.

knowing who or what God is. Nature knows the former — it is inscribed in everybody's heart; the latter is taught only by the Holy Spirit."[44] Accordingly, Luther embraced both a "general knowledge, namely, that God is, that he has created heaven and earth, that he is just, that he punishes the wicked, etc.," and "the particular and the true knowledge" — "what God thinks of us, what he wants to give and to do to deliver us from sin and death and to save us."[45] For Luther, this latter knowledge comes through Scripture.[46] But even the Word of God reveals only a portion of who and what God is. Thus, Luther made a distinction between the hidden God and the revealed God:

> We must discuss God ... preached, revealed, offered to us and worshipped by us, in one way, and God not preached, nor revealed, nor offered to us, nor worshipped by us, in another way. Wherever God hides himself and wills to be unknown to us, there we have no concern. Now, God in his own nature and majesty is to be left alone; in this regard, we have nothing to do with him, nor does he wish us to deal with him. We have to do with him as clothed and displayed in his Word, by which he presents himself to us.[47]

Accordingly, Luther urged that complete and sole attention be given to the Word of God in order to have sure knowledge about God and his will. In conjunction with this, Luther insisted that true knowledge of God can come only through Jesus: "Begin your knowledge and study with Christ, and there let them stay and stick."[48] A key reason for this is that Christ reveals the grace and mercy of God; apart from that, any encounter with God would be disastrous: "God himself is a terrible God if we want to deal with him apart from Christ. He is a God in whom we find no comfort, but only wrath and displeasure."[49]

In the opening pages of the *Institutes of the Christian Religion*, John Calvin set forth his religious epistemology, or theory of how humanity knows God. He began by noting that the knowledge of God and the knowledge that people have of themselves are intimately connected and both direct human attention to God.[50] The first source of knowledge of God is humanity's knowledge of itself: As people consider their very existence and the many gifts — intellectual, social, artistic — they possess, they are inevitably drawn to the conclusion that these blessings have been bestowed on them by a loving, caring creator. Thus, true knowledge of God is available to all people at all times in all places by simple reflection on their wonderful existence and makeup. This is the first aspect of self-knowledge leading to the knowledge of God.

But knowledge of God does not end there. If wonder stirs up the human mind to seek after God, so too does the woe into which human beings have been plunged because of sin: "Our very poverty better discloses the infinitude of benefits reposing in God. The miserable ruin, into which the rebellion of the first man cast us, especially compels us

44. *Exposition of Jonah 1:5*, LW, 19:55.
45. *Explanation of Gal. 4:8–9*, LW, 26:399.
46. *Exposition of John 14:10*, LW, 24:68–69.
47. Martin Luther, *The Bondage of the Will*, 4:10 (684–86), trans. James I. Packer and O. R. Johnston (Old Tappan, N.J.:

Revell, 1957), 169–70.
48. Martin Luther, *WLS*, 2:552.
49. Ibid., 2:554.
50. John Calvin, *Institutes of the Christian Religion*, 1.1.1, LCC, 1:35–36.

to look upward.... Each of us must, then, be so stung by the consciousness of his own unhappiness as to attain at least some knowledge of God."[51] Thus, a second aspect of self-knowledge is the realization of the "miserable ruin" into which people have fallen. As Calvin concluded: "Accordingly, the knowledge of ourselves not only arouses us to seek God, but also, as it were, leads us by the hand to find him."[52]

By the knowledge of God, Calvin intended a personal acquaintance with God the Creator. Far more than mere intellectual recognition that a supreme being exists, this heart knowledge is intended to lead humanity to worship and dependence on God.[53] This is "not that knowledge which, content with empty speculation, merely flits in the brain, but that which will be sound and fruitful if we duly [rightly] perceive it, and if it takes root in the heart."[54] Such sound knowledge of the Creator "ought not only to arouse us to the worship of God but also to awaken and encourage us to the hope of the future life."[55]

Calvin distinguished between two kinds of knowledge: on the one hand, knowledge of God the Creator, and on the other hand, knowledge of God the Redeemer.[56] As for knowledge of God the Creator, self-knowledge is not its only source. A second source is the innate sense of deity within the consciousness of every person: "To prevent anyone from taking refuge in the pretense of ignorance, God himself has implanted in all men a certain understanding of his divine majesty.... [T]herefore, each and every man perceives that there is a God and that he is their Maker."[57] Evidence for this universal, innate, and divinely instilled sense of God is the universal phenomenon of religion: No matter where one might go and observe, people everywhere are engaged in worship. Even if that reverence for a supreme being manifests itself in idolatry, the fact that people acknowledge something greater than themselves confirms the fact of this sense of deity. This innate sense is indelibly written upon human consciousness and provides another source of the knowledge of God the Creator. A third source for the knowledge of God is his revelation in the creation, "in the whole workmanship of the universe. As a consequence, men cannot open their eyes without being compelled to see him.... [T]his skillful ordering of the universe is for us a sort of mirror in which we can contemplate God, who is otherwise invisible."[58] For Calvin it was not only the universe "out there" — the macrocosm — that pointed to God. The universe "within" — the microcosm of the human body — also has telltale signs of God's miraculous work.[59] Thus, his revelation in creation — both the surrounding universe and humanity's own physical existence — testifies to God's existence and deity.

Despite these clear and conclusive testimonies of self-knowledge, the innate sense of deity, and creation, human beings read this data and consistently draw the wrong conclusion. Here Calvin expressed his pessimism toward humanity's ability to gain any benefit from the revelation of the knowledge of God the Creator. However, the fault does not lie with the witness, but with those who refuse to pay attention to the testimony.[60] Calvin

51. Ibid., LCC, 1:36.
52. Ibid., LCC, 1:37.
53. Ibid., 1.2.1, LCC, 1:39–41.
54. Ibid., 1.5.9, LCC, 1:61–62.
55. Ibid., 1.5.10, LCC, 1:62.

56. Ibid., 1.2.1, LCC, 1:40.
57. Ibid., 1.3.1, LCC, 1:43–44.
58. Ibid., 1.5.1, LCC, 1:52 53.
59. Ibid., 1.5.2–3, LCC, 1:53–54.
60. Ibid., 1.5.4, LCC, 1:55.

listed the "madness" into which people fall as they refuse to acknowledge God, who bears witness to himself: Some deny his existence; others attribute his gifts to chance. Some substitute the worship of God with the worship of nature; others consider everything to be the result of evolution. Some are materialists, insisting there is no spiritual reality such as the soul; others are idealists, insisting that a spiritual force having nothing to do with God is the ultimate explanation for all that occurs.[61] Fate, chance, nature, evolution, superstition, empty philosophies — these are the conclusions at which sinful people arrive after looking at the evidence of God all around and within them. The outcome of all of this: humanity is without excuse before God.[62]

With all hope of coming to a right knowledge of God through general revelation removed, humanity is in desperate need of another source of revelation. For Calvin, this fourth source is Scripture:

> It is needful that another and better help be added to direct us aright to the very Creator of the universe. It was not in vain, then, that he added the light of his Word by which to become known unto salvation.... Just as old or bleary-eyed men and those with weak vision, if you thrust before them a most beautiful volume, even if they recognize it to be some sort of writing, yet can scarcely construe two words, but with the aid of spectacles will begin to read distinctly; so Scripture, gathering up the otherwise confused knowledge of God in our minds, having dispersed our dullness, clearly shows us the true God.[63]

The Word of God and the works of God reveal one and the same God. Calvin noted that the list of attributes that one can construct from general revelation is the same list that one can develop from special revelation. The two are not in conflict, even though the latter list is more complete. The difference, however, is that while his works reveal God the Creator, his Word reveals God the Redeemer. Because fallen humanity, due to its own sin, is not benefited by general revelation so as to come to know God the Creator, it needs first to know God the Redeemer in Jesus Christ. Only then can it know God the Creator.[64]

The post-Reformation theologians in both the Lutheran and Reformed traditions continued to affirm traditional church beliefs concerning the existence and knowability of God through general and special revelation.[65] In his masterpiece *Discourses upon the Existence and Attributes of God*, Stephen Charnock maintained, "It is a folly to deny or doubt [the existence] of a sovereign being."[66] He listed numerous reasons, including the universal phenomenon of religion,[67] both the cosmological and teleological arguments

61. Ibid., 1.5.4–5, LCC, 1:55–58; cf. 1.5.11–12, LCC, 1:63–66.

62. Ibid., 1.5.14–15, LCC, 1:68.

63. Ibid., 1.6.1, LCC, 1:69–70.

64. Ibid., 1.6.3, LCC, 1:72–73.

65. E.g., John Andrew Quenstedt, *Theologia Didactico-Polemica sive Systema Theologicum* (Leipzig, 1715), 1.251–68, in Schmid, 105–11; John Gerhard, *Loci Theologici*, 1.96, in

Schmid, 109; Gisbertus Voetius, *Selectarum Disputationum Theologicarum* (Utrecht, 1648–69), 1:167, in Heppe, 47; Amandus Polanus a Polandsdorf, *Syntagma Theologiae Christianae* (Hanover, 1624–25), 2:4, in Heppe, 49–50; *Westminster Confession of Faith*, 1, in Schaff, 3:600–601.

66. Stephen Charnock, *Discourses upon the Existence and Attributes of God* (repr., Grand Rapids: Baker, 1979), 1:29.

67. Ibid.

for God's existence,[68] the constitution of human beings,[69] and "extraordinary occurrences in the world."[70] Charnock also listed the dangers that atheism brings to the world and to atheists themselves, including his conviction that atheism destroys "the foundation of government"[71] and introduces "all evil into the world."[72] Lamenting the increase of atheism in his day, he argued that "it is utterly impossible to demonstrate there is no God."[73] His reasoning included the fact that it is impossible to prove a universal negative: "Can any such person say he has done all that he can to inform himself of the being [existence] of God, or of other things which he denies?"[74] Charnock's wrestling with the problem of atheism was a foretaste of things to come.

THE EXISTENCE AND KNOWABILITY OF GOD IN THE MODERN PERIOD

The modern period witnessed many challenges to the church's traditional belief in God. Yet many Christians continued to affirm God's existence and knowability, even if their arguments and reasons were not of the traditional type. For example, René Descartes (17th cent.), as a precursor to the modern period, offered several arguments for God's existence. In his search for absolute certainty of knowledge, Descartes started by doubting every belief that he held. In this process, he discovered that there was one belief that he could not doubt: his own existence as a thinking being. Thus, Descartes formulated his famous saying, *Cogito, ergo sum* (I think, therefore I am). This was his unshakable starting point for knowledge. As a thinking being, Descartes noted that he had an idea of God in his mind. Pondering the origin of such an idea, he denied that the idea came from himself and concluded that it must come from God; "thus it is absolutely necessary to conclude ... that God exists.... I should not ... have the idea of an infinite substance, seeing that I am a finite being, unless it were given me by some substance in reality infinite."[75] God must exist as the cause for the idea of God in the human mind.

Descartes' second proof of God's existence was based on his understanding that whatever has come into existence and continues to exist does so because God has caused it to come into existence and continues to cause it to exist. He applied this thinking to the fact that he is an existing being who has an idea of God. He dismissed the idea that he could be the cause of himself as a being who has an idea of God.[76] Descartes then concluded that only God could be the cause.[77] In his third argument, Descartes offered an ontological proof for God's existence. Like Anselm's ontological argument, Descartes' proof depended on the notion that existence is a perfection of God, just as his goodness,

---

68. Ibid., 1:42.

69. Ibid., 1:64. Charnock appealed to the existence of the human conscience as a witness to God. He also pointed to the raging sense of dissatisfaction within the human heart—a dissatisfaction that humanity cannot fill on its own—as evidence for God, who alone can satisfy it.

70. Ibid., 1:74.

71. Ibid., 1:77.

72. Ibid., 1:78.

73. Ibid., 1:81.

74. Ibid., 1:83.

75. René Descartes, *Meditations on the First Philosophy*, in John Cottingham, *The Rationalists* (New York: Doubleday, 1990), 137.

76. Ibid., 140.

77. Ibid., 141.

justice, power, and wisdom are perfections.[78] Thus, the idea of God as an infinitely perfect being entails the existence of that infinitely perfect being, for existence is included in those perfections.

William Paley formulated a new teleological argument for the existence of God in his *Natural Theology*. In arguing for the existence of God on the basis of order and design observed in the world, Paley began by imagining that he stumbled across a stone in a field. It would not be wrong, he reasoned, to conclude that the stone had lain there forever. But if the objects were switched—for instance, if he discovered a watch in the field instead of a stone—Paley noted that he could not draw the same conclusion about the watch as he had with the stone, that is, that it had always existed. Accordingly, "the inference ... is inevitable; that the watch must have had a maker; that there must have existed, at some time and at some place or other, an artificer or artificers who formed it for the purpose which we find it actually to answer; who comprehended its construction and designed its use."[79] Paley concluded that the remarkable order and design among living organisms—which are far more complex than any watch—demand acknowledgment of an intelligent Designer, who is God. Similarly, Isaac Newton, the brilliant physicist, also contributed to this discussion. In his work on physics, he attempted to explain where God fits into the creation. Having described the complexity and orderly nature of the solar system, Newton concluded, "This most beautiful system of the sun, planets, and comets could only proceed from the counsel and dominion of an intelligent and powerful Being."[80]

While Descartes, Paley, Newton, and others made important contributions to the long-standing belief in God's existence and knowability, skeptics critiqued the historic arguments and raised serious doubts about this matter. Chief among these were David Hume and Immanuel Kant, who sought to overturn decisively the classic proofs for the existence and knowability of God. Many early modern critics like Hume were strongly influenced by Sextus Empiricus's *Outlines of Skepticism*.[81] Such skepticism infiltrated the church and influenced its perspective on the knowability of God.

David Hume not only attacked the teleological proof, or argument from the order and design in the world.[82] He also marshaled evidence from evil as an argument against God's existence, echoing the classic formulation of the problem of evil by Epicurus:

78. Ibid., 142–43.

79. William Paley, *Natural Theology; or, Evidences of the Existence and Attributes of the Deity, Collected from the Appearances of Nature* (Oxford: Oxford Univ. Press, 2006), 8.

80. Isaac Newton, *Mathematical Principles of Natural Philosophy*, ed. Florian Cajori, ed. and trans. Motte Andrew (Berkeley: Univ. of California Press, 1934 and 1962), 319, in *A Cloud of Witnesses: Readings in the History of Western Christianity*, ed. Joel F. Harrington (Boston and New York: Houghton Mifflin, 2001), 318.

81. Sextus Empiricus lived in the second or third century after Christ. In 1562 his *Outlines of Skepticism* was rediscovered and a Latin translation was made by Henri Étienne. Julia

Annas and Jonathan Barnes, eds., *Sextus Empiricus, Outlines of Skepticism* (Cambridge: Cambridge Univ. Press, 2000), 40–43.

82. He summarized the proof as an argument from experience (we observe that effects have causes) and an argument from analogy. By experience we know that humanly engineered machines—the *effects* that we observe—are the product of great thought and intelligence—the *cause* of those effects. Thus, because the universe resembles a great machine, we conclude—by way of *analogy*—that the designer of the universe must exist and possess great thought and intelligence. Hume criticized a number of the elements in this teleological argument. First, he maintained that because humanly designed machines and the

- Is God willing to prevent evil but not able? Then he is impotent.
- Is he able but not willing? Then he is malevolent.
- Is he both able and willing? Then from where does evil come?[83]

In other words, the dilemma thrust upon the theist by Hume is that one can hold to two of the three affirmations but not to all three. If one acknowledges that evil exists and that God wants to remove it, then one is forced to conclude that God is incapable of removing evil. Thus, God is not all-powerful. If one acknowledges that evil exists and that God is able to do away with it, then one is forced to admit that God himself is evil for not doing anything about it. Thus, God is not good. If one acknowledges that God is both good and all-powerful, then one is forced to come up with some explanation for the presence of evil in the world. Thus, either evil is considered to be good, or one must conclude that God does not exist.

Immanuel Kant also contributed to the demise of the classic proofs for God's existence. He first demonstrated the failure of the ontological argument. In his *Critique of Pure Reason*, Kant argued that existence—which Anselm and Descartes considered to be a predicate (and thus an attribute or perfection of God, like love, truthfulness, justice, wisdom, and grace)—is "evidently not a real predicate; that is, it is not a concept of something which could be added to the concept of a thing." It is merely the exemplification of a thing.[84] Because the ontological argument depends on existence being an attribute, the argument fails. Kant further denied the validity of the cosmological argument, demonstrating that, at some point along the way, the cosmological argument makes an appeal to the ontological argument, which had already shown to be faulty.[85] In a similar

---

world are so different, at best only a weak argument—"which is confessedly liable to error and uncertainty"—from analogy can be made: "The analogy is here [not] entire and perfect. The dissimilarity is so striking, that the utmost you can here pretend is a guess, a conjecture, a presumption concerning a similar cause." Second, Hume noted that whereas we have a great amount of experience observing many cause and effect relationships in the world, we have only one experience of the world. Thus, having only a weak argument from experience, it is not right to conclude something about the cause of the world from the single effect that we observe: "It follows ... that order, arrangement, or the adjustment of final causes is not, in itself, any proof of design." Hume concluded that to draw any conclusions about the cause of the world, we would have to experience the origin of numerous worlds to determine the cause and effect relationship. Third, while admitting that human thought, design, and intelligence are responsible for the engineering of things like houses, ships, furniture, machines, and cities, Hume underscored that such thought "is no more than one of the ... principles of the universe." Hundreds of other foundational principles, or causes, exist. Why, questioned Hume, should we take this one cause, which does indeed explain *some* of the effects we see in the world, and make it the cause of *all* of the effects we see—indeed, of the

world itself? But granting that we take thought as the foundation for the origin of the world, Hume raised another question: "Why select so minute, so weak, so bounded [limited] a principle...? What peculiar privilege has this little agitation of the brain which we call *thought*, that we must thus make it the model of the whole universe?" From these three areas of criticism, Hume concluded that the teleological argument fails. Certainly, there is evidence of order and design in the world. But a weak argument from analogy and a weak argument from experience do not allow us to conclude anything more than that something remotely similar to human thought and intelligence may have caused the world. But the historic argument for God's existence and knowability based on order and design does not prove what people have said it proves. David Hume, *Dialogues Concerning Natural Religion* in *The Empiricists*, (New York: Anchor Books/Doubleday, 1990), 444–49.

83. Ibid., 490. The text has been rendered clearer and divided conveniently into steps.

84. Immanuel Kant, *Critique of Pure Reason*, trans. F. Max Müller (New York: MacMillan, 1896), 483. For scholarly reference: Immanuel Kant, *Critique of Pure Reason*, 2nd ed., trans. J. M. D. Meiklejohn (Knigsberg: Johann Friedrich Hartknock, 1787), 627.

85. Ibid., 486–94. For scholarly reference: 2nd ed., 632–37.

way, he dismissed the teleological argument—he called it the "physico-theological" proof—by showing that it "takes suddenly refuge in the cosmological proof, and as this is only the ontological proof in disguise," it fails for the same reasons the ontological argument fails.[86] Thus, he disposed of all three historic proofs for the existence of God.

Kant himself offered a moral argument for the existence of God in his *Critique of Practical Reason*. He based it on the idea of the *summum bonum*, or highest good, of humanity. As he perceived this through an analysis of the moral law, the highest good is the joining together of moral virtue and happiness. That is, people who conform their will to the moral law will be rewarded with happiness. This expectation does not, and cannot, happen during this earthly existence. If the *summum bonum* cannot take place during this lifetime, then an infinite progress—existence after death—in which the human soul lives on, must be postulated: "This infinite progress is possible only under the presupposition of an infinitely enduring existence and personality of the same rational [human] being; this is called the immortality of the soul. Thus the highest good is practically possible only under the supposition of the immortality of the soul." In addition to existence after death and the immortality of the soul, Kant also believed his argument necessitated the presupposition of the existence of God, because only God is capable of rewarding perfect conformity to the moral law with happiness. Thus, "it must postulate the existence of God as necessarily belonging to the possibility of the highest good."[87]

Ultimately, the philosophy of Kant ended up with a complete denial of any knowledge of God whatsoever. Even his moral argument only led to postulating the existence of God, not to any knowledge of God. This was due to his radical notion that only objects that can be perceived by the senses can be known. All other objects—which Kant called "objects of pure thought," including God, the human soul, and existence after death—can never be known.[88] He saw this as a major step forward for Christianity: "I had to deny *knowledge* in order to make room for *faith*."[89] For Kant, while Christians can never know God and other realities beyond human senses, they still can believe in them. Thus, he initiated the infamous dichotomy between knowledge and faith. The legacy can be observed in the modern world's privileging scientific knowledge over divine revelation and matters of faith, and in the widespread caricature that becoming a Christian involves a leap of faith and eschewing intelligent thinking.

Theologians and philosophers since Kant have been concerned with his banishment of God into a realm beyond the reach of human knowledge. In one sense, much of theology and philosophy following Kant has been a reaction to his views in general and an attempt to "rescue God" from the realm of unknowing in particular. Friedrich Schleiermacher objected to Kant's scheme by locating God within the realm of human experience—indeed, within the human consciousness. According to Schleiermacher, religion is "a feeling of absolute dependence" on the *Geist*, or world spirit that pervades

86. Ibid., 506. For scholarly reference: 2nd ed., 648–58.

87. Immanuel Kant, *Critique of Practical Reason*, 122–24, trans. Lewis White Beck (Chicago: Univ. of Chicago Press, 1949), 226–27.

88. Ibid., 233.

89. Immanuel Kant, "Preface to the Second Edition," xxx, *Critique of Pure Reason*, 2nd ed., trans. Lewis White Beck (Chicago: Univ. of Chicago Press, 1949), 103.

everything. Thus, being in relationship with God comes through intuition; one becomes self-consciously aware of being dependent on this universal being. It is not mediated, or passed on, through the Bible, the church, human morality, or religion, but "it is a universal element of life."[90] Thus, for Schleiermacher, the intuitive feeling of absolute dependence on God, which is a universal experience, provides everyone everywhere with the reality of God. No more proof than this is needed.

Criticizing Schleiermacher as a pantheist—one who believes that God is in everything and everything is God—Karl Barth proposed his neoorthodox response to Kant and Schleiermacher. A key point was the reality of the knowledge of God, which comes from the Word of God, and that Word alone. Specifically, this knowledge is a knowledge of faith and a matter of grace that focuses on Jesus Christ. For Barth, this meant that philosophical proofs for the existence of God and theological systems that seek to establish a foundation for the knowledge of God are off target.[91] Additionally, he rejected the legitimacy of a general revelation of God in creation that is grasped by all people because they are made in the divine image. For Barth, because this knowledge is in distinction from God's own revelation of himself in Jesus Christ, it constitutes a second revelation. In his famous debate with Emil Brunner,[92] Barth angrily critiqued Brunner's view, asserting that it violates the key Protestant principles of *sola Scriptura* (Scripture only) and *sola gratia* (grace only) and is at odds with Paul's statement that the natural man does not and cannot know the things of God (1 Cor. 2:14).[93] Instead, Barth insisted on the knowledge of God coming through one source only: Jesus Christ.

While Barth defended a somewhat traditional view of God's self-disclosure through Jesus Christ, other attacks on the existence and knowability of God surfaced. In the early part of the twentieth century, a movement known as logical positivism, developed by the Vienna Circle, focused on the meaninglessness of any statements about God. Frederick Ferré expressed a key tenet of logical positivism—the *verification principle of meaning*: "The meaning of a sentence is the method of its verification."[94] That is, all statements, to be meaningful, must be verifiable, and they must be verifiable by appeal to empirical tests—tests that necessarily involve one or more of the five human senses. If they cannot be verified by human sense experience—through sight, smell, taste, hearing, or touch—then they cannot be meaningful statements.

Logical positivists applied this verification principle to statements about God, such as "God exists" and "God created the world out of nothing." According to Ferré: "All such claims are logically misguided, according to verificational analysis, since no meaningful statement can in principle be made about 'the supernatural.' Any statement which escapes meaninglessness will be discovered to have as its factual referent only ordinary, natural experiences."[95] Of course, according to logical positivists, there can be no ordinary, natural experience of God; thus, nothing within the human realm of experience

---

90. Friedrich Schleiermacher, *The Christian Faith*, ed. H. R. Mackintosh and J. S. Stewart (Edinburgh: T & T Clark, 1928), sec. 33.

91. *CD*, II/1, 1–68.

92. Karl Barth, "NO!" In *Natural Theology*, trans. John Baillie (London: Geoffrey Bles/Centenary, 1946), 67–128.

93. Ibid., 92.

94. Frederick Ferré, *Language, Logic and God* (New York: Harper & Row, 1961), 12.

95. Ibid., 18.

can either confirm or deny any statements about God. Without the possibility of empirically verifying such theological statements, all of them are meaningless.[96] Thus, whether God exists or not, and whether God created the world out of nothing, the fact remains that all such claims are nonsense.[97]

At the same time as these attacks against the existence and knowability of God were circulating, some Christians continued to support this doctrine in both traditional and new ways. In his highly influential book *Mere Christianity*, C. S. Lewis revived the moral argument for the existence of God.[98] By moving from the fact of human quarrels and the moral law that these presuppose, to the reality of God as the moral Lawgiver whose law people break, Lewis set forth a foundation not only for the existence of God, but for the message that "the Christians are talking about.... They tell you how the demands of this law, which you and I cannot meet, have been met on our behalf, how God himself becomes a man to save man from the disapproval of God."[99]

While Lewis revived the moral argument, Norman Malcolm worked to refresh the ontological argument. He turned to an apparent second form of the argument that Anselm had formulated.[100] According to Malcolm, this second form of Anselm's argument focuses not on *existence* as a perfection of God, but on "*the logical impossibility of non-existence*" as a perfection of God.[101] Employing modal logic (a "mode" is a way that something exists), Malcolm set forth three possible modes of God's existence: (1) God's existence is dependent, or contingent (that is, his existence depends on other things and events); (2) God's existence is impossible (that is, his existence is logically impossible, so God cannot exist); or (3) God's existence is necessary; that is, his existence is logically necessary, so God must exist. Regarding the first mode, Malcolm dismissed the idea that God's existence is contingent, because the term *God* "is incompatible with this meaning that God's existence should *depend* on anything.... God cannot be thought of as being brought into existence by anything or as depending for his continued existence on anything."[102] Thus, Malcolm eliminated contingent existence as a mode of God's existence. This left two modes: impossible or necessary. With regard to the impossible mode of God's existence, Malcolm maintained that the concept of God is not self-contradictory. This left only one mode of God's existence — that of necessary existence — leading to the conclusion "*Necessary existence* is a property of God."[103]

In addition to these revivals of the moral and ontological arguments for God's existence, William Craig reworked the cosmological argument, demonstrating "how reasonable it is to believe that the universe is not eternal but had a beginning and was caused by a personal being; therefore a personal creator of the universe does exist."

---

96. Ibid., 32.

97. Of course, a major criticism of logical positivism is that the verification principle fails to meet its own requirement for verification. No empirical test can be formulated to either verify or falsify the statement "The meaning of a sentence is its method of verification." Thus, it too is meaningless!

98. C. S. Lewis, *Mere Christianity* (New York: Macmillan, 1960), 17–39.

99. Ibid., 39.

100. Norman Malcolm, "Malcolm's Statements of Anselm's Ontological Arguments," in *The Ontological Argument*, ed. Alvin Plantinga (Garden City, N.Y.: Anchor Books/Doubleday, 1965), 141. Malcolm admitted, "There is no evidence that Anselm thought of himself as offering two different proofs."

101. Ibid., 142.

102. Ibid., 143.

103. Ibid., 147.

William Craig's Kalam Cosmological Argument for the Existence of God

The universe had a beginning; two philosophical arguments for this are

1. An actual infinite cannot exist; since a beginningless universe would involve an actually infinite number of past events, the universe must have a beginning.
2. The series of events in time cannot be actually infinite; thus, the universe must have had a beginning.

The universe had a beginning; two scientific confirmations for this are

- The evidence from the expansion of the universe implies that at some point in the past the entire known universe was contracted down to a single point; this event is the "big bang."
- The evidence from the second law of thermodynamics implies that, given enough time, the universe and all its processes will run down and reach heat death. If the universe has existed from eternity, then it should now be in a state of heat death; since this is obviously not the case, the universe must have had a beginning.

Either the universe was caused to exist, or it sprang into existence wholly uncaused out of nothing; the first of these alternatives is eminently more plausible, so the universe was caused to exist.

The cause of the universe is either personal or impersonal; if impersonal, an eternal cause would imply an eternal universe (which has been shown not to be the case from points 1 and 2).

Therefore, the cause of the universe is personal and chose to create a universe in time; this way, the cause could exist changelessly from eternity but choose to create the world in time.

We are justified in calling a personal creator of the universe by the name "God."*

*William Lane Craig, *The Existence of God and the Beginning of the Universe* (San Bernardino, Calif.: Here's Life, 1979). Craig's scholarly discussion of this is found in his book *The Kalam Cosmological Argument* (London: Macmillan, 1979; New York: Barnes & Noble, 1979).

In yet another approach, Alvin Plantinga emphasized that belief in God is a *properly basic belief.* He described a *basic belief* as one that is not accepted as true on the basis of any other beliefs.[104] Plantinga maintained that belief in God is basic, and it is properly basic. Fundamental to a *properly basic belief* in God is that "it is rational to accept it

---

104. Alvin Plantinga, "Reason and Belief in God" in *Faith and Rationality,* ed. Alvin Plantinga and Nicholas Wolterstorff (Notre Dame, Ind.: Univ. of Notre Dame Press, 1983), 46–47.

without accepting it on the basis of any other propositions or beliefs at all."[105] Although some beliefs, like belief in God, are basic, this does not mean that they are groundless: "In each case there is some circumstance or condition that confers justification; there is a circumstance that serves as the ground of justification."[106] Thus, people who believe in God do not do so on the basis of other beliefs, but they are nevertheless justified in believing in God. Such justification lies in the divine revelation in creation, the innate sense of deity, God speaking in Scripture, and so forth.[107] Thus, according to Plantinga, belief in God is properly basic.

Such arguments for the existence of God became particularly important as the third millennium witnessed the onset of a new and virulent form of atheism. Notable scholars offered challenging critiques of theism, among them Richard Dawkins, author of *The God Delusion*;[108] Christopher Hitchens, *God Is Not Great: How Religion Poisons Everything*;[109] and Sam Harris, *Letter to a Christian Nation*.[110] As has been the case throughout the church's history, Christian scholars and apologists have responded with thoughtful rebuttals and well-argued presentations of theism, including Timothy Keller, author of *The Reason for God: Belief in an Age of Skepticism*;[111] David Marshall, *The Truth behind the New Atheism*;[112] and Dinesh D'Souza, *What's So Great about Christianity*.[113]

105. Ibid., 72. For Plantinga, the notion of a properly basic belief in God can trace its origin to Calvin and has been embraced by leading Reformed theologians.

106. Ibid., 79.

107. Ibid., 80.

108. Richard Dawkins, *The God Delusion* (New York: Mariner/Houghton Mifflin, 2008).

109. Christopher Hitchens, *God Is Not Great: How Religion Poisons Everything* (New York: Twelve [Warner], 2007).

110. Sam Harris, *Letter to a Christian Nation* (New York: Knopf, 2006). His first book may also be included in this list: *The End of Faith: Religion, Terror, and the Future of Reason* (New York: Norton, 2004).

111. Timothy Keller, *The Reason for God: Belief in an Age of Skepticism* (New York: Penguin, 2008).

112. David Marshall, *The Truth behind the New Atheism* (Eugene, Ore.: Harvest House, 2007).

113. Dinesh D'Souza, *What's So Great about Christianity* (Washington, D.C.: Regnery, 2007).

10

THE CHARACTER
OF GOD

How has the church come to understand what God is like? How has it defined the various attributes of God?

STATEMENT OF BELIEF

The church has historically sought to understand what God is like by studying and meditating on his attributes. These have included his independence, immutability/ unchangeableness, infinity with respect to time (eternity), infinity with respect to space (omnipresence; God is present everywhere), unity/simplicity, spirituality/invisibility, knowledge (omniscience; God is all-knowing), wisdom, truthfulness (and faithfulness), goodness, love, mercy (grace, patience), holiness, peace (order), righteousness/justice, jealousy, wrath, will, freedom, power (sovereignty, omnipotence; God is all-powerful), perfection, blessedness, beauty, and glory.[1] The early church inherited the concept of the divine attributes from its Jewish roots and expressed them in relation to the teaching of Christ and the apostles. Sophisticated systems for deriving the attributes were developed in the medieval period and beyond. Furthermore, many different ways of classifying the divine attributes arose, one of the most common being the distinction between incommunicable and communicable attributes.

To one degree or another, the church's understanding and discussion of the divine attributes reflected heavily the prevailing philosophies of the day. For example, Aristotle's notion of God as the unmoved mover, and his view that any change indicates a lack of perfection in that evolving being, have resulted in particular views of God's immutability and impassibility—his ability to feel and to experience suffering—that seemed weighted toward philosophical belief at the expense of biblical considerations. In the recent past, theologians have called attention to this fact and have sought to liberate the understanding and discussion of the divine attributes from this close link with Greek philosophy. Of

---

1. This list comes from Wayne Grudem, *Systematic Theology: An Introduction to Biblical Doctrine* (Grand Rapids: Zondervan, 1994, 2000), chaps. 11–13. My thanks to Eric Williamson for his help on this chapter.

course, current philosophies exert their influence on these recent formulations, as seen, for example, in process theology. The church today is not immune to these developments and is giving much attention to reformulating some of the classical ideas of God's attributes. Because these attributes are so numerous, discussion will focus on several particular ones that have come under the greatest scrutiny and provoked significant controversy.

VIEWS OF THE ATTRIBUTES OF GOD IN THE EARLY CHURCH

The early church inherited its concept of God from its Jewish roots. At no point in the New Testament do we find Jesus and the apostles engaging in lengthy descriptions of God or detailed explanations of what he is like. The assumption was that both Jews and Gentiles—at least those who had embraced the Christian faith—were familiar with the attributes of God. On occasion, particular attributes are singled out for attention. Jesus' shocking call to be perfect was based on God's own perfection (Matt. 5:48). In particular, Jesus challenged his followers to "be merciful, just as your Father is merciful" (Luke 6:36). In other interchanges Jesus called attention to the goodness of God (Mark 10:18) and the divine omnipotence (Matt. 19:26). The apostle Paul rehearsed attributes of God, such as wrath (Rom. 1:18), kindness, tolerance, patience (Rom. 2:4), righteousness (Rom 3:21), grace (Rom. 3:23–24), wisdom, knowledge (Rom. 11:33), faithfulness (1 Cor. 1:9), blessedness (1 Tim. 1:11), and self-sufficiency (Acts 17:24–25). James focused on the immutability of God (James 1:17), while the apostle John affirmed divine omniscience (1 John 3:20) and love (1 John 4:8).

The early church developed these ideas about the attributes of God, in most cases in a simple and quite unsystematic way. Aristides described God in terms of his eternity, perfection, self-existence, spiritual nature, omnipresence, omnipotence, and omniscience.[2] Tertullian even offered a "definition" of God, while recognizing the limitations of such an exercise: "So far as a human being can form [write] a definition of God, I adduce [present] one that the conscience of all men will also acknowledge—that God is the great supreme, existing in eternity, unbegotten, unmade, without beginning, without end."[3]

At times, the early church described the various attributes of God. The title "the only unbegotten God" that Justin Martyr[4] gave to the Father was explained by Melito of Sardis: "This being is in no sense made, nor did he ever come into existence; but he has existed from eternity, and will continue to exist for ever and ever."[5] The fact that God is

---

2. "God is not born, not made, an eternal nature without beginning and without end, immortal, perfect, and incomprehensible. Now when I say that he is 'perfect,' this means that there is no defect in him, and he is not in need of anything but all things are in need of him.... He has no name, for everything which has a name is related to created things. He has no form, nor any bodily parts; for whatever possesses these is related to created things. He is neither male nor female. The heavens do not limit him, but the heavens and all things, visible and invisible, receive their limits from him. He has no adversary, for there exists no one who is stronger than he. He does not possess wrath and indignation, for there is nothing which is able to stand against him. There is no ignorance or forgetfulness in his nature, for he is altogether wise and understanding.... He needs nothing from anyone, but all living creatures stand in need of him." Aristides, *The Apology of Aristides*, 1, in *ANF*, 10:263–64. The text has been rendered clearer.

3. Tertullian, *Against Marcion*, 1.3, in *ANF*, 3:273.

4. Justin Martyr, *First Apology*, 14, in *ANF*, 1:167.

5. Melito of Sardis, *Discourse to Antoninus*, in *ANF*, 8:751.

unbegotten was associated with his self-sufficiency, meaning that "service [rendered] to God does not profit him at all, nor has God need of human obedience. But he grants to those who follow and serve him life and incorruption and eternal glory, bestowing benefit upon those who serve [him], because they do serve him, and on his followers, because they do follow him. He does not receive any benefit from them: For he is rich, perfect, and in need of nothing."[6] Such a resourceful God is obviously omnipotent, or all-powerful. Even while affirming that "nothing is impossible for the Omnipotent,"[7] Origen warned not to take the unlimited ability of God too far; otherwise, one could end up affirming absurd things about him: "God can do everything which it is possible for him to do without ceasing to be God, and good, and wise.... [S]o neither is God able to commit wickedness, for the power of doing evil is contrary to his deity and his omnipotence.... Thus, we do not back ourselves into a most absurd corner, saying that with God *all* things are possible."[8]

God is also present everywhere. Even though Scripture speaks of God as dwelling in heaven, several writers offered an important clarification: he is "by no means to be confined in a place; for if he were, then the place containing him would be greater than he; for that which contains is greater than that which is contained. For God is not contained, but is himself the place of all."[9] Clement of Alexandria explained further that God transcends spatial limitations: "God is not in darkness or in place, but above both space and time, and qualities of objects. Therefore neither is he at any time in a [particular] place, either as containing it or as being contained, either by limitation or by section.... And though heaven is called his throne, he is not contained even there."[10] Accordingly, when the presence of God is said to "come" to believers, it does not mean that he moves from one place to another. Neither does God "give [up] his place or vacate his own seat, so that one place should be empty of him, and another which did not formerly contain him be filled."[11]

Because God is everywhere present, he knows everything that occurs: "God is in every country, and in every place, and is never absent, and there is nothing done that he does not know."[12] Indeed, "God knows all things—not those only which [presently] exist, but those also which will exist—and how each thing will be."[13] Tatian even affirmed that God foreknows future contingent events—events that depend on the free will decisions of human beings: "The power of the Word [has] in itself a faculty to foresee future events, not as fated, but as taking place by the choice of free agents."[14]

The early church also believed in the impassibility of God—that God does not experience, and is not affected by, human feelings. Irenaeus complained that false teachers make a mistake on this point: "They endow him [God] with human affections and

---

6. Irenaeus, *Against Heresies*, 4.14.1, in *ANF*, 1:478. The text has been rendered clearer.

7. Origen, *First Principles*, 3.6.5, in *ANF*, 4:346.

8. Origen, *Against Celsus*, 3.70 and 5.23, in *ANF*, 4:492, 553. The text has been rendered clearer.

9. Theophilus, *To Autolycus*, 3, in *ANF*, 2:95.

10. Clement of Alexandria, *Stromata*, 2.2, in *ANF*, 2:348. The text has been rendered clearer. Also, Irenaeus complained about those who imagine God to be like people, who exist in a certain location: "They are ignorant what the expression

means, that heaven is his throne and earth his footstool. For they do not know what God is, but they imagine that he sits the way human beings do, and is contained within bounds, but does not contain." Irenaeus, *Against Heresies*, 4.3.1, in *ANF*, 1:465. The text has been rendered clearer.

11. Origen, *Against Celsus*, 4.5, in *ANF*, 4:499.

12. Melito of Sardis, *Discourse to Antoninus*, in *ANF*, 8:755.

13. Clement of Alexandria, *Stromata*, 6.17, in *ANF*, 2:517.

14. Tatian, *Address to the Greeks*, 7, in *ANF*, 2:67–68. In the context, Tatian explained that God foresaw the fall of humanity.

passions. But if they had known the Scriptures, and had been taught by the truth, they would have known, beyond doubt, that God is not as men are; and that his thoughts are not like the thoughts of men. For the Father of all is at a vast distance from those affections and passions which operate among men."[15] This means, for example, that God does not feel sadness: "We will not serve God as though he stood in need of our service, or as though he would be made unhappy if we ceased to serve him."[16] Indeed, "our salvation is not necessary to him, so that he would gain anything or suffer any loss, if he either made us divine, or allowed us to be annihilated and destroyed by corruption."[17]

The divine impassibility became the basis for the early church's rejection of the heresy of *Patripassianism* (literally, "the Father suffered"), which believed that God the Father was crucified on the cross. Tertullian represented the church's attack against this faulty view that, in order not to appear overtly heretical, cushioned itself by saying the Father was only a cosufferer with the Son: "But how absurd they are even in this foolishness! For what is the meaning of 'fellow-suffering,' but the endurance of suffering along with another. Now if the Father is incapable of suffering, he is incapable of suffering in company with another."[18] Similarly, Arnobius described (his ideal of) the true God: He "should be free from all agitating and disturbing passions; should not burn with anger, should not be excited by any desires.... For it belongs to a mortal race and human weakness to act otherwise."[19] Indeed, for Arnobius, pagan religion is based on the notion that the gods feel emotions, like human beings, and therefore must be appeased.[20] Obviously, if this is pagan religion, Christianity cannot bear any resemblance to it; God must be impassible. Thus, the early church linked the divine impassibility to the incarnation of Jesus Christ: Only in his human nature could the Son of God suffer, for his divine nature, which is impassible, was incapable of suffering.

In an important contribution, Augustine clarified that God's attributes are not characteristics that are added to his essence, nor are they separate parts that, joined together, compose his essence. Rather, each attribute is true of the totality of God's essence; thus, the divine attributes cannot be separated from God's essence. For this reason, discussion of his attributes is somewhat artificial. Nevertheless, Augustine rehearsed the various attributes of God, often using surprising contrasts.[21]

---

15. Irenaeus, *Against Heresies*, 2.13.3, in *ANF*, 1:374.

16. Origen, *Against Celsus*, 8.8, in *ANF*, 4:642.

17. Arnobius, *Against the Heathen*, 64, in *ANF*, 6:458.

18. Tertullian, *Against Praxeas*, 29, in *ANF*, 3:626. *Patripassianism* comes from *pater* (= father) and *passio* (= suffer)—it was the Father who suffered. As Tertullian expressed Praxeas's view: "He asserts that Jesus Christ is God the Father almighty. He contends that the Father was crucified, suffered, and died." Tertullian, *Against All Heresies*, 4.8, in *ANF*, 3:654. Both texts have been rendered clearer. See also Hippolytus, *Against the Heresy of One Noetus*, 1, in *ANF*, 5:223. If the Father and the Son are one and the same, then logic dictates that if Christ suffered, the Father suffered.

19. Arnobius, *Against the Heathen*, 6.2, in *ANF*, 6:507.

20. "We have next to examine the argument coming from the lips of the common people, and find embedded in popular conviction, that sacrifices are offered to the gods of heaven for this purpose, that they may lay aside their anger and passions, and may be restored to a calm and peaceful tranquility, the indignation of their fiery spirits being assuaged." Ibid., 7.5, in *ANF*, 6:519.

21. In a striking passage, Augustine unveiled human sins as cheap imitations of the divine attributes, for in God alone are they perfect and truly expressed. E.g., ambition seeks honor, but God alone is to be honored; philanthropy presents a shadow of generosity, but God is the most generous giver of all; and envy fights for excellence, but nothing is more excellent than God. Augustine, addressing God, admitted that sinful human traits imitate perversely the perfect divine attributes: "The soul commits fornication when it turns away

Augustine on the Attributes of God

Most high, most excellent, most powerful, most all-powerful; most compassionate and most just; most hidden and most near; most beautiful and most strong and stable, yet not contained; unchangeable, yet changing all things; never new, never old; making all things new, yet bringing old age upon the proud ... always working, yet ever at rest; gathering, yet needing nothing; sustaining, pervading, and protecting; creating, nourishing, and developing; seeking, and yet possessing all things. You love but do not burn [with passion]; you are jealous yet free from worry; you repent but have no regrets; you are angry yet peaceful; you change your ways but leave your plans unchanged; you recover what you find, having yet never lost [it in the first place]; you never need anything, but you rejoice in gain; you do not covet, yet you require usury [your stewards to return interest to you]. In order that you may owe, more than enough is given to you; yet who has anything that is not already yours? You pay off debts while owing nothing. And when you forgive debts, you lose nothing.*

*Augustine, *Confessions*, 1.4.4, in *NPNF*[1], 1:46. The text has been rendered clearer.

Augustine also addressed particular attributes of God in some detail. He turned to mathematics to portray the infinite nature of God's knowledge: "The infinity of number, though there is no numbering of infinite numbers, is still not incomprehensible to him whose understanding is infinite. Thus, if everything which is comprehended is defined or made finite by the comprehension of him who knows it, then all infinity is in some inexpressible way made finite to God, for it is comprehensible by his knowledge."[22] In other words, God "comprehends all incomprehensible matters with so incomprehensible a comprehension!"[23] Augustine also addressed the impassibility of God, working hard to affirm certain attributes of God while denying that God suffers any emotion.[24] As many before him, Augustine thought of God as being beyond the realm of passions and feelings: God does not feel anything like human affections.

Addressing the omnipresence of God, Augustine clarified that part of God is not in one place while a different part is in another place: "He is not extended through space by size so that half of him should be in half of the world and half in the other half of it. He is wholly present in the whole of it, as to be wholly in heaven alone and wholly in the earth alone,

---

from you, and seeks apart from you what it cannot find pure and unstained until it returns to you. Thus, everyone pervertedly imitates you who separate themselves far from you and raise themselves up against you. But even by thus imitating you, they acknowledge you to be the Creator of everything." Augustine, *Confessions*, 2.6.13, in *NPNF*[1], 1:58. The text has been rendered clearer.

22. Augustine, *The City of God*, 12.18, in *NPNF*[1], 2:238.
23. Ibid.
24. "We cannot think of patience—or God's jealousy, wrath, and so forth—as it is in us, for it is not that way in God. That is, we cannot feel any of these without disturbance. But far be it from us to imagine that the impassible nature of God is subject to any disturbance! But just as God is jealous without any darkening of spirit, wrathful without any perturbation, merciful without any pain, repentant without any wrong in him to be set right—so God is patient without any passion." Augustine, *On Patience*, 1, in *NPNF*[1], 3:527. The text has been rendered clearer.

and wholly in heaven and earth together; unconfined to any one place, he is in himself everywhere wholly."[25] As for the divine omnipotence, Augustine carefully defined what a person confesses in affirming, "I believe in God the Father almighty": "God is almighty, and yet, though almighty, he cannot die, cannot be deceived, cannot lie; and, as the apostle says, 'cannot deny himself' [2 Tim. 2:13]. How many things that he cannot do, and yet is almighty! Indeed, for this reason, he is almighty because he cannot do these things."[26]

While many in the early church described the attributes of God and discussed them in some detail, others underscored the near futility of such exercises. In their estimation, what *cannot be said* of his characteristics is closer to the truth about God. As a result of this emphasis, an entire tradition — called the *apophatic* approach, or the *via negativa* (negative way) of theology — developed. The story of this development can be found elsewhere.[27]

VIEWS OF THE ATTRIBUTES OF GOD IN THE MIDDLE AGES

The medieval church continued to affirm the traditional attributes of God and developed philosophical and systematic discussions of them. Like those in the early church, Anselm affirmed the impassibility of God. Indeed, he grounded his understanding of the atonement on the divine impassibility: "We say that the Lord Jesus Christ is true God and true man, one person in two natures and two natures in one person. In view of this, when we say that God is suffering some humiliation or weakness, we do not understand this in terms of the exaltedness of his non-suffering [divine] nature, but in terms of the weakness of the human nature that he took upon himself."[28]

Anselm also contributed an important point to the church's belief about God's knowledge of the future. For Anselm, divine foreknowledge and human freedom are compatible; that is, both are true and must be affirmed by the church:

> If something is going to occur freely, God, who foreknows all that shall be, foreknows this very fact. And whatever God foreknows shall necessarily happen in the way in which it is foreknown. So it is necessary that it shall happen freely, and there is therefore no conflict whatsoever between a foreknowledge which entails a necessary occurrence and a free exercise of an uncoerced will. For it is both necessary that God foreknows what shall come to be and that God foreknows that something shall freely come to be.[29]

This divine foreknowledge (of all things that necessarily occur) does not mean that human beings sin or don't sin of necessity (which would remove all freedom and responsibility from people as they sin or don't sin). Anselm corrected this wrong thinking: "You

---

25. Augustine, *Letters*, 187.14, in *Augustine of Hippo: Selected Writings*, ed. Mary T. Clark, Classics of Western Spirituality (Mahwah, N.J.: Paulist, 1984), 409.

26. Augustine, *On the Creed*, 1.2, in *NPNF*[1], 3:369. The text has been rendered clearer.

27. See chap. 9.

28. Anselm, *Why God Became Man*, 1.8, in *Anselm*, 275.

29. Anselm, *The Compatibility of the Foreknowledge, Predestination, and Grace of God with Human Freedom*, 1.1, in *Anselm*, 435–36.

should say: 'God foreknows that I am going freely to sin or not.' From this it follows that I am free to sin or not to sin because God knows that what shall come to pass shall be free. Do you see, then, that it is not impossible for God's foreknowledge (through which he foreknows the future events which are said to happen necessarily) to coexist with freedom of choice (by which much is done freely)?"[30]

Anselm also echoed the early church's idea of divine omnipotence. He questioned God about his inability to do everything: "How are you omnipotent if you cannot do all things? But, how can you do all things if you cannot be corrupted, or tell lies, or make the true into the false (such as to undo what has been done), and many similar things?"[31] Again, Anselm corrected a wrong idea, pointing out that such "power" to do evil is not true power, but impotence instead: "For he who can do these things can do what is not good for himself and what he ought not to do. And the more he can do these things, the more power adversity and perversity have over him and the less he has against them. He, therefore, who can do these things can do them not by power but by impotence."[32] Thus, the divine inability to do absolutely everything—including sin, lie, die, break promises, be thwarted in one's unfailing plans—does not malign the omnipotence of God.

Thomas Aquinas's systematic discussion of the attributes of God exerted a profound impact on the medieval church's understanding of God. To begin with, he emphasized the importance of the *via negativa*, or method of negation: "We must use the method of negative differentiation, particularly in the consideration of the divine substance. For the divine substance, by its immensity, transcends every form that our intellect can realize; and thus we cannot apprehend it by knowing what it is, but we have some sort of knowledge of it by knowing what it is not."[33] By this approach, all attributes that do not belong to God are denied in the search for knowledge about God: "The more we can negatively differentiate it, or the more attributes we can strike off from it in our mind, the more we approach a true knowledge of it."[34]

This approach led Aquinas to affirm the *simplicity* of God: "Now it can be shown how God is not, by denying him whatever is opposed to the idea of him, that is, composition, motion, and the like."[35] This idea meant for Aquinas that God's "nature does not differ from his attributes, nor does his essence differ from his existence. There is no composition of genus and species in him, nor one of subject and accident. Therefore, it is clear that God is in no way composite, but is altogether simple."[36] By saying that God is simple and accordingly does not have accidents, Aquinas denied that God's attributes are accidents such as they are in a human being, i.e., who may be wise and loving, but may be not. Rather, God "has" all of his attributes essentially and necessarily. Furthermore, this divine simplicity affects everything about the way that we ascribe characteristics to God: We may attribute properties to God *analogically*, not *univocally* or *equivocally*: "Univocal terms mean absolutely the same thing, but equivocal terms absolutely different; whereas in analogical terms, a word taken in one sense must be placed in the

30. Ibid., 436.
31. Anselm, *Proslogion*, 7, in *Anselm*, 90.
32. Ibid.
33. Thomas Aquinas, *Summa Contra Gentiles*, 1.14. Cf.

Summa Theologica, pt. 1, q. 2., art. 2.
34. Ibid.
35. *Summa Theologica*, pt. 1, q. 3., prologue.
36. Ibid., pt. 1, q. 3, art. 7.

definition of the same word taken in other senses."[37] Thus, all language about God is analogical language.

Because of this possibility of speaking about God analogically, Aquinas had much to say positively about the attributes of God. Some of the highlights of his theology, which involved a great deal of philosophical reasoning from Aristotle, included the following: God is perfectly *good*: "God is the supreme good.... For good is attributed to God ... inasmuch as all desired perfections flow from him as from the first cause.... Therefore as good is in God as in the first ... cause of all things, it must be in him in a most excellent way; and therefore he is called the supreme good."[38] In addition, God is *omnipresent*, in terms of being present in every place and in all things: "God fills every place; not, indeed, like a body, for a body is said to fill a place inasmuch as it excludes the co-presence of another body; whereas by God being in a place, others are not thereby excluded from it; indeed, by the very fact that he gives being to the things that fill every place, he himself fills every place."[39] Specifically, God is omnipresent by three things: "God is in all things by his power, inasmuch as all things are subject to his power; he is by his presence in all things, as all things are exposed and open to his eyes; he is in all things by his essence, inasmuch as he is present to all as the cause of their being."[40]

God also *knows everything*, which includes knowing himself perfectly and knowing all things. Indeed, God's knowledge is "the cause of all things. For the knowledge of God is to all creatures what the knowledge of the artist is to things made by his art. Now the knowledge of the artist is the cause of the things made by his art from the fact that the artist works by his intellect."[41] This knowledge extends even to things that do not exist,[42] and God has perfect knowledge of future contingent matters—matters that are future from our human point of view and depend on free will decisions and actions of human beings (e.g., what my next book-writing project will be, whether your neighbor will accept Christ when you share the gospel with her, what career change you will make next year, and so forth): "The reason is that his knowledge is measured by eternity ... and eternity, being simultaneously whole, comprises all time.... Hence all things that are in time are present to God from eternity ... because they are eternally present to his vision. Hence it is clear that contingent things are infallibly known by God."[43]

Furthermore, God is *merciful*. By this, Aquinas denied that God feels pity for those in distress; "it is not a property of God to be sorrowful over the misery of others." Still, Aquinas affirmed that God acts in mercy to rescue from this distress.[44] Indeed, God's power is infinite, and as long as the concept is clarified, divine *omnipotence*—"God can do all things"—can be "rightly understood to mean that God can do all things that are possible; and for this reason he is said to be omnipotent.... [Something] cannot come under the divine omnipotence, not because of any defect in the power of God, but because it has not the nature of a feasible or possible thing.... Hence it is better to say that such things cannot be done, than that God cannot do them."[45] Aquinas concluded

37. Ibid., pt. 1, q. 13, art. 10.

38. Ibid., pt. 1, q. 6, art. 2.

39. Ibid., pt. 1, q. 8, art. 2.

40. Ibid., pt. 1, q. 8, art. 3.

41. Ibid., pt. 1, q. 14, art. 8.

42. Ibid., pt. 1, q. 14, art. 9.

43. Ibid., pt. 1, q. 14, art. 13. The text has been rendered clearer.

44. Ibid., pt. 1, q. 21, art. 3.

45. Ibid., pt. 1, q. 25, art. 3.

from all this that God is perfectly blessed: "All of these things belong in a most excellent manner to God, namely, to be perfect.... Thus, God is blessed in the highest degree."[46]

Finally, Aquinas made an important contribution in distinguishing between the divine attributes that have no likeness in human beings and those that do have a likeness.[47] As for this latter category, some divine attributes exhibit some imperfect counterpart in human beings. For example, God is truthful, and people can be truthful; God is merciful, and people can be merciful. For Aquinas (as noted above), the truthfulness and mercy of God, and the truthfulness and mercy of human beings, are not completely different nor completely the same. Rather, they are analogous: "Things said alike of God and of human beings are not said either in quite the same sense, or in a totally different sense, but in an analogous sense."[48]

VIEWS OF THE ATTRIBUTES OF GOD IN THE REFORMATION AND POST-REFORMATION

Unlike many issues debated at the time of the Reformation, the doctrine of God's attributes was not a point of disagreement between Roman Catholicism and Protestantism. In keeping with traditional concepts of the divine characteristics, the *Augsburg Confession* offered a succinct definition of God: "There is one divine essence which is called and is God: eternal, without body, indivisible [without parts], of infinite power, wisdom, [and] goodness."[49] All Christians, whether Protestant or Catholic, could assent to this definition of God.

Searching Scripture for the attributes of God, John Calvin focused on Exodus 34:6–7: "Let us observe that his [God's] eternity and his self-existence are announced by that wonderful name twice repeated. Thereupon his powers are mentioned, by which he is shown to us not as he is in himself, but as he is toward us; so that this recognition of him consists more in living experience than in vain and high-flown speculation."[50] Discussing the Lord's Prayer, Calvin affirmed that the opening line — "Our Father ... in heaven" — does not mean that God is located in one place, but expresses instead the omnipresence of God.[51] Furthermore, that opening line affirms the unchangeableness,

---

46. Ibid., pt. 1, q. 26, art. 1. The text has been rendered clearer.

47. "Because God gives to creatures all their perfections ... he has with all creatures a likeness, and an unlikeness at the same time. For this point of likeness, however, it is more proper to say that the creature is like God than that God is like the creature. For that is said to be like a thing, which possesses its quality or form. Since then that which is found to perfection in God is found in other beings by some manner of imperfect participation, the said point of likeness belongs to God absolutely, but not so to the creature. And thus the creature has what belongs to God, and is rightly said to be like to God: but it cannot be said that God has what belongs to the creature, nor is it fitting to say that God is like the creature; as we do not say that a man is like his picture, and yet his picture

is rightly pronounced to be like him." Aquinas, *Summa Contra Gentiles*, 1.29, *An Annotated Translation*.

48. Aquinas, *Summa Contra Gentiles*, 1.34, *An Annotated Translation*.

49. *Augsburg Confession*, 1, in Schaff, 3:7. This wording was followed by the Anglican Church's *Thirty-nine Articles*: "There is but one living and true God, eternal, without body, parts, or passions; of infinite power, wisdom, and goodness." *Thirty-nine Articles*, 1, in Schaff, 3:487. It must be remembered that Luther's theology was a potent influence on the Reformers working in the Church of England.

50. John Calvin, *Institutes of the Christian Religion*, 1.10.2, LCC, 1:97–98.

51. Ibid., 3.20.40, LCC, 2:902.

sustaining power, and exalted sovereignty of God: "It is as if he had been said to be of infinite greatness or loftiness, of incomprehensible essence, of boundless might, and of eternal immortality. But while we hear this, our thought must be raised higher when God is spoken of, lest we dream up anything earthly or physical about him, lest we measure him by our small measure, or conform his will to our emotions."[52]

Clearly, Calvin was concerned that people not reduce or limit God by their own imagination and desire. Human beings as finite and sinful creatures are far too disposed to, and adept at, remaking God in their image. But God will not and cannot be mocked by those who try to domesticate him by conforming him to their image and whim. Rather, the fullness of God and his glorious attributes breaks out from human molds and demands worship filled with a sense of awe.[53]

As for the troublesome aspects of the divine attributes, Calvin addressed them by some of the traditional means. In dealing with the apparent contradiction between the unchangeableness of God and his repentance, Calvin expressed his preference for biblical statements—for example, Numbers 23:19; 1 Samuel 15:29—that deny change in God and his will.[54] To explain the Bible's description of God as changing his mind, Calvin invoked the necessity for God to accommodate himself to human capacity—"to represent himself to us not as he is in himself, but as he seems to us"[55]—in order to be understood. Thus, Scripture uses *anthropomorphisms*—expressions describing God and his ways in human terms, like "God repents"—to achieve clear communication: "We ought not to understand anything else under the word 'repentance' than change of action.... Therefore, since every change among men is a correction of what displeases them, but that correction arises out of repentance, then by the word 'repentance' is meant the fact that God changes with respect to his actions. Meanwhile, neither God's plan nor his will is reversed, nor his volition altered."[56] Thus, God remains unchangeable as to his being, purpose, and will, but people do see him "repenting"—changing his actions—as circumstances change.

Those who followed Calvin's theology of God continued to set forth the traditional view of the divine attributes. The *Belgic Confession* offered a definition of God: "We all believe with the heart, and confess with the mouth, that there is one only simple and spiritual being, whom we call God; and that he is eternal, incomprehensible, invisible, immutable, infinite, almighty, perfectly wise, just, good, and the overflowing fountain of all good."[57] Similarly, the *Westminster Shorter Catechism* provided a brief description: "God is a Spirit, infinite, eternal, and unchangeable, in his being, wisdom, power, holiness, justice, goodness, and truth."[58] The *Westminster Confession of Faith* expanded on this list:

> There is but one only living and true God, who is infinite in being and perfections, a completely pure spirit, invisible, without body, parts, or passions, immutable, immense, eternal, incomprehensible, almighty, most wise, most holy, most free, most absolute, working all things according to the counsel of

---

52. Ibid., 3.20.40, LCC, 2:903.
53. Ibid., 3.20.41, LCC, 2:903–4.
54. Ibid., 1.17.12, LCC, 1:225–26.
55. Ibid., 1.17.13, LCC, 1:227.

56. Ibid.
57. *Belgic Confession*, 1, in Schaff, 3:383–84.
58. *Westminster Shorter Catechism*, q. 4, in Schaff, 3:676–77.

his own immutable and most righteous will, for his own glory; most loving, gracious, merciful, patient, abundant in goodness and truth, forgiving iniquity, transgression, and sin; the rewarder of those who diligently seek him; and with all, he is wholly just and terrible in his judgments, hating all sin, and who will by no means clear the guilty.[59]

The post-Reformers from both the Lutheran and Calvinist persuasions expanded on the discussion of the divine attributes while also exposing the false beliefs put forward by heretical groups such as the Socinians. A controversy arose concerning God's knowledge of future contingent things—decisions and actions that depend on the free will of human beings. On this issue, the two groups were united in their rejection of the Socinian view, which denied that God could have this kind of knowledge. As Turretin described the Socinian heretics, "They openly withdraw from him [God] the knowledge of future contingencies as not belonging to the class of knowable things, saying either that he does not know them absolutely or only indeterminately and probably."[60] The Socinians held this position because it left the human will free from all causal conditions that could decisively incline it in one direction rather than another. Preservation of this libertarian freedom means that not even God himself—his decree, his call to salvation, the drawing of the Holy Spirit, and so forth—can so influence human decisions and actions that they will always accord with his plan and purpose. Turretin strongly objected to this view. He developed a biblical case (John 21:17; 1 John 3:20) that affirmed the perfect knowledge of God.[61] He also appealed to the many prophecies in Scripture as evidence of God's infallible knowledge of the future.[62]

A key point for Turretin was that God can know contingent decisions and events because his decree has determined what decisions and events will definitely take place. Turretin saw this divine decree as a causal factor that could indeed decisively incline the human will in one direction rather than another. Thus, the divine plan and purpose for all things is determined; and since it is determined, God can know it with perfect certainty.[63] Carefully, Turretin denied that such foreknowledge and predetermination do away with human freedom and responsibility. This is so, because while God's preordained plan comes about necessarily, it comes about without constraint.[64] By such

---

59. *Westminster Confession of Faith*, 2.1, in Schaff, 3:606–7.

60. Francis Turretin, *Institutes of Elenctic Theology*, ed. James T. Dennison Jr., trans. George Musgrave Giger, 3 vols. in 1 (Phillipsburg, N.J.: P & R, 1997), 3rd topic, 12th q., sec. 7, 1:208.

61. Ibid., sec. 11, 1:209.

62. Ibid., sec. 14, 1:209–10. E.g., he referred to Isaiah 46:10 and 41:23 to demonstrate that one mark of the one and only true God, over against false gods, is his perfect knowledge of the future.

63. "Of whatever things there is not a determinate truth, of them there cannot be a certain and infallible knowledge if they are absolutely and in every respect indeterminate. But future contingent things are not such. For if they are indeter-

minate with respect to the second cause [the free will decisions of human beings] and in themselves, they are not so as to the first cause [God] which decreed their future occurrence. If their truth is indeterminate with respect to us (who cannot see in which direction the free second cause [the human will] is about to incline itself), it is not so with respect to God to whom all future things appear as present." Ibid., sec. 19, 1:210–11.

64. "The freedom of the will is indeed overthrown by a physical and coercive necessity, which is at odds with the notion of human freedom, but not by a hypothetical necessity and the infallibility of the event, for the same thing in this respect can be both free and necessary. Thus, although people's actions may be free—because they are done

arguments, Lutheran and Reformed theologians critiqued the Socinian heresy and defended the historical belief of the church.

Luis de Molina, a Roman Catholic, offered a different approach to harmonizing human free will with the doctrines of divine foreknowledge and predestination. He sought to reconcile the two by appealing to a type of divine knowledge that he called *middle* knowledge, because it stands between the *natural* knowledge and the *free* knowledge of God. *Natural* knowledge is the knowledge God possesses of not only all *actual* things—past, present, and future—but all *possible* things as well—what *could* be. Included in this type is knowledge of all *possible future contingent* choices and events—choices and events that involve some act of human will.[65] *Free* knowledge is the knowledge God possesses of all things that he has decreed or ordained will necessarily take place; it is knowledge of what *will* be. Included in this type is knowledge of all *actual future contingent* choices and events—choices and events that involve some act of human will.[66] *Middle* knowledge is the knowledge God possesses of all things that can take place involving an act of human will before God freely chooses to decree something about them. God possesses knowledge of what *would* be if situations and circumstances were different from what they actually are. Included in this type is knowledge of all *conditional future contingent* choices and events—choices and events that involve some act of human will.[67]

For Molina, middle knowledge resolves the apparent tension between human free will and God's foreknowledge and predestination. Indeed, free choice does not stem from divine foreknowledge; rather, "God foreknows it because the being endowed with free choice would freely do that very thing."[68] Neither does free choice stem from divine

---

spontaneously and by a previous decision of the will—they do not cease to be necessary with respect to the divine decree and foreknowledge.... Now the foreknowledge of God implies indeed the infallibility of the future occurrence of the event and the necessity of consequence, and yet does not imply coercion or violence, nor take away from the will its intrinsic liberty." Ibid., sec. 24, 1:211. The text has been rendered clearer. An example may clarify Turretin's important point. Although we human beings might not know whether John and Mary will embrace or refuse salvation because we cannot foresee whether they will say yes or no to Jesus Christ—and from our perspective, their free will could decide either way—God does know it, and he knows it because he has decreed salvation for Mary but not for John. But this does not involve the divine decree in coercion, forcing Mary to say yes rather than no and constraining John to say no rather than yes. That would eliminate all sense of human freedom. But Mary could certainly embrace salvation because God has decreed it, and at the same time say yes to Jesus Christ by a free act of her will. And John could refuse salvation because God has decreed it, and at the same time say no to Jesus Christ by a free act of his will. Mary certainly embraces salvation and John certainly refuses it—that is *necessary* because of the divine decree. And Mary voluntarily says yes to Jesus Christ while John voluntarily says no—that is done *freely*, because Mary and John willingly and

without any constraint make those decisions according to their free will.

65. Luis de Molina, *On Divine Foreknowledge* (pt. 4 of the *Concordia*), disputation 52.9, trans. Alfred J. Freddoso (Ithaca, N.Y., and London: Cornell Univ. Press, 1988), 168. To continue our earlier example, by his natural knowledge God knows that it is possible that Mary will embrace salvation in Christ if she hears the gospel, but that it is possible that she will refuse it. And God knows that it is possible that John will refuse salvation in Christ if he hears the gospel, but that it is possible that he will embrace it.

66. Ibid. To continue with our illustration, by his free knowledge God knows that Mary will actually embrace salvation in Christ when she hears the gospel and that John will actually refuse salvation when he hears the gospel, because God has predestined Mary for her end and John for his end.

67. Ibid. From our example, by his middle knowledge God knows that Mary will embrace salvation on the condition that she hears the gospel and that John will refuse salvation on the condition that he hears the gospel. This is their free choice prior to the divine decree concerning their salvation or damnation, and Mary and John could have chosen other than they chose (and God knows this contrary choice as well).

68. Molina, *On Divine Foreknowledge*, disputation 52.10, 170.

predestination, "from God's willing that the thing in question be done by that being. Rather, it stems from the fact that the being would freely will to do that thing."[69] Still, human free will coheres with divine foreknowledge and predestination.[70]

While agreeing in their affirmation of God's infallible knowledge of future contingent things, Lutheran and Reformed theologians differed on the subject of middle knowledge. On the one hand, Lutheran theologians affirmed the reality of middle knowledge;[71] Reformed theologians, on the other hand, rejected it. Turretin argued against it by relating middle knowledge to the divine decree, emphasizing that middle knowledge concerns "conditional future things by which God knows what human beings or angels will freely do without a special decree that precedes it."[72] He argued that the certainty of divine knowledge can only be grounded on the effective decree of God.[73] For Turretin, this decree logically precedes everything else and establishes the sovereignty of God over everything else. As the sovereign Lord, God predestined everything according to his good pleasure, not because he foreknew people would believe, obey, or do right. Thus, middle knowledge cannot be true: "This middle knowledge takes away the dominion [sovereignty] of God over free acts because according to it the acts of the will are supposed to be antecedent [prior] to the decree and therefore have their future realization not from God, but from it [the will] itself. Indeed God would seem rather to depend on the creature while he could decree or effect nothing," unless the human will makes a decision that God could then see.[74] Turretin's case against middle knowledge stood in contrast with the Lutheran view and marked a significant difference between Reformed and Lutheran positions on the divine attribute of knowledge.

Of course, the attribute of omniscience was only one point of focus, as theologians in the post-Reformed period discussed all the other divine perfections as well. A chief contribution to Protestantism's discussion of God was made by Stephen Charnock in his *Discourses upon the Existence and Attributes of God*. Although he engaged in an extensive discussion of each of the divine attributes, only one is selected here, the holiness of God: "The holiness of God, *negatively*, is a perfect and unpolluted freedom from all evil.... [T]he nature of God is estranged from all shadow of evil, all imaginable disease. *Positively*, it is the rectitude or integrity of the divine nature, or that conformity of it, in affection and action, to the divine will ... whereby he has a delight and complacency in everything agreeable to his will, and a hatred of everything contrary to it."[75] Charnock considered

69. Ibid.

70. "From this it follows with absolute clarity that the knowledge through which God, before he decides to create a being endowed with free choice, foresees what that being would do *on the hypothesis* that it should be placed in a particular order of things—this knowledge depends on the fact that the being would in its freedom do this or that, and not the other way around. On the other hand, the knowledge by which God knows *absolutely, without any hypothesis*, what is *in fact* going to happen because of created free choice is always *free* knowledge in God, and such knowledge depends on the free determination of his will, a determination by which he decides to create such-and-such a faculty of free choice in such-and-such an order of things." Ibid.

71. John Andrew Quenstedt, *Theologia Didactico-Polemica sive Systema Theologicum* (Leipzig, 1715), 1.289, in Schmid, 126–27.

72. Turretin, *Institutes of Elenctic Theology*, 3rd topic, 13th q., sec. 8, 1:214.

73. Ibid., sec. 12, 1:215.

74. Ibid., sec. 13–14, 1:215–16.

75. Stephen Charnock, *Discourses upon the Existence and Attributes of God*, 2 vols. in 1 (repr., Grand Rapids: Baker, 1979), 2:114–15.

holiness to be the supreme attribute of God: "If any, this attribute has an excellency above his other perfections.... As it seems to challenge [claim] an excellency above all his other perfections, so it is the glory of all the rest. As it is the glory of the Godhead, so it is the glory of every perfection in the Godhead.... Should this [attribute] be tarnished, all the rest would lose their honor and their comfortable effectiveness."[76]

VIEWS OF THE ATTRIBUTES OF GOD IN THE MODERN PERIOD

As was generally true of the modern period, critics of Christianity launched many attacks against cardinal doctrines and their traditional formulation. The doctrine of God was no exception to this.

Friedrich Schleiermacher expressed a profound disgust for (his caricature of) the church's historical approaches to listing and defining the attributes of God: "If the list of these attributes is regarded as a complete summary of definitions to be related to God himself, then a complete knowledge of God must be derivable from conceptions, and an explanation in due theoretic form would take the place of that divine ineffability of the divine being."[77] He reformulated the Christian faith in terms of a self-conscious feeling of absolute dependence on God. As could be expected, this notion led to a novel approach to the doctrine of God: "All attributes which we ascribe to God are to be taken as denoting not something special in God, but only something special in the manner in which the feeling of absolute dependence is to be related to him."[78] Thus, Schleiermacher introduced an entirely new approach to the discussion of the attributes of God.

Perhaps the most common practice in modern theology was the elevation of the attribute of love above—and at the expense of—all the other divine attributes. Albrecht Ritschl asserted, "There is no other conception of equal worth beside this which needs to be taken into account."[79] As a consequence for Ritschl, any other attribute—wrath, for example—that seems contrary to the divine love could not be real: "According to the New Testament, God's wrath signifies his determination to destroy those who definitively set themselves against redemption and the final end of the kingdom of God.... From the point of view of theology, therefore, no validity can be assigned to the idea of the wrath of God and his curse upon sinners."[80]

Other theologians, not wanting to dismiss entirely the retributive aspect of God's character, moved to relax the divine justice. Albert Knudson was highly critical of the traditional church's conception of how the love of God and his justice hold together:

> The conviction arose that the divine righteousness and the divine love are logically opposed to each other and that the real genius of Christianity lies in the

---

76. Ibid., 2:112–13. The text has been rendered clearer.

77. Friedrich Schleiermacher, *The Christian Faith*, ed. H. R. Mackintosh and J. S. Stewart (Edinburgh: T & T Clark, 1928), 196. Of course, Schleiermacher failed to note that no theologian or church leader, engaging in a study of God, ever claimed that his presentation was anything even close to being an exhaustive discussion of the divine attributes.

78. Ibid., 194.

79. Albrecht Ritschl, *The Christian Doctrine of Justification and Reconciliation* (Clifton, N.J.: Reference Book Publishers, 1966), 273.

80. Ibid., 323.

way in which this opposition was overcome in the interest of the divine love. Righteousness, it was argued, implies distributive justice, and distributive justice forbids any departure from the strict law of reward and punishment as determined by what one deserves. There can, therefore, be no forgiveness of sins until the demands of the justice have been met. These demands were, however, met by the death of Christ, and thus a new era of divine grace was inaugurated.[81]

Although admitting some truth to this concept, Knudson denied an important aspect of it: "That God is righteous in the sense that he is not indifferent to moral distinctions and does not treat the upright and the wicked alike, and in the further sense that he betrays no favoritism in dealing with men, would be generally accepted as an essential part of Christian teaching. But that his righteousness requires him to mete out rewards and punishments to men in exact proportion to what they deserve is quite another matter."[82] Comparing such an approach to the legalism of the Pharisees, and appealing to the parable of the prodigal son, Knudson argued that Jesus "set forth the highest form of the divine love as that which manifests itself in disregard of the principle of exact distributive justice. Love does not, of course, exclude remuneration and retribution.... But forgiving love cannot be bound by them. It transcends the law of merit and demerit. It bestows favors on men in spite of their demerit."[83] Such forgiveness, grace, and mercy of God can be expressed apart from the sacrificial death of Jesus Christ as a full and exact payment for the sins of people who stand condemned before the perfectly righteous and wrathful God: "No atonement in the ordinary sense of the term is necessary before the forgiving love of God can become operative. This is a point of decisive importance in the Christian conception of the divine character."[84] Thus, the love of God trumps the holiness, righteousness, and wrath of God. This position was far from the traditional doctrines of divine love and divine justice.

Hans Küng was another modern theologian who preempted the righteousness and holiness of God with the divine love. He denied the traditional church doctrine of sacrifice and favored instead a vague notion of the expression of divine love: "The cross is not to be understood as a sacrifice demanded by a cruel God. In the light of Easter it was understood as quite the reverse, as the deepest expression of his love. *Love*, by which God—not so much in an abstract 'nature' as in his activity, his 'style'—can be defined: love not as feeling, but as 'existing for,' 'doing good to' others. A love, that is, which cannot be defined abstractly but only with reference to this Jesus."[85] Thus, by revising the traditional doctrine of the sacrifice of the cross—which historically for the church was the point at which the love, grace, and mercy of God meet the divine holiness, justice, and wrath—modern theologians found it difficult to hold these two aspects of the divine character together. This move resulted in a privileging of the love of God over and above the divine justice.

81. Albert C. Knudson, *The Doctrine of God* (New York: Abingdon, 1930), 342.

82. Ibid., 344. As support, Knudson listed Gen. 2:17; Ex. 34:7; Deut. 27:26; Ezek. 18:4; Rom. 1:32; 2:8; 6:23; 12:19; Gal. 3:10; 2 Thess. 1:8.

83. Ibid., 345.

84. Ibid., 346.

85. Hans Küng, *On Being a Christian*, trans. Edward Quinn (Garden City, N.Y.: Doubleday, 1976), 435.

Echoing a traditional approach to the attributes of God, William G. T. Shedd was typical of those who stood against destructive modern developments in theology. For example, he pointed out a decisive problem for any pantheistic concept of God (the theology that identifies God with everything in the universe):

> The infinite cannot be the perfect if the pantheistic postulate is true. For if the infinite being is passing from lower to higher modes of existence and of consciousness, as finite being is, absolute and immutable perfection cannot be attributed to him. Moreover, since evolution may be from the more perfect to the less perfect, as well as from the less perfect to the more perfect, it follows from the pantheistic theory that the infinite being may tend downward and become evil.[86]

Against those who would make happiness to be the greatest purpose and good of humanity, Shedd reasoned from the attribute of the wisdom of God: "The happiness of the creature cannot be the final end of God's action. There would be no wisdom in this case, because the superior would be subordinated to the inferior. This would be folly, not wisdom. It would be a poor adaptation of means to ends. The end would be made the means, and the means the end. The infinite would exist for the finite." Shedd pointed out that happiness is more a by-product than a purpose or a goal: "Happiness from its very nature cannot be an ultimate end, because to seek it is to fail of getting it: 'He who finds his life will lose it.' To seek holiness as an ultimate end is to attain it. To seek holiness results in happiness, but not vice versa. Happiness is the effect, and holiness is the cause. Hence the command is 'be holy'—not 'be happy.'"[87]

An important development in the doctrine of God was sparked by the process philosophy of Alfred North Whitehead as developed by Charles Hartshorne and others. A motive for the development of process theology was disenchantment with the traditional notion of God—perfect, immutable, static, impassible (unfeeling), removed from the world—as (allegedly) formulated by some classical theologians like Thomas Aquinas. A philosophical influence in this development was existentialism and its emphasis on becoming (a process) rather than being (stability of existence). According to Whitehead's process metaphysic, or philosophy of reality, the basic unity of reality is called an *actual entity* or *actual occasion*. Each actual entity is *dipolar*, consisting of both a physical pole and a mental pole. By means of its *physical pole*, an actual entity *prehends*—grasps, or feels—the physical reality of other actual entities. By means of its *mental pole*, an actual entity prehends eternal objects. Each actual entity prehends many other previous actual entities and unifies these prehensions into itself, while adding some self-creativity.

From his application of process philosophy to God, Whitehead concluded that "the nature of God is dipolar. He has a primordial nature and a consequent nature."[88] In terms of his primordial nature, God "is the unlimited conceptual realization of the absolute

---

86. William G. T. Shedd, *Dogmatic Theology*, 3:5, in *Dogmatic Theology*, ed. Alan W. Gomes, 3rd ed. (Phillipsburg, N.J.: P & R, 2003), 282.

87. Ibid., 288.

88. Alfred North Whitehead, *Process and Reality: An Essay in Cosmology* (New York: Macmillan, 1929), sec. 524.

wealth of potentiality."[89] That is, the primordial nature of God is his abstract, unconditioned, absolute aspect. As for his consequent nature, "He is the presupposed actuality of conceptual operation, in unison of becoming with every other creative act. Thus, by reason of the relativity of all things, there is a reaction of the world on God. The completion of God's nature into a fullness of physical feeling is derived from the objectification of the world in God."[90] That is, the consequent nature of God is his concrete, conditioned, relative aspect that is changed by his relationships with the world.

Developing Whitehead's process proposals, Charles Hartshorne construed God as dipolar with an *abstract essence* (parallel to Whitehead's mental pole) and a *concrete actuality* (parallel to Whitehead's physical pole). According to his abstract nature, God is absolute, immutable, independent, and unsurpassable in perfection. According to his concrete actuality, God is relative, changing, dependent, and always surpassing himself in perfection. In his concrete actuality, God is constantly growing, being responsive to and enriched by his relationships with the world. Hartshorne called his philosophy of the religious idea of God *panentheism* (God in everything).[91] Most evangelicals reacted with alarm to process theology and sought to demonstrate that its intentional distancing of itself from classical theism sowed the seeds of its own destruction.

Karl Barth made further contribution to the development of the doctrine of God. He focused on "the being of God as the one who loves in freedom"[92] and on the idea that God gives himself to human beings: "He does not will to be God for himself nor as God to be alone with himself. He wills as God to be for us and with us who are not God."[93] Barth grounded this divine giving of himself to human beings in God's self-giving, triune nature: "He is Father, Son and Holy Spirit and therefore alive in his unique being with and for and in another.... He does not exist in solitude but in fellowship. Therefore what he seeks and creates between himself and us is in fact nothing else but what he wills and completes and therefore is in himself."[94] The divine loving, then, is "his act as that of the one who loves."[95] This loving is unconditional, "without any reference to an existing aptitude or worthiness on the part of the loved. God's love is not merely conditioned by any reciprocity of love. It is also not conditioned by any worthiness to be loved on the part of the loved, by any existing capacity for union or fellowship on his side."[96] Furthermore, "God loves because he loves; because this act is his being, his essence and his nature."[97] God's love, then, is necessary; yet "for this very reason it is also free from every necessity in respect of its object. God loves us, and loves the world, in accordance with his revelation. But he loves us and the world as he who would still be one who loves without us and without the world; as he, therefore, who needs no other to form the prior ground of his existence as the one who loves and as God."[98]

Focusing on the divine freedom, Barth insisted that God is "unlimited, unrestricted and unconditioned from without. He is the free Creator, the free Reconciler, the free

89. Ibid., sec. 521.

90. Ibid., sec. 523.

91. Charles Hartshorne, *A Natural Theology for Our Time* (LaSalle, Ill.: Open Court, 1967), 25–27.

92. *CD*, II/1, 257.

93. Ibid., 274.

94. Ibid., 275.

95. Ibid.

96. Ibid., 278.

97. Ibid., 279.

98. Ibid., 280.

Redeemer."[99] God is consequently free to reveal himself objectively within the world; that is, he reveals "his *existence*, that is to say his being, independent of our thought about it, preceding and providing the basis for our thought, absolutely objective."[100] For Barth, there are two primary meanings of the divine freedom. The first is God's independence: "Because he is God, as such he already has and is his own being. Therefore this being does not need any origination and constitution."[101] The second meaning is God's freedom from being conditioned by anything outside of himself: "If there is something other, it can exist in its own manner of being only by God and from God. It can exist only in subordination to, and in the service of, God. But God was, is and will be who he is without the being and nature of this other existence having any other possible significance than what God is pleased to assign to it."[102] In this, Barth stood clearly and firmly against process theology, pantheism, panentheism, and any other theology that would limit the freedom of God and make him contingent on the created order.[103]

Moreover, Barth affirmed both the transcendence and immanence of God. As for the divine transcendence, God can "be sufficiently beyond the creature to be its Creator out of nothing and at the same time be free enough partially or completely to transform its being or to take it from it again as first he gave it."[104] But "God can do even more than this," so Barth also affirmed the divine immanence: He can "so indwell the other that, while he is its Creator and the Giver of its life, and while he does not take away this life, he does not withdraw his presence from this creaturely existence which is so different from his own divine life.... He can grant and leave it its own special being distinct from his own, and yet even in this way, and therefore in this its creaturely freedom, sustain, uphold and govern it by his own divine being, thus being its beginning, center and end."[105] Thus, as Barth conceived it, "the being of God as the one who loves in freedom" reaffirmed the historic position of the church—both the divine transcendence and divine immanence—and firmly rejected the modern notions of process theology, pantheism, and panentheism.

One of the newest movements to question the classic notion of God came as a challenge from within the ranks of evangelicals themselves. Known as "open theism," this movement was promoted by evangelicals such as Clark Pinnock, John Sanders, and Gregory Boyd. Although some major tenets of open theism are treated elsewhere, its view of divine omniscience appears here.[106]

John Sanders subscribed to the idea of God's knowledge called *present knowledge* or *presentism*, which "affirms omniscience but denies exhaustive foreknowledge. Although God's knowledge is coextensive with reality in that God knows all that can be known, the future actions of free creatures are not yet reality, and so there is nothing to be known."[107] This limitation does not detract from God's perfection, because these future actions cannot be known. A key belief at the heart of this position is human freedom. According to open theists, humans enjoy the divine gift of libertarian free will, or freedom even

---

99. Ibid., 301.
100. Ibid., 304.
101. Ibid., 306.
102. Ibid., 308.
103. Ibid., 309.

104. Ibid., 313.
105. Ibid., 313–14.
106. See chap. 9.
107. John Sanders, *The God Who Risks: A Theology of Providence* (Downers Grove, Ill.: InterVarsity, 1998), 198–99.

to contradict the will and directing influences of God. Thus, God does not and cannot determine the choices and actions of human beings. Because future human decisions and actions are completely free, God cannot possibly know them. Despite this limitation — not an imperfection, though — God is amazingly resourceful and relational in his future dealings with human beings: "Due to the knowledge of all past and present, as well as God's superior abilities of analysis and inference, God is able to predict with amazing accuracy what he believes will occur."[108]

As far as support for this view that the future is open because of the libertarian free will of human beings, Sanders appealed to four categories of biblical texts: texts that present God as uncertain, as making promises conditioned by human actions, as consulting with human beings about what action he will take, and as responding to human decisions.[109] Gregory Boyd contributed further biblical evidence for open theism: texts that present God as regretting how things turn out, as wondering about the future, as confronting the unexpected, as getting frustrated, as testing human beings to know their character, as speaking in terms of what may or may not be, and the like.[110] Boyd's strongest argument focused on biblical texts that affirm that God changes his mind: "By definition, one cannot change what is permanently fixed. Hence, every time the Bible teaches us that God changes his mind, it is teaching us that God's mind is not permanently fixed.... It means that some of what God knows regarding the future consists of things that *may* go one way or another. He adjusts his plans — changes his mind — depending on what does or does not take place."[111] As for counterevidence in Scripture that God does not change his mind and knows the future exhaustively, Boyd insisted that "the passages that constitute the motif of future openness should be taken just as literally as the passages that constitute the motif of future determinism."[112]

Combining this biblical evidence for the openness of the future with the notion of human libertarian free will, Sanders, Boyd, and other open theists defined divine omniscience as God knowing all that God can know. Because the future decisions and actions of free human beings cannot be known, those items are not part of what God knows; thus, "the future is partly open and partly settled."[113]

Open theism's denial of God's exhaustive foreknowledge and its insistence that the future is partly open was rebuffed by many evangelicals, among whom the most notable was Bruce Ware. He critiqued the biblical support set forth by open theism, emphasizing major problems with both "divine growth-in-knowledge texts and divine repentance texts."[114] As for the first set of texts, Ware agreed that a commendable hermeneutical principle that should generally be followed is to take biblical passages literally. However, he objected that applying that interpretive principle to the divine growth-in-knowledge texts fails miserably.[115] As for the second set of texts, Ware argued these divine repentance

108. Ibid., 199.

109. Ibid., 74. Sanders follows Terence Fretheim, *The Suffering of God: An Old Testament Perspective* (Philadelphia: Fortress, 1984), 45–59.

110. Gregory A. Boyd, *God of the Possible: A Biblical Introduction to the Open View of God* (Grand Rapids: Baker, 2000), 55–71.

111. Ibid., 75.

112. Ibid., 54.

113. Ibid., 86.

114. Bruce A. Ware, *God's Lesser Glory: The Diminished God of Open Theism* (Wheaton: Crossway, 2000), 65.

115. Ibid., 67–86. Understanding the texts literally results in God either knowing what he already knows or still not knowing future free will decisions of human beings — the very thing open theists insist God cannot know.

texts should be understood anthropomorphically: "A given ascription to God may rightly be understood as anthropomorphic when Scripture clearly presents God as transcending the very human or finite features it elsewhere attributes to him."[116] He pointed to two texts (Num. 23:19; 1 Sam. 15:29) that "describe God as *not* capable of repenting."[117] He concluded, "If these biblical statements represent a broad and comprehensive teaching about God's nature, then we have here a case in which Scripture presents God as transcending (i.e., in some sense he does *not* repent because he, as God, transcends human repentance) the very human or finite feature it elsewhere attributes to him (i.e., in some sense he *does* repent)."[118] Thus, when Scripture says that God repents, "it indicates 1) his awareness that the human situation has altered and 2) his desire to act in a way fitting to this changed situation.... [Moreover,] when God is said to repent, it indicates his real experience, in historically unfolding relationships with people, of changed dispositions or emotions in relation to some changed human situation."[119] All of this displays "a very important interpersonal dynamic" between God and his human creatures.[120] Thus, Ware concluded that "neither the divine growth-in-knowledge texts nor the divine repentance texts imply that God has learned something he did not previously know."[121] This argument left open theism with a shaky foundation for its denial of God's exhaustive foreknowledge.

But Ware did more than just critique open theism. He presented scriptural affirmations of exhaustive divine foreknowledge, including the many passages in Isaiah 41–48 that emphasize "God's claim to know and declare the future in purposely *sweeping* and *general* language" and that offer specific predictions that "involve, for their fulfillment, the future free choices and actions of human beings."[122] Specifically, according to Isaiah 41:21–24, "God has chosen to vindicate himself as God by declaring what the future will be, so that when God's predictions come true, people will testify that he is God."[123] From these and many other scriptural affirmations, Ware concluded that "the extensiveness, specificity, and accuracy of God's knowledge of these manifold future actions and events are *fully explicable* in a model that affirms *exhaustive divine foreknowledge*, whereas these examples are fully inexplicable in open theism."[124]

The work of Ware and others was so influential that the Southern Baptist Convention, in its rewrite of the 1963 *Baptist Faith and Message*, changed the wording of its doctrine of God with the addition of one sentence affirming exhaustive divine foreknowledge: "He is all powerful and all knowing; and his perfect knowledge extends to all things, past, present, and future, including the future decisions of his free creatures."[125] In addition, the Evangelical Theological Society dedicated one of its annual meetings to the topic of open theism and conducted an investigation of two of its members, Clark Pinnock and John Sanders, because of their public embrace of open theism.

---

116. Ibid., 86.

117. Ibid.

118. Ibid., 86–87.

119. Ibid., 90–91.

120. Ibid., 92.

121. Ibid., 98.

122. Ibid., 119–20.

123. Ibid., 120 (italics removed).

124. Ibid., 139.

125. *Baptist Faith and Message* (Southern Baptist Convention, 2000), 2. The earlier *BFM* had affirmed the following: "There is one and only one living and true God. He is an intelligent, spiritual, and personal Being, the Creator, Redeemer, Preserver, and Ruler of the universe. God is infinite in holiness and all other perfections. To him we owe the highest love, reverence, and obedience." *Baptist Faith and Message* (1925, 1963), 2, in Lumpkin, 393. The additional affirmation was inserted between the second and third sentences.

Of course, just as the church has never restricted its concern to one or even a few of the attributes of God, the church of the third millennium continues to wrestle not only with divine omniscience, but with all the other attributes as well, including immutability,[126] impassibility,[127] eternity (is God's "eternity timelessness, or is it never-ending existence within time?"[128]), simplicity,[129] and others. At the same time, the attributes of God are not relegated to academic debate but provide great comfort and resources for Christians who worship, pray to, and serve the God who is characterized by all-powerfulness, love, holiness, wrath, jealousy, mercy, and the like. Appropriately, then, J. I. Packer's classical treatment of the divine attributes, *Knowing God*, continues to attract the devotional attention of believers today.[130]

126. Bruce Ware, "An Evangelical Reexamination of the Doctrine of the Immutability of God" (Ph.D. diss., Fuller Theological Seminary, 1984); for a summary, see ibid., "An Evangelical Reformulation of the Doctrine of the Immutability of God," *JETS* 29, no. 4 (December 1986): 431–46.

127. Robert Glenn Lister, "Impassible and Impassioned: Reevaluating the Doctrines of Divine Impassibility and Divine Relationality" (Ph.D. diss., Southern Baptist Theological Seminary, 2007).

128. John S. Feinberg, *No One Like Him: The Doctrine of God*, Foundations of Evangelical Theology, ed. John S. Feinberg (Wheaton: Crossway, 2001), 375. For a discussion of this attribute and the two concepts, see his chapter "God, Time, and Eternity," 375–436.

129. Alvin Plantinga, *Does God Have a Nature?* (Milwaukee, Wis.: Marquette Univ. Press, 1980).

130. J. I. Packer, *Knowing God* (Downers Grove, Ill.: InterVarsity, 1993).

11

GOD IN THREE PERSONS: THE TRINITY

How has the church come to understand that God is three persons yet one God?

STATEMENT OF BELIEF

The church has historically believed that "God eternally exists as three persons, Father, Son, and Holy Spirit, and each person is fully God, and there is one God."[1] This belief about the Trinity has been traditionally regarded as an essential tenet of Christianity for several reasons. "To study the Bible's teaching on the Trinity gives us great insight into the question that is at the center of all of our seeking after God: What is God like in himself? Here we learn that in himself, in his very being, God exists in the persons of the Father, Son, and Holy Spirit, yet he is one God."[2] Moreover, this doctrine distinguishes Christianity from all other religions of the world, including Judaism, Islam, Hinduism, and Buddhism. No other religion comes close to having a belief in a triune God, and some explicitly deny this cardinal truth of Christianity.

The doctrine of the Trinity was hammered out very early in the church's existence in response to a pronounced tension between belief in monotheism (there is only one God) and the New Testament's teaching that Jesus Christ is the Son of God and fully God himself, which the church affirmed. Another piece—the recognition of the deity of the Holy Spirit—came a bit later. As it worked out this doctrine, the church was wracked by dissension and division, but this turmoil gave way to a settled conviction about the triune nature of God by the end of the fourth century. Since then, all three branches of Christendom—Roman Catholic, Orthodox, and Protestant—have agreed on this doctrine. Indeed, a distinguishing characteristic of most sects and cults claiming to be Christian is a heretical belief about this matter.

---

1. Wayne Grudem, *Systematic Theology: An Introduction to Biblical Doctrine* (Grand Rapids: Zondervan, 1994, 2000), 226.
2. Ibid.

Evangelicals share this common Christian heritage. Thus, while tracing the development of the doctrine, this chapter will mark the unity in this belief and contrast it with the various erroneous views that have arisen over the course of the centuries.[3]

THE DOCTRINE OF THE TRINITY IN THE EARLY CHURCH

The early church inherited its strong monotheistic belief from Judaism. The Hebrew Bible (the Christians' Old Testament) affirmed the existence of one and only one God (Deut. 6:4; cf. Isa. 45:5). Jesus and the apostles maintained this monotheistic stance from the very beginning. When asked about the greatest commandment, Jesus replied with an affirmation of Deuteronomy 6:4 (Matt. 22:34–38). The apostle Paul argued against the existence of pagan gods by confessing "there is no God but one" (1 Cor. 8:4). These were strong affirmations of monotheism. At the same time, Jesus Christ claimed that he was the Son of God, and thus fully divine, and taught that the Holy Spirit was fully God as well.[4] The New Testament baptismal formula (Matt. 28:19) and apostolic blessing (2 Cor. 13:14) both placed the Father, Son, and Holy Spirit in coordinate relationship with one another. All this evidence pointed to a unique divine reality that involved all three.

Accordingly, the early church was faced with both belief in monotheism and belief in the deity of the Father, Son, and Holy Spirit—what would later be called Trinitarianism. And the early church affirmed both. Regarding monotheism, Clement of Rome referred to "the name of the true and only God."[5] The first chief tenet of Christianity was the belief that God created the heavens and the earth. Concerning the identity of this Creator, Irenaeus explained: "He is the only God, the only Lord, the only Creator, the only Father, alone containing all things, and himself commanding all things into existence."[6] In deflecting the charge of atheism made against early Christians, Athenagoras clarified that "our doctrine acknowledges one God, the Maker of this universe, who is himself uncreated."[7] The early church affirmed belief in one and only one God.

As for the other reality, the early church developed a "Trinitarian" consciousness, noting the relationships between the Father, the Son, and the Holy Spirit. Following Matthew's gospel, Justin Martyr described a Trinitarian baptismal formula: "In the name of God, the Father and Lord of the universe, and of our Savior Jesus Christ, and of the Holy Spirit, they [new converts] then receive the washing with water."[8] As the doctrine of the Trinity developed, the practice of baptizing in the name of the Father, Son, and Holy Spirit was increasingly understood in the light of this doctrine. Eventually, the

---

3. My thanks to Marc Cortez and Billy Preston for their help on this chapter.

4. For the discussion of the deity of God the Son and God the Holy Spirit, see chaps. 17 and 20.

5. Clement of Rome, *Letter of the Romans to the Corinthians*, 43, in Holmes, 77; *ANF*, 1:17.

6. Irenaeus, *Against Heresies*, 2.1.1, in *ANF*, 1:359. Similarly, the *Shepherd of Hermas* urged: "First of all, believe that God is one, who created all things and set them in order, and made out of what did not exist everything that is, and who contains all things but is himself alone uncontained." *Shepherd of Hermas*, mandate 1.1 (26), in Holmes, 375; *ANF*, 2:20.

7. Athenagoras, *A Plea for the Christians*, 4, in *ANF*, 2:131.

8. Justin Martyr, *First Apology*, 61, in *ANF*, 1:183; cf. *Didache*, 7.1, in Holmes, 259; *ANF*, 7:379.

Trinitarian baptismal formula became so important that baptism was regarded as "not complete except by the authority of the most excellent Trinity."[9]

A Trinitarian consciousness also manifested itself among the early Christians outside of this baptismal formula. As Polycarp was being martyred, he prayed to God the Father: "I glorify you, through the eternal and heavenly High Priest, Jesus Christ, your beloved Son, through whom to you, with him and the Holy Spirit, be glory both now and for the ages to come."[10] This consciousness was carried over to the church's worship, as shown by Justin Martyr's affirmation: "... the most true God, the Father of righteousness and temperance [patience] and the other virtues, who is free from all impurity. But both him, and the Son (who came forth from him and taught us these things ...), and the prophetic Spirit, we worship and adore, knowing them in reason and truth."[11] And Justin affirmed this Trinitarian belief while cognizant of the fact that "we should worship God alone."[12] Ignatius described the church and its members as "stones of a temple, prepared beforehand for the building of God the Father, hoisted up to the heights by the crane of Jesus Christ, which is the cross, using as a rope the Holy Spirit."[13] In his rebuttal of the charge of atheism, Athenagoras wondered: "Who ... would not be astonished to hear men who speak of God the Father, and of God the Son, and of the Holy Spirit, and who declare both their power in union and their distinction in order, called atheists?"[14] In sum, the early church affirmed belief in the triune God in its baptismal formula, its praying, its worship, its ecclesiology, and its apologetics.

An early description of the relationship between the three referred to the Son as the Word of the Father and to the Spirit as the Wisdom of the Father; these two were the two "hands" of the Father as he created.[15] In an interesting reference to the creation of the sun and moon on the fourth day of creation, Theophilus noted: "The three days which were before the lights are types of the Trinity—of God, his Word, and his Wisdom."[16] Appealing to Proverbs 3:19–20 and 8:22–31, Irenaeus "demonstrated that the Word, namely the Son, was always with the Father; and that Wisdom also, which is the Spirit, was present with him, anterior [prior] to all creation.... There is therefore one God, who by the Word and Wisdom created and arranged all things."[17]

The church's first attempts in understanding and explaining the relationship between the Father, Son, and Holy Spirit focused on what would later be called the "economic Trinity" (the different roles or activities of the three in relationship to the world). Irenaeus expressed the cooperating work of the three as "the Father planning everything well and giving his commands, the Son carrying these into execution and performing the work of

9. Origin, *First Principles*, 1.3.2, in *ANF*, 4:252.

10. *Martyrdom of Polycarp*, 14, in Holmes, 239; *ANF*, 1:42.

11. Justin Martyr, *First Apology*, 6, in *ANF*, 1:164.

12. Ibid., 16, in *ANF*, 1:168.

13. Ignatius, *Letter to the Ephesians*, 9, in Holmes, 143; *ANF*, 1:53.

14. Athenagoras, *A Plea for the Christians*, 10, in *ANF*, 2:133. A bit later, Athenagoras stated that Christians "know God and his Logos, what is the oneness of the Son with the Father, what is the communion of the Father with the Son, what is the Spirit, what is the unity of these three, the Spirit, the Son, the Father, and their distinction in unity." Ibid., 12, in *ANF*, 2:134.

15. Irenaeus, *Against Heresies*, 4.20.1, in *ANF*, 1:487.

16. Theophilus, *To Autolycus*, 2.15, in *ANF*, 2:100–101. Theophilus's statement is the first known use of the word *Trinity* in Greek (τριας; *Trias*).

17. Irenaeus, *Against Heresies*, 4.20.3–4, in *ANF*, 1:488.

creating, and the Spirit nourishing and increasing [what is made]."[18] Indeed, through this triadic pattern "was God revealed; for God the Father is shown forth through all these [operations], the Spirit indeed working, and the Son ministering, while the Father was approving, and man's salvation being accomplished."[19]

This understanding of the economic Trinity was further developed over time. Hippolytus noted a certain tension between the oneness of God and the works of the three.[20] He explained how to hold these two truths together: "But if he desires to learn how it is shown still that there is one God, let him know that his power is one. As far as regards the power, therefore, God is one. But as far as regards the economy, there is a three-fold manifestation."[21] Hippolytus then outlined the economy of the three. Referring to John 1:1, he explained:

> If, then, the Word was with God, and was also God, what follows? Would one say that he speaks of two Gods? I shall not indeed speak of two Gods, but of one; of two persons, however, and of a third economy, viz., the grace of the Holy Spirit. For the Father indeed is one, but there are two persons, because there is also the Son; and then there is the third, the Holy Spirit. The Father decrees, the Word executes, and the Son is manifested, through whom the Father is believed on. The economy of harmony is led back to one God; for God is one. It is the Father who commands, and the Son who obeys, and the Holy Spirit who gives understanding: The Father who is *above* all, and the Son who is *through* all, and the Holy Spirit who is *in* all.[22]

Thus, the relationship of the Father, Son, and Holy Spirit was a functional one. While affirming that God is one, the early church also affirmed that the Father, Son, and Holy Spirit could be distinguished by their roles or activities in the world.

The church, however, did not confine its thinking to the economic relationship between the three. Other areas of sophisticated reasoning were explored as well. Appealing to Genesis 1:26–27, Justin Martyr affirmed, "We can indisputably learn that [God] conversed with some one who was numerically distinct from himself and also a rational Being."[23] Thus, the Father and the Son are distinct persons; yet, there is only one God. Furthermore, Tatian explored the idea of the Son's generation: "God was in the beginning.... With him, by Logos-power, the Logos himself also, who was in him, subsists. And by his [God's] simple will, the Logos springs forth; and the Logos, not coming forth in vain, becomes the first-begotten work of the Father." This generation rendered the Son equal with the Father, not of a lesser nature.[24] Clearly, the early church dedicated itself to careful thinking about the Godhead.

This kind of sophisticated thinking was becoming necessary in the church because several errors arose at this time. Two movements in particular presented formidable

18. Ibid., 4.38.3, in *ANF*, 1:521–22.

19. Ibid., 4.20.6, in *ANF*, 1:489.

20. "For who will not say that there is one God? Yet, he will not on that account deny the economy." Hippolytus, *Against the Heresy of One Noetus*, 3, in *ANF*, 5:224.

21. Ibid., 8, in *ANF*, 5:226.

22. Ibid., 14, in *ANF*, 5:228.

23. Justin Martyr, *Dialogue with Trypho, a Jew*, 62, in *ANF*, 1:228; cf. *Dialogue*, 128, in *ANF*, 1:264.

24. Tatian, *Address to the Greeks*, 5, in *ANF*, 2:67.

problems for the church's emerging Trinitarian formulation. The first, called *dynamic monarchianism*, owed its origin to Theodotus in Rome and was spread by Paul of Samosata, bishop of Antioch.[25] The second, called *modalistic monarchianism*, was introduced by Praxeas in Rome, articulated by Noetus of Smyrna and his disciples Zephyrinus and Callistus (both bishops of Rome), and popularized by Sabellius. Both were forms of *monarchianism*, emphasizing the unity of God as the only *monarchia*, or ruler of the universe. If the premise "God is one" is foremost in one's thinking about the Godhead, then the deity of the Son and the deity of the Holy Spirit become problematic. If God (the Father) is God, and Jesus (the Son) is God, it appears that there are two gods. Additionally, if the Holy Spirit is God, then apparently belief in three gods is affirmed. This problem was the underlying difficulty that both movements sought to address.[26]

Hippolytus explained some of the major ideas of dynamic monarchianism:

> Jesus was a (mere) man, born of a virgin, according to the counsel of the Father. After he had lived indiscriminately with all men and had become preeminently religious, he subsequently—at his baptism in the Jordan River—received Christ, who came from above and descended (upon him) in the form of a dove. This was the reason, according to Theodotus, why (miraculous) powers did not operate within him prior to the manifestation in him of that Spirit which descended and which proclaims him to be the Christ.[27]

Dynamic monarchianism believed that Jesus was just an ordinary man, though one who was particularly good and holy. The Spirit (or Christ) descended upon Jesus at his baptism, enabling him to perform miracles without making him divine. Thus, Jesus was a man indwelt in an unusually powerful manner by the Spirit, but he was not God.[28] Thankfully, this form of heresy exerted little influence in the church.

Not so, however, with modalistic monarchianism, also called *modalism* and *Sabellianism*, which became a widespread belief in the early church. Hippolytus explained the major tenets of one of its proponents, Callistus, bishop of Rome: "Callistus alleges that the Logos himself is Son and is himself Father. Although called by a different title, in reality he is one indivisible spirit. And he maintains that the Father is not one person while the Son is another, but that they are one and the same; and that all things are full of the divine Spirit.... And he affirms that the Spirit, which became incarnate in the virgin, is not different from the Father, but is one and the same."[29] Modalistic monarchianism held that there is one God who can be designated by three different names—"Father," "Son," and "Holy Spirit"—at different times, but these three are not distinct persons.

25. To be more precise, there were two proponents of dynamic monarchianism named Theodotus. To distinguish them, one is called Theodotus the Tanner, the other Theodotus the Money-Changer. Tertullian made mention of the two heretics in *Against All Heresies*, 8, in *ANF*, 3:654.

26. Tertullian, *Against Praxeas*, 3, in *ANF*, 3:598–99.

27. Hippolytus, *The Refutation of All Heresies*, 7.23, in *ANF*, 5:114–15. The text has been rendered clearer. We are dependent on Hippolytus and other "orthodox" thinkers, who wrote refutations of early heresies, for our understanding of dynamic monarchianism. We trust that they represented fairly their opponents' positions.

28. For more discussion of early christological heresies, see chap. 17.

29. Hippolytus, *The Refutation of All Heresies*, 9.7, in *ANF*, 5:130. The text has been rendered clearer. For the similar view of Praxeas, see Tertullian, *Against Praxeas*, 1, in *ANF*, 3:597.

Instead, they are different *modes* (thus, *modalism*) of the one God. Thus, God can be called "Father" as the Creator of the world and Lawgiver; he can be called "Son" as God incarnate in Jesus Christ; and he can be called "Holy Spirit" as God in the church age. Accordingly, Jesus Christ is God and the Spirit is God, but they are not distinct persons. Furthermore, this resolution was thought to be the only way to protect Christianity from embracing tritheism—belief in three gods.[30]

The early church rejected both dynamic monarchianism and modalism as being far removed from its traditional understanding of the oneness of God and the threeness of the Father, Son (who is fully divine), and Spirit. Dynamic monarchianism considered Jesus Christ to be a mere man, while modalistic monarchianism emphasized the oneness of the Godhead to such an extent that the three were lost in the one. The church found neither of these views acceptable.

Novatian on Dynamic Monarchianism and Modalism

Both they who say that Jesus Christ himself is God the Father, and they who would have him to be only man, have gathered from Scripture the sources and reasons of their error and perversity. Because when they perceived that it was written that "God is one," they thought that they could not otherwise hold such an opinion than by supposing that it must be believed either that Christ was man only, or really God the Father.... And thus they who say that Jesus Christ is the Father argue as follows: If God is one, and Christ is God, then Christ is the Father, because God is one. If Christ is not the Father, because Christ is God the Son, there appear to be two Gods introduced, contrary to the Scriptures. And they who contend that Christ is man only, conclude on the other hand in this way: If the Father is one, and the Son another, but the Father is God and Christ is God, then there is not one God, but two Gods are at once introduced—the Father and the Son. And if God is one, by consequence Christ must be a man, so that rightly the Father may be one God.*

*Novatian, *Treatise Concerning the Trinity*, 30, in *ANF*, 5:642. The text has been rendered clearer.

Addressing these errors, Tertullian formulated the clearest doctrine of the Trinity that the church had developed up to his time. Like others, he appealed to the plural words in Genesis 1:26 as a hint of the plurality in the Godhead.[31] His formulation of the deity of the Holy Spirit set a precedent for further development.[32] Moreover, his wording of the Trinitarian doctrine demonstrated precision:

---

30. "One cannot believe in only one God in any other way than by saying that the Father, the Son, and the Holy Spirit are the very same person." Tertullian, *Against Praxeas*, 2, in *ANF*, 3:598. From this idea flowed the corollary called *patripassianism* (see ch. 10, n. 18).

31. Tertullian, *Against Praxeas*, 12, in *ANF*, 3:606.

32. "Then there is the Paraclete or Comforter, for which the Lord promises to pray to the Father and to send from heaven after he had ascended to the Father. He is called 'another Comforter' indeed (John 14:16).... 'He shall receive of mine,'

All are of one, by unity ... of *substance*; while the mystery of the economy is still guarded, which distributes the unity into a *Trinity*, placing in their order the three *persons*—the Father, the Son, and the Holy Spirit. Three, however, not in condition, but in degree; not in substance, but in form; not in power, but in appearance. Yet they are of one *substance* and of one condition and of one power, inasmuch as he is one God from whom these degrees and forms and aspects are reckoned under the name of the Father and of the Son and of the Holy Spirit.[33]

Tertullian's wording became the foundation for the church's definition of the Trinity: God is one in essence or substance yet three in persons. This formula meant that the Father is fully God, the Son is fully God, and the Holy Spirit is fully God, and the three are distinct from each other; yet God is only one, inseparable in essence. Furthermore, Tertullian used a number of analogies—root, tree, fruit; fountain, river, stream; sun, ray, apex of ray—to illustrate this reality.[34]

Origen also addressed errors in this doctrine, using the word *hypostases* to refer to the three *persons* of the Trinity. Specifically, God has revealed his nature as consisting of "three hypostases [persons], the Father and the Son and the Holy Spirit,"[35] yet these three persons share the same essence.[36] Origen began to develop the idea of the "ontological Trinity" (the word "ontological" refers to "being"; thus, the "ontological Trinity" refers to the eternal and ordered relationships between the three persons). He affirmed that the Trinitarian relationships are eternal; that is, there was never a time when the Son and the Spirit did not exist. Speaking of the Son, Origen explained: "As light ... could never exist without splendor, so neither can the Son be understood to exist without the Father."[37] Although the Son was generated by the Father, this generation was from all eternity: "God is the Father of his only-begotten Son, who was born indeed of him, and derives from him what he is, but without any beginning."[38] Furthermore, this generation demonstrates "the unity of nature and substance belonging to the Father and Son."[39] Indeed, because of this, the Son is *homoousios* (of the same nature) with the Father.

Similarly, there was never a time when the Holy Spirit did not exist. Origen affirmed that "we have been able to find no statement in holy Scripture in which the Holy Spirit could be said to be made or created."[40] Moreover, he denounced anyone who "should venture to say, that at the time when he was not yet the Holy Spirit, he was ignorant of the

says Christ (John 16:14), just as Christ himself received of the Father's. Thus the connection of the Father in the Son, and of the Son in the Paraclete, produces three coherent persons, who are yet distinct one from another. These three are one essence, not one person, as it is said, 'I and my Father are one' (John 10:30), in respect of unity of substance, not singularity of number." Tertullian, *Against Praxeas*, 25, in *ANF*, 3:621. The text has been rendered clearer.

33. Tertullian, *Against Praxeas*, 2, in *ANF*, 3:598. The text has been rendered clearer. Cf. *Against Praxeas*, 12, 25, in *ANF*, 3:607, 621. Tertullian's statement is the first known use of the word "Trinity" in Latin (*Trinitas*). He was also the first to use the term *persona*, or person, to refer to each of the three members. A key biblical passage for him was John 10:30, from

which he argued that the two subjects ("I and my Father") are joined by a plural predicate ("are") and terminate in an abstract noun ("one" substance or essence), not a personal noun ("one" person). Ibid., 22, in *ANF*, 3:618.

34. Ibid., 8, in *ANF*, 3:603.

35. Origen, *Commentary on the Gospel of John*, 2.6, in *ANF*, 10:328.

36. Origen called it "the fountain of divinity." Origen, *First Principles*, 1.3.7, in *ANF*, 4:255.

37. Ibid., 4.28, in *ANF*, 4:376–77.

38. Ibid., 1.2.2, in *ANF*, 4:246.

39. Ibid., 1.2.6, in *ANF*, 4:248.

40. Ibid., 1.3.3, in *ANF*, 4:252.

Father, but that after he had received knowledge, he was made the Holy Spirit. For if this were the case, the Holy Spirit would never be reckoned in the unity of the Trinity—i.e., along with the unchangeable Father and his Son—unless he had always been the Holy Spirit."[41] Although the Holy Spirit "proceeds from the Father,"[42] this procession is from all eternity.[43] With this reasoning, Origen paved the way for the two affirmations of the eternal generation of the Son and the eternal procession of the Holy Spirit.

At the beginning of the fourth century, the church became embroiled in a fierce controversy concerning the deity of the Son of God, Jesus Christ. Recounted elsewhere,[44] this struggle with Arianism exerted a great impact on the early church's developing Trinitarian doctrine. Specifically, the structure of the Creed of Nicea underscored and formulated the church's Trinitarian consciousness: "We believe in one God the Father all-sovereign, maker of all things visible and invisible; and in one Lord Jesus Christ, the Son of God ...; and in the Holy Spirit."[45] Although it was hoped that this confession of faith would resolve the conflict by putting an end to Arianism, such hope was ill-founded. For the next half century, a few resilient Christians, convinced of the truth and the necessity of the Nicene decision, fought to make the Creed of Nicea the orthodox belief of the church at that time—and for all times.

Athanasius offered a stalwart defense of the Creed of Nicea and its developing Trinitarian theology. Concerning the Father and the Son, he affirmed: "We believe in one unbegotten God, Father almighty ... who has his being from himself. And in one only-begotten Word, Wisdom, Son, begotten of the Father without beginning and eternally ... the true image of the Father, equal in honor and glory."[46] This eternal generation means that the Son is not a created being. Arguing against the Arian heresy and appealing to Scripture, Athanasius explained: "What belongs to the Father, belongs to the Son.... As then the Father is not a creature, so neither is the Son; and as it is not possible to say of him [the Father], 'there was a time when he was not,' nor 'made of nothing,' so it is not proper to say the like of the Son either. But rather, as the Father's attributes are everlastingness, immortality, eternity, and not being a creature, it follows that thus also we must think of the Son."[47] Although eternal and equal with the Father in all things, the Son is also eternally and immutably distinct from him: "Neither is the Father the Son, nor the Son the Father. For the Father is Father of the Son, and the Son, Son of the Father."[48] For Athanasius, then, "the fullness of the Father's Godhead is the being of the Son, and the Son is whole God."[49] In whatever the Father is, so is the Son, with one exception—the Son is not the Father.

In similar fashion, Athanasius discussed the Holy Spirit as the third member of the Trinity—"one with the Godhead which is in the unoriginated Triad"[50]—in relationship with the Father and the Son: "The Holy Spirit, being that which proceeds from the Father, is ever

---

41. Ibid., 1.3.4, in *ANF*, 4:253.

42. Ibid., 3.5.8, in *ANF*, 4:344.

43. Ibid., 4.28, in *ANF*, 4:377.

44. See chap. 17.

45. Creed of Nicea, in Schaff, 2:58–59; Bettenson, 27–28.

46. Athanasius, *Statement of Faith*, 1, in *NPNF*[2], 4:84. The text has been rendered clearer. Cf. *Against the Arians*, 1.14, in *NPNF*[2], 4:314–15.

47. He appealed to Matt. 10:40; John 5:26; and 14:9. Atha-nasius, *On Luke 10:22 (Matthew 11:27)*, 4, in *NPNF*[2], 4:89. The text has been rendered clearer.

48. Athanasius, *Statement of Faith*, 2, in *NPNF*[2], 4:84.

49. Athanasius, *Four Discourses against the Arians*, 3.6, in *NPNF*[2], 4:396.

50. Athanasius, *Letters to Serapion on the Holy Spirit*, 1.21, in *Letters of St. Athanasius Concerning the Holy Spirit*, trans. C. R. B. Shapland (New York: Philosophical Library, 1951), 120.

in the hands of the Father who sends and of the Son who conveys him, by whose means he filled all things."[51] Because the Spirit "has the same oneness with the Son as the Son has with the Father," he cannot be considered a creature.[52] Furthermore, because the Son is in the Spirit and the Spirit is in the Son, the two are never separated and always joined with the Father; thus: "The holy and blessed Triad is indivisible and one in itself. When mention is made of the Father, there is included also his Word, and the Spirit who is in the Son. If the Son is named, the Father is in the Son, and the Spirit is not outside the Word. For there is from the Father one grace which is fulfilled through the Son in the Holy Spirit."[53]

Using precise nonbiblical (but nonetheless important) terms to distinguish the orthodox doctrine of the Trinity from heresy, Athanasius referred to both the Son and the Spirit as *homoousios* and *consubstantial* (of one and the same substance) with the Father.[54] Although eternal and equal, the three are eternally and immutably distinct: "In the Godhead alone the Father is properly Father, and because he is the only Father, he is and was and always will be. The Son is properly Son, and the only Son. And in them it holds good that the Father is always Father, and the Son is always Son, and the Holy Spirit is always Holy Spirit."[55]

Three other church leaders played a critical role in the formulation of the doctrine of the Trinity at this time: Basil the Great, Gregory of Nyssa, and Gregory of Nazianzus, together known as the Cappadocian fathers. They affirmed and defended both the deity of the Son and the deity of the Spirit and clarified the orthodox formulation of one substance (*ousia*) and three persons (*hypostases*): "Ousia has the same relation to hypostasis as the common has to the particular.... The term *ousia* is common, like goodness, or Godhead, or any similar attribute; while hypostasis is contemplated in the special property of Fatherhood, Sonship, or the power to sanctify."[56] As Gregory of Nazianzus formulated it, "The Godhead is one in three, and the three are one, in whom the Godhead is, or to speak more accurately, who are the Godhead."[57]

With these three persons, there is a definite Trinitarian order, expressed by Gregory of Nyssa as "from the Father, through the Son, to the Holy Spirit."[58] At the same time, the three mutually indwell one another. This concept of *perichoresis* was a major Trinitarian contribution of the Cappadocian fathers: "Each of these persons possesses unity, not less with that which is united to him [the other two persons] than with himself, by reason of the identity of essence and power. And this is the account of the unity, so far as we have apprehended it."[59] Because of this perichoretic unity between them, the three

---

51. Athanasius, *Statement of Faith*, 4, in *NPNF²*, 4:85.

52. Athanasius, *Letters to Serapion on the Holy Spirit*, 1.2, in Shapland, *Letters of St. Athanasius Concerning the Holy Spirit*, 64–65.

53. Ibid., 1.14, in Shapland, *Letters of St. Athanasius*, 93–94.

54. Athanasius, *De Decretis*, or *Defense of the Nicene Definition*, 5.19–20, in *NPNF²*, 4:162–64.

55. Athanasius, *Letters to Serapion*, 4.6, in Shapland, *Letters of St. Athanasius Concerning the Holy Spirit*, 188.

56. Basil of Caesarea, *Letter* 214.4, in *NPNF²*, 8:254.

57. Gregory of Nazianzus, *Oration* 39.11, in *NPNF²*, 7:355–56.

58. Gregory of Nyssa, *Against Eunomius*, 1.36, in *NPNF²*, 5:84. Although Gregory addresses this Trinitarian order in the context of how human beings contemplate the Godhead, his assumption is that human contemplation of the divine being corresponds to the triune God as he actually is.

59. Gregory of Nazianzus, "Fifth Theological Oration: On the Holy Spirit," *Oration* 32 (31).16, in *NPNF²*, 7:323. E.g., the Father is united both with the Son and the Holy Spirit, as well as with himself.

engage in mutual and magnificent glory-giving: "You see the revolving circle of the glory moving from like to like. The Son is glorified by the Spirit; the Father is glorified by the Son; again the Son has his glory from the Father; and the only-begotten thus becomes the glory of the Spirit. For with what shall the Father be glorified, but with the true glory of the Son; and with what again shall the Son be glorified, but with the majesty of the Spirit?"[60] What distinguishes the three are "the attributes indicative of the persons" and unique to them.[61] For Basil, these are "fatherhood, sonship, and sanctification."[62] For Gregory of Nazianzus, the three distinguishing characteristics are "the unbegottenness of the Father ... the generation of the Son and the procession of the Spirit."[63] In terms of the persons, "the Father is the begetter and the emitter ... the Son is the begotten, and the Holy Spirit the emission."[64] Gregory of Nyssa distinguished them on the basis of *cause* and *that which is caused*:

> While we confess the unchanging character of the divine nature, we do not deny the difference in respect of *cause* and *that which is caused*. By this alone we understand that one person is distinguished from another. Our belief is that one is *the cause*, and another is *of the cause*. Also, in that which is *of the cause*, we recognize another distinction. For one is directly from the first cause, and another by that which is directly from the first cause. Thus, the attribute of being only-begotten is without doubt in the Son. And the interposition of the Son, while it guards his attribute of being only-begotten, does not shut out the Spirit from his relation by way of nature to the Father.[65]

The one and the three; the unity of essence and diversity of persons. The Cappadocian fathers attempted to maintain a balance between these elements in their development of the doctrine of the Trinity.

Gregory of Nazianzus' Summary of the Doctrine of the Trinity

> This I give you to share, and to defend all your life, the one Godhead and power, found in the three in unity and comprising the three separately; not unequal, in substances or natures, neither increased nor diminished by superiorities or inferiorities; in every respect equal, in every respect the same; just as the beauty and the greatness of the heavens is one; the infinite conjunction of three infinite ones, each God when considered in himself; as the Father so the Son, as the Son so the Holy Spirit; the three one God when contemplated together; each God because consubstantial; one God because of the monarchy. No sooner do I conceive of the one than I am illumined by the splendor of

---

60. Gregory of Nyssa, *On the Holy Spirit against the Followers of Macedonius*, in *NPNF*[2], 5:324.

61. Gregory of Nyssa, *Against Eunomius*, 2.2, in *NPNF*[2], 5:102.

62. Basil, *Letter* 236.6, in *NPNF*[2], 8:278.

63. Gregory of Nazianzus, *Oration* 32 (31).8, in *NPNF*[2], 7:320.

64. Gregory of Nazianzus, "Third Theological Oration: On the Son," *Oration* 29.2, in *NPNF*[2], 7:301.

65. Gregory of Nyssa, *On "Not Three Gods,"* in *NPNF*[2], 5:336. The text has been rendered clearer.

the three; no sooner do I distinguish them than I am carried back to the one. When I think of any one of the three I think of him as the whole, and my eyes are filled, and the greater part of what I am thinking of escapes me. I cannot grasp the greatness of that one so as to attribute a greater greatness to the rest. When I contemplate the three together, I see but one torch, and cannot divide or measure out the undivided light.*

*Gregory of Nazianzus, "On Holy Baptism," *Oration* 40.41, in *NPNF²*, 7:375.

The Council of Constantinople reworked the Creed of Nicea and produced the Nicene (or Nicene-Constantinopolitan) Creed with a clearer affirmation of the deity of both the Son and the Holy Spirit. The church's doctrine of the Trinity was well established with this statement. Further developments awaited the contribution of Augustine.

In the beginning of his treatise *On the Trinity*, Augustine echoed the orthodox doctrine of the Trinity.[66] In terms of the divine nature (e.g., the divine attributes of greatness, goodness, and omnipotence), "Whatever ... is spoken of God in respect to himself, is both spoken singly of each person, that is, of the Father, and the Son, and the Holy Spirit; and together of the Trinity itself, not plurally but in the singular."[67] Thus, God is great, good, and all-powerful; the Father is great, good, and all-powerful; the Son is great, good, and all-powerful; the Holy Spirit is great, good, and all-powerful; the Trinity is great, good, and all-powerful. At the same time, distinctions between the three persons can be discerned because of the diverse relationships that exist between the Father (who begets and is the beginning), the Son (who is begotten and sent), and the Holy Spirit (who proceeds).[68]

While buttressing these elements of the traditional formulation, Augustine also added his unique touches. Specifically, he articulated what would later be called the double procession of the Spirit: the Holy Spirit proceeds from both the Father and the Son. Affirming that it is God the Father "from whom the Holy Spirit principally proceeds," Augustine explained: "I have added the word *principally*, because we find that the Holy Spirit proceeds from the Son also. But the Father gave him this too, not as to one already existing, and not yet having it; but whatever he gave to the only-begotten Word, he gave by begetting him. Therefore, he so begat him as that the common Gift should proceed from him also, and the Holy Spirit should be the Spirit of both."[69] He found biblical warrant for this notion, as Scripture speaks of both the Spirit of God and the Spirit of Christ (e.g., Rom. 8:9). From this, Augustine concluded: "God the Father is not the Father of the Holy Spirit, but of the Son; and God the Son is not the Son of the Holy Spirit, but of the Father;

---

66. "The Father, and the Son, and the Holy Spirit intimate a divine unity of one and the same substance in an indivisible equality; and therefore, they are not three Gods, but one God.... The Father has begotten the Son, and so he who is the Father is not the Son; and the Son is begotten by the Father, and so he who is the Son is not the Father; and the Holy Spirit is neither the Father nor the Son, but only the Spirit of the Father and of the Son, he himself also co-equal with the Father and the Son, and pertaining to the unity of the Trinity." Augustine, *On the Trinity*, 1.4.7, in *NPNF¹*, 3:20; cf. *Letter* 169, in *NPNF¹*, 1:540.

67. Augustine, *On the Trinity*, 5.8.9, in *NPNF¹*, 3:92.

68. Ibid., 5.13.14—14.15, in *NPNF¹*, 3:94.

69. Ibid., 15.17.29, in *NPNF¹*, 3:216.

but God the Holy Spirit is the Spirit not of the Father only, or of the Son only, but of the Father and the Son."[70] This fact led him to affirm the double procession of the Holy Spirit.

Augustine found another implication from this fact: "The Holy Spirit is neither of the Father alone, nor of the Son alone, but of both; and so intimates to us a mutual love, with which the Father and the Son reciprocally love one another."[71] Thus, he referred to the Spirit as "a certain unutterable communion of the Father and the Son"[72] and "the substantial and consubstantial love of both ... the Father and the Son."[73] As both bond between and member of the Trinity, the Spirit unites the three as one.

Given the limits of human language, Augustine developed psychological analogies to describe the Trinity. He culled these from the human soul, because the soul is "the image of God, that is, of the supreme Trinity."[74] One was the analogy of "he that loves, and that which is loved, and love."[75] A second analogy was the interplay between "memory, understanding, and will."[76] Mind, knowledge, and love provided a third analogy.[77] A fourth analogy was the association between human remembering, understanding, and love of God.[78] With regard to these analogies, Augustine admitted their failing; nevertheless, many since him have sought to develop such analogies of the Trinity.

Augustine's doctrine of the Trinity was followed closely by the Western church. The Athanasian Creed expressed the great advancement in this doctrine from the early days of the church to the fourth/fifth century. All deviations from this orthodox formulation of the doctrine of the Trinity were condemned soundly by the church. Joining together the church's doctrine of Christ and its doctrine of the Trinity, the fifth ecumenical council, the Second Council of Constantinople (553), insisted that the second person of the Trinity, begotten of the Father from all eternity, was the very same divine person who became incarnate.[79] Furthermore, this divine person, as incarnate, was the very same person who was crucified.[80] The doctrine of the Trinity had developed to become an essential doctrine of the Christian faith.

70. Augustine, *Sermon* 21 (71).18, in *NPNF*[1], 6:323–24.

71. Augustine, *On the Trinity*, 15.17.27, in *NPNF*[1], 3:215.

72. Ibid., 5.11.12, in *NPNF*[1], 3:93.

73. Augustine, *Tractates on the Gospel of John*, 105.3, in *NPNF*[1], 7:396; cf. Tractate 20.3; *On the Trinity*, 6.5.7.

74. Augustine, *The City of God*, 11.26, in *NPNF*[1], 2:220; cf. Augustine, *On the Trinity*, 14.4.6, in *NPNF*[1], 3:186.

75. Augustine, *On the Trinity*, 8.10.14, in *NPNF*[1], 3:124. He explained: "When I ... love anything, there are three things concerned — myself, and that which I love, and love itself. For I do not love love, except I love a lover; for there is no love where nothing is loved. Therefore there are three things — he who loves, and that which is loved, and love." Ibid., 9.2.2, in *NPNF*[1], 3:126.

76. Augustine, *On the Trinity*, 10.11.17, in *NPNF*[1], 3:142. He explained: "Since ... these three — memory, understanding, will — are not three lives, but one life; nor three minds, but one mind; it follows certainly that neither are they three substances, but one substance." Ibid., 10.11.18, in *NPNF*[1], 3:142.

77. "The mind itself, and the love of it, and the knowledge of it, are three things, and these three are one; and when they are perfect they are equal." Augustine, *On the Trinity*, 9.4.4, in *NPNF*[1], 3:127; cf. ibid., 14.10.13, in *NPNF*[1], 3:190–91.

78. Augustine, *On the Trinity*, 14.12.15, in *NPNF*[1], 3:191.

79. Denial of this brought condemnation: "If anyone will not confess that the Word of God has two nativities, that which is before all ages from the Father, outside time and without a body, and secondly that nativity of these latter days when the Word of God came down from the heavens and was made flesh of holy and glorious Mary, mother of God and ever-virgin, and was born from her: let him be anathema." Second Council of Constantinople, anathema 2, in *Decrees of the Ecumenical Councils*, ed. Norman P. Tanner (Washington: Georgetown University Press, 1990).

80. Denial of this brought condemnation: "If anyone does not confess his belief that our Lord Jesus Christ, who was crucified in his human flesh, is truly God and the Lord of glory and one of the members of the holy Trinity: let him be anathema." Second Council of Constantinople, anathema 10, in Tanner, *Decrees of the Ecumenical Councils*.

The Athanasian Creed

The Catholic Faith is this: That we worship one God in Trinity and Trinity in unity. Neither confounding the persons, nor dividing the substance. For there is one person of the Father, another of the Son, and another of the Holy Spirit. But the Godhead of the Father, of the Son, and of the Holy Spirit is all one; the glory equal, the majesty coeternal. Such as the Father is, such is the Son, and such is the Holy Spirit.... So the Father is God, the Son is God, and the Holy Spirit is God. And yet they are not three Gods, but one God.... The Father is made of none, neither created, nor begotten. The Son is of the Father alone; not made, nor created, but begotten. The Holy Spirit is of the Father and of the Son, neither made, nor created, nor begotten, but proceeding.... And in this Trinity no one is before or after another, no one is greater or less than another. But the whole three persons are coeternal and coequal. So that in all things: the unity in Trinity, and the Trinity in unity, is to be worshipped. He, therefore, that will be saved, must thus think of the Trinity.*

*Athanasian Creed, 3–7, 15–16, 21–23, 25–28, in Grudem, *Systematic Theology*, 1170. The text has been rendered clearer.

THE DOCTRINE OF THE TRINITY IN THE MIDDLE AGES

The Third Council of Toledo (Spain) in 589 introduced a one-word change in the Nicene Creed that sowed the seeds of discord with the doctrine of the Trinity and eventually resulted in the split between what became the Roman Catholic Church and the Eastern Orthodox Church. The word *filioque* ("and the son") was inserted in the final phrase concerning the Spirit so that the new reading became "I believe in the Holy Spirit, the Lord and giver of life; who proceeds from the Father *and the Son*; who, with the Father and the Son together is worshiped and glorified."[81] This affirmation of the double procession of the Spirit was opposed by the Eastern part of the church, led by Photius, bishop of Constantinople. The Western church supported the addition and promoted it to the official teaching of the Catholic Church at the Second Council of Lyons (1274). The division between Eastern and Western Christendom over this issue continues to this day.

A few minor skirmishes over the doctrine of the Trinity—specifically against the Trinitarian views of Abelard, Rosellinus, Joachim of Fiore, and Gilbert de La Porrée—were fought, but for the most part the traditional doctrine was affirmed and developed during the medieval period. Its continuing importance can be seen in Richard of St. Victor's affirmation that "the most sacred and most secret mystery of the Trinity" is "the supreme article of our faith."[82] Whether this doctrine was a revealed truth or could

81. Nicene Creed, in Schaff, 2:59.
82. Richard of St. Victor, *On the Trinity*, 4.5, in Pelikan, 3:279.

also be rationally demonstrated was an ongoing debate. According to Aquinas, whereas natural reason can prove the existence of God and "can know what belongs to the unity of the essence," it cannot know "what belongs to the distinction of the persons." Thus, "it is impossible to attain to the knowledge of the Trinity by natural reason."[83]

From another perspective, Richard averred: "There is no absence not only of probable but also of necessary arguments for the explanation of anything that has necessary being.... It appears moreover that it is entirely impossible for any necessary being to lack a necessary reason."[84] Given that, for Richard, God is a necessary being, certain rational arguments exist to prove, not only his existence, but his triune nature as well. Because the God whose existence can be rationally proved is perfect in goodness and therefore perfect in love, argued Richard, "the perfection of charity [love] requires a Trinity of persons."[85] Only two divine persons could not constitute the Godhead, for "in mutual love and very fervent love nothing is rarer or more magnificent than to wish that another to be loved equally by the one whom you love supremely and by whom you are supremely loved."[86] Thus, a Trinity of divine, loving persons necessarily exists and can be rationally demonstrated.[87]

As for the doctrine itself, Boethius offered the standard view: "Father ... is God; Son is God; and Holy Spirit is God. Therefore, Father, Son and Holy Spirit are one God, not three gods. The explanatory cause of this conjunction [unity] is lack of difference."[88] Differentiating between a substance (the nature of a thing) and its accidents (the changeable characteristics of a thing), he maintained there could be no divine essences "separate in accidents or in substantial differences"; thus, there is unity in God.[89] Accordingly, "even though 'God' is thrice repeated when Father, Son, and Holy Spirit are named, the three unities do not produce a plurality of number in respect to that which they truly are."[90] That is, there is one God, not three. While this statement established the unity of the Godhead, Boethius also explained the distinctions between the three: "The plurality of the Trinity was made by the fact that this is predication of relation"; that is, the relationships between the Father, Son, and Holy Spirit bring "number to the Trinity.... For the Father is not the same as the Son, nor is the Holy Spirit the same as either of them." Yet, because theirs is a relationship of identicals, "God is the same as the Father, the Son, and the Holy Spirit. He is the same as justice, goodness, greatness and all the things which can be predicated of him himself."[91] Unity and diversity, as well as equality and distinction, were firmly maintained in Boethius's doctrine of the Trinity.[92]

---

83. Aquinas, *Summa Theologica*, pt. 1, q. 32, art. 1.

84. Richard of St. Victor, *On the Trinity*, 1.4; ibid., bk. 1, trans. Jonathan Couser, 4. http://pvspade.com/Logic/docs/StVictor.pdf.

85. Ibid., 3.11, 13; idem, *The Twelve Patriarchs; The Mystical Ark; Book Three of the Trinity*, trans. and ed. Grover A. Zinn (New York: Paulist, 1979), 385, 387.

86. Richard of St. Victor, *On the Trinity*, 3.11; idem, *The Twelve Patriarchs*, 384.

87. Richard of St. Victor, *On the Trinity*, 3.15, 25; idem, *The Twelve Patriarchs*, 388–89, 396–97.

88. Boethius, *On the Holy Trinity*, 1; ibid., trans. Erik C.

Kenyon. Available at http://pvspade.com/Logic/docs/BoethiusDeTrin.pdf.

89. Ibid., 3.

90. Ibid.

91. Ibid., 6.

92. A similar idea can be found in Anselm, who, speaking of the Father and the Son, explained: "They are contrasted in terms of their relation such that the one never receives what is proper to the other. They are concordant in terms of their nature such that the essence of one is possessed by the other. What makes one Father and the other Son makes them different, so that the Father is never called the Son, or the Son

Thomas Aquinas applied philosophy to his traditional formulation of the doctrine, which he summarized simply as "one essence of the three persons, and three persons of the one essence."[93] With his notion of "person," Aquinas focused on relationship: "Relation in God is not as an accident in a subject, but is the divine essence itself, and so it is subsistent, for the divine essence subsists.... Therefore a divine person signifies a relation as subsisting."[94] Specifically, he identified four relations of the Godhead: paternity, filiation, spiration, and procession.[95] As a result of an act of the intellect, the Father is characterized by *paternity* in relationship to the Son, and the Son is characterized by *filiation* in relationship to the Father. As a result of an act of the will, the Father and the Son are characterized by *spiration* in relationship to the Holy Spirit, and the Spirit is characterized by *procession* in relationship to the Father and the Son. Being the result of different acts, generation and procession are different relationships.[96] Such differences, however, do not mean inequality between the three members: "If there were any inequality in the divine persons, they would not have the same essence; and thus the three persons would not be one God, which is impossible."[97] While denying inequality between the three persons, Aquinas also affirmed an eternal order between them because the Father is the principal member of the Trinity.[98]

With such discussions, the important doctrine of the Trinity was reaffirmed and developed by the Western church during the Middle Ages. The Catholic Church's defense of the double procession of the Holy Spirit had led to a division with the Eastern church, but at the Council of Florence in 1439 a serious attempt was made to reunite the two churches. The Catholic Church offered this affirmation: "The Latin Church recognizes but *one* principle, *one* cause of the Holy Spirit, namely, the Father. It is from the Father that the Son holds his place in the 'procession' of the Holy Spirit. It is in this sense that the Holy Spirit proceeds from the Father, but he proceeds *also* from the Son."[99] The Eastern church representatives agreed, stating "that they recognized the procession of the Holy Spirit from the Father *and* the Son as from *one* principle ... and from *one* cause."[100] Hopes for reconciliation were dashed soon afterward, however, as other forces came into play.

Father. But through their substance they are the same, so that the essence of the Son is always in the Father and that of the Father in the Son. Not differing but the same, not many but one: such is, of both, the essence." Anselm, *Monologion*, 43, in *Anselm*, 56.

93. Aquinas, *Summa Theologica*, pt. 1, q. 39, art. 2.

94. Ibid., pt. 1, q. 29, art. 4.

95. "Real relations in God can be understood only in regard to those actions according to which there are internal, and not external, processions in God. These processions are two only ... one derived from the action of the intellect, the procession of the Word, and the other from the action of the will, the procession of Love. In respect of each of these processions two opposite relations arise. One of these is the relation of the person proceeding from the principle; the other is the relation of the principle himself. The procession of the Word is called *generation* in the proper sense of the term, by which it is applied to living things. Now the relation of the principle of generation in perfect living beings is called *paternity*, and the relation of the one proceeding from the principle is called *filiation*. But the procession of Love has no proper name of its own, and so neither have the ensuing relations a proper name of their own. The relation of the principle of this procession is called *spiration*, and the relation of the person proceeding is called *procession*—although these two names belong to the processions or origins themselves, and not to the relations." Ibid., pt. 1, q. 28, art. 4.

96. Ibid., pt. 1, q. 27, art. 4.

97. Ibid., pt. 1, q. 42, art. 1.

98. Ibid., pt. 1, q. 33, art. 1.

99. Leon Van der Essen, "The Council of Florence." *The Catholic Encyclopedia*, vol. 6 (New York: Robert Appleton, 1909), 113.

100. Ibid.

THE DOCTRINE OF THE TRINITY IN THE REFORMATION AND POST-REFORMATION

Although the Protestant churches, like the Eastern church, would separate from the Catholic Church, distancing themselves from Rome over many key doctrinal issues, the two shared the traditional doctrine of the Trinity inherited from the early church and advanced by the medieval church. The issue never became a point of contention between the two, and the Reformers added little to the orthodox formulation. Martin Luther explained the traditional view as belief that "in the divine majesty there exists but one individual essence, yet this exists in such mode, that there exists first the person, who is called the Father; and from him exists the second [person], who is the Son, born from eternity; and proceeding from both these is the third, namely, the Holy Spirit. These three persons are not separate from each other, like two or three brothers or sisters; but they subsist in one and the same eternal, undivided, and indivisible essence."[101] The *Augsburg Confession* stated that its Trinitarian doctrine was derived from the early church.[102] Thus, Luther and the Lutheran churches affirmed the traditional doctrine.

John Calvin incorporated this doctrine into the Trinitarian structure of his *Institutes of the Christian Religion*. He maintained that God cannot be truly known apart from his revelation of himself as triune: "God also designates himself by another special mark to distinguish himself more precisely from idols. For he so proclaims himself the sole God as to offer himself to be contemplated clearly in three persons. Unless we grasp these, only the bare and empty name of God flits about in our brains, to the exclusion of the true God."[103] For Calvin, this doctrine is a proper summary of the biblical revelation of God; to deny it, therefore, is to fall into heresy.[104]

Scripture specifically teaches the full deity of both the Son and the Holy Spirit, and Calvin affirmed and defended these truths. When pressed by heretics (e.g., Valentine Gentile) on this issue, Calvin took a rather novel turn by using the term *autotheos* ("God of himself") to express the deity of the Son (and, by implication, the deity of the Holy Spirit).[105] That is, in terms of his essence, the Son is "God of himself" and does not derive his deity from the Father (by implication, the same is true of the Spirit). In affirming this, Calvin diametrically opposed heretics who wrongly believed that "the Father, who is truly and properly the sole God, in forming the Son and the Spirit, infused into them his own deity" such "that he is the only 'essence giver.'"[106] What the Son does receive from the Father is his eternal sonship (and, similarly, the third member receives his eternal personhood as the Holy Spirit from both the Father and the Son). As Calvin explained:

---

101. Martin Luther, "Sermon for Trinity Sunday; Romans 11:33–36," in *Church Postil: Sermons on the Epistles*, 3 vols. (New Market, Va.: New Market Evangelical Lutheran Publishing, 1869), 3:4.

102. *Augsburg Confession*, 1, in Schaff, 3:7. In the *Formula of Concord*, the Lutheran churches affirmed their agreement with the *Apostles'*, *Nicene*, and *Athanasian Creeds* on this (and other) doctrine. Schaff, 3:95.

103. John Calvin, *Institutes of the Christian Religion*, 1.13.2,

LCC, 1:122.

104. Ibid., 1.13.3, LCC, 1:123.

105. This discussion is adapted from Robert Letham, *The Holy Trinity: In Scripture, History, Theology, and Worship* (Phillipsburg, N.J.: P & R, 2004), 256–57. Although Calvin did not employ the term *autotheos* in his *Institutes*, the root idea that the Son (and the Spirit) is God himself is present there. E.g., 1.13.23–25, LCC, 1:149–54.

106. Calvin, *Institutes*, 1.13.23, LCC, 1:149.

"We say that deity in an absolute sense exists of itself; whence likewise we confess that the Son, since he is God, exists of himself, but not in respect of his person; indeed, since he is the Son, we say that he exists from the Father. Thus his essence is without beginning; while the beginning of his person is God himself."[107]

The distinctions between the three persons appear in both the economic Trinity and the ontological Trinity. With regard to the order or economy of the Trinity, Calvin explained: "To the Father is attributed the beginning of activity, and the fountain and wellspring of all things; to the Son, wisdom, counsel, and the ordered disposition of all things; but to the Spirit is assigned the power and efficacy of that activity.... The observance of an order is not meaningless or superfluous, when the Father is thought of as first, then from him the Son, and finally from both the Spirit."[108] With regard to the relationships within the Trinity, Calvin (focusing on the Father and the Son) noted: "When we mark the relation that he has with the Father, we rightly make the Father the beginning of the Son."[109] Thus, the three persons are distinguished from one another on the basis of both the differences in their primary activities and the relationships between them. At the same time, Calvin cautioned against overlooking the unity of the Trinity:

> That passage in Gregory of Nazianzus vastly delights me: "I cannot think on the one without quickly being encircled by the splendor of the three; nor can I discern the three without being straightway carried back to the one." Let us not, then, be led to imagine a trinity of persons that keeps our thoughts distracted and does not at once lead them back to that unity. Indeed, the words "Father," "Son," and "Spirit" imply a real distinction—let no one think that these titles, by which God is variously designated from his works, are empty—but a distinction, not a division.[110]

This widespread agreement between Catholics, Lutherans, and Calvinists on the doctrine of the Trinity did not go unchallenged, however. Certain heretics denounced the doctrine as irrational and called for the church to abandon belief in it. Michael Servetus's anti-Trinitarianism was so dangerous that much of Calvin's writing on the doctrine in his *Institutes* was a defense of the traditional formulation against Servetus's heretical view.[111] Because of his anti-Trinitarianism, Servetus was condemned and executed as a heretic. He was followed by Lelio and Faustus Socinus, who wrote a catechism for Unitarianism called the *Racovian Catechism*. Both Lutheran and Reformed theologians following the Reformation period addressed the Socinian heresy and labeled its anti-Trinitarianism as dangerous because it "blasphemously dared to traduce this most sacred mystery as a figment of the human brain."[112] They also expressed and defended the traditional doctrine.[113] As for the procession of the Holy Spirit, the post-Reformation theologians

---

107. Ibid., 1.13.25, LCC, 1:154.

108. Ibid., 1.13.18, LCC, 1:142–43.

109. Ibid., 1.13.19, LCC, 1:144.

110. Ibid., 1.13.17, LCC, 1:141–42. Calvin's quotation of Gregory of Nazianzus is from his work "On Holy Baptism," *Oration* 40.41 (cited above).

111. Servetus's views were set forth in *On the Trinity* and

On the Errors of the Trinity.

112. Francis Turretin, *Institutes of Elenctic Theology*, ed. James T. Dennison Jr., trans. George Musgrave Giger, 3 vols. in 1 (Phillipsburg, N.J.: P & R, 1997), 3rd topic, 25th q., sec. 3, 1:266.

113. E.g., ibid., 1:253–60.

continued to affirm the Western church's double procession rather than the Orthodox church's view.[114] Besides this disagreement, Catholicism, Orthodoxy, and Protestantism confessed and defended the traditional doctrine of the Trinity

THE DOCTRINE OF THE TRINITY
IN THE MODERN PERIOD

The challenges to this traditional view continued and expanded during the modern period. Although the heresies of Servetus and the Socinians had been fairly easily dismissed by Catholics, Orthodox, and Protestants alike, the seeds of doubt about the Trinity that they had sown began to flower, sometimes with impunity, in this period. The fruit of this development took on several forms. One result was that the doctrine of the Trinity was, for the most part, simply and tragically neglected in Christian theology.[115] As the modern period was characterized by a rise in materialism, agnosticism, and atheism, the doctrine of the Trinity was deemphasized. As Karl Rahner summarized the situation leading up to the middle part of the twentieth century: "We must be willing to admit that, should the doctrine of the Trinity have to be dropped as false, the major part of religious literature could well remain virtually unchanged."[116]

A prime example of this neglect can be found in the theology of Friedrich Schleiermacher. As a result of his reformulation of theology in line with his view that religion is essentially a feeling of absolute dependence on God, Schleiermacher dispensed with abstract Christian dogmas. For this reason, the doctrine of the Trinity could not be essential to the Christian faith: "The assumption of an eternal distinction in the Supreme Being is not an utterance concerning the religious consciousness, for there it never could emerge."[117] Unsurprisingly, then, Schleiermacher relegated his brief discussion of the Trinity to the end of his theological treatise, *The Christian Faith*.

The modern period's neglect of the doctrine of the Trinity came to an abrupt end with Karl Barth, whose formidable articulation of the doctrine also weighed heavily against its critics. In keeping with the historic church position, Barth considered the doctrine to be essential to a right understanding and explication of Christian doctrine. Accordingly,

---

114. "But although the Greeks [the Orthodox Church] should not be indicted for heresy on account of their view, nor should it have been the occasion of a schism, yet the Latins' [Roman Catholic Church's] view is better retained, both because the Holy Spirit is sent by the Son (John 16:7; 'If I go I will send the Comforter to you'), and because he is also called the Spirit of the Son (Gal. 4:6; 'God sent forth the Spirit of the Son into our hearts, crying, "Father"'), and because, whatever he [the Spirit] has, he has it from the Son (John 16:13–14; 'He shall take of mine and shall declare it to you'), and because Christ breathed the Holy Spirit upon the disciples (John 20:22)." The text has been rendered clearer. Leonard Riissen, *Francisci Turretini Compendium Theologiae* (Amsterdam, 1695), 4.13, in Heppe, 131.

115. William Newton Clarke provided an explanation for this neglect: "The prominence of the doctrine of the Trinity at any given time will depend upon the thought of the time. It is not likely to be at the front when the living controversies of the age relate to theism itself. In defending the reality of God against materialism or agnosticism, few will discuss the inner mode of his existence: it is enough to maintain his personality, his character, and his relation to his universe." William Newton Clarke, *Outline of Christian Theology* (Edinburgh: T & T Clark, 1909), 180.

116. Karl Rahner, *The Trinity*, trans. Joseph Donceel (New York: Herder & Herder, 1970, Crossroad, 1997), 10–11.

117. Friedrich Schleiermacher, *The Christian Faith*, ed. H. R. Mackintosh and J. S. Stewart (Edinburgh: T & T Clark, 1928), 739.

in his *Church Dogmatics*, he discussed it in the very first volume, placing "the doctrine of the Trinity at the head of the whole of dogmatics."[118] He argued that the Trinity needed to be the first topic addressed in order to protect theology from the rampant speculation that arises when the doctrine "is first allowed to be articulate only at a later stage, instead of being given the first word, since it has to give us our information on the concrete and decisive question, Who God is."[119] Indeed, for Barth, because the doctrine of the Trinity "fundamentally distinguishes the Christian doctrine of God as Christian,"[120] it should be discussed at the outset of theology.

Barth's starting point for discussion of the Trinity was the biblical testimony: "The statement, 'God reveals himself as the Lord,' understood in this sense, i.e., the meaning intended by this statement, and therefore the revelation itself attested by Scripture, we call 'the root of the doctrine of the Trinity.'"[121] The three parts of this statement—subject ("God"), predicate ("reveals"), and object ("himself")[122]—reveal that there are three aspects to God's being. The very nature of revelation itself shows this as well, as "God himself in unimpaired unity yet also in unimpaired distinction is Revealer, Revelation, and Revealedness";[123] that is, the act of revelation involves the one who reveals, that which is revealed, and the effect that the revelation has on those to whom it is revealed. This self-revelatory act indicates the plurality of God's divine nature, but this does "not mean that revelation is the ground of the Trinity, as if God were the Three-in-one only in his revelation and for the sake of his revelation."[124]

Specifically, the Revealer is "the God who according to his nature cannot be unveiled to man."[125] The only reason that human beings may know about him is that God in his freedom decides to reveal himself. The Revelation is the Revealer who makes himself known through Jesus Christ. Because this self-revelatory act is the only means by which people may have a knowledge of God, it is the emphasis of Scripture and of all history.[126] The Revealedness is the human response to this Revelation.[127] In this Revealedness, God reveals himself "as the Spirit of the Father and of the Son, and so as the same one God, but this time as the same one God in this way as well, namely, in this unity, rather, in this self-disclosing unity, disclosing itself to men, unity with the Father and the Son."[128]

For Barth, Christian theology must hold together both the "oneness in threeness"[129] and the "threeness in oneness"[130] of the Trinity: "The concept of the revealed unity of the revealed God does not exclude but includes a distinction, an arrangement, in the essence of God. This distinction or arrangement is the distinction or arrangement of the three 'persons'—we prefer to say, the three 'modes of being' in God."[131] This affirmation was

---

118. *CD*, I/1,345.

119. Ibid., 346.

120. Ibid.

121. Ibid., 353.

122. Ibid., 361.

123. Ibid., 339.

124. Ibid., 358.

125. Ibid., 362.

126. "The doctrine of the Trinity historically considered, in its origin and construction, has not been interested equally in Father, Son, and Holy Spirit; here also the theme was primarily the second person of the Trinity, God the Son, the divinity of Christ." Ibid., 361.

127. "God's revealedness makes it a relationship between man, the effective meeting between God and man." Ibid., 381.

128. Ibid.

129. Ibid., 400.

130. Ibid., 406.

131. Ibid., 407. The text has been rendered clearer.

not the modalism of earlier heresy, because Barth used the phrase "mode of being" in a way that was synonymous with the classical term *person*. Indeed, Barth insisted that any doctrine of the Trinity that emphasizes the unity of the Godhead over the distinctions of modes or persons, or any doctrine that emphasizes the threeness of the Godhead over the oneness, is incorrect.[132]

Barth is credited with launching the emphasis on what is now being called the social Trinity. In the Godhead itself, the three modes or persons exist in eternal, dynamic, "social" relationship with one another. Importantly, this communitarian reality finds its echo in the dynamic, social relationships of human beings, as Barth explained:

> In God's own being and sphere there is a counterpart: a genuine but harmonious self-encounter and self-discovery; a free co-existence and cooperation; an open confrontation and reciprocity. Man is the repetition of this divine life form; its copy and reflection. He is this first in the fact that he is the counterpart of God, the encounter and discovery in God himself being copied and imitated in God's relation to man. But he is it also in the fact that he is himself the counterpart of his fellows and has in them a counterpart, the co-existence and cooperation in God himself being repeated in the relation of man to man. Thus ... the analogy between God and man is simply the existence of the I and the Thou in confrontation. This is first constitutive for God, and then for man created by God.[133]

Specifically, for Barth, it is in the plurality of gender—male and female—and in the relationship of "man to woman and woman to man"[134] that human beings reflect the plurality of persons—Father, Son, and Holy Spirit—and their Trinitarian relationship with one another. Barth was followed in this social Trinitarian emphasis by theologians like Stanley Grenz.[135]

This turn toward interest in the social Trinity did not overshadow developments in the ontological (or immanent) Trinity and the economic Trinity in the modern period. One of the most important axioms for doing Trinitarian theology was formulated by Karl Rahner and is known as Rahner's Rule: "The 'economic' Trinity is the 'immanent' Trinity and the 'immanent' Trinity is the 'economic' Trinity."[136] From this axiom he argued with specific reference to the incarnation that the Logos, the Son of God, was the only person of the Trinity that could have become a man; neither the Father nor the Spirit could have become incarnate. If the thesis "that every divine person might become man" were true, Rahner contended, "it would create havoc with theology":

> There would no longer be any connection between "mission" and the intra-trinitarian life. Our sonship in grace would in fact have absolutely nothing to

---

132. As he explained his preference for the expression "three-in-oneness" to conceptualize this ultimately unfathomable mystery: "In the doctrine of the Trinity our concern is with God's oneness in threeness and threeness in oneness. Past these two obviously one-sided and unsatisfactory formulations we cannot get. They are both one-sided and unsatisfactory.... The concept of 'three-in-oneness' must be regarded as the conflation of both these formulas, or rather as the indication of that

conflation of the two, which we cannot attain to." Ibid., 423.

133. Ibid., 185.

134. Ibid., 186.

135. Stanley J. Grenz, *Theology for the Community of God* (Nashville: Broadman, 1994); *The Social God and the Relational Self: A Trinitarian Theology of the Imago Dei* (Louisville: Westminster John Knox, 2001).

136. Rahner, *The Trinity*, 22.

do with the Son's sonship, since it might equally well be brought about without any modification by another incarnate person. That which God is for us would tell us absolutely nothing about that which he is in himself, as triune. These and many similar conclusions, which would follow from this thesis, go against the whole sense of holy Scripture.[137]

Thus, Rahner asserted "that the understanding of the 'immanent' Trinity must come from the 'economic' Trinity."[138]

Understood in a certain way, Rahner's Rule is a key axiom for the orthodox doctrine of the Trinity:

> If the axiom is held to reflect the fact that God's self-revelation as triune in the work of creation, providence, and grace is a true revelation of who he is eternally, then it expresses a truth at the heart of the Christian faith. It points to the faithfulness of God. It demonstrates that there is only one Trinity. God is free and did not need to create us, nor to make himself known to us. But, having chosen to do so, his own faithfulness requires that he reveal himself in a manner that reflects who he is. A bifurcation between the economic Trinity and the immanent Trinity undermines our knowledge of God. Our salvation depends on God's revelation of himself in the history of salvation being true and faithful to who he is in himself.[139]

Understood in a different way, Rahner's Rule has been criticized as leading to modalism, pan(en)theism, and an anthropological starting point for theology.[140]

Questions concerning the order of the three persons and relationships of authority and submission also came to the forefront in Trinitarian discussions. Eschewing the traditional ordering that gives primacy to the Father, Wolfhart Pannenberg contended that this notion is inconsistent with the biblical idea of mutual reciprocity within the Godhead,[141] as seen in the Father's handing over of the kingdom to the Son.[142] That is, though the Son is generated and sent by the Father, which makes the Son dependent on the Father, at the same time the Father cannot be the Father without the Son, which

---

137. Ibid., 28, 30.

138. Ibid., 65–66.

139. Letham, *Holy Trinity*, 296.

140. E.g., Jürgen Moltmann's Rahner-like axiom—"The theology of the cross must be the doctrine of the Trinity and the doctrine of the Trinity must be the theology of the cross"—demanded that both the generation of the Son and the creation of the world are eternal and necessary. Indeed, for Moltmann, God's Trinitarian existence is intimately connected with the world and its suffering, which is the heresy of panentheism (God in everything). Jürgen Moltmann, *The Crucified God: The Cross of Christ as the Foundation and Criticism of Christian Theology* (Minneapolis: Fortress, 1993), 241. Other critics of Rahner's axiom include Colin E. Gunton, *Yesterday and Today: A Study of Continuities in Christology*

(Grand Rapids: Eerdmans, 1983), and Paul D. Molnar, *Divine Freedom and the Doctrine of the Immanent Trinity: In Dialogue with Karl Barth and Contemporary Theology* (Edinburgh: T & T Clark, 2002).

141. "The Father is not begotten of the Son or sent by him. These relations are irreversible. But in another way the relativity of fatherhood that finds expression in the designation 'Father' might well involve a dependence of the Father on the Son and thus be the basis of true reciprocity in the trinitarian relations." Wolfhart Pannenberg, *Systematic Theology*, vol. 1, trans. Geoffrey W. Bromiley (Grand Rapids: Eerdmans, 1991), 312.

142. "The self-distinction of the Father from the Son is not just that he begets the Son but that he hands over all things to him, so that his kingdom and his own deity are now dependent upon the Son." Ibid., 313.

makes the Father dependent on the Son. Thus, there is reciprocity between the persons of the Godhead.

This idea of mutual reciprocity was modified to include the denial of any relationships of authority and submission among the members of the Trinity. Kevin Giles denounced the notion of an eternal order in the Godhead, claiming that the notion is a reinvention of the doctrine of the Trinity and an elevation of one divine person over another, who is therefore relegated logically to a position of inferiority.[143] He was countered by J. Scott Horrell, who presented biblical evidence for eternal order in the Godhead and who proposed an eternally ordered social model of the Trinity. He defined this concept "as the social model that, while insisting on equality of the divine nature, affirms 'perpetual distinction of roles within the immanent Godhead'.... This entails something like the generous preeminence of the Father, the joyous collaboration of the Son, and the ever-serving activity of the Spirit."[144]

Even more removed from the traditional doctrine was the denial of the Trinity in "Oneness" Pentecostalism, "[a] religious movement that emerged in 1914 within the Assemblies of God ... stream of the early Pentecostal revival, challenging the traditional Trinitarian doctrine and baptismal practice with a modalistic view of God, a doctrine of the name of Jesus, and an insistence upon rebaptism in the name of the Lord Jesus Christ."[145] This belief is a variety of modalism. "The theological center is Christocentric in that as a human being Jesus *is* the Son, and as Spirit (i.e., in his deity) he reveals, indeed, *is* the Father, and sends, indeed, *is* the Holy Spirit as the Spirit of the risen Jesus who indwells the believer."[146] Clearly, a distinctive feature of oneness Pentecostalism is Jesus—specifically, the name "Lord Jesus Christ"—and this emphasis leads to adherents of the doctrine being baptized (or, in the case of Christians, rebaptized) in that name.

In the modern period, theologians not only concentrated on the Trinity in and for itself but also explored how the doctrine might affect other Christian doctrines. Books such as *Jesus in Trinitarian Perspective: An Introductory Christology*;[147] Catherine LaCugna's *God for Us: The Trinity and Christian Life*;[148] Stanley Grenz's *The Social God and the Relational Self*;[149] and Miroslav Volf's *After Our Likeness: The Church and the Image of the Trinity*[150] reflect the Trinitarian theological turn in the doctrines of Christology, soteriology, and ecclesiology, respectively. Trinitarian doctrine became the lens through which these doctrines were re-visioned; this development has led to a change

143. Kevin Giles, *Jesus and the Father: Modern Evangelicals Reinvent the Doctrine of the Trinity* (Downers Grove, Ill.: InterVarsity, 2006).

144. J. Scott Horrell, "The Eternal Son of God in the Social Trinity," in *Jesus in Trinitarian Perspective*, ed. Fred Sanders and Klaus Issler (Nashville: Broadman Academic, 2007), 44.

145. D. A. Reed, "Oneness Pentecostalism" in *The New International Dictionary of Pentecostal and Charismatic Movements*, ed. Stanley M. Burgess, rev. and exp. ed. (Grand Rapids: Zondervan, 2002), 936. The Oneness movement was soon expelled from the Assemblies of God.

146. Ibid., 942.

147. Sanders and Issler, *Jesus in Trinitarian Perspective: An Introductory Christology*.

148. Catherine Mowry LaCugna, *God for Us: The Trinity and Christian Life* (San Francisco: HarperSanFrancisco, 1992).

149. Stanley J. Grenz, *The Social God and the Relational Self: A Trinitarian Theology of the* Imago Dei (Louisville, Ky.: Westminster John Knox, 2001).

150. Miroslav Volf, *After Our Likeness: The Church and the Image of the Trinity* (Grand Rapids: Eerdmans, 1998).

in the traditional formulations of these (and other) doctrines. Moreover, as Christians and churches in the West came into closer and more prolonged contact with Islam, Hinduism, Buddhism, and the like, the realization that their worship of and allegiance to the God who is triune distinguished Christianity from all other world religions was enhanced. Appropriately, the doctrine of the Trinity continued to be a primary focus in the third millennium.

12

CREATION

How has the church come to understand why, how, and when God created the universe?

STATEMENT OF BELIEF

The church has historically believed that God created the universe ex nihilo—out of nothing—in the relatively recent past, perhaps five or six thousand years ago. As the consensus of the church, this position was affirmed against philosophical theories that were similar in some ways to modern theories of evolution. It was not until the seventeenth century that a major challenge to this belief was set forth, yet on the whole the church continued to affirm and defend its traditional belief. Following that point, other challenges arose, none of which was greater than Charles Darwin's theory of evolution. Since the middle of the nineteenth century, that theory has significantly affected the church's view of divine creation.

Although most believers have traditionally followed the historic position of the church on this issue, several camps representing differing beliefs on creation can be found in the church today. These include naturalistic evolution (though very few Christians hold this idea); theistic evolution; old earth (or progressive) creationism; young earth creationism; and the fully gifted creation perspective. It should be remembered that, even though Christians are divided—even hotly so, at times—on this issue, it has been only in the last few centuries that any significant controversy has existed over divine creation. Thus, the following discussion will be essentially uniform throughout the periods of the early church, the Middle Ages, the Reformation, and the early modern period.[1]

DIVINE CREATION IN THE EARLY CHURCH

Belief in God's creation of the world and all that exists in it was taken over by the early church from its Jewish heritage. Genesis 1:1 affirms divine creation, and the remainder of the chapter sets forth how that creation came about. The first Christians preached this

---

1. My thanks to Bryan Lilly for his help with this chapter.

traditional belief (Acts 14:15; 17:24). According to the apostle John, one of the songs of praise sung in heaven acknowledges God as the Creator (Rev. 4:11). While affirming the marvelous work of God in creation, the apostles also underscored the prominent role of the Son of God in the creative process (John 1:3; Col. 1:15–17). Both the Father and the Son were involved in the creation of the universe, which was brought into existence out of nothing (Heb. 11:3).[2]

The early church continued to affirm this divine creation. Origen explained the relationship between the work of the Father and that of the Son: "The *immediate Creator*, and, as it were, very maker of the world was the Word, the Son of God; while the Father of the Word, by commanding his own Son—the Word—to create the world, is the *primary Creator*."[3] Justin Martyr emphasized this instrumental role of the Word, noting that God "created and arranged all things by him."[4] Irenaeus also acknowledged the work of the Holy Spirit (the "Wisdom" of God) in creation, affirming that the Father is "the Creator, who made those things by himself, that is, through his Word and his Wisdom."[5]

Although it is often thought that evolution did not present a challenge to the church until Charles Darwin's theory, such is not the case. The early church had to confront ancient philosophies that resembled modern evolutionary theories in some ways. Chief among these theories was the position of Epicurus, who set forth a theory that the chance collision of atoms in the limitless void of the universe was the origin of all life.[6] Hippolytus explained that Epicurus's theory included the idea that even God himself was the product of the random crash of atoms. The obvious conclusion was that God is not in control of the universe, but all is left up to chance.[7] The church reacted to Epicurus's ideas in several ways. Some thoroughly critiqued his theory and expressed amazement that anyone in his right mind could believe it.[8] Others carefully drew the distinction between the response of those holding the random chance theory and the response of Christians—which was to give thanks to God for creating everything.[9] The church dismissed such atomistic theories of the origin of the world.

Another false theory of the origin of the universe, against which the early church took a strong stand, was the idea of the *demiurge*. Put forward by Gnosticism, the view had its roots in Plato's notion of demiurge (noted below) and Plotinus's concept of emanation. At the heart of this heresy was the view that matter is inherently evil while spiritual things

2. If we were to consider the teaching of the whole Bible, this statement would also affirm the role of the Holy Spirit in divine creation.

3. Origen, *Against Celsus*, 6.60, in *ANF*, 4:601.

4. Justin Martyr, *Second Apology*, 6, in *ANF*, 1:190.

5. Irenaeus, *Against Heresies*, 2.30.9, in *ANF*, 1:406.

6. Dionysius of Alexandria, *Works*, extant fragment 2.1, in *ANF*, 6:85. Although these proponents used the term "atom" in their theories, their concept of an atom was not the scientifically developed idea with which we are familiar today.

7. Hippolytus, *The Refutation of All Heresies*, 1.19, in *ANF*, 5:21. Epicurus is better known for the Epicurean motto—"Eat, drink, and be merry"—associated with his name.

8. Minucius Felix, *The Octavius*, 17, in *ANF*, 4:182.

9. Origen confronted a proponent of Epicurean atomic theory—Celsus, a staunch enemy of the early church: "Let Celsus then say distinctly that the great diversity among the products of the earth is not the work of providence, but that a certain fortuitous concurrence [accidental collision] of atoms gave birth to qualities so diverse that it was owing [due] to chance that so many kinds of plants, trees, and herbs resemble one another, that no disposing reason gave existence to them, and that they do not derive their origin from an understanding that is beyond all admiration. We Christians, however, who are devoted to the worship of the only God, who created these things, feel grateful for them to him who made them." Origen, *Against Celsus*, 4.75, in *ANF*, 4:531.

are inherently good. In light of this belief, the supreme deity, being spiritual and thus good, could by no means create the world, which is material and thus bad. To explain the reality of the created world, Gnosticism posited a series of emanations, or projections, out of the supreme deity.[10] Those closest to this deity were primarily spiritual in nature; those farther removed from it were primarily material in nature. *Demiurge* was the name given to the emanation possessing sufficient spiritual nature to bring something into existence and sufficient material nature to create a material world. This notion of emanations from God appeared absurd to the church.[11] By contrast, Irenaeus set forth the church's position that "God is the Creator": "That there is nothing either above him or after him, and that he created all things not influenced by anyone but according to his own free will. He is the only God, the only Lord, the only Creator, the only Father. He alone contains all things, and he himself commanded all things into existence."[12]

If God is self-sufficient and entirely sovereign, as the church confessed, why then did he create the universe? Lactantius reasoned: "It cannot even be said that God made the world for his own sake, since he can exist without the world, as he did before it was made. And God himself does not make us of all those things that are contained in it, and which are produced. It is evident, therefore, that the world was constructed for the sake of living beings, since living beings enjoy those things of which it consists."[13] But it was not so much the "why" question that attracted the attention of the early church. Rather, the church focused on two other issues: *How* and *when* did God do his work of creation?

Most early Christians believed that God created ex nihilo — he "made out of what did not exist everything that is."[14] Clement of Alexandria underscored the sovereignty of God — "the sheer exercise of his will" — as being the only explanation for the created order.[15] Hermas added a description of how creation came about: "The God of hosts ... by his invisible and mighty power and by his great wisdom created the world, and by his glorious purpose clothed his creation with beauty, and by his mighty word fixed the heaven and set the earth's foundation upon the waters."[16]

This affirmation put the early church at odds with Plato's philosophy that matter is eternal. As Tatian explained: "Matter is not, like God, without beginning, nor, as having no beginning, is of equal power with God; rather, it is begotten, and not produced by any other being, but brought into existence by the Framer of all things alone."[17] Indeed, the early church was strongly critical of Plato's idea of the eternity of matter, as Theophilus showed:

> If God is uncreated and matter is uncreated, God is no longer, according to the Platonists' own thinking, the Creator of all things, nor, so far as their opinions hold, is the monarchy [the idea of God as the one and only first principle]

---

10. Think of the ripples that expand outwardly along the water's surface after a stone is tossed into a pond.

11. As Irenaeus noted: "Not one of them [emanations] is God. For every one will be defective, because each possesses only a small part when compared with all the rest. Thus, the title *Omnipotent* will be reduced to nothing." Irenaeus, *Against Heresies*, 2.1.5, in *ANF*, 1:360. The text has been rendered clearer.

12. Ibid., 2.1.1, in *ANF*, 1:359. The text has been rendered

clearer.

13. Lactantius, *The Divine Institutes*, 7.4, in *ANF*, 7:198.

14. *Shepherd of Hermas*, mandate 1 (26), in Holmes, 375; *ANF*, 1:20.

15. Clement of Alexandria, *Exhortation to the Heathen*, 4, in *ANF*, 2:189–90. The text has been rendered clearer.

16. *Shepherd of Hermas*, vision 1.3 (3.4), in Holmes, 339; *ANF*, 1:10.

17. Tatian, *Address to the Greeks*, 5, in *ANF*, 2:67.

established. And what great thing is it if God made the world out of existing materials? For even a human artist, when he gets material from someone, makes of it whatever he pleases. But the power of God is manifested in this, that out of things that are not, he makes whatever he pleases.[18]

Irenaeus summarized the early church's belief in creation ex nihilo: God "himself called into being the substance of his creation, when previously it had no existence."[19]

As for biblical support for creation ex nihilo, Tertullian had to admit that "even if the Scripture has not expressly declared that all things were made out of nothing—just as it abstains from saying that they were formed out of matter—there was no such pressing [urgent] need for expressly indicating the creation of all things out of nothing, as there was of their creation out of matter, if that had been their origin."[20] According to his reasoning, in the case of creation ex nihilo, it is to be presupposed that God created out of nothing. However, had it been creation out of something, that case would be left in doubt unless it were clearly stated.[21] Adding to this argument, Tertullian noted how, in Genesis 1, "whenever anything is made out of anything, [the Holy Spirit] mentions both the thing that is made and the thing of which it is made."[22] His examples included the land bringing forth vegetation, plants, and fruit trees after their own kinds (Gen. 1:11–12); the seas bringing forth living creatures and the sky bringing forth birds, all according to their own kinds (Gen. 1:20–21); and the earth bringing forth living creatures according to their own kinds (Gen. 1:24). Accordingly, Tertullian concluded:

> God, when producing other things out of things which had been already made, indicates them by the prophet [Moses], and tells us what he has produced from such and such a source.... If the Holy Spirit took upon himself so great a concern for our instruction, that we might know from what everything was produced, would he not in like manner have kept us well informed about both the heaven and the earth, by indicating for us what it was that he made them of, if their original consisted of any material substance?... He confirms (by that silence our assertion) that they were produced out of nothing. "In the beginning," then, "God made the heaven and the earth."[23]

Not everyone in the church took the Genesis account in such a literal manner. Origen argued that a straightforward interpretation runs counter to history and reason, proposing instead that the narratives "may be accepted in a spiritual signification [meaning]."[24] Rejecting a literal understanding, Origen developed his own bizarre theory of divine creation: Because God is omnipotent, he must always have had a creation over which he could exercise his power.[25] Following his own logic, Origen proposed that God created an invisible spiritual world composed of rational creatures over which he could exercise his

---

18. Theophilus, *Theophilus to Autolycus*, 2.4, in *ANF*, 2:95.

19. Irenaeus, *Against Heresies*, 2.10.4, in *ANF*, 1:370. Irenaeus appealed to Luke 18:27 for biblical support.

20. Tertullian, *Against Hermogenes*, 21, in *ANF*, 3:489.

21. Ibid.

22. Ibid., 22, in *ANF*, 3:489–90.

23. Ibid., in *ANF*, 3:490.

24. Origen, *First Principles*, 4.1.16 (from the Latin ed.), in *ANF*, 4:365. Origen particularly tripped over the fact that the first three days of creation were characterized by the cycle of "evening and morning" before the sun had been created.

25. Ibid., 1.2.10, in *ANF*, 4:249–50.

power. It was this spiritual heaven and earth—not the actual visible world in which we live—to which Moses referred in Genesis 1:1.[26] The actual visible heaven and earth were created by God following the fall of the rational creatures that populated the original spiritual world.[27] A unique notion, Origen's view never caught on in the church.

While affirming creation ex nihilo as the answer to the question of *how* the universe came into existence, the early church was also fascinated with the question of *when* God created it out of nothing. Taking the creation account in Genesis 1 literally, Methodius affirmed that "God [made] heaven and earth, and the things which are in them, in six days,"[28] adding that "the creation of the world in six days was still recent."[29] This latter assertion was tied to calculations of how long the created world would exist. Many Christians interpreted the biblical idea that "a day with the Lord is like a thousand years" as being an indication of just that matter. As Irenaeus reasoned: "In as many days as this world was made, in so many thousand years it shall be concluded.... For the day of the Lord is as a thousand years; and in six days created things were completed. It is evident, therefore, that they will come to an end at the sixth thousand year [mark]."[30] A slight variation on this theory included the sabbath day in the calculations for the expected life span of the world. Thus, with seven days to multiply by one thousand, this placed the entire existence of the world at seven thousand years.[31] This six-thousand- (or seven-thousand-) year view was fairly widespread in the early church. Obviously, many early Christians believed that the world would not exist for a long time. Accordingly, they reasoned that it was not very old; creation had taken place in the not too distant past.

---

26. Ibid., 2.9.1, in *ANF*, 4.289–90.

27. Although endowed with goodness, these rational creatures in the invisible, spiritual world did not possess their goodness as an essential quality: They would enjoy the blessing of God if they remained good. But they also possessed free will, which they could use to go against God. Indeed, this became the case: "Because they neglected and despised such goodness, then each one, by fault of his own laziness, became—one more quickly, another more slowly; one to a greater degree, another to a lesser degree—the cause of his own downfall." Ibid., 1.6.2, in *ANF*, 4:260. Origen found in this view an explanation for the great differences found among God's creatures in the actual visible world today: "God, who deemed it just to arrange his creatures according to their merit, brought down these different rational creatures into the harmony of one world.... Thus, each one—whether heavenly beings, earthly beings, or infernal beings—is said to have the causes of his diversity in himself and antecedent to his bodily birth." Ibid., 2.9.6–7, in *ANF*, 4:292–93. Thus, the actual visible world became the home of fallen beings; that is, beings who had fallen in the invisible spiritual world. Those who had fallen the least became embodied as angels. Those who had fallen more became embodied as human beings. And those who had fallen the most became embodied as demons, with Satan as their head. Thus, this present real world is similar to a prison and a reforming school. Punishment for rebellion has been meted out according to the gravity of each one's fall,

but the world is also a stage for each one, using its free will to reform itself and turn back to God. The texts have been rendered clearer.

28. Methodius, *The Banquet of the Ten Virgins*, 8.11, in *ANF*, 6:339.

29. Ibid., 7.5, in *ANF*, 6:333. Methodius was commenting on a passage from the Song of Solomon (6:8–9). He understood the referents of "sixty queens ... eighty concubines ... and virgins beyond number" to be groups of people who lived after the creation of the world. The "sixty queens" referred to people living between the creation and the time of Noah, while the "eighty concubines" referred to those living from the time of Abraham to the time of Christ. The expression cited above was his comment on the sixty queens—the creation of the world was still recent in relationship to them, and they stretched all the way to the flood. Thus, Methodius did not think a great deal of time passed between creation and the flood, nor (by implication) from the time of Abraham to the time of Christ. Therefore, the use of his expression to summarize his entire idea is justified.

30. Irenaeus, *Against Heresies*, 5.28.3, in *ANF*, 1:557. Cf. *Letter of Barnabas*, 15, in Holmes, 315–16; *ANF*, 1:146–47. Hippolytus used this scheme to calculate both the birth of Jesus Christ and the end of the world. Hippolytus, *Fragments from Daniel*, 2.4–5, in *ANF*, 5:179.

31. Cyprian, *Treatise* 11.11, in *ANF*, 5:503.

The fourth century witnessed the rise of a dangerous heresy—Arianism—that denied the deity of Christ. In responding to this erroneous Christology, the church urged that one piece of evidence for the Son's deity was his involvement in the creation of the world. Specifically, the Creed of Nicea spoke of Jesus Christ, "through whom all things were made, things in heaven and things on the earth; who for us men and for our salvation came down and was made flesh."[32] For supporters of the Christian faith as defined by this creed, the two works of the Son—Creator of the universe and Savior of humankind—went hand in hand. The one who became incarnate to save the world was none other than the one who had created the world in the first place. Thus, the church took a stand against Arianism. As Amphilochius warned, "A man is altogether irreligious and a stranger to the truth if he does not say that Christ the Savior is also the Maker of all things."[33]

Augustine affirmed the early church's teaching on divine creation and added a new approach to the interpretation of Genesis 1. He also addressed the speculation of those who wondered what God was doing *before* he created the universe. At first, Augustine refuted the usual answer that is attributed to him: "He was preparing hell for those who pry into mysteries."[34] His actual answer, then, was that God created time when he created the universe; thus, there was no time *before* the creation. This fact renders the question absurd.[35] As to how God created, like many before him, Augustine affirmed a two-step process in creation: first, God created matter ex nihilo; second, he molded that unformed matter into the world fit for humanity.[36]

Augustine introduced a novelty into the way of approaching the biblical record of creation—an allegorical, or nonliteral, interpretation of Genesis 1.[37] This method resulted in a view that the six days of creation were not literal days but were a device to show the progressive knowledge of creation. He came to this position as a result of trying to determine when the creation of the angels took place. He rejected the idea that they were created after the rest of creation came into existence. Instead, he reasoned that they were created at the very beginning; indeed, they are the "light" mentioned in Genesis 1:3. Noting that their creation took place "not the 'first day' but 'one day,'" and that "the second day, the third, and the rest are not other days," he concluded: "The same 'one' day is repeated to complete the number six or seven, so that there should be knowledge both of God's works and of his rest."[38] So for Augustine, the pattern "and there was morning and evening" expressed the *progressive knowledge* of divine creation by God's angelic creatures, but it did not refer to *actual days of creation*. Even with this allegorical interpretation of Genesis, Augustine believed in a fairly recent creation and explicitly warned against accepting the view that the world is old.[39]

32. Creed of Nicea, in Bettenson, 25.

33. Amphilochius, *Fragment* 16, in Pelikan, 1:204–5.

34. Augustine, *Confessions*, 11.12.14, in *NPNF*[1], 1:167.

35. Ibid., 11.13.15, in *NPNF*[1], 1:167.

36. Ibid., 12.8.8, in *NPNF*[1], 1:178.

37. This approach allowed Augustine to find a reference to the Trinity in the first two verses. Ibid., 13.5.6, in *NPNF*[1], 1:191. He also found a description of fallen humanity that is saved by turning to the Lord. Ibid., 13.12.13, in *NPNF*[1], 1:194. Indeed, Augustine worked through the entire first chapter of Genesis, applying this allegorical method to the text and finding insights about Scripture, spiritual gifts, baptism, the Lord's Supper, and so forth.

38. Augustine, *The City of God*, 11.9, in *NPNF*[1], 2:210.

39. "They are deceived, too, by those highly untrue documents that profess to give the history of many thousand years. If we calculate by the sacred writings, however, we find that not six thousand years have already passed." Ibid., 12.10, in *NPNF*[1], 2:232. The text has been rendered clearer.

Augustine's Interpretation of the Days of Genesis 1

Morning returns when the creature [angel] returns to the praise and love of the Creator. When it does so in the knowledge of itself, that is the first day. When in the knowledge of the firmament, which is the name given to the sky between the waters above and those beneath, that is the second day. When in the knowledge of the earth, and the sea, and all things that grow out of the earth, that is the third day. When in the knowledge of the greater and less luminaries [lights] and all the stars, that is the fourth day. When in the knowledge of all animals that swim in the waters and that fly in the air, that is the fifth day. When in the knowledge of all animals that live on the earth, and of man himself, that is the sixth day.*

*Augustine, *The City of God*, 11.7, in *NPNF¹*, 2:209.

Many in the early church disagreed with Augustine and continued to affirm a literal six-day creation. Basil the Great, commenting on the expression "and there was morning and evening, one day," presented a literal interpretation of the days of creation as twenty-four-hour periods:

Scripture means the space of a day and a night. Why does Scripture say "one day" and not "the first day"? Before speaking to us of the second, the third, and the fourth days, would it not have been more natural to call that one "the first" that began the series? But if it says "one day," it is due to a wish to determine the measure of day and night and to combine the time that they contain. Now twenty-four hours fill up the space of one day — we mean, of a day and a night. It is as though it said: twenty-four hours measure the space of a day, or that, in reality a day is the time that the heavens starting from one point take to return there.[40]

Thus, Basil interpreted the creation account of Genesis 1 in a literal way and discussed the divine creation in terms of six literal twenty-four-hour periods of time. This became the standard view of the early church — and of the church that was to come.

DIVINE CREATION IN THE MIDDLE AGES

Although approaching the subject philosophically, Thomas Aquinas reiterated the standard church teaching on divine creation. Specifically, he affirmed that the Godhead was responsible for the creation of the universe: "To create pertains to God according to his being, that is, his essence, which is common to the three persons. Hence to create is not proper to any one person, but is common to the whole Trinity."[41] At the same time,

40. Basil the Great, *The Hexaemeron*, Homily 2.8, in *NPNF²*, 8:64.

41. Thomas Aquinas, *Summa Theologica*, pt. 1, q. 45, art. 6.

Aquinas noted differences in the roles of creation between the Father, Son, and Holy Spirit: "When treating of the knowledge and will of God, God is the cause of things by his intellect and will, just as the craftsman is cause of the things made by his craft. Now the craftsman works through the word conceived in his intellect, and through the love of his will regarding some object. Hence also God the Father made the creature through his Word, which is his Son, and through his Love, which is the Holy Spirit."[42] He also addressed the issue of whether the days of creation were one day (Augustine's position) or an actual series of days.[43] Aquinas believed that the two views were not that far apart if the different starting points of Augustine and the others were taken into consideration.

Medieval scholastic theologians also attempted to prove creation ex nihilo by means of reason without any appeal to Scripture. An example of this was Anselm's rational argument in his *Monologion*. He raised the question of the origin of created things.[44] Logically, Anselm offered three possible answers: "If ... the totality of things visible and invisible is out of some material, it can only be ... out of either the supreme nature, or out of itself, or out of some third essence."[45] He quickly dismissed the third option because "there just is no third essence."[46] By process of elimination, this left two possibilities. He further dismissed the possibility that matter is from itself, reasoning: "Again, everything that is out of matter is out of something other than itself and is posterior to [after] it. But because nothing is other than itself, or posterior to itself, it follows, therefore, that nothing is out of itself as material."[47] By process of elimination, this left only one option: The totality of things must exist out of the supreme nature.

But this raised a problem: What is the nature of the supreme nature? Anselm reasoned: "Can something less than the supreme nature exist out of the supreme nature as matter? But this would mean that the supreme good could be changed and made less good. One is just not allowed to say this. But everything that is not the supreme nature is less than it. It is therefore impossible than any non-supreme being should exist out of the supreme nature in this way.... No lesser nature, then, exists out of the supreme nature as matter."[48] Only one conclusion could be drawn: "We have therefore established that neither the supreme nature, nor the universe itself, nor anything else, is the matter out of which the universe exists. It is therefore clear that there is no matter out of which the universe exists."[49] And thus is proved the creation of the universe ex nihilo: "It is therefore utterly evident, beyond a shadow of a doubt, that the supreme essence alone and through itself produced so much and so many things of such beauty—things so varied, yet ordered, so different, yet concordant—and produced them out of nothing."[50]

Other medieval writers appealed to Scripture in their affirmations of the creation of the universe about four thousand years before the coming of Christ. For example, John

---

42. Ibid.

43. Ibid., pt. 1, q. 74, art. 2. Aquinas noted that Augustine's position was set forth in his following works: *Gen. ad lit.*, 4:22; *De Civ. Dei*, 11:9; *Ad Orosium*, 26; and *Gen. ad lit.*, 4:28.

44. Anselm, *Monologion*, 7, in *Anselm*, 18–19.

45. Ibid., in *Anselm*, 19.

46. Ibid.

47. Ibid.

48. Ibid., in *Anselm*, 19–20.

49. Ibid., in *Anselm*, 20.

50. Ibid.

Driedo, writing in 1533 and reasoning from Revelation 13:8, concluded: "According to Scripture, if Christ is the true lamb slain from the beginning of the world in the hearts of a faithful people, it follows that the church of Christ has now lasted for five thousand five hundred years."[51]

As the early church had confessed, so the medieval church affirmed creation ex nihilo in the not too distant past.

DIVINE CREATION IN THE REFORMATION AND POST-REFORMATION

Martin Luther addressed the doctrine of divine creation in his *Lectures on Genesis*. He affirmed that "the world was not in existence before 6,000 years ago"[52] and was created ex nihilo. He did not maintain his view against anyone who argued for a lengthy period of creation. Instead, he presented it against philosophers who believed that the universe was eternal. Moreover, Luther appeared disgusted by the fact that "apart from the general knowledge that the world had its beginning from nothing, there is hardly anything about which there is common agreement among all theologians."[53]

His dispute was specifically against two popular ideas. The first was the allegorical view: "Augustine resorts to extraordinary trifling in his treatment of the six days, which he makes out to be mystical days of knowledge among the angels, not natural ones." The second was the framework hypothesis: "I am disregarding the division which some make — into works of creating, [the works] of separating [days one through three] and [the works] of adorning [days four through six]."[54] Luther instead insisted on a literal interpretation: "We assert that Moses spoke in the literal sense, not allegorically or figuratively — i.e., that the world, with all its creatures, was created within six days, as the words read."[55]

Interpreting Genesis literally, Luther believed that Genesis 1:1 referred to the creation of the rough materials from which everything else would be fashioned, part of God's activity on the first day of creation. As for verse 2, Luther explained that both the earth and heaven were empty and void at this point in the creation drama. Now everything was ready for the creative activity of the Word of God: "These are functions of the Second Person, that is, of Christ, the Son of God: to adorn and separate the crude mass which was brought forth out of nothing."[56] Moreover, the Trinitarian work of creation also featured the Holy Spirit: "The Father creates heaven and earth out of nothing through the Son, whom Moses calls the Word. Over these the Holy Spirit broods. As a hen broods her eggs, keeping them warm in order to hatch her chicks, and, as it were, to bring them to life through heat, so Scripture says which the Holy Spirit brooded, as it were, on the waters to bring to life those substances that were to be quickened and adorned. For it is the office of the Holy Spirit to make alive."[57] Thus, Luther championed

---

51. John Driedo, *De Ecclesiasticis Scripturis et Dogmatibus* (1533), pt. 4, folio 280r., in Tavard, 138.

52. Martin Luther, *Lectures on Genesis: Chapters 1–5*, in LW, 1:3.

53. Ibid., LW, 1:4.

54. Ibid., LW, 1:4, 5. Luther critiqued the framework hypothesis of Nicholas of Lyra.

55. Ibid., LW, 1:5.

56. Ibid., LW, 1:6–9.

57. Ibid., LW, 1:9.

a literal reading of Genesis 1 while avoiding allegorical interpretations and refusing to engage in speculation beyond the text.[58] Moreover, he maintained the church's traditional doctrine that the triune God created the world ex nihilo about six thousand years earlier.

Martin Luther on the Nicene Creed's Affirmation of Divine Creation

What is the force of this, or what do you mean by these words: *I believe in God, the Father almighty, maker of heaven and earth*? Answer: This is what I mean and believe—that I am a creature of God. That is, he has given me and constantly preserves my body, soul, and life; members great and small; all my senses, reason, and understanding, and so on; food and drink, clothing and support, wife and children, housekeepers, house and home, etc. In addition, he causes all creatures to serve for the uses and necessities of life. These include the sun, moon and stars in the firmament; day and night; air, fire, water, earth, and whatever it bears and produces; birds and fishes, beasts, grain, and all kinds of produce, and whatever else there is of bodily and temporal goods; and good government, peace, and security. Thus, we learn from this article that none of us has life in himself, nor can he preserve his life or anything that is listed here or can be listed, however small and unimportant a thing it might be. For everything is included in the word Creator.*

*Martin Luther, *The Large Catechism*, 2.1, trans. F. Bente and W. H. T. Dan, in *Triglot Concordia: The Symbolical Books of the Evangelical Lutheran Church* (St. Louis: Concordia, 1921), 681. The text has been rendered clearer.

John Calvin argued for creation ex nihilo on the basis of the Hebrew of Genesis 1:1: "Moses ... has not used the term יָצַר (*yatsar*), which signifies to frame or form, but בָּרָא (*bara*), which signifies to create. Therefore, his meaning is, that the world was made out of nothing. Hence the folly of those is refuted who imagine that unformed matter existed from eternity.... Let this, then, be maintained in the first place, that the world is not eternal but was created by God."[59] Furthermore, on the basis of the numbering of the days, Calvin insisted on a literal six-day creation. He did not make this affirmation against anyone who argued for a lengthy period of creation. Instead, he presented it against those who believed that God instantaneously created the world—in only a moment of time.

---

58. On this latter point, Luther assented that the creation account is highly selective—it does not recount the origin of angels, for example. He explained and defended the divine purpose for this brevity: "Moses wrote nothing about the creation of the angels because, to begin with, he describes only the creation of visible things. In the second place, he did not want to provide an opportunity for speculation. Our God did the right thing in that he did not permit many matters to be written; otherwise, we would have despised what we now have and would have pried into what is beyond us." Martin Luther, *WLS*, 1:23.

59. John Calvin, *Commentaries on the First Book of Moses Called Genesis*, vol. 1, trans. John King (repr., Grand Rapids: Baker, 2005), 70.

As for when the creation took place, Calvin echoed the historic position of the church: "Little more than five thousand years have passed since the creation of the universe."[60] Like many before him, Calvin believed that the duration of the universe's existence would be about six thousand years. Living in the middle of the sixteenth century, he calculated that the end of the world would not be far off: "The duration of the world, now declining to its ultimate end, has not yet attained six thousand years."[61] Interestingly, Calvin seemed to anticipate an objection to this young earth view, a problem that would become pronounced centuries after him. He addressed the difficulty of the first three days of creation having light when as yet the sun, the moon, and the stars had not been created. As he explained with regard to Genesis 1:14:

> God had before created the light, but he now institutes a new order in nature, that the sun should be the dispenser of diurnal light and the moon and the stars should shine by night. And he assigns them to this office to teach us that all creatures are subject to his will and execute what he enjoins on them. For Moses relates nothing else than that God ordained certain instruments to diffuse through the earth, by reciprocal changes, the light that had been previously created. The only difference is that the light was before dispersed, but now proceeds from lucid bodies that, in serving this purpose, obey the commands of God.[62]

For Calvin, the existence of light prior to the creation of the sun presented no problem.

He further developed the doctrine of creation into a robust appreciation for living in the created order accompanied by a moderated use of created things:

> Scripture ... duly informs us what is the right use of earthly benefits—a matter not to be neglected in the ordering of our life. For if we are to live, we have also to use those helps necessary for living. And we also cannot avoid those things that seem to serve delight more than necessity. Therefore, we must hold to a measure so as to use them with a clear conscience, whether for necessity or for delight.... If we must simply pass through this world, there is no doubt we should use its good things in so far as they help rather than hinder our course.[63]

He bemoaned two extreme positions that had become widespread among Christians. One was an overly severe restriction on the use of temporal goods, prohibiting any enjoyment of God's created gifts. For Calvin, such a position "would fetter [bind] consciences more tightly than does the Word of the Lord"; therefore, it was wrong.[64] The opposite position embraced a limitless freedom that could only be moderated by each individual's conscience. Calvin's reply underscored the error of this extreme: "Certainly I admit that

60. John Calvin, *Institutes of the Christian Religion*, 3.21.4, LCC, 2:925. Calvin scoffed at the cosmology of the Egyptians, "who extend their antiquity to six thousand years before the creation of the world!" Ibid., 1.8.4, LCC, 1:84.

61. Ibid., 1.14.1, LCC, 1:160. Actually, Calvin repeated the six-thousand-year figure twice in the same section. Criticizing those who insist that God should have created the world

ages before he did, Calvin exclaimed: "As if within six thousand years God has not shown evidences enough on which to exercise our minds in earnest meditation!" Ibid., LCC, 1:161.

62. Calvin, *Commentaries on Genesis*, 1:83.

63. Calvin, *Institutes*, 3.10.1, LCC, 1:719–20.

64. Ibid., LCC, 1:720.

consciences neither ought to nor can be bound here to definite and precise legal formulas; but inasmuch as Scripture gives general rules for lawful use, we ought surely to limit our use in accordance with them."[65] Therefore, he championed the following principle: "that the use of God's gifts is not wrongly directed when it is referred to that end to which the author himself created and destined them for us, because he created them for our good, not for our ruin. Accordingly, no one will hold to a straighter path than he who diligently looks to this end. Now, if we ponder to what end God created food, we will find that he meant not only to provide for necessity but also for delight and good cheer."[66] Emphasizing this idea of human delight in created beauty, Calvin added:

> Has the Lord clothed the flowers with the great beauty that greets our eyes, the sweetness of smell that is wafted upon our nostrils, and yet will it be unlawful for our eyes to be affected by that beauty, or our sense of smell by the sweetness of that odor? What? Did he not so distinguish colors as to make some more lovely than others? What? Did he not endow gold and silver, ivory and marble, with a loveliness that renders them more precious than other metals or stones? Did he not, in short, render many things attractive to us, apart from their necessary use?[67]

Accordingly, Calvin set forth both the utility and the beauty of divine creation.

So entrenched in the church's consciousness was belief in divine creation that the historic Protestant creeds barely mention it.[68] Although these creeds were written to distinguish Protestantism from Catholicism, their writers did not sense the need to address the issue of creation, because both Protestants and Catholics alike commonly affirmed it. In the midst of so many differences, this doctrine was not a point of dispute. When the post-Reformation theologians addressed the topic, they simply expressed the historic view of the church.[69] Within this context, in 1658, and correlating biblical, ancient Near Eastern and current calendars, Bishop James Ussher of Ireland calculated the precise date of God's creation of the universe: Sunday, October 23, 4004 BC.[70] With this date

---

65. Ibid.

66. Ibid., 3.10.2, LCC, 1:720.

67. Ibid., LCC, 1:721.

68. *Augsburg Confession*, pt. 1, art. 1, in Schaff, 3:7; *Formula of Concord*, Epitome 2, in Schaff, 3:94–95; *Heidelberg Catechism*, q. 26, in Schaff, 3:315; *Belgic Confession*, art. 12, in Schaff, 3:395; *Westminster Confession of Faith*, 4, in Schaff, 3:611.

69. E.g., John Gerhard, *Loci Theologici* (1621), 4.51, in Schmid, 161.

70. James Ussher, *The Annals of the World* (1658), 4. Here are Ussher's calculations: "For as much as our Christian epoch falls many ages after the beginning of the world, and the number of years before that backward is not only more troublesome, but (unless greater care be taken) more liable to error; also it hath pleased our modern chronologers to add to that generally received hypothesis (which asserted the Julian years, with their three cycles by a certain mathematical prolepsis, to have run down to the very beginning of the world)

an artificial epoch, framed out of three cycles multiplied in themselves; for the Solar Cycle being multiplied by the Lunar, or the number of 28 by 19, produces the great Paschal Cycle of 532 years, and that again multiplied by 15, the number of the indiction, there arises the period of 7980 years, which was first (if I mistake not) observed by Robert Lotharing, bishop of Hereford, in our island of Britain, and 500 years after by Joseph Scaliger fitted for chronological uses, and called by the name of the Julian Period, because it contained a cycle of so many Julian years. Now if the series of the three minor cycles be from this present year extended backward unto precedent times, the 4713 years before the beginning of our Christian account will be found to be that year into which the first year of the indiction, the first of the Lunar Cycle, and the first of the Solar will fall. Having placed therefore the heads of this period in the kalends of January in that proleptic year, the first of our Christian vulgar account must be reckoned the 4714 of the Julian Period, which, being divided by 15. 19. 28. [*sic*] will present us with the 4 Roman indiction, the 2 Lunar Cycle, and

incorporated into a 1701 edition of the Bible, the church's historic belief in a fairly recent creation was continued and given precision.

The seventeenth century marked the beginning of critical attacks against the church's historic doctrine of divine creation. Isaac La Peyrére offered a pre-Adamite theory, a view that human beings existed before Adam.[71] Using information gathered from America, China, and Greenland, La Peyrére dated the existence of humans as far back as 50,000 BC. This was in obvious conflict with Bishop Ussher's chronology, a view that the church generally accepted as being in line with biblical data. It also challenged the clear teaching of Genesis 2 that Adam was the first human being created. La Peyrére, a Roman Catholic, sought to avoid the obvious contradiction with Scripture by affirming that Adam was the origin of the Jewish race. However, according to La Peyrére, the Bible is not exhaustive in its discussion of human origins. Other cultures developed independently from Adam, and indeed preceded him and the Jewish people. Because the Bible is silent on these other peoples, La Peyrére insisted that his pre-Adamite theory did not contradict Scripture.

Turretin attacked La Peyrére's theory, though he considered "the Preadamite [*sic*] fiction is so absurd in itself and foreign to all reason (no less than to the Scripture revelation itself) as to deserve the contempt and indignation of believers rather than a laborious [careful] refutation."[72] Most of Turretin's arguments were biblical.[73] He also addressed La Peyrére's contention that the two accounts of creation—Genesis 1 and Genesis 2—are contradictory stories.[74] Thus, a ready answer to the pre-Adamite theory was offered. But this was only the beginning of the church's problems with this issue.

---

the 10 Solar, which are the principal characters of that year. We find moreover that the year of our forefathers, and the years of the ancient Egyptians and Hebrews were of the same quantity with the Julian, consisting of twelve equal months, every of them containing 30 days, (for it cannot be proved that the Hebrews did use lunar months before the Babylonian Captivity) adjoining to the end of the twelfth month, the addition of five days, and every four year six. And I have observed by the continued succession of these years, as they are delivered in holy writ, that the end of the great Nebuchadnezzar and the beginning of Evil-Merodach's (his sons) reign, fell out in the 3442 year of the world, but by collation of Chaldean history and the astronomical canon, it fell out in the 186 year of Nabonasar, and, as by certain connection, it must follow in the 562 year before the Christian account, and of the Julian Period, the 4152, and from thence I gathered the creation of the world did fall out upon the 710 year of the Julian Period, by placing its beginning in autumn: but for as much as the first day of the world began with the evening of the first day of the week, I have observed that the Sunday, which in the year 710 aforesaid came nearest the Autumnal Equinox, by astronomical tables (notwithstanding the stay of the sun in the days of Joshua, and the going back of it in the days of Hezekiah) happened upon the 23 day of the Julian October; from thence concluded that from the evening preceding that first day of the Julian year, both the first day of the creation and the first motion of time are to be deduced."

71. Isaac La Peyrére, *Men before Adam, or A Discourse upon the Twelfth, Thirteenth, and Fourteenth Verses of the Fifth Chapter of the Apostle Paul to the Romans, by Which Are Prov'd That the First Men Were Created before Adam* (Lat. ed., 1655; Eng. ed., 1658). Cf. La Peyrére, *Relation de l'Islande* (1663) and *Relation de Groenland* (1647).

72. Francis Turretin, *Institutes of Elenctic Theology*, ed. James T. Dennison Jr., trans. George Musgrave Giger, 3 vols. in 1 (Phillipsburg, N.J.: P & R, 1997), 5th topic, 8th q., sec. 1, 1:457.

73. Ibid., 1:457–58. The citation from Wisdom is from the apocryphal book. Although Turretin did not regard the book as canonical, he nonetheless believed that it strengthened his case against the Roman Catholic La Peyrére.

74. "The Preadamite is not to be listened to when he maintains that the creation of the first chapter differs from that described in chapter 2 in various particulars [details]: That in the former, God by one act created male and female at the same time, but in the latter the production of Adam and Eve must have been successive.... Two false hypotheses are supposed here: first, that the creation of the male and female (dealt with in the first chapter) was made at the same time by a single act; while two existing substances are clearly intimated in Gen. 1:27: 'Male and female he created them.' Second, that what is related of the creation of Adam and Eve in Gen. 2 could not have occurred on the same day.... Although it is evident

DIVINE CREATION IN THE MODERN PERIOD

Following La Peyrére's lead, the attacks against the church's doctrine of creation multiplied in the modern period. As the new science of geology became established, two competing theories to explain geological observations came to the forefront. Catastrophism was proposed by Georges Cuvier in his *Theory of the Earth* (1813). This theory maintained that the geological history of the earth could be attributed to numerous catastrophic floods— inundations of the land by the sea—that caused massive extinctions that were then followed by renewals of living creatures. Even though Cuvier believed that the last catastrophic flood had occurred five thousand years ago, he did not explicitly consider it to correspond to the flood of Noah. Moreover, he held to a relatively old earth in order to account for the evidence of numerous past floods. Other proponents of this theory included William Buckland, William Conybeare, and Alan Sedgwick, and their "old-earth catastrophist (or diluvial) geology was widely accepted in the 1820s by most geologists and academic theologians.... The catastrophist theory ... greatly reduced the geological significance of the Noachian deluge and expanded earth history well beyond the traditional biblical view."[75]

In opposition to catastrophism, another geological theory was first propounded by James Hutton and popularized by Charles Lyell in his *Principles of Geology* (1830–33):

> His theory was a radical uniformitarianism in which he insisted that only present-day processes at present-day rates of intensity and magnitude should be used to interpret the rock record of past geological activity.... It explained the whole rock record by slow gradual processes (which included very localized catastrophes like volcanoes and earthquakes at their present frequency of occurrence around the world), thereby reducing the [Noachian] Flood to a geological non-event. His theory also expanded the time of earth history even more than Cuvier or Buckland had done.[76]

It was Lyell's uniformitarianism that rather quickly won the day and thus presented a monumental challenge to the traditional reading of Genesis.

Faced with the prospect of developing a new interpretation of the biblical record that could be harmonized with the geological record, Christians responded with several new approaches to Genesis. One of the leading Scottish evangelicals, Thomas Chalmers, proposed the *gap theory*: "The vast geological ages occurred before Genesis 1:3, and the rest of Genesis 1 is an account of recreation in six literal days on the geological ruins of the previously destroyed earth."[77] Anglican clergyman George Stanley Faber articulated the *day-age theory*—"the days of Genesis 1 are figurative, representing the vast geological ages"[78]—that was popularized by the Scottish geologist Hugh Miller. John Fleming, Scottish Presbyterian minister and zoologist, proposed the *tranquil flood theory*: "The Noachian flood was a global historical event, but it was such a peaceful event that it left

---

that Adam and Eve were not created together and at one time (but successively), it is a false inference that they were produced on different days." Ibid., 1:459.

75. Terry Mortenson, *The Great Turning Point* (Green For-est, Alaska: Master Books, 2004), 32, 33.

76. Ibid.

77. Ibid., 12n7.

78. Ibid., 12n8.

no significant and lasting geological effects."[79] Finally, John Pye Smith, an evangelical Congregational theologian, developed the *local flood theory*: "The Flood was catastrophic but affected only the Mesopotamian valley."[80] With the rise of biblical criticism, another approach that viewed Genesis as a myth was added to the mix. Although many Christians continued to interpret Genesis literally and to hold to the traditional church doctrine of divine creation, these theories challenged many with their unsettling implications.

In the first half of the nineteenth century, in Great Britain, "a tenacious and denominationally eclectic band of scientists and clergymen (and some were both) opposed the new geological theories being developed at the time, which said that the earth was millions of years old. These men became known as 'scriptural geologists,' 'Mosaic geologists,' or 'biblical literalists.'"[81] More specifically:

> The scriptural geologists held to the dominant Christian view within church history up to their own time, namely, that Moses wrote Genesis 1–11 (along with the rest of Genesis) under divine inspiration and that these chapters ought to be interpreted literally as a reliable, fully historical account. This conviction led them to believe, like many contemporary and earlier Christians, that the Noachian flood was a unique global catastrophe which produced much, or most, of the fossil-bearing sedimentary rock formations, and that the earth was roughly six thousand years old.

They also attacked prevailing geological ideas and compromise views on this issue:

> From this position they opposed with equal vigor both the "uniformitarian" theory of earth history propounded by James Hutton and Charles Lyell, and the "catastrophist" theory of Georges Cuvier, William Buckland, William Conybeare, Adam Sedgwick, etc. They also rejected, as compromises of Scripture, the gap theory, the day-age theory, the tranquil flood theory, the local flood theory, and the myth theory. Though all but the myth theory were advocated by Christians who believed in the divine inspiration and historicity of Genesis 1–11, the scriptural geologists believed their opponents' theories were unconvincing interpretations of Scripture based on unproven old-earth theories of geology.[82]

Although their work made a significant contribution at the time, by the middle of the nineteenth century the scriptural geologists had faded from the scene.

The publication of Charles Darwin's book *On the Origin of Species* in 1859 marked a watershed for the church's doctrine of creation.[83] Granted, the early church had critiqued the views of the atomists.[84] Furthermore, the scriptural geologists had stood strongly against the new uniformitarian geology and the novel interpretations of Genesis generated by this developing science. Still, the church had never squared off against such a

79. Ibid., 12n9.

80. Ibid., 12n10.

81. Ibid., 11. Mortenson is the undisputed expert on these "scriptural geologists," having written his Ph.D. dissertation on them. *The Great Turning Point* is a summary of his thesis.

82. Ibid., 12.

83. Charles Darwin, *On the Origin of Species by Means of Natural Selection, or the Preservation of Favoured Races in the Struggle for Life* (London: John Murray, 1859).

84. See earlier in this chapter, p. 255.

virulent opponent as it now faced in Darwinian evolution. The final page of Darwin's manifesto presented a direct challenge to everything the church had ever believed:

> Thus, from the war of nature, from famine and death, the most exalted object which we are capable of conceiving, namely, the production of the higher animals, directly follows. There is grandeur in this view of life, with its several powers, having been originally breathed by the Creator into a few forms or into one; and that, while this planet has gone cycling on according to the fixed law of gravity, from so simple a beginning endless forms most beautiful and most wonderful have been, and are being evolved.[85]

The contention that all of life had evolved according to natural selection as random mutations produced changes without purpose or design over a very long period of time, directly contradicted the Genesis account of divine creation ex nihilo. Furthermore, the church had historically read this account as affirming a young earth's development from nonexistence to maturity over the course of a brief period of six (literal) days. All of this was challenged by the publication of Darwin's evolutionary theory.

The church's reaction to this challenge was mixed. One approach was to denounce explicitly Darwinian evolution as atheistic. In his book *What Is Darwinism?* Charles Hodge focused on Darwin's tenet that "natural selection is without design, being conducted by unintelligent physical causes."[86] For Hodge, this element rendered Darwin's theory unacceptable: "It is that Darwin rejects all teleology, or the doctrine of final causes. He denies design in any of the organisms in the vegetable or animal world.... It is this feature of his system which brings it into conflict not only with Christianity, but with the fundamental principles of natural religion."[87] Hodge also rejected the attempt by some to compartmentalize science and religion into separate spheres of knowledge, so that the theory of evolution and Scripture do not appear to be in conflict, though they actually are.[88] Finding fatal flaws in Darwin's theory,[89] he reserved his chief criticism to the theory's banishment of God from the universe.[90] Thus, to the question, "What is Darwinism?" Hodge responded: "It is atheism. This does not mean ... that Mr. Darwin himself and all who adopt his views are atheists; but it means that his theory is atheistic; that the exclusion of design from nature is ... tantamount to atheism."[91]

A second approach explicitly rejected evolution while it sought to reconcile (some aspects of) scientific discoveries with the biblical account. Typical of this approach was that of William G. T. Shedd. He unhesitatingly affirmed creation ex nihilo with careful attention to Scripture.[92] Indeed, Shedd interpreted Genesis 1:1 as the all-encompassing description of God's creation of the spiritual world and the physical world out of nothing,[93] with Genesis 1:2 depicting the original composition of the physical universe.[94]

---

85. Charles Darwin, *On the Origin of Species* and *The Descent of Man* (New York: Modern Library, n.d.), 374.

86. Charles Hodge, *What Is Darwinism?* (New York: Scribner, Armstrong, & Co., 1874), 48.

87. Ibid., 52; cf. 168–69.

88. Ibid., 141–42.

89. Ibid., 142–44, 150, 151.

90. Ibid., 173–74.

91. Ibid., 177.

92. William G. T. Shedd, *Dogmatic Theology*, 3.7, in *Dogmatic Theology*, ed. Alan W. Gomes, 3rd ed. (Phillipsburg, N.J.: P & R, 2003), 367.

93. Ibid., 371.

94. Ibid., 372.

However, "Between the single comprehensive act of the creation … of chaotic matter mentioned in Genesis 1:1, and the series of divine acts in the six days described in Genesis 1:3–31, an interval of time elapsed."[95] The six days of Genesis 1, according to Shedd, were not literal, twenty-four hour days; rather, they were lengthy periods of time.[96] Thus, Genesis 1 demanded a significantly old age for the earth.

Given this, Shedd believed that a harmony could be worked out between the creation account and some aspects of current physical science. Indeed, he maintained that "the order of creation as given in Genesis is corroborated by the best settled results of modern physics."[97] He gave some specific examples of this corroboration from geology, including the formation of the earth's crust and the gradual clearing of the earth's atmosphere.[98] By no means, however, did Shedd accept the naturalistic evolutionary theory of his day—he referred to it as "pseudoevolution."[99] He made a clear distinction between the development of the inorganic world—which took place by mechanical and chemical processes—and the development of biological life—which was originated at each step of the way by divine creative acts. The divine creative acts, therefore, were specifically in the ex nihilo creation of vegetable species, lower animal species (fishes, reptiles, birds), higher animal species (quadrupeds like cattle), and human beings.[100] Thus, Shedd was a critic of Darwinian evolution while still attempting to forge some kind of harmony between the biblical account of creation and current scientific knowledge.

A third approach to the challenge of evolution was to find common ground between biblical creation and evolutionary theory. Viewing evolution as a scientific theory to be tested, B. B. Warfield was "sure that the old faith will be able not merely to live with, but assimilate to itself all facts [of evolution].... The only living question with regard to the doctrine of evolution is whether it is true."[101] In addition to the truthfulness of evolutionary theory, its conformity with Scripture was critical for Warfield. On this matter, he concluded: "I am free to say, for myself, that I do not think that there is any general statement in the Bible or any part of the account of creation, either as given in Genesis 1 and 2 or elsewhere alluded to, that need be opposed to evolution."[102] In the end, Warfield affirmed there is no final conflict between holding a nuanced theory of evolution and being a Christian.[103]

95. Ibid.

96. Ibid., 373.

97. Ibid., 375.

98. Ibid., 375–79.

99. Ibid., 387.

100. Ibid., 378.

101. B. B. Warfield, "The Present-Day Conception of Evolution," *Presbyterian Messenger* (December 5, 1895), 7–8, in *Evolution, Scripture, and Science*, ed. Mark A. Noll and Daniel N. Livingstone (Grand Rapids: Baker, 2000), 165.

102. B. B. Warfield, "Evolution or Development," lecture first delivered at Princeton Seminary on December 12, 1888, in Noll and Livingstone, *Evolution, Scripture, and Science*, 130. Still, Warfield pointed to the creation of Eve (Gen. 2:18–25) as constituting the most serious biblical challenge to Christians' acceptance of evolutionary theory (ibid.).

103. Clearly, what Warfield cautiously entertained was not the naturalistic philosophy that undergirded evolution. Indeed, he explicitly denounced such naturalism because it "leaves no place for the Christian's God, who is not the God afar off of the deist, and not the simple world-ground of the pantheist, but the living God of the Bible." Warfield, "Present-Day Conception of Evolution," 7–8, in Noll and Livingstone, *Evolution, Scripture, and Science*, 162. But what attracted Warfield to the theory was evolution's explanatory ability in certain cases. E.g., Warfield appreciated evolution's tenet that all human beings have a common ancestor. Warfield, "On the Antiquity and Unity of the Human Race," *Princeton Theological Review* 9 (January 1911): 1–25, in Noll and Livingstone, *Evolution, Scripture, and Science*, 279–80. It was with particular reference to this that Warfield found a concurrence between the doctrine of creation and some modified form of

B. B. Warfield on the Harmony between Evolution and Christianity

The upshot of the whole matter is that there is no *necessary* antagonism of Christianity to evolution, *provided that* we do not hold to too extreme a form of evolution. To adopt any form that does not permit God freely to work apart from law and that does not allow *miraculous* intervention (in the giving of the soul, in creating Eve, etc.) will entail a great reconstruction of Christian doctrine, and a very great lowering of the detailed authority of the Bible. But if we condition the theory by allowing the constant oversight of God in the whole process, and his occasional supernatural interference for the production of *new* beginnings by an actual output of creative force, producing something new ... in preceding conditions, we may hold to the modified theory of evolution and be Christians in the ordinary orthodox sense.*

*B. B. Warfield, "Evolution or Development," lecture first delivered at Princeton Seminary on December 12, 1888, in Noll and Livingstone, *Evolution, Scripture, and Science*, 130–31.

Warfield's view entailed that the earth and all it contains is of ancient rather than of recent origin. He dismissed the idea that a conflict exists between the age of the earth as envisioned by scientists and as conceived by "students of the Bible." Addressing the young earth view, which relied upon the genealogies of Genesis 5 and 11 to construct a brief chronology for the earth's earliest period, Warfield asserted: "It is precarious in the extreme to draw chronological inferences from these genealogies. The genealogies of Scripture were not constructed for a chronological purpose, and any appearance they present of affording materials for chronological inferences is accidental and illusory."[104] Thus, Warfield and others cautiously accepted some aspects of evolutionary theory while

evolution, what he termed "a theory of evolution *per saltum* [by leaps]": "If under the directing hand of God a human body is formed at a leap by propagation from brutish parents, it would be quite consonant with the fitness of things that it should be provided by his creative energy with a truly human soul." Warfield, "Review of James Orr, *God's Image in Man and Its Defacement in the Light of Modern Denials* (London: Hodder & Stoughton, 1905)," *Princeton Theological Review* 4 (October 1906): 555–58, in Noll and Livingstone, *Evolution, Scripture, and Science*, 232–33. In other words, Warfield saw no conflict between an evolutionary development of human beings physically from lower life forms (primates, hominids) and the immediate divine impartation of a human soul into these developing creatures so as to constitute human beings made in God's image. One reason why Warfield found no conflict was that he believed in the compatibility of evolutionary processes with teleology—purposeful direction. Warfield, "Review of Vernon L. Kellogg, *Darwinism Today: A Discussion of Present-Day Scientific Criticism of the Darwinian*

Selection Theories, Together with a Brief Account of the Principal and Other Proposed Auxiliary and Alternative Theories of Species-Forming (New York: Henry Holt, 1907)," *Princeton Theological Review* 6 (October 1908): 640–50, in Noll and Livingstone, *Evolution, Scripture, and Science*, 250. Indeed, Warfield held out hope that scientists would move "towards the recognition of the mystery of life and life processes, of their inexplicability on purely physicochemical grounds, of the necessity of the assumption of the working of some higher directive force in the advance of organic development." Warfield, "Review of Vernon L. Kellogg, *Darwinism Today*," in Noll and Livingstone, *Evolution, Scripture, and Science*, 250. While acknowledging that his proposal flew in the face of Darwinian evolutionary theory, Warfield nonetheless naively clung to it as his hope.

104. B. B. Warfield, "The Manner and Time of Man's Origin," *The Bible Student*, n.s., 8, no. 5 (November 1903): 241–52, in Noll and Livingstone, *Evolution, Scripture, and Science*, 217–18.

insisting that there was no ultimate conflict between it and the classical Christian doctrine of divine creation.

Evangelicals gained a heightened sense of the importance of interpreting the biblical record of creation in a responsible and exegetically sound manner. Many were also concerned to formulate a doctrine of creation that either challenged or incorporated—interacted with, if nothing more—the current developments in evolutionary theory. Six major interpretative approaches to the opening chapters of Genesis were the result: the framework hypothesis, the gap theory, the day-age theory, the intermittent-day theory, the fully-gifted creation theory, and the literal approach.

The framework hypothesis, or literary interpretation, had its roots in Augustine and was retrieved by several leading evangelicals, including Henri Blocher, Herman Ridderbos, Bernard Ramm, Meredith Kline, and Ronald Youngblood. Blocher explained the hypothesis: "The literary interpretation takes the form of the week attributed to the work of creation to be an artistic arrangement, a modest example of anthropomorphism that is not to be taken literally.... The text is composed as the author meditates on the finished work, so that we may understand how the creation is related to God and what is its significance for mankind."[105] For Blocher this approach avoids various difficulties[106] and has in its favor "both the genre and the style of the Genesis 1 prologue."[107]

The Framework Hypothesis

Days of Forming	Days of Filling
Day 1: Light and darkness separated	Day 4: Sun, moon, and stars (lights in the heaven)
Day 2: Sky and waters separated	Day 5: Fish and birds
Day 3: Dry land and seas separated, plants and trees*	Day 6: Animals and man

*The NIV Study Bible, ed. Kenneth Barker et al. (Grand Rapids: Zondervan, 1985), 6 (note to Gen. 1:11).

The gap theory, as noted above, was originated by Thomas Chalmers in the nineteenth century. G. H. Pember revived the theory. Wrestling with the reality of the fossil record and its vivid testimony of death and destruction, Pember could not reconcile this report with the biblical account of the created world that God had pronounced "very good." He surmised, "Since, then, the fossil remains are those of creatures anterior [prior] to Adam, and yet show evident tokens of disease, death, and mutual destruction, they must have belonged to another world and have a sin-stained history of their own."[108] He located

---

105. Henri Blocher, *In the Beginning: The Opening Chapters of Genesis*, trans. David G. Preston (Downers Grove, Ill.: InterVarsity, 1984), 50.

106. Ibid., 50, 52.

107. Ibid., 50.

108. G. H. Pember, *Earth's Earliest Ages* (1884; repr., New York: Revell, 1900), 35.

the existence of this other world in the "gap" between Genesis 1:1 and 1:2, a world that the Bible describes as "formless and void." As for how to account for this "gap" in the Genesis story, Pember explained: "There is room for any length of time between the first and second verses of the Bible."[109] Into this gap in Genesis was situated another world of death, decay, and destruction.[110] In the twentieth century, the *Scofield Reference Bible* popularized the theory, which the study notes listed as a possible interpretation of the opening verses of Genesis 1.[111] Arthur Custance's *Without Form and Void* provided the most robust defense of the theory.[112]

As scientific observation and measurement resulted in an ever-increasing body of evidence for an ancient earth, some evangelicals opted for an approach to the Genesis account that interpreted the "days" of Genesis 1 not as literal twenty-four-hour days but as long periods of time (the "day-age" theory) or as twenty-four-hour days that were separated by long periods of time (the "intermittent-day" theory). This evidence for an old earth included the antiquity of sedimentary rock sequences, the slow process of coral reef formation, radiometric dating of rocks and meteorites that indicates an age of 4.5 billion years, the slow cooling of liquid magma, the lengthy time necessary for fossil formation, the lengthy time for light to travel, the expansion of the universe, continental drift, the formation of stars, and others.[113]

The day-age theory was proposed in order to maintain the six-day structure of Genesis 1 and incorporate the vast age of the earth into this biblical framework. In this theory, each "day" of Genesis represents a very long period of time. As noted above, George Stanley Faber and Hugh Miller propounded this theory in the nineteenth century. They were followed by notable theologians and churchmen such as Alexander Maclaren, Charles Hodge, James Orr, and A. H. Strong.[114] Similarly, the intermittent-day theory sought to maintain a literal twenty-four-hour period for the days of Genesis 1 and incorporate the vast age of the earth into this biblical framework. To accomplish this, this theory

109. Ibid., 28.

110. Ibid.

111. C. I. Scofield, ed., *The Scofield Reference Bible* (New York: Oxford Univ. Press, 1917), 3. Specifically, on the expression "without form and void" as a description of the earth in Gen. 1:2, the notes explained: "Jeremiah 4:23–26, Isaiah 24:1 and 45:18 clearly indicate that the earth had undergone a cataclysmic change as the result of a divine judgment. The face of the earth bears everywhere the marks of such a catastrophe. There are not lacking intimations that connect it with a previous testing and fall of angels. See Ezekiel 28:12–15 and Isaiah 14:9–14, which certainly go beyond the kings of Tyre and Babylon." Here, the *Scofield Bible* made a connection between the fall of Satan and his followers and the destruction of the original, perfect creation as God's judgment on the angelic rebellion.

112. Arthur C. Custance, *Without Form and Void: A Study of the Meaning of Genesis 1:2* (Brockville, Ont.: Doorway Papers, 1970).

113. E.g., Davis A. Young, *Christianity and the Age of the Earth* (Grand Rapids: Zondervan, 1982).

114. Young summarized the biblical arguments to which supporters of the day-age theory consistently pointed in its defense: First, "the Hebrew word for 'day' frequently denotes a long period of time rather than an ordinary day ... so that it cannot be dogmatically asserted that the six days must be treated as ordinary days." Second, "at least the first three days cannot be treated as ordinary days inasmuch as the sun ... was not even yet in existence." Third, "the events depicted in the six days are not of such a nature to have occurred within twenty-four hours." Fourth, "the seventh day, the day of God's rest, is still going on and is therefore a long period of time.... [Therefore], the preceding six days might also legitimately be treated as long periods of time of indeterminate length." Ibid., 58–59. Appealing to these arguments, Young concluded, "There are exegetical grounds for maintaining that the six days of creation were long, indeterminate periods of time." Ibid., 161.

proposed that each day of Genesis was separated from the next by a very lengthy period of time.[115]

The fully gifted creation theory, dismissing both naturalistic evolution and special creationism, was proposed by Howard J. Van Till.[116] It embraced (1) creation ex nihilo; (2) the divine gift to all created things of "a being that is defined in part by their 'creaturely properties' ... [and] also defined in a very important way by a characteristic set of 'creaturely capabilities' ... to act and interact in a remarkably rich diversity of ways"; and (3) the idea that these capabilities make it such that "something like biotic evolution" has occurred.[117] Clearly, this last element distinguished Van Till's position from the others. Although accused of embracing theistic evolution, Van Till distanced himself from this label because it focuses primarily on the development of creatures and only secondarily on the divine creative action. So Van Till opted for another label—"*the fully gifted creation perspective*—a vision that recognizes the entire universe as a creation that has, by God's unbounded generosity and unfathomable creativity, been given all of the capabilities for self-organization and transformation necessary to make possible something as humanly incomprehensible as unbroken evolutionary development."[118]

Championing the historical viewpoint of the church, another and final position—called "young earth creationism" or "scientific creationism"—became particularly strong at the turn of the third millennium. Creationists viewed all of the above positions as compromises with scientific findings that were, in their opinion, suspect at best or entirely wrong at worst. At the heart of this position was scientific dismissal of evolutionary theory and scientific support for creationism.

In his seminal work *Scientific Creationism*, Henry Morris contrasted two models of origins—the evolutionary model and the creation model:[119]

---

115. Specifically, Robert C. Newman maintained "that the 'days' of Genesis 1 are twenty-four-hour days, sequential but not consecutive, and that the creative activity largely occurs between days rather than on them. That is, each Genesis day introduces a new creative period." Robert C. Newman and Herman J. Eckelmann Jr., *Genesis One and the Origin of the Earth* (Downers Grove, Ill.: InterVarsity, 1977), 74. As for the anticipated objection that Ex. 20:8–11 demands that the days of the creation week were literal and consecutive twenty-four-hour periods, Newman responded: "This argument is not necessarily valid, because it is an argument from analogy, not from identity. The work-week and Sabbath day differ from the creation week in *at least* one point—the former are repeated again and again, but the latter is not. Because the passage does not explicitly say that 'day' is to be understood the same way in both cases, this may differ also.... Perhaps twenty-four-hour days are used in the work-week to commemorate long periods in creation week." Ibid., 62–63.

116. Howard J. Van Till, *The Fourth Day: What the Bible and the Heavens Are Telling Us about the Creation* (Grand Rapids: Eerdmans, 1986), 249.

117. Howard J. Van Till, "The Fully Gifted Creation," in *Three Views on Creation and Evolution*, ed. J. P. Moreland and John Mark Reynolds (Grand Rapids: Zondervan, 1999), 170–71. Although Van Till's book *The Fourth Day* (see n. 116 above) is a more scholarly work than his article in the *Three Views* anthology, the latter represents his later and more developed perspective; thus, citations from the article are warranted.

118. Van Till, "Fully Gifted Creation," 173.

119. Henry M. Morris, ed., *Scientific Creationism* (San Diego: Creation-Life, 1974), 12.

Evolution Model	Creation Model
Continuing naturalistic origin	Completed supernatural origin
Net present increase in complexity	Net present decrease in complexity
Earth history dominated by uniformitarianism	Earth history dominated by catastrophism

He offered several reasons for the failure of the first model: it contradicts the first and second laws of thermodynamics;[120] it relies on the notion of natural selection, with its emphasis on genetic mutations;[121] and it cannot account for the systematic gaps in the fossil record. Reversing directions, he maintained that the fossil record is evidence of a great catastrophe.[122] Indeed, a scenario from a great, worldwide catastrophe—Noah's flood—is "explicitly confirmed in the geologic column."[123] In addition, Morris maintained that the residual effects of the flood would also account for what one actually observes in the earth's present surface features.[124] Again, this was taken as confirmation of the creation model with catastrophism. Finally, Morris questioned the evidence from different types of dating techniques—for example, radiometric dating and radiocarbon dating—that concluded that the earth is billions of years old. Rather, he pointed to evidence for a young earth.[125] Thus, he concluded the creation model is far superior to the evolution model.[126] Morris pioneered the modern young earth or scientific creationism movement and launched such groups as the Institute for Creation Research and Answers in Genesis.

In another but related development, evangelicals and others launched an aggressive scientific attack against Darwin's theory of evolution, though in a significantly different manner than creationism. Specifically, the *intelligent design movement* (ID) was directed at two fronts: critiquing naturalism, the foundation of evolutionary theory, and establishing the fact that God's work in the world can be empirically detected. As William Dembski explained: "Its fundamental claim is that intelligent causes are necessary to explain the complex, information-rich structures of biology and that these causes are empirically detectable. To say intelligent causes are empirically detectable is to say there exist well-defined methods that on the basis of observational features of the world are capable of reliably distinguishing intelligent causes from undirected natural causes."[127] As for the movement's critique of naturalism, Dembski and ID proponents argued "that Darwinism is *on its own terms* a failed scientific research program—that it does not constitute a well-supported scientific theory, that its explanatory power is

120. Ibid., 25–26.

121. Ibid., 55–57.

122. Ibid., 117–19.

123. Ibid., 120.

124. "Mountain-building, glaciation, pluviation, volcanism, and possible continental drift." Ibid., 28.

125. This evidence included the efflux of gases into the atmosphere, the influx of meteoric material from space, the influx of materials into the ocean, the efflux of materials from the mantle into the crust, and the decay of the earth's magnetic field. Ibid., 149–60.

126. Ibid., 201.

127. William A. Dembski, *Intelligent Design: The Bridge between Science and Theology* (Downers Grove, Ill.: InterVarsity, 1999), 106.

severely limited and that it fails abysmally when it tries to account for the grand sweep of natural history."[128] The intelligent design movement offered a critique of Darwinian evolution and scientific naturalism that undergirds it, and sought ways to establish the fact that God's work in the world is empirically detectable as evidence of an Intelligent Designer.

Into the twenty-first century, evangelicals holding these various views on divine creation lobbied for their positions, often in hotly contested forums. The doctrine continues to be a point of disagreement within the church today.

---

128. Ibid., 112. Specifically, these problems include "the origin of life, the origin of the genetic code, the origin of multicellular life, the origin of sexuality, the scarcity of transitional forms in the fossil record, the biological big bang that occurred in the Cambrian era, the development of complex organ systems and the development of irreducibly complex molecular machines." Ibid., 113. Cf. Michael Behe, *Darwin's Black Box: The Biochemical Challenge to Evolution* (New York: Free Press, 1996).

Chapter 13

PROVIDENCE

How has the church come to understand God's continuing work of preserving and governing his creation? How has it developed its views of God's decrees? How has the church dealt with the problem of evil?

STATEMENT OF BELIEF

The church has historically affirmed that in addition to creating the world, God exercises control over his creation through his providence. This work includes his preservation of all that he created, his cooperation in the ongoing activities of the created order, and his government in directing the creation to fulfill his purposes. Some closely associate this providential care with God's decrees, "the eternal plans of God whereby, before the creation of the world, he determined to bring about everything that happens."[1] According to this view, God's "providential actions are the outworking of the eternal decrees that he made long ago."[2] Of course, one of the major issues raised by this position is the problem of evil: If God is all-powerful and exercises control over everything in his creation, what can explain the presence of evil and suffering in the world? Even those who do not hold such a view have still had to wrestle with this issue.

While the church has substantial agreement over God's providential care of the inanimate universe and the plant and animal kingdoms, great division has historically existed over God's providential relationship to the moral choices and actions of human beings. The Reformed position (and views similar to it) affirms the decrees of God as the foundation for everything that comes to pass. It also holds that every detail of everything that happens is part of the providential plan of God. The Arminian position (and views similar to it) holds "that God's providential involvement in or control of history must not include every specific detail of every event that happens. So God's purpose or plan

---

1. Wayne Grudem, *Systematic Theology: An Introduction to Biblical Doctrine* (Grand Rapids: Zondervan, 1994, 2000), 332.
2. Ibid.

for the world 'is not a blueprint encompassing all future contingencies' but 'a dynamic program for the world, the outworking of which depends in part on man.'"[3] This chapter will trace the development of these two divergent positions while also noting the points of agreement on the doctrine of divine providence.[4]

THE DOCTRINE OF PROVIDENCE IN THE EARLY CHURCH

The writers of the New Testament affirmed divine providence on the basis of Hebrew Scripture (e.g., Prov. 16:33) and the teachings of Jesus about sparrows and other mundane realities of life (Matt. 10:29–30). Practical application of this affirmation included the command not to fear (Matt. 10:31) and the instruction that Christians "ought to say, 'If it is the Lord's will, we will live and do this or that'" (James 4:15).

Following the New Testament period, the early church continued this belief, calling God "the Master of the universe"[5] who "rules over the whole world."[6] An inexhaustible and meticulous divine providence was acknowledged as a general principle: "God does exercise a providence over all things.... Certain of the Gentiles were convinced that they should call the Maker of this universe the Father, who exercises a providence over all things, and arranges the affairs [events] of our world."[7] This applied to the material universe: "The heavens move at God's direction and obey him in peace. Day and night complete the course assigned by him, neither hindering the other. The sun and the moon and the choirs of stars circle in harmony within the courses assigned to them, according to his direction, without any deviation at all.... The seasons, spring and summer and autumn and winter, give way in succession, one to the other, in peace."[8] Irenaeus extended this divine control to human (and angelic) beings.[9] As applied by Origen, this control meant: "Of those events that happen to men, none occur by accident or chance, but in accordance with a plan so carefully considered, and so stupendous, that it does not overlook even the number of hairs on a person's head, not merely of Christians, but perhaps of all human beings. And the plan of this providential government extends even to caring for the sale of two sparrows for a penny."[10]

The church demanded a particular lifestyle from its members in light of God's providence. The *Didache* gave a simple instruction: "Accept as good the things that happen to you, knowing that nothing transpires apart from God."[11] Even death for the cause of Christ—whose own death had been in accordance with the divine plan[12]—was to be recognized as part of the plan of the sovereign God: "Blessed and noble ... are all the

---

3. Ibid. The quote is taken from Clark Pinnock, "Responsible Freedom in the Flow of Biblical History," in *Grace Unlimited*, ed. Clark H. Pinnock (Minneapolis: Bethany, 1975), 18.

4. My thanks to Josh Nelson for his help with this chapter.

5. Clement of Rome, *Letter of the Romans to the Corinthians*, 8.2, in Holmes, 37; *ANF*, 1:7 ("the Lord of all things").

6. *Letter of Barnabas*, 21.5, in Holmes, 325; *ANF*, 1:149.

7. Irenaeus, *Against Heresies*, 3.25.1, in *ANF*, 1:459.

8. Clement of Rome, *Letter of the Romans to the Corinthians*, 20, in Holmes, 53; *ANF*, 1:10.

9. Irenaeus, *Against Heresies*, 5.22.2, in *ANF*, 1:551.

10. Origen, *First Principles*, 2.11.5, in *ANF*, 4:299. The text has been rendered clearer.

11. *The Didache*, 3.10, in Holmes, 255; *ANF*, 7:378.

12. Justin Martyr, *Dialogue with Trypho, a Jew*, 102, in *ANF*, 1:250.

martyrdoms that have taken place in accordance with the will of God (for we must reverently assign to God the power over all things)."[13]

At first glance, this affirmation would appear to involve God in actively willing and doing evil. While preserving his providence, this belief would sacrifice God's goodness. To avoid this possible quandary, some spoke of God's *permission* of such evil events rather than his *willing* of them. Tertullian made this distinction: "Though some things seem to savor of the will of God, seeing that they are allowed by him, it does not necessarily follow that everything which is permitted proceeds out of the mere and absolute will of him who permits [it]."[14] Clement of Alexandria offered a similar idea:

> The Lord did not suffer by the will of the Father, nor are persecuted believers persecuted by the will of God.... But nothing takes place apart from the will of the Lord of the universe. It remains for us to say that such things happen apart from the prevention of God; for this alone saves both the providence and goodness of God. We must not therefore think that he actively produces afflictions (far be it that we should think this!); but we must be persuaded that he does not prevent those that cause them, but overrules for good the crimes of his enemies.[15]

Thus, God's providence does not will evil like it wills good. Rather, it *permits* evil while it *wills* good, as Origen explained:

> We must inquire into the meaning of the statement, that "all things are ordained according to God's will," and ascertain whether sins are or are not included among the things which God ordains. For if God's government extends to sins ... it is for those who speak in this manner to see how incorrect is the expression that "all things are ordained by the will of God." For it follows from it that all sins and all their consequences are ordained by the will of God, which is a different thing from saying that they come to pass with God's permission.... When we say that "the providence of God regulates all things," we utter a great truth if we attribute to that providence nothing but what is just and right. But if we ascribe to the providence of God all things whatsoever, however unjust they may be, then it is no longer true that the providence of God regulates all things.[16]

Therefore, God ordains all the good that occurs in the universe while he permits even the evil that takes place. The early church insisted on this affirmation. Otherwise, its high view of the providence of God could be misunderstood to mean that God is the author of evil.

Obviously, the church's affirmation of divine providence did not entail a belief in the loss of human free will. Origen explicitly denied that human beings "are like pieces of wood and stones, which are dragged about by those causes that act upon them

---

13. *The Martyrdom of Polycarp*, 2, in Holmes, 227; *ANF*, 1:39.

14. Tertullian, *On Exhortation to Chastity*, 3, in *ANF*, 4:51.

15. Clement of Alexandria, *Stromata*, 4.12, in *ANF*, 2:424;

cf. *Stromata*, 1.17, in *ANF*, 2:320. The text has been rendered clearer.

16. Origen, *Against Celsus*, 7.68, in *ANF*, 4:638. The text's "ordered" has been rendered "ordained."

externally."[17] This means that human beings who use their free will in ways that please God—even though such good acts are according to divine providence—are worthy of praise.[18] Oppositely, this means that those who abuse their free will in doing evil—even though such bad acts are according to divine providence—are deserving of punishment.[19] Indeed, this reality of praiseworthiness and blameworthiness became a common apologetic for the existence of human free will, as Athenagoras explained: Human beings "have freedom of choice as to both virtue and vice. For you would not either honor the good or punish the bad, unless vice and virtue were in their own power."[20] Thus, the church affirmed the compatibility of human freedom and divine providence: "We ... maintain that all things are administered by God in proportion to the condition of the free will of each individual ... and that the nature of our free will admits the occurrence of contingent events."[21] In other words, divine providence extends to everything in the universe and functions even in the case of human freedom, which guarantees that various possibilities—for both good and evil—exist whenever people are faced with the choice of decisions and actions.

At times the early church wrestled theologically and philosophically with the problem of evil. Some, like Arnobius, simply admitted that evil is a mystery: "They will ask, 'Why does the almighty God not remove these evils, but allow them to exist and to go on without ceasing through all the ages?' If we have learned of God the supreme ruler, and resolved not to wander in a maze of wicked and mad speculations, then we must answer that we do not know these things."[22] But others attempted to offer solutions to this problem, and several reasons were proposed for the problem of evil.

Tertullian reasoned from the fact that God decided to create human beings with free will. Because of this, God could not intervene to stop people from abusing their freedom by choosing to do evil. Addressing the fall of Adam and Eve into sin, Tertullian framed the problem in this way: "You reason that if God were good, and if he were unwilling that such a catastrophe should happen, and if by his foreknowledge he was not ignorant of the future, and if he were powerful enough to hinder its occurrence, that result would never have come about.... Since, however, it has occurred, the contrary affirmation must certainly be true: God must be neither good, nor knowledgeable of the future, nor powerful."[23] After vindicating the goodness, foreknowledge, and power of God, Tertullian turned to human beings to look for the cause of evil: "I find, then, that God constituted humanity free, ruler of its own will and power.... Upon careful consideration, it can be shown that this human freedom alone is to be blamed for the evil that it committed itself."[24] Because God had constituted humanity free, he could not step in and stop its abuse of freedom; otherwise, "he would have removed human free will, which he had

17. Origen, *First Principles*, 3.1.5, in *ANF*, 4:304. A modern analogy might use robots.

18. Ibid., 4.82, in *ANF*, 4:534.

19. Ibid., 4.70, in *ANF*, 4:528.

20. Athenagoras, *A Plea for the Christians*, 24, in *ANF*, 2:142.

21. Origen, *Against Celsus*, 5.21, in *ANF*, 4:552.

22. Arnobius, *Against the Heathen*, 2.55, in *ANF*, 6:454. The text has been rendered clearer.

23. Tertullian, *Against Marcion*, 2.5, in *ANF*, 3:300–301. The text has been rendered clearer.

24. Ibid., 2.5–6, in *ANF*, 3:301–3. The text has been rendered clearer.

permitted with a set purpose and in goodness.[25] This early solution to the problem of evil would later be termed the "free will defense."

Another solution to the problem of evil was proposed by Origen, who argued that evil is necessary for the spontaneous production of morally upright human beings.[26] Lactantius echoed this idea by underscoring the necessity of the contrast between virtue and vice, good and evil, so as to understand the difference between the two and to promote virtue:

> Virtue cannot be discerned unless it has vices opposed to it, nor can it be developed unless it is exercised by adversity. For God designed that there should be this distinction between good and evil things, that we may know from that which is evil the value of the good, and also know the value of evil from the good. The nature of either one cannot be understood if the other one is removed. God, therefore, did not exclude evil, that the nature of virtue might be evident.[27]

For Lactantius, moral virtues like patience and faithfulness develop if and only if evil exists and persists. Were there no evil, human beings would not develop virtue. As to whether God could have created human beings inherently virtuous, that whole idea is absurd. God could have created human beings in the absence of evil, but they would not have been *virtuous* human beings. For virtue to prosper, evil is necessary; thus, God does not intervene to remove evil from the world.

While wrestling with the problem of evil, the early church did not follow the proposal of Marcion; indeed, it condemned his idea. For Marcion, Jesus' teaching about two types of trees (Matt. 7:18) implied the existence of two gods[28] — "one judicial, harsh, mighty in war; the other mild, placid, and simply good and excellent."[29] Taking it a step further, Marcion identified the evil god with Yahweh of the Old Testament. This was the god who created the world and the evil in it. And this was the just and vengeful god who showed preference for the people of Israel, to the point of encouraging the genocide of the Canaanites. According to Irenaeus, Marcion considered this god "to be the author of evils, to take delight in war, to be weak in purpose, and even to be contrary to himself."[30] The good god, on the other hand, was above the Creator god and became the Father of Jesus Christ. This was the god of the New Testament, who has love and mercy for all people. Thus, Marcion resolved the problem of evil by proposing the existence of two gods, one of whom was responsible for the evil in the world. Not only did the church find this solution unsatisfactory; it condemned it as heresy.

With the theology of Augustine, the church presented its most extensive case for God's inexhaustible and meticulous providence working in conjunction with human free will: "We assert both that God knows all things before they come to pass, and that we do by our free will whatever we know and feel to be done by us only because we will it." He explained how these two affirmations could be compatible:

25. Ibid., 2.7, in *ANF*, 3:303. The text has been rendered clearer.

26. Origen, *Against Celsus*, 4.3, in *ANF*, 4:498.

27. Lactantius, *The Divine Institutes*, 5.7, in *ANF*, 7:142.

The text has been rendered clearer.

28. Tertullian, *Against Marcion*, 1.2, in *ANF*, 3:272–73.

29. Ibid., 1.6, in *ANF*, 3:275.

30. Irenaeus, *Against Heresies*, 1.27.2, in *ANF*, 1:352.

[There is] an order of causes in which the highest effect is attributed to the will of God.... But it does not follow that, though there is for God a certain order of all causes, there must therefore be nothing depending on the free exercise of our own wills, for our wills themselves are included in that order of causes which is certain to God, and is embraced by his foreknowledge, for human wills are also the cause of human actions. And he who foreknew all the causes of things would certainly not have been ignorant of our wills, because they are among those causes.[31]

In one sense, then, the human will decides and acts of necessity, meaning that whatever God foreknows will happen will certainly come to pass. But in another sense, the human will does not act of necessity, if necessity is understood to be a kind of compulsion to decide or act a certain way. Rather, the human will decides and acts according to its own choice: "If we will, it is; if we do not will, it is not."[32] For Augustine, two truths must be affirmed together, and one truth cannot be used to destroy the other: "We are by no means compelled to do away with the freedom of the will by retaining divine foreknowledge, or, by retaining the freedom of the will, to deny that God has foreknowledge of future things—an ungodly idea! But we embrace both."[33] Thus, Augustine affirmed that "whatever is done in the world is done partly by divine agency and partly by our will."[34] And he extended this providential control to include everything that exists.[35]

In dealing with the problem of evil, Augustine offered the free will defense. He came from a background of dualism, which he embraced while attracted to a movement called Manichaeism. According to this view, two eternal principles—one of good, the other of evil—exist eternally and are locked in mortal combat.[36] For Manichaeism, therefore, the problem of evil is an eternal one, just part of the way the universe has always been and always will exist.

Shrugging off this idea as inadequate, Augustine argued that evil is not something that exists; rather, "evil is nothing but a privation [negation, or absence] of good."[37] He worked from the notion that God, who is the supreme good and source of good, created everything good in its original state. But creatures can fall away from their original goodness, and it is in this loss of goodness that evil consists: "Here we see the proper use of the word *evil*; for it is correctly applied not to essence, but to negation or loss."[38] But

31. Augustine, *The City of God*, 5.9, in *NPNF*[1], 2:91. The text has been rendered clearer.

32. Ibid., 5.10, in *NPNF*[1], 2:91.

33. Ibid., in *NPNF*[1], 2:93.

34. Augustine, *Eighty-three Different Questions*, 24, in *St. Augustine: Eighty-three Different Questions*, trans., David L. Mosher, Fathers of the Church (Catholic Univ. of America Press, 2002), 51.

35. Augustine, *City of God*, 5.11, in *NPNF*[1], 2:93.

36. For a current parallel to Manichean dualism, we can think of the battle between the good side and the evil side of the force in the Star Wars series.

37. Augustine, *Confessions*, 3.7.12, in *NPNF*[1], 1:64. The text

has been rendered clearer.

38. Augustine, *On the Morals of the Manicheans*, 4.4.6, in *NPNF*[1], 4:70–71. In his *Confessions*, Augustine demonstrated that the idea of evil being a thing is wrong: "I sought out where evil came from. Evil is not a thing; for if it were a thing, it would be good. For either it would be an incorruptible thing, and so a chief good, or a corruptible thing, which unless it were good [to begin with] it could not be corrupted. I perceived, therefore, and it was made clear to me, that God made all things good, and there are no things whatsoever that were not made by him." Augustine, *Confessions*, 7.12.18, in *NPNF*[1], 1:110. The text has been rendered clearer.

why would creatures originally created good fall away? It was at this point that Augustine introduced the idea of human free will, specifically "a perversion of the will, turned away from God."[39] Yet even this turning away from God and abuse of free will in doing evil did not and could not ultimately frustrate the will of God: "For it would not be done if he did not permit it (and, of course, his permission is not unwilling, but willing)."[40] Indeed, God foreknew and even decreed that Adam and Eve would abuse their free will and plunge all of humanity into sin and death: "For man, by his sin, could not disturb the divine counsel, nor compel God to change what he had decreed."[41] Thus, Augustine offered the free will defense to deal with the problem of evil.

THE DOCTRINE OF PROVIDENCE IN THE MIDDLE AGES

The medieval church continued to affirm the doctrine of divine providence, noting its biblical basis while also exploring the matter from a philosophical perspective. Two notable contributors to the church's doctrine were Anselm and Aquinas.

Like Augustine, Anselm addressed the problem of evil, specifically this issue: "If everything that exists derives its existence from God's knowledge, then God is the Creator and author also of evil works and, by inference, unjustly punishes the wicked."[42] Noting that this idea is unacceptable, and following his predecessor, Anselm explained "that the goodness which consists of uprightness is really something that exists, whereas the evil which is called unrighteousness lacks existence entirely."[43] Concerning God's relationship to both, he noted, "Everything that has existence owes its being at all to God, who is the source of all uprightness but not of unrighteousness. Therefore, although God is a factor in all that is done by a righteous or unrighteous will in its good and evil acts, nevertheless, in the case of its good acts he effects both their existence and their goodness, whereas in the case of its evil acts he causes them to be, but not to be evil."[44]

Anselm anticipated an objection to this apparently unfair notion: "How is it that the goodness of our actions is the result of God's goodness and their evil the result of our own fault alone or the devil's? ... And why is God's contribution to our evil deeds blameless and our part in our own good deeds praiseworthy so that, as a consequence, their goodness is clearly seen to be imputable to God and their evil to us?"[45] In reply, Anselm argued for compatibility between human free choice and the grace of God: "A creature possesses the uprightness ... only by the grace of God.... With God's gracious help ...

---

39. Augustine, *Confessions*, 7.16.22, in *NPNF*[1], 1:111; cf. 7.3.5, in *NPNF*[1], 1:104. The text has been rendered clearer.

40. Augustine, *Enchiridion on Faith, Hope, and Love*, 100, in *NPNF*[1], 3:269.

41. Augustine, *City of God*, 14.11, in *NPNF*[1], 2:271. In this same section, Augustine dealt with scriptural passages indicating that God changes his mind or repents by denying that they mean that God's decree changes: "For though God is said to change his intentions (so that, in one sense, the Holy Scripture even says that God repented) this is said with reference

to man's expectation, or the order of natural causes, and not with reference to that which the Almighty had foreknown that he would do."

42. Anselm, *The Compatibility of the Foreknowledge, Predestination, and Grace of God with Human Freedom*, 1.7, in *Anselm*, 447.

43. Ibid.

44. Ibid.

45. Ibid., 3.3, in *Anselm*, 448–49.

his grace harmonizes with free choice to achieve salvation for people.... Grace always aids one's innate free choice by giving it the uprightness that it may preserve by free choice, because without grace it achieves nothing toward salvation."[46] Thus, good deeds rebound to the praise of God, while at the same time those who do them are praiseworthy because they cooperate with the grace of God by their free will.[47] On the negative side of evil works, however, it is another case: "That God is active in evil ones is the fault of the human being alone; for God would not be active in human evil deeds unless people were freely willing to do them.... [I]n the case of evil deeds people are the sole cause of their evilness because they do them by their independent, unjust choice alone."[48] Thus, Anselm offered a resolution to the problem of evil by placing the blame squarely on the shoulders of human beings, who commit evil actions by their evil will.

Thomas Aquinas addressed divine providence, affirming that everything that God created is kept in existence by divine preservation: "The existence of every creature depends on God, so that not for a moment could it exist, but would fall into nothingness, were it not kept in existence by the operation of the divine power."[49] Such providence also includes God's direction of all things to accomplish their divinely designed purpose. Aquinas supported his contention with an appeal to Aristotle, particularly his philosophy of agents acting toward an end or goal (think of a baker following a recipe to make a pie). For Aquinas, God is the first, or causal, agent, who directs all things to accomplish his purpose: "We must say that all things are subject to divine providence, not only in general but also in their own individual selves.... For since every agent acts for an end, the ordering of effects towards that end extends as far as the causality of the first agent extends.... But the causality of God, who is the first agent, extends to all being [everything that exists].... Hence all things that exist in whatever manner are necessarily directed by God towards some end."[50] Divine providence directs everything to accomplish God's design.

This contention does not mean that God only exercises immediate control over everything. Rather, he also employs secondary means or intermediaries to accomplish his government of the universe (think of the laws of physics — the laws of gravity and entropy, for example — as means that God uses to control the physical universe).[51] For Aquinas, this meant that divine providence does not make everything that takes place happen by necessity. Rather, God's foreknowledge "has prepared for some things necessary causes, so that they happen of necessity. For others [it has prepared] contingent causes, that they may happen by contingency."[52] In this way "the dignity of causality is imparted even to creatures."[53] That is, God has included human beings — their choices and actions — in his providential plan. He accomplishes this plan through the intermediary decisions and works — both good and evil — of responsible human beings.

In treating the problem of evil, Aquinas laid this foundation: "God neither wills evil to be done, nor wills it not to be done, but wills to permit evil to be done, and this is a

46. Ibid., in *Anselm*, 155.
47. Ibid., 3.14, in *Anselm*, 474.
48. Ibid.
49. Thomas Aquinas, *Summa Theologica*, pt. 1, q. 104, art. 1.

50. Ibid., pt. 1, q. 22, art. 2.
51. Ibid., pt. 1, q. 103, art. 6.
52. Ibid., pt. 1, q. 22, art. 4.
53. Ibid., pt. 1, q. 22, art. 3.

good."[54] Following Augustine, Aquinas believed evil to be the absence of good.[55] As for why God permits evil, or the absence of good, his answer began with the notion of the great diversity of the created order, a diversity designed by God[56] and which extends to different degrees of goodness. Indeed, "the universe would not be perfect if only one grade of goodness were found in things."[57] To take an example of these different grades of goodness, Aquinas noted *absolute goodness*—the goodness of things that cannot be corrupted—and *fallible goodness*—the goodness of things that can be corrupted. Continuing his reasoning, he asserted that as "the perfection of the universe requires that there should be some which can fail in goodness ... it follows that sometimes they do fail. Now ... evil consists ... in the fact that a thing fails in goodness. Hence it is clear that evil is found in things, as corruption also is found; for corruption is itself an evil."[58]

Anticipating the objection that this explanation makes God out to be the author of evil, Aquinas pointed out that, in one sense, God is certainly not the cause of evil: "The evil that consists in the defect of action is always caused by the defect of the agent. But in God there is no defect, but the highest perfection.... Hence, the evil which consists in defect of action, or which is caused by defect of the agent, is not reduced to God as to its cause."[59] However, he admitted that, in another sense, God is indeed the cause of evil: "Now, the order of the universe requires that there should be some things that can, and do sometimes, fail. And thus God, by causing in things the good of the order of the universe, consequently and as it were by accident, causes the corruption of things."[60] In other words, God is ultimately the reason for evil's existence, in that he created a world in which some things could and did indeed fall away from the original goodness with which he created them. But he is not the cause of their falling away; they are responsible for the loss of goodness, or evil. For this fault, these fallen things are judged and a penalty is assessed. "And so God is the author of the evil that is the penalty, but he is not the author of the evil that is fault."[61]

THE DOCTRINE OF PROVIDENCE IN THE REFORMATION AND POST-REFORMATION

Martin Luther affirmed the doctrine of providence, though it was not a major point of difference between him and the Catholic Church: "God the Father initiated and executed the creation of all things through the Word; and now he continues to preserve his creation through the Word, and that forever and ever. He remains with his handiwork until he sees fit to terminate it.... Hence, as heaven, earth, sun, moon, stars, man, and all living things were created in the beginning through the Word, so they are wonderfully governed and preserved through the Word."[62] This providential care is not always evident in

---

54. Ibid., pt. 1, q. 19, art. 9.
55. Ibid., pt. 1, q. 48, art. 1.
56. Ibid., pt. 1, q. 47, art. 1.
57. Ibid., pt. 1, q. 47, art. 2.
58. Ibid., pt. 1, q. 48, art. 2.

59. Ibid., pt. 1, q. 49, art. 2.
60. Ibid.
61. Ibid.
62. Martin Luther, *Sermons on the Gospel of St. John, 1-4,* LW, 22:26.

the lives of believers; rather, it must be embraced by faith: "The opposite is what appears to reason, that while [God] says he exercises as great a care for us as he does for the pupil of his eye, he meanwhile puts us into prisons, causes us to lose our property and children, forces us to flee, and finally permits us to be killed.... A great concern God, indeed, for his saints.... Faith feels and believes this when a person is being afflicted and learns that new kind of warfare and that new victory—through the cross."[63]

In *The Bondage of the Will*, Luther addressed the issue of human freedom. He wrote this piece in response to Erasmus, who, in his *Freedom of the Will*, argued that human beings possess sufficiently free will so as to cooperate with the grace of God.[64] Luther's critique of Erasmus's view began with a biblical argument, with particular focus on Romans 1:18.[65] Luther concluded that "even in the most excellent men, however endowed with law, righteousness, wisdom, and all virtues, 'free will', their most excellent part, is nonetheless ungodly, and unrighteous, and merits God's wrath."[66] From this Luther drew the important principle that " 'free will' is nothing but the greatest enemy of righteousness and man's salvation.... 'Free will', when at its best, is then at its worst, and the more it endeavors the worse it grows and is."[67] He also marshaled theological reasons against human freedom.[68]

Qualifying his criticism, Luther did not mean that free will cannot achieve anything whatsoever. Indeed, " 'free will' by its endeavors can advance in some direction, namely, in the direction of good works, or the righteousness of the civil or moral law, yet it does not advance towards God's righteousness, nor does God deem its efforts in any respect worthy to gain his righteousness."[69] Furthermore, he acknowledged that Erasmus's view of free will was not identical with that of Pelagius, who insisted that it is by substantial human effort that people are saved. Yet Luther surprisingly affirmed that Erasmus's view was more dangerous than Pelagianism: "This hypocrisy of theirs [Erasmus and his followers] results in their valuing and seeking to purchase the grace of God at a much cheaper rate than the Pelagians. The latter assert that it is not by a feeble something within us that we obtain grace, but by efforts and works that are complete, entire, perfect, many and mighty; but our friends here tell us that it is by something very small, almost nothing, that we merit grace."[70] In other words, Erasmus's insistence that human free will cooperates only minimally with the grace of God to obtain salvation was, in Luther's calculation, even more devaluing of divine grace than was Pelagius's view. Thus, Luther's theology challenged the prevailing notion of human freedom, according it instead no role in salvation and only a small part in doing good in the civil and moral realms.[71]

---

63. *Lectures on the Minor Prophets III: Zechariah*, LW, 20:31.

64. Erasmus's work was published in September 1524, and Luther's response appeared in December 1525.

65. He also treated Rom. 9:30 and 10:20 (quoting Isa. 65:1).

66. *The Bondage of the Will*, trans. James I. Packer and O. R. Johnston (Old Tappan, N.J.: Revell, 1957), 275; LW, 33:249.

67. Ibid., 276, 278; LW, 33: 250, 252.

68. These arguments are "drawn from the purpose of grace, from the promise, from the power of the law, from original sin, and from God's election;every one of which by itself

could utterly overthrow 'free will.' " Ibid., 297; LW, 33:272.

69. Ibid., 289; LW, 33:264.

70. Ibid., 293-94; LW, 33:268.

71. The *Augsburg Confession* made this affirmation of the Lutheran view of free will: "Concerning free will, the Lutherans teach that man's will has some freedom to work a civil righteousness and to choose such things as reason can attain to, but that it has no power to work the righteousness of God, or a spiritual righteousness, without the Spirit of God.... For although nature is in some way able to do the external works (for it is able to withhold the hands from theft and murder),

John Calvin defined providence as meaning "not that by which God idly observes from heaven what takes place on earth, but that by which, as keeper of the keys, he governs all events."[72] Accordingly, "he so regulates all things that nothing takes place without his deliberation."[73] Such work rules out fortune and luck, to which most people wrongly cling.[74] At the same time, divine providence must not be mistaken for fate, the philosophy that everything necessarily happens according to predetermined laws. The whole process is impersonal, and not even God can intervene to change it. Calvin objected and denied equating fate with providence.[75]

But this doctrine of providence, warned Calvin, should never be allowed to decay into irresponsibility. Addressing people who misunderstood divine providence, he noted: "They cancel all those plans which have to do with the future, as militating against God's providence, which, without their being consulted, has decreed what he would have happen. Then whatever does happen now, they so impute to God's providence that they close their eyes to the man who has clearly done it.... Thus all crimes, because subject to God's ordinance, they call virtues."[76] This warped view fails to consider that in addition to divine sovereignty, there is human responsibility:

> This means that we are not at all hindered by God's eternal decrees either from looking ahead for ourselves or from putting all our affairs in order, but always in submission to his will. The reason is obvious. For he who has set the limits to our life has at the same time entrusted to us its care; he has provided means and helps to preserve it; he has also made us able to foresee dangers; that they may not overwhelm us unaware, he has offered precautions and remedies.... The Lord has inspired in men the arts of taking counsel and caution, by which to comply with his providence in the preservation of life itself.[77]

Thus, Calvin affirmed compatibility between providence and human responsibility. Speaking pastorally, Calvin insisted that the doctrine of providence brings release from worry and great comfort to believers.

At the same time as affirming the comfort that this doctrine brings, Calvin admitted that the interface between God's plan or will — "what he had from eternity foreseen, approved, and decreed"[78] — and biblical statements of God's "repentance" creates a problem. Passages that affirm such repentance "seem to suggest ... that the plan of God does not stand firm and sure, but is subject to change in response to the disposition of things

---

yet it cannot work the inward motions, such as the fear of God, trust in God, chastity, patience, and the like." *Augsburg Confession*, 18, in Schaff, 3:18–19. Although explicitly denying the role of free will in obtaining salvation and, in turn, emphasizing divine sovereignty in salvation, the Lutherans also specifically denied fatalism. The *Formula of Concord* explained: "[We repudiate] ... the insane dogma of the Stoic philosophers, as also the madness of the Manicheans, who taught that all things that come to pass take place by necessity and cannot possibly be otherwise; and that man does all things by constraint, even those things that he transacts in external matters, and that he

is compelled to the committing of evil works and crimes, such as unlawful lusts, acts, rapine, murders, thefts, and the like." *Formula of Concord*, 2, neg. 1, in Schaff, 3:109–10.

72. John Calvin, *Institutes of the Christian Religion*, 1.16.4, LCC, 1:202.

73. Ibid., 1.16.3, LCC, 1:200.

74. Ibid., 1.16.2, LCC, 1:198–99.

75. Ibid., 1.16.8, LCC, 1:207.

76. Ibid., 1.17.3, LCC, 1:215.

77. His biblical support is Prov. 16:9. Ibid., 1.17.4, LCC, 1:216.

78. Ibid., 1.17.13, LCC, 1:227.

John Calvin on the Comfort of Divine Providence

When the light of divine providence has once shone upon a godly man, he is then relieved and set free not only from the extreme anxiety and fear that were pressing him before, but from every care. For as he rightly dreads fortune, so he fearlessly dares to commit himself to God. His comfort, I say, is to know that his heavenly Father so holds all things in his power, so rules by his authority and will, so governs by his wisdom, that nothing can happen except he determine it. Moreover, it comforts him to know that he has been received into God's safekeeping and entrusted to the care of his angels, and that neither water, nor fire, nor iron can harm him, except in so far as it pleases God as governor to give them occasion.... Whence ... do they have this never-failing assurance but from knowing that, when the world appears to be aimlessly tumbled about, the Lord is everywhere at work, and from trusting that his work will be for their welfare? Now, if their welfare is attacked either by the devil or by wicked men, then indeed, unless strengthened through remembering and meditating upon providence, they will certainly and quickly despair. But let them recall that the devil and the whole cohort of the wicked are completely restrained by God's hand as by a bridle, so that they are unable either to hatch any plot against us or, having hatched it, to make preparations or, if they have fully planned it, to lift a finger to carry it out, except so far as God has permitted, indeed commanded. Let them, also, recall that the devil and his crew are not only chained, but also curbed and compelled to do service. Such thoughts will provide them great comfort!*

> *John Calvin, *Institutes of the Christian Religion*, 1.17.11, LCC, 1:224. The text has been rendered clearer. The *Belgic Confession* also recounted the comfort that such a view of God's providence gives to Christians: "We entirely trust in him, being persuaded that he so restrains the devil and all our enemies that they cannot hurt us apart from his will and permission." *Belgic Confession of Faith*, 13, in Schaff, 3:397. Similarly, the *Heidelberg Catechism* rehearsed the practical benefits of belief in God's providential care, "that we may be patient in suffering and thankful in prosperity. Also, in regard to the future, that we have good confidence in our faithful God and Father. For we know that no creature will separate us from his love, since all creatures are in his hand so that apart from his will they cannot so much as even move." *Heidelberg Catechism*, q. 28, in Schaff, 3:316.

below."[79] Calvin offered a solution to this quandary. First, he denounced the idea that God repents because it contradicts the biblical affirmation that God "is not a man, that he can repent" (1 Sam. 15:29).[80] Second, he affirmed that the language of repentance, when applied to God, is anthropomorphic, not realistic.[81] Third, Calvin used two examples—

---

79. Ibid., 1.17.12, LCC, 1:225. These passages are Gen. 6:6; 1 Sam. 15:11; Jer. 18:8; Jonah 3:4, 10; Isa. 38:1, 5; 2 Kings 20:1; and 2 Chron. 32:24.

80. Ibid., 1.17.12, LCC, 1:226.

81. Ibid., 1.17.13, LCC, 1:227. An anthropomorphism (derived from two Greek words, *anthropos*, referring to "man," and *morphe*, having to do with "manner") is a way of speaking about God in the "manner of man," or in human terms.

the divine threats to destroy the people of Nineveh in forty days (Jonah 3:4) and to cut off Hezekiah's life (Isa. 38:1) — to illustrate that these warnings "nonetheless contain a tacit condition. For why did the Lord send Jonah to the Ninevites to foretell the ruin of the city? Why did he through Isaiah indicate death to Hezekiah? For he could have destroyed both the Ninevites and Hezekiah without any messenger of destruction."[82] As Calvin concluded: "Therefore he had in view something other than that, forewarned of their death, they might discern it coming from a distance. Indeed, he did not wish them to perish, but to be changed lest they perish."[83] Thus, God carries out his plan that human beings repent and become saved, thereby accomplishing his will for them. And he by no means repents of his eternal, fixed plan.[84]

Lutheran and Reformed churches in the post-Reformation period developed this doctrine in great detail. Both groups discussed providence under three headings: *preservation, concurrence,* and *government.* As for the first of these: "Preservation is the act of divine providence by which God sustains all things created by him, so that they continue in being [existence] with the properties implanted in their nature and the powers received in creation."[85] Scripture was cited in support (Acts 17:28; Col. 1:17; Heb. 1:3).[86]

The second aspect of providence, concurrence, brings the working of God together with the working of his creation: "God not only gives and preserves to secondary causes the power to act, but immediately influences the action and effect of the creature, so that the same effect is produced not by God alone, nor by the creature alone, nor partly by God and partly by the creature, but at the same time by God and the creature, as one and the same total efficiency — that is, by God as the universal and first cause, and by the creature as the particular and secondary cause."[87] Specifically, "the *first cause* is that which is entirely independent; but upon it all other things, if there are any, depend; this is God. A *second cause* is that which recognizes another cause prior to itself, upon which it depends; such are the efficient created causes that ... depend on the first cause as for their existence so also for their operation."[88] Examples of secondary causes include the law of gravity, the bonding of chemicals to produce amino acids, the orbit of the planets and stars, and the human will exercising its prerogative to either obey God or sin against him. With their doctrine of concurrence, the post-Reformers did not allow for the idea that these secondary causes act independently of God, nor that the secondary causes become primary causes (with God, now the secondary cause, helpless to direct them or dependent on them), nor that God's activity and the activities of secondary causes are completely different.[89] Yet these theologians affirmed the real activity of such secondary

---

82. Ibid., 1.17.14, LCC, 1:227.

83. Ibid., 1.17.14, LCC, 1:227–28.

84. Ibid., 1.17.14, LCC, 1:228.

85. David Hollaz, *Examen Theologicum Acroamaticum* (1707), 441, in Schmid, 170–71. For a Reformed definition, see John Heidegger, *Corpus Theologiae* (Zürich, 1700), 7.20, in Heppe, 257.

86. John Gerhard, *Loci Theologici* (1621), 4.83, in Schmid, 179.

87. John Andrew Quenstedt, *Theologia Didactico-Polemica sive Systema Theologicum* (Leipzig, 1715), 1.531, in Schmid, 180. For a Reformed definition, see Heidegger, *Corpus Theologiae,* 7.28, in Heppe, 258.

88. Quenstedt, *Theologia Didactico-Polemica,* 1.544, in Schmid, 184.

89. John Marck, *Compendium Theologiae Christianae didactico-elencticum* (Amsterdam, 1690), 10.10, in Heppe, 259.

causes.[90] In his work of concurrence, God acts together with all that he has created in a way that is consistent with each thing's nature.[91]

The third aspect of providence is government, which is "an act of divine providence by which God symmetrically arranges each and every creature, in its particular strength, actions, and suffering, to the glory of the Creator and the good of this universe, especially to the salvation of the godly."[92] This government applies to both inanimate (or nonrational) things and living (or rational) beings.[93] Indeed, there is one system of government for inanimate things, another system for living creatures.[94] Furthermore, "The end [purpose] of providence is the glory of God and the salvation of the elect."[95]

The doctrine of providence introduced some important theological questions for the post-Reformation theologians. One was the relationship between divine foreknowledge and the sovereign, eternal decrees of God. For Lutheran theologians, divine foreknowledge is not dependent on or based on a divine decree.[96] By contrast, Reformed theologians closely associated the doctrine of providence with the doctrine of the divine decrees.[97] Specifically, they made a distinction between the providence of God and his divine foreknowledge while acknowledging that God both possesses exhaustive foreknowledge and sovereignly determines all that happens.[98] Thus, the Reformed position was the opposite of the Lutheran position on the relationship between divine foreknowledge and the divine decrees.

A second important theological question was the relationship of God's providence to evil. Post-Reformed theologians denied that their doctrine of providence makes God out to be the author of evil. Some appealed to a distinction between an action, its effects, and the quality or nature (either good or bad) of that action.[99] Others made a distinction between proximate (or near) causes and remote (or far) causes.[100] With God as

---

90. Heidegger, *Corpus Theologiae*, 7.27, in Heppe, 259.

91. Quenstedt, *Theologia Didactico-Polemica*, 1.545, in Schmid, 185.

92. Ibid., 1.533, in Schmid, 187–88. For a Reformed definition, see Heidegger, *Corpus Theologiae*, 7.24, in Heppe, 262.

93. Heidegger, *Corpus Theologiae*, 7.24, in Heppe, 262.

94. Ibid., 7.25, in Heppe, 263. Lutheran theologians detected four specific modes of divine government: permission, hindrance, direction, and determination. See Quenstedt, *Theologia Didactico-Polemica*, 1.533, 534, in Schmid, 189–90; Hollaz, *Examen Theologicum Acroamaticum*, 449, in Schmid, 189.

95. Marcus Wendelin, *Christianae Theologiae Systema* (Cassel, 1656), 1.6.12, in Heppe, 263.

96. As Hollaz explained: "The foreknowledge and decree of God concerning future things are eternal and simultaneous on the part of God; but, according to our mode of conception, the foreknowledge of God precedes the divine decree." Hollaz, *Examen Theologicum Acroamaticum*, 432, in Schmid, 178.

97. As Riissen noted: "The decrees are the norm of the whole of providence." Leonard Riissen, *Francisci Turretini Compendium Theologiae* (Amsterdam, 1695), 8.3, in Heppe,

252; cf. William Bucan, *Institutiones Theologicae seu Locorum Communium Christianae Religionis* (Geneva, 1609), 14.3, in Heppe, 252.

98. "God's providence is not the same as bare foreknowledge but is care in action and will in operation, conjoined with the act of a knowing mind…. Free causes are related to God's providence not only as being foreknown as future and destined to do this or that, but also as moved, roused and applied by God and ordained for their own acts and results…. In short, foreknowledge, which holy Scripture ascribes to God, cannot be separated from his will." John Heidegger, *Corpus Theologiae* (Zürich, 1700), 7.54, in Heppe, 269–70. The text has been rendered clearer.

99. E.g., Quenstedt insisted that God "concurs with the actions and effects, but not with the deficiency of the actions"; such evil actions have no other cause than creatures. Thus, God "concurs in disgraceful acts and is inwardly present to them, yet in such a manner as not to be defiled." Quenstedt, *Theologia Didactico-Polemica*, 1.545, in Schmid, 186.

100. E.g., Hollaz offered: "God concurs with the *remote*, not with the *proximate* material of actions [that are] morally evil. The *former* is an indeterminate act; the *latter* is an act

the remote cause of human actions and human beings as the proximate cause of their own actions, God escapes the charge of complicity or guilt by association with those who commit evil. People do evil, and they alone are held accountable for the evil they commit; God never is. Still others made a distinction between divine action and divine permission: "Divine providence governs the bad as well as the good, the latter by effective action, the former by effective permission."[101] These theologians did not mean that God approves of bad things and thus permits them; rather, God gives his permission by not impeding those bad things from occurring. "Evil, which is sin and which God neither creates nor causes, also cannot be completely and in every way withdrawn from the eternal ordering of God.... But God does not ordain evil as he does good, i.e., as something that pleases him, but as the sort of thing that he hates. Nevertheless, he knowingly and willingly destines it, lets it be in the world, and uses it wonderfully for good."[102]

Within Reformed theological circles, the early consensus about the relationship of divine providence and human freedom came apart in the theology of Jacob Arminius. In one sense, he affirmed a typical Calvinist doctrine of providence.[103] Where Arminius broke ranks with Reformed theology was in his rejection of divine predetermination. Actually, he did affirm a type of predetermination; that is, when a determination has been made by God, "the second cause [e.g., a human being], both with regard to its power and the use of that power, remains free either to act or not to act, so that, if it be the pleasure of this second cause, it can suspend [or defer] its own action."[104] Thus, he opted for absolute human freedom (later to be called libertarian freedom, or contra-causal freedom, because it is always able to act contrary to even the causal influences exerted on it by God).[105] For Arminius, God's predetermination of some event cannot so decisively incline the will of human beings involved in that event as to guarantee its outcome.

---

determinate and applied to a prohibited thing.... Therefore, the determination to this or that object is not from God as from the first and universal cause, but from the second and particular cause." Hollaz, *Examen Theologicum Acroamaticum*, 443, in Schmid, 186–87.

101. John Wolleb, *Christianae Theologiae Compendium* (Basel, 1626), 30, in Heppe, 274. The text has been rendered clearer.

102. *Bremische Bekenntnis*, in Heppe, 274. The text has been rendered clearer. Thus, "if willing to permit is the same as willing the permission of sin, we agree that God willingly permits it. If it is the same as permitting it approvingly or approving the thing permitted, we must not admit that God willingly permits sin." Bartholomew Keckermann, *Systema Sacrosanctae Theologiae* (Geneva, 1611), 115, in Heppe, 275. This approach answered the challenge that the doctrine of providence implicated God as the author of sin. As Bucan explained: "God does not infuse malice into the wills of evil men, as he infuses goodness into the hearts of the godly.... The sin of the wicked is their own; their doing this or that by sinning is of God's power ... and so in the same work God is

ascertained to be righteous, man to be guilty." Bucan, *Institutiones Theologicae*, 19.11, in Heppe, 276.

103. "I place in subjection to divine providence both the free will and even the actions of a rational creature, so that nothing can be done apart from the will of God, not even any of those things that are done in opposition to it." James Arminius, *Declaration of Sentiments*, II, "The Providence of God," in *The Writings of James Arminius*, 3 vols., trans. James Nichols (Grand Rapids: Baker, 1956), 1:251.

104. James Arminius, *The Apology or Defense*, art. 7, in *Writings of James Arminius*, 1:296.

105. He gave an example from Acts 4:27–28 of Herod, Pontius Pilate, and the other coconspirators in the death of Christ. For Arminius, even though the things "necessary for the execution of this 'fore-determination' were all fixed, yet it was possible for this act (the crucifixion of Christ), which had been 'previously appointed' by God, not to be produced by those persons, and they might have remained free and indifferent to the performance of this action, up to the moment of time in which they perpetrated the deed." Ibid., 1:296–97.

The kind of predetermination that Arminius rejected came in two forms. "Hard" determinism denies that human beings possess freedom of any kind, insisting instead that the divine decree constrains them against their will so that they do not act freely. Arminius denounced this notion.[106] He also rejected determinism in its "soft" form: an act can be free yet determined so long as the causal conditions do not constrain the will; rather, human beings act in accordance with their own will and nature and thus possess significant freedom. Arminius believed there is a contradiction between human freedom and causation of any kind.[107] No causal conditions exist that can decisively incline human beings to will one thing rather than another. Thus, though he embraced the Reformed doctrine of providence, Arminius strongly distanced himself from the common linking of divine providence with the doctrine of the divine decree.

His view also became the position against which typical Reformed theology articulated its position. Reformed theologians insisted that "in the matter of free will and its first determination, God is not only occupied in advising and persuading by his moral providence, but by a physical [providence], by bending the will and that directly; not only by illuminating it intellectually, but also by infusing it through the will with a new propensity toward himself and toward spiritual and saving benefits."[108] At the same time, these theologians rejected the criticism that this notion banishes all sense of free will. They maintained that the human will could be free and determined by God at the same time, so long as the divine determination does not constrain but instead moves the human will in such a way that it freely follows the divine determination: "When the will itself determines itself, it is already acting freely; why, then, should it not be acting freely when it is determined by God, because God moves it according to its nature? ... Therefore ... God does not abolish freedom from a cause and from its free action."[109]

THE DOCTRINE OF PROVIDENCE IN THE MODERN PERIOD

Despite these efforts by Reformed theologians, the modern period raised strong objections against the doctrine of providence, not the least of which was that it makes God to be the author of sin. Jonathan Edwards offered a reply to this objection, noting two possible meanings of the phrase "the author of sin": "If by 'the author of sin,' is meant the sinner, the agent, or actor of sin, or the *doer* of a wicked thing; so it would

---

106. Ibid.

107. He explained his problem with this position: "What the proponents of such a doctrine advance about 'that freedom not being taken away that belongs to the nature of the creature' is not sufficient to destroy this contradiction: Because it is not sufficient for the establishment of contingency and freedom to have the presence of a power which can freely act according to nature; but it is requisite that the use and employment of that power and freedom should on no account be impeded." Ibid., 1:297–98.

108. Peter van Mastricht, *Theoretico-practica Theologia*, new ed. (Utrecht and Amsterdam, 1725 [1714]), 3.11.11, in Heppe, 270–71. Cf. Anthony Walaeus, *Loci communes s. Theologiae* (Leiden, 1640), 311, in Heppe, 271.

109. Walaeus, *Loci communes s. Theologiae*, 301, in Heppe, 272; cf. Francis Turretin, *Institutes of Elenctic Theology*, ed. James T. Dennison Jr., trans. George Musgrave Giger, 3 vols. in 1 (Phillipsburg, N.J.: P & R, 1997), 6th topic, 1st q., sec. 9, 1:492–93.

be a reproach and blasphemy to suppose God to be the author of sin."[110] A second meaning exists, however: "But if by 'the author of sin,' is meant the permitter, or not a hinderer of sin; and at the same time, a disposer of the state of events, in such a manner, for wise, holy and most excellent ends and purposes, that sin, if it is permitted or not hindered, will most certainly and infallibly follow: ... I don't deny that God is the author of sin (though I dislike and reject the phrase, as that which by use and custom is apt to carry another sense)."[111] Edwards also considered the problem of providence and freedom. He defined freedom in terms of self-determination, as "that power and opportunity for one to do and conduct as he will, or according to his choice."[112] This is the case no matter how a person comes to have such a will: "whether it was caused by some external motive, or internal habitual bias; whether it was determined by some internal antecedent volition, or whether it happened without a cause; whether it was necessarily connected with something foregoing, or not connected."[113] Edwards argued for the compatibility of this notion of human freedom with the sovereign, determining purpose or will of God.[114]

Such a view was strongly challenged, however. One movement, *Deism*, traded God's personal providential care for the world for a mechanistic model. Deism pictured God as a divine watchmaker who created the universe and everything it in (along with the natural laws—like the laws of gravity and inertia—needed for its successful continuous operation), wound it up, and let it go. And he never intervenes in the day-to-day functioning of the universe. God does not preserve, cooperate with, and govern his creation; rather, he has relegated the ongoing operation of the universe to natural laws that function on a completely mechanistic order. Essentially, the world is a machine.

Friedrich Schleiermacher further hijacked the doctrine of providence, forcing it into his reformulation of the Christian faith as the feeling of absolute dependence on the divine spirit of the world. According to this scheme, divine government is working toward the perfection of the human spirit in unity with this divine spirit through Christ.[115] Thus, there is only one unified goal for everything that exists, and everything that exists must be considered in relation to that unified goal.[116] Schleiermacher did not like the term *providence* to describe this reality, preferring instead biblical words such as *predestination* and *foreordination*.[117] His reformulation of the doctrine was a reduction of the more robust formulations from the church's history.

With the advent of process theology, the doctrine of divine providence became the target of yet another attack. The metaphor of God as "controlling power" was singled out for

---

110. Jonathan Edwards, *Freedom of the Will*, pt. 4, sec. 9, in Perry Miller, gen. ed., *The Works of Jonathan Edwards*, vol. 1 (New Haven and London: Yale Univ. Press, 1957), 399.

111. Ibid.

112. Ibid., pt. 1, sec. 5, in Miller, *Works of Jonathan Edwards*, 164.

113. Ibid.

114. "God's moral government over mankind, his treating them as moral agents, making them the objects of his commands, counsels, calls, warnings, expostulations, promises, threatenings, rewards and punishments, is not inconsistent with a determining disposal of all events, of every kind, throughout the universe, in his providence; either by positive efficiency, or permission." Ibid., conclusion, in Miller, *Works of Jonathan Edwards*, 431.

115. Friedrich Schleiermacher, *The Christian Faith*, ed. H. R. Mackintosh and J. S. Stewart (Edinburgh: T & T Clark, 1928), 724–25.

116. Ibid., 725.

117. Ibid.

critique: "Process theology denies the existence of this God."[118] Specifically, the omniscience, omnipotence, self-sufficiency, and other divine attributes supporting the traditional notions of divine providence came under attack.[119] Against them, process theology formulated its doctrine of divine creativity "as based upon responsiveness to the world. Since the very meaning of actuality involves internal relatedness, God as an actuality is essentially related to the world. Since actuality as such is partially self-creative, future events are not yet determinate, so that even perfect knowledge cannot know the future, and God does not wholly control the world. Any divine creative influence must be persuasive, not coercive."[120] This divine influence cooperates with what Alfred North Whitehead referred to as the "initial aim" or goal of each individual entity, or "occasion," in the world: "This is an impulse, initially felt conformally by the occasion, to actualize the best possibility open to it, given its concrete situation.... God seeks to persuade each occasion toward that possibility for its own existence which would be best for it; but God cannot control the finite occasion's self-actualization. Accordingly, the divine creative activity involves risk."[121]

Clearly, this conception has important implications for the problem of evil: "The obvious point is that, because God is not in complete control of the events of the world, the occurrence of genuine evil is not incompatible with God's beneficence toward all his creatures."[122] Working from an evolutionary perspective, process theology insisted that with the development of more complex beings came a greater possibility for increasing evil.[123] Indeed, God's stimulation of greater complexity is necessary to avoid the evil of "unnecessary triviality," which attempts to "prevent the maximization of enjoyment, which is the one intrinsic good."[124] With such stimulation, however, comes the greater risk of suffering and evil. The problem, then, ultimately goes back to God:

> Had God not led the realm of finitude out of chaos into a cosmos that includes life, nothing worthy of the term "suffering" would occur. Had God not lured the world on to the creation of beings with the capacity for conscious, rational self-determination, the distinctively human forms of evil on our planet would not occur. Hence, God is responsible for these evils in the sense of having encouraged the world in the direction that made these evils possible. But unnecessary triviality is also evil, because it also detracts from the maximization of enjoyment. Hence, the question as to whether God is indictable for the world's evil reduces to the question as to whether the positive values enjoyed by the higher forms of actuality are worth the risk of the negative values, the sufferings.[125]

Thus, "God is responsible for evil but not indictable for it."[126] Clearly, process theology's perspective on divine providence and the concomitant problem of evil is very different from the classical discussion of the doctrine.

118. John B. Cobb Jr. and David Ray Griffin, *Process Theology: An Introductory Exposition* (Philadelphia: Westminster, 1976), 9.

119. Ibid., 32.
120. Ibid., 52–53.
121. Ibid., 53.

122. Ibid.
123. Ibid., 73.
124. Ibid., 70.
125. Ibid., 75.
126. Ibid., 69.

Theologians such as William G. T. Shedd and Paul Helm continued to affirm and defend the traditional church teaching on divine providence. Shedd succinctly presented the classic doctrine while summarizing the biblical evidence for the all-inclusive providential control of God over physical nature generally, the animal creation, the events of human history, individual life, the so-called fortuitous [chance] events, particulars as well as universals, and the free actions of people, including their sin.[127] Helm embraced a view of the relationship between divine providence and human freedom known as *compatibilism*, as he explained: "People perform free acts when they do what they want to do.... That is, they are not constrained or compelled in their actions, but what they do flows unimpededly from their wants, desires, preferences, goals and the like. The great advantage of such a view of human freedom is that, being compatible with determinism, it is also compatible with a full view of divine omniscience and omnipotence, and thus with a 'no-risk' theory of providence."[128]

Helm also addressed the problem of evil, proposing that though "God could have created men and women who freely (in a sense compatible with determinism) did only what was morally right,"[129] God did not do so for an important reason: "that out of that evil a greater good would come, a good that could not have come, or could not have been as great, if there had not been that evil."[130] This was referred to as the greater good defense.[131] The greater good envisioned includes such virtuous traits as "sympathy or compassion or patience. These concepts are defined in terms of some supposed evil or lack or need which calls forth the sympathetic or compassionate response, and without which that response would not be intelligible."[132] Helm concluded that "the evils that occur are ultimately justified by the fact that without them certain good states of affairs could not logically occur."[133] Thus, evil exists in this world because certain greater goods are parasitic on it. This view was Helm's answer to the problem of evil within his compatibilistic view of providence.

As we have seen, throughout its history the church developed various approaches to the problem of evil. In a helpful analysis of these different *theodicies* (or defenses that attempt "to explain why an omnipotent, all-loving God might or would allow evil in our world"), John Feinberg exposed a basic approach at the core of most of them. As he explained: "The strategy involves four basic steps. The theologian begins by adopting a notion of divine omnipotence according to which God can do only what is logically possible. This, of course, means he can't actualize a world that contains contradictory states of affairs."[134] Feinberg continued: "The second step is to argue that in creating a world,

127. William G. T. Shedd, *Dogmatic Theology*, 3.6, in *Dogmatic Theology*, ed. Alan W. Gomes, 3rd ed. (Phillipsburg, N.J.: P & R, 2003), 413–14.

128. Paul Helm, *The Providence of God*, Contours of Christian Theology (Downers Grove, Ill.: InterVarsity, 1993), 67.

129. Ibid., 197.

130. Ibid.

131. As Helm further explained it: "In order for any version of the good reason or greater-good defense to be plausible on moral grounds, the evil (its character, amount and inci-

dence) must be a logically necessary condition of the good that is alleged to follow it. It must be that without which the good could not be achieved, not merely one means among others by which the good may be achieved." Ibid., 202.

132. Ibid.

133. Ibid., 202–3.

134. John S. Feinberg, *The Many Faces of Evil: Theological Systems and the Problem of Evil*, 3rd ed. (Wheaton: Crossway, 2004), 489. E.g., God cannot actualize a world in which I am married to Nora and Nora does not exist.

God had to choose between actualizing one of two good things. The two are mutually contradictory, so God couldn't do both.... Regardless of the theology, one of the two options will be removing evil. Depending on the theology, the other option will specify some other valuable thing God could do in creating a world."[135] Examples of this second option include the free will defense (as seen in Augustine) and the greater good defense (as seen in Helm). The third step "appeals to a commonly held ethical principle. This principle says that no one can be held morally accountable for failing to do what they couldn't do.... But in all the cases in question, God isn't free both to remove evil and to accomplish the other positive goal in our world. Hence, he isn't guilty for failing to do both."[136] The fourth step is the final one: "The theist grants that if God had chosen to remove evil, he would have done something very good. However, the theist argues that the option God chose is a value of such magnitude that it is at least as valuable as removing evil. It either counterbalances or overbalances the evil present in our world. Hence, in choosing this option rather than removing evil, God has done nothing wrong."[137] This, then, is the basic four-step strategy undertaken by most theodicies or defenses of God in relation to the problem of evil.

One of the newest movements to question the traditional notion of divine providence came as a challenge from within the ranks of evangelicalism itself. Known as *open theism*, this movement was promoted by notable evangelicals such as Clark Pinnock, John Sanders, and Greg Boyd. Although some major tenets of this movement are treated elsewhere, its view of divine providence appears here.[138]

In his book *The God Who Risks*, John Sanders presented a "risk" model of divine providence. He contrasted this model with a "no-risk" model (the traditional model throughout most of church history) that maintains "no event ever happens without God's specifically selecting it to happen. Nothing is too insignificant for God's meticulous and exhaustive control.... Thus God never takes any risks and nothing ever turns out differently from the way God desires. The divine will is never thwarted in any respect."[139] He then set forth his "risk" model of divine providence, working from a definition of providence as "the adequacy of God's wisdom and power to the task with which he has charged himself":[140]

> God grants humans genuine freedom to participate in this project, as he does not force them to comply.... God freely chooses to be affected by his creatures—there is contingency in God's relation with creation. Moreover, God is the sovereign determiner of the sort of sovereignty he will exercise. God is free to sovereignly decide not to determine everything that happens in history. He does not have to because God is supremely wise, endlessly resourceful, amazingly creative and omnicompetent in seeking to fulfill his project.[141]

---

135. Ibid.

136. Ibid., 490.

137. Ibid.

138. See chap. 10.

139. John Sanders, *The God Who Risks: A Theology of Prov-*idence (Downers Grove, Ill.: InterVarsity, 1998), 10.

140. Ibid., 169. Sanders's definition is from H. H. Farmer, *The World and God: A Study of Prayer, Providence and Miracle in Christian Experience*, rev. ed. (London: Nisbet, 1955), 236.

141. Ibid., 169.

The divine goal for creation is fixed, but the means to its realization are flexible.[142] This entails that God does not "foreordain everything that comes to pass," that "God grants humans libertarian freedom and does not exercise exhaustive control," and that "God adopts certain overall strategies—for example, the granting of significant freedom—that create the potential for the occurrence of individual instances of evil which are, as such, pure loss and not a means to any greater good."[143] In Sanders's understanding, "God's decision to create this particular sort of world has (1) a great chance of success and little possibility of failure while concomitantly having a (2) high amount of risk in the sense that it matters deeply to God how things go."[144] For Sanders, this view of providence has many advantages in regard to the doctrine of salvation, suffering and evil, prayer, and divine guidance.[145] He summarized his risk-taking view of divine providence:

> First, God loves us and desires for us to enter into reciprocal relations of love with him and with our fellow creatures.... In this we would freely come to collaborate with God toward the achievement of God's goals. Second, God has sovereignly decided to make some of his actions contingent on our requests and actions.... Hence there is conditionality in God, for God truly responds to what we do. Third, God chooses to exercise general rather than meticulous providence, allowing space for us to operate and for God to be creative and resourceful in working with us. Fourth, God has granted us the libertarian freedom necessary for a truly personal relationship of love to develop. In summary, God freely enters into genuine give-and-take relations with us. This entails risk-taking on his part because we are capable of letting God down.[146]

Open theism in general, and Sanders's risk-taking model of providence, with its accompanying denial of God's meticulous sovereignty, in particular, were specifically criticized by Bruce Ware,[147] John Frame,[148] James Spiegel,[149] and others.[150] Most evangelicals denounced the open theism position[151] and championed, with careful exposition of Scripture and sophisticated philosophical arguments, the traditional church doctrine of divine providence.

---

142. Ibid., 170.

143. Ibid., 170–71. Sanders developed these ideas from the following: Helm, *Providence of God*, 40; William Hasker, *God, Time, and Knowledge*, Cornell Studies in the Philosophy of Religion (Ithaca: Cornell Univ. Press, 1989), 197; David Basinger, "Middle Knowledge and Divine Control: Some Clarifications," *International Journal for Philosophy of Religion* 30 (1991): 135.

144. Ibid., 172.

145. Ibid., 237–79.

146. Ibid., 282.

147. Bruce A. Ware, *God's Lesser Glory: The Diminished God of Open Theism* (Wheaton: Crossway, 2000).

148. John M. Frame, *No Other God: A Response to Open Theism* (Phillipsburg, N.J.: P & R, 2001).

149. James S. Spiegel, "Does God Take Risks?" in *God Under Fire: Modern Scholarship Reinvents God*, Douglas S. Huffman and Eric L. Johnson, gen. eds. (Grand Rapids: Zondervan, 2002), 187–210.

150. See the collection of essays in John Piper, Justin Taylor, and Paul Kjoss Helseth, eds., *Beyond the Bounds: Open Theism and the Undermining of Biblical Christianity* (Wheaton: Crossway, 2003).

151. The Evangelical Theological Society addressed this issue at length at its annual meetings in 2002 and 2003 and examined two of its members—John Sanders and Clark Pinnock—for articulating open theism.

14

ANGELS, SATAN, AND DEMONS

How has the church come to understand angels and their roles? How has the church thought about Satan and demons and the spiritual warfare they wage against the church?

STATEMENT OF BELIEF

The church has historically affirmed belief in the reality of another sphere of existence beyond the realm of human beings and the visible world. This spiritual realm is inhabited by (1) angels, which are "created, spiritual beings with moral judgment and high intelligence, but without physical bodies"; and (2) demons, which are "evil angels who sinned against God and who now continually work evil in the world."[1] Questions have abounded about this spiritual realm: When were angels created? How many angels are there? What do angels do? Who was Satan, and what happened to this angel? Why did other angels fall with Satan, and how many of them fell? What do Satan and the demons do? What is spiritual warfare, and how is a Christian to counter evil attacks? Can a Christian be demon possessed?

Given human curiosity and the relatively scarce amount of biblical material devoted to this subject, the church has historically engaged in a great deal of speculation in attempting to answer these questions. Indeed, a common caricature of the medieval church is that it was absorbed with attempts to answer ridiculously irrelevant questions, such as "How many angels can fit on the head of a pin?" Despite this problem, interest in the spiritual realm has always captured the church's attention. On the one hand, the doctrine of angels, Satan, and demons is a relatively minor doctrine, as seen in the fact that no major church council or statement of faith has focused on it. Also, it has never been

---

1. Wayne Grudem, *Systematic Theology: An Introduction to Biblical Doctrine* (Grand Rapids: Zondervan, 1994, 2000), 397, 412.

a point of major contention dividing churches. On the other hand, Scripture presents the reality of the spiritual realm, and the doctrine of angels, Satan, and demons has reminded the church that human beings are not alone in the world of divinely created beings. These beings exist for a purpose, playing an important role in God's plan, and the church's doctrinal understanding of them—even though lacking the details many wish they could have—encourages believers to engage in right relationships with angels, Satan, and demons.[2]

BELIEFS ABOUT THE SPIRITUAL REALM IN THE EARLY CHURCH

The early church inherited a substantial amount of its belief about the spiritual realm from its Jewish roots. Angels appeared commonly in Old Testament stories. For example, Jacob had a dream of a ladder extending from earth to heaven, and "the angels of God were ascending and descending on it" (Gen. 28:12). Also, Satan was a key protagonist in the book of Job. A concentration of angelic visitations accompanied the conception, birth, and early life of Jesus (Matt. 1:18–2:23; Luke 1:26–38; 2:8–20). An important element of his ministry was the casting out of demons (Matt. 8:28–34), and Jesus taught about Satan and his work (John 8:44). The apostle Paul encouraged believers to be on the alert for spiritual battle (Eph. 6:12). The apostle Peter gave practical counsel as to how to face up to the devil and his attacks (1 Peter 5:8–9). Angels are presented as "ministering spirits sent to serve those who will inherit salvation" (Heb. 1:14). In its last book, the New Testament describes a vision of a cosmic battle in which a host of good angels completely defeats Satan and the evil angels (Rev. 12:7–9).

Following the time of Jesus and the apostles, the early church continued to place considerable emphasis on angels and demons. On the one hand, much about angels was clouded in mystery, as Origen noted: "The teaching of the church has laid down that these beings exist indeed; but that what they are, or how they exist, it has not explained with sufficient clearness."[3] On the other hand, much could be known about them. For example, Athenagoras explained that God is not the only being who inhabits the spiritual realm: "We recognize also a multitude of ministering angels, whom God the maker and framer of the world distributed and appointed to their various posts by his Word."[4]

The early church added a good amount of imagination to its biblically based knowledge about angels; indeed, speculation about the nature and number of angels was common. As Tertullian opined: "Every spirit possesses wings. This is a common property of both angels and demons. So they are everywhere in a single moment; the whole world is as one place to them."[5] That is, angels can move everywhere with lightning-swift speed. On occasion, they can even reveal themselves physically by taking on human appearance,

---

2. My thanks to Dave Richards for his assistance with this chapter.

3. Origen, *First Principles*, preface, 6, in *ANF*, 4:240.

4. Athenagoras, *A Plea for the Christians*, 10, in *ANF*, 2:133–34. The text has been rendered clearer.

5. Tertullian, *Apology*, 22, in *ANF*, 3:36. The text has been rendered clearer.

as Tertullian explained: "You have sometimes read and believed that the Creator's angels have been changed into human form. They have carried about so real of a body that Abraham even washed their feet and Lot was rescued from the Sodomites by their hands. An angel, moreover, wrestled with a man so strenuously with his body that Jacob desired to be let loose."[6] Such appearances, however, are the exception rather than the rule, for angels are incorporeal—without a body—by nature. Indeed, the heavenly creation "is incorporeal, since it is called—or is—'fire' and 'spirit' ... 'spirit,' as being a creature of the intellectual sphere; 'fire,' as being of a purifying nature."[7] Furthermore, the early church believed that angels are immense in number.[8]

The early church also thought much about the function of angels. According to Athenagoras, angels were created by God and "entrusted with the control of matter and the forms of matter.... For this is the office of the angels: to exercise providence for God over the things created and ordered by him; so that God may have the universal and general providence of the entirety of the universe, while the particular parts are provided for by the angels appointed over them."[9] Some angels were given responsibilities associated with the nations of the world.[10] According to Origen, this custodial role of angels began at the dispersion of people at the tower of Babel.[11] The purpose of these angels now is to lead the nations under their control back to God, as Eusebius explained: Angels operate so that people would "turn toward realities which they saw in the heavens—the sun, the moon, and the stars. These objects, in fact, which hold a place of eminence in the visible universe, drew the eyes of those who saw them upward, as close as possible to the King of the universe, into his antechamber, so to speak, and by their grandeur and beauty led them to contemplate, by analogy, the Creator of the universe."[12] Thus, some angels have custody of the nations and stimulate their inhabitants to consider God and seek for him.

Beyond helping in this way, "there are certain angels of God ... which are his servants in accomplishing the salvation of men."[13] John Chrysostom found biblical support (Heb. 1:14) for the idea that God "has assigned to angels who are above us this ministry on our

6. Tertullian, *On the Flesh of Christ*, 3, in *ANF*, 3:523. The text has been rendered clearer. His biblical references are Gen. 18:4; 19:16; and 32:24–30.

7. Gregory of Nazianzus, *Oration* 28.31, in *NPNF²*, 7:300. His reference was to Ps. 104:4.

8. Cyril of Jerusalem attempted to communicate the vastness of the multitudes of angels: "Consider how populous is the Roman Empire. Consider how populous are the barbarian tribes at the present, and how many have died within the last hundred years. Consider how many nations have become extinct during the last thousand years. Consider from Adam down to this day. Great indeed is the multitude! But how little it is, for the angels are many more.... It is written [about angels], 'Thousand thousands ministered to him, and ten thousand times ten thousand stood before him' [Dan. 7:10]. This does not mean that the multitude is limited to that size; but the prophet could not express more than these." Cyril of Jerusalem, *Catechetical Lectures*, 15.24, in *NPNF²*, 7:111–12.

The text has been rendered clearer.

9. Athenagoras, *A Plea for the Christians*, 24, in *ANF*, 2:142.

10. Irenaeus supported this belief by appealing to Deut. 32:8 (as found in the Septuagint): "When the Most High divided the nations and scattered the children of Adam, he fixed the boundaries of the nations according to the number of the angels of God." Irenaeus, *Against Heresies*, 3.12.9, in *ANF*, 1:433. Origen also appealed to references in Daniel to the princes of Persia and Greece (Dan. 10:13, 20) for support that angels are over individual nations. Origen, *First Principles*, 3.3.2, in *ANF*, 4:335.

11. Origen, *Against Celsus*, 5.30, in *ANF*, 4:556.

12. By "nations" Eusebius referred to the Gentiles, not the Jews. Eusebius, *Preparation to the Gospel*, 4.7–8, cited in Jean Daniélou, *The Angels and Their Mission: According to the Fathers of the Church*, trans. David Heimann (Allen, Tex.: Christian Classics, 1987), 19–20.

13. Origen, *First Principles*, preface, 10, in *ANF*, 4:241.

behalf. It is as if one should say, 'For this purpose God employs them; this is the office of angels, to minister to God for our salvation.' So that it is an angelic work, to do all for the salvation of the brothers. Or rather it is the work of Christ himself, for he indeed saves as Lord, but they as servants."[14] This service is important for both the assistance and the example angels provide: "It is enough to be assured that the holy angels of God are propitious [favorably disposed] toward us, and that they do all things on our behalf, that our disposition of mind towards God should imitate as far as it is within the power of human nature the example of these holy angels, who again follow the example of their God."[15] Indeed, Origen believed that human beings would eventually become like angels: "We know ... that the angels are superior to men; so that men, when made prefect, become like the angels."[16] Biblical support for this view was found in Jesus' words in Matthew 22:30. If this is the future of believers, then contemplation of angelic reality should characterize Christians throughout their earthly preparation for heaven: "Scripture admonishes our souls to contemplate the stable nature of the angels, so that our stability in virtue will be fortified by their example. For since it has been promised us that the life after the resurrection will resemble the condition of angels ... it follows that our life in this world should [already] be in conformity with that which will follow."[17]

Despite their exalted status, angels should never be worshiped, nor should prayer be directed to them. Origen explained that Christians are never "commanded to honor and worship them in place of God—even though they minister to us and bear God's blessings to us. For every prayer, petition, intercession, and thanksgiving is to be sent up to the supreme God through the High Priest—the living Word and God, who is above all the angels."[18] Cyprian noted that Revelation 19:10 and 22:9 prohibit the worship of angels.[19] Refusing worship, angels are concerned about only one thing, as Lactantius summarized: "The angels neither allow nor wish themselves to be called gods, because they are immortal. For their one and only duty is to submit to the will of God and not to do anything at all except at his command."[20]

Tragically, all the angels did not submit to God. The early church discussed how and why some angels abandoned their divinely appointed position. Athenagoras attributed this fall to the angels' abuse of their free will in rebelling against God: "Just as with human beings, who have freedom of choice with regard to both virtue and vice

14. John Chrysostom, *Homilies on Hebrews*, 3.4, in *NPNF*[1], 14:377.

15. Origen, *Against Celsus*, 5.5, in *ANF*, 4:544–45.

16. Ibid., 4.29, in *ANF*, 4:509.

17. Gregory of Nyssa, *Homilies in Song of Songs*, 4, cited in Daniélou, *Angels and Their Mission*, 89–90.

18. Origen, *Against Celsus*, 5.4, in *ANF*, 4:544. That this refusal to worship angels was the common view of the early church is clear from almost all sources. However, several references may point to a practice on the part of some to worship angels. The apostle Paul, in fact, warned against this in one of his letters (Col. 2:18). Also, in a controversial passage from Justin Martyr, the worship of angels by Christians was proposed as evidence that believers in Christ are not atheists: "Both him [the Father] and the Son (who came forth from him and taught us these things, and the host of the other good angels who follow and are made like him), and the prophetic Spirit, we worship and adore." Justin Martyr, *First Apology*, 6, in *ANF*, 1:164. This passage is controversial because, as it stands, it clearly contradicts other of Justin's affirmations that Christians worship the Father, the Son, and the prophetic Spirit. For Justin's "usual" description of true Christian worship, see *First Apology*, 13, in *ANF*, 1:166–67.

19. Cyprian, *Treatise* 9.24, in *ANF*, 5:491.

20. Lactantius, *The Divine Institutes*, 2.17, in *ANF*, 7:65. The text has been rendered clearer.

(... and some are diligent in the matters entrusted to them, and others faithless), so it is among the angels. They were created free [moral] agents by God. Some have continued in those things for which God made them and over which he ordained them; but some outraged both the constitution of their nature and the government [oversight] entrusted to them."[21] Many in the early church emphasized the terrible sin of some of the angels who had sexual intercourse with human women. The narrative of Genesis 6:2, 4 was the basis for this belief. As Athenagoras explained, some angels "fell into impure love of virgins, and were conquered by the flesh.... Of these lovers of virgins, therefore, those who are called giants were born.... These angels, then, who have fallen from heaven, and haunt the air and the earth, are no longer able to rise to heavenly things, and the souls of the giants, which are the demons who wander about the world, perform similar actions."[22] This sexual sin perverted God's design, as Justin Martyr noted: "The angels transgressed their appointed role and were captivated by the love of women."[23]

Tragic results took place as a result of this angelic sin. According to Irenaeus and Clement of Alexandria, the rebellious angels were hurled out of heaven and cast down to the earth.[24] Citing Jude 6, Clement explained this judgment in greater detail: "'But the angels,' he says, 'who did not keep their own pre-eminence ... but left their own habitation ... [God] has reserved these to the judgment of the great day, in chains, under darkness.' He means the place near the earth, that is, the dark air. Now by 'chains,' he means the loss of the honor in which they had stood, and the lust of feeble things."[25] Ultimately, this sin will result in eternal punishment, as Irenaeus noted: "The Lord has said that there are certain angels of the devil for whom eternal fire is prepared."[26] Although Origen speculated that these fallen angels might ultimately be restored to their original position,[27] Tertullian expressed the belief of the church: "Although there is assigned to angels perdition in 'the fire prepared for the devil and his angels' (Matt. 25:41), yet a restoration is never promised to them. Christ never received any directive from the Father about the salvation of angels."[28]

At the head of this angelic rebellion was the devil, or Satan. Irenaeus explained, "The Hebrew word *Satan* means an apostate."[29] If the devil apostatized or fell away, it implies that he was not created evil. Origen explained the original high position of Satan:

> We find in the prophet Ezekiel two prophecies written to the prince of Tyre....
> The second is clearly of such a kind that it cannot be at all understood about
> a human being, but about some superior power which had fallen away from

---

21. Athenagoras, *A Plea for the Christians*, 24, in *ANF*, 2:142. The text has been rendered clearer.

22. Ibid., 24–25, in *ANF*, 2:142. The text has been rendered clearer.

23. Justin Martyr, *Second Apology*, 5, in *ANF*, 1:190. The text has been rendered clearer.

24. Irenaeus, *Against Heresies*, 4.16.2, in *ANF*, 1:481; Clement of Alexandria, *Stromata*, 3.2; 7.7, in *ANF*, 2:274, 536.

25. Clement of Alexandria, "Comments on the Epistle of Jude," in *Fragments from Cassiodorus*, 2, in *ANF*, 2:573. The text has been rendered clearer.

26. Irenaeus, *Against Heresies*, 4.41.1, in *ANF*, 1:524. His reference is to Matt. 25:41.

27. Origen, *First Principles*, 1.6.3, in *ANF*, 4:261. Speaking of the devil and his evil angels, Origen speculated: "In a future world, will any of these orders who act under the government of the devil, and obey his wicked commands, be converted to righteousness because they possess the faculty of free will? Or may persistent and habitual wickedness be changed by the power of habit into nature? This is a result of which you yourself, reader, may approve."

28. Tertullian, *On the Flesh of Christ*, 14, in *ANF*, 3:533. The text has been rendered clearer.

29. Irenaeus, *Against Heresies*, 5.21.2, in *ANF*, 1:549.

a higher position and had been reduced to a lower, worse condition.... This opposing and evil power was not formed or created that way by nature, but fell from a better to a worse position, and was transformed into a wicked being.... [This opposing power] was formerly holy and happy; from which state of happiness it fell from the time that evil was found in it, and was hurled to the earth, and was not such by nature and creation.[30]

The reason given for the falling away of Satan is this: "When he saw human beings made in the image of God, he broke forth into jealousy and malevolent envy.... How great an evil is that by which an angel fell!"[31] Satan was not alone in his demise, as Irenaeus noted: "Eternal fire was not originally prepared for man, but for him ... who is the leader of the apostasy, and for those angels who became apostates along with him."[32]

Of chief importance was the devil's role in leading humanity astray: "The apostate angel caused the disobedience of humanity by means of the serpent."[33] Tertullian added that Satan is "the angel of evil, the source of error, and the corrupter of the whole world, by whom, in the beginning, man was entrapped into breaking the commandment of God."[34] Thus, even before sin entered into the human realm, it existed in the angelic realm and provoked our first parents to fall, as Theophilus explained: "Because she was in the beginning deceived by the serpent, this Eve became the author of sin. Actually, it was the wicked demon, who is also called Satan, who then spoke to her through the serpent. He is also called 'demon' and 'dragon' on account of his revolting against God. For at first he was an angel."[35]

The early church was keenly aware of the ongoing spiritual battle between angels and demons, and this developed into a belief in guardian angels. According to Origen, "every human soul is put in subjection to some angel."[36] Clement of Alexandria pointed to Matthew 18:10 for biblical support for this idea.[37] Furthermore, Origen reasoned from various biblical passages that angels are involved with individual churches and people: "To one angel, the church of the Ephesians was entrusted; to another, that of the Smyrneans. One angel was to be Peter's; another, Paul's. And so on down to each of the little ones that are in the church. For such and such angels as even daily behold the face of God must be assigned to each one of them. And there must also be some angels who encamp around those who fear God."[38]

The role of this guardian angel was conceived differently by different people. The writer of the *Shepherd of Hermas* actually envisioned two angels influencing each person. One is an angel of righteousness, fostering the good.[39] Opposed to this is an angel

---

30. Origen, *First Principles*, 1.5.4, in *ANF*, 4:258–59. The text has been rendered clearer. His reference is to Ezek. 27 and 28.

31. Cyprian, *Treatise* 10.4, in *ANF*, 5:492.

32. Irenaeus, *Against Heresies*, 3.23.3, in *ANF*, 1:456. The text has been rendered clearer.

33. Ibid., 4.1.4, in *ANF*, 1:462. The text has been rendered clearer.

34. Tertullian, *The Soul's Testimony*, 3, in *ANF*, 3:177.

35. Theophilus, *To Autolycus*, 2.28, in *ANF*, 2:105. The text has been rendered clearer.

36. Origen, *Commentary on Matthew*, 13.5, in *ANF*, 10:478.

37. Clement of Alexandria, *Stromata*, 5.14, in *ANF*, 2:466.

38. Origen, *First Principles*, 1.8.1, in *ANF*, 4:265. His references are Rev. 2–3; Acts 12:15; Matt. 18:10; and Ps. 34:7.

39. *Shepherd of Hermas*, mandate 6.2.36, in Holmes, 391; *ANF*, 2:24.

of wickedness, who prompts its person toward evil.[40] In addition to this angelic role of guiding people toward the good, Origen added the angelic responsibility to lead people to repentance: "We are not at first chastised [reproved] by the Father of the family himself, but by the angels whom he has sent as masters over us with the responsibility of chastising [reproving] and correcting each one of us."[41] Another role for guardian angels is that of helping Christians when they pray: "We must suppose that the angels who are the overseers and ministers of God are present to one who is praying, in order to ask with him for what he petitions [requests]. The angel, indeed, of each one of us ... prays with us and cooperates with us, as far as it is possible, in what we seek."[42]

This guardianship of angels is especially necessary because demons work against God and his will. Between their expulsion from heaven and their final judgment, these evil angels wreak havoc in the earth. According to Tertullian, they illicitly communicate secret knowledge about magic, astrology, and cosmetics; this last element is targeted at women so they become obsessed with external beauty.[43] In addition to these stratagems, fallen angels invent errors and false doctrines to prevent the church's progress.[44] By this trickery, evil angels "strive to turn people away from the worship and knowledge of the true Majesty. Thus, people will not be able to obtain immortality. This is because these angels lost immortality on account of their wickedness."[45]

Some in the early church addressed the issue of demon possession. Tertullian offered biblical support that some people — Mary Magdalene (Mark 16:9), the Gadarene demoniac (Matt. 8:28–34) — were possessed by demons.[46] Origen described how demon possession manifests itself:

> There is a twofold mode of operation of wicked spirits. Sometimes they take complete and entire possession of the mind, so as not to allow their captives the power of either understanding or feeling. For example, this is the case with those who are commonly called "possessed," whom we see to be deprived of reason, and insane (such as those were who are related in the Gospel to have been cured by the Savior). At other times, these evil spirits use their wicked suggestions to deprave a conscious and intelligent soul with thoughts of various kinds — persuading it to do evil — of which Judas is an illustration.[47]

The proper response to demon possession is exorcism. Justin Martyr explained how this takes place in the name of Jesus Christ: "We call him Helper and Redeemer, the power of whose name even the demons fear. Even to this day, when they are exorcised in the name of Jesus Christ ... they are overcome."[48] A particularly powerful illustration of this took place through Gregory Thaumaturgus (whose last name literally means

40. Ibid., in Holmes, 391–93; ANF, 2:24.

41. Origen, Selecta in Psalmos, 37, cited in Daniélou, Angels and Their Mission, 77.

42. Origen, De oratione, 11.5, cited in Daniélou, Angels and Their Mission, 79.

43. Tertullian, On the Apparel of Women, 2, in ANF, 4:14–15.

44. Origen, First Principles, 3.3.4, in ANF, 4:336.

45. Lactantius, The Divine Institutes, 2.17, in ANF, 7:66.

46. Tertullian, A Treatise on the Soul, 25, in ANF, 3:206.

47. Origen, First Principles, 3.3.4, in ANF, 4:336. The text has been rendered clearer.

48. Justin Martyr, Dialogue with Trypho, a Jew, 30, in ANF, 1:209.

"wonder worker"). On one occasion, he encountered a pagan shrine that was under demonic sway and so purged it of demons through the powerful name of Jesus Christ.[49]

Certainly, demons wreak havoc among unbelievers. By contrast, Origen noted: "A Christian—I mean a true Christian, who has submitted to God alone and his Word— will suffer nothing from demons. For he is mightier than demons."[50] Cyprian provided the reason why this is so: "Demons can no longer remain in the body of a person who is baptized and sanctified, in whom the Holy Spirit is beginning to dwell."[51] So, when Satan's fury is directed against believers, they do not need to shrink back from him, as the *Shepherd of Hermas* instructed: "'Fear the Lord,' he said, 'and keep his commandments.... But do not fear the devil, for if you fear the Lord you will rule over the devil, because he has no power. And where there is no power, there is no fear.... But do fear the works of the devil, because they are evil.'"[52] The need to face satanic attacks with complete trust in the Lord was further urged: "All those who are full in the faith resist him mightily and he leaves them alone, because he finds no place where he can gain entrance."[53]

Angels assist in this resistance. To counteract the strategies of Satan and the demons, "God does no less than to set his own angels over his devout servants, so that none of the hostile angels—not even the one who is called 'the prince of this world'—can do anything against those who have given themselves to God."[54] Thus, it is proper for believers to rely on God and ask for angelic protection: "We entrust ourselves to the supreme God through Jesus Christ, who has given us such instruction. We ask for every kind of help from him, and for the guardianship of holy and good angels, to defend us from the earth-spirits intent on lust."[55] This angelic help is directed not only for individuals but also for the church. Using a metaphor of a boat, Hippolytus affirmed: "The church has mariners [sailors] on the port and the starboard sides, helpers like the holy angels, by whom the church is always governed and defended."[56]

Believers in the early church experienced the reality of the spiritual realm vividly and constantly. For many, their entire earthly pilgrimage was devoted to repelling the onslaughts of evil spirits. Perhaps no one embodied this spiritual warfare more than St. Antony, one of the earliest Christian monks. In his *Life of St. Antony*, Athanasius described the fierce attacks against the godly Antony by the devil himself, attacks that were resisted by determination and faith.

Antony also depended on a monastic lifestyle for success in repelling these satanic attacks: "He repressed his body more and more and kept it in subjection, lest haply having conquered on one side, he should be dragged down on the other. He therefore planned to accustom himself to a severer mode of life."[57] As part of this, Antony severely

49. Gregory of Nyssa, *Life of Gregory Thaumaturgus*, in *Paganism and Christianity, 100–425 C.E.*, ed. Ramsay Mac-Mullen and Eugene N. Lane (Minneapolis: Augsburg Fortress, 1992), 207–15.

50. Origen, *Against Celsus*, 8.36, in *ANF*, 4:653.

51. Cyprian, *Letter* 75.15, in *ANF*, 5:402.

52. *Shepherd of Hermas*, mandate 7, 37, in Holmes, 393; *ANF*, 2:24–25.

53. Ibid., mandate 12, 48, in Holmes, 416–17; *ANF*, 2:29–30.

54. Origen, *Against Celsus*, 8.36, in *ANF*, 4:653.

55. Ibid., 8.60, in *ANF*, 4:662.

56. Hippolytus, *Treatise on Christ and Antichrist*, 59, in *ANF*, 5:217.

57. Athanasius, *Life of St. Antony*, 7, in *NPNF*[2], 4:197. The text has been rendered clearer.

Antony's Wrestling with the Devil

The devil, who hates and envies what is good, could not stand to see such determination in a young man, but attempted to carry out against him what he had been unable to accomplish against others. First of all he tried to lead him away from godly discipline, whispering to him the memory of his wealth, care for his sister, claims of family, love of money, love of glory, various sumptuous foods and the leisure of life, and at last the difficulty of virtue and the great effort it demands.... In a word he raised in his mind a great cloud of debate, wishing to deter him from his settled purpose. But the enemy discovered that he was too weak for Antony's determination, and that he instead was conquered by Antony's resolve, overthrown by his great faith, and defeated through his constant prayers.*

*Athanasius, *Life of St. Antony*, 5, in *NPNF*[2], 4:196–97. The text has been rendered clearer.

subjected his body to rigorous discipline in terms of eating only bread and salt, drinking only water, fasting quite often, sleeping on the bare ground, and often forgoing sleep. His example served to promote asceticism in the early church as an antidote to demonic attacks. Engaging in exorcisms of demons, Antony was also victorious over the demonic forces that attacked others.[58]

Clearly, the doctrine of angels and demons held a very important position in the theology and practice of the early church, and Augustine both supported and extended this belief. He explained both angelic nature and function: "'Angel' is the name of their office, not of their nature. If you seek the name of their nature, it is 'spirit'; if you seek the name of their office, it is 'angel.' From what they are, 'spirit'; from what they do, 'angel.'"[59] This term can refer to two varieties: Good angels are called "the angels of God," while the wicked angels are called "the angels of the devil, or demons."[60]

The difference between these two types of angelic beings was part of Augustine's narrative of two cities, recounted in *The City of God*: "Two cities have been formed by two loves: the earthly city, by the love of self, even to the contempt of God; the heavenly [city], by the love of God, even to the contempt of self."[61] For Augustine, "the foundations of these two cities were originally laid in the difference that arose among the angels."[62] Fancifully, he proposed that this difference between good and bad angels is found in the creation account.[63] Some of these created beings remained good while others turned to

---

58. Ibid., 64, in *NPNF*[2], 4:213.

59. Augustine, *Enarrations on the Psalms*, 103, 1, 15, PL, 37:1348, cited in *Catechism of the Catholic Church*, sec. 329, n. 188.

60. Augustine, *The City of God*, 5.9, in *NPNF*[1], 2:91.

61. Ibid., 14.28, in *NPNF*[1], 2:282–83.

62. Ibid., 11.1, in *NPNF*[1], 2:205.

63. "To me, it does not seem inconsistent with the work of God if we understand that the angels were created when that first light was made, and that a separation was made between the holy and the wicked angels when, as is said, 'God divided the light from the darkness; and God called the light "day," and the darkness he called "night" [Gen. 1:4–5].' The light is the holy community of the angels who are spiritually radiant with the illumination of the truth. The opposing darkness is the toxic pollution of the spiritual condition of those angels who are turned away from the light of righteousness." Ibid., 11.19, in *NPNF*[1], 2:215. The text has been rendered clearer. Augustine could not imagine that the opening chapter of Genesis did not include a reference to the

evil, not because some were originally created good and others evil—God created only good essences—but because of "a difference in their wills and desires.... While some resolutely continued in that which was the common good of all, namely, in God himself, and in his eternity, truth and love; others, being enamored rather of their own power, as if they could be their own good, lapsed [fell] to this private good of their own, from that higher and blessed good that was common to all."[64] Thus, the good angels willed to remain obedient, while the evil angels willed to defect from God.

At this point, Augustine added a new twist with his belief that the number of fallen angels will be replaced by an equal number of believing human beings:

> It pleased God ... [that] mankind, who constituted the remainder of the intelligent creation, having perished without exception under sin ... should be in part restored, and should fill up the gap which the rebellion and fall of the devils had left in the company [community] of the angels.... We do not know the number either of the saints [Christians] or of the devils; but we know that the children of the holy mother [Christians] ... shall succeed to the place of the fallen angels, and shall dwell forever in that peaceful abode from which they [the devils] fell.[65]

Thus, Augustine envisioned a restoration of the harmony that existed in the created realm before sin entered into both the spiritual world and the physical world. Those replacing Satan and the demons would not be redeemed angelic beings, but redeemed human beings. In this way, the city of God will one day be fully restored. In the meantime, angels invite human beings to join them in the worship of God.[66]

The greatest contribution to the early church's doctrine of angels was made by Dionysius the Pseudo-Areopagite. He offered an elaborate description of angelic beings, imagining them to be "superior" to human beings and nearer to God because of their "generous communion with the Deity" and their "total intelligence."[67] His predecessor Augustine had showed great restraint in refusing to speculate about the organization, rankings, and nature of the angelic realm.[68] Dionysius, by contrast, did not hesitate to

---

creation of angels: "When all things, which are recorded to have been completed in six days, were created and arranged, how should the angels be omitted, as if they were not among the works of God, from which on the seventh day he rested?" Ibid., 11.9, in *NPNF*[1], 2:209. Although at best there is an implicit reference to angels in the days of creation, Augustine found explicit indication elsewhere in Scripture that angels were created by God (Ps. 148:1–5). Noting that Job 38:7 indicates that the angels existed before the stars, Augustine reasoned backwards from the fourth day (on which the stars were made) to this conclusion: "There is no question that if the angels are included in the works of God during these six days, they are that light that was called 'day.'" Ibid., 11.9, in *NPNF*[1], 2:210. Moreover, Augustine did not discount the view that the angels were created by God prior to the creation of the

world. Ibid., 11.32, in *NPNF*[1], 2:223. For further discussion of Augustine's view on creation, see chap. 12.

64. Ibid., 12.1, in *NPNF*[1], 2:231. Augustine rejected the common view that some angels had engaged in sexual intercourse with human women, as found in Gen. 6:2, 4. Ibid., 3.5; 15.23, in *NPNF*[1], 2:45; 303–5.

65. Augustine, *Enchiridion on Faith, Hope, and Love*, 29, in *NPNF*[1], 3:247.

66. Augustine, *City of God*, 10.25, in *NPNF*[1], 2:196.

67. Dionysius the Pseudo-Areopagite, *The Celestial Hierarchy*, 4.2, in *Pseudo-Dionysius: The Complete Works*, trans. Colm Luibheid and Paul Rorem (New York: Paulist, 1987), 156–57.

68. Augustine, *Enchiridion on Faith, Hope, and Love*, 58, in *NPNF*[1], 3:256.

describe in great detail the hierarchy that exists among the angels.[69] Taking nine biblical terms—*thrones, cherubim, seraphim, authorities, dominions, powers, angels, archangels,* and *principalities*—that refer to members of the heavenly realm, Dionysius offered a detailed description of each of these nine orders.

In the first hierarchy of three orders are *seraphim, cherubim,* and *thrones.*[70] The members of this first hierarchy "are, as it were, in the anteroom of divinity."[71] The second hierarchy of three orders is situated in a middle position, below the seraphim, cherubim, and thrones, yet above the third hierarchy. These are *dominions, powers,* and *authorities.*[72] Below these is the third and lowest hierarchy, which are *principalities, archangels,* and *angels.* According to Dionysius, each of these three hierarchies takes from that which is above it and communicates down the hierarchical ladder to its subordinates. Together, this works toward harmony in the universe. This angelic hierarchy was especially important for Dionysius because it was the model after which God designed the church's hierarchy of bishop, priest, and deacon.[73] Just as there is order, authority, and subordination in the celestial hierarchy, these same realities must be observed within the church.[74]

Because of the authority that became attached to the writings of Dionysius, they exerted an ill-founded yet significant influence over key leaders of the church in the following centuries. At its outset, the early church had been marked by a good deal of biblical restraint as it developed its doctrine of angels, Satan, and demons. Because of the unbounded contributions of Dionysius, however, many nonbiblical elements were added to this doctrine and eventually bequeathed to the medieval church.

BELIEFS ABOUT THE SPIRITUAL REALM IN THE MIDDLE AGES

The medieval doctrine of angels and demons is most commonly associated with Thomas Aquinas, but many others developed a theology of the spiritual realm during the Middle Ages. An important contributor was John of Damascus, whose *Exposition of the Orthodox Faith* deeply influenced later medieval theologians. In his treatment of angels, John relied on Dionysius for his hierarchical classification.[75] John also addressed the fall of the devil, imagining him as the divinely appointed ruler of the world who, though created good and endowed with great privilege, abused his free will in rebellion against God: "[He] became roused against God who created him, and determined to rise in rebellion against him; and he was the first to depart from good and become evil."[76]

The nature of this satanic fall was explained in greater detail by Anselm in his work *On the Fall of the Devil.* He too focused on Satan's abuse of free will, explaining that the devil "sinned by willing something that pleased him and that he did not have and that

69. Dionysius, *Celestial Hierarchy,* 6.2, in *Pseudo-Dionysius,* 160–61.

70. Ibid., 7.1, in *Pseudo-Dionysius,* 162.

71. Ibid., 7.2, in *Pseudo-Dionysius,* 163.

72. Ibid., 8.1, in *Pseudo-Dionysius,* 167.

73. Ibid., 1.3, in *Pseudo-Dionysius,* 146.

74. For further discussion, see chap. 27.

75. John of Damascus, *Exposition of the Orthodox Faith,* 2.3, in *NPNF²,* 9:18–20 (the second pages 18–20 in this volume).

76. Ibid., 2.4, in *NPNF²,* 9:20 (the second page 20 in this volume).

he should not have then willed, but that could increase his happiness. By inordinately willing more than he had received, his will exceeded the limits of justice."[77] The devil's overreaching was nothing other than willing to be like, or even greater than, God himself.[78] Satan was not the only rebel, and all the evil angels "lost the good that they had and did not obtain that which induced them to depreciate justice. Thus, the angels are divided into those who, adhering to justice, can enjoy all the goods they will, and those who, having abandoned justice, are deprived of whatever good they desire."[79]

Anselm also echoed Augustine's idea that the number of fallen angels had to be replaced by an equal number of redeemed human beings; thus, the atonement of Jesus Christ became a necessity to restore perfect harmony in the universe. He began with the idea of a perfect number of reasoning beings, by which he meant both angels and humans.[80] From this starting point, Anselm reasoned to his replacement idea: Because the fallen angels "must have been of that number, either their number was inevitably to be made up, or the number of rational beings will remain smaller than was foreseen previously in that perfect number—and that is impossible. Beyond doubt, they have to be replaced. It is necessary, therefore, that their number should be made up from the human race, because there is no other race from which it can be made complete."[81]

With the publication of his *Sentences*, Peter Lombard promoted the doctrine of angels to a major topic in the academic study of theology. From now on, this doctrine would be part of the theological curriculum of everyone preparing for ministry and teaching.

Thomas Aquinas was nicknamed the "Angelic Doctor" because of the vast treatment he gave to angels. Much of what he wrote on the subject was steeped in the philosophy of Aristotle, but he also relied on biblical teaching in formulating his doctrine. His definition of angels was philosophically derived, based on the idea that God made creatures by his intellect and will. Because God created angels by his intellect, they are completely intellectual beings that lack any physical nature.[82] Thus, angels are the creatures who are most like God. Moreover, their number is immense. Again, Aquinas believed this on the basis of philosophical reasoning: Whereas the perfection of physical things is found in their *immense size*, the perfection of nonphysical things is found in their *immense number*.[83] Aquinas also addressed the difference between physical bodies, angels, and God in terms of their presence in space: "[A] body is in a place in a *circumscribed*—or limited—manner, since it is measured by the place. An angel, however, is not there in a circumscribed manner, since he is not measured by the place. Rather, he is there in a *definitive* manner, because he is in one place in such a way that he is not in another. But God is neither circumscriptively nor definitively there, because he is everywhere."[84] Although angels are not present everywhere like God, they can move instantaneously from place to place—though they do not pass through space, nor do they take time to accomplish

77. Anselm, *On the Fall of the Devil*, 4, in *Anselm*, 202.

78. Ibid., 4, in *Anselm*, 202–3.

79. Ibid., 6, in *Anselm*, 204.

80. Anselm, *Why God Became Man*, 1.16, in *Anselm*, 290.

81. Ibid.

82. Thomas Aquinas, *Summa Theologica*, pt. 1, q. 50, art.

1. In his *Summa Contra Gentiles*, 2.91, Aquinas offered eight proofs for the existence of incorporeal intelligent creatures, or angels.

83. Aquinas, *Summa Theologica*, pt. 1, q. 50, art. 3.

84. Ibid., pt. 1, q. 52, art. 2. The text has been rendered clearer.

their movements.[85] Furthermore, Aquinas affirmed that angels have free will, "and they possess it in a higher degree of perfection than in human beings."[86] This idea means that angels bear the image of God even more than human beings do. Furthermore, this free will is not susceptible to wrongful desires or the lure of temptation, for only creatures with a physical body can be influenced by such things.[87]

As to their origin, Aquinas argued that God created angels, probably at the same time that he created human beings.[88] He believed they were created in the empyrean heaven, the highest of all created realms.[89] The angels were not created perfect, nor in the state of blessedness; that reality came about only as they were influenced by God's grace so that they could merit perfection through love. Having once obtained this blessedness, however, their situation is different: "The blessed angels cannot sin. The reason for this is, because their blessedness consists in seeing God through his essence. Now, God's essence is the very essence of goodness. Consequently, the angel beholding God is disposed towards God.... Therefore, the blessed angels can neither will nor act, except as aiming towards God. Now whoever wills or acts in this manner cannot sin. Consequently, the blessed angel cannot sin."[90]

Aquinas dedicated a significant amount of space to a discussion of the hierarchical order among the angels. Relying heavily on Dionysius and John of Damascus, along with several biblical passages (Eph. 1:20–21; Col. 1:16), Aquinas constructed a "map" of the spiritual realm.

Aquinas's Hierarchy of Spiritual Beings

- first hierarchy (which "contemplates the ideas of things in God himself")

    seraphim (which "excel in what is the supreme excellence of all, in being united to God himself")

    cherubim (which "know the divine secrets supereminently")

    thrones (which are "raised up so as to be the familiar recipients of God in themselves")

- second hierarchy (which "contemplates the ideas of things in the universal causes" and "considers what is to be done")

    dominions (which "appoint those things that are to be done")

    virtues (which "give the power of carrying out what is to be done")

    powers (which "order how what has been commanded or decided to be done can be carried out by others")

---

85. This kind of speculation led critics of scholastic theologians to poke fun at their concern over matters of minutiae. E.g., Rabelais accused the scholastics of arguing over the worthless question of how many angels can dance on the head of a pin. There is no evidence from scholastic writings that this point was ever debated, but Aquinas certainly did have an answer to the question: Only one angel can be in one place at the same time, because the presence of its "power touches the place immediately," thereby making it impossible for another angel to be present. Ibid., pt. 1, q. 52, art. 3.

86. Ibid., pt. 1, q. 59, art. 3.
87. Ibid., pt. 1, q. 59, art. 4.
88. Ibid., pt. 1, q. 61, arts. 1, 3.
89. Ibid., pt. 1, q. 61, art. 4.
90. Ibid., pt. 1, q. 62, art. 8.

- third hierarchy (which "contemplates the ideas of things in their application to particular effects" and "carries out the work")
    principalities (which are "the beginners and leaders" who "preside over the government of peoples and kingdoms")
    archangels (which "hold a middle place" and "announce great things above reason to human beings")
    angels (which "simply execute what is to be done" and "announce small things within the realm of reason to human beings").*

*Thomas Aquinas, *Summa Theologica*, pt. 1, q. 108, art. 6.

In one of the longest treatments of any subject in the *Summa Theologica*, Aquinas positioned the many diverse spiritual beings (as found in Scripture) in an elaborate three-tiered hierarchy with detailed "job descriptions" to identify and distinguish them all. This schema influenced his view of the church, for Aquinas, like Dionysius before him, held that "the church hierarchy is copied from the heavenly."[91] Specifically, "the order of divine providence has so disposed [arranged] not only among the angels, but also in the whole universe, that inferior things are administered by the superior."[92] If the whole cosmos is set up according to a universal hierarchy, then the angelic realm and the church participate in this hierarchical structure. Obviously, then, laypeople must obey the leaders of the church, even as the lower orders of spiritual beings obey the higher ones.

For Aquinas, the future of believers is to be taken up into the order of angels so as to become like them. Using as his starting point Jesus' statement (Matt. 22:30), Aquinas drew his conclusion: Although according to nature, human beings can never be like the angels, according to God's grace, human beings can be transformed to become like them.[93] Before becoming like angels in their future life, human beings are protected by guardian angels in this life. Aquinas believed that "each man has a guardian angel appointed to him. The reason for this is that the guardianship of angels belongs to the execution of divine providence concerning men."[94] This guardian angel has the specific purpose of protecting its assigned human being.[95]

A chief reason that such guardianship is necessary is the presence of demons in the world. These evil angels attempt to thwart God's will from being done among human beings. Aquinas affirmed that the angelic sin was pride—"not to be subject to a superior when subjection is due."[96] Specifically, the object of the devil's pride was becoming like God.[97] This meant that the devil was not created evil. Rather, Aquinas held that this fall of the devil took place the instant after his creation.[98] The devil—created by grace and with a free will, as were all the angels—needed only to exercise his free will once to do good, and he would have merited God's eternal blessing immediately. Because this choice did not take place, Aquinas concluded that the devil abused his freedom by

---

91. Ibid., pt. 1, q. 108, art. 4.
92. Ibid., pt. 1, q. 112, art. 2.
93. Ibid., pt. 1, q. 108, art. 8.
94. Ibid., pt. 1, q. 113, art. 2.

95. Ibid., pt. 1, q. 113, art. 4.
96. Ibid., pt. 1, q. 63, art. 2.
97. Ibid., pt. 1, q. 63, art. 3.
98. Ibid., pt. 1, q. 63, art. 6.

sinning immediately after he was created. In sinning, the devil led a host of other angels with him in rebellion against God. Appealing to Revelation 12:4, Aquinas explained: "It is said that the dragon 'drew' with him 'the third part of the stars of heaven.' I answer that, the sin of the highest angel was the cause of the others sinning."[99] Punishment for this demonic rebellion is twofold: some demons are currently in hell tormenting human souls who are there, while others lurk around earth tempting human beings.[100]

Aquinas's lengthy treatment of the doctrine of angels and demons cemented Catholic belief on this matter for centuries to come. Combining some biblical affirmations about the spiritual realm with speculative reasoning from the philosophy of Aristotle and the imaginative celestial hierarchy of Pseudo-Dionysius, it ensured that medieval belief in angels and demons would be a mixture of fact and fantasy.

While Catholic scholasticism formulated the official position of the church, popular beliefs about angels and demons—some of which bore little or no resemblance to the Roman Catholic Church's approved doctrine—arose and flourished. For example, a very popular theme in medieval literature, sermons, paintings, and woodcuts was "the art of dying." One common version of this pictured a sickly man lying on his deathbed, being tempted by demons and helped by angels. The last temptation of the demons was designed to entice the dying man to yield over his soul to the devil. To accomplish their evil deed, the demons tortured the man with memories of his many former sins—murder, theft, fornication— and with visions of the confiscation and squandering of his property—his home, brewery, livestock—after his death by his greedy heirs. If he would only consign his soul to the evil one, he would find comfort in his dying moments! In reaction to these enticements, the angels reminded the dying man of the many blessings that come to the faithful, represented by the Virgin Mary, the apostle Peter, the throng of saints, and the crucified Jesus Christ. As the demonic torture increased, the angelic comfort was intensified. Finally, at the point of death, the soul of the man left his body and was born heavenward by the angels. Such was the Christian "art of dying." Of course, descriptions of purgatory and hell gave a prominent place to the horrible sufferings that take place in both regions of the dead, sufferings that in part are cruelly administered by the terrifying demons that inhabit those nightmarish places.

BELIEFS ABOUT THE SPIRITUAL REALM IN THE REFORMATION AND POST-REFORMATION

Reflecting the medieval church's view of angels, Martin Luther did little to further this doctrine. He offered a traditional definition: "An angel is a spiritual creature, a personal being without a body, appointed for the service of the divine [heavenly] church."[101] He avoided speculation about the angelic realm, noting that Scripture had little to say on the subject.[102] Luther thought in traditional ways about guardian angels, adding that "the holy servants of God take care of eating, drinking, sleeping, and waking children!

---

99. Ibid., pt. 1, q. 63, art. 8.

100. Ibid., pt. 1, q. 64, art. 4. This does not mean, according to Aquinas, that all sins are due to demonically instigated temptation. Ibid., pt. 1, q. 114, art. 3. But Aquinas underscored the subtle craftiness of the devil and his followers, who can

even perform apparent miracles to lead people astray. Ibid., pt. 1, q. 114, art. 4.

101. Martin Luther, WLS, 1:23.

102. Ibid.

It certainly seems to be an insignificant work. But the angels do it with joy; for it is very pleasing to God, who has commanded them to do it."[103] The good angels are also involved in protecting people from the bad angels, or demons.

Luther was very conscious of the intense spiritual battle that raged around him. He believed that, in addition to meditation on the Word of God and prayer, spiritual warfare was the third key characteristic of a fruitful theologian (as Luther developed Ps. 119): "You see how David complains so often about all kinds of enemies, arrogant princes or tyrants, false spirits and factions, whom he must tolerate because he meditates, that is, because he is occupied with God's Word. For as soon as God's Word takes root and grows in you, the devil will harass you, and will make a real doctor of you, and by his assaults will teach you to seek and love God's Word."[104] Many of Luther's writings were filled with references to battling against Satan and his evil minions. Perhaps none is more widely known and loved than his great hymn, "A Mighty Fortress Is Our God," which features the reality of spiritual warfare and the need to trust wholeheartedly and only in Jesus Christ for victory.

Martin Luther's "A Mighty Fortress Is Our God"

A mighty fortress is our God, a bulwark never failing;
Our helper he amid the flood of mortal ills prevailing.
For still our ancient foe doth seek to work us woe —
His craft and power are great, and, armed with cruel hate,
On earth is not his equal.

Did we in our own strength confide, our striving would be losing,
Were not the right man on our side, the man of God's own choosing.
Dost ask who that may be? Christ Jesus, it is he —
Lord Sabaoth his name, from age to age the same,
And he must win the battle.

And though this world, with devils filled, should threaten to undo us,
We will not fear, for God hath willed his truth to triumph through us.
The prince of darkness grim, we tremble not for him —
His rage we can endure, for lo, his doom is sure:
One little word shall fell him.

That word above all earthly powers, no thanks to them, abideth;
The Spirit and the gifts are ours through him who with us sideth.
Let goods and kindred go, this mortal life also —
The body they may kill; God's truth abideth still:
His kingdom is forever. Amen.*

*Martin Luther, "A Mighty Fortress Is Our God," trans. Frederick H. Hedge, in *The Hymnal for Worship and Celebration* (Waco, Tex.: Word Music, 1986), 26. A "bulwark" is a fortress, "our ancient foe" is Satan, and "Lord Sabaoth" is Lord of hosts, or the angelic realm.

---

103. Ibid., 1:24.

104. Martin Luther, *Preface to the Wittenberg Edition of*

Luther's German Writings, LW, 34:287.

Luther held a traditional view of the fall of the angels. At the head of the rebellion against God, prompted by pride, was the devil, or Satan. Luther relied on Scripture to describe this evil one as a "prince of this world" and "a murderer from the very beginning and a liar."[105] An interesting contribution of Luther was his notion that the devil "apes" God: "The devil is always the imitator of our Lord God, forever poses as divine and creates the impression that he is God."[106] Luther explained how this imitation comes about: "If [the devil] cannot prevent it nor hinder God's Word by force, he opposes it with an illusion of godliness, takes the very words which God has spoken, and so twists them as to peddle his lies and poison under their name."[107] Because of such subtleties, Luther warned believers to be on guard against Satan, who may present himself as either a black devil or a white one, camouflaging himself and counterfeiting the gospel.[108] He also emphasized the need to rebuke the devil with the authority of Christ: "Little is gained against the devil with a lengthy disputation; but a brief word and reply such as this is effective: I am a Christian, of the same flesh and blood as is my Lord Christ, the Son of God. You settle with him [God], devil! Such a retort would soon make him depart."[109] Furthermore, Luther realized that a prime occasion for demonic attack is when Christians have sinned. Although Satan may take advantage of this sin to accuse believers, Luther counseled them to turn the tables on the devil by addressing him:

> If you can tell me that I am a poor sinner, I, on the other hand, can tell you that Christ died for sinners and is their intercessor.... You remind me of the boundless, great faithfulness and goodness of my Lord and Savior Jesus Christ. The burden of my sins and all the trouble and misery that were to oppress me eternally, he very gladly took upon his shoulders and suffered the bitter death on the cross for them. To him I direct you. You may accuse and condemn him. Let me rest in peace; for on his shoulders, not on mine, lie all my sins and the sins of all the world.[110]

As always, Luther championed the grace of God in Christ for overcoming the evil one.

Acknowledging that the Catholic Church—in particular Thomas Aquinas—had fallen into error in its teaching about angels, John Calvin warned against engaging in speculation and urged that attention be paid to Scripture instead.[111] For Calvin, this biblical teaching includes the fact that different names are given to the angels, and each name is important for what it reveals about their character and role.[112] In addition, Scripture

---

105. "Christ says that the devil is a prince of this world (John 14:30; 16:11); and in John 8:44 Christ says that he is a murderer from the very beginning and a liar. If, then, we want to and must live on earth, we must realize that we are guests who lodge in an inn with a criminal as manager. And there is an inscription or a sign over the door that reads *The House of a Murderer* or *The House of a Liar*. For Christ himself has hung such a sign or coat of arms over his door and on his house by saying that the devil is a murderer and a liar. He is a murderer for killing the body, and a liar for misleading the soul. That is the devil's trade and his work. That is the way he keeps house;

that is how business is carried on in his inn." Martin Luther, *A Letter of Consolation to the Christians at Halle*, LW, 43:146.

106. Luther, *WLS*, 1:396.

107. Ibid., 1:397. The text has been rendered clearer.

108. Ibid., 1:395.

109. *Sermons of the Gospel of St. John, 1-4*, LW, 44:106.

110. Luther, *WLS*, 1:403.

111. John Calvin, *Institutes of the Christian Religion*, 1.14.4, LCC, 1:165.

112. Ibid., 1.14.5, LCC, 1:165.

113. Ibid., 1.14.6, LCC, 1:166.

reminds us that angels "keep vigil for our safety, take upon themselves our defense, direct our ways, and take care that some harm may not befall us."[113]

As for the hierarchical order, number, and form of the angels, Calvin distanced himself from Aquinas's speculation. For example, Calvin pointed to the paucity of evidence for the angelic hierarchy and concluded that we cannot know the order of the angels. In terms of the number of angels, he was content to assemble a few passages to demonstrate there is "a huge multitude."[114] He did discuss the appearance of angels, but even here he underscored that much remains shrouded in mystery.[115] Furthermore, Calvin called into question the common belief about guardian angels.[116] Rather than affirming individual guardian angels, Calvin was more persuaded that the entire company of angels has care for believers.[117]

Calvin's solution to the church's error-plagued doctrine of angels was to focus on why God employs angels to carry out his will: "Surely he does not do this out of necessity as if he could not do without them. For as often as he pleases, he disregards them and carries out his work through his will alone."[118] God uses angels, not because he needs them, but because Christians need an extra measure of comfort and assurance in their earthly pilgrimage: "When we see ourselves surrounded by so many dangers ... we would sometimes be filled with fear or yield to despair if the Lord did not make us realize the presence of his grace according to our capacity. For this reason, he not only promises to take care of us, but tells us he has innumerable guardians whom he has commanded to look after our safety."[119] Focusing on the fact that praise belongs to God alone, Calvin chided people who so focus on angels that their attention is led away from God. Yet he emphasized that angels "keep us in the one Mediator, Christ, that we may wholly depend upon him, lean upon him, be brought to him, and rest in him."[120]

Protestant theologians in the post-Reformation period exhibited the tendency both to speculate and to adhere closely to biblical teaching on the doctrine of angels, Satan, and demons. For example, Francis Turretin strongly criticized Thomas Aquinas and Catholic scholasticism on the matter of an angelic hierarchy.[121] Moreover, Turretin distanced himself from Roman Catholic practice by opposing the idea that angels are mediators in the sense of interceding in prayer for believers.[122] And he warned against worshiping angels in the Roman Catholic manner. Having said this, however, Turretin emphasized

---

114. Ibid., 1.14.8, LCC, 1:168.

115. Ibid., 1.14.8, LCC, 1:168–69.

116. Ibid., 1.14.7, LCC, 1:167. Calvin found one passage—the story involving Peter's angel (Acts 12:15)—that did seem to indicate the existence of guardian angels. But even here he cautioned: "Here, also, it can be answered that nothing prevents us from understanding this of any angel at all to whom the Lord had then given over the care of Peter; yet he would not for that reason be Peter's permanent guardian." Ibid.

117. "We should hold as a fact that the care of each one of us is not the task of one angel only, but all with one consent watch over our salvation.... For if the fact that all the heavenly host are keeping watch for his safety will not satisfy a man, I do not see what benefit he could derive from knowing that one

angel has been given to him as his special guardian. Indeed, those who confine to one angel the care that God takes of each one of us are doing a great injustice both to themselves and to all the members of the church." Ibid., 1.14.7, LCC, 1:167–68.

118. Ibid., 1.14.11, LCC, 1:171.

119. Ibid. The text has been rendered clearer.

120. Ibid., 1.14.12, LCC, 1:172.

121. Francis Turretin, *Institutes of Elenctic Theology*, ed. James T. Dennison Jr., trans. George Musgrave Giger, 3 vols. in 1 (Phillipsburg, N.J.: P & R, 1997), 7th topic, 7th q., sec. 2–3, 1:551.

122. Ibid., 7th topic, 9th q., sec. 1–12, 1:560–63.

the respect due to angels: "We do not deny that honor is to be paid to them by reason of their dignity, that we may acknowledge and celebrate their excellence, revere their presence, obey their admonitions, imitate their example and repay their intense love for us by reciprocal affection."[123]

BELIEFS ABOUT THE SPIRITUAL REALM IN THE MODERN PERIOD

The modern period was characterized by two important developments regarding the doctrine of angels, Satan, and demons. First, the more liberal elements within Christianity, displaying a bias against supernatural matters, treated the doctrine with benign neglect at best and with outright contempt at worst. For example, Friedrich Schleiermacher regarded the doctrine of angels as having neither a positive nor a negative value: "It can, therefore, continue to have its place in Christian language without laying on us the duty of arriving at any conclusion with regard to its truth."[124] In dealing with the many biblical passages about angels, Schleiermacher speculated that "Christ and the apostles might have said all these things [about angels] without having had any real conviction of the existence of such beings or any desire to communicate it."[125] Although apparently affirming a neutral stance toward the doctrine, Schleiermacher portrayed his own bias against it by considering it to be a childish belief.[126] Thus, having evolved beyond this original childish belief about angels, the church has little or no need for them; indeed, "the question whether the angels exist or not ought to have no influence on our conduct, and ... revelations of their existence are now no longer to be expected."[127]

In the same way, Schleiermacher addressed the doctrine of the devil, criticizing it as "so unstable that we cannot expect anyone to be convinced of its truth."[128] He called into question all the historical beliefs of the church on this topic, including the fall of the good angels, demonic activity against humanity, and the role of Satan in the fall of Adam and Eve. As before, Schleiermacher dismissed the many biblical affirmations about Satan and demons.[129] Furthermore, "Even if we could regard some or, indeed, all of those passages of Scripture as referring to the devil, there is still no reason for our accepting this notion as a permanent element in Christian doctrine and defining it accordingly so accurately that everything attributed to the devil could be conceived as a consistent whole."[130] Thus, the church has no need to hold on to the notion of the devil in the enlightened world; indeed, such a belief may be quite dangerous: "It would be bad enough if anyone neglected due care for himself and others because of his trust in the protection of angels. But it would certainly be more dangerous if at will, in place of self-examination, he attributed his growing wickedness to the influence of Satan."[131] Despite this, Schleiermacher

123. Ibid., sec. 13, 1:563.
124. Friedrich Schleiermacher, *The Christian Faith*, ed. H. R. Mackintosh and J. S. Stewart (Edinburgh: T & T Clark, 1928), 156.
125. Ibid., 158.
126. Ibid., 159.

127. Ibid., 160.
128. Ibid., 161.
129. Ibid., 163–64.
130. Ibid., 167.
131. Ibid., 168–69.

found a positive use for believing in the devil and teaching on the subject, "in order to make clear the positive godlessness of evil in itself, or to emphasize the fact that it is only in a higher protection that we can find help against an evil the source of whose power our will and intelligence seem unable to reach."[132]

While Schleiermacher held on to the doctrine of angels and demons for some kind of sentimental value, those who followed him were not so disposed and dismissed such belief. David Strauss, for example, applauded the advancement in modern thinking that liberated humanity from its superstitious ideas about angels: "If the modern idea of God and conception of the world are right, there cannot possibly be beings of this kind."[133]

In a second important development, the more conservative elements of Christianity, reacting to these liberal tendencies, relegated the doctrine to the periphery of Christian beliefs. For example, out of the nearly one hundred articles published as *The Fundamentals* of the Christian faith, only one addressed this topic, and it was dedicated to the doctrine of Satan.[134] Only after the midway point of the twentieth century was an interest in angels and demons rekindled.

Karl Barth, more than anyone else, was responsible for this resurgence in attention. Explaining his methodology in developing a doctrine of angels, Barth saw the need to steer clear of two extremes: the modern tendency to dismiss the doctrine completely, and the historical tendency to engage in rampant speculation.[135] He focused on the key passage of Hebrews 1:14. For Barth, the error of earlier theologians was their emphasis on the word "spirits," for it gave rise to an overemphasis on the spiritual *nature* of angels. But for Barth "the main point is not that angels are 'spirits,' but that as such they receive from the adjective λειτουργικα *leitourgika*; 'ministering' and the participle ἀποδτελλομενα [*apostellomena*; 'sent'] a distinctive character and activity."[136] Thus, he emphasized the function of angels, which is to play a mediating role between God and human beings.[137]

With great reluctance, Barth dedicated a small part of his discussion on angels to their "opponents." Noting the menacing nature of such discussion, he commented: "Sinister matters may be very real, but they must not be contemplated too long or studied too precisely or adopted too intensively.... The very thing which the demons are waiting for, especially in theology, is that we should find them dreadfully interesting and give them our serious and perhaps systematic attention."[138] He rejected the traditional notion that bad angels are merely fallen versions of good angels: "It is thus quite inappropriate to speak of God and the devil or angels and demons in the same breath. They have no common denominator. They do not grow from a common root."[139] Barth limited his discussion of demons to their function of antithesis: "Angels and demons are related as creation and chaos, as the free grace of God and nothingness, as good and evil, as life and death, as the light of revelation and the darkness which will not receive it, as redemption and perdition, as *kerygma* [the preaching of the good news of Jesus Christ] and myth...."

132. Ibid., 169.

133. David F. Strauss, *Die Christliche Glaubenslehre*, 1:670–71, cited in *CD*, III/3, 413.

134. Jessie Penn-Lewis, "Satan and His Kingdom," in *The Fundamentals*, vol. 4 (Los Angeles: Bible Institute of Los Angeles, 1917), 183–98.

135. *CD*, III/3, 369.

136. Ibid., 453.

137. Ibid., 478.

138. Ibid., 519.

139. Ibid., 520.

[We insist] on the unconditional antithesis of the two spheres."[140] Concerning the nature of demons, he insisted that they "lie in nothingness": "They [demons] are. As we cannot deny the peculiar existence of nothingness, we cannot deny their existence. They are null and void, but they are not nothing. They are, but only in their own way; they are, but improperly.... They are only as God affirms himself and the creature and thus pronounces a necessary No.... They can only exist in the attempt to rage against God and to spoil his creation."[141]

In a discussion reminiscent of Barth's, C. S. Lewis warned about the two extremes of error to be avoided when considering demons: "One is to disbelieve in their existence. The other is to believe, and to feel an excessive and unhealthy interest in them."[142] If the former error typified the modern period as a whole, the latter more recently surfaced as the modern period gave way to postmodernism. In society in general, an almost medieval obsession with demonic possession and exorcism was revived with the film *The Exorcist* (originally released in 1975, rereleased in 2000). Popular angelology could be seen in the very successful *Touched by an Angel* television program, movies such as *The Preacher's Wife* and *City of Angels*, and the nearly constant appearance of books dedicated to the topic of angels on the *New York Times* bestseller list for literature. In Christian literature, an example of this interest was the staggering popularity of books by Frank Peretti. As recounted in *This Present Darkness* and *Piercing the Darkness*, Peretti's fictitious towns are populated by hordes of demons that wreak havoc with the citizens; these people, in turn, are empowered and ultimately led to glorious triumph by heroic angels. Such tales of spiritual combat between good angels and bad demons captured the popular evangelical imagination by storm.

Even evangelical theology did not escape such fascination with angelic realities. On the one hand, the notion of "spiritual warfare" resulted in numerous theological treatments. These ranged from wide-eyed speculation that a demon lies behind every bad habit (smoking, overeating) and sin (fornication, murder) to the concept of "territorial spirits" that gain a foothold in certain geographical areas of the world and envelop those regions in particularly virulent forms of spiritual darkness. Solutions run the spectrum from casting out demons from everyone and everything—including Christians and those highly resistant territories—to so-called steps to freedom in Christ. Several of these steps include renunciation of involvement in occult practices and repudiating demonic strongholds in one's life.[143] On the other hand, several evangelicals have contributed well-balanced treatments of angels and their roles. Although known for many other things, Billy Graham was one of the first to contribute to this evangelical resurgence in interest with his book *Angels: God's Secret Agents*.[144] Most recent evangelical systematic theologies have dedicated significant attention to the topic, including Wayne Grudem's *Systematic Theology*.[145]

---

140. Ibid.

141. Ibid., 523.

142. C. S. Lewis, *The Screwtape Letters* (London: Geoffrey Bles, 1942), 9.

143. Neil T. Anderson, *The Bondage Breaker* (Eugene, Ore.:

Harvest House, 1990), 185–204.

144. Billy Graham, *Angels: God's Secret Agents* (Garden City, N.Y.: Doubleday, 1975).

145. Grudem, *Systematic Theology*, chaps. 19, 20.

Part 3

THE DOCTRINE OF HUMANITY

Chapter 15

THE CREATION AND NATURE OF HUMANITY

How has the church developed its understanding of human beings? How has it come to view the image of God?

STATEMENT OF BELIEF

The church has historically affirmed that God created human beings in his image. While the precise identity of this image has been a matter of debate and changing conceptions, such disagreement has not silenced the church's affirmation. Furthermore, the church has historically maintained that human nature is complex, a composite of material and immaterial elements. Apart from a very few exceptions, the church has affirmed the reality of the human body, though it has also wrestled with views that disparage the body and treat it as being inherently evil. Also, the church has affirmed the reality of the human soul or the human spirit, though the specific identity of these elements has been a matter of debate. Thus, throughout the church's history, some have insisted that human nature consists of two aspects—a material body and an immaterial soul or spirit—while others have claimed there are three—a material body and two immaterial elements, soul and spirit. In either case, the idea that human nature is complex has been standard belief throughout most of the church's existence.

The modern period has presented several important challenges to the church's historical anthropology. Much of the erosion of this belief has focused on the question of the soul. In a scientifically oriented world with its emphasis on empirical data and materialistic philosophy (or naturalism), the concept of an immaterial aspect of human nature has come under increasingly heavy attack. Through its latest innovative research employing

321

fMRI, PET, SPECT, MRS, and MEG,[1] neuroscience claims to be able to explain all aspects of human behavior—including thoughts, memories, feelings of love, ethical decisions, value judgments, and even faith in Jesus Christ—by recourse to physiological processes in the brain and central nervous system. Such findings have led to the erosion of traditional Christian beliefs about the soul. Even some evangelicals have become monists or materialists, denying the soul's existence. Given this development, theological anthropology has again become an important area of study and reflection for the church.[2]

THE VIEW OF HUMANITY IN THE EARLY CHURCH

The first Christians were deeply influenced by their Jewish roots, especially the Hebrew Bible's teaching about God's creation of human beings in his image (Gen. 1:26–31). Paul picked up this idea in addressing God's work in sanctification of "the new self, which is being renewed in knowledge in the image of its Creator" (Col. 3:9–10; cf. Eph. 4:22–24). Indeed, the apostle described the entire process of Christian growth as being progressively conformed to the image of Jesus Christ (Rom. 8:29; 2 Cor. 3:18). This insistence on renewal of the divine image can only mean that the image, prior to salvation and this sanctification process, is tragically marred and dreadfully corrupted by sin. Thus, the early Christians affirmed both human dignity, because people are created in the image of God, and human depravity, because the image of God in people is warped and perverted by sin. Moreover, the first Christians affirmed the complexity of human nature. Jesus himself had indicated that the human constitution possesses two elements, which he referred to as the body and soul (Matt. 10:28; cf. Mark 12:30). Similarly, Paul indicated a complex human nature—"spirit, soul and body"—in his prayer for the Thessalonians (1 Thess. 5:23). Thus, the New Testament writers affirmed that human nature consists of both material and immaterial aspects.

After this apostolic period, the early church continued to affirm the complexity of human nature and the dignity of human beings made in the image of God. Much attention was dedicated to the nature of the soul and, in particular, to its immortality. This view did not mean that human souls are eternal, in the sense of not having a beginning.[3] Indeed, the church disagreed with Plato that the soul is eternal, appealing to the account of Adam's creation as evidence for the beginning of the human soul.[4] But the immortality of the soul did mean that it would exist forever in the future, because of God's design: "It appears that the soul is not naturally immortal, but is made immortal by the grace of God, through faith and righteousness, and by knowledge."[5] Lactantius offered several pieces of evidence in support of the immortality of the soul, including that "the soul

---

1. That is, functional magnetic resonance imaging, positron emission tomography, single photon emission computed tomography, magnetic resonance spectroscopy, and magnetoencephalography.

2. My thanks to John Lopes for his help with this chapter.

3. As Justin Martyr reasoned, "If the world is begotten,

souls also are necessarily begotten." Justin Martyr, *Dialogue with Trypho, a Jew*, 5, in *ANF*, 1:197.

4. Tertullian, *Treatise on the Soul*, 3–4, in *ANF*, 3:184.

5. Clement of Alexandria, *Fragment of Comments on 1 Peter*, 1:3, in *ANF*, 2:571.

cannot entirely perish, since it received its origin from the Spirit of God, [who] is eternal."[6] To this theological argument was added an appeal to common human intuition.[7]

Beyond this quality of immortality, the nature of the soul includes "rationality, sensibility, intelligence, and freedom of the will."[8] In accordance with the philosopher Aristotle's definition of a human being as the rational animal,[9] the early church focused its discussions of the image of God on human reason and free will. As Justin Martyr asserted, "In the beginning He [God] made the human race with the power of thought and of choosing the truth and doing right."[10] This notion of the image of God as consisting of rationality and free will became dominant in the church's anthropology, as Origen noted in his summary of basic Christian doctrines: It "is clearly defined in the teaching of the church that every rational soul is possessed of free will and volition."[11]

Four theologians of the early church contributed significantly to the development of its doctrine of humanity. Although quite different from each other, Irenaeus, Tertullian, Origen, and Augustine addressed such issues as the identity of the image of God in human beings, human nature, and the origin of the soul.

The basic view of humanity developed by Irenaeus was that "man is a mixed organization of soul and flesh [body], who was formed after the likeness of God and molded by His hands—that is, by the Son and Holy Spirit, to whom also He said, 'Let Us make man' [Gen. 1:26]."[12] More specifically, unbelievers, who are made in God's *image*, possess a twofold nature: body and soul. Believers, however, who are made in God's *image and likeness*, possess a threefold nature: body, soul, and spirit. As for the first group, Irenaeus observed: "If the Spirit of God is missing in the soul, he who is such is certainly of an animal nature. Being left carnal, he is an imperfect being, possessing indeed the image [of God] in his formation, but not receiving the likeness through the Spirit."[13] It seems that, for Irenaeus, the soul particularly consists of human reason and freedom of the will. Unbelievers, being made in the image of God in the sense that they possess a soul, retain their rationality and ability to choose, but only in a corrupted way.[14] When conversion from this sinfulness takes place, a third element—the spirit—is added to the nature of redeemed human beings: "The perfect person consists in the mixing together and the union of the soul receiving the spirit of the Father, together with the body that was molded after the image of God."[15] Irenaeus appealed to Scripture (1 Thess. 5:23) in

6. Lactantius, *The Divine Institutes*, 7.12; cf. 3.9; 7.9, in *ANF*, 7:209; cf. 77, 206.

7. Tertullian, *On the Resurrection of the Flesh*, 3, in *ANF*, 3:547.

8. Tertullian, *Treatise on the Soul*, 38, in *ANF*, 3:219.

9. Aristotle, *On the Soul*, 2.3, in *Aristotle: On the Soul, Parva Naturalia, On Breath*, trans. W. S. Hett, Loeb Classical Library (Cambridge, Mass.: Harvard Univ. Press, 1957), 85. Aristotle contrasted animals, which are able to perceive with their senses, and human beings, who are able to reason or think.

10. Justin Martyr, *First Apology*, 1.28, in *ANF*, 1:172. In his *Dialogue with Trypho*, Justin again linked rationality with freedom and made them constitutive of both human beings

and angels: "God, wishing men and angels to follow his will, resolved to create them free to do righteousness; possessing reason, that they may know by whom they are created, and through whom they, not existing formerly, do now exist; and with a law that they should be judged by him, if they do anything contrary to right reason." *Dialogue with Trypho a Jew*, 141, in *ANF*, 1:270.

11. Origen, *First Principles*, preface, 5, in *ANF*, 4:240.

12. Irenaeus, *Against Heresies*, 4, preface, 4, in *ANF*, 1:463.

13. Ibid., 5.6.1, in *ANF*, 1:532. The text has been rendered clearer.

14. Ibid., 4.4.3, in *ANF*, 1:466.

15. Ibid., 5.6.1, in *ANF*, 1:531. The text has been rendered clearer.

support of this threefold composite nature of Christians.[16] In this anthropology, Irenaeus did not belittle the human body. Indeed, he appealed to Scripture (1 Cor. 3:16–17; cf. 6:13–15) as support for the body being the "handiwork" and "temple" of God.[17] He is credited with originating the *trichotomist view*—that human nature may be distinguished into the three elements of body, soul, and spirit.[18]

The second major theologian of the early church helping to develop its anthropology was Tertullian. He did not follow Irenaeus's trichotomist view. Rather, Tertullian championed the view that human beings are composed of two elements, one being material and the other being immaterial. Indeed, he spoke out against the view that the soul and the spirit are two different realities in human beings.[19] His argument against this position was based on the impossibility of separating the activity of the soul from the activity of the spirit.[20] Tertullian is credited with originating the *dichotomist view*—that human nature may be distinguished into the two elements of body and soul (or spirit).[21]

Furthermore, Tertullian denied that God creates a human soul and then joins it to a human body. This *creationist*[22] view believed "that the soul is not conceived in the womb, nor is formed and produced at the time that the body is molded, but is impressed from outside on the infant before his complete vitality but after the process of childbirth."[23] Instead, Tertullian offered an original idea called *traducianism*[24]—both the soul and the body come into existence by the procreative act of the parents:[25] "The two are no doubt produced by human parents of two substances, but not at two different periods; rather they are so entirely one that neither is before the other in point of time."[26] This simultaneous creation of the soul and body takes place at the moment of conception: "We believe that life begins at conception, because we contend that the soul also begins from conception. Life begins at the same moment and place that the soul does."[27] In support of traducianism, he argued from the definition of death[28] and appealed to the similarities between parents and their offspring.[29] Thus, Tertullian believed that human nature,

16. Ibid., in *ANF*, 1:532.

17. Ibid., 5.6.2, in *ANF*, 1:532.

18. *Trichotomy* is from two Greek words: τριχα (*tricha*), meaning "threefold," and τεμνω (*temnô*), meaning "mark off, cut, or divide"; thus, human nature can be divided into three distinct aspects.

19. Tertullian, *Treatise on the Soul*, 10, in *ANF*, 3:189–90.

20. Ibid., in *ANF*, 3:190.

21. *Dichotomy* is from two Greek words: διχη (*dichē*), meaning "twofold," and τεμνω (*temnô*), meaning "mark off, cut, or divide"; thus, human nature can be divided into two distinct aspects.

22. Not in the sense of the origin of the universe. Creationism in this context refers to the origin of the soul.

23. Tertullian, *Treatise on the Soul*, 25, in *ANF*, 3:205. I have rendered the text clearer.

24. *Traducianism* comes from the Latin word *tradure*, meaning "generation." This view stood in contrast with Plato's notion that the soul—which is eternal—joins with the body when a newborn takes his first breath. "Plato tells us that

the soul, being quite a different formation from the body and originating elsewhere and externally to the womb, is inhaled when the newborn infant first draws breath." Ibid.

25. Ibid., 27, in *ANF*, 3:207.

26. Tertullian, *On the Resurrection of the Flesh*, 45, in *ANF*, 3:578.

27. Tertullian, *Treatise on the Soul*, 27, in *ANF*, 3:208.

28. "As death is defined to be nothing other than the separation of body and soul, so life—the opposite of death—cannot be defined differently than the coming together of body and soul. If the division of the two takes place at one time by means of death, so the principle of their combination should assure us that it occurs simultaneously to the two substances by means of life." Ibid., in *ANF*, 3:207. The text has been rendered clearer.

29. "Pray, tell me, how it comes about that, from similarity of soul, we resemble our parents in disposition ... if we are not produced from the seed of the soul?" Ibid., in *ANF*, 3:206. The text has been rendered clearer.

consisting of a material aspect, or body, and an immaterial aspect, or soul (or spirit), arises intact by transmission from the person's parents.

The *creationist view* of the origin of the soul was articulated and defended over against the traducianist view. Methodius appealed to the origin of Adam (Gen. 2:7), averring that if anyone teaches "that the immortal being of the soul also is sown along with the mortal body, he will not be believed; for the Almighty alone breathes into man the undying and undecaying part, as also it is He alone who is Creator of the invisible and indestructible."[30] Accordingly, Lactantius said, the soul comes directly from God, while the body is derived from physical material.[31] Lactantius further reasoned that "a body may be produced from a body, since something is contributed from both [father and mother]; but a soul cannot be produced from souls.... [T]he manner of the production of souls belongs entirely to God alone.... For nothing but what is mortal can be generated from mortals.... From this it is evident that souls are not given by parents, but by ... God."[32] Moreover, the proponents of creationism argued from the contentious dichotomy between the body and soul: If the body is inherently evil and the soul is inherently good, then God must be responsible for the latter aspect of human nature but cannot be responsible for the former aspect. Thus, God creates specially and directly the soul of each human being, then unites that soul to a body that is produced through the sexual act of the forthcoming person's parents. When this soul, made in the image of God, is joined to a sinful body, the resulting person shares in both the dignity of creation and the depravity of sin.

The third major contributor to the early church's doctrine of humanity was Origen. On the one hand, his discussion of human nature was fairly standard, as he affirmed a trichotomist view of human constitution.[33] On the other hand, he offered a particularly unusual view of the origin of the human soul. He surmised that because God is omnipotent, he must always have had a creation over which he could exercise his power. Following his own logic, Origen proposed that God had an invisible spiritual world composed of rational creatures over which he could exercise his power. Although endowed with goodness, these creatures did not possess their goodness as an essential quality. They would only continue to enjoy the blessing of God if they remained good. But they also possessed free will, which they could use to go against God. Indeed, this abuse of freedom became the case: "They neglected and despised such goodness, then each one, by fault of his own laziness, became—one more quickly, another more slowly; one to a greater degree, another to a lesser degree—the cause of his own downfall."[34] Thus, the

30. Methodius, *The Banquet of the Ten Virgins*, 2.7, in *ANF*, 6:316.

31. Lactantius, *The Divine Institutes*, 2.13, in *ANF*, 7:61.

32. Lactantius, *On the Workmanship of God, or the Formation of Man*, 19, in *ANF*, 7:298–99.

33. Origen, *First Principles*, 4.11 (from the Latin ed.), in *ANF*, 4:359.

34. Ibid., 1.6.2, in *ANF*, 4:260. The text has been rendered clearer. Origen found in this view an explanation for the great differences found among God's creatures today: "Because these rational creatures themselves were endowed with the power of free will, this freedom of will either incited each one to progress by imitation of God or reduced him to failure through negligence. And this is the cause of the diversity among rational creatures.... Now God, who thought it right to arrange his creatures according to their merit, brought down these different rational creatures into the harmony of one world.... Thus, each creature—whether heavenly beings, earthly beings, or infernal beings—is said to have the causes of his diversity in himself. And these causes are antecedent to his bodily birth." Ibid., 2.9.6–7, in *ANF*, 4:292–93.

actual visible world became the home of fallen beings; that is, beings who had fallen in the invisible spiritual world. Those who had fallen the least became embodied as angels. Those who had fallen the most became embodied as demons, with Satan as their head. And those who had fallen to an intermediate degree became embodied as human beings. Thus, human beings consist of a soul that fell in a pre-temporal, invisible universe, and a material body. According to the degree of fallenness of their soul, human beings either suffer much or little during their lifetime. Although unique and offering a vivid explanation for the problem of evil and the differences in suffering among human beings, Origen's view never caught on in the church.

As strange as Origen's doctrine of human nature was, it nevertheless contained an important issue with which early Christians wrestled: the dichotomy between body and soul. In this development, they were deeply influenced by Plato's philosophy that pitted the material aspect of human nature—the body, which is inherently evil—against the immaterial aspect—the soul or spirit, which is inherently good.[35] Indeed, the *Letter to Diognetus* echoed this Platonic viewpoint, speaking of the soul's imprisonment in the body.[36] Cyprian's view was typical: "For since we possess the body from the earth and the spirit from heaven, we ourselves are both earth and heaven; and in both—that is, both in body and spirit—we pray that God's will may be done. For between the flesh and the spirit there is a struggle, and there is a daily strife as they disagree one with the other."[37]

Perceptively, some Christians specified that it is not the body per se that is evil.[38] But others failed to make this distinction, blaming the body for their personal troubles: "The flesh, since it is earthly, and therefore mortal, draws with itself [drags down] the spirit linked to it, and leads it from immortality to death.... [T]he flesh hinders the spirit from following God."[39] A result of such thinking was a disparagement of the body leading to, of all things, a hope for death: "But when a separation shall have been made between the body and the soul [at death], then evil will be disunited from good; and as the body perishes and the soul remains, so evil will perish and good be permanent. Then man, having received the garment of immortality, will be wise and free from evil, as God is."[40]

---

35. More specifically, Greek anthropology had its origin in the "Orphic" myth of the sixth century BC. According to Greek mythology, the Titans—the offspring of heaven and earth—murdered Dionysus, the son of Zeus, and ate his body. Zeus consumed the Titans with a thunderbolt, and out of their remains sprang the race of human beings. Thus, humans come from the Titans, the wicked sons of Earth. Original Titanic sin haunts humans during their lifetime, and this sin is associated with their earthly, physical part; this part is inherently evil. Yet the Titans were also the children of Heaven, and they consumed divine Dionysus, so humans possess a divine or heavenly part as well. Thus, human beings are composed of two independent substances: body and soul, with the former being inherently evil and the latter being divine. Plato (427–347 BC) adopted this "Orphic" myth to produce his view of the transmigration of the soul: souls existed at first in the highest heavens, but some fell and were forced into human bodies. They are condemned to successive reincarnations for ten thousand years. After this, if they have sufficiently purified themselves,

their souls will return to their heavenly realm. The soul can be purified through philosophy, the pursuit of wisdom through reasoning, the contemplation of aesthetic beauty, and the denial of bodily pleasures. As for the body, Plato believed the Greek word for body was derived from a word meaning "to shut up in a prison." Adopted from Frank Bottomley, *Attitudes to the Body in Western Christendom* (London: Lepus, 1979), 20, 178n10.

36. *Letter to Diognetus*, 6, in *ANF*, 1:27.

37. Cyprian, *Treatise*, 4.16, in *ANF*, 5:451.

38. Novatian, *Treatise Concerning the Trinity*, 10, in *ANF*, 5:620.

39. Lactantius, *The Divine Institutes*, 4.25, in *ANF*, 7:127.

40. Ibid., 7.5, in *ANF*, 7:202. There are some significant textual difficulties with this section, so it is very doubtful that Lactantius himself wrote this section. Nevertheless, it reflects his thoughts on human nature in earlier sections of *The Divine Institutes*. Moreover, it certainly communicates the body-soul dichotomy of some writer in the church.

This contentious dualism between body and soul would become a persistent problem in the church.

The fourth major contribution to the early church's anthropology was made by Augustine. On one front, he developed his doctrine of humanity in opposition to the view of Pelagius, whose anthropology he denounced. Augustine began with a strong assertion of the goodness of humanity as created by God.[41] He described the image of God in human beings as being reflective of the Trinity.[42] This divine image was pristine in the original creation of Adam and Eve: "Though they carried about an animal body, they yet felt in it no disobedience moving against themselves. This was the righteous appointment, that inasmuch as their soul had received from the Lord the body for its servant, as it itself obeyed the Lord, even so its body should obey Him, and should exhibit a service suitable to the life given it without resistance."[43] Still, for Adam and Eve in this unfallen, sinless state, "even then there must be the help of God."[44] Of course, after the fall, this situation changed, and each human being is completely depraved and corrupted by sin.[45] And it is this tragic, desperate reality that is changed again by the divine work of salvation.[46]

Regarding his idea of the human constitution, Augustine fluctuated between trichotomy and dichotomy: "There are three things of which man consists—namely, spirit, soul, and body. These are sometimes spoken of as two, because frequently the soul is named along with the spirit. This is the case because a certain rational part of the soul—and animals lack this part—is called the spirit. The principal part of us is the spirit. Next, the life by which we are united with the body is called the soul. Finally, the body itself, because it is visible, is the last part in us."[47] As for the origin of the soul, Augustine pleaded ignorance, noting his indecision with regard to the two predominant theories, traducianism and creationism.[48] But he did not find the biblical case for either position convincing.[49] Indeed, Augustine posited that the origin of the soul is a topic not revealed by God.[50] For this reason, he did not decide one way or the other. Because of his influence, Augustine's anthropology became the church's doctrine of humanity.

---

41. Augustine, *On Marriage and Concupiscence*, 2.36[21], in *NPNF*[1], 5:298.

42. Augustine, *On the Trinity*, 14.19.25, in *NPNF*[1], 3:197.

43. Augustine, *On Forgiveness of Sins, and Baptism*, 2.36[22], in *NPNF*[1], 5:59.

44. Augustine, *On Nature and Grace*, 56[48], in *NPNF*[1], 5:140.

45. See the further discussion in chap. 16.

46. Augustine, *On Man's Perfection in Righteousness*, 4.10, in *NPNF*[1], 5:162.

47. Augustine, *On Faith and the Creed*, 10.23, in *NPNF*[1], 3:331; cf. *On the Soul and Its Origin*, 4.3, in *NPNF*[1], 5:355. The text has been rendered clearer.

48. Referring to an earlier work, *On the Soul and Its Origin*, Augustine explained: "[In] a little work of mine ... concerning the origin of souls in individual people, I had confessed that I did not know whether they are propagated from the primeval soul of the first man, and from that by parental descent, or whether they are individually assigned to each person apart from propagation, as the first [soul] was to Adam." Augustine,

Retractions, bk. 2, chap. 56, on the treatise *On the Soul and Its Origin*, in *NPNF*[1], 5:310. He referred to the following passage in that earlier work: "If inquiry is made into the soul's own origin—of which subject it knows nothing—isn't the matter then too high or beyond one's strength to be capable of apprehension? And you deem it an absurd thing and incompatible with reason for the soul not to know whether it is inbreathed by God, or whether it is derived from the parents, although it does not remember this event as soon as it is past, and reckons it among the things that it has forgotten beyond recall." Ibid., 4.6[5], in *NPNF*[1], 5:356. The text has been rendered clearer. Of course, Augustine admitted, "Concerning the origin of the human soul ... I am not indeed absolutely ignorant even on this point, for I know that God breathed into the face of the first man, and that 'man then became a living soul' [Gen. 2:7]." Ibid., 4.3[2], in *NPNF*[1], 5:354.

49. Augustine, *On the Soul and Its Origin*, 1.17, 21–29, in *NPNF*[1], 5:322, 324–28.

50. Ibid., 4.5, in *NPNF*[1], 5:355–56.

THE VIEW OF HUMANITY IN THE MIDDLE AGES

One of the most dramatic developments for the medieval church was the flourishing of monastic movements. These had originated in the early church, with Antony and Pachomius launching both the individual monastic lifestyle and community monasticism.[51] After his conversion in Italy and return to North Africa, Augustine established a monastic community in association with a parish church, providing a model for centuries to come. In the medieval period, monastic orders like the Cluniacs, the Cistercians, the Franciscans, the Dominicans, the Augustinians, and the Carmelites exerted a profound influence on both church and society.

At the heart of monasticism was asceticism, a worldview that insisted on forgoing physical pleasures such as eating tasteful and expensive food, drinking soothing wine, sleeping in comfortable arrangements, and engaging in sexual intercourse. Asceticism was motivated by a contentious dualism that viewed the body and all things material as being inherently evil, and the spirit and all things spiritual as being inherently good. This denigration of the material aspect of human nature had its roots in Platonic philosophy, and, as noted above, the early church had wrestled with this problem. It continued and was heightened in the Middle Ages, and the church's theology and practice suffered dramatically because of it. Christology suffered because the physical humanity of Jesus clashed with the disparagement of the body. The honor of marriage suffered because sexual intercourse, even between lawfully wedded husbands and wives, was viewed with disgust. The clergy suffered because the imposition of celibacy forced many of them into an unnatural lifestyle, leading to rampant sexual immorality.

The doctrine of humanity suffered as well. Explaining the creation and nature of humanity, John of Damascus placed human beings in a sort of middle position between angels and the material created order of heaven and earth:

> God created angels, the kind of being that is of his own nature (for the nature that has to do with reason is related to God and understandable by the mind alone). He also created the material world, the kind of being that, since it clearly belongs to the realm of the senses, is separated from him by the greatest distance. And it was also right that there should be a mixture of both kinds of being, as a token of still greater wisdom and of the richness of the divine giving as regards natures.... Humanity is to be a sort of connecting link between the visible and invisible natures.[52]

These two natures, according to John, correspond to the body and soul of human beings.[53] Furthermore, this twofold nature is both the dignity and depravity of humanity. On the one hand, the body is the aspect by which human beings are related to the material world, consisting of inanimate things, plants, and animals. On the other hand, the soul connects human beings with the angelic realm, consisting of rational, intelligent

---

51. See chap. 24 for more discussion.

52. John of Damascus, *Exposition of the Orthodox Faith*, 2.12, in *NPNF*[2], 9:30 (the second page 30 in the volume). For

his idea, John relied on Gregory of Nazianzus, *Oration* 38 and *Oration* 42.

53. Ibid.

beings, and enables human beings to relate to God and pursue Godlike behavior. John's exposition seemed to denigrate the body in order to exalt the importance of the soul.[54]

As with most topics, Thomas Aquinas dedicated a significant amount of attention to the doctrine of humanity. He dealt with the image and likeness of God by discussing the key text of Genesis 1:26.[55] Like many before him, Aquinas made a distinction between the image and the likeness of God. Specifically, he associated the immaterial and highest aspect of human beings—the spirit, mind, or intellect—with the divine image and relegated other human dimensions—emotions, desires, even the body—to the likeness of God.[56] Accordingly, human beings bear a resemblance—though a very imperfect resemblance—to God.[57] More specifically, Aquinas spoke of "a threefold image of creation, of re-creation, and of likeness. The first is found in all men, the second only in the just [Christians], the third only in the blessed [in heaven]."[58] In one sense, then, all human beings are made in the image of God because of their natural capacity for knowing God. This reality is true even for fallen humanity, in whom the image of God has been marred due to sin; indeed, Aquinas described the image as "'obscured and disfigured' ... in sinners."[59] The image is more pronounced in Christians, those who truly know God through his grace. And this image is especially strong in those who have been glorified, for they know and love God perfectly in heaven.[60]

For Aquinas, only human beings, not animals or other irrational creatures, are made in the image of God. Indeed, it is God's gift of "'an intellectual soul, which raises him [man] above the beasts of the field.' Therefore things without intellect are not made in God's image."[61] Thus, Aquinas essentially equated the image with rationality. From his biblical support (Eph. 4:23–24; Col. 3:10), he averred that "to be in the image of God belongs to the mind only."[62] From this identification flowed the logical conclusion that angels, who are more intelligent than human beings, are more perfectly made in the divine image.[63]

Discussing the constitution of human beings, Aquinas reasoned that the soul is created by God: "Since it cannot be made of pre-existing matter—whether corporeal, which would render it a corporeal being, or spiritual, which would involve the transmutation of one spiritual substance into another—we must conclude that it cannot exist except by creation."[64] As to the nature of this soul, Aquinas closely followed the philosophy of Aristotle, who defined the soul as the form of the body:

> For the nature of each thing is shown by its operation. Now the proper operation of man as man is to understand, because he thereby surpasses all other animals. From this, too, Aristotle concludes that the ultimate happiness of man

54. Ibid.

55. Thomas Aquinas, *Summa Theologica*, pt. 1, q. 93, art. 1.

56. Ibid., pt. 1, q. 93, art. 9.

57. Ibid., pt. 1, q. 93, art. 1.

58. Ibid., pt. 1, q. 93, art. 4.

59. Ibid., pt. 1, q. 93, art. 8. Aquinas relied on Augustine, *On the Trinity*, 14.6.

60. Still relying on Augustine, Aquinas noted that the image is "'clear and beautiful' ... in the just." Ibid.

61. Ibid., pt. 1, q. 93, art. 2. His citation of Augustine came from *On the Literal Meaning of Genesis*, 6.12.

62. Ibid., pt. 1, q. 93, art. 6.

63. "[The] image chiefly consists ... in the intellectual nature. Thus, the image of God is more perfect in the angels than in man, because their intellectual nature is more perfect." Ibid., pt. 1, q. 93, art. 3.

64. Ibid., pt. 1, q. 90, art. 2. The text has been rendered clear.

must consist in this operation as properly belonging to him. Man must therefore derive his species from that which is the principle of this operation. But the species of anything is derived from its form. It follows therefore that the intellectual principle—or the soul—is the proper form of man.[65]

Because the image of God is essentially reason, Aquinas emphasized the importance of the soul exercising rational control over the body. Indeed, he pictured the state of human beings before the fall as (1) reason being subject to God; (2) the lower powers of the soul—the emotions and desires—being subject to reason; and (3) the body being subject to the soul. And, he added, this original reality was according to grace, not the natural state of human beings: "Now it is clear that such a subjection of the body to the soul, and of the lower powers to reason, was not from nature; otherwise it would have remained after sin. Thus, it is clear that the original submission, by virtue of which reason was subject to God, was not merely a natural gift, but a supernatural gift of grace."[66] In other words, before their fall into sin, Adam and Eve were recipients of the gift of grace that maintained a proper harmony between their reason (the highest faculty of their soul), their emotions and desires (the lower parts of their soul), and their body. As he emphasized this hierarchy of elements even within the unfallen human constitution, Aquinas contributed to the ongoing disparagement of the human body and the elevation of the human soul in the church of the Middle Ages.

THE VIEW OF HUMANITY IN THE REFORMATION AND POST-REFORMATION

In developing his doctrine of humanity, Luther commented on the inadequacy of describing man philosophically as a rational animal—like Aristotle and Aquinas before him. Still, Luther underscored the fact that reason is "the essential difference by which man is distinguished from the animals and other things."[67] But he preferred to address the nature of humanity by means of theology, which "defines man whole and perfect: Namely, that man is a creature of God consisting of body and a living soul, made in the beginning after the image of God, without sin."[68] He summed up this latter concept: "My understanding of the image of God is this: that Adam had it in his being and that he not only knew God and believed that He was good, but that he also lived in a life that was wholly godly; that is, he was without the fear of death or of any other danger, and was content with God's favor."[69] This creation in the image of God gives the highest dignity

---

65. Ibid., pt. 1, q. 76, art. 1. His references to Aristotle are from *On the Soul*, 2.2, and *Ethics*, 10.7.

66. Ibid., pt. 1, q. 95, art. 1. The text has been rendered clearer.

67. Martin Luther, *Disputation Concerning Man*, LW, 34: 137.

68. Ibid., 34:138.

69. *Lectures on Genesis: Chapters 1–5*, LW, 1:62–63. Elsewhere Luther commented: "The image of God, according to which Adam was created, was something far more distinguished and excellent, since obviously no leprosy of sin adhered either to his reason or to his will. Both his inner and his outer sensations were all of the purest kind. His intellect was the clearest, his memory was the best, and his will was the most straightforward—all in the most beautiful tranquility of mind, without any fear of death and without any anxiety. To these inner qualities came also those most beautiful and superb qualities of body and of all the limbs [members], qualities in which he surpassed all the remaining living creatures." Ibid.

to all human beings, no matter what their socioeconomic status or societal standing may be.[70]

For Luther, human nature made in the image of God consists of three elements: spirit, soul, and body (though, as seen above, he also referred to human qualities in terms of two aspects). Turning to Scripture (1 Thess. 5:23), he explained: "The first part, the spirit, is the highest, deepest and noblest part of man. By it he is enabled to lay hold on things incomprehensible, invisible, and eternal. It is, in brief, the dwelling-place of faith and the Word of God." There is some overlap between this aspect and the soul, which has primary reference to the body and reason: "Reason is the light in this dwelling [the soul], and unless the spirit, which is lighted with the brighter light of faith, controls this light of reason, it cannot but be in error." Finally, "The third part is the body with its members. Its work is but to carry out and apply that which the soul knows and the spirit believes."[71]

On the one hand, Luther viewed man in almost an intermediate position between animals and angels, according to God's design: "He had created him for physical life and bodily activity; He nevertheless added intellectual power, which is also in the angels, with the result that man is a living being compounded of the natures of the brute [animal] and of the angels."[72] At this point, Luther seemingly erected a strong dichotomy between the material and immaterial aspects of human nature. On the other hand, human beings hold a unique place in his understanding; indeed, he refused to posit any significant dichotomy between the two aspects: "The soul is of a substance different from that of the body; and yet, there is an intimate union and connection, for the soul loves the body very much."[73] Here, Luther emphasized a holistic dualism. As to the origin of the soul, Luther embraced the traducianist position that the soul is the product of the union of the sperm and egg, as is the body.[74]

Of course, with Adam's fall into sin, the image of God in humanity suffered deeply. Indeed, according to Luther, that which gives humanity its dignity—being made in the image of God—is so corrupted in respect to a relationship with God that it is nearly completely obliterated. All that remains is a trace of the image in the civic realm of human interaction with other humans. Furthermore, only through the gospel can people be remade in the image of God.[75]

---

70. "We do not consider it a special honor that we are God's creatures. Rather, we stare and gape because someone is a prince or a great lord, even though the man's office is merely a human creation and an imitation. For if God had not previously produced his creature and made man, it would be impossible to make any prince. And yet all people grasp for such an office as if it were a precious thing. But the fact that I am God's work and creature is much more glorious and great! Therefore, male servants, female servants, and everybody should interest themselves in this high honor and say: 'I am a human being! This is certainly a higher title than being a prince, for God did not make a prince; human beings made him. That I am a human being is the work of God alone!'" Martin Luther, *WLS*, 2:877.

71. *Magnificat*, LW, 21:303.
72. *Lectures on Genesis: Chapters 1–5*, LW, 1:112.
73. Luther, *WLS*, 2:876.
74. "When a child is born today, the soul is created together with the body, contrary to Plato. Although all others disagree, it's my opinion that the soul isn't added [to the body] from the outside but is created out of the matter of the semen. This is my reason: If the soul came from somewhere else, it would be made bad by contact with the body, but the soul isn't bad by chance but by nature. Consequently the soul must be born out of corrupt matter and seed and must be created by God out of the matter of a man and a woman." *Table Talk Recorded by John Mathesius*, LW, 54:401.

75. *Lectures on Genesis: Chapters 1–5*, LW, 1:64.

The opening lines of John Calvin's *Institutes of the Christian Religion* underscored the importance he attached to the doctrine of humanity: "Nearly all the wisdom we possess—that is to say, true and sound wisdom—consists of two parts: the knowledge of God and of ourselves."[76] Expanding on this idea, Calvin explained: "We cannot have a clear and complete knowledge of God unless it is accompanied by a corresponding knowledge of ourselves. This knowledge of ourselves is twofold: namely, to know what we were like when we were first created and what our condition became after the fall of Adam."[77] Focusing on the first type of knowledge, Calvin developed the doctrine of humanity as originally created in the divine image: "For although God's glory shines forth in the outer man, yet there is no doubt that the proper seat of his image is in the soul. I do not deny, indeed, that our outward form, in so far as it distinguishes and separates us from brute animals, at the same time more closely joins us to God."[78] While Calvin clearly did not limit humanity's creation in the image of God to the human soul, he tended to emphasize the interior qualities of the mind and the heart as primarily bearing the divine image.[79] One reason for this emphasis was his approach to determining the nature of the image in humanity: His method was to observe what is restored when God transforms corrupt human nature through salvation.[80] He cited two key texts (Eph. 4:24; Col. 3:10) that emphasize that "the end of regeneration is that Christ should reform us to God's image."[81] Reasoning from these passages, he concluded that "we are so restored that with true piety, righteousness, purity, and intelligence we bear God's image."[82]

Developing this idea further and taking cues from Augustine, Calvin proposed a twofold notion of the image of God: Before the fall into sin, humanity fully bore the image of God, which consisted of both natural gifts—sound understanding and integrity of heart—and supernatural gifts—faith, love, holiness, and righteousness. Because of the fall and sin, humanity has completely lost its supernatural gifts, while its natural gifts are thoroughly devastated.[83] Through renewal by the Holy Spirit in salvation, the image in all its wondrous aspects is gradually restored. But the fullness of restoration awaits a future existence.[84]

---

76. John Calvin, *Institutes of the Christian Religion*, 1.1.1, LCC, 1:35.

77. Ibid., 1.15.1, LCC, 1:183.

78. Ibid., 1.15.3, LCC, 1:186. In noting the upright posture of human beings, Calvin cited Ovid's observation in *Metamorphoses*, 1.85–86. *Ovid: Metamorphoses*, trans. Frank Justus Miller, 2 vols., Loeb Classical Library (Cambridge, Mass.: Harvard Univ. Press, 1939), 1:9. Going against many who preceded him, Calvin rejected the common view that the image of God and the likeness of God refer to two different matters. Ibid., 1.15.3, LCC, 1:187–88.

79. "Although the soul is not man, yet it is not absurd for man, in respect to his soul, to be called God's image; even though I retain the principle … that the likeness of God extends to the whole excellence by which man's nature towers over all the kinds of living creatures.… And although the

primary seat of the divine image was in the mind and heart, or in the soul and its powers, yet there was no part of man, not even the body itself, in which some sparks did not glow." Ibid., 1.15.3, LCC, 1:188.

80. Ibid., 1.15.4, LCC, 1:189–90.

81. Ibid., LCC, 1:189.

82. Ibid., LCC, 1:190.

83. Ibid., 2.2.12, LCC, 1:270.

84. "God's image is the perfect excellence of human nature which shone in Adam before his defection, but was subsequently so vitiated and almost blotted out that nothing remains after the ruin except what is confused, mutilated, and disease-ridden. Therefore, in some part it now is manifest in the elect, in so far as they have been reborn in the spirit; but it will attain its full splendor in heaven." Ibid., 1.15.4, LCC, 1:190.

Moving beyond theological discussion, Calvin underscored a practical application of the reality that human beings are made in the image of God. This very fact helps Christians to love people as the Bible commands: "Scripture helps in the best way when it teaches that we are not to consider that men merit of themselves, but we are to look upon the image of God in all men, to which we owe all honor and love."[85] He urged that respect for the image of God enables Christians to love even the most unloving and unlovable people they will meet.[86]

Post-Reformation theologians who followed the trail of Luther and Calvin continued to express and defend their positions on human nature and the image of God in humanity. Both Lutheran and Reformed theologians embraced dichotomy, the view that human nature consists of two aspects,[87] and rejected a trichotomist view by both underscoring the lack of any essential difference between soul and spirit[88] and noting that the terms *soul* and *spirit* are used interchangeably in Scripture.[89] In a major point of difference, Lutheran and Reformed theologians took opposing views on the origin of the soul. Lutherans embraced traducianism;[90] Reformed theologians took the creationist position.[91]

---

85. Ibid., 3.7.6, LCC, 1:696.

86. "Whatever man you meet who needs your aid, you have no reason to refuse to help him. Say, 'He is a stranger'; but the Lord has given him a mark that ought to be familiar to you.... Say, 'He is contemptible and worthless'; but the Lord shows him to be one to whom he has deigned to give the beauty of his image. Say that he does not deserve even your least effort for his sake; but the image of God, which recommends him to you, is worthy of your giving yourself and all your possessions. Assuredly there is but one way in which to achieve what is not merely difficult but utterly against human nature: to love those who hate us, to repay their evil deeds with benefits, to return blessings for reproaches [Matt. 5:44]. It is that we remember not to consider men's evil intention but to look upon the image of God in them, which cancels and effaces their transgressions, and with its beauty and dignity allures us to love and embrace them." Ibid., 3.7.6, LCC, 1:696–97.

87. John Andrew Quenstedt, *Theologia Didactico-Polemica sive Systema Theologicum* (1715), 1.513, in Schmid, 166; John Gerhard, *Loci Theologici* (1621), 17.80, in Schmid, 166.

88. Gisbert Voetius, *Selectarum Disputationum Theologicarum* (Utrecht, 1648–69), 1:765, in Heppe, 221.

89. Gerhard, *Loci Theologici*, 17.80, in Schmid, 166.

90. Quenstedt offered the Lutheran position: "The soul of the first man was immediately created by God; but the soul of Eve was produced by propagation, and the souls of the rest of men are created, not daily, nor begotten of their parents as the body or souls of brutes [animals], but, *by virtue of the divine blessing, are propagated, per traducem, by their parents.*" As support, he pointed to the blessing of God (Gen. 1:28; cf. 8:17; 9:1); God's rest and cessation on the seventh day from all work (Gen. 2:2); the production of the soul of

Eve (Gen. 2:21–22); the description of generation (Gen. 5:3); the problem that the other position—creationism—presents for original sin or the justice of God; and Ps. 51:7. Quenstedt, *Theologia Didactico-Polemica*, 1.519, in Schmid, 166–67. Clearly, Leonard Hutter saw this traducianist position in accord with both Luther and Scripture: "If any of our brethren should ask which opinion we think most accordant with the truth, we fearlessly answer that we precisely accord with the opinion of Luther, and hold it to be consonant with Scripture, namely, that the human soul is propagated by traduction; so that, just as everything else produces its like, a lion begetting a lion, a horse begetting a horse, so also man begets man, and not alone the flesh, or the body, but also the soul is propagated essentially from its parents." Leonard Hutter, *Compendium Locorum Theologicorum* (1610), 319, in Schmid, 249.

91. Riissen represented the Reformed view: "We lay it down that all souls are created by God directly and are infused by being created, and so are produced ex nihilo apart from any pre-existent matter." Leonard Riissen, *Francisci Turretini Compendium Theologiae* (Amsterdam, 1695), 7.52.2, in Heppe, 227–28. Polan offered various objections to the traducianist position, among which were the indivisibility of the soul (which cannot divide in the parents and combine in their children) and the fact that God is the Father of spirits or souls (Heb. 12:9), meaning that they are not generated by parents. Amandus Polan, *Syntagma Theologiae Christianae* (Hanover, 1624–1625), 5.23, in Heppe, 229. Positively, Voetius marshaled several biblical passages (Gen. 2:7; Eccl. 12:7 with Heb. 12:9 and Zech. 12:1) in support of creationism. Gisbert Voetius, *Selectarum Disputationum Theologicarum* (Utrecht, 1648–69), 1.798, in Heppe, 229–30.

As for the original image of God, both Lutheran and Reformed theologians empha-sized that Adam and Eve lived in a "state of innocence or integrity":[92] "It is called a state of integrity, because man in it was upright and uncorrupt (Eccl. 7:29) in intellect, will, the corporeal [bodily] affections and endowments, and in all things was perfect. They call it also the state of *innocence* because he was innocent and holy, free from sin and pollution."[93] Reformed theologians specifically spoke of original righteousness and noted an additional element: As created in the image of God and standing before him as the head of all human beings, Adam would have transmitted the divine image and the gift of original righteousness intact had he remained upright before God.[94]

The post-Reformation period was a time for theologians to discourse widely on the nature of human beings. With the Enlightenment came a growing interest in human nature from a philosophical perspective. A chief example of this development was René Descartes, whose *Meditations on First Philosophy* was groundbreaking for future discussions about human nature in general and dualism in particular. His view, often called substance dualism, posited the existence of two very different substances composing human nature:[95] the body, which Descartes defined as an extended substance, and the soul (or mind), which he defined as a thinking substance. For Descartes, "the human body may be considered as a machine," and it is subject to the same laws of nature as all other material substances.[96] The soul, because it is a thinking substance, is not subject to the laws of nature and is completely different from the body. Of course, this proposal raised the obvious question of how these two disparate substances could ever interact with each other so that the mind could influence the body and vice versa. Descartes' answer was to posit the pineal gland as the point of contact. Although this solution would come under sustained attack by antidualists in the centuries to come, Descartes' substance dualism became a key philosophical viewpoint with regard to human nature.[97]

THE VIEW OF HUMANITY IN THE MODERN PERIOD

Just as the modern period witnessed widespread attacks against the church's historical position on most doctrines, so it happened with the doctrine of humanity. In part, this development was the result of factors that led modernists to doubt the truth of Scripture when it addresses the creation of human beings and the constitution of human nature. Another contributing factor was the rise of new "secular" disciplines such as psychology,

---

92. David Hollaz, *Examen Theologicum Acroamati-cum* (1707), 461, in Schmid, 220. Cf. Quenstedt, *Theologia Didactico-Polemica*, 1.518, in Schmid, 166.

93. Abraham Calov, *Systema Locorum Theologicorum* (1655–1677), 4.389, in Schmid, 220.

94. William Bucan, *Institutiones Theologicae seu Locorum Communium Christianae Religionis* (Geneva, 1609), 10.7, in Heppe, 240.

95. René Descartes, *Meditations on First Philosophy*, trans. Laurence J. Lafleur (Indianapolis: Bobbs-Merrill, 1960), 73–74. Descartes published his first edition of the *Meditations*

in Latin in 1641 and the first French edition in 1647.

96. Ibid., 80.

97. William Hasker made this humorous assessment: "The hoariest objection specifically to Cartesian dualism (but one still frequently taken as decisive) is that, because of the great disparity between mental and physical substances, causal interaction between them is unintelligible and impossible. This argument may well hold the all-time record for over-rated objections to major philosophical positions." William Hasker, *The Emergent Self* (Ithaca and London: Cornell Univ. Press, 1999), 150.

sociology, and (nontheological) anthropology. These disciplines, with their nonbiblical (and, often times, unbiblical) foundations, antisupernaturalisitic presuppositions, evolutionary leanings, empirical methodologies, and the like, presented strong challenges to the church's traditional understanding of humanity. In part, the church reacted to reaffirm its position, but many within its ranks capitulated to these secular influences and reconstructed—even deconstructed—the doctrine.

As these secular disciplines became more popular and exerted a growing and widespread influence, some within the church began to incorporate findings from these areas into their doctrine of humanity. Typical was William Newton Clarke, who, in his discussion of sources of Christian theology, noted, "Psychology, the study of man as a spirit, is important to theology, because it is in man the spirit that religion exists: and psychology properly begins with physiology, the study of the human body."[98] Thus, he proposed his view of human nature as consisting of body and spirit not on the basis of any biblical affirmations but "because it is the one that is most naturally and instinctively discerned in common life. It is the division that a man is aware of when he thinks of himself, and that he discerns in others; and it is the only division of human nature that men learn from self-knowledge."[99] On this psychological basis, Clarke summarized his view of human nature: "Personality in man is made up by the combination of these powers of intellect, sensibility, and volition in a self-conscious unity, with moral judgment crowning their action with significance. As for the body, it is the servant of personality for the gathering of sensations, and its organ for the expression of its life and action."[100] His focus on human capacities—particularly self-consciousness, the power of abstract thought, amenableness to moral law, the capacity for religion, the power of choosing one's supreme end, and constructive mastery of things within the world[101]—deeply influenced his discussion of the image of God: "In the capacities of the human spirit is found that image or likeness of God."[102] Clarke exemplified many modern theologians who eschewed the biblical portrait of human nature and embraced in its place the findings of current psychological theories.

Clarke was an example in another area as well, relying on anthropology and other cognate sciences for his doctrine of human origins. As he explained: "The time has come when theology should remand the investigation of the time and manner of the origin of man to the science of anthropology with its kindred sciences, just as it now remands the time and manner of the origin of the earth to astronomy and geology, and should accept and use their discoveries on the subject, content with knowing that the origin of mankind, as of all else, is in God."[103] Of course, this approach resulted in viewing human beings as just another product of evolution, along with all other living beings. Yet Clarke did not embrace the theory as evolutionists presented it, but offered his own modified view: He combined some type of divine direction with evolutionary processes, thus championing theistic evolution as his theory of human origins.[104]

---

98. William Newton Clarke, *Outline of Christian Theology* (Edinburgh: T & T Clark, 1909), 48.
99. Ibid., 182.
100. Ibid., 187–88.

101. Ibid., 188–90.
102. Ibid., 191.
103. Ibid., 223.
104. Ibid., 224–26.

Philosophy—particularly of the existentialist variety—was introduced into theological discussions of humanity by neoorthodox leaders Karl Barth and Emil Brunner. Barth dismissed the historicity of the biblical account of Adam and Eve,[105] depending largely on the "I-Thou" philosophy of Martin Buber[106] in developing his concept of the confrontational and reciprocal relationship of humanity as created in the image of God with its Creator.[107] Consequently, Barth moved away from the classical understanding of the *imago Dei* as something man is or does.[108] Rather than an attribute or an activity, the *imago Dei* is confrontational relationality, first and foremost between the members of the Trinity, then between God and human beings, and finally between people and other people:

> In God's own being and sphere there is a counterpart: a genuine but harmonious self-encounter and self-discovery; a free co-existence and co-operation; an open confrontation and reciprocity. Man is the repetition of this divine form of life; its copy and reflection. He is this first in the fact that he is the counterpart of God, the encounter and discovery in God Himself being copied and imitated in God's relation to man. But he is it also in the fact that he is himself the counterpart of his fellows and has in them a counterpart, the co-existence and co-operation in God Himself being repeated in the relation of man to man. Thus ... the analogy between God and man is simply the existence of the I and the Thou in confrontation. This is first constitutive for God, and then for man created by God.[109]

Barth supported this idea from the fact that nothing is mentioned in Genesis 1:26–27 about the intellectual and volitional aspects of human beings that figured so prominently in the church's historic discussion of the *imago Dei*.[110] Rather, it is in the plurality of gender—male and female—and in the relationship of "man to woman and woman to

---

105. Barth did not believe that Adam and Eve were historical people who existed in some state of innocence in a pristine location known as the garden of Eden. Rather, he regarded the Genesis account as "saga." Contrasting the "historical" with the "non-historical," Barth explained: "In addition to the 'historical' there has always been a legitimate 'non-historical' and pre-historical view of history, and its 'non-historical' and pre-historical depiction in the form of saga.... I am using saga in the sense of an intuitive and poetic picture of a pre-historical reality of history which is enacted once and for all within the confines of time and space." Yet Barth distanced this genre of saga from myth, thus claiming a superiority of the biblical narrative of creation to the Babylonian creation myth *Enuma Elish* (written about 2000 BC) and the Egyptian creation myth. From this, he continued to surmise: "Why did not the imagination of the Israelites turn like others to the wide field of myth?... Why is it that there emerges here, and only here, what might intrinsically have been the object of Babylonian or Egyptian imagination—a real Creator and real creation? To these questions there is no answer. We can only affirm *that*

it is a fact. And this fact alone is the distinctive characteristic of the biblical creation histories.... It is sacred saga, because it speaks of God and because it speaks of Him—this is its peculiar feature—as the Creator." Applying saga to Adam and Eve and the garden of Eden, Barth noted: "Necessarily, therefore, we have to accept both the fact that Paradise was planted and existed somewhere and not just everywhere or nowhere but also the fact that there can be no actual investigation of this 'somewhere.' It is palpable that in these passages we have to do with a genuine consideration of real events, persons and things, but only with a consideration and therefore not with a historical review but with constructions which do not have their origin in observation but in imagination." *CD*, III/1, 81, 92, 252.

106. Martin Buber, *I and Thou*, trans. R. Gregor Smith (Edinburgh: T & T Clark, 1937).

107. *CD*, III/1, 184.

108. Ibid., 184–87.

109. Ibid., 185.

110. Ibid.

man" that human beings reflect the plurality of persons—Father, Son, and Holy Spirit—and their trinitarian relationship with one another.[111] Only secondarily and derivatively does the divine image consist in some attribute or attributes possessed by human beings and/or humanity's activity of ruling and exercising dominion over the rest of the created order.[112] With this, Barth established a new theology of the divine image as consisting not of a substance nor of an activity, but of relationality.

Barth's neoorthodox companion Emil Brunner developed his doctrine of humanity with some similarities to Barth.[113] As Brunner described his concept of human beings made in the divine image: "The being of man as an 'I' is being from and in the Divine 'Thou,' or, more exactly, from and in the Divine Word, whose claim 'calls' man's being into existence.... From the side of God this twofold relation is known as a 'call,' and from that of man as an 'answer'; thus the heart of man's being is seen to be: responsible existence."[114] Relying on existential philosophy, with its emphasis on authentic existence and the need for a free and uncompromised decision, Brunner maintained: "The necessity for decision, an obligation which he can never evade, is the distinguishing feature of man.... [It] is responsive, 'answering,' responsible being.... [I]t is the being created by God to stand 'over-against' Him, who can reply to God, and who in this answer alone fulfills—or destroys—the purpose of God's creation."[115] Human beings, created in God's image for a loving relationship with him, stand in relation to and owe God a response.[116]

More specifically, Brunner distinguished between the image of God in a formal sense and a material sense. In the formal sense, the image of God "describes the human as human, the imperishable structure of man's being which cannot be affected by the conflict between the Original Creation and Sin."[117] He listed "freedom, reason, conscience, language, etc." as the elements of this formal aspect of the divine image,[118] which cannot be lost, even in sinful, unresponsive, or mal-responsive people.[119] While this formal aspect is retained, the material aspect (i.e., in terms of content) has been lost in sinful, unresponsive, or mal-responsive people: "The human element as form, as structure—namely, as responsible being—has remained; the human element as content, that is, as being in love, has been lost. Man does not cease to be 'in the sight of' God; but he is in

111. Ibid., 186.

112. Ibid., 188.

113. Preferring to view the creation account as myth rather than (with Barth) saga, Brunner maintained that the biblical witness could not be taken seriously in light of the assured results of modern science: "The conflict between the teaching of history, natural science and paleontology, on the origins of the human race, and that of the ecclesiastical doctrine, waged on both sides with the passion of a fanatical concern for truth, has led, all along the line, to the victory of the scientific view, and to the gradual but inevitable decline of the ecclesiastical view.... The pitiable comedy which is produced when theology claims that a 'higher, more perfect' human existence of the first generation existed in a sphere not accessible to research, as it retires before the relentless onward march of scientific research, should be abandoned,

once for all, since it has for long provoked nothing but scorn and mockery, and has exposed the message of the Church to the just reproach of 'living at the back of beyond.'... The ecclesiastical doctrine of Adam and Eve cannot compete with the impressive power of this scientific knowledge." Emil Brunner, *Man in Revolt: A Christian Anthropology* (Philadelphia: Westminster, 1947), 85–87.

114. Ibid., 97.

115. Ibid., 97–98.

116. Ibid., 98.

117. Ibid., 513.

118. Ibid., 510.

119. Emil Brunner, *The Christian Doctrine of Creation and Redemption*, trans. Olive Wyon (Philadelphia: Westminster, 1953), 56–57.

the sight of God as a perverted being, and therefore God also appears to be perverted to him."[120] Thus, Brunner concluded with a provocative contradiction: "Even where man revolts against God in titanic rebellion, and with great daring and insolence 'gets rid' of Him or deifies himself, even there, behind the human perversion, the Divine image itself looks forth. Man could not be godless without God; he could not curse God if he were not first of all loved by God."[121]

As biblical scholars made strides in Old Testament studies (specifically on Gen. 1:1–2:3) and conducted extensive research into ancient Near Eastern literature (especially with background studies on the image of God), sympathies for another approach to the image of God arose. Gerhard von Rad, for example, noted: "Just as powerful earthly kings, to indicate their claim to dominion, erect an image of themselves in the provinces of their empire where they do not personally appear, so man is placed upon earth in God's image as God's sovereign emblem."[122] Thus arose a new functional understanding of the divine image: human beings are the image of God as his representatives or co-regents who exercise dominion over the created order.[123]

Along with these modern developments in the doctrine of humanity, many Christians championed the church's historical viewpoint while making significant modifications of it. G. C. Berkouwer, for example, disagreed with the church's tendency to focus its discussion of the image of God on one or two essential human attributes, like reason and free will.[124] In addition, he was critical of approaches that isolated the image of God in terms of some human activity, such as the exercise of dominion over the created order.[125] Moreover, he opposed Barth's idea that the image of God consists in humanity's creation as male and female.[126] Furthermore, Berkouwer questioned the legitimacy of approaches that made a distinction between the formal and material aspects of the image of God.[127]

In place of these approaches, Berkouwer substituted what could be called a holistic approach, based on "Scripture's emphasis on the whole man as the image of God."[128] He developed this view by emphasizing "the importance of the Biblical witness to Christ as the image of God and to the renewal, in communion with Christ, of man according to that image, spoken of in the New Testament."[129] Accordingly, he rejected a piecemeal approach to identifying the divine image, arguing, "No part of man is emphasized as independent of other parts, not because the various parts are not important, but because the Word of God is concerned precisely with the whole man in his relation to God."[130] Thus, it is illegitimate to consider human nature as being divided into higher

120. Brunner, *Man in Revolt*, 170.

121. Ibid., 187.

122. Gerhard von Rad, *Genesis: A Commentary*, trans. John H. Marks et al., rev. ed. (Philadelphia: Westminster, 1972), 60.

123. For an excellent summary of the development of this functionalist interpretation of the divine image, including historical precedents in the early and medieval church and the important contributions from twentieth-century Old Testament scholars, see J. Richard Middleton, *The Liberating Image: The* Imago Dei *in Genesis 1* (Grand Rapids: Brazos,

2005), 24–34.

124. G. C. Berkouwer, *Man: The Image of God* (Grand Rapids: Eerdmans, 1962), 33–36.

125. Ibid., 70–71.

126. Ibid., 72–73.

127. Ibid., 57, 61, 62.

128. Ibid., 77.

129. Ibid., 98. He based his conclusions on several key biblical passages (Gen. 1:26; 2 Cor. 3:18; 4:6; Eph. 4:24; Col. 3:10).

130. Ibid., 200.

and lower parts, "implying that the higher part is holier than the lower and stands closer to God, the lower as such then being impure and sinful and further away from the God of life."[131]

Anthony Hoekema, in his work *Created in God's Image*,[132] maintained that "the concept of man as the *image* or *likeness* of God tells us that man as he was created was to *mirror* God and to *represent* God."[133] With regard to the first, man "was to *mirror* God. As a mirror reflects, so man should reflect God. When one looks at a human being, one ought to see in him or her a certain reflection of God ... something of God's love, God's kindness, and God's goodness." As for the second aspect, "man also *represents* God.... Ancient rulers often set up images of themselves in distant parts of their realms; an image of this sort then represented the ruler, stood for his authority, and reminded his subjects that he was indeed their king.... Man, then, was created in God's image so that he or she might represent God, like an ambassador from a foreign country.... [S]o man must seek to advance God's program for this world."[134] Thus, human beings created in the divine image are to reflect and represent God.

Hoekema also discussed the importance of Jesus Christ, as the true image of God, for formulating a complete and biblical doctrine. He focused on three particular relationships in the life of Christ: "From looking at Jesus Christ, the perfect image of God, we learn that the proper functioning of the image includes being directed toward God, being directed toward the neighbor, and ruling over nature."[135] Thus, "Just as Christ, the true image of God, functioned in three relationships, so also must man.... God has placed man into a threefold relationship: between man and God, between man and his fellowmen, and between man and nature."[136] Additionally, Hoekema outlined the four stages in the doctrine of the image of God: Prior to the fall, the original image; after the fall, the perverted image; through redemption, the renewed or restored image; in the future, with glorification, the perfected image.[137]

With the development of neuroscience, new data was added to the consideration of how human beings function. Specifically, fMRI, PET, SPECT, MRS, and MEG produced an ever-growing body of evidence that much of what used to be considered the realm of the soul—including consciousness, self-awareness, personality, moral sensitivity, cognitive reasoning, memory, volition, even religious aptitude—is intimately tied to neurological processes operating in the brain and central nervous system. As one person explained:

> One widespread tradition has it that we human beings are responsible agents, captains of our fate, *because* we really are *souls*, immaterial and immortal clumps of Godstuff that inhabit and control our material bodies rather like spectral puppeteers.... But this idea of immaterial souls, capable of defying the laws of physics, has outlived its credibility thanks to the advance of the natural

131. Ibid., 203.

132. Anthony A. Hoekema, *Created in God's Image* (Grand Rapids: Eerdmans and Exeter: Paternoster, 1986).

133. Ibid., 67.

134. Ibid., 67–68.

135. Ibid., 75.

136. Ibid., 75.

137. Ibid., 82–95.

sciences. Many people think the implications of this are dreadful: We don't really have "free will" and nothing really matters.[138]

Similarly, Francis Crick, who proposed the double-helix model of DNA, stated, "'You,' your joys and your sorrows, your memories and your ambitions, your sense of personal identity and free will, are in fact no more than the behavior of a vast assembly of nerve cells and their associated molecules."[139] This development led some evangelicals to question seriously the traditional doctrine of humanity, especially as to the reality and nature of the soul and its relationship with the body. Several important scholars offered new perspectives on the topic as a result.

Nancey Murphy was a proponent of a theory called *nonreductive physicalism*, with *physicalism* being a denial of dualism and *nonreductive* being a denial of "the absence of human meaning, responsibility and freedom."[140] As for the essence of her theory, Murphy maintained: "The nonreductive physicalist says ... that if there is no soul, then these higher capacities [human rationality, morality, spirituality] must be explained in a different manner. In part they are explainable as brain functions, but their full explanation requires attention to human social relations, to cultural factors and, most importantly, to God's action in our lives."[141] Thus, she rejected "neurobiological determinism—that is, the possibility that the laws governing neural processes determine all of human thought and behavior."[142] This idea could be called "bottom-up causation." Instead, the whole person—existing in and with social relations, cultural realities, and divine activity—contributes "top-down causation," resulting in meaning, responsibility, and freedom.

William Hasker developed *emergent dualism* or *emergent personalism*, affirming:

> The human mind is produced by the human brain and is not a separate element "added to" the brain from outside. This leads to the further conclusion that mental properties are "emergent" in the following sense: they are properties that manifest themselves when the appropriate material constituents are placed in special, highly complex relationships, but these properties are not observable in simpler configurations nor are they derivable from the laws which describe the properties of matter as it behaves in these simpler configurations. Which is to say: *mental properties are emergent*; they involve emergent causal powers that are not in evidence in the absence of consciousness.[143]

Hasker saw his emergent personalism as having strong advantages over traditional (Cartesian) dualism because of "the close natural connection it postulates between mind

---

138. Daniel C. Dennett, *Freedom Evolves* (New York: Viking, 2003), 1, cited in Nancey Murphy, "Nonreductive Physicalism," in *In Search of the Soul: Four Views of the Mind-Body Problem*, ed. Joel B. Green and Stuart L. Palmer (Downers Grove, Ill.: InterVarsity, 2005), 115.

139. Francis Crick, *The Astonishing Hypothesis: The Scientific Search for the Soul* (New York: Simon & Schuster, 1994), 3, cited in Green and Palmer, *In Search of the Soul*, 13. This latter book omits the word *personal* before "identity," as it is

in Crick's original writing.

140. Murphy, "Nonreductive Physicalism," 115.

141. Ibid., 116.

142. Ibid., 128.

143. Hasker, *Emergent Self*, 189–90. Actually, Hasker's definition is far more complex than this discussion, as he distinguishes his form of emergentism from several others. For the sake of our discussion, however, the above citation provides an adequate presentation of his view.

and brain, as contrasted with the disparity between mind and matter postulated by Cartesianism."[144] Moreover, he claimed that his view goes beyond materialism in being able to account for the teleological nature of many mental processes and for the reality of human free will.[145] Finally, Hasker postulated that his view can account for life after death and personal resurrection; thus, it finds itself in no conflict with Scripture.[146]

John Cooper affirmed and defended "holistic dualism" or "dualistic holism."[147] For Cooper, "some sort of 'dualistic' anthropology is entailed by the biblical teaching on the intermediate state,"[148] the period of existence between death and the resurrection of the body. Accordingly, his holistic dualism maintained "both the unity of human nature and the possibility of personal existence without a body."[149] He believed that "the central issue is whether the soul can survive and function apart from the human body. In other words, is human nature constructed in such a way that at death it can 'come apart,' the conscious personal part continuing to exist while the organism disintegrates?" Giving a positive response, Cooper underscored the implications of his view: "Then the person or soul cannot be the same as a living active human body or necessarily tied to such a body. There must be enough of an ontological difference between the person or soul and the body that they are not only distinct from each other, but also separable at death."[150] Only dualism can account for this reality. Although affirming dualism, Cooper distanced himself from the form of substance dualism historically embraced by the church but which owes its foundation to Plato or René Descartes.[151] Moreover, he carefully constructed his position on the basis of Old and New Testament affirmations of both holism and dualism.[152] His holistic dualism accounted for both the unity of human nature—body and soul—in this earthly life and "personal existence apart from earthly-bodily existence.... When we die, there is a dichotomy of ego [self] and the earthly organism. We are constituted in such a way that we can survive 'coming apart' at death, unnatural as this may be."[153]

With the advent of modern and scientific attacks, the doctrine of humanity has become once again an important topic for theology. Although the focus of discussion has largely moved away from such issues as dichotomy versus trichotomy, the origin of the soul, and the relationship of the divine image to the divine likeness, other issues like the existence of an immaterial human element and the identity of the image of God have risen to paramount theological importance today.

144. Ibid., 192. Other advantages listed by Hasker included the ability of emergentism to account for commissurotomy, the intimate connection between consciousness and the brain, and the souls of animals. Ibid., 192–93.

145. Ibid., 195.

146. Ibid., 232, 235.

147. John Cooper, *Body, Soul and Life Everlasting: Biblical Anthropology and the Monism-Dualism Debate* (Grand Rapids: Eerdmans and Leicester: Apollos, 1989, 2000), xxvii.

148. Ibid., xv.

149. Ibid., xxvii–xxviii.

150. Ibid., 1–2.

151. Ibid., 36–37.

152. Ibid., 37–69, 146–62.

153. Ibid., 162–63.

16

SIN

How has the church come to view sin and its origin? How has it developed various views on what is inherited from Adam?

STATEMENT OF BELIEF

The church has historically affirmed that God's plan of salvation through Jesus Christ is necessitated by and a response to human sin. This sin manifests itself in evil actions, destructive words, improper motivations, wrong attitudes, and a depraved nature. Indeed, "sin is any failure to conform to the moral law of God in act, attitude, or nature."[1] Moreover, from early on the church formulated a doctrine of *original sin*, or "the sin that is ours as a result of Adam's fall ... the guilt and tendency to sin with which we are born."[2] At times the church has given further detail about this inborn tendency to sin, speaking in terms of (1) *total depravity*, meaning "every part of our being is affected by sin — our intellects, our emotions and desires, our hearts (the center of our desires and decision-making processes), our goals and motives, and even our physical bodies"; and (2) *total inability*, meaning "not only do we as sinners lack any spiritual good in ourselves, but we also lack the ability to do anything that will in itself please God and the ability to come to God in our own strength."[3]

Throughout history, different theologians and different churches have placed different emphases on the above-noted elements of sin, leading to different doctrines of sin. One such view — Pelagianism — denies that people bear any relationship whatsoever to Adam and his sin; therefore, original sin, total depravity, and total inability are all denied. Another view — semi-Pelagianism — denies liability for guilt from Adam but agrees that people are corrupted by sin. The Augustinian or Calvinist is the full-orbed doctrine of original sin described above, which includes both guilt and corruption — characterized by both total depravity and total inability — because of Adam's sin.

---

1. Wayne Grudem, *Systematic Theology: An Introduction to Biblical Doctrine* (Grand Rapids: Zondervan, 1994, 2000), 490.
2. Ibid., 494–95.

How these various views of original sin developed will be one focus of this chapter. Another will be the historical development of the church's understandings of both the origin of sin and actual sins.[4]

VIEWS OF SIN IN THE EARLY CHURCH

The first account of sin in the human race is recounted in the third chapter of Genesis. The rest of the Old Testament is like a broken record as it rehearses over and over again the constant fall of humanity into more and greater sins. Brother rises up against brother, the ungodly destroy the godly, and dreadfully evil nations are divine instruments used to punish the wicked people of God. Even the righteous fall into the quagmire of sin. The New Testament is no different. Jesus himself indicated a sin so terrible that it is unpardonable (Matt. 12:31–32). The apostle Paul linked death, judgment, and the condemnation of all humanity to the one sin of Adam (Rom. 5:12–19), and he spoke of the "law of sin" wreaking havoc in human beings (Rom. 7:23). The picture of sin that Paul and the other authors paint is one of universal depravity and corruption.

The early church addressed itself to identifying sin in all of its terrible manifestations and fighting against it on its many fronts. In his letter to the church of Corinth, Clement of Rome sought to combat the same sin of division that the apostle Paul had confronted earlier in his letters.[5] Clement attributed such sin to the failure of each Christian to carry out God's will, giving preference to an evil heart.[6] Similarly, Justin Martyr focused on individual responsibility for sin, affirming that people "become subject to punishment by their own fault." Although Justin linked humanity to Adam, the relationship is one of ancestor to descendants, each of whom sins individually.[7] Thus, sinful people become "like Adam and Eve," but they do so when they "work out death for themselves."[8] Of course, people are "brought up in bad habits and wicked training," and this contributes to their sinfulness, but they are still individually responsible for sin.[9] Irenaeus had a similar focus: "Those people who have fallen away ... have done so through their own fault, since they have been created free agents and exercised power over themselves.... They are destitute of all good things, having become to themselves the cause of their punishment in a place of that nature."[10]

The early church wrestled with and attempted to explain the fall of the human race. In addition to placing a strong emphasis on individual freedom and responsibility, Tatian emphasized the role of Satan in the fall of human beings.[11] Theophilus started from the position that Adam was originally created in a "neutral" situation: Man "was by nature

---

3. Ibid., 497.

4. My thanks to Alex Leung for his help on this chapter.

5. "Your schism has perverted many; it has brought many to despair, plunged many into doubt, and caused all of us to sorrow. And yet your rebellion still continues!" Clement of Rome, *Letter of the Romans to the Corinthians*, 46–47, in Holmes, 81–83; *ANF*, 1:17–18.

6. Ibid., in Holmes, 33; *ANF*, 1:5–6.

7. "The human race ... from Adam had fallen under the power of death and the guile [deceit] of the serpent, and each one had committed personal transgression." Justin Martyr, *Dialogue with Trypho, a Jew*, 88, in *ANF*, 1:243.

8. Ibid., 124, in *ANF*, 1:262.

9. Justin Martyr, *First Apology*, 61, in *ANF*, 1:183.

10. Irenaeus, *Against Heresies*, 4.39.3–4, in *ANF*, 1:523. The text has been rendered clearer.

11. Tatian, *Address to the Greeks*, 7, in *ANF*, 2:68.

neither mortal nor immortal. For if God had made man immortal from the beginning, he would have made man to be God. But if God had made man mortal, God himself would seem to be the cause of man's death. Thus, God did not make man either immortal or mortal ... but capable of both." So Adam faced the choice of two pathways: "If he should incline to the things of immortality, keeping the commandment of God, man should receive immortality as a reward from him and should become God. If, on the other hand, he should incline to the things of death, disobeying God, man should himself be the cause of death to himself. For God made man free and with power over himself."[12] Thus, Theophilus firmly placed the blame for sin on the shoulders of a disobedient Adam and not on God. In doing so, he compared Adam to an infant whom God "wanted to test ... to see if he was submissive to his commandment."[13] As Adam failed the divine test, "disobedience procured [obtained] his expulsion from paradise."[14]

Fuller development of the link between the sin of Adam and the human race occurred with Tertullian. He viewed human beings as being composed of a body and a soul, both of which come into existence at the moment of conception. Thus, "the soul of a human being—which may be compared with the beginning sprout of a tree—has been derived from Adam as its root. It has been propagated among his descendants by means of women, to whom it has been entrusted for transmission."[15] This has tragic results, as "all people are perishing who never even saw a single square foot of ground in paradise."[16] The reason for this tragic situation is that, starting with Adam, by means of the transmission of the soul from generation to generation, all people have a sinful nature: "We have indeed borne the image of the earthly [the image of Adam], by our sharing in his transgression, by our participation in his death, and by our banishment from paradise."[17] Tertullian, then, affirmed that human sin is "evil which arises from its [the soul's] corrupt origin."[18]

Cyprian took this discussion further. His doctrine of infant baptism—by which the Holy Spirit brings renewal "from the filth of the old contagion [infection]"[19]—underscored most clearly the link between Adam's sin and humanity's plight at birth: "This recently born infant has not sinned except that, being born physically according to Adam, he has contracted the contagion [infection] of the ancient death at his birth. Thus, he more easily approaches the reception of the forgiveness of sins, because the sins forgiven are not his own but those of another."[20] For Cyprian, baptism of infants is necessary not because newborn children have committed any personal sin, but because they have inherited sin and death from their first father, Adam.

Although the idea that all of humanity is identified with Adam in his sin was growing in popularity in certain parts of the church, others did not follow suit. Their emphasis continued to be on the individual's responsibility for sin. According to Clement of

---

12. Theophilus, *To Autolycus*, 2.27, in *ANF*, 2:105. The text has been rendered clearer.

13. Ibid., 2.25, in *ANF*, 2:104. The text has been rendered clearer.

14. Ibid.

15. Tertullian, *Treatise on the Soul*, 19, in *ANF*, 3:200. The text has been rendered clearer.

16. Tertullian, *Against Marcion*, 1.22, in *ANF*, 3:287. The

text has been rendered clearer.

17. Tertullian, *On the Resurrection of the Flesh*, 49, in *ANF*, 3:583.

18. Tertullian, *Treatise on the Soul*, 41, in *ANF*, 3:220.

19. Cyprian, *Treatise* 2:23, in *ANF*, 5:436.

20. Cyprian, *Letter* 58.5, in *ANF*, 5:354. The text has been rendered clearer.

Alexandria, Adam fell from this original state by misusing the reason and free will God had given to progress toward perfection. In his fall, Adam lost this God-given ability and thus was given over to death. But this sin of Adam affected him only; no evil or sin was transmitted by him to his descendants.[21] Clement was followed with some modification by other church leaders. For example, Athanasius described Adam in his original state as "having had his mind directed toward God in a freedom unembarrassed by shame."[22] His sin, then, was focusing his attention — especially his body and its physical desires — on the things of the world instead of God.[23] Although he individually lost sight of God, "when Adam sinned, his sin reached to all people,"[24] reaping tragic consequences: "For this reason, death gained ground on all people, and corruption infected them. The whole human race began to perish. Man, rational and made in God's image, began to disappear, and the workmanship of God was in the process of destruction."[25]

Still, these church leaders denied that infants are born with sin inherited from Adam. Gregory of Nazianzus, addressing the case of unbaptized babies, claimed they "will be neither glorified nor punished by the righteous Judge, because they are unsealed yet not evil."[26] Similarly, Gregory of Nyssa affirmed: "The innocent baby has no plague of ignorance before its soul's eyes obscuring its measure of light.... It does not need the soundness that comes from purgation [cleansing], because it never allowed the plague into its soul at all."[27] Thus, there was a reluctance to attribute the guilt of Adam to humanity in general and to children in particular.

At the beginning of the fifth century, a major challenge to the developing positions of the church was put forth by Pelagius. He was incensed by the moral corruption he found in Rome, and he was deeply troubled by a prayer in the *Confessions* of Augustine: (Speaking to God) "Give [me] what you command, and command [me to do] what you will."[28] To Pelagius, the attitude reflected in this prayer was one that encouraged waiting on God for courage, strength, and ability to do his will. But human beings are already designed by God himself to carry out his will — so why rely on God to be encouraged and equipped to do so? Pelagius's reaction reflected his view of human nature and its relationship to Adam and his sin. He believed that whereas God had given human beings the *capacity* to fulfill the commandments, both *volition* and *action* are strictly human faculties.[29] God created

---

21. Commenting on Job 1:21, Clement asserted: "The righteous Job says, 'Naked came I out of my mother's womb, and naked will I return there.' He does not mean naked of possessions, for that would be a trivial and common thing. Rather, he means as a just man: He comes out of the womb naked of evil and sin." Clement of Alexandria, *Stromata*, 4.25, in *ANF*, 2:439. The text has been rendered clearer.

22. Athanasius, *Against the Heathen*, 2, in *NPNF²*, 4:5. The text has been rendered clearer.

23. Ibid., 3, in *NPNF²*, 4:5.

24. Athanasius, *Four Discourses against the Arians*, 1.51, in *NPNF²*, 4:336. The text has been rendered clearer.

25. Athanasius, *The Incarnation of the Word*, 6, in *NPNF²*, 4:39. The text has been rendered clearer.

26. Gregory of Nazianzus, "On Holy Baptism," *Oration*

40:23, in *NPNF²*, 7:367. The text has been rendered clearer.

27. Gregory of Nyssa, *On Infants' Early Deaths*, in *NPNF²*, 5:377. The text has been rendered clearer.

28. Augustine, *On the Gift of Perseverance*, 53: "Although I published [the *Confessions*] before the Pelagian heresy had come into existence, certainly in them I said to my God, and said it frequently, 'Give what you command, and command what you will.' Pelagius at Rome, when they were mentioned in his presence by a certain brother and fellow bishop of mine, could not stand these words of mine." *NPNF¹*, 5:547.

29. Augustine, *On the Grace of Christ*, 1.5, in *NPNF¹*, 5:218–19. It should be noted that much of Pelagius's position must be reconstructed from the writings of Augustine, because few actual writings of Pelagius exist today. We trust that Augustine was fair in presenting his opponent's views.

all human beings with the power to act; it now depends on them to will and to engage in the action. Thus, people act out of a capacity given to them by the grace of God, but their will and action are not assisted by grace.

To Augustine, Pelagius's view of human nature minimized the importance of God's grace. But Pelagius did not deny grace; he simply defined it in a novel way: Grace is God's work to assist the capacity to be able to do the good. But this was not all. In his grace, God also provided people with free will, including the capacity not to sin.[30] Indeed, this absolute free will to choose good—or to choose evil—is the basis for rewarding the choice to do good: "For there would be no virtue for those who always remain good if they had not been able to choose evil. God wished to present to the rational creature the gift of voluntary goodness and the power of free will. So he planted in human beings the possibility of turning itself toward either side."[31] Furthermore, God's grace includes the revelation of right and wrong in the human conscience, which "helps us to turn aside from evil and to do good."[32] To this natural ability, God added grace in the form of an additional revelation of his will—"the law (of Moses) and the teaching (of Jesus Christ)."[33] Thus, God's grace is strictly external.

People only need such external aids, however, because they do not have any internal tendency to sin; they are not inclined toward doing evil. Pelagius held that God creates every human soul (the doctrine of creationism), meaning that no one is born with a corrupt nature inherited from Adam.[34] Thus, there is no sinful nature in people when they are born. It may appear that people have an evil nature, but that is only the result of habitual sin: "Nothing else makes it difficult for us to do good than the long custom of sinning that has infected us since we were children and has gradually corrupted us for many years. Afterwards, it holds us bound to it and delivered over to it, so that it almost seems as if it had the same force as nature."[35] Also, humanity certainly does not bear any guilt for Adam's sin, because no one can be held morally accountable for what another person does. As for the fall of Adam, his sin leaves a bad example for people to follow. But it in no way inclines them to sin.

Pelagius concluded that believers helped by God's grace could live without sin.[36] In support of this view, he cited many examples of holy people in Scripture, saints who had never sinned,[37] and he appealed to the absurdity of God commanding holiness (Lev. 19:2) and perfection (Matt. 5:48) if sinlessness were not possible. To believe otherwise would be blasphemous, as Pelagius reasoned: "No one knows better the measure of our strength

---

30. Augustine, *On the Proceedings of Pelagius*, 22.10, in *NPNF*[1], 5:193.

31. Pelagius, *Letter to Demetrias*, in *A Cloud of Witnesses: Readings in the History of Western Christianity*, ed. Joel F. Harrington (Boston and New York: Houghton Mifflin, 2001), 100.

32. Augustine, *On the Grace of Christ*, 1.45, in *NPNF*[1], 5:233.

33. Ibid., in *NPNF*[1], 5:232–33.

34. "Everything good and everything evil, on account of which we are either praiseworthy or blameworthy, is not born with us, but done by us. For we are born not fully developed,

but with a capacity for either conduct. We are born without virtue or vice. Before we act according to our own will, the only thing in man is that which God has formed." Augustine, *On the Grace of Christ, and On Original Sin*, 2.14, in *NPNF*[1], 5:241. The text has been rendered clearer.

35. Pelagius, *Letter to Demetrias*, in Harrington, *Cloud of Witnesses*, 100.

36. Augustine, *On the Proceedings of Pelagius*, 20, in *NPNF*[1], 5:191.

37. Pelagius, *Letter to Demetrias*, in Harrington, *Cloud of Witnesses*, 100–101.

than he [God] who gave us our strength; and no one has a better understanding of what is within our power than he [God] who endowed us with the very resources of our power. He has not willed to command anything impossible, for he is righteous; and he will not condemn people for what they could not help, for he is holy."[38]

Pelagius attracted a significant following and was joined by a disciple, Celestius, who also promoted his views. Celestius summarized the Pelagian position in six articles: (1) Adam was created mortal and would have died whether he had sinned or not sinned; (2) Adam's sin harmed only himself and not the human race; (3) both the law and the gospel lead us to the kingdom; (4) there were sinless people before the coming of Christ; (5) newborn infants are in the same condition as Adam was before the fall; and (6) the whole human race does not, on the one hand, die through Adam's death or transgression, nor, on the other hand, does the whole human race rise again through the resurrection of Christ.[39]

The church reacted with deep concern and criticism.

The church's action to combat Pelagianism was largely the result of the work of Augustine, whose major tenets were as follows: As originally created, Adam (and Eve) was a magnificent being—intelligent, strong, healthy, upright, and blessed in all his ways by God. He possessed great ability and freedom of will, but not perfection. Augustine distinguished between two conditions: *to be able not to sin*, and *not to be able to sin*. Adam was able not to sin, but he was not yet not able to sin.[40] To Adam, God gave a good will[41] as well as the gift of perseverance to aid him in continuing to exercise his good will: "To the first man who, in that good in which he had been made upright, had received the ability not to sin, the ability not to die, the ability not to forsake that good itself, was given the aid of perseverance."[42]

From this privileged existence and position, Adam and Eve fell. Although seemingly trivial—it was the mere eating of a piece of fruit—the sin was disastrous because our first parents had been given every advantage to steer them away from falling and keep them doing the good.[43] Although living in harmony with God, each other, and themselves, and though possessing a nature that did not lean toward disobedience, Adam and Eve disobeyed. For Augustine, the origin of this first sin was pride: "For 'pride is the beginning of sin' (Ecclesiasticus 10:13). And what is pride but the craving for undue exaltation? And this is undue exaltation, when the soul abandons him [God] to whom it ought to cleave as its end, and becomes a kind of end to itself. This happens when it becomes its own satisfaction."[44] As a result of Adam's fall, humanity lost the freedom of will it once enjoyed: "Accordingly, he who is the servant of sin is free to sin. And hence he will not be free to do right until, being freed from sin, he shall begin to be the servant of righteousness.[45] Indeed, rather than being *able not to sin*, all people after the

38. Ibid., in Harrington, *Cloud of Witnesses*, 101.

39. Augustine, *On the Proceedings of Pelagius*, 23.11, in *NPNF*[1], 5:193.

40. Augustine, *On Rebuke and Grace*, 33, in *NPNF*[1], 5:485.

41. Augustine, *The City of God*, 14.11, in *NPNF*[1], 2:271.

42. Augustine, *On Rebuke and Grace*, 34, in *NPNF*[1], 5:485.

43. Augustine, *City of God*, 14.12, in *NPNF*[1], 2:272–73.

44. Ibid., 14.13, in *NPNF*[1], 2:273. Augustine's citation is from Ecclesiasticus, one of the apocryphal writings he believed should be in the Bible.

45. Augustine, *Enchiridion on Faith, Hope, and Love*, 30, in *NPNF*[1], 3:247.

fall are *not able not to sin.* Augustine did not mean that people have no free will whatsoever. Rather, he meant that whenever unbelievers use their free will, they always use it to choose evil instead of good. Clearly, this was the complete opposite of Pelagius's position.

What is more, the first sin of Adam plunged all of humanity into a hellish nightmare, as affirmed by Romans 5:12: "By his sin the whole race of which he was the root was corrupted in him and therefore subjected to the penalty of death. Thus, all his descendants were tainted with the original sin and were drawn by it through various errors and sufferings into the final and eternal punishment."[46] Indeed, Augustine painted the plight of humanity with horrific detail: "The whole mass of the human race was under condemnation, steeped and drowning in misery, and it was being tossed from one form of evil to another."[47] This tragic situation is true of humanity because "by the evil will of that one man all sinned in him, since all were that one man, from whom, therefore, they all individually derive original sin."[48] Expanding on this, Augustine addressed the nature of humanity's identification with Adam: "In the first man ... there existed the whole human nature, which was to be transmitted by the woman to posterity [offspring], when that conjugal union received the divine sentence of its own condemnation; and what man was made, not when he was created, but when he sinned and was punished, this he propagated [passed down], so far as the origin of sin and death are concerned."[49] Augustine maintained that both death—the punishment for sin—and the corruption of human nature are passed down from Adam: "Human nature was in his person vitiated and altered to such an extent that he suffered in his members the warring of disobedient lust, and became subject to the necessity of dying. And what he himself had become by sin and punishment, such he passed down to those whom he generated."[50] His favorite term for this tendency of human nature to turn away from God and to be attracted to the things of this world—this "battle of disobedient lust"—was *concupiscence*.[51]

By underscoring the identity of Adam and the rest of humanity, Augustine expanded on others before him who posited the solidarity between the first man and all people. As already noted, Augustine appealed to Romans 5:12 as proof of his position. He cited the

---

46. Ibid., 26, in *NPNF*[1], 3:246. His mistranslation of Rom. 5:12—*in quo omnes pecaverunt* ("in whom all sinned")—is found in *Against Two Letters of the Pelagians*, in *NPNF*[1], 5:419. The text has been rendered clearer.

47. Ibid., 27, in *NPNF*[1], 3:246. The text has been rendered clearer.

48. Augustine, *On Marriage and Concupiscence*, 2.15, in *NPNF*[1], 5:288.

49. Augustine, *City of God*, 13.3, in *NPNF*[1], 2:246.

50. Ibid. The text has been rendered clearer.

51. Although it encompasses any and all kinds of wrong desires, concupiscence was nearly equated at times with sexual lust. Thus, for Augustine, it seemed impossible that sexual intercourse in marriage between husband and wife—which indeed is the proper place for the expression of sexual union—could not be tainted by concupiscence. E.g., when speaking of "the evil of concupiscence," Augustine explained that "indeed, marriage uses concupiscence rightly, but even marriage occasionally feels shame at it. Marriage itself is 'honorable in all' (Heb. 13:4) the goods that properly belong to it. But even when the 'marriage bed is undefiled' (Heb. 13:4)—not only by fornication and adultery, which are damnable disgraces, but also by any of those excesses of intercourse that do not arise from [the predominant desire to conceive children, but from] an overbearing lust of pleasure (these are venial sins in husband and wife)—even then, when it comes to intercourse, the act of sex itself, which is lawful and honorable, cannot be engaged in apart from the passion of lust." Augustine, *On Marriage and Concupiscence*, 1.27, in *NPNF*[1], 5:274–75. The text has been significantly paraphrased.

practice of infant baptism as further evidence of original sin.[52] Through his emphasis on the corporate solidarity between Adam and the rest of humanity, the tragic situation of original sin into which all people are born, the liability to condemnation for all unbaptized persons because of the guilt of Adam that they bear, and the inheritance of a corrupt nature that spells the inevitability of actual sins whenever unbelievers will to act, Augustine both defeated Pelagius and left a legacy of a robust theology of sin.

The church followed Augustine's lead. The Council of Carthage in 418 condemned Pelagius's views that death is a natural part of human existence and not the punishment for sin,[53] and that God's grace is limited to providing external help.[54] The Synod of Orange in 529 condemned the notion that the human soul remains unaffected by Adam's fall into sin,[55] while also denouncing the idea that Adam's sin was not passed on through the human race.[56] The church insisted on the thoroughgoing need for God's grace from beginning to end to overcome the disabling effects of Adam's sin, which was passed down from him to the entire human race.

But not everybody in the church agreed with the condemnation of Pelagius and the enthronement of Augustine's view of sin and grace. Another position—often called *semi-Pelagianism*,[57] because it partially embraced Augustine's principles while avoiding what some saw to be its extremes—was championed by people like John Cassian. He set up the debate between Pelagianism and Augustinianism as two horns of a dilemma: "Does God have compassion on us because we have shown the beginning of a good will? Or does the beginning of a good will follow because God has had compassion on us?" He called attention to counterexamples to both positions: "For if we say that the beginning of free will is in our own power, what about Paul the persecutor and Matthew the tax collector? The first was drawn to salvation while eager for bloodshed and the punishment of the innocent, and the second while ready for violence and rape! But if we say that the beginning of our free will is always due to the inspiration of the grace of God, what about the faith of Zacchaeus or the goodness of the thief on the cross?"[58] Cassian then developed a third view in between the two positions. He agreed with Pelagius that the human will is free to do good and not, against Augustine, only free to do evil.[59] Yet, with Augustine, Cassian also insisted on the movement of God's grace to assist the will:

> So great is the Creator's kindness toward his creatures that his providence not only accompanies it but actually constantly precedes it. This is what the prophet experienced and clearly affirmed: "My God will go before me with his mercy" (Psa. 59:9). When he sees in us some beginnings of a good will, he

52. "Infants have committed no sin of their own since they have been alive. Only original sin, therefore, remains, whereby they are made captive under the devil's power, until they are redeemed from it by the laver [bath] of regeneration and the blood of Christ." Augustine, *On Marriage and Concupiscence*, 1.22, in *NPNF*[1], 5:273.

53. The Council of Carthage, "Canons on Sin and Grace," canon 1, Mansi, 3:811; Bettenson, 64.

54. Ibid., canon 5, Mansi, 3:811; Bettenson, 65.

55. Synod of Orange, canon 1.

56. Ibid., canon 2.

57. The term *semi-Pelagianism* was actually coined in the sixteenth century, but its major tenets were already present in the fifth and sixth centuries.

58. John Cassian, *The Third Conference of Abbot Chaeremon*, 11, in *NPNF*[2], 11:427–28.

59. Ibid., 12, in *NPNF*[2], 11:428.

immediately enlightens it and strengthens it and urges it on toward salvation. He increases that which he himself planted or which he sees has arisen from our own efforts.[60]

Thus, in some cases—for example, Paul and Matthew—God gives people a good will that, assisted by his grace, does good. In other cases—for example, Zacchaeus, the thief on the cross—the good will is already present and then is assisted by God's grace. The grace of God and human free will exist harmoniously together. In all cases, however, the human will is good enough so as to cooperate with God's grace. Thus, Cassian ascribed a key, even though minor, role to the will in overcoming sin.[61]

Through the influence of John Cassian and others, the Synod of Arles in 473 condemned certain Augustinian positions, including the denial of cooperation between human obedience and divine grace, and the destruction of human free will after Adam's fall. In their place, the Council affirmed a cooperative effort between God's grace and human freedom and work: "Man's effort and endeavor is to be united with God's grace. Man's freedom of will is not extinct but warped and weakened."[62]

The Council of Orange in 529 put a stop to this drift toward semi-Pelagianism. It condemned the proposition that God's grace comes at human request[63] and denounced the idea that the human will must anticipate God's action in people for him to forgive them.[64] Furthermore, the council condemned the notion that faith, or even a minimal desire to believe, is part of human nature and not the result of divine grace.[65] The semi-Pelagian proposal that God gives some people a good will but others already have a good will—thus enabling them to seek out salvation—was also denounced.[66] Finally, the council positively set forth certain statements about the tragedy of sin in humanity. For example, it affirmed that "the sin of the first man has so impaired and weakened free will that afterward no one can love God as he should. Neither can he believe in God, or do good for God's sake unless the grace of God's mercy goes before him."[67] Thus, a modified Augustinian view of sin became the church's doctrine from the fifth century on.

VIEWS OF SIN IN THE MIDDLE AGES

During the first part of the Middle Ages, few challenges arose to the Augustinian position on sin. Indeed, many repeated his classic articles. For example, Servatus Lupus of Ferrières echoed, "We are not born in the condition in which Adam was created, but

---

60. Ibid., 8, in *NPNF*[2], 11:426. The quotation from Ps. 59:9 introduced a key term into the debate between Pelagius and Augustine that is brought out in chap. 22 on regeneration, conversion, and calling, and chap. 23 on justification. In Latin, the word translated "go before" is *preveniere*. Relying on this word, Augustine coined a type of grace—*prevenient grace*—that is God's goodness to sinners even before they come to salvation. Cassian agreed with this kind of grace and used it in his discussion to emphasize the necessity and reality of grace to act on the human will.

61. "The main share in our salvation is to be ascribed not to the merit of our own works but to heavenly grace." Ibid., 18, in *NPNF*[2], 11:434.

62. Synod of Arles, PL, 53:683; Mansi, 7:1010; Bettenson, 65–66.

63. Council of Orange, canon 3.

64. Ibid., canon 4.

65. Ibid., canon 5.

66. Ibid., canon 8.

67. The Council of Orange, affirmations.

as sinners in our origin."[68] And the theologian and monk Gottschalk underscored again that "none of us is able to use free will to do good, but only to do evil."[69]

Anselm developed a new idea concerning sin in *Why God Became Man*. He worked in a context of feudalism, an economic system in which powerful lords gave protection to their serfs in exchange for food and service. Anselm pictured the relationship between God and people like that between a lord and his servants. Just as the serfs must honor their lord by giving him what is due him, so human beings must give honor to God by giving him what is due him. Accordingly, Anselm defined sin: "To sin is nothing other than not to give God what is owed to him. What is the debt which we owe to God?... This is righteousness or uprightness of the will.... This is the sole honor, the complete honor, which we owe to God and which God demands from us.... Someone who does not render to God this honor due to him is taking away from God what is his, and dishonoring God, and this is what it is to sin."[70]

Thomas Aquinas treated the subject of sin at great lengths. He defined actual sin as "nothing else than a bad human act."[71] Because "an act is a human act because it is voluntary," an act can be sinful if the willful choice behind the act violates either human reason or the moral law of God.[72] In sinning, people choose some created good over the Good. Thus, sin is departing from the proper end or goal of life, which is God himself. This places the responsibility for actual sins squarely on the shoulders of the people who commit them. Indeed, Aquinas rejected the idea that God could be responsible for sins.[73] He also denied that Satan could be the direct or necessary cause of sin.[74] So God does not lead anyone to sin, and Satan does not possess the power to force anyone to sin. Thus, human beings themselves are ultimately responsible for their own sins.

In keeping with Augustine's emphasis on humanity's corporate solidarity with Adam, Aquinas focused his attention on the role of Adam in original sin: "Through origin from the first man, sin entered into the world. According to the Catholic faith, we are bound to hold that the first sin of the first man is transmitted to his descendants, by way of origin."[75] He offered an explanation for the problem of original sin, beginning with the identification of humanity with Adam: "All men born of Adam may be considered as one man, since they have one common nature, which they receive from their first parents....

68. Servatus Lupus of Ferrières, *Additional Epistles*, 3, in Pelikan, 3:83.

69. As quoted by Gottschalk's contemporary, deacon Florus of Lyons, in *On Three Epistles*, 21, PL, 121:1022–23, in Pelikan, 3:83.

70. Anselm, *Why God Became Man*, 1.11, in *Anselm*, 283. Anselm's solution for humanity's sin was the satisfaction of God's honor through the death of the God-man Jesus Christ. See further discussion in chap. 18.

71. Thomas Aquinas, *Summa Theologica*, 1st pt. of pt. 2, q. 71, art. 6.

72. Ibid.

73. "Every sin is a departure from the order [orientation] to God as the end. But God inclines and turns all things to himself as to their last [ultimate] end ... so that it is impossible that he should be either to himself or to another the cause of departing from the order [orientation] to himself. Therefore he cannot be directly the cause of sin." Ibid., 1st pt. of pt. 2, q. 79, art. 1.

74. Ibid., 1st pt. of pt. 2, q. 80, art. 3. Still, Satan does play a role in human sin: "The devil is the occasional and indirect cause of all our sins in so far as he induced the first man to sin, by reason of whose sin human nature is so infected that we are all prone to sin.... He is not, however, the direct cause of all the sins of men, as though each [sin] were the result of his suggestion." Ibid., 1st pt. of pt. 2, q. 80, art. 4.

75. Ibid., 1st pt. of pt. 2, q. 81, art. 1.

Accordingly, the multitude of men born of Adam are as so many members of one body."[76] Aquinas developed this idea into an analogy between the many parts of the body and the soul of a person, on the one hand, and the many descendants of our first parent and Adam himself, on the other hand: "Now the action of one member of the body—for example, the hand—is voluntary, not by the will of that hand, but by the will of the soul, the first mover of the members.... In this way, then, the disorder which is in people born of Adam is voluntary, not by their will but by the will of their first parent. By the process of generation, Adam moves all who originate from him, even as the soul's will moves all the members to their actions."[77] Thus, for Aquinas, "the sin which is transmitted by the first parent to his descendants is called original.... [O]riginal sin is not the sin of the person, except in so far as this person receives his nature from his first parent."[78]

Aquinas further spoke of original sin as a habit, "for it is a disordered disposition, arising from the destruction of the harmony which was essential to original justice."[79] Original justice was God's gift to human beings by which their reason was enabled to control their "lower powers"—feelings, desires, passions, and bodily activities. By falling into sin, human beings lost this gift of original righteousness. As a result, the original harmony was lost as well, so that now the lower nature of people dominates their reason and wreaks havoc in and through them: "[O]riginal justice was forfeited through the sin of our first parent, just as human nature was stricken in the soul by the disorder among the powers.... So also it became subject to corruption, by reason of disorder in the body."[80] Flowing from this loss of original justice and the corruption of human nature came "death and all consequent bodily defects [as God's] punishments of sin."[81] This notion became an important part of the medieval view of original sin: The loss of God's supernatural gifts was the key idea, more important than the corruption of human nature.

Of course, the greatest disruption that sin has caused in people is their loss of orientation toward seeking God as their greatest goal or ultimate end. Aquinas took this idea and used it to make a distinction between mortal sins and venial sins. As for the former type, "He who, by sinning, turns away from his last [ultimate] end, if we consider the nature of his sin, falls irreparably, and therefore is said to sin mortally and to deserve eternal punishment." As for the latter type of sin, "But when a person sins without turning away from God, by the very nature of his sin, his disorder can be repaired, because the principle of the order is not destroyed. Therefore, he is said to commit a venial sin, because he does not sin so as to deserve to be punished eternally."[82] Aquinas's distinction between mortal and venial sins became an important part of the Roman Catholic Church's position on sin.

---

76. Ibid.

77. Ibid. The text has been rendered clearer.

78. Ibid.

79. Ibid., 1st pt. of pt. 2, q. 82, art. 1.

80. Ibid., 1st pt. of pt. 2, q. 85, art. 5.

81. Ibid.

82. Ibid., 1st pt. of pt. 2, q. 72, art. 5. Aquinas cited 1 Cor. 3:15 in support of his idea that venial sins are punished temporally: "'Wood, hay and stubble' designate venial sins that inject themselves into people who are concerned for earthly things. These materials are stored in a house without belonging to the substance of the house, and they can be burned while the house is saved. In a similar way, venial sins increase in a person while his spiritual house remains. The person suffers fire because of them, either in the form of temporal trials in this life or purgatory after this life, but he is saved forever." Ibid., 1st pt. of pt. 2, q. 89, art. 2.

VIEWS OF SIN DURING THE REFORMATION AND POST-REFORMATION

Martin Luther experienced the depths of sin, and his struggle to overcome this enemy influenced all of his theology. As a young man, Luther was struck by lightning, which awakened in him the fear of death and the impending judgment of God for his sins. Enrolling in a strict Augustinian monastery, Luther sought relief from the very real damnation that he so keenly felt. At times confessing his sins for hours on end, he began to hate the God who appeared only to be a judge of his shortcomings: "My situation was that, although an impeccable monk, I stood before God as a sinner troubled in conscience, and I had no confidence that my merit would assuage him. Therefore, I did not love a just and angry God, but rather hated and murmured against him."[83] In the midst of his struggling, Luther discovered the forgiveness of sin through the gospel and embraced the doctrine of justification by faith alone.

At the heart of Luther's idea of sin was his rejection of the common, semi-Pelagian view of free will. In *The Bondage of the Will*, Luther resurrected Augustine's position and denied that the will has such ability and freedom. On the contrary, human will is enslaved to sin and evil and cannot decide to reverse itself and turn toward God.[84] In a vivid analogy, Luther pictured the will as a horse, on which one of only two riders may ride — God or Satan: "If God rides it, it wills and goes where God wills.... If Satan rides, it wills and goes where Satan wills. Nor may it choose to which rider it will run, or which it will seek; but the riders themselves fight to decide who shall have and hold it."[85] Thus, its evil rider, Satan, drives the will of unbelievers to sin, and there is no hope that any good can come from this desperate situation. Only God has the power to intervene, change the perverse will, and direct it toward himself and the good.[86]

This pervasive corruption of human nature is only one aspect of original sin: "By one sin Adam makes all those who are born of him guilty of this same sin of his and gives them what he has, though it is quite foreign to them.... Therefore, we are damned by a foreign sin."[87] Luther admitted the apparent unfairness of the notion that human beings are condemned for Adam's sin.[88] But biblical passages (Ps. 51:5; Eph. 2:3) persuaded Luther

---

83. Martin Luther, *Preface to the Complete Edition of Luther's Latin Writings (1945)*, cited in Roland H. Bainton, *Here I Stand: A Life of Martin Luther* (Peabody, Mass.: Hendrickson, 1977), 49–50; for a slightly different version, see ibid., LW, 34:336–37.

84. Martin Luther, *The Bondage of the Will*, trans. James I. Packer and O. R. Johnston (Old Tappan, N.J.: Revell, 1957), 273–78.

85. Ibid., 103–4.

86. The *Formula of Concord* expressed this strong view of human corruption in terms of total inability: "In spiritual and divine things the intellect, heart, and will of the unregenerate man are utterly unable, by their own natural powers, to understand, believe, accept, think, will, begin, effect, do, work, or concur in working anything, but they are entirely dead to what

is good, and corrupt, so that in man's nature since the Fall, before regeneration, there is not the least spark of spiritual power remaining, nor present, by which, of himself, he can prepare himself for God's grace, or accept the offered grace, nor be capable of it for and of himself, or apply or accommodate himself thereto, or by his own powers be able of himself, as of himself, to aid, do, work, or concur in working anything towards his conversion, either wholly, or half, or in any, even the least or most inconsiderable part." *Formula of Concord*, Solid Declaration 2.7, trans. F. Bente and W. H. T. Dan, in *Triglot Concordia: The Symbolical Books of the Evangelical Lutheran Church* (St. Louis: Concordia, 1921), 883.

87. Martin Luther, *WLS*, 3:1295.

88. Ibid.

of its truth.[89] Moreover, the thoroughgoing corruption within human beings becomes "the source and beginning of all the other sins.... From all this it is now clear and plain that original sin is nothing but the utter maliciousness and the inclination to evil that all human beings feel in themselves."[90] Paraphrasing Matthew 7:17, Luther observed: "We are not sinners because we commit sin—now this one, now that one—but we commit these acts because we are sinners before we do so; that is, bad tree and bad seed produce bad fruit, and from an evil root nothing but an evil tree can grow."[91] Accordingly, he urged: "Diligently learn the doctrine of original sin and do not argue about the reason why God permitted it.... Rather, ask how we may be saved and freed from the evil."[92]

Even as people saved from sin, believers remain thoroughly sinful. Luther explained this phenomenon as "at the same time righteous and a sinner" or "always righteous and a sinner."[93] That is, Christians enjoy salvation in Christ while still being weighed down with sin: "We are in truth and totally sinners, with regard to ourselves and our first birth. On the contrary, in so far as Christ has been given for us, we are totally holy and just. Thus, from different points of view we are said to be just and sinners at one and the same time."[94] Thus, the Lutheran doctrine of sin was well established.

Like Luther, John Calvin emphasized a view of sin that was strongly in line with that of Augustine. Discussing the fall of Adam, Calvin took Augustine's view about the first sin: Pride was at the heart of Adam's disobedience to the will of God. If he had not been puffed up with ambition, Adam would have lived forever in the upright state in which he had been originally created.[95] In addition to pride, another problem at the heart of our first parents' disobedience was unfaithfulness to the Word of God.[96] As a result of the fall, all the wonderful gifts that had characterized Adam as a being created in the image of God were lost. They were replaced by new traits—horrible "gifts" that belong not only to Adam, but to his descendants as well.

> After the heavenly image [the image of God] was obliterated in him [Adam], he was not the only one to suffer this punishment. In place of wisdom, virtue, holiness, truth, and justice—with which gifts he had been clothed—there came forth the most filthy plagues, blindness, impotence, impurity, vanity, and injustice. But he [Adam] also entangled and immersed his offspring in the same miseries. This is the inherited corruption, which the church fathers termed "original sin," meaning by the word "sin" the depravation of a nature previously good and pure.[97]

Citing Romans 5:12[98] and Psalm 51:5,[99] he concluded that "all of us who have descended from impure seed are born infected with the contagion of sin. In fact, before we saw the light of this life we were soiled and spotted in God's sight."[100]

---

89. Ibid., 1295–96.

90. Ibid., 1297.

91. Ibid., 1299.

92. *Lectures on Genesis: Chapters 38–44*, LW, 7:281.

93. *Lectures on Romans*, LW, 15:127; *Lectures on Galatians*, LW 27:230–231.

94. Cited in Timothy George, *Theology of the Reformers* (Nashville: Broadman, 1988), 71.

95. John Calvin, *Institutes of the Christian Religion*, 2.1.4, LCC, 1:245. The text has been rendered clearer.

96. Ibid.

97. Ibid., 2.1.5, LCC, 1:246.

98. Ibid., LCC, 1:247.

99. Ibid.

100. Ibid., LCC, 1:248. Job 14:4 is cited as further support.

But why is this so? Calvin rejected the view that sin is passed on from generation to generation through the transmission of a sinful nature from parents to children. Rather, he pictured Adam as the representative of humanity. As Adam went, so did his descendants:

> The Lord entrusted to Adam those gifts that he willed to be conferred upon human nature. Hence Adam, when he lost the gifts received, lost them not only for himself but for us all.... Adam had received for us no less than for himself those gifts which he lost, and they had not been given to one man but had been assigned to the whole human race. There is nothing absurd, then, in supposing that, when Adam was despoiled, human nature was left naked and destitute, or that when he was infected with sin, contagion crept into human nature. The beginning of corruption in Adam was such that it was conveyed in a perpetual stream from the ancestors into their descendants.[101]

Thus, he defined original sin as "a hereditary depravity and corruption of our nature, diffused into all parts of the soul, which first makes us liable to God's wrath, then also brings forth in us those works which Scripture calls 'works of the flesh' (Galatians 5:19)."[102]

Two important points are contained in this definition. "First, we are so vitiated and perverted in every part of our nature that by this great corruption we stand justly condemned and convicted before God, to whom nothing is acceptable but righteousness, innocence and purity. And this is not liability for another's transgression.... Since we through his sin have become entangled in the curse, he is said to have made us guilty."[103] Original sin renders people—including newborns—so depraved in their whole being that it brings God's judgment upon everyone.[104] Second, original sin is the fountainhead out of which more and more actual sins flow: "This perversity never ceases in us, but continually bears new fruits—the works of the flesh.... For our nature is not only destitute and empty of good, but so fertile and fruitful of every evil that it cannot be idle."[105] In saying this, Calvin clearly distanced himself from those who maintained that sin impacts part of human nature but leaves other aspects—the will, for example, or human reason—untouched. Thus, Calvin attacked the Pelagian view of sin, and the semi-Pelagian view did not escape his criticism either. His view is called *total depravity*: "All parts of the soul were possessed by sin after Adam deserted the fountain of righteousness. For not only did a lower appetite seduce him, but unspeakable impiety occupied the very citadel of his mind, and pride penetrated to the depths of his heart.... The whole man is overwhelmed—as by a deluge—from head to foot, so that no part is immune from sin and all that proceeds from him is to be imputed to sin."[106]

---

101. Ibid., 2.1.7, LCC, 1:249–50.

102. Ibid., 2.1.8, LCC, 1:251.

103. Ibid.

104. Speaking of infants: "For, even though the fruits of their iniquity [sin] have not yet come forth, they have the seed enclosed within them. Indeed, their whole nature is a seed of sin; hence it can only be hateful and abhorrent to God." Ibid.

105. Ibid., LCC, 1:251–52.

106. Ibid., 2.1.9, LCC, 1:252–53.

Like Augustine, Calvin disagreed with the prevailing view that the human will is free; thus, human beings cannot do any good in relationship to God and his kingdom. This view is called *total inability*: "Because of the bondage of sin by which the will is held bound, it cannot move toward good, much less apply itself to it; for a movement of this sort is the beginning of conversion to God, which in Scripture is ascribed entirely to God's grace.... Nonetheless, the will remains, with the most eager inclination disposed and hastening to sin."[107] Accordingly, a fallen person sins necessarily, but not—and Calvin underscores this point—under compulsion:

> For man, when he gave himself over to this necessity, was not deprived of will, but of soundness of will.... [M]an, as he was corrupted by the fall, sinned willingly, not unwillingly or by compulsion; by the most eager inclination of his heart, not by forced compulsion; by the prompting of his own lust, not by compulsion from the outside. Yet so depraved is his nature that he can be moved or impelled only to evil. If this is true, then it is clearly expressed that man is surely subject to the necessity of sinning.[108]

This means that Adam did not sin and fall by necessity. Of all human beings, he was the freest and could have used his will to continue in obedience and trust in God.[109] For Calvin, the reason that Adam misused his freedom was that his will was not firmly settled to choose only the good.[110] Although some may object that God is to blame for failing to give Adam a settled will, Calvin condemned the thought and underscored that the blame falls squarely and solely upon Adam: "It was in his [God's] own choice to give whatever he pleased. But the reason he did not sustain man by the virtue of perseverance lies hidden in his plan.... Yet he [Adam] is not excusable, for he received so much that he voluntarily brought about his own destruction."[111]

At the Council of Trent, the Roman Catholic Church did not distance itself at some points from the Protestant view of sin.[112] The difference showed up, rather, in the Catholic Church's affirmation of a role for the human will in salvation. Thus, the church denied total depravity and total inability, centerpieces of Luther and Calvin's view. The human will, even though fallen, is not totally vitiated by sin and maintains some ability to cooperate with God's grace in salvation. Accordingly, the council condemned key Reformation positions about the human will's role in escaping from sin.[113]

---

107. Ibid., 2.3.5, LCC, 1:294.

108. Ibid., LCC, 1:294–96.

109. Ibid., 1.15.8, LCC, 1:195.

110. Ibid.

111. Ibid., LCC, 1:196. Following Calvin's theology, confessions of faith such as the *Heidelberg Catechism*, the *Belgic Confession*, and the *Thirty-nine Articles* articulated the Reformed doctrine of sin. *Heidelberg Catechism*, 1st pt., q. 6–10, in Schaff, 3:309–10; *Belgic Confession*, art. 15, in Schaff, 3:400; *Thirty-nine Articles*, 9, in Schaff, 3:492.

112. E.g., the council condemned the following position: "If anyone does not confess that the first man Adam, when he had transgressed the commandment of God in paradise, immedi-

ately lost the holiness and righteousness wherein he had been constituted [created]; and that he incurred, through the offense of that prevarication [disobedience], the wrath and indignation of God, and consequently death, with which God had previously threatened him, and, together with death, captivity under his power who henceforth had the empire [power] of death, that is to say, the devil, and that the entire Adam, through that offense of prevarication [disobedience], was changed, in body and soul, for the worse; let him be anathema." *Canons and Decrees of the Council of Trent*, 5th session (June 17, 1546), *Decree Concerning Original Sin*, 1, in Schaff, 2:84–85.

113. *Canons and Decrees of the Council of Trent*, 6th session (January 13, 1547), *Canons on Justification*, 4, in Schaff, 2:111.

The Protestant view of sin was attacked not only by Catholic theology but by some Protestants as well. Socinianism returned to a Pelagian position on sin. Because it contradicts human reason, original sin is to be denied. According to the *Racovian Catechism*, Adam's act affected him and him alone: "The fall of Adam, as it was but one act, could not have power to deprave his nature, much less that of his posterity. I do not deny, however, that by the habit of sinning, the nature of man is infected with a certain stain, and a very strong disposition to wickedness."[114] Moreover, the *Catechism* was critical of the biblical passages used in support of original sin.[115] Furthermore, it denied that "Paul states in Romans 5:12 that all have sinned in Adam. It is not there said 'in Adam' all have sinned.... Paul asserts that 'death passed upon all men *since*, or *for that*, all have sinned.' But he speaks throughout not of original, but actual sin."[116] Thus, Socinianism rejected original sin, total depravity, and total inability.

Another challenge arose with Jacob Arminius and Arminianism. On one hand, Arminianism affirmed that original sin infects all people. Indeed, Arminius underscored the relationship between Adam and the rest of humanity, speaking of "sins that people perpetrated in Adam" and the plight of children who "sinned in the person of their first father Adam" and are "condemned for the sin of Adam."[117] He also expressed a strong view of total inability: "In his lapsed and sinful state, man is not capable, of and by himself, either to think, to will, or to do that which is really good."[118] On the other hand, Arminianism posited that the negative effects of original sin are removed for everyone by God's grace. This idea of prevenient grace was not new, but Arminianism applied it to human sin in a new way. Specifically, Arminius affirmed that original sin condemns no one "because God has taken the whole human race into the grace of reconciliation and has entered into a covenant of grace with Adam and with the whole of his posterity in him. In this he promises the remission of all sins to as many as stand firmly and do not deal treacherously in that covenant. Since infants have not broken this covenant, they do not seem to be liable to condemnation."[119] Thus, Arminianism affirmed humanity's solidarity with Adam in sin, guilt, depravity, and inability, but also posited prevenient grace from God that eliminated all these problems for all people until they reach the age of accountability.

114. *Racovian Catechism*, 5.10, trans. Thomas Rees (London, 1818; repr., Lexington, Ky.: American Theological Library Association, 1962), 326.

115. E.g., it attacked David's expression in Ps. 51:7: "It must be observed that David does not speak here of all men generally but of himself alone. In the next place, though he seems to speak of some innate propensity to sin, yet he does not refer the origin of it to Adam but only to his mother; as indeed, we see that a propensity to certain vices is derived from parents, although the remoter ancestors of those parents were not inclined to them. Nor does he [David] state this propensity to be such, that he was not able to abstain from the sins he is deploring ... had he chosen to create for himself the power." Ibid., 327.

116. Ibid., 328–30.

117. Jacob Arminius, *Apology against Thirty-one Defamatory Articles*, arts. 13–14, especially 13.1, 3, in James Arminius, *The Works of Jacob Arminius*, 3 vols., trans. James Nichols (Whitefish, Mont.: Kessinger, 2006), 1:318, 319. In this apology, Arminius responded to and rejected false doctrines attributed to him. In articles 13 and 14, he addressed the charge leveled against Borius, an accusation that Borius denied original sin. Arminius treated the accusation as an attack against him, so he in turn rebuffed the denial of original sin.

118. Jacob Arminius, "On the Free-Will of Man," *Declaration of Sentiments*, 3, in James Arminius, *Works*, 1:252.

119. Arminius, *Apology against Thirty-one Defamatory Articles*, arts. 13–14, 13.1, in James Arminius, *Works*, 1:318.

VIEWS OF SIN IN THE MODERN PERIOD

John Wesley added to this development with some important modifications. Affirming that Adam was the representative of humanity before God,[120] he explained what this representative role meant: "The state of all mankind so completely depended on Adam that, by his fall, they all fell into sorrow, and pain, and death—spiritual and temporal."[121] More specifically: "(1) Our bodies then became mortal. (2) Our souls died; that is, were disunited from God. Thus, (3) we are all born with a sinful, devilish nature. By reason of this, (4) we are children of wrath, liable to eternal death (Rom. 5:18; Eph. 2:3)."[122] Thus, original sin affects all people, including infants (this is why "they are proper subjects of baptism"[123]), and results in liability of divine condemnation.

Still, Wesley denied that any person "will be damned for this [Adam's sin] alone."[124] Something more than the liability from original sin is needed for God to justly punish people, and Wesley placed the blame on corrupt human nature that results in sinful behavior. As noted above, he affirmed "entire depravity and corruption, which by nature spreads itself over the whole person, leaving no part uninfected."[125] Out of this corrupt human nature, then, flow actual sins—both sins of commission and sins of omission.[126] For these actual sins, human beings become liable to divine punishment.

While affirming these elements, Wesley offered an Arminian modification to the doctrine of sin. He proposed that prevenient grace is given to all humanity to remove the disabilities due to corrupt human nature.[127] By means of overcoming the incapacitating

---

120. John Wesley, *The Doctrine of Original Sin*, 3.6, cited in Robert W. Burtner and Robert E. Chiles, eds., *A Compend of Wesley's Theology* (Nashville: Abingdon, 1954), 116.

121. Ibid.

122. John Wesley, *Minutes of Some Late Conversations*, June 25, 1744 (8:277), cited in Burtner and Chiles, *Compend of Wesley's Theology*, 117.

123. John Wesley, *On Baptism*, 4.2, cited in Albert C. Outler, ed. *John Wesley*. (New York: Oxford Univ. Press, 1966), 324.

124. John Wesley, *Predestination Calmly Considered*, 34, cited in Outler, *John Wesley*, 441.

125. John Wesley, "Romans 6:6," cited in Burtner and Chiles, *Compend of Wesley's Theology*, 120. Elsewhere, in a lengthy description, Wesley painted a picture of total depravity: "Know that you are corrupted in every power, in every faculty of your soul, that you are totally corrupted in every one of these, all the foundations being out of joint. The eyes of your understanding are darkened, so that they cannot discern God or the things of God. The clouds of ignorance and error rest upon you and cover you with the shadow of death. You know nothing yet as you should know—neither God, nor the world, nor yourself. Your will is no longer the will of God but is completely perverse and distorted, hateful of all good, of all which God loves, and prone to all evil, to every abomination that God hates. Your affections are alienated from God and scattered abroad over all the earth. All your passions—both

your desires and hates, your joys and sorrows, your hopes and fears—are out of joint. They are either wrong in degree or directed at wrong objects. So there is no soundness in your soul; rather, 'from the crown of the head to the sole of the foot' (to use the strong expression of the prophet) there are only 'wounds, and bruises, and putrefying sores' (Isa. 1:6)." John Wesley, *The Way to the Kingdom*, 2.1, cited in Burtner and Chiles, *Compend of Wesley's Theology*, 121.

126. Wesley, *Doctrine of Original Sin*, 2, cited in Burtner and Chiles, *Compend of Wesley's Theology*, 122. Wesley also referred to this original sin as "parent-sins, from which all the rest derive their being." John Wesley, *Upon Our Lord's Sermon on the Mount: 11*, 1.3, cited in Burtner and Chiles, *Compend of Wesley's Theology*, 123. In terms of sins of commission and sins of omission, see John Wesley, *The Wilderness State*, 3.2–4, cited in Burtner and Chiles, *Compend of Wesley's Theology*, 125.

127. "Every person has a greater or less measure of this [prevenient grace], which does not wait for his call. Sooner or later everyone has good desires, though the majority of people stifle them before they can strike deep root or produce any considerable fruit. Thus, no one sins because he lacks grace but because he does not use the grace that he has." John Wesley, *On Working Out Our Own Salvation*, 1.1 passim, cited in Burtner and Chiles, *Compend of Wesley's Theology*, 149.

effects of original sin, prevenient grace enables all people to pursue salvation. Commenting on Philippians 2:12–13, Wesley explained: "Given that God works in you, you are now able to work out your own salvation. Because he works in you of his own good pleasure, without any merits of yours, both to will and to do, it is possible for you to fulfill all righteousness."[128]

In keeping with this idea, Wesley embraced the notion of Christian perfection: In this lifetime, and as a result of God's powerful work of grace in one's life, "a Christian is so far perfect as not to commit sin." Part and parcel of this view was Wesley's distinction between "sin properly so called (that is, a voluntary transgression of a known law), but sin improperly so called (that is, an involuntary transgression of a divine law, known or unknown)."[129] Complete freedom from sin applies only to the first category, that of true or actual sin, but is not the case with the second category.[130] Thus, by circumscribing the common definition of sin, Wesley was able to envision a state of grace in this lifetime in which Christians do not willfully break any known laws; thus, they are perfect.

The doctrine of sin continued to be affirmed and explained by many in the church; at the same time, its historic articulation came under attack and was modified in various directions by others in the modern period. On the one hand, some theologians continued to embrace the solidarity of the human race with Adam and the implications of that solidarity for the imputation and transmission of the guilt and corruption of sin to all people. On the other hand, some decried this corporate notion and emphasized the reality of individual sin and guilt. Still others moved away from the theoretical idea of inherited sin that spells sinfulness for everyone and underscored the concrete reality of societal sin that alienates everyone through systemic evils. Finally, others grew weary of the concept of sin and essentially eliminated it as a topic of concern in the church. Modern voices who dissented from the traditional formulation included Immanuel Kant,[131] Friedrich Schleiermacher,[132] Søren Kierkegaard,[133] Paul Tillich,[134] and Jürgen Moltmann.[135]

---

128. John Wesley, *On Working Out Our Own Salvation*, 1.1 passim, cited in Burtner and Chiles, *Compend of Wesley's Theology*, 149.

129. John Wesley, *Thoughts on Christian Perfection*, q. 6, ans. 1, cited in Outler, *John Wesley*, 287.

130. "I believe there is no such perfection in this life as excludes these involuntary transgressions, which I apprehend to be naturally consequent on the ignorance and mistakes inseparable from mortality. Therefore 'sinless perfection' is a phrase I never use lest it should *seem* to contradict myself. I believe a person filled with the love of God is still liable to these involuntary transgressions. Such transgressions you may call sins if you please. I do not for several reasons." John Wesley, *Thoughts on Christian Perfection*, q. 6, ans. 3–6, cited in Outler, *John Wesley*, 287.

131. Immanuel Kant, *Religion within the Limits of Reason Alone*, trans. Theodore M. Greene and Hoyt H. Hudson (San Francisco: Harper & Row, 1960). Kant attempted to offer an a priori argument for the existence of universal sin. His starting point was the original predisposition to good in human nature.

132. Friedrich Schleiermacher, *The Christian Faith*, ed. H. R. Mackintosh and J. S. Stewart (Edinburgh: T & T Clark, 1928). He reconfigured the doctrine in light of his reformation of religion as the feeling of absolute dependence on God; thus, sin became the opposite of such consciousness.

133. Søren Kierkegaard, *The Sickness unto Death*, in Søren Kierkegaard, *Fear and Trembling and the Sickness unto Death*, trans. Walter Lowrie (Princeton: Princeton Univ. Press, 1941). Working within an existentialist framework, he reformulated the doctrine of sin in terms of individual despair.

134. Paul Tillich, *Systematic Theology*, 3 vols. (Chicago: Univ. of Chicago Press, 1957). Tillich recast the doctrine of sin in terms of existentialist philosophy.

135. Jürgen Moltmann, *Theology of Hope: On the Ground and the Implication of a Christian Eschatology*, 5th ed. (repr., San Francisco: HarperSanFrancisco, 1967). Borrowing from Joseph Pieper's *Über die Hoffnung*, Moltmann reformulated the concept of sin in terms of hopelessness.

Of particular note was the modern propensity to address sin more as a social phenomenon than as an individual problem. Walter Rauschenbusch, the father of the social gospel, articulated the view of sin from the standpoint of that gospel: "The social gospel seeks to bring men under repentance for their collective sins and to create a more sensitive and more modern conscience."[136] He claimed that whereas theology focuses on the doctrine of the fall, Jesus and the biblical writers (Paul is an exception) placed little importance on it. The social gospel would correct this misplaced emphasis.[137] Indeed, the element of selfishness—the preference of self to the common good—played an important role in his discussion.[138] Linking sin, selfishness, and antisocial behavior, Rauschenbusch emphasized the social dimension of sin.[139] Echoing some elements of the social gospel, liberation theology developed a concept of sin that was far from traditional, as Gustavo Gutiérrez explained: "In the liberation approach sin is not considered as an individual, private, or merely interior reality.... Sin is regarded as a social, historical fact ... evident in oppressive structures, in the exploitation of man by man, in the domination and slavery of peoples, races, and social classes. Sin appears, therefore, as the fundamental alienation, the root of a situation of injustice and exploitation."[140]

Still, discussions continued on the traditional formulation of the doctrine of sin and its many elements. For example, Charles Hodge and Herman Bavinck addressed the issue of Adam's relationship with the human race. Hodge noted both the natural headship of Adam—he was the physical head of all humanity—and the federal headship exercised by Adam: "Over and beyond this natural relation which exists between a man and his posterity, there was a special divine constitution by which he was appointed the head and representative of his whole race."[141] Corresponding to Hodge's natural headship position, Bavinck affirmed the realist view that "all of us were germinally present in Adam's loins, and all proceeded from that source.... The choice he made and the action he undertook were those of all his descendants. Certainly this physical oneness of the whole of humanity in Adam as such is of great importance for the explanation of original sin."[142] Yet, he explained further, "realism by itself is insufficient as an explanation of original sin.... [I]f Adam's trespass had been ours in this realistic sense, we would also be responsible for all the other sins of Adam, all the sins of Eve, even all the sins of all our ancestors, for we were included in them as much as in Adam when he violated the probationary command."[143] Thus, like Hodge, Bavinck turned to the federalist or representative view

136. Walter Rauschenbusch, *A Theology for the Social Gospel* (Nashville: Abingdon, 1978), 5.

137. Ibid., 42.

138. Ibid., 49.

139. "Sin is essentially selfishness. That definition is more in harmony with the social gospel than with any individualistic type of religion. The sinful mind, then, is the unsocial and antisocial mind. To find the climax of sin we must not linger over a man who swears, or sneers at religions, or denies the mystery of the trinity, but put our hands on social groups who have turned the patrimony of a nation into the private property of small class, or have left the peasant laborers cowed, degraded, demoralized, and without rights in the land. When we find such in history, or in present-day life, we shall know we have stuck real rebellion against God on the higher levels of sin." Ibid., 50.

140. Gustavo Gutiérrez, *A Theology of Liberation*, trans. and ed. Caridad Inda and John Eagleson (Maryknoll: Orbis, 1973), 175.

141. Charles Hodge, *Systematic Theology*, 3 vols. (1872–73; Peabody, Mass.: Hendrickson, 1999), 2:196–97.

142. Herman Bavinck, *Reformed Dogmatics*, ed. John Bolt, vol. 3: *Sin and Salvation in Christ* (Grand Rapids: Baker, 2006), 102.

143. Ibid., 102–3.

of the imputation of Adam's sin to account for the relationship between Adam's sin and the rest of humanity. This view does not rule out the realist view, but it does go beyond it.[144] According to this view, God constituted Adam the representative head of the entire human race; thus, "If Adam fell, humanity would fall."[145] So Bavinck affirmed the divine design: "In one person he [God] declares all guilty, and so humankind is born — unclean and in the process of dying — from Adam."[146]

Evangelicals joined in this discussion. Henri Blocher offered a nuanced interpretation of a key passage, arguing that "the role of Adam and of his sin in Romans 5 is to make possible the imputation, the judicial treatment, of human sins. His role thus brings about the condemnation of all, and its sequel, death."[147] Millard Erickson, while affirming that all people receive both corrupt nature and guilt with condemnation from Adam, distanced himself from the traditional Reformed position: "With this matter of guilt, however, just as with the imputation of Christ's righteousness, there must be some conscious and voluntary decision on our part. Until this is the case, there is only a conditional imputation of guilt."[148] So how do people become guilty before God?

> We become responsible and guilty when we accept or approve of our corrupt nature. There is a time in the life of each one of us when we become aware of our own tendency toward sin. At that point we may abhor the sinful nature that has been there all the time. But if we acquiesce in that sinful nature, we are in effect saying that it is good. By placing our tacit approval upon the corruption, we are also approving or concurring in the action in the Garden of Eden so long ago. We become guilty of that sin without having committed any sin of our own.[149]

Thus, Erickson embraced a conditional imputation of Adam's guilt for sin. Approaching the same issue, David Smith appealed to Ezekiel 18: "The father's sin will not be charged against his children; we may conclude, then, that God does not impute the sin of Adam against his posterity. Consequently, we may rule out the concept of inherited sin."[150] And what of guilt? "The Bible declares that every soul is guilty before God because of that individual's personal sin. Thus, divine condemnation occurs not for hereditary sin, but only for actual, personal sin."[151] Thus, Smith denied the traditional doctrine of the imputation of Adam's guilt for sin.

Moving away from such a focus on original sin, Cornelius Plantinga expanded the evangelical doctrine by looking at sin through new and creative metaphors in *Not the Way It's Supposed to Be*. For Plantinga, the way it is supposed to be, biblically speaking, is called *shalom*, meaning "universal flourishing, wholeness, and delight."[152] Sin, then, is anything that is against shalom. But Plantinga did not downplay the theological

---

144. Ibid., 103–4.

145. Ibid., 106.

146. Ibid. John Murray adopted a similar view in his *The Imputation of Adam's Sin* (Phillipsburg, N.J.: P & R, 1959).

147. Henri Blocher, *Original Sin: Illuminating the Riddle*, New Studies in Biblical Theology, ed. D. A. Carson (Grand Rapids: Eerdmans, 1997), 77 (italics removed).

148. Millard J. Erickson, *Christian Theology*, 2nd ed.

(Grand Rapids: Baker, 1998), 656.

149. Ibid.

150. David L. Smith, *With Willful Intent: A Theology of Sin* (Wheaton: Victor, 1994), 368.

151. Ibid.

152. Cornelius Plantinga, Jr., *Not the Way It's Supposed to Be: A Breviary of Sin* (Grand Rapids: Eerdmans, 1995), 10.

orientation of sin as anything that is against God. Indeed, "all sin has first and finally a Godward force.... Sin is a culpable and personal affront to a personal God."[153] Without minimizing this theological focus, Plantinga insisted there is more to sin: "God hates sin not just because it violates his law but, more substantively, because it violates shalom, because it breaks the peace, because it interferes with the way things are supposed to be.... Shalom is God's design for creation and redemption; sin is blamable human vandalism of these great realities and therefore an affront to their architect and builder."[154] Using several creative metaphors, Plantinga presented sinful corruption as "an unhappy cluster of spiritual perversion, pollution, and disintegration."[155] Furthermore, a dismal reality of corruption is its tendency to progress. According to Plantinga, this progress of corruption results in two seemingly contradictory ends—fatality and fertility.[156] To this discussion, Plantinga added other metaphors for sin: parasite, masquerade, folly, addiction, and attack and flight.[157]

As the third millennium unfolds, evangelicals continue to affirm the doctrine of sin while expressing it in light of new developments in theology, biblical understanding, and social consciousness.[158]

---

153. Ibid., 13.

154. Ibid., 14, 16.

155. Ibid., 29; specifically for each metaphor, see 40–41, 43–45, and 45–47.

156. Ibid., 53–54.

157. Ibid., 87–88, 98, 119, 147, 153, 197.

158. E.g., the evangelical affirmation of the fall has been expressed afresh: "Because of Adam's fall, all became sinners and stand under God's righteous judgement. Human rebellion against God shows itself today in many ways: such as in atheistic denials of God's existence; in functional atheism that concedes God's existence but denies his relevance to personal conduct; in oppression of the poor and helpless; in occult concepts of reality; in the abuse of earth's resources; and in theories of an accidental naturalistic evolutionary origin of the universe and human life; and in many other ways." "Creation and Fall," in *Evangelical Affirmations*, ed. Kenneth S. Kantzer and Carl F. H. Henry (Grand Rapids: Zondervan, 1990), 31.

Part 4

THE DOCTRINES OF CHRIST AND THE HOLY SPIRIT

THE PERSON OF JESUS CHRIST

How has the church developed its understanding that Jesus Christ is fully God and fully man yet one person?

STATEMENT OF BELIEF

The church has historically believed that "Jesus Christ was fully God and fully man in one person, and will be so forever."[1] His deity is demonstrated by his own claims supported by his divine attributes and miraculous activities. His humanity is demonstrated by the virgin birth and his human attributes, activities, relationships, trials, and temptations. One peculiarity of his humanity was sinlessness, but this did not make him something other than human. Along with affirming the two natures of Jesus Christ, the church has also insisted that it was necessary for him to be fully God and fully man if he was to accomplish salvation for all of humanity.

In spite of this consistent and widespread belief, the church has had to face, and continues to face, numerous challenges to its view. At times some have denied the full deity of Christ. At other times, the full humanity of Jesus was denied. At still other times, some have viewed him as a kind of mixture of deity and humanity—a "divinehuman" Jesus Christ, so to speak. However, with each challenge, the church has responded with a defense of its historic belief.

When it comes to the person of Jesus Christ, the Roman Catholic Church, the Orthodox Church, and Protestant churches share a common belief. Although each might have slightly different emphases, a remarkable agreement exists about Jesus Christ. Evangelicals share this common heritage. Thus, while tracing the development of the doctrine of Jesus Christ, this chapter will mark the unity of this belief and contrast it with the various erroneous views that have arisen over the course of the centuries.[2]

---

1. Wayne Grudem, *Systematic Theology: An Introduction to Biblical Doctrine* (Grand Rapids: Zondervan, 1994, 2000), 529.

2. My thanks to Tyler Wittman for his help on this chapter.

VIEWS OF JESUS CHRIST IN THE EARLY CHURCH

The New Testament gives many testimonies about the person of Jesus Christ, from those who knew him best, to his enemies, and even from Jesus himself. Both Matthew (1:18–25) and Luke (1:28–35) recount his virgin birth, or better, his virginal conception. Yet even before he was born as the human Jesus of Nazareth, he had existed—indeed, had always existed—as the Word of God (John 1:1). It was this eternal Word who became incarnate (John 1:14). The incarnation involved the divine Son of God leaving his prerogative of glory shared with the Father in heaven, humbling himself, and becoming a man among humans (Phil. 2:6–11). Thus, Jesus Christ was the God-man.

After the witness of the New Testament, the early church continued to bear testimony to this God-man. Ignatius affirmed that "God appeared in human form to bring the newness of eternal life";[3] thus, he encouraged unity in "Jesus Christ, who physically was a descendant of David, who is Son of man and Son of God."[4] As the *Letter to Diognetus* explained, the Creator did not send "some subordinate, or angel or ruler or one of those who manage earthly matters, or one of those entrusted with the administration of things in heaven, but the Designer and Creator of the universe himself, by whom he created the heavens ... [and] the earth.... He sent him as God; he sent him as a man to men."[5]

Tragically, one of the earliest heresies the church faced was the denial of the full humanity of Jesus. Indeed, the apostle John warned against this erroneous view—the refusal to acknowledge "that Jesus Christ has come in the flesh" (1 John 4:1–3). Known as *Docetism*—from the Greek word for *seem* or *appear*—this view held that Jesus only seemed to be a man. The Docetists believed he was a spirit being, only appearing as a human being. Countering this heresy, Ignatius insisted that Jesus Christ was truly human because he experienced the true activities of human beings: "He really was born, who both ate and drank; who really was persecuted under Pontius Pilate; who really was crucified and died ... who, moreover, really was raised from the dead when his Father raised him up.... But if, as some atheists (that is, unbelievers) say, he suffered in appearance only ... why am I in chains? And why do I want to fight with wild beasts? If that is the case, I die for no reason."[6] Ignatius's last point raised the question of why he, a follower of Jesus, was suffering—in reality!—if Jesus had not been human—in reality. But Jesus "is truly of the family of David with respect to human descent, and the Son of God with respect to the divine will and power."[7]

Docetism became part and parcel of *Gnosticism*, a complex group of movements that focused on a secret *gnosis*, or knowledge, that was reserved for the elite members of its sects. Because Gnosticism drove a wedge between spiritual realities—which are inherently good—and physical realities—which are inherently evil—these movements could

---

3. Ignatius, *Letter to the Ephesians*, 19, in Holmes, 150; *ANF*, 1:57.

4. Ibid., 20, in Holmes, 151; *ANF*, 1:58. Ignatius even concluded one of his letters: "I bid you farewell always in our God Jesus Christ." Ignatius, *Letter to Polycarp*, 8, in Holmes, 201; *ANF*, 1:96.

5. *Letter to Diognetus*, 7, in Holmes, 543–45; *ANF*, 1:27.

6. Ignatius, *Letter to the Trallians*, 9–10, in Holmes, 165; *ANF*, 1:69–70.

7. Ignatius, *Letter to the Smyrnaeans*, 1, in Holmes, 185; *ANF*, 1:86.

not accept the church's contention that the Son of God took on human flesh. This would have meant that God, who is spiritual and thus good, had a body, which is physical and thus evil. To counter the church's affirmation, several heretical gospels were circulated by the Gnostics. These included the *Gospel of Thomas*, the *Gospel of Judas*, and the *Gospel of Peter*. Church leaders rejected these writings, which were falsely attributed to apostles.[8] The early church was united in its strong opposition to Gnosticism and its major tenet Docetism as expressed in these falsely named gospels.

Early Christian writers continually affirmed that Jesus Christ was both fully God and fully man, and that the incarnation did not diminish the deity of the Son of God nor make him a superman. Melito of Sardis described this mystery:

> Though he [the Son of God] was incorporeal, he formed for himself a body like ours. He appeared as one of the sheep, yet he remained the Shepherd. He was esteemed a servant, yet he did not renounce being a Son. He was carried about in the womb of Mary, yet he was clothed in the nature of his Father. He walked on the earth, yet he filled heaven. He appeared as an infant, yet he did not discard his eternal nature. He was invested with a body, but it did not limit his divinity. He was esteemed poor, yet he was not divested of his riches. He needed nourishment because he was man, yet he did not cease to nourish the entire world because he is God. He put on the likeness of a servant, yet it did not impair the likeness of his Father. He was everything by his unchangeable nature. He was standing before Pilate, and at the same time he was sitting with his Father. He was nailed on a tree, yet he was the Lord of all things.[9]

While some critics found this kind of talk to be "not merely paradoxical, but also foolish,"[10] Justin Martyr reaffirmed this view of Jesus: "He was the only begotten of the Father of all things, being begotten in a particular manner as the Word and Power by [God], and having afterwards become man through the Virgin."[11] Thus, the early church affirmed that the Son of God had always existed, owing his eternal existence to the Father—thus, he was the only begotten of the Father. Having existed always, he became incarnate as a man through his birth by the Virgin Mary. Simply put, he was "truly man" and he was "truly God."[12]

The early church insisted that this union of the divine and human was necessary to accomplish the salvation of humanity. Irenaeus countered *Ebionism*, another early heretical movement that denied the incarnation and insisted that Jesus was only a man in whom the presence and power of God worked mightily. Irenaeus wondered: "How can they be saved unless it was God who worked out their salvation upon earth? Or how shall man pass into God, unless God has [first] passed into man?"[13] He added: "For no one

---

8. Eusebius, *Ecclesiastical History*, 6.12.2, in *Eusebius' Ecclesiastical History*, trans. Christian Frederick Cruse (Grand Rapids: Baker, 1962), 231-32.

9. Melito of Sardis, *From the Discourse on the Cross*, in *ANF*, 8:756. The text has been rendered clearer. Cf. Irenaeus, *Against Heresies*, 3.16.6, in *ANF*, 1:443.

10. Justin Martyr, *Dialogue with Trypho, a Jew*, 48, in *ANF*, 1:219.

11. Ibid., 105, in *ANF*, 1:251.

12. Irenaeus, *Against Heresies*, 4.6.7, in *ANF*, 1:469.

13. Ibid., 4.33.7, in *ANF*, 1:507.

can forgive sins but God alone; while the Lord forgave them and healed men, it is clear that he was himself the Word of God made the Son of man, receiving from the Father the power to forgive sins. He was man and he was God, in order that since as man he suffered for us, so as God he might have compassion on us, and forgive our sins."[14] On this basis, Novatian urged people to confess Christ to be God: "Whoever does not acknowledge him to be God would lose salvation, which he could not find elsewhere than in Christ God."[15]

Proof of the deity of Jesus Christ consisted in many points. One was the fact that he is worshiped, an activity that is reserved for God alone.[16] Included in this worship is honoring the Son through directing prayers to him, further evidence of Christ's deity.[17] For biblical support, Old Testament prophecies fulfilled in Jesus were marshaled.[18] Jesus' own testimony and miracles provided additional confirmation.[19] The divine attributes — omnipotence,[20] omniscience,[21] and omnipresence[22] — belonging to the Son were also used to shore up support. Other reasons for considering Jesus Christ to be God included his claim to have come from heaven, his granting of immortality, his preexistence, his eternality, and his claim to be one with the Father. From this evidence about the Son, Novatian concluded: "He is God, but God in such a manner as to be the Son, not the Father."[23] And Hippolytus noted, "He who is over all, the blessed God, has been born; and having been made man, he is still God forever."[24]

Tragically, other heresies in the early church denied the full deity of the Son, including the particularly widespread *Arianism*, named for its founder. Arius believed that God, being one and only one, could never share his being with anyone or anything else.[25] To do so would mean there are two gods, but by definition God is absolutely unique. Moreover, this eternal and unbegotten God created a Son; thus, the Son is a created being: "[God] begat an only-begotten Son before eternal times.... He made him exist at his own will,

---

14. Ibid., 5.17.3, in *ANF*, 1:545. The text has been rendered clearer.

15. Novatian, *Treatise Concerning the Trinity*, 12, in *ANF*, 5:621.

16. Justin Martyr, *First Apology*, 13, in *ANF*, 1:166–67; *Second Apology*, 13, in *ANF*, 1:193.

17. Origen, *Against Celsus*, 5.4, in *ANF*, 4:544. As Origen explained: "We worship with all our power the one God, and his only Son, the Word and the Image of God, by prayers and supplications; and we offer our petitions to the God of the universe through his only begotten Son. To the Son we first present them, and beseech [plead with] him, as 'the propitiation for our sins,' and our High Priest, to offer our desires, and sacrifices, and prayers, to the Most High. Our faith, therefore, is directed to God through his Son, who strengthens it in us.... We honor the Father when we admire his Son." Ibid., 8.13, in *ANF*, 4:644.

18. Justin Martyr, *Dialogue with Trypho*, 76, in *ANF*, 1:237.

19. Origen, *Against Celsus*, 8.9; 8.12, in *ANF*, 4:642–44.

20. Origen, *First Principles*, 1.2.10, 12, in *ANF*, 4:250–51.

21. Origen, *Commentary on the Gospel of John*, 1.27, in *ANF*, 10:313.

22. Origin argued that the Son was never confined to any one place: "This Son of God, in respect of the Word being God, which was in the beginning with God, no one will logically suppose to be contained in any place.... It is distinctly shown that the divinity of the Son of God was not shut up in some place.... We are not to suppose that all the majesty of his divinity was confined within the limits of his slender body, so that all the 'Word' of God ... was either torn away from the Father, or restrained and confined within the narrowness of his bodily person, and is not to be considered to have operated anywhere else." Origen, *First Principles*, 4.1.28–30, in *ANF*, 4:377. The text has been rendered clearer. Biblical evidence cited by Origen included Matt. 18:20 and 28:20. Origen, *Against Celsus*, 2.9, in *ANF*, 4:434.

23. Novatian, *Treatise on the Trinity*, 15, in *ANF*, 5:624–25.

24. Hippolytus, *Against the Heresy of One Noetus*, 6, in *ANF*, 5:225. The text has been rendered clearer.

25. "We acknowledge one God, the only unbegotten, the only eternal, the only one without beginning, the only true, the only one who has immortality, the only wise, the only good, the only sovereign." Arius, *Letter to Alexander*, in *NPNF²*, 4:458. The text has been rendered clearer.

unalterable and unchangeable. He was a perfect creature of God, but not as one of the creatures; he was a perfect offspring, but not as one of things begotten.... At the will of God, he was created before times and before ages, and gaining life and being from the Father."[26] Furthermore, God created the entire universe and all that is in it through the Son. Therefore, "We consider that the Son has this prerogative [to be called 'Son'] over others, and therefore is called Only-begotten, because he alone was brought into existence by God alone, and all other things were created by God through the Son."[27] Despite granting the Son this uniqueness, Arius maintained that the Son is nonetheless a created being.

This idea meant for Arius that there was a time when the Son did not exist: "The Son, being begotten apart from time by the Father, and being created and founded before ages, did not exist before his generation." Accordingly, the Son "is not eternal or co-eternal or co-unoriginate with the Father."[28] Another implication for Arius was that the Son has a different nature than the Father; that is, the Son is *heteroousios*—of a different substance—not *homoousios*—of the same substance—as the Father.[29]

Arius developed "biblical" support for his position. As "the firstborn of all creation," the Son is a created being (Col. 1:15). Moreover, when Jesus prayed to the Father that the disciples "may know you, the only true God," he admitted that there is only one God, and Jesus is not he (John 17:3). Furthermore, Jesus himself affirmed, "the Father is greater than I" (John 14:28). Finally, Jesus admits to an imperfection—he lacks omniscience, not knowing the time of his own return—thus indicating that he is not God (Mark 13:32). As for titles such as "God" and "Son of God," when they are applied by the biblical writers to the Son, they are simply terms of respect and do not indicate that he is divine.[30] Proverbs 8:22–31 was cited because several of its expressions—"the Lord created me" and "before the age he established me"—were understood by Arius to refer to the Son. Arius considered this to be a strong case for his view of the Son of God.

The church became alarmed at Arius's teachings, but it was actually the state that intervened to deal with the situation.[31] When the emperor Constantine became aware of this theological argument, he feared division within the Roman Empire over which he ruled and so convened a meeting to investigate the matter. The Council of Nicea, held in 325, became the first ecumenical, or general, council because it gathered together representatives from churches throughout the empire to decide a theological issue. Three parties were present at the council: a small pro-Arian party, a small anti-Arian party, and

---

26. Ibid. The text has been rendered clearer.

27. Athanasius, *Defense of the Nicene Council*, 3.7, in *NPNF*[2], 4:154. The text has been rendered clearer.

28. Arius, *Letter to Alexander*, in *NPNF*[2], 4:458. The text has been rendered clearer.

29. Arius believed that if the Father and the Son shared the same essence, and the Son received that nature from the Father, it would mean that God is "compounded and divisible and alterable and material." But by definition, God is not like that. Ibid.

30. Thus, Athanasius complained about the Arians calling Christ the "Son of God": "What is this but to deny that he is very Son, and only in name to call him Son at all? Athanasius,

Four Discourses against the Arians, 1.5.15, in *NPNF*[2], 4:315.

31. Prior to the Council of Nicea, early in 325, a synod met in Antioch and set forth the belief that Christ was divine and anathematized the view of Arius. The statement of belief described Christ as "not made but properly an offspring, but begotten in an ineffable, indescribable manner." Indeed, he "exists eternally and did not at one time not exist." The section of condemnation was directed against "those who say or think or preach that the Son of God is a creature or has come into being or has been made and is not truly begotten, or that there was a then [time] when he did not exist." Creed of Antioch, 9, 13, in Pelikan, 1:200–201.

a large undecided party. A creed favorable to Arianism was immediately rejected by the council. Eusebius of Caesarea put forth a baptismal creed recited in his church, and this may have been a basis for the Creed of Nicea that eventually was produced.[32]

The Creed of Nicea (325)

We believe ... in one Lord Jesus Christ, the Son of God, begotten of the Father, only-begotten, that is, of the substance of the Father, God of God, light of light, true God of true God, begotten not made, of one substance with the Father, through whom all things were made, things in heaven and things on earth; who for us men and for our salvation came down and was made flesh, and became man, suffered, and rose again on the third day, ascended into the heavens, is coming to judge the living and dead.*

> *Creed of Nicea, in Schaff, 2:60; Bettenson, 27–28. The Creed of Nicea was crafted to express the full deity of Christ in contrast with the Arian belief. The affirmations that Christ was "begotten of the Father," "only-begotten," and "begotten not made" were intended to distinguish the existence of the Son from that of all creatures: They all had been made, but the Son is not a created being. In a completely unique way, the Father had begotten the Son, and begotten him alone. As Eusebius of Caesarea later explained: "[We allowed the expression] 'begotten, not made,' since the Council alleged that 'made' was an appellative common to the other creatures which came into existence through the Son, to whom the Son had no likeness. Therefore ... he was not a work resembling the things which through him came into existence, but was of an essence which is too high for the level of any work." Eusebius of Caesarea, *Letter* 6, in *NPNF*[2], 4:75. It should be noted that Athanasius appended this letter to his *Defense of the Nicene Council* (written about 350). Similarly, the statements that the Son is "of the substance of the Father" and "of one substance with the Father" were intended to set off the Son from all creatures and to affirm that he shares the same nature as the Father. Again, Eusebius explained: "'One in essence with the Father' suggests that the Son of God bears no resemblance to the originated creatures, but that to his Father alone who begat him is he in every way assimilated, and that he is not of any other existence and essence, but from the Father." Eusebius of Caesarea, *Letter* 7, *NPNF*[2], 4:75–76. Furthermore, being *homoousios*—of the same essence—with the Father means that the Son is fully God. As Athanasius later commented: "They [the council participants] meant that the Son was from the Father, and not merely like, but the same in likeness ... since the generation of the Son from the Father is not according to the nature of men, and not only like, but also inseparable from the essence of the Father, and he and the Father are one." Athanasius, *Defense of the Nicene Council*, 5.20, in *NPNF*[2], 4:163–64. Indeed, the council affirmed that the Son is "God of God, light from light, true God of true God."

Not only did the Council of Nicea affirm the full deity of the Son; it also condemned specific Arian beliefs as heretical.[33] Only two of the more than three hundred theologians attending the council joined Arius in refusing to sign the creed. Arius was banished with

---

32. According to Bettenson, this was the case. Bettenson, 27. But Kelly takes issue with this view. Kelly, 229.

33. Using the words and expressions of Arianism, the council anathematized, or condemned, the following: "And those who say, 'There was [a time] when he did not exist,' and 'Before he was begotten he did not exist,' and that 'He came into existence from nothingness,' or those who allege that the Son of God is 'of another substance or essence' or 'created' or 'changeable' or 'alterable,' these [people] the catholic and apostolic church anathematizes." Creed of Nicea, in Bettenson, 28. The text has been rendered clearer.

the warning to cease and desist from teaching his heretical views. The church would press on with a firmly established belief in the full deity of the Son of God.

In 328 Arius himself avoided further censure by offering a creed that carefully avoided the controversial doctrines about Christ. This eventually led to his reinstatement by the emperor. Also, the change in emperors resulted in the flourishing of the Arian faith.[34] Indeed, Jerome later complained, "The whole world groaned and marveled to find itself Arian."[35] As Arianism dominated, Athanasius championed the Nicene faith and found himself exiled five times for his defense of it. He insisted that if salvation is the forgiveness of sins and the imparting of divine life into sinful people, then the Son had to be fully God in order to become human to save.[36] This conviction led him to denounce the Arian view of Christ as creature: "If the Word were a creature, how could he have power to undo God's judgment and to forgive sin, since ... this is God's prerogative only?"[37] Moreover, Athanasius insisted against the Arians that the Son is eternal.[38] Furthermore, he twisted an Arian argument to prove that, just as parents give birth to children in their image, so also the Son shares the same nature as the Father.[39] Thus, "the Son is different in kind and different in essence from created things. Instead, he is proper to the Father's essence and is one in nature with him."[40] Finally, while affirming that the Son is of the same nature as the Father, Athanasius also insisted that the two are distinct from each other. In saying this, he avoided the heresy of *modalism*, or *Sabellianism*, which believed that "Father" and "Son" are merely different names for the one God who revealed himself at different times by those names. As a consequence, this heresy did not hold that the two are distinct persons.[41] Athanasius avoided this error by emphasizing that the unity of nature between Father and Son did not make them the same.[42] In these ways, Athanasius

---

34. Although Constantine was firmly on the side of the Nicene faith, one of his sons, Constantius, was firmly on the side of Arianism while his other son, Constans, followed in his father's footsteps. Thus, when Constantine died in 337 and the empire was divided into East and West, Constantius encouraged Arianism in the Eastern part of the empire while Constans reinforced the Nicene faith in the western part. After the death of Constans in 350, Constantius took over the entire empire. As a result, the Arian faith flourished.

35. Jerome, *Dialogue against Luciferianos*, 19, in Kelly, 238. The bans against Arianism were lifted and an extreme view of the Son's subordination to the Father reigned. Shockingly, it was argued that "it is the Catholic doctrine that there are two persons of the Father and the Son, and that the Father is greater and that the Son is subordinated to the Father." Second Creed of Sirmium, in Hilary of Poitiers, *On the Synod*, 11, in Kelly, 285–86. Also, the Nicene affirmation that the Son is *homoousios* with the Father was outlawed. Indeed, some Arians insisted that the Son is *anomoios*—unlike—the Father because he is unbegotten, while the Son is begotten.

36. Athanasius, *Councils of Ariminum and Seleucia*, 3.51, in *NPNF*[2], 4:477.

37. Athanasius, *Four Discourses against the Arians*, 2.67, in

NPNF[2], 4:385. The text has been rendered clearer.

38. For Athanasius, the Scriptures prohibit "in every light the Arian heresy, and signify the eternity of the Word, and that he is not foreign but proper to the Father's essence. For when has anyone ever seen a light without radiance? Or who dares to say that the expression can be different from the substance? Or has not a man himself lost his mind who even entertains the thought that God was ever without his Word and Wisdom?" Athanasius, *Four Discourses against the Arians*, 2.32, in *NPNF*[2], 4:365. The text has been rendered clearer.

39. Athanasius, *Four Discourses against the Arians*, 1.26, in *NPNF*[2], 4:322.

40. Ibid., 1.58, in *NPNF*[2], 4:340. The text has been rendered clearer. Indeed, Athanasius affirmed that "the divinity of the Father is identical with the divinity of the Son" and, conversely, that "the divinity of the Son is the divinity of the Father." Athanasius, *Four Discourses against the Arians*, 1.61; 3.41, in *NPNF*[2], 4:341, 416. The text has been rendered clearer.

41. For an extended discussion of this, see chap. 11 on the Trinity.

42. Athanasius, *Four Discourses against the Arians*, 3.4, in *NPNF*[2], 4:395.

did much to champion the Nicene faith and developed the early church's theology of the identity of the divine nature and the distinction between the Father and Son.

But it was the moderate majority of the church, which had been represented by the undecided party at the council itself, which eventually reacted to the excesses of Arianism and embraced Athanasius's theology.[43] This view ultimately gave way to full support for the Nicene faith through the encouragement of the emperors Gratian and Theodosius I. At the second ecumenical, or general, council of the church—the Council of Constantinople, in 381—the Creed of Nicea was modified slightly as the Nicene-Constantinopolitan Creed. The Nicene Creed, as it is called, expressed complete belief in the full deity of the Son. Thus, the Nicene faith was reaffirmed and Arianism was defeated.

The Nicene Creed (381)

We believe ... in one Lord Jesus Christ, the only-begotten Son of God, begotten of the Father before all the ages, Light of Light, true God of true God, begotten not made, of one substance with the Father, through whom all things were made; who for us men and for our salvation came down from the heavens, and was made flesh of the Holy Spirit and the Virgin Mary, and became man, and was crucified for us under Pontius Pilate, and suffered and was buried, and rose again on the third day according to the Scriptures, and ascended into the heavens, and sat down on the right hand of the Father, and will come again with glory to judge living and dead, of whose kingdom there shall be no end.*

*Nicene Creed, in Schaff, 2:58–59; Bettenson, 28–29.

While settling the issue of the deity of the Son, the church soon had to face another one. This issue concerned the relationship between the divine nature of Jesus Christ—now firmly established—and his human nature. As we have seen, the early church had taken a strong stand against Docetism and Ebionism, heresies that denied the humanity of Jesus Christ. But while affirming both his deity and his humanity, the church had not yet addressed how those two natures could exist in one person.

While joining in the fight against Arianism, Apollinarius expressed an unusual idea about the incarnate Son. He referred to Christ as the "flesh-bearing God"[44] and encouraged "a single worship of the Word and the flesh that he assumed."[45] That is, in taking on human nature, the Word became united with a body only.[46] His focus on the assumption

---

43. At first they accepted a compromise view focusing on the word *homoiousios* in place of the key Nicene word *homoousios* (note the change of one letter). Although not ready to agree that the Son was *homoousios*—of the same essence as the Father—they did affirm that the Son was *homoiousios*—of a similar essence as the Father. As Cyril of Jerusalem stated of the Son, "In all things the Son is *like* him who begat him." Cyril of Jerusalem, *Catechetical Lectures*, 11.18, in *NPNF²*, 7:69.

44. Gregory of Nazianzus, *Letter* 102, in *NPNF²*, 7:444.

45. Apollinarius, *Detailed Confession of Faith*, 28. Hans Lietzman, *Appolinaris von Laodicea und Seine Schule: Texte und Untersuchungen* (Tübingen: J. C. B. Mohr [Paul Siebeck], 1904), 177, cited in Pelikan, 1:239.

46. Apollinarius's biblical basis was a woodenly literal understanding of John 1:14. Gregory of Nazianzus, *Letter* 101, in *NPNF²*, 7:442. Gregory complained that Apollinarius had misinterpreted the verse. "They who reason in this way do not

of flesh revealed Apollinarius's restricted view of the human nature of Christ: It consisted of only a human body but not a human soul. Indeed, his soul was replaced with the divine Word.[47] In other words, Jesus was not an ordinary human being. And Apollinarius admitted as much, citing Philippians 2:7–8 as support.[48]

The church's reaction to Apollinarius's view was swift and focused on several key points. Gregory of Nazianzus charged it with bordering on Docetism with an understanding of Christ's flesh "as a phantom rather than a reality."[49] Thus, the humanity assumed by the Word—according to Apollinarianism—was not true human nature. Indeed, if Christ lacked an essential component of human nature—a soul that included the mind and the will—it was incorrect to call him human at all.[50] The church also denied the premise on which Apollinarianism was founded. It was not impossible for two distinct natures—divine and human—to unite together in one person. Instead, the church affirmed the reality of the unity of God and perfect, complete man in the one person Jesus Christ.[51] Most importantly, the church objected that the Apollinarian God-man failed to accomplish the salvation of humanity. Gregory of Nazianzus set forth this important principle: "If anyone has put his trust in him [Christ] as a man without a human mind, he has really lost his mind, and is completely unworthy of salvation. For that which he [Christ] has not assumed he has not healed; but that which is united to his deity is also saved."[52] In other words, if Christ took on only part of human nature in his incarnation, he could only save that part. But the entirety of human nature fell in Adam; thus, salvation of the entire person is necessary. This leads to a need for the Savior to be fully human.[53] By holding forth a Savior who is only partially human—lacking a human soul, with its mind and will—Apollinarianism offered a salvation that was also partial.

The church would not stand for such a view. In several synods and ultimately at the Council of Constantinople in 381, Apollinarianism was condemned as a heresy. As we will see, the Creed of Chalcedon, written in 451, expressly denied the Apollinarian error. The Savior was a true and complete human being, with body, soul, mind, and will.

Others besides Apollinarius did not see the God-man this way. Another controversy broke out involving Nestorius, the patriarch of Constantinople. Nestorius was asked to

know that this expression is a synecdoche, a part of speech that describes the whole by referring to a part of it." The text has been rendered clearer. In other words, "flesh" in John 1:14 did indeed refer to the physical body assumed by Jesus Christ, but it stood for the whole of human nature—soul, mind, will and body—not just part of it, that Christ took on.

47. Apollinarius, *Fragment* 107, in Lietzman, *Appolinaris von Laodicea und seine Schule*, 232; cf. Kelly, 291–92.

48. Gregory of Nazianzus, *Letter* 102, in *NPNF²*, 7:444.

49. Ibid.

50. "But if he [Christ] has a soul, and yet is without a [human] mind, how is he man, for man is not a mindless animal?... But, says [Apollinarius], the deity took the place of the human mind. How does this relate to me? For deity joined to flesh alone is not man." Gregory of Nazianzus, *Letter* 101, in *NPNF²*, 7:440. The text has been rendered clearer.

51. As Gregory affirmed: "We do not sever the humanity from the deity, but we lay down as a sure doctrine the unity and identity of the person. From of old he was not man but God, and the only Son before all ages, unmingled with body or anything physical. However, in these last days he has also assumed manhood [human nature] for our salvation: passible [able to suffer] in his flesh, but impassible in his deity; limited as to space in the body, but omnipresent in the Spirit. At one and the same time he is earthly and heavenly, tangible and intangible, comprehensible and incomprehensible. The purpose was that by one and the same person, who was perfect man and also God, the entire humanity fallen through sin might be recreated." Ibid., in *NPNF²*, 7:439. The text has been rendered clearer.

52. Ibid., in *NPNF²*, 7:440. The text has been rendered clearer.

53. Ibid.

comment on the traditional title for the Virgin Mary—*theotokos*. Literally translated, the word is "God bearer," reflecting the belief that the one who was conceived in the womb and born of Mary was fully divine.[54] Uncomfortable with affirming *theotokos* without also affirming that Mary was *anthropotokos*—"man-bearing"—or, better still, *christotokos*—"Christ-bearing"—Nestorius found himself in trouble. On the one hand, to deny Mary as *theotokos* would fly in the face of a traditional church belief. On the other hand, Nestorius could not allow that God had a mother, that God was conceived and nurtured in a womb for nine months, that God was born, or that God suffered and died.

Nestorius's reluctance to unreservedly affirm Mary as *theotokos* drew the concerned attention of the church. In particular, Cyril of Alexandria attacked him, pinning on Nestorius a heretical view that he vigorously denied holding.[55] Two principal tenets of Nestorianism were eventually condemned. The first was the view that Jesus Christ is composed of two distinct and independent persons who work in conjunction with each other.[56] The second was that a true union of divine and human would have involved God in change and suffering, which is impossible. It also would have made it impossible for Jesus Christ as man to experience true human existence. Cyril responded to this Nestorian position by affirming that in the incarnation, while retaining their respective characteristics,[57] "the two natures being brought together in a true union, there is of both one Christ and one Son."[58] Thus, for Cyril, the eternal Son of God personally united with a human nature—body and soul—conceived by the Virgin Mary:[59] "The holy fathers ... ventured to call the holy virgin the Mother of God [*theotokos*: God bearer], not as if the nature of the Word or his divinity had its beginning from the holy virgin, but because of her was born that holy body with a rational soul, to which the Word being personally united is said to be born according to the flesh."[60] The church followed Cyril,

---

54. It is important to note the historical context in which this title of Mary was affirmed. As originally intended, *theotokos*, or "God bearer," expressed a truth about Jesus Christ himself and had little to do with Mary. Only later, when the idea of *theotokos* became "Mother of God," was the title used to express something about Mary, singling her out for a high status in the church. Thus, evangelicals can and should affirm that Mary is *theotokos*, in the historical sense that the one whom she conceived and gave birth to—Jesus Christ—was fully God.

55. I underscore the fact that Nestorius himself denied the beliefs for which Cyril of Alexandria and the church condemned him. Partly due to poor communication on the part of Nestorius, who was intent on stirring up controversy, and partly due to church politics, he became associated with a position that was clearly not his own.

56. Cyril expressed this idea as he distanced the church from the alleged Nestorian view: "We do not divide the God from the man, nor separate him into parts, as though the two natures were mutually united in him [Jesus Christ] only through a sharing of dignity and authority ... neither do we give separately to the Word of God the name Christ and the same name separately to a different one born of a woman; but

we know only one Christ, the Word from God the Father with his own flesh." Cyril of Alexandria, *The Third Letter of Cyril to Nestorius* (or *The Epistle of Cyril to Nestorius with the 12 Anathemas*), in NPNF[2], 14:202. Thus, Nestorius's idea of God and man working in conjunction was strongly denounced by the church.

57. "Although he assumed flesh and blood, he remained what he was, God in essence and in truth. Neither do we say that his flesh was changed into the nature of divinity, nor that the ineffable nature of the Word of God was laid aside for the nature of flesh [human nature]; for he is unchanged and absolutely unchangeable, being the same always." Ibid.

58. Cyril of Alexandria, *The Fourth Letter of Cyril to Nestorius* (or *The Epistle of Cyril to Nestorius*), in NPNF[2], 14:198.

59. "He who had an existence before all ages and was born [generated] of the Father, is said to have been born according to the flesh of a woman, not as though his divine nature received its beginning of existence in the holy virgin, for it did not need a second generation after that of the Father.... For us and for our salvation, he personally united to himself a human body, and came forth of a woman. He is in this way said to be born after the flesh." Ibid.

60. Ibid.

who brought twelve charges of heresy against Nestorius.[61] These accusations secured his official condemnation at the third ecumenical council of the church, the Council of Ephesus. As we will see, the Creed of Chalcedon, written in 451, expressly denounced the Nestorian error. Jesus Christ is truly the God-man, consisting of a divine nature and a human nature united in one person.[62]

Having addressed Apollinarianism and Nestorianism, the early church still had one more major heresy to counter. Named after the simple monk Eutychus, Eutychianism combined the two natures of Jesus Christ into one different nature after the incarnation. This view is an example of *monophysitism*, or the belief that Jesus Christ possessed only one nature.[63] Of particular concern was Eutychus's belief that before the incarnation, both the divine and human natures of Jesus Christ existed. But after the union of these natures in the incarnation, Jesus Christ possessed only one nature. And somehow this one nature made him different from all other human beings, because Christ was not of the same nature as the rest of humanity.[64]

Once again, the church responded quickly to this challenge to orthodoxy. Two concerns were voiced: First, Eutychianism denied that the incarnate Christ had two distinct natures. According to one interpretation of his view, the divine nature so absorbed the human nature of Christ that essentially the one nature was divine. On another interpretation, the one nature was a fusion or hybrid of the divine and human natures, a "divinehuman" nature, so to speak. In either case, the church objected, insisting that after the incarnation Jesus Christ had two complete natures that maintained their respective properties—the divine nature with its attributes of deity, and the human nature with its attributes of humanity.[65] The second concern was Eutychus's denial that the human nature of Jesus was the same as that of all human beings.[66] This cut across the church's belief in Jesus' full humanity. Flavian offered this formula for understanding the incarnation: "We affirm that Christ is of two natures after the incarnation, affirming one Christ,

---

61. Cyril of Alexandria, *The Twelve Anathemas of Cyril against Nestorius*, in *NPNF*[2], 14:206–18.

62. John of Antioch offered a statement on Christology in a letter to Cyril of Alexandria. Known as the *Symbol of Unity*, this formula did much to unite the church and pave the way for a settlement on the doctrine of Christ: "We confess ... our Lord Jesus Christ, the only-begotten Son of God, perfect God and perfect man composed of a rational soul and a body, begotten before the ages from his Father in respect of his divinity, but likewise in these last days for us and our salvation [he was born] from the virgin Mary in respect of his manhood [humanity]. He is consubstantial [of the same nature] with the Father in respect of his divinity and at the same time consubstantial [of the same nature] with us in respect of his manhood. For a union of two natures has been accomplished. Hence we confess one Christ, one Son, one Lord. In virtue of this conception of a union without confusion we confess the holy Virgin as *theotokos* because the divine Word became flesh and was made man and from the very conception united to

himself the temple taken from her." John of Antioch, *Letter 38 to Cyril of Alexandria*, Kelly, 328–29.

63. The term *monophysitism* is a combination of two words. *Mono* signifies "one" and *physis* signifies "nature." Thus, the term is used to affirm that after the incarnation, Jesus Christ had only one nature. Actually, interpreting Eutychus is quite difficult, because he offered confusing and seemingly different answers to questions posed to him about his view of Christ.

64. "I admit that I have never said that he is consubstantial [of the same nature] with us.... I admit that our Lord was of two natures before the union, but after the union one nature." *The Admissions of Eutychus*, in Bettenson, 53.

65. Flavian, *Letter 26: A Second Letter to Leo*, in *NPNF*[2], 12:36–38.

66. As Flavian explained: "Though he calls it human, he [Eutychus] refuses to say it was consubstantial with us or with her who bore him, according to the flesh." Ibid., in *NPNF*[2], 12:37.

one Son, one Lord, in one subsistence and one person."[67] This "two nature ... one person" affirmation became the standard way of expressing the reality of the God-man.[68]

The fourth ecumenical council, the Council of Chalcedon, was convened in 451 and composed a new statement of faith, the Chalcedonian Creed. It embraced the "two nature ... one person" formula, which became the standard way of expressing the *hypostatic union*, the union of the divine and human natures in the one person Jesus Christ. Against *Eutychianism* it clearly underscored that Jesus Christ is to be "recognized in two natures, without confusion and without change. The distinction of the natures was in no way annulled by the union, but rather the characteristics of each nature were preserved." Also, as we have mentioned, the Creed explicitly denied three earlier heresies with specific wording against their major tenets: Against *Arianism* and its denial of the full deity of the Son, it specifically affirmed that Jesus Christ is "complete in divinity" and "consubstantial—of the same nature—as the Father." Against *Apollinarianism* and its denial of the full humanity of the Word, it expressly affirmed belief in "our Lord Jesus Christ, who is complete in humanity, truly man, having a rational soul and body." Against *Nestorianism* and its view that two distinct and independent persons worked in conjunction with each other in Jesus Christ, it explicitly stated that the "one and the same Christ, Son, Lord, Only-begotten" is to be "recognized in two natures, without division and without separation. They come together in one person and one existence, not as parted or divided into two persons, but one and the same Son and Only-begotten God the Word, Lord Jesus Christ."

The Chalcedonian Creed (451)

Following the holy fathers, we all with one accord teach men to acknowledge one and the same Son, our Lord Jesus Christ, at once complete in divinity and complete in manhood, truly God and truly man, consisting also of a rational soul and body; of one substance [*homoousios*] with the Father as regards his Godhead, and at the same time of one substance with us as regards his manhood; like us in all respects, apart from sin; as regards his Godhead, begotten of the Father before the ages, but yet as regards his manhood begotten [born], for

---

67. Synod of Constantinople (November 8, 448), in Kelly, 331.

68. The chief opponent of Eutychianism was Leo, the bishop of Rome. In his *Tome*, Leo argued against this heresy and presented a summary of the church's belief about the two natures of Jesus Christ. First, the two natures—divine and human—that exist in Jesus Christ are complete natures, and they maintain their respective characteristics in the union. Second, it was the eternal Word, the Son of God, who came to be the God-man, and he did not experience any loss of his divine powers in the incarnation. Third, as to his humanity, Jesus Christ is consubstantial—of the very same nature—with human beings, yet without sin. Fourth, the unity is a real one in which each nature—divine and human—"performs its proper functions in cooperation with the other. The Word performs that which pertains to the Word; the flesh performs that which pertains to the flesh.... The Word does not cease to be on an equality with the Father's glory, so the flesh does not desert the nature of our race." Leo the Great, *Letter* 28, 3–4, *Letter to Flavian*, in *NPNF*[2], 12:40–41; Bettenson, 54–56. The text has been rendered clearer. Despite Leo's efforts to contradict and banish Eutychianism, another church council was convened at Ephesus in 449. Known as the "robber synod," it refused to confirm Leo's *Tome*. Instead, it approved Eutychus and his heretical view!

us men and for our salvation, of Mary the virgin, the God-bearer [*theotokos*]; one and the same Christ, Son, Lord, only-begotten, recognized in two natures, without confusion, without change, without division, without separation; the distinction of natures being in no way annulled by the union, but rather the characteristics of each nature being preserved and coming together to form one person and subsistence [hypostasis], not as parted or separated into two persons, but one and the same Son and only-begotten God the Word, Lord Jesus Christ.*

*Creed of Chalcedon, in Schaff, 2:62–63; Bettenson, 56.

The settlement reached at Chalcedon established the church's Christology to a large degree. Certainly the church in the Western part of the empire fully embraced the Chalcedonian formula.[69] But some from the church in the East reacted negatively to it. This development was due in part to the expression "two natures" sounding very much like Nestorianism. Thus, following the Council of Chalcedon, monophysitism resurfaced and challenged the creed's affirmation of two natures. Monophysitism was officially condemned by the church at the Second Council of Constantinople in 553.[70] Not until the modern period would any serious heresy arise to challenge this orthodox Christology.

VIEWS OF JESUS CHRIST IN THE MIDDLE AGES

The medieval period witnessed little in terms of new developments in Christology. Rather, the church repeated and reinforced its traditional belief as that had been set down

69. This can seen in the Athanasian Creed, which echoed the Chalcedonian Creed. Athanasian Creed, 29–36, in Schaff, 2:68–69. Dating the Athanasian Creed is very difficult. It certainly was not written by Athanasius, so it does not belong to the fourth century. I place it here following the Chalcedonian Creed because it seems to reflect the Christology of that document.

70. One of the anathemas stated: "If anyone affirms that a union was made of the divine and human natures, or speaks about the one nature of God the Word made flesh, but does not understand these things according to what the church fathers have taught—namely, that from the divine and human natures a personal union was made, and that one Christ was formed—but from these expressions tries to introduce one nature or substance made of the divinity and humanity of Christ: let him be anathema. In affirming that the only-begotten God the Word was personally united to humanity, we do not mean that there was a confusion made of each of the natures into the other, but rather that each nature remained what it was, and in this way we understand that the Word was united to humanity. So there is only one Christ, both God and man, consubstantial with the Father in respect to his divinity, and also consubstantial with us in respect to our humanity. Both those who divide or split up the mystery of the divine dispensation of Christ, and those who introduce into that mystery some confusion, are equally rejected and anathematized by the church of God." Second Council of Constantinople, *Anathema* 8. An important modification of monophysitism was a position called *monothelitism*, a term that is a combination of two words. *Mono* signifies "one" and *thelema* signifies "will." The basic idea of this view was that while Jesus Christ possessed two natures, he only had one will. Thus, it formally agreed with the Chalcedonian Creed about the two natures. However, monothelitism balked at the idea of two wills as leading to a division in the unity of the person of Christ. Rather, it maintained that there was one will or—as some put it—one natural principle of operation in Jesus Christ. At one point, even the bishop of Rome, Pope Honorius, fell prey to this view. Officially, the Third Council of Constantinople (680–81) denounced monothelitism and applied the Chalcedonian Creed to the two wills and the two principles of operation in Jesus Christ. Each nature willed and worked that which is proper to itself—miracles by the divine nature, sufferings by the human nature—the two willing and working together in unity. The settlement obtained at the Third Council of Constantinople effectively put a halt to monophysitism and monothelitism.

at the councils of Nicea, Constantinople (I, II, and III), Ephesus, and Chalcedon. Anselm reasoned about the nature of Jesus Christ as he considered the issue of *Why God Became Man*. Starting from a view of sin as robbing God of his honor, and holding that humanity cannot give an adequate satisfaction to God to restore his honor, Anselm concluded that the only one who can save humanity is one who is both God and man: "No one can pay [this satisfaction] except God, and no one ought to pay except a man: it is necessary that a God-man should pay it."[71] Anselm noted that this reality could not be a divine nature becoming a human nature, nor a human nature becoming a divine nature, nor these two natures merely joining together. Rather, it required one who was both fully divine and fully human: "Given ... that it is necessary for a God-man to be found in whom the wholeness of both natures is kept intact, it is no less necessary for these two natures to combine, as wholes, in one person, in the same way as the body and the rational soul coalesce into one human being. For otherwise it cannot come about that one and the same person may be perfect God and perfect man."[72] Thus, reasoning from his doctrine of salvation, Anselm affirmed the traditional belief in the God-man.

Interacting with the various creeds and citing the architects of the historic position of the church, Thomas Aquinas also echoed the traditional belief. He affirmed that after the incarnation, the person of Jesus Christ was composed of two natures.[73] He further rehearsed the two historic heresies of Eutychianism and Nestorianism[74] and centered the historic church's Christology between these two positions.[75] Aquinas also summarized the church's view on the *communication of properties*. This issue centered on whether it is proper to speak of the human experiences of Christ while referring to him as God, and whether it is proper to speak of the divine experiences of Christ while referring to him as man. Some in the church insisted that care must be taken to refer to the man when speaking of Christ's human experiences—in his human nature, Jesus was weak and tired, hungry and thirsty, tempted and subject to death—and to refer to God when speaking of Christ's divine experiences—in his divine nature, he was all-powerful, eternal, and unchangeable. But this was not the church's view, because "words which are said of Christ either in his divine or human nature may be said either of God or of man.... And hence of the man may be said what belongs to the divine nature, as of a hypostasis [person] of the divine nature; and of God may be said what belongs to the human nature, as of a hypostasis [person] of human nature."[76] Aquinas did not affirm that the divine nature of Jesus Christ somehow became human, so that it was weak and tired, hungry and thirsty, temptable and mortal. Nor did he affirm that the human nature somehow became divine, so that it was all-powerful, eternal, and unchangeable. Rather, he meant that while the two natures maintained their respective properties, the church is still right in saying, for example, "they ... crucified the Lord of glory" (1 Cor. 2:8), and calling Mary *theotokos*, the "God bearer." The divine nature did not die, and Mary only contributed the human nature of Jesus. Nevertheless, what is said of either nature may be said

71. Anselm, *Why God Became Man*, 2.6, in *Anselm*, 320.
72. Ibid., 2.7, in *Anselm*, 321.
73. Thomas Aquinas, *Summa Theologica*, pt. 3, q. 2, art. 4.
74. Ibid., pt. 3, q. 2, art. 6.
75. Ibid.
76. Ibid., pt. 3, q. 16, art. 4.

of either God or man, because both "God" and "man" refer to the one person of Jesus Christ.[77] Thus, Aquinas reaffirmed the church's historic view of Jesus Christ.

VIEWS OF JESUS CHRIST IN THE REFORMATION AND POST-REFORMATION

The story was similar during the period of the Reformation, though controversy did flare up between Martin Luther and Huldrych Zwingli. Arguing against each other's view of the Lord's Supper, each charged the other with heresy about Jesus Christ.

At issue was the presence of Christ during the celebration of the Lord's Supper. Luther held that Christ is present everywhere, taking this to demonstrate "at least in one way how God could bring it about that Christ is in heaven and his body in the Lord's Supper at the same time."[78] But how could the human body of Christ be everywhere present? A key point for Luther was that in the incarnation, "since the divinity and humanity are one person in Christ, the Scriptures ascribe to the divinity, because of this personal union, all that happens to humanity, and vice versa."[79] This meant that Jesus Christ, including his human nature—which in and of itself is localized in one space and not present in every space—is ubiquitous, or everywhere present, in virtue of its union with the divine nature.[80] Thus, Luther held to the communication of properties in a strict sense. Specifically, the human body of Christ had picked up the divine property of being omnipresent, receiving this characteristic from its union with his divine nature.

For holding this belief, Luther was charged by his opponents with the ancient heresy of Eutychianism.[81] Zwingli accused Luther of mingling the two natures into one essence.[82] Calvin also complained that Luther's view destroyed the human body of Christ and eliminated the difference between his divine and human nature.[83] Of course, Luther rejected this charge, clarifying: "We do not say that divinity is humanity, or that the divine nature is the human nature, which would be confusing the natures into one essence. Rather, we merge the two distinct natures into one single person, and say: 'God is man and man is God.'"[84]

---

77. Grudem supplies two excellent examples that serve to clarify Aquinas's point on the communication of properties. Grudem, *Systematic Theology*, 562.

78. Martin Luther, *Confession Concerning Christ's Supper*, LW, 37:207. As we will see, Zwingli agreed that the right hand of God is everywhere present, but he believed this to be true of Christ according to his deity, not according to his humanity. LW, 37:213n77. For a more complete presentation of Luther's view, see chap. 29.

79. Ibid., LW, 37:210.

80. "Wherever Christ is according to his divinity, he is there as a natural, divine person and he is also naturally and personally there.... But if he is present naturally and personally wherever he is, then he must be man there, too, since he is not two separate persons but a single person. Wherever this person is, it is the single, indivisible person, and if you can say,

'Here is God,' then you must also say, 'Christ the man is present too.'" Ibid., LW, 37:218.

81. See the earlier discussion of Eutychianism.

82. Huldrych Zwingli, *Christian Answer,* in *Corpus Reformatum*, 92, 933–34. Luther responded to this charge in *Confession Concerning Christ's Supper*, LW, 37:212.

83. Calvin compared Luther's error with "that insane notion of Servetus (which all godly men rightly find abhorrent), that his [Christ's] body was swallowed up by his divinity. I do not say that they think so. But if to fill all things in an invisible manner is numbered among the gifts of the glorified body, it is plain that the substance of the body is wiped out, and that no difference between deity and human nature is left. John Calvin, *Institutes of the Christian Religion*, 4.17.29, LCC, 2:1398–99.

84. *Confession Concerning Christ's Supper*, LW, 37:212.

Huldrych Zwingli took a very different position than Luther on the presence of Christ in the Lord's Supper. He denied that the Lord was physically present in the elements. "According to its proper essence, the body of Christ is truly and naturally seated at the right hand of the Father. It cannot therefore be present in this way in the Supper."[85] Zwingli strengthened this point by focusing on the promise of Christ in John 17:11 and its fulfillment in his ascension: "It is the human nature [of Jesus] which leaves the world.... [A]s regards a natural, essential and localized presence the humanity is not here, for it has left the world."[86] From this line of reasoning, Zwingli concluded that the physical body of Christ cannot be present in the Eucharistic elements. Thus, he stood at odds with Luther.

For his apparent separation between the human nature and divine nature of Christ, Zwingli was charged by his opponents with the ancient heresy of Nestorianism.[87] Little came of this exchange of accusations, and neither Luther nor Zwingli was ever formally charged with heretical Christology. But their sensitivity and responses to the charges demonstrated their profound respect for the early church's creeds as neither wanted to be at odds with these historic confessions about the God-man.

So it was with John Calvin, whose Christology was fully traditional, echoing Anselm's thought in *Why God Became Man*[88] and relying on the Chalcedonian formula.[89] He also affirmed the communication of properties,[90] without allowing this to result in the errors of Nestorianism and Eutychianism, both of which he condemned.[91]

Those who followed Luther, Calvin, and the other Reformers continued to embrace and defend this traditional view of Jesus Christ. The Lutheran *Formula of Concord* opened with a statement affirming the historic creeds of the church and recognizing them as the standard against which all heresies receive their condemnation.[92] Similarly, on the Reformed side, the major Calvinist confessions continued to uphold the church's historic Christology.[93] However, Lutheran and Reformed theologies disagreed about the communication of properties: "The Reformed theologians ... deny that, by the hypostatic union, the properties of the divine nature have been truly and really imparted to the human nature of Christ ... so that the human nature of our Savior is truly omnipresent, omnipotent, and omniscient."[94] According to the Lutheran position, however: "The majesty of the omnipresence of the Word was communicated to the human nature of Christ in the first moment of the personal union, in consequence of which, along with the divine

---

85. Huldrych Zwingli, *An Exposition of the Faith*, in G. W. Bromiley, ed., *Zwingli and Bullinger*, LCC, 24:256.

86. Ibid., 24:257.

87. Luther explained his accusation: "We ... raise a hue and cry against them [Zwingli and his sympathizers] for separating the person of Christ as though there were two persons. If Zwingli's [biblical interpretation] stands, then Christ will have to be two persons, one a divine and the other a human person, since Zwingli applies all the texts concerning the passion only to the human nature and completely excludes them from the divine nature. But if the works are divided and separated, the person will also have to be separated, since all the doing and suffering are not ascribed to natures but to persons. It is the person who does and suffers everything, the one thing

according to this nature and the other thing according to the other nature.... Therefore, we regard our Lord Christ as God and man in one person, 'neither confusing the natures nor dividing the person.'" *Confession Concerning Christ's Supper*, LW, 37:212–13. With his ending quote, Luther appealed to the Chalcedonian formula.

88. Calvin, *Institutes*, 2.12.1–3, LCC, 1:464–67.

89. Ibid., 2.14.1, LCC, 1:482–83.

90. Ibid., 2.14.1–2, LCC, 1:482–84.

91. Ibid., 2.14.4, LCC, 1:486–87.

92. *Formula of Concord*, Epitome 2, in Schaff, 3:94–95.

93. *Belgic Confession*, 18–19, in Schaff, 3:402–4.

94. Ibid.

nature, it [the human nature] is now omnipresent, in the state of exaltation, in a true, real, substantial and effective presence."[95] Besides this one peculiarity, both Lutheran and Reformed theologians in the post-Reformation period embraced and defended the church's historic position on Jesus Christ, the God-man.

VIEWS OF JESUS CHRIST IN THE MODERN PERIOD

The Lutheran communication of properties provoked a reaction in some modern theologians: The incarnation was not about what the church had historically imagined it was, but about the *kenosis*, or self-emptying, of the divine when the Son of God became a man. A chief proponent of this view was Gottfried Thomasius (1802–1875), who explained the incarnation "as the self-limitation of the Son of God."[96] He reasoned that the Son could not have maintained his full divinity during the incarnation.[97] Although a Lutheran theologian, Thomasius rejected the Lutheran explanation of the communication of properties.[98] In his mind, the only way for a true incarnation to take place was if the Son "gave himself over into the form of human limitation,"[99] which involved a divine self-emptying.[100] Biblical support for this was found in Philippians 2:6–8, particularly the expression "he emptied himself" (v. 7).[101] Thomasius thus defined kenosis: "It is the exchange of the one form of existence for the other; Christ emptied himself of the one and assumed the other. It is thus an act of free self-denial, which has as its two moments the renunciation of the divine condition of glory, due him as God, and the assumption of the humanly limited and conditioned pattern of life."[102]

Thomasius specified the divestiture of the divine attributes of the Son of God. He did not give up his immanent divine attributes (which characterize God as he is in himself and as the three members of the Godhead are in relation to each other): "absolute power, truth, holiness and love ... which as such are inseparable from the essence of God, and no more does he, as the incarnate one, withhold their use."[103] But he did divest himself of his relative divine attributes (which characterize God as he is in relation to the world): omnipotence, omniscience, and omnipresence.[104] Thus, in the incarnation, the Son did not—indeed, could not—empty himself of his immanent divine attributes, for he would have ceased to be God. Rather, he emptied himself of the relative divine attributes, not just giving up the use of his omnipotence, omniscience, and omnipresence, but not even possessing them during his incarnation.[105]

95. John Andrew Quenstedt, *Theologia Didactico-Polemica sive Systema Theologicum* (Leipzig, 1715), 3.185, in Schmid, 331.

96. Gottfried Thomasius, *Christ's Person and Work*, 40, in *God and Incarnation in Mid-Nineteenth Century German Theology*, ed. Claude Welch (New York: Oxford Univ. Press, 1965), 46.

97. "The divine then, so to speak, surpasses the human as a broader circle does a smaller one; in its knowledge, life and action the divine extends infinitely far over and above the human, as the extra-historical over the temporal, as that which is perfect in itself over that which becomes, as the all-

permeating and all-determining over the conditioned, over that which is bound to the limits and laws of earthly existence." Ibid., in Welch, *God and Incarnation*, 46–47.

98. Ibid., in Welch, *God and Incarnation*, 47.

99. Ibid., in Welch, *God and Incarnation*, 47–48.

100. Ibid., in Welch, *God and Incarnation*, 48.

101. Ibid., in Welch, *God and Incarnation*, 51–53.

102. Ibid., in Welch, *God and Incarnation*, 53.

103. Ibid., in Welch, *God and Incarnation*, 67–68.

104. Ibid., 43, in Welch, *God and Incarnation*, 70.

105. Ibid., in Welch, *God and Incarnation*, 70–71.

Following his state of humiliation, the Son of God experienced exaltation, "a condition of unlimited freedom and absolute powerfulness of life; as the exalted one he must now be in full possession of the divine glory of which he divested himself.... [W]e say that the glorified Christ is omnipresent, omnipotent and omniscient."[106] This kenotic Christology originated by Thomasius attracted some followers, but most Christians considered it to be at odds with the Chalcedonian understanding of the incarnation. It would be revived and rendered more sophisticated by some later theologians, though it has never been considered to be in accordance with orthodox Christology.

Beyond this kenotic model, the modern period witnessed the undoing of the church's historic consensus on Christology. Friedrich Schleiermacher reinterpreted religion in terms of a feeling of absolute dependence on the world's spirit, which he called God. In keeping with his theological realignment, Schleiermacher presented Jesus as the ideal in whom this God-consciousness reached it apex: "His particular spiritual content cannot ... be explained by the content of the human environment to which he belonged, but only by the universal source of spiritual life in virtue of a creative divine act in which, as an absolute maximum, the conception of man as the subject of the God-consciousness comes to completion."[107] In keeping with this ideal, Schleiermacher revisioned the sinlessness of Christ as the gradual yet complete submission of his self-consciousness to his God-consciousness: "No impression was taken up merely sensuously into the innermost consciousness and elaborated apart from God-consciousness into an element of life, nor did any action ... ever proceed solely from the sense-nature and not from God-consciousness."[108] For Schleiermacher, "The Redeemer, then, is like all men in virtue of the identity of human nature, but distinguished from them all the constant potency of his God-consciousness, which was a veritable existence of God in him."[109] More specifically, "to ascribe to Christ an absolutely powerful God-consciousness, and to attribute to him an existence of God in him, are exactly the same thing."[110] In other words, Christ fully experienced absolute dependence on God-consciousness, and this reality was what rendered him unique yet similar to all human beings in pursuit of such consciousness.

Schleiermacher's reformulated Christology influenced many theologians, who further revised the doctrine, even though the quest for the historical Jesus by liberal Protestants actually began some decades earlier.[111] Hermann Samuel Reimarus drove a wedge

---

106. Ibid., in Welch, *God and Incarnation*, 75–76.

107. Friedrich Schleiermacher, *The Christian Faith*, ed. H. R. Mackintosh and J. S. Stewart (Edinburgh: T & T Clark, 1928), 381.

108. Ibid., 383.

109. Ibid., 385.

110. Ibid., 387.

111. Some scholars roughly group the quest for the historical Jesus into three phases. The first quest, beginning with Hermann Samuel Reimarus and ending with Albert Schweitzer, sought to dehistoricize Jesus, distancing him greatly from his first-century Palestinian world. As N. T. Wright noted, "The 'Quest' began as an explicitly anti-theological, anti-Christian, anti-dogmatic movement. Its initial agenda was not to find a Jesus upon whom Christian faith might be based, but to show that the faith of the church (as it was then conceived) could not in fact be based on the real Jesus of Nazareth." N. T. Wright, *Jesus and the Victory of God* (London: SPCK; Minneapolis: Fortress, 1996), 17. The second or "new quest" began with Schweitzer and ended with Rudolf Bultmann. It focused on Jesus as an eschatological prophet whose message—at its core, a radical call to commitment, once its cultural accoutrements were stripped away—could be twisted and shaped to accommodate many viewpoints (e.g., the call to discipleship of the early church; the call to authenticity of existentialism). The "third quest," beginning with Ernst Käsemann and extending into the third millennium, treats seriously the historical context of Jesus. It seeks to construct

between what the real Jesus of Nazareth was about and what his disciples dreamed and finally wrote that he was about.[112] Following in Schleiermacher's footsteps, David Friedrich Strauss revisioned the Bible as myth and then, having dismissed the portrait of Jesus painted by the New Testament authors, reinterpreted Christ along the theological lines of Schleiermacher's ideal man.[113] Martin Kähler erected a dichotomy between the historical Jesus of Nazareth and the Christ of Scripture, maintaining: "We do not possess any sources for a 'life of Jesus' that a historian can accept as reliable and adequate."[114] Accordingly, "the risen Lord is not the historical Jesus *behind* the Gospels, but the Christ of the apostolic preaching, of the *whole* New Testament.... Therefore, we speak of the historic Christ of the Bible."[115] In the view of Albert Schweitzer, Jesus was steeped in the eschatological doctrine of his time. Fueled by this great expectation, Jesus died by attempting to bring in the kingdom of God violently, yet his hopes for this eschatological event were dashed to pieces:

> In the knowledge that he is the coming Son of Man, Jesus lays hold of the wheel
> of the world to set it moving on that last revolution that is to bring all ordinary
> history to a close. It refuses to turn, and he throws himself upon it. Then it does
> turn; and it crushes him. Instead of bringing in the eschatological conditions,
> he has destroyed them. The wheel rolls onward and the mangled body of the
> one immeasurably great man, who was strong enough to think of himself as the
> spiritual ruler of mankind and to bend history to his purpose, is hanging upon
> it still. That is his victory and his reign.[116]

Rudolph Bultmann erected a dichotomy between the historical Jesus of Nazareth and the "kerygmatic" Christ of faith, asserting that the former was relatively unimportant, and the latter was what really mattered for the church. According to Bultmann, "I do indeed think that we can now know almost nothing concerning the life and personality

---

a Christology that locates him in his first-century Palestinian culture and views his claims to messiahship as both historically relevant for the Judaism of his day and transcending the mistaken political notions often attached to the messianic vision of that contemporary Judaism.

112. Hermann Samuel Reimarus, *Fragments*, 1.30–33, in *Reimarus: Fragments*, ed. Charles H. Talbert, trans. Ralph S. Fraser, Lives of Jesus Series (Philadelphia: Fortress, 1970), 126–34. The fragment—entitled "On the Intentions of Jesus and His Disciples"—here referenced was published in 1778 by Gotthold Ephraim Lessing as part of his *Wolfenbüttel Fragments* (seven fragments published between 1774 and 1778).

113. David Friedrich Strauss, *The Life of Jesus Critically Examined* (Philadelphia: Augsburg Fortress, 1972); idem, *The Christ of Faith and the Jesus of History: A Critique of Schleiermacher's* The Life of Jesus, trans. Leander E. Keck (Philadelphia: Fortress, 1977). As one Strauss scholar put it: "Strauss' *Life of Jesus* was the most intellectually reasoned attack which has ever been mounted against Christianity. There have been other assaults more radical and bitter, others expressed in

more vituperative language ... but no one since Strauss has so acutely concentrated on the crucial cardinal issues that must be dealt with. Strauss confronted theology with an either/or: either show that the Christian faith is historically and intellectually credible, or admit that it is based on myth and delusion. That was the alternative. Nothing less was and is at stake than the whole historical and intellectual basis of Christianity. If Strauss cannot be convincingly answered, then it would appear that Christianity must slowly but surely collapse." Horton Harris, *David Friedrich Strauss and His Theology*, Monograph Supplement to the Scottish Journal of Theology (Cambridge: Cambridge Univ. Press, 1973), 281–82.

114. Martin Kähler, *The So-Called Historical Jesus and the Historic, Biblical Christ*, trans. Carl E. Braaten (Philadelphia: Fortress, 1964), 48.

115. Ibid., 65.

116. Albert Schweitzer, *The Quest of the Historical Jesus: A Critical Study of Its Progress from Reimarus to Wrede*, trans. W. Montgomery (London: Adam and Charles Black, 1910), 368–69.

of Jesus, since the early Christian sources show no interest in either, [and] are moreover fragmentary and often legendary."[117] The "kerygmatic" Christ of faith—the one who was preached by the first disciples—is the product of the early Christian community and is covered with mythology. This encrustation demands that the church engage in *de-mythologizing*,[118] or removing the mythological elements so as to recover the deeper, existential meaning of the New Testament portrait of Jesus.[119]

Rebuffing demythologization, N. T. Wright sought to construct a portrait of Jesus by locating him within first-century Palestinian culture. He averred: "Jesus belonged thoroughly within the complex and multiform Judaism of his day.... Thus his praxis, his stories and his symbols all pointed to his belief and claim that Israel's god was fulfilling his promises and purposes in and through what he himself was doing.... He was, and remains, 'Jesus the Jew.'"[120] As for the goals of this Jesus, Wright offered: "He aimed, then, to reconstitute Israel around himself, as the true returned-from-exile people; to achieve the victory of Israel's god over the evil that had enslaved his people; and, some-how, to bring about the greatest hope of all, the victorious return of YHWH to Zion."[121] Intentionally focusing on these aims, Jesus engaged in his itinerant prophetic ministry, discipled the Twelve and some others, and proclaimed the kingdom of God. Beyond these, however, Jesus had a specific vocation, an obvious calling for any would-be first-century Jewish Messiah: to "go to Jerusalem, fight the battle against the forces of evil, and get yourself enthroned as the rightful king. Jesus, in fact, adopted precisely this strategy. But ... he had in mind a different battle, a different throne."[122]

With this vocation in mind, Jesus went to Jerusalem to die, and he initiated this cli-mactic event by instituting two symbols: the cleansing of the temple and the institution of the Lord's Supper: "The first symbol said: the present system is corrupt and recalci-trant. It is ripe for judgment. But Jesus is the Messiah, the one through whom YHWH, the God of all the world, will save Israel and thereby the world. And the second symbol said: this is how the true exodus will come about. This is how evil will be defeated. This is how sins will be forgiven."[123] According to Wright, Jesus certainly calculated that his words and actions would incense the Jewish leaders and eventually end in his execution by the Romans. But Jesus was primarily motivated by "the unshakable belief ... that if he went this route, if he fought this battle, the long night of Israel's exile would be over at last, and the new day for Israel and the world really would dawn once and for all."[124] Thus, Wright situated Jesus solidly in his first-century Palestinian Jewish world to under-stand his teachings, his miracles, his kingdom stories, and his sufferings and death in that context.

117. Rudolph Bultmann, *Jesus and the Word* (New York: Scribner, 1958), 8.

118. Rudolph Bultmann, *Jesus Christ and Mythology* (New York: Scribner, 1958), 18.

119. Karl Barth, for one, attempted to reverse this direc-tion. He constructed a Christology using the biblical materials and decried all attempts to dismiss the New Testament wit-ness to Christ. *CD*, IV/1, 163. E.g., he borrowed the parable of the prodigal son to express the humiliation and exaltation of Jesus. *CD*, IV/1–2.

120. Wright, *Jesus and the Victory of God* (London: SPCK; Minneapolis: Fortress, 1996), 472–73. Wright's use of the expression "Jesus the Jew" was a deliberate reference to the title of Geza Vermes's book *Jesus the Jew: A Historian's Reading of the Gospels* (London: Collins, 1973).

121. Ibid., 473–74.

122. Ibid., 474, 539.

123. Ibid., 609–10.

124. Ibid., 610.

Other theologians reworked classical Christology in accordance with other criteria. In his *Christianity and the Social Crisis*, Walter Rauschenbusch applied higher critical methods to discover the "revolutionary" Jesus.[125] Marcus Borg revisioned Christ as a Spirit-filled, wise countercultural reformer.[126] John Dominic Crossan presented Jesus as a "peasant Jewish Cynic."[127] In summary, the nineteenth and twentieth centuries witnessed many attempts to reimagine Jesus as historic Christology was being overthrown.

Further attacks against traditional Christology were launched. John Hick, in *The Myth of God Incarnate*, insisted that to affirm "that the historical Jesus of Nazareth was also God is as devoid of meaning as to say that this circle drawn with a pencil on paper is also a square."[128] The obvious charge was that the incarnation is incoherent; to affirm that Jesus Christ is God is to be logically inconsistent. This must be the case because the incarnation claims, for example, that the divine attributes of immutability and omnipotence, and the human attributes of mutability and limitation of power, exist together in one being. Hick and the others argued that because the human and divine attributes are mutually exclusive, they could never exist together in the person of Jesus Christ. To affirm such a thing is absurd and incoherent.

The Problem of Mutually Exclusive Attributes, according to
The Myth of God Incarnate

The person of Jesus Christ is

as to his humanity	as to his deity
finite	infinite
caused to exist	uncaused existence
dependent	independent
mutable	immutable
spatial (local)	nonspatial (omnipresent)
temporal (has a beginning)	nontemporal (eternal)
limited in knowledge	omniscient
limited in power, strength	omnipotent

---

125. Walter Rauschenbusch, *Christianity and the Social Crisis* (1907; repr., New York and Evanston, Ill.: Harper & Row, 1964).

126. Marcus Borg, *Jesus: A New Vision: Spirit, Culture, and the Life of Discipleship* (San Francisco: Harper & Row, 1987).

127. John Dominic Crossan, *The Historical Jesus: The Life of a Mediterranean Jewish Peasant* (San Francisco: Harper & Row, 1991).

128. John Hick, "Jesus and the World Religions," in *The Myth of God Incarnate*, ed. John Hick (London: SCM, 1977), 178.

Evangelicals did not allow this charge of incoherence and inconsistency to go unanswered. In his *The Logic of God Incarnate*, Thomas Morris offered "the two-minds view of Christ"[129] in his incarnation, as an attempt to deal with one aspect of the apparent inconsistency: With regard to knowledge, how can Christ be limited in knowledge while at the same time be omniscient? Specifically, Morris's theory proposed "two distinct ranges of consciousness" in the person of Jesus Christ: "There is first what we can call the eternal mind of God the Son with its distinctively divine consciousness, whatever that might be, encompassing the full scope of omniscience. And in addition there is a distinctly earthly consciousness that came into existence and grew and developed ... [and that] was thoroughly human, Jewish, and first-century Palestinian in nature."[130] Morris proposed that "the divine mind of God the Son contained, but was not contained by, his earthly mind, or range of consciousness. That is to say, there was what can be called an asymmetrical accessing relationship between the two minds." Accordingly, "the divine mind had full and direct access to the earthly, human experience resulting from the incarnation, but the earthly consciousness did not have such full and direct access to the content of the overarching omniscience proper to the Logos [the Son of God], but only such access, on occasion, as the divine mind allowed it to have."[131] This model allowed for intellectual growth of Jesus in his humanity (e.g., Jesus "grew in wisdom"; Luke 2:52). It also accounted for the "unusual" insights into people and situations that distinguished Jesus from other human beings (e.g., Matt. 9:4; John 1:45–51; 6:64; 16:19). Furthermore, the model provided an explanation for such a phenomenon as Jesus not being aware of the time of his own return (Mark 13:32). Thus, Morris affirmed, along the lines of historic Christology, that Jesus Christ was fully human, but not merely human; he was also fully divine. In the incarnation there is one person Jesus Christ with two natures, human and divine, and hence two ranges of consciousness. And Morris's model provided a way to understand the incarnation such that the charge of incoherence fails.

Still, evangelical responses did not stem the tide of attacks against historic Christology; two assaults were particularly virulent. The first came from the Jesus Seminar, which studied the sayings of Jesus. It attempted to apply certain criteria to the Gospels, including the noncanonical *Gospel of Thomas* (see below), in order to discern what Jesus certainly said or what he may have said, and then to distinguish that from what Jesus probably did not say or certainly did not say.[132] Applying the criteria,[133] the seminar

129. Thomas V. Morris, *The Logic of God Incarnate* (Ithaca, N.Y., and London: Cornell Univ. Press, 1986), 102.

130. Ibid., 102–3.

131. Ibid., 103.

132. One such criterion was that of dissimilarity: "If we are to identify the voice of Jesus that made his the precipitator of the Christian tradition, we have to look for sayings and stories that distinguish his voice from other ordinary speakers and even sages of his time." Applying this notion, the Jesus Seminar made this assumption: "Jesus' characteristic talk was distinctive—it can usually be distinguished from common

lore. Otherwise it is futile to search for the authentic words of Jesus." This criterion was applied to the content of the sayings of Jesus, and again the Jesus Seminar developed a test for authenticity: "Jesus' parables and sayings cut against the social and religious grain ... [and] surprise and shock: they characteristically call for a reversal of roles or frustrate ordinary, everyday expectations." Robert W. Funk, Roy W. Hoover, and the Jesus Seminar, *The Five Gospels: The Search for the Authentic Words of Jesus* (New York: Polebridge/Macmillan, 1993), 30–31.

133. Ibid., 36–37.

reached a surprising conclusion: "Eighty-two percent of the words ascribed to Jesus in the gospels were not actually spoken by him, according to the Jesus Seminar."[134] Evangelical responses to the Jesus Seminar decried its theologically liberal bias, its criteria for assessing the sayings of Jesus, and its alleged scientific methodology.

The second thematic variation was the return of Gnostic Christologies, a development that gained impetus by means of a trendy fascination with early Gnostic documents such as the *Gospel of Thomas* and the *Gospel of Judas*. As noted previously, the early church strongly denounced such Gospels because they were steeped in Docetism. In an important work entitled *Orthodoxy and Heresy in Earliest Christianity*, Walter Bauer challenged the notion that early Christianity was divided into an "orthodox" group and various "heretical groups," the latter holding to unbiblical views of Jesus. According to Bauer, it was possible that "certain manifestations of Christian life that the authors of the church renounce as 'heresies' originally had not been such at all, but, at least here and there, were the only form of the new religion—that is, for those regions they were simply 'Christianity.' The possibility also exists that their adherents constituted the majority, and that they looked down with hatred and scorn on the orthodox, who for them were the false believers."[135] If Bauer's thesis was correct, then these Gnostic gospels and their Gnostic Christologies were not heretical; indeed, they should play an important role in the modern church's conviction about Christ.

Accordingly, in the latest development, some saw these Gospels as credible witnesses to Jesus of Nazareth that must be incorporated with the canonical Gospels into the church's Christology.[136] As Stephen Patterson asserted with regard to the *Gospel of Thomas*, "As an independent reading of the Jesus tradition, it provides us with a crucial and indispensable tool for gaining critical distance on the synoptic [Gospels] tradition, which has so long dominated the Jesus discussion."[137] But evangelicals disputed this notion. Norm Perrin demonstrated that the *Gospel of Thomas* was a late second-century document written in Coptic, not a first-century Gospel about Jesus written in Greek. Perrin concluded: "We can no longer hold to our romantic vision of *Thomas* as a naïve, artless compiler of Jesus sayings. More importantly, we can no longer envisage the collection as an early and therefore reliable witness of the Jesus tradition."[138] Although on a more sophisticated level, modern evangelicals followed Christians in the early church in dismissing these Gnostic Christologies as false.

In addition to defending the church's traditional formulation, evangelicals made significant contributions to advancing the doctrine of Christ. Some of these constructive works included Millard J. Erickson, *The Word Became Flesh*;[139] Michael S. Horton,

---

134. Ibid., 5.

135. Walter Bauer, *Rechtgläubigkeit und Ketzerei im ältesten Christentum* (Tübingen: J. C. B. Mohr, 1934); Eng. trans., *Orthodoxy and Heresy in Earliest Christianity*, ed. Robert Kraft, trans. Gerhard Krodel, Philadelphia Seminar on Christian Origins (Philadelphia: Fortress, 1971), xxii.

136. For an example, see Elaine Pagels, *The Gnostic Gospels* (New York: Vintage Books/Random House, 1979/1989); idem, *Beyond Belief: The Secret Gospel of Thomas* (New York:

Random House, 2003).

137. Stephen J. Patterson, *The Gospel of Thomas and Jesus*, Foundations and Facets Reference Series (Sonoma, Calif.: Polebridge, 1993), 241.

138. Norm Perrin, "Thomas: The Fifth Gospel?" *JETS* 49, no. 1 (March 2006), 80.

139. Millard J. Erickson, *The Word Became Flesh: A Contemporary Incarnational Christology* (Grand Rapids: Baker, 1991).

Lord and Servant;[140] Simon J. Gathercole, *The Preexistent Son*;[141] Fred Sanders and Klaus Issler, eds., *Jesus in Trinitarian Perspective*;[142] Oliver D. Crisp, *Divinity and Humanity*;[143] Richard Bauckham, *Jesus and the God of Israel*;[144] and Robert M. Bowman Jr. and J. Ed Komoszewski, *Putting Jesus in His Place*.[145] Through these and other similar efforts, evangelicals continue to express and defend the church's historical doctrine of Jesus Christ.

---

140. Michael S. Horton, *Lord and Servant: A Covenant Christology* (Louisville: Westminster John Knox, 2005).

141. Simon J. Gathercole, *The Preexistent Son: Recovering the Christologies of Matthew, Mark, and Luke* (Grand Rapids: Eerdmans, 2006).

142. Fred Sanders and Klaus Issler, eds., *Jesus in Trinitarian Perspective* (Nashville: Broadman Academic, 2007).

143. Oliver D. Crisp, *Divinity and Humanity*, Current Issues in Theology (Cambridge: Cambridge Univ. Press, 2007).

144. Richard Bauckham, *Jesus and the God of Israel: God Crucified and Other Studies on the New Testament's Christology of Divine Identity* (Grand Rapids: Eerdmans, 2008).

145. Robert M. Bowman Jr. and J. Ed Komoszewski, *Putting Jesus in His Place: The Case for the Deity of Christ* (Grand Rapids: Kregel, 2007).

Chapter 18

THE ATONEMENT

How has the church come to understand
the nature and benefits of the atonement?

STATEMENT OF BELIEF

The church has historically explained the atonement — "the work Christ did in his life and death to earn our salvation" — in various ways.[1] At times, it has viewed the death of Christ as a payment to Satan; at other times, Christ's death has been considered to be a tribute offered to God to restore his honor lost through humanity's sin. Some in the church have focused on the great example of Christ's life as his chief accomplishment; others have underscored how much the death of Christ demonstrates the love of God and prompts humanity to love in return. The number of different views is quite extensive.

Unlike many important doctrines, the atonement has never been the subject of an ecumenical, or general, church council to determine its official doctrinal formulation. The prevalent view among Protestants is called the penal substitutionary view: "Christ's death was 'penal' in that he bore a penalty when he died. His death was also a 'substitution' in that he was a substitute for us when he died."[2] The question "For whom did Christ die?" — a question of the extent of the atonement — has been an important debate among Protestants. Evangelicals have generally held to the penal substitutionary model of the atonement while also highlighting other aspects that Christ's death accomplished. Recently, this view, or the emphasis placed on penal substitution so as to elevate it above other theories of the atonement, has come under strong attack.[3]

THE ATONEMENT IN THE EARLY CHURCH

The early church formulated its understanding of the work of Jesus Christ from the background of the Old Testament sacrificial system and the teachings of Christ himself.

---

1. Wayne Grudem, *Systematic Theology: An Introduction to Biblical Doctrine* (Grand Rapids: Zondervan, 1994, 2000), 568.
2. Ibid., 579.
3. My thanks to Rony Kozman and Micah Carter for their help on this chapter. It has appeared in a shorter format in Gregg Allison, "A History of the Doctrine of the Atonement," The Atonement in Focus issue, *The Southern Baptist Journal of Theology* 11, no. 2 (Summer 2007): 4–19. Permission granted.

The fact that Jesus' sufferings began on the night of the Passover linked his death with the sacrificial lamb offered during that special Jewish festival (Ex. 12; 1 Cor. 5:7; cf. John 1:29). According to the writer to the Hebrews, the entire sacrificial system was inadequate and ultimately unable to remove sin (Heb. 10:1–4). Indeed, those sacrifices looked forward to and found their fulfillment in the sacrifice of Jesus (Heb. 10:11–14).

The New Testament presents the death of Christ as a multifaceted diamond. One facet of the gem is *expiation*: Christ's sacrifice removed the liability to punishment and condemnation under which sinful people suffered (Heb. 9:6–15). A second facet is *propitiation*: Christ's death appeased the wrath of God against his sinful creatures (Rom. 3:25–26; 1 John 2:2). The gem's third facet is *redemption*: The death of Christ is the payment he offered to God to buy captives out of the slave market of sin (Mark 10:45; 1 Peter 1:18–19). The fourth facet of the diamond is *reconciliation*: Christ's death has taken sinners from being enemies of God to being his friends and children (2 Cor. 5:17–21). The fifth facet is *Christ the Victor*: Through his death, Christ achieved ultimate victory over Satan and the demons (Heb. 2:14–15; Col. 2:15). A sixth facet is *example*: Christ's death is both a demonstration of God's love and a model of obedience and suffering for believers to follow (Rom. 5:8; 1 Peter 2:20–21). A final facet of Christ's work is *exchange*: The righteousness of Jesus Christ is imputed, or credited, to the account of those who believe in him, and their sin is imputed to him (2 Cor. 5:21; Rom. 5:19).

Following this multifaceted New Testament approach, the early church offered various descriptions of Christ's sacrificial work. At first, these were quite simple explanations. For example, Clement of Rome described Christ's work of substitution: "Because of the love he had for us, Jesus Christ our Lord, in accordance with God's will, gave his blood for us, and his flesh for our flesh, and his life for our lives."[4] This suffering on behalf of others becomes the example for Christians to follow: "You see, dear friends, the kind of pattern that has been given to us; for if the Lord so humbled himself, what should we do, who through him have come under the yoke of his grace?"[5] In another approach, the *Letter to Diognetus* exalted the transaction that took place between Christ and sinners worthy of punishment and death:

> Oh, the surpassing kindness and love of God! He did not hate us, or reject us, or bear a grudge against us. Instead, he was patient and forbearing; in his mercy he took upon himself our sins. He himself gave up his own Son as a ransom for us—the holy one for the lawless, the guiltless for the guilty, "the just for the unjust" [1 Pet. 3:18], the incorruptible for the corruptible, the immortal for the mortal. For what else but his righteousness could have covered our sins? In whom was it possible for us, the lawless and ungodly, to be justified, except in the Son of God alone? O the sweet exchange! O the incomprehensible work of God! O the unexpected blessings, that the sinfulness of many should be hidden in one righteous man, while the righteousness of one should justify many sinners![6]

---

4. Clement of Rome, *Letter of the Romans to the Corinthians*, 49, in Holmes, 85; *ANF*, 1:18.

5. Ibid., 16, in Holmes, 47–49; *ANF*, 1:9. This is the lesson that Clement drew from descriptions of the Suffering Servant in Isa. 53 and Ps. 22.

6. *The Epistle to Diognetus*, 9, in Holmes, 547; *ANF*, 1:28. The text has been rendered clearer.

The early church focused its discussion on different aspects of Christ's work as well. Rehearsing the themes of the curse and healing, Justin Martyr explained: "The Father of all wished his Christ take upon himself the curses of the whole human family, knowing that, after he had been crucified and was dead, he would raise him up.... His Father wished him to suffer this, in order that by his stripes the human race might be healed."[7] Melito of Sardis developed the theme of redemption by means of sacrifice, playing off the sacrifice of Isaac (Gen. 22): "In place of Isaac the just, a ram appeared for slaughter, in order that Isaac might be liberated from his bonds. The slaughter of this animal redeemed Isaac from death. In like manner, the Lord, being slain, saved us; being bound, he loosed [freed] us; being sacrificed, he redeemed us."[8] Similarly, Irenaeus appealed to Abraham's sacrifice to portray Christ's work of redemption through his sacrificial death: "Abraham, according to his faith, followed the command of the Word of God, and with a ready mind delivered up, as a sacrifice to God, his only-begotten and beloved son, in order that God also might be pleased to offer up for all his seed [offspring] his own beloved and only-begotten Son, as a sacrifice for our redemption."[9]

Irenaeus was also responsible for formulating one of the earliest well-developed views of the atonement, called *the recapitulation theory*: "When he [the Son of God] became incarnate, and made man, he commenced anew the long line of human beings, and furnished us with salvation in a brief, comprehensive manner. So what we had lost in Adam—namely, to be according to the image and likeness of God—that we might recover in Jesus Christ."[10] Irenaeus's view focused on the events in the life of Jesus Christ as the recapitulation, or summation, of all the life events of fallen humanity. However, instead of these being lived out in disobedience to God, Christ lived them obediently. Therefore, he reversed the sinful direction in which people were headed, saved them, and provided them with a new orientation:

> He [Jesus Christ] came to save all [humanity] through means of himself—all, I say, who through him are born again to God—infants, children, boys, young men and old. He therefore passed through every age, becoming an infant for infants, thus sanctifying infants; a child for children, thus sanctifying those who are of this age, at the same time becoming an example of holiness, righteousness, and submission; a youth for youths, becoming an example to youths, and thus sanctifying them for the Lord. So likewise, he was an old man for old men, that he might be a perfect master for all, not merely in respect to the setting forth of the truth, but also as regards age, sanctifying at the same time the aged also, and becoming an example to them as well.[11]

Thus, Christ's life repeated the course of human existence, with this one important exception: the sinful course was reversed, and Christ's obedient life was exchanged for it.

But it was not only the curse-reversing *life* of Jesus Christ that Irenaeus emphasized; he also saw Christ's *death* as undoing human disobedience:

7. Justin Martyr, *Dialogue with Trypho, a Jew*, 137, in *ANF*, 1:268; cf. ibid., 95, in *ANF*, 1:247. The text has been rendered clearer.

8. Melito of Sardis, from the *Catena on Genesis*, 5, in *ANF*, 8:759.

9. Irenaeus, *Against Heresies*, 4.5.4, in *ANF*, 1:467.

10. Ibid., 3.18.1, in *ANF*, 1:446. The text has been rendered clearer.

11. Ibid., 2.22.4, in *ANF*, 1:391. The text has been rendered clearer.

In order to do away with [the effects of] that disobedience of man which had taken place at the beginning by means of a tree, "he became obedient unto death, even the death of the cross" [Phil. 2:8]. By this he rectified that disobedience that had occurred by means of a tree, through that obedience which was [accomplished] upon the tree [of the cross] ... We had offended God in the first Adam, when he did not obey God's commandment. In the second Adam, however, we are reconciled, being made obedient even unto death.[12]

According to Irenaeus's recapitulation theory, what Adam is to disobedience, Christ—through both his life and death—is to obedience: "For as by the disobedience of the one man, who was originally formed from virgin soil, the many were made sinners and forfeited life; so was it necessary that, by the obedience of one man, who was originally born from a virgin, many should be justified and receive salvation."[13]

Another common theme in the early church's understanding of the atonement was rescue from Satan, the enemy of humanity. The person most commonly associated with this view is Origen, who popularized *the ransom to Satan theory* of Christ's work. For Origen, Satan had usurped God's rightful ownership of human beings; thus, all people illegitimately belong to the evil one. Christ's death was the ransom that was paid to release people from this tragic situation, and the ransom was paid to Satan. As Origen reasoned: "To whom did he [Christ] give his life a ransom for many? Assuredly not to God; could it then be to the evil one? For he was holding us fast until the ransom should be given him, even the life of Jesus; being deceived with the idea that he could have dominion over it, and not seeing that he could not bear the torture in retaining it."[14] Origen's wording made it seem as though Satan was the one who dictated the terms of salvation: "If therefore we are bought with a price ... without doubt we are bought by someone, whose slaves we were, who also demanded what price he would, to let go from his power those whom he held. Now it was the devil who held us, to whom we had been sold by our sins. He demanded therefore as our price, the blood of Jesus."[15] Although he demanded Christ for a ransom, Satan did not anticipate the consequences of this transaction, out of his own ignorance.[16] Once Satan had Christ in his clutches, he could not hold him; rather, Satan was forced to let Christ go. Thus, he lost not only his former slaves, who had been ransomed by Christ, but the ransom—Christ himself—as well. The death of Christ dealt "the first blow in the conflict which is to overthrow the power of that evil spirit the devil, who had obtained dominion over the whole world."[17]

---

12. Ibid., 5.16.3, in *ANF*, 1:544. The text has been rendered clearer.

13. Ibid., 3.18.7, in *ANF*, 1:448.

14. Origen, *Commentary on Matthew 16:8*, cited in H. D. McDonald, *The Atonement of the Death of Christ in Faith, Revelation, and History* (Grand Rapids: Baker, 1985), 142.

15. Origen, *Homilies in Romans*, 2:13, cited in McDonald, *Atonement of the Death of Christ*, 142.

16. Origen, *Homilies in Psalm 35 (34)*:8. See R. S. Franks, *The Work of Christ: A Historical Study of Christian Doctrine*,

Nelson's Library of Theology, H. H. Rowley, gen. ed. (London: Thomas Nelson and Sons, 1962), 40.

17. Origen, *Against Celsus*, 7.17, in *ANF*, 4:617. Although certainly a questionable theory of Christ's work, because it lacks extensive biblical support, the ransom to Satan theory was only one aspect of Origen's overall understanding of the death of Christ. He also placed a strong (and biblical) emphasis on Christ's death being a vicarious substitution (e.g., *Homilies in John*, 28.19.165).

Popularized by Origen, the ransom to Satan theory was reworked by many who came after him. Strange twists were often added to the basic view. For example, Gregory of Nyssa conceived of Christ's work as an exquisite deception—with God being credited with tricking Satan and causing the loss of his victim.[18] The deception entered by means of Christ's deity being enclosed in human flesh. Lured by the powerful miracles of Christ, Satan desired to conquer him as the ransom for humanity. But Satan was tricked, for he had no idea that hidden under Christ's flesh was the divine nature. Gregory used the metaphor of bait on a fishing line, luring fish. Concealed inside the bait, however, was the hook, the instrument through which the hungry fish were reeled in to destruction:

> In order to secure that the ransom on our behalf might be easily accepted by him [Satan] who required it, the deity [of Christ] was hidden under the veil of our [human] nature. Thus, as with ravenous [hungry] fish, the hook of the deity might be gulped down along with the bait of flesh. In this way, life would be introduced into the house of death, and light would shine in the darkness. And so that which is diametrically opposed to light and life might vanish; for it is not in the nature of darkness to remain when light is present, or of death to exist when life is active.[19]

Thus, by means of this deceptive divine ploy, the ransom that was to be paid to Satan destroyed him and left him with nothing.

Another modification of the ransom theory was made by those who dissented from the idea that the ransom was paid to Satan. For example, John of Damascus, using the same analogy of bait and hook, proposed that Christ ransomed fallen humanity through his death, but the ransom was given to God the Father because the sin of humanity had been committed against him. Rather than Satan being tricked, it was death that was lured by the bait of Christ's humanity and deceived by his deity.[20]

Although it became the most common view of the work of Christ in the early church, the ransom to Satan theory did not enjoy a monopoly. Some church leaders emphasized the substitutionary nature of the death of Christ. For example, Tertullian presented Christ's death as an atonement for sin, with escape from hell and eternal life in heaven as the results.[21] Similarly, Athanasius described how Christ's sacrifice paid the penalty for the sins of all humanity:

> It was necessary that the debt owed by everyone should be paid, and this debt owed was that everyone should die. For this particular reason, Jesus Christ came

18. Gregory of Nyssa, *The Great Catechism*, 22–23, in *NPNF²*, 5:492–93.

19. Ibid., 24, in *NPNF²*, 5:494. The text has been rendered clearer.

20. Our Lord Jesus Christ "dies because he took on himself death on our behalf, and he makes himself an offering to the Father for our sakes. For we had sinned against him, and it was right that he should receive the ransom for us, and that we should thus be delivered from the condemnation. God forbid that the blood of the Lord should have been offered to the tyrant. Therefore, death approaches and, swallowing up the body as a bait is transfixed on the hook of divinity, and after tasting of a sinless and life-giving body, perishes, and brings up again all whom of old he swallowed up. For just as darkness disappears on the introduction of light, so is death repulsed before the assault of life, and brings life to all, but death to the destroyer." John of Damascus, *Exposition of the Orthodox Faith*, 3.27, in *NPNF²*, 9:72 (this is the second page 72 in the volume).

21. Tertullian, *On Flight in Persecution*, 12, in *ANF*, 4:123.

among us.... He offered up his sacrifice on behalf of everyone, yielding his temple [i.e., his body] to death in the place of everyone.... And so it was that two wonderful things came to pass at once: the death of everyone was accomplished in the Lord's body, and death and corruption were completely done away with by reason of the Word that was united with it. For death was necessary, and death must be suffered on behalf of everyone, so that the debt owed by everyone might be paid.[22]

Thus, Christ "became to us salvation, and became life, and became propitiation" by offering his death as a sacrifice to pay the penalty for sins.[23]

This idea of substitution was joined with various other themes in Augustine's understanding of the atonement. Focusing on Christ as the one mediator between God and humanity, Augustine explained that Christ "is both the priest who offers and the sacrifice offered."[24] In this dual role, Christ fulfills the four aspects of a fitting sacrifice — "*to whom* it is offered, *by whom* it is offered, *what* is offered, [and] *for whom* it is offered: The same one and true Mediator himself, reconciling us to God by the sacrifice of peace, might remain one with him [the Father] to whom he offered [it], might make those [believers] one in himself for whom he offered [it], and he [himself] might be in one both the offerer and the offering."[25] Specifically, this sacrifice was for sin: "[W]e came to death through sin; he [Christ came to it] through righteousness: and, therefore, as our death is the punishment of sin, so his death was made a sacrifice for sin."[26] Furthermore, this sacrificial death brought redemption for sinners: "Christ, though guiltless, took our punishment, that he might cancel our guilt, and do away with our punishment.... Confess that he died, and you may also confess that he, without taking our sin, took its punishment."[27]

In terms of the benefits of Christ's work, Augustine saw his death as delivering sinful people from Satan's evil power.[28] But he did not limit his discussion to this one benefit. Another benefit is escape from the second death, or eternal death that is meted out on the wicked after the resurrection. For believers, the death of Christ rescues from this horrific end.[29] Another benefit is the removal of God's wrath and reconciliation to friendship with God.[30] Furthermore, when Christ's death is viewed as the supreme demonstration of God's love for humanity, a final benefit that flows from it is a stimulus to love God in return.[31] The cross of Christ demonstrates God's love for fallen humanity, and those who see this demonstration are encouraged to respond with love.[32]

Thus, for Augustine, Christ's atoning death rescued sinful human beings by liberating them from Satan, removing the divine wrath, reconciling humanity to God, demonstrat-

---

22. Athanasius, *On the Incarnation of the Word*, 20, in *NPNF*[2], 4:47. The text has been rendered clearer.

23. Athanasius, *Four Discourses against the Arians*, 1:64, in *NPNF*[2], 4:343.

24. Augustine, *The City of God*, 10.20, in *NPNF*[1], 2:193.

25. Augustine, *On the Trinity*, 4.14.19, in *NPNF*[1], 3:79 (italics added). The text has been rendered clearer.

26. Ibid., 4.12.15, in *NPNF*[1], 3:77.

27. Augustine, *Reply to Faustus the Manichaean*, 14:4, 7, in *NPNF*[1], 4:208–9.

28. Augustine, *Sermon* 163.1; in Alister McGrath, *Iustitia Dei: A History of the Christian Doctrine of Justification* (Cambridge: Cambridge Univ. Press, 1986), 29.

29. Augustine, *City of God*, 13.11, in *NPNF*[1], 2:250.

30. Augustine, *Enchiridion on Faith, Hope, and Love*, 33, in *NPNF*[1], 3:249.

31. Augustine, *On the Trinity*, 13.10.13, 14, in *NPNF*[1], 3:174.

32. Augustine, *On the Catechizing of the Uninstructed*, 4.7, in *NPNF*[1], 3:286–87.

ing the love of God, and providing escape from death. In short, it cured the fallen world of its many miseries.

THE ATONEMENT IN THE MIDDLE AGES

After many centuries of domination by the ransom to Satan theory, Anselm offered a fresh view of the atonement, *the satisfaction theory*. In his book *Why God Became Man*, he set forth the major aspects of his model, beginning with the problem of sin:

> To sin is nothing other than not to give God what is owed to him. What is the debt which we owe to God?... This is righteousness or uprightness of the will. It makes individuals righteous or upright in their heart, that is, their will. This is the sole honor, the complete honor, which we owe to God and which God demands from us.... Someone who does not render to God this honor due to him is taking away from God what is his, and dishonoring God, and this is what it is to sin.[33]

Anselm lived in a feudal system in which overlords provided protection for their serfs, who in turn provided food and services for their lords. In this feudal system, restitution of honor was a key concept. If a serf dishonored his lord by stealing ten chickens, for example, the satisfactory solution to this problem was not merely restoration of what had been stolen—ten chickens. Satisfaction demanded a payment that went beyond what was due, so the serf owed, say, fifteen chickens to his lord. Anselm picked up on this concept of satisfaction, and viewed the solution to human sin in the same light:

> As long as he does not repay what he has taken away, he remains in a state of guilt. And it is not sufficient merely to repay what has been taken away: rather, he ought to pay back more than he took, in proportion to the insult which he has inflicted.... One should also observe that when someone repays what he has unlawfully stolen, what he is under an obligation to give is not the same as what it would be possible to demand from him, were it not that he had seized the other person's property. Therefore, everyone who sins is under an obligation to repay to God the honor which he has violently taken from him, and this is the satisfaction which every sinner is obliged to give to God.[34]

At this point, Anselm denied that "it is fitting for God to forgive a sin out of mercy alone, without any restitution of the honor taken away from him."[35] Two options remained: "It is a necessary consequence, therefore, that either the honor which has been taken away should be repaid, or punishment should follow."[36] To not restore God's honor is unthinkable, so Anselm focused on a satisfactory payment for sin:

> It is impossible for God to lose his honor. For either a sinner of his own accord repays what he owes or God takes it from him against his—the sinner's—will.

---

33. Anselm, *Why God Became Man*, 1.11, in *Anselm*, 283.
34. Ibid.

35. Ibid., 1.12, in *Anselm*, 284.
36. Ibid., 1.13, in *Anselm*, 287.

This is because either a man of his own free will demonstrates the submission which he owes to God by not sinning, or alternatively by paying recompense for his sin, or else God brings him into submission to himself against his will, by subjecting him to torment, and in this way he shows that he is his Lord, something which the man himself refuses to admit voluntarily.[37]

Perhaps, then, God could simply punish all humanity—each person—for his or her sins, and not save anyone. Such retribution would satisfy his justice. But Anselm could not accept this idea for a reason that he picked up from Augustine: God cannot punish every human being, because a number of human beings equal to the number of fallen angels must be saved.[38] This would restore the original creation to its balance and harmony. So satisfaction for sin—in one way or another—is necessary.[39]

Could it be that a man could pay the debt himself? Anselm imagined what could be offered to God as a payment for sin: "Penitence, a contrite and humbled heart, fasting and many kinds of bodily labor, the showing of pity through giving and forgiveness, and obedience."[40] But Anselm quickly dismissed these as things owed to God already.[41] Thus, if owed to God, these things cannot be given to him in payment for sin. And there is another problem as well:

> Because of the man who was conquered [Adam, in the fall], the whole of humanity is rotten and, as it were, in a ferment with sin—and God raises up no one with sin to fill up the complement of the renowned heavenly city. Correspondingly, supposing a man were victorious, because of him as many humans would be brought out of sin into a state of righteousness as would make up that full number ... for the completion of which mankind was created. But a man who is a sinner is in no way capable of doing this, for one sinner cannot make another sinner righteous.[42]

So man is helpless to save himself.

For Anselm, the only one who can save humanity is one who is both God and man:

> [Satisfaction] cannot come about unless there should be someone who would make a payment to God greater than everything that exists apart from God.... It is also a necessity that someone who can give to God from his own property something which exceeds everything which is inferior to God, must himself be superior to everything that exists apart from God.... Now, there is nothing superior to all that exists which is not God—except God.... But the obligation rests with man, and no one else, to make the payment.... Otherwise mankind is not making recompense. If, therefore,... no one can pay except God, and no one ought to pay except man: it is necessary that a God-man should pay it.[43]

37. Ibid., 1.14, in *Anselm*, 287.

38. Ibid., 1.16, in *Anselm*, 290. Augustine expressed this idea in his *Enchiridion on Faith, Hope and Love*, 29, in *NPNF¹*, 3:247.

39. Ibid., 1.19, in *Anselm*, 300–303.

40. Ibid., 1.20, in *Anselm*, 303.

41. Ibid.

42. Ibid., 1.23, in *Anselm*, 309.

43. Ibid., 2.6, in *Anselm*, 319–20.

Therefore, Jesus Christ, the God-man, is the only one who can offer satisfaction for the sin of humanity:

> He ought to possess something ... which he may give to God voluntarily and not in payment of a debt.... If we say that he will make a present of himself as an act of obedience to God ... this will not constitute giving something which God does not demand from him in repayment of a debt. For every rational creature owes this obedience to God.... [But] to hand himself over to death, for the honor of God ... is not something which God will demand from him in repayment of a debt, given that, since there will be no sin in him, he will be under no obligation to die.[44]

Thus, the death of Christ is the sufficient and necessary satisfaction that he willingly offered to God. In doing so, Christ obtained a reward, but it was a reward that he did not need. It only makes sense that Christ would give this reward to fallen human beings, "for whose salvation ... he made himself a man."[45] So Christ directs that his reward should be given to sinners so as to provide satisfaction for their sins, and the Father gives redemption to all who embrace the Son.[46] In this way, Anselm explained the work of Christ in terms of the satisfaction theory of the atonement.

While reaction to Anselm's theory was generally positive, dissenters expressed contempt for his view. Chief among these was Abelard, who originated *the moral influence theory* of the atonement. Actually, he rejected both of the prevalent theories of his time—the ransom to Satan theory and Anselm's satisfaction view. In their place he proposed another position: "The purpose and cause of the incarnation was that he [Christ] might illuminate the world by his wisdom and excite it to the love of himself."[47] What people need, according to Abelard, is for their love for God to be stimulated. God does not require the death of Christ as a payment for sin; Abelard distanced himself from that idea. Instead, a persuasive exhibition of God's love is necessary. Christ provided this demonstration by his life and especially by his death, the crowning act of love: "Our redemption is that supreme love shown in our case by the passion of Christ which not only liberates from slavery to sin, but [also] wins for us the true liberty of the sons of God, so that we may fulfill all things from love rather than from fear."[48] The work of Christ, being an exhibition of divine love, stimulates people to love God.[49] In short, Abelard did not minimize the death of Christ, but he denied that it has a necessary connection to the forgiveness of sins. Also, he removed the atonement from an objective reality—what Christ accomplished on the cross—to a subjective influence on people—it kindles within them a love for God. Thus, the death of Christ is the supreme example of divine love and influences sinners to respond to God with a reciprocating

44. Ibid., 2.11, in *Anselm*, 329–30.

45. Ibid., 2.19, in *Anselm*, 353.

46. Ibid., 2.20, in *Anselm*, 354.

47. Council of Sens, in McDonald, *Atonement of the Death of Christ*, 174.

48. Peter Abelard, *Exposition of the Epistle to the Romans*,

The Epitome of Christian Doctrine, comment on Rom. 3:26, in McDonald, *Atonement of the Death of Christ*, 175.

49. "Kindled by so great a benefit of divine grace, charity should not be afraid to endure anything for his [Christ's] sake." Ibid.

love. This, for Abelard, is the heart of the Christian faith: "Christ died for us in order to show how great was his love for humanity and to prove that love is the essence of Christianity."[50]

In discussing Christ's atoning work, Aquinas developed Anselm's idea that Christ went beyond the call of duty in dying—his was a work of *supererogation*.[51] For Anselm, this had meant that Christ's infinite satisfaction through his death could be applied to the infinite penalty accumulated by humanity's sin. But Aquinas viewed both the life and the death of Christ as "a superabundant atonement for the sins of the human race."[52] This atonement, according to Aquinas, has to be appropriated by several means: "Christ's passion [suffering] works its effect in them to whom it is applied, through faith and charity [love] and the sacraments of faith."[53] Specifically, these sacraments are baptism—to remove original sin and actual sins committed before baptism—and penance—to deal with actual sins committed after baptism.[54] Thus, while affirming that Christ's death was a superabundant atonement, Aquinas held that a human cooperation with the work of Christ is necessary. Faith, love, and participation in the sacraments unite people to the atonement of Christ and become a necessary part of it. It is easy to see how this idea could turn into a system of human works designed to merit the grace and forgiveness of God. This was one of the reasons that people like Martin Luther and John Calvin sought to reform the church.

THE ATONEMENT IN THE REFORMATION AND POST-REFORMATION

The Reformers introduced another view of the atonement, generally called the *penal substitutionary theory*. In some ways, it was similar to Anselm's satisfaction theory, but with this major difference: instead of grounding the atonement in the honor of God—

---

50. Peter Abelard, *Sentences*, 23; and *Exposition of the Epistle to the Romans*, LCC, 10:283–84, cited in Bruce Demarest, *The Cross and Salvation: The Doctrine of Salvation*, Foundations of Evangelical Theology, John S. Feinberg, gen. ed. (Wheaton: Crossway, 1997), 153. Reaction to Abelard's view was quick. Its chief opponent was Bernard of Clairvaux, who wrote to the pope with his concerns: "What profit is there for Christ to instruct us by example if he did not first restore us by his grace? Are we not instructed in vain if the body of sin is not first destroyed in us, that we should no more serve sin? If all the benefit that we derive from Christ consists in the example of his virtuous life, it follows that Adam must be said to harm us only by the example of sin. But truly the medicine given us was proportional to the disease. 'For as in Adam all die, even so in Christ shall all be made alive' (1 Cor. 15:22). As is the one, so is the other. If the life which Christ gives is nothing other than his instruction, the death which Adam gave is in the same way only his instruction; so that the one by his example leads men to sin, the other by his example and his

Word leads them to a holy life and to love him. But if we rest in the Christian faith, and not in the heresy of Pelagius [this is Abelard's view], and confess that by generation [birth] and not by example was the sin of Adam imparted to us, and by sin death, let us also confess that it is necessary for righteousness to be restored to us by Christ, not by instruction, but by regeneration [new birth] and by righteousness of life (Rom. 5:18)." Bernard of Clairvaux, "To Pope Innocent, against Certain Heads of Abelard's Heresies," *Letter* 60.9.23, in *Some Letters of Saint Bernard, Abbot of Clairvaux*, ed. Francis Aiden Gasquet, trans. Samuel J. Eales (London: John Hodges, 1904), 290–91. The text has been rendered clearer. In keeping with these concerns, the Council of Sens, in 1140, condemned Abelard's moral influence theory for being incomplete.

51. *Supererogation* comes from two Latin words indicating "a work that goes beyond" what is required.

52. Thomas Aquinas, *Summa Theologica*, pt. 3, q. 48, art. 2.

53. Ibid., pt. 3, q. 49, art. 3.

54. Ibid.

that of which God had been robbed by the sin of humanity—the Reformers grounded it in the justice of God. Because he is holy, God hates sin with wrathful anger and acts against it by condemning and punishing sin. Thus, there is an eternal penalty to pay for sin. Humanity could not atone for its own sin, but Christ did: as the substitute for humanity, he died as a sacrifice to pay the penalty, suffered the divine wrath against sin, and removed its condemnation forever.

Martin Luther expressed the penal substitutionary theory in this way:

> Because an eternal, unchangeable sentence of condemnation has passed upon sin—for God cannot and will not regard sin with favor, but his wrath abides upon it eternally and irrevocably—redemption was not possible without a ransom of such precious worth as to atone for sin, to assume the guilt, pay the price of wrath and thus abolish sin. This no creature was able to do. There was no remedy except for God's only Son to step into our distress and himself become man, to take upon himself the load of awful and eternal wrath and make his own body and blood a sacrifice for sin. And so he did, out of the immeasurably great mercy and love towards us, giving himself up and bearing the sentence of unending wrath and death.[55]

Luther emphasized the dreadful state in which sinful humanity finds itself, due specifically to its failure to obey God's law. This breakdown results in a curse on all people. Christ accomplished salvation by bearing the curse for everyone: "Putting off his innocence and holiness and putting on your sinful person, he bore your sin, death, and curse; he became a sacrifice and a curse for you, in order thus to set you free from the curse of the Law."[56] Luther specified that Christ became this sacrifice and curse by dying on the cross as a substitute for sinful human beings.[57] This sacrifice, then, was a propitiation: "Christ suffered for us and became a place of propitiation through suffering, except that we are unrighteous, for whom he took on that nature, and must seek our righteousness from God alone, having our sins forgiven through a propitiation of that kind."[58] Thus, Luther contributed to the development of the doctrine of the atonement.

John Calvin located the penal substitutionary atonement within Christ's larger work of exercising the three offices of prophet, king, and priest.[59] As priest, Christ reconciles sinful people to God by his sacrificial death:

> As a pure and stainless Mediator he [Christ] is by his holiness to reconcile us to God. But God's righteous curse bars our access to him, and God in his capacity as judge is angry toward us. Hence, an expiation must intervene in order that Christ as priest may obtain God's favor for us and appease his wrath. Thus Christ to perform this office had to come forward with a sacrifice. . . . The

55. Martin Luther, "Epistle Sermon: Twenty-fourth Sunday after Trinity," cited in John Nicholas Lenker, ed., *The Precious and Sacred Writings of Martin Luther* (Minneapolis: The Luther Press, 1909), 9:43–45.

56. Martin Luther, *Lectures on Galatians*, LW, 26:288.

57. Ibid., LW, 26:279.

58. *Lectures on Romans*, LW, 25:32–33n25.

59. John Calvin, *Institutes of the Christian Religion*, 2.15.1–2, LCC, 1:495.

priestly office belongs to Christ alone because by the sacrifice of his death he blotted out our own guilt and made satisfaction for our sins.[60]

In discussing the details of Christ's atonement, Calvin emphasized several key points: Atonement is necessary because of God's righteous wrath against sin. Calvin described the situation of a typical sinner: "Scripture teaches that he was estranged from God through sin, is an heir of wrath, subject to the curse of eternal death, excluded from all hope of salvation, beyond every blessing of God, the slave of Satan, captive under the yoke of sin, destined finally for a dreadful destruction and already involved in it."[61] The atoning work of Christ intervened into this human nightmare. Involved in this work, according to Calvin, were substitution, cleansing, expiation (removing the liability to suffer punishment through satisfaction), and propitiation (appeasing the divine wrath).[62]

According to Calvin, it was not only by his death that Christ accomplished all of this; his life of obedience was also involved: "From the time when he took on the form of a servant, he began to pay the price of liberation in order to redeem us."[63] But this life of obedience was not the key element: "To define the way of salvation more exactly, Scripture ascribes this particularly and properly to Christ's death."[64] Calvin underscored the voluntary nature of this death. And he emphasized that Christ died as an innocent and righteous man, in place of sinful humanity. For Calvin, Christ's condemnation before Pontius Pilate taught this lesson:

> The curse caused by our guilt was awaiting us at God's heavenly judgment seat. Accordingly, Scripture first relates Christ's condemnation before Pontius Pilate ... to teach us that the penalty to which we were subject had been imposed upon this righteous man. We could not escape God's dreadful judgment. To deliver us from it, Christ allowed himself to be condemned before a mortal man.... To take away our condemnation, it was not enough for him to suffer any kind of death: to make satisfaction for our redemption a form of death had to be chosen in which he might free us both by transferring our condemnation to himself and by taking our guilt upon himself.[65]

Thus, "the guilt that held us liable for punishment has been transferred to the head of the Son of God."[66]

Furthermore, the very form of death suffered by Christ—crucifixion—was meaningful for Calvin. By dying on a cross, Christ became the curse for humanity: "The cross was accursed, not only in human opinion but by decree of God (Deut. 21:23). Hence, when Christ is hanged upon the cross, he makes himself subject to the curse. It had to happen in this way in order that the whole curse—which on account of our sins awaited us, or rather lay upon us—might be lifted from us, while it was transferred to him."[67]

---

60. Ibid., 2.15.6, LCC, 1:501–2.
61. Ibid., 2.16.2, LCC, 1:505.
62. Ibid.
63. Ibid., 2.16.5, LCC, 1:507.

64. Ibid. The text has been rendered clearer.
65. Ibid., 2.16.5, LCC, 1:508–9.
66. Ibid., 2.16.5, LCC, 1:509–10.
67. Ibid., 2.16.6, LCC, 1:510.

And by dying as a sacrifice, as pictured in the sacrifices under the old covenant, Christ removed the wrath of God against humanity:

What was figuratively represented in the Mosaic sacrifices is manifested in Christ, the archetype of the figures. Therefore, to perform a perfect expiation, he gave his own life as an *Asham*, that is, as an expiatory offering for sin … upon which our stain and punishment might somehow be cast, and cease to be imputed to us…. The Son of God, utterly clean of all fault, nevertheless took upon himself the shame and reproach of our iniquities, and in return clothes us with his purity…. Here, then, is the meaning of this saying: Christ was offered to the Father in death as an expiatory sacrifice that when he discharged all satisfaction through his sacrifice, we might cease to be afraid of God's wrath.[68]

Thus, in terms of benefits for humanity, "we have in his death the complete fulfillment of salvation, for through it we are reconciled to God, his righteous judgment is satisfied, the curse is removed, and the penalty paid in full."[69]

Calvin and Luther focused on the atonement as a penal substitution, Christ paying the penalty of death as a substitute for sinful humanity. Lutheran and Reformed theology following them continued to develop this theory. For example, the *Formula of Concord*, speaking about a condemned man, affirmed, "[I]t is necessary for him to believe that Jesus Christ has expiated all his sins, and made satisfaction for them, and has obtained remission of sins, righteousness which avails before God, and eternal life without the intervention of any merit of the sinner."[70] Similarly, the *Belgic Confession* described the multifaceted nature of the atonement:

We believe that Jesus Christ is ordained with an oath to be an eternal high priest … who has presented himself on our behalf before his Father, to appease his wrath by his full satisfaction, by offering himself on the tree of the cross, and pouring out his precious blood to purge away our sins…. And he has suffered all this for the remission of our sins. It is not necessary to seek or invent any other means of being reconciled to God than this only sacrifice, once offered, by which believers are made perfect forever.[71]

Furthermore, the *Heidelberg Catechism* echoed much of Anselm's satisfaction theory, with the key difference introduced by the Reformers: instead of grounding the atonement in the honor of God, it focused on the holiness of God as its foundation.[72] Thus, the penal substitutionary theory of the atonement was developed during the Reformation.

Although this theory became the standard view of the atonement among Protestants, it did not go unchallenged. The heretical Socinians developed a view similar in some ways to Abelard's moral influence theory; it is called the *example theory* of the atonement. Like Abelard's position, it rejected the idea that God, because he is just, punishes sin by meting out judgment. Faustus Socinus, founder of the movement, complained:

---

68. Ibid.
69. Ibid., 2.16.13, LCC, 1:520.
70. *Formula of Concord*, art. 4, in Schaff, 3:127. The text has

been rendered clearer.
71. *Belgic Confession*, art. 21, in Schaff, 3:406–7.
72. *Heidelberg Catechism*, q. 12–18, in Schaff, 3.311–13.

"If we could just get rid of this [idea of] justice ... this fiction of Christ's satisfaction would be thoroughly exposed, and should vanish."[73] Indeed, for Socinus, justice leading to punishment, and mercy leading to forgiveness, are completely contradictory. Thus, if Jesus Christ suffered punishment to satisfy the justice of God, there can be no mercy leading to forgiveness. However, we know that God is merciful. This means that he forgives sin without demanding that his justice is satisfied. This is possible because divine justice and mercy are a matter of the will, and so God can simply choose not to exercise his justice:

> There is no such justice in God that absolutely and inexorably requires that sin is punished and that God himself cannot repudiate.... There is a kind of justice which we are accustomed to call by this name, and which is seen only in punishment of sin, but the Scriptures by no means dignify this with the name of justice; rather, they call it wrath or anger.... Hence they greatly err who, deceived by the common use of the word justice, suppose that justice in this sense is a perpetual attribute of God and affirm that it is infinite.[74]

Because God could choose not to exercise his justice, he willed to exercise his mercy instead. Therefore, Christ did not have to offer himself as a satisfaction to God: "Why should God have willed to kill his innocent Son by a cruel and damnable death when there was no need of satisfaction? If this were the way, both the generosity of God would perish and we would invent for ourselves a God who is base and sordid."[75]

Socinianism also maintained that Jesus was an unusually holy man who was equipped with the power of God, but who was not God himself. It pointed to this powerful example of virtue and integrity in the life of Jesus as the model for all humanity to follow. The crowning moment of his exemplary life was Jesus' death, the supreme act of obedience. Thus, by his life and death, Jesus provides a wonderful example that moves people to break with their sins and live holy lives: "Christ takes away sins because by heavenly and most ample promises he attracts and is strong to move all men to repentance, by which sins are destroyed.... He takes away sins because by the example of his most innocent life, he very readily draws all who have not lost hope, to leave their sins and zealously to embrace righteousness and holiness."[76] Thus, the cross of Christ is not about a substitutionary death undertaken by the Son of God. Rather, it is the supreme example of a righteous man and is intended to lead others to embrace forgiveness: "Although the intervention of the blood of Christ did not move God to grant us exemption from punishment of our sins, nevertheless it has moved us to accept the pardon offered and to put our faith in Christ himself—our justification comes from this—and has also in the highest way commended to us the ineffable love of God."[77] Like Abelard's moral influence theory, the Socinian example theory removed the atonement from an objective reality—what Christ

---

73. Faustus Socinus, *De Jesu Christo Servatore*, 3.1, in McDonald, *Atonement of the Death of Christ*, 197.

74. Ibid., 1.2, in McDonald, *Atonement of the Death of Christ*, 198. The text has been rendered clearer.

75. Ibid. The text has been rendered clearer.

76. Faustus Socinus, *Praelectiones Theologia*, 591, cited in L. W. Grensted, *A Short History of the Doctrine of the Atonement* (1920; repr., Eugene, Ore.: Wipf & Stock, 2001), 287.

77. Faustus Socinus, *De Jesu Christo Servatore*, 1.4, in McDonald, *Atonement of the Death of Christ*, 198–99.

accomplished on the cross—to a subjective influence—it moves people to receive the forgiveness of God, which he wills to exercise instead of his justice.

Hugo Grotius disagreed with the Socinians that God does not require a payment for sin, for he could not will to set aside his justice and simply show mercy by forgiving sinful people. But Grotius also rejected the Reformers' idea that Christ's death is a propitiation that removes God's wrath from sinners. So he developed a new view of Christ's work of atonement.

Grotius's position envisioned God as Governor of the universe—thus, the name *the governmental theory*. As Governor, God could choose to relax his standards and forgive sinful people through his mercy. This was due to the fact that as the Lawgiver, God himself was not subject to his law. Actually, God as Governor could eliminate the law or relax it. The former was the option that Socinus had chosen. Grotius opted for the latter. And he based God's relaxation of the law on two goods, both of which would have been eliminated had God as Judge strictly upheld the law: "If all mankind had been given over to eternal death as sinners, two most beautiful things would have perished from the earth—reverential piety towards God on the part of man, and the manifestation of a wonderful benevolence [goodness] towards man on the part of God."[78] But why didn't God simply eliminate the law entirely and be merciful toward sinful people? Grotius cited Isaiah 42:21: "It pleased the LORD for the sake of his righteousness to make his law great and glorious." From this, Grotius drew two conclusions: upholding the law to some degree underscored the holiness of God as Governor, and it was in the best interests of the governed for God to support the law in some measure. Grotius called this the "common good—the conservation and example of order."[79]

At this point, Grotius introduced the work of Christ as meeting the requirements of the relaxed law. His death underscored the terrible nature of sin and emphasized that the law must be respected. And Christ's sharing in human nature allied him closely enough with people so that God could mete out punishment on him instead of sinners: "There is nothing unjust in this, that God whose is the highest authority in all matters not in themselves unjust, and is himself subject to no law, willed to use the sufferings and death of Christ to establish a weighty example against the immense guilt of us all, with whom Christ was most closely allied by nature, by sovereignty, by security."[80] But Christ's sufferings and death did not meet the exact requirements of the divine law; they only satisfied the less stringent demands of the relaxed law. Thus, Christ's work is only "some sort" of satisfaction. More than anything else, it protected the interests of God's government of the universe.

Grotius summarized his governmental theory:

> Among all the attributes of God, love of the human race stands first. Therefore God, though he could justly punish the sins of all men by a worthy and legiti-

78. Hugo Grotius, *Defense of the Catholic Faith on the Satisfaction of Christ, against F. Socinus*, 3, in McDonald, *Atonement of the Death of Christ*, 204.

79. Ibid., 4, in McDonald, *Atonement of the Death of Christ*, 204.

80. Ibid., in McDonald, *Atonement of the Death of Christ*, 205.

mate punishment, that is, by eternal death, and was moved to do so, willed to spare those who believe in Christ. But when it was determined to spare them, either by instituting or not some example against so many and so great sins, he most wisely chose that way by which the greatest number of his attributes might be manifested at the same time; namely, both his mercy and his severity or hatred of sin, and his concern for maintaining the law.[81]

By placing God's government of the world and his love for humanity as the highest priorities of God, Grotius developed a theory that dismissed the atonement of Christ as an exact payment of the penalty demanded by the justice of God and expressed in his law. Christ suffered and died, not as a satisfaction for the exact penalty, but as a token of God's concern to uphold his moral law.

Despite challenges from Socinianism and Hugo Grotius, and in some respects in reaction to them, the post-Reformers continued to defend the penal substitutionary view of the atonement inherited from Luther and Calvin.[82] While agreeing on most points, Lutheran and Reformed theologies of the atonement separated on the issues of the extent of the atonement. The debate dealt with the question, "For whom did Christ die and provide atonement for sins?" The Lutheran position held that Christ died for all people—including the reprobate, those who would never turn to Christ and be saved.[83] This unlimited atonement position was also embraced by Reformed theologian Jacob Arminius and expressed in the *Five Articles of the Remonstrants*: "Jesus Christ, the Savior of the world, died for all men and every man, so that he has obtained for them all, by his death on the cross, redemption and the forgiveness of sins. Yet, no one actually enjoys this forgiveness of sins except the believer."[84] Thus, both Lutheran and Arminian theology embraced the unlimited atonement position.

Although the position of John Calvin on this issue is debatable,[85] later Reformed theologians embraced a limited view of the atonement of Christ; that is, Christ did not die

---

81. Ibid., 5, in McDonald, *Atonement of the Death of Christ*, 206.

82. E.g., see *Westminster Confession of Faith*, 8.5, in Schaff, 3:621.

83. Quenstedt explained: "The personal object of atonement comprises each and every sinful person, without any exception whatsoever. For Christ suffered and died for all, according to the serious and sincere good pleasure and kind intention of God the Father and himself. According to this, he truly wills the salvation of each and every person, even of those who fail to embrace salvation." John Andrew Quenstedt, *Theologia Didactico-Polemica sive Systema Theologicum* (Leipzig, 1715), 3.238, in Schmid, 363; cf. John Gerhardt, *Loci Theologici* (1621), 4.178, in Schmid, 363.

84. *Five Arminian Articles*, art. 2, in Schaff, 3:546. The text has been rendered clearer. The last phrase specified that the application of the atonement is to believers only; thus, universalism—that all people will actually be saved—was avoided.

85. For a cautious, well-reasoned perspective on this issue, see Robert A. Peterson Sr., *Calvin and the Atonement: What the Renowned Pastor and Teacher Said about the Cross of Christ*, rev. ed. (Fearn, Ross-Shire, UK: Mentor, 1999). Peterson called attention to writers who found Calvin supporting unlimited atonement—R. T. Kendall, *Calvin and English Calvinism to 1649* (Carlisle, Pa., and Cumbria: Paternoster, 1979, 1999); Paul Van Buren, *Christ in Our Place: The Substitutionary Character of Calvin's Doctrine of Reconciliation* (Grand Rapids: Eerdmans, 1975)—and others who believed that Calvin held to a limited atonement—A. A. Hodge, *The Atonement* (1867; repr., Grand Rapids: Eerdmans, 1953); W. Robert Godfrey, "Reformed Thought on the Extent of the Atonement 10 1618," *WTJ* 37 (1975): 137–38; Roger Nicole, "John Calvin's View of the Extent of the Atonement," *WTJ* 47 (1985): 208; Jonathan Rainbow, "Redemptor Ecclesiae, Redemptor Mundi: An Historical and Theological Study of John Calvin's Doctrine of the Extent of the Atonement" (Ph.D. diss., Univ. of California), 1986.

for the sins of every person, but only for the sins of the elect. The classic statement of this was set down in the *Five Articles of Calvinism* at the Synod of Dort in 1619, composed in response to the *Five Articles of the Remonstrants*. Against Arminianism's unlimited view of the atonement, the *Five Articles of Calvinism* offered the limited atonement position:

> This was the sovereign counsel and most gracious will and purpose of God the Father, that the enlivening and saving effectiveness of the very precious death of his Son should extend to all the elect, for giving them alone the gift of justifying faith, by which to bring them infallibly to salvation. It was the will of God that Christ, by the blood of the cross, by which he confirmed the new covenant, should effectively redeem out of every people, tribe, nation and language, all those, and those only, who were chosen from eternity for salvation, and given to him by the Father.[86]

The classical defense of the limited atonement view was voiced by John Owen in his *Death of Death in the Death of Christ* (1647).

Notably, some Reformed theologians, the "Amyraldians"[87] of the French theological school of Saumur, dissented from this common limited atonement perspective. They believed that Christ died for the sins of all people, an unlimited atonement made in accordance with God's will that all people would be saved on the condition of believing in Christ. Because no one is capable of responding in faith, due to sinful depravity, God instituted a covenant of salvation only with the elect, in whom he produces faith. This "hypothetical universalism," as the view came to be known, was a minority position among Reformed theologians.

Thus, a major theological difference arose in the Reformation and post-Reformed period: the limited atonement position versus the unlimited atonement view.

THE ATONEMENT IN THE MODERN PERIOD

The penal substitutionary theory of the atonement, originated by the Reformers and developed by their successors, was embraced by most Protestants. Challenges like those of the Socinians and Hugo Grotius were fairly uncommon and repudiated by most Protestant theologians. But new challenges to the position arose in the modern period and were accepted by more and more churches. Able apologists for the penal substitutionary view also defended and developed that position against these new theories.

William G. T. Shedd was a stalwart defender of this doctrine of the atonement. Affirming that "the atonement of Christ is represented in Scripture as vicarious,"[88] Shedd demonstrated both its substitutionary nature and penal character, the penalty in this case being the sufferings endured by Christ as substitute for sinful human beings.[89] He

---

86. *Canons of the Synod of Dort*, 2.8, in Schaff, 3:587. The text has been rendered clearer. Cf. *Westminster Confession of Faith*, 8.8, in Schaff, 3:622.

87. The name reflects the founder of the position, Moise Amyraut (1596-1664).

88. William G. T. Shedd, *Dogmatic Theology*, 8.2, in *Dogmatic Theology*, ed. Alan W. Gomes, 3rd ed. (Phillipsburg, N.J.: P & R, 2003), 690.

89. Ibid., 711–20.

also joined in the debate about the extent of the atonement, bringing helpful and needed clarity by distinguishing between *atonement* and *redemption*:[90] "Atonement is unlimited, and redemption is limited. This statement includes all the scriptural texts: those that assert that Christ died for all men, and those that assert that he died for his people. He who asserts unlimited atonement and limited redemption cannot well be misconceived. He is understood to hold that the sacrifice of Christ is unlimited in its value, sufficiency, and publication, but limited in its effectual application."[91] Still, Shedd closely united the sufficiency of the atonement and the divine intention to apply it in redemption in the divine decree, so his position is rightly classified as limited atonement.[92]

Charles Hodge was another outstanding defender of the penal substitutionary theory of the atonement, which he summarized in the following:

> It is the plain doctrine of Scripture that ... Christ saves us neither by the mere exercise of power, nor by his doctrine, nor by his example, nor by the moral influence which he exerted, nor by any subjective influence on his people, whether natural or mystical, but as a satisfaction to divine justice, as an expiation for sin and as a ransom from the curse and authority of the law, they reconciling us to God, by making it consistent with his perfections to exercise mercy toward sinners, and then renewing them after his own image, and finally exalting them to all the dignity, excellence, and blessedness of the sons of God.[93]

Hodge addressed numerous possible objections that had been and would continue to be offered against his view of the atonement. One such objection emphasized the love of God to the exclusion of all the other divine attributes—including the divine justice: "It is objected that there can be no antagonism in God. There cannot be one impulse to punish and another impulse not to punish. All God's acts or manifestations of himself toward his creatures must be referred to one principle, and that principle is love. And, therefore, his plan of saving sinners can only be regarded as an exhibition of love, not of justice in any form."[94] Hodge countered this objection: "It is true God is love. But it is no less true that love in God is not a weakness, impelling him to do what ought not to be done. If sin ought to be punished, as conscience and the word of God declare, then there is nothing in God which impels him to leave it unpunished. His whole nature is indeed harmonious, but it has the harmony of moral excellence."[95]

A second objection was that "the idea of expiation, the innocent suffering for the guilty and God being thereby propitiated, is declared to be pagan and revolting."[96] Hodge responded: "No man has the right to make his taste or feelings the test of truth. That a doctrine is disagreeable is no sufficient evidence of its untruth.... Besides, the idea of expiation is not revolting to the vast majority of minds, as is proved by its being incorporated in all religions.... So far from being revolting, it is cherished and delighted in as the only hope of the guilty."[97] Thus, in a full-orbed presentation of the penal substitutionary

90. Ibid., 739–50.
91. Ibid., 743.
92. Ibid., 746–50.
93. Charles Hodge, *Systematic Theology*, 3 vols. (Grand Rapids: Eerdmans, 1946), 2:520.

94. Ibid., 2: 540.
95. Ibid.
96. Ibid., 2:541.
97. Ibid.

theory, Charles Hodge echoed the Reformed doctrine of the atonement and defended it against its many critics.

One such critic was Friedrich Schleiermacher, who offered a new theory of the atonement in line with his vision of religion as a feeling of absolute dependence on God. However, God, for Schleiermacher, is not a personal, transcendent being. Rather, he is the infinite spiritual reality that flows through all that exists. Christianity, therefore, is not about doctrines and beliefs; rather, it is about the heart, nurturing the intuitive awareness of being united with, and dependent on, this world spirit that pervades everything. With this notion of religion, Schleiermacher maintained that Christ redeemed humanity by providing the supreme example of a man in whom the intuitive sense of dependence on God was nurtured. He was not the God-man; rather, "the Redeemer ... is like all men in virtue of the identity of human nature, but distinguished from them all by the constant potency of his God-consciousness, which was a real existence of God in him."[98] Because of this reality, "the Redeemer assumes believers into the power of his God-consciousness, and this is his redemptive activity."[99] Hence, Schleiermacher developed a subjective idea of the atonement.

In the twentieth century, Gustaf Aulen rehabilitated the ancient *Christ as Victor theory*. "Its central theme is the idea of the atonement as a divine conflict and victory; Christ—*Christus Victor*—fights against and triumphs over the evil powers of the world, the 'tyrants' under which mankind is in bondage and suffering, and in him God reconciles the world to himself."[100] The powers holding humanity in slavery include sin, death, the law, and demonic forces. Joining together sin and death, Aulen offered: "Sin takes the central place among the powers that hold man in bondage; all the others stand in direct relation to it. Above all, death, which is sometimes almost personified as 'the last enemy that will be destroyed' (1 Cor. 15:26), is most closely connected with sin. Where sin reigns, there death reigns also."[101] As for the law enslaving humanity, Aulen explained: "The way of legal righteousness which the law recommends or, rather, demands, can never lead to salvation and life. It leads, like the way of human merit, not to God, but away from God, and deeper and deeper into sin."[102] The final group that holds humanity in its sway is the demonic realm: "The array of hostile forces includes also the complex of demonic 'principalities,' 'powers,' 'thrones,' 'dominions,' which rule in 'this present evil age' (Gal. 1:4) but over which Christ has prevailed. There is comparatively little direct mention of the devil, but he is without doubt regarded as standing behind the demonic hosts as their chief."[103] In support of his view, Aulen appealed to many passages of Scripture (e.g., Col. 2:15; 1 John 3:8; 5:19) that emphasize Christ's victory over evil forces. He also marshaled historical evidence in support of his view. For example, he reinterpreted the recapitulation theory of Irenaeus and the penal substitutionary theory of Martin Luther so that they agreed with his position. Of course, he also pointed to the

98. Friedrich Schleiermacher, *The Christian Faith*, ed. H. R. Mackintosh and J. S. Stewart (Edinburgh: T & T Clark, 1928), 385.

99. Ibid., 425.

100. Gustaf Aulen, *Christus Victor: An Historical Study of the Three Main Types of the Idea of Atonement* (London: SPCK, 1931), 20.

101. Ibid., 83.

102. Ibid., 84.

103. Ibid., 85.

many ransom to Satan theories, insisting that his Christ the Victor theory was at the core of all of these.

Not surprisingly, the debate over limited versus unlimited atonement continued in the modern period, with important modification being developed. Bruce Demarest, for example, sought to clarify the real issue under discussion:

> Older theologians enquired into the *extent* of the atonement and debated whether it was limited or unlimited. More recent scholars have focused on the *intent* of Christ's death, with the discussion centering on whether the atonement was particular or universal. We choose to ask the question, *For whom did Christ intend to provide atonement through his suffering and death?* Accordingly, we will divide the question in two parts: We inquire, first, into the *provision* Christ made via his death on the cross. And we explore, second, the *application* of the benefits gained by Calvary to sinners.[104]

He presented numerous passages in support of the provision that Christ made by being an atonement for the sins of all people.[105] According to Demarest, "Other texts stating that Christ died for the disciples, the apostles, the sheep, the church, etc ... do not exclude other biblical teachings to the effect that the Savior atoned for the sins of the world at large. What is true for the universal set is also true of a sub-set thereof."[106] As he summarized: "We conclude that in terms of the atonement's *provision*, Christ died not merely for the elect but for all sinners in all times and places.... Christ, in other words, provided salvation for more people than those to whom he purposed to apply its saving benefits."[107] Demarest also noted Scripture that "emphasizes the particularity of the application side of the atonement."[108] Accordingly, he proposed viewing the issue from the vantage point of a double intention, "God's purpose regarding the *provision* of the atonement and his purpose concerning the *application* thereof":

> Scripture leads us to conclude that God loves all people he created and that Christ died to provide salvation for all. The *provision* side of the atonement is part of the general will of God that must be preached to all. But beyond this, the Father loves the "sheep" with a special love, and in the divine will the Spirit applies the benefits of Christ's death to the "sheep," or the elect. The *application* side of the atonement is part of the special will of God shared with those who come to faith.[109]

Demarest's view, therefore, underscored "that by divine *intention* Christ's suffering and death are universal in its provision and particular in its application."[110]

At the turn of the third millennium, the doctrine of the atonement came under fierce attack. Particularly singled out for criticism was the penal substitutionary theory

---

104. Demarest, *The Cross and Salvation*, 189.
105. Ibid., 189–91.
106. Ibid., 191.
107. Ibid.
108. Ibid., 193.

109. Ibid.
110. Ibid. The "unlimited limited atonement" position, a variation of Demarest's view, was articulated in Mark Driscoll and Gerry Breshears, *Death by Love: Letters from the Cross* (Wheaton: Crossway, 2008), 163–82.

because, according to its detractors, it privileges one (outmoded) metaphor of the atonement, it fosters passivity in the face of evil and oppression, and it even encourages child abuse. Some evangelicals, disturbed by these criticisms, undertook a revisioning of the traditional doctrine.[111] This was a frontal attack against the historic Protestant and modern evangelical position of the church's doctrine of the atonement.

Attacks such as these concerning the nature of the atonement led many evangelicals to rehearse and defend the penal substitutionary model.[112] Although not written specifically in response to these attacks, J. I. Packer's "What Did the Cross Achieve? The Logic of Penal Substitution" stood as one of the most important expressions of this theory of the atonement. According to Packer, the classical model is anchored

> within the world of moral law, guilty conscience, and retributive justice. Thus is forged a conceptual instrument for conveying the thought that God remits our sins and accepts our persons into favor not because of any amends we have attempted, but because the penalty which was our due was diverted on to Christ. The notion which the phrase "penal substitution" expresses is that Jesus Christ our Lord, moved by a love that was determined to do everything necessary to save us, endured and exhausted the destructive divine judgment for which we were otherwise inescapably destined, and so won us forgiveness, adoption and glory. To affirm penal substitution is to say that believers are in debt to Christ specifically for this, and that this is the mainspring of all their joy, peace and praise both now and for eternity.[113]

The penal substitutionary model continued to find able defenders. Even more fundamentally, many evangelicals turned to a rearticulation of the gospel message itself:

> The Father sent the Son to free us from the dominion of sin and Satan, and to make us God's children and friends. Jesus paid our penalty in our place on his cross, satisfying the retributive demands of divine justice by shedding his blood in sacrifice and so making possible justification for all who trust in him (Rom. 3:25–26). The Bible describes this mighty substitutionary transaction as the

111. Joel B. Green and Mark D. Baker, *Recovering the Scandal of the Cross: Atonement in New Testament and Contemporary Contexts* (Downers Grove, Ill.: InterVarsity, 2000); Hans Boersma, *Violence, Hospitality, and the Cross: Reappropriating the Atonement Tradition* (Grand Rapids: Baker Academic, 2004); J. Denny Weaver, *The Nonviolent Atonement* (Grand Rapids: Eerdmans, 2001); S. Mark Heim, *Saved from Sacrifice: A Theology of the Cross* (Grand Rapids: Eerdmans, 2006); René Girard, *Violence and the Sacred*, trans. Patrick Gregory (Baltimore: Johns Hopkins Univ. Press, 1979); Brad Jersak and Michael Hardin, eds., *Stricken by God? Nonviolent Identification and the Victory of Christ* (Grand Rapids: Eerdmans, 2007); John Sanders, ed., *Atonement and Violence: A Theological Conversation* (Nashville: Abingdon, 2006).

112. Steve Jeffery, Michael Ovey, and Andrew Sach, *Pierced for Our Transgressions: Rediscovering the Glory of Penal Substitution* (Wheaton: Crossway, 2007); J. I. Packer and Mark Dever, *In My Place Condemned He Stood: Celebrating the Glory of the Atonement* (Wheaton: Crossway, 2008); Charles E. Hill and Frank A. James III, eds., *The Glory of the Atonement: Biblical, Historical, and Practical Perspectives* (Downers Grove, Ill.: InterVarsity, 2004); Mark Driscoll and Gerry Breshears, *Death by Love: Letters from the Cross* (Wheaton: Crossway, 2008); Garry Williams, "Justice, Law, and Guilt," Evangelical Alliance: Symposium on Penal Substitution (2005), available at www.eauk.org/theology/key_papers/Atonement/upload/garry_williams.pdf. For a multiple perspectives approach, see James Beilby and Paul R. Eddy, *The Nature of the Atonement: Four Views* (Downers Grove, Ill.: InterVarsity, 2006).

113. J. I. Packer, "What Did the Cross Achieve? The Logic of Penal Substitution," Tyndale Biblical Theology Lecture, 1973, *Tyndale Bulletin* 25 (1974): 3–45.

achieving of ransom, reconciliation, redemption, propitiation, and conquest of evil powers (Matt. 20:28; 2 Cor. 5:18–21; Rom. 3:23–25; John 12:31; Col 2:15). It secures for us a restored relationship with God that brings pardon and peace, acceptance and access, and adoption into God's family (Col. 1:20; 2:13–14; Rom. 5:1–2; Gal. 4:4–7; 1 Peter 3:18). The faith in God and in Christ to which the Gospel calls us is a trustful outgoing of our hearts to lay hold of these promised and proffered benefits.[114]

And so evangelicals sought to express the good news of Jesus Christ in such a way that the multifaceted biblical teachings on the atonement would be reflected in a message of salvation that is quite expansive.

---

114. John N. Akers, John H. Armstrong, and John D. Woodbridge, gen. eds., *This We Believe: The Good News of* *Jesus Christ for the World* (Grand Rapids: Zondervan, 2000), 242.

Chapter 19

RESURRECTION AND ASCENSION

How has the church come to understand the reality and significance of the resurrection and ascension of Jesus Christ?

STATEMENT OF BELIEF

The church has historically believed that Jesus Christ rose on the third day following his crucifixion and then ascended into heaven forty days later. It has pointed to the resurrection as God's seal of approval on the death of Christ as complete payment for humanity's sin and as a promise of the final bodily resurrection of all believers. And the church has underscored the importance of the ascension as a guarantee that Christ has received glory and honor and now rules with authority over the entire universe.

The church has had to defend this conviction against many challenges ranging from denials of Christ's actual death to charges that the disciples merely hallucinated in believing Christ to be alive. Other attacks have focused on the impossibility of such a miraculous occurrence or poked fun at the idea of a physical ascension into heaven. While unique in its claim to a resurrection and ascension of its founder, the church has historically maintained that Christianity stands or collapses on the reality of these events.

There is widespread agreement on the resurrection and ascension among Roman Catholics, Orthodox, and Protestants. Evangelicals share this common heritage. Thus, while tracing the development of the church's belief about Christ's resurrection and ascension, this chapter will highlight this doctrine and contrast it with the various challenges to it that have arisen across the span of two thousand years.[1]

THE RESURRECTION AND ASCENSION IN THE EARLY CHURCH

Each of the four gospels narrates the events surrounding the resurrection of Jesus Christ. Of course, no human observer actually saw the resurrection itself, so the New

---

1. My thanks to Bradley Davis for his help on this chapter.

Testament does not provide an eyewitness account of it. Rather, the stories focus on the reality of Christ's death three days before, the discovery of the empty tomb on Easter morning, and the appearances of the risen Christ to his followers (Luke 23:44–24:49 and parallels). In addition to recounting Jesus' resurrection, Luke's gospel and his book of Acts narrate his ascension (Luke 24:50–51; Acts 1:6–11). In his sermon on the day of Pentecost, the apostle Peter addressed the importance of both the resurrection and ascension as fulfillment of Old Testament prophecy (Pss. 16:8–11; 110:1) and concluded with this challenge for his hearers: "Therefore, let all Israel be assured of this: God has made this Jesus, whom you crucified, both Lord and Christ" (Acts 2:36; see vv. 24–36).

In addition to these narratives of the resurrection and ascension and the crucial role these events played in the church's preaching, the rest of the New Testament discusses their importance for doctrinal and ethical matters. Peter links the resurrection to regeneration (1 Peter 1:3), while the apostle Paul joins it with justification (Rom. 4:25). In his great passage on the resurrection, Paul links the resurrection of believers from the dead with that of Jesus Christ (1 Cor. 15:12–17). Additionally, Paul explained that because of God's powerful work of resurrection and ascension on behalf of his Son (Eph. 1:19–21), Jesus' disciples are also raised up with him and seated with him (Eph. 2:6–7).

Following the period of the apostolic witness to the resurrection and ascension, the early church continued to insist on the reality of those events and to explain their significance. Polycarp simply urged Christians to believe in God, "who raised our Lord Jesus Christ 'from the dead and gave him glory' and a throne at his right hand."[2] Tertullian underscored that "belief in the resurrection" of Christ was "firmly settled."[3] So true was Tertullian's observation that even a Jewish historian, Josephus, noted:

> About this time there lived Jesus, a wise man, if indeed one ought to call him a man. For he was one who wrought surprising feats and was a teacher of such people as accept the truth gladly. He won over many Jews and many of the Greeks. He was the Christ. When Pilate, upon hearing him accused by men of the highest standing among us, had condemned him to be crucified, those who had in the first place come to love him did not give up their affection for him. On the third day he appeared to them restored to life, for the prophets of God had prophesied these and countless other marvelous things about him. And the tribe of the Christians, so called after him, has still to this day not disappeared.[4]

Confronting an early heresy that denied the true humanity of Jesus Christ — *Docetism*, which held that Christ only appeared to be a real human being — the early Christians insisted on his physical resurrection and ascension. Ignatius affirmed that Jesus Christ "truly suffered just as he truly raised himself — not, as certain unbelievers say, that he suffered in appearance only.... For I know and believe that he was in the flesh even after the resurrection; and when he came to Peter and those with him, he said to them,

---

2. Polycarp, *Letter to the Philippians*, 2.1, in Holmes, 207; *ANF*, 1:32. Polycarp's reference is to 1 Peter 1:21.

3. Tertullian, *On the Flesh of Christ*, 1, in *ANF*, 3:521.

4. Flavius Josephus, *Antiquities of the Jews*, 18.3.63–64

(3), in Josephus, *Jewish Antiquities: Books 18–19*, trans. L. H. Feldman, 10 vols., Loeb Classical Library (Cambridge, Mass.: Harvard Univ. Press, 1963), 9:49–50.

'Take hold of me; handle me and see that I am not a disembodied demon.' And immediately they touched him and believed, being closely united with his flesh and blood."[5] In an imaginary dialogue, Tertullian cited Paul's discussion (1 Cor. 15) as proof that believers will physically rise from the dead because of Christ's physical resurrection:

> What is the point that Paul evidently works hard to make us believe throughout this passage? The resurrection of the dead, you say, which some deny. Paul certainly wished it to be believed on the strength of the example that he cited—the Lord's resurrection. Certainly, you say. Well now, is an example borrowed from different circumstances or from similar ones? From similar ones, by all means, is your answer. How then did Christ rise again? In the flesh or not? No doubt, since you are told that he "died according to the Scriptures" (1 Cor. 15:3) and that "he was buried according to the Scriptures" (1 Cor. 15:4), he without doubt rose in the flesh. Thus, you will also allow that it was in the flesh that Christ was raised from the dead. Because the very same body that fell in death, and which lay in the tomb, also rose again. If, therefore, we are to rise again after the example of Christ—who rose in the flesh—we will certainly not rise according to that example unless we ourselves will also rise again in the flesh.[6]

Thus, against Docetism's denial of the physical reality of Christ, the early church believed in his bodily resurrection and ascension.

The pagan critics of Christianity enjoyed poking fun at such an incredible belief. Celsus, one of the earliest opponents of Christianity, laughed at the audacity of the idea of a resurrection and attempted to discredit the belief by questioning its eyewitnesses:

> But who witnessed this? A hysterical woman—as you state—and someone else who was caught up in the same pattern of delusion! This person either dreamed it, owing to a peculiar state of mind, or he was under the influence of an overactive imagination and so concocted an appearance of Jesus according his own wishes. This kind of wishful thinking has been verified in countless cases. Or perhaps what is more probable, this person desired to impress others with this sign, and by such a lie wanted to create an opportunity for imposters like himself.[7]

According to Celsus, "If Jesus desired to show that his power was really divine, he ought to have appeared to those who had ill-treated him, and to the one who had condemned him, and to all men universally."[8] Celsus proposed that the alleged appearances of the risen Christ were nothing but dreams or the products of a wild imagination.[9] Other attacks raised against the exaltation of Christ accused his followers of deception. According to Justin Martyr, the Jews maintained that "his disciples stole him by night from the

---

5. Ignatius, *Letter to the Smyrnaeans*, 2–3, in Holmes, 186–87; *ANF*, 1:87. Ignatius's citation is Luke 24:39.
6. Tertullian, *On the Resurrection of the Flesh*, 48, in *ANF*, 3:581. The text has been rendered clearer.
7. Origen, *Against Celsus*, 2.55, in *ANF*, 4:453.
8. Ibid., 2.63, in *ANF*, 4:456.
9. Ibid., 2.60, in *ANF*, 4:455.

tomb, where he was laid when unfastened from the cross, and now deceive men by asserting that he has risen from the dead and ascended into heaven."[10]

The early church offered defenses against these attacks. In responding to Celsus' criticisms, Origen noted that "there was ... no obligation for Jesus to appear either to the judge who condemned him or to those who ill-treated him."[11] Gregory of Nyssa pointed to the biblical description of Christ's grave clothes (John 20:7–8) as proof that the disciples did not steal the body: "The arrangement of the clothes in the tomb—the cloth that was around our Savior's head was not lying with the linen clothes but was wrapped together in a place by itself—did not testify to the terror and hurry of thieves. It therefore refutes the story that the body was stolen."[12] Similarly, John Chrysostom argued from the account of Jesus' burial (John 19:38, 39–40) that the stolen body theory was unlikely:

> What does it mean that the grave linens were stuck on with the myrrh? For Peter saw these lying [in the tomb]. For if the disciples were interested in stealing, they would not have stolen the body naked, not only because of dishonoring it, but also in order not to delay and lose time in stripping it, and not to give them who were interested an opportunity to awake and seize them. Especially when it was myrrh, a drug that adheres tightly to the body and cleaves to the clothes; thus, it was not easy to take the clothes off the body and would require much time. From this again, the tale of the theft is improbable.[13]

In addition to these defenses, the church continued to press its traditional faith. In a summary of the early church's belief in the resurrection and ascension, Cyprian affirmed the following about Christ:

> On the third day, he freely rose again from the dead. He appeared to his disciples as he had been. He presented himself for recognition by those who saw and associated with him. Being evident by the nature of his bodily existence, he delayed for forty days so they might be instructed by him in the precepts of life and might learn what they were to teach. Then, in a cloud spread around him, he was lifted up into heaven, that as a conqueror he might bring to the Father, man whom he loved, whom he put on, and whom he shielded from death.[14]

This belief was further summarized in the early church's creeds. The Nicene Creed made this simple confession of faith about Jesus Christ: "[I believe that] he suffered and

10. Justin Martyr, *Dialogue with Trypho, a Jew*, 108, in *ANF*, 1:253. Tertullian confronted the same idea: "Without a single disciple near, the grave was found empty of all but the clothes of the buried one. But nevertheless, the leaders of the Jews, whom it nearly concerned both to spread abroad a lie and keep back a people tributary and submissive to them from the faith, gave it out that the body of Christ had been stolen by his followers." Tertullian, *Apology*, 21, in *ANF*, 3:35. Sarcastically, Tertullian exclaimed: "This is he [Jesus] whom his disciples secretly stole away, that it might be said he had risen again, or the gardener removed so that his crop of lettuce might come to

no harm from the crowds of visitors!" Tertullian, *The Shows*, 30, in *ANF*, 3:91. The text has been rendered clearer.

11. Origen, *Against Celsus*, 2.67, in *ANF*, 4:458.

12. Cited in John F. Whitworth, *Legal and Historical Proof of the Resurrection of the Dead* (Harrisburg, Pa.: Publishing House of the United Evangelical Church, 1912), 64–65.

13. John Chrysostom, *Homilies on the Gospel of Saint Matthew*, homily 90 on Matthew 28:11–14, in *NPNF*[2], 10:530–31. The text has been rendered clearer.

14. Cyprian, *Treatise* 6.14, in *ANF*, 5:468. The text has been rendered clearer.

was buried, and the third day he rose again, according to the Scriptures, and he ascended into heaven and sat at the right hand of the Father."[15]

Moreover, this faith was lived out concretely. As the church developed its liturgy, or formal order of worship to be followed in its services, special days in the calendar year were set aside to commemorate the significant events in the life of Jesus. Resurrection sermons (delivered on Easter Sunday) and ascension sermons (delivered forty days after Easter) became standard elements in all the churches. For example, John Chrysostom delivered a message on Christ's ascension as the first fruits of the ascension for all Christians.[16] Appealing to Romans 6:4 and Colossians 3:1–3, Augustine linked all the events of Christ's death, burial, resurrection, and ascension with the earthly life of a believer, "that the life which the Christian leads here might be modeled upon them."[17]

THE RESURRECTION AND ASCENSION IN THE MIDDLE AGES

The medieval church repeated this belief and celebrated it in particular ways during its liturgical year. Highlights of this calendar were Good Friday and Easter Sunday. The drama of Christ's death and then his resurrection following were reenacted by focusing on Good Friday as a day of mourning that then turned to a joyful celebration on Easter Sunday. As Rupert of Deutz explained: "The joy of such a great salvation and of such a necessary redemption, of such a price by whose value the captivity of the world has been redeemed, is to be deferred until the third day. For then, by his resurrection, the Victor has announced his victory to us, and has shown us in himself what we are to hope for about ourselves."[18] Bernard of Clairvaux expressed the clear dichotomy between Good Friday and Easter Sunday when he said, "He who had been a lamb in his passion became a lion in his resurrection."[19] Moreover, the medieval writers insisted on the necessity of the ascension following the resurrection. Bernard of Clairvaux, alluding to Hebrews 4:14 ("we have a great high priest who has gone through the heavens"), reasoned: "If my Lord Jesus had indeed risen from the dead but had not ascended into heaven, it could not be said of him that he had 'gone through,' but only that he had passed away."[20]

Thomas Aquinas continued to uphold the traditional doctrines of the resurrection and ascension while probing deeper into the two events. Appealing to Luke 24:46, he offered five reasons for the necessity of the resurrection. The first has to do with the principle of God lifting up the humble: "Because Christ humbled himself even to the death of the cross, from love and obedience to God, it behooved him to be lifted up by God to a glorious resurrection."[21] The second reason is that the Christian "belief in Christ's

---

15. Nicene Creed, in Schaff, 2:59. Similar affirmations are found in the Apostles' Creed, the Creed of Nicea, and the Athanasian Creed.

16. John Chrysostom, in Peter Toon, *The Ascension of Our Lord* (Nashville: Nelson, 1984), 130.

17. Augustine, *Enchiridion on Faith, Hope, and Love*, 53, in *NPNF*[1], 3:255.

18. Rupert of Deutz, *On Divine Offices*, 6.3, in Pelikan, 3:133–34.

19. Bernard of Clairvaux, *Sermons on Various Topics*, 57.2, in Pelikan, 3:153.

20. Bernard of Clairvaux, *Sermons on the Song of Songs*, 79.1.3, in Pelikan, 3:153.

21. Thomas Aquinas, *Summa Theologica*, pt. 3, q. 53, art. 1.

Godhead [deity] is confirmed by his rising again."[22] Aquinas's third reason focused on the hope the resurrection gives to believers, because "through seeing Christ, who is our head, rise again, we hope that we likewise shall rise again."[23] Fourth, the resurrection encourages believers to holy living.[24] The fifth reason that Aquinas offered has to do with the justification of believers, which for Aquinas signified progress in good works.[25]

Turning to the ascension, Aquinas explained that "Christ's ascension is the cause of our salvation in two ways: first of all, on our part; secondly, on his."[26] As to the part of Christians, Aquinas offered: "On our part, in so far as by the ascension our souls are uplifted to him; because … his ascension fosters first, faith; secondly, hope; thirdly, love. Fourthly, our reverence for him is thereby increased, since we no longer deem him an earthly man, but the God of heaven."[27] As to Christ's part in the ascension being a cause of salvation, Aquinas presented three areas. First, Christ's ascension prepared the way for the ascension of believers: "since Christ is our head, then what was bestowed on Christ is bestowed on us through him."[28] Second, Christ's ascension initiated his ministry of prayer for all believers: "because as the high priest under the Old Testament entered the holy place to stand before God for the people, so also Christ entered heaven 'to make intercession for us' (Heb. 7:25). Because the very showing of himself in the human nature which he took with him to heaven is a pleading for us."[29] Finally, Christ's ascension paved the way for his endowments of spiritual gifts: "Thirdly, when he was established in his heavenly seat as God and Lord, he sent down gifts upon humanity: 'He ascended above all the heavens, that he might fill all things' (Eph. 4:10) — that is, 'with his gifts,' as someone interprets the passage."[30]

In summary, the medieval church continued to confess and honor the traditional church doctrines of the resurrection and ascension.

THE RESURRECTION AND ASCENSION IN THE REFORMATION AND POST-REFORMATION

The principal Reformers — Martin Luther, Huldrych Zwingli, and John Calvin — continued to affirm the church's historic position on the resurrection and ascension. Thus, no doctrinal rift with Roman Catholicism broke out over this issue. This peaceful situation did not mean, however, that the matter was completely without controversy, for Martin Luther and Huldrych Zwingli drew different conclusions about the human body of Christ from this doctrine. These divergent implications were then marshaled to support Luther and Zwingli's opposing views of the presence of Christ in the Lord's Supper.

For Zwingli, belief in the resurrection and ascension demanded recognition that Christ's human body is located at the right hand of the Father; therefore, it cannot be present during the celebration of the Lord's Supper. He argued this from the church's confession of faith:

22. Ibid.
23. Ibid.
24. Ibid.
25. Ibid.
26. Ibid., pt. 3, q. 57, art. 6.

27. Ibid.
28. Ibid., pt. 3, q. 58, art. 4.
29. Ibid., pt. 3, q. 57, art. 6.
30. Ibid. The text has been rendered clearer.

They [the false teachers] are confronted by the articles of our Christian creed: "He [Christ] ascended into heaven and sat at the right hand of God the Father almighty; from here he will come to judge the living and the dead." Therefore, they must either abandon the false doctrine of the presence of the essential body of Christ in this sacrament, or else they must at once renounce these three articles of faith, which — God forbid! — anyone should ever dream of doing.[31]

Zwingli attacked his opponents' idea that because Christ is God, and God is everywhere, then Christ — including his human nature — can be everywhere. "But," he added, "it is not the property [nature] of the body."[32] Furthermore, he pointed to the biblical evidence that Christ has left this world (John 16:28) to support his view that it is Christ's body — not his divine presence — that is no longer on earth: "How then does he leave the world? With his divine presence and protection and grace and goodness and lovingkindness? God forbid: it is not for any creature to say that. But necessarily he has left us, for he said so himself, and he cannot lie. It follows, then, that he has departed from us at any rate in the body, he has left us in the body."[33] Given this truth, "the body and the blood of Christ cannot be present in the sacrament.... [H]e sits at the right hand of the Father, he has left the world, he is no longer present with us. And if these words are true, it is impossible to maintain that his flesh and blood are present in the sacrament."[34] Thus, Zwingli imagined Christ saying, "When you see me ascend up to heaven, you will see clearly that you have not eaten me literally and I cannot be eaten literally."[35]

Of course, Luther agreed with Zwingli about the basic truth of the resurrection and ascension of Christ. Specifically, Luther underscored the importance of the resurrection: "This is the chief article of the Christian doctrine. No one who claims to be a Christian or a preacher of the gospel may deny that.... Whoever denies this article must simultaneously deny far more, namely, first of all, that you believe properly; in the second place, that the Word which you believe has been true; in the third place, that we apostles [Paul and the others] preach correctly and that we are God's apostles; in the fourth place, that God is faithful; in brief, that God is God. "[36]

The difference between Luther and Zwingli over these doctrines came in their understanding of Christ's sitting at the right hand of God. For Luther, the right hand does not refer to a place but to the power of God; therefore, it means that Christ is present everywhere. The ascended Jesus Christ, including his human nature — which in and of itself is localized in one space and not present in every space — is everywhere present in virtue of the union of the divine and human natures: "Wherever Christ is according to his divinity, he is there as a natural, divine person and he is also naturally and personally there. But if he is present naturally and personally wherever he is, then he must be man there, too, since he is not two separate persons but a single person. Wherever this person

---

31. Huldrych Zwingli, *On the Lord's Supper*, preface, in G. W. Bromiley, ed., *Zwingli and Bullinger*, LCC 24:186. The text has been rendered clearer.

32. Zwingli, *On the Lord's Supper*, art. 2, ibid., LCC 24:214.

33. Ibid.

34. Ibid., LCC 24:214–15.

35. Ibid., LCC 24:206.

36. Martin Luther, *Commentary on 1 Corinthians 15*, LW, 28:94-95.

Luther on the ascended Christ: "Christ Lay in Death's Bands"

Christ Jesus lay in death's strong bands,
For our offenses given;
But now at God's right hand he stands
And brings us life from heaven;
Therefore let us joyful be
And sing to God right thankfully
Loud songs of hallelujah.
Hallelujah! *

> * Luther composed this hymn in 1524. Translated by Richard Massic in 1854, it appears in *The Handbook to the Lutheran Hymnal* (St. Louis: Concordia, 1942), 148, and *The Lutheran Hymnal*, The Evangelical Lutheran Synodical Conference of North America (St. Louis: Concordia, 1941), no. 195.

---

is, it is the single, indivisible person, and if you can say, 'Here is God,' then you must also say, 'Christ the man is present too.' "[37] Luther took this to demonstrate "at least in one way how God could bring it about that Christ is in heaven and his body in the Lord's Supper at the same time."[38]

Thus, a basic disagreement arose between Zwingli and Luther on this issue. In accord with the church, both affirmed belief in the resurrection and ascension of Jesus Christ. But the implication of those events for the human nature of Christ divided the two. For Zwingli, on the one hand, it meant that the ascended Christ could not be physically present in the Lord's Supper. Luther, on the other hand, held that the ascended Christ was indeed present bodily in that celebration.

John Calvin echoed the historic belief of the church in the resurrection and ascension of Christ while focusing his discussion of these events on the great benefit they bring to believers. He first explained how the work of salvation is divided between Christ's death and resurrection: "Through his death, sin was wiped out and death extinguished; through his resurrection, righteousness was restored and life raised up, so that—thanks to his resurrection—his death manifested its power and efficacy [effectiveness] in us."[39] This restoration of a holy life takes place as believers put to death the works of their sinful nature, and the ability to walk in newness of life is a second benefit of the resurrection. Referencing Romans 6:4 and Colossians 3:1–5, Calvin commented: "By these words we are not only invited through the example of the risen Christ to strive after newness of life; but we are taught that we are reborn into righteousness through his power."[40] Moreover, "we also receive a third benefit from his resurrection: we are assured of our own resurrection by receiving a sort of guarantee substantiated by his."[41]

---

37. *Confession Concerning Christ's Supper*, LW, 37:218.
38. Ibid., LW, 37:207.
39. John Calvin, *Institutes of the Christian Religion*, 2.16.13, LCC, 1:521.
40. Ibid., 2.16.13, LCC, 1:522.
41. Ibid.

Turning to the ascension, Calvin emphasized Christ's gift of the Holy Spirit as one of its key aspects: "Christ left us in such a way that his presence might be more useful to us—a presence that had been confined in a humble abode of flesh so long as he sojourned on earth."[41] After the ascension, this more "useful" presence is none other than the Holy Spirit. The ascension also brought greater power and ruling energy to Christ:

> We see how much more abundantly he advanced his kingdom, how much greater power he displayed both in helping his people and in scattering his enemies. Carried up to heaven, therefore, he withdrew his bodily presence from our sight (Acts 1:9), not to cease to be present with believers still on their earthly pilgrimage, but to rule heaven and earth with a more immediate power. But by his ascension he fulfilled what he had promised: that he would be with us even to the end of the world. As his body was raised up above all the heavens, so his power and energy were diffused and spread beyond all the bounds of heaven and earth.[43]

Christ's ascension resulted in three benefits for believers. First, "the Lord by his ascent to heaven opened the way into the heavenly kingdom, which had been closed through Adam.... So that we do not await heaven with a bare hope, but in our head already possess it."[44] Calvin listed as a second benefit the intercession and advocacy work of Christ before the Father's throne: "He turns the Father's eyes to his own righteousness to avert his gaze from our sins. He so reconciles the Father's heart to us that by his intercession he prepares a way and access for us to the Father's throne. He fills with grace and kindness the throne that for miserable sinners would otherwise have been filled with dread."[45] As the third benefit of the ascension, Calvin underscored the many different spiritual riches that Christ pours out on his church: "He therefore sits on high, transfusing us with his power, that he may enliven us to spiritual life, sanctify us by his Spirit, adorn his church with various gifts of his grace, keep it safe from all harm by his protection, restrain the raging enemies of his cross and of our salvation by the strength of his hand, and finally hold all power in heaven and on earth."[46]

Those who followed after Luther, Zwingli, and Calvin continued to affirm the historic belief of the church. From a Lutheran perspective, Hollaz summarized the resurrection in this way: "The resurrection is the act of glorious victory by which Christ, the God-man, through the same power as that of God the Father and the Holy Spirit, brought forth his body, reunited with the soul and glorified, from the tomb, and showed it alive to his disciples by various proofs, for the confirmation of our peace, fellowship, joy, and hope in our own future resurrection."[47] And Quenstedt underscored that the resurrection applied to the human nature of Christ: "He was raised up by God not according to his divine nature but only according to his human nature. Yet the divine nature is not, therefore, altogether excluded from this act; for it has imparted to the human nature the

---

42. Ibid., 2.16.14, LCC, 1:522.

43. Ibid., 2.16.14, LCC, 1:523.

44. Ibid., 2.16.16, LCC, 1:524.

45. Ibid., 2.16.16, LCC, 1:524–25.

46. Ibid., 2.16.16, LCC, 1:525. The text has been rendered clearer.

47. David Hollaz, *Examen Theologicum Acroamaticum* (1707), 779, in Schmid, 380.

power to rise again and has made its resurrection of advantage to us, i.e., that the resurrection might be victor over death, sin, and hell, and our justifier."[48]

From a Reformed perspective, the *Heidelberg Catechism* summarized the benefits of Christ's resurrection for believers: "First, by his resurrection he has overcome death, so that he might make us partakers of the righteousness which by his death he has obtained for us. Secondly, we also are now by his power raised up to a new life. Thirdly, the resurrection of Christ is to us a sure pledge of our blessed resurrection."[49] Similarly, the *Catechism* noted the benefits that come to believers from Christ's ascension: "First, that he is our advocate in the presence of his Father in heaven. Secondly, that we have our flesh in heaven, as a sure pledge that he, as the head, will also take us, his members, up to himself. Thirdly, that he sends us his Spirit, as a down payment, by whose power we seek those things which are above, where Christ sits at the right hand of God, and not things on the earth."[50]Helpfully, the *Westminster Shorter Catechism* contrasted the two states of Christ: his *humiliation* (including his lowly birth, submission to the divine law, sufferings, death, and burial) and his *exaltation*: "Christ's exaltation consists in his rising again from the dead on the third day, in ascending up into heaven, his sitting at the right hand of God the Father, and in coming to judge the world at the last day."[51]

THE RESURRECTION AND ASCENSION IN THE MODERN PERIOD

The modern period witnessed the undoing of the church's historic consensus regarding the resurrection and ascension of Christ. The eighteenth century marked the beginning of the quest for the historical Jesus by liberal Protestants. Developments in biblical criticism (leading to questions concerning the reliability of the Gospel accounts of Christ), the presupposition of antisupernaturalism (with the concomitant dismissal of the accounts of the miracles of Christ), the elevation of reason (exemplified in English Deism, which did away with much of historic Christian belief), and many other factors stirred up this search for the real Jesus Christ. Proponents of this quest offered numerous challenges to the resurrection and ascension; a small sample follows.

Hermann Samuel Reimarus is credited with initiating the quest when he alleged a discrepancy between the good news preached by Jesus and the proclamation of the apostles about spiritual salvation through Christ. He explained this transformation of messages by insisting that the disciples stole the body of the dead Jesus and later announced his resurrection and ascension.

Reimarus claimed that Jesus preached a message about the kingdom of God and repentance that was intended to bring redemption to Israel. It was a moral and political salvation that Jesus attempted to achieve, not a spiritual salvation. According to Reimarus, Jesus never predicted his resurrection. It was unthinkable that if Jesus had

---

48. John Andrew Quenstedt, *Theologia Didactico-Polemica sive Systema Theologicum* (Leipzig, 1715), 3.377, in Schmid, 401.

49. *Heidelberg Catechism*, q. 45, in Schaff, 3:321–22.
50. *Heidelberg Catechism*, q. 49, in Schaff, 3:323.
51. *Westminster Shorter Catechism*, q. 28, in Schaff, 3:682.

actually announced this, "such a vivid promise would not have been remembered by a single disciple, apostle, evangelist, or woman when he really did die and was buried. Here all of them speak and act as if they had never heard of such a thing in their whole lives. They wrap the corpse in a shroud, try to preserve it from decay and putrefaction by using many spices."[52] For Reimarus, this could only mean that Christ's disciples "know nothing of such a promise; they are thinking only that Jesus is dead and will stay dead and that he will decay and stink like anyone else. They completely abandon all hope of salvation through him and do not show the least trace of any other hope of a resurrection or spiritual redemption."[53] This led him to the obvious question: "Did Jesus, after he had been put to death, actually rise from the dead?"[54] He answered his own question: "It is always possible and extremely probable, if one looks into the matter, that the disciples came to the tomb at night, stole the body, and afterwards said that Jesus had risen."[55]

But why and how did the disciples fabricate such a story of victory over the grave? According to Reimarus, they were power-hungry and greedy men all along and would not allow Jesus' death to interfere with their long-standing plans for fame and fortune: "We see how impossible it is that the apostles could have had any other object in promulgating a new doctrine than their old one, namely, that of ultimately obtaining power and worldly advantage. For an intentional, deliberate fabrication of a false occurrence can only spring from a preconceived resolve and from an object or motive harbored in the mind."[56] To promote their deception, the disciples stole the body of Jesus:

> Above all things, it was necessary to get rid of the body of Jesus as speedily as possible, in order that they might say he had risen and ascended into heaven.... They made away with the corpse in little more than twenty-four hours, before corruption had well set in, and when it became known that the body of Jesus was gone, they pretended to be full of astonishment, and ignorant of any resurrection, and proceeded with others to the spot in order to survey the empty tomb.[57]

At just the right moment, then, the disciples announced Jesus' resurrection and ascension.[58] Reimarus bolstered his view by noting that Jesus allegedly appeared only to the disciples. They furthered their deception by appealing to Old Testament texts that purportedly prophesied the resurrection. Thus, the whole thing was a sham. Albert

---

52. Hermann Samuel Reimarus, *Fragments*, ed. Charles H. Talbert, trans. Ralph S. Fraser (Philadelphia: Fortress, 1970), 131.

53. Ibid., 131.

54. Ibid., 153.

55. Ibid., 172. He substantiated his answer with several moves. Reimarus rejected Matthew's account of the sealing of the tomb and the posting of the guard around it. The disciples' lack of appeal to these events, which they could have used as evidence that Jesus did indeed rise from the dead on the third day, was Reimarus's proof that such events did not actually occur but were fabricated by Matthew. Furthermore,

he underscored the numerous discrepancies between the four Gospel accounts of the empty tomb and the appearances of the risen Lord. He then appealed: "Reader, you who are conscientious and honest: tell me before God, could you accept as unanimous and sincere this testimony concerning such an important matter that contradicts itself so often and so obviously in respect to person, time, place, manner, intent, word, story?" Ibid., 197.

56. Ibid., 243.

57. Ibid., 249–50.

58. Ibid., 250.

Schweitzer, who later followed Reimarus's direction, praised the *Fragments* as "perhaps the most splendid achievement in the whole course of the historical investigation of the life of Jesus."[59]

Reimarus's theory that the disciples were deceivers was offset by another theory that the disciples were actually deceived into thinking that Jesus died and rose from the dead. Karl Bahrdt and Karl Venturini pioneered the modern idea that Jesus did not indeed die but instead faked his death and then proclaimed his resurrection.[60] H. E. G. Paulus popularized this theory, claiming that Jesus only appeared to be dead when he was taken from the cross and laid in the tomb, where the cool temperature, careful wrapping of his body in spices and oils, the earthquake, and other factors caused him to resuscitate.[61]

Rather than explaining away the resurrection as the product of the disciples' deception[62] or of their being deceived,[63] David Friedrich Strauss appealed to the Gospel writers' use of myth to dismiss the reality of these miraculous events. He defined the term in the following way: "We distinguish by the name *evangelical myth* a narrative relating directly or indirectly to Jesus, which may be considered not as the expression of a fact, but as the product of an idea of his earliest followers."[64] For Strauss, the resurrection and ascension of Jesus were not historical events but mythological ideas concocted by his followers. Strauss described the possible process the disciples underwent in forming these ideas. It first involved their departure from Jerusalem—where the resurrection of Jesus could be refuted simply by pointing to the body in the tomb—to their home in Galilee:

59. Albert Schweitzer, *The Quest of the Historical Jesus: A Critical Study of Its Progress from Reimarus to Wrede*, trans. W. Montgomery (New York: Macmillan, 1961), 22–23.

60. Karl Bahrdt, *Ausführung des Plans und Zwecks Jesu* (1784–92); Karl Venturini, *Natürliche Geschichte des Grossen Propheten von Nazareth* (1800–1802), cited in William Lane Craig, *The Historical Argument for the Resurrection of Jesus during the Deist Controversy* (Lewiston, N.Y.: Edwin Mellen, 1985), 392–93.

61. Heinrich Eberhard Gottlob Paulus, *Das Leben Jesu, als Grundlage Einer Reinen Geschichte des Urchristentums* (*The Life of Jesus as the Basis of a Purely Historical Account of Early Christianity*), 2 vols. (Heidelberg: C. F. Winter, 1828).

62. David Friedrich Strauss, "Hermann Samuel Reimarus and His Apology," in *Reimarus: Fragments*, ed. Charles H. Talbert (Philadelphia: Fortress, 1970), 49.

63. "It is impossible that a being who had been stolen half-dead out of the tomb, who crept about weak and ill, needing medical treatment, who required bandaging, strengthening and understanding, and who still at last yielded to his sufferings, could have given to his disciples the impression that he was a conqueror over death and the grave, the prince of life, an impression which lay at the bottom of their future ministry. Such a resuscitation could only have weakened the impression which he had made upon them in life and in death, at the most could only have given it a mournful voice, but could

by no possibility have changed their sorrow into enthusiasm, have elevated their reverence into worship." David Friedrich Strauss, *A New Life of Jesus*, 2nd ed., 2 vols. (London: Williams & Norgate, 1879), 1:412.

64. Some of Strauss's criteria for myth were negative: "I. *Negative.* That an account is not historical—that the matter related could not have taken place in the manner described is evident: *First.* When the narration is irreconcilable with the known and universal laws which govern the course of events... *Secondly.* An account which shall be regarded as historically valid, must neither be inconsistent with itself, nor in contradiction with other accounts." Other criteria were positive: "II. *Positive.* The positive characters of legend and fiction are to be recognized sometimes in the form, sometimes in the substance of a narrative. If the form is poetical, if the characters converse in hymns and in a more diffuse and elevated strain than might be expected from their training and situations, such discourses ... are not to be regarded as historical... If the contents of a narrative strikingly accords [*sic*] with certain ideas existing and prevailing within the circle from which the narrative proceeded, which ideas themselves seem to be the product of preconceived opinions rather than of practical experience, it is more or less probable ... that such a narrative is of mythical origin." David Friedrich Strauss, *The Life of Jesus Critically Examined*, ed. Peter C. Hodgson, trans. George Eliot (Philadelphia: Fortress, 1972), 87–89.

Here was the place where they gradually began to breathe freely, and where their faith in Jesus, which had been temporarily depressed, might once more expand with its former vigor. But here also, where no body lay in the grave to contradict bold suppositions, might gradually be formed the idea of the resurrection of Jesus; and when this conviction had so elevated the courage and enthusiasm of his adherents that they ventured to proclaim it in the metropolis [of Jerusalem], it was no longer possible by the sight of the body of Jesus either to convict [refute] themselves, or to be convicted [refuted] by others.[65]

While in Galilee, the disciples "conceived that, as it was not possible that Jesus should be held by the bonds of death (Acts 2:24), he passed only a short time in the grave."[66] Three days were determined to be the exact amount of time between death and resurrection, and the myth grew.[67] Wanting to honor Jesus as the risen Lord, the disciples also concocted the idea of the ascension.[68] Thus, Strauss dismissed the resurrection and the ascension of Jesus as the products of the vivid imagination of the disciples. As myths, they have no basis in reality; "these data having been called in question in their historical form, assume that of a mental product, and find a refuge in the soul of the believer."[69]

Albert Schweitzer denounced all earlier quests for the historical Jesus that asserted that Jesus was the product of the imagination of his followers. Specifically, he criticized theories that removed the messiahship of Jesus from his self-consciousness and attributed the concept to his followers, as something they projected onto the teacher Jesus only later, as they wrote the Gospels.[70] For Schweitzer, the only way to account for the messianic consciousness of Jesus was to recognize that he was steeped in the eschatological doctrine and expectations of his time.[71] It was, then, this "eschatological worldview" that determined the ministry of Jesus, prompting him to predict his imminent return prior to the completion of his disciples' ministry (Matt. 10:23).[72] Jesus' eschatological expectations were mistaken, however: "It is equally clear ... that this prediction was not fulfilled. The disciples returned to him; and the appearing of the Son of Man had not taken place.... An event of supernatural history which must take place, and must take

---

65. Strauss, *Life of Jesus Critically Examined*, 743.

66. Ibid., 743–44.

67. Ibid., 744.

68. Ibid., 755.

69. Ibid., 758.

70. "The positive difficulty which confronts the skeptical theory is to explain how the Messianic beliefs of the first generation of disciples arose if Jesus, throughout his life, was for all—even for the disciples—merely a "teacher" and gave even his intimates [friends] no hint of the dignity which he claimed for himself. How can the appearances of the risen Jesus have suggested to the disciples the idea that Jesus, the crucified teacher, was the Messiah?... How did the appearance of the risen Jesus suddenly become for them a proof of his Messiahship and the basis for their eschatology?" Schweitzer, *The Quest of the Historical Jesus*, 343. In this section of his

book, Schweitzer specifically critiqued the "Messianic secret" theory of W. Wrede, *The Messianic Secret in the Gospels* (1901; English ed., trans. J. C. G. Grieg [Cambridge: James Clarke & Co., 1971]).

71. Ibid., 348. Schweitzer emphasized the intensity of the eschatological hope present at Jesus' time. Elsewhere he stated: "We must always make a fresh effort to realize to ourselves that Jesus and his immediate followers were, at that time, in an enthusiastic state of intense eschatological expectation. We must picture them among the people who were filled with repentance for their sins and with faith in the kingdom, hourly expecting the coming of the kingdom and the revelation of Jesus as the Son of Man, seeing in the eager multitude itself a sign that their reckoning of the time was correct." Ibid.

72. Ibid., 357.

place at that particular point of time, failed to come about."[72] Because of this delay in or nonoccurrence of his return, Jesus changed his attitude and direction of ministry: He restricted himself to interaction with his twelve disciples and spoke openly of the sufferings—specifically, his own passion and atoning death for the world—that would precede and usher in the coming of the kingdom of God. The resurrection was also part of this changed expectation.[74] Despite his great expectation, Jesus died by attempting to bring in the kingdom of God violently; tragically, his hopes for this eschatological event were dashed to pieces:

> Jesus ... in the knowledge that he is the coming Son of Man, lays hold of the wheel of the world to set it moving on that last revolution which is to bring all ordinary history to a close. It refuses to turn, and he throws himself upon it. Then it does turn; and it crushes him. Instead of bringing in the eschatological conditions, he has destroyed them. The wheel rolls onward and the mangled body of the one immeasurably great man, who was strong enough to think of himself as the spiritual ruler of mankind and to bend history to his purpose, is hanging upon it still. That is his victory and his reign.[75]

Rudolph Bultmann began his *Theology of the New Testament* with the assertion, "The message of Jesus is a presupposition for the theology of the New Testament rather than a part of that theology itself."[76] With this, he affirmed the dichotomy between the historical Jesus of Nazareth and the "kerygmatic" Christ of faith; the former was relatively unimportant, and the latter was what really mattered for the church. According to Bultmann, "I do indeed think that we can now know almost nothing concerning the life and personality of Jesus, because the early Christian sources show no interest in either and also are fragmentary and often legendary."[77] The "kerygmatic" Christ of faith—the one who was preached by the first disciples—is the product of the early Christian community and is covered with mythology. This conviction led Bultmann to adopt his method of interpreting the Bible: "We must ask whether the eschatological preaching and the mythological sayings as a whole contain a still deeper meaning that is concealed under the cover of mythology. If that is so, let us abandon the mythological conceptions precisely because we want to retain their deeper meaning. This method of interpretation of the New Testament, which tries to recover the deeper meaning behind the mythological conceptions, I call *de-mythologizing*."[78] Given this approach, he could not accept the resurrection and ascension of Jesus as historical events, "for the resurrection, of course, simply cannot be a visible fact in the realm of human history,"[79] and "a historical fact that involves a resurrection from the dead is utterly inconceivable."[80] As the product of

---

73. Ibid.

74. Ibid., 364.

75. Ibid., 368–69.

76. Rudolf Bultmann, *Theology of the New Testament*, 2 vols., trans. Kendrick Grobel (New York: Scribner, 1951), 1:3.

77. Rudolf Bultmann, *Jesus and the Word* (New York: Scribner, 1958), 8.

78. Rudolf Bultmann, *Jesus Christ and Mythology* (New York: Scribner, 1958), 18.

79. Bultmann, *Theology of the New Testament*, 1:295.

80. Rudolf Bultmann, "New Testament and Mythology," in *Kerygma and Myth*, ed. H. W. Bartsch, trans. Reginald H. Fuller (London: SPCK, 1953), 39.

the disciples' reflection on Jesus and his message, the proclamation of the resurrection and ascension may induce faith in the risen and ascended Christ, but the events themselves have no basis in history. But this is what matters anyway, according to Bultmann: "Christ meets us in the preaching as one crucified and risen.... The faith of Easter is just this—faith in the word of preaching."[81]

Kirsopp Lake attempted to offer a natural explanation behind the church's faith in the empty tomb and the resurrection of Christ on the third day. He proposed that the women went to the wrong tomb:

> It is seriously a matter for doubt whether the women were really in a position to be quite certain that the tomb that they visited was that in which they had seen Joseph of Arimathea bury the Lord's body. The neighborhood of Jerusalem is full of rock-tombs, and it would not be easy to distinguish one from another without careful notes.... Moreover, it is very doubtful if they were close to the tomb at the moment of burial.... It is likely that they were watching from a distance, and that Joseph of Arimathea was a representative of the Jews rather than of the disciples.... The possibility, therefore, that they came to the wrong tomb is to be reckoned with, and it is important because it supplies the natural explanation of the fact that whereas they had seen the tomb closed, they found it open.[82]

Only after the belief developed that Jesus had somehow risen from the dead, the women viewed their visit to this tomb as proof of the resurrection.[83] This view allowed Lake and others like him to believe in some kind of resurrection of Christ without holding to the miracle of the empty tomb. This was important according to Lake because "the empty tomb is for us doctrinally indefensible and is historically insufficiently accredited."[84]

The Passover Plot, by Hugh Schonfield, renewed a centuries-old hypothesis that Jesus plotted with his followers to fake his death and deceive the world. Schonfield portrayed Jesus as a thoroughgoing master schemer.[85] This held true as Jesus prepared for his rescue from death: "Two things ... were indispensable to the success of a rescue operation. The first was to administer a drug to Jesus on the cross to give the impression of premature death, and the second was to obtain the speedy delivery of the body to Joseph."[86] In hatching this plot, Jesus deliberately did not involve his closest disciples but chose a handful of trusted outsiders instead. Through their help, the deception unfolded, beginning with administering the secret drug to Jesus by means of a sponge soaked in vinegar. Follow-

---

81. Ibid., 41.

82. Kirsopp Lake, *The Historical Evidence for the Resurrection of Jesus Christ* (New York: G. P. Putnam's Sons, 1912), 250.

83. Ibid., 251–52.

84. Ibid., 253. Specifically, Lake considered the resurrection "not as the resurrection of a material body, but as the manifestation of a surviving personality." Ibid., 274-75. Lake further sought to explain the appearances of the risen Jesus by means of thought transference, telepathy, and subliminal consciousness. From a psychological point of view, Lake conjec-

tured, "Perhaps they are proofs that personality survives death in a form that does not exclude the possibility of communication. Perhaps they are proofs of as yet unfathomed possibilities of the influence of living personality and of unconscious thought that suddenly reaches the plane of consciousness and manifests itself there in the form of 'appearances' or 'messages.'" Ibid., 275–76.

85. Hugh J. Schonfield, *The Passover Plot* (London: Hutchinson, 1965), 162.

86. Ibid., 166.

ing this, "Jesus lapsed quickly into complete unconsciousness. His body sagged. His head lolled on his breast, and to all intents and purposes he was a dead man."[87] Immediately afterward, Joseph of Arimathea, one of Jesus' coconspirators, secured the body and laid it in his tomb. Schonfield continued his conjecturing: "Jesus lay in the tomb over the Sabbath. He would not regain consciousness for many hours, and in the meantime the spices and linen bandage provided the best dressing for his injuries.... What seems probable is that in the darkness of Saturday night when Jesus was brought out of the tomb by those concerned in the plan he regained consciousness temporarily, but finally succumbed."[88] He then accounted for the missing body of Jesus: "Before dawn the mortal remains of Jesus were quickly yet reverently interred, leaving the puzzle of the empty tomb."[89] As for what happened that first Easter Sunday, Schonfield proposed: "It impresses as true that the women did find someone in the tomb, who could have been the gardener or the other unknown man ... who administered the drugged drink to Jesus on the cross. If he spoke to the women, which is quite likely, they were in no state to take in what he said. All that registered at the time was that the body of Jesus was gone and that a strange man was there.... The story progressed in the light of belief in the resurrection of Jesus."[90]

The responses of Christians to this onslaught of attacks against the resurrection and ascension of Jesus were many and varied. William Craig summarized the apologetic approach of eighteenth-century writers as they defended the resurrection:

> The orthodox thinkers argued that both internal and external evidence confirms the authenticity of the gospels, so that the reports we have of the resurrection stem from the apostles themselves or the apostolic circle. Therefore, if these accounts are not true, then their authors and the disciples were either deceivers or deceived. But the perspicuity of the events of the resurrection makes it impossible for the disciples to have been misled into thinking that Jesus had been raised from the tomb when in fact he had not. And it is equally futile to try to dismiss the apostles as base charlatans who had conspired together to invent the whole affair. Therefore, the accounts must be true, and Jesus did rise from the dead and appear to his disciples, leaving an empty grave behind him. This fact alone allows us to account for the otherwise unexplainable phenomena of the origin, spread, and steadfastness of primitive Christianity. Objections to the evidence for the resurrection can be refuted; in particular the resurrection narratives can be shown to be complementary, not contradictory, in nature. Therefore, the resurrection of Jesus is firmly established as historical fact.[91]

In terms of specific arguments, Christian apologists presented the case against the disciples deceiving people by stealing the body or making up the stories of Jesus' appearances. William Paley reasoned: "Would men in such circumstances pretend to have seen what they never saw; assert facts which they had no knowledge of; go about lying to teach virtue; and though not only convinced of Christ's being an imposter, but having seen the

87. Ibid., 167.
88. Ibid., 170, 172.
89. Ibid., 172.

90. Ibid., 174.
91. Craig, *Historical Argument for the Resurrection of Jesus*, 350.

success of his imposture in his crucifixion, yet persist in carrying on; and so persist, as to bring upon themselves, for nothing, and with full knowledge of the consequence, enmity and hatred, danger and death?"[92] The lawyer Simon Greenleaf authored *Testimony of the Evangelists, Examined by the Rules of Evidence Administered in Courts of Justice*. Investigating the testimonies of the writers of the four Gospels to the resurrection of Christ, Greenleaf concluded:

> It was ... impossible that they could have persisted in affirming the truths they have narrated, had Jesus not actually risen from the dead, and had they not known this fact as certainly as they knew any other fact.... To have persisted in so gross a falsehood, after it was known to them, was not only to encounter, for life, all the evils which man could inflict from the outside, but to endure also the pangs of inward and conscious guilt; with no hope of future peace, no testimony of a good conscience, no expectation of honor or esteem among men, no hope of happiness in this life, or in the world to come.[93]

At the same time, many in the church affirmed the traditional doctrine. Writing in *The Fundamentals*, R. A. Torrey reemphasized that "the resurrection of Jesus Christ from the dead is the cornerstone of Christian doctrine. The crucifixion loses its meaning without the resurrection. Without the resurrection, the death of Christ was only the heroic death of a noble martyr. With the resurrection, it is the atoning death of the Son of God. It shows that death to be of sufficient value to cover all our sins, for it was the sacrifice of the Son of God."[94] Furthermore, Torrey insisted that the entire supernatural or miraculous nature of Christianity stood or fell on the reality of Christ's resurrection: "If the Scriptural assertions of Christ's resurrection can be established as historic certainties, the claims and doctrines of Christianity rest upon an impregnable foundation. On the other hand, if the resurrection of Jesus Christ from the dead cannot be established, Christianity must go."[95]

Beginning in the middle of the twentieth century, a movement arose among German theologians—including Hans von Campenhausen and Hans Grass—who began to defend the historicity of the resurrection of Jesus Christ.[96] Wolfhart Pannenberg became the most widely recognized theologian in this movement. He was particularly critical of the well-entrenched view that one's personal encounter with the living Christ becomes the basis for one's certainty about the resurrection of Jesus. According to Pannenberg, this perspective was wrongheaded: "One cannot achieve such knowledge about the living, present Lord through direct, present-day experience in association with the exalted Lord—an immediate experience of the Lord that establishes the certainty, not only of the reality of his

---

92. William Paley, *A View of the Evidences of Christianity*, 2 vols., 5th ed. (London: R. Faulder, 1796; repr., Westmead, U.K.: Gregg International, 1970), 1:327–28, cited in Craig, *Historical Argument for the Resurrection of Jesus*, 336.

93. Simon Greenleaf, *Testimony of the Evangelists, Examined by the Rules of Evidence Administered in Courts of Justice* (1847; repr., Grand Rapids: Baker, 1965, 1984), 29–30.

94. R. A. Torrey, "The Certainty and Importance of the Bodily Resurrection of Jesus Christ from the Dead," in idem, *The Fundamentals*, vol. 2 (Los Angeles: Bible Institute of Los Angeles, 1917), 298–99.

95. Ibid., 299–300.

96. Hans von Campenhausen, *Der Ablauf der Osterereignisse und das Leere Grab* (Heidelberg, 1952), and Hans Grass, *Ostergeschehen und Osterberichte* (Göttingen: Vandenhoeck and Ruprecht, 1956).

resurrection, but also of his historical existence."[97] He underscored the error in this way of thinking:

> But who can be certain of such experiences? How can one distinguish them from self-delusion? Further, the New Testament testifies that through his exaltation Jesus has been removed from the earth and from his disciples. Only on the basis of what happened in the past, not because of present experiences, do we know that Jesus lives as the exalted Lord. Only in trust in the reliability of the reports of Jesus' resurrection and exaltation are we able to turn in prayer to the one who is exalted and now lives, and thus to associate with him in the present.[98]

Furthermore, Pannenberg dismissed the centuries-old view that the appearances of Jesus were merely the product of disciples' overactive imagination. Indeed, he regarded this notion as "problematic precisely in psychological terms":[99] "To maintain ... that the appearances were produced by the enthusiastically excited imagination of the disciples does not hold, at least for the first and most fundamental appearance. The Easter appearances are not to be explained from the Easter faith of the disciples; rather, conversely, the Easter faith of the disciples is to be explained from the appearances."[100] On the contrary, the resurrection was a historical reality, not a psychological event in the minds of the followers of Jesus.[101] Two complementary traditions—one affirming Jesus' appearances after his resurrection, the other recounting the conditions in the tomb after his resurrection (it was empty)—provided the foundation for Pannenberg's insistence on the historicity of the resurrection: "If the appearance tradition and the grave tradition came into existence independently, then by their mutually complementing each other they let the assertion of the reality of Jesus' resurrection ... appear as historically very probable, and that always means in historical inquiry that it is to be presupposed until contrary evidence appears."[102]

American evangelicals wrote both popular and scholarly apologetics for the resurrection. On a popular level, Josh McDowell authored the bestselling book *Evidence That Demands a Verdict,* with a lengthy chapter titled "The Resurrection—Hoax or History?"[103] William Lane Craig published several scholarly works on the topic, including *The Historical Argument for the Resurrection of Jesus during the Deist Controversy* and *Assessing the New Testament Evidence for the Historicity of the Resurrection of Jesus.*[104] In this latter writing, he concluded: "The most reasonable historical explanation for the facts of the empty tomb, the resurrection appearances, and the origin of the Christian Way would therefore seem to be that Jesus rose from the dead." He then raised a key question: "Now it has become part of conventional theological wisdom that such is a

97. Wolfhart Pannenberg, *Jesus—God and Man,* trans. Lewis L. Wilkins and Duane A. Priebe, 2nd ed. (Philadelphia: Westminster, 1968, 1977), 27–28.

98. Ibid., 28.
99. Ibid., 96.
100. Ibid.
101. Ibid., 98.

102. Ibid., 105.
103. Josh McDowell, *Evidence That Demands a Verdict* (San Bernardino, Calif.: Here's Life, 1972).
104. Craig, *Historical Argument for the Resurrection of Jesus*; and idem, *Assessing the New Testament Evidence for the Historicity of the Resurrection of Jesus* (Lewiston/Queenston/Lampeter: Edwin Mellen, 1989).

conclusion that must not be drawn. But why not? If it is the case that the evidence can only be plausibly explained by the historical fact of the resurrection of Jesus, why are we debarred from that conclusion?"[105] Craig answered by distinguishing between the resurrection *event* and its *cause*: "The event of the resurrection occurs within human history, but the cause of the resurrection is outside human history."[106] For Craig, the resurrection as event can be verified historically. He noted, however: "The real problem comes when we inquire concerning the cause of the resurrection. The historian *qua* historian could conclude that the best explanation of the fact is that 'Jesus rose from the dead'; but he could not conclude, 'God raised Jesus from the dead.' But what I wish to suggest ... is that the historian 'in his off hours,' to paraphrase Bertrand Russell, that is, the historian as a human being, may indeed rightly infer from the evidence that God has acted here in history."[107] This conclusion is the historic position of the church that Christians embrace.

105. Craig, *Assessing the New Testament Evidence*, 418.   107. Ibid., 419.
106. Ibid.

20

THE HOLY SPIRIT

***How has the church come to understand the person
and work of the Holy Spirit? How did it develop
various views on his distinctive activities?***

STATEMENT OF BELIEF

The church has historically believed that the Holy Spirit is the third person of the Trinity, fully God and coequal with God the Father and God the Son. When the deity of the Spirit was denied, the early church marshaled biblical and theological support, along with appeals to the church's worship of the Spirit and its baptism in the name of the Spirit, in support of his deity. The church has also historically embraced the multifaceted ministry of the Holy Spirit, including his conviction of sin and his work of regeneration in the lives of unbelievers, and in the lives of believers, his sealing ministry, distribution of spiritual gifts, empowerment for service, work of sanctification, illumination of Scripture, personal guidance, and much more.

Relatively little disagreement has existed among Christians about the person and work of the Holy Spirit. Some points of debate include the relationship of the Holy Spirit to the Father and the Son. The Roman Catholic Church and Protestant churches are set apart from the Orthodox churches in the belief that "the Holy Spirit proceeds from both the Father and the Son." Orthodox theology holds that the Spirit proceeds from the Father only. Further disagreement exists over the relationship of the Holy Spirit to the sacraments or ordinances of Christianity. Some churches—for example, the Roman Catholic Church—link the Spirit's work directly and exclusively to the sacraments. That is, the Holy Spirit does not work outside of those channels of God's grace. Other churches, while administering baptism and the Lord's Supper, do not limit the Spirit's work to those and other formal church activities. Additionally, since the beginning of the Pentecostal movement, disagreement is found as to the baptism of the Holy Spirit, the so-called "sign gifts" of the Spirit (e.g., prophecy and miracles), and the role of speaking in tongues as evidence of the Holy Spirit's work in a believer's life.

Evangelicals hold to the historical beliefs about the Holy Spirit's deity and ministry (including the position that the Spirit proceeds from both the Father and the Son), but they reflect a significant amount of disagreement on the Spirit's link to the sacraments and his role in Spirit baptism and distribution of miraculous gifts.[1]

THE VIEW OF THE HOLY SPIRIT IN THE EARLY CHURCH

The early church was dependent on the Old Testament and the teaching of Jesus for understanding the new covenant ministry of the Holy Spirit. Jesus himself had been conceived by the Holy Spirit (Luke 1:35) and filled with the Spirit without measure (John 3:34–35), enabling him to engage in powerful ministry (Luke 4:14–19). But Jesus also anticipated a future new outpouring of the Spirit in fulfillment of Old Testament prophecies (Jer. 31:31–34; Ezek. 36:24–27; Joel 2:28–32). Indeed, the apostle John explained that this fresh work of the Spirit awaited Jesus' death and resurrection (John 7:35–37). Even after his resurrection, Jesus told the apostles: "Do not leave Jerusalem, but wait for the gift my Father promised, which you have heard me speak about. For John baptized with water, but in a few days you will be baptized with the Holy Spirit" (Acts 1:4–5). This prophecy was fulfilled on the day of Pentecost, when the disciples were "filled with the Holy Spirit" as the prophet Joel had predicted (Acts 2:1–21).

Empowered by this Spirit, the early church began to multiply and disperse throughout the world. It realized that the way to please God was to be filled with the Holy Spirit (Eph. 5:18), walk in him (Gal. 5:16–26), and not grieve (Eph. 4:30) or quench the Spirit (1 Thess. 5:19). Clement of Rome congratulated the Corinthians for the powerful working of the Spirit in their midst: "A profound and rich peace was given to all, together with an insatiable desire to do good, and an abundant outpouring of the Holy Spirit fell upon everyone as well."[2] A chief role of the Holy Spirit was to bring comfort to Christians, as the term *Paraclete* (the apostle John's preferred word for him) emphasized. As Origen noted: "The Paraclete, who is called the Holy Spirit, is so called from his work of consolation.... For if anyone has deserved to participate in the Holy Spirit by the knowledge of his ineffable mysteries, he undoubtedly obtains comfort and joy of heart."[3] This knowledge was communicated by the apostles and teachers in the early church, and these instructors taught rightly because of the Holy Spirit in them. The *Shepherd of Hermas* described "apostles and teachers who preached to the whole world and who reverently and purely taught the word of the Lord, and who misappropriated nothing for evil desire, but always walked in righteousness and truth, just as they had also received the Holy Spirit."[4] The Spirit was also the giver of power and gifts, both of which had equipped the original apostles and now enabled the church to carry out its ministry.[5]

---

1. My thanks to Rony Kozman for his help on this chapter.

2. Clement of Rome, *Letter of the Romans to the Corinthians*, 2, in Holmes, 31; *ANF*, 1:5. Barnabas praised a similar powerful outpouring among his readers: "I truly see that the Spirit has been poured out upon you from the riches of the Lord's fountain." *Letter of Barnabas*, 1, in Holmes, 275; *ANF*, 1:137.

3. Origen, *First Principles*, 2.7.4, in *ANF*, 4:285–86.

4. *Shepherd of Hermas*, parable 9.25, in Holmes, 509; *ANF*, 2:51–52.

5. "For this is he [the Holy Spirit] who strengthened their [the disciples'] hearts and minds, who marked out the gospel sacraments, who was in them the enlightener of divine things; and they being strengthened, feared, for the sake of the Lord's

This issue of the Holy Spirit's role in miraculous works became an early topic of debate concerning the Spirit. Montanus, along with two prophetesses, Priscilla and Maximilla, founded the movement called *Montanism* in the region of Phrygia (part of Asia Minor).[6] The claim of Montanus and these prophetesses to be the mouthpiece of the Holy Spirit was denounced by the early church, especially as it became clear that some of the "Spirit communications" were far from the truth. For example, Montanus claimed, "I am the Father and the Son and the Paraclete,"[7] and Maximilla prophesied, "After me there will be no more prophecy, but the end."[8] Indeed, Montanism stirred up hope of the immediate return of Christ and identified the location of the New Jerusalem, claiming this revelation as part of a prophecy of Priscilla: "Appearing as a woman clothed in a shining robe, Christ came to me [in my sleep]; he put wisdom into me and revealed to me that this place [Phrygia] is sacred and that here Jerusalem will come down from heaven."[9] For obvious reasons, the early church did not tolerate such nonsense. In addition, it became suspicious of any overemphasis on the Holy Spirit.

The early church also acknowledged the newness of the Holy Spirit's ministry in its midst as compared with his work before the Christian era. At the same time, the church took pains to clarify that he was not somehow a different Spirit from the one before: "It is the same Holy Spirit ... in those who believed in God before the advent of Christ, or in those who by means of Christ have sought refuge in God."[10] It is not two Holy Spirits that account for the change, but a difference in his ministry from before the coming of Christ to after it, as Origen explained: "The chief advent of the Holy Spirit is ... after the ascension of Christ to heaven, rather than before his coming into the world. For, before that, it was upon the prophets alone, and upon a few individuals.... But after the advent of the Savior," the Spirit is poured out on all Christians.[11] Novatian emphasized a similar idea, giving more detail about the difference in the Holy Spirit's ministry before Christ (the first column below) and his work after Christ (the second column below):

With regard to the prophets:	*With regard to the apostles:*
He was not always in them.	He remained with them always.
He was distributed in a limited way.	He was poured out on everyone.
He was given sparingly.	He was given freely.[12]

name, neither dungeons nor chains, nay [indeed], even trod under foot the very powers of the world and its tortures, since they were henceforth armed and strengthened by the same Spirit, having in themselves the gifts which this same Spirit distributes, and appropriates to the church, the spouse of Christ, as her ornaments. This is he who places prophets in the church, instructs teachers, directs [speaking in] tongues, gives powers and healings, does wonderful works, offers discrimination [discernment] of spirits, affords powers of government, suggests counsels, and orders and arranges all the other gifts there are of *charismata*, and thus makes the Lord's church everywhere, and in all, perfected and completed." Novatian, *Treatise Concerning the Trinity*, 29, in *ANF*, 5:640–41.

6. Hippolytus, *The Refutation of All Heresies*, 8.12, in *ANF*, 5:123–24.

7. Didymus, *On the Trinity*, 3.41.1, in Petry, 90.

8. Epiphanius, *Heresies*, 48.11, in Petry, 90.

9. Ibid., 49.1, in Petry, 90.

10. Origen, *First Principles*, 2.7.1, in *ANF*, 4:284.

11. Ibid., 2.7.2, in *ANF*, 4:285.

12. Novatian, *Treatise Concerning the Trinity*, 29, in *ANF*, 5:640.

In both its ministry and theology, the early church closely associated this unprecedented ministry of the Holy Spirit with the work of the Father and the Son. From very early on, the Christian rite of baptism was done in the name of all three persons, in keeping with Jesus' instructions (Matt. 28:18–20). The *Didache* prescribed this same threefold baptismal formula,[13] as did Justin Martyr.[14] Also, the church's earliest theology took on a Trinitarian format that acknowledged the Holy Spirit right alongside the Father and the Son. For example, Tertullian's "rule of faith" began with a focus on the uniqueness of God, then spoke of the Son of God, then addressed the third person: "We believe that Jesus Christ also sent from heaven from the Father—according to his own promise—the Holy Spirit, the Paraclete. He is the sanctifier of the faith of those who believe in the Father, and in the Son, and in the Holy Spirit. This rule of faith has come down to us from the beginning of the gospel."[15] On the basis of biblical evidence,[16] Origen concluded that the Holy Spirit has always been the Holy Spirit and a member of the Trinity: "It was not by progressive advancement that he came to be the Holy Spirit.... For if this were the case, the Holy Spirit would never be reckoned in the unity of the Trinity, i.e., along with the unchangeable Father and his Son, unless he had always been the Holy Spirit."[17]

Such careful work in understanding the Holy Spirit became essential for the early church as various errors concerning him arose. Two movements in particular challenged the traditional view of the Spirit. Both were forms of *monarchianism*, which means that they emphasized the unity of God as the only *monarchia*, or ruler of the universe. If the premise "God is one" was foremost in one's thinking about the Godhead, then the deity of the Son and the deity of the Holy Spirit become problematic. If God (the Father) is God, and Jesus (the Son) is God, it appears that there are two gods. On top of this, if the Holy Spirit is God, then apparently belief in three gods is affirmed. This belief was the underlying difficulty that both movements sought to address.

The first movement, called *dynamic monarchianism*, was originated by Theodotus in Rome and championed by Paul of Samosata, bishop of Antioch.[18] Both proponents of dynamic monarchianism viewed the Holy Spirit as being little more than a divine influence.[19] Fortunately, this form of heresy exerted little influence in the church.

Not so, however, with the second heresy, called *modalistic monarchianism*, which became a widespread belief in the early church. It was founded by Praxeas in Rome, car-

13. *Didache*, 7, in Holmes, 259; *ANF*, 7:379.

14. Justin Martyr, *First Apology*, 61, in *ANF*, 1:183.

15. Tertullian, *Against Praxeas*, 2, in *ANF*, 3:598. The text has been rendered clearer. Similarly, Irenaeus summed up these major points in the early church's belief about the Holy Spirit: "The Holy Spirit, through whom the prophets prophesied, and the fathers learned the things of God, and the righteous were led forth into the way of righteousness; and who in the end of the times was poured out in a new way ... renewing man unto God.'" Irenaeus, *The Demonstration of the Apostolic Preaching*, 6, in St. Irenaeus, *The Demonstration of the Apostolic Preaching*, trans. J. Armitage Robinson (Suffolk, England: Richard Clay and Sons, 1919), 75.

16. E.g., he appeals to Christian baptism and makes an argument from the unpardonable sin. Origen, *First Principles*, 1.3.2, in *ANF*, 4:252.

17. Ibid., 1.3.4, in *ANF*, 4:253.

18. To be more precise, there were two proponents of dynamic monarchianism named Theodotus. To distinguish them, one is called Theodotus the Tanner, the other Theodotus the Money-Changer. Tertullian, *Against All Heresies*, 8.8, in *ANF*, 3:654.

19. Hippolytus, *The Refutation of All Heresies*, 7.23, in *ANF*, 5:114–15. We are dependent on Hippolytus and other "orthodox" thinkers, who wrote refutations of early heresies, for our understanding of dynamic monarchianism. We trust that they represented fairly their opponents' positions.

ried on by Noetus of Smyrna and his followers Zephyrinus and Callistus (both bishops of Rome), and popularized by Sabellius. Hippolytus described Callistus's view: "Callistus alleges that the Logos himself is Son and is himself Father. Although called by a different title, in reality he is one indivisible spirit. And he maintains that the Father is not one person while the Son is another, but that they are one and the same; and that all things are full of the divine Spirit.... And he affirms that the Spirit, which became incarnate in the virgin, is not different from the Father, but is one and the same."[20] Modalistic monarchianism held that there is one God who can be designated by three different names — "Father," "Son," and "Holy Spirit" — at different times, but these three are not distinct persons. Instead, they are different *modes* (thus, *modal*ism) of the one God. Thus, God can be called "Father" as the Creator of the world and Lawgiver; he can be called "Son" as God incarnate in Jesus Christ; and he can be called the "Holy Spirit" as God in the church age. According to modalistic monarchianism, Jesus Christ is God and the Spirit is God, but they are not distinct persons.

The early church rejected modalism, affirming instead that the Father, Son, and Holy Spirit are three distinct persons. Speaking of the Holy Spirit, Tertullian explained:

> There is the Paraclete or Comforter, for whom the Lord promises to pray to the Father and to send from heaven after he had ascended to the Father. He is called "another Comforter" indeed (John 14:16).... "He shall receive of mine," says Christ (John 16:14), just as Christ himself received of the Father's. Thus the connection of the Father in the Son, and of the Son in the Paraclete, produces three coherent persons, who are yet distinct one from another. These three are one essence, not one person.[21]

Tertullian's wording became the foundation for the church's definition of the Trinity: God is one in essence yet three in persons.[22] This means that the Holy Spirit is fully God, just as the Father and the Son are; yet he is also distinct from those two. Modalistic monarchianism emphasized the oneness of the Godhead and did not do justice to the distinctions in persons. For this reason, the church considered it to be wrong.

Another doctrinal challenge — Arianism, named after its founder Arius — confronted the church in the fourth century. In 325 the first ecumenical, or general, council of the church was convened by the emperor Constantine to refute the Arian denial of the deity of Jesus Christ. The Council of Nicea focused its attention on this issue of the Son's divine nature. But Arius had expressed his views on the Holy Spirit as well. Just as he denied that the Son was of the same divine substance as the Father (and, thus, something other than fully divine), so Arius insisted that the Holy Spirit was not of the same substance of the Father and the Son (and, thus, not fully divine).[23] The council did not take up this latter

20. Ibid., 9.7, in *ANF*, 5:130. For the similar view of Praxeas, see Tertullian, *Against Praxeas*, 1, in *ANF*, 3:597. The text has been rendered clearer.

21. Tertullian, *Against Praxeas*, 25, in *ANF*, 3:621. The text has been rendered clearer.

22. For further discussion, see chap. 11.

23. "The essences of the Father and the Son and the Holy Spirit are separate in nature, and estranged, and disconnected, and alien, and without participation of each other ... utterly unlike [different from] each other in essence and glory, unto infinity." Athanasius, *Four Discourses against the Arians*, discourse 1.2.6, in *NPNF²*, 4:309.

challenge, but the Creed of Nicea did affirm belief in the Holy Spirit.[24] This Trinitarian formula at least implied a disagreement with Arius's view.

Not long after the Council of Nicea was completed, debate about the Holy Spirit broke out. On the one hand, those who sympathized with Arianism considered the Spirit to be a created being. For example, Eusebius of Caesarea, citing John 1:3, affirmed that the Holy Spirit is "one of the things which have come into existence through the Son."[25] On the other hand, champions of the traditional view of the Holy Spirit convincingly argued that position. Cyril of Jerusalem explained that "the only-begotten Son, together with the Holy Spirit, is a partaker of the Father's Godhead."[26] He attributed deity to the Spirit: "The Holy Spirit is a power most mighty, a divine and unsearchable being."[27] Moreover, the Spirit is a person, not just a powerful force.[28] Against the Arian view, Cyril argued that the awesome Spirit can never be considered a created being: "Nothing among created things is equal in honor to him. For the families of the angels, and all their hosts assembled together, have no equality with the Holy Spirit. The all-excellent power of the Comforter overshadows all of these. Indeed, angels are sent forth to serve [Heb. 1:14], but the Spirit searches even the deep things of God [1 Cor. 2:10–11]."[29]

In a similar way, Athanasius set forth the orthodox view of the Holy Spirit. He affirmed that the Spirit "belongs to and is one with the Godhead which is in the Triad."[30] Because this Triad is eternal, and because the Holy Spirit is part of the Triad, he must share the same substance as the Father and the Son. Athanasius also argued the deity of the Holy Spirit from the fact that Christians become "partakers of God" through him: "If the Holy Spirit were a creature, we would have no participation in God through him; we would be united to a creature and alien [separated] from the divine nature.... If he makes men divine, his nature must undoubtedly be that of God."[31] And just as Athanasius campaigned tirelessly for the expression "the Son is *homoousios* — of the same substance — with the Father," so he affirmed that the Holy Spirit is *homoousios* with the Father and the Son.[32] Thus, Athanasius placed the three persons of the Godhead in the closest possible relationship as sharers in the one divine essence.[33] In 362, at the Council of Alexandria, the church — through the urging of Athanasius — agreed "to anathematize those who say that the Holy Spirit is a creature and separate from the essence of Christ.... For we believe that there is one Godhead, and that it has one nature, and not that there is one nature of the Father, from which that of the Son and of the Holy Spirit are distinct."[34] This development contributed significantly to the demise of Arianism and its heretical view of the Holy Spirit.

---

24. "And [we believe] in the Holy Spirit." Creed of Nicea, in Bettenson, 25.

25. Eusebius of Caesarea, *Praeparatio evangelica*, 11.20, in Kelly, 255.

26. Cyril of Jerusalem, *Catechetical Lectures*, 6.6, in *NPNF*², 7:34.

27. Ibid., 16.3, in *NPNF*², 7:115.

28. "Though the titles of the Holy Spirit are many, he is one and the same; living, existing, and always present together with the Father and the Son. He was not uttered or breathed from the mouth and lips of the Father or the Son, nor dispersed into the air, but he has a real substance. He himself speaks, works, gives gifts, and sanctifies." Ibid., 17.5, in *NPNF*², 7:125. The text has been rendered clearer.

29. Ibid., 16.23, in *NPNF*², 7:121. The text has been rendered clearer.

30. Athanasius, *Letters to Serapion*, 1.21, in Kelly, 257.

31. Ibid., 1.24, in Kelly, 257–58. At the heart of this argument is the biblical affirmation in 2 Peter 1:4.

32. Ibid., 1.27, in Kelly, 258.

33. Ibid., 1.14, in Kelly, 258.

34. Athanasius, *Letter to the Church of Antioch*, 3, 6, in *NPNF*², 4:484, 485.

The next major contribution to the orthodox doctrine of the Holy Spirit was made by three key church leaders: Gregory of Nyssa, Gregory of Nazianzus, and Basil the Great, known as the Cappadocian fathers from their place of origin — Cappadocia, in Asia Minor. Their view came to the forefront against the erroneous position of the Macedonians or Pneumatomachians ("Spirit fighters"), who denied the deity of the Spirit but who also did not call him a creature.[35] In countering this error, the Cappadocian fathers set forth the definitive theology of the Holy Spirit. Basil denounced the view that the Spirit was created by God and insisted instead on the identity of the Spirit's essence with that of the Father and of the Son.[36] Gregory of Nazianzus raised the question openly: "What then? Is the Spirit God? Most certainly. Well then, is he consubstantial [of the same nature as the Father and the Son]? Yes, if he is God."[37]

If the Holy Spirit is consubstantial (or *homoousios*, of the same divine nature), and the Son is as well, what is there to distinguish the two? Could one not conclude that the Father has two Sons? In order to differentiate the Son and the Spirit who share the divine nature, Basil emphasized the importance of distinguishing several key terms: "We do not speak of the Holy Spirit as *unbegotten*, for we recognize one who is unbegotten and one origin of all things, the Father of our Lord Jesus Christ. Nor do we speak of the Holy Spirit as *begotten*, for by the tradition of the faith we have been taught one [i.e., the Son] who is *only-begotten*. The Spirit of truth we have been taught to *proceed* from the Father, and we confess him to be of God without creation."[38] Thus, God the Father is *unbegotten*, God the Son is the *only-begotten*, and the Holy Spirit is not begotten, but *proceeds*. The exact meaning of those terms touched on an incomprehensible mystery, the pursuit of which would only make people "frenzy-stricken for prying into the mystery of God. And who are we to … supply an account of the [divine] nature which is so unspeakable and transcending all words?"[39] But the generation, or begottenness, of the Son, and the procession of the Holy Spirit, both indicate that neither the Son nor the Spirit is created. Also, the Son and Spirit are differentiated by the mode of their origin: the Son is generated, or begotten, but the Spirit proceeds. As Basil explained, the Holy Spirit is said to be of God "in the sense of proceeding out of God, not by generation, like the Son, but as breath of his mouth."[40]

From whom does the Holy Spirit proceed? Gregory of Nazianzus echoed the above idea of Basil that the Holy Spirit proceeds from the Father.[41] Yet Basil also indicated that the Holy Spirit is joined "to the one Father *through* the one Son" and that "the natural goodness and the inherent holiness and the royal dignity extend *from* the Father *through* the only-begotten [Son] to the Spirit."[42] Similarly, Gregory of Nyssa emphasized,

35. Eustathius simply expressed this heresy: "I can neither admit that the Holy Spirit is God, nor can I dare affirm him to be a creature." The expression is attributed to Eustathius by the historian Socrates Scholasticus, *The Ecclesiastical History*, 2.45, in *NPNF*[2], 2:74. In other words, the position was firmly in the middle of the road. One of the arguments used to support the Pneumatomachian position was the absence of any reference to the deity of the Holy Spirit in Scripture. Gregory of Nazianzus addressed this objection in "Fifth Theological Oration: On the Holy Spirit," *Oration* 32.23–28, in *NPNF*[2], 7:325–27.

36. Basil of Caesarea, *Letters*, 125.3, in *NPNF*[2], 8:195.

37. Gregory of Nazianzus, *Oration* 32.10, in *NPNF*[2], 7:321.

38. Basil, *Letters*, 125.3, in *NPNF*[2], 8:195. The text has been rendered clearer.

39. Gregory of Nazianzus, *Oration* 32.8, in *NPNF*[2], 7:320.

40. Basil of Caesarea, *On the Spirit*, 18.46, in *NPNF*[2], 8:29.

41. Gregory of Nazianzus, *Oration* 32.8, in *NPNF*[2], 7:320.

42. Basil, *On the Spirit*, 18.45, 47, in *NPNF*[2], 8:28–29.

"[T]he Holy Spirit is indeed *from* God, and *of* the Christ, according to Scripture. He should not be confused with the Father in never being originated nor with the Son in being the only-begotten. And while he should be regarded separately in certain distinctive properties, he has in all else an exact identity with them."[43] Thus, for Gregory of Nyssa, it was proper to speak of the Spirit as "proceeding from the Father, receiving from the Son."[44] Again, using the difference between *the cause* (God the Father) and *from the cause* (the Son and the Spirit), he distinguished between the Son, who is *directly* from the cause, and the Spirit, who is *indirectly* from the cause.[45]

The danger in these discussions was that an imbalance would be created between two important truths: the Godhead is of one essence, yet the three members eternally exist as distinct persons. Gregory of Nyssa insisted on holding together both the unity of the divine nature and the diversity of the divine persons: "In personality, the Spirit is one thing and the Word another, and yet again that from which the Word and Spirit are [i.e., God the Father] is another. But when you have understood the concept of what the distinction is in these, the oneness of the nature does not allow division. Thus, the supremacy of the one First Cause is not split and cut up into differing Godships."[46] Although distinguishable in terms of personhood, they share the divine essence and, consequently, are to be equally honored: "We glorify the Holy Spirit together with the Father and the Son, from the conviction that he is not separated from the divine nature."[47]

This development of the theology of the Holy Spirit eventually led to the formal statement of the second ecumenical, or general, council of the church: the Council of Constantinople, in 381. On the point about the Holy Spirit, the Nicene Creed now read: "I believe in the Holy Spirit, the Lord and giver of life, who proceeds from the Father; who with the Father and the Son together is worshiped and glorified; who also spoke through the prophets."[48] It should be noted that this original Nicene Creed affirmed belief in the procession of the Spirit from the Father alone.

Augustine applied the finishing touches to the early church's theology of the Holy Spirit. He insisted with those before him that the Spirit is fully God, equal in essence with the Father and the Son and united with them: "The effect of the same substance in Father and Son and Holy Spirit is, that whatever is said of each in respect to themselves, is to be taken of them, not in the plural in sum, but in the singular. For as the Father is God, and the Son is God, and the Holy Spirit is God, which no one doubts to be said in respect to substance, yet we do not say that the very supreme Trinity itself is three Gods, but one God."[49] The Spirit is related personally to the Father and the Son in the following way:

> The Holy Spirit is the Spirit both of the Father and of the Son. But the relationship is not itself apparent in that name, but it is apparent when he is called the gift of God. For he is the gift of the Father and of the Son, because "he proceeds

---

43. Gregory of Nyssa, *On the Holy Spirit against the Followers of Macedonius*, 2, in *NPNF*², 5:314–15. The text has been rendered clearer.

44. Ibid., 11, in *NPNF*², 5:319.

45. Gregory of Nyssa, *On "Not Three Gods,"* 15, in *NPNF*², 5:336.

46. Gregory of Nyssa, *The Great Catechism*, 3, in *NPNF*², 5:477. The text has been rendered clearer.

47. Basil, *Letters*, 159.2, in *NPNF*², 8:212.

48. Nicene-Constantinopolitan Creed, in Schaff, 2:59.

49. Augustine, *On the Trinity*, 5.8/9, in *NPNF*¹, 3:91.

from the Father" (as the Lord says [John 15:26]) and because of what the apostle says, "Now if any man does not have the Spirit of Christ, he does not belong to him" [Rom. 8:9].... Therefore the Holy Spirit is a certain inexpressible communion of the Father and the Son.... In order, therefore, that the communion of both may be signified from a name which is suitable to both, the Holy Spirit is called the gift of both.[50]

For Augustine, the Spirit is the gift of both the Father and the Son. But if the Holy Spirit comes from the Father, why, then, is he not a son? In response, Augustine again emphasized the generation of the Son from the Father alone and the procession of the Spirit from both Father and Son.[51] Thus, Augustine affirmed the double procession of the Holy Spirit more clearly than anyone before him. This did not mean that there are two agents as the source of the Holy Spirit. Rather, through the one action of the Father and Son together, the Spirit proceeds. Indeed, in begetting the Son, the Father made it such that the Spirit would proceed from both of them:

It is not to no purpose that in this Trinity the Son and none other is called the Word of God, and the Holy Spirit and none other is called the Gift of God, and God the Father alone is he from whom the Word is born, and from whom the Holy Spirit principally proceeds. And therefore I have added the word *principally*, because we find that the Holy Spirit proceeds from the Son also. But the Father gave him this too, not as to one already existing, and not yet having it; but whatever he gave to the only-begotten Word, he gave by begetting him. Therefore he so begat him as that the common Gift should proceed from him also, and the Holy Spirit should be the Spirit of both.[52]

Augustine summarized the position of the double procession of the Holy Spirit: "The Son is from the Father, the Spirit also is from the Father. But the former is begotten, the latter proceeds. So the former is Son of the Father from whom he is begotten, but the latter is the Spirit of both since he proceeds from both.... The Father is the author of the Spirit's procession because he begot such a Son, and in begetting him made him also the source from which the Spirit proceeds."[53]

Augustine's position was not officially sanctioned by the church until the Third Council of Toledo (Spain) in 589. Actually, only the Western Church—corresponding to what are today called the Roman Catholic Church and the Protestant churches—affirmed the double procession of the Spirit. This was written as an insertion of one word—*filioque* ("and the Son")—into the Latin version of the Nicene Creed. Thus, the creed was changed to read: "I believe in the Holy Spirit, the Lord and giver of life, who proceeds from the Father *and the Son*."[54] This would soon become a major point of contention between the Western and Eastern portions of the church. Indeed, Christianity would become, and continues to be, divided over this issue.

---

50. Ibid., 5.11/12, in *NPNF*[1], 3:93. The text has been rendered clearer.

51. Ibid., 5.14/15, in *NPNF*[1], 3:94.

52. Ibid., 15.17/29, in *NPNF*[1], 3:216.

53. Augustine, *Collattio cum Maximino Arianorum episcopo*, 2.14.1, in Kelly, 275–76.

54. Nicene-Constantinopolitan Creed (later version), in Schaff, 2:59.

THE VIEW OF THE HOLY SPIRIT
DURING THE MIDDLE AGES

The division between Eastern and Western Christianity over the procession of the Holy Spirit did not happen all at once. Because of the strength of Augustine's theology, the West unanimously repeated his view. For example, the historian Venerable Bede recorded a common medieval creed "glorifying God the Father, who is without beginning, and his only begotten Son, begotten of the Father before all worlds, and the Holy Spirit, ineffably proceeding from the Father and the Son."[55] Similarly, the standard wording was echoed at the Fourth Lateran Council in 1215: "The Father is from no one, but the Son is from the Father only, and the Holy Spirit is equally from both, always without beginning and end; the Father begetting, the Son begotten, and the Holy Spirit proceeding; consubstantial and coequal, co-omnipotent and co-eternal."[56]

The Eastern church, however, could not agree with the Western church on the issue of the double procession of the Holy Spirit. Because representatives of the Eastern church were not in attendance at Toledo, Photius, bishop of Constantinople, excommunicated Pope Nicholas I. His reason: the addition of *filioque* had corrupted the Nicene Creed. Moreover, Photius averred, "[N]either in the divine words of Scripture nor in the human words of the holy Fathers was it ever verbally enunciated that the Spirit proceeds from the Son."[57] The counterevidence from Scripture affirms instead that the Spirit "proceeds from the Father [alone]" (John 15:26, as Photius understood the passage).[58] Another objection raised by the Eastern church against this view was that it could not guard against making the Son a second source or principle of the Holy Spirit. If the Father was a source of the Holy Spirit, and the Son was a source of the Holy Spirit, the unity of the Trinity would be destroyed. Eastern theologians could even point to actual examples of proponents of double procession falling into error. For example, Hilary of Poitiers insisted that "we are bound to confess him [the Holy Spirit], proceeding from Father and Son as authors.' "[59] If Hilary could speak of plural "authors," then the conclusion was obvious: "The Father and the Son are not one principle of the Holy Spirit."[60] Western theologians, however, explicitly denied this charge, affirming with Augustine that "the Father and the Son are not two principles, but one principle of the Holy Spirit."[61] As Aquinas explained: "The Father and the Son are in everything one, wherever there is no distinction between them of opposite relation. Hence since there is no relative opposition between them as the principle of the Holy Spirit, it follows that the Father and the Son

55. Venerable Bede, *Ecclesiastical History*, 4.17, in *Bede: The Ecclesiastical History of the English People*, ed. Judith McClure and Roger Collins (Oxford: Oxford Univ. Press, 1999), 200. According to Boniface, the catholic faith acknowledged that "the Father has the Son, the Son has the Father, and the Holy Spirit proceeds from the Father and the Son." Boniface, *Sermon* 1.2, PL, 89:844–45, in Pelikan, 3:22.

56. Fourth Lateran Council, canon 1, in Petry, 322.

57. Photius, *Mystagogia Spiritus Sancti*, 91, cited in Edmund J. Fortman, *The Triune God: A Historical Study of the Doctrine of the Trinity* (London: Hutchinson, 1972), 94.

58. Photius, *Mystagogia Spiritus sancti*, 2, cited in Fortman, *Triune God*, 94.

59. Hilary of Poitiers, *On the Trinity*, 2.29, in *NPNF²*, 9:60. Aquinas quoted Hillary's view as a key objection to the double procession. Thomas Aquinas, *Summa Theologica*, pt. 1, q. 36, art. 4.

60. Aquinas, *Summa Theologica*, pt. 1, q. 36, art. 4.

61. Augustine, *On the Trinity*, 5.14, in *NPNF¹*, 3:94.

are one principle of the Holy Spirit."[62] Thus, the Western church had a ready answer for the Eastern church's objections to double procession.

Anselm mounted the most formidable response to the Eastern church's rejection of the procession of the Spirit from both the Father and the Son. He underscored several points: Consistent with biblical texts that call the third person "the Spirit of God" and the "Spirit of Christ," Anselm affirmed that "the Holy Spirit is the Spirit of God and the Spirit of the Father and the Son."[63] For Anselm, this meant that "the Holy Spirit exists and proceeds from God and the Father. And so the Holy Spirit exists and proceeds from the Son."[64] Moreover, though "the Son and the Holy Spirit have from the Father what constitutes the Son or the Holy Spirit ... the Son is from his Father, that is, from God who is his Father, while the Holy Spirit is not from God as his Father but only from God who is Father."[65] Thus Anselm defined the unique relationships between the three persons of the Godhead while affirming the traditional difference between the generation of the Son and the procession of the Spirit. He also noted, "[W]hen we profess that the Holy Spirit is from God the Father, it follows from the same unity of the divine nature, if the same God is Father and Son, that the Holy Spirit is from the Son."[66] Anselm's reasoned conclusion was that "the Holy Spirit is from the Son as well as from the Father."[67] Given the truth of this last point, Anselm concluded that the Holy Spirit "is proved also to exist and proceed from the Son. For the Holy Spirit proceeds from the one from whom he exists, and he originates from the one from whom he proceeds."[68]

Anselm marshaled several biblical arguments as well. Reasoning from Jesus' teaching that the Father would send the Spirit in his (that is, Jesus') name (John 14:26) and that Jesus would send the Spirit from the Father (John 15:26), he concluded that Jesus' "sending of the Spirit and the Father's sending of the Spirit are one and the same."[69] In response to the Eastern church's contention that the Holy Spirit proceeds from the Father through the Son, he appealed to the one divine nature of the Father and the Son and concluded: "Therefore, we cannot understand how, if the same divine nature belongs to the Son, the Holy Spirit proceeds from the divine nature of the Father through the divine nature of the Son and not from the divine nature of the Son."[70] While affirming the double procession of the Holy Spirit, Anselm, like others before him, denied that this entails two causes or two sources for the Spirit.[71] In summary, Anselm's *On the Procession of the Holy Spirit* was a robust, Western church refutation of the Eastern church's doctrine.

For some, the conflict between the two theologies was due to a misunderstanding of terms. To others, the Eastern church, from the perspective of the West, was committing unpardonable sin. At the heart of the matter was the question of authority. The Eastern

---

62. Aquinas, *Summa Theologica*, pt. 1, q. 36, art. 4.

63. Anselm, *On the Procession of the Holy Spirit*, 1, in *Anselm*, 391.

64. Ibid., 12, in *Anselm*, 424.

65. Ibid., 1, in *Anselm*, 391.

66. Ibid., in *Anselm*, 404.

67. Ibid., in *Anselm*, 398. Anselm also worked from this line of thought: If the Holy Spirit is from God, then because God is the Father and the Son and the Holy Spirit, the Spirit

must be from all three. Anselm rejected this, arguing that "the Holy Spirit cannot be from his very self, since no person can originate from the person's very self." He concluded, therefore, that the Holy Spirit is from both the Father and the Son. Ibid., 2, in *Anselm*, 401.

68. Ibid., in *Anselm*, 403.

69. Ibid., 4, in *Anselm*, 406.

70. Ibid., 9, in *Anselm*, 415.

71. Ibid., 10, in *Anselm*, 419.

church was unwilling to acknowledge the supreme authority of the Roman pope, and it dissented from the change to the original Nicene Creed. Indeed, it pointed out that the word *filioque* had been inserted into the creed at a council at which none of its representatives were present. Such a unilateral and authoritative decision was unacceptable to the East.

This matter of church authority was seen in another medieval emphasis: the identification of the saving and sanctifying work of the Holy Spirit with the Roman Catholic Church. For centuries the church had linked reception of the Spirit with baptism and its accompanying rite of confirmation.[72] This practice became even more pronounced in the Middle Ages.[73] Indeed, it was through the Holy Spirit's work in its midst—and in it alone—that the Roman Catholic Church considered itself to be the sole source of salvation for the world: "The sixth [article of faith] is the sanctification of the church by the Holy Spirit, and by the sacraments of grace, and by all those things in which the Christian Church communicates. By which is understood that the Church, with its sacraments and discipline, is, through the Holy Spirit, sufficient for the salvation of every sinner; and that outside the Church there is no salvation."[74] In this way, the saving and sanctifying work of the Holy Spirit was decisively linked to the Roman Catholic Church, and especially to its sacraments. The church went on to claim further that through the infallibility granted by the Holy Spirit to the pope, the church that was led by him could not err in matters of faith.

THE VIEW OF THE HOLY SPIRIT DURING THE REFORMATION AND POST-REFORMATION

Of course, this notion was directly and vigorously challenged by Martin Luther. Chief among his arguments against the Roman Catholic Church was that Catholicism had long ago abandoned Scripture and the truth contained in it; therefore, whatever it might claim, it could not be in the right. But Luther's appeal was not only to the Bible; rather, he urged a fine balance between the Word of God and the Spirit of God. Here, then, we see one aspect of Luther's practical doctrine of the Holy Spirit:

> Because God has now permitted his holy gospel to go forth, he deals with us in two ways: First, outwardly, and second, inwardly. Outwardly he deals with us through the preached Word, or the gospel, and through the visible signs of baptism and the Lord's Supper. Inwardly he deals with us through the Holy Spirit and faith. But this is always in such a way and in this order that the outward

---

72. See chap. 28 on baptism.

73. E.g., Pope Eugenius IV insisted on the sacrament of confirmation being performed by a bishop of the church. His reason, based on Acts 8:14–18, was: "It is written of the apostles alone that by the laying on of hands they gave the Holy Spirit, and the bishops hold the office of the apostles.... Now, in place of this laying on of hands, confirmation is given in the Church.... In this sacrament the Holy Spirit is

given to strengthen us, as it was given to the apostles on the day of Pentecost, that the Christian may confess boldly the name of Christ." Pope Eugenius IV, *Exultate Deo*, in H. Denzinger, *Enchiridion Symbolorum et Definitionum*, 201ff.; Petry, 325–26.

74. Archbishop John Peckham, "On the Ignorance of Priests; Pastoral Delinquency in Instruction and Preaching," in *Constitutions on Clerical Responsibility*; Petry, 338.

means must precede the inward means, and the inward means comes after through the outward means. So, then, God has willed that he will not give to anyone the inward gifts [of the Spirit and faith] except through the outward means [of the Word and the sacraments].[75]

Thus, the Spirit of God carries out his ministry in believers through the Word of God. And the Spirit of God was absolutely necessary for understanding the Word of God: "No one can correctly understand God or his Word unless he has received such understanding immediately from the Holy Spirit."[76] In this way, Luther closely linked the Word of God and the Spirit of God.

As so much of Luther's theology was oriented to the reality of salvation in Jesus Christ, it is not surprising to find that he emphasized the role of the Holy Spirit in this experience. In his *Small Catechism*, Luther appealed to the absolute necessity of the Spirit for salvation:

I believe that I cannot, by my own reason or strength, believe in Jesus Christ my Lord, or come to him. But the Holy Spirit has called me through the gospel, enlightened me by his gifts, and sanctified and preserved me in the true faith. In the same way, he calls, gathers, enlightens, and sanctifies the whole Christian Church on earth, and preserves it in union with Jesus Christ in the one true faith. In this Christian Church he daily and richly forgives all my sins, and the sins of all believers. And he will raise up me and all the dead at the last day, and he will grant eternal life to me and to all who believe in Christ. This is most certainly true.[77]

For Luther, the fact that the Spirit is the *Holy* Spirit underscores one of his primary works—sanctification[78]—which Luther considered to be the application of the benefits of Christ's saving work:

The work is done and accomplished; for Christ has acquired and gained the treasure for us by his suffering, death, resurrection, etc. But if the work remained concealed so that no one knew of it, then it would be in vain and lost. That this treasure, therefore, might not lie buried, but be appropriated and enjoyed, God has caused the Word to go forth and be proclaimed, in which he gives the Holy Spirit to bring this treasure home and appropriate it to us. Therefore, sanctifying is nothing else than bringing us to Christ to receive this good, to which we could not attain of ourselves.[79]

Like Luther, Calvin insisted that the Spirit of God and the Word of God are inseparably linked, criticizing the Catholic Church for boasting "of the Holy Spirit solely to commend with his name strange doctrines foreign to God's Word—while the Spirit wills

---

75. Martin Luther, *Against the Heavenly Prophets in the Matter of Images and Sacraments*, LW, 40:83.

76. *Magnificat*, LW, 21:299.

77. Martin Luther, *Small Catechism*, pt. 2, art. 3, in Schaff, 3:80. The text has been rendered clearer.

78. Martin Luther, *Large Catechism*, 2.3, in *Triglot Concordia: The Symbolical Books of the Evangelical Lutheran Church*, trans. F. Bente and W. H. T. Dau (St. Louis: Concordia, 1921), 687.

79. Ibid., 2.3, in *Trigot Concordia*, 689.

to be conjoined with God's Word by an indissoluble bond."[80] This link means "we are to expect nothing more from his [God's] Spirit than that he will illumine our minds to perceive the truth of his [Christ's] teachings." For Calvin, a principal error of the Catholic Church was its preference for the Spirit of God over against the Word of God. Its claim to infallibility, then, because of its neglect of Scripture, was both in vain and bogus.[81] But Calvin's church would give heed to the Spirit of God linked closely to the Word of God.

Beyond these polemical areas, Calvin gave extensive treatment to the person and work of the Holy Spirit. In addition to expressing and defending the orthodox view of his deity and relationship to the Father and the Son, Calvin introduced several new emphases on the ministry of the Spirit. None is more important than what he called "the witness of the Spirit." This work has particular reference to the authority of Scripture[82] as it meets the need of Christians to be absolutely sure the Bible is the Word of God.[83] On one hand, Calvin noted, the Roman Catholic Church claimed that it alone could confer such authority on the Bible. For Calvin, this church-ascribed authority was precarious, resting on the decision of mere human beings. On the other hand, Calvin admitted that even legitimate arguments for biblical authority—and he himself rehearsed a number of these (including its majesty, antiquity, fulfilled prophecy, and others)—could not provide the certainty necessary for believers to embrace Scripture with absolute confidence.

Calvin's answer to this dilemma was the conviction of the authority of Scripture provided by "the secret testimony of the Spirit."[84] He explained why this is the case: "The testimony of the Spirit is more excellent than all reason. For as God alone is a fit witness of himself in his Word, so also the Word will not find acceptance in men's hearts before it is sealed by the inward testimony of the Spirit. The same Spirit, therefore, who has spoken through the mouths of the prophets must penetrate into our hearts to persuade us that they faithfully proclaimed what had been divinely commanded."[85] This witness of the Spirit goes beyond all human ability to authenticate Scripture, and as his testimony is sealed upon the hearts of believers, they obtain the certainty needed:

> For even if it [Scripture] wins reverence for itself by its own majesty, it seriously affects us only when it is sealed upon our hearts through the Spirit. Therefore, illumined by his power, we believe neither by our own nor by anyone else's judgment that Scripture is from God. But above human judgment we affirm with utter certainty (just as if we were gazing upon the majesty of God himself) that it has flowed to us from the very mouth of God by the ministry of men.[86]

As Calvin appealed to the Holy Spirit to bring conviction of biblical authority, some of his opponents took that appeal to an extreme. They ended up emphasizing the Spirit of God to such a degree that they disregarded the Word of God. In a sense, their claim was that because they had the Holy Spirit, they did not need Scripture. Calvin had to refute these "fanatics" or "mystics" and their concentration on the Holy Spirit to the exclusion of the Bible. He did so by underscoring the need for balance between the Word of God

---

80. John Calvin, *Institutes of the Christian Religion*, 4.8.14, LCC, 2:1163.

81. Ibid., 4.8.13, LCC, 2:1162–63.

82. Ibid., 1.7.1, LCC, 1:74.

83. Ibid.

84. Ibid., 1.7.4, LCC, 1:78.

85. Ibid., LCC, 1:79.

86. Ibid., 1.7.5, LCC, 1:80.

and the Spirit of God: "Under the reign of Christ the new church will have this true and complete happiness: to be ruled no less by the voice of God than by the Spirit."[87] If the Spirit works in conjunction with the Bible, the application for believers is quite evident: "From this we readily understand that we ought zealously to apply ourselves both to read and to hearken [pay attention] to Scripture if indeed we want to receive any gain and benefit from the Spirit of God."[88] This agreement of Spirit and Scripture provides great comfort and also helps the church to guard against mistaking an evil spirit for the Holy Spirit. Indeed, Calvin noted that the Holy Spirit "would have us to recognize him in his own image, which he stamped upon the Scriptures. He is the author of the Scriptures: he cannot vary and differ from himself. Hence he must ever remain just as he once revealed himself there."[89] Thus, the Word of God and Spirit of God are inseparably linked together:

> The Holy Spirit so inheres in his truth, which he expresses in Scripture, that only when its proper reverence and dignity are given to the Word does the Holy Spirit show forth his power.... For by a kind of mutual bond the Lord has joined together the certainty of his Word and of his Spirit so that the perfect religion of the Word may abide in our minds when the Spirit, who causes us to contemplate God's face, shines; and that we in turn may embrace the Spirit with no fear of being deceived when we recognize him in his own image, namely, in the Word. So indeed it is. God did not bring forth his Word among men for the sake of a momentary display, intending at the coming of his Spirit to abolish it. Rather, he sent down the same Spirit by whose power he had dispensed the Word, to complete his work by the efficacious confirmation of the Word.[90]

This conviction meant that the fanatics, who claimed to have "graduated" from Scripture to the Spirit, were wrong and refuted by Calvin.

The Protestant churches that followed Luther and Calvin echoed the traditional doctrine of the Holy Spirit,[91] making an important addition: the ministry of the illumination of the Holy Spirit. David Hollaz defined this work of the Spirit:

> Illumination is the act of applying grace by which the Holy Spirit, through the ministry of the Word, teaches a man who is a sinner and called to the church, and continues to instruct him in an ever-increasing measure. The earnest purpose is to remove the darkness of ignorance and error, and imbue him with the knowledge of the Word of God by instilling from the Law the conviction of sin, and from the Gospel the understanding of divine mercy, founded on the merit of Christ.[92]

Appealing to Scripture (Ps. 119:18; Eph. 1:17–19),[93] John Owen insisted that this work of the Spirit is necessary in order for Christians to understand Scripture with full assur-

---

87. Ibid., 1.9.1, LCC, 1:93.

88. Ibid., 1.9.2, LCC, 1:94.

89. Ibid., LCC, 1:94–95.

90. Ibid., 1.9.3, LCC, 1:95.

91. See, e.g., *Heidelberg Catechism*, q. 53, in Schaff, 3:324; *Belgic Confession*, 11, in Schaff, 3:395.

92. David Hollaz, *Examen Theologicum Acroamaticum*

(1707), 819, in Schmid, 451. The text has been rendered clearer.

93. John Owen, *The Causes, Ways, and Means of Understanding the Mind of God as Revealed in His Word, with Assurance Therein* (London, 1687), chap. 2, in *The Works of John Owen*, ed. William H. Goold, 16 vols. (Edinburgh: Banner of Truth Trust, 1967), 4:130, 133. Owen's other support included Luke 24:45; John 14–16; and 2 Cor. 3:13–18.

ance.[94] He carefully distinguished between the Holy Spirit's work of inspiring Scripture and illuminating Scripture: "When the Holy Spirit gave *new revelations* of old unto the prophets and penmen of the Scripture by *immediate inspiration*, he did therein and therewith communicate unto them an infallible evidence that they were from God; and when he *illumines our minds* in the knowledge of what is revealed, he does therein himself bear witness unto, and assure us of, the truth which we do understand."[95] As to what specifically is illumined by the Spirit, Owen noted "all divine truths necessary to be known and to be believed, that we may live unto God in faith and obedience, or come unto and abide in Christ, as also [to] be preserved from seducers."[96] This careful explanation of the illumination of the Holy Spirit sought to counter the rampant subjectivism of so-called mystics and groups such as the Quakers, because it insisted that when the Word of God is preached, the Spirit of God works to illumine people by means of that Word—and not apart from it.[97]

That the doctrine of the Holy Spirit was not a major point of difference between Protestants and Catholics at the time of the Reformation can be seen by the fact that the Council of Trent does not dedicate any discussion to it. Furthermore, the *Profession of the Tridentine Faith* does not include an article on the doctrine. On the personhood and deity of the Holy Spirit, and on his procession from both the Father and the Son, Catholics and Protestants were in complete agreement.

THE VIEW OF THE HOLY SPIRIT IN THE MODERN PERIOD

John Wesley's special contribution to the doctrine of the Holy Spirit was his teaching on the witness of the Holy Spirit to provide believers with the assurance of their salvation. Based on Romans 8:16, Wesley offered this definition: "By the testimony of the Spirit, I mean, an inward impression on the soul, by which the Spirit of God immediately and directly witnesses to my spirit, that I am a child of God; that Jesus Christ has loved me, and given himself for me; that all my sins are blotted out, and I, even I, am reconciled to God."[98] Not a theoretical notion, this witness of the Spirit had been Wesley's own experience at his conversion.[99]

Complaints raised against this doctrine were its seeming lack of verification and susceptibility to being counterfeited: How could people know that what they experienced

---

94. Ibid., chap. 1, in Goold, *Works of John Owen*, 4:126.

95. Ibid., chap. 3, in Goold, *Works of John Owen*, 4:150.

96. Ibid., 4:148.

97. Hollaz, *Examen Theologicum Acroamaticum*, 847, in Schmid, 453–56.

98. John Wesley, *The Witness of the Spirit: II*, 2.2, in *Wesley's Standard Sermons*, ed. E. H. Sugden, 2 vols. (London: Epworth, 1921), 2:345. Cf. Albert C. Outler, *John Wesley* (New York: Oxford Univ. Press, 1964), 211.

99. As he himself recounts: "In the evening I went very unwillingly to a society in Aldersgate Street, where one was reading [Martin] Luther's preface to the *Letter to the Romans*. About a quarter before nine, while he was describing the change which God works in the heart through faith in Christ, I felt my heart strangely warmed. I felt I did trust in Christ, Christ alone for salvation; and an assurance was given me that he had taken away *my* sins, even *mine*, and saved *me* from the law of sin and death." John Wesley, *Journal*, "May 24, 1738," cited in Robert W. Burtner and Robert E. Chiles, *A Compend of Wesley's Theology* (Nashville: Abingdon, 1954), 101–2. The reading that Wesley heard was Luther's preface to his commentary on Romans.

was the authentic witness of the Spirit and not some delusion—either human or demonic? On the one hand, Wesley saw this testimony as so foundational that no explanation could be given for it; it is intuitively sensed with certainty.[100] On the other hand, he emphasized that the testimony of the Spirit is attested to by the fruit of a changed life in those who have experienced such assurance.[101] Indeed, for Wesley, there was the closest possible connection between the witness of the Spirit and the fruit of the Spirit.[102] Thus, the privilege of all believers is the full assurance of faith through the inner witness of the Spirit. Faith may exist without this assurance; that is, Christians may lack this confidence and experience doubts about their salvation.[103] But all have the privilege of "full assurance [that] excludes all doubt" as a wonderful gift of the Holy Spirit.[104]

Karl Barth also addressed the testimony of the Holy Spirit as being essential for knowing divine revelation.[105] This comes as the objective revelation of God in Christ as an act of divine majesty, to which corresponds a subjective appropriation.[106] Thus, this self-revelation creates knowing subjects of those who attend to Jesus Christ. It was at this juncture that Barth invoked the assistance of the Holy Spirit: "It is by the Holy Spirit, by whom Jesus Christ is, that he is also known as the one he is."[107] Indeed, "the process in which all knowledge of Jesus Christ, and therefore of the history in which as very God he also became very man, is grounded, the process of cognition which underlies Christology and is executed in it, is identical with ... the witness of the Holy Spirit."[108] Specifically, the Spirit "is the finger of God which opens blind eyes and deaf ears for the truth, which quickens dead hearts by and for the truth, which causes the reason of man, so concerned about its limitations and so proud within those limitations, to receive the truth notwithstanding its limitations."[109] But Barth urged caution toward any undue attention on the Holy Spirit. To focus on him is to miss entirely the point, which is the witness that the Spirit renders to Jesus Christ.[110]

The classic doctrine of the procession of the Holy Spirit continued to be affirmed by the church in the modern period. As historically had been the case, attempts at definition proved to be rather elusive because of the mysterious nature of this relationship between the Spirit and the other two members of the Trinity. Louis Berkhof defined procession as "that eternal and necessary act of the first and second persons in the Trinity whereby they, within the divine Being, become the ground of the personal subsistence of the Holy Spirit, and put the third person in possession of the whole divine essence, without any

100. John Wesley, *The Witness of the Spirit: I*, 2.9–10, in Sugden, *Wesley's Standard Sermons*, 1:216–17.

101. Ibid., 2.11–12, in Sugden, *Wesley's Standard Sermons*, 1:217.

102. Wesley, *The Witness of the Spirit: II*, 5.3–4, in Sugden, *Wesley's Standard Sermons*, 2:358–59. Cf. Outler, *John Wesley*, 219-20.

103. Under the influence of the Moravians, Wesley originally believed that apart from the assurance of salvation, there could be no true justifying faith. However, when charged with "enthusiasm" (a derogatory term usually reserved for mystics and fanatics; see above discussion about Calvin), Wesley backed off from linking the two so closely. His revised view

was that assurance normally accompanies justifying faith and is the privilege of all believers through the witness of the Spirit. But he recognized that exceptions to this normal pattern do occur. Cf. Outler, ed., *John Wesley*, 209.

104. John Wesley, *Letters*: "To Richard Tompson," cited in Burtner and Chiles, *Compend of Wesley's Theology*, 100.

105. *CD*, IV/2, 118.

106. Ibid., 119–22.

107. Ibid., 125.

108. Ibid.

109. Ibid., 126.

110. Ibid., 130.

division, alienation or change."[111] William G. T. Shedd differentiated between procession and spiration.[112] Due in part to difficulties understanding the complicated notion of procession, some theologians opted to drop this aspect of the doctrine of the Holy Spirit. For example, John Feinberg underscored the lack of clarity in conceptualizing the procession as the Father and the Son communicating the divine essence to the Spirit, with such communication being eternal.[113] Feinberg, along with others, dismissed the traditional biblical support for procession of the Holy Spirit, maintaining that the key passages (esp. John 15:26) focus mainly on the future sending of the Spirit at Pentecost and do not "say anything about the relationship that has held between the Father and Son for all eternity."[114]

Without doubt, the most important modern development in regard to the doctrine of the Holy Spirit originated at the beginning of the twentieth century and eventually led to three movements: Pentecostalism, the charismatic movement, and "third wave" evangelicalism. It began when an itinerant evangelist, Charles Fox Parham, became convinced that every instance of baptism in the Holy Spirit in the book of Acts was accompanied by speaking in tongues. In a revival in Topeka, Kansas, in 1901, Parham taught that speaking in tongues was the initial evidence that one had been baptized in the Holy Spirit, an experience that should be normative for all Christians. Parham came into contact with William J. Seymour, who was instrumental in the Azusa Street revival in Los Angeles in 1906.[115] From this event, new churches and new denominations—called Pentecostal because of the similarity between their experience of the Holy Spirit and that of the Christians on the day of Pentecost—arose and multiplied throughout the world. These include the Assemblies of God, Church of God (Cleveland, Tenn.), Church of God in Christ, Pentecostal Holiness Church, International Church of the Foursquare Gospel, and others.

Pentecostal theology of the baptism of the Holy Spirit accompanied by speaking in tongues (together with the conviction that miraculous spiritual gifts are active in the church today) did more than just launch new churches and denominations. It also infiltrated already existing churches and denominations, producing the charismatic movement. Baptists, Lutherans, Methodists, Anglicans—even Roman Catholics—claimed a renewal through coming into contact with Pentecostalism. Typified by enthusiastic devotion to Jesus Christ and possessing a tireless energy for evangelism and missions, Pentecostalism and the charismatic movement have turned the church's attention to the doctrine of the Holy Spirit.

One of the most important contributors to the systematic formulation of Pentecostal-charismatic doctrine was J. Rodman Williams. In his *Renewal Theology*, Williams

---

111. Louis Berkhof, *Systematic Theology*, 4th ed. (Grand Rapids: Eerdmans, 1939), 97. See also William G. T. Shedd, *Dogmatic Theology*, 3:4, in *Dogmatic Theology*, ed. Alan W. Gomes, 3rd ed. (Phillipsburg, N.J.: P & R, 2003), 242–45.

112. Ibid., 242. Spiration is the act of the Father and Son with regard to the Spirit; they spirate the Spirit. Procession is the result of spiration; the Holy Spirit proceeds from the Father and the Son.

113. John S. Feinberg, *No One Like Him: The Doctrine of God*, Foundations of Evangelical Theology, John S. Feinberg, gen. ed. (Wheaton: Crossway, 2001), 489.

114. Ibid., 491. Robert Reymond agreed that this passage does not refer to the immanent Trinity. Robert L. Reymond, *A New Systematic Theology of the Christian Faith* (New York: Nelson, 1998), 331–32.

115. An engaging account of this is Cecil M. Robeck Jr., *The Azusa Street Mission and Revival: The Birth of the Global Pentecostal Movement* (Nashville: Nelson, 2006).

devoted hundreds of pages to the doctrine of the Holy Spirit and spiritual gifts.[116] He distinguished between two experiences involving the Spirit. For the first, which takes place at a person's salvation, Jesus Christ is the one who baptizes, and he baptizes believers in the Holy Spirit (Mark 1:8; 1 Cor. 12:13).[117] The second experience is the coming of the Holy Spirit. He is said to be "poured out" (Acts 2:33), and to "come on" believers (Acts 1:8; cf. 10:44; 11:15). These believers are said to be "baptized with" (Acts 1:5; 11:16) or "filled with" (Acts 2:2–4; 4:31; 9:17; 13:9; 13:52; Eph. 5:18) the Holy Spirit. Williams specified: "Along with the initial reception of the gift of the Holy Spirit described as 'filling,' there are later repetitions of being filled as well as emphasis on continuing fullness. Such fillings in no way invalidate the initial filling but serve to show that the concept of filling is quite complex in richness and meaning."[118] He underscored the importance of this reality and described it as "a profoundly internal experience of the Spirit of God moving throughout like wind or fire until all barriers are breached and the Holy Spirit pervades everything."[119] This powerful outpouring of the Holy Spirit is a second blessing subsequent to a believer's salvation.[120]

Accompanying this work of the Spirit is the phenomenon of speaking in tongues (Gk. *glossolalia*). Analyzing the data from Acts (2:4; 10:45–46; 8:17–19; 19:6), Williams concluded: "It is clear that the *primary activity* consequent to the reception of the Holy Spirit was that of speaking in tongues. We focus on the word 'primary,' because although other things were mentioned, speaking in tongues was first.... It follows that speaking in tongues was clear evidence that the Holy Spirit had been given."[121]

Closely associated with this blessing are the *charismata* of the Spirit, or spiritual gifts, "for the Holy Spirit who is given bestows gifts in turn."[122] This intimate link between the gift of the Spirit and the gifts of the Spirit explains why a common criticism of charismatics is so off target: "Criticism is sometimes made that participants [in the charismatic renewal] are preoccupied with 'the sensational.' Rather than being satisfied with their salvation and a 'normal' Christian walk, they are caught up in such things as tongues, prophecies, healings, and the like. Moreover, the criticism sometimes continues, charismatics exhibit a lot of carnality and therefore would do well to leave the gifts and be more concerned with holiness and righteousness."[123] While admitting that some need to make strides in godliness and some do exaggerate certain gifts, Williams denounced the solution that is typically proposed: "But the answer cannot be to forget the spiritual gifts, for they and they alone are *the* manifestation of the Spirit."[124] Thus, the gifts of the Spirit — word of wisdom, word of knowledge, faith, gifts of healings, workings

---

116. This stands in stark contrast with other systematic theologies of both past and present.

117. J. Rodman Williams, *Renewal Theology*, vol. 2: *Salvation, the Holy Spirit, and Christian Living* (Grand Rapids: Zondervan, 1990), 199. While some within the Pentecostal and charismatic movements make a distinction between a baptism *in* the Holy Spirit of Acts 2 and a baptism *by* the Holy Spirit in 1 Cor. 12:13, Williams did not. Noting that the Greek preposition (*en*) is the same in both cases, Williams argued: "It would seem preferable to translate it [1 Cor. 12:13] thus: 'In

one Spirit we were all baptized....' Accordingly, the Holy Spirit is again seen as element and not agent, and Christ (though not mentioned directly) is implied to be the agent." Ibid.

118. Ibid., 202.

119. Ibid., 203.

120. Ibid., 205–6, 211.

121. Ibid., 211.

122. Ibid., 323.

123. Ibid., 331.

124. Ibid.

of miracles, prophecy, distinguishing of spirits, kinds of tongues, and interpretation of tongues—constitute the ninefold manifestation of the Holy Spirit.[125]

To Pentecostalism and the charismatic movement, a new movement emphasizing the Holy Spirit was added in the latter part of the twentieth century. It was given the name "*third wave* evangelicalism" by C. Peter Wagner because it followed the *first wave*— Pentecostalism—and the *second wave*—the charismatic movement. Wayne Grudem described the characteristics of third wave evangelicalism: " 'Third wave' people encourage the equipping of all believers to use New Testament spiritual gifts today, and say that the proclamation of the gospel should ordinarily be accompanied by 'signs, wonders, and miracles,' according to the New Testament pattern. They teach, however, that baptism in the Holy Spirit happens to all Christians at conversion, and that subsequent experiences are better called 'filling' with the Holy Spirit."[126] Clearly this movement took some of its doctrine of the Spirit from Pentecostal/charismatic theology—the emphasis on the continuation of all the spiritual gifts in the church[127]—while modifying it in accordance with traditional evangelical theology—the baptism with the Spirit occurs at conversion. Third wave evangelicalism exercised an important influence through people such as John Wimber, Wayne Grudem, and Sam Storms.

As a result of Pentecostalism, the charismatic movement, and third wave evangelicalism, the doctrine of the Holy Spirit has been elevated to its appropriate place among Christian doctrines.

125. Ibid., 347–409.

126. Wayne Grudem, *Systematic Theology: An Introduction to Biblical Doctrine* (Grand Rapids: Zondervan, 1994, 2000), 763–64n2.

127. Grudem, however, excluded the office of apostleship as a continuing reality after the age of the apostles. Ibid., 911.

THE DOCTRINE OF THE APPLICATION OF REDEMPTION

ELECTION AND REPROBATION

How has the church developed various views on God's predestining work of election and reprobation?

STATEMENT OF BELIEF

One of the most important yet controversial issues with which the church has historically wrestled is the doctrine of *predestination*, or God's decree regarding the eternal destinies of people. Included in this debate is the common breakdown of predestination into two component parts: *election* and *reprobation*. According to the Reformed or Calvinist perspective, "Election is an act of God before creation in which he chooses some people to be saved, not on account of any foreseen merit in them, but only because of his sovereign good pleasure."[1] Calvinism specifies that God's choice of some for eternal life is *unconditional*, not based on any human merit or a positive response of faith to the gospel as foreseen by God. Rather, election is according to God's sovereign will and good pleasure purposed before the creation of the world. Some Calvinists, in addition to embracing election, also affirm reprobation. "Reprobation is the sovereign decision of God before creation to pass over some persons, in sorrow deciding not to save them, and to punish them for their sins, and thereby to manifest his justice."[2] This view is commonly called *double predestination*, though some believe that the term "is not a helpful term because it gives the impression that both election and reprobation are carried out in the same way by God and have no essential differences between them, which is certainly not true."[3] This view is challenged by the Arminian and/or Wesleyan view of predestination. This perspective affirms divine election and specifies that such election is *conditional*—it is based on God's foreknowledge of a person's positive response to the gospel of Jesus Christ. Furthermore, double predestination is denied.

To these two historical and divergent perspectives on the doctrine of predestination, the modern development by Karl Barth must be added. His doctrine of election focuses

---

1. Wayne Grudem, *Systematic Theology: An Introduction to Biblical Doctrine* (Grand Rapids: Zondervan, 1994, 2000), 670.

2. Ibid., 684.

3. Ibid., 670; cf. 686.

attention on Jesus Christ, who is both the *elected man* and the *electing God* (this, for Barth, is double predestination).[4] Throughout this chapter, these views will be the focal point of attention.[5]

VIEWS OF PREDESTINATION IN THE EARLY CHURCH

The early church was the recipient of the Jewish Scripture—our Old Testament— which had a strong predestinarian element in it: The nation of Israel was presented as the quintessential example of divine, gracious election (Deut. 7:6–8). Moreover, in his eschatological teaching, Jesus spoke of "the elect" (Matt. 24:22, 24, 31), and the apostle Paul addressed Christians as those "predestined" and "chosen" by God (Rom. 8:29–30; 9:14–24; Eph. 1:3–6, 11–12; 2 Thess. 2:13–14).

As the early church considered these and other biblical passages, its development of a doctrine of predestination took place in a historical and philosophical context that featured such notions as fatalism and absolute determinism. Not surprisingly, therefore, the church placed a strong emphasis on human free will and self-determination. At the same time, it affirmed the sovereignty of God. Tertullian, for example, understood divine power and grace as the explanation for the transformation of people from unbelievers to believers.[6] Some Christians extended this idea of sovereignty to God's predestination of certain people, called "the elect." Clement of Rome commended his readers: "You struggled day and night on behalf of all the brotherhood, that through fear and conscientiousness the number of his elect might be saved."[7] And Clement of Alexandria noted that God "has dispensed his goodness both to Greeks and barbarians, even to those of them who were predestined, and in due time called, the faithful and elect."[8]

While speaking like this, however, the early church generally associated divine predestination with God's foreknowledge of what people would be or do. For example, Justin Martyr affirmed, "he foreknows that some are to be saved by repentance, some even that are perhaps not yet born,"[9] adding as well that "the people foreknown to believe in him [Christ] were foreknown to pursue diligently the fear of the Lord."[10] Given this framework, it was believed that predestination is based on divine foreknowledge; that is, God elects some "knowing before the foundation of the world that they would be righteous."[11] Oppositely, God passes over others, knowing their personal sinfulness: "He ... has given them over to unbelief and turned away his presence from people of this mold, leaving them in the darkness which they have ... chosen for themselves."[12]

Recognizing that certain portions of Scripture seem to ascribe to God a much greater role in humanity's salvation or damnation than simple foreknowledge, some in the early

---

4. Some of this material is adapted from my article "Divine Election," in *The Evangelical Dictionary of World Missions*, ed. A. Scott Moreau (Grand Rapids: Baker, 2000), 285–86.

5. My thanks to David Campbell for his help with this chapter.

6. Tertullian, *Treatise on the Soul*, 21, in *ANF*, 3:202.

7. Clement of Rome, *Letter of the Romans to the Corinthians*, 2, in Holmes, 31; *ANF*, 1:5.

8. Clement of Alexandria, *Stromata*, 7.2, in *ANF*, 2:524.

9. Justin Martyr, *First Apology*, 28, in *ANF*, 1:172.

10. Justin Martyr, *Dialogue with Trypho, a Jew*, 70, in *ANF*, 1:234.

11. Clement of Alexandria, *Stromata*, 7.17, in *ANF*, 2:555.

12. Irenaeus, *Against Heresies*, 4.29.2, in *ANF*, 1:502. The text has been rendered clearer.

church attempted to treat those passages so as to clear up possible misunderstanding. In particular, Origen addressed these difficult passages. Interpreting the Exodus account (used by Paul in Rom. 9) of the hardening of Pharaoh's heart by God, Origen explained that the divine "hardening follows as a result of the inherent principle of wickedness in such persons, and so God is said to harden him who is hardened."[13] As for Paul's statement that "it does not ... depend on man's desire or effort, but on God's mercy" (Rom. 9:16), Origen emphasized that "what is done by God is infinitely greater than what is done by ourselves."[14] But this divine, eminent power does not do away with human cooperation in salvation. As for Paul's inquiry, "Does not the potter have the right to make out of the same lump of clay some pottery for noble purposes and some for common use?" (Rom. 9:21), Origin countered: "The Creator does not make vessels of honor and vessels of dishonor from the beginning according to his foreknowledge, since he does not condemn or justify beforehand according to it. Rather, he makes into vessels of honor those who cleanse themselves, and he makes into vessels of dishonor those who allow themselves to remain polluted. Thus, it [God's creation of vessels for honor or dishonor] results from preceding causes."[15] In this way, Origen sought to avoid the position that God predestines people in the sense of electing some for salvation and passing over others for damnation. On the contrary, whatever God makes of people is the consequence of "preceding causes"—their own responsible and free decisions and actions to be holy or to continue doing evil. Indeed, for Origen, there are no conditions—either good or bad—that can decisively influence the human will toward doing either good or bad.[16] For Origen and many others, human free will and self-determination were of crucial importance.

Given this strong role for human freedom, the early church presented salvation in terms of a cooperative effort between God and human beings. Ignatius put it simply: "If you want to do well, God is ready to help you."[17] This synergy consisted of human desire and will to be and do right, matched as a consequence by the grace of God, yet also anticipated by his foreknowledge: "To those ... whose hearts the Lord saw were about to become pure, and who were about to serve him with all their heart, he gave repentance; but to those whose deceit and wickedness he saw, who were about to repent hypocritically, he did not give repentance, lest they should somehow again profane his name."[18] Thus, it is not the human will and determination on its own; that would be futile. Nor is it God alone; that would be constraint. Rather, the two work together.[19]

---

13. Origen, *First Principles*, 3.1.10, in *ANF*, 4:310.

14. Ibid., 3.1.18, in *ANF*, 4:322.

15. In treating Rom. 9:21, Origen cited 2 Tim. 2:20–21 and, cautioning against bringing Scripture into conflict with itself, blended the two passages. Origen, *First Principles*, 3.1.20, in *ANF*, 4:325–26. The text has been rendered clearer.

16. Ibid., 3.2.4, in *ANF*, 4:332.

17. Ignatius, *Letter to the Smyrnaeans*, 11, in Holmes, 193; *ANF*, 1:91.

18. *Shepherd of Hermas*, parable 8.6.72, in Holmes, 461; *ANF*, 1:41.

19. According to Clement of Alexandria, "a man by himself working and toiling at freedom from passion achieves nothing. But if he clearly shows himself very desirous and earnest about this, he attains it by the addition of the power of God. For God conspires with willing people. But if they abandon their eagerness, the Spirit which is given by God is also restrained. For to save the unwilling is the role of one exercising compulsion; but to save the willing is the role of one showing grace." Clement of Alexandria, *Who Is the Rich Man Who Will Be Saved?* 21, in *ANF*, 2:597. The text has been rendered clearer.

A serious challenge to this notion of divine and human cooperation was put forward by Pelagius. He held that people are not born with a corrupt nature inherited from Adam.[20] They may indeed fall into sin, but that is by their choice, and they do not have to do so. Furthermore, God has provided grace, which Pelagius defined in a novel way: Grace is God's work to assist the capacity to be able to do the good. But this was not all: "What he [Pelagius] meant by God's grace was that, when our nature was created, it received the capacity of not sinning, because it was created with free will."[21] Within this framework, Pelagius worked out his concept of predestination: "To predestine is the same as to foreknow. Therefore, those he [God] foresaw would be conformed [to the image of Christ] in life, he intended to be conformed in glory.... So too, then, he has now chosen those whom he foreknew would believe from among the Gentiles, and has rejected those whom he foreknew would be unbelieving out of Israel." Interpreting God's promise "I will have mercy on whom I have mercy" (Rom. 9:15), Pelagius rendered it, "I will have mercy on him whom I have foreknown will be able to deserve compassion."[22]

This development was challenged and the doctrine reformulated when Augustine refuted Pelagian theology and worked through his doctrines of grace, original sin, merit, foreknowledge, and sovereignty, and in the midst of all of this, predestination.

Augustine defined predestination in close relationship to God's foreknowledge: "The ordering of his future works in his foreknowledge, which cannot be deceived and changed, is absolute, and nothing but, predestination."[23] This predestination includes the election of some to eternal life and the reprobation of others to eternal punishment. It was set in the context of grace and original sin (doctrines on which Augustine was at polar opposites from Pelagius), as Augustine explained: "He [God] has appointed them [people condemned in Adam] to be regenerated, before they die physically, whom he predestined to eternal life, as the most merciful giver of grace. To those whom he has predestined to eternal death, however, he is also the most righteous awarder of punishment, not only on account of the sins which they add in the indulgence of their own will, but also because of their original sin, even if, as in the case of infants, they add nothing to it."[24]

Predestination was also set in the context of free will and merit—a combination favored by Pelagius but soundly denounced by Augustine as contrary to the way God graciously works.[25] Rather than being merited by the proper exercise of human free will, eternal life is the gift of divine grace alone.[26] For Augustine, the closest possible relationship exists between this grace and God's predestination: "There is only this difference, predestination is the preparation for grace, while grace is the donation itself ... the effect of that predestination."[27] So it all depends on God's sovereign will to choose some and pass over others. Based on his choice, people will either turn to Christ and persevere in

20. Augustine, *On the Grace of Christ, and On Original Sin*, 2.14, in *NPNF¹*, 5:241.

21. Augustine, *On the Proceedings of Pelagius*, 22.10, in *NPNF¹*, 5:192–93.

22. Pelagius, *Pelagius's Commentary on St. Paul's Epistle to the Romans*, 8:29; 9:10; 9:15, trans. Theodore de Bruyn (Oxford: Clarendon, 1993), 112, 116, 117.

23. Augustine, *On the Gift of Perseverance*, 41, in *NPNF¹*, 5:542.

24. Augustine, *On the Soul and Its Origin*, 16, in *NPNF¹*, 5:361. The text has been rendered clearer.

25. Augustine, *Against Two Letters of the Pelagians*, 16, in *NPNF¹*, 5:423–24.

26. Ibid., in *NPNF¹*, 5:424.

27. Augustine, *On the Predestination of the Saints*, 19.10, in *NPNF¹*, 5:507.

the faith, or they will fall away from the religious obedience that they currently practice.[28] Moreover, election is purposeful: it is so that divinely chosen people will believe in Christ, live holy lives, and give God praise.[29]

To the charge that predestination contradicts the biblical statement that God "wants all men to be saved and to come to a knowledge of the truth" (1 Tim. 2:4), Augustine responded with his interpretation of that passage "as meaning that no man is saved unless God wills his salvation: not that there is no man whose salvation he does not will, but that no man is saved apart from his will; and that, therefore, we should pray [to] him to will our salvation, because if he wills it, it must necessarily be accomplished."[30] To the charge that selective election seems totally unfair, Augustine appealed to the mystery of God's plan (Rom. 11:33; Ps. 25:10) and affirmed with Scripture that there is no unrighteousness with God (Rom. 9:14).[31] Indeed, though he related all these elements—sovereignty, foreknowledge, original sin, grace, merit, human freedom—Augustine ultimately admitted that predestination is largely mysterious and a cause for wonderment.

Given the fact that the predestining work of God is inscrutable and mysterious, the question arose about who belongs to the elect and who belongs to the reprobate. For Augustine, it was not as simple a matter as pointing to the members of the church as being chosen by God and everyone else as being passed over by God. Certainly, only true believers, or the elect, belong to the true church, "in whom is the fixed number of the saints predestined before the foundation of the world."[32] But only God perfectly knows who constitutes the true church. As for those who look at the visible church, the situation can be quite confusing: "For, in that unspeakable foreknowledge of God, many who seem to be outside [the church] are in reality inside it, and many who seem to be inside [the church] yet really are outside it."[33] In other words, many who are predestined to eternal life may not be part of the (local or visible) church. Similarly, many who are predestined to eternal punishment may be part of the (local or visible) church. But this perspective did not cause Augustine to dispense with the church, for God had appointed its means of grace—the preaching of the Word, church authority, baptism, the Lord's Supper—as helps for the elect.[34]

VIEWS OF PREDESTINATION IN THE MIDDLE AGES

Even in his own writing *On the Predestination of the Saints*, Augustine acknowledged that certain people, though agreeing with him on many matters, parted company when it came to this issue.[35] These Christians, who would later become known as the semi-Pelagians,[36] agreed with him about the fall of Adam, original sin, the necessity of and

---

28. Augustine, *On the Gift of Perseverance*, 58, in *NPNF*[1], 5:549.

29. Augustine, *On the Predestination of the Saints*, 34.17, 37, in *NPNF*[1], 5:514–15, 516.

30. Augustine, *Enchiridion on Faith, Hope, and Love*, 103, in *NPNF*[1], 3:270.

31. Augustine, *On the Gift of Perseverance*, 25.11, in *NPNF*[1], 5:534.

32. Augustine, *On Baptism, against the Donatists*, 5.27.38, in *NPNF*[1], 4:477.

33. Ibid. The text has been rendered clearer.

34. Augustine, *On the Gift of Perseverance*, 56, in *NPNF*[1], 5:548–49.

35. Augustine, *On the Predestination of the Saints*, 2, in *NPNF*[1], 5:498.

36. Although the descriptive name was coined in the sixteenth century, the semi-Pelagian theological position originated in the fifth century. For further discussion of this view, see chap. 16.

salvation by grace, and so forth. Despite Augustine's hope that they would come to their senses concerning predestination, these semi-Pelagians continued to dissent from his specific formulation of that doctrine. This clash between the Augustinian doctrine of predestination and the corresponding semi-Pelagian doctrine set the tone for and would characterize in part the theological world of the Middle Ages, which was on the threshold.

Chief among the semi-Pelagian objections was that Augustine's view of predestination was, according to Faustus of Rhegium, "a fatalistic theory."[37] God was seen as the one responsible for human sin, blamable for human evil, and accountable for human condemnation and misery. Faustus's solution was to invoke divine foreknowledge and permission and distinguish them from divine predestination: "What God wills is one thing; what God permits is another thing. Therefore he wills the good, permits the evil, and foreknows both. He assists righteous deeds with his goodness; he permits unrighteous deeds in accordance with the freedom of the [human] will."[38] Thus, while God certainly foreknows everything that comes to pass, predestination pertains only to what is good while permission pertains to what is bad. For the good, God receives the credit and praise. But human beings are responsible for their own sin and blamable for human evil; they bring condemnation and misery upon themselves. In this way, semi-Pelagianism sought to escape the "fatalism" of Augustinian predestination.

But there was another objection. As seen above, according to Augustine, God did not will all people to be saved; rather, he chose the elect, and them only, for salvation. Against this notion, John Cassian complained: "How can we imagine without grievous blasphemy that he [God] does not generally will *all* men, but only *some* instead of *all*, to be saved? Those then who perish, perish against his will."[39] Cassian found Augustine's selective election in conflict with Paul's statement in 1 Timothy 2:4.[40] But again, Augustine interpreted this passage not as affirming the divine will for the salvation of *all* people, but as expressing the necessity of the divine will for the salvation of *any and all types* of people. But semi-Pelagians decried this as a poor interpretation and emphasized God's desire that all people be saved.

That stage having been set for the Middle Ages, in 529 the church convened the Synod of Orange to resolve the conflict between Augustinianism, Pelagianism, and semi-Pelagianism. On many issues the synod sided with Augustinian theology and took a decidedly anti-Pelagian stance. However, on the doctrine of predestination, it was reluctant to embrace Augustinian theology. Indeed, the synod distanced itself from what apparently had become a common (mis)understanding of Augustine's doctrine of reprobation: "We not only do not believe that any are foreordained to evil by the power of God, but even state with utter abhorrence that if there are those who want to believe so evil a thing, they are anathema [cursed]."[41] Furthermore, the synod was more positive about the salvation of those who are members of the church than Augustine had been: "We also believe that

---

37. Faustus of Rhegium, *On Grace*, 1.16, in Pelikan, 1:320.

38. Ibid., 2.2, in Pelikan, 1:321. The text has been rendered clearer.

39. John Cassian, *Conferences of John Cassian*: "Third Conference of Bishop Chaeremon," 7, in *NPNF*², 11:425.

40. Although he does not mention Augustine by name, it is clear that Cassian is disagreeing with him.

41. Synod of Orange, concluding statement of faith. Available at http://www.reformed.org/documents (accessed August 6, 2009).

after grace has been received through baptism, all baptized persons have the ability and responsibility, if they desire to work faithfully, to perform with the aid and cooperation of Christ what is of essential importance in regard to the salvation of their soul.... God himself first inspires in us both faith in him and love ... so that we may both faithfully seek the sacrament of baptism, and after baptism are able by his help to do what is pleasing to him."[42] With this statement, the church established an identity between those whom God elects for salvation and those who are its baptized members. Certainly, this stance was far removed from Pelagianism and, to a lesser extent, from semi-Pelagianism. However, the Synod of Orange, in its hesitancy toward Augustine's doctrine of predestination, developed what could be called semi-Augustinianism.

As the early church had done, the medieval church engaged in discussions concerning predestination and human free will. In keeping with the scholastic emphasis of this period, Anselm approached the matter from a philosophical perspective in his work *The Compatibility of God's Foreknowledge, Predestination, and Grace with Human Freedom*. As discussed elsewhere, Anselm resolved the apparent problem between divine foreknowledge and human freedom.[43] In a similar manner, he demonstrated the compatibility of divine predestination and human freedom. He stated the problem: "To say that God predestines means that he pre-ordains, that is, to bring it about that something happen in the future. But it seems that whatever God decrees to happen in the future shall necessarily happen. Therefore, whatever God predestines shall happen of necessity. If then he predestines the good and evil acts that we do, no room is left for the action of a free choice but all occur of necessity."[44] Anselm's solution was to begin by embracing the position that divine predestination includes not only the good deeds of people but their evil deeds as well, "in the sense that it is by permitting the latter that God is said to be the cause of evils which he does not actually cause. In fact he is said to harden people when he does not soften them and to lead them into temptation when he does not release them from it. Therefore there is no problem in saying that in this sense God predestines evil people and their evil acts when he does not straighten them out along with their evil acts."[45]

As for his solution, Anselm made a distinction between God causing something to happen by forcing or constraining it to take place, and God causing something to happen as a consequence of something else taking place. In the latter case, "he causes them not by compelling or constraining the will but by leaving it to its own devices. And even though the will employs its own power, it still causes nothing which God does not also cause by his grace in the case of good deeds. In the case of evil ones, however, the evil is not due to any fault of God, but to the same free choice."[46] For example, God does not predestine people to eternal punishment against their will (by constraint), but he predestines them so that of necessity (not by compulsion) they are condemned as a consequence of their evil deeds (in which they engage freely). Likewise, God does not predestine people to eternal life against their own will (by constraint), but he predestines them so that of

---

42. Ibid.

43. See the discussion in chap. 10.

44. Anselm, *The Compatibility of God's Foreknowledge, Predestination, and Grace with Human Freedom*, 2.1, in

Anselm, 449.

45. Ibid., 2.2, in *Anselm*, 450.

46. Ibid., 2.3, in *Anselm*, 451.

necessity (not by compulsion) they are saved as a consequence of their faith in Christ (in which they engage freely). As Anselm concluded: "Predestination does not exclude free choice and that free choice is not opposed to predestination."[47]

Thomas Aquinas joined biblical support to philosophical reasoning in his affirmation of predestination, which he considered to fall under the general category of providence. According to Aquinas, divine providence directs human beings toward their end, which is twofold. The first end "exceeds all proportion and power of created nature; and this end is eternal life.... Now if a thing cannot attain to something by the power of its nature, it must be directed to it by another.... A rational creature, capable of eternal life, is led towards it, directed, as it were, by God.... Hence the type of this direction of a rational creature towards the end of eternal life is called predestination."[48] The second end "is proportionate to created nature, to which end created being can attain according to the power of its nature."[49] Citing God's love for Jacob but hatred for Esau (Mal. 1:2–3), Aquinas also affirmed this second end: "Thus, as men are ordained to eternal life through the providence of God, it likewise is part of that providence to permit some to fall away from that end; this is called reprobation.... Therefore, as predestination includes the will to confer grace and glory, so also reprobation includes the will to permit a person to fall into sin, and to impose the punishment of damnation on account of that sin."[50]

Citing Ephesians 1:4, Aquinas closely associated love with God's election of people.[51] Accordingly, God's foreknowledge of people's faith and good works is ruled out as the basis for the divine election. Appealing to Titus 3:5, he reasoned: "As he [God] saved us, so he predestined that we should be saved. Therefore, foreknowledge of merits is not the cause or reason of predestination."[52] With this, Aquinas specifically dissented from others before him — Origen, Pelagius — who held to a doctrine of predestination based on divine foreknowledge of human merit.[53] For Aquinas, this idea confuses effect and reason (or cause): "It is clear that what is of grace is the effect of predestination; and this cannot be considered as the reason of predestination.... It is impossible that the whole effect of predestination in general should have any cause as coming from us, because whatever is in man disposing him towards salvation is all included under the effect of predestination — even the preparation for grace."[54] Rather, it is in the goodness of God that the reason for predestination must be found: "God wills to reveal his goodness in men: in respect to those whom he predestines, by means of his mercy, as sparing them; and in respect of others, whom he reprobates, by means of his justice, in punishing them. This is the reason why God elects some and rejects others."[55]

Aquinas made a distinction between the decree of predestination and the actualization of that decree.[56] He applied this distinction to the question of "whether predestination can be furthered by the prayers of the saints."[57] Considering the question as it

47. Ibid.
48. Thomas Aquinas, *Summa Theologica*, pt. 1, q. 23, art. 1. The text has been rendered clearer.
49. Ibid., pt. 1, q. 23, art. 1.
50. Ibid., pt. 1, q. 23, art. 3.
51. Ibid., pt. 1, q. 23, art. 4.

52. Ibid., pt. 1, q. 23, art. 5.
53. Ibid.
54. Ibid. The text has been rendered clearer.
55. Ibid. The text has been rendered clearer.
56. Ibid., pt. 1, q. 23, art. 2.
57. Ibid., pt. 1, q. 23, art. 8.

regards the decree itself, Aquinas firmly denied that "predestination be furthered by the prayers of the saints. For it is not due to their prayers that anyone is predestined by God."[58] Considering the question as it regards the actualization of the decree, he affirmed that predestination is aided by prayer: "Because providence, of which predestination is a part, does not do away with secondary causes but so provides effects that the order of secondary causes falls also under providence. So ... the salvation of a person is predestined by God in such a way that whatever helps that person toward salvation falls under the order of predestination."[59] Thus, in the actualization of salvation, human efforts like prayer are the means appointed by God to help the elect move toward the salvation to which God predestined them.

VIEWS OF PREDESTINATION IN THE REFORMATION AND POST-REFORMATION

Being trained as an Augustinian monk, Martin Luther adapted much of his mentor's doctrine of predestination. This was especially the case in Luther's debate with Erasmus on the freedom or bondage of the will. Although Erasmus championed (limited) human freedom, Luther, like Augustine, maintained "there can be no 'free-will' in man."[60] As an important consequence of this situation, however, "our salvation may be taken entirely out of our hands and put into the hand of God alone. And this too is utterly necessary, for we are so weak and uncertain that if it depended on us, not even a single person would be saved; the devil would surely overpower us all. But since God is dependable—his predestination cannot fail, and no one can withstand him—we still have hope in the face of sin."[61]

Luther was aware of how distressed people are concerning whether they are elect or not: "When a man is assailed by thoughts regarding his election, he is being assailed by hell."[62] Accordingly, he tried to guide people in how to think about their election so it becomes a comfort to them, pointing people to the gospel:

> If you follow this advice, if you first recognize that you are a child of wrath by nature, guilty of eternal death and damnation, from which no creature, either man or angel, is able to save you, and if you then grasp God's promise, believing that he ... has sent Christ, his only Son, to render satisfaction for your sin, to give you his innocence and righteousness, and finally to redeem you from all danger and death, then do not doubt that you belong to the little flock of the elect.[63]

Thus, the antidote for both foolish speculation about the doctrine of predestination and distressful concern about one's own predestination is paying careful attention to and trusting in the gospel of Jesus Christ for salvation.

---

58. Ibid.

59. Ibid.

60. Martin Luther, *The Bondage of the Will*, trans. James I. Packer and O. R. Johnston (Old Tappan, N.J.: Revell, 1957), 317.

61. Martin Luther, *Preface to the New Testament*, LW, 35:378.

62. *A Sermon on Preparing to Die*, LW, 42:103.

63. Martin Luther, *WLS*, 1:457.

Luther embraced *unconditional election*. Indeed, he located this decision in "the dreadful hidden will of God, who, according to his own counsel, ordains such person as he wills to receive and partake of the mercy preached and offered. This will is not to be inquired into, but to be reverently adored, as by far the most awesome secret of the Divine Majesty."[64] Commenting on 1 Peter 1:2, Luther emphasized the sovereign purpose in God's election of some for salvation: "They are chosen ... not by themselves but according to God's arrangement.... The human doctrine of free will and of our powers no longer amounts to anything. Our will is unimportant; God's will and choosing are decisive."[65] This is the opposite of *conditional election*, the idea that God foreknows who will have faith in Christ and *on that basis* elects them for salvation. Rather, according to Luther, faith is the result of divine election, not the basis for it.[66]

More than any other Reformation leader, John Calvin is associated with the doctrine of predestination. The idea of the centrality and dominance of God's predestining work in the theology of Calvin has become part and parcel of the common portrayal of his position.[67] Added to this portrait is the view that Calvin's understanding of predestination is a logical outcome of his doctrine of the sovereignty of God. Good reasons exist to dispute this caricature, however.[68]

---

64. Luther, *Bondage of the Will*, 168. Luther added: "But God hidden in Majesty neither deplores nor takes away death, but works life, and death, and all in all; nor has he set bounds to himself by his Word, but has kept himself free from all things." Ibid., 170. His election cannot be conditioned by anything or anyone.

65. *The Catholic Epistles*, LW 30:6.

66. *WLS*, 1:461. Following Luther, the *Formula of Concord* formally addressed the doctrine "of the eternal predestination and election of God" while also explaining divine foreknowledge: "The foreknowledge of God is nothing other than this, that God knows all things before they come to pass.... This foreknowledge of God extends both to good and evil." Concerning predestination, the *Formula* affirmed: "The predestination or eternal election of God extends only to the good and beloved children of God, and this is the cause of their salvation.... This predestination of God is not to be searched out in the hidden counsel of God, but is to be sought in the Word of God in which it is revealed. But the Word of God leads us to Christ." The *Formula* balanced the exclusive nature of divine election with the universal call to salvation and the divine wish for all to be saved. Furthermore, it denounced common perversions of this doctrine of election, especially those that relax human responsibility: "If (they say) God has elected me to eternal salvation; I cannot be damned; let me do what evil I will. But, on the other hand, if I am not elected to eternal life, all the good that I may do will give me no advantage at all, for all my endeavors will be in vain." But for those who give their attention to the teaching on predestination in the Word of God and who turn to Christ through repentance and faith, there is a "sweet comfort which we may draw from this most whole-some doctrine: inasmuch as by it we are rendered certain that by mere grace, without any merit of our own, we are chosen in Christ for eternal life, and that no one can pluck us out of his hands." *Formula of Concord*, 11.2–3, 4–6, 7, 8, 12, in Schaff, 3:165–70. The text has been rendered clearer.

67. This notion seems to have been first articulated by Alexander Schweizer, *Die Glaubenslehre der Evangelisch-Reformierten Kirche* (Zürich, 1844–45), and F. C. Baur, *Lehrbuch der Christlichen Dogmengeschichte*, 3rd ed. (Stuttgart, 1867). The idea is now largely discounted. See the fine summary in Charles Partee, "Calvin's Central Dogma Again," *The Sixteenth Century Journal*, 18, no. 2 (Summer 1987), 191–99.

68. In Calvin's first edition of the *Institutes of the Christian Religion* (1536), the word *predestination* never occurs. In the second and third editions, Calvin placed his discussion of the topic under the doctrine of God. But in his final edition (1559), Calvin moved the discussion of predestination to the very end of book 3, under the doctrine of the application of salvation. In this position, it follows Calvin's treatment of faith and repentance, sanctification, justification, and prayer. It is not found under the doctrine of God, where seemingly it would need to be if predestination were the logical conclusion of divine sovereignty. It is not found at the beginning of his doctrine of salvation, where seemingly it would need to be if it were the central and dominant theme of Calvin's theology. Rather, for Calvin, predestination is the answer to a practical ministry question: Why, "among those to whom it is preached, it [the gospel] does not gain the same acceptance either constantly or in equal degree." John Calvin, *Institutes of the Christian Religion*, 3.21.1, LCC, 2:920–21. In other words, Calvin addressed the doctrine of predestination as the reason why

As Calvin put it simply, predestination is that "by which God adopts some to hope of life, and sentences others to eternal death."[69] In a more developed definition, he expanded his thought: "We call predestination God's eternal decree, by which he compacted with himself what he willed to become of each person. For all are not created in equal condition; rather, eternal life is foreordained for some, eternal damnation for others. Therefore, as any man has been created to one or the other of these ends, we speak of him as predestined to life or to death."[70]

In his detailed discussion of the topic, Calvin underscored numerous points. Foremost in importance is the fact that predestination is a biblical teaching. Rather than depending on logical implications of his doctrine of God—for example, because God is completely sovereign over all things, he must be in control of people's eternal destinies as well—Calvin used many biblical passages (e.g., Rom. 9–11; Eph. 1) in unfolding his doctrine of predestination. Furthermore, predestination is part of the eternal and unchangeable decree of God. It is not something that God makes up as time and history move on, but his plan was established before the creation of the world and prior to the existence of those whom the decree affects. It is also based on his gracious and free decision, not on anything in the elect or the reprobate.[71] In other words, predestination is unconditional.

Moreover, predestination is individual. While presenting the reality of the divine election of the people of Israel, Calvin also affirmed that God's choice extends to actual individuals, who will most certainly experience salvation.[72] Indeed, there are two types of human beings—the elect and the reprobate—and each individual is assigned to one or the other by the decree of God: "When he [Christ] declares that he knows whom he has chosen (John 13:18), he denotes in the human genus a particular species, distinguished not by the quality of its virtues but by heavenly decree."[73] Accordingly, predestination is double. Calvin clearly affirmed that predestination involves both election and reprobation. Specifically, he cited Paul's metaphor of the potter and the clay in support (Rom. 9:22–23).[74] So people are distinguished by God's choice, which includes both election and reprobation.[75] Calvin dismissed the view that affirms that God chooses the elect but denies that he has anything to do with reprobation: "It will be highly absurd to say that others acquire by chance or obtain by their own effort what election alone confers on a few. Therefore, those whom God passes over, he condemns; and this he does for no other reason than that he wills to exclude them from the inheritance which he predestines for his own children."[76]

---

some people embrace Jesus Christ when they hear the gospel presented and others do not. He also found great comfort in this doctrine to share with believers, to encourage them in their Christian faith. This is hardly reason to elevate Calvin's view of predestination to the heights that the common caricature of his position ascribes to it.

69. Ibid., 3.21.5, LCC, 2:926.

70. Ibid.

71. Ibid., 3.21.summary, LCC, 2:931–32.

72. Ibid., 3.21.7, LCC, 2:930.

73. Ibid., 3.22.7, LCC, 2:941.

74. Ibid., 3.23.1, LCC, 2:948.

75. Calvin anticipated an objection, implied in Paul's own discussion: "They add also that vessels of wrath are for good reason said to be 'made for destruction' but that 'God has prepared vessels of mercy' [Rom. 9:22]; for in this way, Paul ascribes to, and claims for, God the credit for salvation, while he casts the blame for their perdition upon those who of their own will bring it upon themselves. But though I should admit to them that Paul, using a different expression, softens the harshness of the former clause, it is utterly inconsistent to transfer the preparation for destruction to anything but God's secret plan." Ibid.

76. Ibid., 3.23.1, LCC, 2:947.

For Calvin, predestination is not based on God's foreknowledge of human worth or unworthiness — the common view of many people,[77] yet a view that was patently wrong for several reasons. First, divine election came before the world ever existed (Eph. 1:4), which "takes away all regard for worth. For what basis for distinction is there among those who did not yet exist, and who were subsequently to be equals in Adam?"[78] Second, election is grounded on "God's good pleasure" (Eph. 1:5): "By these words he [Paul] does away with all means of their election that men imagine in themselves."[79] Third, election is for the sake of people becoming holy, not because they are holy.[80] For Calvin, even reprobation is not grounded on God's foreknowledge. Citing the example of Jacob and Esau, Calvin concluded that God does not decide for reprobation on the basis of people's evil works that he foreknows.[81] So predestination is not based on people's faith, or lack thereof, good or evil deeds, or any other kind of human merit or demerit. God does not elect certain people because he foreknows what kind of people they will turn out to be, nor does God pass over others for the same reason.

Taking his discussion of foreknowledge one step further, Calvin denied that God merely foreknows with certainty all things that take place. Rather, God actually determines all things: "I will freely admit that foreknowledge alone imposes no necessity upon creatures.... [But] both life and death are acts of God's will more than of his foreknowledge.... But since he foresees future events only by reason of the fact that he decreed that they take place.... it is clear that all things take place rather by his determination and bidding."[82] Thus, election and reprobation are not the result of God's foreknowledge alone. Rather, they are both determinations of his sovereign will.

Concerning reprobation, Calvin emphasized the finality of the divine decision: God simply decides to do this, and there is no more fundamental reason than the divine will.[83] But this opens the door to a possible objection: If the reprobate are predestined to this end, they cannot help but sin, and such determination excuses them from punishment. Anticipating this objection, Calvin insisted that "the sufferings they bear are all inflicted upon them by God's most righteous judgment."[84] In his final analysis, Calvin underscored both the will of God and the evil of the reprobate as the reason for their disastrous end: "The fact that the reprobate do not obey God's Word when it is made known to them will be justly charged against the evil and depravity of their hearts. But it must be added

77. Ibid., 3.22.1, LCC, 2:932. A bit later, Calvin noted that Augustine originally held to God's foreknowledge as a basis for the divine election. However, "after he had gained a better knowledge of Scripture, he not only retracted it as patently false, but stoutly refuted it." Calvin offered Augustine's refutation based on John 15:16: "Here, surely, is rendered void the reasoning of those who defend God's foreknowledge against God's grace, and therefore say that we were chosen before the establishment of the world because God foresaw that we would be good, not that he himself would make us good. He who says, 'You did not choose me, but I chose you' [John 15:16] does not speak of foreseen goodness." Ibid., 3.22.8, LCC, 2:941–42.

78. Ibid., LCC, 2:934.

79. Ibid.

80. Ibid., 3.22.3, LCC, 2:935.

81. Ibid., 3.22.11, LCC, 2:946–47.

82. Ibid., 3.23.6, LCC, 2:954–55.

83. Commenting on Paul's conclusion of Rom. 9:18, Calvin offered: "If, then, we cannot determine a reason why he grants mercy to his own, except that it so pleases him, neither shall we have any reason for rejecting others, other than his will. For when it is said that God hardens or shows mercy to whom he wills, men are warned by this to seek no cause outside his will." Ibid., 3.22.11, LCC, 2:946–47. Recognizing the stark nature of his position, Calvin offered, "The decree is dreadful indeed, I confess." Ibid., 3.23.7, LCC, 2:955.

84. Ibid., 3.23.9, LCC, 2:957.

at the same time that they have been given over to this depravity because they have been raised up by the just but inscrutable judgment of God to show forth his glory in their condemnation."[85] Thus, Calvin affirmed that the reprobate are held accountable for the evil they do. At the same time, he affirmed that they are predestined as such and come to destruction because of God's will: "They were left in their stubbornness, even though the Lord could have softened their hearts—because his immutable decree had once for all destined them to destruction."[86]

Calvin anticipated and responded to possible objections to his doctrine of predestination.[87] Moreover, he raised the issue of how to treat this matter practically, urging that two errors should be avoided. The first error is careless speculation about predestination. For Calvin, it must be acknowledged that predestination is a great mystery, and God has wisely decided to reveal some things, but not many things, about it. Thus, one safeguard that Calvin enjoined on people was to avoid foolish speculation,[88] meaning that they are safe only when they restrict their study of predestination to God's revelation in the Bible.[89] Using an oxymoron, Calvin urged: "And let us not be ashamed to be ignorant of something in this matter, in which there is a certain *learned ignorance*. Rather, let us willingly refrain from inquiring into a kind of knowledge, the ardent desire for which is both foolish and dangerous, indeed, even deadly."[90]

The second error is avoiding saying anything about the matter. Calvin recognized that, for many reasons, people refused to deal with predestination. Pointing to his above guideline—follow the contours of the biblical revelation—he urged those who prefer to be silent not to withhold God's truth from others:

> For Scripture is the school of the Holy Spirit, in which, as nothing is omitted that is both necessary and useful to know, so nothing is taught but what is expedient to know. Therefore, we must guard against depriving believers of anything disclosed about predestination in Scripture. Otherwise, we seem either wickedly to defraud them of the blessing of their God, or to accuse and scoff at the Holy Spirit for having published what it is in any way profitable to suppress.[91]

Indeed, Calvin highlights the benefits of understanding this doctrine. It magnifies the grace of God, encourages humility on the part of believers, and grounds confident hope.[92] Finally, he emphasized that "election is to be understood and recognized in Christ alone."[93]

The Reformed churches that developed from Calvin and his theology continued to embrace and repeat his view of predestination.[94]

---

85. Ibid., 3.24.14, LCC, 2:981. The text has been rendered clearer.

86. Ibid.

87. Ibid., 3.22.10–3.23.12, LCC, 2:943–60.

88. Ibid., 3.21.1, LCC, 2:922–23.

89. Ibid., 3.21.2, LCC, 2:923–24.

90. Ibid., LCC, 2:923. Emphasis added.

91. Ibid., 3.21.3, LCC, 2:924. The text has been rendered clearer.

92. Ibid., 3.21.1, LCC, 2:921–22.

93. "First, if we seek God's fatherly mercy and kindly heart, we should turn our eyes to Christ, on whom alone God's Spirit rests.... Christ, then, is the mirror wherein we must, and without self-deception may, contemplate our own election." Ibid., 3.24.5, LCC, 2:970.

94. *French Confession of Faith*, 12, in Schaff, 3:366–67; *Belgic Confession*, 16, in Schaff, 3:401; *Heidelberg Catechism*, 54, in Schaff, 3:324–25; *Thirty-nine Articles*, 10, 17, in Schaff, 3:493–94, 497–99.

A negative reaction to this Calvinist doctrine arose from Roman Catholic quarters. The Council of Trent repudiated the "rash presumption" of predestination: "No one ... so long as he is in this mortal life, ought so far to presume with regard to the secret mystery of predestination, as to determine for certain that he is assuredly in the number of the predestined.... [F]or except by special revelation, it cannot be known whom God has chosen for himself."[95] Indeed, the council condemned those who are convinced that they are elect: "If anyone says that a man who is born again and justified is bound by faith to believe that he is assuredly in the number of the predestined, let him be anathema."[96]

Dissention was also voiced by the new movement of Anabaptists. Although its earliest document, the *Schleitheim Confession*, did not address the issue, the *Waterland Confession* denounced unconditional election and reprobation.[97] But it did affirm a conditional election—one based on faith and remaining a believer.[98] This Anabaptist theology of conditional election and a denial of reprobation would become widespread among Protestants in the centuries to come through the development of Arminian theology in the post-Reformed period and Wesleyan theology in the modern period.

The legacy of Calvinism was furthered by Theodore Beza, who did much to place predestination at the center of Calvinist theology. Beza's doctrine of predestination is often considered the classical expression of its supralapsarian form, that is, the form that asserts that the divine decree of election and reprobation precedes the divine decree to create human beings and to permit the fall of humanity (thus, the decree of predestination comes before—*supra*—the decree of the fall—*lapsis*).

Beza's doctrine affirmed divine creation of human beings "according to two kinds, completely different from each other"—the elect and the reprobate.[99] Concerning "the damnation of the reprobate, although the whole fault for it is in themselves ... Scripture ... leads us to this high secret, which by order is the first cause of their damnation, of which secret no other cause is known to men than God's just will."[100] To actualize his decree, God ordained that all those whom he would create would also fall into sin, so that he might demonstrate both his mercy and his justice.[101] But this did not entail the creation of human beings as sinful from the start, "for then he [God] should have been ... the author of sin, which afterwards he could not justly have punished. Rather, God made man after his own image."[102] Adam, so created, fell according to his own will and—quite remarkably—also according to the will of God, "whom it pleased by a marvelous and incomprehensible means, that the thing that he does not allow (for as much as it is sin) should not happen apart from his will."[103]

95. *Canons and Decrees of the Council of Trent*, 6th session (January 13, 1547), *Decree on Justification*, chap. 12, in Schaff, 2:103. The text has been rendered clearer.

96. Ibid., in Schaff, 2:113. The text has been rendered clearer.

97. *Waterland Confession*, 7, in Lumpkin, 47.

98. Ibid., 47–48.

99. Theodore Beza, *A Brief Declaration of the Chief Points of Christian Religion, Set Forth in a Table*, 2. The text has been rendered clearer. Available at www.covenanter.org/Beza/

besas_table.html.

100. Ibid. The text has been rendered clearer.

101. Ibid., 3. As we will see, this formulation by Beza was often (disparagingly) referred to as an absolute decree (*decretum absolutum*) because it focused solely on the will of God and did not allow for any other considerations—the work of Christ, foreseen faith and good works, and so forth—to be a part of his decree.

102. Ibid. The text has been rendered clearer.

103. Ibid. The text has been rendered clearer.

So as to rescue the elect from this disastrous situation of sin, God also decreed the accomplishment of salvation through Jesus Christ. Moreover, God ordained the means of communicating this salvation to the elect.[104] As for the reprobate, however: "God makes them go to their own place, those whom he created to that end that he might be glorified in their just condemnation.... He orderly disposes the causes and means by which it might come to pass that the whole cause of their damnation might be of themselves."[105] Thus, Beza expressed a view of double predestination that came to be marked out for attack because it conceived of an absolute decree dependent only on the will of God and nothing else. Furthermore, because it appeared to place the decree for both election and reprobation before (*supra*) the decrees of creation and permission of the fall (*lapsis*), many opposed Beza's doctrine—*supralapsarianism* ("before the fall")—on the grounds that it made God the author of sin and that it was unjust, unloving, and unworthy of God.

Indeed, fifty years after Calvin, the Reformed theologian Jacob Arminius objected to the Calvinist doctrine of predestination. While affirming election, Arminius claimed that it is based on God's foreknowledge of those who will believe in Christ and remain believers throughout their lifetime.

Specifically, Arminius rejected several forms of Calvinist predestinarian doctrine with regard to the order of salvation. His main contention was against supralapsarianism, which he defined: "God by an eternal and immutable decree has predestined from among men (whom he did not consider as being then *created*, much less as being *fallen*) certain individuals to everlasting life, and others to eternal destruction, without any regard whatever to righteousness or sin, to obedience or disobedience, but purely of his own good pleasure, to demonstrate the glory of his justice and mercy."[106] Thus, the decree of predestination was logically prior to (*supra*) the decree to create human beings and the decree to permit the fall of Adam (*lapsis*). By implication, the decree to reprobation preceded the decree to allow humanity to fall into sin. Furthermore, "from this decree of divine election and reprobation ... it follows that the elect are necessarily saved, it being impossible for them to perish, and that the reprobate are necessarily damned, it being impossible for them to be saved; and all this from the absolute purpose [or determination] of God, which is altogether antecedent to all things."[107] In no uncertain terms, Arminius rejected this supralapsarian view of predestination.[108]

But Arminius was not finished. He further denounced both a modified supralapsarianism and *sublapsarianism*, the latter of which he described in the following:

> Because God willed within himself from all eternity to make a decree by which he might elect certain men and reprobate others, he viewed and considered the human race not only *as created* but likewise *as fallen* or corrupt, and on that account obnoxious to cursing and malediction. Out of this lapsed and accursed state God determined to liberate certain individuals and to save them freely by

---

104. Ibid., 4. The text has been rendered clearer.

105. Ibid., 5. The text has been rendered clearer.

106. James Arminius, *The Writings of James Arminius*, 3 vols., trans. James Nichols (Grand Rapids: Baker, 1956),

1:211–12.

107. Ibid., 1:215.

108. Ibid., 1:215–41.

his grace, for a declaration of his mercy; but he resolved in his own just judgment to leave the rest under the curse [or malediction] for a declaration of his justice. In both these cases God acts without the least consideration of *repentance* and *faith* in those whom he elects, or of *impenitence* and *unbelief* in those whom he reprobates.[109]

Thus, the decree of predestination was logically subsequent to (*sub*) the decree to create human beings and the decree to permit the fall of Adam (*lapsis*). By implication, the decree to reprobation followed the decree to allow humanity to fall into sin. According to Arminius, though these other forms of predestination "outwardly pretend" to differ from supralapsarianism,[110] they should be rejected.[111]

Having dispensed with these forms of Calvinist predestination, Arminius articulated his own understanding of the doctrine under four headings. The first addressed God's purpose to save people through Jesus Christ. The second addressed election and reprobation: God "decreed to receive into favor *those who repent and believe*, and, in Christ, for his sake and through him, to effect the salvation of such penitents and believers as persevered to the end; but to leave in sin, and under wrath, *all impenitent persons and unbelievers*, and to damn them as aliens from Christ."[112] The third addressed the means of effecting the first two decrees. The fourth addressed the divine foreknowledge concerning which specific individuals would be chosen — or not — for salvation: "This decree has its foundation in the foreknowledge of God, by which he knew from all eternity those individuals who *would*, through his prevenient grace, *believe*, and, through his subsequent grace *would persevere*."[113] Arminius's views were expressed in the *Five Articles of the Remonstrants*, the first of which addressed this issue:

> God, by an eternal, unchangeable purpose in Jesus Christ his Son, before the foundation of the world, determined, out of the fallen, sinful race of men to save in Christ, for Christ's sake, and through Christ, those who, through the grace of the Holy Spirit, shall believe on his Son Jesus, and shall persevere in this faith and obedience of faith, through this grace, even to the end. On the other hand, he determined to leave the disobedient and unbelieving in sin and under wrath, and to condemn them as alienated from Christ.[114]

Thus was born the Arminian theology of predestination.

The Calvinist reply to this Arminian theology in general, and the Remonstrants in particular, was blunt in its dissent. The Synod of Dort affirmed both the decree of election and the decree of reprobation. As for the former: "Election is the unchangeable purpose of God by which, before the foundation of the world, out of sheer grace, accord-

---

109. Ibid., 1:243.

110. Arminius explained, "Neither of them lays down *the creation* or *the fall* as a mediate cause foreordained by God for the execution of the preceding decree of predestination.... They have desired to use the greatest precaution, lest it might be concluded from their doctrine that *God is the author of sin*." Ibid., 1:244.

111. Ibid., 1:247.

112. Ibid.

113. Ibid., 1:247–48. I have substituted the word *prevenient* for the text's *preventing* for clarity's sake.

114. *Five Arminian Articles*, 1, in Schaff, 3:545–46. The text has been rendered clearer.

ing to the sovereign good pleasure of his own will, he has chosen from the whole human race (which had fallen through their own fault from their original state of uprightness into sin and destruction) a certain number of persons to redemption in Christ."[115] This was a statement of belief in *unconditional* election, which became the second element in the acronym *TULIP*, or the five points of Calvinism.[116] Moreover, the Synod denied *conditional* election — God's choice is based on something in those whom he elected. Furthermore, the synod affirmed the doctrine of reprobation.[117]

In other post-Reformation developments, theologians of the Reformed churches carried on this debate. Although some opted for and defended *supralapsarianism*,[118] the majority championed *infralapsarianism* or *sublapsarianism*.[119] The earliest Baptist churches were split between Anabaptist (and the new Arminian) theology and the Calvinist doctrine of predestination. On the one hand, a fully Calvinist theology of predestination was affirmed in both the *First London Confession* and the *Second London Confession* of the Particular Baptists.[120] On the other hand, an anti-Calvinist theology of predestination was affirmed by the General Baptists.[121]

VIEWS OF PREDESTINATION IN THE MODERN PERIOD

Like many before him, John Wesley denounced the doctrine of predestination. In *Predestination Calmly Considered*, he contemptibly linked "unconditional election" with "the cloven foot of reprobation."[122] Still, he acknowledged that election is a biblical idea. Accordingly, he affirmed two types: "First, a divine appointment of some particular

---

115. *Canons of the Synod of Dort*, 1.7, in Schaff, 3:582. The text has been rendered clearer.

116. *TULIP* stands for *T*otal depravity, *U*nconditional election, *L*imited atonement, *I*rresistible grace, and *P*erseverance of the saints.

117. "Out of his sovereign, completely just, irreprehensible and unchangeable good pleasure, he [God] decreed to leave [these] in the common misery into which they have willfully plunged themselves, and not to give them saving faith and the grace of conversion. Rather, he permitted them in his just judgment to follow their own way, finally, for the declaration of his justice, to condemn and punish them forever, not only on account of their unbelief, but also for all their other sins." *Canons of the Synod of Dort*, 1.15, in Schaff, 3:584. The text has been rendered clearer.

118. E.g., John Braun, *Doctrina Foederum sive Systema Theologiae Didacticae et Elencticae* (Amsterdam, 1688), 1.2.9.24–26, in Heppe, 160–61.

119. E.g., John Heidegger, *Corpus Theologiae* (Zürich, 1700), 5.33–34, in Heppe, 157–59. See also Leonard Riissen, *Francisci Turretini Compendium Theologiae* (Amsterdam, 1695), 6.19.1, in Heppe, 159–60.

120. *London Confession*, 3, in Lumpkin, 157; *Second London Confession*, 3, in ibid., 254–55.

121. John Smyth authored his *Short Confession of Faith in Twenty Articles* (1610), the second of which affirmed "that God has created and redeemed the human race to his own image, and has ordained all men (no one being reprobated) to life." John Smyth, *Short Confession of Faith in Twenty Articles*, 2, in Lumpkin, 100. That same year, Smyth signed an English translation of the *Waterland Confession* (cited above), which denied unconditional election and reprobation. *Short Confession of Faith*, 7, in Lumpkin, 104. Furthermore, an anti-Calvinist theology of predestination was affirmed by some early Baptists in "A Declaration of Faith of English People Remaining at Amsterdam in Holland," sec. 5, in Lumpkin, 118. Moreover, in response to the London confessions of the Particular Baptists, the General Baptists published the Orthodox Creed. Interestingly, this creed approached a Calvinist theology of predestination, undoubtedly because of its purpose of attempting to unify Protestants. The Orthodox Creed, 9, in Lumpkin, 302–4.

122. John Wesley, *Predestination Calmly Considered*, 15, in *The Works of John Wesley*, 3rd ed., vols. 9–10 (repr., Grand Rapids: Baker, 2002), 10:209.

men to do some particular work in the world. And this election I believe to be not only personal, but absolute and unconditional. Thus Cyrus was elected to rebuild the temple, and St. Paul, with the twelve, to preach the gospel."[123] Of greater importance was a second type of election, "a divine appointment of some men to eternal happiness. But I believe this election to be conditional, as well as the reprobation opposite to it. I believe the eternal decree concerning both is expressed in those words: 'He who believes will be saved; he who does not believe will be damned.' "[124] Specifically, then, Wesley linked election with faith in Christ,[125] thus championing conditional, not unconditional, election. This latter election could claim no biblical support, and "it necessarily implies unconditional reprobation,"[126] which Wesley denied.[127]

As for Paul's treatment of election and reprobation (Rom. 9), Wesley paraphrased the key ideas: " 'He has mercy on whom he will have mercy,' namely, those that truly believe; 'and whom he will,' namely, obstinate unbelievers, he suffers to be 'hardened.'... 'Has not' the great 'Potter power over his own clay to make,' or appoint, one sort of 'vessels,' namely, believers, 'to honor,' and the others 'to dishonor'?"[128] That is, Wesley interpreted the passages in a way that emphasized that the election of believers to salvation was conditioned on their faith in Christ and that the reprobation of unbelievers was conditioned on their persistent unbelief. Moreover, he emphatically denied that divine sovereignty is "the ground of unconditional reprobation.... No, no; in this awful work, God proceeds according to the known rules of his justice and mercy, but never assigns his sovereignty as the cause why any man is punished with everlasting destruction."[129]

As he progressed in *Predestination Calmly Considered*, Wesley revealed that he was objecting specifically against a hyper-Calvinist view of the doctrine.[130] Over against it, he offered his own system—a measure of human freedom supplied by universal grace, unlimited atonement, conditional election, and conditional reprobation—and warned: "The doctrine of absolute predestination naturally leads to the chambers of death."[131]

In *Free Grace*, Wesley addressed specific problems that would result if the doctrine of predestination were true: It would render the preaching of the gospel superfluous;[132] it would have a numbing effect on the pursuit of holiness;[133] it would lead to the complete

---

123. Ibid., 16, in *Works of John Wesley*, 10:209–10.

124. He modified Mark 16:16 for his citation. Ibid., 17, in *Works of John Wesley*, 10:210.

125. Ibid., 18, in *Works of John Wesley*, 10:210.

126. Ibid., 19, in *Works of John Wesley*, 10:210–11.

127. Wesley claimed that reprobation conflicts with four types of biblical passages: (1) those that place the responsibility for condemnation on the shoulders of people who commit personal sin (Ezek. 18; Matt. 25); (2) passages that "declare God's willingness that all should be saved" (e.g., 1 Tim. 2:3–4; 2 Peter 3:9); (3) passages that "declare that Christ came to save all men; that he died for all; that he atoned for all, even for those who finally perish" (e.g., Matt. 18:11; 1 Tim. 2:6); and (4) passages that "declare the justice of God" and that Wesley felt could not possibly be reconciled with reprobation. Ibid., 20, 21, 22, in *Works of John Wesley*, 10:214–16.

128. Ibid., 27, 28, in *Works of John Wesley*, 10:219–20.

129. Ibid., 29, in *Works of John Wesley*, 10:220.

130. Ibid., 30, 37, 43, in *Works of John Wesley*, 10:220, 224, 228–29.

131. Ibid., 88, in *Works of John Wesley*, 10:258.

132. "It is needless to those who are elect; for they, whether with preaching or without it, will infallibly be saved.... It is also useless to those who are not elect, for they cannot possibly be saved: They, whether with preaching or without it, will infallibly be damned." John Wesley, *Free Grace*, 10, in *The Works of John Wesley*, 3rd ed., vols. 7–8 (repr. Grand Rapids: Baker, 2002), 7:376–83.

133. "It wholly takes away those first motives to follow after holiness, so frequently proposed in Scripture, the hope of future reward and fear of punishment, the hope of heaven and fear of hell." Ibid., 11, in *Works of John Wesley*, 7:376–83.

hopelessness of those whom God has decreed to pass over through reprobation;[134] it would exercise a numbing effect on one's motivation for good works toward the reprobate and the marginalized;[135] it would render the Christian revelation unnecessary and therefore false;[136] and it would be open to the charge of blasphemy because it portrays Christ as a liar and pictures God as crueler and more unjust than Satan.[137] Thus, Wesley stood against the Calvinist doctrine of predestination.

Despite Wesley's insistence on a logical link between election and reprobation, the practice of embracing the former while rejecting the latter had appeared before in the development of the doctrine of predestination. In this regard, the modern period was no different. For example, the *New Hampshire Confession* of the Baptists contained an article on election but made no mention of reprobation.[138] Among Southern Baptists, this trend was followed by the *Baptist Faith and Message*.[139] Although Baptist theologian A. H. Strong affirmed a doctrine of reprobation, he did nothing to develop it.[140] Similarly, Millard Erickson mentioned reprobation in his explanation of God's plan,[141] but in his specific discussion of predestination, he did not address the doctrine of reprobation.[142]

The modern period saw a very significant development in the doctrine of predestination through the theology of Karl Barth. Rejecting the historic view of predestination as the absolute, unconditional, unsearchable decree of God, Barth instead placed Jesus Christ squarely in the middle of the discussion: "Jesus Christ is himself the divine election of grace."[143] Barth explained: "In the beginning, before time and space as we know them, before creation, before there was any reality distinct from God which could be the object of the love of God or the setting for his acts of freedom, God anticipated and determined within himself ... that the goal and meaning of all his dealings with the as yet non-existent universe should be the fact that in his Son he would be gracious towards man, uniting himself with him."[144]

Specifically for Barth, the church must make "the two assertions that Jesus Christ is the electing God, and that he is also elected man."[145] First, in terms of his being the electing God, Jesus Christ "himself is this good pleasure, the will of God in action.... He is not merely the revelation of the mystery of God. He is the thing concealed within this mystery, and the revelation of it is the revelation of himself and not of something else."[146] Moreover, as the electing God, as the active elector, Christ elects all humanity in himself.[147] This is Jesus Christ the electing God. Second, he is also the elected man,

134. Ibid., 10–27, in *Works of John Wesley*, 7:376–83.

135. "For what help is there to relieve the temporal needs of those who are just dropping into eternal fire?" Ibid.

136. Ibid.

137. Ibid.

138. *New Hampshire Confession*, 9, in Lumpkin, 364.

139. *Baptist Faith and Message* (Southern Baptist Convention), 5, in Lumpkin, 395–96. The text of this 1963 revision of the original 1925 *Confession* reflects the latest changes as made in the 2000 edition.

140. Augustus Hopkins Strong, *Systematic Theology: A Compendium*, 3 vols. in 1 (Philadelphia: Judson, 1907), 355.

Indeed, Strong presented at length the doctrine of election while making only a brief mention of reprobation, relegating his discussion of it to an objection to the doctrine of election. Ibid., 789–90.

141. Millard J. Erickson, *Christian Theology*, 2nd ed. (Grand Rapids: Baker, 1998), 373.

142. Ibid., 936–40.

143. *CD*, II/2, 95.

144. Ibid., 101.

145. Ibid., 103.

146. Ibid., 104.

147. Ibid., 105–6.

the one passively elected: "Jesus Christ, then, is not merely one of the elect but *the* elect of God. From the very beginning (from eternity itself), as elected man he does not stand alongside the rest of the elect, but before and above them as the one who is originally and properly the Elect."[148] "In Christ" is the election of all humanity: " 'In him' means in his person, in his will, in his own divine choice, in the basic decision of God which he fulfills over against every man. What singles him out from the rest of the elect, and yet also, and for the first time, unites him with them, is the fact that as elected man he is also the elect-ing God, electing them in his own humanity."[149] Of course, "the election of the man Jesus is specifically his election to suffering," and ultimately this accomplishes salvation for humanity: "The rejection that all men incurred, the wrath of God under which all men lie, the death which all men must die, God in his love for men transfers from all eternity to him in whom he loves and elects them, and whom he elects at their head and in their place."[150] Thus, Jesus Christ is both the electing God and the elected man.

In addition to the election of Jesus Christ, Barth's doctrine of election included "the election of the community," by which he meant Israel, the church, and ultimately all humanity. Barth saw this community aspect as an advancement over earlier, individual-istic-oriented formulations of the doctrine.[151] Two communities — Israel and the church, very different from each other — compose the community of Jesus Christ.[152] More spe-cifically, "Israel is the people of the Jews which resists its divine election.... The church is the gathering of Jews and Gentiles called on the ground of its election."[153] Both, therefore, perform important service for the elect community.

Finally, Barth treated the "election of the individual," affirming, "[T]hat which has been eternally determined in Jesus Christ is concretely determined for every individual man ... to the extent that in his Word the electing God enters with him into the relation-ship of Elector to elected, and by his Word makes him an elected man."[154] Within the framework of election and grace, the individual "predestined man is simply forgiven man."[155] This sinful, godless, unrighteous predestined man rebelliously rejects the elec-tion of God through Jesus Christ, but even this rebellious rejection will be rejected and reversed by "the divine election of grace."[156] Indeed, the announcement of the impos-sibility of this choice of rejecting God and his election in Jesus Christ is the gospel of the church for man: "It testifies to him, in opposition to his own choice, the gracious choice of God in Jesus Christ as the beginning of all God's ways and works, and therefore the futility of his own desire and undertaking.... He cannot reverse or change the eternal decision of God — by which he regards, considers and wills man, not in his isolation over against him, but in his Son Jesus."[157] Thus, God's election of grace of all people means ultimately that each person — even the one who persists in his rejection of Jesus Christ — will be saved. As Barth noted in regard to the persistently rebellious person, "the divine pre-decision, by which he is elected and not rejected, never has been or is or will be inef-

148. Ibid., 116.
149. Ibid., 117.
150. Ibid., 122–24.
151. Ibid., 195–96.
152. Ibid., 198.

153. Ibid., 198–99.
154. Ibid., 309–10.
155. Ibid., 315.
156. Ibid., 316.
157. Ibid., 316–17.

fective.... In Jesus Christ his rejection, too, is rejected, and his election consummated."[158] For this reason, Barth was charged with embracing universalism, which he attempted to deny by appeal to God's ultimate freedom.

Despite the creative proposal of Barth, most evangelicals lined up along the traditional lines of either the Calvinist/Reformed or Arminian/Wesleyan views of predestination. For example, Jack Cottrell affirmed conditional election based on divine foreknowledge: "Through his foreknowledge God sees who will believe upon Jesus Christ as Savior and Lord, and become united with him in Christian baptism; then even before the creation of the world he predestines these believers to share the glory of the risen Christ."[159] J. Rodman Williams dissented from this position, reasoning that if "one misapprehends foreknowledge by viewing it as the foreseeing of faith, the result will be that of exaggerating human freedom."[160] Similarly, appealing to Romans 8:29, Wayne Grudem spoke out against this common view of conditional election: "This verse can hardly be used to demonstrate that God based his predestination on foreknowledge of *the fact that a person would believe.* The passage speaks rather of the fact that God knew *persons* ('*those whom* he foreknew'), not that he knew some *fact about them*, such as the fact that they would believe. It is a personal, relational knowledge that is spoken of here."[161] Citing other passages (Rom. 9:11–13; 11:5–6; Eph. 1:5–6; 2 Tim. 1:9) that address the reason for divine election, Grudem noted that "Scripture never speaks of our faith or the fact that we would come to believe in Christ as the reason God chose us."[162] Rather, the reasons given in Scripture include the divine purpose, will, grace, and love.[163] This election, then, "is 'unconditional' because it is not *conditioned upon* anything that God sees in us that makes us worthy of his choosing us."[164]

Most Christians, then, fell into one or the other camp on the issue of predestination. As important as the debate was between proponents of unconditional election and advocates of conditional election, the divine work of electing sinful people for salvation continued to be underscored. As Dietrich Ritschl emphasized, the reality of divine election as revealed in Scripture was "the most radical theological statement" ever imagined and constituted "the strongest of all thinkable counterstatements to the postulate of the senselessness of the world and the godlessness of humanity."[165]

---

158. Ibid., II/2, 322.

159. Jack W. Cottrell, "Conditional Election," in *Grace Unlimited*, ed. Clark H. Pinnock (Minneapolis: Bethany, 1975), 62.

160. J. Rodman Williams, *Renewal Theology*, 3 vols. in 1 (Grand Rapids: Zondervan, 1996), 2:22.

161. Grudem, *Systematic Theology*, 676.

162. Ibid., 677.

163. Ibid., 677–78.

164. Ibid., 679. Interestingly, while Grudem and Williams agreed about election, they disagreed about reprobation. Williams firmly denied a divine decree to reprobation. According to Williams, "There is *no* predestination to death. God's purpose is never destruction." Williams, *Renewal Theology*, 2:20. But Grudem just as strongly, yet also circumspectly, affirmed

the doctrine, pointing to Jude 4; Rom. 9:17–22; 11:7; and 1 Peter 2:8: "In many ways the doctrine of reprobation is the most difficult of all the teachings of Scripture for us to think about and to accept, because it deals with such horrible and eternal consequences for human beings made in the image of God.... It is something that we would not want to believe, and would not believe, unless Scripture clearly taught it." Grudem, *Systematic Theology*, 685.

165. Dietrich Ritschl, *Zur Logik der Theologie: Kurze Darstellung der Zusammenhänge Theologischer Grundgedanken* (Munich: Kaiser, 1988), 163, cited in Christian Link, "Election and Reprobation," in *John Calvin's Impact on Church and Society, 1509–2009*, ed. Martin Ernst Hirzel and Martin Sallmann (Grand Rapids: Eerdmans, 2009), 105.

Chapter 22

REGENERATION, CONVERSION, AND EFFECTIVE CALLING

How has the church come to understand what it means to be born again and how people respond to the gospel through faith and repentance? How has the church understood the gospel message and how it becomes effective?

STATEMENT OF BELIEF

The church historically has acknowledged that the proclamation of the death and resurrection of Jesus Christ—the gospel (1 Cor. 15:1–8)—is the one and only message by which sinful human beings may experience salvation. It is this gospel call that is the first step and foundational reality for the application of salvation in the lives of those who will become Christians. Another aspect of the application of salvation is the divine work of regeneration, "a secret act of God in which he imparts new spiritual life to us. This is sometimes called 'being born again' (using language from John 3:3–8)."[1] Linked to regeneration is the human act of conversion, "our willing response to the gospel call, in which we sincerely repent of sins and place our trust in Christ for salvation."[2]

From its outset, the church has associated regeneration and conversion with the preaching of the gospel, the mysterious work of the Holy Spirit (the effective call), repentance, faith, and baptism. But how these activities are related to one another in the process of salvation has become and continues to be a contested issue. The Roman Catholic Church insists on baptismal regeneration; that is, water baptism is the means of grace by which the new birth is effectively accomplished for those being baptized.

---

1. Wayne Grudem, *Systematic Theology: An Introduction to Biblical Doctrine* (Grand Rapids: Zondervan, 1994, 2000), 699.
2. Ibid., 709.

Thus, the gospel, regeneration, and faith are necessarily tied in with this sacrament. Protestant churches deny baptismal regeneration but nonetheless insist on the necessity of both regeneration and conversion, involving repentance and faith. In addition, many Protestants acknowledge not only a call to salvation that is extended to everyone who hears the gospel, but also an effective call that summons those who will become Christians to salvation. Some believe that regeneration precedes (logically, not temporally) conversion, while others reverse the order. Evangelicals follow Protestant theology in these areas but demonstrate a remarkable diversity of opinions on the relationship between the gospel, the effective call, regeneration, conversion, faith, repentance, and baptism.[3]

REGENERATION, CONVERSION, AND CALLING IN THE EARLY CHURCH

Jesus' dialogue with Nicodemus presented the necessity of regeneration for salvation (John 3:3–8). This new birth comes about through the Holy Spirit's personal agency and the instrumentality of the Word of God (1 Peter 1:23–25; James 1:18). As the disciples proclaimed this Word, they called for people to convert (Acts 3:19–20), which entailed both repentance (Luke 24:46–48) and faith in Christ (Acts 16:30–33). The powerful work of God in calling people to salvation is an essential aspect of this (Rom. 8:28–30) and comes through the gospel (2 Thess. 2:13–14).

Church leaders following the apostles continued this emphasis on regeneration and conversion (with minimal attention to calling) as part of the divine work of salvation. Cyprian emphasized that regeneration was completely a work of God: "The new man is born again and restored to his God by his grace."[4] Barnabas associated this regeneration with faith, divine revelation, and repentance: "By receiving the forgiveness of sins and setting our hope on the name, we became new, created again from the beginning. Consequently, God truly dwells in our dwelling-place—that is, in us. How? The word of his faith, the call of his promise, the wisdom of his righteous decrees, the commandments of his teaching, he himself prophesying in us, he himself dwelling in us.... Granting to us repentance, he leads us into the incorruptible temple."[5]

As for the role of faith in God's work of bringing salvation to people, Clement of Alexandria commented on 1 John 2:29: "John says, 'Everyone who does righteousness is born of God'—being regenerated, that is, according to faith."[6] This faith is a gift from God: "Such a change from unbelief to faith—and to trust in hope and fear—is divine. And truly we discover that faith is the first movement towards salvation."[7] Furthermore, this faith is rooted in Christ's words: "Faith is, so to speak, a comprehensive knowledge of the

---

3. My thanks to Tyler Gordon for his help with this chapter. Because I discuss baptism in a separate chapter, I will address that matter here only as it directly relates to the other doctrines of regeneration, conversion, and calling. But it is not possible to remove the discussion of baptism from these other topics, because all of them have been intimately associated throughout the history of the church.

4. Cyprian, *Treatise* 4.9, in *ANF*, 5:449.

5. *Letter of Barnabas*, 16.7–9, in Holmes, 291; *ANF*, 1:319.

6. Clement of Alexandria, *Fragments from Cassiodorus*, "Comments on the First Epistle of John," 2:29, in *ANF*, 2:576.

7. Clement of Alexandria, *Stromata*, 2.6, in *ANF*, 2:354.

essentials. And knowledge is the strong and sure demonstration of what is received by faith, built upon faith by the Lord's teaching."[8]

As for the role of repentance, Tertullian explained the meaning of the word itself: "In Greek, the word for 'repentance' (*metanoia*) is formed, not from the confession of sin, but from a change of mind."[9] He emphasized the necessity of repentance for "amendment" of life, or conversion: "Where there is no fear [of God], in like manner there is no amendment. Where there is no amendment, repentance is of necessity vain. For it lacks the fruit for which God sowed it — that is, man's salvation."[10] Repentance entails the acknowledgment that one has committed grievous acts against God, followed by a change of life, as Origen explained: "Those who have passed severe condemnation upon themselves because of their sins, and who — as on that account — lament and bewail themselves as lost — so far as their previous conduct is concerned — and who have manifested a satisfactory change, are received by God on account of their repentance."[11] For Clement of Alexandria, this meant "repentance is an effect of faith. For unless a man believes that to which he was addicted is sin, he will not abandon it. And if he does not believe that punishment looms over the transgressor, and that salvation belongs to the one who lives according to the commandments, he will not reform."[12] In a biblical theology of repentance, Cyprian listed nearly four dozen passages to demonstrate "that all sins may be forgiven him who has turned to God with his whole heart."[13]

The notion that the new birth brings a radical reformation of life was a continuous theme in the church: "All that is dead or weak in her [the soul] has been taken away."[14] Clement of Alexandria added simply: "He that repents of what he did no longer does or says as he did.... He who has received the forgiveness of sins ought to sin no more."[15] Cyprian associated this change with the Holy Spirit: "By the agency of the Spirit breathed from heaven, a second birth had restored me to a new man."[16] Of course, this radical transformation of life provoked amazement among those both outside and inside the church. Tertullian noted, "Some persons wonder that those whom they had known to be unsteady, worthless, or wicked before they bore this name [of Christian] have been suddenly converted to virtuous courses."[17] And Origen stated, "The multitude of the church is astonished at beholding transformations which have taken place from so great evils to that which is better."[18]

Some of these converts to Christianity recounted their testimonies. For example, Justin Martyr emphasized that, as one who had thoroughly studied philosophy, he discovered Christianity to be his only satisfaction: "Immediately a flame was kindled in my soul, and a love for the prophets, and of those men who are friends of Christ, possessed me. And while revolving [pondering] his words in my mind, I found this philosophy alone to be

8. Ibid., 7.10, in *ANF*, 2:539.

9. Tertullian, *Against Marcion*, 2.24, in *ANF*, 3:316.

10. Tertullian, *On Repentance*, 39–40, in *ANF*, 3:657.

11. Origen, *Against Celsus*, 3.71, in *ANF*, 4:492.

12. Clement of Alexandria, *Stromata*, 2.6, in *ANF*, 2:353.

13. Cyprian, *Exhortation to Repentance*, in *ANF*, 5:592–95. Scholars are not sure that Cyprian was the author of this treatise. His biblical references are from the Psalms, Isaiah, Jeremiah, Lamentations, Ezekiel, Daniel, Micah, Zephaniah, Zechariah, Hosea, Ecclesiasticus (the Apocryphal book), Acts, 2 Corinthians, 2 Timothy, and Revelation.

14. Origen, *Commentary on the Gospel of John*, 2.12, in *ANF*, 9:334.

15. Clement of Alexandria, *Stromata*, 2.12, in *ANF*, 2:360.

16. Cyprian, *Letter* 1.4, in *ANF*, 5:276.

17. Tertullian, *To the Nations*, 1.4, in *ANF*, 3:112.

18. Origen, *Commentary on Matthew*, 11.18, in *ANF*, 9:447.

safe and profitable."[19] Tatian's conversion was prompted by a study in which he contrasted the contradictory and unethical writings of the ancient Greeks and Romans with

> certain "barbaric" writings [Scripture], too old to be compared with the opinions of the Greeks and too divine to be compared with their errors. I was led to put faith in these by the unpretentious nature of the language, the authentic character of the writers, the foreknowledge displayed of future events, the excellent quality of the precepts, and the declaration of the government of the universe as centered in one Being. As my soul was being taught by God, I discerned that the former class of writings leads to condemnation, but that these put an end to the slavery that is in the world and rescue us from a multiplicity of rulers and ten thousand tyrants.[20]

Prophetic Scripture played the decisive role in the conversion of Theophilus: "I met with the sacred Scriptures of the holy prophets, who also by the Spirit of God foretold the things that have already happened, just as they came to pass, and the things now occurring as they are now happening, and things future in the order in which they will be accomplished. Admitting, therefore, the proof which events happening as predicted afford, I do not disbelieve, but I believe, obedient to God."[21] Cyprian's conversion was marked by his baptism. He related how difficult the concept of conversion was for him to grasp,[22] and how baptism clarified the idea: "By the help of the water of new birth, the stain of former years had been washed away, and a light from above, serene and pure, had been infused into my reconciled heart—after that, by the agency of the Spirit breathed from heaven, a second birth had restored me to a new man."[23]

A very important development in the early church, strengthened by Cyprian, was the belief that baptism regenerates, or brings the new birth. This baptismal regeneration eventually became closely associated with infant baptism. (Because this development is thoroughly recounted in chapter 28, it will not be repeated here.) A chief architect of this theology was Augustine, but his own conversion was as dissimilar to this theological position as can be imagined. Although his godly mother, Monica, prayed for her son to turn to Christ, Augustine became deeply embedded in sexual sin. Following the heresy of Manichaeism for a period of time, then studying the philosophy of neo-Platonism, Augustine eventually met Ambrose, the bishop of Milan, and became intrigued by this preacher's allegorical interpretation of the Old Testament. Finally, one of the most widely known conversions in the history of the church took place. Augustine was converted from his sexually immoral lifestyle and became a theologian and leader of the church.

Augustine's Account of His Conversion, in His *Confessions* to God

I flung myself down somehow under a certain fig-tree and gave free rein to the tears that burst from my eyes like rivers, as an acceptable sacrifice to you. Many things I had to say to you, and the gist of them, though not the precise words,

---

19. Justin Martyr, *Dialogue with Trypho, a Jew*, 8, in *ANF*, 1:198.

20. Tatian, *Address to the Greeks*, 29, in *ANF*, 2:77. The text has been rendered clearer.

21. Theophilus, *To Autolycus*, 1.14, in *ANF*, 2:93.

22. Cyprian, *Letter* 1.3, in *ANF*, 5:275.

23. Cyprian, *Letter* 1.4, in *ANF*, 5:276.

was, "O Lord, how long? How long? Will you be angry forever? Do not remember our age-old sins" [Pss. 6:3; 79:5, 8]. For by these I was conscious of being held prisoner. I uttered cries of misery: "Why must I go on saying, 'Tomorrow … tomorrow?' Why not now? Why not put an end to my depravity this very hour?"

I went on talking like this and weeping in the intense bitterness of my broken heart. Suddenly I heard a voice from a house nearby—perhaps a voice of some boy or girl, I do not know—singing over and over again, "Pick it up and read, pick it up and read." My expression immediately altered, and I began to think hard whether children ordinarily repeated a ditty like this in any sort of game, but I could not recall ever having heard it anywhere else. I stemmed the flood of tears and rose to my feet, believing that this could be nothing other than a divine command to open the Book and read the first passage I chanced upon; for I had heard the story of how Antony had been instructed by a gospel text. He happened to arrive while the gospel was being read, and took the words to be addressed to himself when he heard, *Go and sell all you possess and give the money to the poor: you will have treasure in heaven. Then come, follow me.* So he was promptly converted to you by this plainly divine message. Stung into action, I returned to the place where Alypius [Augustine's friend] was sitting, for on leaving it I had put down there the book of the apostle's [Paul's] letters. I snatched it up, opened it and read in silence the passage on which my eyes first lighted: *Not in dissipation and drunkenness, nor in debauchery and lewdness, nor in arguing and jealousy; but put on the Lord Jesus Christ, and make no provision for the flesh or the gratification of your desires* [Rom. 13:13–14]. I had no wish to read further, nor was there need. No sooner had I reached the end of the verse than the light of certainty flooded my heart and all dark shades of doubt fled away.*

*Augustine, *Confessions*, 8.12 (28–29), in John E. Rotelle, *The Confessions*, The Works of Saint Augustine: A Translation for the 21st Century, pt. 1, vol. 1 (Hyde Park, N.Y.: New City Press, 1997), 206–7. Cf. *NPNF*[1], 1:127–28. Augustine referred to the *Life of St. Antony*, written by Athanasius, specifically the section in which Antony's call to ministry was recounted. Antony had entered into a church and heard the reading of Jesus' challenge to the rich young ruler (Matt. 19:21). He took this to be God's call to ministry.

By means of his doctrine of predestination, Augustine introduced another idea into this discussion. Given that God has chosen certain people for salvation, they will certainly respond with repentance and faith to the message of salvation by means of a special grace: "This grace by which strength is perfected in weakness conducts all who are predestined and called according to the divine purpose to the state of the highest perfection and glory. By such grace it is effected, not only that we discover what ought to be done, but also that we do what we have discovered; not only that we believe what ought to be loved, but also that we love what we have believed."[24] Specifically, Augustine posited two

24. Augustine, *On the Grace of Christ, and On Original Sin*, 1.12[11], in *NPNF*[1], 5:222. His statement echoes parts of Rom. 8:28–30 and 2 Cor. 12:9.

calls—one that goes out to all people indiscriminately and does not result in salvation, and a second call that goes out only to the elect and that does result in their salvation with guarantee: "God calls many predestined children of his, to make them members of his only predestined Son, not with the calling with which they [others] were called who would not come.... [We know] that there is a certain sure calling of those who are called according to God's purpose, whom he has foreknown and predestined before to be conformed to the image of his Son.... [This is] not any sort of calling whatever, but that calling with which a man is made a believer."[25]

Augustine emphasized the effectiveness of the divine call and its assisting grace so that the elect come to Christ:

> Who can fail to see that a man's coming or not coming is by the determination of his will? This determination, however, may stand alone, if the man does not come; but if he does come, it cannot be without assistance, and such assistance that he not only knows what it is he ought to do, but also actually does what he thus knows.... [God] so teaches [by the grace of the Spirit] that whatever a man learns, he not only sees with his perception, but also desires with his choice and accomplishes in action.[26]

Accordingly, "Everyone who has learned of the Father not only has the possibility of coming, but comes; and in this result are already included the motion of the capacity, the affection of the will, and the effect of the action."[27]

In all this discussion, Augustine stood opposed to the view of human free will and divine grace as put forth by Pelagius. According to Pelagius, God created all human beings with the power to act; it now depends on them to will and to engage in the action. Indeed, in his grace, God provided people with free will, including the capacity not to sin.[28] Moreover, this absolute free will to choose what is right—or to choose what is wrong—is the very essence of human dignity and the basis for rewarding the choice to do good and punishing the choice to do evil: "For there would be no virtue for those who always remain good if they had not been able to choose evil. God wished to present to the rational creature the gift of voluntary goodness and the power of free will. So he planted in human beings the possibility of turning itself toward either side."[29] Furthermore, people do not have any internal tendency to sin; people are not inclined in any way toward doing evil. Pelagius held that God creates every human soul (the doctrine of creationism), meaning that no one is born with a corrupt nature inherited from Adam.[30] Also, humanity certainly does not bear any guilt for Adam's sin, because no one can be held morally accountable for what another person does. For Pelagius, the conclusion of

25. Augustine, *On the Predestination of the Saints*, 32, in *NPNF*[1], 5:513. The text has been rendered clearer.

26. Augustine, *On the Grace of Christ, and On Original Sin*, 1.15[14], in *NPNF*[1], 5:223. Augustine worked from the key text of John 6:45.

27. Ibid. For a similar treatment, see *On the Predestination of the Saints*, 13[8]–14, in *NPNF*[1], 5:504–5.

28. Augustine, *On the Proceedings of Pelagius*, 22.10, in *NPNF*[1], 5:193.

29. Pelagius, *Letter to Demetrias*, in *A Cloud of Witnesses: Readings in the History of Western Christianity*, ed. Joel F. Harrington (Boston and New York: Houghton Mifflin, 2001), 100.

30. Augustine, *On Original Sin*, 2.14, in *NPNF*[1], 5:241.

this was that believers helped by God's grace could live without sin.[31] This position was far removed from the church's traditional understanding of original sin; the need for regeneration, faith, repentance, and baptism; and Augustine's insistence on divine election and the necessity of grace. The church, through Augustine's influence, condemned Pelagius and his views.

As noted already, Augustine made a distinction between a general call—which is extended to all people through the message of the gospel—and a particular call—which is extended only to the elect and ensures their response for salvation. In doing so, Augustine anticipated and provided the foundation for a very important development, the fruit of which would not be seen until the Reformation. At that point, the effective call of God would become an important topic situated in the discussion of regeneration and conversion, repentance and faith. But until then, infant baptism—with its power to regenerate—was the official rite of the church.[32]

REGENERATION, CONVERSION, AND CALLING IN THE MIDDLE AGES

The emphasis on infant baptism for regeneration and salvation should not be taken to mean that the church restricted its efforts to expand only to children of professing Christians. Major missionary efforts like Gregory the Great's commissioning of Augustine (not the one discussed above) and almost forty monks to evangelize King Ethelbert of Kent (modern-day England) and Irish monastic missions—to name only two—sought to convert the heathen populace. Some of these efforts were enormously successful and included mass conversions to Christianity. This concept of mass movement to Christ is vividly presented in the account of the conversion of the heathen king of the Franks. Clovis was married to Clotilde, a Christian princess who repeatedly urged her husband to forsake his worthless gods and turn to Christ. As forcefully as Clotilde pressed him to convert, Clovis resisted, until he and his troops met their military match in the army of the Alemanni. Threatened with destruction, Clovis prayed fervently:

> Jesus Christ, whom Clotilde declares to be the son of the living God, who it is said gives aid to the oppressed and victory to those who put their hope in you, I beg the glory of your aid. If you should grant me victory over these enemies and I test which power that people consecrated to your name say they have proved concerning you, I will believe in you and be baptized in your name. For I have called upon my gods, but as I have proved, they are far removed from my aid. So I believe that they have no power, for they do not help those who serve them.

---

31. Augustine, *On the Proceedings of Pelagius*, 20, in *NPNF*[1], 5:191.

32. As expressed by the Council of Carthage in 417: "If anyone says that newborn children do not need to be baptized, or that they are baptized for the forgiveness of sins, but that no original sin is derived from Adam to be washed away in the laver of regeneration—so that in their case the baptismal formula 'for the forgiveness of sins' is to be taken in a fictitious and not in its true sense—let him be anathema (condemned to hell)." The Council of Carthage, canon 2, in Bettenson, 59. The text has been rendered clearer.

Now I call upon you, and long to believe in you—all the more that I may escape my enemies.[33]

As can be anticipated, the Alemanni miraculously began to flee from the battle, and Clovis and his army were victorious. Clovis maintained his promise to Christ and was baptized along with more than three thousand of his soldiers.

The Conversion of Clovis

The queen sent to the blessed Remigius, bishop of the city of Rheims, begging him to bring to the king the gospel of salvation. The priest, little by little and secretly, led Clovis to believe in the true God, maker of heaven and earth, and to forsake idols, which could not help him nor anybody else. But the king said, "Willingly I will hear you, father; but one thing is in the way—that the people who follow me are not content to leave their gods. I will go and speak to them according to your word." When he came among them, the power of God went before him, and before he had spoken all the people cried out together, "We cast off mortal gods, righteous king, and we are ready to follow the God whom Remigius tells us is immortal." These things were told to the bishop. He was filled with joy and ordered the [baptismal] font to be prepared. Of Clovis's army there were baptized more than three thousand.*

*Ecclesiastical History of France, 2.27–31, in Petry, 202–3. The text has been rendered clearer.

In another miraculous account, some Saxon pagans were converted as a result of a power encounter between the true God and the Saxon god Thor.

Many of the people of Hesse were converted [by Boniface] to the Catholic faith.... [Some] cast aside all heathen profanation ... and it was with the advice and consent of these men that Boniface sought to fell [cut down] a certain tree of great size at Geismar and called, in the ancient speech of the region, the oak of Jove [i.e., Thor]. The man of God was surrounded by the servants of God. When he would cut down the tree, a great mob of pagans who were there cursed him bitterly among themselves because he was the enemy of their gods. And when he had cut into the trunk a little way, a breeze sent by God stirred overhead, and suddenly the branching top of the tree was broken off, and the oak in all its huge bulk fell to the ground. And it was broken into four parts, as if by the divine will, so that the trunk was divided into four huge sections without any effort of the brothers who stood by. When the pagans who had cursed saw this, they stopped cursing and, believing, blessed God.[34]

---

33. *Ecclesiastical History of France*, 2.27–31, in Petry, 202. The text has been rendered clearer.

34. Willibald, *Life of Boniface*, 6, in Petry, 205–6. The text has been rendered clearer.

Through these miraculous conversions of the heathens, and in many other ways, the medieval church expanded. Still, the theology and practice of the church identified baptism with regeneration. Although this baptismal regeneration was for adults in areas previously untouched by the message of Christ, wherever the church became established, the baptism of infants became the norm.

Theologically, the medieval church debated the merits of Augustine's doctrine of salvation, particularly as it addressed the issue of how the human will is related to the grace of God. John Cassian expressed the central issue in the following set of questions: "Does God have compassion on us because we have shown the beginning of a good will? Or does the beginning of a good will follow because God has had compassion on us? Many people, believing each of these and asserting them more strongly than is right, become entangled in all kinds of contradictions." Noting contrasting biblical examples, Cassian underscored the problem with both extreme positions: "For if we say that the beginning of free will is in our own power, what about Paul the persecutor and Matthew the tax collector? The first was drawn to salvation while eager for bloodshed and the punishment of the innocent, and the second while ready for violence and rape! But if we say that the beginning of our free will is always due to the inspiration of the grace of God, what about the faith of Zacchaeus or the goodness of the thief on the cross?"[35] Accordingly, Cassian insisted on both human free will and the necessity of divine grace. Against Augustine, he denied that the human will beset by sin is only capable of doing evil.[36] Yet Cassian also insisted on the movement of God's grace to assist the will: "So great is the Creator's kindness toward his creatures that his providence not only accompanies it but actually constantly precedes it. This is what the prophet experienced and clearly affirmed: 'My God will go before me with his mercy' (Psa. 59:9). When he sees in us some beginnings of a good will, he immediately enlightens it and strengthens it and urges it on toward salvation. He increases that which he himself implanted or which he sees has arisen from our own efforts."[37]

Accordingly, in some cases—for example, Paul and Matthew—God gives people a good will that, assisted by his grace, does good. In other cases—for example, Zacchaeus and the thief on the cross—the good will is already present and then is assisted by God's grace. So Cassian concluded that "these two then—the grace of God and free will—seem opposed to each other but really are in harmony, and we gather from the system of goodness that we ought to have both of them.... For when God sees us inclined to will what is good, he meets, guides and strengthens us.... Again, if he finds that we are unwilling or have grown cold, he stirs our hearts with healing encouragement, by which

35. John Cassian, *The Third Conference of Abbot Chaeremon*, 11, in *NPNF*[2], 11:427–28. The text has been rendered clearer.

36. "We should not hold that God made man such that he can never will or be capable of what is good. Otherwise, he has not granted him a free will, if he has allowed him only to will or be capable of evil, but not to will or be capable of what is good by himself." Ibid., 12, in *NPNF*[2], 11:428.

37. Ibid., 8, in *NPNF*[2], 11:426. The text has been rendered

clearer. The quotation from Ps. 59:9 introduced a key term into the discussion, as will be seen later. In Latin, the word translated "go before" is *praevenire*. Relying on this word, Augustine coined a type of grace—*prevenient grace*—that is God's goodness to sinners even before they come to salvation. Cassian agreed with this kind of grace and used it in his discussion to emphasize the necessity and reality of grace to act on the human will.

a good will is either renewed or formed in us."[38] In all cases, however, the human will is good enough so as to cooperate with God's grace: "It cannot be doubted that there are by nature some seeds of goodness in every soul implanted by the kindness of the Creator, but unless these are quickened by the assistance of God, they will not be able to attain to an increase of perfection."[39] Thus, Cassian ascribed a key, though minor, role to the will in salvation.[40] Although terms such as regeneration and conversion were not featured in his discussion, his view that salvation is a synergistic work—a cooperation between divine grace and human free will—would influence both the Roman Catholic Church and some expressions of Protestantism in the centuries to follow.

REGENERATION, CONVERSION, AND CALLING IN THE REFORMATION AND POST-REFORMATION

One of the most significant conversions in the history of the church was that of Martin Luther. As an Augustinian monk, he was disturbed by the phrase "the justice of God" in Romans 1:17; indeed, the idea struck terror in his soul, and his many attempts to please and satisfy God through prayers, vigils, good works, confession, and the like left him with a tormented conscience: "I did not love, indeed I hated, that God who punished sinners; and with a monstrous, silent, if not blasphemous, murmuring I fumed against God." Then, over time and through a study of Scripture, particularly Romans, Luther came to understand the precise nature of the meaning of the phrase "the justice of God" and was converted. As the founder of the Protestant Reformation, Luther worked through such doctrines as regeneration and conversion.

The Conversion of Martin Luther

I greatly longed to understand Paul's *Epistle to the Romans*, and nothing stood in the way but that one expression "the justice of God," because I took it to mean that justice whereby God is just and deals justly in punishing the unjust. My situation was that, although an impeccable monk, I stood before God as a sinner troubled in conscience, and I had no confidence that my merit would assuage him. Therefore, I did not love a just and angry God, but rather hated and murmured against him. Yet I clung to the dear Paul and had a great yearning to know what he meant. Night and day I pondered until I saw the connection between the justice of God and the statement that "the just shall live by his faith." Then I grasped that the justice of God is that righteousness by which through grace and sheer mercy God justifies us through faith. Thereupon I felt myself to be reborn and to have gone through open doors into paradise. The whole of Scripture took on a new meaning, and whereas before the "justice

---

38. Ibid., 11, in *NPNF*[2], 11:427–28. The text has been rendered clearer.

39. Ibid., 12, in *NPNF*[2], 11:428.

40. "The main share in our salvation is to be ascribed not to the merit of our own works but to heavenly grace." Ibid., 18, in *NPNF*[2], 11:434.

of God" had filled me with hate, now it became to me inexpressibly sweet in greater love. This passage of Paul became to me a gate to heaven.*

*Martin Luther, *Preface to the Complete Edition of Luther's Latin Writings* (1945), cited in Roland H. Bainton, *Here I Stand: A Life of Martin Luther* (New York and Scarborough, Ontario: Mentor, 1977), 49–50; LW, 34:336–37.

As those who for centuries before him did, Luther continued to link regeneration with baptism. Although his concept of baptism was significantly different from that of Roman Catholicism — "baptism is not common water only, but it is water comprehended in God's command, and connected with God's Word"[41] — he still practiced infant baptism and still viewed it as regenerating infants. Expanding on this definition of baptism, Luther explained that it is not the water that works forgiveness of sins, delivers from death and the devil, and gives eternal salvation to all who believe, "but the Word of God which is with and in the water, and faith which trusts in the Word of God in the water. For without the Word of God, the water is nothing but water and no baptism. But with the Word of God, it is a baptism, that is, a gracious water of life and a washing of regeneration in the Holy Spirit."[42] Baptism was to be administered to infants so that it would accomplish its great work in their lives.

At the same time, Luther linked regeneration with saving faith; indeed, he emphasized that apart from faith in Christ through his Word, regeneration does not take place. He defined faith as "a divine work in us which changes us and makes us to be born anew of God, John 1[:12-13]. It kills the old Adam and makes us altogether different men, in heart and spirit and mind and powers; and it brings with it the Holy Spirit. O it is a living, busy, active, mighty thing, this faith."[43] For Luther, faith is a gift of divine grace: "Faith, the work of the Holy Spirit, fashions a different mind and different attitudes, and makes an altogether new human being. Therefore, faith is an active, difficult, and powerful thing. If we want truly to consider what it really is, it is something done to us rather than something that we do; for it changes the heart and the mind."[44] Specifically, faith "is a work of God, not of man, as Paul teaches [Eph. 2:8]. The other works he [God] works through us and with our help, but this one alone he works in us and without our help."[45]

Furthermore, conversion involves awareness of sin before God does his unilateral work. Indeed, Luther insisted: "It is necessary, if you would be converted, that you become terrified, that is, that you have an alarmed and trembling conscience. Then, after this condition has been created, you must grasp the consolation that comes not from any work of your own, but from the work of God. He sent his Son Jesus Christ into this world in order to proclaim to terrified sinners the mercy of God. This is the way conversion is brought about; other ways are wrong ways." Then this graciously given faith and the regenerating work of God radically alters the person who is saved by it for good works:

---

41. Martin Luther, *Small Catechism*, 1, in Schaff, 3:85.

42. Luther's reference was to Titus 3:5. Ibid., 3, in Schaff, 3:86.

43. Martin Luther, *Prefaces to the New Testament*, LW, 35:370.

44. *Lectures on Genesis: Chapters 6-19*, LW, 2:267.

45. *The Babylonian Captivity of the Church*, LW, 36:62.

The real faith, of which we are speaking, cannot be brought into being by our own thoughts. On the contrary, it is entirely God's work in us, without any cooperation on our part.... Therefore it also is a very mighty, active, restless, busy thing, which at once renews a man, gives him second birth, and introduces him to a new manner and way of life, so that it is impossible for him not to do good without ceasing. For as naturally as a tree bears fruit, good works follow upon faith.[46]

With words echoing what was just stated about faith, Luther addressed the sacrament of baptism: "Man is not born again of his own choice and idea; but a new birth must take place through holy baptism without man's contributing anything. The Holy Spirit is bestowed through the divine will and grace by means of the externally preached Word and the water. These are the father and the mother of this new birth, through which man becomes new, pure, and holy before God, an heir of the kingdom of heaven."[47] Furthermore, Luther held that baptism includes "repentance, which is really nothing else than baptism."[48] Repentance, therefore, is part and parcel of baptism. Thus, faith, a terror-stricken conscience, repentance, and regeneration leading to reformation of life — together with baptism — were inextricably linked in Luther.

Luther also affirmed a distinction between an outward call to salvation that goes to all people and an inward call that goes to people who actually experience salvation through Christ. His discussion of this was placed in the context of his debate about the freedom or the bondage of the will. Given the fact that all people are sinful, Luther maintained that their wills are completely bound by sin and not free to embrace the gospel. Referring to Christ's words in John 6:44, Luther explained: "What he is talking about is your 'power whereby man can make some endeavor towards Christ'. In things that pertain to salvation, he asserts that power to be null."[49] Accordingly, the only hope for this desperate situation is for God himself to inwardly draw sinners to himself: "But the ungodly does not 'come,' even when he hears the word, unless the Father draws and teaches him inwardly; which he does by shedding abroad his Spirit. When that happens, there follows a 'drawing' other than that which is outward; Christ is then displayed by the enlightening of the Spirit, and by it man is rapt to Christ with the sweetest rapture, he being passive while God speaks, teaches and draws, rather than seeking or running himself."[50]

John Calvin developed the Reformed doctrines of regeneration and conversion. Like Luther, he emphasized the necessary work of the Holy Spirit in drawing spiritually dead sinners to Christ through the Word of God:

---

46. Martin Luther, *WLS*, 1.475.

47. Ibid., 1:344.

48. Martin Luther, *Larger Catechism*, 4.74, trans. F. Bente and W. H. T. Dau, in *Triglot Concordia: The Symbolical Books of the Evangelical Lutheran Church* (St. Louis: Concordia, 1921), 751. In this context, Luther linked baptism with the third sacrament of the Roman Catholic Church, namely, penance. In his *Ninety-five Theses*, Luther distanced himself from the Roman Catholic notion of penance. In his first two theses,

Luther noted: "1. Our Lord and master Jesus Christ, in saying 'Repent' [Matt. 4:17], meant the whole life of the faithful to be an act of repentance. 2. This saying cannot be understood of the sacrament of penance ... which is administered by the priesthood." Bettenson, 206.

49. Martin Luther, *The Bondage of the Will*, trans. James I. Packer and O. R. Johnston (Old Tappen, N.J.: Revell, 1957), 311. Cf. LCC, 33:284.

50. Ibid. Cf. LCC, 33:285.

As we cannot come to Christ unless we are drawn by the Spirit, so when we are drawn we are lifted up in mind and heart above our understanding. For the soul, illumined by him, takes on a new keenness, as it were, to contemplate the heavenly mysteries, whose splendor had previously blinded it. And man's understanding, thus beamed by the light of Holy Spirit, then at last begins to taste those things which belong to the kingdom of God, having formerly been quite foolish and dull in tasting them.... Accordingly, it [the Word] cannot penetrate into our minds unless the Spirit, as the inner teacher, through his illumination makes entry for it.[51]

This illumination by the Spirit affects the cognitive powers of the convert, but the work of the Spirit also includes his confirmation, which affects the heart of the person:

It now remains to pour into the heart itself what the mind has absorbed. For the Word of God is not received by faith if it flits about in the top of the brain, but when it takes root in the depth of the heart that it may be an invincible defense to withstand and drive off all the stratagems [strategies] of temptation. But if it is true that the mind's real understanding is illumination by the Spirit of God, then in such confirmation of the heart his power is much more clearly manifested, to the extent that the heart's distrust is greater than the mind's blindness. It is harder for the heart to be furnished with assurance than for the mind to be endowed with thought. The Spirit accordingly serves as a seal, to seal up in our hearts those very promises, the certainty of which it has previously impressed upon our minds.[52]

Having set forth his doctrine of faith, Calvin insisted that the view "that repentance not only constantly follows faith, but is born of faith, ought to be a fact beyond controversy."[53] He defined repentance as "the true turning of our life to God, a turning that arises from a pure and earnest fear of him; and it consists in the mortification of our flesh and of the old man, and in the vivification of the Spirit."[54] This repentance consists of three elements: a transformation of the soul;[55] fear of God, and especially the divine judgment;[56] and mortification of the flesh and vivification of the spirit.[57] Put simply, this reality is what is known as regeneration, "whose sole end is to restore in us the image of God that had been disfigured and all but obliterated through Adam's transgression."[58] The fruit of such repentance includes "piety toward God, charity toward men, and in the whole of life, holiness and purity."[59] Calvin warned against an overemphasis on external signs of repentance such as fasting and mourning, and called for constant confession of sin. But he also underscored "that repentance is a special gift of God" and that the effectiveness of the gospel call to repentance "depends on the Spirit of regeneration."[60]

51. John Calvin, *Institutes of the Christian Religion*, 3.2.34, LCC, 1:582.

52. Ibid., 3.2.36, LCC, 1:583–84.

53. Ibid., 3.3.1, LCC, 1:593.

54. Ibid., 3.3.5, LCC, 1:597.

55. Ibid., 3.3.6, LCC, 1:598.

56. Ibid., 3.3.7, LCC, 1:599.

57. Ibid., 3.3.8, LCC, 1:600.

58. Ibid., 3.3.9, LCC, 1:601.

59. Ibid., 3.3.16, LCC, 1:609.

60. Ibid., 3.3.21, LCC, 1:615.

It was at this point that Calvin resurrected Augustine's notion of the general call and the effective call to salvation. He explained the latter in terms of a "special grace, which only the elect receive through regeneration. For I do not tarry over those fanatics who babble that grace is equally and indiscriminately distributed."[61] This special grace or effective call is extended to the elect at the same time that the gospel is communicated to both the elect and the wicked.[62] Furthermore, this "grace, which is secretly bestowed on human hearers, is not received by any hard heart. It is given for this purpose: that hardness of heart may first be taken away."[63] So there is both a general call extended to everyone through the gospel, and a particular call extended only to the elect at the same time; specifically, "all are called to repentance and faith by outward preaching; yet, the spirit of repentance and faith is not given to all."[64] Only the elect receive this call, which "consists not only in the preaching of the Word but also in the illumination of the Spirit." The result of this is salvation for the elect, but "a heavier judgment remains upon the wicked because they reject the testimony of God's love. And God also, to show forth his glory, withdraws the effectual working of his Spirit from them. This inner call, then, is a pledge of salvation that cannot deceive us."[65]

Intermixed into this discussion was the doctrine of baptism. Because he continued the tradition of infant baptism, Calvin had to address how that practice relates to regeneration and conversion. Calvin affirmed an unusual work of God to cause regeneration: "Those infants who are to be saved—as some are surely saved from that early age—are previously regenerated by the Lord. For if they bear with them an inborn corruption from their mother's womb, they must be cleansed of it before they can be admitted into God's kingdom, for nothing polluted or defiled may enter there."[66] As for repentance and faith, elements necessary for conversion and to receive baptism, Calvin appealed to the circumcision of Jewish infants: "Since God communicated circumcision to infants as a sacrament of repentance and faith, it does not seem absurd if they are now made participants in baptism. For although infants, at the very moment they were circumcised, did not comprehend with their understanding what that sign meant, they were truly circumcised for the putting to death of their corrupt and defiled nature, a putting to death that they would afterward practice in mature years." He then drew a conclusion about the parallel sign of baptism for infants: "Infants are baptized into future repentance and faith. And even though these have not yet been formed in them, the seed of both lies hidden within them by the secret working of the Spirit."[67] Thus, Calvin offered a way to reconcile infant baptism with the doctrine of regeneration and with the necessity of faith and repentance for conversion.

The Roman Catholic Church denounced these Protestant views of salvation. Mixing together justification, sanctification, regeneration, conversion, and baptism, the Council of Trent asserted this view of salvation: "Justification itself ... is not remission of sins merely, but also the sanctification and renewal of the inward man, through the voluntary

---

61. Ibid., 2.2.6, LCC, 1:262.
62. Ibid., 3.24.1, LCC, 2:965.
63. Ibid.
64. Ibid., 3.22.10, LCC, 2:944.

65. Ibid., 3.24.2, LCC, 2:967.
66. Ibid., 4.16.17, LCC, 2:1340.
67. Ibid., 4.16.20, LCC, 2:1343.

reception of the grace, and of the gifts, by which an unjust man becomes just.... Of this justification, the ... instrumental cause is the sacrament of baptism, which is the sacrament of faith, without which [faith] no man was ever justified."[68] Relying upon the concept of prevenient grace, the council insisted that this salvation is the result of a cooperative effort between God, who supplies grace, and human beings who take advantage of that grace: "They, who by sins were alienated from God, may be disposed through his quickening and assisting grace, to convert themselves to their own justification, by freely assenting to and cooperating with that grace."[69] This cooperation is most clearly seen in the preparatory works—belief in revealed truth, hope, repentance, and purposing to be holy—that adults are to engage in before their baptism.[70] As for infants, the council continued the tradition that baptism brings about their regeneration.[71]

One group of Protestants developed a view of salvation that interrupted this centuries-old link between regeneration and baptism. The Anabaptists repudiated infant baptism, demanding that only those people who could repent of their sins and make a credible profession of faith in Christ could be baptized. In the *Waterland Confession*, a clear distinction and separation between regeneration[72] and baptism was drawn. It declared the origin, instrumentality, and necessity of regeneration: "This regeneration has its rise from God through Christ. The medium or instrument through which it is generated in us is the Holy Spirit with all his fiery virtues, apart from any cooperation of any creature. Here, concerning the regenerate, we affirm that they are born not out of anything whatsoever that the creature does, but from God; and by it we become children of God.... We believe and teach that this regeneration is necessary to salvation."[73] As for the rite of baptism, the *Confession* affirmed: "Holy baptism is an external, visible and evangelical action, in which, according to Christ's precept and the practice of the apostles, for a holy end, are baptized with water in the name of the Father and of the Son and of the Holy Spirit, those who hear, believe and freely receive in a penitent heart the doctrine of the holy gospel. Christ commands such people to be baptized, but by no means infants."[74] This theology unlinking regeneration from baptism and denouncing infant baptism was continued by the Baptists, who believed that "those who do actually profess repentance towards God, faith in and obedience to our Lord Jesus, are the only proper subjects of this ordinance."[75] For Baptists, baptism does not cause regeneration, nor can it be viewed as a

---

68. *Canons and Decrees of the Council of Trent*, 6th session (January 13, 1547), *Decree on Justification*, chap. 7, in Schaff, 2:94–95.

69. Ibid., chap. 5, in Schaff, 2:92.

70. Ibid., chap. 6, in Schaff, 2:93.

71. *Canons and Decrees of the Council of Trent*, 5th session (June 17, 1546), *Decree on Original Sin*, chap. 4, in Schaff, 2:87.

72. "Regeneration is a certain divine quality in the mind of a man truly come to himself, an erection of the image of God in man, a renovation of the mind or soul, a true illumination of the mind with the knowledge of the truth, bringing with it a change of will and of carnal desires and lusts, a sincere mortification of internal wickedness, and of the old man delighting

himself in lust, wickedness and sin. It is, moreover, a vivification that manifests itself in an honest life according to God, in true goodness, justice and holiness. It is a removal of the heart of stone, full of vanity, stolidity, blindness, ignorance, sin and perverse pleasures and, on the contrary, is the gracious gift of the promised heart of flesh, replete with [full of] the law of God, light, sight, wisdom, understanding, virtue and holy desires." *Waterland Confession*, 22, in Lumpkin, 56.

73. Ibid. In support of the necessity of regeneration, appeal was made to John 3:3, 5.

74. Ibid., 31, in Lumpkin, 60.

75. *Second London Confession*, 29.2, in Lumpkin, 291.

sign of some future repentance and faith. It is reserved for those who have been regenerated by the Holy Spirit through the Word of God and who have repented of their sins and placed their faith in Christ.

One of the most important developments in the post-Reformation period was the disagreement among Reformed leaders who closely followed Calvin's theology and the Remonstrants who followed the dissenting theology of Jacob Arminius. To settle the conflict, the Synod of Dort was convened in 1618, and the *Canons of the Synod of Dort* were issued in 1619. One key issue was whether the grace of God for regeneration is resistible, as the Remonstrants maintained, or irresistible, which was the position taken by traditional Calvinists. In settling this matter, the *Canons of Dort* addressed in great detail the doctrine of salvation.

The *Canons* recovered the notion, first proposed by Augustine a millennium earlier and revived by Calvin, of a divine call that exists in two forms—an external call and an effective call: "When God accomplishes his good pleasure in the elect, or works in them true conversion, he not only causes the gospel to be externally preached to them, and powerfully illuminates their minds by his Holy Spirit, that they may rightly understand and discern the things of the Spirit of God, but by the efficacy [effectiveness] of the same regenerating Spirit, he pervades the inmost recesses of the man."[76] Thus, every person who is confronted with the gospel is "called" by God to salvation; this call is the external or outward call. At the same time that they are confronted with the gospel, the elect are "called" by God in an additional way; this call is the internal call, which is always effective: All "in whose hearts God works in this marvelous manner are certainly, infallibly, and effectively regenerated and do actually believe. Whereupon the will thus renewed is not only actuated and influenced by God, but in consequence of this influence, becomes itself active. Therefore also, man is himself rightly said to believe and repent, by virtue of that grace received."[77] Even this faith is a gift of God, "because he who works in man both to will and to do ... produces both the will to believe and the act of believing also."[78] At the same time, this mighty work of God is closely associated with specific God-appointed means—the preaching of the gospel, the sacraments, and the exercise of church discipline.[79]

REGENERATION, CONVERSION, AND CALLING IN THE MODERN PERIOD

Following these developments in Lutheran, Reformed, and Baptist churches, the theology of Jacob Arminius and the Remonstrants—called Arminianism or Wesleyan-Arminianism, after John Wesley's modification of Arminian theology—was an important theological addition in the modern period. It posited a kind of grace—*prevenient* grace, from a Latin word *praevenire*, meaning "to precede" or "to go before"—that is

---

76. *Canons of the Synod of Dort*, "Third and Fourth Heads of Doctrine," 11, in Schaff, 3:590.

77. Ibid., 12, in Schaff, 3:590.

78. Ibid., 14, in Schaff, 3:591.

79. Ibid., 17, in Schaff, 3:592.

active in the salvation of sinful people. This grace overcomes the dreadful effects of original sin and enables all people everywhere to respond positively to God's work of salvation. The existence of this universal prevenient grace means that no special work of God—the effective call—is necessary in the lives of people who actually embrace salvation.

John Wesley articulated the idea of prevenient grace as God's provision to help completely sinful human beings: "The condition of man after the fall of Adam is such that he cannot turn and prepare himself, by his own natural strength and works, to faith and calling upon God; therefore, we have no power to do good works, pleasant and acceptable to God, without the prevenient grace of God by Christ [going before] us, that we may have a good will, and working with us, when we have that good will."[80] All people everywhere, therefore, are recipients of prevenient grace to enable them to meet the conditions for salvation: "Salvation begins with ... prevenient grace, including the first wish to please God, the first dawn of light concerning his will, and the first slight transient conviction of having sinned against him. All these imply some tendency towards life; some degree of salvation; the beginning of a deliverance from a blind, unfeeling heart, quite insensible of God and the things of God."[81] Wesley turned to John 1:9 for his biblical support for prevenient grace: "Everyone has some measure of that light, some faint glimmering ray, which, sooner or later, more or less, enlightens every man who comes into the world. And everyone, unless he is one of the small number whose conscience is seared as with a hot iron, feels more or less uneasy when he acts contrary to the light of his own conscience. So that no man sins because he lacks grace, but because he does not use the grace that he has."[82] But anyone who cooperates with prevenient grace is enabled to repent of sin and believe in Christ for salvation.

Wesley also believed in baptismal regeneration: "By water ... as a means—the water of baptism—we are regenerated or born again."[83] Qualifying himself, Wesley did not equate baptism with the new birth in the case of adults who are baptized, but did so in the case of infant baptism. However, he also noted that each and every infant eventually grows up to commit personal sin and reject the grace of God. As a result, they lose the eternal life given to them in baptism. This desperate situation calls for them to be born again through an adult conversion to Jesus Christ. Thus, Wesley challenged those who had been baptized as infants not to rely upon that experience for their present salvation.[84] While effective at the time, their infant baptism had lost its benefits through their fall into personal sin. Thus, those who were baptized as infants yet have fallen away must be born again—again.

The Wesleyan-Arminian notion of prevenient grace stood in opposition to Calvinist theology. Although they did not deny the reality of some kind of grace that is common to everyone, Calvinists rejected many of the alleged benefits of prevenient grace. A propo-

80. *Methodist Articles of Religion*, 8, in Schaff, 3:809.

81. John Wesley, *Working Out Our Own Salvation*, in *The Works of John Wesley*, 14 vols. (Grand Rapids: Zondervan, 1958), 6:509.

82. Ibid., in *Works of John Wesley*, 6:512.

83. John Wesley, *A Treatise on Baptism*, 1, in *Works of John Wesley*, 10:188–201.

84. John Wesley, *The Marks of the New Birth*, 4.1-5, in *Works of John Wesley*, 10:193-94.

nent of a twofold notion of grace was Jonathan Edwards, who referred to the two types as common grace and special, or saving, grace. As for the first, "the phrase *common grace* is used to signify that kind of action or influence of the Spirit of God to which are owing [due] those religious or moral attainments that are common to both saints and sinners, and so signifies as much as common assistance." As for the second, "the phrase *special* or *saving grace* is sometimes used to signify that particular kind or degree of operation or influence of God's Spirit, by which saving actions and attainments do arise in the godly or—which is the same thing—special and saving assistance."[85] According to Edwards, God's grace that is at work in conversion is of this second type.[86] He used the term *conversion* interchangeably with the terms *regeneration* and *calling*.[87] From this, he drew the inference "*that necessarily conversion is wrought at once. That* knowledge, that reformation and conviction that is preparatory to conversion may be gradual, and the work after conversion may be gradually carried on, yet that work of grace on the soul by which a person is brought out of a state of total corruption and depravity into a state of grace, to an interest in Christ, and to be actually a child of God, is in a moment."[88] As for the nature of this divine work of conversion/regeneration/calling, Edwards identified it as "a principle of divine love."[89] Furthermore, he demonstrated that this principle "comes into existence in the soul by the power of God in the influence of the Holy Spirit, the third person in the blessed Trinity."[90] Thus, he concluded "that true saving grace is nothing other than that very love of God—that is, God, in one of the persons of the Trinity—uniting himself to the soul of a creature, as a vital principle, dwelling there and exerting himself by the faculties of the soul of man, in his own proper nature, after the manner of a principle of nature."[91]

Edwards was not only interested in a theoretical understanding of regeneration and conversion. He was also involved in the Great Awakening, a series of revivals affecting many churches—Dutch Reformed, Presbyterian, Congregational—in the American colonies in the 1740s. Edwards himself published an account of the revival in his town. Entitled *A Faithful Narrative of the Surprising Work of God in the Conversion of Many Hundred Souls in Northampton*, the publication sparked many other churches to seek similar revivals. Two other works by Edwards—*The Distinguishing Marks of a Work of the Spirit of God* and *Some Thoughts Concerning the Present Revival*—attempted to make revivalism theologically understandable and to defend it from its critics. In his *Treatise Concerning Religious Affections*, Edwards further sought to distinguish between true and false signs of conversion. Being nurtured in a Calvinist theological atmosphere, conversions and revivals during the Great Awakening were seen as "the surprising work of God." Nothing of human origin could help prepare for or contribute to this miraculous operation of God in saving people and renewing churches.

---

85. Jonathan Edwards, *Treatise on Grace*, 1, in *Treatise on Grace and Other Posthumously Published Writings by Jonathan Edwards*, ed. Paul Helm (Greenwood, S.C.: Attic, 1971), 25.

86. Ibid., in Helm, *Treatise on Grace*, 32–33.

87. Ibid., in Helm, *Treatise on Grace*, 33–35.

88. Ibid., in Helm, *Treatise on Grace*, 33–34.

89. Edwards appealed to Matt. 22:36; Luke 10:25–28; Rom. 13:8, 10; 1 Cor. 13; 1 Tim. 1:5; and James 2:8 for biblical support for this notion. Ibid., 2, in Helm, *Treatise on Grace*, 40–45.

90. Ibid., 3, in Helm, *Treatise on Grace*, 51.

91. Ibid., in Helm, *Treatise on Grace*, 72.

John Owen sounded this same theme while exposing several false views of regeneration that had become popular in his time. He asserted that "regeneration does not consist in a participation in the ordinance of baptism and a profession of the doctrine of repentance";[92] "a moral reformation of life and conversation";[93] and "enthusiastic raptures, ecstasies, voices, or anything of the kind."[94] Furthermore, he was critical of certain well-intentioned people who engaged in overanalysis of the mysterious work of regeneration. Although studies of the doctrine were good and proper, Owen was fearful that such studies were degenerating into a mockery of the work of regeneration.[95] Owen also set forth his doctrine of regeneration, formulated along classical Calvinist lines: "From the whole it appears that our regeneration is a work of the Spirit of God, and that not any act of our own, which is only so, is intended by it."[96] When he addressed conversion, Owen used the term as a synonym for regeneration.

Rather than using the terms interchangeably, as Edwards and Owen had done, other theologians maintained that regeneration and conversion are related to each other as two sides of the same coin. According to this understanding, the coin is redemption; one side — the "divine" side — is regeneration, the other — the "human" side — is conversion. Samuel Hopkins insisted that the two be distinguished and expressed their relationship in terms of cause and effect: "In this renovation, there is the operation of the cause, which is the work done by the Spirit of God; and there is the effect, which consists in the exercises of the regenerate, in which they are active and agents."[97] The former is regeneration; the latter, conversion. Breaking from the traditional view that regeneration affects both the intellect and the will, Hopkins insisted instead that regeneration does not affect the mind, which is incapable of moral depravity, but the will only; thus, "regeneration is in Scripture represented as consisting in giving *a new heart*."[98] Furthermore, Hopkins offered the controversial notion that the Holy Spirit works immediately on the heart, apart from any means (i.e., the Word of God) in regenerating sinners.[99]

Other controversial ideas about regeneration and conversion were under way, none of which was more important and influential than the theology of Charles Finney. Because of this, the Calvinist theology that typified the Great Awakening in the 1740s gave way to a Wesleyan-Arminian framework in the American revivals of the nineteenth century.

In particular, Finney articulated his view of regeneration, including repentance and faith, in opposition to the prevailing Calvinistic views. He opposed the usual distinction

---

92. John Owen, *Pneumatologia: A Discourse Concerning the Holy Spirit*, 3.1, in *The Works of John Owen*, ed. William H. Goold, 16 vols. (Edinburgh: Banner of Truth Trust, 1965), 3:216.

93. Ibid., in *Works of John Owen*, 3:217–20.

94. Ibid., in *Works of John Owen*, 3:224–25.

95. Ibid., in *Works of John Owen*, 3:227. Owen quoted from Samuel Parker, *Defense and Continuation of the Ecclesiastical Polity* (London,1671), 306–7.

96. Owen, *Pneumatologia*, 3.5, in *Works of John Owen*, 3:336.

97. Samuel Hopkins, "Application of Redemption," 2, in

The Works of Samuel Hopkins, vol. 1 of *American Religious Thought of the 18th and 19th Centuries*, ed. Bruce Kuklick (1865; repr., New York: Garland, 1987), 367.

98. Ibid., 2.3, in *Works of Samuel Hopkins*, 369.

99. He appealed to the example of Lydia in Acts 16:14. Ibid. 2.4, in *Works of Samuel Hopkins*, 371–72. Hopkins addressed a possible counterargument to his view: "St. James says, 'Of his own will he begat us, *with the word of truth*' (James 1:18). But here in regeneration he includes the effect wrought, or conversion, and does not mean only the act by which the effect is produced, as distinguished from the effect, which is intended by the regeneration now under consideration." Ibid., 372.

made between regeneration and conversion, a distinction that he considered to be "arbitrary and theological, rather than biblical.... In both alike God and man are both active, and their activity is simultaneous. God works or draws, and the sinner yields or turns or—which is the same thing—changes his heart or, in other words, is born again."[100] Finney underscored one reason for his strong objection to this distinction: "It leads the sinner to wait to be regenerated, before he repents or turns to God. It is of most fatal tendency to represent the sinner as under a necessity of waiting to be passively regenerated, before he gives himself to God."[101]

Finney's emphasis on human activity rather than passivity had implications for his practice of renewing the church and evangelizing outsiders. As opposed to the Calvinist tradition that considered revival and conversion to be the results of a miraculous work, Finney explained: "Revival is not dependent on a miracle in any sense.... It is a result we can logically expect from the right use of God-given means, as much as any other effect produced by applying tools and resources. A miracle might or might not precede a revival ... But the miracle [is] not the revival."[102] Still, Finney did not discount the necessity of God's work to bring about revival: "I said that a revival is the result of the right use of the appropriate means given by God. The means which God has enjoined for the production of a revival, doubtless have a natural tendency to produce a revival—otherwise, God would not have enjoined them. But means will not produce a revival without the blessing of God."[103]

Some of Finney's suggested means to promote revival were standard: self-preparation, prevailing prayer, being filled with the Spirit, personal testimony, witnessing, preaching the gospel, and the like. But he introduced several other means, which became known as "new measures." He admitted that "the strategies of the latest revivals have proven very useful, but are attacked as innovations. There things in particular have attracted criticism: anxious meetings, extended meetings, and the anxious seat."[104] Specifically, anxious meetings were held "to converse with sinners seeking Christ and to instruct sinners individually to lead them immediately to Christ." Extended meetings had as their purpose "to devote a period of days to religious services to powerfully bring people to grapple with spiritual matters." And the anxious seat was "a seat set aside at a meeting where the spiritually anxious can come and be addressed specifically and be prayed for and talked with individually."[105] Finney's theology of regeneration and his new measures for conversion resulted in a major paradigm shift in the Protestant approach to ministry. A much more aggressive call to conversion through publicity of church revival meetings and invitations to come forward to deal seriously with God at the anxious bench were employed. Furthermore, an almost formulaic approach to evangelism—(1) have faith, (2) repent, and (3) be baptized for the remission of sins, then (4) one would be forgiven and (5) receive the gift of the Holy Spirit—became standard fare in many churches

100. Charles Grandison Finney, *Lectures on Systematic Theology* (1878), lecture 17, in *Finney's Systematic Theology: New Expanded Edition*, ed. Dennis Carroll, Bill Nicely, and L. G. Parkhurst Jr. (Minneapolis: Bethany, 1994), 271.
101. Ibid.

102. Charles Grandison Finney, *Lectures on Revival* (Minneapolis: Bethany, 1988), 13.
103. Ibid., 14.
104. Ibid., 167.
105. Ibid., 167–71.

beginning in the nineteenth century. Finney's anxious bench also became a major contributor to the development of the altar call, or public appeal for nonbelievers to respond to the gospel in a visible way.[106]

Intense renewal spilled outside the churches in America, creating frontier revivals. Called the Second Great Awakening, these series of revivals began with the Gasper River revival in south-central Kentucky in 1800. In the most famous of the camp meetings (as the revivals came to be known), the Cane Ridge (Kentucky) revival of 1801, led by Barton W. Stone, was characterized by lively preaching, cooperation between denominations (Baptists, Methodists, Presbyterians), and emotionalism.[107]

Barton W. Stone's Description of the Cane Ridge Revival

Many, very many, fell down as men slain in battle, and continued for hours together in an apparently breathless and motionless state, sometimes for a few moments reviving and exhibiting symptoms of life by a deep groan or piercing shriek, or by a prayer for mercy fervently uttered. After lying there for hours, they obtained deliverance. The gloomy cloud that had covered their faces seemed gradually and visibly to disappear, and hope, in smiles, brightened into joy. They would rise, shouting deliverances and then would address the surrounding multitude in language truly eloquent and impressive. With astonishment did I hear men, women and children declaring the wonderful works of God and the glorious mysteries of the gospel.*

*Cited in Peter Toon, *Born Again: A Biblical and Theological Study of Regeneration* (Grand Rapids: Baker, 1987), 167. Stone was a leader of this frontier revival.

The revivals that began on the American frontier at the start of the nineteenth century continued to exert a large influence on American churches and life throughout the century. The New England revival featured such notable Christians as Timothy Dwight, president of Yale; Asahel Nettleton, a Congregational Church evangelist; and Lyman

---

106. David Bennett defined the altar call in the following way: "A method of evangelism, within which a regular or frequent, planned invitation is given to 'unbelievers' to respond to Jesus Christ publicly at the conclusion of a sermon or other gospel presentation, in such ways as calling out a response, raising a hand, standing, or walking to a designated spot in the evangelistic setting. A response to such an invitation would normally be followed by immediate counseling and later by some form of follow-up. It often incorporates an appeal to Christians for such issues as rededication and call to missions. It is not a theology, though it does reflect and support particular theologies." David Bennett, *The Altar Call: Its Origins and Present Usage* (Lanham, Md.: Univ. Press of America, 2000), xvi.

107. One of the most significant developments growing out of these frontier revivals was the beginning of a new church called the Disciples of Christ. One of the doctrinal distinctives was this church's linking of regeneration, conversion, faith, repentance, and baptism (by immersion). Its founder, Alexander Campbell, maintained that "scripturally, no one can be converted to God until he is immersed"; thus, for the Disciples of Christ, baptism is necessary for salvation. Although formally in agreement with the Roman Catholic Church, it differed in its insistence on actual conversion as being part of the process (thus, there can be no baptism of infants). And while it had certain similarities to the Protestant heritage, including the Baptist emphasis on baptism by immersion for believers and not infants, Campbellite theology differed in its insistence on baptism for salvation. Alexander Campbell, *Christian System*, prop. 10 (Nashville: Gospel Advocate, 2001).

Beecher, who experienced the revival through the influence of Timothy Dwight. The Third Great Awakening in America was sparked by the preaching of lay businessmen such as D. L. Moody. Arising out of this revival were noontime prayer meetings in major metropolitan centers such as New York City and Chicago, the Young Men's Christian Association, the Sunday school, and the Chicago Evangelization Society (later to be renamed Moody Bible Institute in honor of its founder).

In theological discussion, further attention was given to the relationship of regeneration and conversion. Among Reformed theologians, it was fairly well settled that regeneration is a direct, unmediated work of God, while conversion takes place through a human response of faith and repentance. Given this, theologians such as William G. T. Shedd emphasized the *logical priority* of regeneration to conversion. By logical priority, he did not mean that regeneration takes place *temporally* prior to conversion, which *temporally* follows regeneration. Rather, "regeneration precedes conversion in the order of nature, not of time."[108] Given the sinful state of non-Christians, it is not *logically* possible for them to repent of their sins and place their faith in Christ (be converted). The *logical* order is instead regeneration—the imparting of new spiritual life—that enables people to repent and believe: "Regeneration is the cause of conversion. The Holy Spirit acts in regeneration, and as a consequence the human spirit acts in conversion."[109]

Shedd has been followed by most Reformed theologians in his insistence on the logical priority of regeneration to conversion. John Murray concurred: "As sinners we are dead in trespasses and sins. Faith is a whole-souled act of loving trust and self-commitment. Of that we are incapable until renewed by the Holy Spirit.... Hence regeneration must be prior to faith.... Repentance is the twin sister of faith—we cannot think of the one without the other—and so repentance would be conjoined with faith."[110] Thus, "we are not born again by faith or repentance or conversion; we repent and believe because we have been regenerated."[111] But Murray also insisted on the logical priority of the effective call in the order of salvation, for this reason: "Salvation in actual possession takes its start from an effective summons on the part of God and ... this summons, since it is God's summons, carries in its bosom all of the operative efficacy by which it is made effective. It is calling and not regeneration that possesses that character. Hence, there is more to be said for the priority of calling."[112] With God as its author, the call is a summons to the elect according to the eternal divine purpose. It is this effective call "by which we are actually united to Christ ... which unites us to the inwardly operative grace of God." Regeneration, then, is "that which is wrought inwardly by God's grace in order that we may yield to God's call the appropriate and necessary response. In that case the new birth would come after the call and prior to the response on our part [conversion]."[113]

One theologian who disagreed with the logical priority of regeneration to conversion was Millard Erickson. His logical order was first conversion, then regeneration, because

---

108. William G. T. Shedd, *Dogmatic Theology*, sup. 6.3.6, in *Dogmatic Theology*, ed. Alan W. Gomes, 3rd ed. (Phillipsburg, N.J.: P & R, 2003), 785.

109. Ibid., in Gomes, *Dogmatic Theology*, 772.

110. John Murray, *Redemption Accomplished and Applied*

(Grand Rapids: Eerdmans, 1955, 1984), 86–87.

111. Ibid., 103.

112. Ibid., 86.

113. Ibid., 93–94.

repentance and faith (the elements of conversion) are the conditions for regeneration. But from where does the ability to repent of sins and believe in Christ come? Erickson appealed to the effective call or special calling of God, which, he explained, "involves an extraordinary presentation of the message of salvation. It is sufficiently powerful to counteract the effects of sin and enable the person to believe. It is also so appealing that the person will believe." He noted further that "special calling is in many ways similar to the prevenient grace of which Arminians speak. It differs from that concept, however, in two respects. It is bestowed only upon the elect, not upon all humans, and it leads infallibly or efficaciously to a positive response by the recipient."[114] As Erickson concluded: "Although no one is capable of responding to the general call of the gospel, in the case of the elect, God works intensively through a special calling so that they do respond in repentance and faith. As a result of this conversion, God regenerates them.... Thus the logical order of the initial aspects of salvation is special calling — conversion — regeneration."[115]

Throughout the second half of the twentieth century, American evangelicalism became identified with the evangelist Billy Graham and his work. Through his worldwide crusades, Graham preached the gospel to nearly three hundred million people and called them to come to Christ; millions credit Graham's message as key to their conversion. His book *How to Be Born Again* expressed his view of regeneration (or conversion). Appealing to Jesus' words concerning the necessity of the new birth (John 3:7),[116] Graham underscored the impossibility of sinners bringing about their own regeneration.[117] Still, he insisted: "All you have to do to be born again is to repent of your sins and believe in the Lord Jesus as your personal Lord and Savior."[118] Indeed, he summarized in four guidelines how a person can be born again: recognition of the love of God, repentance from sin, reception of Christ as Savior and Lord, and public confession of Christ. All of this should be expressed in prayer. "O God, I acknowledge that I have sinned against you. I am sorry for my sins. I am willing to turn from my sins. I openly receive and acknowledge Jesus Christ as my Savior. I confess him as Lord. From this moment on I want to live for him and serve him. In Jesus' name. Amen."[119] Graham's simple and direct approach was typical of the evangelistic efforts of many evangelical churches and movements such as Campus Crusade for Christ.[120]

Through the efforts and encouragement of Graham and many other evangelicals, the twentieth century witnessed an explosion of missions and a new discipline of missiology. This in turn contributed to changing perceptions of conversion, particularly when dealing with people who have never had contact with the Christian gospel — Muslims, Buddhists, Taoists, Hindus — and hardened secularists. In such cases, a direct presentation of the message of Christ is not possible, because the listeners have no concept of the

114. Millard J. Erickson, *Christian Theology*, 2nd ed. (Grand Rapids: Baker, 1998), 943–44.

115. Ibid., 945.

116. Billy Graham, *How to Be Born Again* (Waco: Word, 1977), 147.

117. Ibid., 150.

118. Ibid., 156.

119. Ibid., 168–69.

120. The Campus Crusade for Christ booklet *Have You Ever Heard of the Four Spiritual Laws?* and the many variations on it have been effective tools in the evangelization of millions of people around the world.

Christian God, Christian Scripture, and so forth, or have forcefully rejected such ideas. To confront this reality, missiologists began to focus on the (at times) lengthy process that is needed for people to convert to Christianity. James Engel, for example, developed the *Engel Scale*, consisting of eight stages through which non-Christians may need to progress before their conversion: awareness of a supreme being; some knowledge of the gospel; knowledge of the fundamentals of the gospel; grasp of personal implications of the gospel; positive attitude toward the act of becoming a Christian; recognition of a problem and intention to act; decision to act; repentance and faith in Christ.[121] Thus, energetic and pleading calls for people to convert to Christ may in many cases need to follow a process that moves non-Christians progressively along the way to becoming Christians.

In summary, evangelical churches generally follow (most of) Protestant theology's doctrine of regeneration, conversion, effective calling, repentance, faith, and grace (both prevenient and special) — with its many variations on those themes. But one thing can be said in terms of a common evangelical view of this, as formulated by the National Association of Evangelicals: "We believe that for the salvation of lost and sinful people, regeneration by the Holy Spirit is absolutely essential."[122]

---

121. James F. Engel, *Contemporary Christian Communications: Its Theory and Practice* (Nashville: Nelson, 1979), 80.
122. National Association of Evangelicals, Statement of Faith. www.nae.net/about-us/statement-of-faith. Accessed 29 October 2010.

Chapter 23

JUSTIFICATION (RIGHT LEGAL STANDING BEFORE GOD)

How has the church come to understand how and when people gain right legal standing before God?

STATEMENT OF BELIEF

The church historically has affirmed that one aspect of God's work of salvation on behalf of sinful humanity is justification. Few doctrines are better known than this one because of the intense debate that was waged over it during the Reformation. Before that debate, however, the doctrine of justification by divine grace through faith alone had been championed by Augustine over against the view of grace as external help as articulated by Pelagius. Even with Augustine's strong presentation, the medieval church was reluctant to accept his entire view and opted for a middle course between Augustine and Pelagius, often called semi-Pelagianism.

With the rediscovery of Augustine's doctrine during the Reformation, justification once again came to the center of theological attention. Indeed, the *material principle* of Protestantism was the doctrine of justification.[1] In contrast with Roman Catholic theology, which viewed justification as a process of divine grace being infused into people to make them actually righteous, Protestant theology insisted that justification is a legal act of God who, as Judge, declares sinners not guilty but righteous instead. He does so by crediting the righteousness of Christ to their account, so while they are not actually righteous, God views them as being so because of Christ's righteousness. And all of this is appropriated by faith in Christ alone. The Catholic Church vehemently denounced this view of justification, condemning it as heresy.

This debate remained essentially unchanged until the modern period. With the general thawing of tensions between the Catholic Church and many Protestant churches

---

1. The *formal principle* of Protestantism is *sola Scriptura* (Scripture alone), the framework that shaped the Reforma- tion. By the *material principle* is meant the content at the heart of the Reformation.

in the twentieth century, the doctrine of justification was revisited. Some kind of rapprochement was reached between the Catholic Church and some Lutheran churches as well as between Catholics and Anglicans. Even some evangelicals and Catholics reached some agreement on the doctrine. Beyond this, new questions arose as to the exact nature of justification, leading to a "new perspective" on Paul and his doctrine. Indeed, the material principle of Protestantism has become the center of theological attention once again.[2]

VIEWS OF JUSTIFICATION IN THE EARLY CHURCH

Although the apostle Paul is generally thought of as the New Testament author who devoted considerable space to the theme of justification, he is not the only one who treated it. Jesus himself on several occasions addressed the topic (Matt. 12:33–37; Luke 18:9–14). Also, because of its alleged contradictions with Paul's teaching, James's discussion of justification is well known (James 2:18–26). As for Paul, his letter to the Romans is the richest exposition of the topic. A key theme is the contrast between justification by the works of the law and justification by faith, as detailed in Romans 3:21–28 and as illustrated by the example of Abraham (Rom. 4:1–5, 13–25). This same idea is echoed in Paul's letter to the Galatians (Gal. 2:15–21; 3:15–29). Beyond justification, this divine work is all of one piece with God's other mighty works of salvation—foreknowledge, predestination, calling, and glorification (Rom. 8:29–30).

After the apostolic period, the church continued to affirm this doctrine. Contrasting self-effort with faith, Clement of Rome underscored that "having been called through his [God's] will in Christ Jesus, [we] are not justified through ourselves or through our own wisdom or understanding or piety or works which we have done in holiness of heart, but through faith, by which the almighty God has justified all who have existed from the beginning."[3] Like the apostle Paul, Justin Martyr appealed to Abraham as the supreme example of justification.[4] Other biblical examples included the prostitute who ministered to Christ and Habakkuk's affirmation.[5] In the *Letter to Diognetus*, such justification was placed in the context of the removal of sins and the gift of the righteousness of Christ: "For what else but his righteousness could have covered our sins? In whom was it possible for us, the lawless and the ungodly, to be justified, except in the Son of God alone? O the sweet exchange, O the incomprehensible work of God, O the unexpected blessings, that the sinfulness of many should be hidden in one righteous man, while the righteousness of one should justify many sinners!"[6]

These limited comments reflected some of the biblical emphases on justification. Some in the early church, however, took the discussion of justification in a different—

---

2. My thanks to Bradley Cochran for his help on this chapter.

3. Clement of Rome, *Letter of the Romans to the Corinthians*, 32.4, in Holmes, 63, 65; *ANF*, 1:13. Cf. Irenaeus, *Against Heresies*, 4.27.2, in *ANF*, 1:499. Clement of Alexandria, *Stromata*, 1.7, in *ANF*, 2:308.

4. "Abraham was declared by God to be righteous, not on account of circumcision, but on account of faith." Justin Martyr, *Dialogue with Trypho, a Jew*, 92, in *ANF*, 1:245.

5. Tertullian referred to Luke 7:36–50 and Habakkuk 2:4. Tertullian, *Against Marcion*, 4.18, in *ANF* 3:376.

6. *Letter to Diognetus*, 9.3–5, in Holmes, 547; *ANF*, 1:28.

and, some would say, unbiblical—direction. Due to their need to address such current issues as fatalism—the view that human beings have no freedom, but everything has been predetermined by fate—these church leaders placed the discussion of justification in the context of free will and self-determination. For example, Tertullian explained: "The power of the grace of God, more potent indeed than nature, exercises its influence over the faculty that underlies itself within us—even the freedom of our will, which is described as self-determination."[7] Here, divine grace for salvation was affirmed in a context in which Scripture did not address it.

Without this biblical context, the discussion could go off in several directions. For some it slipped into the direction of encouraging people to do their best with what God has given to them.[8] For others the discussion moved in the direction of merit, as it did with Theophilus: "God made man free, and with power over himself.... For as man, disobeying, drew death upon himself; so, obeying the will of God, he who desires is able to obtain eternal life for himself."[9] Support for this idea of free will and self-determination came primarily from the Old Testament and philosophy, as Justin Martyr argued: "We have learned from the prophets ... that punishments, rebukes, and good rewards are rendered according to the merit of each man's actions.... Unless human beings have the power of avoiding evil and choosing good by free choice, they are not accountable for their actions, no matter what kind they are.... For human beings would not be worthy of reward or praise if they of themselves did not choose the good."[10] Thus, free will and self-determination were affirmed, together with the belief that the proper use of these would result in reward, while neglect or abuse would result in judgment. Indeed, Tertullian envisioned God as a "debtor" to human deeds: "God accepts good works, and if he accepts them, he also rewards them.... So a good work has God as its debtor, just as an evil deed has also; for a judge is one who rewards every cause."[11] Thus, some within the early church linked God's gracious work of justification with human free will and self-determination, opening the door for a system of meriting divine favor through the proper use of human freedom.

As his title "the doctor of grace" indicates, Augustine had much to say about divine grace in general and the doctrine of justification in particular. In part, Augustine's theology was expressed in opposition to the teachings of Pelagius, a monk who developed the idea of grace as external helps for people.[12] Only this type of help is necessary, argued

---

7. Tertullian, *Treatise on the Soul*, 21, in *ANF*, 3:202. The text has been rendered clearer.

8. As Irenaeus offered: "If you will deliver up to him what is yours—that is, faith towards him and subjection—you will receive his handiwork, and will be a perfect work of God." Irenaeus, *Against Heresies*, 4.39.2, in *ANF*, 1:523. The text has been rendered clearer.

9. Theophilus, *To Autolycus*, 2.27, in *ANF*, 2:105.

10. Justin Martyr, *First Apology*, 43, in *ANF*, 1:177. The text has been rendered clearer.

11. Tertullian, *On Repentance*, 2, in *ANF*, 3:658. The text has been rendered clearer.

12. As Alister McGrath pointed out, "Augustine's doctrine

of justification underwent significant development.... When did Augustine change his mind on this crucial matter? Fortunately, we have his own answer to this question: it was 'in the first of two books written to Simplicianus,' written in late 396 or early 397.... In view of the fact that the Pelagian controversy would not break out until early the following century, it is important to appreciate that Augustine appears to have developed his new understanding of justification—which would henceforth bear the epithet 'Augustinian'—in a non-polemical context. It is not correct to suppose that Augustine's doctrine of justification is merely a reaction against Pelagianism." *Iustitia Dei: A History of the Christian Doctrine of Justification* (Cambridge: Cambridge Univ. Press, 1986), 24.

Pelagius, because the sin of Adam had not exerted a terrible influence on humanity.[13] Augustine's theology was completely different: Grace cannot be restricted to external aids; rather, it is an internal work of God on the human soul. Even in their upright state, Adam and Eve needed this grace so they could continue to will to do the good: humanity was "made upright that, though unable to remain in its uprightness without divine help, it could of its own mere will depart from it."[14] And depart it did. Now that the human race is fallen, the absolute need for grace is magnified all the more. After rehearsing the terrible miseries with which people are tormented during their earthly existence—grief at the loss of loved ones, crimes committed by evil people, natural disasters, accidents, physical diseases, demonic activity—Augustine offered the only hope of relief: "From this hell upon earth there is no escape, except through the grace of the Savior Christ, our God and Lord."[15]

Augustine defined grace and its relationship to justification:

> What is grace? That which is freely given. What is "freely given"? Given, not paid. If it was due, wages would be given, but grace would not be bestowed. But if it was really due, then you were good. But if, as is true, you were evil but believed on him who justifies the ungodly (What is, "who justifies the ungodly"? the ungodly is made righteous), consider what by right hung over you by the law and you have obtained by grace. But having obtained that grace by faith, you will be just by faith—"for the just lives by faith."[16]

Thus, justification involves God making sinners righteous.[17] According to Augustine, this gift of righteousness is received by faith. But even the faith to receive God's grace is nothing other than his gift, so all discussion of merit in salvation is ended: "For you did not obtain favor by yourself, so that anything should be owed to you. Therefore, in giving the reward of immortality, God crowns his own gifts, not your merits."[18]

Conscientiously, Augustine wrestled with the relationship of grace, law, free will, and good works. He constantly pointed out that people enslaved to sin are not able to obtain righteousness by themselves: "For what good work can a lost person perform, except so far as he has been delivered from damnation? Can they do anything by the free determination of their own will?... When man by his own free will sinned, then sin was victorious over him, and the freedom of his will was lost."[19] In saying this, Augustine did not deny free will. Rather, he stressed that unbelievers always use their free will to

13. For a discussion of Pelagius's view of sin, see chap. 16.

14. Augustine, *Enchiridion on Faith, Hope, and Love*, 107. *NPNF*[1], 3:272. The text has been rendered clearer.

15. Augustine, *The City of God*, 22.22, in *NPNF*[1], 2:500–501.

16. Augustine, *Tractates on the Gospel of John*, John 1:15–18, Tractate 3.9, in *NPNF*[1], 7:21. Augustine makes reference to Rom. 4:5 and Hab. 2:4. The text has been rendered clearer.

17. Augustine, *On the Spirit and the Letter*, 18, in *NPNF*[1], 5:90. As McGrath pointed out, "It is utterly alien to Augustine's thought to speak of a forensic doctrine of justification,

or of imputed righteousness in the Reformed sense of the term." Alister E. McGrath, "Forerunners of the Reformation? A Critical Examination of the Evidence for Precursors of the Reformation Doctrines of Justification," *Harvard Theological Review* 75, no. 1 (1982): 220. As we will see later, the Reformers harkened back to Augustine as they developed their doctrine of justification, but they also significantly modified his formulation.

18. Augustine, *Tractates on the Gospel of John*, John 1:15–18, Tractate 3.10, in *NPNF*[1], 7:22.

19. Augustine, *Enchiridion on Faith, Hope, and Love*, 30, in *NPNF*[1], 3:247. The text has been rendered clearer.

sin, because it is enslaved.[20] But once justified by faith, believers are liberated to live righteously and carry out the law. Speaking of the good commandments of God, Augustine explained:

> Everyone who is incorporated into him [Christ] and made a member of his body is able, by God giving the increase within, to work righteousness.... The righteousness of the law is proposed in these terms—that whoever does it will live in it. And the purpose is that when each [person] has discovered his own weakness, he may not by his own strength, nor by the letter of the law (which cannot be done), but by faith, satisfy the Justifier, attain, do, and live in it. For the work in which he who does it will live, is not done except by the one who is justified. His justification, however, is received by faith.... Accordingly, as the law is not made void, but is established by faith, since faith obtains grace by which the law is fulfilled; so free will is not made void through grace, but is established, since grace heals the will by which righteousness is freely loved.[21]

For the Christian, then, "this is true freedom, for he has pleasure in the righteous deed; and it is at the same time a holy bondage, for he is obedient to the will of God."[22] Indeed, Augustine insisted that believers will engage in doing good: "We shall be made truly free, then, when God fashions us, that is, forms and creates us new, not as men—for he has done that already—but as good men, which his grace is now doing, that we may be a new creation in Christ Jesus."[23] Specifically, Augustine emphasized Paul's concept of "faith working through love" (Gal. 5:6) as the outcome of justification by faith.[24] Freed by grace and driven by love, believers acquire merits, again through divine grace. Ultimately, God will reward these merits, but only as he recognizes in them his own work: "When God crowns our merits, he will crown nothing else than his own gifts."[25]

To whom is *justifying grace* given? Augustine underscored that those whom God predestined are the recipients of his grace.[26] This does not mean, however, that those who are not predestined are completely without any benefit of divine grace whatsoever, for Augustine posited grace that belongs to the realm of nature, a kind of *natural* or *common grace*.[27] Furthermore, the divine preparation of people before salvation is the operation of

20. "The free will taken captive does not avail for anything except for sin." Augustine, *A Treatise against Two Letters of the Pelagians*, 3.24.8, in *NPNF*[1], 5:414.

21. Augustine, *On the Spirit and the Letter*, 50–52, in *NPNF*[1], 5:105–6. The text has been rendered clearer.

22. Augustine, *Enchiridion on Faith, Hope, and Love*, 30, in *NPNF*[1], 3:248.

23. Ibid., 31, in *NPNF*[1], 3:248. Augustine appealed to Eph. 2:10.

24. Augustine, *Tractates on the Gospel of John*, John 7:14–18, Tractate 29.6, in *NPNF*[1], 7:185.

25. Augustine, *Epistle* 194.19. Indeed, Augustine spoke of eternal life as "surely the reward of good works." At the same time, he concluded: "We are to understand, then, that man's good deserts are themselves the gift of God, so that when these obtain the recompense of eternal life, it is simply grace given for grace." Augustine, *Enchiridion on Faith, Hope, and Love*, 107, in *NPNF*[1], 3:272.

26. This discussion is taken up in chap. 21.

27. "Let the grace ... by which we are living and reasonable creatures, and are distinguished from cattle, be attributed to nature. Let that grace also by which, among men themselves, the handsome are made to differ from the deformed, or the intelligent from the stupid, or anything of that kind, be ascribed to nature." Augustine, *On the Predestination of the Saints*, 10, in *NPNF*[1], 5:503. The text has been rendered clearer.

still another type of grace — *prevenient grace*.[28] And the continuation in the state of faith leading on to ultimate salvation is due to yet another kind of grace — *persevering grace*:

> We are fellow workers with him [God] who does the work, because his mercy goes before us. He goes before us, however, that we may be healed; but then he will also follow us, that being healed we may grow healthy and strong. He goes before us that we may be called; he will follow us so that we may be glorified. He goes before us so that we may lead godly lives; he will follow us so that we may always live with him, because apart from him we can do nothing.[29]

Thus, grace in its many varieties accomplishes justification. Prevenient grace prepares the recipient for justification, justifying grace accomplishes the act of justification, and persevering grace works throughout the process of justification so as to preserve it.[30]

Augustine's powerful refutation of Pelagianism and his dynamic exposition of divine grace and justification carried the day. The church condemned the Pelagian position at several councils (e.g., the Council of Carthage in 418; the Council of Ephesus in 431) insisting on the thoroughgoing need for God's grace from beginning to end.[31]

Despite the church's affirmation of Augustine's view, some church leaders believed he had gone too far in tying grace so tightly with predestination. This close association seemed to them to destroy any sense of significant human free will. Although they also rejected classical Pelagianism, these leaders had some leanings in that direction; thus, their position is called *semi-Pelagianism*.[32] It could also be termed *semi-Augustinianism*, because they partially embraced Augustine's principles while avoiding what they saw to be its extremes. A key example of this was John Cassian;[33] others included Vincent of Lerins and Faustus of Rhegium. Through their influence, the Synod of Arles in 473 affirmed a cooperative effort between God's grace and human freedom and work: "Man's effort and endeavor is to be united with God's grace; man's freedom of will is not extinct but attenuated and weakened."[34] The church began walking down the path of semi-Pelagianism.

---

28. From the Latin *praevenire* ("to go before"), prevenient grace is God's activity in preparing people for faith leading to justification. Referencing the Latin translation of Psalm 59:10, Augustine explained prevenient grace: "We read in Holy Scripture ... that God's mercy 'shall meet me' [*praevenient*].... It goes before the unwilling to make him willing." Augustine, *Enchiridion on Faith, Hope, and Love*, 32, in *NPNF*[1], 3:248.

29. Augustine, *On Nature and Grace*, 35 [31], in *NPNF*[1], 5:133. The text has been rendered clearer. Augustine found biblical support for prevenient and persevering grace: "There is both this: 'The God of mercy will go before me' (Psalm 59:10) and again this: 'Your mercy will follow me all the days of my life' (Psalm 23:6)." Ibid. He also cited Psalm 21:3 ("For you have gone before him with the blessings of sweetness") as evidence for prevenient grace. He commented: "What is here more properly understood than that actual desire for the good ...? For good begins to be longed for when it has begun to grow sweet.... Therefore, the 'blessing of sweetness' is God's grace,

by which is caused in us that what he prescribes to us delights us, and we desire it — that is, we love it. If God does not go before us, not only is it not finished, but it is not ever started, from us. For if apart from him we are able to do actually nothing, we are able neither to start nor finish, because to begin, it is said, 'His mercy will go before me' (Psa. 59:10); to finish, it is said, 'His mercy will follow me' (Psa. 23:6)." *A Treatise against Two Letters of the Pelagians*, 2.21, in *NPNF*[1], 5:401. The text has been rendered clearer.

30. For a further discussion of Augustine's notion of persevering grace, see chap. 25.

31. Council of Carthage, canons on sin and grace, canons 5 and 6, in Mansi, 3:811; Bettenson, 64–65.

32. The term *semi-Pelagianism* was actually coined in the sixteenth century, but its major tenets were already present in the fifth and sixth centuries.

33. Cassian's view is discussed in chap. 22.

34. Synod of Arles, in Mansi, 7:1010; Bettenson, 65–66.

The Synod of Orange in 529 put a stop to this drift, taking a firm stand against the semi-Pelagian position that the human will initiates the request for grace, the wish for forgiveness of sins, and the desire to believe.[35] The council also positively set forth the absolute need for God's prevenient grace. For example, it affirmed that "the sin of the first man has so impaired and weakened free will that afterward no one can either love God as he ought or believe in God or do good for God's sake, unless the grace of divine mercy goes before him."[36] Thus, the Augustinian view of grace and justification, with some significant modifications, became the standard view of the church.

VIEWS OF JUSTIFICATION IN THE MIDDLE AGES

The influence of Augustine was most clearly seen in the medieval period in the writings of the Augustinians, church leaders who echoed and defended his theology. For example, the Venerable Bede insisted that "grace should be the starting point, grace should be the consummation, grace should be the crown" of human existence.[37] He was critical of Pelagianism, particularly condemning Julian of Eclanum's overly optimistic view of human goodness. For Bede, this position relegated grace to the role of "an accessory support" instead of "a prevenient inspiration and originator of good works and merits" in sinful people.[38] Similarly, Ildefonsus explained that "apart from the grace of God, the [human] free will is not capable of anything good."[39] So prevenient grace, changing the will to desire the good and to seek God, is absolutely necessary.

These medieval Augustinians emphasized that grace was received by faith alone. For example, Julian of Toledo insisted that "all effort of human argument must be suspended where faith alone is sufficient." Faith alone in Christ results in justification, according to Ildefonsus: "The beginning of human salvation comes from faith, which, when it is in Christ, is justification for the believer."[40] Julian spoke of "the righteousness of faith, by which we are justified. This faith is that we believe in him whom we cannot see, and that, being cleansed by faith, we will eventually see him in whom we now believe."[41] And good works play no role in justification, as Ildefonsus underscored: "God, who makes the unclean clean and removes sins, justifies the sinner apart from works."[42]

At the same time, Ildefonsus insisted that the fruit of justification consists in good works, so "faith unadorned with works is not only lacking in beauty, but is in fact dead."[43] Therefore, no contradiction exists between Paul's teaching on justification by faith alone and James's teaching that justification is by faith and works: "If someone believes in Christ, he can be saved by faith alone." But he cannot turn this into an excuse for "refusing to do good works," which is James's point.[44] Indeed, Isidore of Seville issued a

---

35. Synod of Orange, canons 3, 5, 6. Available at http://www.reformed.org/documents.

36. Ibid., conclusion.

37. Venerable Bede, *Allegorical Exposition of the Song of Songs*, 1, in Pelikan, 3:25.

38. Ibid., in Pelikan, 3:25.

39. Ildefonsus, *On the Knowledge of Baptism*, 100, in Pelikan, 3:26–27.

40. Ildefonsus, *Journey through the Desert*, 89, in Pelikan, 3:27.

41. Julian of Toledo, *The Sixth Age*, 2.14, in Pelikan, 3:27.

42. Ildefonsus, *The Virginity of Mary*, in Pelikan, 3:27.

43. Ildefonsus, *Journey through the Desert*, 83, in Pelikan, 3:27.

44. Julian of Toledo, *Antithesis*, 2.77, in Pelikan, 3:27–28.

stern warning for the person who "flatters himself uselessly about faith alone if it is not adorned with good works."[45] While reflecting biblical teaching, this theology left the door open to a popular spirituality that primarily viewed righteousness not as a state but as a continuous process. For example, Boniface urged that "we never imagine that we are righteous enough, but we constantly plead with God to increase our merits."[46]

More than anyone else, Thomas Aquinas set down the medieval Catholic notion of justification and its corollaries of grace, human effort, and merit. Although a substantial departure from Augustine and the Augustinians of the Middle Ages, his theology became determinative for the Roman Catholic Church.

Working from Aristotelian philosophy, Aquinas envisioned justification as a movement or "a change from the state of unrighteousness to a state of righteousness."[47] Just as any physical movement in nature must be brought about by some mover—an arrow is launched by an archer, for example—so justification as a spiritual movement must be brought about by spiritual resources from God. Given this, Aquinas dispensed with the belief that people can merit eternal life apart from God's grace. He showed the futility of this quest by noting that a human action leading to a goal or an end must be adapted to that end in the sense that it must be able to achieve that goal. Applying this idea to meriting salvation, he concluded: "Now eternal life is an end exceeding the proportion of human nature.... Hence man, by his natural gifts, cannot produce meritorious works proportionate to eternal life; and for this a higher force is needed, viz. the force of grace. And thus without grace man cannot merit eternal life; yet he can perform works conducting to a good which is natural to man."[48]

Accordingly, Aquinas echoed the view, prevalent in the church for centuries, that emphasized the grace of God yet prescribed an important role for human cooperation in obtaining salvation. Certainly, God exercises the primary role in achieving and applying salvation, but people have their part to play as well. God moves by initiating grace in a person's life; then that person moves toward God and moves away from sin, resulting in the forgiveness of sins. Thus, Aquinas believed in a synergy, or cooperative effort, between God and people in justification.

He explained this synergy, beginning with this principle: "Man, by his will, does works meriting eternal life; but ... for this it is necessary that the person's will should be prepared with grace by God."[49] So part of God's objective is to initiate the grace that prepares a person's will for salvation. In this way, the divine work involves the free will of those who are justified. Specifically, God "so infuses the gift of justifying grace that at the same time he moves free choice to accept the gift of grace."[50] This movement of the free will is the act of faith; included in it is a movement away from sin.[51] The effect of this process, finally, is the forgiveness of sins; that is the end or goal of the infusion of divine grace. Thus, "there are four things which are accounted to be necessary for the justifi-

---

45. Isidore of Seville, *Sentences*, 2.2.8, in Pelikan, 3:28.

46. Boniface, *Sermon*, 4.4, in Pelikan, 3:28.

47. Thomas Aquinas, *Summa Theologica*, 1st pt. of pt. 2, q. 113, art. 1. The text has been rendered clearer. For Aquinas, because justification can be defined by its goal or end, he at

times described justification as the forgiveness of sins. Ibid.

48. Ibid., 1st part of pt. 2, q. 109, art. 5; cf. q. 114, art. 5.

49. Ibid.

50. Ibid., 1st part of pt. 2, q. 113, art. 3.

51. Ibid., 1st part of pt. 2, q. 113, arts. 4, 5.

cation of the ungodly, viz. the infusion of grace, the movement of the free will towards God by faith, the movement of the free will away from sin, and the forgiveness of sins."[52]

According to Aquinas, justifying grace is infused, or poured, into the person who by faith accepts that gift of grace. So justification goes beyond a mere work of imputation — declaring that a person is not guilty but righteous before God instead. It includes an infusion of grace that actually makes the person's nature righteous. He defended this idea by appealing to the divine love: "As God's love consists not merely in the act of the divine will [in declaring a person righteous] but also implies a certain effect of grace, so likewise, when God does not impute sin to a man, there is implied a certain effect in him to whom the sin is not imputed."[53] Thus, the one who is justified is both *declared* righteous and *made* righteous. Then, with this God-given ability, Christians carry out their responsibility to cooperate with God: "Grace is given to us that we may do good and keep from sin."[54] In this discussion, Aquinas was influenced by the popular theological conviction that "God does not deny grace to the man who does what is in him." Furthermore, by engaging in good deeds, people accumulate merits. Here, Aquinas distinguished between two kinds of merits: (1) *Condign merits* are real merits, or merits of worthiness, accomplished by a righteous person through divine grace. (2) *Congruous merits*, or merits of fitness, are not strictly merits; rather, they are human works reckoned as merits, because in doing them, people do what is in them to do.[55] Considered in and of themselves, good works do not achieve any real merit — condign merit — before God, because those who do good works have received everything — especially grace — from him in the first place. But as long as people do what is within their ability to accomplish — according to the way God has designed them to use their free will to do good — they are rewarded with congruous merit. But Aquinas went beyond this, considering human work done with the assistance of the Holy Spirit. For Aquinas, this can and does achieve true condign merit resulting in eternal life.[56]

But what about those who do not merit eternal life? For Aquinas, the souls of people are immediately upon death conveyed to heaven — where they receive their deserved reward — or hell — where they are eternally punished for not having merited life. But in keeping with church doctrine, Aquinas offered a third alternative — purgatory — for those whose soul needs further cleansing from venial, or forgivable, sins.[57] Purgatory is a place where "there is only temporal punishment,"[58] by which the stain of venial sin is purged. After this period of cleansing, the soul is transferred to heaven to receive its

---

52. "The justification of the ungodly is a movement by which the soul is moved by God from a state of sin to a state of righteousness. Now in the movement by which one thing is moved by another, three things are required: first, the motion of the mover; secondly, the movement of the moved; thirdly, the consummation of the movement, or the attainment of the end. On the part of the divine motion, there is the infusion of grace; on the part of the free will that is moved, there are two movements — of departure [from sin] ... and of approach [toward God]; but the consummation of the movement or the attainment of the end of the movement is implied in the forgiveness of sins; for in this is the justification of the ungodly completed."

Ibid., 1st part of pt. 2, q. 113, art. 6. Although Aquinas spoke of "the movement of the free will towards sin," I have rendered his expression "the movement of the free will away from sin" because this notion was his intent, according to q. 113, art. 5.

53. Ibid., 1st part of pt. 2, q. 113, art. 2. Still, Aquinas considered justification to be an instantaneous act. 1st pt. of pt. 2, q. 113, art. 7.

54. Ibid., 1st pt. of pt. 2, q. 109, art. 9.

55. Ibid., 1st pt. of pt. 2, q. 114, art. 3.

56. Ibid.

57. Ibid., sup., q. 69, art. 2.

58. Ibid., sup., q. 69, art. 7.

proper reward of eternal life. To aid this movement from purgatory to heaven, living believers provide help for the souls in purgatory. Aquinas based this on "the words of 2 Maccabees 12:46: 'It is ... a holy and wholesome thought to pray for the dead that they may be released from sins.' But this would not be profitable unless it were a help to them. Therefore the sufferings of the living profit the dead."[59] The unity between the living and the dead, and the fact that "the dead live in the memory of the living," is the mechanism of this help.[60] Indeed, the sufferings of the living can help the souls in purgatory but do not have any benefit for those in hell.[61] In addition to their sufferings, the living may also offer prayers, masses, and alms on behalf of the souls in purgatory. For Aquinas, "these three are reckoned the principal means of benefiting the dead."[62] The church practiced interceding for the dead at its services, praying for the release of these souls from purgatory. Indeed, for a sum of money, masses—celebrations of the Eucharist—were offered for the dead. And the poor were helped financially through almsgiving, and the merits of this good work could benefit those in purgatory.

Another aid for the souls in purgatory was an indulgence, which is the remission of the temporal punishment due to sin. The two kinds were a partial indulgence, which removes some of the temporal punishment, and a plenary, or full, indulgence, which removes the entire punishment. Aquinas explained the operation of indulgences to help souls in purgatory: "The reason why they help is the oneness of the mystical body in which many have performed works of satisfaction exceeding the requirements of their debts.... So great is the quantity of such merits that it exceeds the entire debt of punishment due to those who are living at this moment: and this is especially due to the merits of Christ."[63] These merits accumulate in a "treasury of the saints" and can be allocated to those who need them.[64] The pope has the authority to distribute these merits on behalf of the souls in purgatory, thereby releasing them from their temporal punishment.

This doctrine of purgatory was further developed in the following centuries, and the church made several pronouncements concerning it. In particular, the Second Council of Lyons (1274) and the Council of Florence (1438) officially made purgatory part of the institution of the Roman Catholic Church. Thus, justification was not confined to this life but could be completed after death.

The use—and abuse—of indulgences also developed further in the latter medieval period. The high point came when Pope Clement VI issued the bull *Unigenitus* in 1343

---

59. Ibid., sup., q. 71, art. 2. Second Maccabees is considered to be part of the Old Testament canon by the Roman Catholic Church, but it is rejected as canonical by Protestant churches. See the discussion in chap. 2. The quote from Augustine is from *De Cure pro Mortuis*, 1 (trans. H. Browne [Cambridge: N.p., n.d.]).

60. "The sufferings of the living benefit the dead in two ways even as they benefit the living, both on account of the bond of love and on account of the prayers being directed to them. Nevertheless, we must not believe that the sufferings of the living benefit them so as to change their state from unhappiness to happiness or vice versa. But they help for the lessening of punishment or something of the kind that involves no

change in the state of the dead." The text has been rendered clearer. Ibid.

61. Ibid., sup., q. 71, art. 5, 6.

62. Ibid., sup., q. 71, art. 9.

63. Ibid., sup., q. 25, art. 1.

64. "Now one man can satisfy for another.... And the saints in whom this super-abundance of satisfactions is found, did not perform their good works for this or that particular person, who needs the remission of his punishment.... but they performed them for the whole church in general.... Now those things which are the common property of a number [i.e., the church] are distributed to the various individuals according to the judgment of him who rules them all." Ibid.

defining the theology of indulgences. He contended that the treasury of the church was at first entrusted to Peter, to whom were given the keys of the kingdom (Matt. 16:18–19). This means that he and his successors, the bishops of Rome—as the vicar of Christ on earth—have the right and duty to dispense the ever-increasing supply of merits.[65]

This proclamation by the church was applied in various ways to the actual dispensing of indulgences. On the eve of the Reformation, the monk John Tetzel sold indulgences according to the instructions of Albert of Mainz, archbishop of that city.[66] These instructions provided the rationale for paying money for what essentially is free—God's grace for the forgiveness of sins and release from purgatory—and further set forth how the faithful could obtain full remission of their own sins.[67] The rules called for the faithful to engage in prayer in certain selected churches.[68] These Christians were also instructed in the benefits of indulgences "so that they may be more easily induced to contribute," that is, purchase indulgences.[69] Moreover, "because the conditions of people, and their occupations, are so various and different," the church decided what rates to charge different groups.[70] A "sliding scale" of payment was laid down, and the faithful were encouraged based on their socioeconomic status.[71] Finally, provision was made for the poor to "supply their contribution with prayer and fasting."[72] In addition to purchasing indulgences for themselves, people were urged to obtain them for souls in purgatory.[73]

The selling of indulgences became a highly successful money-making operation for the Catholic Church. "A penny in the coffer rings, a soul from purgatory springs" was the publicity jingle employed by John Tetzel to stimulate the faithful to buy indulgences for those in purgatory. Such crass promotional techniques, feeding off the ignorance of church members, induced many to give beyond their financial means. Still, the foreboding sense of divine judgment and punishment after death was strong among the common

---

65. Clement VI, *Unigenitus*, in Bettenson, 203. "Vicar" means representative.

66. Albert announced that the money raised from the sale of indulgences would be sent to Rome for the building of St. Peter's Basilica. Actually, however, only half the money was used for that construction. The other half was transferred from Albert to the bank to pay off the debt he had incurred in buying the office of archbishop of Mainz.

67. "The first grace is the complete forgiveness of all sin. Nothing greater than this can be named, since sinful man, deprived of the grace of God, obtains complete forgiveness by these means and once more enjoys God's grace. Moreover, through this forgiveness of sins, the punishment which one is obligated to undergo in purgatory on account of the injury done to the divine majesty is all forgiven, and the pains of purgatory are completely blotted out. And although nothing is precious enough to be given in exchange for such a grace—since it is a free gift and grace is beyond price—yet in order that Christian believers may be more easily induced to procure it, we establish the following rules." Albert of Mainz, *Instructions*, in Bettenson, 203–4. The text has been rendered clearer.

68. "In the first place, everyone who is contrite in heart and has made verbal confession shall visit at least the seven

churches indicated for this purpose, those in which the papal arms [seal] are displayed, and in each church shall say five 'Our Fathers' and five 'Hail Mary's' in honor of the five wounds of our Lord Jesus Christ, by whom our salvation is won." Ibid., in Bettenson, 204. The text has been rendered clearer.

69. Ibid.

70. Ibid.

71. Kings and bishops were assessed the greatest amount, followed by abbots (heads of monasteries), counts, and barons. Next in line came nobles and church leaders of lesser rank. Self-employed workers paid a nominal amount, and those who had little income were charged even less.

72. "For the kingdom of heaven should be open to the poor as much as the rich." Ibid., in Bettenson, 204.

73. The instructions set forth how contributions could be made for the souls in purgatory so they could have forgiveness: "The same contribution shall be placed in the chest by a living person as one would make for himself.... It is, furthermore, not necessary that the persons who place their contributions in the chest for the dead should be contrite in heart and have verbally confessed, since this grace is based simply on the state of grace in which the dead departed, and on the contribution of the living." Ibid., in Bettenson, 205.

people, and they recognized the need to make satisfaction to God. They chased after justification, but the church offered the faithful little more than empty promises that the pope could draw upon the treasury of the saints to relieve them and those in purgatory of the temporal punishment due to sin.

VIEWS OF JUSTIFICATION IN THE REFORMATION AND POST-REFORMATION

Into this dismal situation, a young monk by the name of Martin Luther dared to enter. On October 31, 1517,[74] he nailed his Ninety-five Theses to the door of the Castle Church in Wittenberg (Germany). This action was the typical way of indicating a desire to debate the posted items, so Luther was calling upon the Wittenberg University community to address the topic of indulgences. There is little doubt that he had no idea that his posting of the Ninety-five Theses would be a spark of revolution over the issue of justification.

Several key themes were rehearsed in the theses: Luther denied that the pope had "power to forgive guilt, except by declaring and confirming that it has been forgiven by God";[75] justification belongs to God alone. He thus criticized the promise of indulgences for deceiving purchasers.[76] Furthermore, Luther criticized the way indulgences were sold, scolding their hawkers as "preaching an invention of man" and "preaching doctrines inconsistent with Christianity."[77] Moreover, he was concerned that the emphasis on buying and selling indulgences would detract from people helping the poor. He countered with this thesis: "Christians are to be taught that to give to the poor or to lend to the needy is a better work than the purchase of indulgences."[78] Indeed, he worried that the poor were being induced to spend what little money they had on indulgences, thus plunging them and their families into financial ruin.[79] Giving the benefit of the doubt to the pope, Luther assured the faithful that if the pope were only aware of the tremendous cost of indulgences to the poor, he would suspend the practice.[80] Finally, Luther emphasized: "Every Christian who is truly contrite has plenary remission both of penance and of guilt as his due, even without an indulgence."[81] It was for this reason that he countered the Church's claim to the "treasure of the saints" with another treasure, "the holy gospel of the glory and grace of God."[82]

The reaction to Luther's Ninety-five Theses was quick and widespread. The idea of questioning the church's system of obtaining forgiveness of sins and satisfying God brought the issue of justification to the forefront in the years to come. More than anything else, Luther became known as the champion of justification by grace through faith alone.

Addressing the specific elements of justification, Luther distinguished between "two kinds of Christian righteousness.... The first is alien righteousness, that is, the righteousness of another, instilled from outside. This is the righteousness of Christ by which he

---

74. This date is generally considered to be the start of the Protestant Reformation.

75. Martin Luther, *The Ninety-five Theses*, 6, in Bettenson, 206.

76. Ibid., 24, in Bettenson, 207.

77. Ibid., 27, 35; cf. 33, in Bettenson, 207, 208, 210.

78. Ibid., 43, in Bettenson, 208.

79. Ibid., 46, in Bettenson, 209.

80. Ibid., 50, 51, in Bettenson, 209.

81. Ibid., 36, in Bettenson, 208.

82. Ibid., 62, in Bettenson, 210.

justifies through faith."[83] This alien righteousness "is primary; it is the basis, the cause, the source of all our actual righteousness."[84] As for the second type: "The second kind of righteousness is our proper righteousness, not because we alone work it, but because we work with that first and alien righteousness. This is that manner of life spent profitably in good works, in the first place, in slaying the flesh and crucifying the desires with respect to the self.... In the second place, this righteousness consists in love to one's neighbor, and in the third place, in meekness and fear toward God."[85]

Luther's concept of an alien righteousness was a particularly important contribution he made to the doctrine of justification. When combined with the forgiveness of sins — which was synonymous with justification[86] — the result was what Luther (like Clement of Rome), called "the sweet exchange" between Jesus Christ and a sinner. He explained this in the form of a prayer: "You, Lord Jesus, are my righteousness and I am your sin. You have taken on yourself what you were not, and you have given me what I am not."[87] Thus, in exchange for his sins, which are transferred to Christ and borne by him, the sinner receives the righteousness of Christ — an alien righteousness.

In his *Freedom of a Christian*, Luther presented alien righteousness and actual righteousness in a paradoxical way: "I shall set down the following two propositions concerning the freedom and the bondage of the spirit: A Christian is a perfectly free lord of all, subject to none. A Christian is a perfectly obedient servant of all, subject to all. These two theses seem to contradict each other."[88] Luther addressed the first thesis: Christian freedom is established by justification by grace through faith alone and not works. Such divine action frees the Christian from the law of God.[89] In the strongest possible language, Luther urged: "If works are sought after as a means to righteousness ... and are done under the false impression that through them one is justified, they are made necessary and freedom and faith are destroyed; and this addition to them makes them no longer good but truly damnable works."[90] As for the second thesis, Christian service and obligation to engage in good works for the sake of all people is established by justification.[91] Luther turned to Paul for support for this idea: "This is a truly Christian life. Here, faith is truly active through love [Gal. 5:6], that is, it finds expression in works of the

83. Martin Luther, *Two Kinds of Righteousness*, LW, 31:297.

84. Ibid., LW, 31:298.

85. Ibid., LW, 31:299.

86. "To attain the remission of sins is to be justified." Martin Luther, *Apology for the Augsburg Confession*, 4.76, in *Triglot Concordia: The Symbolical Books of the Evangelical Lutheran Church*, trans. F. Bente and W. H. T. Dau (St. Louis: Concordia, 1921), 143.

87. Preserved Smith, ed., *Luther's Correspondence and Other Contemporary Letters* (Philadelphia: Lutheran Publication Society, 1913), 1:34, cited in Timothy George, *Theology of the Reformers* (Nashville: Broadman, 1988), 69–70.

88. "A Christian has all that he needs in faith and needs no works to justify himself. If he has no need of works, he has no need of the law. And if he has no need of the law, surely he is free from the law.... Christian liberty ... makes the law and works unnecessary for any man's righteousness and salva-

tion." Luther, *The Freedom of a Christian*, LW, 31:344.

89. Ibid., LW, 31:349–50.

90. Ibid., LW, 31:363.

91. "Here the works begin; here a man cannot enjoy leisure; here he must indeed take care to discipline his body by fastings, watchings, labors, and other reasonable discipline and to subject it to the Spirit.... In doing these works, however, we must not think that a man is justified before God by them." The control a Christian exercises over his body is ultimately aimed at service for others: "A man does not live for himself alone in this mortal body to work for it alone, but he lives also for all men on earth; rather, he lives only for others and not for himself.... This is what makes caring for the body a Christian work, that through its health and comfort we may be able to work, to acquire, and lay by funds with which to aid those who are in need." Ibid., LW, 31:358–59, 364–65.

freest service, cheerfully and lovingly done, with which a man willingly serves another without hope of reward."[92] From this discussion, Luther underscored: "We do not reject good works; on the contrary, we cherish and teach them as much as possible."[93]

As much as Luther tried to emphasize the importance of good works following faith, some of his opponents latched onto his rallying cry "justification by faith alone" and accused him of denying any role for good works. His *Treatise on Good Works* was intended to set the record straight, addressing the relationship between faith and works. In a surprising opening, Luther noted the most important good work of all—faith. From this preeminent work of faith, all other good works must flow.[94] As narrowly defined by the Roman Catholic Church, good works consisted solely of religious deeds—"praying in church, fasting, and almsgiving."[95] Luther revolutionized the concept of good works by insisting that even common activities—working, eating, drinking, and sleeping—could qualify as real good works before God.[96] It is faith—confidence that what one does pleases God because it is according to his will—that qualifies an activity as a good work before God. This work is joyfully done without regard for the merit that it acquires: "Thus a Christian man who lives in this confidence toward God knows all things, can do all things, ventures everything that needs to be done, and does everything gladly and willingly, not that he may gather merits and good works, but because it is a pleasure for him to please God in doing these things. He simply serves God with no thought of reward, content that his service pleases God."[97]

Luther's pointed break with the Roman Catholic Church's notion of merit was a corollary of his doctrine of justification. He strongly condemned Aquinas's notion of condign and congruous merits, because the teaching renders the grace of God in the death of Christ unnecessary.[98] Another corollary of Luther's doctrine of justification was his paradoxical statements "simultaneously righteous and a sinner" and "always righteous and a sinner." Again, he distanced himself from the Catholic notion that a person is partly righteous (to the degree that infused grace has transformed his character into holiness) and partly sinful (to the degree that this sanctifying grace needs to accomplish more renewal). Rather, for Luther, a person is both completely justified by God, and thus righteous, and completely sinful at the same time. Luther explained this paradoxical idea: "For inasmuch as the saints are always aware of their sin and implore God for the merciful gift of his righteousness, they are for this very reason also always reckoned righteous by God. Therefore, they are before themselves and in truth unrighteous, but before God they are righteous because he reckons them so on account of this confession of their sin; they are sinners in fact, but by virtue of the reckoning of the merciful God they are righteous."[99]

Thus, Luther's doctrine of justification undercut the merit system of the Roman Catholic Church and called for a new church—the Protestant Church—to focus on God's

---

92. Ibid., LW, 31:365.

93. Ibid., LW, 31:363.

94. *Treatise on Good Works*, 2, LW, 44:23.

95. Ibid., 3, LW, 44:24.

96. Ibid., LW, 44:24–25.

97. Ibid., 6, LW, 44:27.

98. *Lectures on Galatians*, LW, 26:124. Reflecting this emphasis of Luther, the *Augsburg Confession* emphasized the futility of human merit before God. *Augsburg Confession*, art. 4, in Schaff, 3:10.

99. Martin Luther, *Lectures on Romans*, in *Luther: Lectures on Romans*, ed. Wilhelm Pauck; LCC 15:125.

grace received through faith alone. As he explained, "If the doctrine of justification is lost, the whole of Christian doctrine is lost."[100]

John Calvin systematically set forth the doctrine of justification, echoing Luther's conviction by calling it "the main hinge on which religion turns" and urging the church to "devote the greatest attention and care to it."[101] He explained "justification simply as the acceptance with which God receives us into his favor as righteous people. And we say that it consists in the remission of sins and the imputation of Christ's righteousness."[102] He contrasted justification by works and by faith: "He in whose life that purity and holiness will be found which deserves a testimony of righteousness before God's throne will be said to be justified by works, or else he who, by the wholeness of his works, can meet and satisfy God's judgment. On the contrary, justified by faith is he who, excluded from the righteousness of works, grasps the righteousness of Christ through faith, and clothed in it, appears in God's sight not as a sinner but as a righteous man."[103]

Like Luther before him, Calvin criticized the Roman Catholic Church's insistence that justification is the result of faith joined together with good works. Indeed, the Protestant view of justification by faith alone automatically excludes justification by faith plus works.[104] Anticipating a Catholic response—that the works upon which the Roman Catholic Church insists are not done by a person himself, but are "the gifts of Christ and the fruit of regeneration"—Calvin still rejected any role for such works in justification.[105] Key to this dissent was the fact that "the benefits of Christ—sanctification and righteousness—are different."[106] With this point, he underscored a major problem with the Catholic theology of justification: it mixed together the declarative work of God—justification, by which a person is credited with righteousness—and the transforming works of God—regeneration and sanctification, by which a person actually becomes righteous. For Calvin, though these works of God are inseparable, they are distinguishable; indeed, they must be differentiated: "to be justified means something different from being made new creatures,"[107] and confounding the two results in a false notion of justification. By confusing justification and sanctification, the Roman Catholic Church emphasized the infusion of righteousness rather than the imputation of righteousness, and it viewed justification as a reward that could be merited.[108] But

---

100. *Lectures on Galatians: Chapters 1-4*, LW, 26:9. The *Smalcald Articles* addressed the importance of it in this way: "Of this article nothing can be yielded or surrendered, even though heaven and earth, and whatever will not abide [all created things], should sink to ruin. *For there is no other name under heaven given among men by which we must be saved*, says Peter (Acts 4:12). *And with his stripes we are healed* (Isa. 53:5). And upon this article all things depend which we teach and practice in opposition to the pope, the devil, and the world. Therefore, we must be sure concerning this doctrine, and not doubt; for otherwise all is lost, and the pope and devil and all things gain the victory and suit [rule] over us." *Smalcald Articles*, 2.1.5, in Bente and Dau, *Triglot Concordia*, 463.

101. John Calvin, *Institutes of the Christian Religion*, 3.11.1,

LCC, 1:726.

102. Ibid., 3.11.2, LCC, 1:727. In other words: "He is said to be justified in God's sight who is both reckoned righteous in God's judgment and has been accepted on account of his righteousness.... Now he is justified who is reckoned in the condition not of a sinner, but of a righteous man; and for that reason, he stands firm before God's judgment seat while all sinners fall." Ibid., LCC, 1:726.

103. Ibid., LCC, 1:726–27.

104. Ibid., 3.11.13, LCC, 1:743.

105. Ibid., 3.11.14, LCC, 1:744.

106. Ibid.

107. Ibid., 3.11.6, LCC, 1:732.

108. Ibid., 3.11.14, LCC, 1:745.

justification is not about merit, nor is it about infusion of grace, even with the help of the Holy Spirit. Thus, the Roman Catholic Church had missed the point of justification by grace through faith alone.[109]

As critical as he was of good works done to achieve righteousness before God, Calvin positively presented good works that follow justification.[110] At the same time, he insisted that even those good deeds should never be viewed as works done by believers themselves. To do so would rob God of his honor and the rightful thanks due him, because the only valid works done are carried out through his grace.[111] This emphasis on good works rebuffed the Catholic charge that the Protestant doctrine of justification by faith alone was a hindrance to good works.[112] Calvin reasoned: "What if, rather, these [good works] were encouraged and strengthened? For we dream neither of a faith devoid of good works nor of a justification that stands without them."[113] To support this position, he reemphasized the inseparable link between justification and sanctification: "Do you wish, then, to attain righteousness in Christ? You must first possess Christ; but you cannot possess him without being made partaker in his sanctification, because he cannot be divided into pieces.... [H]e gives both of them at the same time, the one never without the other."[114] Calvin concluded that, by receiving both justification and sanctification, believers will indeed engage in good works, though they are not saved by them.[115]

The Lutheran and Reformed churches that developed out of the theology of Luther and Calvin continued to emphasize the doctrine of justification and defend it against Catholic attacks. The title of a book by Heinrich Bullinger indicated the precise wording of the Protestant doctrine: *The Grace of God That Justifies Us for the Sake of Christ through Faith Alone, without Good Works, While Faith Meanwhile Abounds in Good Works.*[116] All of the historic Protestant confessions presented the doctrine in that way.

109. So Calvin offered this order of God's working: Scripture "presents this order of justification: To begin with, God deigns [consents] to embrace the sinner with his pure and freely given goodness, finding nothing in him except his miserable condition to prompt him to mercy, since he sees man totally void and empty of good works; and so he seeks in himself the reason to benefit man. Then God touches the sinner with a sense of his goodness in order that he, despairing of his own works, may ground the whole of his salvation in God's mercy. This is the experience of faith through which the sinner comes into possession of his salvation when from the teaching of the gospel he acknowledges that he has been reconciled to God: that with Christ's righteousness interceding and forgiveness of sins accomplished he is justified. And although regenerated by the Spirit of God, he ponders the eternal righteousness laid up for him not in the good works to which he inclines but in the sole righteousness of Christ." Ibid., 3.11.16, LCC, 1:746.

110. Ibid., 3.14.8, LCC, 1:775–76.

111. Thus, Calvin had a pessimistic view even of those good works performed by Christians: "The best work that can be brought forward from them [works] is still always spotted and corrupted with some impurity of the flesh, and has, so to speak, some dirt mixed with it.... We have not a single work going forth from the saints that if it is judged in itself does not deserve shame as its just reward." Ibid., 3.14.9, LCC, 1:776–77. Thus, the true value of good works is due to God's grace. Yet these works please God and bring reward to those who perform them: "Let the Lord, then, call to judgment the best in human works: he will indeed recognize in them his own righteousness but man's dishonor and shame! Good works, then, are pleasing to God and are not unfruitful for their doers. But they receive by way of reward the most ample benefits of God, not because they so deserve but because God's kindness has of itself set this value on them." Ibid., 3.15.3, LCC, 1:791.

112. Ibid., 3.16.1, LCC, 1:797.

113. Ibid., LCC, 1:798.

114. Ibid.

115. "Thus it is clear how true it is that we are justified not without works yet not through works, since in our sharing in Christ, which justifies us, sanctification is just as much included as righteousness." Ibid.

116. Heinrich Bullinger (1554).

The Council of Trent strongly denounced this Protestant doctrine. In its decree on justification,[117] the council stated and supported the Catholic doctrinal emphases. These included the necessity of baptism for justification;[118] the idea of justification as the cooperative work between God, who gives prevenient grace, and people who embrace that grace;[119] the necessity of preparation for justification;[120] a definition of justification as "not only forgiveness of sins but also the sanctification and renewal of the inward man, through the voluntary reception of the grace and the gifts";[121] the insistence that justification can and must increase daily in the lives of the justified;[122] and the conviction that justification can be lost, through unfaithfulness and any and all mortal sins.[123] In the second place, the council denounced the Protestant ideas of justification as heresy, condemning to hell anyone embracing those notions.[124] The Roman Catholic Church and Protestant churches were at complete odds over this doctrine.

VIEWS OF JUSTIFICATION IN THE MODERN PERIOD

The modern period featured several important developments with the doctrine of justification. Many Protestants continued to assert the Reformation notion of justification against the Roman Catholic idea. Other Protestants, like John Wesley, altered the doctrine from its historic Reformation formulation. Still others dismissed the idea of justification as fiction, subjecting the historic Protestant view to searing attacks. This called forth a fresh defense of the doctrine. Questions concerning the nature of the doctrine led to a reexamination of the Pauline and Lutheran formulations of justification. Finally, ecumenical dialogue resulted in some startling agreements on the doctrine by churches that historically had strongly opposing viewpoints.

While the historic formulation continued to be expressed and defended by most Protestants, some affirmed the Reformation doctrine to some degree but made substantial modifications to it as well. John Wesley expressed the typical Protestant distinction between justification and regeneration[125] and between justification and sanctification.[126] Specifically, he underscored that "the plain scriptural notion of justification is pardon, the forgiveness of sins" that comes through "the propitiation made by the blood" of Jesus Christ.[127] Despite this apparent expression of the historic Protestant view, Wesley made

117. *Canons and Decrees of the Council of Trent*, 6th session (January 13, 1547), *Decree on Justification*, in Schaff, 2:89–118.

118. Ibid., 4, in Schaff, 2:91.

119. Ibid., 5, in Schaff, 2:92.

120. Ibid., 6, in Schaff, 2:93.

121. Ibid., 7, in Schaff, 2:94. The text has been rendered clearer.

122. Ibid., 10, in Schaff, 2:99.

123. Ibid., 15, in Schaff, 2:106. This justifying grace can be recovered, however, through the sacrament of penance.

124. Over thirty canons of anathema, or condemnation, were included in the *Decree on Justification*. These included denunciations of the Protestant principles that justification is by faith, and faith alone; that justification is only about the removal of sins and the imputation of Christ's righteousness; that justification is a once-and-for-all declarative act of God that is either true of a person or not, but cannot be increased; and that justification entirely removes any and all penalties acquired because of sin (instead, the council affirmed its belief in purgatory). Ibid., canons 9, 11, 24, 30, in Schaff, 2:112, 115, 117.

125. John Wesley, *The Great Privilege of Those Who Are Born of God*, in *The Works of John Wesley*, ed. Thomas Jackson, 14 vols. (Grand Rapids: Zondervan, 1958), 5:224.

126. John Wesley, *Justification by Faith*, 2.1–3.2, in *Wesley's Standard Sermons*, ed. Edward H. Sugden, 2 vols. (London: Epworth, 1921), 1:119–22.

127. Ibid., 2.5, in Sugden, *Wesley's Standard Sermons*, 1:120.

a key change to the doctrine. This stemmed from his close association between justification and regeneration/sanctification. Although the Reformers before him insisted on the association of these two works, Wesley joined them together in a tighter fashion than his predecessors ever did. Specifically, he rejected the idea that God justifies sinners simply by reckoning them as righteous: "Least of all does justification imply, that God is deceived in those whom he justifies; that he thinks them to be what, in fact, they are not; that he accounts them to be otherwise than they are. It does by no means imply, that God ... believes us righteous when we are unrighteous."[128] Accordingly, he tied the two divine works closely together: "In the moment a sinner is justified, his heart is cleansed in a low degree."[129] That is, "God sanctifies as well as justifies all them who believe in him. They to whom the righteousness of Christ is imputed are made righteous by the Spirit of Christ; they are renewed in the image of God."[130] Thus, justification is not only about the imputation of Christ's righteousness, but the forgiveness of and the cleansing from sin. By this, then, God sees the person as righteous because he actually is righteous.[131]

Wesley's concern about the traditional formulation of the doctrine of justification was the ease with which it opens the door to a disregard for sanctification and ongoing engagement in good works. Both Luther and Calvin had been forced to confront these misunderstandings and misapplications of the doctrine. Wesley and others following him found themselves needing to confront them as well. An example of this was Charles Finney, who claimed, "There is scarcely any question in theology that has been encumbered with more injurious and technical mysticism than that of justification.... For sinners to be forensically pronounced just, is impossible and absurd."[132] He explicitly denied the traditional notion of justification "as a forensic or judicial proceeding."[133] Rather, justification "consists in a governmental decree of pardon or amnesty—in arresting and setting aside the execution of the incurred penalty of law—in pardoning and restoring to favor those who have sinned, and those whom the law had pronounced guilty, and upon whom it had passed the sentence of eternal death, and rewarding them as if they had been righteous."[134] He also rejected the imputation of Christ's righteousness to sinners.[135] Throughout his discussion, he made it clear that he was reacting to a certain view of justification, which he described as "certainly another gospel"[136] because "it is antinomianism."[137] With this

---

128. Ibid., 2.4, in Sugden, *Wesley's Standard Sermons,* 1:120.

129. John Wesley, *An Answer to the Rev. Mr. Church*, in *The Works of the Rev. John Wesley*, ed. John Emory, 7 vols. (New York: B. Waugh and T. Mason, 1835), 5:284.

130. John Wesley, *The Lord Our Righteousness*, in Jackson, *Works of John Wesley*, 5:241.

131. By his own admission, Wesley was fearful of the common abuse of the historic Protestant formulation of justification and imputation: "What we are afraid of is this—lest anyone should use the phrase, 'The righteousness of Christ,' or 'The righteousness of Christ is imputed to me,' as a cover for his unrighteousness. We have known this done a thousand times. A man has been reproved, suppose for drunkenness. 'O,' he said, 'I pretend to no righteousness of my own; Christ

is my righteousness.' ... And thus, though a man be as far from the practice as from the tempers of a Christian; though he neither has the mind which was in Christ, nor in any respect walks as he walked; yet he has armor of proof against all conviction, in what he calls 'the righteousness of Christ.'" Ibid., in Jackson, *Works of John Wesley*, 5:244.

132. Charles Grandison Finney, *Lectures on Systematic Theology* (1878), lecture 25, in *Finney's Systematic Theology: New Expanded Edition*, ed. Dennis Carroll, Bill Nicely, and L. G. Parkhurst Jr. (Minneapolis: Bethany, 1994), 360, 361–62.

133. Ibid., in Carroll et al., *Finney's Systematic Theology*, 360.

134. Ibid., in Carroll et al., *Finney's Systematic Theology*, 361.

135. Ibid., in Carroll et al., *Finney's Systematic Theology*, 362.

136. Ibid., in Carroll et al., *Finney's Systematic Theology*, 369.

137. Ibid.

criticism, Finney referred to the idea that "being once justified, he [the sinner] is always thereafter justified, whatever he may do."[138] Obviously, some people were taking advantage of the doctrine and, while claiming to have been justified by faith alone, were not living out that faith in love. It is quite doubtful that Luther, Calvin, and the post-Reformers would recognize the doctrine of justification that they articulated and defended in Finney's description. Nevertheless, this common misperception of the traditional Reformation doctrine was perpetuated and held up for ongoing attacks by Finney and others.

Typical of some other Protestants was a reinterpretation of the traditional doctrine in line with modern concerns, developments, and worldviews. For example, Friedrich Schleiermacher reformulated the doctrine of justification in accordance with his view of religion as the self-consciousness of absolute dependence on God. Accordingly, the event of justification is not an objective reality, but a subjective reality in the consciousness of people.[139] As a second example, Shailer Matthews challenged the traditional idea of justification because of the modern struggle to understand God as a sovereign Judge who acquits sinners of their sin. For Matthews, modern man's "fundamental conception of the universe makes it difficult for him to respond to the forensic conception of God as a monarch who establishes days of trial and passes individual sentences upon millions of lives. His idea of law makes it hard for him to think of a remitted penalty in a moral world, where relations are genetic and only figuratively to be conceived of in terms of the law court and a king."[140] Thus, salvation does not involve justification but is instead about moral living: "The loving God of the universe will save a man who tries to live as Jesus did."[141] This same type of re-visioning of the doctrine of justification can be found in a third example, Paul Tillich, for whom the modern human plight was doubt and despair. Thus, he reformulated the doctrine as the divine response to this human predicament. As a final example, Rudoph Bultmann reformulated the doctrine of justification in accordance with existentialist philosophy. Within this framework, he viewed the gospel as offering people the possibility to turn from their inauthentic existence to authentic existence through faith in Christ. All of these formulations were clear departures from the Reformation doctrine of justification.

Toward the close of the twentieth century, several new developments arose in conjunction with discussions between churches that historically have taken very different views on the doctrine of justification. One of these, an ecumenical effort on the part of the Catholic Church and the Lutheran Church, resulted in the publication of *A Joint Declaration on the Doctrine of Justification*.[142] It affirmed that "the subscribing Lutheran churches and the Roman Catholic Church are now able to articulate a common understanding of our

---

138. Ibid.

139. "We can as little ... admit an act in time eventuating at a particular moment or an act directed upon an individual. All that can be individual or temporal is the effect of a divine act or decree, not the act or decree itself. Only in so far as the dogmatic treatment makes its starting point the self-consciousness of the individual, and therefore in this case the consciousness of an alteration in the relation to God, can we think of the justifying action of God as bearing on the individual." Friedrich Schleiermacher, *The Christian Faith*, ed.

H. R. Mackintosh and J. S. Stewart (Edinburgh: T & T Clark, 1928), 501.

140. Shailer Matthews, *The Gospel and the Modern Man* (New York: Macmillan, 1912), 182.

141. Ibid., 184.

142. A product of years of study and dialogue, the document was signed officially by members of the World Lutheran Federation and the Roman Catholic Church on October 31, 1999, the 482nd anniversary of the Reformation.

justification by God's grace through faith in Christ."[143] The document followed a standard format: First, the common understanding of justification, encompassing the consensus in the basic truth of the doctrine, was set forth.[144] Second, the particular Lutheran explications of the doctrine were set forth and declared to be compatible with this common understanding. Third, the particular Roman Catholic explications of the doctrine were set forth and declared to be compatible with this common understanding. The far-reaching consequences of this document included the removal of the historic condemnations that the Lutheran churches and the Catholic Church pronounced against each other in regard to their opposing views on this doctrine.[145] Despite the official consensus reached by the World Lutheran Federation and the Catholic Church, a significant minority of Lutheran churches—including the Lutheran Church, Missouri Synod—refused to sign the *Joint Declaration*. At the heart of their objection was the conviction that the document did not indicate a significant change in the Roman Catholic theology of justification. What it did represent, according to those who rejected the agreement, was a tragic willingness on the part of most Lutheran churches to accept the Catholic view as a valid interpretation of Scripture.[146] Many evangelicals who were not Lutherans supported this minority view, rejecting the *Joint Declaration* as a bona fide consensus on justification.[147]

A second development in this area was the initiative on the part of several leading Roman Catholics and important evangelicals. To date, this effort has resulted in the publication of six significant statements under the rubric "Evangelicals and Catholics Together,"[148] the first two of which addressed the doctrine of justification. "The Christian Mission in the Third Millennium" made a brief and ambiguous affirmation about justification.[149] Intense criticism of it led to a second statement, "The Gift of Salvation,"

---

143. *A Joint Declaration on the Doctrine of Justification*, 5. Available at http://www.vatican.va/roman_curia/pontifical_councils/chrstuni/documents/rc_pc_chrstuni_doc_31101999_cath-luth-joint-declaration_en.html; and http://www.lutheranworld.org/LWF_Documents/EN/JDDJ_99-jd97e.pdf.

144. The common understanding embraced the complete helplessness of sinful human beings to achieve any merit toward their justification; the relationship between justification and regeneration; a certain agreement on justification by faith and through grace; and other elements. Ibid., 19–27.

145. "Thus the doctrinal condemnations of the sixteenth century, in so far as they relate to the doctrine of justification, appear in a new light: The teaching of the Lutheran churches presented in this *Declaration* does not fall under the condemnations from the Council of Trent. The condemnations in the Lutheran Confessions do not apply to the teaching of the Roman Catholic Church presented in this *Declaration*." Ibid., 41.

146. At its 1988 national convention, the LCMS took the following action: "To Express Deep Regret and Profound Disagreement with ELCA Actions RESOLUTION 3-08A Adopted in Convention by The Lutheran Church--Missouri Synod, July 1998." Available at http://www.lcms.org/pages/internal.asp?NavID=2144.

147. A similar initiative between the Roman Catholic Church and the Anglican Church produced a joint statement on the doctrine of justification: ARCIC-II, *Salvation and the Church. An Agreed Statement by the Second Anglican–Roman Catholic International Commission* (London, 1987). Available at http://www.prounione.urbe.it/dia-int/arcic/doc/e_arcicII_salvation.html. Because this statement is nonauthoritative, I prefer to discuss in detail the Roman Catholic–Lutheran *Joint Declaration*. Many of the same issues are addressed in both statements.

148. "Evangelicals and Catholics Together: The Christian Mission in the Third Millennium," *First Things* 43 (1994): 15–22; "The Gift of Salvation," *First Things* 79 (1998): 20–23; "Your Word Is Truth," *First Things* 125 (2002): 38–42; "The Communion of Saints," *First Things* 131 (2003): 26–33; "The Call to Holiness," *First Things* 151 (2005): 23–26; "That They May Have Life," *First Things* 166 (2006): 18–27.

149. "We affirm together that we are justified by grace through faith because of Christ. Living faith is active in love that is nothing less than the love of Christ, for we together say with Paul: 'I have been crucified with Christ; it is no longer I who live, but Christ who lives in me; and the life I now live in the flesh I live by faith in the Son of God, who loved me and gave himself for me' (Galatians 2)." "Evangelicals and Catholics Together," 16.

written in an attempt to clarify the nature of the agreement reached on the doctrine of justification. This document affirmed the following:

> We agree that justification is not earned by any good works or merits of our own; it is entirely God's gift, conferred through the Father's sheer graciousness, out of the love that he bears us in his Son, who suffered on our behalf and rose from the dead for our justification (Romans 4:25). In justification, God, on the basis of Christ's righteousness alone, declares us to be no longer his rebellious enemies but his forgiven friends, and by virtue of his declaration it is so.[150]

Because of the issue of how this justification is to be received—by faith alone, according to the historical Protestant understanding, or by some other means in addition to faith—the statement addressed the nature of faith and affirmed that justification is by faith alone, specifying, "We understand that what we here affirm is in agreement with what the Reformation traditions have meant by justification by faith alone (*sola fide*)."[151] Despite this widespread and significant agreement on the doctrine of justification, the statement recognized that numerous questions still remain for discussion.[152]

With the increased interest in the doctrine of justification at the turn of the third millennium, several other developments came to the forefront of theological debate. The first, dubbed the "new perspective," raised serious doubts that Luther's understanding of justification was a rediscovery of the apostle Paul's doctrine. Instead, it maintained that "the Protestant reading of Paul was a reading back of Luther's own experience into Paul."[153] In this new perspective,[154] the condemnation leveled by Jesus against the Pharisees and other religious leaders was aimed at their transposing their covenantal relationship with God into covenantal privilege that proudly separated them from the Gentiles. An attitude of exclusive favoritism developed: the Jews enjoyed a special status before God, and everyone else was not so favored. This attitude of superiority was accompanied by meticulous attention to the details of the law in order for the Jews to distinguish themselves externally from the Gentiles. Paul followed Jesus in condemning such attitudes

---

150. "Gift of Salvation," 21.

151. Ibid.

152. Ibid., 22.

153. J. D. G. Dunn and A. M. Suggate, *The Justice of God: A Fresh Look at the Old Doctrine of Justification* (Carlisle, Pa.: Paternoster, 1993), 14. For further discussion, see Paul O'Callahan, *Fides Christi: The Justification Debate* (Dublin: Four Courts, 1997). I am indebted to O'Callahan's work for part of my discussion on this topic.

154. Two developments contributed to this new perspective. Ernst Käsemann's study of Paul's concept of "the righteousness of God" placed it in the context of intertestamental Judaism—the Judaism that developed between the end of the writing of the Old Testament and that which is presented in the New Testament. Käsemann concluded that the term *righteousness*, while "originally signifying trustworthiness in regard to the community, came to mean the rehabilitated standing of a member of the community who had been acquit-

ted of an offense against it." "'The Righteousness of God' in Paul," in Ernst Käsemann, *New Testament Questions of Today* (Philadelphia: Fortress, 1969), 172, cited in O'Callahan, *Fides Christi*, 189. That is, the righteousness of God had to do with his relationship of grace and faithfulness toward those in his covenant community. Working from this background, biblical scholars such as E. P. Sanders denied that the Judaism confronted by Jesus was legalistic and oriented toward works righteousness. Instead, it could be described as "covenantal nomism." According to Sanders, the election of the people of Israel, the giving of the law, the provision of atonement for sin by means of sacrifices, and ultimate salvation were all part of a covenant of grace established by God. Nomism, or obedience to the law, kept individual Jews in the covenant; it was not a legalistic means to earn favor and forgiveness before God so as to become part of the covenant. E. P. Sanders, *Paul and Palestinian Judaism: A Comparison of Patterns of Religion* (London: SCM, 1977), 427.

and actions—what Paul called "the works of the law." Indeed, this was the heart of the Pauline doctrine of justification by faith: "The Christian doctrine of justification began as Paul's protest not as an individual sinner against a Jewish legalism, but as Paul's protest on behalf of Gentiles against Jewish exclusivism."[155]

This "new perspective" was popularized by N. T. Wright, who maintained that the Protestant Reformers missed the point on key issues like the righteousness of God and the doctrine of justification. The former is not about the imputation of Christ's righteousness to sinners,[156] but God's own covenant faithfulness to his promises.[157] Justification, then, is not about sinners being accepted by God, but about identifying the true members of the covenant community: "Justification was not so much about 'getting in,' or indeed about 'staying in,' as about 'how you could tell who was in.'"[158] The Pauline doctrine of justification is not about "legalistic works-righteousness."[159] Rather, it stands against Jewish nationalistic pride that was manifested in keeping the law so as to be distinguished from the Gentiles, whom the Jewish people deemed outside of the covenant community. Evangelicals reacted to Wright and the "new perspective" in several ways, with some being swayed by the position and others offering strong criticism.[160] Without a doubt, the material principle of Protestantism has become the center of theological attention once again.

---

155. Dunn and Suggate, *Justice of God*, 25. As Dunn concluded: "The added factor against which Paul himself was protesting was not individual human effort, but the assumption that ethnic origin and identity is a factor in determining the grace of God and its expression. Ethnic origin and identity is a different way of assessing human worth, but one more fundamental than the question of ability to perform good works. What Paul protested against was even more insidious—the assumption that the way people are constituted by birth rules them in or rules them out from receiving God's grace. Paul's protest was not against a high regard for righteousness, against dedicated devotion to God's law. It was rather against the corollary to such devotion: that failure to share in that devotion meant exclusion from the life of the world to come, and that the majority of peoples of the world were in principle so excluded. J. D. G. Dunn, "The Influence of Galatians in Christian Thought," in *The Theology of Paul's Letter to the Galatians* (Cambridge: Cambridge Univ. Press, 1993), 143–44, cited in O'Callahan, *Fides Christi*, 185.

156. N. T. Wright, *What Saint Paul Really Said* (Minneapo-

lis: Fortress, 2005), 98–99.

157. N. T. Wright, *The Climax of the Covenant: Christ and the Law in Pauline Theology* (Edinburgh: T & T Clark, 1991), 36.

158. Wright, *What Paul Really Said*, 119.

159. Ibid., 18. Cf. Sanders, *Paul and Palestinian Judaism*, 550.

160. D. A. Carson, Peter O'Brien, and Mark A. Seifrid, eds., *Justification and Variegated Nomism*, vol. 1: *The Complexities of Second Temple Judaism* (Grand Rapids: Baker Academic, 2001), and vol. 2: *Justification and Variegated Nomism: The Paradoxes of Paul* (Grand Rapids: Baker Academic, 2004); Brian Vickers, *Jesus' Blood and Righteousness: Paul's Theology of Imputation* (Wheaton: Crossway, 2006); John Piper, *The Future of Justification: A Response to N. T. Wright* (Wheaton: Crossway, 2007). The 2010 national meeting of the Evangelical Theological Society was devoted to the theme of "Justification by Faith," with N. T. Wright and Thomas R. Schreiner facing off on the new perspective debate.

Chapter 24

SANCTIFICATION (GROWTH IN LIKENESS TO CHRIST)

How has the church come to understand how believers grow in Christian maturity?

STATEMENT OF BELIEF

The church has historically affirmed that part of the believers' experience of salvation is growing in Christian maturity. This *sanctification* is "a progressive work of God and man that makes us more and more free from sin and like Christ in our actual lives."[1] In this cooperative work, God does his part and Christians do their part. Among the roles that God performs is setting believers apart from sin, providing the example of Jesus Christ's obedience, and supplying the power and resources of the Holy Spirit to lead Christians into deepening holiness of life. God has also given tools of sanctification to believers for their role in progressing in Christian maturity. Sometimes called *means of grace*, these include prayer, reading and meditating on Scripture, the mortification of the flesh, confession of sin, and self-discipline. The expectation is that believers will yield themselves to God and employ these divinely given means to progress in sanctification.

At times in the church's history, one side of this divine-human cooperation has been emphasized more than the other. Thus, different approaches to sanctification have been proposed and used in the church. This variety continues today. There is disagreement, for example, as to the extent of Christian maturity attainable in this life. Whereas most believers affirm that sanctification is never completed in this life, some insist on Christian perfectionism, even speaking of a "second blessing" following an initial conversion that brings a definitive break with willful sin and complete holiness. Indeed, Pentecostal churches have insisted that this "second blessing" consists of the baptism of the Holy Spirit accompanied by speaking in tongues. The place of so-called spiritual disciplines—

---

1. Wayne Grudem, *Systematic Theology: An Introduction to Biblical Doctrine* (Grand Rapids: Zondervan, 1994, 2000), 746.

fasting, meditation, contemplative prayer, and so forth—is also a debatable point. There are Christians from all of these different persuasions.

Given these historical differences, this chapter will trace the development of the church's views on sanctification. Because widespread agreement exists on many essential elements, the focus will be on those common points. However, the diversity of positions will also be noted when those differences exerted a significant impact on the church.[2]

VIEWS OF SANCTIFICATION IN THE EARLY CHURCH

Jesus Christ and the disciples had much to say about sanctification. In a startling statement, Jesus commanded his followers, "Be perfect, therefore, as your heavenly Father is perfect" (Matt. 5:48). Similarly, the apostle Peter, citing Leviticus 11:44, urged believers on toward holiness (1 Peter 1:13–16). In accordance with the divine will for sanctification (1 Thess. 4:3), the apostle Paul prayed for the church: "May God himself, the God of peace, sanctify you through and through. May your whole spirit, soul and body be kept blameless at the coming of our Lord Jesus Christ" (1 Thess. 5:23). Key to this progress in holiness is the example of Jesus Christ (1 John 2:6) and the sanctifying work of the Holy Spirit (1 Peter 1:2) that produces good fruit (Gal. 5:22–23). Together with this emphasis on God's role in sanctification, the responsibilities of Christians in this progressive work were also enumerated. Their part consists in yielding to God (Rom. 6:13); being filled with the Spirit (Eph. 5:18); mortification of the flesh (Rom. 8:13); reading, meditating on, and obeying the Bible (John 17:17; 1 Peter 2:2); prayer (Eph. 6:18); and confession of sin (1 John 1:9). Paul expressed this cooperative effort between God and Christians in sanctification: "[M]y dear friends, as you have always obeyed ... continue to work out your salvation with fear and trembling, For it is God who works in you to will and to act according to his good purpose" (Phil. 2:12–13).

Sanctification continued to be a major concern and practice of the early Christians following the time of the apostles. Indeed, progress in Christian maturity was demanded as evidence for genuine faith in Christ, as Justin Martyr noted: "Let it be understood that those who are not found living as Christ taught are not Christians, even though they profess with the lips the teachings of Christ. For not those who make profession, but those who do the works, shall be saved."[3] Numerous descriptions of a genuine Christian lifestyle have come down to us. Taking a composite from the writings of Clement of Alexandria, the following traits were among those recognized as characteristic of mature believers: discreet laughter,[4] calmness and composure,[5] simplicity and thriftiness,[6] reverence and thankfulness,[7] edifying and chaste conversation,[8] self-discipline (with impassibility),[9] wise servanthood (especially toward the needy and enemies),[10] forgiveness,[11]

---

2. My thanks to Eron Plevan for his help with this chapter.

3. Justin Martyr, *First Apology*, 16, in *ANF*, 1:168. He cited Matt. 7:21 as support. The text has been rendered clearer.

4. Clement of Alexandria, *The Instructor*, 2.5, in *ANF*, 2:250.

5. Ibid., 2.7, in *ANF*, 2:253.

6. Ibid., 3.7, in *ANF*, 2:280–81.

7. Clement of Alexandria, *Stromata*, 7.7, in *ANF*, 2:533.

8. Clement of Alexandria, *Instructor*, 2.6–7, in *ANF*, 2:250–51.

9. Clement of Alexandria, *Stromata*, 7.11, in *ANF*, 2:542.

10. Ibid., 7.12, in *ANF*, 2:542.

11. Ibid., 7.13, in *ANF*, 2:546.

and Christ-centeredness.[12] Similarly, Tertullian listed the characteristics of believers as discipline, goodness, wisdom, temperance, chastity, compassion, truthfulness, and freedom. He concluded: "Whoever wishes to understand who the Christians are, must seek to employ these marks for their discovery."[13]

Those who lived as mature believers were so different from the unbelievers around them that the testimony of a genuine Christian lifestyle became a powerful apology, or defense, for Christianity. The apologists argued for the excellence of the Christian faith and demanded understanding of, and tolerance for, Christians. Significantly, one of their chief points of evidence was the transformed lives that believers exhibited. Indeed, Aristides wrote an apology to the Emperor Hadrian and offered the lives of the early Christians as a witness to the superiority of Christianity over other religions:

> They do not commit adultery or fornication, nor bear false witness, nor embezzle what is held in pledge, nor covet that which is not theirs. They honor father and mother, and show kindness to those near to them; and whenever they are judges, they judge uprightly. They do not worship idols (made) in the image of man. Whatever they would not want others to do to them, they do not do to others.... They comfort their oppressors ... and make them their friends; they do good to their enemies. Their women ... are pure as virgins, and their daughters are modest. Their men keep themselves from every unlawful union and from all uncleanness.... Falsehood is not found among them. They love one another. From widows they do not turn away their esteem; and they rescue orphans from anyone who treats them harshly. The one who has, gives to him who does not have, without boasting.... If there is anyone among them who is poor and needy, and if they do not have any extra food, they fast two or three days in order to supply to the needy their lack of food. They obey the commands of their Messiah with much care, living justly and seriously as the Lord their God commanded them.[14]

Eventually, living according to such high standards of conduct became a prerequisite for incorporation into the church at baptism. Indeed, if any of the following people— whether men or women—came to be baptized, they first had to leave their job, or they would be rejected: pimps, prostitutes, idol makers, actors or actresses in the theater, charioteers, duelers, racers, gamblers, Olympic athletes, musicians (specifically, those who played the pipe, lute, or harp at the Olympic games), dance masters, or hucksters.[15]

Of course, not everyone was impressed with the godly lifestyle of the early Christians. Apparently, raising the bar of moral living pricked the conscience of unbelievers, who in turn ridiculed believers for their holiness.[16] Another complaint raised against the early Christians was that their holy lifestyle demanded that they remove themselves from worldly matters and live as recluses; hence, they were useless in the real world. Tertullian pointed out the patent absurdity of this charge:

12. Ibid., 7.12, in *ANF*, 2:546.
13. Tertullian, *To the Nations*, 4, in *ANF*, 3:112.
14. Aristides, *Apology*, 15, in *ANF*, 10:276–77. The text has been rendered clearer.
15. *Apostolic Constitutions*, 8.32, in *ANF*, 7:495.
16. Tertullian, *Apology*, 39, in *ANF*, 3:46.

How in all the world can that be the case with people who live among you, eat the same food, wear the same clothes, have the same habits, and endure the same necessities of life? We are not Indian Brahmans or Gymnosophists, who dwell in woods and exile themselves from ordinary human life. Rather, we sojourn [live our short lives] with you in the world, abstaining from neither forum, meat market, bath, booth, workshop, inn, weekly market, nor any other place of business. We sail with you, fight [serve in the military] with you, and till the ground [farm] with you.... [E]ven in the various arts, we make public property of our works for your benefit. How it is that we seem useless in your ordinary course of life—living with you and by you as we do—I am not able to understand.[17]

Tertullian articulated an important principle regarding Christians being *in*, but not *of*, the world: "It is not merely by being in the world ... that we lapse [fall away] from God, but by touching and tainting ourselves with the world's sins.... The places in themselves do not contaminate, but what is done in them; from this, even the places themselves ... become defiled. The polluted things pollute us."[18] Thus, not withdrawal from the world, but caution and discipline in the world, was demanded of believers who would be holy and leave their mark on the world. As Tertullian accentuated, Christians "are remarkable only for reformation of our former vices."[19]

At the same time, many in the early church urged what could be described as a very suspicious and loose association with the world and its attractions. This attitude verged on asceticism, or disdain for anything physical and pleasurable. Tatian's motto was, "Die to the world, repudiating the madness that is in it! Live to God, and by apprehending him lay aside your old nature!"[20] Clement of Alexandria urged believers to wean themselves from the world: "For if you would loose, withdraw, and separate (for this is what the cross means) your soul from the delight and pleasure that is in this life, you will possess it, found and resting in the looked-for hope."[21] Cyprian was typical of those holding this view, as he explained:

The one peaceful and trustworthy tranquility, the one solid, firm, and constant security is this: For a man to withdraw from these whirlpools of a distracting world, and, anchored on the ground of the harbor of salvation, to lift his eyes from earth to heaven.... He who is actually greater than the world can crave or desire nothing from the world. How stable, how free from all shocks is that safeguard! How heavenly the protection in its constant blessings! To be loosed from the traps of this entangling world, to be purged from earthly garbage, and be fitted for the light of eternal immortality![22]

Cyprian thus urged believers that "whatever things are earthly, and have been received in this world, ought to be scorned, even as the world itself is scorned."[23]

---

17. Ibid., 42, in *ANF*, 3:49. The text has been rendered clearer. In Hinduism, *Brahmans* were the priests who made up the highest caste, or social class, in Indian society. *Gymnosophists* were Indian philosophers who went about naked.

18. Tertullian, *On the Shows*, 8, in *ANF*, 3:83.

19. Tertullian, *To Scapula*, 2, in *ANF*, 3:106.

20. Tatian, *Address of Tatian to the Greeks*, 11, in *ANF*, 2:69.

21. Clement of Alexandria, *Stromata*, 2.20, in *ANF*, 2:371.

22. Cyprian, *Letter* 1.14, in *ANF*, 5:279. The text has been rendered clearer.

23. Cyprian, *Treatise* 2.7, in *ANF*, 5:432. The text has been rendered clearer.

In one sense, this early form of asceticism had biblical grounds (Luke 14:33; 1 Cor. 6:19–20; 7:29–31; 1 John 2:15–17).[24] In another sense, however, asceticism was the product of Platonic philosophy, which denigrated anything physical or material while emphasizing the spiritual and immaterial. Not surprisingly, Clement of Alexandria cited the philosopher as a foundation for repudiating the world and its pleasures and pains: "According to Plato ... 'each pleasure and pain nails to the body the soul' of the man, who does not sever and crucify himself from the passions."[25] Here Clement highlighted Plato's view of human nature: the soul has been imprisoned in the body, and salvation consists in the soul's escape from the body. This release could only be achieved by disengaging from the world and pursuing the life of the soul. Plato's philosophy exerted a strong impact on the view of sanctification in the early church.

As to the extent of sanctification in this life, the church had various views. On the one hand, Clement of Alexandria insisted: "It is in this way that one truly follows the Savior, by aiming at sinlessness and at his perfection."[26] He defined what this looked like: "He who merely abstains from evil conduct is not just, unless he also adds goodness and knowledge.... [A]bstinence from sins is not sufficient for perfection, unless in addition he assumes the work of righteousness—activity in doing good."[27] Clement envisioned a mature Christian who would not be affected by temptation, lust, or any passion or activity in this world.[28] Thus, through "training, the exercise of will, and by the force of reason, and knowledge, and providence," the spiritual Christian's knowledge of God reaches the point of becoming "incapable of being lost."[29] At this point, "In all circumstances ... the soul of the spiritual Christian is strong, in a condition of extreme health and strength, like the body of an athlete.... Certainly, then, the ... soul, adorned with perfect virtue, is the earthly image of the divine power ... being unconquered by pleasure and ruler over irrational desires. For he well knows what is and what is not to be done."[30]

On the other hand, many distanced themselves from the idea of human sinlessness or perfection in the Christian life. Clement himself tempered his own position: A person is "perfected as godly, and as patient, and as self-controlled, and as a worker, and as a martyr, and as a spiritual Christian. But I know of no one [who is] perfect in all things at the same time, as long as he is still human.... The only exception is Christ alone, who clothed himself with humanity for us."[31] Cyprian went even farther, insisting that Scripture indicates the impossibility of perfection: "Lest anyone should flatter himself that he is innocent—and should perish more terribly by exalting himself—he is instructed and taught that he sins daily. For he is told to pray daily for his sins."[32]

---

24. E.g., Cyprian, *Treatise* 12, third book, testimonies, 11, in *ANF*, 5:536.

25. Clement of Alexandria, *Stromata*, 2.20, in *ANF*, 2:371.

26. Clement of Alexandria, *Who Is the Rich Man Who Will Be Saved?* 21, in *ANF*, 2:597.

27. Clement of Alexandria, *Stromata*, 6.12, in *ANF*, 2:504. The text has been rendered clearer.

28. Ibid., 6.9, in *ANF*, 2:497.

29. Ibid., 7.7, in *ANF*, 2:536.

30. Ibid., 7.11, in *ANF*, 2:541. The text has been rendered

clearer. Clement was deeply influenced by Gnosticism, even borrowing the term *gnostic* to refer to a spiritual Christian. I have avoided the use of that language.

31. Ibid., 7.7, in *ANF*, 2:433. The text has been rendered clearer. Cf. Clement, *Instructor*, 2, in *ANF*, 2:210.

32. Cyprian, *Treatise* 4.22, in *ANF*, 5:453. The text has been rendered clearer. Cyprian referred to the Lord's Prayer, in which Christ urged daily prayer for forgiveness from sins. Elsewhere, he cited Prov. 20:9 and 1 John 1:10. Cyprian, *Treatise* 8.3, in *ANF*, 5:476.

A curious but serious challenge in the debate over Christian perfection was brought forth by Pelagius, who denied that divine grace working on human hearts was necessary for believers to please God. Indeed, Pelagius was scandalized by a prayer of Augustine: "Give what you command, and command what you will." To Pelagius, this passive attitude seemed to encourage believers to wait upon God for strength, patience, courage, or whatever else was needed to obey his commands. According to Pelagius, however, command implies capability: because God directed believers to do his will, they should just go ahead and do it.[33] Moreover, given his view of human ability, he insisted that Christians could be perfect in this life. Through the intervention of Augustine, this Pelagian view was exposed as false.[34]

Regarding the means for spiritual growth, Clement of Alexandria proposed that the "sacrifices" of Christians are "prayers, praises, readings in the Scriptures before meals, psalms and hymns during meals and before bed, and prayers once again during the night."[35] The importance of the Word of God was emphasized: "Let no day pass without reading some portion of the Sacred Scriptures, at a time that is most convenient; and give some space to meditation. Never get out of the habit of reading in the Sacred Scriptures, for nothing feeds the soul and enriches the mind so well as those sacred studies do."[36] Reading Scripture and prayer were closely associated, as Cyprian noted: "Be constant in both prayer and reading; now speak with God, now let God speak with you. Let him instruct you in his teachings, let him direct you."[37] Prayer was offered on behalf of oneself, particularly for divine protection, as Tertullian emphasized: "Prayer is the wall of faith: her arms and missiles against the foe, who keeps watch over us on all sides. So we never walk unarmed."[38] And prayer was offered on behalf of others, as Cyprian explained: "With mutual prayers, let us by turns cherish, guard, and arm one another."[39]

So important was prayer that the early church initiated set times for its practice, as Tertullian described: "Concerning the time for prayer, the outward observance of certain hours will not be unprofitable. I refer to these common hours that mark the intervals of the day — the third, the sixth, and the ninth hours — which we may find in the Scriptures to have been more solemn than the rest."[40] Thus, the pattern of praying at three set times

33. Pelagius, *Letter to Demetrias*, 16, cited in Alister E. McGrath, *Christian Spirituality: An Introduction* (Oxford: Blackwell, 1999), 43.

34. For further discussion of Pelagianism, see chap. 16.

35. Clement of Alexandria, *Stromata*, 7.7, in *ANF*, 2:537.

36. Theonas of Alexandria, *Letter to Lucianus*, 9, in *ANF*, 6:161. The text has been rendered clearer.

37. Cyprian, *Letter* 1.15, in *ANF*, 5:279–80. The text has been rendered clearer.

38. Tertullian, *On Prayer*, 29, in *ANF*, 3:691. The text has been rendered clearer.

39. Cyprian, *Letter* 30.6, in *ANF*, 5:310. The text has been rendered clearer.

40. Tertullian, *On Prayer*, 25, in *ANF*, 3:689. The text has been rendered clearer. He was aware of the absence of any biblical commandment for these appointed times of prayer but found a pattern set forth: "The first infusion of the Holy

Spirit into the disciples gathered together took place 'at the third hour' [Acts 2:1–4]. Peter, on the day in which he experienced the vision of the universal church ... had gone onto the roof of the house to pray 'at the sixth hour' [Acts 10:9]. The same apostle was going into the temple with John 'at the ninth hour,' when he restored the lame man to health [Acts 3:1]. Although these practices stand simply without any biblical instruction about their observance, still it may be considered a good thing to establish some definite expectation. This may add strictness to the command to pray, and it may, as it were by a law, tear us away from our businesses so we can carry out our duty." Ibid. The text has been rendered clearer. In his work *On Fasting*, Tertullian expanded on this prayer pattern: "In Luke's book on Acts, the third hour is demonstrated to be an hour of prayer, for it was about this hour that they who had received the initial gift of the Holy Spirit were mistaken for being drunk. The same is true for the sixth hour, at which

during the day was set down in the early church. This structure was eventually expanded to seven times of prayer daily—called *offices* (from the Latin *officium*, or *obligation*).

The Church's Seven Times of Prayer

- Prime, or early morning prayer
- Matins, or morning prayer
- Terce (third), or prayer at 9:00 a.m.
- Sext (sixth), or prayer at noon
- None (ninth), or prayer at 3:00 p.m.
- Vespers, or evening prayer
- Compline, or prayer before going to bed

Another important element in sanctification that was introduced in the early church was devotion to celibacy. Athenagoras noted: "You would find many among us, both men and women, growing old unmarried, in hope of living in closer communion with God. Remaining in virginity and in the state of eunuchs brings one closer to God, while the indulgence of carnal thought and desire leads one away from him."[41] Many underscored the fact that a commitment to celibacy was not a requirement, but a voluntary act of devotion instead, as Tertullian noted: "We do not reject marriage, but simply refrain from it. Nor do we prescribe celibacy as the rule, but only recommend it. We observe it as a good state—indeed, even the better state—if each person uses it carefully according to his ability. But at the same time, we earnestly vindicate marriage."[42]

Celibacy was considered to be superior to marriage for several reasons. According to Origen: "Christians who maintain a perpetual virginity do not do so for any human honor, for any fee or reward, nor from any motive of vainglory.... They are preserved by God in a spirit that is well-pleasing to him, and in the exercise of every responsibility, being filled with all righteousness and goodness."[43] A particular emphasis was placed on the future reward for celibates: "What else is virginity than the glorious preparation for the future life?"[44] Cyprian detailed this future reward: "When he [the Lord] says that in his Father's house there are many mansions, he indicates there are dwellings of better habitation, which you virgins are seeking. Cutting away the desires of the flesh, you obtain the reward of a greater grace in the heavenly home."[45]

Peter went up on the roof, and the ninth hour, at which they entered the temple. We should certainly understand that, with absolutely perfect indifference, we must pray always, everywhere, and at all times [Eph. 6:18]. Yet, these three hours are clearly more marked in human affairs. They divide the day, distinguish businesses, and echo in the public ear. Similarly, they have been of special solemnity in divine prayers. This practice is further sanctioned by the corroborative fact that Daniel prayed three times a day [Dan. 6:10]." *On Fasting*, 10, in *ANF*, 4:108. The text has been rendered clearer.

41. Athenagoras, *A Plea for the Christians*, 33, in *ANF*, 2:146. The text has been rendered clearer.

42. Tertullian, *Against Marcion*, 1.29, in *ANF*, 3:294. The text has been rendered clearer.

43. Origen, *Against Celsus*, 7.48, in *ANF*, 4:631.

44. Novatian, *On the Discipline and Advantage of Chastity*, 7, in *ANF*, 5:589.

45. Cyprian, *Treatise* 2.23, in *ANF*, 5:436. The text has been rendered clearer.

Support for this elevation of celibacy as a crucial element in devotion to God and holiness of life was found in Scripture, specifically Paul's own preference for celibacy (1 Cor. 7:8–9).[46] Appeal was made to Jesus' teaching about the future resurrection life, in which there will be no married people (Luke 20:34–35): "That which we shall be, you have already begun to be. You possess already in this world the glory of the resurrection. You pass through the world without the deadly disease of the world. As you continue chaste and virgins, you are equal to the angels of God."[47] Jesus' words about eunuchs were also cited (Matt. 19:11–12).[48] Furthermore, Methodius cited the example of Jesus, who was a virgin, along with the vision of virgins in the age to come (Rev. 14:1–4).[49] In addition to this biblical support, other "practical" reasons were given for "the immense advantage of chastity, including avoidance of pain in childbirth, release from suffering arising from the death of children, freedom from spousal responsibilities, and fearlessness in the face of persecution."[50]

By the middle of the third century, celibacy as a superior way of holiness was well established in the church. Cyprian spoke of the honor with which virgins were regarded: "This is the flower of the church's seed, the grace and ornament of spiritual endowment, a joyous disposition, the wholesome and uncorrupted work of praise and honor, God's image reflecting the holiness of the Lord, the more illustrious portion of Christ's flock. The glorious fruitfulness of mother church rejoices by their means, and in them abundantly flourishes."[51] A parallel between celibacy and martyrdom developed, as Methodius noted: "Virgins are martyrs. It is not that they bear the pains of the body for a brief moment of time, but they endure them throughout all of their life."[52] Indeed, the prize for virgins was second only to that of martyrs, as Cyprian outlined in his address to virgins: "The reward for the martyrs is a hundred-fold; the second is yours, sixty-fold.... With you, whose reward is second in grace [next to that of the martyrs], let there be the strength in endurance next to theirs."[53] It is not surprising, then, that when persecution of the church was officially ended at the beginning of the fourth century, celibacy replaced martyrdom as the highest calling for believers to follow. Thus, the order of virgins became an established part of the church (though it was not like the ordained offices of bishop, elder, and deacon).[54]

This elevation of celibacy and the ever-present attitude of disdain for the world and what it offers coalesced into a new phenomenon in the early church: monasticism. Because martyrdom for the faith no longer existed, the question arose: How can sincere Christians live holy lives on earth so as to achieve the greatest reward in heaven? The answer was found in monastic movements. The notion of disengaging from the world and dedicating one's entire life to the pursuit of God and his holiness appealed to the most serious-minded believers, and monasticism became a characteristic of the church.

---

46. Tertullian, *To His Wife*, 1.3, in *ANF*, 4:40.

47. Cyprian, *Treatise* 2.22, in *ANF*, 5:436. The text has been rendered clearer.

48. Ibid., *Treatise* 12, testimony 32, in *ANF*, 5:543.

49. Methodius, *The Banquet of the Ten Virgins*, 1.5, in *ANF*, 6:313.

50. Cyprian, *Treatise* 2.22, in *ANF*, 5:436. Cf. Novatian, *On the Discipline and Advantage of Chastity*, 7, in *ANF*, 5:589.

51. Ibid., 2.23, in *ANF*, 5:431. The text has been rendered clearer.

52. Methodius, *The Banquet of the Ten Virgins*, 7.3, in *ANF*, 6:332.

53. Cyprian, *Treatise* 2.21, in *ANF*, 5:436. The text has been rendered clearer.

54. *Apostolic Constitutions*, 8.24, in *ANF*, 7:493.

Several types of monasticism developed. One type, called *anchoritism*, involved individuals living a hermit-style existence on their own. An example was St. Antony, who gave up a comfortable life and lived in a rough cave in the desert of Egypt. This happened as a result of hearing Jesus' words in the gospel (Matt. 19:21).[55] To encourage the large number of monks who had joined themselves to his monastic lifestyle, Antony urged: "We should not think, as we look [back] at the world, that we have renounced anything of much consequence, for the whole earth is very small compared with all the heaven. Therefore, even if by chance we were rulers of all the earth, and gave it all up, that would be worth nothing in comparison with the kingdom of heaven."[56]

A second kind of monasticism, called *cenobitism*, brought individuals together into a community of monks. A noted example was St. Benedict of Nursia, who founded the order of Benedictines in a monastery at Monte Cassino near Rome. The *Rule of St. Benedict*, written about 529 for the order that he founded, became the standard for later monastic orders. In it, Benedict explained the philosophy for the discipline he imposed on the monks: "If we want to escape the sufferings of hell and reach eternal life, we must hurry to do now what may benefit us for eternity.... Never abandoning God's rule, but persevering in his teaching in the monastery until death, we will patiently share in the sufferings of Christ, so that we may deserve to be sharers in his kingdom as well."[57]

Fairly rapidly, monasticism became a characteristic of the church. Its most influential leaders were trained in monasteries, and monastic movements became the chief organ of the church for evangelism. Specifically, St. Patrick evangelized the entire island of Ireland. Following Patrick and other early Irish monks—Aidan, Columba, and others—Irish monasticism carried the gospel to previously unreached peoples in the British Isles and the continent of Europe. Monasteries became the sole center of education and culture in the Dark Ages.[58] And monasticism periodically brought renewal to the church.

Besides Augustine's contribution to monasticism—he originated the pattern of a community of priests attached to a particular church (the origin of the parish system)—he exerted an influence on the church's doctrine of sanctification. He clarified the biblical concept of "living according to the flesh" (Gal. 5:19–21), noting that it is not just about engaging in physical pleasures so as to commit bodily sins. Such living also involves "vices of the soul."[59] He also underscored the fact that sin is not the result of the physical body exerting a negative influence on the soul, causing the person to engage in evil actions: "It was not the corruptible body that made the soul sinful, but the sinful soul

55. Athanasius, *Life of Antony*, 2, in *NPNF²*, 4:196.

56. Ibid., 17, in *NPNF²*, 4:200. The text has been rendered clearer.

57. Benedict, *The Rule of St. Benedict*, prologue, from Coleman J. Barry, *Readings in Church History: From Pentecost to the Protestant Revolt* (Westminster, Md.: Newman, 1960), 166.

58. An example of this was the role of the monasteries during the Carolingian Renaissance beginning in the eighth century. Charlemagne and his chief adviser, Alcuin, encouraged an emphasis on education and the preservation of Christian culture, as shown in the following instructions to "ministers of the altar of God, the other orders who observe a rule, and the congregations of monks": "Let them join and associate to themselves not only children of servile condition, but also sons of freemen. And let schools be established in which boys may learn to read. Correct carefully the Psalms, the signs in writing, the songs, the calendar, the grammar, in each monastery or bishopric, and the Catholic books. Because often men desire to pray to God properly, but they pray badly because of incorrect books." Charlemagne, *General Admonition* (789), 72, in Bettenson, 106.

59. Augustine, *The City of God*, 14.2, in *NPNF¹*, 2:263.

that made the body corruptible. And though from this corruption of the body there arise certain incitements to vice, and indeed, even vicious desires, yet we must still not blame all the vices of an evil life on the body."[60] He concluded: "It is not by having a body ... but by living according to himself—that is, according to man—that man became like the devil."[61] In keeping with this, Augustine cautioned against viewing the body as inherently evil and the spirit or soul as inherently good—this was an error propounded by Plato and was not biblical teaching. So sanctification does not consist in focusing solely on spiritual matters while denying bodily needs and desires. Rather, it involves "living according to God"—in both body and soul—instead of "living according to man"—or sinful human nature, which affects both body and soul.[62]

For Augustine, this reality demands an entrenched battle lasting one's entire lifetime; at no time during this protracted war can complete victory over sin ever be declared.[63] The primary reason why the battle never ceases is the constant indwelling presence of concupiscence, or the sinful nature.[64] Nonetheless, Christians should never cease to strive against sin and to pursue holiness. For this, Augustine urged reliance on the grace of God, which restores humanity's fallen nature to be once again the righteous image of God:

> It is the Spirit of grace that works in order to restore in us the image of God, in which we were created. Sin, indeed, is contrary to nature, and it is grace that heals it.... In consequence of this sinfulness, the law of God is erased out of people's hearts. But when sin is being healed, the law is written on their hearts and the prescriptions of the law are done by nature—not that grace is denied by nature, but rather nature is repaired by grace. By God's grace, the righteousness which sin had blotted out is written on the renewed inner man.[65]

For Augustine, this grace of God is a grace that cooperates with the human will so that it desires to do the good and obey him. Indeed, God

> prepares the will, and perfects by his cooperation what he initiates by his operation.... [I]n the beginning he works in us that we may have the will, and in perfecting works with us when we have the will.... He operates, therefore, apart from us, in order that we may will. But when we will, and so will that we may act, he cooperates with us. We ourselves can, however, do nothing to work good works of godliness apart from God either working that we may will or co-working [with us] when we will.[66]

Just as salvation is the unilateral work of God to intervene and rescue people when their will is not directed toward him, so sanctification is God's cooperative work to assist believers as their will is directed toward him and desires to do good. From beginning to

---

60. Ibid., 14.3, in *NPNF*[1], 2:263–64. The text has been rendered clearer.

61. Ibid., in *NPNF*[1], 2:264. The text has been rendered clearer.

62. Ibid., 14.4–5, in *NPNF*[1], 2:264–66.

63. Augustine, *On the Spirit and the Letter*, 65, in *NPNF*[1], 5:113. Augustine cited 1 Kings 8:46; Ps. 143:2; Matt. 6:12; and

1 John 1:8 in support of this idea.

64. Augustine, *On Nature and Grace*, 72, in *NPNF*[1], 5:147.

65. Augustine, *On the Spirit and the Letter*, 47, in *NPNF*[1], 5:103. The text has been rendered clearer.

66. Augustine, *On Grace and Free Will*, 33, in *NPNF*[1], 5:458. The text has been rendered clearer.

end, therefore, the grace of God is necessary for any and all good that believers do. In all this, love is supreme, with love being a gift that God gives to believers through the Holy Spirit. This love, then, becomes "the root of good things"[67] that believers do:

> The human will is so divinely helped in the pursuit of righteousness, that he [the believer] receives the Holy Spirit, by whom there is formed in his mind a delight in, and a love of, that supreme and unchangeable good, which is God. By this gift to him of the down payment, as it were, of the free gift, he [the believer] conceives a burning desire to cleave to his Maker. A man's free will, indeed, does not help at all except to sin, if he does not know the way of truth. And even after he begins to know his duty and proper aim, unless he also takes delight in and feels a love for it, he neither does his duty, nor sets about it, nor lives rightly. Now, in order that such a course may engage our affections, God's "love is shed abroad in our hearts," not through the free will which arises from ourselves, but through "the Holy Spirit, who is given to us" [Rom 5:5].[68]

The grace of God and the power of the Holy Spirit cooperate with the free will of believers, filling it with love that in turn longs for God and does the good that pleases him. By this process, lasting their entire lifetime, believers are remade in the image of God and carry out their sanctification.

VIEWS OF SANCTIFICATION IN THE MIDDLE AGES

The medieval church developed new approaches to sanctification. The *lectio divina* (sacred reading), introduced in the fifth century by John Cassian, became an essential part of the medieval religious orders. It was popularized in the eleventh century by Guigo de Castro in a letter (known as the *Scala Paradisi*) in which he recounted a vision of a ladder to paradise consisting of the four rungs of "reading, meditation, prayer, and contemplation."[69] Guigo interpreted the four rungs as the four elements in the *lectio divina*: "Reading, or lesson, is busily looking on holy Scripture with all one's will and wit. Meditation is a studious searching with the mind to know what was before concealed through desiring proper skill. Prayer is a devout desiring of the heart to get what is good and avoid what is evil. Contemplation is the lifting up of the heart to God tasting somewhat of the heavenly sweetness and flavor. Reading seeks, meditation finds, prayer asks, contemplation feels."[70] Guigo referred his reader to the words of Jesus in Matthew 7:7: "Seek through reading, and you will find holy meditation in your thinking; and knock through praying and the doors will be opened to you to enter through heavenly contemplation to feel what you desire."[71] The rigorous practice of *lectio divina* promoted sanctification.

---

67. Augustine, *On the Grace of Christ*, 21, in *NPNF*[1], 5:225.
68. Augustine, *On the Spirit and the Letter*, 5, in *NPNF*[1], 5:84–85. The text has been rendered clearer.
69. "Letter of Dom Guigo the Carthusian to Brother Gervase about the Contemplative Life," chap. 1. Available at

http://fisheaters.com/guigo.html. Guigo was also referred to as Guigues du Chastel.
70. Ibid.
71. Ibid.

About the same time, another approach to sanctification was presented by Bernard of Clairvaux, who emphasized loving God in an important book bearing that title. He discussed four stages in the love of God. The first is love of oneself for one's own sake. Such love "must begin with the flesh."[72] The second stage is loving God for one's own sake, in which a Christian "begins to seek for God by faith and to love him as necessary to himself."[73] Bernard's third stage is loving God for God's sake. As a Christian begins to honor God through praying, thinking, and reading about him, and obeying his commands, "God reveals himself gradually in this kind of familiarity and consequently becomes lovely. When a man tastes how sweet God is … [he] loves God not now because of himself but because of God."[74] The fourth stage, considered by Bernard only to be a slight possibility during this lifetime, is loving only for God's sake: "In some wondrous way he forgets himself and, ceasing to belong to himself, he passes entirely into God and becomes one with him."[75]

Yet another medieval approach to sanctification was the so-called *threefold path* of pursuing God. Hugh of Balma gave an example of this in *The Roads to Zion*: "This way to God is threefold; that is, it consists of a way of cleansing (*via purgativa*), in which the human mind is disposed so that it may discern true wisdom; a way of illumination (*via illuminativa*), in which the mind is set on fire as it reflects with the fire of love; and the way of unity (*via unitiva*), in which the mind is carried upwards by God alone, and is led beyond all reason, understanding and intelligence." For Hugh of Balma, these three are successive stages leading to mystical union of love with God.[76]

New religious orders came into existence and breathed renewed spirituality into the church of the Middle Ages. The most famous of all was the Franciscans, or the Order of Brothers Minor, followers of St. Francis of Assisi.[77] Three vows—poverty, obedience, and celibacy—formed the heart of Francis' *Rule* and were taken by the monks.[78] Focusing on the poor, sick, and marginalized people of society, the Franciscans, clothed in rough brown tunics and wearing sandals (if needed), preached about Christ and begged for alms in support of the order and the poor.[79] The Dominicans, Augustinians, and others joined the Franciscans as mendicant (or begging) orders.

One of the most important medieval movements emphasizing the cultivation of Christian spirituality was the *Devotio Moderna*, or modern way of serving God. One aspect of this movement was the Brothers of the Common Life, a group of laypeople who organized themselves into a community that bore some resemblance to monastic orders. Although its participants did not take monastic vows, the Brothers of the Common Life

---

72. Bernard of Clairvaux, *On Loving God*, 15, in Bernard of Clairvaux, *On Loving God: An Analytical Commentary by Emero Stiegman*, Cistercian Fathers Series (Kalamazoo, Mich.: Cistercian, 1995), 40.

73. Ibid.

74. Ibid., 41.

75. Ibid.

76. Hugh of Balma, *The Roads to Zion*, prologue, 5–7, in Francis Ruello and Jeanne Barbet, eds., *Theologia Mystica* (Paris: Editions du Cerf, 1995), 1:130–32, cited in McGrath, *Christian Spirituality*, 151–52.

77. In Latin, *Ordo Fratrum Minorum*, or O.F.M. These initials still indicate a Franciscan monk today.

78. "This is the Rule and way of life of the brothers minor: to observe the holy gospel of our Lord Jesus Christ, living in obedience, without personal possessions, and in chastity." St. Francis of Assisi, *The Rule of St. Francis*, 1, in Bettenson, 141–42. This rule was actually the second one written by Francis and was approved by Pope Honorius III in 1223.

79. Francis, *Rule of St. Francis*, 6, in Bettenson, 143–44.

did live together and pursue holiness of life through regular times of community prayer, reading of Scripture, fasting, and so forth. A very important participant in the *Devotio Moderna* was Thomas à Kempis, author of one of the most famous bestsellers of all times, *The Imitation of Christ*. He rejected the sterility of the scholastic theology of his day and urged his readers to follow Christ in humility, love for God and others, virtue, and contempt for the praises of the world. As he stated his thesis: "The Lord states, 'He who follows me does not walk in darkness' (John 8:12). These, Christ's words, advise us that if we wish to be really enlightened and to be freed from spiritual blindness, we must imitate the lifestyle of Christ. Our deepest desire should be to reflect on Christ's life."[80] To accomplish this, Thomas underscored the need to move beyond mere intellectual learning.[81] Holiness of life—especially denial of oneself—must keep pace with knowledge: "If you want to know and learn something worthwhile, seek to be unknown and ignored. A true knowledge and evaluation of self is the best and most worthwhile sort of learning. Perfect wisdom is having no great opinion of self and a good and high regard for others."[82] Key to all of this for Thomas was "the inward conversation of Christ with the faithful soul":

> Happy is the soul who listens to the Lord speaking to her. She receives words of comfort from his mouth. Happy are the ears that catch the drift of the divine whispers and ignore the whispers of the world.... Happy are those eyes that are closed to outward things and open to what is inward. Happy are those who try to empty themselves for God and cut themselves off from every worldly hindrance. Note this, my soul. Shut the door on your passions. Let yourself hear what your Lord God says to you.... Leave what is passing. Choose the everlasting. What are the things of time but deceits? If the Creator leaves you, what good can any created thing do for you? Leave everything. Make yourself pleasing to your Creator. Then you will be able to grasp the true happiness.[83]

The teachings and proposals by Guigo de Castro, Bernard of Clairvaux, Hugh of Balma, St. Francis, Thomas à Kempis, and others contributed to the doctrine and practice of sanctification in the Middle Ages.

VIEWS OF SANCTIFICATION IN THE REFORMATION AND POST-REFORMATION

In an important critique of the practice of sanctification in place at this time, the *Augsburg Confession* exposed the errors of the current Roman Catholic system of monasticism. For the Lutheran Reformers, the Catholic Church's emphasis on monasticism—especially its elevation of celibacy, or singleness—confused the common people, giving them the wrong idea of how to live a holy life. Indeed, this misplaced emphasis on monas-

---

80. Thomas à Kempis, *The Imitation of Christ*, 1.1, trans. John Rooney (London: Staples, 1979), 1.

81. Ibid., 1.1, trans. Rooney, 1–2.

82. Ibid., 1.2, trans. Rooney, 3.

83. Ibid., 3.1, trans. Rooney, 67–68.

ticism communicated to laypeople that they could not please God.[84] To clarify this confusion, the *Confession* emphasized the rightness and purity of marriage "for anyone who is not adapted for a single life." It pointed to Paul's command to married people (1 Cor. 7:2) and to the creation ordinance (Gen. 2:18) "that compels marriage for all those who are not exempted by the special work of God. Therefore, those who are obedient to this commandment and ordinance of God do not sin [by getting married]."[85] This still allowed for some to take a vow of celibacy, but such a commitment was to be completely voluntary and never a result of constraint.[86] At the heart of the *Confession*'s rejection of monasticism was its theology, which contradicted justification by grace through faith alone in Jesus Christ: "Paul teaches everywhere that righteousness is not to be sought by our own observances and services that are devised by men. Rather, righteousness comes by faith to those who believe that they are received into favor by God for Christ's sake."[87] For the Lutheran Reformers, the entire monastic system contradicted this important truth, and thus was rendered null and void.[88]

John Calvin linked his discussion of initial salvation (regeneration and adoption) with his treatment of sanctification by emphasizing the fact that the latter flows from, and confirms, the former: "The object of regeneration ... is to manifest in the life of believers a harmony and agreement between God's righteousness and their obedience, and thus to confirm the adoption that they have received as sons."[89] The focal point for this gradual transformation is the life of Jesus Christ, "whose pattern we ought to express in our life.... For we have been adopted as sons by the Lord with this one condition: that our life express Christ, the bond of our adoption."[90] This imitation of Christ is no mere formality, expressed outwardly only: "But it must enter our heart and pass into our daily living, and so transform us into itself that it may not be unfruitful for us."[91] While desiring that all believers eagerly pursue and attain this inward conformity to Christ, Calvin was a realist. He recognized that most Christians fall far short of this lofty goal.[92] His counsel, therefore, was quite practical and reasonable:

> Let each one of us, then, proceed according to the measure of his puny capacity and set out upon the journey we have begun. No one shall set out so inauspiciously as not daily to make some headway, though it may be slight. Therefore, let us not cease so to act that we may make some unceasing progress in the way of the Lord. And let us not despair at the slightness of our success; for

---

84. "The people imagine many harmful ideas from these false commendations of the monastic life. They hear celibacy praised with great exaggeration; therefore, they live as married people with a guilty conscience. They hear that mendicants [those who beg for money] are the only ones who are perfect; therefore, they have possessions, buy and sell with a guilty conscience. They hear that the gospel only gives counsel not to take revenge when wrong; therefore, some in private life are not afraid to avenge themselves, because they hear it is a counsel [only for monks], not a commandment [for all Christians]. Others think that all political and civil positions are illegitimate jobs for Christians to hold." *Augsburg Confession,*

2.6, in Schaff, 3:57. The text has been rendered clearer.
85. Ibid., in Schaff, 3:52. The text has been rendered clearer.
86. Ibid., in Schaff, 3:53.
87. Ibid., in Schaff, 3:55. The text has been rendered clearer.
88. Ibid.
89. John Calvin, *Institutes of the Christian Religion*, 3.6.1, LCC, 1:684.
90. Ibid., 3.6.3, LCC, 1:686.
91. Ibid., 3.6.4, LCC, 1:688.
92. Ibid., 3.6.5, LCC, 1:688.

even though attainment may not correspond to desire, when today outstrips yesterday, the effort is not lost. Only let us look toward our mark with sincere simplicity and aspire to our goal; not fondly flattering ourselves, nor excusing our own evil deeds, but with continuous effort striving toward this end: that we may surpass ourselves in goodness until we attain to goodness itself.[93]

For Calvin, two elements were key for this process of sanctification. The first was self-denial, which he described practically through a series of contrasts:

We are not our own: let not our reason nor our will, therefore, sway our plans and deeds. We are not our own: let us therefore not set it as our goal to seek what is expedient for us according to the flesh. We are not our own: insofar as we can, let us therefore forget ourselves and all that is ours. Conversely, we are God's: let us therefore live for him and die for him. We are God's: let his wisdom and will, therefore, rule all our actions. We are God's: let all the parts of our life accordingly strive toward him as our only lawful goal.[94]

Following denial of self, the second crucial element was devotion to God: "That we do not seek the things that are ours but those which are of the Lord's will and will serve to advance his glory."[95] For Calvin, such self-denial and pursuit after God enables believers to consider others more highly than themselves, do good for others, place their trust only in God's blessings, and peacefully and thankfully endure adversity.[96]

Part and parcel of this self-denial was bearing the cross of Christ: Those whom "the Lord has adopted and deemed worthy of his fellowship ought to prepare themselves for a hard, toilsome, and unquiet life, crammed with very many and various kinds of evil."[97] Calvin listed several reasons for believers having to face adversity in bearing the cross. These included the destruction of self-reliance and self-effort, the encouragement of believers to experience God's faithfulness and have hope for the future, the testing of the patience of believers so as to teach them obedience, the restraint of fleshly desires, and correction of believers as part of God's disciplinary action.[98]

In dealing with bearing one's cross, Calvin made it a point to distance himself from those who urged Christians to face adversity with a Stoic attitude, which "count[s] it depraved not only to groan and weep but also to be sad and care-ridden."[99] Calvin was critical of this view: "Patiently to bear the cross is not to be utterly stupefied [anesthetized] and to be deprived of all feeling of pain. It is not as the Stoics of old foolishly described 'the great-souled man': one who, having cast off all human qualities, was affected equally by adversity and prosperity, by sad times and happy ones—indeed, who like a stone was not affected at all."[100] To contradict this Stoic approach to suffering, Calvin turned to Christ, who "groaned and wept both over his own and others' misfortunes."[101] Thus, Calvin recognized the legitimacy of trusting God in the midst of

---

93. Ibid., 3.6.5, LCC, 1:689.
94. Ibid., 3.7.1, LCC, 1:690.
95. Ibid., 3.7.2, LCC, 1:690–91.
96. Ibid., 3.7.4–10, LCC, 1:693–701.
97. Ibid., 3.8.1, LCC, 1:702.

98. Ibid., 3.8.2–6, LCC, 1:704–7.
99. Ibid., 3.8.9, LCC, 1:709.
100. Ibid.
101. Ibid.

tears and pain and envisioned that "the conclusion will always be: The Lord so willed, therefore, let us follow his will. Indeed, amid the very pricks [pangs] of pain, amid groaning and tears, this thought must intervene: to incline our heart to bear cheerfully those things which have so moved it."[102]

While the Reformers were developing their doctrine and practice of sanctification, a strong disagreement arose with the prevailing notions of sanctification in their day. The Roman Catholic reaction at the Council of Trent reflected the difference between Protestant and Catholic understandings of justification[103] and sanctification. For Protestants, growth in sanctification, not justification, is to be the lifelong pursuit of believers. But for Catholics, progress in obtaining greater and greater degrees of justification is the goal. Still, both groups emphasized the need to mature spiritually.

To this end, important Catholic approaches to sanctification were developed by Ignatius of Loyola in his *Spiritual Exercises* (encouraging the development of an indifference to worldly things so attention could be firmly given to the worship of God), Teresa of Avila in *The Way of Perfection* and *Interior Castle* (encouraging the pursuit of mystical union of the soul with Christ through detachment from self and the world), and John of the Cross in *The Dark Night of the Soul* and *The Night of the Spirit*.[104]

Protestant approaches to sanctification took a very different direction from Catholic mysticism. Careful doctrinal formulations were, of course, articulated, as seen in the *Westminster Confession of Faith*, which linked sanctification to Christ's work of salvation and to the Word and Spirit of God:

> They who are effectively called and regenerated, having a new heart and a new spirit created in them, are further sanctified, really and personally, through the virtue of Christ's death and resurrection, by his Word and Spirit dwelling in them. The dominion of the whole body of sin is destroyed, and the several [various] lusts thereof are more and more weakened and mortified, and they are sanctified more and more quickened [enlivened] and strengthened, in all saving graces, to the practice of true holiness, without which no man will see the Lord.[105]

Furthermore, the *Confession* highlighted that, despite occasional and temporary setbacks, believers are marked by continual progress in sanctification. However, this steadily increasing pattern of victory always falls short of perfection.[106]

In addition to these doctrinal formulations, Protestants emphasized the experience of sanctification. This was portrayed in the form of an allegory in John Bunyan's *Pilgrim's Progress*. It traced the journey of the main character, Christian, from the "City of Destruction" to the "Heavenly City," rehearsing the many constant trials and temptations

---

102. Ibid., 3.8.10, LCC, 1:710–11.

103. See the discussion in chap. 23.

104. Ignatius of Loyola, *The Spiritual Exercises of Saint Ignatius: A New Translation from the Authorized Latin Text*, trans. Pierre Wolff (Liguori, Mo.: Triumph, 1997); Teresa of Avila, *The Way of Perfection*, trans. and ed. E. Allison Peers (Garden City, N.Y.: Image, 1991); Teresa of Avila, *Interior Cas-* tle, trans. and ed. E. Allison Peers (Garden City, N.Y.: Image, 1972); John of the Cross, *The Dark Night of the Soul* and *The Night of the Spirit*, in *The Complete Works of St. John of the Cross*, ed. E. Allison Peers (Westminster, Md.: Newmann, 1957).

105. *Westminster Confession of Faith*, 13.1, in Schaff, 3:629.

106. Ibid., 13.2–3, in Schaff, 3:629–30.

that he had to face along the way. Jonathan Edwards also developed this theme of pilgrimage in his sermon *The Christian Pilgrim*:

> We should not rest in the world and its enjoyments, but should desire heaven. We should above all things desire a heavenly happiness: to be with God and be well with Jesus Christ. Though surrounded with outward enjoyments, and settled in families with desirable friends and relationships; though we have companions whose company is delightful and children in whom we see many promising characteristics; though we live by good neighbors and are generally loved when we are known; yet, we should not take our rest in these things as our inheritance. We should possess, enjoy and use them, with no other perspective than we are ready to give them up, whenever we are called to do so, and to exchange them willingly and cheerfully for heaven.[107]

Like their Catholic counterparts, Protestants also emphasized the important element of dying to sin as part of the process of sanctification. For example, John Owen wrote several treatises on this element, including *On the Mortification of Sin in Believers, Of Temptation*, and *The Nature, Power, Deceit, and Presence of Indwelling Sin*. As he defined it (from Rom. 8:13): "*To mortify* ... [is] a metaphorical expression, taken from the putting of any living thing to death.... Indwelling sin is compared to a person, a living person, called 'the old man,' with his faculties and properties, his wisdom, craft, subtlety, strength; this ... must be killed, put to death, mortified—that is, have its power, life, vigor, and strength to produce its effects taken away by the Spirit ... utterly mortified and slain by the cross of Christ."[108] For Owen, this mortification consists in three things: it is a habitual weakening of sin, it is constant fighting and contending against sin, and it is evidenced by frequent success against sin.[109] Exposing several false ideas of what it is, he denied that mortification ever produces the death and final elimination of sin, and that it is accomplished by merely pretending that sin is eliminated, by self-improvement, by simply diverting sin, or by occasionally conquering sin.[110] Of utmost importance in the mortification of sin is reliance upon the assistance of the Holy Spirit.[111] Indeed, Owen underscored the hopelessness of those who tenaciously fight again sin apart from this help of the Holy Spirit:

> Being strangers to the Spirit of God, all [their effort is] in vain. They combat without victory, have war without peace, and are in slavery all their days.... The law drives them on, and sin beats them back. Sometimes they think, indeed, that they have foiled sin, when they have only raised a dust that they see it not; that is, they distemper [weaken] their natural affections of fear, sorrow, and anguish, which makes them believe that sin is conquered when it is not touched.

---

107. Jonathan Edwards, "The Christian Pilgrim," in *Jonathan Edwards: Basic Writings*, ed. O. E. Winslow (New York: New American Library, 1966), 136–37, cited in McGrath, *Christian Spirituality*, 92.

108. John Owen, "Of the Mortification of Sin in the Believer," in *Overcoming Sin and Temptation*, ed. Kelly M. Kapic and Justin Taylor (Wheaton: Crossway, 2006), 48–49.

109. Ibid., 73–78.

110. Ibid., 69–73.

111. "He works in us and with us, not against us or without us; so that his assistance is an encouragement as to the facilitating of the work, and no occasion of neglect as to the work itself." Ibid., 62.

By that time they are cold, they must go to the battle again; and the lust which they thought to be slain appears to have had no wound.[112]

During the post-Reformation period, a complaint arose about the dry and sterile spiritual environment that typified many of the churches. Although it was engaged in defending the Reformation against attacks from Catholic apologists and various heretical groups, Protestant scholasticism was seen by some as emphasizing the cognitive element of Christianity while neglecting matters of the heart. A reaction against this intellectualizing of the faith set in, particularly in Germany, through a renewal movement called *pietism*. An influential book, *Pia Desideria (Pious Desire)* by Philip Jacob Spener, offered six proposals for correcting the current lukewarm conditions in the church: (1) a more extensive use of the Word of God in the church (including family Bible reading, Scripture reading without comment in the church service, and discussion of Scripture in church meetings); (2) the establishment and exercise of the priesthood of all believers (the involvement of the entire congregation in use of their spiritual gifts); (3) putting knowledge of the Christian faith into practice (aided by believers being held accountable to, and being counseled by, confessors); (4) attention to conducting oneself properly in religious controversies (many had grown sick and tired of the wars of religion that had decimated a sizable part of Europe); (5) reformation of the pastoral training in schools and universities (sparked by the model of theology professors who live serious and devout Christian lives and who offer better preparation for practical church ministry); and (6) sermons that go beyond homiletical brilliance to touch the hearts and lives of those who hear them.[113] Pietism became a mighty force within Protestantism, giving rise to schools, orphanages, and an extensive missionary movement.

VIEWS OF SANCTIFICATION IN THE MODERN PERIOD

Despite the general historical consensus that sanctification is never completed in this lifetime, John Wesley took a different view. He championed the cause of Christian perfection, carefully attempting to explain what he meant, clarifying his position against its detractors, and encouraging believers to pursue it. He defined Christian perfection, or holiness (Wesley's objection to it being called "sinless perfection"[114] should be noted): "The loving God with all our heart, mind, soul and strength. This implies that no wrong temper, none contrary to love, remains in the soul and that all the thoughts, words and actions are governed by pure love."[115] For Wesley, this state is attainable by believers in their earthly lifetime, but he did not envision that "there is any absolute perfection on earth."[116] Indeed, he set forth "in what sense Christians are not perfect," noting that they

---

112. Ibid.

113. Philip Jacob Spener, *Pia Desideria*, pt. 3, trans. Theodore G. Tappert (Philadelphia: Fortress, 1964), 87–122.

114. "'Sinless perfection' is a phrase I never use lest it should *seem* to contradict myself." John Wesley, *Thoughts on*

Christian Perfection, q. 6, ans. 4, in *John Wesley*, ed. Albert C. Outler (New York: Oxford Univ. Press, 1964), 287.

115. Ibid., q. 6, ans., in Outler, *John Wesley*, 284.

116. Wesley, *Christian Perfection*, 1.9, in Outler, *John Wesley*, 258.

are not free from ignorance, mistakes, infirmities, and temptation.[117] Yet he affirmed that Christians are free from sin, in this sense: "By sin, I here understand outward sin, according to the plain, common acceptance of the word; an actual, voluntary transgression of the law; of the revealed, written law of God; of any commandment of God acknowledged to be such at the time it is transgressed."[118] And Wesley did not view perfection as a static state, rather: "However much any man has attained, or in however high a degree he is perfect, he still needs to 'grow in grace' and daily to advance in the knowledge and love of God his Savior."[119]

Biblical support marshaled by Wesley in defense of his position consisted in the following: He appealed to the distinctions among Christians set forth by John in his first letter: "dear children ... fathers ... young men" (1 John 2:12–14). For Wesley, the last group is perfect. Moreover, he cited numerous passages—1 John 3:9; 5:18—that affirm that believers have made a complete break with sin.[120] Furthermore, he disputed the biblical examples of holy people falling into sin, which were commonly used to show that even giants of the faith inevitably fail. As for any Old Testament examples—Abraham, Moses, David—Wesley dismissed them as not belonging to the Christian era of unprecedented sanctifying grace.[121] And he refused to accept the argument that New Testament examples of sin on the part of the apostles—Peter, Paul—imply that all Christians must commit sin.[122]

In affirming that "a Christian is so far perfect as not to commit sin," Wesley averred that "this is the glorious privilege of every Christian."[123] Practically speaking, "in a state of perfection every desire is in subjection to the obedience of Christ. The will is entirely subject to the will of God and the affections wholly fixed on him."[124] Proof of having achieved this state can be detected, but knowledge of it is not infallible. But Wesley offered guidance as to how a person can judge for himself that he has attained perfection:

> When, after having been fully convinced of inbred [indwelling] sin by a far deeper and clearer conviction than that he experienced before justification and after having experienced a gradual mortification of it, he experiences a total death to sin and an entire renewal in the love and image of God, so as to rejoice always, to pray without ceasing and in everything to give thanks.... Not that the feeling all love and no sin is a sufficient proof.... No one, therefore, ought to believe that the work is done until there is added the testimony of the Spirit, witnessing his entire sanctification as clearly as his justification.[125]

For Wesley, this experience was both continuous and critical, in the sense that a lengthy period of preparation leading up to it could take place, but the experience itself would

---

117. Ibid., 1.1–9, in Outler, 254–58.

118. John Wesley, *The Great Privilege of Those Who Are Born of God*, in *The Works of John Wesley*, ed. Thomas Jackson, 14 vols. (Grand Rapids: Zondervan, 1959), 5:227.

119. Wesley, *Christian Perfection*, 1.9, in Outler, *John Wesley*, 258.

120. Ibid., 2.4–6, in Outler, *John Wesley*, 259–60. He also included verses from Rom. 6.

121. Ibid., 2.13, in Outler, *John Wesley*, 263.

122. Ibid., 2.14–20, in Outler, *John Wesley*, 263–67.

123. Ibid., 2.20–21, in Outler, *John Wesley*, 267.

124. Wesley, *Thoughts on Christian Perfection*, q. 5, ans., in Outler, *John Wesley*, 286.

125. Ibid., q. 26, ans., in Outler, *John Wesley*, 293.

be instantaneous.[126] This crisis experience comes by faith, but continuous preparation for it is demanded. In answering the question, "How are we to wait for this change?" he noted:

> Not in careless indifference or indolent inactivity, but in vigorous and universal obedience; in a zealous keeping of all the commandments; in watchfulness and painfulness; in denying ourselves and taking up our cross daily; as well as in earnest prayer and fasting and a close attention to all the ordinances of God.... It is true that we receive it by simple faith; but God does not, will not, give that faith unless we seek it with all diligence in the way which he has ordained.[127]

In his view on entire sanctification, Wesley was followed by Charles Finney.[128] Later the Holiness movement and churches would accept Wesley's theology on this matter as well.

In 1875 a call was issued to attend a "Convention for the Promotion of Practical Holiness" in Keswick, England. This launched a series of annual conventions, held in Keswick and elsewhere in the world, that championed a new approach to sanctification, called the Keswick approach: "We believe the Word of God teaches that the *normal* Christian life is one of uniform sustained victory over known sin; and that no temptation is permitted to happen to us without a way of escape being provided by God, so we may be able to bear it."[129] Additionally, "the normal experience of the child of God should be one of victory instead of constant defeat, one of liberty instead of grinding bondage, one of 'perfect peace' instead of restless worry. It shows that in Christ there is provided for every believer victory, liberty, and rest, and that this may be obtained not by a life-long struggle after an impossible ideal, but by the surrender of the individual to God, and the indwelling of the Holy Spirit."[130] Keswick conventions[131] focused on one distinctive thing: Jesus' promise of an abundant life (John 10:10), which goes beyond "life" (eternal life, which is shared by all Christians), but that is experienced by few people: "Not all Christians have entered into the experience of abounding life.... Abounding life is just the fullness of life in Christ, made possible by his death and resurrection, and made actual by the indwelling and infilling of the Holy Spirit."[132] The blessing of this abundant life for Christ is, according to the Keswick perspective, both instantaneous and progressive:

---

126. Ibid., q. 28, ans., in Outler, *John Wesley*, 294.

127. Ibid., q. 29, ans., in Outler, *John Wesley*, 294.

128. Charles Grandison Finney, *Lectures on Systematic Theology* (1878), lecture 26, in *Finney's Systematic Theology: New Expanded Edition*, ed. Dennis Carroll, Bill Nicely, and L. G. Parkhurst Jr. (Minneapolis: Bethany, 1994), 381–96.

129. Steven Barabas, *So Great Salvation* (Eugene, Ore.: Wipf & Stock, 1952), 84. Barabas was a chronicler of the Keswick movement. His citation is from an editorial in the first issue of *The Christian's Pathway to Power*.

130. Ibid.

131. These followed a certain topical pattern. Day 1 focused on sin, while day 2 underscored identification with Christ and reliance on the indwelling power of the Holy Spirit to overcome sin. Day 3 called Christians to consecrate their lives in complete and unconditional surrender to God, and day 4 gave instructions on how to be filled, or controlled, by the Holy Spirit. Although not originally part of Keswick conventions, a fifth day was added in order to call believers to a life of service—evangelism and world missions.

132. W. Graham Scroggie, *Abounding Life*, in *Life More Abundant: Spirit-Filled Messages from the Keswick Convention*, ed. Herbert F. Stevenson (Grand Rapids: Zondervan, 1987), 14–15. Scroggie spoke at Keswick conventions from 1912 to 1954.

The sense of rest, the sense of all-sufficiency of grace in Christ, has come to them with a wonderful instantaneousness. But this has been followed by an experience of its progressiveness that they never knew before. Sanctification in the sense of conformity to the life and character of Christ is a process, a gradual process, a continuous process, an endless process. But sanctification, in the sense of a definite decision for holiness, a thorough and whole-hearted dedication to God, the committal [commitment] of the whole being to him, is a crisis; and the crisis must take place before we really know the process.[133]

To assist people to experience this moment, the movement prescribed a seven-step process. Many authors promoted this distinctive Keswick sanctification, including Hannah Whithall Smith, Andrew Murray, R. A. Torrey, and Major Ian Thomas.

Keswick Sanctification

1. Immediate abandonment of every known sin and doubtful indulgence.
2. Surrender of the whole being to Jesus Christ as not only Savior, but Master and Lord.
3. Appropriation by faith of God's promise and power for holy living.
4. Voluntary mortification of the self-life, that God may be all in all.
5. Gracious renewal or transformation of the inmost temper and disposition.
6. Separation unto God for sanctification and service.
7. Empowerment and filling with the Holy Spirit.*

*E. H. Johnson, *The Highest Life: A Story of Shortcoming and a Goal, Including a Friendly Analysis of the Keswick Movement*, 2nd ed. (New York: A. C. Armstrong & Son, 1901), 46.

The Keswick approach left a lasting legacy on many evangelical leaders, churches, and movements. Bill Bright and Campus Crusade for Christ encouraged Christians to confess their sins and be filled with the Holy Spirit. Specifically, he contrasted three kinds of people: the *natural man* or person who does not yet believe in Jesus Christ; the *spiritual man* or Christian who lives victoriously in the power of the Holy Spirit as a way of life; and the *carnal Christian* or believer who lives a defeated Christian life because he relies on his own effort and strength and does not appropriate the Spirit-filled life. For Bright, most Christians fall into the third category, and a principal ministry of Campus Crusade for Christ became that of explaining to believers everywhere the basic truth of living in the power of the Holy Spirit through experiencing his filling.[134]

---

133. Evan H. Hopkins, *Crisis and Process*, in Stevenson, *Life More Abundant*, 61.

134. Bill Bright, *Have You Made the Wonderful Discovery of the Spirit-Filled Life?* (Orlando, Fla.: Bright Media Foundations and Campus Crusade for Christ, 2008).

Another essential of evangelical spirituality is the daily "quiet time." Various programs and aids were developed to encourage and guide Christians in their daily exercise of reading the Bible, reflecting on it, and praying. For example, *Our Daily Bread* was introduced, a small booklet published monthly that includes a Bible passage, brief meditation, and prayer for the day.

Some evangelicals developed the theology and practice of sanctification with recourse to the ancient spiritual disciplines employed in the church since its inception. Richard Foster's *Celebration of Discipline* organized these in three categories: *inward disciplines* of meditation, prayer, fasting, and study; *outward disciplines* of simplicity, solitude, submission, and service; and *corporate disciplines* of confession, worship, guidance, and celebration.[135] Dallas Willard's *The Spirit of the Disciplines* used the two divisions of *disciplines of abstinence* (including solitude, fasting, chastity, and sacrifice) and *disciplines of engagement* (including study, worship, prayer, and fellowship).[136] Evangelicals are thus reaching back to the classic spiritual disciplines for progress in sanctification.

135. Richard J. Foster, *Celebration of Discipline* (San Francisco: Harper and Row, 1978).

136. Dallas Willard, *The Spirit of the Disciplines* (San Francisco: Harper and Row, 1988), 159–90.

25

PERSEVERANCE OF THE SAINTS (REMAINING A CHRISTIAN)

How has the church developed different views on the security of a believer's salvation?

STATEMENT OF BELIEF

The church has historically been divided over the issue of the perseverance of the saints and its corollary, eternal security or the assurance of salvation. Perseverance "refers to the continuation of the work of God in the life of a true believer. To the question 'Will the operation of divine grace begun in a true believer's life certainly continue and be brought to completion such that a genuine Christian can never completely fall away from Christ and fail to obtain eternal salvation?' two different answers—one positive, one negative—have historically been offered."[1]

The first position is generally associated with John Calvin and similar views that flowed into and out of his theology. It maintains that genuine believers will certainly persevere in the Christian faith. The second view is generally associated with Arminianism and related views that flowed into and out of that theology. It holds that even genuine Christians can apostatize and fall away from the true faith. As for the corollary of perseverance, eternal security or the assurance of salvation is "the subjective confidence which genuine Christians are privileged to possess that they truly belong to God as his children and heirs of eternal life."[2] Again, two opposing views—Calvinism and Arminianism (along with their associated positions)—exist. The first position maintains that genuine Christians may possess "the confidence that they will continue as believers throughout

---

1. Gregg R. Allison, "Eternal Security," in *Evangelical Dictionary of World Missions*, ed. A. Scott Moreau (Grand Rapids: Baker, 2000), 318. My thanks to John Lopes for his help on this chapter.

2. Gregg R. Allison, "Assurance of Salvation," in *Evangelical Dictionary of World Missions*, 92.

their life and when they die they will certainly go to be with Christ in heaven forever."[3] The second view "focuses on the reality of the present state of grace of Christians and the assurance that engenders."[4] The church today is divided on this issue.

VIEWS OF PERSEVERANCE IN THE EARLY CHURCH

This division of perspective on the perseverance of the saints was apparent in the early church. Many church leaders emphasized the need to continue firmly in the Christian faith and not fall away. This message was sounded with particular urgency because of the intense persecutions that the early church faced. When threatened with loss of property, imprisonment, or even death, the first believers had to confront honestly the possibility of abandoning their Christian profession. To urge them on to continued faithfulness, early church leaders issued dire warnings of the tragic consequences that would follow from denying the faith. Even when persecution waned, the reality of temptation and the possibility of reverting to their former sinful lifestyle constantly threatened to undo Christians. Added to this was the spiritual battle waged against believers by Satan and his demons, who attempted to lure unsuspecting people into error and heresy.

Given these dangers, early church writers urged Christians to faithfulness and obedience and warned them against apostasy. Barnabas offered this exhortation:

> Let us be on guard in the last days, for the whole time of our faith will do us no good unless now, in the age of lawlessness, we resist as well the coming stumbling blocks, as befits God's children.... Let us never fall asleep in our sins, as if being "called" was an excuse to rest, lest the evil ruler gain power over us and thrust us out of the kingdom of the Lord. Moreover, consider this as well, my brothers: when you see that after such extraordinary signs and wonders were done in Israel, even then they were abandoned, let us be on guard lest we should be found to be, as it is written, "many called, but few chosen."[5]

In light of such warnings, it should not be surprising to find the early church condemning those who began to follow Christ but later abandoned him. For example, the *Shepherd of Hermas* condemned "the apostates and traitors to the church, who by their sins have blasphemed the Lord, and in addition were ashamed of the Lord's name by which they were called. These, therefore, utterly perished to God."[6] Among these heretics were those who directed Christians to embrace the Mosaic law. And Justin Martyr warned that those who "have confessed and known this man to be Christ, yet have returned to the legalism of the old covenant, "and have denied that this man is Christ, and have not repented" before they die will "not be saved."[7]

As an example of people who began well but in the end failed to stay on course, the early church pointed to Israel. Irenaeus focused on Old Testament stories of the

---

3. Ibid.

4. Ibid.

5. *Letter of Barnabas*, 4, in Holmes, 283; *ANF*, 1:139. The citation is from Matt. 20:16 or 22:14.

6. *Shepherd of Hermas*, parable 8.6.72, in Holmes, 463; *ANF*, 2:41.

7. Justin Martyr, *Dialogue with Trypho, a Jew*, 47, in *ANF*, 1:218.

disobedience and unfaithfulness of Israel—as Paul did, for example, in 1 Corinthians 10:1–12. Irenaeus warned Christians that the same tragic end—condemnation and punishment—awaits them if they revert to their sinful ways:

> It is for our instruction that their actions have been committed to writing, in order that we might know, in the first place, that our God and theirs is one, and that sins do not please Him although committed by men of renown, and in the second place, that we should keep from wickedness. For if these men of old time, who preceded us in the gifts (bestowed upon them), and for whom the Son of God had not yet suffered, when they committed any sin and served fleshly lusts, were rendered objects of such disgrace, what shall the men of the present day suffer, who have despised the Lord's coming, and have become the slaves of their own lusts? ... We should not be proud, nor look severely on the people of old. Rather, we should fear that, after coming to the knowledge of Christ, we do things that displease God so as to obtain no further forgiveness of sin, but indeed, we find ourselves shut out of the kingdom of God.[8]

Just as the people of Israel were chosen by God for privilege but ended up with punishment, so Christians who embrace Christ and his salvation could lose their grip and forfeit that great treasure.

Something can be detected in Irenaeus's writing that became typical in other writings in the early church: an emphasis on fearing the loss of salvation as a preventive against pride. In one sense, the church created a climate of fear and insecurity with its constant warnings against falling away from Christ. As Irenaeus noted, this uncertainty acted as a deterrent against pride, presumption, and carelessness. The reasoning was that if believers could be kept in a state of worry and doubt, then they would be less likely to drift away from the faith because of inattentiveness. Tertullian underscored this point:

> We should walk with such holiness and such certainty of faith so as to be confident and secure in regard to our own conscience, desiring that it may continue in us to the end. Yet, we should not be presumptuous that it will. For the one who presumes feels less apprehension. The one who feels less apprehension takes less precaution. The one who takes less precaution runs more risk. But fear is the foundation of salvation, while presumption is an impediment to fear. It is more useful, therefore, to be apprehensive that we may possibly fail than to be presumptuous that we cannot. For apprehension will lead us to fear, fear to caution, and caution to salvation. On the other hand, if we are presumptuous, there will be neither fear nor caution to save us.[9]

---

8. Irenaeus, *Against Heresies*, 4.27.2, in *ANF*, 1:499. The last sentence has been rendered clearer.

9. Tertullian, *On the Apparel of Women*, 2.2, in *ANF*, 4:19. The text has been rendered clearer. Similarly, Cyprian urged: "Let fear be the keeper of innocence, that the Lord, who of his mercy has flowed into our hearts in the access of celestial [heavenly] grace, may be kept by righteous submissiveness in the hostelry [home] of a grateful [thankful] mind, that the assurance we have gained may not beget carelessness, and so the old enemy creep upon us again." Cyprian, *Letter* 1.4, in *ANF*, 5:276.

Those in the early church who emphasized the dangerous possibility of believers falling away from the faith did so for several reasons. One we have already mentioned: it was seen as a deterrent to pride, which could ultimately lead to sin and apostasy. A second reason was the belief that sins committed after baptism could not be forgiven. In light of this view, a practice developed in the church of postponing baptism until right before one's death, so that one could be sure to leave this life with all sins washed away. For those who were already baptized but fell into sin afterward, no hope remained. Thus, Hippolytus criticized certain heretics, who promised their followers a second baptism—called "redemption"—to remove sins committed after their first baptism: "And by this (other baptism) they wickedly subvert those that remain with them in expectation of redemption, as if persons, after they had once been baptized, could again obtain remission."[10] No wonder that some writers issued warnings against returning to sin and evil after committing oneself to Christ through baptism.

A third reason for this emphasis on the danger of falling away was that supporters viewed the biblical evidence as pointing in its direction. In addition to the example of Israel, Solomon served as another prominent exhibit of one who began well but ended poorly. Indeed, in light of several key passages of Scripture, Cyprian viewed Solomon as issuing a clear warning for Christians:

> Whoever has confessed Christ is not greater, or better, or dearer to God than Solomon. As long as he walked in God's ways, he retained the grace that he had received from the Lord. But after he abandoned the Lord's way, he also lost the Lord's grace. Therefore, it is written, "Hold tightly to what you have, so that no one will take your crown" (Rev. 3:11). But certainly the Lord would not threaten that the crown of righteousness could be taken away, were it not true that the crown must depart when righteousness departs.... It is also written, "He who stands firm until the end will be saved" (Matt. 10:22). Thus, whatever comes before "the end" is a step by which we ascend to the summit of salvation. But it is not the finish, where the full result of the ascent is finally gained.[11]

Cyprian rehearsed other biblical passages—for example, 2 Chronicles 15:2; Ezekiel 33:12; Matthew 3:10; 7:22–23; Luke 9:62; 17:31–32; John 5:14; and 1 Corinthians 3:16–17—that emphasized the dangers of abandoning Christ and the need for perseverance to continue in the faith.[12] For Cyprian and many others, Scripture was one of several lines of evidence for the possibility of believers falling away from Christ. This danger demanded strong warnings to Christians about the perils of returning to their former way of life and departing from the faith. That urgent message was sounded again and again in the early church.

But this was not the only perspective. If some in the church threatened believers, others offered hope even for Christians who gave in to temptation. The *Shepherd of Hermas*

---

10. Hippolytus, *The Refutation of All Heresies*, 6.36, in *ANF*, 5:92.

11. Cyprian, *Treatise* 1.20–21: "On the Unity of the Church," in *ANF*, 5:428. The text has been rendered clearer.

12. Cyprian, *Treatise* 11: "Exhortation to Martyrdom, Addressed to Fortunatus," 7; ibid., *Treatise* 12: "Three Books of Testimonies against the Jews," 3rd book, 26–27, in *ANF*, 5:500, 542.

underscored the merciful character of God to help wayward believers: "God is not like men, who bear grudges; no, he is without malice and has compassion on his creation."[13] This gracious God could be asked to preserve Christians from falling away. Appealing to Scripture (1 Cor. 6:9; John 5:14), Cyprian urged this very thing:

> He [Paul] says that we are sanctified in the name of our Lord Jesus Christ and by the Spirit of our God. We pray that this sanctification may abide in us; and because our Lord and Judge warns the man that was healed and quickened by Him to sin no more lest a worse thing happen unto him, we make this supplication in our constant prayers, we ask this day and night, that the sanctification and quickening which is received from the grace of God may be preserved by His protection.[14]

And Cyprian marveled at the depths of God's mercy that not only gives redemption but also makes "provision that more abundant care should be taken for preserving man after he is already redeemed!... Nor would the infirmity and weakness of human frailty have any resource, unless the divine mercy, coming once more in aid, should open some way of securing salvation, by pointing out works of justice and mercy."[15]

Even greater testimonies to the early church's conviction that salvation is the certain treasure that awaits faithful believers are the stories of perseverance in the face of death on the part of its martyrs. As his name implies, Justin Martyr was one of the early believers who died for their faith. His martyrdom at the hands of Rusticus, the prefect of Rome, in 165 provides a stirring example of confident hope in obtaining salvation:

> Rusticus: "If you are scourged and beheaded, do you believe you will ascend into heaven?"

> Justin: "I hope that, if I endure these things, I shall have his [God's] gifts. For I know that, to all who have thus lived, there abides the divine favor until the completion of the whole world."

> Rusticus: "Do you suppose, then, that you will ascend into heaven to receive some recompense?"

> Justin: "I do not suppose it, but I know and am fully persuaded of it."[16]

The early church's view of the perseverance of the saints reached its most thorough and systematic formulation with Augustine. The title of his book *On the Gift of Perseverance* emphasized one of the key tenets of his position: "The perseverance by which we persevere in Christ even to the end is the gift of God."[17] Augustine's key support was the Lord's Prayer, particularly the last petition for deliverance from evil. Understanding this to be a prayer of Christians for perseverance, he commented: "When that gift of God is granted to them—which is sufficiently plainly shown to be God's gift, since it is asked of Him—...

---

13. *Shepherd of Hermas*, mandate 9.39, in Holmes, 399; *ANF*, 2:26.

14. Cyprian, *Treatise* 4: "On the Lord's Prayer," 12, in *ANF*, 5:450.

15. Cyprian, *Treatise* 8: "On Works and Alms," 1, in *ANF*, 5:476.

16. *The Martyrdom of the Holy Martyrs*, 4, in *ANF*, 1:306. I have varied the format for clarity.

17. Augustine, *On the Gift of Perseverance*, 1, in *NPNF*[1], 5:526.

none of the saints fails to keep his perseverance in holiness even to the end."[18] He bolstered his case by appealing to Ephesians 1:11 (with Ps. 80:17–18), explaining that "As [God] works so that we come to him, so he works that we do not depart.... So, by the work of God, we are caused to continue in Christ with God. Thus, it is by God's hand, not ours, that we do not depart from God."[19] Because this is a divine work, if a person has the gift, he perseveres; if he does not have the gift, he does not persevere. Also, "since no one has perseverance to the end except he who does persevere to the end, many people may have it, but none can lose it.... This gift of God, therefore, may be obtained by prayer, but when it has been given, it cannot be lost by contumacy."[20] Thus, perseverance is a divine gift that God has designed for believers to receive through prayer, and this gift cannot be lost.

For Augustine, no one in this life can know if he has or does not have this gift. Indeed, until one's life is finished, "there is peril of falling. Therefore, it is uncertain whether any one has received this gift so long as he is still alive. For if he fall [sic] before he dies, he is, of course, said not to have persevered; and most truly is it said. How, then, should he be said to have received or to have had perseverance who has not persevered?"[21] Accordingly, even people who are devoted to Christ and committed to honoring God cannot know if they will continue on that path to the very end of their lives. And Augustine appealed to 1 John 2:19 to underscore this view.[22] Still, he admitted that it seems counterintuitive. But as many before him did, Augustine believed that this lack of certainty keeps people humble and fearful so they will not drift away.[23]

But why is there this difference — that some faithful and obedient people will continue in faith and obedience, while others will not? Augustine appealed to the secret predestination of God, highlighting the fact that "the judgments of God are unsearchable." The former group of Christians who persevere are those who were chosen by God for salvation; the latter group was not so predestined.[24] So it all depends on God's sovereign will to choose some and condemn others. Based on his choice, people will either turn to Christ and persevere in the faith, or fall away from the religious obedience that they currently practice:

> The definite determination of God's will concerning predestination is like this: Some people who don't currently believe receive the will to obey and are converted to the faith or persevere in the faith. Other people now live in the pleasures of damnable sins, even if they have been predestined, and have not yet arisen, because the aid of compassionate grace has not yet lifted them up. For if God by his grace has predestined them to be elected but they have not yet been called, they will receive that grace by which they can choose to be elected and will be elected. If any people currently obey but have not been predestined to his kingdom and glory, they do so for a time but will not continue in that obedience to the end.[25]

---

18. Ibid., 9, in *NPNF*[1], 5:529.

19. Ibid., 14, in *NPNF*[1], 5:530. The text has been rendered clearer.

20. Ibid., 10, in *NPNF*[1], 5:529.

21. Ibid., 1, in *NPNF*[1], 5:526.

22. Ibid., 19, in *NPNF*[1], 5:531–32.

23. Ibid., 19, in *NPNF*[1], 5:532.

24. Ibid., 21, in *NPNF*[1], 5:532–33.

25. Ibid., 58, in *NPNF*[1], 5:549. The text has been rendered clearer.

To the charge that God is unfair toward the nonelect, Augustine appealed again to the mystery of the plan of God, who always acts righteously: "He wills not to come to their help, since in His predestination He, secretly, indeed, but yet righteously, has otherwise determined concerning them."[26] Thus, those who receive the gift of perseverance will certainly continue in the faith to the very end, but they can take no credit for receiving this gift from God. And those to whom the gift is not given can never blame God for his failure to grant them perseverance. As the sovereign and incomprehensible God, he does as he pleases. And no one can grasp the "why" of his perfect plan.

VIEWS OF PERSEVERANCE IN THE MIDDLE AGES

Thomas Aquinas leaned heavily on Augustine's theology to develop his view of perseverance yet differed from his predecessor in significant ways. With his forerunner, Aquinas believed that perseverance is a divine gift.[27] But by perseverance, Aquinas meant something different from Augustine: "Perseverance is called the abiding in good to the end of life."[28] This perseverance requires "not only habitual grace but also the gracious help of God sustaining a person in good until the end of life."[29] Why was habitual grace, infused by means of the sacraments of the church, not adequate to ensure continuation in the faith? Aquinas drew attention to the constant problem with human free will in this lifetime: "Free will is changeable by its very nature, and this changeableness is not removed by the habitual grace given in this present life. Thus, it is not in the power of free will, even when it is repaired by grace, to remain unchangeably in good, though it is in its power to choose this. For it is often in our power to choose yet not to accomplish."[30] Thus, the habitual grace provided by the church through its sacraments helps the human will to desire, choose, and do what is right. And these things are necessary for continuing in the Christian life. But such grace does not completely reform the will so that it always wishes, selects, and works what is right. That requires additional gracious help from God: "In order to have this perseverance, man ... needs the divine assistance guiding and guarding him against the attacks of the passions.... And hence after anyone has been justified by grace, he still needs to beseech God for [this] gift of perseverance, that he may be kept from evil till the end of his life. For to many grace is given to whom perseverance in grace is not given."[31] On this point, Aquinas was at odds with Augustine, who held that to all who are given grace to begin salvation, God gives persevering grace.

Aquinas's view was tied closely to his idea that ultimate salvation, though certainly a work of God's grace, must be merited by believers: "Now everlasting life is an end exceeding the proportion of human nature.... Hence man, by his natural endowments, cannot produce meritorious works proportionate to everlasting life, but for this a higher power is needed, namely, the power of grace. And thus without grace man cannot merit everlast-

---

26. Ibid., 25, in *NPNF*[1], 5:534. He specifically referenced Ps. 25:10 and Rom. 9:14, 16.

27. Thomas Aquinas, *Summa Theologica*, 2nd pt. of pt. 2, q. 137, art. 4.

28. Ibid., 1st pt. of pt. 2, q. 109, art. 10.
29. Ibid., 2nd pt. of pt. 2, q. 137, art. 4.
30. Ibid.
31. Ibid., 1st pt. of pt. 2, q. 109, art. 10.

ing life."[32] For Aquinas, the cooperation between the powerful grace of God and human effort to break from sin and do what is right is the formula for eternal life. In terms of God's side of the venture, his grace enabling believers to persevere is infallible. But such grace is not given to everyone who begins on the cooperative journey toward salvation. And on the human side, free will makes perseverance at best a possibility, because it can give in to human passions and choose against doing what is right. This reality dashes the hope of continuing firmly to the end. Aquinas brought these two elements together as he explained that a sinful person needs divine grace "in order to be moved by God to act rightly, and this for two reasons: first, for the general reason that no created thing can put forth any act, unless by virtue of the Divine motion. Secondly, for this special reason—the condition of the state of human nature."[33] Fallen human nature, though healed in part by grace, "remains corrupted and poisoned";[34] thus, certainty of perseverance is not possible even for redeemed—yet still sinful—human beings.

VIEWS OF PERSEVERANCE DURING THE REFORMATION AND POST-REFORMATION

Martin Luther tenderly and compassionately addressed the unsettling reality of doubting one's salvation, recognizing it as one of the most devastating problems that Christians face: "God could be the most foolish of all beings if he had given his Son and Scriptures and the Prophets and, in spite of these gifts, wanted us to remain uncertain and in doubt about our salvation. This notion is the work of the devil; its purpose is to make unbelievers and doubters out of us."[35] He blamed this situation not only on Satan but the Catholic Church as well, which he denounced as abusing conscience-stricken people through its appeal to Ecclesiastes 9:1: "The Catholic Church explains this passage in this way: 'Even though a person is holy and righteous, he does not know whether he is in favor or in disfavor with God, but everything remains uncertain until the future, that is, until the final judgment.'"[36] Luther was so attuned to this problem because as a (very devout) Catholic monk, he had experienced it firsthand for himself.[37] In no uncertain terms, Luther denounced this Catholic "monster of uncertainty":[38] "that they teach doubt and take away from righteousness its substantial form, which is confidence."[39] He warned: "There certainly is no reason for us to think that God is pleased with that doubt and mistrust in us. Indeed, this one sin is by far the gravest of all the sins which will condemn the world and the unbelievers. For the magnitude of the sin can be gauged from the magnitude of God's promise, oath, pledge, and imprecation."[40] To not believe, therefore, but to be filled with doubt instead, is a heinous sin against God. Thus, Luther distanced himself from the centuries-old denial of the assurance of salvation held by the Catholic Church.

---

32. Ibid., 1st pt. of pt. 2, q. 109, art. 5.

33. Ibid., 1st pt. of pt. 2, q. 109, art. 9.

34. Ibid.

35. Martin Luther, *WLS*, 1:457.

36. Ibid., 1:426.

37. Ibid.

38. Martin Luther, *Lectures on Galatians: Chapters 1-4*, LW, 26:386.

39. *Lectures on Genesis: Chapters 21-25*, LW, 4:171.

40. Ibid.; LW, 4:147.

By way of contrast, Luther encouraged Christians to trust God and his Word, assuring them that by so doing, they would have "a joyous heart that can say with certainty and assurance: 'I know of no more sins, for they are all lying on Christ's back. Now, they can never lie both upon him and upon us.'"[41] Luther noted that in addition to the promises of God's Word, baptism and the Lord's Supper—"seals" of God's pledge—are helps for this assurance of salvation.[42] Furthermore, Luther encouraged him who is doubting to "exercise his faith, struggle against the doubt, and strive for certainty."[43] Clearly, Luther compassionately championed the assurance of salvation against the reigning conviction that such assurance was presumptuous and evil.

Following Luther, the *Formula of Concord* expressed its doctrine of perseverance: "Christ ... promises that he will bestow the virtue and operation of the Holy Spirit and divine aid, to the end that we may abide steadfast in the faith and attain eternal life."[44] The *Formula* warned strongly about abusing this truth as a license to live carnally, reasoning presumptuously that because one is eternally saved, one can do evil with impunity.[45] Accordingly, the *Formula* encouraged the proper approach to this doctrine: Attention should be focused on the Word of God—especially on Jesus Christ himself.[46] Thus, Luther and the early Lutheran churches articulated the doctrines of perseverance and assurance of salvation while attempting to avoid abuses associated with them.

It is with John Calvin that the doctrine of the perseverance of the saints is most commonly associated, due at least in part to the fact that one of the "Five Points of Calvinism" includes a statement on perseverance. Before that belief was formalized as one of the critical elements, however, Calvin himself laid down its foundation.

According to Calvin, the perseverance of the saints, and its corollary of assurance, was of great benefit and comfort to believers; thus, it warrants careful consideration and should be practically preached in the church. For Calvin, perseverance rests on God's grace in bringing people to salvation in Christ, an act that is wholly of God and nothing of human effort or merit. Alluding to Paul's statement in Philippians 2:13, he noted that "the apostle does not teach that the grace of a good will is bestowed upon us if we accept it, but that He wills to work in us. This means nothing else than that the Lord by his Spirit directs, bends, and governs our heart and reigns in it as in his own possession.... [T]he hearts of the pious [saints] are so effectively governed by God that they follow him with unwavering intention."[47] Thus, perseverance is entirely a work of God. It is not helped by human willingness, nor is it given as a reward for faithfulness and obedience.

In his affirmation, Calvin confronted a well-established error in the church: that God works in the lives of believers to the extent that they cooperate with his grace.[48]

---

41. *Sermons at the Baptism of Bernhard Von Anhalt*, LW, 51:317.

42. Luther, *WLS*, 3:1265–66.

43. *Lectures on Galatians: Chapters 1-4*, LW, 26:379.

44. This doctrine is tied to the doctrine of predestination. *Formula of Concord*, 11.7, in Schaff, 3:167.

45. Ibid., 11.8, in Schaff, 3:167.

46. Ibid., 11.12, in Schaff, 3:169–70.

47. John Calvin, *Institutes of the Christian Religion*, 2.3.10, LCC 1:303–4.

48. "However, there is here a two-fold error. For besides teaching that our gratefulness for the first grace and our lawful use of it are rewarded by subsequent gifts, they add also that grace does not work in us by itself, but is only a co-worker with us." Ibid., 2.3.11, LCC, 1:304–5.

He did not deny that grace increases in their lives as they rightly respond to God's grace. But he underscored that some common errors have to be avoided concerning this teaching:

> [H]ere we ought to guard against two things: (1) not to say that lawful use of the first grace is rewarded by later graces, as if man by his own effort rendered God's grace effective; or (2) so to think of the reward as to cease to consider it of God's free grace. I grant that believers are to expect this blessing of God: that the better use they have made of the prior graces, the more may the following graces be thereafter increased. But I say this use is also from the Lord and this reward arises from his free benevolence.[49]

And Calvin did not deny that believers must exercise their faith and remain obedient to God. But again, he qualified this truth: "It is very certain that where God's grace reigns, there is readiness to obey it. Yet whence does this readiness come? Does not the Spirit of God, everywhere self-consistent, nourish the very inclination to obedience that he first engendered, and strengthen its constancy to persevere?"[50]

Thus, Calvin removed perseverance from the category of cooperative effort between God and believers. Even the faith and obedience that come forth from believers as they experience God's grace are fruits of the Holy Spirit's work in them. This position effectively deflected the attack of his opponents that believers cannot be sure of continuing in the faith throughout their life because they may fail to cooperate with God's grace; thus, they may fall away from Christ, but they will bear the blame. For Calvin, perseverance is entirely the work of God; thus, believers cannot fail to do a work in which they have no part. If they cannot short-circuit God's grace, then perseverance will continue throughout their lifetime.

Ultimately, Calvin grounded the perseverance of the saints in God's election of them. This truth provides great assurance for believers.[51] Specifically, perseverance is a gift of God that is part and parcel of his election. To his elect, God grants salvation as a gracious gift, and included in that gift is perseverance:

> Though all of us are by nature suffering from the same disease, only those whom it pleases the Lord to touch with his healing hand will get well. The others, whom he, in his righteous judgment, passes over, waste away in their own rottenness until they are consumed. There is no other reason why some persevere to the end, while others fall at the beginning of the course. For perseverance itself is indeed also a gift of God, which he does not bestow on all indiscriminately, but imparts to whom he pleases. If one seeks the reason for the difference—why some steadfastly persevere, and others fail out of instability—none occurs to us other than that the Lord upholds the former, strengthening them by his own power, so that they may not perish; while to the latter, that they may be examples of inconstancy, he does not impart the same power.[52]

---

49. Ibid., LCC, 1:305.
50. Ibid., LCC, 1:306.
51. Ibid., 3.24.6, LCC, 2:971–72.
52. Ibid., 2.5.3, LCC, 1:320.

To heighten their sense of assurance, Calvin rehearsed the biblical promises of Christ to believers (e.g., John 6:37, 39; 10:27–29; Rom. 8:38–39; Phil. 1:6) and emphasized the intercessory work of Christ on their behalf—"that their faith may never fail (Luke 22:32). From this we infer that they are out of danger of falling away because the Son of God, asking that their godliness be kept constant, did not suffer a refusal."[53]

Calvin had to confront the reality that some—perhaps even many—people who profess to be Christians do not remain believers all their lives. Instead, they deny the faith and depart from Christ. Does not this empirical fact argue against the perseverance of the saints? Appealing to 1 John 2:19, Calvin replied that these people were not genuine believers in the first place.[54] But, the rejoinder went, these people were, at times, models of good works, pillars of the faith—even pastors and teachers and leaders of the church. Certainly, they were true Christians! Calvin countered: "I do not deny that they have signs of a call that are similar to those of the elect, but I by no means concede to them that sure establishment of election which I bid believers to seek from the word of the gospel. So then, let not such instances induce us at all to abandon a quiet reliance upon the Lord's promise."[55] This assurance of salvation should not engender "crass and sheer confidence of the flesh, which bears in its train [wake] haughtiness [pride], arrogance, and contempt of others, snuffs out humility and reverence for God, and makes one forget grace received."[56] Rather, this certainty "requires fear, not that we may be dismayed and waver but that … in preparing us humbly to receive God's grace, our trust in him may in no wise [way] be diminished."[57] Thus, the assurance of salvation rests on God's work of perseverance, and it is a wonderful privilege available to all genuine believers. Unsurprisingly, then, "Satan has no more grievous or dangerous temptation to dishearten believers than when he unsettles them with doubt about their election."[58] Calvin attempted to counter the enemy's disruptive attacks by furnishing the church with a clear doctrine of the perseverance of the saints.

Following the theology of Calvin, the *Heidelberg Catechism* pronounced a firm and confident Christian hope:

> *Question 1*: What is thy only comfort in life and in death?
>
> *Answer*: That I, with body and soul, both in life and in death, am not my own, but belong to my faithful Savior Jesus Christ, who with his precious blood has fully satisfied for all my sins, and redeemed me from all the power of the devil; and so preserves me that without the will of my Father in heaven not a hair can fall from my head; yea, that all things must work together for my salvation. Wherefore, by his Holy Spirit, he also assures me of eternal life, and makes me heartily willing and ready henceforth to live unto him.[59]

And the *Belgic Confession* addressed perseverance in its discussion of election and the gift of faith that embraces salvation: "We believe also that faith is not given to the elect only

---

53. Ibid., 3.24.6, LCC, 2:972–73.
54. Ibid., 3.24.7, LCC, 2:973.
55. Ibid.
56. Ibid.

57. Ibid.
58. Ibid., 3.24.4, LCC, 2:968.
59. *Heidelberg Catechism*, q. 1, in Schaff, 3:307–8.

to introduce them into the right way, but also to make them continue in it to the end. For as it is God who began the work, he will also perfect it."[60]

The Catholic Church dissented from this Protestant doctrine of the perseverance of the saints and assurance of salvation. This opposition stemmed from several points. One was the denial that people could ever know God's election of them in this lifetime. A second was the important role that Catholic theology assigned to human cooperation in salvation. Because salvation is a joint effort on the part of God and human beings, believers could use their free will to turn totally away from Christ and deny the faith. Thus, God's persevering efforts could be thwarted, and no living person could ever claim to be certain of his salvation.

This position was formalized at the Council of Trent. Assurance of salvation was denounced as a heresy:

> It should not be said that sins are forgiven, or have been forgiven, for anyone who boasts of his confidence and certainty of the forgiveness of his sins, and rests on that alone. This view may exist—indeed, it does exist—among heretics and schismatics. Certainly, no saint should have doubts about the mercy of God, the merits of Christ, and the virtue and effectiveness of the sacraments. Even so, each person, when he considers himself and his own weakness and unwillingness, should have fear and anxiety about his own reception of grace. For no one can know with a certainty of faith—a certainty that cannot be subject to error—that he has obtained the grace of God.[61]

Accordingly, anyone claiming the assurance of salvation was condemned to hell by the council.[62]

It was not as though the council denied the reality of perseverance. On the contrary, it was affirmed as the gift of God, and the council insisted that Christians can have strong hope that they will remain believers until the very end.[63] What was denounced, however, was the assurance of any particular individual that this gift irrevocably belongs to him. Such certainty smacks of boasting. As the early church did, the council encouraged fear and uncertainty to keep its members from falling into the sin of pride, which could lead them to abandon the faith.[64]

Furthermore, the council insisted that people lose the justifying grace of God—that is, lose their salvation—when they commit mortal sin.[65] This abandoned grace can only be recovered by participation in the sacrament of penance.[66] This view was a far cry from the view of the Reformers, who insisted that perseverance was part and parcel of the gift of salvation, the assurance of which was the privilege of all believers. Such certainty does not lead to pride or moral laxness. On the contrary, Christians possessed by a con-

---

60. *Belgic Confession*, 21, in Schaff, 3:371.

61. *Canons and Decrees of the Council of Trent*, 6th session (January 13, 1547), *Decree on Justification*, chap. 9, in Schaff, 2:98–99. The text has been rendered clearer.

62. Ibid., canon 16, in Schaff, 2:113–14.

63. Ibid., chap. 13, in Schaff, 2:103–4.

64. Ibid., in Schaff, 2:104.

65. Ibid., chap. 15, in Schaff, 2:106.

66. Ibid., chap. 14, in Schaff, 2:105–6. In the 14th session (November 25, 1551), which dealt with the sacraments of penance and extreme unction, the council (*On the Most Holy Sacrament of Penance*, canon 3) condemned anyone who dissented from this understanding of John 20:22–23. In Schaff, 2:164.

fident assurance were willing to risk everything—homes, property, families, even life itself—for the sake of Christ and his cause, because their eternal destiny was sure. Not surprisingly, in Calvin's day and afterward, Geneva produced a "race of martyrs" who spread the gospel despite persecution by Catholics and the threat of death at their hands.

Half a century after Calvin's death, a controversy erupted among some Calvinist theologians in Holland. Led by Jacob Arminius, the Remonstrants took issue with several key doctrinal points, including Calvin's views of perseverance and assurance. Arminius articulated his own view of these doctrines as a counterpoint to the Calvinist position. On the matter of the subjective assurance of believers, Arminius affirmed:

> With regard to the certainty of salvation, my opinion is that it is possible for him who believes in Jesus Christ to be certain and persuaded and, if his heart does not condemn him, he is now in reality assured that he is a son of God and stands in the grace of Jesus Christ. Such a certainty is wrought in the mind both by the action of the Holy Spirit inwardly actuating the believer and by the fruits of faith, as well as from his own conscience and the testimony of God's Spirit witnessing together with his conscience. I also believe that it is possible for such a person, with an assured confidence in the grace of God and his mercy in Christ, to depart out of this life and to appear before the throne of grace without any anxious fear or terrible dread. Still, this person should constantly pray, "O Lord, do not enter into judgment with your servant!"[67]

While affirming the possibility of such subjective assurance, Arminius also urged caution:

> Since "God is greater than our hearts and knows all things," and since a man does not judge himself—indeed, though a man knows nothing against himself, yet he is not by that justified, but he who judges him is the Lord (1 John 3:19; 1 Cor. 4:3)—I dare not [on this account] place this assurance [or certainty] on an equality with that by which we know there is a God, and that Christ is the Savior of the world. Yet it will be proper to make the extent of the boundaries of this assurance a subject of inquiry.[68]

This was hardly controversial material. But when Arminius turned to the doctrine of the perseverance of the saints, he unleashed a storm of controversy. His viewpoint was incorporated into the *Five Articles of the Remonstrants* (1610) as its fifth affirmation. The beginning of the article affirmed that Christians are fully supplied with everything necessary for them to live as faithful and obedient believers throughout their lifetime:

> Those who are incorporated into Christ by a true faith, and have thereby become partakers of his life-giving Spirit, have thereby full power to strive against Satan, sin, the world, and their own flesh, and to win the victory; it being well understood that it is ever through the assisting grace of the Holy Spirit; and that Jesus Christ

---

67. James Arminius, *The Writings of James Arminius*, 3 vols., trans. James Nichols (Grand Rapids: Baker, 1956), 1:255.

The text has been rendered clearer.
68. Ibid.

assists them through his Spirit in all temptations, extends to them his hand, and if only they are ready for the conflict, and desire his help, and are not inactive, keeps them from falling, so that they, by no craft [trick] or power of Satan, can be misled nor plucked out of Christ's hands, according to the Word of Christ (John 10:28).[69]

To this point, there was little to stir up debate. But the article concluded with an issue that would later become a lightning rod for controversy: "But whether they [believers] are capable, through negligence, of forsaking again the first beginnings of their life in Christ, of again returning to this present evil world, of turning away from the holy doctrine which was delivered to them, of losing a good conscience, of becoming devoid of grace—that must be more particularly determined out of the Holy Scripture, before we ourselves can teach it with the full persuasion of our minds."[70] Arminius himself was forthright as to his own belief: "I never taught that a true believer can either totally or finally fall away from the faith and perish; yet, I will not conceal that there are passages of Scripture which seem to me to bear this aspect."[71] But the possibility of entertaining this idea was clearly at odds with the Reformed position on perseverance.

A response to the Remonstrants' position—called Arminianism—was given at the Synod of Dort and articulated in the *Canons of Dort*. Five Calvinist canons were adopted, the last of which treated the doctrine of perseverance. Some of its key tenets included the following: first and foremost, perseverance is a work of God: "By reason of these remains [remnants] of indwelling sin, and the temptations of sin and of the world, those who are converted could not persevere in a state of grace if left to their own strength. But God is faithful, who having conferred grace, mercifully confirms and powerfully preserves them therein, even to the end."[72] Moreover, true believers can be seduced by temptation, their sinful nature, Satan, and the world so as to fall deeply into sin for a time: "They must therefore be constant in watching and prayer, that they be not led into temptation. When these are neglected, they are not only liable to be drawn into great and heinous sins by Satan, the world, and the flesh, but sometimes by the righteous permission of God actually fall into these evils."[73] This backslidden state does not mean, however, that these Christians lose their salvation, for God does not allow "them to proceed so far as to lose the grace of adoption and forfeit the state of justification, or to commit the sin unto death; nor does he permit them to be totally deserted, and to plunge themselves into everlasting destruction."[74] Rather, this state of carnality is and can only be temporary, for "by his Word and Spirit, he [God] certainly and effectively renews them to repentance, to a sincere and godly sorrow for their sins, that they may seek and obtain remission [of sins] in the blood of the Mediator, may again experience the favor of a reconciled God, through faith adore his mercies, and henceforward more diligently work out their own salvation with fear and trembling."[75] Accordingly, God himself is the one who is ultimately responsible for the perseverance of the saints:

69. *Five Arminian Articles*, art. 5, in Schaff, 3:548; cf. Arminius, *The Writings of James Arminius*, 1:254.

70. Ibid., in Schaff, 3:548–49; cf. Arminius, *The Writings of James Arminius*, 1:254.

71. Arminius, *The Writings of James Arminius*, 1:254.

72. *Canons of the Synod of Dort*, 5.3, in Schaff, 3:593.

73. Ibid., 5.4, in Schaff, 3:593.

74. Ibid., 5.6, in Schaff, 3:593.

75. Ibid., 5.7, in Schaff, 3:594.

Thus, it is not in consequence of their own merits or strength, but of God's free mercy, that they do not totally fall from faith and grace, nor continue and perish finally in their backslidings; which, with respect to themselves, is not only possible, but would undoubtedly happen; but with respect to God, it is utterly impossible, since his counsel cannot be changed nor his promise fail, neither can the call according to his purpose be revoked, nor the merit, intercession, and preservation of Christ be rendered ineffective, nor the sealing of the Holy Spirit be frustrated or obliterated.[76]

This fifth canon of the *Canons of Dort* formalized the Calvinist doctrine of the perseverance of the saints and clearly distanced it from the Arminian view.

The *Westminster Confession of Faith* echoed Calvin's theology of perseverance and the fifth canon from the Synod of Dort: "They whom God has accepted in his Beloved, effectively called, and sanctified by his Spirit, can neither totally nor finally fall away from the state of grace, but will certainly persevere in it to the end and be eternally saved." That is, perseverance is a reality for genuine believers—and for them only. Most certainly, it is not the result of human effort but depends on the gracious work of the triune God. Realistically, however, the *Confession* admitted that some believers—and this should be the exception, not the norm—can fall into a state of carnality for a time. Even if it is only temporary, its consequences are devastating: "They may ... for a time, continue therein [in this state]: whereby they incur God's displeasure, and grieve his Holy Spirit; come to be deprived of some measure of their graces and comforts; have their hearts hardened, and their consciences wounded; hurt and scandalize others, and bring temporal judgments upon themselves."[77]

Having established the perseverance of the saints, the *Confession* turned to the assurance of salvation as an outcome of this divine work in the lives of believers. It explained the true nature of assurance, affirming that this certainty is a wonderful privilege reserved for all genuine Christians:

Although hypocrites and other unregenerate men may vainly deceive themselves with false hopes and carnal presumptions of being in the favor of God and estate [state] of salvation, which hope of theirs shall perish; yet such as truly believe in the Lord Jesus, and love him in sincerity, endeavoring to walk in all good conscience before him, may in this life be certainly assured that they are in a state of grace, and may rejoice in the hope of the glory of God, which hope shall never make them ashamed.[78]

Such assurance goes far beyond wishful thinking and self-talk; on the contrary, it is "an infallible assurance of faith" because it is based on both the Word of God and the Spirit of God.[79] Moreover, the *Confession* did not reserve the assurance of salvation for those who have continued for a long time and matured in the Christian faith. Rather,

---

76. Ibid., 5.8, in Schaff, 3:594.

77. *Westminster Confession of Faith*, 17.1–3, in Schaff, 3:636–37.

78. Ibid., 18.1, in Schaff, 3:637–38.

79. Ibid., 18.2, in Schaff, 3:638.

even brand-new believers may lay claim to this certainty, if they will simply grasp the work of God on their behalf, the promises of the Word regarding salvation, and the ministry of the Holy Spirit. All of these resources are available to any Christian who seeks to understand and live by them.[80] The *Confession* concluded with a realistic assessment of this privilege: For various reasons, true believers may live without this certainty, but it can never be completely snuffed out from their life:

> True believers may have the assurance of their salvation shaken, diminished, and interrupted in various ways: by neglect of preserving their assurance, by falling into some special sin which wounds the conscience and grieves the Spirit; by some sudden or violent temptation; by God's withdrawing the light of his countenance, and suffering even those who fear him to walk in darkness without any light. Yet, they are never utterly destitute of that seed of God, and life of faith, that love of Christ and other believers, that sincerity of heart, and consciousness of duty. Out of these things, by the operation of the Spirit, this assurance may, in due time, be revived. By these things, in the meantime, they are supported from utter despair.[81]

Post-Reformation theologians continued to affirm these doctrines, the order of which, they insisted, is important: first comes the perseverance of the saints, then comes the assurance of salvation, because the former is the foundation for the latter.[82] Numerous supports for these doctrines were offered, among which were the effect of Christ's sacrifice, his intercessory ministry, his reigning at the Father's right hand, the eternal love of God and his election,[83] the impossibility of tearing the members of Christ's body from their head, the ongoing infusion of spiritual life by Christ the head into his body,[84] the sanctifying and sealing work of the Holy Spirit,[85] the promise of God, the persevering nature of justifying faith, baptism and the Lord's Supper as offers of assurance, examples of persevering saints, and Scripture's rebuke of doubt and uncertainty.[86]

VIEWS OF PERSEVERANCE IN THE MODERN PERIOD

A modification of the Arminian view of perseverance was introduced by John Wesley. Addressing biblical passages that seem to offer unconditional promises of salvation and perseverance, Wesley maintained that they all must be tempered by other biblical passages that warn about the loss of salvation and the failure to persevere. For example, taking the classical text (Rom. 8:29–30) appealed to by Calvinists in support of their doctrine, Wesley offered this paraphrase: *"And whom he [God] justified—Provided they*

---

80. Ibid., 18.3, in Schaff, 3:638–39.

81. Ibid., 18.4, in Schaff, 3:639–40. The text has been made clearer.

82. John Heidegger, *Corpus Theologiae* (Zürich, 1700), 24.3, in Heppe, 582.

83. *Bremen Confession*, 9.3, in Heppe, 583.

84. Herman Witsius, *De Oeconomia Foederum Dei*, 3rd ed.

(Utrecht, 1694), 3.13.25, in Heppe, 583.

85. Heidegger, *Corpus Theologiae*, 24.9, 12, 44, in Heppe, 584–85.

86. Martin Chemnitz, *Examination of the Council of Trent*, part 1, trans. Fred Kramer (St. Louis: Concordia, 1971), 593-604.

'continued in his goodness' (Rom. 11:22), *he* in the end *glorified*—St. Paul does not affirm, either here or in any other part of his writings, that precisely the same number of men are called, justified, and glorified. He does not deny that a believer may fall away and be cut off between his special calling and his glorification (Rom. 11:22)."[87]

Interestingly, while standing against the classical Calvinist doctrine of perseverance, Wesley treated actual people with deep pastoral concern as they found themselves straying from the Christian faith. In his *A Call to Backsliders*,[88] Wesley attempted to ease the consciences of professing believers who had stumbled in their walk with Christ. He urged that the church not give up on them, even though for various reasons they have given up on themselves. He even went so far as to address the biblical arguments that are used to condemn backsliders and (illegitimately) steal from them any and all hope: they commit the sin unto death (1 John 5:16); they are threatened with impending judgment and fiery indignation (Heb. 10:26–31); they cannot be renewed to repentance (Heb. 6:4–6); and they blaspheme the Holy Spirit and can never be forgiven (Matt. 12:31–32).[89] Wesley dismissed each of these biblical arguments.[90] In turn, the comfort that he offered to his audience of backsliders was based on them not being genuine believers who had lost their salvation and on them not having committed unpardonable sins. Yet Wesley also held out hope for people who once were genuine believers and yet apostatized from the Christian faith, pointing to thousands of actual examples of such people who were renewed to salvation: "In one moment, they received anew both remission of sins, and a lot among them ... were sanctified."[91]

Over and against this Wesleyan perspective, the traditional Calvinist doctrine of perseverance was echoed and defended. One approach was to focus on the *ordo salutis*—the order of salvation, referring to the various mighty works of God in the order in which they are applied to believers for their salvation. By linking glorification—the last divine act—with the previous divine acts that initiate and continue salvation—election, effective calling, regeneration, justification, adoption, union with Christ, and sanctification—Calvinist theologians identified perseverance as part and parcel of the ongoing work of God in saving people. Thus, to affirm these other salvific acts in the lives of believers is, of necessity, to affirm perseverance as well.

In the twentieth century, leading theologians championed the Wesleyan-Arminian doctrine. For example, I. Howard Marshall wrote *Kept by the Power of God: A Study of Perseverance and Falling Away* to address the issue of "whether it is possible for a man who has truly become a Christian and an heir of the life of heaven to fall away from his faith and be finally lost."[92] He rejected the Calvinist doctrine of perseverance: "We must rule out

87. John Wesley, *Explanatory Notes upon the New Testament* (London: Epworth, 1952), 551.

88. John Wesley, *A Call to Backsliders*, in *The Works of John Wesley*, vols. 5–6 (repr., Grand Rapids: Baker, 2002), 6:514–26.

89. Ibid., 1.1–2, in *Works of John Wesley*, 6:516–18.

90. Ibid., 2.5.1–2; 2.8.1–2; 2.9.2, in *Works of John Wesley*, 6:520–24.

91. Ibid., 2.10.1, 2, 5, in *Works of John Wesley*, 6:525–26.

92. I. Howard Marshall, *Kept by the Power of God: A Study of Perseverance and Falling Away* (London: Epworth, 1969), 4.

Elsewhere (p. 91), he framed the question in this way: "Does the verdict that we have been justified by grace through faith mean that we are certain to be justified on the day of judgment or must there remain an element of doubt until the final sentence of acquittal or of guilt is passed?" Although Marshall imagined his approach to avoid the extremes of both Calvinism and Arminianism, I am placing his view under the rubric of Wesleyan-Arminianism because it ultimately agrees with that position that genuine believers—even though, by Marshall's own admission, a small number—can lose their salvation.

the view that God foreordains a certain number of elect to salvation with its logical consequence that they are bound to persevere to the end and attain final salvation. On the other hand, it is not foreclosed that when a man responds to God with faith and commits his life to Him a divine plan comes into action which includes his perseverance."[93] Working with the warnings against apostasy and the admonitions to remain faithful, he reasoned, "The need for exhortation shows that there is a possibility of failure to work out salvation."[94] Furthermore, he drew attention to the many hazards that Christians face during their earthly pilgrimage, dangers that threaten their walk with Christ.[95] While emphasizing that sin puts Christians in grave danger—a peril that is "real and not 'hypothetical'"[96]—Marshall also noted that "the New Testament refers in an admittedly small number of cases to Christians falling into apostasy."[97] This is due to the fact that "God cares for believers and preserves them from falling away."[98] Thus, "it is apparent that believers may be confident of persevering through the power of God, and the majority of believers do persevere."[99]

But what of the individual Christian who wonders about his own continuation in the faith? Marshall offered: "The way to persevere is simply—by persevering. There is no way of telling whether a given person in the church will persevere to the end; the fact of his perseverance at any given moment is shown in the fact that he is persevering.... One is commanded not to speculate but to believe!"[100] Still, recognizing the agonizing nature of the personal questions, Marshall offered a measured hope to believers: "While the New Testament knows the possibility of failure to persevere, it also knows the fact of growth in grace and the knowledge of Jesus Christ so that the Christian can attain to a confidence which lifts him above the fear of falling away. It is perhaps in this idea of growth and development in faith that the key to the problem is to be found."[101]

In another approach, Robert Shank affirmed that the gift of perseverance (like the gift of election) is indeed given by God, but it is certainly and unconditionally given to the church and only contingently and conditionally to individual believers.[102] Accordingly, Shank dissented from the idea that individual Christians are definitely elect and will surely persevere in salvation.[103] Perseverance, yes—for the church. But, according to Shank, this truth should not lead individuals to become presumptuous of the grace of God and ignore "the many warnings and exhortations to persevere in the faith."[104]

In a thoroughgoing biblical theology of perseverance and assurance, Thomas Schreiner and Ardel Caneday identified and analyzed various types of passages that must be considered in treating this subject,[105] then concluded that four popular formulations of the doctrines of perseverance and assurance are wrong: the Wesleyan-Arminian position, or *loss-of-salvation view*;[106] the Grace Evangelical Society position, or *loss-of-rewards*

---

93. Ibid., 195.
94. Ibid., 114.
95. Ibid., 195–96.
96. Ibid., 196–97.
97. Ibid., 197.
98. Ibid.
99. Ibid., 198.
100. Ibid., 205.
101. Ibid., 205–6.

102. Robert Shank, *Life in the Son: A Study of the Doctrine of Perseverance* (repr., Minneapolis: Bethany, 1989), 366.
103. Ibid.
104. Ibid., 367.
105. Thomas R. Schreiner and Ardel B. Caneday, *The Race Set before Us: A Biblical Theology of Perseverance and Assurance* (Downers Grove, Ill.: InterVarsity, 2001), 11–13.
106. Ibid., 21–24.

view;[107] the common evangelical view popularized by John MacArthur, or *tests-of-genuineness view*;[108] and the position based principally on the warnings in the letter to the Hebrews, or *hypothetical-loss-of-salvation view*.[109]

Unconvinced by these views, Schreiner and Caneday reframed the discussion around "the primary question that determines the shape one's doctrine of perseverance and assurance will take": "How do God's warnings and admonitions relate to his promises of assured salvation for his people?"[110] They maintained the compatibility of the divine promises with the divine warnings and admonitions;[111] specifically, they related these to the original proclamation of the gospel with its offer of salvation: "Warnings and admonitions function to extend the initial call of the gospel on throughout our lives, relentlessly calling us to be faithful to Jesus Christ and as road signs always pointing out the narrow pathway to salvation but also clearly marking the wide road to destruction."[112] Consequently, these warnings and admonitions do not function as appeals to Christians to work furiously to earn rewards from God.[113] Rather, they serve to encourage Christians to conceive rationally of the consequences of their actions and, by so doing, urge them to persevere with Christ.[114] Schreiner and Caneday emphasized that when it issues threats about drifting away from the faith or abandoning Christ, "the Bible warns of conceivable consequences, not of probable consequences."[115] To Christians, God promises salvation as the end of trusting in Christ throughout their life; this goal is assured. God also issues warnings and admonitions as the means to accomplish that assured end.[116] "Indeed, the admonitions are one of the means God uses by which we continue to run the race, and thus they must be conceived as strengthening and confirming our assurance."[117]

D. A. Carson, offering some "reflections on assurance," urged a compatabilist approach to this doctrine. Rejecting the idea that genuine Christians can lose their salvation, he addressed the tragic reality of inauthentic faith. Given the existence of spurious or transitory faith, he averred, "The [biblical] passages that speak of falling away do not force us to conclude that the defection is from *genuine* faith."[118] Indeed, working

---

107. "The loss that a Christian may encounter concerns 'rewards' only, not salvation or eternal life, which comes to us only by faith in Jesus Christ.... Loss-of-rewards advocates agree that biblical warnings address true Christians, but because believers cannot lose their salvation, the threat of loss concerns rewards that would otherwise be received in the age to come." Ibid., 24–29.

108. "Those who advocate the tests-of-genuineness view believe that the biblical warnings are addressed to people who profess faith in Jesus Christ but who prove to be false or disingenuous in their confession. Second, this view does not regard the threatened loss to be a possible loss of something already possessed. Rather, the warnings function as tests to prove that the 'disingenuous believer' never possessed true salvation. Thus, biblical admonitions and warnings distinguish pseudobelievers from true believers." Ibid., 29–35.

109. "Succinctly expressed, this interpretive viewpoint claims that any believer who fails to persevere in faithfulness to the gospel (and this is impossible) will not be saved." Ibid., 35–37.

110. Ibid., 142.

111. Ibid., 205–6.

112. Ibid., 206.

113. Ibid., 206–7.

114. Ibid., 207–8.

115. Ibid., 209.

116. Ibid., 212.

117. Ibid., 308. For additional work on this perspective, see: Tom Schreiner, *Run to Win the Prize: Perseverance in the New Testament* (Wheaton: Crossway, 2010).

118. D. A. Carson, "Reflections on Assurance," in *The Grace of God, The Bondage of the Will: Biblical and Practical Perspectives on Calvinism*, ed. Thomas Schreiner and Bruce Ware, 2 vols. (Grand Rapids: Baker, 1995), 2:400–401.

with 1 John 2:19, he reasoned, "Genuine faith, by definition, perseveres; where there is no perseverance, by definition the faith cannot be genuine."[119] That is, perseverance is a constitutive element of saving faith. But what is the nature of the inauthentic faith from which those who have not fully and unequivocally embraced Jesus Christ turn? Carson defined this "apostasy" as "the decisive turning away from a religious position and stance once firmly held. It differs from ordinary unbelief in that it involves turning away from a position of belief; it differs from backsliding in that it is calculated, decisive, and irrevocable; it differs from merely changing one's mind over some relatively minor theological point in that it involves the rejection of an entire position and stance."[120] But such apostasy is not the loss of salvation; genuine Christians with true saving faith persevere until the end. From a compatibilistic perspective,[121] the sovereignty and power of God are at work to preserve genuine Christians as they walk with faith (1 Peter 1:5), and divine admonitions and warnings addressed to morally responsible Christ-followers are a means to encourage such perseverance.

Though Christians may be divided on this doctrine, the importance of the persevering work of God and the subjective sense of assurance of salvation continues for the church as it looks forward to the return of Jesus Christ.

---

119. Ibid., 2:400. The verse can be reconfigured as a *modus tollens* argument (that is, a destructive hypothetical syllogism). Major premise: "If they had belonged to us"—that is, if they had been genuine believers—"they would have remained with us"—that is, they would have persevered. Minor premise (a denial of the consequent): "but their going"—that is, they did not remain with us. Conclusion: "showed that none of them belonged to us"—that is, they were not genuine believers.

120. Ibid., 2:396.

121. Ibid., 2:409.

Part 6

THE DOCTRINE
OF THE CHURCH

Chapter 26

THE CHURCH: ITS NATURE, ITS MARKS, AND ITS PURPOSES

How has the church developed its concept of what constitutes the/a church? How has it come to recognize the marks of a true church? How has its idea of the purposes of the church developed?

STATEMENT OF BELIEF

The church has historically sought to (1) define itself as the body of believers in Jesus Christ, (2) exhibit the characteristics through which the Holy Spirit exercises his mission, and (3) function in a way that pleases God in worship, edifies its members through the proclamation of the Word and the celebration of the sacraments/ordinances, and missionally engages nonbelievers through evangelism and good works. Concretely, the diversity of the ways in which the church has shown its understanding of itself is nearly endless—and quite amazing! One need only consider the difference between the pageantry of an Easter mass in St. Peter's Basilica and the unadorned service of a small rural Baptist church.

Other differences can be noted as well. Some hold that the church began with Abraham or possibly Adam, while others place the beginning of the church at Pentecost. Paralleling this distinction is another difference: the first group finds a great amount of continuity between Old Testament laws and Christians, while the second group finds a great amount of discontinuity between the two. The issue of who constitutes the church is another point of diversity. Some believers maintain that it consists of both believers and unbelievers. Others insist that only regenerate members may belong to the church. Manifestations of these notable differences include diverse practices of baptism—infant baptism as opposed to believer's baptism, and more formal liturgies led by clergy who mirror the Levitical priesthood over against simple worship services modeled after "the New Testament church." Another of the many differences between churches has to do with their relationship to the state. Some churches sustain an interdependent relationship with the governments of the nations in which they exist, while others eschew state involvement in ecclesiastical affairs, adhering to the principle of the separation of church and state.

Despite these evident differences, most churches are characterized by certain essential elements: the worship of God through singing hymns along with verbal and bodily expressions of praise, the reading and preaching of the Word of God, the celebration of the sacraments or ordinances, intercession for members and others who are in need, evangelistic appeals to believe in the gospel, financial giving, missionary zeal and engagement, pastoral leadership, members serving one another through a variety of ministries, the exercise of church discipline, works of mercy among the poor and marginalized, and so forth. It is not too simplistic nor naïve to say that the earliest churches and those of the twenty-first century share some remarkable similarities.

Because widespread agreement exists on many essential elements, this chapter on ecclesiology—Greek ἐκκλησια (*ekklēsia*); thus, the doctrine of the church—will focus on those common points.[1] However, the diversity of positions will also be noted when those differences exerted a significant impact on the church and its understanding of itself, its characteristics, and its purposes.[2]

ECCLESIOLOGY IN THE EARLY CHURCH

The New Testament is replete with references to and instructions about the church. In the first gospel, we read about Jesus' promise to build his church (Matt. 16:18–19). The book of Acts provides a snapshot of the church formed immediately after Pentecost (Acts 2:42). This first church at Jerusalem was named "the Way" (Acts 9:2; 19:9, 23; 22:4; 24:14, 22), probably because of its association with Jesus (who himself is "the Way"; John 14:6). Because this church was "in 'the Way,'" it was opposed and fiercely persecuted. The apostle Paul engaged in three missionary journeys, establishing churches in such places as Iconium, Lystra, and Derbe (Acts 13–14); Philippi, Thessalonica, Berea, and Corinth (Acts 15:36–18:22); and Ephesus (Acts 18:23–21:16). It was to several of these churches that Paul wrote some of his letters, including in them instructions and exhortations, and he was joined in this by the other writers of the New Testament.

As the church of Jesus Christ expanded rapidly and matured, questions concerning the nature, characteristics, and purposes of the church became one of its major concerns. This was especially the case as the church faced another opponent: not persecution from

---

1. My thanks to Josh Nelson for his help on this chapter.

2. Much of the diversity among churches is due to differences in church government, but church government will be treated separately in chap. 27. Another reason for the great diversity is the differences in the sacraments or ordinances, but the discussion of these rites will be treated in chaps. 28 and 29. A final point of diversity is the concept and practice of worship, which will be discussed in chap. 30.

the outside, but heresy from the inside. The Nicene Creed defined the church by means of four adjectives: "We believe ... in one, holy, catholic, and apostolic church." This characterization reflected several centuries of thought that developed as the churches of the second and third centuries sought to identify and distinguish the true Christian church from heretical groups that split from it yet claimed to be genuinely Christian.

Oneness or *unity* characterized the true church of Jesus Christ: "The church, though dispersed throughout the whole world, even to the ends of the earth, has received from the apostles and their disciples this faith ... [and] as if occupying one house, carefully preserves it. It also believes these points [of doctrine] just as if it had only one soul, and one and the same heart. It proclaims them, teaches them, and hands them down, with perfect harmony, as if it possessed only one mouth."[3] Only the true church held to this common faith that united individual churches into one.[4] For Clement of Alexandria, this oneness was the outstanding characteristic of the church of Jesus Christ: "The preeminence of the church, as the principle of unity, is its oneness. In this, it surpasses all other things and has nothing like or equal to itself."[5]

A second characteristic of the church was *holiness*: "God has given to the world, which is driven and tempest-tossed by sins, assemblies—we mean holy churches—in which survive the doctrines of the truth."[6] Although cherished as an essential characteristic, this element presented an embarrassing problem for the church because, in reality, some of its members did not exhibit a lifestyle of purity. One way of confronting such a problem was to make a distinction between those professing to be Christians and those who are genuine Christians, as Justin Martyr did: "Let it be understood that those who are not found living as Christ taught are not Christians, even though they profess with the lips the teachings of Christ."[7] In keeping with this approach, Hippolytus decried the perverse actions of some so-called Christians, specifically denouncing sexual immorality, contraception, and abortion, and lamenting, "After such audacious acts, they lose all sense of shame, yet still attempt to call themselves a catholic church!"[8]

Biblical support for this stance toward non-Christians in the midst of the church was offered, especially Jesus' parable of the wheat and the tares (Matt. 13:24–30). This story was understood by some to indicate that throughout its earthly existence, the church would be populated by both genuine Christians and false members; thus, holiness applied only to the true followers of Christ in a mixed congregation. Regrettably, some used this to excuse sinfulness in the church.[9] Oppositely, Cyprian's counsel for dealing with this

3. Irenaeus, *Against Heresies*, 1.10.1–2, in *ANF*, 1:330–31. The text has been rendered clearer.

4. "All [churches] receive one and the same God the Father. All believe in the same dispensation regarding the incarnation of the Son of God. All are cognizant of the same gift of the Spirit and are familiar with the same commandments. All preserve the same form of ecclesiastical constitution. All expect the same advent of the Lord. All await the same salvation of the complete man, that is, the soul and body. And undoubtedly the preaching of the church is true and steadfast, in which one and the same way of salvation is shown throughout the whole world." Ibid., 5.20.1, in *ANF*, 1:548. The text has been rendered clearer.

5. Clement of Alexandria, *Stromata*, 7.17, in *ANF*, 2:555. The text has been rendered clearer.

6. Theophilus, *To Autolycus*, 2.14, in *ANF*, 2:100.

7. Justin Martyr, *First Apology*, 16, in *ANF*, 1:168. The text has been rendered clearer.

8. Hippolytus, *The Refutation of All Heresies*, 9.7, in *ANF*, 5:131. The text has been rendered clearer.

9. Ibid.

mixed membership was to urge true Christians to strive more urgently for holiness: "Although there seem to be tares in the church, yet neither our faith nor our love ought to be hindered. Because we see that there are tares in the church, we ourselves should not withdraw from the church. Rather, we only should labor that we may be wheat."[10] The church was called to holiness, which was an essential characteristic.

The true church was also *catholic*, meaning "universal."[11] For Clement of Alexandria, this catholicity or universal expansion of the church was the subject of Jesus' parable of the mustard seed (Matt. 13:31–32).[12] According to Augustine, the origin of the word was a saying of Christ—"the *whole* earth"—in Acts 1:8.[13] For Cyril of Jerusalem, the church is "catholic" because "it extends over all the world ... and because it teaches universally and completely one and all the doctrines which ought to come to men's knowledge ... and because it brings into subjection to godliness the whole race of mankind ... and because it universally treats and heals the whole class of sins ... and possesses in itself every form of virtue which is named, both in deeds and words, and in every kind of spiritual gifts."[14] It was to this catholic church that true Christians were to belong; failure to do so meant devastating consequences: "Whoever does not meet with the congregation [Gr. ἐκκλησια (*ekklēsia*; church)] thereby demonstrates his arrogance and has separated [or judged] himself."[15] For Ignatius, the catholic church could be identified by the authoritative presence of a bishop, around whom all true Christians must rally: "Wherever the bishop appears, there let the congregation be; just as wherever Jesus Christ is, there is the catholic church. It is not permissible either to baptize or to hold a love feast without the bishop."[16] This early characterization of the church as "catholic" continued to function as a means of distinguishing the true church from splinter groups in the following centuries.

A final characterization of the church was its *apostolicity*, as explained by Tertullian:

> From this we draw up our rule. Since the Lord Jesus Christ sent the apostles to preach, our rule is that no others ought to be received as preachers than those whom Christ appointed.... Now, what they preached—in other words, what Christ revealed to them—can ... properly be proved in no other way than by those very churches which the apostles founded in person. They declared the gospel to them directly themselves, both *viva voce* [by live voice] ... and

10. Cyprian, *Letter* 50.3, in *ANF*, 5:327. The text has been rendered clearer.

11. One of the earliest uses of this word was the following: "Our Lord Jesus Christ [is] the Savior of our souls and Helmsman of our bodies and Shepherd of the catholic church throughout the world." *The Martyrdom of Polycarp*, 19, in Holmes, 243; *ANF*, 1:43. Cf. *Martyrdom*, 8, in which Polycarp is said to have prayed for "all the catholic church throughout the world." In Holmes, 233; *ANF*, 1:40.

12. "The growth of the Word increased to such a great size that the tree which sprang from it (that is, the church of Christ, established over the whole earth) filled the world." Clement of Alexandria, *Fragments from Nicetas*, 4, in *ANF*, 2:578. The text has been rendered clearer.

13. Augustine, *The Letters of Petilian, the Donatist*, 2.38.391, in *NPNF*[1], 4:554. Actually, Augustine was quite mistaken, as the last phrase of Acts 1:8 is ἑως ἐδχατου της γης (*hēos eschaton tēs gēs*; the end of the earth).

14. Cyril of Jerusalem, *Catechetical Lectures*, 18.23, in *NPNF*[2], 7:139–40.

15. Ignatius, *Letter to the Ephesians*, 5, in Holmes, 141; *ANF*, 1:51.

16. Ignatius, *Letter to the Smyrnaeans*, 8, in Holmes, 189–91; *ANF*, 1:89–90. This is the first occurrence of the adjective *catholic* in Christian literature. For further discussion of Ignatius's elevation of the office of bishop, see chap. 27 on church government.

subsequently by their writings. If, then, these things are so, it is equally clear that all doctrine which agrees with the apostolic churches — those matrixes and original sources of the faith — must be considered as truth, as undoubtedly containing that which the churches received from the apostles, the apostles from Christ, and Christ from God.[17]

True churches could be readily identified as those that adhere to the teachings of the apostles, while heretical groups could be recognized as those that invent and then follow other teachings. True churches, therefore, were either (1) Type 1 apostolic churches, those planted by the apostles; or (2) Type 2 apostolic churches, those founded by Type 1 apostolic churches.[18] But heretical groups were not able to trace back their lineage to the apostles and to apostolic churches, and so true Christians were warned not to associate with these false sects.[19] Practically, then, apostolicity meant adherence to the doctrine of the apostles as expressed in Scripture. Tertullian was thus able to maintain: "We hold communion with the apostolic churches because our doctrine is in no respect different than theirs."[20]

For the early church, then, the confession "We believe ... in one, holy, catholic, and apostolic church" summarized the four essential characteristics of the church. Assemblies of true Christians that possessed these four attributes, and these assemblies alone, were worthy of being called the church of Jesus Christ.

This true church was described in yet another way in the early church — as the mother of all faithful followers of Christ. Tertullian drew this parallel: "Our one Father, God, lives; and so does our mother, the church."[21] Methodius found biblical support in Revelation 12:1–6.[22] In addition to bringing forth her children, the church as mother "draws the children to herself; and we seek our mother, the church."[23] It was not a great leap from this concept of the church as mother to the important assertion of Cyprian: "He can no longer have God for his Father, who has not the church for his mother."[24] With Cyprian,

17. Tertullian, *Prescription against Heretics*, 21, in *ANF*, 3:252. The text has been rendered clearer.

18. Tertullian noted: "[The apostles] founded churches in every city, from which all the other churches, one after another, derived [received] the tradition of the faith, and the seeds of doctrine, and are every day deriving [receiving] them, that they may become churches. Indeed, it is on this account only that they will be able to deem themselves apostolic, as being the offspring of apostolic churches.... In this way all are primitive, and all are apostolic." Ibid., 20, in *ANF*, 3:252. He further explained with reference to heretics: "Their very doctrine, after comparison with that of the apostles, will declare, by its own diversity and contrariety [discrepancy], that it had for its author neither an apostle nor an apostolic man.... To this test, therefore will they [the heretics] be submitted for proof by those churches, which, although they do not have as their founder the apostles or apostolic men (as being of much later date, for churches are in fact being founded daily), yet, since they agree in the same faith, they are accounted as not less apostolic because they are akin [alike] in doctrine." Ibid.,

32, in *ANF*, 3:258. The text has been rendered clearer.

19. Irenaeus, *Against Heresies*, 5.20.1–2, in *ANF*, 1:548.

20. Tertullian, *Prescription against Heretics*, 21, in *ANF*, 3:252–53.

21. Tertullian, *On Monogamy*, 7, in *ANF*, 4:64.

22. "Just as a woman, receiving a man's sperm, within a certain time gives birth to a perfect man, in a parallel way the church conceives those who flee to the Word and, forming them according to the likeness and image of Christ, after a certain time produces them as citizens of that blessed state." Methodius, *The Banquet of the Ten Virgins*, 7.4–6, in *ANF*, 6:336–37.

23. Clement of Alexandria, *The Instructor*, 1.5, in *ANF*, 2:214. At the same time: "The virgin mother is one. I love to call her the church.... She is both virgin and mother — pure as a virgin, loving as a mother. And calling her children to herself, she nurses them with holy milk." Ibid., 1.6, in *ANF*, 2:220. Tertullian used a similar idea: "Our lady mother, the church, makes provision from her bountiful breasts." *To Martyrs*, 1, in *ANF*, 3:693.

24. Cyprian, *Treatise* 1.6: "On the Unity of the Church," in *ANF*, 5:423.

the exclusivity of the church for redemption—"there is no salvation out[side] of the church"[25]—comes to the forefront in the development of ecclesiology:

> The spouse of Christ cannot be adulterous; she is uncorrupted and pure. She knows one home; she guards with chaste modesty the sanctity of one couch [bed]. She keeps us for God. She appoints the sons whom she has born for the kingdom. Whoever is separated from the church and is joined to an adulteress, is separated from the promises of the church; nor can he who forsakes the church of Christ attain to the rewards of Christ. He is a stranger; he is profane; he is an enemy. He can no longer have God for his Father, who has not the church for his mother. If anyone could escape who was outside the ark of Noah, then he also may escape who shall be outside of the church.[26]

In the centuries following, the church would adopt Cyprian's exclusivistic claim as an essential element of its developing ecclesiology.[27]

With its legalization by Constantine early in the fourth century, the church began a new relationship with the state, one that included many privileges but that also allowed the state to play a role in its theology and practice. Moreover, the church became increasingly identified with the Roman Empire, such that most of the members of the church were Roman citizens and most Roman citizens belonged to the church. At the start of the fifth century, Augustine faced a new reality as the Roman Empire began to collapse and opponents of the church blamed its demise on Christianity. His response was to author a definitive Christian view of world history that divided civilization into the church and the world. *The City of God* presented human history as an epic struggle between the people of God—the heavenly city, identified as the church, the spiritual descendants of Abel—and the people of the devil—the earthly city, identified with the worldly descendants of Cain. For Augustine, the collapse of the empire was to be blamed on its failure to relate rightly to the church. This city of God, the church, was to develop throughout the millennium (Rev. 20:1–6) as the kingdom of God squared off against the kingdom of Satan. Many implications for ecclesiology flowed from this.

For his definition of the church, Augustine broadened the concept to include not only the gatherings of believers on earth but also the angelic beings in heaven.[28] This

---

25. Cyprian, *Letter* 72.21, in *ANF*, 5:384.

26. Cyprian, *Treatise* 1.6, in *ANF*, 5:423.

27. A half century after Cyprian, Lactantius explicitly generalized his claim: "When they are called Phrygians, Novatians, Valentinians, Marcionites, Anthropians, or Arians, or by any other name, they have ceased to be Christians. They have lost the name of Christ and have assumed human and external names. It is the catholic church alone that retains true worship. This is the fountain of truth; this is the house of faith; this is the temple of God. If anyone will not enter into it, or if anyone will abandon it, he is estranged from the hope of life and eternal salvation." Lactantius, *The Divine Institutes*, 4:30, in *ANF*, 7:133. All these are names of early heretical groups

that the catholic church was forced to confront.

28. "And we are here to understand the whole church, not that part of it only which wanders as a stranger on the earth ... but that part also which has always from its creation remained steadfast to God in heaven, and has never experienced the misery consequent upon a fall. This part is made up of the holy angels, who enjoy uninterrupted happiness; and (as it is bound to do) it renders assistance to the part which is still wandering among strangers; for these two parts shall be one in the fellowship of eternity, and now they are one in the bonds of love, the whole having been ordained for the worship of the one God." Augustine, *Enchiridion on Faith, Hope, and Love*, 56, in *NPNF*[1], 3:255.

"heavenly" aspect of the church consists only of the good angels.[29] The "earthly" aspect of the church consists of redeemed human beings. Peculiarly, Augustine believed that "by the redemption of man, the gaps that the great apostasy left in the angelic host are filled up."[30] His novel idea was that the salvation of human beings had a purpose of replacing the void left in the heavenly realm through the fall of a large number of angels—now called Satan and demons—into sin.[31]

This meant for Augustine that all redeemed human beings—from the time of Adam to the present time—are members of the church: "All the saints who lived upon the earth previous to the birth of our Lord Jesus Christ, although they were born antecedently, were nevertheless united under the Head with that universal body of which he is the Head."[32] Furthermore, all these redeemed saints had been predestined by God to be saved and to become members of the church of Jesus Christ. Indeed, Augustine defined the church as that "in whom is the fixed number of the saints predestined before the foundation of the world."[33] Given the mysterious nature of predestination, only God perfectly knows who constitutes the true church. As for those who look at the visible church, the situation can be quite confusing: "For in that unspeakable foreknowledge of God, many who seem to be outside the church are in reality inside it, and many who seem to be inside the church are really outside it."[34] In other words, the visible church is composed of both genuine Christians and false members.[35]

Augustine did not despair of the church because of its mixed character, nor did he dispense with it. On the contrary, like Cyprian before him, Augustine maintained the necessity of the church for the salvation of sinful human beings, primarily because of its administration of baptism.[36] At the same time, however:

> It is possible ... that some who have been baptized outside the church may be considered, through the foreknowledge of God, to have been really baptized

---

29. "Of that part of the church which is in heaven what can we say, except that no wicked one is found in it, and that no one has fallen from it, or shall ever fall from it." Ibid., 57, in *NPNF*¹, 3:256.

30. Ibid., 57–58, in *NPNF*¹, 3:256.

31. Augustine found biblical support for his idea: "The holy angels, taught by God, in the eternal contemplation of whose truth their happiness consists, know how great a number of the human race are to supplement their ranks and fill up the full tale [measure] of their citizenship. Therefore, the apostle says, 'all things are gathered [united] in one in Christ, both which are in heaven and which are on earth' [Eph. 1:10]. The things which are in heaven are gathered together [united] when what was lost from it in the fall of the angels is restored from among men; and the things that are on earth are united when those who are predestined to eternal life are redeemed from their old corruption. And thus, through that single sacrifice in which the Mediator was offered up ... heavenly things are brought into peace with earthly things, and earthly things with heavenly. Therefore, as the same apostle says: 'For it pleased the Father that in him [Christ] should all fullness

dwell; and, having made peace through the blood of his cross, by him to reconcile all things to himself: by him, I say, whether they be things in earth or things in heaven' [Col 1:19–20]." Ibid., 62, in *NPNF*¹, 3:257. Cf. chap. 14, pp. 306–7.

32. Augustine, *On the Catechizing of the Uninstructed*, 19.33, in *NPNF*¹, 3:304.

33. Augustine, *On Baptism, against the Donatists*, 5.27.38, in *NPNF*¹, 4:477.

34. Ibid. The text has been rendered clearer.

35. "As long as she is a stranger in the world, the city of God has in her communion, and bound to her by the sacraments, some who shall not eternally dwell in the destiny of the saints.... Today, you may see these men thronging the churches with us, tomorrow crowding the theaters with the godless." Augustine, *The City of God*, 1.35, in *NPNF*¹, 2:21.

36. He spoke of "the church in which the sins are remitted ... and outside the church sins are not remitted. For the church alone has received the pledge of the Holy Spirit, without which there is no remission of sins—such, at least, as brings the pardoned to eternal life." Augustine, *Enchiridion on Faith, Hope, and Love*, 65, in *NPNF*¹, 3:258.

inside the church, because inside the water begins to be profitable to them for salvation. Still, it cannot be said that they were saved in the ark except by water. Again, some who seem to have been baptized inside the church may be considered, through the same foreknowledge of God, more truly to have been baptized outside because, making a bad use of baptism, they die by water. At the time of Noah, this happened to no one who was not outside the ark.[37]

Furthermore, the church is the fellowship of love, whose bond of love is created and sustained by the Holy Spirit and nurtured by genuine believers. Membership in this church is essential for love. Indeed, it is this gift of love that more than anything else distinguishes "the sons of the eternal kingdom and the sons of eternal damnation."[38]

Augustine's position—that the church could be composed of both genuine believers and false members—was directly opposed to a schismatic group against which he argued. The Donatists insisted that the church is truly and completely holy; thus, it is composed only of genuine believers. And it was to this church, and this holy church alone, that the title *catholic* could be rightfully ascribed. So, according to their own thinking, the Donatists were the true "catholic" church. It was precisely at this point that Augustine was most critical of the Donatists: in their misinformed zeal for purity, they had separated themselves from the one and only catholic church; therefore, they were "openly guilty of the manifest sacrilege of schism."[39] Clearly, this violated the nature of the church as the community of love. Because of this, their end would be eternal punishment.[40] The only way that this condemnation could be avoided was for the Donatists to repent and return to the catholic church.[41] This poignant challenge would become the demand of the church to all heretical groups for centuries to come. Because the catholic church is the one and only true church, all heretics and schismatics must denounce their views and practices and become aligned with the catholic church.

In this one, holy, catholic, and apostolic church, the authority and power of the Church of Rome grew. Because of this development, the church became increasingly characterized by its hierarchical structure with the pope at its head.[42]

ECCLESIOLOGY IN THE MIDDLE AGES

Beginning with the sack of Rome by Alaric in 410, the Roman Empire crumbled and gave way to a series of barbarian rulers in what is now Western Europe. This period, referred to as the Dark Ages, was characterized by a spiritual and moral weakening of the

37. Augustine, *On Baptism, against the Donatists*, 5.28.39, in *NPNF*[1], 4:478. The text has been rendered clearer.

38. Augustine, *On the Trinity*, 15.18.32, in *NPNF*[1], 3:217.

39. Augustine, *On Baptism, against the Donatists*, 1.14, in *NPNF*[1], 4:418.

40. Augustine, *Letters of Petilian, the Donatist*, 2.23.54, in *NPNF*[1], 4.544–45.

41. Augustine's challenge to the Donatists and their converts was forceful: "Return with them to the church. Bring those whom you have wounded to be healed by the medicine of peace; bring those whom you have slain to be brought to life again by the life of love. Brotherly union has great power in propitiating God." Augustine, *On Baptism, against the Donatists*, 2.13–18, in *NPNF*[1], 4:433–34. Some of the development of this section reflects ideas in Jaroslav Pelikan, *The Emergence of the Catholic Tradition (100–600)*. See Pelikan, 1:302–12.

42. For more discussion, see chap. 27.

church and a political and economic devastation of the former empire. Still, the church had its advocates, including kings of the Franks (modern-day France) such as Clovis, Pepin the Short (who gave military aid to Pope Stephen, then gave to the popes in Rome the lands that he had conquered during the rescue, giving birth to the papal states), and his son and successor, Charlemagne.

Deeply influenced by Augustine's *City of God*, the newly crowned (December 25, 800) holy Roman emperor Charlemagne self-consciously governed his vast territory as its divinely appointed ruler.[43] This Holy Roman Empire was to be a political entity like its predecessor, the Roman Empire, but ruled by Christian emperors in place of the former pagan Caesars. This empire would give due recognition to the church—that is, to the Roman Catholic Church.[44] This relationship of the church to the state would dominate the ecclesiology of the Middle Ages.

But the medieval church would do more than flower politically. Although monasticism had been an important part of the church from early on,[45] as the new millennium progressed, new monastic movements injected life into the church—the Cluniacs, the Cistercians, the Franciscans, the Augustinians, the Dominicans, and the Carmelites. These last four were mendicant orders that begged for money while preaching the gospel. Indeed, the "evangelical counsels" of the church—the vows of poverty, chastity, and obedience—became a common characteristic of these monastic movements. Alongside these was the institutional church, now even more identified with the Church of Rome.[46]

An important development occurred at this time—the split between the Catholic Church in the West and the Orthodox Church in the East. The two had been characterized by different theological emphases and liturgies from early on, not to mention two different languages (thus the reference to the "Latin" Church—the Catholic Church in the West—and the "Greek" Church—the Orthodox Church in the East). More important, a theological issue separated the two: the Latin Church affirmed the

---

43. To the pope, Charlemagne set forth his vision for the relationship between the state and the church: "I desire to make with you an inviolable treaty of mutual fidelity and love. On the one hand, you will pray for me and give me the apostolic benediction; on the other hand, with the help of God, I will always defend the most holy seat of the holy Roman church. For it is our part to defend the holy church of Christ from the attacks of pagans and infidels from the outside, and from the inside to enforce the acceptance of the Catholic faith. It is your part, most holy father, to aid us in the good fight by raising your hands to God like Moses did [Ex. 17:11], so that by your intercession the Christian people under the leadership of God may always and everywhere be victorious over the enemies of his holy name, and the name of our Lord Jesus Christ may be glorified throughout the world." Charlemagne, "Letter to Pope Leo," in *Monumenta Germaniae Historica, Epistolae* 4, 137, in Petry, 208. The text has been rendered clearer.

44. As Alcuin, Charlemagne's adviser, noted: "We take our stand firmly within the borders of the apostolic doctrine and of the holy Roman church, following their established

authority and clinging to their sacred doctrine, introducing nothing new and accepting nothing apart from what we find in their catholic writings." Alcuin, *Against Felix*, 1.4, in Pelikan, 3:46. One result of this state-church alliance was that the pope would crown the emperor-elect with the symbols of civil authority, and the emperor (and other members of the state) would crown bishops-elect, including the pope, with the symbols—a ring and staff—of spiritual and ecclesiastical authority.

45. For further discussion, see chap. 24.

46. Central to this identification was the ongoing appeal to Matt. 16:18–19. And the early ecclesiology that compared the church to a mother continued to develop in the Middle Ages, as represented by Hincmar of Reims: "The catholic, apostolic, and holy Roman church ... has given birth to us in faith, fed us with catholic milk, nourished us with breasts full of heaven until we were ready for solid food, and led us by her orthodox discipline to perfect manhood." Hincmar of Reims, *On the Divorce of Lothair and Tetberga*, preface, in Pelikan, 3:48.

procession of the Spirit from both the Father and the Son;[47] the Greek Church believed in the procession of the Spirit from the Father only.[48] These differences were fueled by conflict between the churches during the iconoclastic controversy.[49] In 1054, when Michael Cerularius, the patriarch of Constantinople, closed the Latin churches there, the pope's representatives in Constantinople excommunicated the partriarch, who acted in kind. Thus, the schism between the Roman Catholic Church and the Orthodox Church was inaugurated.

Such political developments were matched by theological developments in the church. For example, Thomas Aquinas noted that the word "'church' is the same [in meaning] as 'congregation.' Thus the holy church is the same as the congregation of the faithful."[50] He defined this church by rehearsing the four traditional attributes[51] and popularizing a threefold concept of the church: "This church has three divisions: one on earth, another in heaven, and a third in purgatory."[52] The first concept was also known as *the church militant* (the church on earth, which faces and must overcome trials); the second, *the church triumphant* (the church in heaven, composed of all the saints); and third, *the church expectant* (the church in purgatory, composed of all the souls that are being purged of sin and awaiting transfer into heaven). Aquinas also opposed the growing encroachment of the Catholic Church in secular matters.[53] But his view of restricted papal authority would go unheeded by the power-hungry popes who followed him. Indeed, the latter half of the Middle Ages witnessed an ever-increasing involvement of the Catholic Church in political/social/economic affairs, an egregious growth in immorality, and a seemingly unstoppable bankruptcy in terms of spirituality.[54]

Faced with these devastating and embarrassing developments, people both inside and outside the Catholic Church dissented. Most significantly, this dissent took the form of new ecclesiologies. Indeed, ecclesiology became "the first and the most universal prin-

---

47. "I believe in the Holy Spirit, who proceeds from the Father and the Son" was the affirmation of the Nicene Creed (381), with the addition of the *filioque* clause ("and the Son") by the Council of Toledo (589). For further discussion, see chap. 11.

48. The Greek Church refused to acknowledge the addition of the *filioque* clause.

49. Some within the Greek Church affirmed the use of icons as a stimulus to proper worship, while others denounced this practice. The Latin Church blasted this intrachurch debate, and tensions between East and West were heightened.

50. Thomas Aquinas, *Exposition of the Apostles' Creed*, 12, in *The Sermon-Conferences of St. Thomas Aquinas on the Apostles' Creed*, ed. and trans. Nicholas Ayo (Notre Dame: Univ. of Notre Dame Press, 1988), 125.

51. Ibid., in Ayo, *Sermon-Conferences*, 125–31.

52. Ibid., in Ayo, *Sermon-Conferences*, 129. In this he was expanding on the ecclesiology of Augustine.

53. He asserted that "the secular power is subject to the spiritual power insofar as God has subjected the former to the latter, namely, in matters pertaining to the salvation of souls. And

so we should obey the spiritual power rather than the secular power in such matters. But in matters pertaining to civic welfare, we should obey the secular power rather than the spiritual power." Thomas Aquinas, *Commentary on the Sentences*, bk. 2, distinction 44, reply to obj. 4, in *Aquinas: On Law, Morality, and Politics*, ed. William P. Baumgarth and Richard J. Regan, trans. Richard J. Regan, 2nd ed. (Indianapolis: Hackett, 2002), 196.

54. For further discussion, see chap. 27. As Bernard of Clairvaux observed with shame, "Now that we have peace from the pagans and peace from the heretics, there is still no peace from the false sons [of the church].... Almost all Christians are looking after their own interests, not those of Jesus Christ." Bernard of Clairvaux, *Exposition of Psalm Ninety*, 6.7, in Pelikan, 3:233. And William of Ockham lamented the political involvement of the papacy and denounced its role in state matters: "I think it should be maintained that the papacy instituted by Christ in no way regularly includes temporal and secular affairs.... And indeed what he does in such matters is not valid, because 'those things that are done by a judge are null and void if they do not belong to his office.'" William of Ockham, *On the Imperial and Pontifical Power* (1346–47), 2, in Petry, 515.

ciple of doctrine and of the science of faith."[55] Many of these ecclesiologies aimed at distancing their proponents from the empirical reality of the church. As could be expected, some were considered to be in accordance with Catholic Church theology and practice, while others were ruled out of bounds.

Two ecclesiologies in particular were considered to be consistent with the reigning conception of the Catholic Church. Following some earlier commentators, Bernard of Clairvaux interpreted the Song of Solomon as an allegory of the church. In a spiritual sense, the Song's woman character represents something else: "the bride is the church."[56] Also present is the figure of mother. From this, Bernard concluded that the bride belongs to the bridegroom—the church belongs to Christ—and the mother gives birth to her children—the church brings forth Christians.

The second ecclesiology was developed by Joachim of Fiore. It was based on his conception of history, which was divided into three ages: (1) the first is the age of the Old Testament and corresponds theologically to God the Father; (2) the second is the age of the New Testament and corresponds theologically to God the Son; and (3) the third is the age still to come and corresponds theologically to God the Holy Spirit.[57] According to Joachim, the second period—the age of the Son—was drawing to an end during his own life. To guide the church through the upcoming tribulation that the Antichrist would soon unleash against it, God would raise up two new orders of monks—one being preachers, the other being hermits. Despite the prayers of the hermit order and the testimony of the preaching order, the Antichrist would conquer the church and turn it into an instrument of evil.[58] This dreadful situation would come to a conclusion, however, with the return of Christ. This would issue in the third age—that of the Spirit. Out of this a new reality, the Order of the Just, characterized by spiritual understanding and holiness, would rise. This new spiritual church would preach the gospel, heal the split between the Eastern and Western factions, and bring about the conversion of the Jews.[59] Joachim's apocalyptic vision of a new, spiritual church fit well with the disquieting state of the existing Catholic Church and offered hope for a change.[60]

Three other ecclesiologies were ruled to be heretical visions by the Roman Catholic Church. The first of these, the Cathari (the "pure") or Albigensians (from Albi, their place of origin), clearly held heretical doctrines and engaged in heretical practices.[61] To

---

55. John of Ragusa, *Oration on Communion under Both Kinds*, in Pelikan, 4:71.

56. Bernard of Clairvaux, *Song of Songs, Sermon 14:4.6*, in *The Works of Bernard of Clairvaux*, vol. 2: *On the Song of Songs 1*, trans. Kilian Walsh (Kalamazoo, Mich.: Cistercian, 1977), 103.

57. Joachim of Fiore, *Exposition of the Apocalypse*, f. 5r–v, cited in Bernard McGinn, *Visions of the End: Apocalyptic Traditions in the Middle Ages* (New York: Columbia Univ. Press, 1979), 133–34.

58. Joachim's view later led to the identification of the Roman Catholic Church with the Antichrist. John Wycliffe, John Hus, and Martin Luther were just several who made this connection.

59. The figure forty-two generations was taken from Matt. 1:17: There were forty-two generations from Abraham to Christ,

so Joachim calculated that this would be true for the other two ages. For more discussion of Joachim's scheme of world history, see chap. 31.

60. Unlike the ecclesiology of Augustine's *City of God*, which presented a largely pessimistic view of history because the church would always battle against sin and evil, Joachim's eschatology optimistically envisioned a renewal of the church within history.

61. Among these were a radical metaphysical dualism; a belief in two gods, one of which is good and the other of which is evil; a denial of the humanity of Jesus Christ; a dismissal of the value of the Old Testament and the exclusive use of the New Testament; a denial of the resurrection of the body; and an insistence on rigorous ascetic practices.

stamp out this heresy, Pope Innocent III launched the Albigensian Crusade, followed by a papal inquisition. Extreme measures, including extermination of the Cathari heretics, were ordered by the church and justified by its leading theologians.[62] The second group did not embrace the clearly heretical doctrines of the Cathari. Nonetheless, the Waldensians—named either for their founder, Peter Waldo, or for the *vaux* or valleys to which they fled so as to escape their attackers—were fiercely persecuted by the Catholic Church.[63] Among the beliefs and practices for which the Waldensians were condemned were a refusal to submit to bishops and to obey the pope, whom they denied was the head of the Catholic Church because of his corruption; a denial of masses for the dead, prayer by the saints for Christians on earth, and the doctrine of purgatory; establishment of their own hierarchy; and a ministry in which even laypeople could pray, hear confessions of sin, and administer the sacraments. Even though they were clearly different from the heretical Cathari, the Waldensians were persecuted by the Catholic Church for their ecclesiology.

The third ecclesiology, based on Augustine's concept of the church, was formulated by John Wycliffe and developed by John Hus. In one sense, Wycliffe's view was traditional: the church is a threefold reality—the church in heaven, in purgatory, and on the earth[64]—made up of the elect.[65] However, his idea of the church as composed of the elect meant that membership in the empirical Catholic Church provides no guarantee that people are truly saved or members of the church: God "wills it with good reason that we do not know whether we are of the church. But in proportion as a man may hope that he shall be saved in bliss, so he should suppose that he is a limb of holy church; and thus he should love holy church and worship it as his mother."[66] Of course, Wycliffe's concept of the church meant that the Catholic Church could not guarantee salvation for anyone—not even for its own pope.[67] But he did not stop there; he called the pope the Antichrist.[68]

---

62. E.g., Thomas Aquinas provided warrant for the inquisition. He argued that heretics "deserve not only to be separated from the church by excommunication, but also to be severed from the world by death. For it is a much graver matter to corrupt the faith which quickens the soul, than to forge money, which supports temporal life. Wherefore if forgers of money and other evil-doers are forthwith condemned to death by the secular authority, much more reason is there for heretics, as soon as they are convicted of heresy, to be not only excommunicated but even put to death." *Summa Theologica*, pt. 2, q. 11, art. 3.

63. An early Waldensian catechism set forth their ecclesiology: "The church must be thought of in two ways: one in terms of its substance or nature, the other in terms of the ministry. As for its substance, the holy catholic church is made up of all God's elect, from the beginning to the end, who have, according to the grace of God by the merits of Christ, been gathered together by the Holy Spirit and previously ordained to eternal life, their number and names being known only to the one having chosen them.... But the church with regard to the ministry, comprises the ministers of Christ with the people submitted to them, profiting from the ministry of faith, hope, and love." Petry, 353.

64. John Wycliffe, *The Church and Her Members*, 1, in Petry, 519–20.

65. "It contains no men as members except those who will be saved." Ibid., in Petry, 520.

66. Ibid.

67. "For no pope that lives knows whether he is a member of the church or whether he is a limb of the devil, destined to be damned with Lucifer." Ibid.

68. "The true vicar of Christ should be the poorest man of all, and the meekest man of all men, and the man of most labor in Christ's church. (But choosing of cardinals and dividing of benefices and taking of new names are very far from such a portrait.) Thus lived Peter, after Christ.... All these things that the popes do teach us that they are Antichrists, for Christ himself might not take a name—unless it were meekness and truth. If you say that Christ's church must have a head here on earth, you say truly; for Christ is the head, who must be here with his church until the day of doom, as well as everywhere by reason of his Godhead.... And if you say that Christ must necessarily have such a vicar here on earth, you deny Christ's power and place this devil above Christ.... God willing, these popes shall destroy themselves, yes, even here—for no doubt they shall be destroyed in hell by the judgment of Christ." Ibid., in Petry, 520–21.

Following Wycliffe's lead, John Hus drew out the implication of his ecclesiology: The predestined continue to be part of the true church despite "a temporary exclusion from the church."[69] That is, even if a person predestined for salvation does not belong to the Catholic Church, that person is still a member of the true Christian church. For Hus one could be "of the church"—a genuine member of the elect, belonging to the church of Christ—yet not "in the church"—part of the Church of Rome.[70] The ecclesiology of Wycliffe and Hus proved to be such a threat that it was condemned by the church.

For its part, the Church of Rome attempted to defend itself as the "one, holy, catholic and apostolic church" against the very evident deterioration of unity and holiness in its midst. It even added two correlative attributes to the description of the essence of the church—infallibility and indefectibility. John of Ragusa claimed infallibility for the church, arguing that "it cannot err in those things that are necessary for salvation, because at the time in which it would err in these things it would no longer be holy."[71] Indefectibility—that is, being immune to failure—was claimed for the church even if the pope were to be proven heretical.[72]

In the chaos of the latter Middle Ages, the proper subject to which these characteristics could be attributed was a matter of controversy. On the one hand, Guido Terrena could claim that "where the supreme pontiff with the college of the lord cardinals or with a general council are gathered together in the Lord's name and on behalf of his faith, there is Christ, who is the truth without error." On the other hand, he could make another claim that "in the determination of the things that pertain to faith, the pope is directed by the Holy Spirit and the Holy Spirit speaks in him."[73] To this was added the claim of Henry of Langenstein: "The universal church, which is not able to err or to be exposed to mortal sin, is indeed superior to the college of cardinals and the pope because he does not have this prerogative."[74] So when it was said of the church that it was indefectible and infallible, to what church was reference being made? To the pope alone? To the pope together with the cardinals? To a general council apart from the pope and the cardinals? In reality, this so-called infallible and indefectible church was wracked by immorality, carnality, political manipulation, schism, and heresy.

And so came a frank admission—and a claim by supporters of the church: "On account of her many secret faults, and especially on account of her public and scandalous sins, the church of Christ can be called spotted and wrinkled, and yet, out of reverence for Christ, whose spouse she is, she may, indeed, must be called catholic, holy, and immaculate as regards her form."[75] Along with such urgent cries for help, many people in the latter medieval period clamored for an authentic spirituality in the midst of a seriously compromised Catholic Church. This created a situation that was ripe for reformation.

---

69. John Hus, *Commentary on the Sentences*, 4.21.3, in Pelikan, 4:75.

70. John Hus, *On the Church*, 3.E, in Pelikan, 4:75.

71. John of Ragusa, *Oration on Communion under Both Kinds*, in Pelikan, 4:86.

72. Some church leaders appealed to the words of Jesus in Matt. 23:2–3. Others appealed to the example of Judas, whom Christ did not remove immediately from his apostleship. Nicholas of Cusa appealed to the promise of "the assistance of Christ until the consummation of the age" to support the church's indefectibility and infallibility. Nicholas of Cusa, *Catholic Concordance*, 2.18, in Pelikan, 4:100.

73. Guido Terrena, *Questions on the Infallible Magisterium of the Roman Pontiff*, in Pelikan, 107.

74. Henry of Langenstein, *Letter on Behalf of a Council of Peace*, 13, LCC, 14:118.

75. Heinrich Toke, *On the Church*, conclusion, 2, in Pelikan, 4:97.

ECCLESIOLOGY IN THE
REFORMATION AND POST-REFORMATION

In his efforts at reforming the church, Martin Luther faced a desperate situation: All around him existed—as it had for many centuries—the Roman Catholic Church, yet he was attempting to establish a new and true church. How could he explain to the common person what the church really is? Believing that "a child seven years old knows what the church is,"[76] he turned to the expression "I believe in one holy Christian church, the communion of saints," found in the Children's Creed. He commented: "Here the creed clearly indicates what the church is, namely, a communion of saints, that is a crowd or assembly of people who are Christians and holy."[77] Luther still wondered, "But how will or how can a poor confused person tell where such Christian holy people are to found in this world?"[78] He responded by listing the seven marks of a true church:

- "First, the holy Christian people are recognized by their possession of the holy Word of God."[79]
- "Second, God's people or the Christian holy people are recognized by the holy sacrament of baptism, wherever it is taught, believed, and administered correctly according to Christ's ordinance."[80]
- "Third, God's people, or the Christian holy people, are recognized by the holy sacrament of the altar, wherever it is rightly administered, believed, and received, according to Christ's institution."[81]
- "Fourth, God's people or holy Christians are recognized by the office of the keys exercised publicly. That is, as Christ decrees in Matthew 18[:15–20], if a Christian sins, he should be reproved; and if he does not mend his ways, he should be bound in his sin and cast out. If he does mend his ways, he should be absolved. That is the office of the keys."[82]
- "Fifth, the church is recognized externally by the fact that it consecrates or calls ministers, or has offices that it is to administer."[83]

---

76. Martin Luther, *Smalcald Articles*, 3,12., in *Triglot Concordia: The Symbolical Books of the Evangelical Lutheran Church*, trans. F. Bente and W. H. T. Dau (St. Louis: Concordia, 1921), 499.

77. Martin Luther, *On the Councils of the Church*, LW, 41:143.

78. Ibid., LW, 41:148.

79. Ibid. Luther spoke not only of the "external Word"— that which is preached in the church—but also of the Word that "is sincerely believed and openly professed before the world." For Luther, "this is the principal item, and the holiest of holy possessions"; it is the most important mark of the church. "And even if there were no other sign than this alone, it would suffice to prove that a Christian, holy people must exist there, for God's Word cannot be without God's people, and conversely, God's people cannot be without God's Word." Ibid., LW, 41:149–50.

80. Ibid., LW, 41:151. Luther believed that baptism cleanses people of their sins and should be administered to infants. See the further discussion on Luther's view of baptism in chap. 28.

81. Ibid., LW, 41:152. Luther believed that the Lord's Supper is a last will or testament setting forth the forgiveness of sins. As was true for the Word of God, "wherever baptism and the sacrament of the Lord's Supper are, God's people must be, and vice versa." Ibid. See the further discussion on Luther's view of the Lord's Supper in chap. 29.

82. Ibid., LW, 41:153. Luther called for careful and proper use of church discipline, depending on the tender conscience or stubborn heart of the sinning believer. He also blasted the misuse of the keys by the pope. The true church exercises discipline rightly in order to bring back fallen sinners.

83. Ibid., LW, 41:154. Although a champion of the priesthood of all believers, Luther recognized that Christ himself had instituted certain church leaders to carry out the ministry.

- "Sixth, the holy Christian people are externally recognized by prayer, public praise, and thanksgiving to God."[84]
- "Seventh, the holy Christian people are externally recognized by the holy possession of the sacred cross. They must endure every misfortune and persecution, all kinds of trials and evil from the devil, the world, and the flesh … in order to become like their head, Christ."[85]

Ultimately, the first three marks became the focal points of the Lutheran understanding of the church. According to the *Augsburg Confession*: "The church is the congregation of the saints in which the gospel is rightly taught and the sacraments rightly administered. And unto the true unity of the church, it is sufficient to agree concerning the doctrine of the gospel and the administration of the sacraments."[86] The emphatic statement "It is sufficient" underscored that these two elements—and these two elements alone—constitute a church.

In formulating his concept of the church, John Calvin turned to the expression "I believe (in) the church," found in the Nicene Creed. He distinguished between the invisible church and the visible church. Taking inspiration from Augustine, he noted that God alone perfectly knows the true members—the elect—who constitute the invisible church.[87] By contrast, the visible church, like the field that is a mixture of wheat and tares, is composed of both genuine believers and unsaved members. Because the two groups are often indistinguishable—they have been baptized, profess faith in Christ, attend church, and so forth—Calvin urged the church to exercise a "charitable judgment"—to give professing Christians the benefit of the doubt—and not engage in a witch hunt to rid itself of inauthentic members.[88]

Like Luther before him, Calvin discussed the marks of the true church. "From this the face of the church comes forth and becomes visible to our eyes. Wherever we see the Word of God purely preached and heard, and the sacraments administered according to Christ's institution, there, it is not to be doubted, a church of God exists. For his promise cannot fail."[89] One notes these are the same as Luther's first three marks. Other Calvinists—indeed, Martin Bucer, Calvin's colleague in Strasbourg, France—added

---

84. Ibid., LW, 41:164. He continued: "Where you see and hear the Lord's Prayer prayed and taught; or psalms or other spiritual songs sung, in accordance with the Word of God and the true faith; also the creed, the Ten Commandments, and the catechism used in public, you may rest assured that a holy Christian people of God are present." Ibid. For Luther, these prayers and songs were to be spoken and sung in a language that the common person could understand. Thus, he led church services in German, rather than Latin (the language of the church, which most people could not understand), even composing hymns in German to be sung by the entire congregation. His most notable hymn is "A Mighty Fortress Is Our God."

85. Ibid., LW, 41:164. Thus, suffering of all types marks the true church, for it contributes to the sanctification of God's people, and through it, God blesses his church.

86. *Augsburg Confession*, 7, in Schaff, 3:11–12. Melanchthon, the writer of the *Confession*, echoed this idea in his *Loci Communes*: "The marks that point out the church are the pure gospel and the proper use of the sacraments." Philipp Melanchthon, *Loci Communes*, trans. J. A. O. Preus (St. Louis: Concordia, 1992), 137.

87. He noted Eph. 1:13 and 2 Tim. 2:19 as biblical support for God's perfect knowledge of genuine Christians. John Calvin, *Institutes of the Christian Religion*, 4.1.2, LCC, 2:1013.

88. Ibid., 4.1.8, LCC, 2:1022.

89. He cited Matt. 18:20 in support. Ibid., 4.1.9, LCC, 2:1023. In his *Genevan Catechism*, Calvin formulated his first mark in a negative way: "Where the gospel is not declared, heard, and received, there we do not acknowledge the form of the church." *Genevan Catechism*, 18, LCC, 22:31.

church discipline to this list.[90] Following Calvin, some Reformed statements of faith—the *Thirty-nine Articles* of the Anglican Church[91]—continued to list two marks of the church, while others—the *Belgic Confession*, the *Scottish Confession of Faith*—expanded the list to include the third mark of church discipline.[92]

All three of these Protestant churches—Lutheran, Reformed, and Anglican—preserved the centuries-old relationship between church and state; for this reason, they are referred to as composing the *magisterial* Reformation.[93] Another Protestant church, however, developed at this same time and repudiated this notion. Specifically, Anabaptist ecclesiology was characterized by the separation of church and state. Anabaptists were decidedly against personal involvement in the civil government (specifically, serving in office) for several reasons: "The government magistracy is according to the flesh, but the Christians' is according to the Spirit. Their houses and dwelling remain in this world, but the Christians' are in heaven. Their citizenship is in this world, but the Christians' citizenship is in heaven. The weapons of their conflict and war are carnal and against the flesh only, but the Christians' weapons are spiritual, against the fortification of the devil."[94] Practically speaking, this meant that Anabaptists could not swear allegiance to the state and its rulers.[95] Furthermore, they would have nothing to do with the state churches—both the Catholic Church and the magisterial Protestant churches.[96]

90. Although he had much to say on this matter, Calvin did not list discipline as one of the marks of the church. But these gave great assurance to Calvin regarding the progress of the church, and he solemnly warned that any church possessing these marks stood out as a serious force with which people had to reckon: "No one is permitted to spurn its authority, flout its warnings, resist its counsel, or make light of its chastisements—much less desert it and break its unity. For the Lord esteems the communion of his church so highly that he counts as a traitor and apostate from Christianity anyone who arrogantly leaves any Christian society, provided it cherishes the true ministry of Word and sacrament." Calvin, *Institutes.*, 4.1.10, LCC, 2:1024.

91. *Thirty-nine Articles*, 19, in Schaff, 3:486.

92. *Belgic Confession*, 29, in Schaff, 3:383; *Scottish Confession of Faith*, 18, in Schaff, 3:461–62.

93. The Lutheran theologian John Gerhard explained the importance of the state: "The magistracy has been established by God, no less than the ministry, for the collection, preservation, and extension of the church, inasmuch as by means of it both outward discipline and public peace and tranquility are preserved. Without this, the ministry of the church could not readily perform its duty and the collection and extension of the church could hardly take place." Indeed, the civil government is "a wall and shield for the church" for its protection from persecution and a help for its ministry. John Gerhard, *Loci Theologici* (1621), 13.225, in Schmid, 618. Reformed theologian Francis Burmann listed the responsibilities incumbent upon the state in relationship to the church. These included the proper ordering of church services, financial support for the ministry and its ministers, the discipline of erring ministers, building and supporting seminaries, and the trial and punish-

ment of heretics. Condensed from Francis Burmann, *Synopsis Theologiae* (Amsterdam, 1699), 8.10.15, in Heppe, 693–94. For a similar Lutheran perspective, see John William Baier, *Compendium Theologiae Positivae* (1685), 809, in Schmid, 619.

94. *Schleitheim Confession*, 6, in Lumpkin, 28.

95. Biblical support, specifically Jesus' own teaching in Matt. 5:34–37, was offered. Ibid., 7, in Lumpkin, 29.

96. "We are agreed on separation: A separation shall be made from the evil and from the wickedness that the devil planted in the world.... Everything that is not united with our God and Christ cannot be other than an abomination that we should shun and flee from. By this is meant all popish and antipopish works and church services, meetings and church attendance." Ibid., 4, in Lumpkin, 26. As was to be expected, both the Protestant churches and the Roman Catholic Church condemned the Anabaptists. E.g, the Lutheran *Formula of Concord* denounced them for the following views: "(1) That the office of the magistrate is not, according to the New Testament, a condition of life that pleases God. (2) That a Christian man cannot discharge the office of a magistrate with a safe [good] and quiet [clean] conscience. (3) That a Christian man cannot with a good conscience administer and execute the office of a magistrate, if matters so require, against the wicked, nor subjects [i.e., citizens] implore for their defense that power which the magistrate has received from God. (4) That a Christian man cannot with a safe [good] conscience take an oath, nor swear obedience and fidelity [loyalty] to his prince or magistrate. (5) That the magistrate, according to the New Testament, cannot with a good conscience punish criminals with death. *Formula of Concord*, art. 12, "Anabaptist Articles That Are Intolerable in the Commonwealth," 1–5, in Schaff, 3:176.

Of course, the Roman Catholic Church denounced the Protestant churches and their ecclesiology that denied that the pope is the supreme authority. As the *Catechism of the Council of Trent* (1566), citing Ambrose, explained:

> Should anyone object, that the church is content with one Head and one Spouse, Jesus Christ, and requires no other; the answer is obvious.... [Christ] placed over his church, which he governs by his invisible Spirit, a man to be his vicar, and the minister of his power: a visible church requires a visible head, and, therefore, the Savior appointed Peter head and pastor of all the faithful ... desiring that he, who was to succeed him [Peter] should be invested with the very same power of ruling and governing the entire church.[97]

The very essence of the church, therefore, was defined in terms of the papacy; there could be no church where the Catholic hierarchy with the pope in Rome does not preside.[98] These two diametrically opposed doctrines of the church meant that the Catholic Church and the Protestant churches would be separated.

Beginning in the early seventeenth century, a new church — the Baptist church — with a distinctive ecclesiology came into existence.[99] The conviction that only regenerate people may be members of the church was echoed in John Smyth's *Short Confession of Faith in XX Articles* (1609) — "the church of Christ is a company of the faithful; baptized after confession of sin and of faith, endowed with the power of Christ"[100] — and his *Short Confession of Faith* (1610) — "faithful, righteous people, scattered in several parts of the world, [are] the true congregations of God, or the church of Christ."[101] To these people, and these people alone, baptism should be administered.[102] Thomas Helwys, Smyth's close associate, further linked baptism with church membership.[103] Thus, baptism of regenerated people was essential for Baptist church membership.

Accordingly, Smyth defined the church: "A visible communion of saints is of two, three, or more saints joined together by covenant with God and themselves, freely to use all the holy things of God, according to the Word, for their mutual edification and God's glory.... This visible communion of saints is a visible church."[104] Thus, besides

---

97. *Catechism of the Council of Trent*, trans. Jeremy Donovan (Baltimore: Fielding Lucas, Jr., 1829), 75.

98. Indeed, the following pledge of allegiance was demanded by the *Profession of the Tridentine Faith:* "I acknowledge the holy Catholic Apostolic Roman Church for the mother and mistress of all churches; and I promise and swear obedience to the Bishop of Rome, successor to St. Peter, Prince of the Apostles, and Vicar of Jesus Christ." *Profession of the Tridentine Faith* (1564), 10, in Schaff, 2:209.

99. The pioneering Baptist John Smyth was influenced by the Mennonites, in particular by their *Waterland Confession* of 1580. Hans de Ries and Lubbert Gerrits, *The Waterland Confession*, art. 24, in Lumpkin, 57.

100. John Smyth, *Short Confession of Faith in XX Articles* (1609), art. 12, in Lumpkin, 101.

101. John Smyth, *Short Confession of Faith*, art. 22, in Lumpkin, 108.

102. "Holy baptism is given to these in the name of the Father, the Son, and the Holy Spirit, who hear, believe, and with repentant hearts receive the doctrines of the holy gospel. For these, the Lord Jesus has commanded to be baptized, and no unspeaking children." Ibid., art. 29, in Lumpkin, 109–10.

103. "Every church is to receive in all their members by baptism upon the confession of their faith and sins wrought by the preaching of the gospel, according to the primitive institution (Matt. 28:19) and practice (Acts 2:41). Therefore, churches constituted after any other manner or of any other people are not [churches] according to Christ's testament." Thomas Helwys, *English Declaration at Amsterdam* (1611), art. 13, in Lumpkin, 120. The text has been rendered clearer.

104. John Smyth, *Principles and Inferences Concerning the Visible Church*, in *The Works of John Smyth*, ed. W. T. Whitley, 2 vols. (Cambridge: Cambridge Univ. Press, 1915), 1:252. The text has been rendered clearer.

regenerate church membership and believer's baptism, a church covenant was a third element in Smyth's ecclesiology: "The outward part of the true form of the true visible church is a vow, promise, oath, or covenant between God and the saints."[105] A fourth element—the church is a visible spiritual kingdom—was added to the definition of a church by the Baptistic *London Confession of Faith*: "Christ has here on earth a spiritual kingdom, which is the church, which he has purchased and redeemed to himself, as a particular inheritance. The church, as it is visible to us, is a company of visible saints, called and separated from the world, by the Word and Spirit of God, to the visible profession of the faith of the gospel, being baptized into that faith, and joined to the Lord and each other, by mutual agreement, in the practical enjoyment of the ordinances commanded by Christ their head and king."[106] According to Baptist ecclesiology, each local church is autonomous; it possesses authority directly from Christ himself. Furthermore, this power is not mediated through any hierarchy above the local church level, as demonstrated by each church choosing its own officers.[107] Church membership—including both the reception of new members and the expulsion of erring people from membership—is also the prerogative of each congregation.[108]

In 1658 another group of local, autonomous churches—the Congregational Church—was formed. The *Savoy Declaration of Faith and Order* articulated its idea of the church as people "called (through the ministry of the Word by his Spirit)" and "commanded to walk together in particular [local] societies or churches for their mutual edification and the due performance of that public worship which he requires of them in this world."[109] Each church possesses its own authority, and no authoritative entity above the local church exists.[110] Moreover, each church consists of members who are authentic Christians and officers chosen by those members.[111] These church members have the responsibility of accepting new members and disciplining erring members.[112] Furthermore, the Congregational Church denied any role for authoritative governing bodies above the local church level in church disciplinary matters[113] and accorded a very limited role for the civil authorities.[114] In many respects, the Congregational Church and the Baptist movements were quite similar. Indeed, the *Savoy Declaration* significantly influenced the *Second London Confession of Faith*.[115]

---

105. Ibid., in Whitley, *Works of John Smyth*, 1:254.

106. *London Confession of Faith*, 33, in Lumpkin, 165. The text has been rendered clearer.

107. Ibid., 36, in Lumpkin, 166.

108. Ibid., 42–43, in Lumpkin, 168.

109. *Savoy Declaration*, 1–3, in Schaff, 3:724.

110. Ibid., 4, 6, in Schaff, 3:724.

111. Ibid., 7–8, in Schaff, 3:724–25.

112. Ibid., 17–18, in Schaff, 3:726–27.

113. Ibid., 22, in Schaff, 3:727.

114. Ibid., 24.3, in Schaff, 3:720.

115. The influence is seen in the following areas: Christians living in the same geographical vicinity had the responsibility to join a local church: "All believers are bound to join themselves to particular [local] churches, when and where they have opportunity to do so; so all who are admitted to the privileges of a church, are also under its censures [correction] and government, according to the rule of Christ." As members, they were responsible for regular attendance at church meetings. Prayer for and fellowship with other (Baptist) churches was another responsibility. Mutual cooperation with other churches could also be of help in the case of entrenched church problems that defied quick solution. Thus, cooperation with other churches, but no control of one church by another, was encouraged in Baptist ecclesiology. *Second London Confession of Faith*, 26.12–15, in Lumpkin, 288–89. The text has been rendered clearer. Cf. *Savoy Declaration*, 24–26, in Schaff, 3:728–29.

ECCLESIOLOGY IN THE MODERN PERIOD

New Protestant churches arose in the modern period. For example, as he preached in churches and open-air forums, John Wesley organized his converts into groups, thus preserving the fruits of his ministry. After ordaining his own bishops in America, he caused a breach with his own Anglican Church, and the Methodist Church was founded. He drew up the *Methodist Articles of Religion* (1784) for the American Methodists.[116]

Another important contribution to ecclesiology was the missiological emphasis of William Carey. In his pamphlet *Enquiry into the Obligation of Christians to Use Means for the Conversion of the Heathen* (1791), the "father of Protestant missions" confronted churches that were theologically paralyzed from considering their role in the evangelization of the peoples of the world.[117] The immediate results of Carey's work were the formation of the Particular Baptist Missionary Society for Propagating the Gospel among the Heathen and his career as a missionary in India. The long-term results included the launching of hundreds of Protestant foreign missionary societies and innumerable missionaries to take the gospel to the entire world. Indeed, many Protestant churches and denominations became characterized by their missionary orientation.

Disturbed by centuries of division, a growing number of Protestant churches called for some action or structure that could address this disheartening situation and work toward unity among churches. One result of this concern was the ecumenical movement. The initial impetus for this movement was the World Missionary Conference that met in Edinburgh in 1920. This was followed by a series of world conferences on "Faith and Order" (Lausanne, 1927; Edinburgh, 1937) and "Life and Work" (Stockholm, 1925; Oxford, 1937), but the most important development was the creation of the World Council of Churches in 1948.[118] Although the original member churches were all Protestant denominations, the WCC expanded to include the Russian Orthodox Church and official observers from the Roman Catholic Church. From the beginning of the WCC, most

---

116. For his definition of the church, he simply cited the *Thirty-nine Articles* (art. 19): "The visible church of Christ is a congregation of faithful men in which the pure Word of God is preached, and the sacraments duly [rightly] administered according to Christ's ordinance, in all those things that of necessity are requisite to the same." *Methodist Articles of Religion*, 13, in Schaff, 3:810.

117. William Carey, *An Enquiry into the Obligation of Christians to Use Means for the Conversion of the Heathen*. Carey was deeply influenced by Jonathan Edwards's *Account of the Life of the Late Rev. David Brainerd*, the travel journals of the explorer James Cook, and Andrew Fuller's pamphlet *The Gospel Worthy of All Acceptation*. Carey also appealed to the Moravians—descendants of German Pietism—as an example of Christian missionaries who had taken seriously the Great Commission of Christ.

118. The basis for the WCC was as follows: "The World Council of Churches is a fellowship of churches which confess the Lord Jesus Christ as God and Savior according to the Scriptures and therefore seek to fulfill together their common calling to the glory of one God, Father, Son and Holy Spirit." *Constitution of the World Council of Churches* (1948 with 1961 amendment), in Bettenson, 426–27. The vision of the WCC was for the visible unity of all churches: "We believe that the unity which is both God's will and his gift to his church is being made visible as all in each place who are baptized into Jesus Christ and confess him as Lord and Savior are brought by the Holy Spirit into one fully committed fellowship, holding the one apostolic faith, preaching the one gospel, breaking the one bread, joining in common prayer, and having a corporate life reaching out in witness and service to all, and who at the same time are united with the whole Christian fellowship in all places and all ages in such ways that ministry and members are accepted by all, and that all can act and speak together as occasion requires for the tasks to which God calls his people." W. A. Visser't Hooft, ed., *The New Delhi Report: The Third Assembly of the World Council of Churches, 1961* (New York: Association Press, 1962), 116.

evangelicals have not attended. This decision has been motivated by concern about the minimization of doctrine, an increasing marginalization of evangelism, and the support of the WCC for liberation theology and socialist political reform.

Rather than join themselves with the ecumenical movement, evangelical churches in the United States formed their own National Association of Evangelicals in 1942. Worldwide, evangelicals assembled together to form the World Evangelical Fellowship. Evangelical ecumenical efforts, for the most part, have been oriented to evangelism and missions (World Congress on Evangelism, Berlin, 1966; International Congress on World Evangelization, Lausanne, 1974; Pattaya, 1980; Lausanne II, 1989; Pattaya II, 2004; Lausanne III, 2010). The Lausanne Covenant (1974) is a clear example of these evangelical ecumenical efforts.

Perhaps the most radical break with historic ecclesiologies of all types was the doctrine of the church articulated by dispensationalists. Two contributors to this development were J. N. Darby and Lewis Sperry Chafer. Darby insisted on a complete separation between the remnant of the Jewish people and the church—each has its own history, destiny, and hope. Concerning the church, Darby believed that it was a mystery that was not revealed until the apostle Paul wrote his letters[119] and concluded that the doctrine of the church "was thus wholly unknown to the saints of the Old Testament."[120] More specifically, the entire doctrine of the church was communicated by the apostle Paul—it is found nowhere else, even in the New Testament.[121] According to Chafer, some of the key differences between the Jewish people and the church include the baptism and permanent indwelling of Christians by the Holy Spirit, earthly promises to Israel versus heavenly promises to the church, law as the rule of life for the Jews versus grace for Christians, and incorporation into the body of Christ for Christians.[122] Furthermore, Chafer argued that the church began at Pentecost and did not exist for the old covenant people of God because its existence was dependent on the death, resurrection, and ascension of Jesus Christ and the descent of the Holy Spirit to regenerate, baptize, and seal people as part of the church.[123] This church finds its instructions for doctrine, worship, ministry, ordinances, and government solely in (parts of) the New Testament and not at all in the Old Testament.[124]

While all these developments were occurring in Protestant churches, Catholic theology continued to articulate its ecclesiology along the lines of its centuries-old traditions: The Roman Catholic Church—one, holy, catholic, apostolic, indefectible, and infallible—is the only true church. A notable defender of this was John Henry Newman, himself a convert from the Anglican Church, particularly in his signal work *Essay on the Development of Christian Doctrine* (1854).[125] This view was further cemented by the (first) Vatican Council (1870) when it proclaimed the dogma of papal infallibil-

119. J. N. Darby, "The Rapture of the Saints," in *The Collected Writings of J. N. Darby*, ed. William Kelly, 34 vols. (repr., Sunbury, Pa.: Believers Bookshelf, 1972), 11:149.

120. Ibid. He listed Rom. 16:25–26; Eph. 3:4–5, 9; and Col. 1:24 in support.

121. Ibid., 11:150–51.

122. Lewis Sperry Chafer, *Systematic Theology*, 4 vols. (Dallas: Dallas Seminary Press, 1948), vol. 4: *Ecclesiology–Eschatology*, 34.

123. Ibid., 45–46. 124. Ibid., 16, 19, 28, 29.

125. John Henry Newman, *Essay on the Development of Christian Doctrine* (New York: Longmans Green, 1927).

ity.[126] As the Roman Catholic Church was buffeted by the growing tide of modernism, the popes denounced atheism, agnosticism, evolution, liberalism, biblical criticism, secularism, fascism, communism, and the like while trying to hold off those influences from coming inside its own walls. As political developments turned against it, the church found that its relationship with new secular states like Italy was severed. The Second Vatican Council stood in many ways in strong continuity with centuries of Roman Catholic doctrine, but it was also an *aggiornamento* ("updating") of the church's theology. This was particularly evident in its doctrine of the church, which was further elaborated in post-conciliar documents and the *Catechism of the Catholic Church* (1994).

One of the most dynamic developments in the modern period was the beginning and expansion of Pentecostalism and the charismatic movement, which began early in the twentieth century. From this, new churches and new denominations—called Pentecostal, because of the similarity between their experience of the Holy Spirit and that of the Christians on the day of Pentecost—arose and multiplied throughout the world.[127] This drive also infiltrated already existing churches and denominations, producing the charismatic movement. Baptists, Lutherans, Methodists, Anglicans—even Roman Catholics—claimed a renewal through Pentecostal theology. Typified by enthusiastic devotion to Christ and possessing a tireless evangelistic energy, Pentecostalism and the charismatic movement have contributed to the greatest expansion of the church in its history.[128]

Alongside the rapid growth of Pentecostal churches and the influence of the charismatic movement, "one of America's most prominent religious movements in the 1990s [was] 'effective evangelism' through such modern means of 'growing churches' as management, marketing, and megachurches.... Megachurches, churches-for-the-unchurched with congregations over two thousand, are widely touted as 'the inside track to fast growth' and a 'leading trend of the coming millennium.'"[129] Numerous elements contributed to the development of this movement. One was mass media, especially radio and television, which broadcasted megachurch pioneers like Robert Schuller, Oral Roberts,

---

126. As seen earlier, the issue regarding who or what is infallible—the pope, a general council, the church—was debated for centuries, with papal infallibility winning out. But the church itself had never declared an official position in this regard. According to Vatican I: "We teach and define that it is a dogma divinely revealed: that the Roman pontiff, when he speaks *ex cathedra*, that is, when in discharge of the office of pastor and doctor of all Christians, by virtue of his supreme apostolic authority, he defines a doctrine regarding faith or morals to be held by the universal church, by the divine assistance promised to him in blessed Peter, is possessed of that infallibility with which the divine Redeemer will that his church should be endowed for defining doctrine regarding faith or morals; and that therefore such definitions of the Roman Pontiff are irreformable of themselves, and not from the consent of the church." *Dogmatic Decrees of the Vatican*

Council Concerning the Catholic Faith and the Church of Christ, 4th session (July 18, 1870), *First Dogmatic Constitution on the Church of Christ*, 4, in Schaff, 2:270–71.

127. These denominations included the Assemblies of God, the Church of God in Christ, the Church of God (Cleveland, Tenn.), the Pentecostal Holiness Church, the International Church of the Foursquare Gospel, and others. For a history of the founding of Pentecostalism, see Cecil M. Robeck Jr., *The Azusa Street Mission and Revival: The Birth of the Global Pentecostal Movement* (Nashville: Nelson, 2006).

128. For an example of Pentecostal theology, see J. Rodman Williams, *Renewal Theology*, 3 vols. (Grand Rapids: Zondervan, 1996).

129. Os Guinness, *Dining with the Devil: The Megachurch Movement Flirts with Modernity* (Grand Rapids: Baker, 1993), 12.

and Jerry Falwell.[130] A second factor was the application of business strategies to the church. Demographic studies, which identified a church's potential audience, combined with marketing techniques that targeted that audience, were used to determine the church's outreach and programming. Indeed, Robert Schuller identified "the secrets of successful religious retailing" as a key to megachurch development:[131] accessibility, surplus parking, inventory, service, visibility, possibility thinking, and good cash flow.[132] A third contributor was the church growth movement, founded by Donald McGavran and popularized by the Institute of Church Growth at Fuller Theological Seminary. McGavran defined a church growth principle as "a universal truth which, when properly interpreted and applied, contributes significantly to the growth of churches and denominations."[133] Over the years, numerous church growth principles were identified, including purpose, effective evangelism, scientific research, receptivity, homogeneity, lay ministry, and leadership.[134] More than any other church, Willow Creek Community Church and its pastor, Bill Hybels, were identified with this megachurch trend.[135]

In part a reaction against megachurch ecclesiology, a new paradigm developed out of the emergent church conversation. This "postmodern" ecclesiology incorporated several elements, including a protest against traditional churches, a search for authenticity, relationality, contextualization of the gospel for postmoderns, an emphasis on the arts and the imagination, an antifoundational epistemology, experientialism, a preference for narrative over didactic, an emphasis on feelings over cognition, and a sense of connection with the ancient church and its forms. Although young and intentionally non- (or anti-) theological, the emergent church conversation has given birth to several notions of ecclesiology. For Erwin McManus, for example, the church of the twenty-first century must be *EPIC*—*e*xperiential, *p*articipatory, *i*mage-driven, and *c*onnected. Based on research of two hundred emergent churches in the United States and Great Britain, Eddie Gibbs and

130. Mass media gave high visibility to these pastors and their congregations, and dynamic pastoral personalities became a staple of megachurches. Mass media also dictated what kind of "programming"—a media-induced term that replaced the traditional notion of liturgy—could be included in (or excluded from) the broadcasted service. E.g., times of silent prayer, as well as the collection of the offering, became awkward moments for a listening or watching public, and so they were dropped out of broadcasted megachurch services. Whether they were broadcasted or not, megachurch worship services were influenced by these successful media churches. Elements that entertained and emotionally connected with the viewing public became premium marks of megachurches. As one observer noted, "Instead of turning people away from the church, televangelism is changing their very conception of the church and its functions." Quentin J. Schultze, *Televangelism and American Culture: The Business of Popular Religion* (Grand Rapids: Baker, 1991), 205.

131. Robert Schuller, *Your Church Has Real Possibilities!* (Glendale, Calif.: Regal, 1974), 18.

132. Ibid., 19–29. Although contributing greatly to the

success of megachurches, market-driven strategies also contributed to a consumer-oriented approach to church. Potential church members, or customers, had to be enticed by creative advertising, made to feel comfortable and secure by "Disney-like" facilities, satisfied by the "product" on stage, and kept as faithful consumers by churches.

133. Donald A. McGavran and Win Arn, *Ten Steps for Church Growth* (San Francisco: Harper and Row, 1977), 15.

134. These principles are variously found in R. Daniel Reeves and Ron Jenson, *Always Advancing* (San Bernardino, Calif.: Here's Life, 1984); Delos Miles, *Church Growth: A Mighty River* (Nashville: Broadman, 1981); and McGavran and Arn, *Ten Steps for Church Growth*. This summary was taken from Scott Lee Guffin, "An Examination of Key Foundational Influences on the Megachurch Movement in America, 1960–1978," Ph.D. diss., Southern Baptist Theological Seminary, 1999, 297–315.

135. Lynne and Bill Hybels, *Rediscovering Church: The Story and Vision of Willow Creek Community Church* (Grand Rapids: Zondervan, 1995).

Ryan Bolger offered this definition: "Emerging churches are communities that practice the way of Jesus within postmodern cultures." Specifically, they identified nine practices: "Emerging churches (1) identify with the life of Jesus, (2) transform the secular realm, and (3) live highly communal lives. Because of these three activities, they (4) welcome strangers, (5) serve with generosity, (6) participate as producers, (7) create as creative beings, (8) lead as a body, and (9) take part in spiritual activities."[136]

At the same time these creative expressions are challenging long-standing notions of the church, traditional ecclesiologies continue to be expressed and flourish. This growing interest in ecclesiology in the third millennium can be seen not only in a fresh emphasis on church planting (e.g., Acts 29) and scholarly treatments of the doctrine of the church,[137] but also in a host of practical books on the nature, marks, and purposes of the church.[138]

---

136. Eddie Gibbs and Ryan K. Bolger, *Emerging Churches: Creating Christian Community in Postmodern Cultures* (Grand Rapids: Baker, 2005), 44–45.

137. E.g., see my forthcoming volume on ecclesiology to be published by Crossway as part of the Foundations of Evangelical Theology series.

138. Many of these popular offerings have a single adjective — e.g., missional, multisite — attached to the noun "church" in their title: Mark Driscoll and Gerry Breshears, *Vintage Church: Timeless Truths and Timely Methods* (Wheaton: Crossway, 2008); Thom S. Rainer and Eric Geiger, *Simple Church: Returning to God's Process for Making Disciples* (Nashville: Broadman, 2006); Robert D. Dale, *Cultivating Perennial Churches: Your Guide to Long-Term Growth* (Danvers, Mass.: Chalice, 2008); Rodney Harrison, Tom Cheyney, and Don Overstreet, *Spin-off Churches: How One Church Successfully Plants Another* (Nashville: Broadman, 2008); Leonard Sweet, *AquaChurch 2.0: Piloting Your Church in Today's Fluid Culture* (Colorado Springs: Cook, 2008); Brian Bailey and Terry Storch, *The Blogging Church: Shaping the Story of Your Church through Blogs* (San Francisco: Jossey-Bass, 2007); Ed Stetzer, *Planting Missional Churches* (Nashville: Broadman, 2006); Rick Rusaw and Eric Swanson, *The Externally Focused Church* (Loveland, Colo.: Group, 2004); Robert Lewis and Rob Wilkins, *The Church of Irresistible Influence: Bridge-Building Stories to Help Reach Your Community* (Grand Rapids: Zondervan, 2001); Mark Dever, *Nine Marks of a Healthy Church* (Wheaton: Crossway, 2004); Tim Chester and Steve Timmis, *Total Church: A Radical Reshaping around Gospel and Community* (Wheaton: Crossway, 2008).

Chapter 27

CHURCH GOVERNMENT

How has the church developed various views of its governing structure? How has it distinguished between the various church offices?

STATEMENT OF BELIEF

Churches have historically had many different forms of government. The Roman Catholic Church and the Anglican or Episcopal Church, for example, are governed by a three-tiered leadership structure consisting of bishops, presbyters (or priests), and deacons. Priests and deacons serve in a local church, while bishops exercise authority over a number of churches in a diocese. (In the Roman Catholic Church, cardinals—with the pope at their head—hold important positions in the worldwide government of the church.) Presbyterian churches and Reformed churches are governed by elders and deacons at the local level, but they also have regional and national assemblies that exercise authority through selected elders. Still other churches—for example, congregational churches and many Baptist churches—are governed by a two-tiered leadership structure, consisting of pastors (or elders) and deacons. These elders have no formal governing authority above the local congregational level. Evangelicals have been and are found in churches with all three of these governing structures—and in churches with governments that refuse categorization into these three models.[1]

FORMS OF CHURCH GOVERNMENT IN THE EARLY CHURCH

The most obvious leaders of the early church were the *apostles*. Jesus himself appointed twelve of his followers and gave them authority to carry out ministry (Mark 3:13–18). According to the apostle Paul, it was upon these men that the church was founded (Eph.

---

1. My thanks to Chuck Joiner for his help on this chapter.

2:19–20). So important are these twelve that their names are etched on the foundation stones of the New Jerusalem (Rev. 21:14).

Beside the apostles, *elders*—also referred to as *presbyters* (πρεσβυτεροι; *presbuteroi*), *overseers*, *bishops* (ἐπισκοποι; *episkopoi*), and *pastor-teachers* (Eph. 4:11)—exercised important leadership in the early church. When the church of Antioch faced a controversy, Paul and Barnabas were sent "to Jerusalem to see the apostles and elders about this question" (Acts 15:2; cf. vv. 4, 6, 22). At the end of their missionary journey, Paul and Barnabas returned to the churches they had recently planted and "appointed elders... in each church" (Acts 14:23). The responsibilities of the elders included authoritatively leading the church (1 Tim. 2:12–3:7; 5:17), teaching sound doctrine (1 Tim. 3:2; 5:17; Titus 1:9), shepherding the people of God (1 Peter 5:1–4), and praying for healing (James 5:13–16). In addition to elders, another group called *deacons*—including female deacons, or *deaconesses* (1 Tim. 3:8–13)[2]—assisted in the functioning of the church. Thus, the leadership pattern that marked the early church was a twofold order of elders (bishops) and deacons (Phil. 1:1; 1 Tim. 3:1–13).

This twofold order of church leadership was repeated in some churches in the late first century into the second century. Clement of Rome referred to the apostolic practice of choosing church leaders as being in line with Isaiah 60:17, which reads in the Septuagint, "I will appoint their bishops in righteousness and their deacons in faith."[3] The *Didache* gave instructions to Christians to "appoint for yourselves bishops and deacons worthy of the Lord,"[4] and Polycarp encouraged the Philippian church to be "obedient to the presbyters and deacons as to God and Christ."[5] Thus, a two-tiered system of church government featured elders/bishops and deacons.

ELDERS (or BISHOPS)
(plurality)

DEACONS
(plurality)

The distinction between these two offices developed over the course of time. In the New Testament, it seems that the responsibilities not carried out by the elders fell to the deacons (though this is not stated anywhere).[6] Ignatius hinted at one of their serving

---

2. Verse 11 can be taken as referring to either *deaconesses* or *wives* (of deacons, since it is located in a discussion of the qualifications of deacons). For a discussion of these alternatives, see Wayne Grudem, *Systematic Theology: An Introduction to Biblical Doctrine* (Grand Rapids: Zondervan, 1994, 2000), 919–20. While Grudem argues for the second alternative, I believe Paul addresses female deacons, or deaconesses. See my forthcoming book on ecclesiology to be published by Crossway as part of the Foundations of Evangelical Theology series.

3. Clement of Rome, *Letter of the Romans to the Corinthians*, 42, in Holmes, 75; *ANF*, 1:16. Clement's reference is to Isa. 60:17 in the Septuagint, which here mistranslates the Hebrew.

4. *Didache*, 15, in Holmes, 267; *ANF*, 7:381.

5. Polycarp, *Letter to the Philippians*, 5, in Holmes, 213; *ANF*, 1:34.

6. According to many, the narrative of Acts 6:1–7 is instructive for distinguishing between the role of elders—prayer and ministry of the Word of God—and that of deacons—waiting on tables. Thus, elders give attention to the spiritual oversight of the church, whereas deacons occupy themselves with the practical tasks and physical concerns of the church. Although the noun "service" (διακονια; *diakonia*) and the verb "to serve" (διακονειν; *diakonein*) appear in this text, it is not clear if this is a specific example of deacons exercising their role or a more general illustration of men being selected for and carrying out service in the church. Also, as a "deacon" or "servant" (διακονος; *diakonos*) of the church of Cenchreae, Phoebe engaged in important ministries, including being responsible for delivering Paul's letter from Corinth to the church in Rome (Rom. 16:1–2).

tasks when he reminded the "deacons of the 'mysteries' of Jesus Christ" that "they are not merely 'deacons' of food and drink, but ministers of God's church."[7] Clement of Alexandria compared two types of service—one of improvement, the other of ministry—in order to contrast the roles of these two offices: "In the church, the elders attend to the department [service] which has improvement [of the soul] for its object; the deacons attend to the ministerial [service]."[8] For Irenaeus, the elders (or bishops) were to be obeyed in the church as "those who ... possess the succession from the apostles; those who, together with the succession of the episcopate [bishops], have received the certain gift of truth, according to the good pleasure of the Father."[9] Thus, a major responsibility of the bishops was teaching sound doctrine. They were also to give leadership, as it was "the elders who preside over the church."[10] Yet no hard-and-fast rule to distinguish these offices was formulated early on. Indeed, much attention was given to making sure that elders and deacons met the high standards of godliness required by their position.[11]

As already noted, the terms for *elders* (or *presbyters*) and *bishops* (or *overseers*) were used interchangeably in the New Testament (Acts 20:17, 28; Titus 1:5–7). This linguistic practice continued in later church writings well into the third century. Clement of Rome wrote of "the bishop's office" and immediately spoke of those holding that office as "presbyters,"[12] and Irenaeus paralleled the "successions of presbyters" with "the successions of the bishops."[13] Even the noted bishop Cyprian, who did much to solidify the three-tiered structure of church government (see following discussion), addressed the bishop of Rome as "our co-presbyter"[14] and used the terms associated with elders (*presbyters*) and bishops (*episcopacy*) as synonyms.[15] As late as the end of the fourth century, Jerome held that the apostle Paul clearly taught that presbyters are the same as bishops. After appealing to Philippians 1:1 and Acts 20:28 in support, he explained: "Of the names *presbyter* and *bishop*, the first denotes age, the second rank. In writing both to Titus and Timothy, the apostle speaks of the ordination of bishops and deacons, but does not say a word about the ordination of presbyters; for the fact is that the word *bishops* includes presbyters also."[16]

Despite this continued use of *elders* and *bishops* as interchangeable terms, some leaders in the church began to separate these into two distinct offices. Faced with a dangerous heresy and confronted with potential divisions in churches, Ignatius responded with a new form of church government. He made a distinction between the offices of overseer/

---

7. Ignatius, *Letter to the Trallians*, 2, in Holmes, 161; *ANF*, 1:67.

8. Clement of Alexandria, *Stromata*, 7.1, in *ANF*, 2:523.

9. Irenaeus, *Against Heresies*, 4.26.2, in *ANF*, 1:497.

10. *The Shepherd of Hermas*, vision 2.4.8, in Holmes, 347; *ANF*, 2:12.

11. "The presbyters, for their part, must be compassionate, merciful to all, turning back those who have gone astray, visiting all the sick, not neglecting a widow, orphan, or poor person, but 'always aiming at what is honorable in the sight of God and of men.'" Polycarp, *Letter to the Philippians*, 6, in Holmes, 213; *ANF*, 1:34. Note that Polycarp is addressing elders as those who visit the sick and care for the poor.

12. Clement, *Letter of the Romans to the Corinthians*, 44, in Holmes, 79; *ANF*, 1:17.

13. Irenaeus, *Against Heresies*, 2.2 and 3.2, in *ANF*, 1:415.

14. Cyprian, *Letter 40.1*, in *ANF*, 5:319.

15. Cyprian, *Letter 5.4*, in *ANF*, 5:283.

16. Jerome's reference is to Titus 1:5–9 and 1 Tim. 3:1–13. Jerome, *Letter 146, to Evangelus*, 1–2, in *NPNF*², 6:289. In another letter, Jerome argued on the same basis. *Letter 69, to Oceanus*, 3, in *NPNF*², 6:143. Also, in his commentary on Titus, Jerome urged: "If anyone thinks the opinion—that the bishops and presbyters are the same—to be not the view of Scripture but my own—let him study the words of the apostle to the Philippians."

bishop and presbyter/elder and called for "one bishop, together with the presbytery and the deacons, my fellow servants" to lead the churches.[17] In one sense, both the bishop and elders exercised authority over the church,[18] which meant practically that "as the Lord did nothing without the Father, either by himself or through the apostles (for he was united with him), so you [the church] must not do anything without the bishop and the presbyters."[19] However, Ignatius also elevated the office of bishop over that of elder; the position of deacon was under both of these offices. He set up a parallel: "Be eager to do everything in godly harmony, the bishop presiding in the place of God and the presbyters in the place of the council of the apostles and the deacons."[20] Thus, a three-tiered hierarchy featuring one bishop, elders, and deacons was erected.

BISHOP
(one)

ELDERS
(plurality)

DEACONS
(plurality)

Unity with and obedience to the bishop was indispensable.[21] Indeed, because he exercised such authority, the bishop was to be the rallying point for all the activities of the church. Without his supervision and approval, the church could do nothing:

> You must all follow the bishop, as Jesus Christ followed the Father, and follow the presbytery as you would the apostles; respect the deacons as the commandment of God. Let no one do anything that has to do with the church without the bishop. Only that Eucharist that is under the authority of the bishop (or whomever he himself designates) is to be considered valid. Wherever the bishop appears, there

17. Ignatius, *Letter to the Philadelphians*, 4, in Holmes, 179; *ANF*, 1:81. Cf. *Letter to the Magnesians*, 13: "Be eager … to be firmly grounded in the precepts of the Lord and the apostles … together with your most distinguished bishop and that beautifully woven spiritual crown which is your presbytery and the godly deacons." In Holmes, 157; *ANF*, 1:64.

18. Ignatius, *Letter to the Ephesians*, 2, in Holmes, 139; *ANF*, 1:50. Cf. *Letter to the Ephesians*, 20: "Continue to gather together … in order that you may obey the bishop and the presbytery with an undisturbed mind." In Holmes, 149–51; *ANF*, 1:57.

19. Ignatius, *Letter to the Magnesians*, 7, in Holmes, 155; *ANF*, 1:62.

20. Ibid., 6, in Holmes, 153; *ANF*, 1:61. He changes the parallelism in his *Letter to the Trallians*, 2: "For when you are subject to the bishop as to Jesus Christ, it is evident to me that you are living not in accordance with human standards but in accordance with Jesus Christ…. It is essential, therefore, that

you continue your current practice and do nothing without the bishop, but be subject also to the presbytery as to the apostles of Jesus Christ, our hope…. Furthermore, it is necessary that those who are deacons of the 'mysteries' of Jesus Christ please everyone in every respect…. Similarly, let everyone respect the deacons as Jesus Christ, just as they should respect the bishop, who is a model of the Father, and the presbyters as God's council and as the band of the apostles. Without these no group can be called a church." In Holmes, 160–61; *ANF*, 1:66–67.

21. "I congratulate you who are united with him [the bishop], as the church is with Jesus Christ and as Jesus Christ is with the Father, that all things might be harmonious in unity…. Let us, therefore, be careful not to oppose the bishop, in order that we may be obedient to God…. It is obvious, therefore, that we must regard the bishop as the Lord himself." Ignatius, *Letter to the Ephesians*, 5–6, in Holmes, 139–41; *ANF*, 1:51.

let the congregation be; just as wherever Jesus Christ is, there is the catholic church. It is not permissible either to baptize or to hold a love feast without the bishop.[22]

In summary, by placing a single bishop over a church and urging submission to him in doctrine and church practice, Ignatius developed a structure that would counteract heresy and maintain church unity. Looking back at this development, Jerome underscored the reactive nature of the elevation of the office of bishop: "When subsequently one presbyter was chosen to preside over the rest, this was done to remedy schism and to prevent each individual from rending the church of Christ by drawing it to himself."[23] But this three-tiered structure overlooked the fact that the earliest churches founded by the apostles and others were governed by a plurality of bishops—also called elders or overseers—and deacons.

As the church developed in the third and fourth centuries, the threefold structure introduced by Ignatius became the standard government. Cyprian was a key contributor to this development when he was faced with the problem of a rival church founded by Novatian. Novatian and his followers separated from the Catholic Church because they considered it to have compromised the Christian faith.[24] Because this breakaway church was sound in its doctrine, Cyprian could not focus his attack against it on theological grounds. The unity of the church, which the Novatian schism had destroyed, could not only depend on holding to the true faith.

Cyprian's response centered on the office of the bishop as the key to the unity of the church. That is, if someone—like Novatian and his group—was not joined in harmony to the bishops of the Catholic Church, that person or group was heretical: "Whoever he may be, and whatever he may be, he who is not in the church of Christ is not a Christian.... He who has not maintained brotherly love or ecclesiastical [church] unity has lost even what he previously had been.... There is one church, divided by Christ throughout the whole world into many members, and also one episcopate diffused through a harmonious multitude of many bishops."[25]

---

22. Ignatius, *Letter to the Smyrnaeans*, 8, in Holmes, 190–91; *ANF*, 1:89. The Lord's Supper was administered in the context of a "love feast," so Ignatius's point was to prohibit the celebration of the supper apart from the bishop. Also, this is the first recorded use of the phrase "catholic church." At this point, it refers to the *universal* church, but it will soon come to be used to distinguish the *true* church—the (Roman) Catholic Church—from heretical groups. For further discussion of the Lord's Supper, see chap. 29.

23. Jerome, *Letter 146, to Evangelus*, 1, in *NPNF*[2], 6:288. In his commentary on Titus, Jerome was not so deferential to historical factors as the explanation for this development: "A presbyter ... is the same as a bishop, and before dissensions were introduced into religion by the instigation of the devil and it was said among the peoples, 'I am of Paul, I am of Apollos, and I of Cephas' [1 Cor. 1:12; cf. 3:4], churches were governed by a common council of the presbyters acting together; afterwards, when everyone thought that those whom he had baptized were his own, and not Christ's, it was decreed in the whole world that one chosen out of the presbyters should be placed over the rest, and to whom all care of the church should belong, that the seeds of schism might be plucked up [removed]." *Commentary on Titus*, 1.6–7, in John Harrison, *Whose Are the Fathers?* (London: Longmans, Green and Co., 1867), 488.

24. The issue at stake was the possibility of the restoration of Christians who had lapsed, or fallen, from the faith during the persecution of the church. Novatian and his party took a hard-line position: It was not possible to restore apostate believers to membership in the church. Cyprian and the Catholic Church held the opposite view: After sufficient confession of their sin of apostasy and penance for evil done, lapsed believers could be readmitted into the church. For this weak position, Novatian and his followers denounced the Catholic Church as compromising the faith. They broke from the Catholic Church and founded their own, more rigorist church.

25. Cyprian, *Letter* 51.24, in *ANF*, 5:333.

According to Cyprian's concept of the church, the office of bishop is foundational to the very existence of the church, so that without the episcopacy, there can be no church: "You ought to know that the bishop is in the church and the church is in the bishop; and if anyone is not with the bishop, that he is not in the church…. The church, which is catholic and one, is not cut nor divided, but is indeed connected and bound together by the cement of priests, who cohere with one another."[26] This essential role of the office of bishop was "founded on the divine law" as set forth by Jesus Christ himself in Matthew 16:18–19.[27] Moreover, the foundational nature of bishops means that Christians have to live in obedience to their authoritative government. Separation from them—and this was the case with Novatian and his renegade church—spells eternal disaster. Being apart from the church and obtaining salvation is like being outside of Noah's ark and not perishing in the flood—both are impossible. Cyprian made membership in the church necessary for salvation, and the church was none other than the Catholic Church with its bishops at its heart.

This elevation of the office of bishop also gained strength as the concept of the Christian ministry became more and more associated with the old covenant priesthood. As early as Clement of Rome, this parallel was found, forging a distinction between the clergy and the laity.[28] Cyprian referred to the ministry as "the office of our priesthood."[29] Three centuries later, the *Apostolic Constitutions* spelled out which offices of the church correspond to the various old covenant priestly positions, and the elevation of the office of bishop continued: "For these [the bishops] are your high priests, as the presbyters are your priests, and your present deacons instead [are in the place of] of your Levites; but he [Jesus Christ] who is above all these is the High Priest."[30]

As the high priest, the bishop was to be respected and obeyed,[31] and he was responsible for conducting the ministry of the church: "The bishop … is the minister of the word, the keeper of knowledge, the mediator between God and you in the several [various] parts of your divine worship. He is the teacher of piety; and, next after God, he is your father, who has begotten you again to the adoption of sons by water and the Spirit. He is your ruler and governor; he is your king and potentate [chief]."[32] Moreover, as high priest, the bishop had the sole right to ordain the other officers of the church: "We do not permit presbyters to ordain deacons, or deaconesses, or readers, or ministers, or singers, or porters, but only bishops [may ordain]; for this is ecclesiastical [church] order and harmony."[33] Oppositely, only bishops could remove members of the clergy (except in the case of a fellow bishop, who could not be dismissed by a bishop working alone).[34]

Still, at this point, the priests were chosen with the approval of the members of the church: "A people obedient to the Lord's precepts, and fearing God … have the power either of choosing worthy priests, or of rejecting unworthy ones. This very thing, too, we observe to come from divine authority, that the priest should be chosen in the presence

26. Cyprian, *Letter* 68.8, in *ANF*, 5:374–75.

27. Cyprian, *Letter* 26.1, in *ANF*, 5:305.

28. Clement, *Letter of the Romans to the Corinthians*, 40, in Holmes, 73; *ANF*, 1:16.

29. Cyprian, *Letter* 62.19, in *ANF*, 5:363.

30. *Apostolic Constitutions*, 2.4.25, in *ANF*, 7:410.

31. Ibid., 2.3.20, in *ANF*, 7:404.

32. Ibid., 2.4.26, in *ANF*, 7:410.

33. Ibid., 3.2.11, in *ANF*, 7:430.

34. Ibid., 8.3.28, in *ANF*, 7:494.

of the people under the eyes [in the sight] of all and he should be approved worthy and suitable by public judgment and testimony."[35] This practice was also observed in the selection of bishops: "For the proper celebration of ordinations, all the neighboring bishops of the same province [region] should assemble with that people for which a prelate [bishop] is ordained. And the bishop should be chosen in the presence of the people, who have most fully known the life of each one, and have looked into the doing [activities] of each one as respects his habit of life."[36] Thus, the bishop as high priest exercised the highest office in the church.

As the priests of the church, the elders (along with the bishops) had the responsibility to baptize: "We do not permit the rest of the clergy to baptize — for instance, readers, singers, porters, and ministers — but only the bishops and presbyters."[37] But the elders could not ordain, only bless (and receive the blessing from colleagues or their superior).[38]

As Levites, the deacons were not considered to be part of the priesthood; this consisted of the bishops and elders only. Rather, deacons were "ministers of their episcopacy (bishop) and of the church:"[39] "But the deacon is not ordained to the priesthood but to serve the bishop and to carry out the bishop's commands. He does not take part in the council of the clergy.... He receives only what is confided in him under the bishop's authority."[40] Thus, the deacon is to "minister to the bishop, as Christ does to his Father. Let the deacon serve him without blame in everything, as Christ does nothing of himself, but always does those things that please his Father."[41] Part of this was to ease the burden of the bishop: "Let the bishop judge the weighty matters. But let the deacon be the bishop's ear, eye, mouth, heart and soul. In this way, the bishop will not be distracted with trivial things but only the more considerable matters."[42] One key responsibility of the deacons was the distribution of the elements of the Lord's Supper: "He does not baptize, nor does he administer the Lord's Supper. But when a bishop or presbyter has administered the Supper, the deacon distributes the elements to the people, not as a priest but as one who ministers to the priests."[43] Deacons also had the responsibilities of caring for the weak and of doing visitation.[44]

Deaconesses also ministered to the church. Appealing to the example of Phoebe (Rom. 16:1–2), Origen offered biblical support for this ministry: "This text teaches ... two things: that there are ... women deacons in the church, and that women, who have given assistance to so many people and who by their good works deserve to be praised by the apostle, should be accepted in the diaconate."[45] A key requirement for serving in this capacity was to be a virgin or a (once married) widow.[46] Deaconesses were closely asso-

35. Cyprian, *Letter* 67.3–4, in *ANF*, 5:370.

36. Ibid., 67.5, in *ANF*, 5:371 (with reference back to *Letter* 67.4; in *ANF*, 5:370–71). The biblical basis cited for this selection process was Num. 20:25–26; Acts 1:15; and Acts 6:2.

37. *Apostolic Constitutions*, 3.2.11, in *ANF*, 7:430.

38. Ibid., 8.3.28, in *ANF*, 7:494.

39. Cyprian, *Letter* 64.3, in *ANF*, 5:366.

40. Hippolytus, *The Apostolic Tradition of Hippolytus*, 43.9, in Petry, 29.

41. *Apostolic Constitutions*, 2.4.26, in *ANF*, 7:410. The text

has been rendered clearer.

42. Ibid., 2.6.44, in *ANF*, 7:410. The text has been rendered clearer.

43. Ibid., 8.3.28, in *ANF*, 7:494. The text has been rendered clearer.

44. Ibid., 3.2.19, in *ANF*, 7:432.

45. Origen, *Commentary on the Epistle to the Romans*, 16:1–2, cited in Ruth Tucker and Walter Liefeld, *Daughters of the Church* (Grand Rapids: Zondervan, 1987), 106.

46. *Apostolic Constitutions*, 6.3.17, in *ANF*, 7:457.

ciated with the deacons and were to accompany women who had to talk with the male clergy: "Honor the deaconess in the place of the Holy Spirit. She should not do or say anything without the deacon, as the Comforter does not say or do anything of himself but gives glory to Christ by waiting for his pleasure. And as we cannot believe in Christ without the teaching of the Spirit, so do not let any woman address herself to the deacon or bishop without the deaconess."[47] An important reason for this duty was to avoid bringing reproach upon the church because of possible sexual scandal between the male clergy and women: "Ordain a deaconess who is faithful and holy for ministry toward women. For sometimes the bishop cannot send a deacon—who is a man—to the women on account of unbelievers. Therefore, send a woman—a deaconess—on account of the vain imaginations of the wicked."[48] They also were needed for "the baptism of women":

> The deacon will anoint only their forehead with the holy oil; afterwards, the deaconess will anoint them. For there is no necessity that the women should be seen by the men. Only in the laying on of hands will the bishop anoint her head. After that, either you the bishop or a presbyter who is under you will, according to the solemn rite, name over them the Father, Son, and Holy Spirit, and then dip them in the water. Then let a deacon receive the man [who has] been baptized and a deaconess receive the woman. In this way, the conferring of this unbreakable seal will take place with a proper decency.[49]

Thus, by the fourth century the church had become a highly organized, hierarchical institution with the responsibilities of its offices of bishop, elder, deacon, and deaconess specifically delineated. And the unity of the church was found to exist in its bishops, whose office was thus elevated and accorded great authority.

Another source of justification for the church hierarchy of bishops, priests, and deacons was found in the hierarchy that exists within the angelic realm. The early church's chief contributor to this notion was Dionysius the Pseudo-Areopagite. In a very influential book on angels entitled *The Celestial Hierarchy*, Dionysius set forth a threefold hierarchy within the heavenly realm; for Dionysius, this angelic hierarchy was the model after which God designed the church's hierarchy.[50] Accordingly, writing in his other important work, *The Ecclesiastical Hierarchy*, he emphasized that the perfect harmony, order, authority, and subordination that characterizes the angelic hierarchy is to typify the church's hierarchy as well. In practical terms, the power of the church is ultimately found in the bishop, the first and highest in its hierarchy, to whom the priests and deacons—not to mention the laity—are to submit.[51] By erecting this parallel between the celestial hierarchy and the ecclesiastical hierarchy, Dionysius did much to solidify the authority structure of the bishops over the priests and deacons in the church.

47. Ibid., 2.4.26, in *ANF*, 7:410. The text has been rendered clearer.

48. Ibid., 3.2 (between 15 and 16), in *ANF*, 7:431. The text has been rendered clearer.

49. Ibid. The text has been rendered clearer.

50. Dionysius the Pseudo-Areopagite, *The Celestial Hierarchy*, 1.3, in *Pseudo-Dionysius: The Complete Works*, trans. Colm Luibheid and Paul Rorem (New York: Paulist, 1987), 146.

51. Dionysius the Pseudo-Areopagite, *The Ecclesiastical Hierarchy*, 5.5–6, in Luibheid and Rorem, *Pseudo-Dionysius*, 236.

EXCURSUS: THE EARLY DEVELOPMENT OF THE PAPACY

One of the most important developments in the maturing of the hierarchical government in the Catholic Church was the elevation of the bishop of Rome to a position of supremacy among the other bishops. A key point of departure for this evolution was a debate (254–56) between Cyprian, the bishop of Carthage, and Stephen, the bishop of Rome, over the Novatian schism. As we have seen, Cyprian opposed the Novatianists by underscoring that their separation from the Catholic Church placed them outside of the realm of salvation. As a consequence of this division—so Cyprian argued—the administration of the sacraments performed by the ministers of the Novatian churches was invalid. Thus, the baptism of the members of the Novatian churches was worthless. Should any Novatianists convert and desire to enter the Catholic Church, they would have to undergo Catholic baptism.

Stephen took the opposite position. He held that as long as the sacraments were performed according to Christian form, they were valid. Thus, even if people were baptized in the Novatian churches by Novatian ministers, their baptism brought them God's grace. Should any Novatianists convert and desire to enter the Catholic Church, they would not have to undergo Catholic baptism.

In debating the merits of their differing positions on this issue, both bishops appealed to Peter's confession (Matt. 16:15–19). According to Cyprian, this passage demonstrated that Jesus Christ had given authority to his church, and this authority rested in all his apostles—together with their successors, the bishops—as a unity.[52] This Christ-conferred authority was shared equally by the bishops, who act in unity.[53] Still, each bishop was responsible for his own jurisdiction.[54] According to Cyprian, then, the bishop of Rome had responsibility for the ministry of his own church, but he did not exercise any authority over church matters in North Africa. Stephen interpreted the Matthean passage in a very different way. He believed that Jesus had conferred a unique authority on the apostle Peter and his successors. Thus, the bishop of the Church of Rome held the position of primacy among all the other bishops of the world. In the matter at hand, Stephen demanded on this basis that Cyprian submit to him. As the chief bishop, Stephen had the authority to decide the controversy about the baptism of heretics.

52. He argued this interpretation by combining Matt. 16:15–19 with two verses from the gospel of John: "After his resurrection, the Lord again says to Peter, 'Feed my sheep' (John 21:15). Certainly, he gives an equal authority to all the apostles after his resurrection when he says, 'As the Father has sent me, even so I send you. Receive the Holy Spirit. If you forgive anyone his sins, they will be forgiven; and if you retain anyone's sins, they will be retained' (John 20:21). Still, in order to set forth unity, he arranged by his authority the origin of that unity as beginning from one. Certainly the rest of the apostles were also the same as Peter was, gifted with an equal partnership of both honor and authority; but the beginning proceeds from unity." Cyprian, *Treatise* 1.4: "On the Unity of the Church," in *ANF*, 5:422. The text has been rendered clearer.

53. Ibid., treatise 1.5, in *ANF*, 5:423.

54. Cyprian, *Letter* 51.21, in *ANF*, 5:332; cf. *Letter* 71.3., in *ANF*, 5:379. "In the leadership of the church, each bishop exercises his free will, for he will give an account of his conduct to the Lord.". The text has been rendered clearer.

Cyprian refused to submit. He disputed Stephen's contention that Peter was the chief apostle.[55] Thus, the bishop of Rome appealed to Matthew 16 as a proof text for his place of primacy among all the bishops. But those other bishops, while acknowledging the importance of Peter, would not concede any place of honor to his successors. The unity of the church existed because of the equality of all the bishops of the world.

As the number of churches increased, the bishops of five key cities — Alexandria (Egypt), Rome, Antioch (Syria), Jerusalem, and Constantinople — gained authority over the churches in their geographical area.[56] For both historical and administrative reasons, these five cities became the patriarchies, or major centers, of Christianity. Alexandria was the home of the famous catechetical school featuring the theologians Clement and Origen. Antioch was the first Gentile church, the place from which the apostle Paul had embarked on his missionary journeys. Jerusalem was the "mother city" of the faith. Rome and Constantinople were the imperial cities.

Given the inherent instability of such a structure, it was not long before disagreement broke out concerning the equality or superiority of the five bishops. According to the Council of Constantinople (381), "The bishop of Constantinople ... shall have the prerogative (primacy) of honor after the bishop of Rome; because Constantinople is New Rome."[57] Thus, the ranking of importance was Rome, followed by Constantinople, followed by the other three. The Council of Chalcedon (451), attempting to clarify the Council of Constantinople's decision, affirmed the *equality* of position and authority of the bishops of Rome and Constantinople.[58] Of course, the Church of Rome rejected this clarification.

The elevation of Peter and his successors — the bishops of Rome — had developed gradually during the early centuries of Christianity. For example, Irenaeus called attention to the importance of "the very great, the very ancient, and uni-

---

55. "We refute this by reason. For Peter — whom the Lord chose first and upon whom he built his church — did not proudly claim anything to himself, when Paul later disputed with him about circumcision. Nor did he arrogantly assume anything, so as to say that he held the primacy and that he needed to be obeyed by novices and those who had become apostles after him." Cyprian, *Letter* 70.3, in *ANF*, 5:377. The text has been rendered clearer.

56. The Council of Nicea in 325 discussed Alexandria, Rome, and Antioch: "Let the ancient customs prevail which are in Egypt and Libya and Pentapolis, according to which the bishop of Alexandria has authority over all these places. For this is also customary to the bishop of Rome. In like manner in Antioch and in the other provinces, the privileges are to be preserved in the churches." Council of Nicea, canon 6, in *Documents Illustrating Papal Authority, A.D. 96–454*, ed. E. Giles (London: SPCK, 1952), 93. Cf. *NPNF*[2], 14:15 To these three cities were later added Jerusalem and Constantinople.

57. Council of Constantinople, canon 3, in *NPNF*[2], 14:178.

58. "We, following in all things the decisions of the holy fathers, and acknowledging the canon of the one hundred and fifty most religious bishops which has just been read, do also determine and decree the same things respecting the privileges of the most holy Church of Constantinople, New Rome. For the fathers properly gave the primacy to the throne of the elder Rome, because that was the imperial city. And the one hundred and fifty most religious bishops, being moved with the same intention, gave equal privileges to the most holy throne of New Rome, judging with reason, that the city which was honored with the sovereignty and senate, and which enjoyed equal privileges with the elder royal Rome, should also be magnified like her in ecclesiastical [church] matters, being the second after her." The Canons of Chalcedon on the Church of Constantinople, canon 28, in *Creeds, Councils, and Controversies: Documents Illustrating the History of the Church A.D. 337–461*, ed. James Stevenson (London: SPCK, 1972), 333.

versally known church founded and organized at Rome by the two most glorious [famous] apostles, Peter and Paul.... For it is a matter of necessity that every church should agree with this church, on account of its preeminent authority, that is, the faithful everywhere, inasmuch as the apostolic tradition has been preserved continuously by those [faithful men] who exist everywhere [in the church of Rome] that no one would dare dispute its judgment."[59] Damasus, bishop of Rome from 366 to 384, asserted that the ecumenical creeds possessed authority because they were endorsed by the bishop of Rome. Zosimus (417–18)[60] appealed to church tradition that "has assigned such great authority to the apostolic see [the church in Rome] that no one would dare dispute its judgment."[61] Leo the Great (440–61) elevated Peter to a position of great height, focusing on him as the key to Christ's ministry in his church.[62] Indeed, it was through Peter that Christ transferred his authority to the apostles.[63] Furthermore, according to Leo, Peter continues to exercise this mediating role in the church through the bishop of Rome.[64] Gelasius (492–96) claimed that God had willed that the Roman bishop was "to be preeminent over all other bishops."[65] During the tenure of Gregory the Great (590–604), the term *pope* was applied almost exclusively to the Roman bishop. Gregory himself argued that the bishop of Rome exercised supreme authority throughout the world.[66] Thus, these early Roman bishops contributed to the development of the supremacy of the bishop of Rome.

FORMS OF CHURCH GOVERNMENT IN THE MIDDLE AGES

Being so well established with theological justification and after centuries of use, the three-tiered hierarchical structure continued with little change into and throughout the Middle Ages. By far the most important development in church government was the expansion of the powers of the papacy. The height of papal power was reached during the reign

59. Irenaeus, *Against Heresies*, 3.3.2, in *ANF*, 1:415–16.

60. The following men were all bishops of Rome whose tenure as bishop is indicated by the dates.

61. Zosimus, *The Indisputable Authority of the Roman See: Letter 12 to Aurelius and the Council of Carthage*, 1, in Giles, *Documents Illustrating Papal Authority*, 212.

62. Leo the Great, *Sermon 4.2*, in Giles, *Documents Illustrating Papal Authority*, 279.

63. "It was not in vain that what was imparted to all was entrusted to one.... In Peter the strength of all is fortified, and the help of divine grace is so ordered that the stability that is given to Peter through Christ is conveyed to the apostles through Peter." Leo the Great, *Sermon 4.3*, in Giles, *Documents Illustrating Papal Authority*, 279. The text has been rendered clearer.

64. Leo the Great, *Sermon 5.4*, in Giles, *Documents Illustrating Papal Authority*, 281–82.

65. Gelasius, *To the Emperor Anastasius*, in Eric G. Jay, *The Church: Its Changing Image through Twenty Centuries*, vol. 1: *The First Seventeen Centuries* (London: SPCK, 1977), 98.

66. "Certainly Peter, the first of the apostles, himself a member of the holy and universal church, Paul, Andrew, John—what were they but heads of particular communities?... Was it not the case, as your fraternity knows, that the leaders of the apostolic see, which by the providence of God I serve, had the honor offered them of being called universal?" Gregory the Great, *Letter 18*.

of Pope Innocent III (1198–1216), who articulated the superiority of the papacy to the emperor in an allegorical commentary on Genesis 1:14–18. [67]

The unbounded papal superiority over the state claimed by Innocent III would not continue unchallenged by the secular leaders. Less than a century later, Boniface VIII (1294–1303) attempted to intervene in national affairs to prevent the kings of England and France (countries locked in incessant warfare with each other) from taxing the clergy of their lands to raise money for war. Boniface threatened that any government official "who shall impose, exact, or receive [taxes from the church] ... should [would] incur the sentence of excommunication."[68] As might be anticipated, both Edward I of England and Philip IV of France were deeply offended by the pope's prohibition and defied him.

Boniface responded by reiterating papal supremacy. For support, he appealed to various biblical passages and images,[69] the most interesting of which was an allegorical reference to the two swords brandished when Jesus was taken captive at the garden of Gethsemane (Luke 22:38; John 18:11). In bitter response, Philip IV sent an emissary, William of Nogaret, and a mob of mercenaries to capture Boniface and force him to resign his papacy. Although rescued by sympathizers, Boniface VIII died several weeks later. After a brief interim papacy that was followed by lengthy indecision as to whom to elect, Clement V was chosen pope by a pro-French minority. At Philip IV's urging, Clement moved the papacy to Avignon in France, thus initiating what came to be called the "Babylonian captivity of the church."[70] For nearly seventy years, the papacy was characterized by waging war, luxurious living, extravagant spending, and immorality, and became little more than a puppet in the hands of French kings.

Pope Boniface VIII's Claim of Papal Superiority

And we learn from the words of the gospel that in this church and in her power are two swords, the spiritual and the temporal. For when the apostles said, "Behold, here" (that is, in the church, since it was the apostles who spoke) "are two swords"—the Lord did not reply, "It is too much," but "It is enough" [Luke 22:38]. Truly he who denies that the temporal sword is in the power of Peter, misunderstands the words of the Lord, "Put up your sword into the sheath" [John 18:11]. Both are in the power of the church, the spiritual and the material. But the latter is to be used for the church, the former by it; the former by the priest, the latter by kings and captains but at the will and the permission of the priest. The one sword, then, should be under the other, and temporal authority subject to spiritual. For when the apostle says, "there is no power but

---

67. Pope Innocent III, "Letter to Acerbius" (1198), in Bettenson, 123 (in which the document is entitled "The Moon and the Sun").

68. Pope Boniface VIII, *Clericis Laicos* (February 25, 1296), in Bettenson, 124–25.

69. Song 6:9; the ark of Noah; Ps. 22:20; John 10:16; 19:23; 21:16. Boniface VIII, *Unam Sanctam* (1302), in Jay, *The Church*, 1:110–11.

70 0. This disparaging title was a reference to the seventy-year captivity suffered by the people of Israel in Babylonia from 605 to 537 BC. Martin Luther would pick up on this disastrous period in the church's history in his polemical anti-Catholic writing *The Babylonian Captivity of the Church* (1520).

of God, and the powers that be are ordained by God" [Rom. 13:1], they would not be so ordained were not one sword made subject to the other.... Furthermore, we declare, state, define and pronounce that it is altogether necessary to salvation for every human creature to be subject to the Roman pontiff.*

*Boniface VIII, *Unam Sanctam* (1302), in Bettenson, 126–27. Boniface cemented his case by appealing to a prophecy of Jeremiah, Paul's instructions, and Jesus' words: "Thus, concerning the church and her power, is the prophecy of Jeremiah fulfilled, 'See, I have this day set you over the nations and over the kingdoms' [Jer. 1:10], etc. If, therefore, the earthly power err, it shall be judged by the spiritual power; and if a lesser power err, it shall be judged by a greater. But if the supreme power err, it can only be judged by God, not by man; for the testimony of the apostle is 'The spiritual man judges all things, yet he himself is judged by no man' [1 Cor. 2:15]. For this authority, although given to a man and exercised by a man, is not human, but rather divine, given at God's mouth to Peter and established on a rock for him and his successors in him whom he confessed, the Lord saying to Peter himself, 'Whatsoever you shall bind,' etc. [Matt. 16:19]. Whoever therefore resists this power thus ordained of God, resists the ordinance of God [Rom. 13:2]."

It was not until the last year of his reign (1378) that Pope Gregory XI succeeded in transferring the Catholic hierarchy back to Rome. While restoring the papacy to its home, this move did little to resolve the church's problems. Upon Gregory's death in that year, the cardinals who gathered in conclave in Rome to elect his successor were disrupted by unruly mobs of Romans who insisted that an Italian cardinal be chosen. They got their wish: Urban VI, an Italian, was elected pope. His manic personality alienated him from the rest of the hierarchy, however, and the French cardinals pronounced his election invalid. In his place, they elected Clement VII. Urban refused to comply with his deposition by the French cardinals and forcefully inserted himself in Rome, leaving Clement little option but to take his papacy back to Avignon (1379).

Now the church had two popes, and the various countries of Europe sided with one pope or the other. This period (1378–1417) became known as the "Great Schism" and found the church almost hopelessly divided. Although several solutions were unsuccessfully proposed and attempted, the schism was widened when the Council of Pisa (1409) deposed both the pope in Rome and the pope in Avignon and elected Pope Alexander V in their place. Neither deposed pope accepted the council's decision, so instead of two popes, the church now had three. Then Alexander died after only ten months as pope. The Council of Constance (1414–18) was convened as another attempt to end the schism and reform the church. After deposing both the Roman pope and Avignon pope, the council elected Martin V, declaring "that all men, of every rank and condition, including the pope himself, is bound to obey it [the council] in matters concerning the faith, the abolition of the schism, and the reformation of the Church of God in its head and its members."[71] Thus, the conciliar movement was launched in the Roman Catholic Church, a movement that was characterized by the view that general church

71. Council of Constance, *Sacrosanta* (April 1415), in Bettenson, 149.

councils, rather than the papacy, exercise supreme authority in the church. This development broke significantly with the papal-dominated model of the church prevalent in the preceding centuries.

Although elected by the Council of Constance, thus ending the Great Schism, Martin refused to submit to *Sacrosancta* and its proclamation of the supremacy of general church councils above the papacy. He was constrained by the conciliar declaration *Frequens* (1415) — which required the frequent convening (every five years) of a general council — to call the Council of Pavia/Siena (1424–25); yet, he himself refused to attend. After a series of reforming councils — Basel (1431), Ferrara (1438), and Florence (1439) — and the weakening of the papacy, Pope Pius II issued a declaration that made appeals to general church councils illegitimate.[72] These and other developments resulted in the end of the conciliar movement. The Roman Catholic Church would continue to be led by a pope with broad powers and sweeping authority.

Significant people strongly objected to this accumulation of power, wealth, and prestige by the church and its leaders. One such critic was John Wycliffe, who sought to rectify the decrepit state of church leadership by proposing an alternative model focused on "the holiness of the pastor and the wholesomeness of his teaching."[73] As for pastoral holiness, Wycliffe urged that pastors should live frugally, supported exclusively by the giving of their church members. Concerning the teaching ministry, Wycliffe emphasized that "the special office of the pastor seems that of sowing the Word of God among his sheep."[74] In a startling statement, Wycliffe asserted: "Preaching the gospel exceeds prayer and administration of the sacraments, to an infinite degree.... Spreading the gospel has far wider and more evident benefit; it is thus the most precious activity of the church."[75] Despite the many protests lodged against it, the medieval Roman Catholic Church continued to be characterized by a hierarchical government with the papacy at its head.

FORMS OF CHURCH GOVERNMENT IN THE REFORMATION AND POST-REFORMATION

In establishing his churches, Martin Luther's main concern was to distance Lutheran congregations from the Roman Catholic structure and its elevation of the pope as supreme ruler over all Christian churches. In setting forth seven marks that distinguish a true church from the false (Catholic) church, he included the office of ministry:

---

72. "There has sprung up in our time an execrable abuse, unheard of in earlier ages, namely that some men, imbued with the spirit of rebellion, presume to appeal to a future council from the Roman pontiff, the Vicar of Jesus Christ, to whom in the person of blessed Peter it was said, 'Feed my sheep' [John 21:17] and 'Whatsoever you shall bind on earth shall be bound in heaven' [Matt. 16:19]. And that not from a desire for a sounder judgment but to escape the penalties of their misdeeds. Anyone who is not wholly ignorant of the laws can see how this contravenes the sacred canons and how detrimental it is to Christendom. And is it not plainly absurd to appeal to what does not now exist and the date of whose future existence is unknown? Wishing therefore to cast out from the church of God this pestilent poison and to take measures for the safety of the sheep committed to our care, and to ward off from the sheepfold of our Savior all that may offend ... we condemn appeals of this kind and denounce them as erroneous and detestable." Pope Pius II, *Execrabilis* (January 1460), in Bettenson, 150.

73. John Wycliffe, *On the Pastoral Office*, 1.1, LCC, 14: 32.

74. Ibid., 2.1, LCC, 14:48.

75. Ibid., 2.2, LCC, 14:49.

Fifth, the church is recognized externally by the fact that it consecrates or calls ministers, or has offices that it is to administer. There must be bishops, pastors, or preachers, who publicly and privately give, administer, and use the previously mentioned four things [the preaching of the Word of God, the administration of baptism, the administration of the Lord's Supper, and the exercise of church discipline] or holy possessions on behalf of and in the name of the church, or rather by reason of their institution by Christ.[76]

He emphasized that these bishops or pastors were to be called by God and chosen by the church.[77] Giving themselves to spiritual responsibilities, bishops should not be about the matters of the civil government and disturbingly mingle together "the ecclesiastical power and the power of the sword."[78] Besides these general comments, Luther did not offer a developed doctrine of church government. In those areas that became Lutheran during the Reformation, the churches were led by bishops. The state-church relationship that had typified those areas when they were under the Roman Catholic Church continued. Thus, for example, the Scandinavian countries forced the Catholic bishops from their church posts and replaced them with Lutheran bishops.

In transforming the government of the church in Geneva, Switzerland, John Calvin underscored the fact that God could have chosen to rule directly over the church.[79] Yet God opted to govern the church through ministers in order to foster humility, godliness, obedience, teachability, mutual love, and unity.[80] As his biblical basis for church government, Paul's list of apostles, prophets, evangelists, pastors, and teachers (Eph. 4:11) served Calvin well: "Of these, only the last two have an ordinary office in the church; the Lord raised up the first three at the beginning of his kingdom, and now and again revives them as the need of the times demands."[81] He therefore focused on pastors and teachers, and the "difference between them: teachers are not put in charge of discipline, or adminis-

---

76. Martin Luther, *On the Councils and the Church*, LW, 41:154.

77. "No bishop should institute anyone without the election, will, and call of the congregation. Rather, he should confirm the one whom the congregation chose and called." *That a Christian Assembly or Congregation Has the Right and Power to Judge All Teaching and to Call, Appoint, and Dismiss Teachers: Established and Proved by Scripture*, LW, 39:312.

78. *Augsburg Confession*, 2.7, in Schaff, 3:59.

79. John Calvin, *Institutes of the Christian Religion*, 4.3.1, LCC, 2:1053.

80. Ibid., LCC, 2:1054. Calvin issued a clear warning against parishioners who despised the teaching of the Bible through divinely appointed ministers: "Those who think the authority of the Word is dragged down by the baseness of the men called to teach it disclose their own ungratefulness. For, among the many excellent gifts with which God has adorned the human race, it is a singular privilege that he deigns to consecrate to himself the mouths and tongues of men in order that his voice may resound in them. Let us accordingly not

in turn dislike to embrace obediently the doctrine of salvation put forth by his command and by his own mouth. For, although God's power is not bound to outward means, he has nonetheless bound us to this ordinary manner of teaching. Fanatical men, refusing to hold fast to it, entangle themselves in many deadly snares. Many are led either by pride, dislike, or rivalry to the conviction that they can profit enough from private reading and meditation; hence they despise public assemblies and deem preaching superfluous. But, since they do their utmost to sever or break the sacred bond of unity, no one escapes the just penalty of this unholy separation without bewitching himself with pestilent errors and foulest delusions. In order, then, that pure simplicity of faith may flourish among us, let us not be reluctant to use this exercise of religion which God, by ordaining it, has shown us to be necessary and highly approved." Ibid., 4.1.5, LCC, 2:1018.

81. Ibid., 4.3.4, LCC, 2:1056. Today many biblical scholars acknowledge that the final two nouns—*pastors* and *teachers*—actually refer to one and the same office: pastor-teachers.

tering the sacraments, or warnings and exhortations, but only of Scriptural interpretation—to keep doctrine whole [sound] and pure among believers. But the pastoral office includes all these functions within itself."[82] *Teachers*—Calvin also called them *doctors*—focus on educating people in the Bible and good theology. Much of their work was done in the school system in Geneva. *Pastors* are called by God and affirmed by the congregation: "This call of a minister is lawful according to the Word of God, when those who seemed fit are created by the consent and approval of the people; moreover, other pastors ought to preside over the election in order that the multitude may not go wrong either through fickleness, through evil intentions, or through disorder."[83] As pastors, they engage in preaching the Word in the church, baptizing people, conducting the Lord's Supper, and carrying out church discipline. Those who exercise these responsibilities could be called "*bishops, presbyters, pastors and ministers*, according to Scriptural usage, which interchanges these terms."[84] Calvin thus broke with the three-tiered *episcopalian* government of the Catholic Church. According to Calvin's concept, the presbyters rule the church; thus, his system is called *presbyterian* government.

To the offices of pastor and teacher (or doctor), Calvin added two others (based on Rom. 12:7–8 and 1 Cor. 12:28): "government and caring for the poor."[85] *Elders* engage in the first of these roles: Together with the pastors, they have the responsibility of exercising church discipline.[86] Every Thursday the Consistory of Geneva was convened and the pastors and elders together judged the cases of immorality, neglect of church attendance, prayers to Mary, family disputes, and the like.[87] *Deacons* were in charge of caring for the poor and were of two types: "deacons who distribute the alms [money]" and deacons who devote themselves "to the care of the poor and sick.... [T]here will be two kinds of deacons: one to serve the church in administering the affairs of the poor; the other, in caring for the poor themselves."[88] The efforts of the deacons were highly successful: they managed the hospital, aided the thousands of refugees fleeing to Geneva from religious persecution throughout Europe, and provided for the needs of the poor.[89]

Following Calvin's ecclesiology, the *Westminster Confession of Faith* further defined church government, calling for "assemblies as are commonly called synods or councils.... It is their ministerial prerogative to determine controversies concerning the faith and cases of conscience; to set down rules and directions for the better ordering of the

---

82. Ibid., LCC, 2:1057.

83. Ibid., 4.3.15, LCC, 2:1066.

84. Ibid., 4.3.8, LCC, 2:1060. Calvin appealed to the synonymous use of the terms *bishops* and *presbyters* in Titus 1:5–7 and Acts 20:17, 28. Furthermore, commenting on the historical distinction between the offices of bishop and presbyter or elder, Calvin appealed to Jerome (cited earlier). Ibid., 4.4.2, LCC, 2:1069.

85. Ibid., 4.3.8, LCC, 2:1061.

86. "Governors were, I believe, elders chosen from the people, who were charged with the censure of morals and the exercise of discipline along with the bishops. Each church, therefore, had from its beginning a senate, chosen from godly, serious and holy men, which had jurisdiction over the correct-

ing of faults." Ibid., LCC, 2:1061.

87. A new multi-volume series, containing the transcripts of the consistory's meetings, beginning in 1542, is scheduled for publication. For those who are unfamiliar with church discipline, or who simply want an intimate look at the life of common people in Geneva in the sixteenth century, this makes fascinating reading. David Kingdon, gen. ed., *The Registers of the Consistory of Geneva at the Time of Calvin, Volume 1:1542–1544* (Grand Rapids: Eerdmans, 2000).

88. Calvin, *Institutes*, 4.3.9, LCC, 2:1061.

89. For another discussion by Calvin on these four offices, see *Draft Ecclesiastical Ordinances* (September and October 1541), LCC, 22: 58–66.

public worship of God, and government of his church; to receive complaints in cases of wrong administration and to determine authoritatively such cases."[90] More specifically, the *Westminster Assembly Directory for Church Government* made a distinction between different levels of church government:

SYNOD
(national level)

———————————

CLASSIS
(regional level)

———————————

PRESBYTERY
(local level)

At the local church level, the *Directory* called for the government of a *presbytery*. At a regional level involving many churches, the *Directory* called for the government of a *classis*. At the national level, it called for the government of a *synod*.[91]

Yet another development in church government occurred at this time. Spearheaded by the Anabaptists, this movement rejected the church-state reality of the Catholic Church and the new Protestant churches. In one sense, it can be seen as an early form of congregationalism, encouraging the establishment of individual congregations. The earliest expression of this was the Anabaptists' *Schleitheim Confession*, which described the office of pastor as having the responsibilities "to read, admonish and teach, warn, discipline, excommunicate from the church, lead in prayer for the advancement of all the brothers and sisters, serve communion, and in all things see to the care of the body of Christ, in order that it may be built up and developed, thereby silencing its detractors."[92] The *Confession* also emphasized the congregation's ordination and support of its own pastor.[93] With this development, the seeds of *congregational* government were sown.

In England, political and theological developments led to the rejection of the Roman Catholic Church and its replacement with the Anglican Church, or Church of England. King Henry VIII was incensed by the pope's refusal to grant him an annulment of his marriage to Catherine of Aragon. In retaliation, the king proclaimed that England had the right to decide such matters for itself. In 1531 Parliament recognized Henry as the "Supreme Head of the Church of England as far as the law of Christ allows."[94] By two acts passed by Parliament in 1534, the Church of England officially broke away from

---

90. *Westminster Confession of Faith*, 31, in Schaff, 3:668–69. The text has been rendered clearer.

91. *The Westminster Assembly Directory for Church Government* (1645, 1771), in *Paradigms in Polity: Classic Readings in Reformed and Presbyterian Church Government*, ed. David W. Hall and Joseph H. Hall (Grand Rapids: Eerdmans, 1994), 263.

92. *Schleitheim Confession*, art. 5, in Lumpkin, 27. The text has been rendered clearer.

93. The pastor will be "supported by the church which has chosen him, in whatever he may need, so that he who serves the gospel may live from the gospel, as the Lord has commanded. But should it happen that through the cross this pastor is banished or brought home to the Lord through martyrdom, another will be ordained in his place in the same hour so that God's little flock and people may not be destroyed." Ibid. The text has been rendered clearer.

94. *Convocation of 1531*, in Bettenson, 252.

Rome. One act denounced the pope's jurisdiction in England.[95] In the second act—*The Supremacy Act* of 1534—Parliament acknowledged that "the king's majesty justly and rightly is and ought to be the supreme head of the Church of England."[96]

Although the progress of the Reformation in England followed the ebb and flow of the theological leanings of the king or queen on the throne, Queen Elizabeth put her own impress on the Church of England. She combined Catholic and Protestant elements into the one church and maintained its separation from Rome. Although it still had an episcopalian government, the Anglican Church did not look to the pope as its leader. The archbishop of Canterbury was its highest church official, and the queen (or king) was its supreme governor.[97] This was incorporated into the *Thirty-nine Articles*.[98] Thus, the Church of England developed a Protestant episcopalian form of government.

Although this "middle way" solution of Queen Elizabeth satisfied the majority of the English people, an important minority remained quite dissatisfied with the Anglican Church. Because of their voiced opposition to the remnants of Roman Catholicism and their desire to purify the Church of England, they became known as the *Puritans*. One group of these insisted that the church should be completely separate from the state; they were called the *Separatists*. Another movement called for reform of the Anglican Church government along the lines of presbyterianism or congregationalism—a new structure of leadership that gave the members of the local congregation the responsibility for the church. This group was called the *Independents*.

Various separatist and independent congregations arose. For example, Robert Browne fled with his congregation from Norwich, England, to Holland about 1580 to escape persecution for his separatist views. He articulated his ideas for what would eventually become the congregational form of government. Two points emphasized that the members of each local church should choose their own officers and that, as an autonomous entity, each congregation should decide its own matters. Another example was the congregational assembly in Scrooby, England, headed by John Robinson. Also having been forced to flee to Holland, a portion of this group returned to England, embarked on the *Mayflower*, and set sail for America in 1620. The Pilgrims settled in Plymouth Colony and established congregationalism as the form of church government.

A third example was the first Baptist church that came into existence. Members of a separatist assembly—led by John Smyth and Thomas Helwys—from Gainsborough, England, fled to Holland in 1607. While in England, the church had practiced infant baptism, but influenced by some Anabaptists, this church changed its view of baptism and began administering this ordinance to believers only. Smyth wrote a short confession of faith (1609) in which he described a church government composed of two officers:

95. *Abjuration of Papal Supremacy by the Clergy*, 1, in Bettenson, 253.

96. *The Supremacy Act*, 1534, in Bettenson, 252. In 1531 the king had been recognized as the supreme head "as far as the law of Christ allows." With this *Supremacy Act* of 1534, that qualification was removed.

97. The *Supremacy Act* of 1559 recognized Elizabeth as "the only *supreme governor* [not *supreme head*, as the act of 1534 proclaimed] of this realm, and of all other her highness's dominions and countries, as well in all spiritual or ecclesiastical [church] things or causes, as [in all] temporal matters." Bettenson, 261.

98. *Thirty-nine Articles*, 37, in Schaff, 3:512–13.

"The ministers of the church are not only bishops ('*episcopos*'), to whom the power is given to dispense both the word and the sacraments, but also deacons, men and widows, who attend to the affairs of the poor and sick brothers."[99] Helwys's *Declaration of Faith* (1611) specified "that the officers of every church or congregation are either elders, who by their office do especially feed the flock concerning their souls (Acts 20:28; 1 Peter 5:2–3) or deacons, men and women who by their office relieve the necessities of the poor and impotent brothers concerning their bodies (Acts 6:1–4)."[100] Furthermore, Helwys urged that "these officers are to be chosen when there are persons qualified according to the rules in Christ's Testament (1 Tim. 3:2–7; Titus 1:6–9; Acts 6:3–4) by election and approbation of that church or congregation of which they are members (Acts 6:3–4 and 14:23) with fasting, prayer, and laying on of hands (Acts 13:3 and 14:23)."[101] When Helwys returned to England in 1611, he founded the first Baptist church in London. This church was a General Baptist church, being Arminian in theology. Other Particular Baptist churches, holding to a Calvinist theology, arose about this same time.

The number of Baptist churches in London increased, and in 1644 (modified, 1646) the *London Confession of Faith* of the Particular Baptists became their charter, setting forth congregationalism as their form of government: "Every church has power given them from Christ for their well-being, to choose among themselves qualified people for the office of elders and deacons, being qualified according to the Word, as those whom Christ has appointed in his testament for the feeding, governing, serving, and building up of his church. No one else has power to impose on them either these or any other leader."[102] The *Second London Confession of Faith* specified that "a local church, gathered and completely organized according to the mind of Christ, consists of officers and members. The officers appointed by Christ to be chosen and set apart by the church (so called and gathered) … are bishops or elders, and deacons."[103] The *Confession* stipulated that a qualified and gifted pastoral candidate is to "be chosen by the common vote of the church itself"; the same was true for a deacon.[104] Each local church was an independent congregation. Still, the *Confession* called for (nonauthoritative) representative assemblies beyond local church meetings for the purpose of resolving entrenched problems among church members and local churches.[105]

Of course, there were other Independents in England who were not Baptists. During the period of the Commonwealth of England under Oliver Cromwell (who was an Independent), a conference of independent ministers was convened to define their position. This group wrote *The Savoy Declaration of Faith and Order* in 1658. The statement embraced the *Westminster Confession of Faith* with an addendum setting forth the principles of congregationalism. These included the independence of each local church,[106] the right of each congregation to select its own officers, and the two church offices of

99. John Smyth, *A Short Confession of Faith in XX Articles* (1609), 16, in Lumpkin, 101. The text has been rendered clearer.

100. Thomas Helwys, *A Declaration of Faith of English People Remaining at Amsterdam in Holland* (1611), 21, in Lumpkin, 121–22. The text has been rendered clearer.

101. Ibid., in Lumpkin, 122. The text has been rendered clearer.

102. *London Confession of Faith*, 33, 36, in Lumpkin,

165–66. The text has been rendered clearer.

103. *Second London Confession of Faith*, 26.8, in Lumpkin, 287. The text has been rendered clearer.

104. Ibid., 26.9, in Lumpkin, 287. The text has been rendered clearer.

105. Ibid., 26.15, in Lumpkin, 289.

106. *The Savoy Declaration of Faith and Order*, "Of the Institution of Churches and the Order Appointed in Them by Jesus Christ," 4, 5, 6, in Bettenson, 330.

pastor/teacher elder and deacon.[107] Similarly, the Pilgrims in America drew up the *Cambridge Platform* (1648) for the churches in New England.[108] Through these developments, congregationalism became an established structure of church government alongside of episcopalianism and presbyterianism.

FORMS OF CHURCH GOVERNMENT IN THE MODERN PERIOD

One of the strongest supporters of Baptist congregationalism, A. H. Strong presented various arguments that the church should be "democratic or congregational": "proof from the duty of the whole church to preserve unity in its action" (Rom. 12:16; 1 Cor. 1:10; 2 Cor. 13:11); "proof from the responsibility of the whole church for maintaining pure doctrine and practice" (1 Tim. 3:15; Jude 3; Rev. 2–3); "proof from the committing of ordinances to the charge of the whole church to observe and guard" (Matt. 28:19–20; 1 Cor. 11:2, 23–24); "proof from the election by the whole church of its own officers and delegates" (Acts 1:23–26; 6:3–5; 13:2–3; 15:2, 4, 22, 30; 2 Cor. 8:19); and "proof from the power of the whole church to exercise discipline" (Matt. 18:17; 1 Cor. 5:4–5, 13; 2 Thess. 3:6, 14–15).[109] He explicitly opposed the episcopalianism of the Catholic Church[110] and refuted the state-church form of government.[111] In place of these two forms, Strong presented a case for congregational government with a single pastor leading the church. He noted that "in certain of the New Testament churches, there appears to have been a plurality of elders (Acts 20:17; Phil. 1:1; Titus 1:5)."[112] But he softened the impact of this fact: "There is, however, no evidence that the number of elders was uniform, or that the plurality which frequently existed was due to any other cause than the size of the churches for which these elders cared. The NT example, while it permits the multiplication of assistant pastors according to need, does not require a plural eldership in every case."[113] And Strong marshaled counterevidence for a single pastor as head of the church, pointing to biblical passages (Acts 12:17; 15:13; 21:18; Gal. 1:19; 2:12) that "seem to indicate that James was the only pastor or president of the church at Jerusalem"; the singular term "bishop" (NIV "overseer"; 1 Tim. 3:2; Titus 1:7) in contrast with the plural "deacons" (1 Tim. 3:8, 10, 12); the "angel of the church" (Rev. 2:1, 8, 12, 18; 3:1, 7, 14), which Strong took to be the (sole) pastor of those churches; and the unlikelihood that small churches could be required to have a plural eldership, which would be advantageous only in large churches.[114] Strong's position of congregational government with a single pastor leading the church exercised a great influence. Still, a movement developed

---

107. Ibid., 7, 9, in Bettenson, 330–31.

108. *Cambridge Platform*, 10.3, in *The Cambridge Platform: Contemporary Reader's Edition*, ed. Peter Hughes (Boston: Skinner House, 2008).

109. A. H. Strong, *Systematic Theology*, 3 vols. (Philadelphia: Judson, 1912), 3:904–8.

110. Ibid., 3:908–11. Strong's critique could also be taken to include presbyterianism, with its organizational structures

that have authority over local churches.

111. Ibid., 3:912–14.

112. Ibid., 3:915.

113. Ibid., 3:915–16.

114. Ibid. As Grudem points out, Strong's arguments are not very convincing when carefully analyzed and compared with other biblical data. Grudem, *Systematic Theology*, 928–31.

in some congregational churches to replace the solo pastor (with a board of deacons) model with a plurality-of-elders polity.[115]

Two Models of Leadership in Congregational Churches

PASTOR (solo)	ELDER ELDER ELDER
BOARD OF DEACONS	ELDER ELDER ELDER

| CONGREGATION | CONGREGATION |

In terms of modern defenders of the presbyterian form of church government, two are of note: Charles Hodge and Louis Berkhof. Hodge argued for presbyterianism on the basis of three key principles: "What we hold is that the leading principles laid down in Scripture regarding the organization and action of the church are the parity of the clergy, the right of the people [to participate in church government through their representatives, the elders], and the unity of the church."[116] Berkhof noted the problems of congregationalism: "This theory of popular government, making the office of the ministry altogether dependent on the action of the people, is certainly not in harmony with what we learn from the Word of God. Moreover, the theory that each church is independent of every other church fails to express the unity of the Church of Christ, has a disintegrating effect, and opens the door for all kinds of arbitrariness in church government."[117] Positively, he noted: "Reformed churches do not claim that their system of church government is determined in every detail by the Word of God, but do assert that its fundamental principles are directly derived from Scripture." Some of these principles are as follows: Christ is the head of the church and the source of all its authority, which authority he exercises by means of his Word; Christ has endowed the church with power and provided for the specific exercise of this authority by representative structures; and the authority of the church resides primarily in the governing body of the local church.[118] In terms of the major assemblies called for in the presbyterian system, Berkhof maintained that these should be composed of the ministers and elders of local churches who regularly come together as representatives from their churches. Such assemblies both provide visibility to the inner unity shared by local churches[119] and exercise jurisdiction over the doctrines and practices of those churches that they represent.[120]

---

115. E.g., Grudem advocated this position. Grudem, *Systematic Theology*, 932–35. Mark Dever also strongly endorsed this plurality-of-elders model. Mark Dever, *Nine Marks of a Healthy Church* (Wheaton: Crossway, 2004), 219–43.

116. Charles Hodge, *The Church and Its Polity*, chap. 8, in Hall and Hall, *Paradigms in Polity*, 451–53.

117. Louis Berkhof, *Systematic Theology* (Grand Rapids: Eerdmans, 1938), 580–81.

118. Ibid., 581–84. On this last point, Berkhof specified that "the power or authority of the church does not reside first of all in the most general assembly of any church, and is only secondarily and by derivation from this assembly, vested in the governing body of the local church; but that it has its original source in the consistory or session of the local church, and is by this transferred to the major assemblies."

119. Ibid., 590.

120. Ibid., 591.

All of these developments took place in historical Protestant denominations and must be viewed as slight variations on traditional church government doctrine and practice. The turn of the third millennium, however, witnessed several large shifts in these areas as well. One that took place in independent churches and denominations that feature congregational government, as well as in megachurches, was the remaking of church leadership structures along the lines of businesses or corporations. In this retooling, pastors became something like the chief operating officer (COO) of a company, and an important responsibility of theirs became that of managing a large team of staff members, who made the important decisions and ran the ministries of the church. Church growth experts, relying on business models of efficiency and marketing strategies that promote growth in number of customers, encouraged the dismantling of traditional (and biblical) leadership structures in favor of these new advances.[121]

Another significant shift was the development of multisite churches: "A multi-site church is one church meeting in multiple locations—different rooms on the same campus, different locations in the same region, or in some instances, different cities, states, or nations. A multi-site church shares a common vision, budget, leadership, and board."[122] As this definition indicates, this phenomenon is composed of several varieties of multisite churches: "For some churches, having multiple sites involves only a worship service at each location; for others, each location has a full range of support ministries. Some churches use video-cast sermons (recorded or live); others have in-person teaching on-site. Some churches maintain a similar worship atmosphere and style at all their campuses, and others allow or invite variation."[123] Claiming biblical, theological, historical, and missional support, this new polity developed among various kinds of churches and across denominational lines.[124]

Another important recent development in the church was the increasing role taken by women in leadership ministries in churches. True, women like Aimee Semple McPherson, founder of the International Foursquare Gospel Church, had been very active in such roles in Pentecostal churches from the beginning of the twentieth century. In fact, some denominations had begun to ordain women as pastors as early as the latter part of the nineteenth century: Methodist Episcopal Church (1869), Church of God (Anderson, Indiana; 1880), Christian Church/Disciples of Christ (1888), Church of the Nazarene (1908), Free Methodist Church (1911), International Foursquare Gospel Church (1927). But most long-established churches and denominations had minimized leadership opportunities for women until the latter half of the twentieth century. This changed

121. E.g., see Robert Schuller, *Your Church Has Real Possibilities!* (Glendale, Calif.: Regal, 1974).

122. Geoff Surratt, Greg Ligon, and Warren Bird, *The Multi-site Church Revolution* (Grand Rapids: Zondervan, 2006), 18.

123. Ibid.

124. Mark Driscoll and Gerry Breshears, *Vintage Church: Timeless Truths and Timely Methods* (Wheaton: Crossway, 2008), 243–63; Scott McConnell, *Multi-site Churches: Guidance for the Movement's Next Generation* (Nashville: Broad-

man, 2009); Geoff Surratt, Greg Ligon, and Warren Bird, *A Multi-Site Church Road Trip: Exploring the New Normal* (Grand Rapids: Zondervan, 2009); Thomas White and John M. Yeats, *Franchising McChurch: Feeding Our Obsession with Easy Christianity* (Colorado Springs: Cook, 2009), 151–66; Gregg R. Allison, "Theological Defense of Multi-site," *9Marks eJournal* 6, no. 3 (May–June 2009), www.9marks.org. Also see my forthcoming ecclesiology book to be published by Crossway for the Foundations of Evangelical Theology series.

when, in 1956, Methodists and Presbyterians began to ordain women to the ministry; these were the precursors of the United Methodist Church and the Presbyterian Church (USA). The first woman was ordained to ministry in a Southern Baptist church in 1964. The Episcopal Church granted such ordination beginning in 1976.[125] Some denominations have elected women as bishops. For example, the Episcopal Church elected Barbara C. Harris suffragan (assisting) bishop of Massachusetts in 1988.[126]

Many churches and denominations, however, have resisted women's ordination, both for theological reasons, such as the order of creation (Gen. 2),[127] and in application of biblical passages (e.g., 1 Cor. 14:33b–35; 1 Tim. 2:11–15).[128] For example, the Southern Baptist Convention's *Baptist Faith and Message* 2000 revision stated: "While both men and women are gifted for service in the church, the office of pastor is limited to men as qualified by Scripture."[129]

Among evangelicals, the debate over women in church leadership became an important issue, expressed by the formation of two divergent groups: The Council of Biblical Manhood and Womanhood (CBMW), representing the position called complementarianism, maintained that some governing and teaching responsibilities, usually associated with the office of pastor, are restricted to qualified men and are not open to women. The Council for Biblical Equality (CBE), representing the position called egalitarianism, insisted that such restrictions on women are illegitimate and that all ministries, including the office of pastor, are open to men and women alike.[130]

Churches in the third millennium have been challenged to consider seriously how they should be governed. While several diverse polities have characterized church history, new issues are giving rise to a growing number of new models of government in the contemporary scene. Relying on Scripture and tradition, together with cultural developments from both religious and secular sources, churches are changing how they are governed in unprecedented ways.

---

125. Actually, on July 29, 1974, at the Church of the Advocate in Philadelphia, four Episcopal bishops ordained eleven female deacons to the priesthood. One month later the Episcopal house of bishops censured this act: "That the House of Bishops ... express our understanding of their feelings and concern, but express our disagreement with their decision and action. We believe they were wrong; we decry their acting in violation of the collegiality of the House of Bishops, as well as the legislative process of the whole church." *Resolution on the Philadelphia Actions* (1974), cited in J. Gordon Melton, *The Churches Speak On: Women's Ordination* (Detroit: Gale Research, 1991), 64–65.

126. Various justifications for women's ordination have been offered. Some of these pointed to sociological developments ("an increasing cooperation between men and women in business, industry, government, professional life and the church"), including leadership opportunities for women. Others focused on biblical teaching, such as Galatians 3:28, the early church's employment of deaconesses, and theological considerations ("equality of status for men and women both in terms of their creation and their redemption") and their implications for ministry. *Report of the Special Committee on the Ordination of Women* (1955), in Melton, *The Churches Speak On: Women's Ordination*, 189.

127. E.g., *Women in the Church: Scriptural Principles and Ecclesial Practice* (1985), in Melton, *The Churches Speak On: Women's Ordination*, 142–43.

128. Ibid., 143–45.

129. *Baptist Faith and Message* (2000), "The Church."

130. John Piper and Wayne Grudem's edited volume *Recovering Biblical Manhood and Womanhood: A Response to Evangelical Feminism* (Wheaton: Crossway, 1991), along with the Council on Biblical Manhood and Womanhood's "Danvers Statement," became the classic expressions of the first view, while Ronald W. Pierce and Rebecca Merrill Groothuis's *Discovering Biblical Equality: Complementarity without Hierarchy* (Downers Grove, Ill.: InterVarsity, 2004) expressed the other position.

Chapter 28

BAPTISM

How has the church developed various views on the meaning and practice of baptism?

STATEMENT OF BELIEF

Baptism and the Lord's Supper are two rites that Jesus Christ himself commanded his church to perform. Historically, the church has been obedient to this command, celebrating both wherever it has existed. Among churches, however, significant disagreement exists over these rites. One disagreement concerns the term that should be applied to them. Some churches refer to baptism and the Lord's Supper as *sacraments*. The word *sacrament* (Latin *sacramentum*) is associated with the Greek term *mystery*; thus, these two rites are mysteries of the Christian faith. Other churches prefer to call them *ordinances* because baptism and the Lord's Supper were ordained by Christ for the church. For some Protestants, *ordinance* is also used in place of *sacrament* to distance the observance of these two rites from the Roman Catholic understanding that grace is actually conveyed to people through the administration of the sacraments.

A specific disagreement on the issue of baptism is *the mode of baptism*. Some churches administer baptism by sprinkling or pouring with water, while others immerse into water. Another disagreement is found over *the proper recipients of baptism*. Some churches usually confer baptism on infants, while others reserve baptism for those who can give a credible profession of faith in Christ.

Because division exists among believers on this issue, the various views on baptism will be traced throughout the history of the church to show how each perspective began and developed.[1]

BAPTISM IN THE EARLY CHURCH

Even before Jesus began his ministry, baptism was an important element in the Judaism of his time. Anyone who was not born a Jew yet wanted to follow the Jewish religion

---

1. My thanks to Isaac Sumner for his help on this chapter.

had to undergo a *proselyte baptism*.[2] The predecessor of Messiah was called John *the Baptist*; obviously, baptism was a key part of his preparatory ministry (Mark 1:4–5; Luke 3:16; John 1:31; 3:23). When Jesus began his messianic ministry, his first act was to be baptized by John (Matt. 3:13–17), and baptism was an important aspect of his ministry (John 4:1–2). After his resurrection, Jesus commissioned his disciples with the task of continuing his work. Again, baptism was to play an essential role in this endeavor (Matt. 28:19). The early church took seriously this responsibility to baptize. At Pentecost, at the end of his sermon, Peter urged the crowd: "Repent and be baptized, every one of you, in the name of Jesus Christ for the forgiveness of your sins. And you will receive the gift of the Holy Spirit" (Acts 2:38). The response was impressive: "Those who accepted his message were baptized, and about three thousand were added to their number that day" (Acts 2:41). This pattern of hearing and responding to the gospel accompanied by baptism was repeated throughout the early years of the church's expansion in the lives of various groups and individuals (from the book of Acts): Samaritans (8:12); an Ethiopian eunuch (8:36, 38); the persecutor Saul (9:18; 22:16); Gentiles (10:47–48; 11:16–17); a business-woman and her household (16:15); a jailer and his family (16:33); many Corinthians (18:8); a dozen disciples of John the Baptist (19:3–7). The missionary enterprise focused on repentance, faith in Christ, and baptism as the steps of initiation.

The earliest documents outside of our New Testament picture the continuing importance of baptism. Specifically, baptism was the initial rite of Christianity, followed by the Lord's Supper: "Let no one eat or drink of your Eucharist except those who have been baptized into the name of the Lord."[3] The *Didache* also provided this instruction:

> Concerning baptism, baptize as follows: after you have reviewed all these things [with those who are about to be baptized], baptize "in the name of the Father and of the Son and of the Holy Spirit" in running water [e.g., a river of cold water]. But if you have no running water, then baptize into some other water; and if you are not able to baptize in cold water, then do so in warm [e.g., a warm lake]. But if you have neither, then pour water upon the head three times "in the name of the Father and Son and Holy Spirit." And before the baptism, let the one baptizing and the one who is to be baptized fast, as well as any others who are able. Also, you must instruct the one who is to be baptized to fast for one or two days beforehand.[4]

Such was the instruction for the administration of baptism in the second century.

---

2. A *proselyte* is a new convert to a religion, philosophy, or way of life. Non-Jews (called Gentiles) who embraced the Jewish faith were proselytes, and part of their conversion process was proselyte baptism. As many scholars point out, the link between proselyte baptism and Christian baptism is a tenuous one. As Andreas Kostenberger concludes, "The early Church's practice of baptism cannot be adequately explained by, or accounted for, by appealing to proselyte baptism as a precedent. Apart from the question of whether or not proselyte baptism predates Christian baptism (which is far from certain), there are important theological distinctions in the way

in which baptism was conceived that makes a link between these two kinds of baptism tenuous at best and illegitimate at worst." Andreas J. Kostenberger, "Baptism in the Gospels," in Thomas R. Schreiner and Shawn D. Wright, *Believer's Baptism: Sign of the New Covenant*, New American Commentary Studies in Bible and Theology (Nashville: B&H Academic, 2007), 12–13. Cf. Scot McKnight, *A Light among the Gentiles: Jewish Missionary Activity in the Second Temple Period* (Minneapolis: Fortress, 1991), 82–85.

3. *Didache*, 9.5, in Holmes, 261; *ANF*, 7:380.

4. Ibid., 7, in Holmes, 259; *ANF*, 7:379.

How was baptism understood in the early church? Tertullian listed four purposes that baptism serves: (1) the forgiveness of sins, (2) deliverance from death, (3) regeneration, or the new birth, and (4) the gift of the Holy Spirit.[5] To this list, another two will be added: (5) the renunciation of Satan, and (6) identification with Jesus Christ. These themes were given different emphases by the various leaders during the first few centuries, but all six ends played a key role in the theology of baptism in the early church.

First, "in the baptism of water is received the forgiveness of sins."[6] Justin Martyr explained: "At our birth we were born without our own knowledge or choice.... In order that we may ... become the children of choice and knowledge, and may obtain in the water the forgiveness of sins previously committed, there is pronounced over him who chooses to be born again, and has repented of his sins, the name of God the Father and ... of Jesus Christ ... and of the Holy Spirit."[7] In keeping with this emphasis, Barnabas described the wonderful effect of baptism: "Blessed are those who, having set their hope on the cross, descended into the water.... While we descend into the water laden with sins and dirt, we rise up bearing fruit in our heart and with fear and hope in Jesus in our spirits."[8] So common and important was this link between baptism and forgiveness that it was engraved in the Nicene Creed: "I acknowledge one baptism for the forgiveness of sins."[9]

Second, baptism delivers from death: "Is it not wonderful, too, that death should be washed away by bathing?"[10] Cyprian noted this rescue from certain doom, "from that death which once the blood of Christ extinguished, and from which the saving grace of baptism and of our Redeemer has delivered us."[11] Another penalty from which baptism delivers is the judgment of hell, as Cyprian explained: "In the laver [bath] of saving water, the fire of Gehenna is extinguished."[12]

Third, baptism regenerates or brings the new birth: "'By the laver [bath] of regeneration' ... they were born 'as new-born babes.'"[13] Two biblical passages were appealed to in support of this effect of baptism. Citing Paul in Titus 3:5, Cyprian noted: "The blessed apostle sets forth and proves that baptism is the means by which the old man dies and the new man is born, saying, 'He saved us by the washing of regeneration.'"[14] By far the most common verse cited was John 3:5. Irenaeus, finding an analogy in Naaman, who

---

5. Tertullian, *Against Marcion*, 1.28, in *ANF*, 3:293.

6. Cyprian, *Treatise* 11.4, preface, in *ANF*, 5:497.

7. Justin Martyr, *First Apology*, 61, in *ANF*, 1:183.

8. *Letter of Barnabas*, 11, in Holmes, 305–7; *ANF*, 1:144.

9. Nicene Creed, in Schaff, 2:59.

10. Tertullian, *On Baptism*, 2, in *ANF*, 3:669.

11. Cyprian, *Letter* 51.22, in *ANF*, 5:332. Contrasting the water in the pool of Bethesda (John 5:1–9) with the water of baptism, Tertullian set forth this benefit of baptism: "The water that used to remedy bodily defects now heals the spirit. The water that used to bring temporal health now renews eternal health. The water that set free only once a year now daily saves many people, death being removed through the washing of sins. Once the guilt is removed, the penalty—death—is of course removed as well." Tertullian, *On Baptism*, 5, in *ANF*,

3:672. The text has been rendered clearer.

12. Cyprian, *Treatise* 8:2, in *ANF*, 5:476.

13. Origen, *Commentary on Matthew*, 13.27, in *ANF*, 9:491. Origen was citing Titus 3:5.

14. Cyprian, *Letter* 73.6, in *ANF*, 5:388. Citing the same expression in Titus 3:5 and appealing to Jesus' healing of the blind man (John 9:1–11), Irenaeus described this benefit of baptism: "The descendants of Adam, having been formed by God but also fallen into sin, needed the bath of regeneration. Therefore, the Lord said to the blind man after he had smeared his eyes with the clay, 'Go to Siloam and wash.' By this means he restored to him the regeneration that takes place by means of the bath." Irenaeus, *Against Heresies*, 5.15.3, in *ANF*, 1:543. The texts have been rendered clearer.

was cleansed of leprosy when he washed in water (2 Kings 5:14), explained: "This was a symbol for us. For as we are lepers in sin, we are made clean from our old sins by means of the sacred water and the invocation of the Lord. We are spiritually regenerated as newborn babes, just as the Lord has declared: 'Unless a man is born again through water and the Spirit, he shall not enter into the kingdom of heaven.' "[15] John 3:5 became foundational for the necessity of baptism for salvation, as Tertullian explained: "The precept [teaching] is laid down that 'without baptism, salvation is attainable by no one.' "[16] Tying baptism with regeneration and linking it to John 3:5 led to the necessity of baptism for salvation.[17]

Fourth, baptism provides the gift of the Holy Spirit: "What is called the laver [bath] of regeneration takes place with the renewal of the Spirit, for the Spirit now comes in addition since he comes from God and is over and above the water."[18] Tertullian linked this reception of the Spirit to the restoration of the image of God[19] and noted that this gift follows after baptism, anointing with oil (called *unction*), and laying on of hands: "We don't receive the Holy Spirit in the water. Rather, in the water we are cleansed and prepared for the Holy Spirit. After this, when we have come from the baptismal font, we are thoroughly anointed with a blessed unction. Next, the hand is laid upon us, invoking and inviting the Holy Spirit through benediction. To our body, as it emerges from the font, after its old sins, flies the dove of the Holy Spirit, bringing us the peace of God."[20]

Fifth, baptism involves a decisive break from Satan: "When entering the water, we make profession of the Christian faith in the words of its rule: we bear public testimony that we have renounced the devil, his pomp, and his angels."[21] This practice was based on the belief that before becoming believers, people are enslaved to the service of another

---

15. Irenaeus, *Fragment* 34, in *ANF*, 1:574. The text has been rendered clearer.

16. Tertullian, *On Baptism*, 12, in *ANF*, 3:674–75.

17. But what about biblical characters like Abraham, for whom faith was sufficient for salvation? Tertullian granted that "in days gone by, there was salvation by means of bare faith, before the passion and resurrection of the Lord. But now that faith has been enlarged and has become a faith that believes in his nativity, passion and resurrection, there has been an amplification added to the sacrament, that is, the sealing act of baptism; the clothing, in some sense, of the faith which before was bare, and which cannot exist now without its proper law. For the law of baptism has been imposed." Tertullian, *On Baptism*, 13, in *ANF*, 3:676. In further discussion, he cited the baptismal formula (Matt. 28:19) and John 3:5: " 'Unless a man has been reborn of water and Spirit, he shall not enter into the kingdom of the heavens' has tied faith to the necessity of baptism. Thus, all who became believers [after Christ gave this command] were baptized." Tertullian, *On Baptism*, 13, in *ANF*, 3:676. The text has been rendered clearer.

18. Origen, *Commentary on the Gospel of John*, 6.17, in *ANF*, 10:367.

19. The man who is baptized "will be restored for God to

his 'likeness,' for he receives again that Spirit of God whom he had first received from God's breath, but had afterwards lost through sin." Tertullian, *On Baptism*, 5, in *ANF*, 3:672. The text has been rendered clearer.

20. Ibid., 6–8, in *ANF*, 3:672–73. The text has been rendered clearer. By means of an allegorical interpretation of the apocryphal story of Suzanna in the (extended) book of Daniel, Hippolytus noted the practice of anointing with oil: "And what was the oil, but the power of the Holy Spirit, with which believers are anointed as with ointment after the laver of washing?" Hippolytus, *Fragments from Commentaries*: "Fragment on Suzanna," 6:17, in *ANF*, 5:192. And Cyprian concurred that baptism prepares the one being baptized to receive the Spirit: "One is not born by the laying on of hands when he receives the Holy Spirit, but in baptism, so that, being already born, he may receive the Holy Spirit, even as it happened in the first man Adam. For first God formed him, and then breathed into his nostrils the breath of life. For the Spirit cannot be received unless he who receives him first has an existence." Cyprian, *Letter* 73.7, in *ANF*, 5:388. The text has been rendered clearer.

21. Tertullian, *The Shows*, 4, in *ANF*, 3:81; cf. Tertullian, *The Chaplet (Crown)*, 3, in *ANF*, 3:94.

master, Satan. He opposes their conversion and therefore must be renounced before they can embrace Jesus Christ, their new Master.[22]

Sixth, baptism symbolizes one's identification with Jesus Christ. According to Basil the Great, the imitation of Christ is necessary for an intimate relationship with God. This involves being made like Christ in his death so as to put a halt to one's previously sinful life. And this is accomplished through baptism: "Before beginning the second [or new life], it is necessary to put an end to the first.... How then do we achieve the descent into hell? By imitating, through baptism, the burial of Christ. For the bodies of the baptized are, as it were, buried in the water. Baptism, then, symbolically signifies the putting off of the works of the flesh."[23] Identification with Christ's resurrection is also included in the act of baptism: "This is what it is to be born again of water and of the Spirit: being made dead is effected in the water, while our life is worked into us through the Spirit."[24]

In conclusion, the early church understood baptism in various ways: as the forgiveness of sins, deliverance from death, regeneration or the new birth, the gift of the Holy Spirit, the renunciation of Satan, and identification with Jesus Christ.

As the theology of baptism developed in the third and fourth centuries, various practices were added to the rite. One concerned the water. Before it could be used for baptisms, the water had to be consecrated, or set apart, for this activity.[25] Yet Basil the Great warned against seeing the water of baptism in a magical way: "If there is any grace in the water, it is not of the nature of the water, but of the presence of the Spirit."[26] A second addition, already noted, was anointing with oil, or *chrismation* (from the Greek *chrisma*, or oil). Tertullian tied the origin of this practice to the Old Testament practice of anointing men as they entered the Levitical priesthood.[27] Of course, chief among the "anointed" was Jesus the *Christ*, or Anointed One. As Christians who are baptized in Christ, believers should be anointed like the Anointed One.[28] A third addition, already

---

22. See 2 Cor. 4:4; Eph. 2:2. This baptismal denunciation of Satan has important implications for the future life of believers: "Now the covenant you have made concerning the devil is to renounce him, his pomp, and his angels. Such is your agreement in this matter.... You must never think of getting back any of the things that you have renounced and have restored to him, lest he should summon you as a fraudulent man, and a transgressor of your agreement, before God the Judge." Tertullian, *Treatise on the Soul*, 35, in *ANF*, 3:216. The text has been rendered clearer.

23. Basil the Great, *On the Spirit*, 15.35, in *NPNF*[2], 8:21.

24. Ibid., in *NPNF*[2], 8:22. The text has been rendered clearer.

25. Cyprian appealed to Ezek. 36:25 for this practice. Cyprian, *Letter* 69.1, in *ANF*, 5:376. Ultimately, it was Jesus Christ himself who, through his baptism, consecrated the water of baptism so that it possesses effective power. Ignatius put it simply: Jesus Christ "was born and was baptized in order that by his suffering he might cleanse the water." Ignatius, *Letter to the Ephesians*, 18.2, in Holmes, 149; *ANF*, 1:57. To this, Narsai of Syria added: "The high priest [Jesus] descended into

the water and bathed and sanctified it and conferred upon it the power of the Spirit to give life. The holy one drew near to the weak and inanimate element and made it a womb that begets men spiritually." Narsai, *A Homily on the Epiphany of Our Lord*, 289–91, in *Narsai's Metrical Homilies on the Nativity, Epiphany, Passion, and Resurrection*, ed. and trans. Frederick G. McLeod, cited in Thomas M. Finn, *Early Christian Baptism and the Catechumenate: West and East Syria* (Collegeville, Minn.: Liturgical, 1992), 181.

26. Basil the Great, *On the Spirit*, 15.35, in *NPNF*[2], 8:22.

27. Tertullian, *On Baptism*, 7, in *ANF*, 3:672.

28. "As he [Christ] was anointed with an ideal oil of gladness, that is, with the Holy Spirit, called oil of gladness because he is the author of spiritual gladness, so you were anointed with ointment, having been made partakers and fellows of Christ." Cyril of Jerusalem, *Five Catechetical Lectures to the Newly Baptized*, Lecture 21: *Third Lecture on the Mysteries: On Chrism*, 2, in *NPNF*[2], 7.149. Cyprian underscored the necessity of this unction so that the one baptized "may be anointed of God and have in him the grace of Christ." Cyprian, *Letter* 69.2, in *ANF*, 5:376. Various modifications of this practice developed later.

noted, was the laying on of hands. Again, Tertullian appealed to Old Testament precedents.[29] New Testament passages were also cited as a justification for the laying on of hands to receive the Holy Spirit following baptism.[30]

Although the New Testament pattern demonstrates that those who professed faith in Jesus Christ were immediately baptized, this practice gave way to a fourth addition—a period of *catechesis*, or teaching the elements of the Christian faith—prior to baptism. The people who were instructed were referred to as *catechumens*. As they abandoned their former sinful life[31] and moved toward incorporation into the Christian faith, people were enrolled in the book of the church. As catechumens, they were then instructed in the faith before being baptized.[32] According to Hippolytus, the normal length of catechesis was three years, with a qualification: "If a person is earnest and perseveres well in the matter," he should be received earlier "because it is not the time that is judged, but the conduct."[33] In order to instruct the catechumens, *catechists*—or teachers—unfolded the Old and New Testaments and commented on the Nicene Creed. This latter part came to be called "handing over the creed."[34] As they advanced in their

---

In one, the anointing with oil came first, followed by baptism, and the rite was concluded with the application of ointment. *Apostolic Constitutions*, 7.2.22, in *ANF*, 7:469. Eventually, various elaborate practices of anointing were developed, so that different parts of the body were covered with oil in this ceremony. These included the forehead, the ears, the nostrils, and the breast. Each of these symbolized some specific new reality: the gift of the Holy Spirit to restore believers to the image of God, attentiveness to the gospel message, participation in Christ as his sweet fragrance, and protection from the devil by the breastplate of righteousness. Cyril of Jerusalem, *Mystagogical Catecheses* and *Baptismal Catecheses*, cited in Hugh M. Riley, *Christian Initiation: A Comparative Study of the Interpretation of the Baptismal Liturgy in the Mystagogical Writings of Cyril of Jerusalem, John Chrysostom, Theodore of Mopsuestia, and Ambrose of Milan*, Studies in Christian Antiquity 17, ed. Johannes Quasten (Washington, D.C.: Catholic Univ. of America Press, 1974), 372–75.

29. He explained its origin as being "derived from the old sacramental rite in which Jacob blessed his grandsons ... with his hands laid on them and interchanged [crossed]." Tertullian, *On Baptism*, 8, in *ANF*, 3:672.

30. Cyprian appealed to Acts 8:17 and John 3:5 while insisting that people both be baptized and receive the Spirit by the laying on of hands. Cyprian, *Letter* 71.1, in *ANF*, 5:378. Specifically, the new birth comes about by baptism, and the reception of the Holy Spirit comes through the laying on of hands. As he applied the story in Acts (8:14–19) of Peter and John laying hands on the Samaritans who had been baptized: "This [same thing] now too is done among us, so that they who are baptized in the church are brought to the prelates [bishops] of the church, and by our prayers and by the laying on of hands obtain [receive] the Holy Spirit and are perfected with the Lord's seal." Cyprian, *Letter* 72.9, in *ANF*, 5:381.

31. Hippolytus listed the professions that catechumens were required to give up before they could be baptized. Accordingly, candidates could not be pimps, painters and sculptors (of idols), actors, school teachers (of worldly knowledge), participants in Roman circuses (charioteers, athletes, spectators), gladiators or those associated with the profession, idolatrous priests, soldiers and others in the military, prostitutes, magicians, concubines, etc. Hippolytus, *The Apostolic Tradition*, 16.9–25, in *The Apostolic Tradition of Hippolytus*, ed. Gregory Dix (London: Society for the Promotion of Christian Knowledge, 1968), 24–28.

32. At this point, they were considered part of the class of catechumens called the *hearers*. The *Apostolic Constitutions* outlined a very specific curriculum to be imparted to them. This included the knowledge of God (Father, Son, and Holy Spirit); creation, providence, and the divine laws; God's purpose in creating the world and human beings; human nature; divine punishment of the wicked and rewarding of the righteous; and salvation from sin. And hearers were commanded: "Let him that offers himself to baptism learn these and similar things during the time that he is a catechumen." *Apostolic Constitutions*, 7.3.39, in *ANF*, 7:475–76. It would be wrong to draw the conclusion that the catechism was a rigidly prescribed teaching program. As Gregory of Nyssa showed, a good deal of contextualization was required, given the diverse backgrounds from which the catechumens came. Thus, catechetical instruction was not a "one size fits all" approach. Rather, the instruction was to be tailored to the particular catechumen. Gregory of Nyssa, *The Great Catechism*, prologue, in *NPNF*[2], 5:473–74. Cf. Augustine, *On the Catechizing of the Uninstructed*, 15.23, in *NPNF*[1], 3:298–99.

33. Hippolytus, *Apostolic Tradition*, 17.1–2, in Dix, *Apostolic Tradition of Hippolytus*, 28.

34. Augustine, *On the Creed: A Sermon to the Catechumens*, 1, in *NPNF*[1], 3:369.

learning, the hearers became part of the class of catechumens called the *competents*. With the creed memorized, they made a public confession of the faith; then they were baptized.[35]

One reason for the delay of baptism was the changing circumstance in which the church of the fourth century found itself. Now that it was a legal institution, a large influx of new people moved to join it, and not always for the right reasons. One way of ensuring that only people intent on being committed Christians could join the church was to make entrance into it a rather long and difficult process. Another important reason for postponing baptism until after instruction was the growth of the view that baptism cleanses people from their previous sins, but not from the sins committed after baptism. Given this notion, it would be rash for people to be baptized before they had achieved a certain level of maturity in holiness.[36]

A fifth addition was an elaboration of the renunciation of Satan, which could include a profession of faith. According to Ambrose, two questions were asked of the baptismal candidates, to which they responded: "'Do you renounce the devil and his works?' *I do renounce*. 'Do you renounce the world and its pleasures?' *I do renounce*."[37] According to the baptismal practice of Cyril of Jerusalem, the rite took the form of two movements, one renouncing Satan,[38] the other professing belief in the Trinity and baptism.[39] Facing the West, the candidates would first address the following words directly to Satan: "I renounce you Satan, and all your works, and all your pomp, and all your cult [worship]." Turning to the East, the candidates would then profess: "I believe in the Father, and in the

---

35. In some baptismal ceremonies, the candidates were questioned about the faith as part of the act of baptism itself. Ambrose followed the rite of asking three questions to which the candidates replied, "I believe," in conjunction with the three times they were immersed:

"Do you believe in God the Father almighty?"

I believe. (The candidate is submerged for the first time in the water.)

"Do you believe in our Lord Jesus Christ and in his cross?"

I believe. (The candidate is submerged for the second time in the water.)

"Do you believe also in the Holy Spirit?"

I believe. (The candidate is submerged for the third time in the water.)

Ambrose, *On the Sacraments*, 2.20; *On Mysteries*, 28. Paraphrased from Riley, *Christian Initiation*, 150. Yet even the catechumens did not have access to the deep truths of the Christian faith. This privilege was reserved for them after their baptism, when they could be instructed in the great mysteries. Indeed, this postbaptismal instruction was called *mystical catechesis*. This practice was modeled on Christ's own relationship with the disciples, on the one hand, and the masses of people to whom he ministered, on the other hand: "The Lord spoke in parables to those who were incapable of hearing, but to his disciples he explained these parables in private. For the illumination of the glory [of God] is for those who have been enlightened, while blinding is for those who do not believe. These mysteries, which the church now declares to you who are transferred from the lists of the catechumens, are not commonly taught to the Gentiles. For we do not declare the mysteries about the Father and the Son and the Holy Spirit to a Gentile; neither do we speak of the mysteries plainly in the presence of the catechumens." Archelaus, *Disputation with Manes*, fragment, in *ANF*, 6:235. The text has been rendered clearer.

36. Thus, baptism had to follow a significant period of repentance, in which those wishing to be baptized made a definitive break with sin. As Tertullian noted: "We are not washed *in order that* we may cease sinning, but *because* we have ceased. So it is becoming [right] that learners desire baptism but do not hastily receive it: for he who desires it, honors it; he who hastily receives it, disdains it. Hasty reception of baptism is part of disrespect; it inflates the seeker and despises the giver [God]." Tertullian, *On Repentance*, 6, in *ANF*, 3:662. The text has been rendered clearer. Cf. *Shepherd of Hermas*, mandate 4.3, in Holmes, 383; *ANF*, 2:22.

37. Ambrose, *On the Sacraments*, 1.5, cited in Riley, *Christian Initiation*, 27–28.

38. This renunciation was called the *apotaxis* or *abrenuntio*.

39. This second stage was called the *syntaxis* or *profession*.

Son, and in the Holy Spirit, and in one baptism of repentance."[40] In this way, candidates for baptism denounced Satan and decisively broke with his power over them. Church leaders also laid hands on them to exorcise that evil influence.[41]

Finally, fasting was added as a preparation for baptism. This practice dates back at least to the second-century *Didache* and was reinforced in the following centuries.[42] Immediately after their baptism, the newly initiated broke their fast by taking the Lord's Supper. From early on in the church's history, this celebration of baptism leading to receiving communion for the first time took place at Easter time.[43]

It goes without saying that only people who were willing to break with their sins while learning the teachings of the Christian faith could be catechumens, preparing themselves for baptism. This practice seemed to rule out infants and little children from participating. Yet the church began to debate a conflicting practice at the same time.

One of the most important developments in the early church's view of baptism was its switch from baptizing people who could consciously participate in the rite to baptizing infants. At the end of the second century, Tertullian objected to involving children in baptism. The practice was for sponsors to stand in the place of the infants being baptized. During the ceremony, these sponsors would make promises, both to raise the children in the Christian faith and to ensure that the children would live wholeheartedly for the Lord. Tertullian objected that such promising could not—and should not—take place. Baptism should be administered later on in the children's lives, when they are believers.

Tertullian's Denunciation of Infant Baptism

According to the circumstances, disposition, and even age of each individual, the delay of baptism is preferable; principally, however, in the case of little children. For why is it necessary ... that the sponsors should be thrust into danger? They themselves, by reason of death, may fail to fulfill their promises and may be disappointed by the development of an evil disposition in those children for whom they stood. Certainly, the Lord does say about children, "Do not forbid them to come to me". Let them "come," then, while they are growing up. Let them "come" while they are learning, while they are learning *where* to come.

---

40. Cyril of Jerusalem, *Mystagogical Catecheses*, 1.8–9, cited in Riley, *Christian Initiation*, 25. The text has been rendered clearer. Several reasons were given for turning from the West to the East. First, the West was generally associated with darkness and the East with light, because of the sun rising in the East and setting in the West. Second, Scripture indicates that the garden of Eden was planted in the East; thus, candidates would face paradise when making their profession. Finally, an early tradition held that Christ would return from the East; thus, the candidates would affirm their belief in the one still to come by turning in that direction. Indeed, there was an early church practice of praying toward the East. Riley, *Christian Initiation*, 82–83.

41. "Hands shall be laid on them [the candidates] daily in exorcism and, as the day of their baptism draws near, the bishop himself shall exorcise each one of them that he may be personally assured of their purity.... And, laying his hands upon them, he shall exorcise all evil spirits to flee away and never to return." Hippolytus, *The Apostolic Tradition*, 44.20, in Dix, *Apostolic Tradition of Hippolytus*, 31.

42. Tertullian was one who insisted upon a rigorous time of fasting so that those to be baptized had thoroughly dealt with their sins. Tertullian, *On Baptism*, 20, in *ANF*, 3:678–79. Justification for this practice was found in the baptism and fasting of Christ. *Apostolic Constitutions*, 7.2.22, in *ANF*, 7:469.

43. Later, Pentecost was added as another period for baptismal services to take place.

Let them become Christians when they become able to know Christ. Why does innocent infancy rush to the forgiveness of sins? Let them know how to "ask" for salvation, that you may seem at least to have given "to him who asks."*

> *Tertullian here references Matt. 19:14 and Luke 6:30. Tertullian, *On Baptism*, 18, in *ANF*, 3:678. The text has been rendered clearer. Some consider the earliest reference to infant baptism to come in Irenaeus's theory of recapitulation: "He [Jesus] came to save all through means of himself—all, I say, who through him are born again to God—infants, and children, and boys, and youths, and old men." Irenaeus, *Against Heresies*, 2.22.4, in *ANF*, 1:391. If the phrase "born again to God" refers to baptism, then infants would here be said to be baptized.

At the same time, Origen averred: "The church has received a tradition from the apostles to give baptism even to little children."[44] Yet he, too, objected to the practice for the reason that innocent people—children—do not need forgiveness. So why did the church practice infant baptism? Origen offered the explanation that no one—not even an infant who has yet to commit personal sins—is pure: "No one is clean of filth, not even if his life on earth has only been for one day.... Because the filth of birth is removed by the sacrament of baptism, for that reason infants, too, are baptized."[45]

This link between baptism and original sin was made specific by Cyprian. He confronted a controversial situation in which the church, modeling its baptismal practice after the rite of circumcision in the Old Testament, regularly baptized infants on the eighth day following their birth.[46] Cyprian objected to this practice because it was too long a delay, given the dreadful situation into which children are born: "This recently born infant has not sinned except that, being born physically according to Adam, he has contracted the contagion/infection of the ancient death at his birth. Thus, he more easily approaches the reception of the forgiveness of sins, because the sins forgiven are not his own but those of another."[47] Augustine later cited this letter of Cyprian—Augustine called it the "book on the baptism of infants"—as a defining statement on this practice.[48] As Augustine expressed it, "What we are discussing concerns the obliteration of original sin in infants."[49] Because baptism brings the forgiveness of sins, and because infants are born with original sin, the baptism of infants became the church's practice. Although they had not yet personally sinned, infants would still be condemned because of their association with the sin of Adam. Thus, they were to be baptized soon after they were born. By the fifth century, infant baptism was the official church rite.[50]

44. Origen, *Commentary on Romans*, 5.9.3, in Origen, *Commentary on the Epistle to the Romans*, trans. Thomas P. Scheck, The Fathers of the Church: A New Translation (Washington, D.C.: Catholic Univ. of America Press, 2001), 1:367.

45. He appealed to John 3:5 for biblical support. Origen, *Homilies on the Gospel of Luke*, 14:5, in Pelikan, 1:291.

46. Cyprian, *Letter* 58.2, in *ANF*, 5:353–54.

47. Cyprian, *Letter* 58.5, in *ANF*, 5:354. The text has been rendered clearer.

48. Augustine, *On Marriage and Concupiscence*, 2.51, in *NPNF¹*, 5:304.

49. Augustine, *On the Grace of Christ, and On Original Sin*, 21, in *NPNF¹*, 5:244.

50. The Council of Carthage (417), canon 2, made it explicit: "If anyone says that newborn children do not need to be baptized, or that they are baptized for the remission of sins, but that no original sin is derived from Adam to be washed away in the laver of regeneration, so that in their case the baptismal formula 'for the remission of sins' is to be taken in a fictitious and not in its true sense, let him be anathema [condemned to hell]." Bettenson, 64.

In this way, baptism became the most important sacrament of the church prior to the medieval period. It was the one means by which original sin was removed and, in the case of adults, the way in which all their actual sins committed up to that point were forgiven.[51] Indeed, because of its great importance, baptism was considered necessary for salvation. Moreover, as salvation in Jesus Christ became linked with the Catholic Church, baptism in the church became necessary for salvation. This rendered any baptism by any church other than the Catholic Church invalid.[52] Ultimately, however, the church decided that any baptism—even those administered by churches that had broken away from it—was a valid baptism, as long as it conformed in its administration to Christian baptism.

The chief proponent of this view was Augustine. In one sense, he repeated the standard view of baptism. Citing Titus 3:5, he emphasized that baptism brings the new birth leading to eternal life.[53] He also urged that baptism washes away all sins, but it does not remove the sinful nature from those who are baptized.[54] Furthermore, like Cyprian before him, Augustine linked the practice of infant baptism to the need for rescue from original sin.[55] Indeed, for Augustine, the baptism of infants was absolutely essential. Citing 1 John 5:9–12, he reasoned that infants need the Son of God, "whom they can only have by his baptism."[56] Regarding the fate of unbaptized babies, Augustine affirmed that infants who die without being baptized will be involved in the mildest condemnation of all. Thus, the person who teaches that they will not be condemned greatly deceives both himself and others.[57] Accordingly, Augustine commended his fellow Christians for their expression "Baptism is nothing else than 'salvation.'"[58]

But Augustine did not link the effectiveness of baptism as closely to the Catholic Church as others before him had. Indeed, he set forth the possibility that some outside of the church would be saved and many inside the church would be damned.[59] The reason

---

51. As for sins committed after baptism, a new rite—penance—was developed to deal with lapsed Christians, those who had fallen away from the faith or committed particularly bad sins like immorality. Thus, "the deeds done [before baptism] are forgiven [in baptism], and those done after [baptism] are purged [through discipline]." Clement of Alexandria, Stromata, 4.24, in ANF, 2:438. For Tertullian, this "second repentance" could be administered only once after baptism and had to be accompanied by external acts of penance expressing repentance for sin and humility before God. Tertullian, On Repentance, 9, in ANF, 3:663, 364. During this period of penance, people were not allowed to participate in the Lord's Supper. Only after careful observation to make sure that their penance was sincere, the penitents were restored to full fellowship in the church. Apostolic Constitutions, 2.39, in ANF, 7:41. By these two means—baptism and penance—people could effectively deal with their sin. Baptism provided forgiveness and cleansing for original sin and all actual sins committed prior to receiving the rite. Penance addressed sins committed afterwards. But the key event was still baptism because it introduced its recipients into the way of salvation

provided by the church.

52. Seventh Council of Carthage, Concerning the Baptism of Heretics, in ANF, 5:566.

53. Augustine, A Treatise on the Merits and Forgiveness of Sins, and on the Baptism of Infants, 1.23, in NPNF[1], 5:23–24.

54. Augustine, Against Two Letters of the Pelagians, 3.5, in NPNF[1], 5:404.

55. Augustine, A Treatise on the Grace of Christ, and on Original Sin, 2.45, in NPNF[1], 5:253–54.

56. Augustine, A Treatise on the Merits and Forgiveness of Sins, and on the Baptism of Infants, 1.42, in NPNF[1], 5:31. From John 12:46 he further argued that "infants, unless they pass into the number [company] of believers through the sacrament [of baptism] which was divinely instituted for this purpose, will undoubtedly remain in this darkness." Ibid., 1.35, in NPNF[1], 5:29.

57. Ibid., 1.21, in NPNF[1], 5:22–23.

58. Ibid., 1.34, in NPNF[1], 5:28.

59. Augustine, On Baptism, against the Donatists, 5.28.39, in NPNF[1], 4:478. For further discussion on Augustine's doctrine of the church, see chap. 26.

Augustine could affirm this is the principle of *ex opere operato*—literally, by the work performed. The sacraments—in this case baptism—are effective by the simple fact that they are administered. This means that their validity is not dependent on the minister who performs the ceremony. Indeed, for Augustine the baptism administered by the Catholic Church is not a baptism that belongs to the church. In a similar way, the baptism performed by a heretical group is not a baptism that belongs to the heretics. Rather, "baptism belongs to Christ, regardless of who may give it."[60] Accordingly, all people possess baptism who have received it in any place from any sort of person, as long as it was "consecrated in the words of the gospel, and received without deceit on their part with some degree of faith."[61] In affirming this, Augustine emphasized the objectivity of the sacrament—baptism accomplishes forgiveness, regeneration, the promise of eternal life, and the giving of the Holy Spirit—by the simple act of being performed. The character and conduct of the one administering baptism does not and cannot affect it. Neither can the character and conduct of the recipient impede the divine grace.[62]

Ultimately, Augustine's view of the effectiveness of the sacraments—*ex opere operato*—won the day. He thus gave the definitive shape to the Catholic Church's theology of baptism. Although the official position of the church, it was not a view that went unchallenged, as the next sections underscore.

BAPTISM IN THE MIDDLE AGES

A major change in sacramental theology in the medieval period was the elevation of the Lord's Supper to be the preeminent sacrament.[63] Although that honor had previously gone to baptism, the eucharistic sacrifice gradually eclipsed baptism as the most important. Thus, while much attention was given to developing the church's view of the Mass, the practice of baptism remained much like it was from the fifth century on.

One change that did take place during the medieval period was the practice of celebrating baptisms at any time throughout the church year and not only at Easter and Pentecost. The primary reason for this change was the high infant mortality rate. Because children were commonly in grave danger of death at any time, to withhold baptism until the two traditional baptismal seasons was to place infants in danger of condemnation. Thus, the *Constitutions of Padua* (1339) required parents to present their children for baptism within eight days of their birth. This became the generally accepted practice.

Given that, in most areas where Christianity existed, most of the inhabitants identified themselves with the church, little attention was given to adult baptism and its accompanying elaborate ceremonies. The lengthy period for catechism prior to candidacy for baptism, the detailed preparatory events—fasting, and interrogation about the candidates' life and correct belief—for the baptismal service, the baptism of hundreds of adults by the bishop at Easter and Pentecost, and the first reception of the Eucharist

---

60. Ibid., 6.10.15, in *NPNF*[1], 4:484. The text has been rendered clearer.
61. Ibid., 7.53.102, in *NPNF*[1], 4:513.
62. Ibid., 3.14.19, in *NPNF*[1], 4:441.
63. For further discussion, see chap. 29.

by the new group of Christians, fell out of use. They were replaced by simple ceremonies conducted by parish priests almost weekly.

Although the church's baptismal practice had been consistent over the centuries, various challenges to the church's position arose. Hugh of Amiens noted: "The heretics say that the sacraments are of benefit only to those who know about them, not to ignorant adults, and that they do not confer anything at all on little children. Therefore, they condemn the baptism of little children and infants."[64] A major reason offered for rejecting this practice was the inability of infants to have faith, a necessary part of salvation: "Infants, even though they are baptized by you, are simply not saved, because their age prevents them from believing."[65] But the church was not swayed from infant baptism.[66]

Thomas Aquinas summed up the medieval church's view of baptism, first addressing its nature: "Baptism is both reality and sacrament. It is something real signified by the outward washing, and a sacramental sign of the inward justification [grace], which is the only reality in this sacrament."[67] Although he noted that immersion was still commonly practiced, he argued for the validity of other modes: "In the sacrament of baptism, water is put to use for a washing of the body, whereby to signify the inward washing away of sins. Now washing may be done with water not only by immersion, but also by sprinkling or pouring. Therefore, although it is safer to baptize by immersion, because this is the more ordinary fashion, yet baptism can be conferred by sprinkling or also by pouring."[68]

Although baptism by immersion is not necessary, what about baptism itself? Is it necessary for salvation? Aquinas carefully framed his answer, looking at two different cases in which someone has not been baptized. One case involves the person who is not baptized nor desires to be baptized: "This clearly indicates contempt for the sacrament, in regard to those who have free will. Consequently, those to whom baptism is lacking cannot obtain salvation, since neither sacramentally nor mentally are they incorporated in Christ, through whom alone can salvation be obtained." The second case involves the person who is not baptized but wants to be, though hindered from it: "Such a man can obtain salvation without being actually baptized, because of his desire for baptism. This desire is the result of 'faith that works in love,' by which God, whose power is not tied to

64. Hugh of Amiens, *Against the Heretics of His Time*, 1.11, in Pelikan, 3:234.

65. Peter the Venerable, *Against the Petrobrusians*, 10, in Pelikan, 3:234. Similarly, Hugh of Speroni objected: "An infant cannot believe or know anything"; thus, "a faith that he cannot have does not do him any good." Hugh of Speroni, writing against Vacarius's *Against Many and Various Errors*, 13.2, in Pelikan, 3:234.

66. As Anselm defended it against its opponents: "In baptism the sins as far as those that existed before baptism are wiped out, and so the original inability to have justice is not imputed a sin in those already baptized as it was before.... Therefore, if they [infants] die in this [baptized] state, they are not unjust and therefore are not condemned; but they are saved through the justice of Christ who gave himself for them,

and the justice of the faith of their mother the Church, which keeps the faith for them as if they were just." Anselm, *The Virgin Conception and Original Sin*, 29, in *Anselm*, 388–89.

67. Thomas Aquinas, *Summa Theologica*, pt. 3, q. 66, art. 1. The text has been rendered clearer.

68. Ibid., pt. 3, q. 66, art. 7. The text has been rendered clearer. These other modes are particularly useful in urgent cases: "because there is a great number to be baptized ... through there being but [only] a small supply of water; or through feebleness [weakness] of the minister, who cannot hold up the candidate for baptism; or through feebleness [weakness] of the candidate, whose life might be endangered by immersion. We must therefore conclude that immersion is not necessary for baptism." He cited Ezek. 36:25 in support. Ibid.

visible sacraments, sanctifies the man inwardly."[69] Practically speaking, then, in the case of infants, "baptism should not be deferred. First, because in them we do not look for better instruction or fuller conversion. Secondly, because of the danger of death, for no other remedy is available for them besides the sacrament of baptism."[70] Thus, Aquinas supported the continuation of infant baptism by appeal to original sin.[71] However, in the case of adult converts, a delay in baptism should be observed so that the church can ensure they are genuinely converted and so those being baptized can be catechized and show greater reverence for baptism.[72] This adult baptism continued to be accompanied by an exorcism and a briefer catechism as had been the custom of the church.[73]

Aquinas therefore affirmed the Catholic Church's theology and practice of baptism, a position that had been solidly in place for many centuries. Despite some opposition to it, the view seemed quite unshakable. But this situation would change.

BAPTISM IN THE REFORMATION AND POST-REFORMATION

Although he challenged many of the views of the Roman Catholic Church, Martin Luther did not oppose the church's practice of infant baptism. However, he presented it in a significantly different way by intimately linking baptism with the Word of God and faith. As for the benefits of baptism, Luther explained: "It works forgiveness of sins, delivers from death and the devil, and gives eternal salvation to all who believe, as the Word and promise of God declare."[74] The key in all this was not the baptismal ceremony

---

69. Ibid., pt. 3, q. 68, art. 2. The text has been rendered clearer. He cited a specific example: "Hence Ambrose says of Valentinian, who died while yet a catechumen: 'I lost him whom I was to regenerate, but he did not lose the grace he prayed for.'" Ibid.

70. Ibid., pt. 3, q. 68, art. 3.

71. "Now children contract original sin from the sin of Adam. This is made clear by the fact that they are under the penalty of death, which 'passed to everyone' because of the sin of the first man (Rom. 5:12).... But our Lord himself said: 'Unless a man be born again of water and the Holy Spirit, he cannot enter into the kingdom of God' (John 3:5). Consequently it became necessary to baptize children so that, as in birth they incurred damnation through Adam, so in a second birth they might obtain salvation through Christ. Moreover it was fitting for children to receive baptism in order that, being reared from childhood in things pertaining to the Christian way of life, they may the more easily continue in them." Ibid., pt. 3, q. 68, art. 9. The text has been rendered clearer.

72. Aquinas proposed two exceptions to this general rule of delaying baptism for adults: in the case of those who "appear to be completely instructed in the faith and ready for baptism," and when there is present "sickness or some kind of danger of death." Here Aquinas relied on Leo the Great, *Letter* 16. Otherwise, Aquinas urged a delay in baptism: "Baptism should not be conferred on adults as soon as they are converted, but it should

be deferred until some fixed time. First, as a safeguard to the church, lest it be deceived by baptizing those who come to it under false pretenses (1 John 4:1).... And those who approach baptism are put to this test, when their faith and morals are subjected to proof for a period of time. Secondly, this [delay] is necessary as being useful for those who are baptized; for they require a certain period of time in order to be fully instructed in the faith and to be drilled in those things concerning the Christian way of life. Thirdly, a certain reverence for the sacrament demands a delay so that men ... receive the sacrament with greater devotion." Ibid., pt. 3, q. 68, art. 3. The text has been rendered clearer.

73. Ibid., pt. 3, q. 71, arts. 1, 2.

74. Martin Luther, *Small Catechism*, 4.2, in Schaff, 3:85. In his *Large Catechism*, Luther echoed this idea: "Since we know now what baptism is, and how it is to be regarded, we must also learn why and for what purpose it is instituted; that is, what it profits, gives and works. And this also we cannot discern better than from the words of Christ...: *He who believes and is baptized will be saved* [Mark 16:16]. Therefore state it most simply thus, that the power, work, profit, fruit, and end [purpose] of baptism is to save.... But to be saved, we know, is nothing else than to be delivered from sin, death, and the devil, and to enter into the kingdom of Christ, and to live with him forever." Martin Luther, "Of Baptism," *The Large Catechism*, 4.23, in *Triglot Concordia: The Symbolical Books of the Evangelical Lutheran Church*, trans. F. Bente and W. H. T. Dan (St. Louis: Concordia, 1921), 737-38.

itself: "It is not water ... that does it, but the Word of God which is with and in the water, and faith, which trusts in the Word of God in the water. For without the Word of God the water is nothing but water, and no baptism; but with the Word of God it is a baptism."[75] With regard to the element of faith, Luther explained: "Faith clings to the water, and believes that it is baptism, in which there is pure salvation and life; not [salvation] through the water ... but through the fact that it is embodied in the Word and institution of God, and the name of God inheres in it."[76]

But how is faith possible in an infant? Luther offered various answers to this question. He emphasized the faith of the sponsors of the children to be baptized. Because the sponsors believe in their place, the infants are baptized. This view of vicarious faith gave way to an emphasis on the faith of the infants: The children to be baptized do indeed believe when they are baptized. Here, Luther argued from the validity of the sacrament to the faith of the children: Because the sacrament is valid, there must be faith on the part of those being baptized. Moreover, this faith is a gift of Jesus Christ, into whom infants are baptized.[77] Luther bolstered this view with Scripture that demonstrates faith on the part of infants. Luther cited John the Baptist as an illustration of one who believed while still in his mother's womb. Yet, Luther insisted, even if one is not certain that children believe, infant baptism should still be practiced because the sacrament is not based on infant faith. Here, he argued that infant baptism was the practice of the apostles and the historical position of the Christian church. To say that infant baptism is wrong would be to say that there has been no true baptism—thus, no true church—for well over a thousand years. Of course, Luther rejected this absurd conclusion. And, he added, God would never have allowed such a practice to continue in his church for all this time if it were an error.[78] Moving beyond this, Luther eventually denied the importance of faith for the validity of the sacrament: "For not on that account [i.e., the lack of faith] does baptism become invalid; but everything depends upon the Word and command of God.

---

75. Luther, *Small Catechism*, 4.3, in Schaff, 3:86.

76. Luther, "Of Infant Baptism," *Large Catechism*, 4.28, in Bente and Dan, *Triglot Concordia*, 739. According to Luther, a person's baptism in water also emphasizes sanctification: "It signifies that the old Adam in us is to be drowned by daily sorrow and repentance, and perish with all sins and evil lusts; and that the new man should daily come forth again and rise, who shall live before God in righteousness and purity forever." *Small Catechism*, 4.4, in Schaff, 3:86–87. Thus, the sacramental act that took place once in a person's life must be daily relived and progressively realized. Baptism also provides comfort for a guilty conscience: "When our sins and conscience oppress us, we strengthen ourselves and take comfort and say: Nevertheless I am baptized; but if I am baptized, it is promised me that I shall be saved and have eternal life, both in soul and body." "Of Infant Baptism," *Large Catechism*, 4,44, in Bente and Dan, *Triglot Concordia*, 743,

77. Discussed in Timothy George, *Theology of the Reformers* (Nashville: Broadman, 1988), 94–95.

78. "That the baptism of infants is pleasing to Christ is sufficiently proved from his own work, namely, that God sanctifies many of them who have been thus baptized, and has given them the Holy Spirit; and that there are yet many even today in whom we perceive that they have the Holy Spirit both because of their doctrine and life; as it is also given to us by the grace of God that we can explain the Scriptures and come to the knowledge of Christ, which is impossible without the Holy Spirit. But if God did not accept the baptism of infants, He would not give the Holy Spirit nor any of his gifts to any of them; in short, during this long time unto this day no man upon earth could have been a Christian. Now, since God confirms baptism by the gifts of his Holy Spirit as is plainly perceptible in some of the church fathers, as St. Bernard, Gerson, John Hus, and others, who were baptized in infancy, and since the holy Christian church cannot perish until the end of the world, they must acknowledge that such infant baptism is pleasing to God. For he can never be opposed to himself, or support falsehood and wickedness, or for its promotion impart his grace and Spirit." Luther, "Of Infant Baptism," *Large Catechism*, in Bente and Dan, *Triglot Concordia*, 745.

Baptism is nothing else than water and the Word of God in and with each other; that is, when the Word is added to the water, baptism is valid, even though faith be lacking. For my faith does not make baptism, but receives it."[79]

Ultimately, Luther grounded his position on Scripture. For him the Bible does not explicitly command infant baptism. There would not be an adequate biblical basis for starting the practice were infant baptism not practiced already. But Scripture had enough to say about infant baptism that the church could not discontinue it. In particular, Luther appealed to Christ's command to let children come to him. To deny baptism to children would be disobedience to this order. Also, Christ commands the church to baptize "all nations" (Matt. 28:19–20), and this all-encompassing group obviously includes infants. This is confirmed by the baptism of entire family units in the book of Acts: Those household baptisms (Acts 16:14–15, 29–34) undoubtedly included infants being baptized. Thus, Luther expressed hope: "We bring the child to be baptized with the conviction and the hope that he will believe, and we pray that God will give him faith. But we do not baptize on the strength of this belief, but only on the fact that God has commanded it."[80] And so Luther continued the traditional practice of infant baptism.[81]

Huldrych Zwingli also continued this practice, although he justified it in a different way. Actually, early in his career, Zwingli entertained the idea that only adults should be baptized. This idea flowed from his view of the sacraments: they are external signs by which people respond to what God has done. Accordingly, "Baptism is an initiatory sign which introduces or pledges us to Christ, that in him we may be new men and live a new life.... Your outward baptism ought to show you that you cannot continue the old life."[82] Making a strong distinction between "inner baptism"—the baptism of the Holy Spirit, which only God could accomplish—and "outer baptism," the ceremony involving water,[83] Zwingli lamented the fact that water baptism is given to some who have not experienced the inward baptism.[84] Furthermore, baptism is a pledge on the part of those

---

79. Ibid.

80. Ibid.

81. In a point of difference from the Roman Catholic theology of baptism, Luther denied the absolute necessity of baptism in order to be saved: "A man may believe even though he is not baptized. For baptism is no more than an outward sign to admonish us concerning the divine promise. If one can have it, it is good to take it, for no one should despise it. If one cannot have it, or is refused it, he is not damned if he only believes the gospel. For where the gospel is, there is baptism and everything a Christian needs." Cited in *CD*, IV/4, 155. On the other hand, taking a stand against those who denied the importance of baptism—they maintained that "baptism is an external thing, and that external things are of no benefit"—Luther insisted on its necessity: "Baptism is no human trifle, but instituted by God himself. Moreover, it is most solemnly and strictly commanded that we must be baptized or we cannot be saved, lest any one regard it as a trifling matter." "Of Infant Baptism." *Large Catechism*, 4.6, in Bente and Dan, *Triglot Concordia*, 733. Thus, Luther rejected the necessity of

baptism for salvation against the Catholic insistence on the sacrament, while he underscored its necessity against those who would dispense with it.

82. Huldrych Zwingli, *Of Baptism*, in *Zwingli and Bullinger*, ed. G. W. Bromiley, LCC, 24:151. This sign of identification is not for those being baptized, but "for the benefit of other believers." Ibid., LCC, 24:137.

83. Ibid., LCC, 24:133.

84. "Many who have no faith allow themselves to be baptized.... It is evident, then, that the two need not be concurrent: for nothing is more foolish than to say that when a man is baptized, he necessarily becomes a believer." Ibid., LCC:135. It is interesting to note that the Anabaptists capitalized on Zwingli's distinctions to support their position on baptism. If, as Zwingli seemed to imply, outward baptism should correspond to inner baptism, then water baptism should be administered only to believers, who have experienced the work of the Holy Spirit, and not to children, in whom this work has not yet taken place. See later discussion.

baptized to be faithful members of the church. Once God has worked in people's lives and they have repented of sins, they proclaim their commitment to Christ and his church.[85] Obviously, if this is the concept of baptism, only people who can consciously decide for Christ and his cause can be baptized. Children are therefore excluded. But what about the problem of original sin, according to which the church urged the baptism of infants so that it would be removed? Zwingli departed from the traditional idea of original sin, which "is not of itself sinful for him who has it. The defect cannot condemn one ... until he acts out of the defect against the law of God. And one can do that only if he knows the law."[86] Thus, infant baptism was unnecessary to deal with the problem.

However, Zwingli eventually returned to the practice of baptizing infants,[87] through his confrontation with a group of radical Reformers — the Anabaptists. They denied infant baptism and insisted instead that baptism was only for people who could consciously repent and believe in Christ. Their doctrine clearly excluded infants. Zwingli fought against their view and developed several defenses for the traditional practice.

First, he found an analogy between the old covenant practice of circumcision and the new covenant practice of infant baptism. Just as Israel had two signs or seals of their covenant with God — circumcision and the Passover — so the church has two signs or seals of its new covenant with God — baptism and the Lord's Supper.[88] Because circumcision was applied the eighth day after an infant's birth, so baptism should be administered to infants. Unlike circumcision, it should be applied to infant girls as well as boys.

Second, Zwingli pointed to the baptism of John the Baptist, not the command of Jesus Christ to baptize, as the foundation for Christian baptism. This view supported infant baptism in two ways. First, John's baptism of Christ addresses the need of baptism for those who have not sinned.[89] Zwingli secondly drew upon John's practice (Matt. 3:1–12) of first preaching and then baptizing, reasoning: "It cannot be denied that once his hearers had been taught, they had their untaught children baptized as well, that is, they dedicated them to God in baptism."[90] For Zwingli, this confirmed the correctness of infant baptism. But what about the impossibility of children confessing their sins as adult converts did? He refused to "argue the point: for if the text does not establish infant baptism, it does not disprove it."[91]

The third reason for infant baptism is its support from Scripture. Zwingli listed Jesus' welcoming of little children (Luke 18:15–17) and household baptisms (Acts 16) as the biblical basis for the practice. He also cited John the Baptist and Jeremiah as examples of infants still in their mothers' womb who had the Holy Spirit. Thus, Zwingli refuted the Anabaptists' insistence that only those who have the Holy Spirit should be baptized.[92]

---

85. Ibid., LCC:147–48. Zwingli turned to the baptism of John the Baptist in support of this idea.

86. Huldrych Zwingli, *Sämtliche Werke*, 4.308, cited in George, *Theology of the Reformers*, 138. Indeed, Zwingli denounced the church's long-standing error on this matter. Zwingli, *Of Baptism*, in Bromiley, *Zwingli and Bullinger*, LCC, 24:153.

87. He admitted his former error: "For some time I myself was deceived by the error and I thought it better not to baptize children until they came to years of discretion." Ibid., LCC, 24:139.

88. Ibid., LCC, 24:132.

89. "Christ, the very Son of God, took to himself baptism in order that he might give us an example of unity, that we may all enter under the one sign. Therefore, we ought not to say that infants do not need baptism, for Christ did not need it." Ibid., LCC, 24:167. The text has been rendered clearer.

90. Ibid., LCC, 24:146.

91. Ibid., LCC, 24:147.

92. Ibid., LC, 24:149.

Also, their novel practice would go against Scripture, which does not permit rebaptism.[93] Finally, he argued against changing from infant baptism to baptizing only those who could consciously repent and believe in Christ, because to do so would divide the church. He was highly critical of the attitude of the Anabaptists: "The root of the trouble is that the Anabaptists will not recognize any Christians except themselves or any church except their own."[94] For Zwingli, to follow the Anabaptist belief on baptism would destroy the unity of the church. He urged them not to withdraw from the current practice of infant baptism, "for if we do, the result will be a sect and not faith."[95]

But how did the Anabaptists originate? Despite the continuation of infant baptism by Luther and Zwingli, some of those who broke from the Catholic Church at the same time abandoned that practice in favor of the baptism of believers. In Zürich, Felix Manz, Conrad Grebel, and George Blaurock became convinced that only people who could consciously repent of their sins and believe in Jesus Christ for salvation should be baptized, and then only by immersion. Therefore, they did not bring their infant children to the church to be baptized. The Council of Zürich, following Zwingli's theology, denounced this novelty and enacted the *Order to Baptize Infants* on January 18, 1525.

Order to Baptize Infants (January 18, 1525)

Whereas an error has arisen respecting baptism, as if young children should not be baptized until they come to years of discretion and know what the faith is: and whereas some have accordingly neglected to have their children baptized, our Lords the Burgomaster, Council, and Great Council, have had a disputation held about this matter to learn what Holy Scripture has to say about it. As they have learned from it that, notwithstanding this error, children should be baptized as soon as they are born, all those therefore who have hitherto allowed their children to remain unbaptized, must have them baptized within the next week: and whosoever will not do this, must with wife and child, goods and chattels, leave our city, jurisdiction, and dominions, or await what will be done with him. Every one will accordingly know how to conduct himself.*

Order to Baptize Infants, in *Documents Illustrative of the Continental Reformation*, ed. B. J. Kidd (Oxford: Clarendon, 1911), 211.

The response of those targeted by this order was swift and decisive. On January 21, 1521, during a meeting in Manz's home, Blaurock asked Grebel to baptize him. Once baptized, Blaurock in turn baptized others; thus began the Anabaptist movement.[96] The city leaders of Zürich would not tolerate such blatant disobedience and decreed that the

---

93. "There is no basis for rebaptizing in the Word of God. The only outcome of rebaptism is a constraint which provokes opposition." Ibid., LCC, 24:152.

94. Ibid., LCC, 24:158.

95. Ibid., LCC, 24:148.

96. Literally, the word means "to rebaptize." However, because the Anabaptists denied the validity of their infant baptism, they did not see themselves practicing rebaptism, but baptism instead.

Anabaptists should be executed for heresy. The penalty prescribed was death by drowning, a terrible mockery of the Anabaptist belief. Felix Manz was the first to suffer this capital punishment. With Zwingli and the other Zürich ministers as observers, Manz was drowned in the Limmat River, which ran through the city.

The baptismal position of the Anabaptists was built on several arguments. Some of these were presented to disqualify the practice of baptizing children. First, no explicit biblical warrant could be found for infant baptism. Whereas Zwingli and others interpreted the lack of such specific teaching as meaning that Scripture does not prohibit the practice, the Anabaptists understood the silence to mean that Scripture forbids baptizing infants.[97] Second, the Anabaptists noted that none of the New Testament accounts of baptism make any mention of infants participating in the ceremony. Whereas Zwingli and others argued that infant baptisms could be assumed in these accounts, the Anabaptists denied that such a case could legitimately be made.[98] Third, Balthasar Hubmaier turned Zwingli's view of baptism as an initiatory sign against him. What could it possible signify in the case of baptized children? Not the reception of the Holy Spirit, nor the beginning of faith, and certainly not the beginning of a new life. So if the baptism of infants did not symbolize any initial event, the practice should be discontinued.[99]

As a positive case for the baptism of believers, the Anabaptists pointed to all the New Testament passages about baptism and underscored that, in every case, faith preceded water baptism. Zwingli was critical of this view, but only because he twisted the Anabaptist position. He took it to mean that they insisted on a perfect faith before one could be baptized. Hubmaier responded to this criticism by detailing what faith entailed: "You ask, 'What or how much must I know if I want to be baptized?' The answer is that you must know this much of the Word of God before you receive baptism: you must confess yourself a miserable sinner and consider yourself guilty; you must believe in the forgiveness of your sins through Jesus Christ and begin a new life ... before baptism."[100] To bolster the case for the Anabaptist view, Hubmaier capitalized on Zwingli's distinction between outer and inner baptism. Indeed, Hubmaier quoted Zwingli in developing this point: "No physical element or external thing in this world can cleanse the soul,' but faith cleanses the hearts of men. Thus, it follows that baptism cannot wash away sin."[101] Inner baptism—the work of God on the soul—is linked to the grace of God and to faith, according to Zwingli and Hubmaier. Furthermore, both agreed that outer baptism—the ceremony involving water—should be closely connected to the inner reality. For Hubmaier and the Anabaptists, that meant that people must experience the work of God and have faith before they can be baptized with water: "[Water baptism is] an outward and public testimony of the inner baptism of the Spirit."[102] This established the practice

97. Thus, Balthasar Hubmaier noted that he searched in vain for a biblical text stating, "Go into all the world and baptize young infants, teaching them some years later." Balthasar Hubmaier, *On the Christian Baptism of Believers*, 146, cited in Rollin Stely Armour, *Anabaptist Baptism: A Representative Study*, Studies in Anabaptist and Mennonite History, 11 (Scottsdale, Pa.: Herald, 1966), 28.

98. Ibid., 127–31, in Armour, *Anabaptist Baptism*, 28.

99. Ibid., 137, in Armour, *Anabaptist Baptism*, 28–29.

100. Ibid., 122, 136, in Armour, *Anabaptist Baptism*, 29.

101. Balthasar Hubmaier, *Gespräch*, 210, cited in Armour, *Anabaptist Baptism*, 30. The only difference between the two statements was that Zwingli attributed cleansing power to grace rather than faith: "The cleansing of the soul is the property of the unique grace of God alone." Zwingli, *Sämtliche Werke*, 4.333, cited in Armour, *Anabaptist Baptism*, 30.

102. Balthasar Hubmaier, *Eine Christliche Lehrtafel*, 313, cited in Armour, *Anabaptist Baptism*, 31.

of baptizing believers. Added to this—and most important—was the fact that Christ himself commanded the baptism of believers (Matt. 28:18–20).[103]

This Anabaptist belief was stated in the *Schleitheim Confession*: "Baptism shall be given to all those who have learned repentance and amendment [change] of life, and who believe truly that their sins are taken away by Christ, and to all those who walk in the resurrection of Jesus Christ, and wish to be buried with him in death, so that they may be resurrected with him, and to all those who with this significance request it [baptism] of us and demand it for themselves. This excludes all infant baptism."[104] Believer's baptism was introduced by the Anabaptists.

Like Luther and Zwingli before him, John Calvin continued to embrace the practice of infant baptism. He defined baptism as "the sign of the initiation by which we are received into the society of the church, in order that, engrafted into Christ, we may be reckoned among God's children."[105] He specified two purposes for baptism: "First, to serve our faith before him [God]; secondly, to serve our confession before men."[106] In relation to the first purpose, Calvin explained three benefits to faith that baptism brings: it is a confirmation of the forgiveness of sins,[107] it unites believers with Christ in his death and resurrection,[108] and it brings all the blessings of Christ to believers.[109] Although he disagreed with Zwingli's view that limited baptism to a pledge of allegiance to Christ, Calvin nevertheless considered a second purpose for baptism to be "a symbol for bearing witness to our religion before men."[110] In more detail, he explained: "Baptism serves as our confession before men. Indeed, it is the mark by which we publicly profess that we wish to be reckoned God's people; by which we testify that we agree in worshipping the same God, in one religion with all Christians; by which finally we openly affirm our faith."[111] Thus, according to Calvin, baptism serves both the faith of believers and their public confession of that faith before others.

Like Zwingli, Calvin justified infant baptism on the analogy between the old covenant sign of circumcision and the new covenant sign of baptism.[112] He noted that the benefits of both signs are the forgiveness of sins and the putting to death of the sinful nature. This led him to see the analogy between the two and to conclude: "Apart from the difference

---

103. Gunnar Westin and Torsten Bergsten, eds., *Balthasar Hubmaier: Schriften*, 140–46, cited in Armour, *Anabaptist Baptism*, 29.

104. *Schleitheim Confession*, art. 1, in Lumpkin, 25. The *Confession* specifically critiqued the practice of infant baptism as "the highest and chief abomination of the pope" and the Protestants.

105. John Calvin, *Institutes of the Christian Religion*, 4.15.1, LCC, 2:1303.

106. Ibid., LCC, 2:1304.

107. "It is like a sealed document to confirm to us that all our sins are so abolished, forgiven and effaced that they can never come to God's sight, be recalled or charged against us. For he wills that all who believe be baptized for the forgiveness of sins." Ibid. It was not that Calvin identified the water of baptism with some special power in and of itself to effect

forgiveness of sin. On the contrary, citing Scripture (Eph. 5:26–27; Titus 3:5), he noted: "Paul did not mean to signify that our cleansing and salvation are accomplished by water, or that water contains in itself the power to cleanse, regenerate and renew; nor that here is the cause of salvation, but only that in this sacrament are received the knowledge and certainty of such gifts." Ibid., 4.15.2, LCC, 2:1304. Because of this benefit, Calvin criticized Zwingli's view of baptism as being only a declaration of people's faith before others.

108. Ibid., 4.15.5, LCC, 2:1307.

109. Ibid., 4.15.6, LCC, 2:1307–8.

110. Ibid., 4.16.2, LCC, 2:1325.

111. Ibid., 4.15.13, LCC, 2:1313, 1314.

112. Calvin did not appeal to the need to remove original sin as a reason for infant baptism.

in the visible ceremony, whatever belongs to circumcision pertains likewise to baptism.... By this it appears incontrovertible that baptism has taken the place of circumcision to fulfill the same office among us."[113] In this analogy, he found the reason for the baptism of children of Christians: to mark them out as holy, different from the children of unbelievers.[114] He also supported this practice by appeal to Christ's receiving the little children and proclaiming that the kingdom of heaven belongs to them.[115] He further underscored the benefits that accrue "both to the believers who present their children to be baptized, and to the infants themselves who are baptized with the sacred water."[116] For the parents, the benefit is seeing God's covenant of mercy being extended to their children.[117] As for the benefit for the infants: "Being engrafted into the body of the church, they are somewhat more commended to the other members. Then, when they have grown up, they are greatly spurred to an earnest zeal for worshipping God, by whom they were received as children through a solemn symbol of adoption before they were old enough to recognize him as Father."[118] Accordingly, "infants are baptized into future repentance and faith."[119]

To summarize, the three principal Reformers—Martin Luther, Huldrych Zwingli, and John Calvin—continued the centuries-old practice of infant baptism. Their approaches to this sacrament differed from each other, and they all distanced themselves in certain ways from the Roman Catholic observance of the rite. At the same time, the Anabaptists broke from this practice. They believed that only people who can understand the gospel, repent of their sins, and believe in Christ for salvation should be baptized. Luther, Zwingli, and Calvin decried this view of baptism. Of course, the Roman Catholic Church reacted to all of these positions, seeing them as being in error in one way or another. The Council of Trent condemned all views that denied that the church had a true position on baptism[120] and denounced the Anabaptist practice of withholding baptism from children.[121]

Following the trajectory of the Anabaptists, the early Baptists disavowed the legitimacy of any type of infant baptism, whether it was administered in the Catholic Church or paedobaptist Protestant churches.[122] The *London Confession of Faith* detailed baptism for believers:

---

113. Ibid., 4.16.4, LCC, 2:1327.

114. Ibid., 4.16.6, LCC, 2:1328–29.

115. Matt. 19:13–15. Ibid., 4.16.7, LCC, 2:1330.

116. Ibid., 4.16.9, LCC, 2:1331.

117. "God's boundless generosity, in showing itself there, first gives men ample occasion to proclaim his glory, then floods godly hearts with uncommon happiness, which quickens men to a deeper love of their kind Father, as they see his concern on their behalf for their posterity." Ibid., LCC, 2:1332.

118. Ibid. This theology was simply stated in the *Heidelberg Catechism*'s answer to the question, "Are infants to be baptized?" "Yes; for since they, as well as their parents, belong to the covenant and people of God, and both redemption from sin and the Holy Spirit, who works faith, are through the blood of Christ promised to them no less than to their parents, they are also by baptism, as a sign of the covenant, to be engrafted into the Christian church, and distinguished from the children of unbelievers, as was done in the Old Testament by Circumcision, in place of which in the New Testament Baptism is appointed." *Heidelberg Catechism*, q. 74, in Schaff, 3:331.

119. Calvin, *Institutes*, 4.16.20, LCC, 2:1343.

120. *Canons and Decrees of the Council of Trent*, 7th session (March 3, 1547), *Decree on Baptism*, canon 3, in Schaff, 2:122–23.

121. Ibid., canon 13, in Schaff, 2:124–25.

122. This sentiment was expressed by John Smyth in a pamphlet directed at a separatist church: "The true constitution of the church is of a new creation baptized into the Father, the Son, and the Holy Spirit. The false constitution is of baptized infants. We profess, therefore, that all those churches that baptize infants are of the same false constitution." John Smyth, *The Character of the Beast*, in *The Works of John Smyth*, ed. W. T. Whitley, 2 vols. (Cambridge: Cambridge Univ. Press, 1915), 2:565. The text has been rendered clearer.

Baptism is an ordinance of the New Testament, given by Christ, to be dispensed upon persons professing faith, or who are made disciples. These, upon profession of faith, ought to be baptized (and after to partake of the Lord's Supper). The way and manner of dispensing this ordinance is dipping or plunging the body under water. Being a sign, it must answer the things signified; which is, that interest the saints have in the death, burial, and resurrection of Christ. And, as certainly as the body is buried under water, and risen again, so certainly shall the bodies of the saints be raised by the power of Christ, in the day of the resurrection, to reign with Christ.[123]

The *Second London Confession* underscored that "immersion, or dipping of the person in water, is necessary to the due [proper] administration of this ordinance."[124] Thus, the Baptist movement developed and offered an alternative to the tradition of infant baptism.

BAPTISM IN THE MODERN PERIOD

Reformation developments did not signal the end of the rise of different views on baptism. John Wesley offered his own unique position, defining baptism as "the initiatory sacrament, which enters us into covenant with God. It was instituted by Christ, who alone has power to institute a proper sacrament, a sign, seal, pledge, and means of grace, perpetually obligatory on all Christians."[125] He believed that baptism "wash[es] away the guilt of original sin"[126] and effects regeneration.[127] Specifically, he did not equate baptism with the new birth in the case of adults who are baptized, but did so in the case of infant baptism.[128] However, he also noted that every infant eventually grows up to commit personal sin and reject the grace of God. As a result, they lose the eternal life given to them in baptism. This desperate situation calls for them to be born again through an adult conversion to Christ. Thus, Wesley challenged those who had been baptized as infants: "Lean no more on the staff of that broken reed, that you *were* born again in baptism."[129] While effective at the time, their infant baptism had lost its benefits through their fall into personal sin. An adult conversion, then, was needed.

Adding to the variety of views already present, the Quakers denied that water baptism should be observed; rather: "This baptism is a pure and spiritual thing; that is, the baptism of the Spirit and fire, by which we are buried with him, that being washed and purged from our sins, we may 'walk in newness of life.' "[130] For the Quakers, any physi-

---

123. *London Confession of Faith*, 39, 40, in Lumpkin, 167. The text has been rendered clearer.

124. *Second London Confession of Faith*, 29, in Lumpkin, 291.

125. John Wesley, *A Treatise on Baptism*, 1.1, in *The Works of the Rev. John Wesley*, 10 vols. (New York: Harper, 1927), 9:155.

126. Ibid., 2.1, in *Works of the Rev. John Wesley*, 9:157.

127. "This regeneration, which our church in so many places ascribes to baptism, is more than barely being admit-

ted into the church.... By water, then, as a means, the water of baptism, we are regenerated or born again." Ibid., 2.4, in *Works of the Rev. John Wesley*, 9:158.

128. John Wesley, *Sermon 18: The Marks of the New Birth*, 4.1–2, in *Sermons on Several Occasions*, 2 vols. (New York: G. Lane and C. B. Tippett, 1845), 1:160.

129. Ibid., 4.5, in *Sermons on Several Occasions*, 1:161.

130. *Confession of the Society of Friends, Commonly Called Quakers*, 12, in Schaff, 3:797.

cal type of baptism—whether that of infants or of believers—is wrongheaded, because only spiritual realities—in this case, the baptism of the Spirit—counts for anything. Oppositely, Baptist churches insisted on baptism both for membership in the church and for participation in the Lord's Supper.[131] John Dagg supported this position: "As profession [of faith] is necessary to church membership, so is baptism, which is the appointed ceremony of profession. Profession is the substance, and baptism is the form; but Christ's command requires the form as well as the substance."[132] Going still further, Alexander Campbell and the Disciples of Christ argued for the necessity of baptism for salvation itself. The biblical passages used in support (Acts 2:38; 3:19; 22:16) associate salvation with baptism. His opponents challenged Campbell by noting that in many places in the biblical accounts of salvation, no mention of baptism is found. He countered that, similarly, in some biblical discussions of salvation, no mention of faith is found either. "Now, if they have any reason and right to say, that faith is understood in the one case; we have the same reason and right to say, that water or immersion is understood in the other. For their argument is, that in many places this matter [of faith] is made plain enough. This is, also, our argument—in many places this matter [of baptism] is made plain enough."[133] Thus, Campbellite theology insisted on the necessity of baptism for salvation.

A major contribution to the doctrine of baptism was made by Karl Barth. He closely associated the baptism with the Holy Spirit and baptism with water as the foundation of the Christian life.[134] For Barth the baptism with the Holy Spirit is the divine change that transforms a person who once rejected God into a Christian. As this event takes place, another foundational element—water baptism—accompanies it as the required human response to the divine activity.[135] While he was critical of the "bitter conflict" over the mode of baptism, Barth did not hesitate to affirm the necessity of baptism itself.[136] Chief among the biblical supports for baptism was Jesus' command to baptize in Matthew 28:19, but Barth also linked this command to Jesus' own baptism.[137]

Turning to a discussion of the goal of baptism, Barth continued his criticism of the prevailing views of baptism that focused on the people, action, and water involved.[138]

---

131. Baptism "is prerequisite to the privileges of a church relation; and to the Lord's Supper, in which the members of the church, by the [sacred] use of bread and wine, are to commemorate together the dying love of Christ." *New Hampshire Baptist Confession*, 14, in Lumpkin, 366.

132. John L. Dagg, *Manual of Theology: Treatise on Church Order* (repr., Harrisonburg, Va.: Gano Books, 1990), 95.

133. Alexander Campbell, *Christian System*, prop. 10 (Nashville: Gospel Advocate, 2001). Campbell further expressed the issue as two horns of a dilemma pitting "grace, faith, the blood of Jesus, the name of the Lord, and immersion" as "all essential to immediate pardon and acceptance" on one side, and "faith only, grace only, the blood of Christ only, and the name of the Lord only—and not immersion at all" on the other. He argued for the first horn by appealing to Mark 16:16; Acts 22:16; Heb. 9:13; 1 Peter 3:21; and Rev. 7:14. Ibid.

134. *CD*, IV/4, 2.

135. Ibid., 41.

136. From his study of the Greek words for baptism, Barth concluded that "it possibly, or even probably, took the form of immersion, though this is not absolutely certain. There is no proof that it had to take this form in the primitive community.... From the very beginning it might equally well have taken the form of affusion [pouring] or sprinkling. The only sure point is that it entails washing with water; no significance is to be attached to the form of application." Still, despite this apparent ambiguity over the mode of baptism, the New Testament was absolutely clear and insistent on the need for baptism. Ibid., 43, 45.

137. "The direct command to baptize is not a new thing, but an explication and proclamation of the institution of baptism already effected previously in the history of Jesus Christ, namely, in his baptism in the Jordan ... [River, in which] he had himself baptized by John." Ibid., 52, 53.

138. Ibid., 70–71.

By contrast, for Barth, "the goal of baptism is God's act of reconciliation in Jesus Christ through the Holy Spirit, God's act of judgment and grace, of salvation and revelation."[139] This meant that baptism is not a sacrament, with its emphasis on God's work in, with, and through the water. Rather, it is a thoroughly human response to what God has done.[140] Obviously, he stood at odds with the three common and influential views of Roman Catholicism, Lutheranism, and the Reformed tradition stemming from John Calvin.[141] Barth saw his position as approximating that of Huldrych Zwingli. Even though he did not rely on Zwingli for the development of his view, Barth welcomed the label "neo-Zwinglian" to describe his doctrine of baptism.[142]

Yet Barth broke even with Zwingli in what was perhaps his most sustained and earnest criticism of the prevailing view of this doctrine: infant baptism. Lamenting the historical development of this practice, he underscored the lack of biblical evidence for it.[143] Moreover, he saw the doctrine of infant baptism that came to full expression at the time of the Reformation as a reaction to attacks against the practice.[144] Thus, for Barth, the proofs for infant baptism were a late addition to the doctrine, and thus foreign to any proper doctrine of baptism. The historical reality of infant baptism, and the Reformers' wholehearted acceptance of the practice, compelled them to justify it without ever questioning its legitimacy in the first place. Barth found the Reformers woefully lacking in their attempts to formulate such a bona fide doctrine.[145]

So where does the doctrine and practice of baptism stand at the beginning of the third millennium? The historic positions embodied in Roman Catholicism, Lutheranism, Calvinism, and Anabaptism continue to provide the framework for baptismal views in most cases. Evangelicals continue to reject the Catholic view of baptismal regeneration. Infant baptism continues to be practiced among Lutheran, Reformed, Presbyterian, Methodist, Anglican/Episcopalian, and other evangelicals. Those with a baptistic view—all Baptist denominations, Evangelical Free churches, Bible churches, independent churches, and others—baptize people who can consciously understand the gospel, repent of their sins, and make a clear profession of faith in Jesus Christ as Savior and Lord.

139. Ibid., 72.

140. Ibid., 101–2.

141. Considering them together, Barth criticized the common core at the heart of these positions: "Our present interest is in the consensus that the meaning of baptism is to be sought and found in a divine action which is concealed in the administration by men and which makes use of this. What concerns us is the consensus that baptism is to be defined, described and explained as a mystery. This consensus needs to be demythologized. We oppose it. Against it we set the principle that the water baptism which is given by the community and desired and received by the candidates is the human action which corresponds to the divine action in the founding of the Christian life, which [the human action] goes to meet this [divine action] which responds to baptism with the Holy Spirit and cries out for it." Ibid., 105.

142. Ibid., 128–30.

143. Ibid., 165–66.

144. Ibid., 167.

145. Specifically, Barth criticized Luther for contradicting himself when he emphasized the importance of faith then dispensed with faith when infant baptism is performed. Ibid., 172. For Barth, this apparent contradiction called into question the legitimacy of Luther's defense of infant baptism. Similarly, Barth examined Calvin's explanation for the practice and found it lacking to an even greater degree. Specifically, Barth denounced Calvin's parallelism between circumcision and baptism, underscoring the vast difference between the old covenant people of God—physical descendants of Israel—and Christians—who are not the people of God by physical descent. Thus, Barth noted that Calvin "evaded or skipped proving the decisive minor premise, which is in his case that everything that applies to circumcision applies also to baptism. Thus his conclusion that Christians are also to be baptized as infants is left hanging in the air." The doctrine of infant baptism formulated by the Reformers—in particular, Luther and Calvin—fell short in Barth's estimation. Ibid., 178–79.

At the same time, a number of factors have led to less attention being paid to the historic divisions over the doctrine and practice of baptism. Through developments such as cooperative evangelistic efforts, the multidenominational allegiances of the staff members of parachurch ministries, ecumenical missionary endeavors, and the need to withstand the attacks of common opponents to the gospel, evangelicals have united in an unprecedented manner. While together they have championed the "essentials" of evangelical Christianity, these cooperating evangelicals have been forced to consider the essentialness of their opposing baptismal views. In some cases, their decision has been to relegate these conflicting positions to a matter of secondary importance. For example, in *This We Believe: The Good News of Jesus Christ for the World*, leading evangelicals set forth their idea of the central issues for propagating the gospel. At only one point was baptism mentioned.[146] In ecumenical developments spurred on by the World Council of Churches, *Baptism, Eucharist and Ministry* sought to settle some of the most highly entrenched points of dispute among churches. In its article on baptism, the *Baptism, Eucharist and Ministry (BEM)* report offered: "In order to overcome their differences, believer baptists and those who practice infant baptism should reconsider certain aspects of their practices. The first may seek to express more visibly the fact that children are placed under the protection of God's grace. The latter must guard themselves against the practice of apparently indiscriminate baptism and take more seriously their responsibility for the nurture of baptized children to mature commitments to Christ."[147] Although evangelicals have paid little heed to the World Council of Churches and its ecumenical endeavors, the sentiments expressed in the *BEM* report capture to some extent the realities that evangelicals and evangelical churches face as they engage in mission together.

---

146. This mention is in a paraphrase of Matt. 28:18–20: "To share the joy and hope of this gospel is a supreme privilege. It is also an abiding obligation, for the Great Commission of Jesus Christ still stands: proclaim the gospel everywhere, he said, teaching, baptizing, and making disciples." John Akers, John H. Armstrong, and John Woodbridge, eds., *This We Believe: The Good News of Jesus Christ for the World* (Grand Rapids: Zondervan, 2000), 240.

147. The World Council of Churches' Faith and Order Commission, *The Lima Report: Baptism, Eucharist and Ministry* (1982), 16, in Bettenson, 433.

Chapter 29

THE LORD'S SUPPER

How has the church developed various views of the meaning and observation of the Lord's Supper?

STATEMENT OF BELIEF

In addition to baptism, the other ordinance (or sacrament) instituted by Jesus Christ to be observed by the church is the Lord's Supper. Baptism is the initiatory rite of the Christian faith; the Lord's Supper is its continuing rite. The church has historically been faithful to obey the Lord's command to observe this rite but has done so with various understandings of the meaning, purpose, and results of its observation. The Catholic Church celebrates the Eucharist[1] according to a view called *transubstantiation*, which contends that the elements of bread and wine are changed in substance into Christ's body and blood. Lutheran churches celebrate the Lord's Supper according to a view called *consubstantiation*, which holds that the bread and the wine do not actually become the body and blood of Jesus Christ, but that the true body and blood of Christ are present "in, with, and under" the elements. Other churches celebrate communion as a *memorial* of the death of Jesus Christ. The bread and wine are symbols that help believers remember the body that was broken and the blood that was shed by Christ for their sins. Still other churches administer the Lord's Supper with a belief in the *spiritual presence* of Jesus Christ. The bread and wine are still symbols, but not empty symbols. Although the elements do not become the body and blood of Christ, they are a sign that Christ himself is really present.

Other differences exist as well. Some churches restrict the administration of this rite to members of the clergy; others place no such limitations. Some churches celebrate the Lord's Supper weekly (or even daily); others do it once a month, every quarter, or only once a year. The observation of the Lord's Supper by evangelicals is as varied as the above

---

1. The Greek word εὐχαριστια (*eucharistia*) is often translated "thanksgiving." When this rite is referred to as the Eucharist, it reflects the fact that Jesus *gave thanks* for the bread and the cup as part of the original celebration (Matt. 26:27; Mark 14:23; Luke 22:17, 19).

diversity presents, though they all have rejected the Catholic view of transubstantiation. Because such division exists, the various views will be traced throughout history to show how each perspective originated and developed.[2]

THE LORD'S SUPPER IN THE EARLY CHURCH

On the night in which he was betrayed, Jesus commemorated the Passover—his last supper—with his disciples. During that occasion, he instituted a new celebration (Matt. 26:26–29). The apostle Paul communicated divinely received instructions about this act to the church at Corinth (1 Cor. 11:23–26) and firmly rebuked the Corinthians for their abuse of the Lord's Supper while detailing how this practice should be observed (1 Cor. 11:27–32). Apparently, all the early churches regularly observed this rite (Acts 2:42).

The earliest Christian communities continued to observe the Lord's Supper initiated by Jesus himself and explained by Paul. The *Didache* gives us the earliest glimpse into its celebration, explaining that it must involve prayers of thanksgiving and giving this restriction: "But let no one eat or drink of your Eucharist except those who have been baptized into the name of the Lord, for the Lord has also spoken concerning this: 'Do not give what is holy to dogs.'"[3] Justin Martyr gave further details of this celebration. It began with thanksgiving for the bread and for the cup, which contained "wine mixed with water."[4] Deacons distributed the elements to all the baptized faithful, including those present at church as well as the sick and others who could not attend. Again, a restriction was enforced: "And this food is called among us εὐχαριστια [*eucharistia*; the Eucharist], of which no one is allowed to partake but the man who believes that the things we teach are true, and who has been washed with the washing that is for the remission of sins, and unto regeneration, and who is living as Christ has enjoined."[5]

Several points should be underscored. First, only baptized believers could participate in the Lord's Supper. As Cyprian explained: "For by baptism the Holy Spirit is received; and thus those who are baptized, and have received the Holy Spirit, are allowed to drink of the Lord's cup."[6] As for non-Christians in attendance at church: "We receive the heathen [pagans], when they wish to repent, into the church indeed to hear the word, but do not receive them to communion until they received the seal of baptism, and are made complete Christians."[7] Second, only baptized believers who were in proper relationship to Jesus and his church were allowed to participate. Referring to Paul's warning (1 Cor. 11:27–32), Origen urged Christians to observe the Lord's Supper in a worthy manner.[8]

---

2. My thanks to Christopher Newkirk for his help with this chapter.

3. *Didache*, 9, in Holmes, 261; *ANF*, 7:380. The reference is to Jesus' words (Matt. 7:6).

4. Justin Martyr, *First Apology*, 65, in *ANF*, 1:185.

5. Ibid., 65–66, in *ANF*, 1:185.

6. Cyprian, *Letter* 62.8, in *ANF*, 5:360. The text has been rendered clearer.

7. *Apostolic Constitutions*, 2.39, in *ANF*, 7:414.

8. Origen, *Commentary on Matthew*, 11:14, in *ANF*, 10:443. See further discussion in footnote 32. On the basis of this same passage (1 Cor. 11:27–32), Cyprian decried the fact that many lapsed believers—Christians who had denied the faith during intense persecution—were so quickly allowed to participate in communion, before they could adequately repent of abandoning the faith. He warned that this practice "profane[s] the sacred body of the Lord." Cyprian, *Letter* 10.1, in *ANF*, 5:291.

Third, celebration of the Lord's Supper was part and parcel of every weekly church gathering. In his description of a typical Sunday worship service, Justin Martyr noted: "When our prayer is ended, bread and wine and water are brought, and the president in like manner offers prayers and thanksgivings, according to his ability, and the people assent, saying 'Amen!' Then the Eucharist is distributed to each one, and each one participates in that over which thanks have been given. And a portion of it is sent by the deacons to those who are absent."[9] Fourth, the elements of this rite were bread and a cup containing a mixture of wine and water. Cyprian defended this practice as originating with the Lord himself.[10] Thus, as Jesus himself celebrated the first communion with bread and a cup containing both wine and water, so the church must "maintain the plan of evangelical truth and of the tradition of the Lord."[11]

The early church understood the Lord's Supper in a variety of ways. First, the concept of the Lord's Supper as a sacrifice is found very early on. Some linked the eucharistic sacrifice to the prophecy of Malachi, who rebuked the people of Israel for their worthless offerings and looked forward to a true sacrifice — "incense and pure offerings" — among the Gentiles (Mal. 1:10–11). The *Didache* appealed to this passage to encourage proper participation in the "sacrifice" of the Lord's Supper: "On the Lord's own day gather together and break bread and give thanks, having first confessed your sins so that your sacrifice may be pure. But let no one who has a quarrel with a companion join you until they have been reconciled, so that your sacrifice may not be defiled."[12] Justin Martyr saw Malachi as a prophet announcing the contrast between the Jews and the Gentile church: The Jews would continue to bring worthless offerings to God, while the church would offer a true sacrifice — the Lord's Supper — to glorify God.[13] This sacrificial view was also tied to Jesus' words about offering one's gift on the altar (Matt. 5:23–24).[14]

---

9. Justin Martyr, *First Apology*, 67, in *ANF*, 1:186. The text has been rendered clearer.

10. Cyprian, *Letter* 62.9, in *ANF*, 5:360–61.

11. Cyprian, *Letter* 62.1, in *ANF*, 5:359. Cyprian marshaled many scriptural examples to further support this practice. These included Noah (who "did not drink water but wine, and thus expressed the figure of the passion of the Lord"; Gen. 9:20–21), Melchizedek (who "brought out bread and wine"; Gen. 14:18), Solomon (whose wisdom "mixed her wine"; Prov. 9:2), Jacob's blessing of Judah (who "will wash his garments in wine, his robes in the blood of grapes"; Gen. 49:11), and Isaiah's prophecy of the Lord's passion ("Why are your garments red, like those of one treading the winepress?" Isa. 63:2). He seems to get these from Tertullian, *Against Marcion*, 4.40, in *ANF*, 3:418–19.

12. *Didache*, 14, in Holmes, 267; *ANF*, 7:381.

13. "God speaks by the mouth of Malachi ... about the sacrifices at that time presented by you: 'I have no pleasure in you, says the Lord; and I will not accept the sacrifices of your hands. For from the rising of the sun till the setting of the same, my name has been glorified among the Gentiles, and in every place incense is offered to my name, and a pure offering. For my name is great among the Gentiles, says the Lord, but you profane it.' Thus, he speaks of those Gentiles — namely, us — who in every place offer sacrifices to him, i.e., the bread of the Eucharist, and also the cup of the Eucharist, affirming both that we glorify his name, and that you profane it." Justin Martyr, *Dialogue with Trypho, a Jew*, 41, in *ANF*, 1:215. The text has been rendered clearer. Cf. ibid., 117, in *ANF*, 1:257. Irenaeus continued to link the Malachi passage with the sacrifice of the Eucharist: "Again, giving directions to his disciples to offer to God the first fruits of his own created things ... he [Jesus] took that created thing — bread — and gave thanks, saying, 'This is my body.' And the cup likewise — which is part of the creation to which we belong — he confessed to be his blood, and taught the new oblation [sacrifice, offering] of the new covenant. Receiving this from the apostles, the church offers it to God throughout all the world, to him who gives us as the means of existence the first fruits of his own gifts in the New Testament. Concerning this, Malachi ... spoke beforehand [he cites the Malachi text], indicating in the clearest manner by these words that the former people [the Jews] would stop making offerings to God, but that in every place a sacrifice — a pure one — would be offered to him. And his name is glorified among the Gentiles." Irenaeus, *Against Heresies*, 4.17.5, in *ANF*, 1:484. The text has been rendered clearer.

14. Irenaeus, *Against Heresies*, 4.18.1, in *ANF*, 1:484.

Second, while it is clear that sacrificial language was associated with the Lord's Supper, it is not as clear what the early church believed about the nature of the sacrifice. According to Irenaeus, the sacrifices are the bread and the cup of wine, the firstfruits of the divine creation.[15] Yet he held another view as well. In arguing against the heresy of Docetism, which denied the reality of the incarnation and the resurrection of the body, Irenaeus spoke of the Lord's Supper in terms of the actual body of Christ: "For as the bread, which is produced from the earth, when it receives the invocation from God, is no longer common bread, but the Eucharist, it consists of two realities, earthly and heavenly; so also our bodies, when they receive the Eucharist, are no longer corruptible, having the hope of the resurrection to eternity."[16] Thus, when the bread is offered to God during the celebration, it is not only common bread but the body of Jesus Christ as well. This latter heavenly reality nourishes the human flesh that feeds on the offering, and it makes the body a participant in Christ's resurrection life. Cyprian made a parallel between Jesus Christ the High Priest and the church's ministers as priests: As Christ the High Priest offered himself a sacrifice to the Father, so the priests offer a real sacrifice to God when celebrating the Lord's Supper.[17] For Cyprian, this parallel was warranted because "the Lord's passion is the sacrifice which we offer."[18]

Third, this idea rested on a belief in the reality of the presence of Christ in the Eucharist. Addressing the heresy of the Docetists, Ignatius noted a crucial error: "They abstain from the Eucharist and prayer, because they refuse to acknowledge that the Eucharist is the flesh of our Savior Jesus Christ, which suffered for our sins and which the Father by his goodness raised up."[19] Thus, just as these heretics denied the reality of the body of Jesus in his incarnation, so they denied the reality of his body in the Eucharist. Ignatius, however, held to a one-to-one correspondence between the bread and cup and the body and blood: "I want the bread of God, which is the flesh of Christ who is of the seed of David; and for drink I want his blood, which is incorruptible love."[20]

Others made this identification as well. Justin Martyr explained the church's teaching on the elements: "We do not receive these as common bread and common drink. But in like manner as Jesus Christ our Savior, having been made flesh by the Word of God, had both flesh and blood for our salvation, so likewise we have been taught that the food which is blessed by the prayer of his word, and from which our blood and flesh by transmutation are nourished, is the flesh and blood of that Jesus who was made flesh."[21] Irenaeus associated this transformation of the bread and the cup with the "consecration from God" during the eucharistic celebration. He further explained that the wine and the bread, "having received the Word of God, become the Eucharist, which is the body and

---

15. Irenaeus, *Fragment 37*, in *ANF*, 1:574.

16. Irenaeus, *Against Heresies*, 4.18.5, in *ANF*, 1:486.

17. As Cyprian reasoned, "If Jesus Christ, our lord and God, is himself the chief priest of God the Father, and has first offered himself a sacrifice to the Father, and has commanded this to be done in commemoration of himself, certainly that priest truly discharges the office of Christ, who imitates that which Christ did; and he then offers a true and full sacrifice in the church to God the Father, when he proceeds to offer it according to what he sees Christ himself to have offered." Cyprian, *Letter 62.14*, in *ANF*, 5:362.

18. Ibid., 62.17, in *ANF*, 5:363.

19. Ignatius, *Letter to the Smyrnaeans*, 6 (2), in Holmes, 189; *ANF*, 1:89 (the *ANF* edition numbers this citation as the opening part of sec. 7 in the *Letter to the Smyrnaeans*).

20. Ignatius, *Letter to the Romans*, 7.3, in Holmes, 175; *ANF*, 1:77.

21. Justin Martyr, *First Apology*, 66, in *ANF*, 1:185.

blood of Christ."[22] He also associated this change with the Holy Spirit, who was called upon after the church gave thanks for the elements and offered them to God: "We invoke the Holy Spirit, that he may exhibit this sacrifice, both the bread — the body of Christ — and the cup — the blood of Christ — in order that the receivers of these antitypes may obtain remission of sins and life eternal."[23] Thus, through the Word and the Spirit of God, the elements became associated with the body and blood of Christ.

Fourth, this belief in the reality of Christ's presence was tied to the act of commemoration, a key aspect of the rite. Justin Martyr saw the eucharistic elements alluded to in Isaiah 33:13–19: "Now it is evident that in this prophecy [allusion is made] to the bread which our Christ gave us to eat, in remembrance of his being made flesh for the sake of his believers, for whom he also suffered; and to the cup which he gave us to drink, in remembrance of his own blood, with giving of thanks."[24] He emphasized the commemorative aspect of the Eucharist, "the celebration of which our Lord Jesus Christ prescribed, in remembrance of the suffering which he endured on behalf of those who are purified in soul from all iniquity."[25] In the midst of realistic language about the bread and cup, even Cyprian underscored that Christ "has first offered himself a sacrifice to the Father, and he has commanded this to be done in commemoration of himself."[26]

Fifth, the Lord's Supper was viewed by some in symbolic terms. Tertullian used the eucharistic elements to demonstrate the wrongness of the heretic Marcion's denial of the true body of Jesus Christ: "Having taken the bread and given it to his disciples, Jesus made it his own body, by saying, 'This is my body,' that is, the symbol of my body. There could not have been a symbol, however, unless there was first a true body. An empty thing or phantom is incapable of a symbol. He likewise, when mentioning the cup and making the new covenant to be sealed 'in his blood,' affirms the reality of his body. For no blood can belong to a body that is not a body of flesh."[27] Still, for Tertullian, the elements were not empty symbols, for he also affirmed that "the flesh — the human body — feeds on the body and blood of Christ."[28]

The early church also noted several benefits of participation in the Lord's Supper. According to Ignatius, the eucharistic bread is "the medicine of immortality, the antidote we take in order not to die but to live forever in Jesus Christ."[29] Irenaeus believed that the Supper nourishes believers and encourages them to give thanks and serve God.[30] Moreover, Origen emphasized the fact that the very term emphasizes this benefit: "We

---

22. Irenaeus, *Against Heresies*, 5.2.3, in *ANF*, 1:528. Irenaeus used this reality to refute his Gnostic opponents: "As we are his members, we are also nourished by means of the creation. Christ has acknowledged the cup (which is a part of the creation) as his own blood, from which he refreshes our blood. And he has established the bread (also a part of the creation) as his own body, from which he gives increase to our bodies. Therefore, when the mingled cup and the baked bread receive the Word of God, and the Eucharist of the blood and the body of Christ is made (from which things the substance of our flesh is increased and sustained), how can the Gnostics maintain that the flesh is incapable of receiving the gift of God?" Ibid., 5.2.2–3, in *ANF*, 1:528.

23. Irenaeus, *Fragment 37*, in *ANF*, 1:574.

24. Justin Martyr, *Dialogue with Trypho*, 70, in *ANF*, 1:234.

25. Ibid., 41; in *ANF*, 1:215.

26. Cyprian, *Letter* 62.14, in *ANF*, 5:362.

27. Tertullian then gives examples of wine as a symbol for blood. Tertullian, *Against Marcion*, 4.40, in *ANF*, 3:418. The text has been rendered clearer, especially substituting the word *symbol* for *figure*.

28. Tertullian, *On the Resurrection of the Flesh*, 8, in *ANF*, 3:551.

29. Ignatius, *Letter to the Ephesians*, 20, in Holmes, 151; *ANF*, 1:57.

30. Irenaeus, *Against Heresies*, 4.18.6, in *ANF*, 1:486.

have a symbol of gratitude to God in the bread which we call the Eucharist."[31] Further-more, Clement of Alexandria underscored the sanctifying benefit of participation in the Supper.[32] This sanctification demands a radical break from sinful activities, as Cyprian urged: "The sanctified body and temple of God is not polluted by adultery, nor is the innocence dedicated to righteousness stained with the contagion of fraud; neither, after the Eucharist carried it, is the hand spotted with the sword and blood."[33]

Augustine's contribution to the theology of the sacraments was determinative for the church for centuries to come. He defined a sacrament generally as an outward and vis-ible sign of an invisible yet genuine grace.[34] Furthermore, the sacraments are effective in communicating this grace *ex opere operato*—literally, by the work performed. This perspective stood in stark contrast with heretics like the Donatists, who insisted that sac-raments are valid only when administered in a true church by a duly ordained minister. Augustine argued instead that Christ himself is actually the one who baptizes, serves the Lord's Supper, and administers other grace. Accordingly, even when heretics baptize, serve the Supper, and perform other such actions, God's grace is effectively channeled through those sacraments. For this reason, the sacraments of baptism and the Lord's Supper are necessary for salvation.[35]

Specifically, Augustine offered two perspectives on the Lord's Supper. On the one hand, he maintained that Christ is truly present in the elements: "That bread that you see on the altar, sanctified by the Word of God, is Christ's body. That cup, or rather the contents of that cup, sanctified by the Word of God, is Christ's blood. By these ele-ments the Lord Christ willed to convey his body and his blood, which he shed for us."[36] Augustine's notion of *ex opere operato* meant that grace is communicated through the sacrament regardless of who gives it and who receives it, because Christ is truly present. Thus, Augustine held a realistic view of the Lord's Supper: Christ is objectively present in the bread and the cup of wine.

On the other hand, he held a symbolic position, in accordance with his view of what a sacrament is. Augustine denied that the body and blood of the Lord's Supper are identi-

---

31. Origen, *Against Celsus*, 8.57, in *ANF*, 4:661.

32. "And to drink the blood of Jesus is to become partaker of the Lord's immortality; the Spirit being the energetic prin-ciple of the Word, as blood is of flesh. Accordingly, as wine is blended with water, so is the Spirit with man. And the one, the mixture of wine and water, nourishes to faith; while the other, the Spirit, conducts [leads] to immortality. And the mixture of both—of the water and of the Word—is called *Eucharist*, renowned and glorious grace; and they who by faith partake of it are sanctified both in body and soul." Clement of Alexandria, *The Instructor*, 2.2, in *ANF*, 2:242–43. As Ori-gen pointed out, this benefit of personal sanctification is not automatic for the one participating in the Lord's Supper. It is profitable only for those who participate in a worthy manner: "That which is sanctified through the word of God and prayer does not, in its own nature, sanctify him who uses it, for, if this were so, it would sanctify even him who eats unworthily of the bread of the Lord, and no one on account of this food would

become weak or sickly or asleep [Origen's reference is to 1 Cor. 11:29–30].... And in the case of the bread of the Lord, there is advantage to him who uses it, when with undefiled mind and pure conscience he partakes of the bread." Origen, *Commen-tary on Matthew*, 11.14, in *ANF*, 10:443.

33. Cyprian, *Treatise 9: On the Advantage of Patience*, 14, in *ANF*, 5:488.

34. Augustine, *On the Catechizing of the Uninstructed*, 26.50, in *NPNF*[1], 3:312.

35. "No one will enter into his kingdom who is not born again of water and the Spirit; nor shall anyone attain salvation and eternal life except in his kingdom—since the man who does not believe in the Son, and does not eat his flesh, shall not have life, but the wrath of God remains upon him." Augustine, *On the Merits and Forgiveness of Sins, and On the Baptism of Infants*, 1.33, in *NPNF*[1], 3:28. The text has been rendered clearer.

36. Augustine, *Sermon 227*, in Kelly, 447; cf. *On the Trin-ity*, 3.10.21.

cal with Christ's historical body, as seen in his interpretation of the words Jesus spoke to his disciples at the institution of the Supper: "Understand spiritually what I said; you are not to eat this body which you see; nor to drink that blood which they who will crucify me shall pour forth.... Although it is needful that this be visibly celebrated, yet it must be spiritually understood."[37] Indeed, Christ explained "what it is to eat his body and to drink his blood.... This it is, therefore, for a man to eat that meat [food] and to drink that drink, to dwell in Christ, and to have Christ dwelling in him."[38]

Augustine did not stop here. Appealing to Paul's instructions (1 Cor. 10:17), he challenged Christians to live what the Lord's Supper communicates — the unity of the members of the body of Christ:

> One bread; what is this one bread? The one body which we, being many, are. Remember that bread is not made from one grain, but from many.... Be what you can see, and receive what you are.... [S]o too with the wine. Brothers and sisters, just remind yourselves what wine is made from; many grapes hang in the bunch, but the juice of the grapes is poured together in one vessel. That too is how the Lord Christ signified us, how he wished us to belong to him, how he consecrated the sacrament of our peace and unity on his table.[39]

So, for Augustine the Lord's Supper portrays the unity of church members and challenges them to live genuinely as members of the body of Christ.

THE LORD'S SUPPER IN THE MIDDLE AGES

Augustine's view held sway for several centuries, but in the ninth century a controversy erupted over the nature of the presence of Christ in the Lord's Supper. Paschasius Radbertus, a Benedictine abbot, wrote a treatise *On the Body and Blood of the Lord* in 831, affirming a real presence of Christ: "Though the body and blood of Christ remain in the figure of bread and wine, yet we must believe them to be simply a figure and, after consecration, they are nothing else than the body and blood of Christ.... [We must believe them] to be clearly the very flesh which was born of Mary, and suffered on the cross and rose from the tomb."[40] This identification takes place when the words of institution are pronounced during the communion celebration, creating "not some other blood nor the blood of someone else, but the blood of Jesus Christ."[41] He supported his position with Christ's words of institution — "This is my body" (Matt. 26:26) — when he took the bread. Christ did not say, "This is the figure of my body," so Radbertus questioned how anyone could believe that "it is not in fact the reality of the flesh and blood of Christ" that exists in the Eucharist.[42] Radbertus carefully distinguished between reality — "the

---

37. Augustine, *Exposition of the Psalms*, 99.8, in *NPNF*[1], 8.485-86.

38. Augustine, *Tractates on the Gospel of John*, John 6:41-59, Tractate 26.18, in *NPNF*[1], 7.173.

39. Augustine, *Sermon 272*, in *Works of St. Augustine*, ed. John E. Rotelle, vol. 7: Sermons, trans. Edmund Hill (Hyde Park, N.Y.: New City, 1993), pt. 3, 300–301.

40. Paschasius Radbertus, *On the Body and Blood of the Lord*, 1, in Bettenson, 162.

41. Ibid., 15, in Pelikan, 3:75.

42. Ibid., 12, in Pelikan, 3:75–76.

true flesh and blood of Christ"—and figure—the bread and the wine. These elements do not undergo any change during the celebration. The figure still looks and tastes like bread and wine, but the reality is the body and blood of Christ.[43] Thus, "the substance of bread and wine is efficaciously changed within into the flesh and blood of Christ, in such a way that after the consecration the true flesh and blood of Christ is truly believed [to be present]."[44]

This perspective was immediately challenged. Rabanus Maurus strongly opposed the identification of Christ's body in the Eucharist with the incarnate body of the Lord. The key opponent of Radbertus, however, was Ratramnus, a monk from the same abbey who wrote a work also entitled *On the Body and Blood of the Lord*. Like Radbertus, he too distinguished carefully between reality and figure, but in a different way. For Ratramnus, reality is empirical reality perceived by the senses, a "representation of clear fact, not obscured by any shadowy images." Figure is "a kind of overshadowing that reveals its intent under some sort of veil."[45] Applying this discussion to the Lord's Supper, Ratramnus considered the presence of the body and blood of Christ in the Eucharist to be a figure, because the eucharistic mystery "exhibits one thing outwardly to the human senses and proclaims another thing inwardly to the minds of the faithful."[46] The historical body of Jesus Christ, on the other hand, is reality.

In light of this, Ratramnus addressed the key question: "whether that very body which was born of Mary, suffered, died, and was buried, and which sits at the right hand of the Father is daily eaten in the church by the mouth of the faithful through the mystery of the sacraments."[47] Ratramnus replied that "they are not the same."[48] Rather, there is "a great difference"[49] between the historical body of Christ—"the real flesh of Christ"—and the eucharistic body—"the sacrament of the real flesh."[50] So as not to be misunderstood, however, Ratramnus noted that "it should not be supposed that in the mystery of the sacrament either the body of the Lord or his blood is not received by the faithful."[51] But this is the figure of the body and the blood in the Eucharist, not the reality of the empirical body and blood of the historical Jesus Christ.[52]

Paschasius Radbertus's view was adopted. Following his lead, the church began to emphasize the reality of the presence of the body and blood of Christ in the sacrifice of the Lord's Supper. Julian of Toledo explained that "even if it were not mentioned anywhere at all in the ancient Scriptures, the authority of the universal church, which is evident in this practice, must not be regarded lightly."[53]

---

43. Ibid., 10–11, in Pelikan, 3:76.

44. Ibid., 8, in Pelikan, 3:79.

45. Ratramnus, *On the Body and Blood of the Lord*, 8, in Pelikan, 3:76.

46. Ibid., 9, in Pelikan, 3:76–77.

47. Ibid., 50, in Pelikan, 3:77.

48. Ibid., 72, in Pelikan, 3:77.

49. Ibid., 69, in Pelikan, 3:77.

50. Ibid., 57, in Pelikan, 3:77.

51. Ibid., 101, in Pelikan 3:77.

52. In support of his view, Ratramnus turned to the book of Hebrews and its insistence that the sacrifice offered by Christ was "once for all" (7:27; 9:26). This fact precluded a daily repetition of the sacrifice in the Lord's Supper. Radbertus, however, understood this "once for all" sacrifice differently: "Although Christ, having suffered once for all in the flesh, saved the world once for all through one and the same suffering unto death, this offering is nevertheless repeated daily." His reasoning was simple: where there is daily sin, there must be daily sacrifice. Radbertus, *On the Body and Blood of the Lord*, 9, in Pelikan, 3:79.

53. Julian of Toledo, *Prognostications of the Future*, in Pelikan, 3:80.

A similar controversy flared up in the eleventh century. Like Ratramnus before him, Berengar of Tours opposed the identification of the bread and the wine in the Lord's Supper with the historical body and blood of Christ. In support of his view, Berengar appealed to the early church fathers.[54] He noted Ambrose's view that Christ, who has been resurrected and ascended into heaven, is in an exalted state and cannot undergo any change. Thus, he cannot once again become a suffering victim in the Eucharist.[55] Berengar's denial that "the empirical ... bread consecrated on the altar is, after the consecration, truly the body of Christ that exists above"[56] sounded like heresy and was quickly opposed by the church.[57] In 1059 he was forced to repudiate his view by signing a statement affirming that "the bread and wine which are placed on the altar are, after consecration, not only a sacrament but the true body and blood of our Lord Jesus Christ, and that these are sensibly handled and broken by the hands of priests and crushed by the teeth of the faithful, not only sacramentally but in reality."[58] Only this view could ensure that the eucharistic sacrifice was different from the old covenant sacrifices.[59] And only this position could elevate the Lord's Supper above the other sacraments of the church.

This development resulted in much discussion concerning how the elements become the body and blood of Christ. Some articulated a view called *impanation*: While the substance of the bread and wine remain, "the body and blood of the Lord are contained there in a manner that is true but hidden."[60] The church did not accept this theory. Rather, it held that "before the consecration, the bread set forth on the Lord's table is nothing but bread, but in the consecration, by the ineffable power of God, the nature and substance of the bread are converted into the nature and substance of the flesh of Christ."[61] This transformation takes place when the words of consecration are pronounced, resulting in the bread and wine ceasing to exist as such and the body and blood of Christ being present in the sacrament.[62] Rather than the invocation of the Holy Spirit (the key part of the Lord's Supper in the early church), the words of institution became the turning point in the celebration of the sacrament by the medieval church.

At this time, the word *substance* came to hold special significance in the church's doctrine of the Lord's Supper.[63] In particular, Aristotle's use of the term *substance* to refer

54. Berengar of Tours, *Epistle to Adelmannus*, in Pelikan, 3:192.

55. Berengar of Tours, *On the Holy Supper*, 21, 37, 41, 42, in Pelikan, 3:192.

56. Ibid., 21, in Pelikan, 3:192.

57. He was "accused of saying that the Eucharist is not the true body of Christ nor his true blood, but some sort of figure and likeness." Adelmannus of Brescia, *Epistle to Berengar*, in Pelikan, 3:186.

58. Berengar of Tours, *Fragments*, appearing in Lanfranc of Bec, *On the Body and Blood of the Lord*, 2, in Bettenson, 163, and Pelikan, 3:187. Berengar later repudiated this recantation, and was again condemned in 1079.

59. Alger, *On the Sacraments*, 2.3, in Pelikan, 3:188.

60. Guitmond of Aversa, *On the Reality of the Body and Blood of Christ in the Eucharist*, 1, in Pelikan, 3:199. Cf. Berengar of Tours, *Opusculum*, appearing in Lanfranc of Bec, *On the Body and Blood of the Lord*, 9, in Pelikan, 3:198. Cf. Berengar of Tours, *Apologia: On the Holy Supper*, 21, in Pelikan, 3:199.

61. *Life of Saint Maurilius*, 11, in Pelikan, 3:199.

62. Durandus of Troarn, *On the Body and Blood of Christ*, 5.15, in Pelikan, 3:200.

63. Paschasius Radbertus had said the body and blood of Christ were "produced from the substance of bread and wine" when "the substance of bread and wine is changed into the flesh and blood of Christ, effectively and inwardly." Radbertus, *On the Body and Blood of the Lord*, 4, 8, in Pelikan, 3:202. But Ratramnus could also write of the "bread and wine that have been converted into the substance of Christ's body and blood"—though he meant something different by the term. Ratramnus, *On the Body and Blood of the Lord*, 30, in Pelikan, 3:202.

to the essence or defining nature of a thing was taken up in discussions of the Eucharist: The change that took place at the words of institution was a change in the substance of the bread and wine. According to Lanfranc, "earthly substances are changed in the essence of the Lord's body," and Baldwin of Ford explained that "the substance of the bread is changed into the substance of the flesh of Christ."[64]

Aristotle had spoken of both *substance*—the essence or nature of a thing—and *accidents*—the characteristics of a thing that can be perceived by the senses: the appearance, taste, smell, texture, and sound of a thing. Guitmond of Aversa parlayed this distinction into the definitive formula for the eucharistic transformation: While the *accidents* of the bread and wine remain the same—the elements still look like, taste like, smell like, and feel like bread and wine—their *substance* is transformed into the body and blood of Jesus Christ. Rolando Bandinelli, later to become Pope Alexander III, coined the term *transubstantiation* in 1140 to refer to this substantial change.[65]

The Fourth Lateran Council in 1215 made the official pronouncement of the church's position regarding the eucharistic presence of Jesus Christ, "whose body and blood are truly contained in the sacrament of the altar under the forms of bread and wine. The bread is transubstantiated into the body and the wine into the blood by the power of God, so we may receive from him what he has received from us."[66] Thus, the doctrine of transubstantiation was officially affirmed in the church. This council also established the law that people should participate in the sacrament at least once a year after the confession of sins.[67]

Following the official decree of the Fourth Lateran Council, Thomas Aquinas offered the definitive theological and philosophical framework to support transubstantiation. He explained how conversion of one substance into another—something that is naturally impossible—can take place by divine power with the Eucharist. Although the substance changes, the accidents of the bread and wine remain.[68] By joining Aristotelian philosophy with the church's theology of the Lord's Supper, Aquinas set forth the definitive Roman Catholic view of the presence of Christ during the celebration of the Eucharist.

Thomas Aquinas's Explanation of Transubstantiation

God is infinite act; thus, his action extends to the whole nature of being. Therefore, he can work not only formal conversion, so that diverse forms succeed each other in the same subject; but also the change of being itself, so

---

64. Lanfranc of Bec, *On the Body and Blood of the Lord*, 18, in Pelikan, 3:203; Baldwin of Ford, *The Sacrament of the Altar*, 2.1.3, in Pelikan, 3:203.

65. Pope Alexander III, *The Sentences of Roland*, in Pelikan, 3:203. The term also appeared in the writing of Stephen of Autun about the same time. *On the Sacrament of the Altar*, in Pelikan, 3:203.

66. Fourth Lateran Council, canon 1, in Petry, 322–23.

67. Ibid., canon 21, in Petry, 323. Although proclaimed by this council, the rule stipulating participation in communion

at least once a year was not followed by other councils in the thirteenth century. For example, the Council of Toulouse in 1229 and the Council of Albi in 1254 ruled that the faithful should participate in the Eucharist at least three times a year—Christmas and Pentecost, in addition to Easter. The Council of Toulouse, canon 13, in Mansi, 23:197; The Council of Albi, canon 29, in Mansi, 23:840; George Park Fisher, *History of Christian Doctrine* (New York: Scribner's, 1896), 101.

68. Thomas Aquinas, *Summa Theologica*, pt. 3, q. 75, art. 5.

that the whole substance of one thing be changed into the whole substance of another. And this is done by divine power in this sacrament. For the whole substance of the bread is changed into the whole substance of Christ's body, and the whole substance of the wine into the whole substance of Christ's blood. Thus, this is not a formal, but a substantial conversion; nor is it a kind of natural movement. Rather, with a name of its own, it can be called *transubstantiation.**

*Thomas Aquinas, *Summa Theologica*, pt. 3, q. 75, art. 4.

During the latter part of the Middle Ages, the church's position on the Lord's Supper became standardized. Several changes, however, did take place. An important modification had to do with the correctness of the centuries-old tradition of giving communion to infants immediately after they were baptized.[69] One development was to give infants only one of the elements—the cup. The reason for this was a view called *concomitance*, which was explained by Bonaventura: "Because the blessed and glorious body of Christ cannot be divided into its parts and cannot be separated from the soul or from the highest divinity, so under each species there is the one, entire, and indivisible Christ—namely, body, soul, and God. Thus, in each is present the one and most simple sacrament containing the entire Christ."[70] Because the entire Christ is present in each of the elements, taking only one of them still provides a person with all of Christ. The usual manner of celebrating the Lord's Supper was by serving both the bread and the cup, but now an exception was made: "We teach and urge that this custom should always be maintained in the holy church, except in the case of infants and sick people who cannot swallow bread."[71] But the church still held that the cup should be given to infants after their baptism "because, as it is not possible for anyone to enter into life without baptism, so is it not possible without this life-giving viaticum [the Eucharist given to those in mortal danger]."[72] This practice ceased, however, and communion was not given to children recently baptized. This modification was due to a second development.

In the thirteenth century, the church began to give the bread but not the cup to the laity. Again, this practice was justified theologically by the doctrine of concomitance. If laypeople receive only one of the elements, they still receive all of Christ. Practically, this change was instituted out of concern for profaning the holy sacrament. The church feared that the frequent serving of the cup could result in some of the wine being spilled, desecrating the blood of Christ. To prevent this from happening, the church restricted the drinking of the cup to the priest who celebrated the Mass. This was called *communion*

69. This practice was reflected in the following church law: "The presbyter must always have the Eucharist ready, so that when somebody is ill, or an infant is ill, he may immediately communicate him, lest he die without communion." Regino of Prum, *On Church Discipline*, 1.69, in Fisher, *History of Christian Doctrine*, 101.

70. Bonaventura, *Breviloquium*, 6.9 (5), in *Breviloquium of*

St. Bonaventura, trans. E. E. Nemmers (St. Louis: B. Herder, 1946), 199–200.

71. Pope Paschal II, *Letter* 85, *To Pontius*, in Fisher, *History of Christian Doctrine*, 102.

72. William of Champeaux, *Fragment*, in Fisher, *History of Christian Doctrine*, 103.

in one kind because only one element—the bread—was given to the laity during the eucharistic service.[73]

While the Catholic Church settled into its observance of the Lord's Supper with the understanding of transubstantiation, several voices raised strong opposition to its belief. Chief among these was John Wycliffe, who attacked the church's view with a fury[74] and offered several reasons for his rejection of transubstantiation. First and foremost, he decried the lack of a biblical and rational foundation for the idea.[75] A second reason was that transubstantiation did not enjoy the support of church history.[76] Third, transubstantiation was defeated by the recognition of the senses and human judgment that the bread is bread before being consecrated and remains bread after it is consecrated.[77] Finally, Wycliffe drew attention to the disastrous consequences of belief in transubstantiation. He was particularly critical of the idolatry that resulted from the idea, which he saw in two areas: people's worship of the consecrated bread, and the absolute power claimed by the priests to transform the bread into the body of Christ.[78]

On another front, the Catholic Church's practice of communion in one kind was attacked by John Hus and his followers. Hus decried the giving of the eucharistic bread to laypeople while withholding the eucharistic cup from them. He urged the church to rehabilitate the practice of communion of both species, supporting his idea with the conviction that "not custom, but the example of Christ"[79] must be authoritative.[80]

73. It was only a small step from this development to completely prohibiting infants recently baptized from taking communion. Because it was too difficult for them to swallow the eucharistic bread, and because this was the only element given to the laity during the Mass, baptized children were not given communion. This opened up the question of the proper interpretation of the ruling set down by the Fourth Lateran Council (noted above): "After they have reached the age of accountability, all the faithful of both genders will ... reverently receive the sacrament of the Eucharist at least at Easter." What was meant by the "age of accountability"? At what age could children begin to receive communion? This question would not be finally answered for several more centuries, when the Council of Trent made this pronouncement: "This holy Synod teaches that little children who have not arrived at the use of reason are not required by any necessity to participate in the sacramental communion of the Eucharist. Forasmuch as, having been regenerated by the bath of baptism and being incorporated into Christ, they cannot at that age lose the grace of being the sons of God, which they have already acquired." *Canons and Decrees of the Council of Trent*, 21st session (July 16, 1562), *Decree on Communion under Both Species, and the Communion of Infants*, chap. 4, in Schaff, 2:174. The text has been rendered clearer.

74. "I maintain that among all the heresies which have ever appeared in the church, there was never one that was more cunningly smuggled in by hypocrites than this [tran-

substantiation], or which in more ways deceives the people; for it plunders them [the people], leads them astray into idolatry, denies the teaching of Scripture, and by this unbelief provokes the Truth himself oftentimes to anger." John Wycliffe, *Trialog*, 4.2.248, in Gotthard Lechler, *John Wycliffe and His English Precursors* (London: Religious Tract Society, 1878), 343.

75. "Neither upon Scripture nor reason nor revelation can the [Catholic] Church base ... transubstantiation. Therefore, we are not any more obligated to believe this than was the primitive church." John Wycliffe, *On the Eucharist*, 3.13, LCC 14:81.

76. John Wycliffe, *On the Eucharist*, 2.31, LCC, 14:73.

77. John Wycliffe, *Trialog*, 4.4.257, in Lechler, *John Wycliffe and His English Precursors*, 346.

78. Ibid., 4.5.261; 4.6.264; 4.7.279, in Lechler, *John Wycliffe and His English Precursors*, 347.

79. John Hus, *Epistle* 141, in Pelikan, 4:123.

80. His follower John of Rokycana echoed Hus on this, underscoring that "the communion of the divine Eucharist under both species, namely, bread and wine, is of great value and aid to salvation and is necessary for the entire people of believers, and it was commanded by our Lord and Savior." John of Rokycana, *The Position That Communion under Both Kinds Is Necessary and Commanded by the Lord Our Savior*, in Pelikan, 4:123.

THE LORD'S SUPPER IN THE REFORMATION AND POST-REFORMATION

Martin Luther and Consubstantiation[81]

With the publication of *The Babylonian Captivity of the Church* in 1520, Martin Luther attacked the sacramental system and the eucharistic practices of the Roman Catholic Church.[82] In particular he addressed three "captivities" to which the church had subjected the Lord's Supper. The first captivity was the church's withholding of the cup from the laity and the administration of communion in one kind. Luther passionately opposed this practice. He emphasized Jesus' insistence that the cup be drunk by "all" of his disciples.[83] He also dissented logically, reasoning that if the Lord's Supper is given "to the laity, it inevitably follows that it ought not to be withheld from them in either form."[84] Most important, Luther focused on the fact that "the blood is given to all those for whose sins it was poured out. But who will dare to say that it was not poured out for the laity?"[85] Finally, Luther questioned why the church, if it concedes that the laity receive divine grace (the more important matter) through the sacrament, would not concede the sacrament itself (a lesser matter).[86] He called for a general council of the church to put a halt to this tyranny.

The second captivity was the church's decree that transubstantiation—based on Aquinas's use of Aristotle's philosophy—was the only legitimate view of the presence of Christ in the Eucharist. Like Wycliffe before him, Luther underscored the lack of biblical evidence for this position, concluding: "What is asserted without the Scriptures or proven revelation may be held as an opinion but need not be believed."[87] Moreover, Luther, knowing that Aristotle held substance and accidents to be inseparable, criticized Aquinas for misunderstanding and misusing Aristotelian philosophy to explain transubstantiation, with the result that Aquinas built "an unfortunate superstructure [philosophical, rather than biblical, support for transubstantiation] upon an unfortunate foundation [a misunderstanding of Aristotle's philosophy]."[88]

More important, at the heart of his rejection of transubstantiation was the essential principle of interpreting the words of Scripture according to "their grammatical and

---

81. The term *consubstantiation* is used with advisement. The Lutherans did not use it; indeed, Calov denied that the Lutheran view was "consubstantiation, which the Calvinists calumniously charge upon us." Abraham Calov, *Systema Locorum Theologicorum*, 9.307, in Schmid, 564. This being said, however, the term has become so widely associated with the Lutheran position that I will use it here as I explain the historical development of the position.

82. "To begin with, I must deny that there are seven sacraments, and for the present maintain that there are but three: baptism, penance, and the bread. All three have been subjected to a miserable captivity by the Roman curia, and the church has been robbed of all her liberty." Martin Luther, *The Babylonian Captivity of the Church*, LW, 36:18. When he said "for the present," Luther was nearly exaggerating, because by the end of this writing he had excluded penance from being a sacrament: "Never-

theless, it has seemed proper to restrict the name of sacrament to those promises which have signs attached to them. The remainder, not being bound to signs, are bare [mere] promises. Hence there are, strictly speaking, but two sacraments in the church of God—baptism and the bread. For only in these two do we find both the divinely instituted sign and the promise of forgiveness of sins." Ibid., LW, 36:124. Thus, the Protestant position that there are only two sacraments, not seven, was originated.

83. Ibid., LW, 36:20. His appeal was to Matt. 26:27 and Mark 14:23.

84. Ibid., LW, 36:21.

85. Ibid., LW, 36:22. His appeal was to Matt. 26:28 with Luke 22:20.

86. Ibid., LW, 36:23.

87. Ibid., LW, 36:29.

88. Ibid.

proper sense."[89] Applying this to the discussion of the Lord's Supper, Luther noted: "It is an absurd and unheard-of juggling with words to understand 'bread' to mean 'the form or accidents of bread,' and 'wine' to mean 'the form or accidents of wine....' [It is not] right to enfeeble the words of God in this way, and by depriving them of their meaning to cause so much harm."[90] Luther also appealed to the history of the church: "The church kept the true faith for more than twelve hundred years, during which time the holy fathers never, at any time or place, mentioned this transubstantiation (a monstrous word and a monstrous idea), until the pseudo philosophy of Aristotle began to make its inroads into the church in these last three hundred years."[91] Luther could not subscribe to such a recent doctrine. To conclude the matter, he pointed out that "the laymen have never become familiar with their fine-spun philosophy of substance and accidents, and could not grasp it if it were taught to them."[92]

The third captivity was the church's view of the Lord's Supper as "a good work and a sacrifice."[93] As a result, "this abuse has brought an endless host of other abuses in its train, so that the faith of this sacrament has become utterly extinct and the holy sacrament has been turned into mere merchandise, a market, and a profit-making business."[94]

To counter this illegitimate view, Luther offered his own understanding of the Lord's Supper. It is Christ's testament, a promise made by him who was about to die, designating his inheritance — the forgiveness of sins — and naming his heirs — those who believe the promise of the testator.

Martin Luther's View of the Lord's Supper as a Testament

A testament, as everyone knows, is a promise made by one about to die, in which he designates his bequest and appoints his heirs. A testament, therefore, involves first, the death of the testator, and second, the promise of an inheritance and the naming of the heir.... Christ testifies concerning his death when he says, "This is my body, which is given, this is my blood, which is poured out" [Luke 22:19–22]. He names and designates the bequest when he says "for the forgiveness of sins" [Matt. 26:28]. But he appoints the heirs when he says "for you [Luke 22:19–20; 1 Cor. 11:24] and for many" [Matt. 26:28; Mark 14:24], that is, for those who accept and believe the promise of the testator. For here it is faith that makes men heirs.... You see, therefore, that what we call the mass is a promise of the forgiveness of sins made to us by God, and such a promise as has been confirmed by the death of the Son of God.*

*Martin Luther, The Babylonian Captivity of the Church, LW, 36:38.

Luther's view had ramifications for how the Lord's Supper was to be observed: "If the mass is a promise ... then access to it is to be gained, not with any works, or powers, or

---

89. Ibid., LW, 36:30.
90. Ibid., LW, 36:31.
91. Ibid.

92. Ibid.
93. Ibid., LW, 36:35.
94. Ibid.

merits of one's own, but by faith alone."[95] The one who participates in the Lord's Supper hears the Word of God with its promise of the forgiveness of sins and by faith confidently relies on this promise.[96] This also meant that the Lord's Supper is valid for believers only. Its blessings could not be applied to another person, so masses said for the dead were worthless.[97] Finally, this meant that the Lord's Supper is not a sacrifice. A sacrifice is given; a promise is received. Ultimately, Luther challenged the church to rethink its entire eucharistic practice: "The more closely our mass resembles that first mass of all, which Christ performed at the Last Supper, the more Christian it will be."[98]

Although he dissented from the official doctrine of transubstantiation and formulated his own view of the Lord's Supper as a testament, Luther continued to uphold the view that Christ was truly and completely present in the sacrament. Indeed, the sacrament "is the true body and blood of our Lord Jesus Christ, under the bread and wine, given to us Christians to eat and to drink, as it was instituted by Christ himself."[99] He gave several reasons for this view. First, Christ's words of institution—"This is my body"—were to be taken literally, not figuratively. Second, on the basis of biblical statements that Christ is seated at the right hand of God (the expression refers to the ruling power of God, which is everywhere), Luther held that Christ is present everywhere. This shows "at least in one way how God could bring it about that Christ is in heaven and his body in the Supper at the same time."[100] Third, this reality occurs in the incarnation: "Since the divinity and humanity are one person in Christ, the Scriptures ascribe to the divinity, because of this personal union, all that happens to humanity, and vice versa."[101] This union resulted in Jesus' human nature—which in and of itself is localized in one space—becoming ubiquitous (everywhere present). "Wherever Christ is according to his divinity, he is there as a natural, divine person and he is also naturally and personally there.... But if he is present naturally and personally wherever he is, then he must be man there, too, since he is not two separate persons but a single person. Wherever this person is, it is the single, indivisible person, and if you can say, 'Here is God,' then you must also say, 'Christ the man is present too.'"[102]

The view of Luther and his followers eventually came to be called (by its opponents) *consubstantiation*: the body of Christ is present "in, *with* (*con*), and under" the *substance* of the bread.[103] According to the *Formula of Concord*: "We maintain and believe, accord-

95. Ibid., LW, 36:38–39.

96. This meant that Christ's words of institution must be clearly and publicly announced, so that people may hear the promise. Here Luther challenged the church's practice of saying the words softly so that the people could not help but participate in the Eucharist superstitiously. Ibid., LW, 36:41.

97. At this point, Luther challenged the centuries-old tradition of the church by which it gained a great amount of income, as it required and received payment for these masses. Ibid., LW, 36:49.

98. Ibid., LW, 36:51–52.

99. Martin Luther, *Small Catechism*, 6, in Schaff, 3:90.

100. *Confession Concerning Christ's Supper*, LW, 37:207. As we will see, on these points Luther clashed with Huldrych Zwingli.

101. Ibid., LW, 37:210.

102. Ibid., LW, 37:218. For holding this belief, Luther was charged by his opponents with the ancient heresy of Eutychianism, or the fusion of the divine and human natures into one nature. Ibid., LW, 37:212. For a discussion of Eutychianism, see chap. 17.

103. Specifically, the body of Christ is "under the bread, with the bread, and in the bread." *The Solid Declaration of the Formula of Concord*, 7.35, in *Triglot Concordia: The Symbolical Books of the Evangelical Lutheran Church*, trans. F. Bente and W. H. T. Dau (St. Louis: Concordia, 1921), 983. Ursinus is credited with coining the term *consubstantiation*. *Explanations of the Heidelberg Catechism*, 2.78.4; cf. Theodore Beza, *Against Matthias Flacius Illyricus*, 29–30, in Pelikan, 4:200–201.

ing to the simple words of the testament of Christ, the true, yet supernatural eating of the body of Christ, as also the drinking of His blood, which human senses and reason do not comprehend."[104] Consubstantiation became the Lutheran contribution to the controversies regarding the Lord's Supper at the time of the Reformation.

Huldrych Zwingli and the Memorial Oath

Huldrych Zwingli developed a different notion of the Lord's Supper. Like his contemporary Luther, he dissented from the Roman Catholic idea of transubstantiation, offering several arguments against it.[105] First, relying on Augustine, Zwingli noted that Christ's body is located at the right hand of God the Father: "The body of Christ has to be in some particular place in heaven by reason of its character as a true body. And again: Seeing that the body of Christ rose from the dead, it is necessarily in one place. The body of Christ is not in several places at one and the same time any more than our bodies are."[106] In particular, "According to its proper essence, the body of Christ is truly and naturally seated at the right hand of the Father. It cannot therefore be present in this way in the Supper."[107] From this line of reasoning, Zwingli concluded that the eucharistic elements cannot be transubstantiated into the body and blood of Christ.[108]

For his second point against transubstantiation, Zwingli defined a sacrament as "the sign of a holy thing.... Now the sign and the thing signified cannot be one and the same. Therefore the sacrament of the body of Christ cannot be the body itself."[109] Thus, there is no one-to-one correspondence between the eucharistic elements and the body and blood of Christ. Third, Zwingli underscored the proper way to interpret the words of institution. They should not be taken literally, but figuratively,[110] as proved by Christ's own words in John 6:63: "The flesh profits nothing."[111] In the Lord's Supper, therefore, "the words of Christ cannot refer to physical flesh and blood."[112]

Zwingli also voiced opposition to Luther's view of the Lord's Supper, which he considered to be based on a (mistaken) literal interpretation of Matthew 26:26.[113] Zwingli insisted that a literal interpretation would mean that transubstantiation is the correct view, a point he had already proved wrong.[114]

---

104. *Epitome of the Formula of Concord*, 42.21, in Bente and Dau, *Triglot Concordia*, 817.

105. Huldrych Zwingli, *An Exposition of the Faith*, in *Zwingli and Bullinger*, ed. G. W. Bromiley, LCC, 24: 254–55.

106. Ibid., 24:255. His citation of Augustine is a paraphrase from *Tractates on the Gospel of John*, John 7:19-24, Tractate 30.1, in *NPNF¹*, 7:186. Zwingli strengthened this point by focusing on the promise of Christ in John 17:11 and its fulfillment in his ascension: "'Again, I leave the world and go to the Father.' Truth itself compels us to refer this saying primarily and quite literally to Christ's humanity.... Which nature is it that leaves the world? Not the divine, for the divine nature is not confined to one place and therefore does not leave it. Consequently, it is the human nature that leaves the world.... As regards a natural, essential and localized presence, the humanity is not here, for it has left the world. Hence, the body

of Christ is not eaten by us naturally or literally ... but sacramentally and spiritually." Zwingli, *Exposition of the Faith*, 24:257.

107. Ibid., 24:256.

108. For his apparent separation between the human nature and divine nature of Christ, Zwingli was charged by his opponents with the ancient heresy of Nestorianism, or the division of the divine and human natures in Christ. Luther, *Confession Concerning Christ's Supper*, LW, 37:212–13. For a discussion of Nestorianism, see chap. 17.

109. Huldrych Zwingli, *On the Lord's Supper*, LCC, 24:188.

110. Ibid., LCC, 24:189–90.

111. Ibid., LCC, 24:190.

112. Ibid., LCC, 24:191.

113. Ibid.

114. Ibid.

In formulating his own view over against transubstantiation and consubstantiation, Zwingli was influenced by Cornelius Hoen, who argued that a better rendering of "This is my body" would be "This signifies my body." Additionally, Zwingli noted, "For immediately afterwards [after saying 'This is my body'] in Luke 22[:19] Christ adds: 'This do in remembrance of me,' from which it follows that the bread is only a figure of his body to remind us in the Supper that the body was crucified for us."[115] Thus, Zwingli emphasized the Lord's Supper as a memorial.

Huldrych Zwingli on Christ's Words, "This Is My Body"

It has already become clear enough that in this context the word "is" cannot be taken literally. Hence it follows that it must be taken metaphorically or figuratively. In the words: "This is my body," the word "this" means the bread, and the word "body" means the body that is put to death for us. Therefore, the word "is" cannot be taken literally, for the bread is not the body and cannot be.... Necessarily, then, it must be taken figuratively or metaphorically; "This is my body," means, "The bread signifies my body," or "is a figure of my body."*

*Huldrych Zwingli, *On the Lord's Supper*, LCC, 24:225.

Because the Supper is a memorial, the key to its observance is remembering what Christ had accomplished on the cross, and this require faith. Returning to John 6, Zwingli noted (v. 47) "that by eating his flesh and blood Christ simply means believing in the one who gave his flesh and blood that we might live. It is not eating or seeing or perceiving him which saves, but believing on him."[116] Still, the sacrament is necessary because, as an oath, it was God's pledge of his faithfulness to keep his promise of forgiveness for his people.[117]

As his position developed, Zwingli switched from viewing the Lord's Supper as a pledge of a divine oath to viewing it as a pledge of believers to Christ and his church, a pledge "by which someone proves to the church that he either intends to be, or already is, a soldier of Christ, and which informs the whole church, rather than himself, of his faith."[118] Thus, the Lord's Supper as a sacrament is "a demonstration of allegiance" by a believer to the church,

---

115. Ibid., 24:225.

116. Ibid., 24:203.

117. Alister E. McGrath, *Reformation Thought: An Introduction*, 2nd ed. (Grand Rapids: Baker, 1993), 171.

118. Huldrych Zwingli, *Commentary on True and False Religion*; cited in McGrath, *Reformation Thought*, 171. From his service as a chaplain in the Swiss army, Zwingli drew upon two analogies to explain the Lord's Supper in terms of a military oath. First, a Swiss soldier was marked by a white cross (think of the Swiss flag with a white cross on a red background), indicating his loyalty to the Swiss Confederacy. Second, a Swiss citizen went on a pilgrimage to Nahenfels, the site of a battle between Swiss and Austrian forces in 1388 that marked the beginning of the Swiss Confederacy: "If a man sews on a white cross, he proclaims that he is a soldier. And if he makes the pilgrimage to Nahenfels and gives God praise and thanksgiving for the victory granted to our forefathers, he testifies that he is a soldier indeed. Similarly ... the man who in the remembrance or Supper gives thanks to God in the congregation testifies to the fact that from the very heart he rejoices in the death of Christ and thanks him for it." Huldrych Zwingli, *Of Baptism*, LCC, 24:131.The text has been rendered clearer.

by which he swore obedience to it. And it is a memorial of the death of Christ, the event that gave birth to the church. By it, the Christian calls to mind what Christ did, as though Christ said: "I entrust to you a symbol of this my surrender and testament, to awaken in you the remembrance of me and of my goodness to you, so that when you see this bread and this cup, held forth in this memorial supper, you may remember me as delivered up for you, just as if you saw me before you as you see me now, eating with you."[119]

Luther and Zwingli faced off against each other at the Marburg Colloquy in 1529. At issue were fifteen points of disagreement between Luther and his sympathizers (chief among whom was Philipp Melanchthon) and Zwingli and his followers (including Oecolampadius and to some extent Martin Bucer). On fourteen of the points, these theologians of the Reformation arrived at agreement. On the fifteenth point, however, the colloquy only served to widen the chasm. There would be no consensus on the Lord's Supper: "We have not agreed at this moment whether the true body and blood of Christ be corporeally present in the bread and wine."[120] The memorial view became Zwingli's contribution to the controversies regarding the Lord's Supper at the time of the Reformation.

John Calvin and Real Presence

The third leading figure of the Reformation, John Calvin, presented yet another perspective on the Lord's Supper. Because this rite is a sacrament, Calvin sought to define that term carefully as "an outward sign by which the Lord seals on our consciences the promises of his good will toward us in order to sustain the weakness of our faith. And we in turn attest our piety toward him in the presence of the Lord and of his angels and before men."[121] The sacraments do not confirm God's Word for us, but instead help us

---

119. McGrath, *Reformation Thought*, 172. Borrowing another analogy from Cornelius Hoen, Zwingli presented the Lord's Supper as a pledge similar to a ring given by a groom to his bride as they marry. The ring is special because of the context in which it is presented. Zwingli specifically addressed a ring worn by a queen, a present from her king: "The ring with which your majesty was betrothed to the queen your consort is not valued by her merely according to the value of the gold: it is gold, but it is also beyond price, because it is the symbol of her royal husband. For that reason she regards it as the king of all her rings, and if ever she is naming and valuing her jewels, she will say: This is my king, that is, the ring with which my royal husband was betrothed to me. It is the sign of an indissoluble union and fidelity. In the same way the bread and wine are the symbols of that friendship by which God is reconciled to the human race in and through his Son. We do not value them according to their intrinsic worth, but according to the greatness of that which they represent. The bread is no longer common, but consecrated. It is called bread, but it is also called the body of Christ. Indeed, it is in fact the body of Christ, but only in name and signification, or, as we now say, sacramentally." Zwingli, *Exposition of the Faith*, LCC, 24:262–63.

120. G. R. Potter, *Zwingli* (Cambridge: Cambridge Univ. Press, 1976, 1984), 330 2n., in Timothy George, *Theology of the Reformers* (Nashville: Broadman, 1988), 150. Some recent scholarship on Zwingli dissents from the traditional understanding of his view of the Lord's Supper as merely a memorial celebration. One passage from Zwingli that indicates this asserts that Christians come to "the Lord's Supper to feed spiritually upon Christ." Zwingli, *Exposition of the Faith*, LCC, 24:259. See Gottfried W. Lochner, *Zwingli's Thought: New Perspectives* (Leiden: E. J. Brill, 1981).

121. John Calvin, *Institutes of the Christian Religion*, 4.14.1, LCC, 2:1277. Simplifying this idea and giving a nod to Augustine, Calvin stated further: "Here is another briefer definition: one may call it a testimony of divine grace toward us, confirmed by an outward sign, with mutual attestation of our piety toward him. Whichever of these definitions you may choose, it does not differ in meaning from that of Augustine, who teaches that a sacrament is 'a visible sign of a sacred thing,' or 'a visible form of an invisible grace,' but it better and more clearly explains the thing itself." Ibid. The citations from Augustine are from *On the Catechizing of the Uninstructed*, 26.50, in *NPNF¹*, 3:312.

to believe in it: "By this means God provides first for our ignorance and dullness, then for our weakness."[122] One of Calvin's key doctrines was God's accommodation: Due to human weakness and ignorance, God in his mercy accommodated himself to our level, stooping down to address us in a manner that we can understand. For Calvin, the sacraments were an example of this divine condescension: "He condescends to lead us to himself even by these earthly elements, and to set before us in the flesh a mirror of spiritual blessings."[123] The church is made aware of these "spiritual blessings" through the preached word, which must always accompany the sacraments so as to explain them.[124] The church is thus characterized by the *preached* word, which comes first, and the *visible* word, or the sacraments, which follow.

Also crucial to this observance is the work of the Holy Spirit. Calvin rejected any magical force in the sacraments but emphasized the power of the Spirit in them.[125] Indeed, the two are intimately associated: "What increases and confirms faith is precisely the preparation of our minds by his [the Spirit's] inward illumination to receive the confirmation extended by the sacraments."[126] In addition to serving the faith of believers, the sacraments attest to their faith. But Calvin specifically distanced himself from this view—the one held by Zwingli—by underscoring that this attestation of faith is a secondary purpose of the sacraments, in contrast to the primary end of bolstering faith.[127]

Calvin relied chiefly on John 6 for his theology of this sacrament, noting: "Just as bread and wine sustain physical life, so are souls fed by Christ. We now understand the purpose of this mystical blessing, namely, to confirm for us the fact that the Lord's body was once for all so sacrificed for us that we may now feed upon it, and by feeding feel in ourselves the working of that unique sacrifice; and that his blood was once so shed for us in order to be our perpetual drink."[128] Thus, Christ himself is spiritually present in the Lord's Supper.[129] The tokens of the bread and wine are surely symbols, admitted Calvin. But, he argued, in the Supper, God does not present "a vain and empty sign but manifests there the effectiveness of his Spirit to fulfill what he promises."[130]

---

122. Calvin, *Institutes*, 4.14.3, LCC, 2:1278.

123. Ibid. Calvin added: "The sacraments, therefore, are exercises which make us more certain of the trustworthiness of God's Word. And because we are of flesh, they are shown us under things of flesh, to instruct us according to our dull capacity, and to lead us by the hand as tutors lead children.... For by them God manifests himself to us ... as far as our dullness is given to perceive, and attests his good will and love toward us more expressly than by word." Ibid., 4.14.6, LCC, 2:1281.

124. Ibid., 4.17.39, LCC, 2:1416.

125. Ibid., 4.14.9, LCC, 2:1284. He added that the sacraments "do not bestow any grace of themselves, but announce and tell us, and (as they are guarantees and tokens) ratify among us, those things given us by divine bounty. The Holy Spirit ... is he who brings the graces of God with him, gives a place for the sacraments among us, and makes them bear

fruit." Ibid., 4.14.17, LCC, 2:1293.

126. Ibid., 4.14.10, LCC, 2:1285.

127. Ibid., 4.14.13, LCC, 2:1288–89. In this section, Calvin criticized Zwingli's view of the sacraments as oaths. Although Calvin did not deny this aspect of the sacraments, he put it in its proper priority: "We do not tolerate that what is secondary in the sacraments is regarded by them as the first and even the only point. Now, the first point is that the sacraments should serve our faith before God; after this, that they should attest our confession before men." Cf. 4.17.37, LCC, 2:1414. In 4.17.38 Calvin added a third purpose for the Lord's Supper: to encourage mutual love among believers. LCC, 2:1414–16.

128. Ibid., 4.17.1, LCC, 2:1361.

129. Ibid., 4.17.3, LCC, 2:1362.

130. Ibid., 4.17.10, LCC, 2:1370. The text has been rendered clearer.

John Calvin on Christ's Spiritual Presence in the Lord's Supper

I indeed admit that the breaking of bread is a symbol; it is not the thing itself. But having admitted this, we shall nevertheless duly infer that by the showing of the symbol the thing itself is also shown. For unless a man means to call God a deceiver, he would never dare assert that an empty symbol is set forth by him. Therefore, if the Lord truly represents the participation in his body through the breaking of bread, there ought not to be the least doubt that he truly presents and shows his body.*

*John Calvin, *Institutes of the Christian Religion*, 4.17.10, LCC, 2:1371.

How could Christ himself be truly present in the Lord's Supper? Calvin agreed with Zwingli—and strongly disagreed with Luther—that the glorified body of Christ is now in heaven, seated next to the Father. Accordingly, participation in the body and blood of Christ is a mystery; however, the Spirit makes such fellowship possible.[131] Yet, agreeing with Luther, Calvin underscored that Christ, because he sits at the right hand of the Father, reigns everywhere. Thus, he can be powerfully present to give his body and blood in his Supper.[132] Indeed, communion with Christ takes place when we "soar up to heaven" to be with Christ through the power of the Spirit.[133] Elsewhere, Calvin expressed this communion in terms of descent: "We say Christ descends to us both by the outward symbol and by his Spirit, that he may truly quicken our souls by the substance of his flesh and of his blood."[134] Whether by ascent or descent, such communion is both a miracle and a mystery: "It is a secret too lofty for either my mind to comprehend or my words to declare. And, to speak more plainly, I rather experience than understand it."[135]

In addition to articulating his own position, Calvin clearly distinguished his view from the Catholic view,[136] Lutheran consubstantiation,[137] and Zwingli's position.[138] Taking into consideration all of these wayward views, Calvin expressed contentment with any belief that affirmed the true presence of Christ in the eucharistic elements.[139]

---

131. "Even though it seems unbelievable that Christ's flesh, separated from us by such great distance, penetrates to us, so that it becomes our food, let us remember how far the secret power of the Holy Spirit towers above all our senses, and how foolish it is to wish to measure his immeasurableness by our measure. What, then, our mind does not comprehend, let faith conceive: The Spirit truly unites things separated in space." Ibid.

132. Ibid., 4.17.18, LCC, 2:1381.

133. Ibid., 4.17.24, LCC, 2:1390.

134. Ibid.

135. Ibid., 4.17.31, LCC, 2:1403.

136. Ibid., 4.17.12, LCC, 2:1372–73.

137. Ibid., 4.17.16–17, LCC, 2:1379–80.

138. Ibid., 4.17.5, LCC, 2:1365.

139. For Calvin, the observation of the Lord's Supper must

be expressed in such a way that Christians "may be understood not to receive it solely by imagination or understanding of mind, but to enjoy the thing itself as nourishment of eternal life." Ibid., 4.17.19, LCC, 2:1382. Calvin urged frequent celebration of the Lord's Supper in the churches. In his proposal to the Council of Ministers in Geneva, he believed weekly observance to be right but asked for monthly administration of the sacrament. The council did not go along with Calvin's proposal; rather, observance was ordered to be quarterly. John Calvin, *Articles Concerning the Organization of the Church and of Worship at Geneva Proposed by the Ministers at the Council* (January 16, 1537), LCC, 22: 49–50. He envisioned the celebration to take place in the following way: "First, then, it should begin with public prayers. After this a sermon should be given. Then, when bread and wine have been placed on the Table, the minister should repeat the words of institution of

The Anabaptists' "Breaking of Bread"

Although certainly not as noted as Luther, Zwingli, and Calvin in the development of the Lord's Supper during the Reformation, the Anabaptists contributed yet another view. Their *Schleitheim Confession* stipulated: "All those who wish to break one bread in remembrance of the broken body of Christ, and all who wish to drink of one drink as a remembrance of the shed blood of Christ, shall be united beforehand by baptism in one body of Christ, which is the church of God and whose Head is Christ."[140] Zwingli was incensed at this position, because the baptism referred to was the baptism by immersion of those who can repent of sin and believe in Christ for salvation. Furthermore, the article concluded with an exposé of the illegitimacy of all other observances of the Lord's Supper.[141] Only the Anabaptists, so they claimed, observed a true "breaking of bread." Eventually, all the Reformers denounced the Anabaptists' belief about the Lord's Supper.

The Council of Trent and Transubstantiation

In opposition to the various Protestant views of the Lord's Supper, the Council of Trent reaffirmed the traditional Roman Catholic position. Its *Decree Concerning the Most Holy Sacrament of the Eucharist* affirmed the real presence of Christ in the elements and transubstantiation.[142] An important corollary of this transformation was that Christ should be worshiped when the consecrated elements are displayed to the public after the Mass is completed.[143] Trent also reaffirmed that the Mass is a sacrifice—the same Christ who offered himself on the cross as a bloody sacrifice is offered again in the Mass as a bloodless sacrifice. As a propitiation, this sacrifice appeases the wrath of God, who hates sin.[144] By no means does this re-presentation of the sacrifice of Christ detract from his once-and-for-all sacrifice on Calvary. On the contrary, it brings his grace of forgiveness

---

the Supper. Next, he should recite the promises that were left to us in it; at the same time, he should excommunicate [dismiss] all who are debarred from it by the Lord's prohibition. Afterward, he should pray that the Lord, with the kindness with which he has bestowed this sacred food upon us, also teach and form us to receive it with faith and thankfulness of heart, and, inasmuch as we are not so of ourselves, by his mercy make us worthy of such a feast. But here either psalms should be sung, or something be read, and in proper order the believers should partake of the most holy banquet, the ministers breaking the bread and giving the cup. When the Supper is finished, there should be an exhortation to sincere faith and confession of faith, to love and behavior worthy of Christians. At the last, thanks should be given and praises sung to God. When these things are ended, the church should be dismissed in peace." Calvin, *Institutes*, 4.17.43, LCC, 2:1421–22.

140. *Schleitheim Confession*, 3, in Lumpkin, 25.

141. "Whoever has not been called by one God to one faith, to one baptism, to one Spirit, to one body, with all the children

of God's church, cannot be made [into] one bread with them, as indeed must be done if one is truly to break bread according to the command of Christ." *Schleitheim Confession*, 3, in Lumpkin, 26.

142. *Canons and Decrees of the Council of Trent*, 13th session (October 11, 1551), *Decree Concerning the Most Holy Sacrament of the Eucharist*, chaps. 1, 4, in Schaff, 2:126.

143. "All Christ's faithful should in their veneration display toward this most holy sacrament the full worship of adoration which is due to the true God. This is in accordance with the custom always received in the Catholic Church. For it is not to be adored less because it was instituted by Christ the Lord that it might be taken and eaten." Ibid., chap. 5, in Schaff, 2:131. It is customary for the consecrated elements to be exhibited in the tabernacle, a holy receptacle placed in an important location in Catholic churches.

144. *Canons and Decrees of the Council of Trent*, 22nd session (September 17, 1562), *Doctrine of the Sacrifice of the Mass*, chap. 2, in Schaff, 2:179.

"not only for the sins, punishments, satisfactions and other necessities of the faithful who are living, but also for those who are departed [the dead] in Christ, and who are not as yet fully purified."[145]

Over against Protestant beliefs about the Lord's Supper, the council pronounced *anathemas*, curses excommunicating and damning to hell all who subscribed to erroneous views. It specifically condemned those who did not hold to transubstantiation[146] and believed that the Mass is a sacrifice.[147] It also pronounced anathemas against errors in administering the rite. One condemned communion in two kinds, while a second denounced serving communion to infants—a long-time practice of the church.[148]

The Baptistic View

Another important development in the post-Reformation period was the emergence of the Baptists. Their view of the Lord's Supper was first expressed by John Smyth: "The Lord's Supper is the external sign of the communion of Christ and of the faithful among themselves by faith and love."[149] Thomas Helwys added the purpose of the observance: "The Lord's Supper is the outward manifestation of the spiritual communion between Christ and the faithful mutually (1 Cor. 10:16–17) to declare his death until he comes (1 Cor. 11:26)."[150] Since this observance should be part of every worship service, the Lord's Supper should be administered every Sunday.[151]

In its article on baptism, the *London Confession* restricted participation in the Lord's Supper to those who had been baptized.[152] According to Benjamin Keach, "the worthy receivers are, not after a corporeal and carnal manner, but by faith, made partakers of his body and blood, with all his benefits, to the spiritual nourishment and growth in grace."[153] Although originally observing the Lord's Supper weekly, Baptists soon switched to monthly administration out of concern that frequent celebrations would result in a sacramental ritualism similar to that of the Catholic Mass, and for fear that frequent observation of the Lord's Supper would detract from the central element of preaching the Word of God.[154]

---

145. Ibid., in Schaff, 2:179–80.

146. *Decree Concerning the Most Holy Sacrament of the Eucharist*, canon 2, in Schaff, 2:136.

147. *Doctrine of the Sacrifice of the Mass*, canons 1, 3, in Schaff, 2:184–85.

148. *Canons and Decrees of the Council of Trent*, 21st session (July 16, 1562), *Decree on Communion under Both Species, and the Communion of Infants*, canons 1, 4, in Schaff, 2:174–75.

149. John Smyth, *Short Confession of Faith in XX Articles* (1609), 15, in Lumpkin, 101.

150. *A Declaration of Faith of English People Remaining at Amsterdam in Holland* (1611), 15, in Lumpkin, 120–21. The text has been rendered clearer.

151. Ibid., 19, in Lumpkin, 121.

152. *London Confession of Faith*, 39, in Lumpkin, 167. The actual phrase "and after to partake of the Lord's Supper" was added in later editions of the *Confession*.

153. Benjamin Keach, *The Baptist Catechism* (Philadelphia: American Baptist Publication Society, n.d.), 101. Concerning other requirements for worthy participation, Keach added: "It is required of those who would worthily (that is, suitably) partake of the Lord's Supper, that they examine themselves of their knowledge to discern the Lord's body; of their faith, to feed upon him; of their repentance, love and new obedience; lest coming unworthily, they eat and drink judgment to themselves." *Baptist Catechism*, 103.

154. Interestingly, the *Orthodox Creed* (1679) did not hesitate to use the term *sacraments* to refer to what Baptists were increasingly calling *ordinances*: "Those two sacraments, viz. baptism, and the Lord's Supper, are ordinances of positive, sovereign, and holy institution, appointed by the Lord Jesus Christ." *Orthodox Creed*, 27, in Lumpkin, 317.

THE LORD'S SUPPER IN THE MODERN PERIOD

John Wesley viewed the Lord's Supper as a means of conversion for unbelievers: "Inasmuch as we come to his table not to give him anything, but to receive whatsoever he sees best for us, there is no previous preparation indispensably necessary, but a desire to receive whatsoever he pleases to give.... No fitness is required ... but a sense of our state—of our utter sinfulness and helplessness."[155] For believers, the Lord's Supper spurs them on to greater sanctification: "As our bodies are strengthened by bread and wine, so are our souls by these tokens of the body and the blood of Christ. This is the food of our souls; this gives strength to perform our duty and leads us on to perfection."[156]

Baptists increasingly engaged in the practice of "closed communion," restricting participation to only those who had been immersed. Paedobaptists were excluded because "to commune at the Lord's table with any who were only sprinkled in infancy is departing from truth by practically saying that they are baptized when we do not believe that they are."[157] Later, with the advent of Landmarkism, churches that embraced this isolationist movement restricted participation to their own members only. Other Baptist churches disagreed with this view and permitted participation for all Christians who professed faith in Jesus Christ.[158]

In the middle of the nineteenth century, Baptists altered the ordinance by replacing the element of wine with unfermented grape juice. A strong influence in this direction came from the American temperance movement, which aimed at the complete prohibition of alcoholic beverages. While some Baptists continued to urge the use of wine, arguing that the Lord himself commanded that wine be one of the elements, others protested that its use was a stumbling block for alcoholics. The *Baptist Faith and Message* described the elements as "the bread and the fruit of the vine."[159]

While steadily holding to its historic doctrine and practice of the Eucharist, the Roman Catholic Church was faced by challenges to this tradition. Although continuing

---

155. John Wesley, *Journal Entry* (Saturday, June 28, 1740), in *The Works of John Wesley*, ed. Thomas Jackson, 14 vols., vol. 1: *Journals 1735–1745* (1872; repr., Grand Rapids: Baker, 2002), 280.

156. John Wesley, *The Duty of Constant Communion*, 2nd ser., sermon 101, in Jackson, *Works of John Wesley*, vol. 7: *Sermons* (1872; repr., Grand Rapids: Baker, 2002), 148.

157. Isaac Backus, *A History of New England with Particular Reference to the Denomination of Christians Called Baptists*, 2 vols. (Newton, Mass.: Backus Historical Society, 1871), 2:116.

158. In his *An Essay in Defense of Strict Communion*, John Dagg defended closed communion while noting arguments for open communion. The strongest arguments for closed communion, according to Dagg, include the priority of baptism in point of institution; Jesus' insistence (Matt. 28:19–20) on baptism immediately following a profession of faith demands baptism prior to the Lord's Supper; the order of activities in Acts 2:38–47 places baptism before the Lord's Supper; what is symbolized by each ordinance—union and communion

with Christ through baptism, spiritual nourishment through the Lord's Supper—demands baptism precedes the other; and the historical practice of the church. As for the strongest arguments in support of open communion, Dagg noted that the exclusion of nonbaptized Christians from the Lord's Supper excludes them from all Christian instruction; participation in the Lord's Supper is still an obligation for nonbaptized Christians and thus must be obeyed; in Jewish law, circumcision was necessary prior to celebration of the Passover, but Scripture never instills baptism as a preparation for the Lord's Supper; and toleration—manifested in allowing celebration of the Lord's Supper before baptism—is permissible in the case of people improperly taught about baptism. John L. Dagg, *An Essay in Defense of Strict Communion* (Penfield, Ga.: Benjamin Brantly, 1845), 6–12.

159. *Baptist Faith and Message* (Southern Baptist Convention), 7, in Lumpkin, 396–97. This same wording was carried over to the most recent revision of *Baptist Faith and Message* (2000).

to affirm the sacrifice of the Mass, it did so in terms of a re-presentation of the sacrifice of the cross: "The Eucharist is thus a sacrifice because it *re-presents* (makes present) the sacrifice of the cross, because it is its *memorial* and because it *applies* its fruits."[160] This new element emphasized the Eucharist as the sacrifice that the church makes.[161]

The ecumenical movement sought to bring historically separated Protestant churches together. *Baptism, Eucharist and Ministry* (BEM), issued by the Faith and Order Commission of the World Council of Churches, sought to settle some of the most highly entrenched points of dispute among churches. In terms of the Eucharist, *BEM* noted: "The eucharist is a sacramental meal which by visible signs communicates to us God's love in Jesus Christ.... Its celebration continues as the central act of the church's worship."[162] Specifically, it expressed five key aspects: thanksgiving to the Father; anamnesis, or memorial of Christ; invocation of the Spirit; communion of the faithful; and meal of the kingdom.[163] Furthermore, it did not avoid addressing the most controversial issues that divide churches.[164] Many regarded *BEM* as a milestone in addressing centuries-old controversies and in bringing separated churches back together.

Few evangelicals were influenced by *Baptism, Eucharist and Ministry*. Depending on their ecclesiastical identity, Presbyterian evangelicals, Lutheran evangelicals, Methodist evangelicals, Baptist evangelicals, and so forth continued to adopt the theology and practice of the Lord's Supper of that church or denomination with which they were affiliated. While united in their rejection of transubstantiation, evangelicals are found in churches that embrace views on the Lord's Supper from consubstantiation to spiritual presence to memorial and variations on all three of these historic themes.

---

160. *Catechism of the Catholic Church* (New York: Image/Doubleday, 1995), sec. 1364–66.

161. Ibid., sec. 1368.

162. World Council of Churches, "Faith and Order Paper No. 111," *Baptism, Eucharist and Ministry*, E1 (Geneva: World Council of Churches, 1982), 10.

163. Ibid., E3–E26, 10–15.

164. Ibid., E13, 12. Commentary (E15) added: "In the history of the church there have been various attempts to under-

stand the mystery of the real and unique presence of Christ in the eucharist. Some are content merely to affirm this presence without seeking to explain it. Others consider it necessary to assert a change wrought by the Holy Spirit and Christ's words, in consequence of which there is no longer just ordinary bread and wine but the body and blood of Christ. Others again have developed an explanation of the real presence which, though not claiming to exhaust the significance of the mystery, seeks to protect it from damaging interpretations." Ibid., 13.

30

WORSHIP

How has the church developed its concept and practice of worship?

STATEMENT OF BELIEF

The church has historically gathered together regularly (at least every Sunday, if not more frequently) for the purpose of worship, which may be defined as "the activity of glorifying God in his presence with our voices and hearts."[1] Included in these services of worship are activities such as praising and thanking God through song and prayer, reading and preaching the Word of God, celebrating the sacraments, interceding for needs, and giving financially. While these elements seem to be standard activities in most churches, many differences also characterize the churches of Jesus Christ.

One major difference is due to the division between liturgical and nonliturgical churches. According to the former, worship services are to be well ordered and arranged with close attention to historical liturgical practices. Indeed, in some churches—the Roman Catholic Church, for example—the liturgy varies only slightly from that employed in the church well over a millennium ago. According to the latter churches, though worship services are to be ordered generally, allowance should be made for spontaneity and variety. Such churches often believe that a liturgical approach may hinder the leading of the Holy Spirit and encourage religious formalism rather than heartfelt worship.

Within Protestant churches, another major difference in worship patterns can be traced to the incorporation of different principles for ordering worship. One the one hand, the regulative principle holds that God alone, as revealed through his Word, determines what constitutes worship that is acceptable to him. Thus, unless some liturgical element—e.g., biblical hymn singing, reading of Scripture, and preaching—has either explicit or implicit warrant from Scripture, it cannot be incorporated into the church's

---

1. Wayne Grudem, *Systematic Theology: An Introduction to Biblical Doctrine* (Grand Rapids: Zondervan, 1994, 2000), 1003.

worship. On the other hand, the normative principle holds that unless Scripture explicitly or implicitly prohibits them, other worship elements may be incorporated and the church's liturgy is still pleasing to God.

Historically, evangelical churches have exhibited a wide diversity in worship styles in their regular services. Generally speaking, a much more ordered, historically regulated approach to worship characterized evangelical churches prior to the middle of the twentieth century. For various reasons, at that time the growth of evangelical churches began to be accompanied by experimentation with new and creative worship elements and approaches. This chapter traces the development of both the traditional elements of worship and these recent innovations.[2]

WORSHIP IN THE EARLY CHURCH

From the New Testament, we learn of key practices that characterized the meetings of the early churches gathered together to worship God ("we have no other practice—nor do the churches of God"; 1 Cor. 11:16; cf. 14:33). These included reading, preaching, and teaching Scripture (1 Tim. 4:13) so as to admonish one another (Col. 3:16); singing psalms, hymns, and spiritual songs with thanksgiving to God (Col. 3:16); prophesying and praying (1 Cor. 11:3–16), which included making "requests, prayers, intercession and thanksgiving ... for everyone—for kings and all those in authority" (1 Tim. 2:1–2); the exercise of spiritual gifts (1 Cor. 12–14), including speaking in tongues and its interpretation and prophecy and its evaluation (1 Cor. 14), carried out "for the common good" (1 Cor. 12:7); financial giving (1 Cor. 16:2; 2 Cor. 8–9); the exercise of church discipline (1 Cor. 5; cf. 2 Cor. 2:1–11); baptism of new converts (Acts 2:38–41); and the Lord's Supper, which was celebrated in the context of an agape meal or love feast (1 Cor. 10:14–22; 11:17–34; cf. Jude 12). The expectation was that Christians were to come together regularly (Heb. 10:25)—they met at least every Sunday (1 Cor. 16:2), often assembling in homes (Rom. 16:5; 1 Cor. 16:19; Col. 4:15)—as the church of Jesus Christ. Indeed, separation from the church was a tragic step, yet also a clear indication of a bogus faith in Jesus (1 John 2:19).

Many of these practices continued to characterize the meetings of the early churches after the apostolic period. One snapshot of early Christian worship was offered by Justin Martyr. This church, consisting of believers from both urban centers and rural areas (he portrays a rather substantial congregation), gathered together on Sunday because it was both the first day of divine creation and the day of Christ's resurrection. The service consisted of the reading of (what we now call) the Old Testament and the Gospels.[3] This apparently lengthy reading of Scripture was followed by teaching and admonition by the leader of the church, congregational prayer, the celebration of the Eucharist, or Lord's Supper, and financial giving.

---

2. My thanks to Micah Carter and Christopher Newkirk for their research and help on this chapter.

3. "The memoirs of the apostles" was earlier explained by Justin in the section of his *First Apology* immediately preceding the above-cited section: "For the apostles, in the memoirs composed by them, which are called Gospels, have thus delivered unto us what was enjoined upon them." Justin Martyr, *First Apology*, 66, in *ANF*, 1:185.

Justin Martyr's Description of Early Church Worship

On the day called Sunday, all who live in cities or in the country gather together in one place, and the memoirs of the apostles or the writings of the prophets are read, as long as time permits. Then, when the reader has ceased, the president verbally instructs, and exhorts to the imitation of these good things. Then we rise together and pray, and ... when our prayer is ended, bread and wine and water are brought, and the president [presider] in the manner offers prayers and thanksgivings, according to his ability, and the people assent, saying Amen! And there is a distribution [of the Eucharist] to each, and a participation of that over which thanks have been given, and to those who are absent a portion is sent by the deacons. And they who are well to do, and willing, give what each thinks fit; and what is collected is deposited with the president, who gives aid to the orphans and widows, and those who, through sickness or any other cause, are in want, and those who are in bonds [prison], and the strangers sojourning among us, and in a word takes care of all who are in need. But Sunday is the day on which we all hold our common assembly, because it is the first day on which God, having wrought a change in the darkness and matter, made the world; and Jesus Christ our Savior on the same day rose from the dead.*

> *Justin Martyr, *First Apology*, 67, in *ANF*, 1:186. The text has been rendered clearer. For another snapshot, see the *Didache*, 14, in Holmes, 267; *ANF*, 7:381. From an outsider's perspective, Pliny the Younger, the Roman governor of Bithynia-Pontus from AD 111 to 113, described a Christian worship service: "On an appointed day, they had been accustomed to meet before daybreak and to recite a hymn antiphonally to Christ, as to a god, and to bind themselves by an oath, not for the commission of any crime but to abstain from theft, robbery, adultery and breach of faith, and not to deny a deposit when it was claimed. After the conclusion of this ceremony it was their custom to depart and meet again to take food, but it was ordinary and harmless food, and they had ceased this practice after my edict in which ... I had forbidden secret societies." Pliny, *Letter 10, to Trajan*, 46, in Bettenson, 4.

As the church in its early centuries developed, its service of worship was increasingly formalized into a standard, universal liturgy that included the reading of Scripture (the Old Testament, the Gospels, and other portions of the New Testament), singing of the Psalms, preaching, praying, kissing one another (restricted according to gender), and celebrating the Eucharist. Following a set liturgy for the worship service became common practice in the churches.

An Early Standardized Liturgy

In the middle [of the church], let the reader stand upon some high place and let him read the books [of the Old Testament].... When there have been two different lessons read, let some other person sing the hymns of David [the Psalms], and let the people join at the conclusion of the verses. Afterwards, let our Acts be read, and the letters of Paul ... and afterwards let a deacon or presbyter read the Gospels.... Next, let the presbyters, one by one, not all together, exhort the people, followed by the bishop as the commander.... After this, let all rise up with one consent and, looking towards the east ... pray to God eastward, who ascended up to the heaven of heavens to the east.... As to the deacons, after the prayer is over, let some of them attend to the sacrifice of the Eucharist, ministering to the Lord's body with fear.... Then let the men give the men, and the women give the women, the Lord's kiss.... After this let the deacon pray for the whole church, for the whole world,... for the priests and the rulers, for the high priest [the bishop] and the king, and the peace of the universe. After this, let the high priest [the bishop] pray for peace upon the people, and bless them.... After this, let the sacrifice follow, the people standing and praying silently; and when the sacrifice has been made, let every rank [men, young people, old people, children with parents, younger women, mothers, virgins, widows] by itself partake of the Lord's body and precious blood in order, approaching with reverence and holy fear, as to the body of their king.*

*Apostolic Constitutions, 2.7, in ANF, 7:421–22. The text has been rendered clearer.

With the increasing importance of the Church of Rome and Latin as the language of the Roman Empire, a specific Roman liturgy was developed in Latin. This liturgy is often referred to as the *Roman Mass* (or *missal*). "Mass" became the standard word for the Eucharist by the middle of the fifth century, developing from the statement at the end of the liturgy—*Ite missa est*—which dismissed the church. The Roman Mass was highly structured and featured the celebration of the Eucharist. It became a liturgical template for the church's worship services beginning with the fifth century.

The Roman Mass

- An introit ("entrance") psalm (sung at the entrance of the clergy)
- Kyrie eleison ("Lord have mercy")
- The collect (said by the celebrant of the Mass)
- Scripture readings: New Testament letter and gospel (interposed by a psalm)
- Sermon (if included in the Mass)
- Recitation of the Creed (if included in the Mass)
- The offertory, in which laypeople presented the gifts of bread and wine by bringing them forward and placing them on the altar (the choir sang another psalm during this presentation)
- The collect (said by the celebrant, commending the gifts to God)
- The eucharistic celebration (conducted by the celebrant)

    The preface
    Celebrant: "The Lord be with you."
    Response: "And with you."

Celebrant: "Let us lift up our hearts."

Response: *"We life them up to the Lord." (sursum corda)*

Celebrant: "Let us give thanks to the Lord our God."

Response: "It is just and right."

Celebrant: "Just it is indeed and fitting, right, and for our lasting good that we should always and everywhere give thanks to you, Lord, holy Father, almighty and eternal God; who with your only-begotten Son and the Holy Spirit are one God, one Lord, not one as being a single person but three persons in one essence. Whatsoever by your revelation we believe concerning your glory, that too we hold, without difference or distinction, of your Son and also of the Holy Spirit, so that in acknowledging the true, eternal Godhead, we adore in it each person, and yet a unity of essence, and a co-equal majesty; in praise of which the angels and archangels, the cherubim and the seraphim too, lift up their endless hymn, day by day with one voice singing":

Singing of the *Sanctus*: "Holy, holy, holy are you, Lord God of hosts. Your glory fills all heaven and earth. Hosanna in high heaven! Blessed be the one who is coming in the name of the Lord. Hosanna in high heaven!"

The canon of the Mass, including the Lord's Prayer, the consecration of the bread and wine, and the sacrifice

The kiss of peace (exchanged among the clergy)

The reception of the Eucharist by the people (who said "Amen" when the elements were received)

- The collect (said by the celebrant in thanksgiving to God)
- The dismissal.*

*The Missal in Latin and English, being the text of the *Missale Romanum* with English rubrics and a new translation (Westminster: Newman, 1959), 676–720.

WORSHIP IN THE MIDDLE AGES

Besides the Roman missal, a few other liturgies were adopted in the Middle Ages.[4] For example, the *Leonine* liturgy may be dated from the seventh century, perhaps earlier, and it drew upon a variety of sources. The *Gelasian* liturgy may be dated to the time of Gelasius (492–96) and may have been used in churches in the Frankish kingdom

4. Some of this material is adapted from Bard Thomson, ed., *Liturgies of the Western Church* (Philadelphia: Fortress, 1961), 35–46.

(modern-day France) after being revised by Gregory the Great (590–604).[5] The *Gregorian* liturgy was the work of Gregory the Great, with eighth-century additions made by Alcuin or some other assistant to Charlemagne. Although it originated in Rome, the Gregorian liturgy was significantly changed by this Frankish/Gallican addition, and the entire work contributed to the Roman-Gallican liturgy from which the modern missal arose. As this Roman-Gallican liturgy settled into the lands conquered by Charlemagne, many modifications were made. These included touches of dramatic buildup, a heavy use of incense, extended introspection prior to the eucharistic celebration, a Trinitarian orientation in prayers (the number of which was increased significantly), an increased sense of mystery, a view of the Mass as a sacrifice explicable by transubstantiation,[6] and a (physical) distancing of the priest celebrating the Mass from the congregation.

At the height of papal influence, the Catholic Church adopted a simplified Roman missal reworked by the papal administration under Innocent III (1198–1216). When the printing press made standardization of texts possible, this Roman missal theoretically became the liturgy for all the churches; in reality, however, great diversity continued to prevail. Of particular importance was the missal's requirement for the host (the eucharistic bread) to be elevated at the moment of consecration. This further emphasized the already growing trend of conceiving the Mass as the sacrifice of Jesus Christ.

Actually, few laypeople participated in the reception of the Eucharist, preferring to express their devotion to the sacrificial victim by adoring the host—now, the transubstantiated body of Christ—that was conserved in the tabernacle after the Mass was completed. To rectify this, the Fourth Lateran Council in 1215 stipulated that Catholics must participate in the sacrament at least once a year following the confession of sins:

> All the faithful of both genders shall after they have reached the age of discretion faithfully confess all their sins at least once a year to their own (parish) priest and perform to the best of their ability the penance imposed, receiving reverently at least at Easter the sacrament of the Eucharist, unless perhaps at the advice of their own priest they may for a good reason abstain for a time from its reception; otherwise they shall be cut off from the church (excommunicated) during life and deprived of Christian burial in death.[7]

In the thirteenth century, the church began to give the bread but not the cup to the laity. Theologically, this practice was justified by the doctrine of *concomitance*, as explained by Bonaventura:

> Because the blessed and glorious body of Christ cannot be divided into its parts and cannot be separated from the soul or from the highest divinity, so under each species [the bread is one species; the cup, the other] there is the one, entire, and indivisible Christ—namely, body, soul, and God. Thus, in each is present

---

5. "Gregory collected the book of Gelasius for the solemnities of the Mass into one volume, leaving out much, changing little, adding something for the exposition of the lessons of the Gospel." But other internal evidence points to later revisions by Gregory II (d. 731). John the Deacon, *Biography of Gregory the Great*, in Thomson, *Liturgies of the Western Church*, 36.

6. For further discussion of the Catholic view of transubstantiation, see chap. 29.

7. Fourth Lateran Council, canon 21, in Petry, 323. See also footnote 67 in chapter 29.

the one and most simple sacrament containing the entire Christ. And because every part of the species signifies the body of Christ, the whole body so exists in the whole species and it is in any part of it, whether it be undivided or separated.[8]

So if laypeople receive only one of the elements, they still receive all of Christ. Practically, this change was instituted out of fear of profaning the holy sacrament by spilling the blood—the wine-water mix—of Christ. To prevent this from happening, the church restricted the drinking of the cup to the priest who celebrated the Mass. This was called *communion in one kind* because only one element—the bread—was given to the laity during the eucharistic service. Moreover, with all the changes in the liturgy over the last centuries, the eucharistic aspect became the focal point of the entire Mass.

WORSHIP IN THE REFORMATION AND POST-REFORMATION

Between transubstantiation, the sacrificial nature of the eucharistic celebration, the minimization of preaching the Word of God, and the trafficking of indulgences during the Mass, the Reformers had plenty to attack with regard to Roman Catholic worship services. In addition to criticizing, they also constructively contributed new ideas for Protestant worship. Luther himself composed a liturgy as an example for Lutheran churches to imitate in conducting worship services. His *German Mass and Order of Divine Service* (1526) broke with the centuries-old practice of using Latin in the Roman Catholic Mass. Luther radically altered the canon of the Mass so that it excluded any notion of sacrifice, which he vehemently denounced.[9] Furthermore, he targeted his German Mass for "those who are yet to become Christians or to become stronger.... But most of all it [the *Order*] is done on account of the simple and the young, who are to be and must be exercised daily and educated in the Scripture and God's Word."[10] Luther's German Mass became a liturgical template for the Lutheran churches.

Luther's German Mass for Sundays

- Singing a hymn or a German psalm
- Kyrie eleison ("Lord have mercy"), three times
- A Collect
- Reading of the Epistle, followed by the singing of a German hymn

---

8. Bonaventura, *Breviloquium*, 6.9 (5), in *Breviloquium of St. Bonaventura*, trans. E. E. Nemmers (St. Louis: B. Herder, 1946), 199–200.

9. "That utter abomination follows which forces all that precedes in the Mass into its service and is, therefore, called the offertory. From here on almost everything smacks and savors of sacrifice. And the words of life and salvation [the words of institution] are imbedded in the midst of it all.... Let us, therefore, repudiate everything that smacks of sacrifice, together with the entire canon, and retain only that which is pure and holy, and so order our mass." Martin Luther, *An Order of Mass and Communion*, LW, 53:25–26.

10. *German Mass and Order of Divine Service*, LW, 6:171.

- Reading of the Gospel, followed by the congregation singing the Creed
- The sermon, on the Gospel for the Sunday
- A public paraphrase of the Lord's Prayer and admonition about the Lord's Supper
- Administration of the Lord's Supper, accompanied by the singing of the *Sanctus* and other hymns or the *Agnus Dei* ("the Lamb of God")
- The Collect and the Benediction.*

*Martin Luther, *German Mass and Order of Divine Service*, LW, 6:178–86.

John Calvin prepared a service of worship for the Reformed churches in Geneva. The minister opened the service with these words: "Our help is in the name of the Lord." This was immediately followed by a general confession of sin, for which Calvin found biblical warrant and practical usefulness.[11] This, then, was the public confession instituted by Calvin, which began with the invitation of the minister: "My brothers, let each of you present himself before the face of the Lord, and confess his faults and sins, following my words in his heart":

O Lord God, eternal and almighty Father, we confess and acknowledge truthfully before your holy majesty that we are poor sinners, conceived and born in iniquity and corruption, prone to do evil, incapable of any good, and that in our depravity we transgress your holy commandments without end or ceasing; therefore, we purchase for ourselves, through your righteous judgment, our ruin and damnation. Nevertheless, O Lord, we are grieved that we have offended you, and we condemn ourselves and our sins with true repentance, begging your mercy to relieve our distress. O God and Father most gracious and full of compassion, have mercy on us in the name of your Son, our Lord Jesus Christ. And as you blot out our sins and stains, magnify and increase in us day by day the grace of the Holy Spirit, that as we acknowledge our unrighteousness with all our heart, we may be moved by that sorrow that shall bring forth true repentance in us, mortifying all our sins and producing in us the fruit of righteousness and innocence that are pleasing to you, through the same Jesus Christ our Lord. Amen.[12]

Public confession of sin was followed by pastoral absolution. For Calvin, this was a function of the power of the keys given by Christ to the church (Matt. 18:18) and was

---

11. "A willing confession among men follows that secret confession that is made to God, as often as either divine glory or our humiliation demands it. For this reason, the Lord ordained of old among the people of Israel that, after the priest recited the words, the people should confess their iniquities publicly in the temple [Lev. 16:21]. For he foresaw that this help was necessary for them in order that each one might better be led to a just estimation of himself. And it is fitting that,

by the confession of our own wretchedness, we show forth the goodness and mercy of our God, among ourselves and before the whole world." John Calvin, *Institutes of the Christian Religion*, 3.4.10, LCC, 1:634–35.

12. John Calvin, *The Form of Church Prayers and Hymns*, in Thomson, *Liturgies of the Western Church*, 197–98. The text has been rendered clearer.

properly carried out by ministers: "When the whole church stands, as it were, before God's judgment seat, confesses itself guilty, and has its sole refuge in God's mercy, it is no common or light solace to have present there the ambassador of Christ, armed with the mandate of reconciliation, by whom it hears proclaimed its absolution."[13] Coming to Geneva from Strasbourg, Calvin attempted to import the absolution he had used in Strasbourg: "To all those who repent in this way, and look to Jesus Christ for their salvation, I declare that the absolution of sins is effected in the name of the Father, and of the Son, and of the Holy Spirit. Amen."[14] But the Genevan Christians spurned this novelty, and Calvin was forced to dispense with this element of the service.

Confession was followed by a reading of the Ten Commandments to remind the participants of the moral will of God. The congregation sang a song, then the minister prayed for the grace of the Spirit of God as he preached the Word of God to the people who were listening. This was followed by the reading of the biblical text and the sermonic exposition of the text. In response, the pastor led the congregation in the "Great Prayer." This consisted of prayers for rulers in authority, pastors of other congregations, the salvation of nonbelievers, the healing of the sick, and the spiritual and physical needs of the participants. A paraphrase of the Lord's Prayer was then repeated, followed by the congregational recital of the Apostles' Creed. This concluded the liturgy focused on the Word and marked the transition to the liturgy focused on the Lord's Supper.

This ordinance was celebrated once a quarter in Geneva. The pastor read the account of the institution of the Lord's Supper (1 Cor. 11:23–29), and, on the basis of Paul's warning against taking part in an unworthy manner, he prohibited disqualified people from participating.[15] The minister urged those participating to examine themselves for personal sins. This led into the *Sursum Corda*, which began, "Let us lift our spirits and hearts on high where Jesus Christ is in the glory of his Father."[16] The minister distributed the bread and the cup of wine to the participants as they came forward in an orderly and reverential manner. During the distribution, psalms were sung or passages of Scripture were read. The concluding event was the giving of thanks to God.

Calvin's legacy of church liturgy would continue in the following centuries through the Presbyterian and Reformed churches. Furthermore, Calvin articulated what is generally referred to as the regulative principle for worship:

> The rule that distinguishes between pure and vitiated worship is of universal application, in order that we may not adopt any device that seems fit to ourselves, but look to the injunction of Him who alone is entitled to prescribe.

---

13. Calvin, *Institutes*, 3.4.14, LCC, 1:638.

14. Calvin, *Form of Church Prayers and Hymns*, in Thomson, *Liturgies of the Western Church*, 198.

15. "Following that precept, in the name and by the authority of our Lord Jesus Christ, I excommunicate all idolaters, blasphemers and despisers of God, all heretics and those who create private sects in order to break the unity of the church, all perjurers, all who rebel against father and mother or superior, all who promote sedition or mutiny; brutal and disorderly persons, adulterers, lewd and lustful men, thieves, ravishers, greedy and grasping people, drunkards, gluttons, and all those who lead a scandalous and dissolute life. I warn them to abstain from this Holy Table, lest they defile and contaminate the holy food that our Lord Jesus Christ gives to none except they who belong to his household of faith." Ibid., in Thomson, *Liturgies of the Western Church*, 205–6.

16. Ibid., in Thomson, *Liturgies of the Western Church*, 207.

Therefore, if we would have Him to approve our worship, this rule, which he everywhere enforces with the utmost strictness, must be carefully observed. For there is a twofold reason why the Lord, in condemning and prohibiting all fictitious worship, requires us to give obedience only to His own voice.[17]

He offered the regulative principle in order (1) to establish the sovereign God's authority and (2) to help the church avoid presumptuous and superstitious worship.[18] In terms of application of this principle, Calvin forbade the use of choirs, musical presentations, and musical instruments in public worship. This put him at odds with the Old Testament pattern of worship, which included—indeed, even commanded—the employment of musical instruments. In response, Calvin asserted that this practice was only a shadow of the true worship enjoined by the New Testament, which also commands the church (1 Cor. 14:13) to "praise God and pray to him only in a known tongue."[19] This regulative principle would be highlighted and developed over the following centuries by churches that would insist on warrant from Scripture for anything and everything that should be included in their worship services.

Another service of worship to which the Reformation gave birth was that of the Anglican Church. This liturgy was formalized in both the *First Prayer Book* of 1549 and the *Second Prayer Book* of 1552. Although both were written during the reign of Edward VI and deeply influenced by Thomas Cranmer, the first featured changes provoked by Lutheran theology while the second was modified by the encouragement of John Calvin.

The *First Prayer Book* generally followed the structure of the Catholic Mass that had been in place for centuries.[20] When introduced in 1549, it caused an uproar. Protestants complained that it was still essentially a Catholic Mass, many priests introduced changes to return it to a Mass, and laypeople were disturbed by its novelty. At this same time, important Reformed theologians, including Peter Martyr, Martin Bucer, and John à Lasco, took refuge in England, and Calvin interacted with both Cranmer and Edward VI. Through this Calvinist influence (that of Bucer was particularly strong), a revision of the *First Prayer Book* was undertaken, resulting in the *Second Prayer Book* in 1552. Specifically, all traces of the Catholic Mass that could be construed as adoration of the transubstantiated elements (because they were the body and blood of Christ) were eliminated.[21]

With the death of Edward VI and the enthronement of Mary as Queen of England, the Anglican Church reverted back to the Catholicism of Henry VIII, which was embraced by Mary. This came to an end with Queen Elizabeth's coronation and subsequent publication of the *Elizabethan Prayer Book*. With only a few modifications, this was the *Second Prayer Book* as it had been written during Edward's reign.

17. John Calvin, *The Necessity of Reforming the Church* (Audubon, N.J.: Old Paths, 1994), 6.

18. Ibid.

19. John Calvin, *Commentary on the Book of Psalms*, 5 vols., trans. James Anderson (repr., Grand Rapids: Baker, 2005), 3:98.

20. *The Book of the Common Prayer and Administration of the Sacraments, and Other Rites and Ceremonies of the Church of England. Londini in Officina Edward Whitchurch. March, 1549. The Supper of the Lord, and the Holy Communion, Commonly Called the Mass*, in Thomson, *Liturgies of the Western Church*, 245–68.

21. Ibid., in Thomson, *Liturgies of the Western Church*, 269–84.

In reaction to these Protestant changes to the church's worship service, and to ward off Protestant attacks against the Mass, the Council of Trent entrusted the reform of the Roman Catholic missal to Pope Pius IV and (upon his death) to his successor. In 1570 the papal bull *Quo primum tempore* imposed the Roman missal of Pius V on all Catholic churches. Based on the Roman missal of Innocent III (see above), its goal was to restore the Mass to "the pristine norm and rite of the holy Father."[22] The missal harkened back to the early church's notion of the Lord's Supper as a fulfillment of Malachi (1:10–11)— an idea also embraced by the Council of Trent.[23] Thus, the missal envisioned the Mass as a perpetual sacrifice given by Christ to his church: "that he might leave to his own beloved spouse the church a visible sacrifice, such as the nature of man requires, whereby that bloody sacrifice, once to be accomplished on the cross, might be represented, and the memory thereof remain even unto the end of the world, and its salvific virtue be applied to the remission of those sins which we daily commit."[24] Because "the nature of man requires" him to offer sacrifices to God, the sacrifice of the Mass fulfills this obligation.

Within the Anglican Church, growing dissent with Elizabeth's *via media*, or middle way approach, to ecclesiology resulted in the ascendancy of two important groups: the *Separatists and Independents* (whose story will be taken up below with the Baptists and John Owen), and the *Puritans*, who were Christians wishing to reform the Church of England while remaining faithful to it. One revision that the Puritans wanted to instigate was a change in the government of the Anglican Church from episcopalianism to presbyterianism. After a failed attempt by England to impose *The Book of Common Prayer ... for the Use of the Church of Scotland* (1638) on the Scottish people, and the abolition of episcopalianism in favor of presbyterianism during the English civil war, the English Parliament appointed the Westminster Assembly to reform the church. An interesting mixture of interests—Puritan presbyterianism was in the majority, independents were a significant minority pushing for congregationalism, and five nonvoting Scots were observers—the Westminster Assembly produced *A Directory for the Public Worship of God* in 1644. The goal was for this *Directory* to be the standard form for worship in the kingdoms of England, Scotland, and Ireland.

After acknowledging the benefit introduced into the Church of England by the *Prayer Book*, the *Directory*'s preface bemoaned the fact that the established liturgy had also thwarted even more progress toward a full reformation of the church: "Long and sad experience has made it manifest that the liturgy used in the Church of England (not-

---

22. Pope Pius V, *Quo Primum Tempore* (July 14, 1570), introduction, in Thomson, *Liturgies of the Western Church*, 47.

23. E.g., Justin Martyr explained: "Hence God speaks by the mouth of Malachi ... about the sacrifices at that time presented by you: "I have no pleasure in you, says the Lord; and I will not accept the sacrifices of your hands; for 'from the rising of the sun until the setting of the same, my name has been glorified among the Gentiles, and in every place incense is offered to my name, and a pure offering. For my name is great among the Gentiles, says the Lord, but you profane it.' He

then speaks of those Gentiles, namely us, who in every place offer sacrifices to him; that is, the bread of the Eucharist, and also the cup of the Eucharist, affirming both that we glorify his name and that you profane it." Justin Martyr, *Dialogue with Trypho, a Jew*, 41, in ANF, 1:215. The Council of Trent appealed to Mal. 1:11 in *Canons and Decrees of the Council of Trent*, 22nd session (September 17, 1562), *Doctrine of the Sacrifice of the Mass*, 1, in Schaff, 2:178.

24. Ibid., in Schaff, 2:177.

withstanding all the pains and religious intentions of the compilers of it) has proved an offense, not only to many of the godly at home, but also to the Reformed churches abroad."[25] These offenses included the reading of prayers, cumbersome ceremonies, hindrances to the preaching of the Word, and ritual formalism. The purpose of the *Directory*, therefore, was "to hold forth such things as are of divine institution in every ordinance" so that in the "sense and scope of the prayers and other parts of public worship" there "may be a consent of all the churches, in those things that contain the substance of the service and worship of God."[26] The *Directory* gave instructions for six areas: the assembling of the congregation and their behavior in the public worship of God; the public reading of the Holy Scriptures; public prayer before the sermon; the preaching of the Word; prayer after the sermon; and the celebration of the communion, or sacrament of the Lord's Supper.[27]

The Westminster *Directory* was followed by the *Westminster Confession of Faith* (1647). In several of its sections, the *Confession* articulated the key elements of the regulative principle that should govern the church's worship of God. The first element focused on the sufficiency of Scripture. This attribute of Scripture demands that the worship of God in terms of its substance is to be regulated solely by the explicit or implicit instruction of the Word of God. In terms of its form, the worship of God is to be regulated in accordance with general biblical principles, but human wisdom is also to be taken into consideration.[28]

The second element concerned the freedom of conscience: "God alone is Lord of the conscience and has left it free from the doctrines and commandments of men which are in any way contrary to his Word or beside it in matters of faith or worship."[29] This article was expressed in opposition to Catholicism's insistence on its many (nonbiblical) liturgical elements as necessary for the proper worship of God. The *Confession* objected that any such element, because it is merely a human invention and cannot be derived from Scripture, cannot be binding on true worshipers of God. Any such element, because it either stands in opposition to Scripture or is in addition to Scripture, cannot be incorporated into the church's worship.

Third, the *Confession* expressly devoted an article to religious worship that became grounds for the regulative principle: "The acceptable way of worshipping the true God is instituted by himself, and so is limited to his own revealed will that he may not be worshipped according to the imaginations and devices of men, or the suggestions of Satan, under any visible representations or any other way not prescribed in the Holy

---

25. *A Directory for the Public Worship of God throughout the Three Kingdoms of England, Scotland, and Ireland. London, 1644*, preface, in Thomson, *Liturgies of the Western Church*, 354. The text has been rendered clearer.

26. Ibid., in Thomson, *Liturgies of the Western Church*, 356.

27. Ibid., in Thomson, *Liturgies of the Western Church*, 356–71.

28. "The whole counsel of God, concerning all things necessary for his own glory, man's salvation, faith and life, is either expressly set down in Scripture, or by good and neces-

sary consequence may be deduced from Scripture: unto which nothing at any time is to be added, whether by new revelations of the Spirit, or traditions of men.... There are some circumstances concerning the worship of God, and government of the church, common to human actions and societies, which are to be ordered by the light of nature and Christian prudence, according to the general rules of the Word, that are always to be observed." *Westminster Confession of Faith*, 1.6, in Schaff, 3:603–4.

29. Ibid., 20.2, in Schaff, 3:644.

Scriptures."[30] That is, God and God alone determines what is pleasing to him in terms of worship. Furthermore, God's revelation of acceptable worship is found in Scripture and Scripture alone.

Although the *Westminster Confession*'s contribution to the regulative principle of worship would continue, the Westminster *Directory* was short-lived. In 1660, with the end of the civil war and the restoration of the monarchy, Charles II set into motion a series of events that resulted in the Presbyterians being ejected from the Anglican Church. Two important developments in this series were the Savoy Conference (April–July 1661) and Richard Baxter's *Reformation of the Liturgy*. This latter publication became known as the *Savoy Liturgy*. It was the epitome of Puritan insistence that the proper worship of God must both reflect and repeat the Word of God—that is, worship is to be governed by the regulative principle.[31]

The second group of dissenters from Elizabeth's Church of England were the *Independents* (named so because they championed congregationalism, or the independence of each local church) and *Separatists* (aptly named due to their separation from the Anglican Church). The first independent congregation was formed in the winter of 1580–81 by Robert Browne and Robert Harrison in Norwich. The worship service of this congregation was described as follows:

> All being gathered together, the man appointed to teach stands in the midst of the room with his audience gathered around him. He prays for about half an hour, and part of his prayer is that, regarding those who come to scoff and laugh, God would be pleased to change their hearts, by which means they think to escape undiscovered. His sermon is about an hour, and then another stands up to make the text more clear. And at the end, he entreats everyone to go home.[32]

Moving his congregation to Holland in pursuit of religious freedom, Browne described the worship service in this new location: "An order was agreed on for their meetings together, for their exercises in them, as for prayer, thanksgiving, reading of the Scriptures, for exhortation and edification, either by all men who had the gift, or others. And for the lawfulness of putting forth questions to learn the truth, as if anything seemed doubtful and hard, to require some to show it more clearly, or for any to show it himself and to cause the rest to understand."[33] These worship services were heavily oriented to preaching and to prayer, which unlike the set prayers prescribed for worship by the *Prayer Book*, was to be extemporaneous. Clearly, these independent congregations intended to engage in worship in a different way than the Anglican Church.

With the advent of Baptist churches in the early part of the seventeenth century, a major renewal in worship took place. Numerous factors contributed to this change,

---

30. Ibid., 21.1, in Schaff, 3:646.

31. *The Reformation of the Liturgy as It Was Presented to the Right Reverend Bishops by the Divines Appointed by His Majesty's Commission to Treat with Them about the Alteration of It. London, 1661*, in Thomson, *Liturgies of the Western Church*, 385–404.

32. *The Brownist Synagogue*, cited in Horton Davies, *The Worship of the English Puritans* (London: Dacre, 1948), 87. The text has been rendered clearer.

33. Robert Browne, *A True and Short Declaration*, cited in *The Writings of Robert Browne and Robert Harrison*, ed. A. Peel and L. H. Carlson (London: Allen & Unwin, 1953), 422.

including the conviction that doctrine and practice should return to and reflect the doctrine and practice of the New Testament church, and the regulative principle that only elements that have biblical warrant may be included in the church's worship. Accordingly, the English Baptist confession of faith, written by Thomas Helwys in 1611, outlined a very simple service of worship: "Every church, according to the example of Christ's disciples and primitive churches, on every first day of the week (being the Lord's day), should assemble together to pray, prophesy [preach sermons based on Scripture], praise God, break bread, and perform all other parts of spiritual communion for the worship of God, their own mutual edification, the preservation of true religion, and piety in the church."[34]

A more detailed explanation of worship was presented in the *Second London Confession of Faith*. Repeating the three key articles from the *Westminster Confession*, it confirmed that worship must be governed by the regulative principle. The *Second London Confession* affirmed several biblically warranted worship activities. Worship is directed to the triune God.[35] Prayer is singled out as a special part of worship.[36] The usual worship elements were included as well: "The reading of the Scriptures, preaching and hearing the Word of God, teaching and admonishing one another in psalms, hymns, and spiritual songs, singing with grace in our heart to the Lord; as also the administration of baptism and the Lord's Supper are all parts of the religious worship of God."[37]

Furthermore, the *Second London Confession* acknowledged that the place of worship has no importance: "Neither prayer, nor any other part of religious worship, is now under the gospel tied to, or made more acceptable by, any place in which it is performed or toward which it is directed; but God is to be worshipped everywhere in Spirit, and in truth."[38] But it did emphasize that a time for worship has been set down by God in the Ten Commandments: "The Sabbath is kept holy unto the Lord, when men ... do not only observe for the entire day a holy rest from their own works, words, and thoughts about their worldly [i.e., secular] employment and recreation, but also are taken up the whole time in the public and private exercises of his [God's] worship, and in the duties of necessity and mercy."[39]

It was the English Baptists who had begun the regular practice of singing hymns during the worship service. An important contributor to this was Benjamin Keach, who introduced his London congregation to the singing of a hymn to conclude the Lord's Supper. Over time this practice became accepted by most members.[40] But the dissenters in Keach's church led a revolt that split the church into two congregations—a hymn-singing congregation and a non-hymn-singing congregation. Keach published a response entitled *The Breach Repair'd in God's Worship: or Singing of Psalms, Hymns, and Spiritual Songs Proved to Be a Holy Ordinance of Jesus Christ* (1691), which was an apologetic for

---

34. *A Declaration of Faith of English People Remaining at Amsterdam in Holland* (1611), 19, in Lumpkin, 121.

35. *Second London Confession of Faith*, 22.2, in Lumpkin, 280–81.

36. Ibid., 22.3–4, in Lumpkin, 281.

37. Ibid., 22.5, in Lumpkin, 281.

38. Ibid., 22.6, in Lumpkin, 281.

39. Ibid., 22.7–8, in Lumpkin, 282. The text has been rendered clearer.

40. Thomas Crosby, *The History of the English Baptists*, 4 vols. (London: Aaron Ward, 1739), 4:298–300.

the inclusion of singing hymns in the worship service. Keach appealed to Scripture (Eph. 5:19; Col. 3:16; James 5:13) for explicit warrant for the practice; he himself published hundreds of hymns. Keach was followed shortly after by Isaac Watts, and hymn singing was cemented as an important element in Baptist worship services. In America, the *Philadelphia Confession* (1742), reflecting the influence of Keach, included an article on singing hymns during the worship service.[41]

John Owen furthered this discussion by developing the key elements of the regulative principle. He too argued against the incorporation of extra elements that have no biblical warrant into the church's service.[42] Specifically, he denied that the observance of such rites and ceremonies enhances the devotion of the worshipers, renders the worship itself more attractive and beautiful, and helps to preserve the order of church worship.[43] He explicitly condemned the Roman Catholic Church for its violation of the regulative principle.[44] Moreover, Owen constructively set forth what elements are to be incorporated into the worship of God: "The calling, gathering, and settling of churches, with their officers, as the seat and subject of all other solemn instituted worship; prayer, with thanksgiving; singing of psalms; preaching the Word; administration of the sacraments of baptism and the supper of the Lord; discipline and rule of the church collected and settled."[45]

Another group moved far beyond a principle in regulating its worship of God. The Quakers, or Society of Friends, had peculiar ideas of revelation and an individualized "inner light." These particular doctrines influenced the Quaker notion of worship, as seen in the *Confession of the Society of Friends* (1675):

> All true and acceptable worship to God is offered in the inward and immediate moving and drawing of his own Spirit, which is neither limited to places, times, or persons. For though we be [are] to worship him always, in that we are to fear before him, yet as to the outward signification of this in prayers, praises, or preachings, we ought not do it where and when we will, but where and when we are moved thereunto by the secret inspiration of his Spirit in our hearts. This God hears and accepts, and he never fails to move us to it when it is needed; and of this he himself is the only proper judge.[46]

Thus, it was not a principle, but an individualized inspiration of the Spirit, that should regulate the worship of God. As to be expected, the *Confession* denounced the formal liturgical worship that typified most churches at the time.[47] All churches—Catholic, Anglican, Presbyterian, independent congregations—condemned the Quaker notion as being hopelessly subjective and consequently dangerous.

---

41. *Philadelphia Confession of Faith* (1742), 23, in Lumpkin, 351.

42. John Owen, *A Short Catechism*, ans. to q. 14, in *The Works of John Owen*, ed. William H. Goold (Carlisle, Pa.: Banner of Truth Trust, 1965), 15:467.

43. Ibid., explication of q. 14, in Goold, *Works of John Owen*, 15:467–70.

44. Ibid., in Goold, *Works of John Owen*, 15:470–71.

45. John Owen, *A Short Catechism*, q. 17, in Goold, *Works of John Owen*, 15:477.

46. *Confession of the Society of Friends, Commonly Called the Quakers* (1675), 11, in Schaff, 3:796. The text has been rendered clearer.

47. Ibid.

WORSHIP IN THE MODERN PERIOD

This subjective orientation, focusing attention on the individual, came to leave its mark on certain strains of American Protestantism in the modern period, particularly churches caught up in revivalism. If Protestant services were concentrated historically on the worship of God, the services of these revivalistic churches were newly oriented toward evangelism and personal renewal. A major contributor to this new emphasis was Charles Finney. In neither his *Systematic Theology* nor his *Lectures on Revival* does worship play any role. For example, in Finney's discussion of what constitutes genuine evidence of regeneration, he lists such matters as disinterested goodness, reasoned morality, peace of mind before God, involvement in social reform, self-denial, victory over sin, and purposefulness.[48] These may be true and even biblical marks of individual regeneration, but the absence of any mention of desire for and involvement in worship—either corporate or individual—is striking.

Baptist churches, especially in the southern United States, influenced by this revivalism, introduced and emphasized the invitation to convert to Christ at the end of worship services. For some, this development seemed strange and difficult to reconcile "with the due operation and concurrence of the understanding and the heart in this momentous matter (of conversion)."[49] But this closing invitation—to conversion or, additionally, to join the church—became standard fare in Baptist worship services. Furthermore, "it shaped a kind of religious thinking that was intensely individual, making the apex of Christian experience for each separate man and woman a personal change of heart which came about suddenly and publicly and under excruciating emotional pressure."[50] This individualistic strain became a principled part of Baptist churches: "Our notion of worship is simply this. We meet together on the Sabbath to offer up to God, each one for himself, the sacrifice of prayer and praise and to cultivate holy affections by the reading and explanation of the Word of God and by applying its truth to our own souls."[51] Churches following in the train of Finney and revivalism tended to be committed enthusiastically to evangelism, missions, and revival, but this admirable emphasis tended to overshadow corporate worship directed toward God in their services.

Another major contribution to the development of worship services came in the twentieth century through the Pentecostal/charismatic movement. Although the variety of expressions of worship was great, one characteristic that was common within these circles was a conscious sensitivity to the leading of the Holy Spirit. Although this often manifested itself in speaking (or singing) in tongues, such was not always the case. According

48. Charles Grandison Finney, *Lectures on Systematic Theology* (1878), lecture 19, in *Finney's Systematic Theology: New Expanded Edition*, ed. Dennis Carroll, Bill Nicely, and L. G. Parkhurst Jr. (Minneapolis: Bethany, 1994), 293–302. See chap. 22 for discussion of regeneration.

49. F. A. Cox and J. Hoby, *The Baptists in America: A Narrative of the Deputation from the Baptist Union in England to the United States and Canada* (New York: Leavitt, Lord & Co., 1836), 468, cited in Carlton Turner Mitchell, "Baptist Worship

in Relation to Baptist Concepts of the Church, 1608–1865," (Ph.D. diss., New York University, 1962), 181.

50. Bernard A. Weisberger, *They Gathered at the River* (Boston: Little, Brown, 1958), 21, in Mitchell, "Baptist Worship," 182.

51. Francis Wayland, *Notes on the Principles and Practices of Baptist Churches* (New York: Sheldon, Blakemore, & Co., 1857), 160, in Mitchell, "Baptist Worship," 229.

to J. Rodman Williams, the characteristic element of Pentecostal worship is spontaneity. Although orderliness is both necessary and biblical, spontaneity should characterize the church's worship of God as well. Taking his lead from Ephesians 5:19, Williams offered: "These 'spiritual songs' are songs inspired by the Holy Spirit, that is, spontaneous songs in which both the melody and the words are given by the Spirit.... This is an act of free and spontaneous worship that cannot be programmed ahead of time, nor can its contents be previously known."[52] Such spontaneity was particularly noticeable in mainline churches, renewed through the charismatic movement, as they sought to follow the leading of the Spirit while engaged in their traditional liturgical service. As one description explained:

> The charismatic renewal of the mid 20th century has brought about a revival of emphasis on praise and worship in American religious life. Freedom in worship, joyful singing, both vocal and physical expressions of praise, instrumental accompaniment of singing, and acceptance of a wide variety of music styles are all characteristic of this renewal. As in the early days of the pentecostal revival, it is not unusual to find charismatic worshipers singing, shouting, clapping hands, leaping, and dancing before the Lord as they offer him sincere praise and thanksgiving.[53]

The Roman Catholic Church also made significant changes to its liturgy. Vatican II, an *aggiornamento* (or updating) of the church, specifically addressed this aspect in its *Constitution on the Sacred Liturgy*. Specifically, Vatican II gave instructions concerning both the nature of the liturgy and the reform of the liturgy. In his office as priest, Jesus Christ acts through the liturgy to save and to sanctify:

> Just as Christ was sent by the Father, so also he sent the apostles, filled with the Holy Spirit ... so that they might preach the Gospel.... But he also willed that the work of salvation which they preached should be set in train through the sacrifice and sacraments, around which the entire liturgical life revolves.... The liturgy, then, is rightly seen as an exercise of the priestly office of Jesus Christ. It involves the presentation of man's sanctification under the guise of signs perceptible by the senses and its accomplishment in ways appropriate to each of these signs. In it full public worship is performed by the Mystical Body of Jesus Christ, that is, by the Head and his members.[54]

It is through the liturgy that the grace of God flows to sinful people.[55] While reiterating the historic Catholic doctrine of the nature of the liturgy, Vatican II also called for

52. J. Rodman Williams, *Renewal Theology: Systematic Theology from a Charismatic Perspective*, 3 vols. in 1 (Grand Rapids: Zondervan, 1996), 3:104.

53. Delton L. Alford, "Pentecostal and Charismatic Music," in *The New International Dictionary of Pentecostal and Charismatic Movements*, ed. Stanley M. Burgess, rev. and exp. ed. (Grand Rapids: Zondervan, 2002), 918.

54. *Constitution on the Sacred Liturgy* (December 4, 1963), 1.1.6–7, in Vatican Council II, vol. 1: *The Conciliar and Post-Conciliar Documents*, ed. Austin Flannery (New York: Costello, 1975), 4–5.

55. Ibid., 1.1.9–10, in Flannery, *Conciliar and Post-Conciliar Documents*, 6.

a revision in the form of the liturgy: "For the liturgy is made up of unchangeable elements divinely instituted, and of elements subject to change. These latter not only may be changed, but should be changed with the passage of time, if they have suffered from the intrusion of anything out of harmony with the inner nature of the liturgy or have become less suitable."[56]

After the conclusion of Vatican Council II in 1965, the Catholic Church undertook to put into practice the many reforms called for by the council. By the next decade, most Catholic masses worldwide were being celebrated in languages other than Latin. The revision of the liturgy, called for by the council, was described by Pope Paul VI's *Apostolic Constitution on the Roman Missal* (1969) and concretely applied in the Sacred Congregation for Divine Worship's *General Instruction on the Roman Missal* (1970). The *Constitution* drew attention to three important changes in the Roman liturgy: the Eucharistic Prayer,[57] the order of the Mass,[58] and the Scripture readings.[59] The Sacred Congregation for Divine Worship enacted these three major changes, and many other lesser changes, in its *General Instruction on the Roman Missal*. This *aggiornamento* of the Mass featured a balance between the liturgy of the Word and the liturgy of the Eucharist, more readings from Scripture, a near requirement of a homily, greater lay participation, and a service in the language of the people.[60] The response, as could be anticipated, was diverse: Catholics both enthusiastically praised the changes as contributing effectively to a modernization of the church and stridently denounced them as fostering a liberalization of the church.

Following these changes in the Catholic Church, mainline Protestant denominations also updated their worship services. A combination of hymns and directions for liturgy was published by the Lutheran churches, a revised *Book of Common Prayer* was introduced by the Episcopal Church in 1979, and the *Book of Services* was created by the Presbyterian churches in 1993.

The theology of worship became a major interest for evangelicals. William Temple authored a definition that became a standard for evangelical reflection on the topic: "Worship is the submission of all our nature to God: It is the quickening of conscience by his holiness, the nourishment of mind with his truth, the purifying of imagination by his beauty, the opening of the heart to his love, the surrender of will to his purpose."[61] This idea of worship as exerting an all-encompassing impact on Christians was extended by David Peterson, whose *Engaging with God: A Biblical Theology of Worship* concluded that all activities in which Christians participate may constitute genuine worship of God:

---

56. Ibid., 1.3.21, in Flannery, *Conciliar and Post-Conciliar Documents*, 9.

57. *Apostolic Constitution on the Roman Missal* (April 3, 1969), in Flannery, *Conciliar and Post-Conciliar Documents*, 139.

58. Ibid., in Flannery, *Conciliar and Post-Conciliar Documents*, 139–40.

59. Ibid., in Flannery, *Conciliar and Post-Conciliar Documents*, 140.

60. *General Instruction on the Roman Missal* (March 26,

1970), in Flannery, *Conciliar and Post-Conciliar Documents*, 168–79.

61. William Temple, *Readings in St. John's Gospel* (1939; repr., Wilton, Conn.: Morehouse Barlow, 1985). Interestingly, Temple's definition made no mention of the body or physical posture in worship. Included in "the submission of all our nature to God" must be something like "the engagement of body in accordance with the act of worship" (raising of hands in praise, kneeling in humility, etc.).

Throughout the Bible, acceptable worship means approaching or engaging with God on the terms that he proposes and in the manner that he makes possible. It involves honoring, serving and respecting him, abandoning any loyalty or devotion that hinders an exclusive relationship with him. Although some of Scripture's terms for worship may refer to specific gestures of homage, rituals or priestly ministrations, worship is more fundamentally faith expressing itself in obedience and adoration. Consequently, in both Testaments, it is often shown to be a personal and moral fellowship with God relevant to every sphere of life.[62]

D. A. Carson, editor of *Worship by the Book*, authored this definition:

Worship is the proper response of all moral, sentient beings to God, ascribing all honor and worth to their Creator-God precisely because he is worthy, delightfully so. This side of the Fall, *human worship* of God properly responds to the redemptive provisions that God has graciously made. While all true worship is God-centered, *Christian worship* is no less Christ-centered. Empowered by the Spirit and in line with the stipulations of the new covenant, it manifests itself in all our living, finding its impulse in the gospel, which restores our relationship with our Redeemer-God and therefore also with our fellow image-bearers, our co-worshipers. Such worship therefore manifests itself both in adoration and in action, both in the individual believer and in *corporate worship*, which is worship offered up in the context of the body of believers, who strive to align all the forms of their devout ascriptions of all worth to God with the panoply of new covenant mandates and examples that bring to fulfillment the glories of antecedent revelation and anticipate the consummation.[63]

Allen Ross, in *Recalling the Hope of Glory: Biblical Worship from the Garden to the New Creation*, offered this detailed definition:

True worship is the celebration of being in covenant fellowship with the sovereign and holy triune God, by means of the reverent adoration and spontaneous praise of God's nature and works, the expressed commitment of trust and obedience to the covenant responsibilities, and the memorial reenactment of entering into covenant through ritual acts, all with the confident anticipation of the fulfillment of the covenant promises in glory.[64]

These and other definitions urged evangelical churches to think biblically and theologically about their practice of worship.

For the most part, worship services in evangelical churches featured the traditional elements of the ministry of the Word, the singing of hymns of praise and thanksgiving to God, the administration of baptism and the Lord's Supper, and so forth. Evangelical

---

62. David Peterson, *Engaging with God: A Biblical Theology of Worship* (Downers Grove, Ill.: InterVarsity, 1992), 283.

63. D. A. Carson, "Worship under the Word," in *Worship by the Book*, ed. D. A. Carson (Grand Rapids: Zondervan, 2002), 26.

64. Allen P. Ross, *Recalling the Hope of Glory: Biblical Worship from the Garden to the New Creation* (Grand Rapids: Kregel, 2006), 67–68.

churches strongly influenced by revivalism also incorporated elements of evangelism and calls to personal spiritual commitment and renewal.

By far the most serious challenge to the traditional worship service in evangelical churches came from the introduction of innovative elements such as contemporary Christian music. Historically, most Protestant churches had incorporated new and fresh styles of music in their service, as the likes of Benjamin Keach, Isaac Watts, Charles Wesley, Fanny Crosby, and many others could attest. Moreover, many churches had seriously and fervently debated the legitimacy and utility of such innovative music for the proper worship of God. But contemporary Christian music spawned a significant increase in interest in the doctrine and practice of worship among evangelicals. And it led to new and innovative worship services.

Several factors contributed to this development. One was the origin and growth of parachurch movements, such as Campus Crusade for Christ, that targeted young people. Such movements exerted a particularly powerful influence as parachurch worship infiltrated traditional churches.[65] The church growth movement, with its emphasis on "a celebrative, energetic, or exciting worship style," also contributed to innovative worship services.[66] Another factor was the development of the genre of "Christian popular music." "Christian" musicians composed and recorded "Christian" music that was broadcast on radio and television just like folk songs, rock and roll, heavy metal, country-and-western ballads, and the like. Christian recording artists and groups such as Larry Norman, Love Song, Andraé Crouch and the Disciples, Evie Tornquist, B. J. Thomas, Bill Gaither, Keith Green, Amy Grant, Phil Keaggy, 2nd Chapter of Acts, Michael W. Smith, Michael Card, Petra, Twila Paris, dc Talk, Third Day, Rich Mullins, Jars of Clay, Chris Rice, Point of Grace, Caedmon's Call, the Katinas, Kirk Franklin, Casting Crowns, and many others became heroes for many church members who were thankful for such talent, which rivaled that of secular music while offering Christians a safe musical alternative.

As this new genre of music was ushered into church worship services, it raised an important question and offered a challenge: "How entertaining should worship be … especially now that Christianity had its own popular music and artists?…Worship is about God and entertainment is about us. If we allow 'entertaining' to mean 'engaging,' we welcome the dynamic to worship. If, however, 'entertaining' means distraction or amusement, the focus of worship is in jeopardy."[67] As many churches incorporated contemporary Christian music as part of their worship services, more traditional church members—who considered such music as entertainment at best and demonic at worst—and more progressive church members—who considered such music as enhancing true worship—squared off in those churches in what became known as the "worship wars."

Faced with what they considered to be a serious deterioration in the worship of God in many churches, a growing number of evangelicals directly addressed the crisis. Robert Webber offered a particular challenge to evangelicals and their worship services:

> A biblical theology of worship … defines worship in terms of the Gospel. This
> theology recognizes that the content of worship is the story of God's redeeming

---

65. Terry W. York, *America's Worship Wars* (Peabody, Mass.: Hendrickson, 2003), 26–27.

66. Ibid., 51.
67. Ibid., 43–44.

his creatures from the Evil One. This is expressed in his initiating grace toward Adam, Abraham, the patriarchs, Israel, and the prophets and culminating in the life, death, resurrection, and return of Jesus Christ. This message lies at the heart of everything done in the worship of the church. The voice of the Gospel is heard in preaching, in baptism, in the Lord's Supper, in hymns, psalms and spiritual songs, in prayers, in anointing, and in every conceivable act of worship. The content of worship is not negotiable. It cannot be changed, altered, or added to. A true biblical worship is this story of God's initiating a relationship with fallen creatures, a story that is remembered by God's people and for which they give thanks.[68]

Webber rebuked evangelicals for neglecting this gospel story as the heart of worship.[69] He called for a structure for worship services that has four biblically derived and historically practiced elements: entrance into worship, the proclamation of the Word of God, the church's thanksgiving in the Lord's Supper, and dismissal.[70] Similarly, in her book *Reaching Out without Dumbing Down*, Marva Dawn exposed the shortsighted responses of many evangelical churches to the challenges presented at the close of the twentieth century. Among her criticisms were the churches' capitulation to a media-oriented society; postmodern rootlessness; the idols of personal choice, power, fame, and fortune; a therapeutic culture; emotionalism and anti-intellectualism; and rampant individualism.[71] Dawn offered an alternative: "We could plan worship that keeps God as the subject, that nurtures the character of the believer, that forms the Christian community to be a people who reach out in God's purposes to the world."[72]

As another example, the Alliance of Confessing Evangelicals devoted part of the Cambridge Declaration to the topic of the deterioration of the church's worship:

> The loss of God's centrality in the life of today's church is common and lamentable. It is this loss that allows us to transform worship into entertainment, gospel preaching into marketing, believing into technique, being good into feeling good about ourselves, and faithfulness into being successful.... God does not exist to satisfy human ambitions, cravings, the appetite for consumption, or our own private spiritual interests. We must focus on God in our worship, rather than the satisfaction of our own personal needs. God is sovereign in worship; we are not. Our concern must be for God's kingdom, not our own empires, popularity or success.[73]

Not surprisingly, many of these evangelicals reclaimed the regulative principle for worship. John L. Girardeau's classic definition was reemphasized: "A divine warrant is necessary for every element of doctrine, government and worship in the church; that is,

---

68. Robert Webber, *Worship Old and New: A Biblical, Historical, and Practical Introduction*, rev. ed. (Grand Rapids: Zondervan, 1994), 261–62.

69. Ibid., 262.

70. Ibid., 263.

71. Marva J. Dawn, *Reaching Out without Dumbing Down:* *A Theology of Worship for the Turn-of-the-Century Culture* (Grand Rapids: Eerdmans, 1995), 303.

72. Ibid., 304.

73. *The Cambridge Declaration: A Statement by the Alliance of Confessing Evangelicals* (1996). Available at the movement's website: http://www.alliancenet.org.

whatsoever in these spheres is not commanded in the Scriptures, either expressly or by good and necessary consequence from their statements, is forbidden."[74] J. Ligon Duncan refreshed the definition: "The regulative principle, in short, states that worship in its content, motivation, and aim is to be determined by God alone. He teaches us how to think about him and how to approach him. The further we get away, then, from his directions, the less we actually worship."[75] Other evangelicals sought to embrace both the regulative and normative principles. For example, Mark Driscoll claimed the freedom to incorporate new worship elements that are not prohibited by Scripture (i.e., the normative principle). At the same time he emphasized that the church's commitment to the key elements expressly commanded for its worship is so all-consuming that newly added elements will not be allowed to crowd out the other essential elements.[76]

At the turn of the third millennium, with traditional worship patterns and contemporary trends vying for consideration, the church's worship faces important challenges. While the debate may at times become heated, and innovative elements may be introduced with little or no theological consideration, the church of Jesus Christ still continues to emphasize its worship of the triune God.

---

74. John L. Girardeau, *Instrumental Music in the Public Worship of the Church* (1888; repr., Edmonton, Canada: Still Water Revival, 2000), 9.

75. J. Ligon Duncan III, "Does God Care How We Worship?" in *Give Praise to God*, ed. Philip Graham Ryken, Derek W. H. Thomas, and J. Ligon Duncan III (Phillipsburg, N.J.:

P & R, 2003), 27; cf. 23.

76. Mark Driscoll, "Regulative Principle," in Religion Saves sermon series, Mars Hill Church (Seattle), March 2, 2008. Available at church's website: http://www.marshill-church.org/media/religionsaves.

Part 7

THE DOCTRINE
OF THE FUTURE

Chapter 31

CHRIST'S RETURN AND THE MILLENNIUM

How has the church developed various views on the return of Jesus Christ and its relationship to the millennium?

STATEMENT OF BELIEF

Eschatology, from the Greek word ἔσχατος (*eschatos*; "last"), is the study of last things or the future. From its inception, the church has clung to and developed a hope of God's final intervention in the world to put an end to all opposition and ungodliness, reward his faithful followers, and make all things new. Specifically, the church has historically believed in a personal, visible, sudden, and bodily return of Jesus Christ—called his "second coming" to distinguish it from his first advent two thousand years ago—for which believers should eagerly long. Although enjoying great agreement about the fact of this event, Christians have had significant disagreement over "specific details leading up to and immediately following Christ's return. Specifically, they disagree over the nature of the millennium and the relationship of Christ's return to the millennium, the sequence of Christ's return and the great tribulation period that will come to the earth."[1] The evangelical church continues to reflect this essential agreement on Christ's return and a broad spectrum of diverse views concerning its details. In particular, there have been four major views concerning the second coming, the millennium, and the tribulation: amillennialism, classic or historic premillennialism (with a posttribulation view of Christ's return), dispensational premillennialism (with a pretribulation view of Christ's return), and postmillennialism.[2]

---

1. Wayne Grudem, *Systematic Theology: An Introduction to Biblical Doctrine* (Grand Rapids: Zondervan, 1994, 2000), 1095.

2. My thanks to Bryan Lilly for his help with this chapter.

ESCHATOLOGICAL BELIEFS IN THE EARLY CHURCH

From its very outset, the church has looked forward to the return of Christ and a new existence that would be initiated by that event. Jesus himself prophesied his return (Matt. 24:29–30), and the apostle Paul urged this truth as a comfort for believers who were concerned about their loved ones who had died (1 Thess. 4:13–18). The earliest believers eagerly anticipated "the blessed hope—the glorious appearing of our great God and Savior, Jesus Christ" (Titus 2:13).

This hope continued to characterize the church during its first few centuries of growth. An important theme was the contrast between the two comings of Christ, which was seen as being foretold in Old Testament Scripture: "The prophets have proclaimed two advents of [Christ]: the [first] one, that which is already past, when he came as a dishonored and suffering man; but the second, when, according to prophecy, he shall come from heaven with glory, accompanied by his angelic host."[3] This hope was an essential element of the "rule of faith," as Irenaeus attested to the belief of the church in Christ's future "manifestation from heaven in the glory of the Father."[4]

Many Christians believed Christ's return to be imminent, as Cyprian expressed: "Already his second coming draws near to us."[5] The sense of imminency was not equated with immediacy, however. According to Cyprian, Christ gave instructions about events that must precede his return in order to prepare the church to be strong in perseverance, "lest an unexpected and new dread of mischief" would shake the church. He underscored Jesus' teaching that "wars, famines, earthquakes and pestilence would arise everywhere, and adversity would increase more and more in the last times." This fact made the return of Christ imminent, not in the sense of immediate, but as not far off: "Behold, the very things occur which were spoken; and since those occur which were foretold before, whatever things were promised will follow; as the Lord himself promises, saying, 'But when you see all these things come to pass, know that the kingdom of God is at hand' [Luke 21:31]. The kingdom of God ... is beginning to be at hand."[6]

Accordingly, the early church believed that the return of Christ would be linked with several other cataclysmic events. These would include a period of intense tribulation associated with the appearance of the Antichrist, the judgment of believers and unbelievers, and the end of the world as it is currently known. Addressing the great tribulation, Hippolytus interpreted the end-times vision of Daniel (chap. 7) to mean that this tribulation period would precede the return of Christ: "The fourth beast, as being stronger and mightier than all that went before it, will reign five hundred years. When the times are fulfilled, and the ten horns spring from the beast in the last times, then the Antichrist will appear among them. When he makes war against the saints, and persecutes them, then we may expect the manifestation of the Lord from heaven."[7] He also believed

---

3. Justin Martyr, *First Apology*, 52, in *ANF*, 1:180. See also his *Dialogue with Trypho, a Jew*, 110, in *ANF*, 1:253.

4. Irenaeus, *Against Heresies*, 1.10.1, in *ANF*, 1:330.

5. Cyprian, *Letter* 62.18, in *ANF*, 5:363.

6. Cyprian, *Letter* 7.2, in *ANF*, 5:469.

7. Hippolytus, *Fragments from Commentaries: Daniel*, 2.7, in *ANF*, 5:179. See also *Treatise on Christ and Antichrist*, 64: "These things, then, being come to pass, beloved, and the one week being divided into two parts, and the abomination of desolation being manifested then, and the two prophets and

that the church would experience intense persecution during the period leading up to the Lord's return.[8] Justin Martyr expressed a similar view when he spoke of the second coming: "He shall come from heaven with glory, when the man of apostasy, who speaks strange things against the Most High, shall venture to do unlawful deeds on the earth against us Christians."[9] Specifically, Irenaeus offered: "When this Antichrist shall have devastated all things in this world, he will reign for three years and six months, and sit in the temple at Jerusalem; and then the Lord will come from heaven in the clouds, in the glory of the Father, sending this man and those who follow him into the lake of fire."[10]

The early church also looked forward to its reward—the "rapture"—for its perseverance through this tribulation, as Irenaeus expressed: "When in the end the church will suddenly be caught up from this, it is said, 'There shall be tribulation such as has not been since the beginning, neither shall be' (Matt. 24:21). For this is the last contest of the righteous, in which, when they overcome, they are crowned with incorruption."[11] Tertullian described the instantaneous transformation that awaits persecuted believers who are raptured during the tribulation: "These [people] also shall, in the crisis of the last moment and from their instantaneous death, while encountering the oppression of antichrist, undergo a change. They will obtain by this not so much a divestiture of the body as a clothing superimposed upon it with the garment which is from heaven. They shall put on this heavenly garment over their bodies."[12] He contrasted this change with what will happen to those who are already deceased: The dead in Christ will receive their resurrected bodies at the Lord's return.[13] Thus, the early church placed the return of Christ after the period of great tribulation. This is called a *posttribulation* position.[14]

The early church associated another important event with the second coming: a reign of Christ upon the earth for one thousand years. In his Revelation (20:1–6), the apostle John described this "millennium."[15] Many Christians interpreted this to refer to a literal one-thousand-year reign of Christ, beginning immediately after his glorious return. This position is called *premillennialism*.[16] The first reference to this view was Papias, who believed "that there will be a period of a thousand years after the resurrection from the dead when the kingdom of Christ will be set up in material form on this earth."[17] Similarly,

---

forerunners of the Lord having finished their course, and the whole world finally approaching the consummation, what remains but the coming of our Lord and Savior Jesus Christ from heaven, for whom we have looked in hope?" *ANF*, 5:218.

8. Hippolytus, *Treatise on Christ and Antichrist*, 60–64, in *ANF*, 5:217–18.

9. Justin Martyr, *Dialogue with Trypho*, 110, in *ANF*, 1:253–54.

10. Irenaeus, *Against Heresies*, 5.30.4, in *ANF*, 1:560.

11. Ibid., 5.29.1, in *ANF*, 1:558.

12. Tertullian, *Against Marcion*, 5.12, in *ANF*, 3:455. The text has been rendered clearer.

13. Ibid.

14. *Post* is a prefix indicating "after." Thus, the *posttribula-tion* position holds that Christ will return *after* the tribulation.

15. In the Latin, the number "one thousand" is *mille*; hence, the *millennium* is the one-thousand-year reign of

Christ. Another indicator of this event was the statement of Jesus following his institution of the cup during the Lord's Supper: "I tell you, I will not drink of this fruit of the vine from now on until that day when I drink it anew with you in my Father's kingdom" (Matt. 26:29).

16. *Pre* is a prefix indicating "before." Thus, the *premillen-nial* position holds that Christ's second coming will take place *before* the one-thousand-year period. As noted above, historic premillennialism is also posttribulation. Thus, the order of events is as follows: the great tribulation, the return of Christ, the millennium.

17. *Fragments of Papias* 3.12, in Holmes, 567. Eusebius made reference to Papias's belief in Eusebius, *Ecclesiastical History*, 3.39, in *Eusebius' Ecclesiastical History*, trans. Christian Frederick Cruse (Grand Rapids: Eerdmans, 1962), 126; cf. *NPNF*[2], 1:154.

Justin Martyr expressed this hope: "I and others who are right-minded Christians on all points, are assured that there will be a resurrection of the dead and a thousand years in Jerusalem, which will then be built, adorned and enlarged."[18] But he did not consider this belief a key element in orthodox Christian doctrine, noting that "many who belong to the pure and pious faith and are true Christians think otherwise."[19] However, Irenaeus's end-times presentation was held by many in the early church: Christ will return, Antichrist will be defeated, Christians will be resurrected bodily, these believers will reign with Christ on the earth for one thousand years, unbelievers will be resurrected after the millennium, the final judgment will occur, and God will establish the eternal state of heaven and hell.[20]

The Old Testament prophets—Isaiah, Ezekiel, and others—were frequently cited in support of this hope.[21] At times this belief was also based on the calculation that the world would exist for six thousand years, followed by another millennium of rest. At the heart of this view was the Genesis account of six days of creation followed by rest: "Observe, children, what 'he finished in six days' means. It means this: that in six thousand years the Lord will bring everything to an end, for with him a day signifies a thousand years.... Therefore, children, in six days—that is, in six thousand years—everything will be brought to an end."[22] Corresponding to the seventh day, the millennium—a period of one thousand years—will follow: "When the six days—that is, the six thousand years of labor and pain for the saints—have passed, the seventh day, the true sabbath, will come for all of them who have existed from the beginning of the world."[23] Some Christians, like Hippolytus, used this six-thousand-year framework to calculate the time of Christ's return: "For the first appearance of our Lord in the flesh took place in Bethlehem, under Augustus, in the year 5500.... And 6000 years must be accomplished, in order that the Sabbath [the millennium] may come.... From the birth of Christ, then, we must reckon that 500 years remain to make up the 6000, and thus the end shall be."[24] So Hippolytus (writing at the beginning of the third century) anticipated that the millennium would be established about 250 years after his time.

Interpreting the Old Testament prophets literally, some early Christians engaged in elaborate descriptions of the millennium:

> The days will come when vines will grow, each having ten thousand shoots, and
> on each shoot ten thousand branches, and on each branch ten thousand twigs,

18. Justin Martyr, *Dialogue with Trypho*, 80, in *ANF*, 1:239. Tertullian echoed this hope: "We do confess that a kingdom is promised to us upon the earth, although before heaven, only in another state of existence; insomuch as it will be after the resurrection for a thousand years in the divinely-built city of Jerusalem." *Against Marcion*, 3.25, in *ANF*, 3:342.

19. Ibid.

20. Irenaeus, *Against Heresies*, 5.32–36, in *ANF*, 1:561–67.

21. E.g., Irenaeus cites Isa. 11:6–9; 26:19; 30:25–26; as well as Ezek. 28:25–26 and 37:12–14.

22. *Epistle of Barnabas*, 15.3–4, in Holmes, 315; *ANF*, 1:146. For the author of this work, the six days of creation correspond to the six thousand years of human history. This period would soon come to a close, and the seventh day of rest,

corresponding to the millennium, would begin. This would be followed by the eighth day, corresponding to the new heaven and new earth.

23. Quintus Julius Hillarianus, *The Progress of Time*, cited in Bernard McGinn, *Visions of the End: Apocalyptic Traditions in the Middle Ages* (New York: Columbia Univ. Press, 1979), 53.

24. Hippolytus, *Fragments from Commentaries*, in *ANF*, 5:179. Hippolytus calculated 5500 for the beginning of the world by taking the measurements for the ark of the covenant prescribed in Ex. 25:10 ("you shall make its length two and half cubits, its breadth one and half cubits, and its height one and a half cubits") and multiplying their total (5.5) by 1,000 to arrive at 5,500.

and on each twig ten thousand clusters, and in each cluster ten thousand grapes, and each grape when crushed will yield twenty-five measures of wine.... Similarly, a grain of wheat will produce ten thousand heads, and every head will have ten thousand grains, and every grain ten pounds of fine flour, white and clean. And the other fruits, seeds, and grass will produce in similar proportions.[25]

Lactantius added more details to this millennium portrait: "Throughout this time beasts shall not be nourished by blood, nor birds by prey; but all things shall be peaceful and tranquil. Lions and calves shall stand together at the manger [hay trough]. The wolf shall not carry off the sheep, nor the hound wolf [dog] hunt for prey; hawks and eagles shall not injure; the infant shall play with serpents."[26] Because nature will be set free from sin and evil, Satan will be bound, and unbelievers will be held in check by the ruling Christ, Christians can look forward to an unprecedented golden age of righteousness, peace, and prosperity. This premillennial hope—that Christ would return to establish a one-thousand-year millennium kingdom—was strong in the early church.

By the fifth century, premillennialism had given way to another eschatological framework known as *amillennialism*.[27] Several developments contributed to the demise of the former view. One was its emphasis on the luxurious material blessings that awaited believers in the millennium. Eusebius labeled this notion "strange" and considered it "legendary."[28] A second reason was the change in relationship between the church and the state, put into motion by the emperor Constantine and his legalization of Christianity in the Roman Empire early in the fourth century. Another stemmed from attempts to predict precisely the time of Christ's return and the beginning of the millennium. An extreme example of this was the movement known as Montanism, which stirred up hope in the imminent second coming of Christ and the descent of the "New Jerusalem" to Phrygia, the movement's hometown. Such fanaticism soured some Christians on premillennial eschatology.

Theologically, church leaders from Alexandria, Egypt—Clement and Origen— offered an alternative eschatology that undermined premillennialism. Origen particularly criticized the literal interpretation of Scripture upon which premillennialism was based.[29] Moving beyond a literal interpretation, Origen approached Scripture to find its spiritual meaning. According to this sense, Christians would not eat actual luxurious food, but "the bread of life, which may nourish the soul with the food of truth and wisdom."[30] Thus, Christians could still hope for the fulfillment of the promises of the future, but the hope was not for physical goods but spiritual blessings.

---

25. *Fragments of Papias*, 14, in Holmes, 581. Irenaeus made reference to Papias in *Against Heresies* 5.33.3–4; *ANF*, 1:563.

26. Lactantius, *The Divine Institutes*, 24, in *ANF*, 7:219. His reference to Isa. 11:6–9 is clear. See also Tertullian, *Against Hermogenes*, 11, in *ANF*, 3:483. See also Commodianus, *Instructions*, 44, in *ANF*, 4:212.

27. *A* is a prefix indicating "no." Thus, amillennialism holds there is *no* (future) millennium.

28. *Fragments of Papias*, 3.12–13, in Holmes, 567. As noted above, Eusebius made specific reference to the millennial view of Papias, whom he charged with "misunderstanding the apostolic accounts" while drawing attention to the fact that Papias "was a man of very limited intelligence." *Ecclesiastical History*, 3.39, in Cruse, *Eusebius's Ecclesiastical History*, 126; cf. *NPNF*[2], 1:154.

29. Origen, *First Principles*, 2.11.2, in *ANF*, 4:297.

30. Ibid., 2.11.3.

Tyconius and his chief follower Augustine established amillennialism as the reigning eschatological view. Tyconius paved the way for this new understanding by means of his *Book of Rules* for correctly interpreting the prophecies of Scripture: They will be fulfilled *spiritually*, not *literally* as premillennialists imagined. When he applied this method to Revelation 20:1–6, Tyconius focused on a spiritual millennium corresponding to the current church period. Those pictured as reigning with Christ are believers who overcome sin and live righteously.[31]

Augustine was at first attracted to the premillennial view.[32] However, the emphasis of premillennialists on the luxury and prosperity of the millennial kingdom scandalized him; for Augustine, such a hope went beyond the bounds of belief. Influenced by Tyconius, Augustine established the amillennial understanding of Revelation 20. Specifically, he linked the binding of Satan for a thousand years (vv. 2–3) with Jesus' words about binding the strong man (Mark 3:27). This event took place "when the church began to be more and more widely extended among the nations beyond Judea," and it "bridled and restrained [Satan's] power so that he could not seduce and gain possession" of people who are to become Christians.[33] Furthermore, Augustine considered the one thousand years to extend "from the first coming of Christ to the end of the world, when he shall come the second time." There is thus no *future* millennium to which the church looks forward; rather, the millennium of Revelation 20 describes the *present* church age.[34] On the one hand, the first resurrection (vv. 5–6) takes place for the Christian who hears "the voice of the Son of God and passes from death to life" and also "continues in this renewed life." This resurrection is a spiritual one and applies both to the faithful who are alive and to the dead who enjoy their rest in heaven.[35] On the other hand, the second resurrection (v. 5) is the dreadful fate of unbelievers: "When the day of the bodily resurrection arrives, they will come out of their graves, not to life but to judgment, that is, to damnation; this is called the second death." Unlike the first, this second resurrection is a physical one.[36]

Augustine's amillennial interpretation of Revelation 20 superseded the premillennial understanding so prevalent in the early church. With this development, amillennialism became the dominant eschatological belief for well over the next millennium.

ESCHATOLOGICAL BELIEFS IN THE MIDDLE AGES

Although they never succeeded in dethroning amillennialism, several developments in the medieval period challenged that prevailing eschatology. One was the Crusades. Exasperated by the continued expansion of Islam and appalled by the conquest of Jerusalem—the Holy City of Christianity—by the Muslims, the Catholic Church organized the Crusades as a military response to these threats.[37] Eschatological hopes fanned the

---

31. The writings of Tyconius no longer exist, but his position can be adequately reconstructed by studying the writings of Augustine, who took over his views and popularized them. See chap. 8 for a discussion.

32. Augustine, *The City of God*, 20.7, in *NPNF*[1], 2:426.

33. Ibid., 20.8, in *NPNF*[1], 2:428; and 20.7, in *NPNF*[1], 2:427.

34. Ibid., 20.8, in *NPNF*[1], 2:428.

35. Ibid., 20.9, in *NPNF*[1], 2:431.

36. Ibid.

37. The word *crusade* comes from the Latin *crux*, or *cross*; crusaders took up the cross of Christ and fought on behalf of Christianity against the "infidels," or Muslims. The First Crusade took place from 1096 to 1099; the Eighth Crusade failed in 1270.

flame of enthusiasm for the Crusades: If Islam and its far-reaching empire was the Antichrist, it had to be challenged—literally, physically—before the end could come and Christ could return.[38] Therefore, participation in the Crusades would contribute to the fulfillment of end-times prophecies.[39] A second development was the onset of natural disasters, which also served to heighten eschatological expectations. Famines in Europe and the bubonic plague—the so-called Black Death—wiped out a significant percentage of European society, and some saw these tragic events as evidence of God's displeasure with the church, a precursor to the end of the world.[40]

A fanciful yet popular challenge to the amillennialism of the medieval church came from a twelfth-century monk by the name of Joachim of Fiore. He divided history into three ages, with the first corresponding to the Old Testament, the second to the New Testament, and the third to a future spiritual understanding. He then outlined the time periods corresponding to these three ages: "The first age, which flourished under the Law and circumcision, began with Adam. The second, which flourished under the gospel, began with Uzziah [eighth century BC]. The third ... began at the time of St. Benedict [sixth century AD]. Its surpassing excellence is to be expected near the end."[41] Joachim also noted the members of the Trinity corresponding to these three ages: "The first age is ascribed to the Father, the second to the Son, the third to the Holy Spirit."[42]

According to Joachim, the second period—the age of the Son—was drawing to an end. To guide the church through the upcoming tribulation that the Antichrist would soon unleash against it, God would raise up two new orders of monks—one being preachers, the other being hermits—corresponding to the two witnesses of Revelation (11:3–12). These two orders are described in Revelation 14:14–15 as the Son of Man with a sickle and an angel who directs him to use the sickle:

38. In keeping with this, Guibert of Nogent underscored the motivation for the Crusades: "You ought to consider with deep deliberation whether, as a result of your pains, with God acting through you, it should happen that the mother church of all churches [Jerusalem] begins to bloom again to the Christian religion. You ought also consider whether perhaps he may not wish other parts of the East restored to the faith against the approaching times of the Antichrist. For it is clear that Antichrist will not wage war against Jews and pagans, but, according to the etymology of his name, he will attack Christians. If he finds no Christians there (as today there are scarcely any), there will be no one to oppose him or whom he may legally overcome.... This could not happen at all unless Christianity is found where now there is only paganism. If then you are forward in waging holy war, just as you once received the seed of the knowledge of God from Jerusalem, so now you will return a repayment of grace borrowed there, so that the Catholic name will be propagated, that name which is opposed to the treachery of Antichrist and his followers." Guibert of Nogent, *The Deeds of God through the Franks*, 4.20, cited in McGinn, *Visions of the End*, 91. Also, the legend of Merlin the Magician contained his prophecies that a mighty conqueror would recapture the Holy Land from the Muslims; this "good

champion" would be the last world emperor before Christ's return. See Richard Kyle, *The Last Days Are Here Again: A History of the End Times* (Grand Rapids: Baker, 1998), 47.

39. "According to prophecies, before the coming of the Antichrist it is first necessary that the Christian empire be renewed in those parts, either through you or through those whom God pleases, so that the head of all evil who will have his imperial throne there may find some nourishment of faith against which he may fight. Think then that the Almighty has perhaps prepared you to rescue Jerusalem from such subjugation! I ask you to consider what hearts could conceive the joys when you have seen the Holy City raised up by your aid, and the prophetic, even divine, oracles fulfilled in our times!" Guibert of Nogent, *Deeds of God through the Franks*, 4.20, cited in McGinn, *Visions of the End*, 92.

40. The famine in the early part of the fourteenth century, and the plague that peaked about 1350, destroyed nearly half of the European population.

41. Joachim of Fiore, *Exposition of the Apocalypse*, f. 5r–v, cited in McGinn, *Visions of the End*, 134. The text has been rendered clearer.

42. Ibid.

Just as in him who was like the Son of Man there is to be understood a future order of perfect men preserving the life of Christ and the apostles, so in the angel ... is to be seen an order of hermits imitating the life of the angels.... An order will arise that seems new but is not. Clad in black garments and bound with a belt from above, they will increase and their fame will be spread abroad. In the spirit of Elijah they will preach the faith and defend it until the consummation of the world. There will also be an order of hermits imitating the angels' life. Their life will be like a fire burning in love and zeal for God to consume thistles and thorns, that is, to consume and extinguish the wicked life of evil men so they do not abuse the patience of God any longer.[43]

Despite the prayers of the hermit order and the testimony of the preaching order, the Antichrist would conquer the church and turn it into an instrument of evil.[44] This dreadful situation would come to a conclusion, however, with the return of Christ. This event would issue in the third age—that of the Spirit—which would be characterized by spiritual rest and blessing. Joachim calculated that each age lasts forty-two generations of thirty years each, a fact that placed the onset of the third period in the year 1260.[45]

Joachim of Fiore died in 1202, and his prophetic ideas were taken over and modified by others. The two orders predicted by Joachim were identified as the Franciscan order—established by St. Francis in 1209—and the Dominican order—established by St. Dominic in 1216. Rather than seeing the age of the Spirit as a spiritual reality, some of Joachim's followers envisioned a new ideal church that was soon to come and displace the corrupt church currently in existence. One example of this was the Spiritual Franciscans. As the initiators of the age of the Spirit, these barefooted monks clashed with the corrupt institutional Catholic Church, rejecting the sacraments and priesthood and identifying the pope as the Antichrist. This "ideal" church challenged the prevailing amillennialism of the established church. Rejecting an allegorical interpretation of the book of Revelation and its events, it viewed this as an unfolding of history and the future. This understanding would continue for centuries to come and stand alongside the official amillennial perspective.

ESCHATOLOGICAL BELIEFS IN THE REFORMATION AND POST-REFORMATION

Despite their challenges to many of the doctrines of Roman Catholicism, the Protestant Reformers did not oppose the amillennial eschatology of the Catholic Church. Martin Luther did adapt the current view that the pope was the Antichrist. His modification of this idea consisted in his identification of the institution of the papacy—not just

43. Ibid., ff. 175v–176r, cited in McGinn, *Visions of the End*, 136–37.

44. Joachim's view later led to the identification of the Roman Catholic Church with the Antichrist. John Wycliffe, John Hus, and Martin Luther were just several who made this connection.

45. The figure forty-two generations was taken from Matthew 1:17: There were forty-two generations from Adam to Christ, so Joachim calculated that this would be true for the other two ages.

individual corrupt popes—with the Antichrist. This conviction led to his demand that the Roman Catholic Church had to be destroyed for the sake of the true church.

Like most amillennialists, Luther rejected the notion of a future golden age, specifically denouncing premillennialism.[46] But Luther did emphasize the church's hope of the second coming of Christ. At times, Luther even thought this would happen within his lifetime: "It is my firm belief that the angels are getting ready, putting on their armor and girding their swords about them, for the last day is already breaking, and the angels are preparing for the battle, when they will overthrow the Turks [Muslims] and hurl them, along with the pope, to the bottom of hell. The world will perish shortly."[47]

Like Luther, John Calvin was critical of the "chiliasts," the Anabaptist proponents of premillennialism, who believed that the second coming of Christ would result in the destruction of evil and the establishment of his millennial kingdom. Although most Anabaptists went quietly about their work of evangelism and discipleship, several radical incidents took place that saddled the Anabaptist movement with a reputation for violent millenarianism. First, Thomas Müntzer stirred up unrest in the Peasants' War in southern Germany in 1525. He linked his hope in a future golden age to a violent war that would usher in the millennium, but he and his followers were violently crushed through a military effort.[48] Second, Anabaptists in northwestern Germany engaged in the Münster Rebellion in 1534 and 1535. Forsaking the usual pacifism of Anabaptism, Jan Matthys and John of Leyden, the extremist leaders of the rebellion, stirred up apocalyptic expectations that the New Jerusalem would descend on Münster. Through fiery sermons and prophetic visions, the leaders of the rebellion encouraged their followers to take up arms and violently usher in the new world order. Münster was forcibly taken, John of Leyden publicly proclaimed himself to be the Messiah, and an Old Testament type of theocracy, complete with polygamy, was instituted in the conquered city. A joint Catholic-Protestant army was marshaled and crushed the rebellion. Although not at all typical of Anabaptism, the Münster Rebellion tarnished the movement's reputation and tainted premillennialism with an association with violence. As a result, Calvin and the other Reformers decried premillennial eschatology.

This antipremillennial sentiment continued for the most part during the post-Reformation period. Some theologians spoke out directly against the view. Quenstedt contrasted the eschatology of the Lutheran Church with premillennialism: "The second coming of Christ, the general resurrection, the final judgment, and the end of the world are immediately united, and one event follows the other without an interval of time. It is clear that before the completion of the judgment, no earthly kingdom and life abounding in all spiritual and bodily pleasures—as the chiliasts or millennarians dream—is to be expected."[49] Even the recognition of several strands of premillennialism—with

---

46. *Augsburg Confession*, 17, in Schaff, 3:18.

47. Martin Luther, *Conversations with Luther*, ed. and trans. Preserved Smith and H. P. Gallinger (Boston: Pilgrim, 1915), 250–51.

48. It is questionable to place Müntzer in our discussion of the Anabaptists. He was initially a Lutheran but disagreed

with Luther over the slow pace of the Reformation. He was not an Anabaptist either, and should probably be placed in a class by himself.

49. John Andrew Quenstedt, *Theologia Didactico-Polemica sive Systema Theologicum* (Leipzig, 1715), 4.649, in Schmid, 650. The text has been rendered clearer.

some types (referred to as crass chiliasm) better than others—did not give this eschatological view favor with most post-Reformers.[50] Specifically, the reliance of premillennialists upon Revelation 20:1–6 was not a convincing argument in its favor, as Hollaz underscored: "Because the Apocalypse is a prophetic book, full of very puzzling visions, as well as allegorical and quasi-enigmatic forms of speech, [it is] difficult to understand and therefore should be interpreted according to the analogy of the faith, based upon clear and perspicuous Scripture passages."[51] Apparently, the rest of Scripture—all of it outside of Revelation 20—did not affirm premillennial eschatology; thus, according to Hollaz, "the chiliasts cannot clearly show from the cited passage the solemn advent of Christ to establish a millennial kingdom."[52] Still, the churches that developed from the Reformation continued to affirm the great hope of his second coming, as expressed in the *Westminster Confession of Faith*: "As Christ would have us to be certainly persuaded that there shall be a day of judgment, both to deter all men from sin, and for the greater consolation of the godly in their adversity: so will he have that day unknown to men, that they may shake off all carnal security, and be always watchful, because they know not at what hour the Lord will come; and may be ever prepared to say, Come Lord Jesus, come quickly, Amen."[53]

A change in eschatological perspective was noted with the book *The Beloved City*,[54] by the post-Reformation theologian Johann Heinrich Alsted (1588–1638). Breaking with the rejection of chiliasm, Alsted defended premillennialism through a detailed interpretation of Revelation 20. He supported his belief in a future earthly kingdom by appealing to Old Testament passages (Isa. 2:1–4 and 34:1–17) that picture a future time of peace on earth following the wholesale destruction of the nations that are hostile to God. Alsted placed the fulfillment of these prophecies in the millennium. One of his contemporaries, Joseph Mede (1586–1638), popularized Alsted's premillennial view in the book *The Key of the Revelation*.[55] Mede divided Revelation into three periods, the last being a prophecy of the future of the church. This future included the destruction of the papacy (identified as the Antichrist) during the battle of Armageddon, the return of Christ, and the one-thousand-year millennium. In one sense, the works of Alsted and Mede directed Protestant eschatology back to the premillennial view of the early church.

ESCHATOLOGICAL BELIEFS IN THE MODERN PERIOD

This resurgence of premillennialism received strong support in the modern period. The destruction of the Catholic Church during the French Revolution contributed to this renewal in the nineteenth century. Furthermore, it was promoted by prophetic con-

50. John Gerhard, *Loci Theologici* (1621), 20.109, in Schmid, 650–51. Indeed, for Gerhard, the division of opinions among premillennialists was a strong argument against the position.

51. David Hollaz, *Examen Theologicum Acroamaticum* (1707), 1259, in Schmid, 653. The text has been rendered clearer.

52. Ibid.

53. *Westminster Confession of Faith*, 33.3, in Schaff, 3:671-72.

54. The Latin original, *Diatribe de Mille Annis Apocalypticis*, was published in 1627. William Burton translated the English edition, published in 1643.

55. The Latin original, *Clavis Apocalypticae*, was published in 1632. Richard More translated the English edition (London: Philemon Stephens), published in 1650.

ferences convened by premillennialists like Henry Drummond, who added new details to the premillennial scheme. For example, this age or "dispensation" would end with terrible and decisive judgment on the church as well as a return of the Jews to a restored homeland, followed by the return of Christ to institute the millennium kingdom. Premillennialism eventually spread to every Protestant denomination.

Despite this new show of support for premillennialism, amillennialism remained strong in the modern period. Charles Hodge and William G. T. Shedd, like others, defended amillennialism against premillennialism. Hodge summarized what he took to be the historic (amillennial) view of the church: "The common doctrine of the church ... is that the conversion of the world, the restoration of the Jews, and the destruction of Antichrist are to precede the second coming of Christ, which event will be accompanied by the general resurrection of the dead, the final judgment, the end of the world, and the consummation of the church."[56] Furthermore, he voiced objections to the premillennial position, charging it with being a Jewish doctrine, noting its inconsistencies with biblical teaching (specifically on the matters of the last judgment, the eternal state, the resurrection of believers, and the kingdom of God), and accusing it of disparaging the gospel.[57] To Hodge's objections, Shedd added the Apostles' Creed, which makes no mention of "a premillennial advent of Christ."[58] The main points of Hodge and Shedd against the premillennial viewpoint were typical of amillennial objections to it.

Beginning in the modern period, a third eschatological view arose and rivaled amillennialism and premillennialism for consideration. Daniel Whitby and Jonathan Edwards developed *postmillennialism*: Christ will return to judge the world after the millennium.[59] Actually, the seventeenth-century Puritans—for example, Thomas Brightman, John Cotton, and John Owen—had earlier embraced something similar to this position with their doctrine of the "latter-glory." At the end of history, the kingdom of God will come in power, people everywhere will convert to Christ, governments worldwide will support the church, and Christianity will be characterized by purity in faith and practice. After this period of prosperity, Christ will return. This hopeful view came to a crashing end in England with the turbulent political situation. But it found fertile ground in New England.

Whitby and Edwards developed this view further. Whitby stated that the gospel will be spread throughout the earth and the world will be saved. In conjunction with this, the Jews will be restored to the Holy Land, and a thousand-year golden age will be ushered in and bring universal peace and blessing; this will be followed by the second coming. Edwards supported a similar view: The Protestant Reformation had set in motion numerous elements that would ultimately lead to the demise of the papacy (identified as the Antichrist). This development, together with the spread of the gospel through

56. Charles Hodge, *Systematic Theology*, 3 vols. (1872–73; Peabody, Mass.: Hendrickson, 1999), 3:861.

57. Ibid., 3:862–66.

58. William G. T. Shedd, *Dogmatic Theology*, 7.2, in *Dogmatic Theology*, ed. Alan W. Gomes, 3rd ed. (Phillipsburg, N.J.: P & R, 2003), 863. A rejoinder to Shedd's objection is that the phrases of the Apostles' Creed that he believes preclude a pre-

millennial position do not actually address the chronological issue of *when* Christ will return and thus are patient of being accommodated within all three—amillennial, premillennial, and postmillennial—eschatological schemes.

59. *Post* is a prefix indicating "after." Thus, the *post*millennial position holds that Christ will return *after* the millennium.

the power of the Holy Spirit, would usher in the millennium; indeed, the outpouring of revival during the Great Awakening of the 1740s was a harbinger of the approaching millennium. During this golden age of unprecedented peace and prosperity, the gospel would convert the heathen throughout the world. At the end of this period—now characterized by sin and evil, due to the abuse of the millennial prosperity—Christ would return to judge the world then destroy it.

Postmillennialism was encouraged in America by the defeat of King George III and the British in the Revolutionary War. In the nineteenth century, it gained momentum from the Second Great Awakening—Charles Finney embraced this eschatological perspective—and it was fueled by the prosperity and expansionism during the presidency of Andrew Jackson. It also led to Christians championing numerous reform causes like the abolition of slavery, the prohibition of alcoholism through the temperance movement, and the suffrage movement to give women the right to vote.

A major theologian who defended postmillennialism was A. H. Strong. Key elements of his view included the preaching of the gospel in all the world, leading to the steady enlargement of the kingdom of God; the containment of evil; and the return of Christ after a final battle pitting evil against righteousness.[60] His interpretation of Revelation 20 provided the biblical basis for his postmillennialism:[61]

> We may best interpret Revelation 20:4–10 as teaching, in highly figurative language, not a preliminary resurrection of the body, in the case of departed saints, but a period in the later days of the church militant when, under special influence of the Holy Spirit, the spirit of the martyrs shall appear again, true religion is greatly quickened and revived, and the members of Christ's churches become so conscious of their strength in Christ that they shall, to an extent unknown before, triumph over the powers of evil both within and without [internal and external].... In short, we hold that Revelation 20:4–10 does not describe the events commonly called the second advent and resurrection, but rather describes great spiritual changes in the later history of the church, which are typical of, and preliminary to, the second advent and resurrection, and therefore, after the prophetic method, are foretold in language literally applicable only to those final events themselves.[62]

Despite proponents such as Strong, postmillennialism largely fell out of favor by the beginning of the twentieth century. The American Civil War, industrialization, urbanization, and the disillusionment due to the failures of social reform led to a strong sense of pessimism. The hopeful vision of postmillennialism gave way to a new version of premillennialism.[63]

Historic premillennialism as thus far presented was challenged by a new premillennial viewpoint in the nineteenth century, resulting in a division among premillennialists.

---

60. A. H. Strong, *Systematic Theology*, 3 vols. (Philadelphia: Judson, 1912), 3:1008–9.

61. Ibid., 3:1011–12.

62. Ibid., 3:1013.

63. Stanley N. Gundry, "Hermeneutics or Zeitgeist as the Determining Factor in the History of Eschatologies?" *JETS* 20, no. 1 (March 1977): 47–48.

John Nelson Darby and the Plymouth Brethren were the originators of *dispensational premillennialism*. A key distinguishing element in this was its insistence that the church has not replaced Israel as the people of God; rather, the two are distinct groups, each with its own history, destiny, and hope. Another essential belief was that the church would be caught up with Christ—an event called the "rapture" of the church—and removed to heaven immediately before the period of seven years of the great tribulation.[64] Indeed, Darby cleanly separated the church—which was not present in the Old Testament, came into existence at Pentecost, would experience the rapture, and was promised heavenly blessings—from the remnant of Jewish saints—which was prophesied in the Old Testament, would go through the great tribulation, would be present at Christ's return, and was promised earthly blessings in the Promised Land. According to Darby, "two great subjects present themselves to us in Scripture: the church, that sovereign grace that gives us a place along with Christ himself in glory and blessing; and God's government of the world, of which Israel forms the center and the immediate sphere."[65]

This complete separation between the Jewish people and the church had great ramifications for Darby in terms of the proper hope of both groups. The church's hope is for the rapture: "The thing it has to expect for itself is not—though sure of that also—Christ's appearing, but her being taken up where he is [1 Thess. 4:16–17]. We go to meet Christ in the air. Nothing clearer, then, than that we are to go up to meet him, and not await his coming to earth."[66] Darby was emphatic on two points concerning the rapture. First, "as to the time of this rapture, no one, of course, knows it."[67] Second, the rapture will occur before the time of the great tribulation. Citing Revelation 3:10 and 12:10–12, Darby explained that they "show our exemption from the tribulation predicted, a position in which the world will find itself, and in a special manner the Jewish people restored to their land."[68] Clearly, this distinction between the Jewish remnant and the church dictated a complete separation between the two at the end of history. Accordingly, the church will be raptured so as to receive its heavenly blessings, and the Jewish remnant will experience the period of the tribulation, giving way to its earthly blessings.[69]

Dwight L. Moody and most other evangelists in Moody's mold supported premillennialism and even added strong dispensational elements to it. Its worldview stood in stark contrast to the hopeful vision of postmillennialism, which it was replacing: The world is not getting better, but worse, and its end is fast approaching. As Moody urged: "I look on this world as a wrecked vessel. God has given me a life-boat, and said to me, 'Moody, save all you can.' God will come in judgment and burn up this world, but the children of God don't belong to this world; they are in it but not of it, like a ship in the water. This world

---

64. Attempts have been made to trace the origin of the pretribulational rapture to the prophecies of Margaret Mac-Donald. Dave MacPherson, in particular, has insisted on this idea. Dave MacPherson, *The Unbelievable Pre-Trib Origin* (Kansas City, Mo.: Heart of America Bible Society, 1973); idem, *The Rapture Plot* (Simpsonville, S.C.: Millennium III, 1994). Rebuttals of this idea include F. F. Bruce, "Review of *The Unbelievable Pre-Trib Origin*," *Evangelical Quarterly* 47

(January–March 1975): 58.

65. J. N. Darby, "The Rapture of the Saints," in *The Collected Writings of J. N. Darby*, ed. William Kelly, 34 vols. (repr., Sunbury, Pa.: Believers Bookshelf, 1972), 11:125.

66. Ibid., 11:153–54.

67. Ibid., 11:155.

68. Ibid., 11:162.

69. Ibid., 11:163–64.

is getting darker, and its ruin is coming nearer and nearer. If you have any friends of this wreck unsaved, you had better lose no time in getting them off."[70] Through his participation in the Niagara Bible conferences, Moody encouraged the spread of premillennialism. As these conferences ended in 1900, they gave way to the Sea Cliff Bible conferences and their explicitly pretribulational premillennialism.

William Blackstone's *Jesus Is Coming* thoroughly supported the dispensational premillennial position over against postmillennialism.[71] Like Darby and Moody, he argued for the rapture of the church before the seven-year period of tribulation that was to precede immediately the return of Christ. He made a distinction between rapture and revelation: "*Rapture* means to be caught up, or away. *Revelation* means appearing or shining forth or manifestation (Rom. 8:19). The rapture occurs when the church is caught up to meet Christ in the air (1 Thess. 4:14, 17), before the tribulation; and the revelation occurs when Christ comes, with his saints, to end the tribulation, by the execution of righteous judgment upon the earth (2 Thess. 1:7-10; Jude 14). At the rapture, Christ comes into the air for his saints. At the revelation, he comes to the earth with them (1 Thess. 3:13; Zech. 14:5)."[72]

A further distinction concerned the timing of the two events: "The rapture may occur any moment. The revelation can not occur until Antichrist be revealed.... The revelation ushers in the day, the Day of the Lord."[73] Clearly, this pretribulational rapture of the church meant that "the church is to escape the Tribulation, which precedes the Revelation (Matt. 24:29–30)."[74] Further support for Blackstone's position was Christ's promise in Revelation 3:10: "A special hour, or time, of temptation — i.e., trial — is here mentioned, which shall come upon all the world.... Jesus promises to keep the church from, or (*ek*) out of, this tribulation, or hour of temptation, that is, the watchful and prayerful believers will escape it (Luke 21:36). Now, as it covers the whole earth, there is no way of escape from it except to be taken out of the world, and this is accomplished by the rapture."[75] Moreover, Blackstone listed numerous "signs of the times" — the prevalence of travel and knowledge, perilous times, spiritualism, apostasy, worldwide evangelism, and the accumulation of wealth — that indicated that the second coming of Christ (including the rapture) was about to take place.[76] He enthusiastically focused on one last sign — the restoration of Israel to Palestine — the fulfillment of which he saw in "Zionism, the present movement of the Jews to return to the land of their fathers."[77] Because this event was so crucial to the end-times drama, Blackstone petitioned the United States government on several occasions to exercise leadership in establishing a Palestinian homeland for the Jews. In his thinking, not until this development was in place could the Jewish nation be restored, Jesus Christ return, and the millennium start.

Finally, as a contributor to the burgeoning dispensational theology movement, Blackstone divided history into seven periods or dispensations:

---

70. D. L. Moody, *New Sermons* (St. Louis: N. D. Thompson, 1877), 535, cited in Gundry, "Hermeneutics or Zeitgeist...?" 52.

71. William E. Blackstone, *Jesus Is Coming*, 3rd rev. ed. (Chicago, New York, Toronto: Revell, and Los Angeles: The Bible House, 1908), 41–66.

72. Ibid., 75–78.
73. Ibid., 76–78.
74. Ibid., 79.
75. Ibid., 79–80.
76. Ibid., 228–36.
77. Ibid., 236.

- Eden, the age of *innocence* (the time in the garden prior to the fall)
- Antediluvian, the age of *freedom* (from expulsion from the garden until the flood of Noah)
- Postdiluvian, the age of *government* (from the flood until the destruction of Sodom and Gomorrah)
- Patriarchal, the *pilgrim* age (the people of God in Egypt until the Exodus)
- Mosaic, the *Israeliteish* age (the nation until the ascension of Christ)
- Christian, the age of *mystery* (the church age until the rapture, tribulation, the second coming, and the judgment of the nations)
- Millennium, the age of *manifestation* (the millennium kingdom until the release of Satan and the great white throne judgment).[78]

According to Blackstone, after this seven-aged history would come the new heavens and new earth.[79] His dispensational chart was typical of end-times schemes developed by subsequent dispensationalists.

C. I. Scofield was a contemporary of Blackstone and furthered the popularity of dispensationalism through his *Rightly Dividing the Word of Truth* (1885) and especially *The Scofield Reference Bible* (1909; rev. ed. 1917). Millions of people were taught to read the King James Version of the Bible with a dispensational mind-set, thus anchoring that type of interpretation and eschatological perspective among American evangelicals.[80] Like Blackstone, Scofield divided world history into seven dispensations:

- *Innocence* (from the creation of Adam [Gen 2:7] to the expulsion from Eden)
- *Conscience* (from Eden to the flood)
- *Human authority over the earth* (from the flood to Abraham)
- *Promise* (from the promises to Abraham to the judgment of bondage in Egypt)
- *Law* (from the wilderness of Sinai and the covenant of law to the coming of Christ)
- *Pure grace* (from the sacrificial death of Christ to the descent of the Lord from heaven; then follows a brief period called "the great tribulation"; after this comes the personal return of the Lord)
- *The personal reign of Christ* (the millennium, including the battle against the Lord and his saints, the "great white throne" judgment, and the new heaven and new earth).[81]

---

78. Ibid., 222–23. In this list, "age" replaces Blackstone's "aion."

79. Ibid., 223.

80. James Barr commented that the *Scofield Reference Bible* was "perhaps the most important single document in all fundamentalist literature." James Barr, *Fundamentalism* (Philadelphia: Westminster, 1977), 45. J. Barton Payne said, "Of greater influence than any other single factor was the *Scofield Reference Bible* (improved edition, 1917), which inculcated the eschatology of dispensationalism, even while making its primary contribution as a popular defense of evangelicalism, when all else seemed to be falling before the flood of twentieth-century modernism." J. Barton Payne, *The Imminent Appearing of Christ* (Grand Rapids: Eerdmans, 1962), 35.

81. C. I. Scofield, *Rightly Dividing the Word of Truth, Being Ten Outline Studies of the More Important Divisions of Scripture* (Chicago: Bible Institute, 1885), 18–23.

Scofield's dispensational eschatology became commonplace among evangelicals.

Pretribulationism and its emphasis on the rapture of the church was further developed and defended as an essential element in dispensational premillennialism. Lewis Sperry Chafer contributed much to this development with his theology of the great tribulation. For Chafer the issue was "a disagreement that obtains between premillenarians of equal sincerity over whether the church will enter or pass through the great tribulation.... It is contended in this [pretribulational] work that the church never enters or passes through the tribulation and for certain reasons."[82] One reason was the parenthetical nature of the church: it is strictly a phenomenon that began at Pentecost and that will end before the consummation of the times of the Gentiles. Thus, the church will not go through the tribulation: "Those who would thrust the church into the last 7 years of Gentile times are guilty of introducing an element into that period that has no place in that period since it is not to be on earth during the eventful years which that period consummates."[83] Another of Chafer's reasons had to do with the purpose of the tribulation, which he considered to "be for the final judgments of God upon a God- and Christ-rejecting world."[84] Such divine judgment is out of keeping with the nature of the church, which is the recipient of "the measureless grace of God in Christ"[85] and not designed for condemnation. The most important scriptural support for this reason is Revelation 3:10, according to Chafer: "The church is promised complete exemption from this hour of trial [the great tribulation].... Besides, we should note that the promise is not merely to be kept from the trial, but from the hour of trial, i.e., it holds out exemption from the period of trial, not only from the trial during that period.... We conclude, therefore, that ... the whole church will be taken away before the hour of temptation begins, and not merely an assurance of protection in it."[86] In summary, then, "the church will not, because she could not, either enter or pass through the great tribulation."[87]

Through the influence of Darby, Blackstone, Moody, Chafer, and many other proponents of dispensationalism, dispensational (or pretribulational) premillennialism became widely embraced by evangelicals. This position was further enhanced by several bestselling popular books, such as Hal Lindsey's *The Late Great Planet Earth*. Through this book, the notion of the pretribulational rapture of the church became widely known even among the secular public in the United States.[88] This pretribulational-rapture, pre-millennial-return-of-Christ schema continued with the hugely successful Left Behind series, consisting of sixteen volumes, by Tim LaHaye and Jerry Jenkins.[89]

Despite the popularity of dispensational premillennialism, historic premillennialism continued to be championed by many. Even though many of those who contributed to the writing of it were dispensationalists, *The Fundamentals* included an article entitled "The Coming of Christ," written by a posttribulational premillennialist. In his discus-

---

82. Lewis Sperry Chafer, *Systematic Theology*, 4 vols. (Dallas: Dallas Seminary Press, 1948), vol. 4: *Ecclesiology–Eschatology*, 364.

83. Ibid.

84. Ibid., 4:365.

85. Ibid., 4:365–66.

86. Ibid., 4:369–70. Chafer relied upon an important article by Henry C. Thiessen in *BSac* 92 (1935): 201–3.

87. Chafer, *Systematic Theology*, 4:373.

88. Hal Lindsey, with C. C. Carlson, *The Late Great Planet Earth* (Grand Rapids: Zondervan, 1970).

89. Tim LaHaye and Jerry B. Jenkins, Left Behind series (Wheaton: Tyndale, 1995–2007).

sion of Christ's return, Charles Erdman stated: "The Bible further describes the coming of Christ as *imminent*. It is an event that may occur in any lifetime. Whatever difficulties the fact involves, there is no doubt that all the biblical writers and their fellow Christians believed that Christ might return in their generation.... However, 'imminent' does *not* mean '*immediate*'.... 'Imminence' as related to our Lord's return indicates *uncertainty* as to time, but *possibility* of nearness."[90] Although he did not marshal support for the church going through the tribulation, Erdman's definition of imminency as "occurring in any lifetime" rather than as "immediate" or at any time placed him unmistakably in the post-tribulational camp. At the same time, he was firmly committed to premillennialism. Thus, historic premillennialism, with its conviction of the posttribulational return of Christ, continued as a viable eschatological position.

Due to increasing scholarly interest in eschatology, several leading evangelicals contributed to a book setting forth three views on the rapture entitled *The Rapture: Pre-, Mid-, or Post-Tribulational?* Paul Feinberg, defending the pretribulational rapture position, concluded:

> The church will not go through the Tribulation because of the character of that entire period as a time of the outpouring of penal, retributive, divine wrath, as well as the promises of God to the church that exempt it from both the time and the experience of wrath. Further, it is necessary to separate the Rapture of the church from the Second Advent of Christ because of the need for an interval for people to be saved, so that they can enter into the kingdom age in natural, nonglorified bodies. Finally, the differences between Rapture passages and Second Coming passages lead me to believe that there are two separate events referred to in the passages.[91]

Gleason Archer described the midtribulation view, or "the mid-seventieth-week theory of the rapture":

> If the Great Tribulation is to be identified with the second half of the final seven years prior to Armageddon, during which the bowls of divine wrath will be poured out upon the earth, then the view we are about to advocate is really a form of pretribulation Rapture. It simply regards the first three and a half years, during which the Antichrist will increase his power and mount his persecution against the church, as a lesser tribulation, not nearly as terrifying or destructive of life as those fearsome plagues that will dominate the last three and a half years. In other words, this interpretation makes a clear division between the first half as the period of the wrath of man, and the second half as the period of the wrath of God.... The final generation of the pre-Rapture church will be subjected to the wrath of man, but spared from the wrath of God.[92]

---

90. Charles R. Erdman, "The Coming of Christ," in *The Fundamentals*, ed. R. A. Torrey, 14 vols. (Los Angeles: The Bible Institute of Los Angeles, 1917), 4:309–10.

91. Gleason Archer Jr. et al., *Three Views on the Rapture: Pre-, Mid-, or Post-Tribulational?* (Grand Rapids: Zondervan,

1984), 86. For a more recent version of the debate, see Craig Blaising et al., *Three Views on the Rapture: Pre-Tribulation, Pre-Wrath, or Post-Tribulation* (Grand Rapids: Zondervan, 2010).

92. Archer, *Three Views on the Rapture*, 139.

Working with key texts (John 14:1–4; 1 Cor. 15:51–52; 1 Thess. 4:13–18), Douglas Moo dismissed the pretribulational rapture position and defended the posttribulational view:

> We have discovered that the terms used to describe the Second Advent are all applied to a posttribulational coming and that believers are exhorted to look forward to that coming. Any indication that this coming is to be a two-stage event, in which the rapture is separated from the final manifestation, would have to come from passages describing that event. We can now conclude that no evidence for such a separation is found in any of the three principal texts on the rapture. On the contrary, such evidence as exists is in favor of locating the rapture *after* the tribulation, at the same time as the final Parousia [the return of Christ].[93]

While dispensational, or pretribulational, premillennialism was gaining a wider audience, many evangelicals continued to embrace amillennialism and historic premillennialism, with a few committed to postmillennialism. Many churches and denominations did not specify a specific millenarian viewpoint in their statements of faith. For example, the *Baptist Faith and Message* of the Southern Baptist Convention stated simply: "God, in His own time and in His own way, will bring the world to its appropriate end. According to His promise, Jesus Christ will return personally and visibly in glory to the earth."[94] The National Association of Evangelicals offered only the briefest of affirmations of eschatological belief, incorporated into its statement about Jesus Christ: "We believe … in his personal return in power and glory."[95]

Still, evangelicals continued to embrace the church's historic position that Jesus Christ will one day return personally and gloriously. This affirmation had important implications for the church's mission in the present time, as the Lausanne Committee for World Evangelization made specific in its 1974 *Lausanne Covenant*:

> We believe that Jesus Christ will return personally and visibly, in power and glory, to consummate his salvation and his judgment. This promise of his coming is a further spur to our evangelism, for we remember his words that the gospel must first be preached to all nations. We believe that the interim period between Christ's ascension and return is to be filled with the mission of the people of God, who have no liberty to stop before the end. We also remember his warning that false Christs and false prophets will arise as precursors of the final Antichrist. We therefore reject as a proud, self-confident dream the notion that people can ever build a utopia on earth. Our Christian confidence is that God will perfect his kingdom, and we look forward with eager anticipation to that day, and to the new heaven and earth in which righteousness will dwell and God will reign forever. Meanwhile, we rededicate ourselves to the service

---

93. Ibid., 182.

94. *Baptist Faith and Message*, 10. This statement is identical in all three versions of the *Baptist Faith and Message*: 1925,

1963, and 2000. In Lumpkin, 397.

95. National Association of Evangelicals, *Statement of Faith*, 3.

of Christ and of people in joyful submission to his authority over the whole of our lives.[96]

Accordingly, evangelicals are united in their hope of the second coming of Jesus Christ but divided over that event's relationship to the tribulation and (for some) the millennial reign of Christ on earth.

96. Lausanne Committee for World Evangelization, *Lausanne Covenant* (1974), 15.

Chapter *32*

THE FINAL JUDGMENT AND ETERNAL PUNISHMENT

How has the church come to view the judgment of all people and the eternal punishment of unbelievers?

STATEMENT OF BELIEF

From its inception, the church has believed that there will be a final judgment of both believers and unbelievers. This evaluation will take place before the judgment seat of Christ, and both groups will hear his proclamation of their eternal destiny. On the one hand, this judgment will usher believers into the presence of Christ and the blessedness of heavenly reward forever. On the other hand, following their judgment of condemnation, unbelievers will experience eternal conscious punishment in hell. Only a few Christians deviated from this understanding of the last judgment and eternal punishment.

This consensus began to unravel in the modern period, which witnessed attacks against most classical beliefs of the church. The attacks against these two doctrines were particularly strong and took three primary forms: *Universalism* maintained that all people will eventually be saved by the love of God in Jesus Christ. *Conditional immortality* claims that, whereas Christians receive the gift of immortality from God (who alone possesses it), non-Christians do not; thus, their existence ends at death. *Annihilationism*, overlapping significantly with conditional immortality, held that non-Christians will experience conscious punishment for a time after they die but eventually will be annihilated. Most evangelicals continue to embrace the historical position of the church. Only a few hold to the possibility of universal salvation, but some follow conditional immortality and annihilationism, denying that the conscious punishment of unbelievers will be eternal.[1]

---

1. My thanks to Bradley Cochran for his help on this chapter.

JUDGMENT AND PUNISHMENT
IN THE EARLY CHURCH

Jesus and the apostles taught the reality of a final judgment and eternal punishment, continuing a long line of similar belief found in Judaism. Following Old Testament affirmations (e.g., Dan. 12:1–2), Jesus described a future division of the righteous and unrighteous (John 5:28–29), identifying himself as the Judge who will separate and judge the two groups (Matt. 25:31–46). The apostle John pictured this "great white throne" judgment with vivid detail (Rev. 20:11–15). Similar graphic portraits were painted—"their worm does not die and the fire is not quenched" (Mark 9:48), "weeping and gnashing of teeth" (Matt. 8:12), "the fire of hell" (Matt. 18:9)—by other New Testament writers concerning the dreadful fate of the wicked. The apostle Paul spoke of "the day of God's wrath" (Rom. 2:5) and "everlasting destruction" (2 Thess. 1:9) in warning of the destiny of unbelievers. Jesus and the apostles had quite a bit to say about the judgment and final punishment; indeed, this was part of the "elementary teachings" of the faith (Heb. 6:1).

The early church repeated these teachings. Polycarp applied Paul's affirmation about the judgment seat of Christ (Rom. 14:10–12; 2 Cor. 5:10), urging, "Let us serve him [Christ] with fear and all reverence…. Let us be eager with regard to what is good."[2] Irenaeus expressed the reason for this judgment: "The advent of the Son comes indeed alike to all, but is for the purpose of judging, and separating the believing from the unbelieving."[3] The distinction between these two groups is not evident during their earthly existence, as Hermas noted: "Neither the righteous nor sinners are distinguishable in this world, but they are alike. For this life is winter to the righteous, and they cannot be distinguished, because they live with the sinners. For just as in winter the trees, having shed their leaves, are all alike, and it is not apparent which are withered and which are living, so also in this world neither the righteous nor the sinners can be distinguished, but all are alike."[4] By contrast, the world to come will be quite different:

> The age to come is summer to the righteous, but winter to the sinners. So when the mercy of the Lord shines forth, then those who serve God will be revealed; indeed, all people will be revealed. For just as in summer the fruit of each one of the trees appears, and so it is known what kind they are, so also the fruit of the righteous will be revealed, and all will be known because they are flourishing in that world. But the heathen and the sinners, the withered trees that you saw, such people will be found to be withered and fruitless in that world, and will be burned as firewood, and will be obvious because their conduct in their life was evil.[5]

This idea that the coming judgment will be based on deeds done in this life was widespread.[6] Indeed, the Athanasian Creed summarized the belief of the church that Christ

---

2. Polycarp, *Letter to the Philippians*, 6, in Holmes, 213; *ANF*, 1:34.

3. Irenaeus, *Against Heresies*, 5.27.1, in *ANF*, 1:556.

4. *Shepherd of Hermas*, parable 3, in Holmes, 425; *ANF*,

2:32.

5. Ibid., parable 4, in Holmes, 425, 427; *ANF*, 2:32–33.

6. One example is Tertullian. Tertullian, *Apology*, 48, in *ANF*, 3:54.

"will come to judge the living and the dead. At his coming all people will rise again with their bodies and will give account for their own works. Those who have done good will go into eternal life, and those who have done evil will go into eternal fire."[7] This distinction between the rewards for the righteous and the unrighteous was also underscored: "The Lord will judge the world without partiality. Each person will receive according to what he has done: if he is good, his righteousness will precede him; if he is evil, the wages of doing evil will go before him."[8] Ignatius assured the righteous that the "prize set before you is incorruptibility and eternal life."[9] But Justin Martyr emphasized the dreadful plight of the wicked: they go "to the everlasting punishment of fire."[10] Similarly, Barnabas noted, "The way of the black one is crooked and completely cursed. For it is a way of eternal death and punishment."[11] Cyprian vividly described the misery awaiting the wicked: "The damned will burn forever in hell. Devouring flames will be their eternal portion [reward]. Their torments will never decrease or end. Their lamentations will be vain and entreaties ineffective. Their repentance comes too late. They will have to believe in an eternal punishment, as they refused to believe in the eternal life."[12] Athenagoras specifically denied the idea of annihilationism — that after death people cease to exist — explaining that "God has not made us as sheep or beasts of burden, a mere by-product, and that we should perish and be annihilated."[13] In summary, Hippolytus set forth the belief of the early church:

> For all, the righteous and the unrighteous, shall be brought before God the Word. For the Father has committed all judgment to him; and in fulfillment of the Father's counsel, he comes as Judge whom we call Christ…. He, in administering the righteous judgment of the Father to all, assigns to each person what is righteous according to his works. And being present at his judicial decision, all, both men and angels and demons, shall utter one voice, saying, "Righteous is your judgment." The justification of this voice will be seen in the awarding to each person that which is just. To those who have done good will be justly assigned eternal blessing and to the lovers of wickedness shall be given eternal punishment. And the fire which is unquenchable and without end awaits these latter.[14]

This issue of the continuation of punishment for the wicked became a point of debate with the theology of Origen. We have already seen his view on the preexistence of souls: Before the creation of this present world, there existed a spiritual world populated by

---

7. Athanasian Creed, 40–43, in Schaff, 2:69–70.

8. *Letter of Barnabas*, 4, in Holmes, 284; *ANF*, 1:139.

9. Ignatius, *Letter to Polycarp*, 2, in Holmes, 197; *ANF*, 1:94.

10. Justin Martyr, *First Apology*, 12, in *ANF*, 1:166. This seems to be a favorite theme of his writings. In *First Apology*, 16, Justin quoted Jesus' words from Matt. 7:15–16, 19, 21; 13:42; Luke 13:26. He spoke of eternal punishment in chapters 18, 19, and 28 of his *First Apology*; he opened with the idea in the first chapter of his *Second Apology*; and he repeated it

several times in his *Dialogue with Trypho, a Jew*.

11. *Letter of Barnabas*, 20, in Holmes, 323; *ANF*, 1:149.

12. Cyprian, *To Demetrius*, c. 24f., cited in Josef Staudinger, *Life Hereafter*, trans. John J. Coyne (Dublin: Clonmore & Reynolds; London: Burns & Oates, 1964), 211.

13. Athenagoras, *A Plea for the Christians*, 31, in *ANF*, 2:146.

14. Hippolytus, *Against Plato, On the Cause of the Universe*, 3, in *ANF*, 5:222. The text has been rendered clearer.

spirit beings, all of whom possessed free will that they abused so as to fall into sin.[15] Divine punishment—figuratively presented in Scripture as "fire"—serves to rehabilitate these fallen beings.[16] From this, Origen concluded that the action of God is designed to "thoroughly cleanse away the evil that is intermingled throughout the whole soul" and thus purify these sinful beings.[17] Given this transformative nature of divine punishment, Origen held out hope that God's action would eventually restore all fallen beings—angels, humans, perhaps even Satan and the demons—to their original state of communion with him, that "God may be all in all" (1 Cor. 15:28).[18]

Given this view of the restoration of all things, Origen appeared to embrace universal salvation[19] and was charged with denying the church's belief in the eternal punishment of the wicked.[20] Ultimately, a church council held in Alexandria, Egypt, in 400 condemned Origen's doctrine of universal salvation.[21] The pronouncement of condemnation of his view by the synod of Constantinople in 543 was very clear: "If anyone says or thinks that the punishment of demons and of wicked people is only temporary, and will one day have an end, and that a restoration will take place of demons and of wicked people, let him be anathema [cursed]."[22] The church would not tolerate any view denying the reality of a future eternal punishment for the wicked.

---

15. See the discussion in chap. 15.

16. Origen cited Deut. 4:24; 9:3; Dan. 7:10; Mal. 3:2; and 1 Cor. 3:13–15 in support. Origen, *Against Celsus*, 4.13, in *ANF*, 4:502.

17. Ibid.

18. Of course, the question is whether Origen envisioned Satan among the "enemies" of the Son of God. Origen, *First Principles*, 3.5.7, in *ANF*, 4:343–44. Origen hoped that all things, "after their apprehension and punishment for the offenses which they have undergone by way of purgation, may, after having fulfilled and discharged every obligation, deserve a habitation in heaven." Ibid., 2.3.7, in *ANF*, 4:275. This would mean that the end of the creation reflects its beginning: "For the end is always like the beginning; therefore, as there is one end to all things, so should we understand that there was one beginning. And as there is one end to many things, so there spring from one beginning many differences and varieties that again, through the goodness of God, and by subjection to Christ, and through the unity of the Holy Spirit, are recalled to one end, which is like the beginning: all those, that is, who, bending the knee at the name of Jesus, make known by so doing their subjection to him." Ibid., 1.6.2, in *ANF*, 4:260.

19. I have presented here the "received" viewpoint on Origen. Recent studies, however, call for a careful reconsideration of his position. For example, there is a letter from Origen to his friends in Alexandria in which he denies the ultimate restoration of Satan. This is the position of which his enemies accuse him, but he rejects the idea: "Some of those who take pleasure in finding [occasions for] disputes ascribe to us and to our doctrine a blasphemy. On that matter let them consider the way in which they pay attention [to the Scripture] 'Nei-

ther drunkards nor slanderers [or blasphemers] will possess the kingdom of God,' even though they say that the father of malice and perdition, who will be excluded from the kingdom of God, is able to be saved. Even one who has lost his mind cannot say this." Jerome, *Apology against the Book of Rufinus*, 2.18, cited in Frederick W. Norris, "Universal Salvation in Origen and Maximus," in *Universalism and the Doctrine of Hell*, ed. Nigel M. de S. Cameron (Grand Rapids: Baker, 1992), 47.

20. On the one hand, this accusation was not completely true. Origen did not entirely do away with this belief, because it served a useful purpose—to keep very evil people in this world in line. Origen, *Against Celsus*, 6.26, in *ANF*, 4:585. On the other hand, Origen did indeed speculate about the restoration of all things and offered it to the church for consideration. Origen, *First Principles*, 1.6, in *ANF*, 4:260–62.

21. This condemnation can be traced through the letters of Theophilus, bishop of Alexandria, as translated by Jerome. See Jerome's *Letters* 92, 93, 96, 98, and 100, in *NPNF²*, 6:185, 186, 188, 189 (only the first two letters in this list are translated).

22. Synod of Constantinople, 9th anathema, cited in Daniel Pickering Walker, *The Decline of Hell: Seventeenth Century Discussions of Eternal Torment* (Chicago: Univ. of Chicago Press, 1964), 21. The text has been rendered clearer. Many of the anathemas from this council were included in the anathemas of the Second Council of Constantinople in 553: "If anyone says or thinks that the punishment of demons and of wicked men is only temporary and will one day have an end ... let him be anathema [cursed].... If anyone teaches the mythical doctrine of the pre-existence of the soul and the restoration that follows from it, let him be anathema [cursed]." Second Council of Constantinople, canon 1, in *NPNF²*, 14:320.

Affirming the traditional view of the church, Augustine described the first death—physical death—as consisting of the separation of body and soul, and the second death—eternal death—as consisting of the uniting of those two elements in eternal death. Regarding this latter, hellish nightmare that awaits all those who refuse to embrace Christ in this lifetime, he offered: "There, in striking contrast to our present conditions, people will not exist *before* or *after* death, but always *in* death—never living, never dead, but eternally dying. And never can a person be more disastrously in death than when death itself will be deathless."[23] Accordingly, he spoke of two distinct groups—"one Christ's, the other the devil's ... one consisting of the good, the other of the bad"—following the final judgment:

> The former shall have no will, the latter no power, to sin, and neither shall have any power to choose death. But the former shall live truly and happily in eternal life, the latter shall drag a miserable existence in eternal death without the power of dying; for both shall be without end. But among the former there shall be degrees of happiness, one being more preeminently happy than another; and among the latter there shall be degrees of misery, one being more endurably miserable than another.[24]

In his *City of God*, Augustine dealt with the doctrine of eternal punishment in great detail, attempting to counter various opponents' attacks against it. One such objection claimed that, because physical torment eventually destroys embodied human beings, endless physical torment is impossible. Augustine responded by proposing a substantive difference between the current physical body and the future physical body,[25] a change brought about by a divine miracle:[26] "So in the resurrection of the dead shall it [the body] be constituted differently from its present well-known condition."[27] This paves the way for embodied wicked people to experience endless punishment in hell.[28]

But Augustine had to confront another attack. In this case, opponents objected that it is "unjust that any man be doomed to an eternal punishment for sins which, no matter how great they were, were perpetrated in a brief span of time."[29] He responded with amazement: "As if any law ever regulated the duration of the punishment by the duration of the offense punished!"[30] For Augustine, the only way to appreciate the punishment of eternal duration is to grasp the enormity of the crime committed by Adam: "The more enjoyment man found in God, the greater was his wickedness in abandoning him; and he who destroyed in himself a good that might have been eternal, became worthy of eternal evil. Hence the whole mass of the human race is condemned."[31]

---

23. Augustine, *The City of God*, 13.12, 11, in *NPNF*[1], 2:251. The text has been rendered clearer.

24. Augustine envisioned these two groups to consist of both human beings and angels. Augustine, *The Enchiridion on Faith, Hope, and Love*, 111, in *NPNF*[1], 3:273.

25. Augustine, *City of God*, 21.3, in *NPNF*[1], 2:453–54.

26. Ibid., 21.7, in *NPNF*[1], 2:457–59.

27. Ibid., 21.8, in *NPNF*[1], 2:459.

28. Ibid., 21.9, in *NPNF*[1], 2:460–61.

29. Ibid., 21.11, in *NPNF*[1], 2:462.

30. Ibid. He provided some examples: "[No one] would suppose that the pains of punishment should occupy as short a time as the offense; or that murder, adultery, sacrilege, or any other crime should be measured, not by the enormity of the injury or wickedness, but by the length of time spent in its perpetration." Ibid.

31. Ibid., 21.12, in *NPNF*[1], 2:463.

The next two objections addressed by Augustine were similar in that they both imagined an end to the punishment of the wicked; that is, both views allowed for divine punishment of the wicked but denied that such punishment is eternal. The first of these objections was the view that the divine punishments are therapeutic and restorative rather than punitive.[32] Augustine dissented, asserting instead that all punishments come as "just retribution" for sins.[33] The second objection was the view that after a time, God will cease to punish the wicked. Augustine responded with some sympathy because of the compassion at the heart of the objection.[34] He nonetheless criticized it by following the argument to its (il)logical conclusion: "Let, then, this fountain of mercy be extended and flow forth even to the lost angels, and let them also be set free, at least after as many long ages as seem fit!... And yet they dare not extend their pity further and propose the deliverance of the devil himself."[35] In this way, Augustine exposed the error of this position by making it similar to the view of Origen—a view that was condemned by the church as heresy. He further rejoined that the view would extend the divine mercy beyond where God extends it.

In the midst of offering counterarguments against opponents of the doctrine, Augustine made frequent appeals to Scripture in support of eternal conscious punishment in hell. Specifically, he called attention to the biblical phrases "eternal fire" and "torment that lasts forever" (Matt. 25:41; Rev. 20:10—NIV: "tormented day and night for ever and ever"): "In the former, 'eternal' is used; in the latter, 'forever.' By these words Scripture commonly means nothing other than endless duration. Therefore ... the devil and his angels will never return to the justice and life of the saints ... being reserved for the judgment of the last day, when eternal fire will receive them, in which they will be tormented, world without end."[36] Immediately, Augustine linked the future punishment of wicked human beings with that of the devil and his angels, as Jesus had done (Matt. 25:41). He reasoned that if the punishment of the latter is eternal, then the punishment of the former is eternal as well.[37] But Augustine's strongest argument was still to come, as he called attention to the parallel expressions "eternal life" and "eternal punishment" in the same sentence (Matt. 25:46):

> If both destinies are "eternal," then we must either understand both as long-continued but at last terminating, or both as endless. For they are correlated: On the one hand, punishment eternal; on the other hand, life eternal. And to say in one and the same sense "life eternal will be endless, punishment eternal will come to an end," is the height of absurdity. Therefore, as the eternal life of the saints will be endless, so too the eternal punishment of those who are doomed to it will have no end.[38]

32. Ibid., 21.13, in *NPNF*[1], 2:463–64.

33. Ibid., 21.17, in *NPNF*[1], 2:466.

34. "I must now ... enter the lists [arena] of amicable controversy with those tender-hearted Christians who decline to believe that any, or that all, of those whom the infallibly just Judge may pronounce worthy of the punishment of hell, shall suffer eternally, and who suppose that they shall be delivered after a fixed term of punishment, longer or shorter according to the amount of each man's sin.... The error we speak of ...

is dictated by the tenderness of these Christians who suppose that the sufferings of those who are condemned in the judgment will be temporary, while the blessedness of all who are sooner or later set free will be eternal." Ibid.

35. Ibid.

36. Ibid., 21.23, in *NPNF*[1], 2:469. The text has been rendered clearer.

37. Ibid.

38. Ibid. The text has been rendered clearer.

Although a few exceptions would arise over the course of the next millennium and a half, the position of Augustine, which reflected the position of most Christians prior to him, would stand as the classic doctrine of the last judgment and eternal punishment.

JUDGMENT AND PUNISHMENT IN THE MIDDLE AGES

The medieval church faithfully passed on these doctrines as it had inherited them from the early church. The Bible was read as clearly teaching these truths, and even philosophy was co-opted to support them. Although these doctrines were not the object of heretical attacks, the Fourth Lateran Council in 1215 summarized and repeated the long-held position of the church about the judgment to come: "Christ will render to every man, be he damned or elect, according to his works. The damned will go into eternal punishment with the devil, and the elect will go with Christ into eternal glory."[39]

Anselm appealed to reason in his argument for "eternal unhappiness for the soul that rejects the supreme essence." He faced the objection that, rather than meriting eternal damnation, such souls should be more fittingly annihilated. Countering this, he expressed the unreasonableness of the idea of the destruction of a guilty soul: "Suppose that the soul that rejects the end it was made for dies and so becomes non-sentient or completely non-existent. Then the guiltiest soul would be in the same state as the most guiltless, and supremely wise justice would be failing to distinguish between that which, being incapable of any good, desires no evil, and that which, while capable of the greatest good, desires the greatest evil. But the contrariness of this is quite clear enough."[40] He thereby demonstrated what he set out to prove: "Man's soul is created such that it will suffer eternal unhappiness if it disdains to love the supreme essence. Love will enjoy eternal reward, but disdain will suffer eternal punishment. Love will taste unalterable abundance, but disdain unassuageable indigence."[41]

Development of this topic took place with Thomas Aquinas, who investigated many issues related to divine judgment and subsequent eternal punishment. One possible objection that he faced was that "fault is temporal; therefore, the punishment should not be eternal."[42] He anticipated another objection: Because of the heinousness of their sin, the wicked should forfeit their very existence: "But if sinners are destroyed, their punishment cannot be eternal. Therefore it would seem out of keeping with divine justice that sinners should be punished forever."[43] In support for his own position, Aquinas appealed to Jesus' teaching on the eternal punishment of the wicked (Matt. 25:46). He also adapted the view of "the philosopher" Aristotle:

According to the philosopher, punishment is meted out according to the dignity of the person sinned against, so that a person who strikes one in authority

---

39. Fourth Lateran Council, canon 1, cited in Peter Toon, *Heaven and Hell: A Biblical and Theological Overview* (Nashville: Thomas Nelson, 1986), 164.

40. Anselm, *Monologion*, 71, in *Anselm*, 76.

41. Ibid.

42. Thomas Aquinas, *Summa Theologica*, sup., pt. 3, q. 99, art. 1.

43. Ibid. The text has been rendered clearer.

receives a greater punishment than one who strikes anyone else. Now, whoever sins mortally, sins against God—whose commandments he breaks and whose honor he gives another—by placing his end [or ultimate purpose] in someone other than God. But God's majesty is infinite. Therefore, whoever sins mortally deserves infinite punishment; consequently, it seems just that for a mortal sin a person should be punished forever.[44]

Aquinas further reasoned, "Because punishment cannot be infinite in intensity, because the creature is incapable of an infinite quality, it must be infinite at least in duration."[45] Moreover, he drew a conclusion from the fact that a person sins mortally by having as his ultimate end or purpose in life something other than God: "It clearly appears, then, he would have much more willed the enjoyment of that temporal good for all eternity. Therefore, according to the divine judgment, he should be punished as though he had gone on sinning for eternity. Thus beyond question, eternal punishment is due for eternal sin."[46] Aquinas concluded, "By this the error of them who say that the punishment of the wicked will at some time come to an end is excluded."[47]

Beyond this, Aquinas reflected on the nature of and purpose for eternal punishment. As for the former, he made a distinction between "the pain of loss" and "the pain of sense." What is lost in the first pain is the beatific vision of God; what is sensed in the second pain is torment of both body and soul. Thus, "those who sin against God are not only to be punished by their exclusion from perpetual happiness, but also by the experience of something painful."[48] This was the twofold nature of eternal punishment.

Furthermore, Aquinas offered several reasons for the eternal punishment of the wicked. One reason was salvific, "so that by the fear of eternal punishment others may cease to sin."[49] Beyond this, eternal punishment serves the justice of God, and it stimulates gratitude for grace in God's people.[50] Finally, according to Aquinas, the wicked's awareness of the endlessness of their punishment is part of their misery: "The eternity of damnation is part of the punishment of the damned, and it would not have the true nature of punishment unless it were repugnant to their will. Now the eternity of damnation would not be repugnant to their will unless the damned were aware that their punishment was everlasting. It is therefore a condition of their misery that they know they can in no way escape damnation and reach blessedness."[51] Aquinas echoed and advanced the church's historic doctrines of last judgment and eternal punishment.

Theologians and church leaders were not the only ones to describe the torments of eternal punishment. Artists such as Michelangelo painted frighteningly dramatic scenes titled *The Last Judgment*—with the damned being condemned by a furiously wrathful Christ—in churches throughout Christendom. Poets and writers also composed numerous works detailing the future of the damned in hell. For example, in his *Divine Comedy*,

44. Ibid. The text has been rendered clearer.
45. Ibid.
46. Thomas Aquinas, *Summa Contra Gentiles*, 3.145. Aquinas cited key theologians—e.g., Augustine and Gregory the Great—who had previously defended this view.
47. Ibid.

48. Thomas Aquinas, *On the Truth of the Catholic Faith*, 218, cited in Robert A. Peterson, *Hell on Trial: The Case for Eternal Punishment* (Phillipsburg, N.J.: P & R, 1995), 109.
49. Aquinas, *Summa Contra Gentiles*, 3.145.
50. Aquinas, *Summa Theologica*, sup., pt. 3, q. 99, art. 1.
51. Ibid., 2nd pt. of pt. 2, q. 18, art. 3.

Dante Alighieri vividly portrayed "the inferno." Influenced by Dante's writings, John Milton composed *Paradise Lost* and reinforced the vividness of torment in hell.

"The Inferno," in Dante's *Divine Comedy*

Enormous herds of naked souls I saw,
lamenting till their eyes were burned of tears;
they seemed condemned by an unequal law,
for some were stretched supine upon the ground,
some squatted with their arms about themselves,
and others without pause roamed round and round.
Most numerous were those that roamed the plain.
Far fewer were the souls stretched on the sand,
But moved to louder cries by greater pain.
And over all that sand on which they lay
or crouched or roamed, great flakes of flame fell slowly
as snow falls in the Alps on a windless day.*

> *Dante Alighieri, *Divine Comedy: The Inferno*, trans. John Ciardi (New York: Mentor, 1954), 128.

Satan's First Impression of Hell, in John Milton's *Paradise Lost*

At once, as far as angels ken, he views
The dismal situation waste and wild:
A dungeon horrible on all sides round
As one great furnace flamed; yet from those flames
No light; but rather darkness visible
Served only to discover sights of woe,
Regions of sorrow, doleful shades, where peace
And rest can never dwell, hope never comes
That comes to all; but torture without end
Still urges, and a fiery deluge, fed
With ever-burning sulfur unconsumed,
Such place Eternal Justice had prepared
For those rebellious; here their prison ordained
In utter darkness, and their portion set,
As far removed from God and light of heaven
As from the center thrice to the utmost pole.
Oh, how unlike the place from which they fell!*

> *John Milton, *Paradise Lost* (Chicago: Scott, Foresman & Co., 1898), bk. 1, lines 59–75, p. 79.

Such popular portrayals of hell and the eternal punishment experienced by its residents established themselves in the imaginations of the common people as actual descriptions of the future that is in store for the wicked.

JUDGMENT AND PUNISHMENT IN THE REFORMATION AND POST-REFORMATION

Like those who went before him, Martin Luther upheld the doctrines of the last judgment and eternal punishment. He noted how strange the divine punishment is, because "God is friendly ... inclined and willing ever to help and to do good; and he does not like to be angry and punish unless he must do so and is actually forced and obliged to do so by the ceaseless, impenitent, hardened wickedness of men. When he must show anger and mete out punishment, he does so later than a man would."[52] While acknowledging the patience of God to judge and punish, Luther pointed out that this should not be misconstrued as tolerance of evil: "Beware and do not be deceived: Although the punishment is hidden, it is nonetheless certain and will not fail to come."[53] Luther described the torments of the coming punishment: "The fiery oven is ignited merely by the unbearable appearance of God and endures eternally. For the Day of Judgment will not last for a moment only but will stand throughout eternity and will thereafter never come to an end. Constantly the damned will be judged, constantly they will suffer pain, and constantly they will be a fiery oven—that is, they will be tortured within by supreme distress and tribulation."[54]

John Calvin continued the church's historic belief in the last judgment and eternal punishment. Indeed, he looked to the Apostles' Creed as the classical and biblically supported affirmation of this doctrine. Taking the creed's confession concerning Christ— "from whence he will come to judge the living and the dead"—he explained: "He will separate the lambs from the goats, the elect from the reprobate [Matt. 25:31–33]. No one—living or dead—will escape his judgment. The sound of the trumpet will be heard from the ends of the earth, and by it all will be summoned before his judgment seat, both those still alive at that day and those whom death had previously taken from the company of the living [1 Thess. 4:16–17]."[55] After the judgment, believers will experience the eternal blessedness of God's presence. Calvin was almost at a loss for words to describe what is to come, and he felt the biblical descriptions were inadequate to capture this future reality as well: "Though we very truly hear that the kingdom of God will be filled with splendor, joy, happiness, and glory, yet when these things are spoken of, they remain utterly remote from our perception and, as it were, wrapped in obscurities, until that day comes when he will reveal to us his glory, that we may behold it face to face (cf. 1 Cor. 13:12)."[56] Refusing to follow the common path of engaging in speculation about the future, he focused on the blessing of being united with God himself by which "the Lord will share his glory, power, and righteousness with the elect."[57]

52. Martin Luther, *Commentary on Psalm 118*, LW, 14:47.
53. Martin Luther, *WLS*, 3:1154.
54. Ibid., 2:627.
55. John Calvin, *Institutes of the Christian Religion*, 2.16.17, LCC, 1:525.
56. Ibid., 3.25.10, LCC, 2:1004–5.
57. Ibid., LCC, 2:1005.

In a similar manner, Calvin cautiously addressed the postjudgment future of nonbelievers. He took up the debate on the nature of the future punishment, denouncing the idea that the biblical description of the eternal fire should be taken literally.[58] He found reason for the Bible's use of such figurative language—"darkness ... weeping, and gnashing of teeth" (Matt. 8:12; 22:13), "unquenchable fire" (Matt. 3:12; Mark 9:43; Isa. 66:24), and "undying worm gnawing at the heart" (Isa. 66:24; NIV "their worm will not die"): "As by such details we should be enabled in some degree to conceive the lot [destiny] of the wicked, so we ought especially to fix our thoughts upon this: how wretched it is to be cut off from all fellowship with God."[59] Such metaphorical language should also evoke a deep sense of the fury of God's might bearing down against the wicked.[60]

The two results of judgment—the blessing of eternal life and the torment of eternal punishment—were addressed at length by the post-Reformers. Quenstedt underscored two aspects of eternal life: "privative" blessings, which remove what is weak and evil from the experience of Christians, and "positive" blessings, which enrich the experience of believers. As for the former, "the privative blessings are the absence of sin and its causes: the fleshly nature that incites sin, the devil who suggests sin, the world that seduces to sin, and the punishments of sin, such as various sufferings ... temporal death ... [and] eternal death." As for the latter, positive blessings, some are internal: among the internal blessings, "the beatific and immediate vision of God is prominent." Others include "the perfect enlightenment of the intellect ... the complete integrity of the will and the emotions ... the absolute assurance of the eternal duration of this blessedness," and the immortality and incorruptibility of the body. Other positive blessings are external: "Of these, two are prominent: the most delightful relationship with God, the angels, and all the blessed, consisting in mutual presence and most agreeable conversations, and rendering of mutual honor joined with mutual love; and a most beautiful and magnificent home."[61] This gift of eternal life will be enjoyed equally by all Christians; there is no essential difference in the salvation of believers. However, in terms of "accessory rewards"—blessings that accompany eternal life—believers will experience different degrees of blessing.[62]

Turning to the fate of the ungodly, the post-Reformers affirmed that the final judgment would result in eternal conscious punishment in hell. Quenstedt insisted that such eternal duration "will augment the punishments of the damned beyond measure. The *sufferings* will be continuous, *i.e.*, they will have no interval, no interruption; they will be *eternal*, they will have no end."[63] Hollaz denied that "eternal destruction" (2 Thess. 1:9) means "an annihilation of substance"; rather, "it is the forfeiture or the lack of happiness, and shame and everlasting contempt (Dan. 12:2), since there is nothing more contemptible—in the eyes of God, the angels, and the blessed—than the damned."[64]

58. John Calvin, *Commentary on a Harmony of the Evangelists, Matthew, Mark, and Luke*, vol. 1 (repr., Grand Rapids: Baker, 2005), 200–201.

59. Calvin, *Institutes*, 3.25.12, LCC, 2:1007–8.

60. Ibid., LCC, 2:1008.

61. John Andrew Quenstedt, *Theologia Didactico-Polemica sive Systema Theologicum* (Leipzig, 1715), 1.553, in Schmid,

661–62. The text has been rendered clearer.

62. Quenstedt held that this was the belief of the church throughout its history. Ibid., 1.559, in Schmid, 660.

63. Ibid.

64. David Hollaz, *Examen Theologicum Acroamaticum* (1707), 979, in Schmid, 657. The text has been rendered clearer.

Confronting a denial of eternal punishment, Riissen noted: "The punishment of hell is not mere annihilation, as the Socinians would like; or punishment of loss, as though it consisted in simple deprivation of good without any sense of evils."[65]

As he did with eternal life, Quenstedt underscored two aspects of eternal death: privative and positive. In the former, he included "forfeiture of the beatific vision of God ... separation from the society of all the good ... exclusion from heavenly light, rest, and happiness ... entire denial of pity, divine as well as human ... [and] despair of every kind."[66] The "positive" aspect of eternal death was divided into internal elements—the evil that "the damned experience in themselves, viz., the inexplicable pains and tortures of soul"[67]—and external elements. Hollaz described some of the internal evils awaiting the damned: "Their *intellect* will recognize God as the most just judge and most severe avenger of sins.... Their *will* will be tortured by hatred to God, the greatest sorrow, and raging impatience."[68] Quenstedt listed the external sufferings as "those most sorrowful evils, outside of themselves, that they [the damned] deeply feel, namely, association with devils ... a most foul dwelling place ... and most painful burning without being consumed."[69] Thus, the post-Reformers warned vividly of the torments of eternal death that awaited those who in this life refused the salvation offered by Jesus Christ.

Exceptions to this historic consensus of the church were rare. Samuel Richardson, pastor of London's first Particular Baptist church, published a book entitled *Of the Torments of Hell: The Foundations Thereof Discover'd, Search'd, Shaken and Remov'd, with Many Infallible Proofs That There Is Not to Be a Punishment after This Life for Any to Endure That Shall Never End* (1658). Obviously, Richardson did not affirm the traditional doctrine of eternal punishment, but this was a very uncommon position.

JUDGMENT AND PUNISHMENT IN THE MODERN PERIOD

To put the following historical discussion in perspective, Richard Bauckham offers these sobering introductory words:

> Until the nineteenth century almost all Christian theologians taught the reality of eternal torment in hell. Here and there, outside the theological mainstream, were some who believed that the wicked would be finally annihilated.... Even fewer were the advocates of universal salvation, though these few included some major theologians of the early church [as we saw with Origen]. Eternal punishment was firmly asserted in official creeds and confessions of the churches. It must have seemed as indispensable a part of universal Christian belief as the doctrines of the Trinity and the incarnation. Since 1800 this situation has

65. Leonard Riissen, *Francisci Turretini Compendium Theologiae* (Amsterdam, 1695), 18.20, in Heppe, 710.

66. Quenstedt, *Theologia Didactico-Polemica*, 1.562, in Schmid, 659.

67. Ibid., 1.562, in Schmid, 659.

68. Hollaz, *Examen Theologicum Acroamaticum*, 982, in Schmid, 659.

69. Quenstedt, *Theologia Didactico-Polemica*, 1.562, in Schmid, 659; cf. Hollaz, *Examen Theologicum Acroamaticum*, 983, in Schmid, 659.

entirely changed, and no traditional Christian doctrine has been so widely abandoned as that of eternal punishment.[70]

What follows is a summary of this drastic change.

Although he formally treated the doctrines of judgment and punishment in his theology, Jonathan Edwards also preached these in sermons. In this homiletical practice, he was typical of those in his day. In one sermon, he described the utter hopelessness of those in hell, listing five reasons this is so: the wicked in hell will not be able to overcome their enemy—God—so as to deliver themselves; they will have no strength to appease God or to abate the fierceness of his wrath; they will have no friends in hell (or in heaven); they will never be able to escape hell; and they will never be able to find anything to relieve them in hell.[71] In one of the most famous sermons in America, "Sinners in the Hands of an Angry God," Edwards vividly described the fate of those in hell. He affirmed the eternal duration of the divine punishment: "There will be no end to this exquisite horrible misery. When you look forward, you shall see a long forever, a boundless duration before you, which will swallow up your thoughts, and amaze your soul; and you will absolutely despair of ever having any deliverance, any end, any mitigation, any rest at all. . . . Your punishment will indeed be infinite."[72]

Jonathan Edwards's "Sinners in the Hands of an Angry God"

The God that holds you over the pit of hell, much as one holds a spider, or some loathsome insect, over the fire, abhors you, and is dreadfully provoked; his wrath towards you burns like fire; he looks upon you as worthy of nothing else, but to be cast into the fire; he is of purer eyes than to bear to have you in his sight; you are ten thousand times so abominable in his eyes as the most hateful venomous serpent is in ours. You have offended him infinitely more than ever a stubborn rebel did his prince; and yet 'tis nothing but his hand that holds you from falling into the fire every moment; 'tis to be ascribed to nothing else, that you did not go to hell the last night; that you were suffered to awake again in this world, after you closed your eyes to sleep. And there is no other reason to be given why you have not dropped into hell since you arose in the morning, but that God's hand has held you up. There is no other reason to be given why you haven't gone to hell since you have sat here in the house of God, provoking his pure eyes by your sinful wicked manner of attending his solemn worship. Yea, there is nothing else that is to be given as a reason why you don't this very moment drop down into hell.*

*Jonathan Edwards, "Sinners in the Hands of an Angry God," in *A Jonathan Edwards Reader*, ed. John E. Smith, Harry S. Stout, and Kenneth P. Minkema (New Haven and London: Yale Univ. Press, 1995), 97–98.

---

70. Richard Bauckham, "Universalism: A Historical Survey," *Themelios* 4, no. 2 (January 1979): 48.

71. Jonathan Edwards, "The Future Punishment of the Wicked: Unavoidable and Intolerable," in *The Works of President Edwards*, 4 vols. (New York: Leavitt and Allen, 1852), 4:258-59.

72. Jonathan Edwards, "Sinners in the Hands of an Angry God," in *A Jonathan Edwards Reader*, ed. John E. Smith, Harry S. Stout, and Kenneth P. Minkema (New Haven and London: Yale Univ. Press, 1995), 102.

During the nineteenth century, the church's uniform historic position on judgment and eternal punishment began to splinter. Friedrich Schleiermacher reinterpreted religion in terms of a feeling of absolute dependence on God. In keeping with this emphasis, notions of a last judgment and of eternal punishment found little place. Indeed, Schleiermacher maintained that divine punishments "cannot be ordained by God as reformative"[73] nor "merely vengeful or retributive."[74] This left only one possible purpose for divine punishment: "to prevent or to deter. Punishment is, in fact, that which must of necessity be interposed wherever and in so far as the power of the God-consciousness is as yet inactive in the sinner, its object being to prevent his dominant sensuous tendencies from meanwhile attaining complete mastery through mere unchecked habit."[75]

Within this framework, Schleiermacher dismissed the traditional idea of a last judgment.[76] He could envision no purpose for a final separation between believers and unbelievers, and he appealed to the example of Christ—who "partook in the common life shared by sinners"—to argue against the entire idea.[77] Still, with regard to the last judgment, Schleiermacher felt that "in view of its almost universal prevalence in Christendom, we must try to elicit its essential meaning."[78] He dismissed the notion of "vengeful desire to enhance the misery of unbelievers, and to exclude them from all the redemptive influences of the good." He denied that the last judgment had to do with "a fear lest, even after attaining perfected fellowship with Christ, we might be pained by the company of the bad."[79] Rather, its meaning has to do with complete freedom from evil,[80] and it points to the hope that eventually all people would experience the feeling of absolute dependence on God.[81]

Schleiermacher also dismissed the doctrine of eternal damnation, asserting that "the figurative sayings of Christ, which have led to a state of irremediable misery for those who die out of fellowship with Christ being accepted as the counterpart of eternal blessedness, will, if more closely scrutinized, be found insufficient to support any such conclusion."[82] Moreover, he imagined that any type of eternal punishment that involves misery cannot help but result in less and less misery as time goes on.[83] Beyond this, Schleiermacher reasoned that if the punishment of the wicked were spiritual, it would result in a "quickened conscience" that would "issue in some good." This would mean that the wicked "are better by far in their damnation than they were in this life."[84] Schleiermacher's last reason

73. "If the God-consciousness could be strengthened by punishment, a system of divine penalties as perfect as possible could have been made to serve instead of redemption." Friedrich Schleiermacher, *The Christian Faith*, ed. H. R. Mackintosh and J. S. Stewart (Edinburgh: T & T Clark, 1928), 351.

74. "Divine penalties of such a type could be believed in only at a very primitive stage of development—a stage at which the Deity is still thought of as susceptible to irritation, and as not above feeling an injury or having other passive states." Ibid.

75. Ibid., 351–52.

76. He interpreted the traditional view to refer to "the complete separation of the church from the world, inasmuch as the consummation of the former excludes all influences of

the latter upon it.... Christ will utterly separate the believing and the unbelieving from each other, so that they are consigned to quite different places and can exert no further influence on each other." Ibid., 714.

77. Ibid., 715–16.

78. Ibid., 716.

79. Ibid.

80. Ibid., 716–17.

81. Ibid., 717–20.

82. Ibid., 720. He appealed to Matt. 24:26; Mark 9:44; and John 5:29.

83. Ibid.

84. Ibid., 720–21.

for dismissing eternal damnation focused on the empathy that the saved who are blessed would have for their fellow beings who are suffering eternal misery in hell.[85] Recognizing the entrenched nature of the historical position of the church on eternal damnation, Schleiermacher did not call for a complete dismissal of that view. Rather, he urged that "we ought at least to admit equal rights of the milder view, of which likewise there are traces in Scripture; the view, namely, that through the power of redemption, there will one day be a universal restoration of all souls."[86]

Alfred Tennyson's Dream of "the Larger Hope"

The Romantic movement produced writers whose works expressed a deep-seated longing for the Schleiermacher-like universal salvation. For example, the Victorian romanticist Alfred Lord Tennyson articulated the dream of "the larger hope."

The wish, that of the living whole
No life may fail beyond the grave,
Derives it not from what we have
The likest God within the soul?
I stretch lame hands of faith, and grope,
And gather dust and chaff, and call
To what I feel is Lord of all,
And faintly trust the larger hope.*

*Alfred Lord Tennyson, *In Memoriam*, cited in Carl F. H. Henry, *Fundamentals of the Faith* (Grand Rapids: Zondervan, 1969, Baker, 1975), 242.

The nineteenth century witnessed a further erosion of the church's traditional teaching. The theories of universalism, annihilationism, and conditional immortality were championed by more people, yet the church always had defenders of its classical doctrine of the last judgment and eternal punishment. For example, Edward Pusey's *What Is of Faith, as to Everlasting Punishment?* was a defense of the church's historical position — specifically, "the supposition of its necessarily endless duration for all who incur it" — against attacks leveled by Frederick Farrar.[87] In his *Eternal Hope*[88] Farrar had denounced both universalism and conditional immortality, yet held out hope for a salvation that was broader than the historical church doctrine allowed. One of Farrar's reasons for this was that "none of the first four general councils lay down any doctrine whatever concerning the eternal misery of the wicked, or directly or indirectly give any interpretation of the Scriptural expressions that describe their condition."[89] Pusey's objection to Farrar's

85. Ibid., 721.

86. Ibid., 722.

87. Edward Bouverie Pusey, *What Is of Faith, as to Everlasting Punishment? In Reply to Dr. Farrar's Challenge in His*

"Eternal Hope," 1897 (Oxford: James Parker, 1880), 172–77.

88. Frederick W. Farrar, *Eternal Hope* (London and New York: Macmillan, 1897).

89. Ibid., 167.

expanded hope focused on the reason for the silence of early church councils on the doctrine of eternal punishment of the wicked in hell: it was simply not an issue, as the clear majority of the church held to a consensus view.[90]

Other developments were afoot as well. With the advent of liberal Protestant theology came a challenge to the traditional view of a public last judgment in which all humanity would appear together before the judgment seat of Christ to witness God's vindication of himself and his judgments. William Newton Clarke was typical of this challenge. In arguing against the historical doctrine, he asserted: "No Scripture is quoted in support of this view of the purpose of final judgment. The coming judgment that is known to Scripture is intended for the assignment of destiny to men; there is no hint that it is intended for vindication of God."[91] Furthermore, for Clarke, God vindicates himself; thus, he has no reason to involve people in such a vindication.[92] "Moreover, the ordinary conception of the general judgment as a vindication of God reverses the relations of the parties concerned. God is the judge of men, but this idea makes man the judge of God."[93] Thus, he concluded: "All these reasons dissuade us from expecting that God will provide an occasion for the public vindication of his righteousness."[94] Clarke tied in this idea of the judgment with a denial of a visible return of Jesus Christ to judge. This view reduced the last judgment to a private evaluation of each person's life at death rather than a public, cataclysmic event.[95]

At the same time, some momentum for the doctrine of universalism was built. John A. T. Robinson encapsulated this belief in his book *In the End, God....* Several passages (e.g., Rom. 5:18; 1 Cor. 15:22) were important,[96] but Robinson's strongest appeal was made to 1 Corinthians 15:24–28, which concludes, after a rehearsal of the future subjection of all things to Christ, with the affirmation "that God may be all in all."[97] Thus, he embraced the doctrine of universalism. Aware of its ongoing condemnation by the church, he sought to defend the view in a way that was different from all previous (failed) attempts: "The sole basis for such a doctrine, as more than wishful thinking, is the work of God in Christ.... It is solely the Divine 'nevertheless,' intervening beyond any expectation and merit, on which the Christian hope rests."[98]

Furthermore, Robinson insisted that universalism "can finally establish itself only if it also preserves intact two other truths upon which the Bible is equally insistent. These are

90. Pusey, *What Is of Faith, as to Everlasting Punishment?* 136–37. A bit later, William G. T. Shedd would take up Pusey's line of argument, maintaining that the absence of treatment of this doctrine by the first four ecumenical councils has another and better explanation: "Long controversies ending in ecumenical councils and formulated statements were the consequence of the trinitarian errors, but no ecumenical council and no authoritative counter-statement was required to prevent the spread of the tenet of restoration." In the early church, other and very virulent heresies having to do with the Trinity and the person of Christ required the attention of church councils. By comparison, the denial of eternal punishment had "so little even seeming support in Scripture and reason" and was held by so few people that it did not warrant specific

consideration by these councils. William G. T. Shedd, *Dogmatic Theology*, 7:6, in *Dogmatic Theology*, ed. Alan W. Gomes, 3rd ed. (Phillipsburg, N.J.: P & R, 2003), 884.

91. William Newton Clarke, *Outline of Christian Theology* (Edinburgh: T & T Clark, 1909), 463–64.

92. Ibid., 464.

93. Ibid.

94. Ibid., 465.

95. Ibid.

96. John A. T. Robinson, *In The End, God...: A Study of the Christian Doctrine of the Last Things* (London: James Clarke, 1950), 99.

97. Ibid., 99–100.

98. Ibid., 108.

the realities of human freedom and the seriousness of hell."[99] Addressing universalism and the reality of freedom, Robinson held out hope "that an all-compelling love could possibly leave it [freedom] intact."[100] For Robinson, the ultimate compelling love that conquers everything and everybody is nothing other than the infinite love of God. Thus, he appealed to people's experience of coming to "the knowledge of this strange compulsion of God's love and to the assurance that its necessary victory would not abrogate, but simply release, our freedom."[101] Through this experience, he brought universalism and human freedom together.

Addressing universalism and the seriousness of hell, Robinson focused on an existentialist urgency of choice between heaven and hell that each person must feel. He noted that critiques of universalism commonly point to this lack of urgency as a serious flaw with that doctrine: if everyone will only go to heaven and no one will go to hell, where is the sense of urgency in choosing one path or the other?[102] Robinson therefore had to seek for a presentation and defense of universalism that avoided this criticism. He did so by confessing that, from God's point of view, there is no reality of hell.[103] The nonreality of hell is the "true" metaphysical reality. But, insisted Robinson, from the human point of view, the choice between heaven (that is reality) and hell (that is another reality) must be seriously felt.[104] That is, the reality of hell must be the "true" epistemological reality. Nothing must be allowed to weaken the seriousness of this existential choice—especially the "true" metaphysical reality known to God and to believers that hell is not real.[105] He insisted on the serious truth, subjectively perceived by sinful people confronted with the gospel, of the reality of hell despite the truth, objectively perceived by both God and believers, that hell is not real.[106] Robinson thus defended universalism.

In a more modest way, Karl Barth championed the probability of universal salvation, which he asserted would surely be the work of the undeserved grace of God in Christ.[107] He offered two considerations, the first of which focused on the unexpectedness of any such gracious, universal rescue.[108] Barth's second consideration paradoxically urged the expectation of such gracious, universal salvation. This hope was based on the present gracious work of God against sin, from which Barth asked: "Does it not point plainly in the direction of the work of a truly eternal divine patience and deliverance and therefore of an *apokatastasis* or universal reconciliation?"[109] Accordingly, Barth offered hope for the salvation of all human beings through Jesus Christ, thus embracing universalism.

Numerous defenders of the historic doctrine of the last judgment and eternal punishment stepped forward at this time. William Shedd confronted a new form of universalism, which "concedes the force of the biblical and rational arguments respecting the

99. Ibid., 109.

100. Ibid., 110.

101. Ibid., 114.

102. Ibid., 119.

103. Ibid.

104. Ibid., 119–20.

105. Ibid., 120. Robinson said nothing about the "most damnable lie" of confronting sinful people with a choice between heaven and hell when the latter is not an actual—that is, metaphysical—reality. It becomes an epistemological "untruth" with no metaphysical basis.

106. Ibid., 121.

107. *CD*, 476–77.

108. Ibid., 477.

109. Ibid., 477–78.

guilt of sin and its intrinsic desert of eternal punishment, but contends that redemption from it through the vicarious atonement of Christ is extended into the next world."[110] Specifically, "the advocates of this view assert that between death and the final judgment, the application of Christ's work is going on, that the Holy Spirit is regenerating sinners in the intermediate state, and they are believing and repenting as in this life. This makes the day of judgment, instead of the day of death, the dividing line between 'time' and 'eternity.'"[111] Shedd marshaled numerous biblical arguments against this notion of postmortem salvation, appealing particularly to the scriptural affirmation that a person's destiny in judgment is settled immediately after death (Heb. 9:27) and "the parable [of the rich man and Lazarus, which] proves that death is the turning point in human existence and fixes the eternal state of the person."[112] Shedd concluded that no revelation of postmortem salvation has been given; indeed, Scripture indicates the opposite.[113]

Noting that "the chief objections to the doctrine of endless punishment are not biblical, but speculative,"[114] Shedd offered rational arguments for the doctrine of eternal conscious damnation. For his first point, Shedd appealed to the reality of the human conscience.[115] He argued that a guilty conscience expects endless punishment, there is a universal (and, hence, real) fear of endless punishment, and such conscience manifests itself in the demand for justice against wickedness and evildoers.[116] For his second point, Shedd argued, "Endless punishment is rational because of the endlessness of sin.... One sin makes guilt, and guilt makes hell. But while this is so, it is a fact to be observed that sin is actually being added to sin in the future life, and the amount of sin is accumulating."[117] He explained his concept of the eternal reality of sin by noting that sin is so obstinate that it will intensify itself eternally, it will hold the sinful will in bondage eternally, and it will be exacerbated by sinful rejection of the righteous punishment of sin.[118] Shedd's third reason for eternal conscious punishment focused on the nature of evil: "Endless punishment is rational because sin is an infinite evil: infinite, not because committed by an infinite being, but against one."[119] Having affirmed this, Shedd anticipated the typical objection that such punishment is cruel and unjust. He responded to this by reprising Aquinas's argument.[120] Shedd's fourth reason emphasized that when wicked people are punished eternally, their choice is actually being honored: "The finally lost are not to be conceived of as having faint desires and aspirations for a holy and heavenly state and as feebly but really inclined to sorrow for their sin, but are kept in hell contrary to their yearning and petition. There is not a single

110. Shedd, *Dogmatic Theology*, 7.6, in Gomes, *Dogmatic Theology*, 900.

111. Ibid.

112. Ibid., 900–901.

113. Ibid., 902–3.

114. Ibid., 911.

115. Ibid., 920.

116. Ibid., 920–22.

117. Ibid., 922.

118. Ibid., 923–24.

119. Ibid., 925.

120. "The objection that an offense committed in a finite time cannot be an infinite evil and deserve an infinite suffering implies that crime must be measured by the time that was consumed in its perpetration. But even in human punishment, no reference is had to the length of time occupied in the commission of the offense. Murder is committed in an instant, and theft sometimes requires hours. But the former is the greater crime and receives the greater punishment." Ibid., 926.

throb of godly sorrow or a single pulsation of holy desire in the lost spirit.... Sin ultimately assumes a fiendish form and degree."[121] So William Shedd offered both biblical and rational arguments for the endless duration of the conscious punishment of the wicked in hell.

But the issue was not closed. Influenced by numerous factors, some evangelicals began to speak vaguely about a last judgment and eternal punishment of the wicked in hell. Donald Bloesch's discussion of hell intentionally eschewed any dogmatism on this issue. As a consequence, it left open the possibility of salvation after death.[122] Other evangelicals explored the possibility of annihilationism and conditional immortality (these two terms are often but not always used interchangeably). One such example was John Stott, who broke ranks with what he admitted was "traditional orthodoxy for most of the church fathers, the medieval theologians and the Reformers ... and probably most Evangelical leaders."[123] He called attention to the conflict inherent in considering this doctrine of eternal conscious punishment: "Emotionally, I find the concept intolerable and do not understand how people can live with it without either cauterizing their feelings or cracking under the strain." At the same time, he acknowledged: "But our emotions are a fluctuating, unreliable guide to truth and must not be exalted to the place of supreme authority in determining it. As a committed evangelical, my question must be—and is—not what does my heart tell me, but what does God's word say?"[124]

Stott presented four arguments in support of "the possibility that Scripture points in the direction of annihilation, and that 'eternal conscious torment' is a tradition that has to yield to the supreme authority of Scripture."[125] The first argument was linguistic, focusing on the connotation of the biblical word "destruction" as "deprivation of both physical and spiritual life, that is, extinction of being."[126] Stott's second argument examined the biblical imagery—especially fire—used to describe hell: "The main function of fire is not to cause pain, but to secure destruction."[127] The third was an argument from justice, with Stott appealing to the traditional objection to eternal punishment as being cruel and unjust.[128] His fourth argument, borrowed from arguments for universalism, was that "the eternal existence of the impenitent in hell would be hard to reconcile with the promise of God's final victory over evil" and with biblical affirmations of the summation of all things in Christ.[129] After presenting these four arguments,

121. Ibid.

122. "We do not wish to build fences around God's grace,... and we do not preclude the possibility that some in hell might finally be translated into heaven. The gates of the holy city are depicted as being open day and night (Isaiah 60:11; Revelation 21:25), and this means that access to the throne of grace is possible continuously. The gates of hell are locked, but they are locked only from within." Donald G. Bloesch, *Essentials of Evangelical Theology*, 2 vols. (San Francisco: Harper & Row, 1979), 2:226–27.

123. David L. Edwards, with a response from John Stott, *Evangelical Essentials: A Liberal-Evangelical Dialogue* (Downers Grove, Ill.: InterVarsity, 1989), 314.

124. Ibid., 314–15.

125. Ibid., 315.

126. Ibid., 315–16. Stott also acknowledged that "'annihilation' is not quite the same as 'conditional immortality.' According to the latter, nobody survives death except those to whom God gives life (they are therefore immortal by grace, not by nature), whereas according to the former, everybody survives death and will even be resurrected, but the impenitent will finally be destroyed." Ibid.

127. Ibid., 316.

128. Ibid., 318–19.

129. Stott listed John 12:32; 1 Cor. 15:28; Eph. 1:10; and Phil. 2:10–11 in support. Ibid., 319.

Stott admitted hesitancy in offering this view as a viable possibility, acknowledging that annihilationism was a break from the traditional church and evangelical doctrine. Nevertheless, he believed that "the ultimate annihilation of the wicked should at least be accepted as a legitimate, biblically founded alternative to their eternal conscious torment."[130]

A second example of changing evangelical perspectives was John Wenham, who built "the case for conditional immortality,"[131] "the belief that God created man only potentially immortal. Immortality is a state gained by grace through faith when the believer receives eternal life and becomes a partaker of the divine nature, immortality being inherent in God alone." He clearly distinguished this view from universalism, adding: "It shares the doctrine of judgment held by the upholders of everlasting torment in almost every particular—except for one tremendous thing: it sees no continuing place in God's world for human beings living on in unending pain, not reconciled to God. The wrath of God will put an end to sin and evil."[132] His biblical case for this view focused on "the fate of the lost"[133] not being eternal torment but destruction.[134] Wenham critiqued the traditional doctrine of unending conscious punishment of the wicked in hell, and a major reason was that it is "wedded to a belief in the immortality of the soul. A fierce fire will destroy any living creature, unless that creature happens to be immortal."[135] Wenham dissented from this belief because "God alone has immortality" (1 Tim. 6:16), and a Christian "gains immortality . . . when he gains eternal life and becomes partaker of the divine nature."[136] According to Wenham, the immortality of the soul is a Greek philosophical idea, not a biblical teaching.[137] Furthermore, he confessed that he found the traditional doctrine unpalatable, especially as that doctrine and its image of a wrathful, vengeful God were often wildly and distastefully preached by evangelicals.[138] With caution, then, he opted for conditional immortality.[139]

One of the most able modern proponents of conditionalism or annihilationism was Edward Fudge,[140] who offered a lengthy biblical case in support of his position.[141] While affirming that God is "absolutely holy and perfectly just," he questioned: "But are we to believe that God, who 'so loved' the world that he gave his only Son to die for our sins (John 3:16), will also keep millions of sinners alive forever so he can torment them

---

130. Ibid., 320.

131. I have chosen to excerpt Wenham's position from his article "The Case for Conditional Immortality" rather than from his earlier book *The Goodness of God* (Downers Grove, Ill.: InterVarsity, 1974), especially the second chapter on hell. The reason is that the article reflects his mature thinking on this doctrine, the rudimentary elements of which he was only beginning to explore when he wrote the book. In the article, Wenham himself noted: "I am grateful for the opportunity of expounding this case, for it is seventeen years since I tentatively committed myself to it in print. This was in my book *The Goodness of God.* . . . I could do little more than outline the main points of the case for unending conscious torment and for conditional immortality (the latter in seven pages)." John W. Wenham, "The Case for Conditional Immortality," in

Cameron, *Universalism and the Doctrine of Hell,* 162.

132. Ibid.

133. Ibid., 171.

134. Ibid., 174.

135. Ibid., 175.

136. Ibid.

137. Ibid.

138. Ibid., 183–84.

139. Ibid., 190.

140. Edward Fudge, *The Fire That Consumes: A Biblical and Historical Survey of the Doctrine of Final Punishment* (1982; repr., Lincoln, Neb.: iUniverse.com, 2000), 425.

141. Edward William Fudge and Robert A. Peterson, *Two Views of Hell: A Biblical and Theological Dialogue* (Downers Grove, Ill.: InterVarsity, 2000), 24–79.

endlessly throughout all eternity?"[142] Fudge's reply to his own question was emphatically negative: "He [God] will punish those who refuse his salvation, and not one of them will escape. There will be degrees of punishment, and the destructive process will allow plenty of opportunity for that. But whatever conscious suffering may be involved, the unrighteous will all finally die.... The final end of the lost is the lake of fire, which is the second death. Life or death—these are the final two alternatives. Both that life and that death will last forever."[143]

Robert Peterson responded to Edward Fudge, both critiquing his position and defending the historical doctrine of eternal conscious punishment.[144] He clarified the nature of Fudge's position, maintaining that Fudge combines annihilationism with conditional immortality: "He does not hold that human beings are created immortal by God. Instead he believes that only regenerate persons receive the gift of immortality. Fudge combines his belief in conditional immortality with the view that God will raise the dead. Because Fudge holds that the ultimate judgment of God upon the lost will be their extinction of being, he is an annihilationist."[145] Peterson listed eleven other significant theologians—Tertullian, Augustine, Thomas Aquinas, Martin Luther, John Calvin, Jonathan Edwards, John Wesley, Francis Pieper, Louis Berkhof, Lewis Sperry Chafer, and Millard Erickson—who have articulated and defended the historical position of the church on this issue. Peterson then set forth biblical support for the consensus view, often citing passages also used by Fudge in support of his position but demonstrating how they more accurately support the traditionalist view.[146] He therefore offered a thoroughgoing historical and biblical case for the doctrine of the eternal conscious punishment of the wicked in hell. The vast majority of evangelicals agreed with Peterson and continued to affirm the church's historic stance on this issue.

---

142. Ibid., 81.

143. Ibid., 81–82.

144. As far as I know, the only time the two met publicly to debate each other was at Western Seminary's spring lecture-ship in March 2001. But the two engaged in "debate" through the book *Two Views of Hell*.

145. Ibid., 102.

146. Ibid., 130–68.

Chapter 33

THE NEW HEAVENS AND NEW EARTH

How did the church develop its vision of the end of this world followed by a new heavens and a new earth?

STATEMENT OF BELIEF

The church has historically held out the hope that "after the final judgment, believers will enter into the full enjoyment of life in the presence of God forever.... There will be a new heavens and a new earth—an entirely renewed creation—and we will live with God there."[1] Life after death with the Lord in heaven, and even the return of Christ (together with his earthly reign in the millennial kingdom, according to some evangelicals), do not compose the fullness of God's plan for the created order and believers. The destruction or renewal of all that currently exists, together with its replacement by a new universe in which the blessings of God will be experienced in an eternal state, is the ultimate hope toward which all exists. While general agreement about this hope is found among Christians, disagreement exists over how this final event will come about. As one theologian has wondered: "Will the present universe be totally annihilated, so that the new universe will be completely other than the present cosmos, or will the new universe be essentially the same cosmos as the present, only renewed and purified?"[2] Furthermore, recent developments have influenced some Christians to emphasize the spiritual nature of life in the eternal state, while other Christians continue to champion the physical nature of existence in the new heavens and new earth.[3]

---

1. Wayne Grudem, *Systematic Theology: An Introduction to Biblical Doctrine* (Grand Rapids: Zondervan, 1994, 2004), 1158.

2. Anthony Hoekema, *The Bible and the Future* (Grand Rapids: Eerdmans, 1979), 279–80.

3. My thanks to Eron Plevan for his help on this chapter.

THE IDEA OF THE ETERNAL
STATE IN THE EARLY CHURCH

The destruction of the world as we now know it, which is to be replaced by new heavens and a new earth, was addressed on several occasions in the New Testament. Peter linked it with the future "day of the Lord" and underscored the motivation it should provide for godly living (2 Peter 3:10). This "day of the Lord" is a predominant Old Testament theme, especially in the prophetic books. The New Testament authors picked up and developed this end-of-the-world focus from earlier biblical writers such as Isaiah (Isa. 65:17–19; cf. 66:22–24). The apostle John, in his Revelation, saw the fulfillment of these prophecies in a vision of the end: "Then I saw a new heaven and a new earth, for the first heaven and the first earth had passed away, and there was no longer any sea. I saw the Holy City, the new Jerusalem, coming down out of heaven from God, prepared as a bride beautifully dressed for her husband" (Rev. 21:1–2). Although not often emphasized, the hope of a new order of reality to replace the old heavens and earth with their sin, pain, and death was nurtured by the biblical writers of both the Old and New Testaments.

The early church continued to foster this hope:

> But what a spectacle is that fast approaching advent of our Lord...! What exultation of the angelic hosts! What glory of the rising saints! What kingdom of the righteous that will follow! What city of New Jerusalem! Yes, and there are other sights: that last day of judgment, with its eternal issues; that day unlooked for by the nations, the theme of their derision, when the world gray with age, and all its many products, shall be consumed in one great flame![4]

The early church believed in a series of eschatological events that would be initiated by the second coming: Christ will return, Antichrist will be defeated, Christians will be resurrected bodily, these believers will reign with Christ on the earth for one thousand years, unbelievers will be resurrected after the millennium, the final judgment will take place, and God will establish the eternal state of heaven and hell.[5] According to the early church, this final, remarkable change will be preceded by clear and unmistakable signs:

> As the end of this world approaches, the condition of human affairs must undergo a change, and through the prevalence of wickedness become worse. The result will be that our current times, in which sin and ungodliness have increased even to the highest degree, may be judged happy and almost golden in comparison with that incurable evil. For righteousness will so decrease, and ungodliness, greed, desire, and lust will so greatly increase, that if there will happen to be any good people, they will fall prey to the wicked and will be harassed on all sides by the unrighteous. The wicked alone will live in luxury, but the good will be afflicted with trials and deprivation.... There will be no faith among people, nor peace, nor kindness, nor shame, nor truth; thus, there

---

4. Tertullian, *The Shows*, or *De Spectaculis*, 30, in *ANF*,
3:91.

5. For details, see chap. 31.

will be neither security nor government nor rest from evil. For all the earth will be in a state of tumult; wars will rage everywhere.[6]

As the world and everything in it spirals downward, cosmic chaos will occur.

Wonderful signs in heaven will confound the minds of people with the greatest terrors—the trails of comets, the darkness of the sun, the color of the moon, and the gliding of the falling stars. Nor, however, will these things take place in the usual manner. Instead, there will suddenly appear stars unknown and unseen by the eyes; the sun will be continually darkened so that there will be scarcely any distinction between the night and the day. The moon will now disappear, not for three hours only; covered with constant blood, it will go through extraordinary movement so that it will not be easy for people to ascertain the orbits of the stars or the seasons of the year; for there will be either summer in the winter, or winter in the summer.... The stars will fall in great numbers, so that the sky will appear dark without any light. The highest mountains also will fall and be level with the plains; the sea will be rendered unnavigable.[7]

A final divine judgment will be announced: "The trumpet from heaven shall utter its wailing voice. Then all will tremble and quake at that mournful sound. But then, through the anger of God against the people who have not known righteousness, the sword and fire, famine and disease, will reign; and above everything else, fear will hang always."[8] And so the end will come, ushering in the new heavens and new earth. Apparently, because the early church considered that most people were ill prepared for the judgment of all things, it prayed "for the delay of the final consummation."[9]

Some in the early church denied that this final, convulsive event would come about by the annihilation of the current heavens and earth. For example, Irenaeus explained:

Neither is the substance nor the essence of the creation annihilated (for faithful and true is he who has established it), but "the form of the world passes away" [1 Cor. 7:31]; that is, those things among which transgression has occurred, because man has grown old in them.... But when this [present] form [of things] passes away, and man has been renewed and flourishes in an incorruptible state, so as to preclude the possibility of becoming old, [then] there will be the new heavens and the new earth, in which the new man will remain, continually enjoying new communion with God.[10]

Similarly, for Origen, the biblical descriptions of the future destruction of the world could not mean that the heavens and the earth would literally be destroyed. Rather, these descriptions pictured a transformation of all that exists. Reasoning from Paul's statement that "this world in its present form is passing away" (1 Cor. 7:31), Origen maintained: "If the form of the world passes away, it is by no means an annihilation or destruction of

---

6. Lactantius, *The Divine Institutes*, 7.16, in *ANF*, 7:213. The text has been rendered clearer.

7. Ibid., in *ANF*, 7:213–14. The text has been rendered clearer.

8. Ibid., in *ANF*, 7:214. The text has been rendered clearer.

9. Tertullian, *Apology*, 39, in *ANF*, 3:46.

10. Irenaeus, *Against Heresies*, 5.36, in *ANF*, 1:566–67. The text has been rendered clearer.

their material substance that is shown to take place, but a kind of change of quality and a transformation of appearance."[11] Methodius took the same position that the end of the present universe would be transformative, not destructive.

> It is not satisfactory to say that the universe will be completely destroyed, and sea and air and sky will be no longer. For the whole world will be deluged with fire from heaven and burned for the purpose of purification and renewal. It will not, however, come to complete ruin and corruption.... After being restored to a better and more fitting state, the creation remains.... The earth and the heavens must exist again after the fiery destruction of the elements and the shaking of all things.[12]

Others were not so persuaded; they held instead to a total annihilation of the current heavens and earth. Melito of Sardis spoke of "a flood of fire" that would come in the future so that "the earth will be burned up, together with its mountains."[13] Looking to the future, Tertullian knew that "a mighty cataclysm hangs over the whole earth. In fact, the very end of all things threatens dreadful woes."[14] Tertullian linked creation out of nothing with a future destruction into nothing: "The belief that everything was made from nothing will be impressed upon us by that ultimate dispensation of God which will bring back all things to nothing.... I return, therefore, to the principle which defines that all things which have come from nothing will return ultimately to nothing."[15] After this annihilation of what exists, the new heavens and new earth will be established by God.

In summary, the early church held to the hope of a new heavens and new earth in the future. Whether that would come about through a miraculous divine renewal of the existing heavens and earth, or by means of a total annihilation of the existing universe followed by a divine re-creation out of nothing, was a point of disagreement.

THE IDEA OF THE ETERNAL STATE IN THE MIDDLE AGES

As eschatology was not of pressing importance to the church in the Middle Ages, few medieval theologians and church leaders had much to say on the doctrine of the eternal state. Two who did were Anselm and Thomas Aquinas. Believing that God designed to elect and save a number of human beings equal to the number of fallen angels so as to restore the universe wracked by sin, Anselm concluded: "We believe that the present

11. Origen, *First Principles*, 1.6.4, in *ANF*, 4:262. He also cited Ps. 102:27.

12. Methodius, *The Discourse on the Resurrection*, 1.8, in *ANF*, 6:365–66. The text has been rendered clearer. By affirming this, however, Methodius was forced to respond to a possible criticism that, in light of Matt. 24:35 and Isa. 51:6, his view was unbiblical: "It is useful for the Scriptures to call the change of the world from its present condition to a better and more glorious one, 'destruction.' Its original form will be lost in the change of all things to a state of greater splendor; for there is no contradiction nor absurdity in the Holy Scriptures.

For not 'the world,' but the 'form of this world,' will pass away, it is said.... We may expect that the creation will pass away, as if it were to perish in the burning fire, in order that it may be renewed; not, however, that it will be destroyed." Ibid., 1.9, in *ANF*, 6:366. The text has been rendered clearer.

13. Melito of Sardis, *Apology*, 1, in *ANF*, 8:755–56.

14. Tertullian, *Apology*, 32, in *ANF*, 3:42–43. The text has been rendered clearer.

15. Tertullian, *Against Hermogenes*, 34, in *ANF*, 3:490–91. The text has been rendered clearer.

physical mass of the universe is to be changed anew into something better. We believe that this will not come to pass until the number of elect humans has reached its final total, and the blessed city ... has been brought to completion; also that, after the completion of the city, the renewal will follow without delay."[16]

Thomas Aquinas affirmed the doctrine of new heavens and new earth while engaging in speculation about the nature of that renewal. To the question of whether the world will be renewed, he responded positively, citing Scripture (Isa. 65:17; Rev. 21:1). He also applied reason to the issue: "The dwelling should befit the dweller. But the world was made to be man's dwelling; therefore, it should be fitting for man. Now, man will be renewed; therefore, the world will be likewise." He also appealed to the idea of correspondence: "Now man has some likeness to the universe by which he is called 'a little world.' Thus, man loves the whole world naturally and consequently desires its good. Therefore, so that man's desire is satisfied, the universe must also be made better." As for the objection that God had ceased his creative activity on the seventh day (making the renewal of the universe—a creative, divine act—impossible), Aquinas proposed "that the future renewal of the world preceded in the works of the six days by way of a remote likeness, namely in the glory and grace of the angels."[17] Furthermore, he speculated that when this restoration will occur, the heavenly bodies—the sun, moon, and stars—will cease their movement, yet their brightness will be increased. At the same time, the earth and its elements will be renewed by an additional brightness, yet plants and animals will cease to exist after the renewal.[18]

THE IDEA OF THE ETERNAL STATE IN THE REFORMATION AND POST-REFORMATION

As was true of the medieval period, the major contributors in the Reformation had little sustained interest in eschatology. John Calvin, for example, interpreted the prophecy of new heavens and new earth (Isa. 65:17) metaphorically of the church.

> By these metaphors he promises a remarkable change of affairs; as if God had said that he has both the inclination and the power not only to restore his church, but to restore it in such a manner that it shall appear to gain new life and to dwell in a new world. These are exaggerated modes of expression; but the greatness of such a blessing, which was to be manifested at the coming of Christ, could not be described in any other way. Nor does he mean only the first coming, but the whole reign, which must be extended as far as the last coming.... [E]ven now we are in the progress and accomplishment of it [this restoration], and those things will not be fulfilled till the last resurrection.[19]

---

16. Anselm, *Why God Became Man*, 1.18, in *Anselm*, 295.

17. Thomas Aquinas, *Summa Theologica*, sup., 3rd pt., art. 91, q. 1.

18. Ibid., q. 2–5.

19. John Calvin, *Commentary on the Prophet Isaiah*, vol. 3, trans. William Pringle (repr., Grand Rapids: Baker, 2005), 397–98. Martin Luther narrowed this prophecy even further,

referring it to the spiritual and physical renovation of Christians—which still had a long way to go: "I do not see a new heaven and a new body in us, but only the one born of our parents. Yet we believe it. We must turn the sack inside out, and then they will appear." Martin Luther, *Lectures on Isaiah: Chapters 40-66*, LW, 17:388.

Concerning Peter's prophecy (2 Peter 3:6–13) of the destruction of the present heavens and earth by fire, Calvin explained:

> [What is said concerning] the burning of heaven and earth, requires no long explanation, if indeed we duly consider what is intended. For it was not his [Peter's] purpose to speak refinedly [in detail] about fire and storm, and other things, but only that he might introduce an exhortation, which he immediately adds [verse 11], even that we ought to strive after newness of life. For he thus reasons, that as heaven and earth are to be purged by fire, that they may correspond with the kingdom of Christ, hence the renovation of men is much more necessary. Mischievous, then, are those interpreters who consume much labor on refined [detailed] speculations, since the apostle applies his doctrine to godly exhortations.[20]

Still, Calvin maintained that life as it exists now will undergo a future renewal:

> Heaven and earth, he [Peter] says, will pass away for our sakes; is it right, then, for us to be engrossed in the things of earth, and not, on the contrary, to attend to a holy and godly life? The corruption of heaven and earth will be purged by fire, while yet as the things created by God they are pure. What, then, ought to be done by us who are full of so many pollutions?... Of the elements of the world I shall only say this one thing, that they are to be consumed, only that they may be renovated, their substance remaining the same, as it may be easily gathered from Romans 8:21, and from other passages.[21]

Besides this orientation of their commentaries to the practical effects this passage should have for godly Christian living, the Reformers typically had nothing more to say about the eschatological event of the new heavens and new earth.

Post-Reformation theology affirmed that the end of the world would bring about wholesale destruction and transformation. Many Lutheran theologians held the annihilationist perspective, as articulated by Quenstedt: "The form of this consummation consists not in the mere change, alteration, or renewing of qualities, but in the total abolition and reduction of the world's substance itself to nothing."[22] Agreeing with this view, Hollaz proposed a purpose for this divine destruction: "The consummation of the world is an action of the triune God, by which, to the glory of his truth, power, and justice, and the deliverance of the elect, he will destroy with fire and annihilate the entire fabric of heaven and earth, and all created things, except intelligent creatures [i.e., human beings, angels]."[23] Besides magnifying the glory and power of God, another purpose for this destruction will be to restore the creation to its original pristine condition: "The present age will be accomplished and created things redeemed from the vanity to which they are subjected because of sin, to be restored to their pristine state of integrity."[24] Other

---

20. John Calvin, *Commentaries on the Catholic Epistles*, ed. and trans. John Owen (repr., Grand Rapids: Baker, 2005), 420.

21. Ibid., 420–21.

22. John Andrew Quenstedt, *Theologia Didactico-Polemica sive Systema Theologicum* (Leipzig, 1715), 4.638, in Schmid, 656.

23. David Hollaz, *Examen Theologicum Acroamaticum* (1707), 1273, in Schmid, 656. The text has been rendered clearer.

24. Nicholas Guertler, *Institutiones Theologiae* (Marburg, 1732), 33, in Heppe, 706.

theologians affirmed the opposing view that this change will entail a transformation, not a destruction: "The elements will not be removed but changed. For we expect not other heavens and another earth, but new heavens and a new earth."[25]

The Reformed theologian Francis Turretin engaged in a careful study of which view was the more probable. He framed the debate carefully by posing key questions: "What will the destruction of the earth be like? Will it be annihilated by the final conflagration [fiery destruction of the elements] or will it be restored and renewed?" Recognizing the nonessential nature of this doctrine, he urged allowance for disagreement between the opposing views.[26] Still, Turretin opted for "the transformative perspective." He maintained that descriptions of the destruction of the world, using verbs such as "to alter" and "to change" (Ps. 102:25–27), "do not designate abolition or annihilation, but only a change." Furthermore, he turned to 2 Peter 3:6–12, from which "various arguments to prove the renovation of the world are drawn." These arguments included "the comparison with the former world overwhelmed by the flood" (which did not destroy, but purged, that world) and Peter's use of words such as "melt" and "burn up" (2 Peter 3:12): "Now these things imply a change and not an annihilation.... What fire melts and burns up is not usually annihilated; yea they are only purged of dross and impurities, as in the metallic kingdom the metal is not annihilated but purged, and comes forth purer after being subjected to fire."[27] Turretin concluded his discussion with wise words: "We think we ought not to curiously pry into the things which, as God has chosen to conceal from us, are both safely unknown and are defined dangerously. The certain knowledge of these is to be looked for at length on the happy day when that restoration will take place."[28]

THE IDEA OF THE ETERNAL STATE IN THE MODERN PERIOD

Like most other doctrines, the traditional church doctrine of the eternal state came under attack in the modern period. One of the most pervasive influences undermining the historic church position was the modernist reduction of religion to an inner state of peace or an internal sense of God. Friedrich Schleiermacher contributed to this reorientation by means of his redefinition of the Christian faith as God-consciousness, specifically, a self-awareness of absolute dependence on God. In Schleiermacher's subjective approach to religion, no place remained for an external, physical transformation of this current world order into a renewed universe; the whole idea was completely meaningless. For this reason, Schleiermacher was reduced to writing about "God-consciousness present and future" in his systematic theology's section on eschatology.[29] His rejection of biblical revelation of this doctrine led him to conclude: "We therefore always remain

---

25. William Ames (Amesius), *Medullas Theologiae* (*The Marrow of Theology*) (Amsterdam, 1634 [1628]), 31, in Heppe, 706.

26. Francis Turretin, *Institutes of Elenctic Theology*, ed. James T. Dennison Jr., trans. George Musgrave Giger, 3 vols. in 1 (Phillipsburg, N.J.: P & R, 1997), 18th–20th topics, 3:590.

27. Ibid., 3:591. Turretin also anticipated and answered objections to his view (3:594).

28. Ibid., 3:596.

29. Friedrich Schleiermacher, *The Christian Faith*, ed. H. R. Mackintosh and J. S. Stewart (Edinburgh: T & T Clark, 1928), 719–20.

uncertain how the state which is the church's highest consummation can be gained or possessed in this form by individual personalities emerging into immortality."[30]

Against Schleiermacher, many echoed the traditional doctrine. For A. A. Hodge, the divine teleology—God's purpose for human existence in the world—demanded that the new heavens and new earth would be thoroughly adapted for human existence:

> Heaven, as the eternal home of the divine man and of all the redeemed members of the human race, must necessarily be thoroughly human in its structure, conditions, and activities. Its joys and occupations [activities] must all be rational, moral, emotional, voluntary, and active. There must be the exercise of all the faculties, the gratification of all tastes, the development of all latent capacities, the realization of all ideals. The reason, the intellectual curiosity, the imagination, the aesthetic instincts, the holy affections, the social affinities, the inexhaustible resources of strength and power native to the human soul, must all find in heaven exercise and satisfaction.... Heaven will prove the consummate flower and fruit of the whole creation and of all the history of the universe.[31]

Charles Hodge presented a standard exposition of this doctrine, citing much biblical evidence for it (Ps. 102:25–26; Isa. 51:6; 65:17; Rom. 8:19–21; 2 Peter 3:6–13; Rev. 20:11; 21:1).[32] Working in a context in which science was achieving a preeminent place, he appealed to scientific discoveries to bolster his theological conviction: "Scientists tell us that there is abundant evidence that the earth was once in a state of fusion, and there are causes in operation that are adequate to reduce it to that state again, whenever God sees fit to put them into operation."[33] Appealing to biblical texts and scientific evidence, Hodge sided with the view that not annihilation, but renovation of the existing universe, was the correct perspective.[34] Expressing an interpretation of biblical texts that could only come in a scientific age, he specified the extent of this renovation: it does not pertain to the entire universe, but to the earth only. Although he acknowledged that the entire universe appears to be the reference of the biblical affirmation "heaven and earth will pass away," Hodge explained why this could not be the case: "It was natural that this interpretation should be put upon the language of the Bible so long as our earth was regarded as the center of the universe.... The case however assumes a different aspect when we know that our earth and even our solar system is a mere speck in the immensity of God's works."[35] So he concluded:

---

30. Ibid., 720.

31. A. A. Hodge, *Evangelical Theology: A Course of Popular Lectures* (Edinburgh: Banner of Truth Trust, 1976), 400–401.

32. Charles Hodge, *Systematic Theology*, 3 vols. (Grand Rapids: Eerdmans, 1946), 3:851–52.

33. Ibid., 3:852.

34. "The destruction here foretold is not annihilation. (a.) The world is to be burned up; but combustion is not a destruction of substance. It is merely a change of state or condition. (b.) The destruction of the world by water and its destruction by fire are analogous events; the former was not annihilation, therefore, the second is not. (c.) The destruction spoken of is elsewhere called a παλιγγενσια, regeneration (Matt. 19:28); an ἀποκαταστσια, a restoration (Acts 3:21); a deliverance from the bondage of corruption (Rom. 8:21).... (d.) There is no evidence either from Scripture or experience, that any substance has ever been annihilated. If force is motion, it may cease; but cessation of motion is not annihilation, and the common idea in our day, among scientists, is that no force is ever lost; it is, as they say, only transformed." Ibid.

35. Ibid., 853. The text has been rendered clearer.

The *à priori* probability is overwhelmingly in favor of the more limited interpretation. Anything so stupendous as the passing away of the whole universe as the last act of the drama of human history would be altogether out of keeping.... The Bible concerns man. The earth was cursed for his transgression. That curse is to be removed when man's redemption is completed. The κτισις [*ktisis*; creation] that was made subject to futility for man's sin, is our earth; and our earth is the κτισις which is to be delivered from the bondage of corruption. The change to be effected is in the dwelling place of man.[36]

Against this focus on a future existence that is physical, some modern theologians turned to an emphasis on the spiritual reality to come. Indeed, William G. T. Shedd noted that "the modern church maintains the doctrine of the eternal blessedness but in a more spiritual form than prevailed in either the ancient or medieval church."[37] Continuing in this tradition, Shedd described "the scriptural representation of the heavenly state" as being marked by "sinless perfection ... impeccability or indefectibility ... mental happiness — the vision of the divine perfections and delight in them[— and] ... the personal presence of the mediator with his redeemed people."[38] Similarly, Donald Guthrie, in developing a New Testament eschatology, maintained: "We shall not expect ... to find a description of a place, so much as the presence of a person.... Paul does not think of heaven as a place, but thinks of it in terms of the presence of God."[39]

Slightly modifying the discussion, Millard Erickson did note the concreteness of the eternal state, explaining: "Humanity's original dwelling was in the paradisiacal setting of the Garden of Eden; his final dwelling will also be in a perfect setting — the new Jerusalem. Part of the glorification of the human will be the provision of a perfect environment in which to dwell. It will be perfect, for the glory of God will be present."[40] This concreteness is also demanded by the reality of resurrection bodies inhabiting the new universe. Furthermore, Erickson noted, "Parallel references to heaven and earth suggest that, like earth, heaven must be a locale."[41] But in further discussion of this eschatological reality, he emphasized the hope of being in the presence of God almost to the neglect of further development of the concrete reality of the universe to come:

Heaven is, first and foremost, the presence of God.... Sometimes, especially in popular presentations, heaven is depicted as primarily a place of great physical pleasures, a place where everything we have most desired here on earth is

---

36. Ibid., 854.

37. William G. T. Shedd, *Dogmatic Theology*, 7.5, in *Dogmatic Theology*, ed. Alan W. Gomes, 3rd ed. (Phillipsburg, N.J.: P & R, 2003), 882.

38. Ibid., 882–83. It is interesting to note that Shedd made reference to Isaiah 65:17 and Revelation 21:1 only once in his systematic theology, and that was part of his lexical study of the word *creation* to demonstrate that it does not always refer to creation ex nihilo in Scripture. At no point did he make reference to the 2 Peter 3 texts about the destruction of the current universe and the establishment of the new heavens

and new earth.

39. Donald Guthrie, *New Testament Theology* (Downers Grove, Ill.: InterVarsity, 1970), 875, 880.

40. Millard J. Erickson, *Christian Theology*, 2nd ed. (Grand Rapids: Baker, 1998), 1013. It is interesting to note that Erickson made reference to the 2 Peter 3 texts only twice, and that was in regard to the certainty both of judgment and of the Lord's return, but without any discussion of the destruction of the current universe and its replacement by the new heavens and new earth. He made no reference to Isa. 65:17.

41. Ibid., 1239.

fulfilled to the ultimate degree. Thus heaven seems to be merely earthly (and even worldly) conditions amplified. The correct perspective, however, is to see the basic nature of heaven as the presence of God, from which all the blessings of heaven follow.[42]

Furthermore, because "God does not occupy space, which is a feature of our universe, it would seem that heaven is a state, a spiritual condition, rather than a place."[43] Between these two emphases, Erickson opted for a more spiritual notion of the world to come (the eschaton):

> We must be mindful, however, that heaven is another realm, another dimension of reality, so it is difficult to know what features of the world apply as well to the world to come, and what the term *place* means in relation to the eschaton. It is probably safest to say that while heaven is both a place and a state, it is primarily a state. The distinguishing mark of heaven will not be a particular location, but a condition of blessedness, sinlessness, joy, and peace. Life in heaven, accordingly, will be more real than our present existence.[44]

Other twentieth-century theologians gave more attention to the physical texture of the new heavens and new earth. Analyzing the biblical data from the book of Revelation, Gordon Lewis and Bruce Demarest pointed to four images employed in its presentation of the eternal state: city, temple, garden, and the wedding supper of the Lamb.[45] These images call for understanding the future universe as being a concrete reality. Using sanctified imagination, Lewis and Demarest described life in a new physical universe: "In glorified bodies we will enjoy a restored and improved Eden, a place of pristine beauty and unbroken fellowship.... The new heaven and earth will provide an environment conducive to the most precious values we now know — just and loving relationships, fellowship, beauty, and significant activity."[46] Thus, Lewis and Demarest maintained a strongly physical nature for the new heavens and new earth.

Wayne Grudem directly addressed the growing evangelical drift that emphasized the spiritual nature of the eternal state at the expense of a very real, physical new heavens and new earth.[47] He offered several lines of support for the physical reality of heaven: The biblical narrative of Jesus' ascension into heaven demands that it must be a place that exists in time and space. This is confirmed by Stephen's sighting of Jesus at the right hand of God (Acts 7:55–56): "He did not see mere symbols of a state of existence. It seems rather that his eyes were opened to see a spiritual dimension of reality which God has hidden from us in this present age, a dimension which nonetheless really does exist in our space/time universe."[48] The resurrection of bodies is further support that heaven is a physical place. Indeed, that is the sense of Jesus' promise, "I go to prepare a *place* for you"

---

42. Ibid., 1235.

43. Ibid., 1239.

44. Ibid.

45. Gordon R. Lewis and Bruce A. Demarest, *Integrative Theology: Historical, Biblical, Systematic, Apologetic, Practical*, 3 vols. in 1 (Grand Rapids: Zondervan, 1996), 3:469.

46. Ibid., 3:480–81.

47. Grudem, *Systematic Theology*, 1159. Grudem specifically mentioned Guthrie and Erickson as examples of this evangelical view.

48. Ibid.

(John 14:2).[49] He concluded: "These texts lead us to conclude that heaven is even now a place—though one whose location is now unknown to us and whose existence is now unable to be perceived by our natural senses. It is this place of God's dwelling that will be somehow made new at the time of the final judgment and will be joined to a renewed earth."[50] Still, Grudem balanced this emphasis with another one:

> But more important than all the physical beauty of the heavenly city, more important than the fellowship we will enjoy eternally with all God's people from all nations and all periods in history, more important than our freedom from pain and sorrow and physical suffering, and more important than our reigning over God's kingdom—more important by far than any of these will be the fact that we will be in the presence of God and enjoying unhindered fellowship with him.[51]

In his book *Heaven*, Randy Alcorn exposed the growing tendency among evangelicals to emphasize the spiritual reality of the eternal state and, like Grudem, attempted to underscore the physical reality of the new heavens and new earth. For example, he reasoned: "The biblical doctrine of the New Earth implies something startling: that if we want to know what the ultimate Heaven, our eternal home, will be like, the best place to start is by looking around us. We shouldn't close our eyes and try to imagine the unimaginable. We should open our eyes, because the present Earth is as much a valid reference point for envisioning the New Earth as our present bodies are a valid reference point for envisioning our new bodies."[52] Indeed, Alcorn emphasized, this is the divine design for creation: "The idea of the New Earth as a physical place isn't an invention of short-sighted human imagination. Rather, it's the invention of a transcendent God, who made physical human beings to live on a physical Earth, *and* who chose to become a man himself on that same Earth. He did this that he might redeem mankind *and* Earth. Why? In order to glorify himself and enjoy forever the company of men and women in a world he's made for us."[53]

It is to the magnificent future reality of new heavens and a new earth that Christians, following the traditional hope of the church, look forward.

49. Ibid., 1160.
50. Ibid.
51. Ibid., 1164.

52. Randy Alcorn, *Heaven* (Wheaton: Tyndale, 2004), 81.
53. Ibid.

GLOSSARY OF MAJOR CHURCH LEADERS, WRITINGS, AND MOVEMENTS

Abelard, Peter (1079–1142)*

Medieval philosopher, professor of philosophy and theology at the University of Paris, and scholastic theologian. His most famous work, *Sic et Non* (*Yes and No*), was a juxtaposition of passages from Scripture, the early church fathers, and other authorities who were apparently in contradiction to each other. His intent was to provoke independent thinking leading to a reconciliation of the conflicting positions, but he offered no synthesis of his own. He developed the moral influence theory of the atonement over against the ransom to Satan theory and Anselm's satisfaction theory. Abelard's disposition and methodology of doubt were denounced by Bernard of Clairvaux. He is infamously known for a scandalous love affair with Héloïse.

Ambrose (c. 339–397)

Bishop of Milan, famous for his exposition of Scripture and for being a defender of orthodoxy against the Arian heresy. Augustine's conversion was partly the result of Ambrose's preaching.

Anabaptists/Anabaptism (16th cent.–present)

Churches associated with an uncompromising reform movement that began in the early part of the Reformation. The name comes from two words that literally mean new or re-baptism, and the term became associated with these churches because of their repudiation of infant baptism—whether by the Roman Catholic Church or Protestant churches—and their insistence on baptizing people who could give a credible profession of faith in Jesus Christ. Anabaptism was a free-church movement developing out of a different tradition from the magisterial Reformation (Lutheran, Reformed, and Anglican churches). Anabaptist churches emphasized believers' baptism, the new birth, non-violence, discipleship, separation from the world, and care for the poor.

Andrew of St. Victor (d. 1175)

A follower in the tradition of Hugh of St. Victor and the Victorine school of biblical interpretation, who focused on the literal sense of Scripture more so than any other medieval interpreter. He wrote commentaries on portions and books of the Old Testament, including one on the Octateuch (the five books of Moses along with Joshua, Judges, and Ruth).

---

*My thanks to David Campbell, Brian Hubert, Alex Leung, and Isaac Sumner for their help in compiling this glossary.

Anselm of Canterbury (c. 1033–1109)

Archbishop of Canterbury and an early promoter of scholasticism, one of the first theologians to explain and defend Christianity through reason and logic as opposed to arguing from Scripture and the church fathers. His dictum "faith seeking understanding" underscored his belief that truth from revelation and the church is capable of rational demonstration and can be supported by reason. He is most known for his ontological argument for the existence of God and for his work on the atonement, in which he articulated the satisfaction theory of Christ's death, overturning the ransom to Satan theory held by most theologians prior to Anselm.

Apollinarius (c. 310–c. 390)/Apollinarianism

Bishop of Laodicea and friend of Athanasius who developed the heretical view that now bears his name. Apollinarianism denies that the incarnate Son of God assumed a human soul, insisting that the only aspect of human nature he took on was a human body. This view was condemned at the second ecumenical Council of Constantinople in 381, as the church insisted that if Jesus Christ lacked a human soul, then he was not a real and fully human being, and therefore human beings could not be saved.

Apologists (2nd cent.)

Intellectually capable guardians of Christianity, leaders who defended the faith against false accusations—atheism, incest, and cannibalism—and persecutions by the Roman Empire while arguing for the superior nature of the Christian faith. Among them were Justin Martyr, Athenagoras, Aristides, Theophilus of Antioch, Tatian, Melito of Sardis, Apollinaris of Hierapolis, Quadratus, and the author of the *Epistle to Diognetus*.

Apostles' Creed (4th–8th cent.)

An early Christian creed that emerged in the fourth century (yet containing earlier material) and came into its present form several centuries later. Although not written by the apostles, it summarizes the Christian faith as they articulated it in their biblical writings. Like many creeds, it is structured in a Trinitarian form.

Apostolic Constitutions (4th cent.)

Although not written by the apostles, writings that set forth church doctrine, liturgical practices, and religious observances common in the third and fourth centuries.

Apostolic Fathers (end 1st–mid-2nd cent.)

Authors of the earliest non-canonical writings after the New Testament, some of whom knew the apostles and guided the church in the post-apostolic period. They are Clement of Rome, *Letter of the Romans to the Corinthians* (c. 96); Ignatius of Antioch, six letters to churches (the Ephesians, Magnesians, Trallians, Romans, Philadelphians, and Smyrnaeans) and one letter to Polycarp; Polycarp of Smyrna, *Letter to the Philippians*; *The Martyrdom of Polycarp*; the *Didache*; *Letter of Barnabas*; *Shepherd of Hermas*; *Letter to Diognetus*; and fragments of Quadratus and Papias.

Aristides (2nd cent.)

An apologist who composed an *Apology* addressed to the Emperor Hadrian. Praised by Eusebius and Jerome, the work was popular and widely circulated among Christians.

Arius (c. 250 – c. 336)/Arianism

An Alexandrian presbyter whose Christological beliefs placed him and his supporters at odds with the church. Among other tenets, Arius believed that the Son of God was a created being and denied that he is of the same essence as God the Father. Although the Council of Nicea (325) officially condemned Arius and his ideas as heretical, Arianism flourished for the next half century until again condemned and marginalized at the Council of Constantinople (381). Arianism in modified form continues today in sects and cults that deny the full deity of Jesus Christ.

Arminius, James (1559 – 1609)/Arminianism

Protestant professor of theology at the University of Leiden, who broke from the Reformed position on predestination. He emphasized that God chose whom he would save based on his foreknowledge of who would repent and believe in Jesus Christ. Corresponding to the centrality of human action in salvation was a view of grace that assisted the sinner but was resistible. After his death, his successors synthesized his views into the Five Articles of the Remonstrants, a protest against Reformed orthodoxy on the doctrines of predestination, the atonement of Christ, grace and its resistibility, and the perseverance of the saints. These Arminian positions were denounced by the Synod of Dort.

Arnobius (late 3rd – early 4th cent.)

Bishop in Gaul (modern-day France), during the period of fierce persecution during the reign of Emperor Diocletian, whose seven-volume apologetic work, *Against the Nations*, addresses monotheism, the deity of Christ, rapid Christian expansion, heathen idolatry, and many other topics.

Athanasian Creed (c. 500)

Confessional statement broadly used in the Western church that is neither considered a creed nor written by Athanasius, written most likely around 500 in southern France. This work is different from the more popular Apostles' Creed and Nicene Creed in form and its inclusion of "anathemas," or condemnations of aberrant viewpoints. It is divided into two portions: an orthodox section on the Trinity and another section that presents a Chalcedonian view of the incarnation.

Athanasius (c. 296 – 373)

Bishop of Alexandria, whose work as a secretary at the Council of Nicea (325) exposed him to the Arian heresy, against which he later fought for many decades. Suffering five exiles for his defense of the Nicean faith, Athanasius contributed significantly to the ultimate defeat of Arianism and the victory of orthodox Christology. He insisted that the Son of God is not a created being and is of the same essence as God the Father.

Athenagoras of Athens (2nd cent.)

An Apologist who defended Christianity against the common charges of cannibalism, atheism, and incest and offered a philosophical explanation of physical resurrection.

Augsburg Confession (1530)

One of Lutheranism's primary confessions of faith, written by Philip Melanchthon and approved by the Lutheran churches as a defense of Protestantism that could be broadly supported at the beginning of the Reformation. Although it failed to convince Emperor Charles V and the Catholic Church at the Diet of Augsburg in 1530, in 1550 the Peace of Augsburg allowed estates to adhere either to the *Augsburg Confession* or to Roman Catholicism.

Augustine of Hippo (354–430)

Bishop of Hippo in North Africa, who stands as one the greatest theologians in church history. He played a crucial role in the Donatist and Pelagian controversies, contributed significantly to the orthodox doctrine of the Trinity, wrote the first "autobiography" (his *Confessions*, a prayer to God in which he recounted his conversion), articulated a philosophy of history from a Christian perspective (*The City of God*), and explained many theological issues such as the nature of the sacraments, original sin, grace, and predestination. His works contributed to both Roman Catholic and Protestant theologies.

Barnabas (late 1st–early 2nd cent.)/*Letter of Barnabas*

An Apostolic Father—not to be confused with the apostle (Acts 14:14) and traveling companion of Paul—who wrote *The Letter of Barnabas* to address Christianity's relationship to Judaism and understanding of the Jewish Scriptures.

Barth, Karl (1886–1968)

Swiss pastor and theologian, acknowledged as one of the most important church leaders, especially for his contribution to the origin and development of neo-orthodoxy. Although deeply influenced by Schleiermacher, von Harnack, and Herrmann, he came to reject his liberal Protestant training and drew from the existentialism of Kierkegaard. The neo-orthodox theology that emerged was characterized by a dialectical approach, a rejection of general revelation and natural theology, a view of the Bible as becoming the Word of God, a consideration of God as radically transcendent, a dismissal of any remnant of the image of God in sinful human beings, and a doctrine of election for which he was charged with embracing universalism. His many contributions include his commentary on Romans (1919; revised 1921), the Barmen Declaration (1934), and his massive *Church Dogmatics* (first vol., 1932; unfinished at the time of his death).

Basil the Great (c. 330–379)

One of the Cappadocian Fathers and the brother of Gregory of Nyssa, succeeding Eusebius as the bishop of Caesarea and playing a major role in the Arian and Pneumatomachian controversies. The defeat of Arianism at the second ecumenical Council of Constantinople in 381 was an acknowledgment of his success as a defender of orthodoxy, particularly the doctrines of the Trinity and the Holy Spirit.

Bede ("Venerable Bede") (672/673–735)

Monk, biblical commentator, and church historian whose *Ecclesiastical History of the English People* is a crucial source for understanding the history of Christianity in England.

Belgic Confession (1561)

The first confession of faith of the Reformed churches in the Netherlands, written by Guy de Brey to demonstrate the legitimacy of Protestant doctrine that was being assailed by the Roman Catholic Church. The Synod of Dort confirmed the *Belgic Confession* as a doctrinal standard of the Reformed churches in the Netherlands along with the *Heidelberg Confession* and the Canons of Dort (the Three Forms of Unity).

Bellarmine, Robert (1542–1621)

Jesuit theologian, professor, and polemical writer, best known for refuting Reformation doctrines as part of the post-Tridentine Roman Catholic Church. Among his many authoritative roles were serving as archbishop, settling theological controversies, and participating in the Inquisition (in which capacity he forbade Galileo to teach a heliocentric view of the universe).

Bernard of Clairvaux (1090–1153)

The Abbot of Clairvaux who exercised great influence in ecclesiastical and political affairs. He was a supporter of the Second Crusade and preached throughout Europe to raise money for the military campaign. He wrote a number of important works on monasticism, but he is best known for an unfinished series of sermons on the Song of Songs. He also urged that Abelard be condemned by the church.

Beza, Theodore (1519–1605)

A close disciple and co-worker of John Calvin who preserved Calvin's work and legacy after the Reformer's death. As preacher and teacher of theology, he established a strict lifestyle in Geneva, laying the foundations of Puritanism. He also labored to strengthen French Huguenots and advised many Protestant rulers.

Bonaventura, Giovanni (1217–1274)

Monk and second founder of the Franciscan order, and a scholastic theologian standing in the Augustinian (and neo-Platonic) tradition and resisting the Aristotelian renaissance popular among many of his contemporaries (e.g., Thomas Aquinas).

Brunner, Emil (1889–1966)

Swiss pastor, theologian, and professor, associated with the dialectical theology, or neo-orthodoxy, of Karl Barth, though the two were noted for their strong disagreement on natural theology. His theology, as expressed in important writings such as *The Mediator, God and Man, The Divine Imperative, Man in Revolt, Truth as Encounter*, and *Christian Doctrine*, was directed at the challenges to Christianity posed by an increasingly secular world.

Bullinger, Heinrich (1504–1575)

Huldrych Zwingli's successor in Zurich and author of the *Second Helvetic Confession*, creating an international standard of Reformed doctrine. Along with Calvin, he signed the *Consensus Tigurinus*, which unified Reformed churches in regard to the Lord's Supper.

Bultmann, Rudolph (1884–1976)

German Lutheran biblical scholar, whose approach of demythologization strongly influenced biblical studies. Considering the Bible as myth, he advocated peeling back its mythological accretions so as to uncover its essential meaning, which he viewed in terms of existentialist philosophy. He also made a strong dichotomy between history and faith.

Calov, Abraham (1612–1686)

Professor and strict defender of Lutheran orthodoxy, who was strongly critical of less dogmatic Lutherans and stood against Roman Catholic, Reformed, and Remonstrance theologians. His most notable works are *Systema Locorum Theologicorum*, his twelve-volume systematic theology, and *Biblia Illustrata*, his commentary on the whole Bible.

Calvin, John (1509–1564)

Swiss reformer, theologian, and pastor, whose leadership of the burgeoning church in Geneva helped transform it into an exemplary Protestant city. Due to his ability to skillfully assimilate, systematize, and communicate Reformation ideas, he has had a lasting impact, illustrated by the fact that his name became synonymous with Reformed theology, particularly as it pertains to predestination. His two most important works are the *Institutes of the Christian Religion* and his biblical commentaries.

Canons (of the Synod) of Dort (1619)

The theological decisions of the Dutch national synod held to address the Arminian protest, its positions becoming known as the five points of Calvinism (*TULIP: T*otal depravity, *U*nconditional election, *L*imited atonement, *I*rresistible grace, *P*erseverance of the saints) in contrast to the Five Articles of the Remonstrants. The Canons of Dort is an accepted doctrinal standard of many Reformed churches throughout the world as part of the Three Forms of Unity.

Cappadocian Fathers (4th cent.)

Three theologians—Gregory of Nazianzus, Basil (the Great) of Caesarea, and Gregory of Nyssa (brother of Basil)—all from the region of Cappadocia and known for their work on the orthodox doctrines of the Trinity and Christology.

Cassian, John (c. 360–c. 430)

A monk who greatly influenced monastic life, rules, and order and is best known for his uneasiness concerning Augustine's doctrine of grace. He attacked Augustine's view and took a different view of the relationship between human responsibility and divine grace, a position that later came to be known as semi-Pelagianism.

Chemnitz, Martin (1522–1586)

Foremost German theologian in the generation after Luther who helped preserve the Reformation legacy in Germany, largely by mediating between conflicting views within Lutheranism, most notably by contributing to the *Formula of Concord* (1577). He also denounced the Roman Catholic Church and its theology in his *Examination of the Council of Trent* (1565–1573).

Chicago Statement on Biblical Inerrancy (1978)

Formulated by approximately three hundred evangelical scholars representing a wide spectrum of denominations and churches, the culmination of the International Council on Biblical Inerrancy Summit I that convened October 26–28, 1978, in Chicago. The papers from the summit were later published as the book *Inerrancy*. The statement presented the evangelical consensus on the inspiration, authority, and truthfulness (inerrancy) of Scripture.

Chicago Statement on Biblical Hermeneutics (1982)

Formulated by approximately one hundred evangelical scholars, the culmination of the International Council on Biblical Inerrancy Summit II that convened November 10–13, 1982, in Chicago. The proceedings from the summit were later published as the book *Hermeneutics, Inerrancy, and the Bible*. The statement clarified important hermeneutical issues and principles such as the necessity of interpreting the Bible literally, or according to its grammatical-historical sense, while considering its various genre; the role of both preunderstandings and the Holy Spirit in interpreting and applying Scripture; an affirmation of objective biblical truth; and an emphasis on a single, determinate meaning of Scripture.

Chrysostom, John (c. 347–407)

Bishop of Constantinople whose surname means "golden-mouthed," most noted for sound biblical exegesis and the eloquent preaching in which he engaged both as a bishop and later as patriarch of Constantinople. His writing on the priesthood was devoted to the responsibilities of pastoral care.

Clarke, William Newton (1840–1912)

Pastor, theologian, and professor whose *An Outline of Christian Theology* (1894) represented typical liberal Protestant theology. Together with Walter Rauschenbusch and others, he helped develop the Brotherhood of the Kingdom that gave rise to the social gospel movement.

Clement of Alexandria (d. 215)

An influential Christian thinker who was trained in the catechetical school founded in Alexandria by Pantaenus and later became its headmaster. His works explore the relationship between Christianity and culture, present Christ as the instructor offering Christian moral guidance, and combat the heresy of gnosticism.

Clement of Rome (late 1st cent.)

Bishop of Rome and an Apostolic Father, who wrote the *Letter of the Romans to the Corinthians* (c. 96) to address some of the same problems that the apostle Paul had treated in two of his New Testament letters (1 and 2 Corinthians). It gives the first post–New Testament snapshot of the early church.

Council of Chalcedon (451)/Creed of Chalcedon

The fourth ecumenical council, presided over by Leo the Great and the Emperor Marcion and attended by more than 350 bishops. It condemned the heresies of Arianism, Apollinarianism, Nestorianism, and Eutychianism and articulated the orthodox doctrine of the hypostatic union—that is, the union of two natures (divine and human) in the one person of Jesus Christ.

Council of Constantinople I (381)

The second ecumenical council (and first of three held at Constantinople), convened by Emperor Theodosius and attended by more than 150 bishops. It upheld the doctrines of the Council of Nicea (325), condemned Apollinarianism, and defended the deity of the Holy Spirit against the Macedonians or Pneumatomachians ("Spirit fighters").

Council of Constantinople II (553)

The fifth ecumenical council, convened by the Emperor Justinian and attended by more than 150 bishops. It was called to settle the bitter controversy of the Three Chapters—that is, whether Theodore of Mopsuestia, Theodoret, and Ibas of Edessas should be condemned as Nestorians or whether, in agreement with the Council of Chalcedon, they should be accepted. The council also condemned the theologically controversial views of Origen.

Council of Constantinople III (680–681)

The sixth ecumenical council, convened by the Emperor Constantine IV and attended by nearly 175 bishops. Its sole purpose was settling the Monothelite (literally, "one will") controversy in the Eastern Church. Monothelitism stated that after the incarnation, Jesus Christ had only one will by which he performed his divine and human actions. The council produced a Definition of Faith that contains a reproduction of the Chalcedonian belief concerning the two natures of Christ and concludes that because Christ had two natures, he must by necessity have two wills.

Council of Ephesus (431)

The third ecumenical council, presided over by Cyril of Alexandria and attended by more than two hundred bishops. It condemned Nestorianism, defended Mary as *theotokos* (literally, "God-bearer"), and upheld the unity of the one person of Jesus Christ.

Council of Nicea (325)/Creed of Nicea

The first ecumenical council, convened by the Emperor Constantine and attended by 318 bishops. It condemned Arianism and defended the deity of the Son of God, using the term *homoousios* to affirm that the Son is of the same nature as the Father.

Council of Trent (mid–16th cent.)

The nineteenth ecumenical council as recognized by the Roman Catholic Church, held in three phases between 1545 and 1563. It articulated the church's positions on the doctrines challenged by the Reformers, whose views were condemned. Trent also corrected abuses regarding clerical offices, required clergy to exercise greater pastoral care, ordered the establishment of seminaries, and endorsed the theology of Thomas Aquinas. It set the trajectory for Roman Catholic theology and practice for the next four centuries.

Cyprian of Carthage (d. 251)

Bishop of Carthage during Emperor Decius's persecution (249–251), who fled from his seat and continued to wield leadership of the church via correspondence from hiding. Following the persecution, he addressed the question of what to do with lapsed Christians, those who had apostatized under persecution. His many writings, notably *On the Unity of the Church*, contributed significantly to the development of the Catholic Church's structure and hierarchy. Cyprian was publicly executed by Valerian in 258 A.D.

Cyril of Alexandria (378–444)

Bishop of Alexandria and defender of orthodox Christology, known mostly for his denunciation of Nestorianism. Offering his *Twelve Anathemas* against Nestorius, through political intrigue he managed to have Nestorianism condemned at the third ecumenical Council of Ephesus in 431.

Cyril of Jerusalem (c. 315–386)

Bishop of Jerusalem from 349 until his death, whose stand against Arianism cost him banishment three times. His twenty-four *Catechetical Instructions* were used for training new converts and young believers in the Christian faith. He particularly emphasized baptism and the Eucharist.

Descartes, René (1596–1650)

French philosopher, called the father of modern philosophy because of his revolutionary impact on epistemology and metaphysics. He sought an unshakable basis for all knowledge. In his *Meditations on First Philosophy* (1641), he concluded, *cogito ergo sum* ("I think, therefore I am"); that is, because he was thinking, he could be certain of his existence. From that starting point he defended the existence of God and the outside world. He also explored the relationship between the mind/soul and the body.

Didache (c. 150)

A handbook commonly known as *The Teaching of the Twelve (Apostles)* and catalogued with the writings of the Apostolic Fathers. It is of unknown origin but provides one of the earliest snapshots of early church worship. It consists of a moral treatise setting forth the "two ways" of life and death and instructions on topics such as baptism, prayer, fasting, the Lord's Supper, church officials, and standing firm against worldly living.

Dionysius the pseudo-Areopagite (6th cent.)

Allegedly the convert of the apostle Paul in Athens (Acts 17:34), a mystical theologian who authored several important treatises that were considered highly authoritative by important church leaders such as Aquinas because of their purported origin. Engaging in much speculation, he described in great detail the angelic hierarchy and insisted that the church's hierarchy parallel the celestial order. Much later, in the Renaissance, his writings were demonstrated to have originated in the sixth century.

Docetism (started 1st cent.)

From the Greek δοκεω (*dokeô*; to seem or appear), a heresy maintaining that Jesus Christ only appeared to be a real and fully human being. It held that because matter is essentially evil, the Son of God could not have become incarnate, so his physical nature was only an illusion. It was condemned by the early church but has resurfaced in various expressions throughout church history.

Dominic (c. 1174 – 1221)

Spanish founder of the Dominican Order, whose purpose for establishing this Order of Preachers was to win back the heretical Albigensians (or Cathari) to the Catholic Church through missionaries who were contentedly poor, spiritually strong, and capable of persuasive itinerant preaching. Dominic began to dispatch his monks to other parts of the world to preach itinerantly. In 1217 Pope Honorius III granted official approval to the Order, and through contact with Francis of Assisi the Dominicans adopted poverty and begging as a major element.

Eck, John (1486 – 1543)

Roman Catholic theologian considered one of the most prominent polemicists against the Reformation. In public debate with Luther, Eck forced him to admit that his rejection of indulgences was an implicit rejection of the infallibility of the pope. He helped compose the papal bull, "Exsurge Domine," that excommunicated Luther in 1521.

Edwards, Jonathan (1703 – 1758)

One of the foremost American theologians and philosophers, whose preaching and writing contributed significantly to the (First) Great Awakening. Through a series of sermons on divine sovereignty, justification, and genuine conversion, his church in Northhampton, Massachusetts, experienced revival, which then spread to many other churches. Edwards described and defended the revival in *A Faithful Narrative of the Surprising Work of God, Distinguishing Marks of a Work of the Spirit of God*, and *Some Thoughts Concerning the Present Revival*. In addition to his theological works on sin and the human will, his *Treatise Concerning Religious Affections* analyzed religious experience and drew conclusions about true and false signs of conversion.

Erasmus, Desiderius (1466 – 1536)

Roman Catholic monk and scholar who applied a humanist emphasis to Scripture to produce a Greek New Testament (*Novum Instrumentum*, 1516) and the first Latin translation since the Vulgate. He strongly satirized the Roman Catholic Church and its pope in works such as *Handbook of the Christian Soldier, The Praise of Folly*, and *Julius Exclusus*. He also engaged in polemics against Luther in favor of the freedom of the will, which Luther contradicted in his *Bondage of the Will*.

Eriugena, John Scotus (9th cent.)

Irish (as "Eriugena" indicates) theologian, biblical scholar, and philosopher who lived much of his life in France. His writings treated a wide variety of topics such as a Latin translation of the works of Dionysius the pseudo-Areopagite, a Neoplatonic philosophy of nature, the freedom of the will versus severe predestination, and the nature of the Eucharist.

Eusebius of Caesarea (c. 263 – c. 340)

One of the early church's greatest scholars, whose most enduring and important work is *Ecclesiastical History*, a history of the Christian church up to 324 A.D. As bishop of Caesarea and advisor to Constantine, Eusebius was a key figure in the Arian controversy.

Eutychus (c. 378 – 454)/Eutychianism

Abbot of a monastery, who held that after the incarnation, the divine and human natures of Christ fused to form a hybrid nature or, more simply understood, the divine nature completely overpowered the human nature. Denounced by Leo the Great, Eutychianism was officially condemned as a heresy at the fourth ecumenical Council of Chalcedon in 451, as the church insisted that Christ must be recognized as having both a fully human and a fully divine nature.

Finney, Charles Grandison (1792 – 1875)

Pastor, itinerant evangelist, and professor who was a major contributor to the Second Great Awakening in America and is considered to be the father of modern revivalism. His innovative approach to revivals included techniques such as publicity for the events, a new style of pulpit oratory, protracted evening meetings, exhortations by women, and the "anxious bench" for people considering conversion. After his Erie Canal revivals (1825 – 1830), he was a pastor, became president of Oberlin College (Ohio), and promoted temperance, abolitionism, and perfectionism.

Formula of Concord (1577)

One of Lutheranism's primary confessions of faith, uniting most of the disputing factions of Lutheranism after the Reformer's death. The *Formula of Concord*, along with the *Augsburg Confession* and several other documents, was included in the *Book of Concord*, which serves as an authoritative doctrinal guide for most Lutherans.

Fourth Lateran Council (1215)

Convened by Pope Innocent III and attended by nearly fifteen hundred participants, the most important of the Lateran councils (named after one of the chief churches in Rome). Treating a wide range of issues, it is known for its statement concerning the Eucharist that contains the first official definition of the doctrine of transubstantiation, and for its call for annual confession of sins and reception of communion.

Francis of Assisi (1181/82 – 1226)

Founder of the Franciscan Order and one of the best-known of medieval saints. After hearing Matthew 10:7 – 14 read during Mass, he understood the words of Christ as being a personal call to ministry. Forsaking wealth and comfort, he lived a life of total poverty and eventually founded a mendicant (begging) order that was approved by Pope Innocent III in 1210. He is known for the "Prayer of St. Francis" and the stigmata (the wounds of the crucified Christ).

Gallican (French) Confession (1559)

A summary of the Bible's teaching adopted by the first national synod of the Reformed churches of France. It served as a unifying doctrinal standard. It distinguished Huguenots (French Calvinists) from Catholics as well as Anabaptists and Spiritualists.

Gerhard, John (1582–1637)

Lutheran theologian and professor whose most important contribution is *Loci Theologici* (1621), a comprehensive and clear treatment of all the Christian doctrines exemplifying the best of Protestant scholasticism.

Gnosticism (started 2nd cent.)

A matrix of heresies that was promoted by people such as Marcion, Saturinus, and Valentinus. It differentiated the god of the Old Testament and the god of the New Testament, embraced metaphysical dualism, held a docetic view of Jesus Christ, and claimed to possess a secret gnosis (Gr. γνωσις; *gnōsis*) knowledge regarding salvation. It has resurfaced in modified form throughout church history.

Great Awakening, First (1730s–1740s)

Led by luminaries such as Theodore Jacob Frelinghuysen, Gilbert Tennent, George Whitefield, and Jonathan Edwards, a series of revivals in colonial America that led to an increased number of people making professions of faith, a resurgence in Calvinism, a deepening of piety, and a greater concern for education. It also resulted in divisions among detractors and supporters of revival. Some historians regard the Great Awakening as a significant contributor to the American Revolution.

Great Awakening, Second (first part of 19th cent.)

A series of revivals of quite different tenor that took place on the American frontier and in New England. The first of these revivals, centered particularly in Kentucky, was characterized by persuasive preaching, unchecked emotionalism, cooperation between various denominations, and controversy between opponents and supporters of revival. Revivalism in New England, which affected such leaders as Timothy Dwight, Asehel Nettleton, and Lyman Beecher, took on a much more serene and dignified tone.

Great Awakening, Third (second half of 19th cent.)

A series of revivals that took on many forms, including businessmen and union prayer meetings (in Chicago and New York City, for example), the formation of the Young Men's Christian Association (YMCA), the evangelistic preaching of D. L. Moody, new missionary agencies, cults such as Christian Science and Jehovah's Witnesses, and the development of social movements such as temperance and woman suffrage.

Gregory of Nazianzus (c. 330–c. 390)

One of the Cappadocian Fathers and known as "the Theologian." He combated the heresies of Eunomianism and Apollinarianism while championing orthodox Christology and developing orthodox Trinitarian theology. He provided leadership for the second ecumenical Council of Constantinople in 381, in which his insistence that if Jesus Christ did not take on full humanity, then human beings cannot be saved ("What he has not assumed, he has not healed") was decisive for articulating orthodox Christology.

Gregory of Nyssa (c. 331 – c. 395)

One of the Cappadocian Fathers, contributing much to the development of the orthodox doctrine of the Trinity while fighting against Christological heresies. Additionally, he focused on the doctrine of God, explored the contemplative and mystical life, and provided a systematic theology for the church.

Gregory the Great (c. 540 – 604)

Bishop of Rome from 590 and a passionate promoter of evangelization and monasticism. He was a gifted administrator and contributed significantly to the development and power of the papacy.

Grotius, Hugo (1583 – 1645)

Politician, jurist, theologian, apologist, and one of Holland's greatest minds. He had to flee to France because he was an Arminian. He is widely known for originating the governmental theory of the atonement.

Heidegger, John (1633 – 1698)

Swiss theologian and professor whose many writings were largely polemical and addressed against the Roman Catholic Church. He contributed significantly to the *Helvetic (Swiss) Formula Consensus* that defended the Synod of Dort's understanding of the atonement against Amyraldianism.

Heidelberg Catechism (1563)

The most important and widely distributed doctrinal standard of Reformed theology, written by Zacharias Ursinus (with possible contribution by Casper Olevianus) as a defense of the Reformed faith after the Peace of Augsburg. The document takes the form of 129 questions answered in a uniquely kind and personal tone. It spread throughout Europe and was adopted as one of the Three Forms of Unity by the Synod of Dort.

Hippolytus (c. 170 – c. 236)

A leader in the church of Rome who contributed much to the church's developing interpretation of Scripture and theology while chronicling the many doctrinal heresies from the end of the first century up to his time.

Hodge, Charles (1797 – 1878)

Theologian, professor, and editor who taught exegesis and theology for more than fifty years at Princeton Theological Seminary. His many writings include commentaries on books of the Bible, a three-volume *Systematic Theology* (1871 – 1873), and numerous articles in *Biblical Repertoire and Princeton Review*, of which he was editor for several decades.

Hollaz, David (c. 1647 – 1713)

German Lutheran pastor and educator, whose most popular work is his *Examen Theologicum Acroamaticum* (1707), a systematic theology written for his students in preparatory school. He incorporated earlier Lutheran theology while contributing to the doctrines of Scripture, salvation, and the church.

Hugh of St. Victor (d. 1142)

Medieval theologian and biblical interpreter who gave a new emphasis to historical study of Scripture using the literal sense in interpreting the text. His approach to Scripture launched the Victorines, a new school of biblical interpretation. His work on the sacraments was the first medieval *summae* of theology.

Huss, John (c. 1372–1415)

Professor of philosophy and rector of the University of Prague as well as rector and preacher at the main church in Prague. He is best known for his work as a pre-Reformer. Drawing much from the works of John Wycliffe, he attacked clerical corruption in the Catholic Church, criticized transubstantiation, and denounced some popes as heretics. As a result, he was excommunicated by the church, and his followers were placed under an interdict. Although promised safe travel to the Council of Constance, Huss was burned at the stake there in 1415. He became a national hero, and his Hussite movement spread throughout Bohemia.

Ignatius (d. 110/115)

Disciple of the apostle John and an Apostolic Father, who as bishop of Antioch was arrested and escorted by imperial soldiers through Asia Minor to his martyrdom in Rome. During his trip he wrote seven letters — six to churches (letters to the Ephesians, Magnesians, Trallians, Romans, Philadelphians, and Smyrneans) and one to Polycarp — that combated docetism and church factions, calling for one bishop to rule over each church (the origin of monoepiscopacy).

Ignatius of Loyola (1491–1556)

Founder of the Jesuit order, whose mystical experience following a serious leg injury led him to zealously pursue religion. He mentored six men based on the principles in his *Spiritual Exercises*, and together they founded an order, also known as the Society of Jesus, devoted to the service of the papacy. This rapidly growing group of educators, missionaries, and preachers was an important part of the Roman Catholic response to the Reformation.

Irenaeus of Lyons (c. 130–c. 200)

Trained under Polycarp, a missionary to Gaul (modern-day France) and bishop of Lyons. He systematically refuted heresy, particularly gnosticism, in his lengthy writing *Against Heresies*. His doctrine of recapitulation maintained that Jesus Christ recapitulated, or retraced, the life cycle of human beings, undoing the disobedience of Adam and accomplishing salvation through his obedient life and death.

Isidore of Seville (c. 560–636)

Archbishop of Seville and a prolific author whose writings include an encyclopedia, a Christology for a Jewish audience, and exegetical works promoting an allegorical interpretation of Scripture.

Jerome (c. 345–420)

Monk, biblical scholar, and theologian also known as Hieronymus, most noted for his translation of the Bible from Hebrew and Greek into Latin, known as the Latin Vulgate. He argued that the church should use the Hebrew canon of Scripture that does not contain the Apocryphal writings.

Joachim of Fiore (c. 1135–1202)

Cistercian monk and abbot of the monastery he founded in Fiore (Italy). His chief contribution is the revolutionary idea of dividing history into three periods (as opposed to the common two-period division of "before Christ" and "after Christ"), each of which corresponds to a different person of the Trinity. The Spiritual Franciscans deeply appreciated his theory, which was also lauded by many mystics.

Justin Martyr (d. 165)

An Apologist who sought to defend the Christian faith against the charges of atheism, incest, and cannibalism. He was converted as a philosopher to Christianity, which he considered to be the true philosophy, and as an apologist he drew parallels between Christian and Platonic worldviews. He also offered a defense of Christianity against Jewish beliefs. As his last name indicates, he was martyred around 165.

Kant, Immanuel (1724–1804)

Considered to be one of history's greatest philosophers, whose many writings transformed the field of epistemology, breaking with both empiricism and rationalism. In *Critique of Pure Reason* he offered his transcendental idealism, conceiving the mind as containing innate categories with which to process the data received through sense experience. In *Critique of Practical Reason* and *Foundation of the Metaphysics of Morals*, he articulated his moral philosophy centered around the categorical imperative. He also postulated the existence of God based on the idea of the *summum bonum*, or highest good. His *Religion within the Limits of Reason Alone* was an attempt to erect a religious system based solely on human reason.

Knox, John (c. 1513–1572)

Scottish reformer, pastor, historian, and disciple of John Calvin who sought to do for the kingdom of Scotland what Calvin had done in Geneva. Through several key documents—the Book of Discipline (1561) and the Book of Common Order (1562/1564)—he helped establish the Reformed Church of Scotland, with a government that became known as presbyterianism. Although Mary Queen of Scots sought to undo Knox's reforming efforts, she was forced to abdicate the throne, and Protestantism was officially established by Parliament in 1567.

Lactantius (c. 250–c. 324)

Born in North Africa, a teacher of rhetoric who was involved with the political and societal concerns of his day. His key work, *The Divine Institutes* (c. 309), though problematic in terms of some of its theological assertions, linked the prosperity and endurance of Rome to its allegiance to God. This work was still influential at the time of the Reformation.

Leo the Great (d. 461)

Bishop of Rome, who persuaded Attila the Hun not to attack the city as had been planned. Theologically, he opposed Pelagianism, and his *Tome* came to be regarded as the standard of Christological orthodoxy against Eutychianism and was influential at the fourth ecumenical Council of Chalcedon in 451. His influence contributed to the establishment of the papacy.

Letter to Diognetus (2nd cent.)

Written to a pagan, exposing the stupidity of idolatry and the superstitions of Judaism. It provided an explanation of the Christian faith and the work of Christ for salvation and exhorted its reader to convert to Christianity. It is classified among the works of the Apologists.

Locke, John (1632–1704)

British professor whose philosophy had an immeasurable impact on the Western world. He explained his empiricist views in his *Essay on Human Understanding*, championing reason as being more certain than faith. However, in *The Reasonableness of Christianity*, he argued that Christianity is the clearest body of truths, all of which can be arrived at by natural means. He also wrote influential works of political and social philosophy.

Luther, Martin (1483–1546)

German theologian, pastor, and leading Reformer, whose *Ninety-five Theses* (1517) questioned the sale of indulgences, provoked the indignation of the Roman Catholic Church, and sparked the Protestant Reformation. His many contributions include a German translation of the Bible, commentaries on many books of Scripture, the book *The Bondage of the Will*, and both small and large catechisms. Luther is best known for his emphases on the authority and clarity of Scripture (which does not include the Apocrypha), justification by faith alone, the priesthood of all believers, the two sacraments of baptism and the Lord's Supper, and a courageous stance against doctrinal error.

Marcion (d. c. 154)

Born in Pontus and later a teacher in Rome who was condemned as a heretic after coming under the influence of gnosticism. He provided one of the earliest canons of Scripture, rejecting the entire Old Testament and containing a New Testament consisting of a mutilated version of Luke's gospel and ten Pauline letters. The church was spurred on to consider the proper canon of Scripture.

Melanchthon, Philip (1497–1560)

German humanist professor and theologian. Aside from Luther, he was the chief influence on the Reformation in Germany. His important writings include the *Loci communes theologici* (1521), the first systematic presentation of Protestant theology, and the *Augsburg Confession* and its *Apology* (1530). He further developed the Lutheran distinction between law and gospel by distinguishing between three uses of the law: one that demands perfection, one that directs civil affairs, and another that guides Christian living.

Melito of Sardis (d. c. 180)

Bishop of Sardis, classified as an Apologist, who urged Antoninus Caesar to condemn idolatry and polytheism. He also appealed to Antoninus's successor, Marcus Aurelius, to investigate more carefully the Christian faith and rescind persecution against the church.

Molina, Luis de (1535–1600)/Molinism

Spanish Jesuit theologian and professor, most commonly known for his identification of one type of God's omniscience, different from his natural knowledge and free knowledge, called "middle knowledge." That is, God's knowledge of the future actions of free agents is based upon his perfect knowledge of how those agents will act in specific circumstances. This view led to conflicts between the Jesuits and Dominicans, who more closely adhered to the theology of Augustine. In the twentieth century, Molinism began to experience a revival among analytical philosophers and evangelicals such as Alvin Plantinga and William Lane Craig.

Montanus (fl. mid – 2nd cent.)/Montanism

A self-proclaimed prophet who joined with two prophetesses, Prisca and Maximilla (who called themselves the mouthpiece of the Holy Spirit), and emphasized visions, speaking in tongues, asceticism, and other intense religious experiences. They established the movement that bears his name (Montanism), and stirred up hope in the imminent second coming of Christ, and prophesied that the New Jerusalem would descend from heaven to Phrygia. Montanism was labeled as a heresy by the church, but it persisted until the fifth century.

Nestorius (end of 4th – mid-5th cent.)/Nestorianism

Bishop of Constantinople whose career lasted only three years, until 431, when he was condemned as a heretic for his aberrant Christology, labeled Nestorianism. He was charged with affirming a view (which he later denied holding) that there were two persons—one divine, one human—who cooperated together in Jesus Christ. This brought about the censure of Cyril of Alexandria, who pressed to have Nestorius's view condemned at the third ecumenical Council of Ephesus in 431.

Nicene (or Nicene-Constantinopolitan) Creed (381)

A creed, produced at the second ecumenical Council of Constantinople in 381, that was a reworking of the earlier Creed of Nicea (325) and put an end to the nearly half-century of ascendency of the Arian heresy following the first ecumenical Council of Nicea. It affirmed the full deity of both God the Son and God the Holy Spirit.

Nicholas of Lyra (c. 1270 – 1349)

Franciscan monk and biblical scholar who was regent master at the University of Paris and head of the Franciscan order in France. His major work is a best-selling commentary on the whole Bible that focuses on its literal meaning.

Origen (c. 185 – 254)

The greatest biblical scholar and most prolific writer in the early church, who combated Celsius's attacks against Christianity, engaged in textual criticism, composed the first significant systematic treatment of Christian doctrine, and contributed significantly to the doctrine of the Trinity. He also held several controversial viewpoints, including an allegorical interpretation of Scripture, belief in the pre-existence of the soul, a model of the work of Christ known as the "ransom to Satan" theory, and (possibly) a hope of universal salvation.

Owen, John (1616 – 1683)

One of the most significant Puritan theologians, who was favored by Lord Protector Oliver Cromwell and then King Charles II and so contributed widely to the English Commonwealth and Protectorate. He is best known for his classical defense of limited atonement in *The Death of Death in the Death of Christ* (1647). Later, when he was called upon by the Council of State to defend the deity of Christ against the Socinians, he developed a view that the humanity of Christ carried out his ministry through the power of the Holy Spirit.

Papias (late 1st – early 2nd cent.)

Bishop of Hierapolis, whose work is counted among the Apostolic Fathers. Although only fragments of his writings survive, they provide details concerning the origins of the Gospels and express belief in a future millennium.

Pelagius (354 – 420/440)/Pelagianism

British monk and ascetic who took offense at a prayer of Augustine and championed heretical doctrines in Carthage, North Africa. He disagreed with original sin by denying solidarity between the sin of Adam and the human race, he viewed divine grace more as external help than as a work of God on the human soul, and he emphasized human free will. His positions were countered by Augustine, Jerome, and others and were denounced by the Council of Carthage. Pelagianism has continued in modified form in various liberal understandings of Christianity.

Peter Lombard (c. 1100 – 1160)

Medieval theologian, whose chief work was *Four Books of Sentences* (written 1147 – 1151), a compilation of "sentences" from the Bible, the church fathers, and other authorities that he attempted to reconcile or choose between. The *Sentences* became a standard textbook of theology until the time of the Reformation. He was the first to give the standard list of seven sacraments — baptism, confirmation, the Eucharist, penance, marriage, holy orders, and last rites — of the Roman Catholic Church.

Photius (c. 810 – c. 895)

Patriarch of Constantinople who was involved in numerous disagreements between the Eastern and Western churches, particularly the Western church's affirmation that the Holy Spirit proceeds from both the Father and the Son.

Polycarp (d. c. 155)

Disciple of the apostle John, mentor of Irenaeus, and bishop of the church of Smyrna, whose *Letter to the Philippians* emphasizes living the Christian life. It is included among the works of the Apostolic Fathers, as is the *Martyrdom of Polycarp*, a document attributed to his church in Smyrna that records Polycarp's public burning at the stake when he was more than eighty years old.

Quadratus (early 2nd cent.)

One of the earliest Apologists, whose writing (of which only a fragment survives) was an apology addressed to the Roman emperor Hadrian sometime between 120 – 130.

Quenstedt, John Andrew (1617 – 1688)

Lutheran professor and dogmatician whose systematic theology, *Theologia Didactico-Polemica sive Systema Theologicum* (Lipsiae, 1715), is one of the greatest Lutheran writings because it clearly addressed every issue of that time, drew from vast and varied sources, and contained impressive amounts of Scriptural exegesis. He earned a reputation for being humble and kind toward his opponents.

Richard of St. Victor (d. 1173)

Student of Hugh of St. Victor and medieval theologian who continued the Victorine emphasis on the literal interpretation of Scripture. His work on the Trinity offers a complex argument of necessary reasons for a triune God, and he contributed significantly to the development of mystical theology. His teachings greatly influenced Bonaventure and the Franciscan school of thought.

Riissen, Leonard (c. 1636 – c. 1700)

Dutch Reformed pastor and theologian who opposed Arminianism and promoted the work of Francis Turretin through his *Francisci Turretini Compendium Theologiae* (Amsterdam, 1695).

Schleiermacher, Friedrich (1763 – 1834)

Philosopher, pastor, and theologian who is considered to be the father of liberal Protestant theology. While a chaplain in Berlin, he became involved in the German Romantic movement and sought to explain the Christian religion, in such a way that his brilliant friends would consider it, in *On Religion: Speeches to its Cultured Despisers* (1799). Reacting to Kant's contention that God is utterly transcendent, Schleiermacher re-imagined religion as the feeling of absolute dependence on the world spirit, an intuition of immediate self-consciousness possessed by all human beings. In his *Christian Faith* (1821/22; revised 1830/31), he reshaped Christian doctrines around his notion of religion as subjective feeling or intuition. He also contributed significantly to the development of philosophical hermeneutics. His theology provided the foundation for liberal Protestantism and evoked strong reaction from such luminaries as Karl Barth and Emil Brunner.

Schlethheim Confession (1527)

The original Anabaptist confessional document, which helped define the movement by addressing seven concerns of Anabaptists in Switzerland and southern Germany. Michael Sattler, later martyred in Zurich, was the primary author of the confession, which was widely distributed and to which response was given by both Zwingli and Calvin.

Scholasticism (Catholic) (11th – 16th cent.)

A scholarly approach and method employed by many theologians during the latter part of the medieval period, the term being derived from the Latin *scholasticus*, meaning "learned." As an approach, it joined together Christian theology and philosophy (especially that of Aristotle), seeking to find compatibility between faith and reason. As a method, it involved composing lists of contradictory statements from several authoritative sources and applying logic to find their agreement. The main figures associated with scholasticism are Anselm, Peter Abelard, Duns Scotus, William of Ockham, Bonaventura, and Thomas Aquinas.

Scholasticism (Protestant) (late 16th – early 18th cent.)

The theological approach and framework of classical Protestant orthodoxy. Although often caricaturized as an intellectualist distortion of the theologies of Luther and Calvin, it is more accurately a conservative attempt to preserve the legacy of the Reformation in changing circumstances and an ardent concern for the purity of Protestant doctrine against a revived Roman Catholicism and the heresy of Socinianism. Vast and meticulous theological works were produced by the Lutheran and Reformed post-Reformation theologians, often of a polemical nature, in response to attacks against Protestant theology and as an attempt to systematize that theology.

Scotus, John Duns (c. 1265–1308)

Scottish (as "Scotus" indicates) Franciscan monk and scholastic philosopher-theologian who taught in Oxford, Paris, and Cologne. His writings treated a wide range of topics, including Aristotelian philosophy, commentaries on Peter Lombard's *Sentences*, natural theology (including a proof for the existence of God), the realist-nominalist debate, and a defense of the immaculate conception of Mary.

Second Helvetic Confession (1566)

The most influential and thorough Reformed confession of the sixteenth century, written by Heinrich Bullinger to help defend the faith of elector Frederick III of the Palatinate and to explain Reformed theology for the imperial assembly in Germany. While the *First Helvetic Confession* united the Swiss Reformed, the *Second* was also adopted by those in France, Hungary, Poland, and Scotland.

Shedd, William G. T. (1820–1894)

Professor of theology who articulated and defended Calvinism in his three-volume *Dogmatic Theology* (1888–1894). His work was influenced by the methodology of Francis Bacon and by Scottish common sense realism.

Shepherd of Hermas (c. 150)

An allegory written by a member of the church of Rome, included among the writings of the Apostolic Fathers. It consists of five *Visions,* twelve *Mandates* (commandments), and ten *Similitudes* (parables). The "shepherd" is an angel of repentance who calls the church to holiness. The work was considered worthy of canonical status by some in the early church.

Socinianism (16th–17th cent.)

A heretical movement launched by Faustus Socinus (1539–1604) and his uncle, Lelio Socinus (1525–1562), two Italian humanists. Faustus, living in Rakow, Poland, wrote the *Racovian Catechism* (published after his death in 1605), setting forth the major tenets of the movement: an emphasis on reason, a denial of the deity of Christ, a repudiation of original sin and predestination, an attack on the satisfaction theory of the atonement, and anti-Trinitarianism. Despite being short-lived due to attacks against it by both Roman Catholics and Protestants, Socinianism had a widespread liberalizing influence across Europe.

Spinoza, Baruch (1632–1677)

Dutch businessman, philosopher, and theologian who was banished from his Jewish community for heresy. Shorty afterward, he published the *Tractatus Theologico-Politicus* (*Theological-Political Treatise*; 1670). Foundational to modern biblical criticism, the book distinguishes between the superstitions found in Scripture and the universal truths that pertain to love and other virtues. In his work *Ethics* he identified God with his creation, a pantheistic view that would be central to liberalism and condemned by many, including Karl Barth.

Tatian (d. c. 185)

Disciple of Justin Martyr and an Apologist, who repudiated his philosophical roots and became a defender of the Christian faith. His *Diatesseron* is the first harmony of the Gospels. Later in life he apostasized and became an adherent of gnosticism.

Tertullian (160–240)

North African theologian, the first Christian leader to employ Latin. As an Apologist he argued for the toleration of Christianity and denounced gnosticism. As a philosopher he originated traducianism, the doctrine of the transmission of the soul from parents to their offspring. As a theologian he addressed such doctrines as baptism and post-baptismal sins, Christology, and the initial Trinitarian understanding of God (for which he coined the term *trinitas*). He converted to Montanism later in life.

Theodore of Mopsuestia (c. 350–428)

Bishop of Mopsuestia, who rejected the Alexandrian school of allegorical interpretation, advocating instead a more literal approach to Scripture. His doctrine of the incarnation was condemned at the Council of Ephesus (431) and the Council of Constantinople II (533).

Theodoret (c. 393–c. 460)

Bishop of Cyrus, whose major contribution was his teaching about the person of Jesus Christ and his support of Nestorius in the Nestorian controversy. His early support of the view that Christ had two natures and two persons gave way to his embrace of the orthodox belief that Christ is one person with two natures. This position was affirmed at the fourth ecumenical Council of Chalcedon (451).

Theophilus of Antioch (d. c. 185)

Bishop of Antioch and one of the Apologists. His *To Autolycus* was written to a pagan and relied on natural proofs and the Hebrew Bible to defend Christianity against Greek philosophy and myth. He also wrote the first known Christian commentary on the *Hexaemeron*, the six days of the creation account in Genesis, in which he affirmed that God created the world ex nihilo, literally, "out of nothing."

Thirty-nine Articles (1562)

The doctrinal standard for the Church of England beginning in the reign of Elizabeth I. It is also known as the *Articles of Religion*. Not intended to be a systematic work and written to permit some doctrinal diversity, it developed out of a concern for national unity as well as doctrinal continuity with the historic church and the Reformers.

Thomas Aquinas (1225–1274)

Medieval philosopher, Dominican monk, and eminent scholastic theologian, who is best known for the integration of Christian theology and Aristotelian philosophy. His many works include commentaries on Scripture and Peter Lombard's *Sentences*, discussions of Aristotle's writings, and theological treatises, among which pride of place goes to his *Summa Theologica*. This widely influential work treats such matters as the multiple senses of Scripture, proofs for the existence of God, the Trinity, angels, Christian virtues, and the sacraments, including Aquinas's philosophical foundation for the doctrine of transubstantiation. In 1879 Pope Leo XIII declared Thomism (Aquinas's teachings) to be eternally valid for the Roman Catholic Church.

Turretin, Francis (1623 – 1687)

Reformed theologian and professor at the University of Geneva during the height of Protestant scholasticism. He underscored the importance of grounding theology on divine revelation rather than philosophy (as held by Catholic Scholasticism) or reason (as held by Socinianism). He contributed significantly to the *Helvetic (Swiss) Formula Consensus,* which emphasized divine providence in preserving biblical writings. His systematic theology, *Institutes of Elenctic Theology* (Geneva, 1679 – 1685), was used by Princeton Theological Seminary as its primary instructional text until the 1870s, significantly influencing that school's doctrine of biblical inerrancy.

Tyconius (4th cent.)

African Donatist theologian, whose seven rules for the interpretation of Scripture (*Book of Rules*) and spiritual interpretation of the book of Revelation (especially Rev. 20:1 – 6) influenced Augustine's hermeneutic and eschatological view.

Ursinus, Zacharias (1534 – 1583)

German Reformed professor and scholar best remembered for his contribution to and defense of the *Heidelberg Catechism*. He contributed significantly to the Reformed understanding of the covenants between God and human beings and helped to spread Calvinist doctrine in Germany.

Ussher, James (1581 – 1656)

Professor, Archbishop of the Church of England, and Primate of all Ireland, well known as a church historian while also writing popular chronologies of world events, including the creation. Although he agreed with Puritan theology, he disagreed with its rejection of the Church of England's ceremony and ecclesiology, believing it to be modeled after the early church.

Vatican Council I (1869 – 1870)

The council considered the twentieth ecumenical council by the Roman Catholic Church, convened by Pope Pius IX to deal with the disturbing trends of modernism, rationalism, liberalism, and the like. It is most remembered for its promulgation of the dogma of papal infallibility (*Pastor Aeternus*, July 18, 1870).

Vatican Council II (1962 – 1965)

The council considered the twenty-first ecumenical council by the Roman Catholic Church, convened by Pope John XXIII and completed by Pope Paul VI. It served as an *aggiornamento*, or updating, of the Catholic Church and addressed such important issues as divine revelation, the structure of the Mass (which should emphasize both the Liturgy of the Word and the Liturgy of the Eucharist), ecumenism, the salvation of non-Catholics, and ecclesiology.

Vincent of Lerins (d. c. 450)

Author of the *Commonitorium* (an aid for memory) written under the pseudonym "Peregrinus." He explained orthodoxy as "that faith which has been believed everywhere, always, and by everyone." He held that the final ground and authority of Christian truth is Scripture while insisting that church tradition and authority are not in opposition to it.

Warfield, Benjamin Breckenridge (1851–1921)

Professor of theology at Princeton Theological Seminary and a defender of the orthodox doctrines of the inspiration and inerrancy of Scripture. His many writings cover such topics as evolution, liberal theology, revivalism, cessationism, and sanctification.

Wesley, John (1703–1791)

Pastor, missionary, and evangelist whose open-air itinerant preaching and Arminian-influenced doctrine contributed to the Evangelical Revival in Great Britain and became the basis for the Methodist Church and Wesleyan-Arminian theology. A devout Anglican and missionary to the colony of Georgia in America, he was later (May 24, 1738) converted through the influence of the Moravians and the testimony of Martin Luther. His theology was characterized by a rejection of the Calvinist doctrine of predestination and an affirmation of conditional election, an emphasis on prevenient grace and a view of justification that includes the impartation of new life, and an insistence on the reality of Christian living that includes entire sanctification or Christian perfection.

Westminster Confession of Faith (1647)

A confession commissioned by the Puritan Parliament to guide the reform of the Church of England and written by the Westminster Assembly, consisting of more than 120 Puritan theologians, some independents, and Scottish commissioners. While treating the broad spectrum of Christian doctrines, it gives particular emphasis to the sovereignty of God, covenant theology (specifically, the covenant of works and the covenant of grace), worship, and exposure of false Roman Catholic theology. Although the confession fell out of use among Anglicans, it had an enduring influence in Scotland and among Presbyterian churches. The *Confession of Faith* is joined by a *Larger Catechism* and a *Shorter Catechism*. It was later modified by the Congregationalists in their *Savoy Declaration* (1658) and by the Baptists in their *Second London Confession* (1688).

Wycliffe, John (c. 1330–1384)

Professor at Oxford and English theologian, best known for his work as a pre-Reformer. He was highly critical of the papacy, insisted that salvation does not depend on association with the visible (i.e., Catholic) church, and attacked the doctrine of transubstantiation and other church practices. He also broke with Catholic teaching and tradition by affirming Scripture as the supreme and final authority and, in fact, translated much of the New Testament into English. Wycliffe's teaching greatly influenced the Czech reformer John Huss, and his followers in

England were called the Lollards. The Council of Constance (1415) condemned him (posthumously) as a heretic. In 1428, Wycliffe's remains were dug up and burned, and his ashes thrown into the river.

Zwingli, Huldrych (1484 – 1531)

Swiss theologian, pastor and chaplain, and Reformer in Zurich, who arrived at the Reformation principles of justification by faith alone and of Scripture alone independently of, but in parallel with, Martin Luther. At the same time, he contended with Luther—both through his writings as well as at the Marburg Colloquy—against consubstantiation in favor of a memorial view of the Lord's Supper. He also denounced the Anabaptists, developing a theological case for infant baptism.

GENERAL INDEX

Historical Theology Video Lectures

An Introduction to Christian Doctrine

Gregg R. Allison

Most historical theology studies follow Christian beliefs chronologically, discussing notable doctrinal developments for all areas of theology according to their historical appearance. While this may be good history, it can make for confusing theology, with the classic theological doctrines scattered throughout various time periods, movements, and controversies.

In *Historical Theology Video Lectures* and its accompanying textbook, Gregg Allison offers students the opportunity to study the historical development of theology by a topical-chronological arrangement, setting out the history one doctrine at a time. This approach allows students to concentrate on one tenet of Christianity and its formulation in the early church, through the Middle Ages, Reformation, and post-Reformation era, and into the modern period.

Historical Theology Video Lectures is a superb resource for students and self-learners wanting to better understand the development of Christian theology.

Available in stores and online!

Systematic Theology

An Introduction to Biblical Doctrine

Wayne Grudem

The Christian church has a long tradition of systematic theology, that is, studying theology and doctrine organized around fairly standard categories such as the Word of God, redemption, and Jesus Christ. This introduction to systematic theology has several distinctive features:

- A strong emphasis on the scriptural basis for each doctrine and teaching
- Clear writing, with technical terms kept to a minimum
- A contemporary approach, treating subjects of special interest to the church today
- A friendly tone, appealing to the emotions and the spirit as well as the intellect
- Frequent application to life
- Resources for worship with each chapter
- Bibliographies with each chapter that cross-reference subjects to a wide range of other systematic theologies.

Every Christian "does theology." With over 300,000 copies in print, *Systematic Theology: An Introduction to Biblical Doctrine* is a proven, trusted resource for introducing biblical doctrine, and instructing theological application.

Available in stores and online!

Making Sense of the Bible

One of Seven Parts from Grudem's Systematic Theology

Wayne Grudem

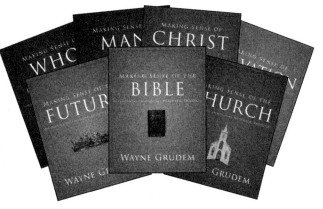

With a strong emphasis on the scriptural basis for each doctrine—what the whole Bible teaches us today about a particular topic; clear writing, with technical terms kept to a minimum; and a contemporary approach, emphasizing how each doctrine should be understood and applied by present-day Christians—the Making Sense of Series is required reading for anyone interested in understanding all aspects of systematic theology.

Taken from the bestselling *Systematic Theology* text, the Making Sense of Series offers people bite-size pieces of seven core biblical doctrines. Volumes are affordably priced and perfect for small groups, Sunday school classes, or Bible studies. Volumes include:

Making Sense of the Bible (Vol. 1)
Making Sense of Who God Is (Vol. 2)
Making Sense of Man and Sin (Vol. 3)
Making Sense of Christ and the Spirit (Vol. 4)
Making Sense of Salvation (Vol. 5)
Making Sense of the Church (Vol. 6)
Making Sense of the Future (Vol. 7)

Written in a friendly tone, appealing to the emotions and the spirit as well as the intellect, the Making Sense of Series helps readers overcome wrong ideas, make better decisions on new questions, and grow as Christians.

Available in stores and online!